HOLLYWOOD CREATIVE DIRECTORY

52ND EDITION

FALL 2004

The Only Call You Have To Make

Fast & Easy Online Quoting
Call our 24-hour charter hotline at:

800-519-6283

www.myaircraftquote.com

- Worldwide charter service
- Wide variety of aircraft
- 24-hour service
- Centralized national management team
- Backed by Raytheon Aircraft Company with 70 years of business aviation experience

Raytheon Aircraft Charter & Management has earned the ARG/US gold rating exceeding safety, equipment and crew standards for FAA 135 charter operators.

Contact John E. Martin
Van Nuys Airport: (818) 756-2182

Raytheon Aircraft Charter & Management

www.raytheonaircraftcharter.com

Senior Vice President,
IFILM Publishing
JEFF BLACK

Editorial
Vice President, IFILM Publishing
LAUREN ROSSINI

Senior Editor
STEVE ATINSKY

Director, Research
L. M. SIEGEL

Director, Online Product Development
SHARON BORDAS

Editor
MATT HAYES

Production Manager
CARLA GREEN

Software Engineer
SAMIRA MAHJOUB

Directory Sales
Senior Director, Sales
VALENCIA MCKINLEY

Manager, Inside Sales
AMELIA HAYES

Marketing
Director, Marketing
BETSY AHLSTRAND

Ad Sales
AFM Advertising Inc.
6700 Fallbrook Ave., Suite 222
West Hills, CA 91307
818.999.9356

Ad Sales Directors
JEFF BRUNER, KEN ROSE, BILL BUCK
ELIZABETH FERRIS

Founder
ALEKS HORVAT

Telephone
323.308.3490 • 800.815.0503

Fax
323.308.3492 (Research)
323.308.3493 (Sales)

Web Site
www.hcdonline.com

Customer Service
hcdcustomerservice@ifilm.com

Directory Sales
hcdsales@ifilm.com

Listings
hcdlistings@ifilm.com

52ND EDITION • FALL 2004

CONTENTS

1024 N. Orange Dr.
Hollywood, CA 90038
Phone: 323.308.3490 or 800.815.0503
Fax: 323.308.3492
www.hcdonline.com

COPYRIGHT NOTICE

Copyright © 1987-2004 by *Hollywood Creative Directory.* ALL RIGHTS RESERVED. No part of this publication may be reproduced, transmitted, transcribed, stored in a retrieval system, or translated into any human or computer language, in any form or by any means whatsoever, without the express permission of the *Hollywood Creative Directory*, 1024 N. Orange Dr., Hollywood, CA 90038.

TRADEMARK

The name *Hollywood Creative Directory* is a trademark (TM) of the *Hollywood Creative Directory, Inc.*

DISCLAIMER

The information contained in the *Hollywood Creative Directory* is provided to us directly by the companies listed. *Hollywood Creative Directory* cannot be held responsible for the veracity of a particular listing or misrepresentation by a listee. *Hollywood Creative Directory* is not responsible for information that has changed after the book has gone to press.

STUDIOS

The Walt Disney Company
500 S. Buena Vista St.
Burbank, CA 91521
Phone 818-560-1000
www.disney.com

DreamWorks SKG
1000 Flower St.
Glendale, CA 91201
Phone 818-695-5000
www.dreamworks.com

Metro-Goldwyn-Mayer (MGM)
10250 Constellation Blvd.
Los Angeles, CA 90067
Phone 310-449-3000
www.mgm.com

Miramax Films
New York
375 Greenwich St.
New York, NY 10013-2338
Phone 212-941-3800
Los Angeles
8439 Sunset Blvd.
West Hollywood, CA 90069
Phone 323-822-4100
www.miramax.com

New Line Cinema
116 N. Robertson Blvd., Ste. 200
Los Angeles, CA 90048
Phone 310-854-5811
www.newline.com

Paramount Pictures
5555 Melrose Ave.
Los Angeles, CA 90038-3197
Phone 323-956-5000
www.paramount.com

Sony Pictures Entertainment
10202 W. Washington Blvd.
Culver City, CA 90232-3195
Phone 310-244-4000
www.sony.com

Twentieth Century Fox
10201 W. Pico Blvd.
Los Angeles, CA 90035
Phone 310-369-1000
www.fox.com

Universal Pictures
100 Universal City Plaza
Universal City, CA 91608-1085
Phone 818-777-1000
www.universalstudios.com

Warner Bros.
4000 Warner Blvd.
Burbank, CA 91522-0001
Phone 818-954-6000
www.warnerbros.com

NETWORKS AND MAJOR CABLE CHANNELS

ABC
500 S. Buena Vista St.
Burbank, CA 91521
Phone 818-460-7777
www.abc.com

CBS
7800 Beverly Blvd.
Los Angeles, CA 90036-2188
Phone 323-575-2345
www.cbs.com

Fox
10201 W. Pico Blvd.
Los Angeles, CA 90035
Phone 310-369-1000
www.fox.com

HBO
1100 Avenue of the Americas
New York, NY 10036
Phone 212-512-1000
www.hbo.com

NBC
3000 W. Alameda Ave.
Burbank, CA 91523-0001
Phone 818-840-4444
www.nbc.com

Showtime
1633 Broadway
New York, NY 10019
Phone 212-708-1600
www.sho.com

UPN
11800 Wilshire Blvd.
Los Angeles, CA 90025
Phone 310-575-7000
www.upn.com

The WB Television Network
4000 Warner Blvd., Bldg. 34-R
Burbank, CA 91522-0001
Phone 818-977-5000
www.thewb.com

STATE FILM COMMISSIONS

ALABAMA

Alabama Film Office
Alabama Center for Commerce
401 Adams Ave., Ste. 630
Montgomery, AL 36104
Phone 334-242-4195
Fax 334-242-2077
www.alabamafilm.org
Brenda Hobbie – Film Office Coordinator

ALASKA

Alaska Film Program
550 W. Seventh Ave., Ste. 1770
Anchorage, AK 99501-3510
Phone 907-269-8190
Fax 907-269-8125
www.alaskafilm.org
Margy Johnson - Director

ARIZONA

Arizona Film Commission
1700 W. Washington St., Ste. 220
Phoenix, AZ 85007
Phone 602-771-1193
800-523-6695
Fax 602-771-1211
www.azcommerce.com
Robert Detweiler - Director

ARKANSAS

Arkansas Film Office
One Capitol Mall, Ste. 4B-505
Little Rock, AR 72201
Phone 501-682-7676
Fax 501-682-3456
www.1800arkansas.com/film
Joe Glass - Film Commissioner

CALIFORNIA

California Film Commission
7080 Hollywood Blvd., Ste. 900
Hollywood, CA 90028
Phone 323-860-2960
800-858-4749
Fax 323-860-2972
www.film.ca.gov
www.cinemascout.com
www.filmcafirst.com
Karen R. Constine - Director

COLORADO

Colorado Tourism Office – Film Support
www.coloradofilm.org

CONNECTICUT

Connecticut Film, Video & Media Office
805 Brook St., Bldg. 4
Rocky Hill, CT 06067
Phone 860-571-7130
800-392-2122
Fax 860-721-7088
www.ctfilm.com
Guy Ortoleva - Executive Director

DELAWARE

Delaware Film Office
Delaware Tourism Office
99 Kings Highway
Dover, DE 19901
Phone 302-739-4271,x6823
Fax 302-739-5749
www.state.de.us/dedo
Cheryl Heiks - Film Office Coordinator

DISTRICT OF COLUMBIA

Office of Motion Picture & TV Development
441 Fourth St. NW,
Ste. 760 North
Washington, DC 20001
Phone 202-727-6608
Fax 202-727-3246
www.film.dc.gov
Crystal Palmer - Director

FLORIDA

Governor's Office of Film & Entertainment
Executive Office of the Governor
400 S. Monroe St., Ste. 2002
Tallahassee, FL 32399-0001
Phone 850-410-4765
877-352-3456
818-508-7772 (LA Office)
Fax 850-410-4770
www.filminflorida.com
Susan Albershardt – Film Commissioner

GEORGIA

Georgia Department of Film, Video & Music
285 Peachtree Center Ave.,
Ste. 1000
Atlanta, GA 30303
Phone 404-656-3591
877-746-6842
Fax 404-656-3565
www.filmgeorgia.org
Greg Torre - Director

HAWAII

Hawaii Film Office (State of Hawaii)
250 S. Hotel St., 5th Fl.
Honolulu, HI 96813
Phone 808-586-2570
Fax 808-586-2572
Email info@hawaiifilmoffice.com
www.hawaiifilmoffice.com
Donne Dawson – Film Commissioner

Maui County Film Office (Islands of Maui, Molokai, Lanai)
200 S. High St., 6th Fl.
Wailuku, HI 96793
Phone 808-270-7415
Fax 808-270-7995
Email info@filmmaui.com
www.filmmaui.com
Benita Brazier - Film Commissioner

Honolulu Film Office (Island of Oahu)
530 S. King St., Rm. 306
Honolulu, HI 96813
Phone: 808-527-6108
Fax: 808-527-6102
Email info@filmhonolulu.com
www.filmhonolulu.com
Walea Constantinau – Film Commissioner

Kauai Film Commision (Island of Kauai)
4444 Rice St., Ste, 200
Lihue, HI 96766
Phone 808-241-6386
Fax 808-241-6399
Email info@filmkauai.com
www.filmkauai.com
Tiffani Lizama – Film Commissioner

Big Island Film Office (Island of Hawaii)
25 Aupuni St., Rm 219
Hilo, HI 96720
Phone 808-326-2663
Fax 808-935-1205
Email film@bigisland.com
www.filmbigisland.com
Marilyn Killeri – Film Commissioner

IDAHO

Idaho Film Bureau
700 W. State St.
PO Box 83720
Boise, ID 83720-0093
Phone 208-334-2470
800-942-8338
Fax 208-334-2631
www.filmidaho.com
Peg Owens - Director

ILLINOIS

Illinois Film Office
100 W. Randolph, Ste. 3-400
Chicago, IL 60601
Phone 312-814-3600
Fax 312-814-8874
www.filmillinois.state.il.us
Brenda Sexton – Film Commissioner

INDIANA

Indiana Film Commission
Indiana Department of Commerce
1 N. Capitol Ave., Ste. 700
Indianapolis, IN 46204-2288
Phone 317-232-8829
Fax 317-233-6887
www.filmindiana.com
Jane Rulon - Director

IOWA

Iowa Film Office
200 E. Grand Ave.
Des Moines, IA 50309
Phone 515-242-4726
Fax 515-242-4809
www.state.ia.us/film
Wendol Jarvis - Contact

KANSAS

Kansas Film Commission
1000 SW Jackson, Ste. 100
Topeka, KS 66612
Phone 785-296-2178
888-701-FILM
Fax 785-296-3490
Email pjasso@kansascommerce.com
www.filmkansas.com
Peter Jasso - Film Commissioner

KENTUCKY

Kentucky Film Commission
500 Mero St.
2200 Capitol Plaza Tower
Frankfort, KY 40601
Phone 502-564-3456
800-345-6591
Fax 502-564-7588
www.kyfilmoffice.com
Todd Cassidy - Director

LOUISIANA

Louisiana Film Commission
PO Box 94185
Baton Rouge, LA 70804-4320
Phone 225-342-8150
888-655-0447
Fax 225-342-5349
www.lafilm.org
Mark Smith - Film Commissioner

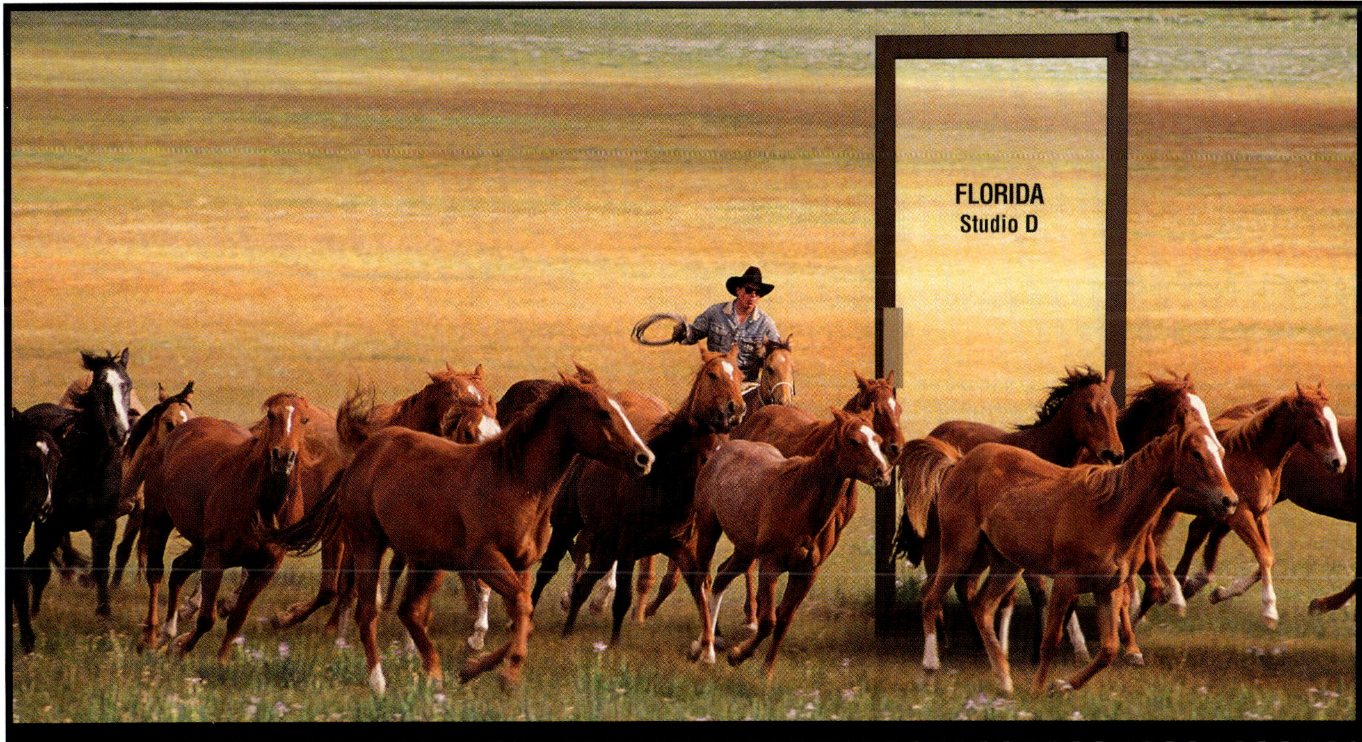

Governor's Office of Film and Entertainment
Toll Free (877) FLA-FILM • (818) 508-7772

MAINE

Maine Film Office
59 State House Station
Augusta, ME 04333
Phone 207-624-7631
Fax 207-287-8070
www.filminmaine.com
Lea Girardin - Director

MARYLAND

Maryland Film Office
217 E. Redwood St.
Baltimore, MD 21202
Phone 410-767-6340
800-333-6632
410-767-0067 (Hotline)
Fax 410-333-0044
Email filminfo@marylandfilm.org
www.marylandfilm.org
Jack Gerbes - Director

MASSACHUSETTS

Massachusetts Sports & Entertainment Commission
One Fleet Center Pl., Ste. 200
Boston, MA 02114
Phone 617-624-1237
Fax 617-624-1239
Email info@masportsandfilm.org
www.masportsandfilm.org
Marc R. Drago – President

MICHIGAN

Michigan Film Office
702 W. Kalamazoo St.
Lansing, MI 48915
Phone 517-373-0638
800-477-3456
Fax 517-241-2930
www.michigan.gov/hal
Janet Lockwood - Director

MINNESOTA

Minnesota Film & TV Board
401 N. Third St., Ste. 460
Minneapolis, MN 55401
Phone 612-332-6493
Fax 612-332-3735
www.mnfilm.org
Craig Rice - Executive Director

MISSISSIPPI

Mississippi Film Office
PO Box 849
Jackson, MS 39205
Phone 601-359-3297
Fax 601-359-5048
www.visitmississippi.org/film
Ward Emling - Manager

MISSOURI

Missouri Film Commission
301 W. High St., Ste. 720
PO Box 118
Jefferson City, MO 65102
Phone 573-751-9050
Fax 573-522-1719
www.missouridevelopment.org/film
Jerry Jones - Director

MONTANA

Montana Film Office
301 S. Park Ave.
Helena, MT 59620
Phone 406-841-2876
800-553-4563
Fax 406-841-2877
www.montanafilm.com
Sten Iversen - Director

NEBRASKA

Nebraska Film Office
PO Box 94666
301 Centennial Mall South, 4th Fl.
Lincoln, NE 68509-4666
Phone 402-471-3680
800-228-6505
Fax 402-471-3365
www.filmnebraska.org
Laurie J. Richards - Nebraska Film Officer

NEVADA

Nevada Film Office
555 E. Washington Ave., Ste. 5400
Las Vegas, NV 89101
Phone 702-486-2711
877-638-3456
Fax 702-486-2712
Email lvnfo@bizopp.state.nv.us
www.nevadafilm.com
Charles Geocaris - Director

NEW HAMPSHIRE

New Hampshire Film & Television Office
172 Pembroke Rd.
PO Box 1856
Concord, NH 03302-1856
Phone 603-271-2665
Fax 603-271-6870
www.filmnh.org

NEW JERSEY

New Jersey Motion Picture & Television Commission
153 Halsey St., 5th Fl.
PO Box 47023
Newark, NJ 07101
Phone 973-648-6279
Fax 973-648-7350
www.njfilm.org
Joseph Friedman - Executive Director

FrameForge 3D Studio

DON'T DRAW YOUR STORYBOARDS – DIRECT THEM!

Communicate your vision like never before. Easily create realistic 3D storyboards in a virtual set or exterior location as if you were actually shooting your project, but without the pressures of an expensive cast and crew waiting for your next setup.

- ★ **Props and characters move as easily as pieces on a chess board**
- ★ **Complete Pose Control** lets the user define and store exactly the pose they want
- ★ **Intuitive Set Building** with walls, doors, windows, etc that can be stored for reuse in other projects
- ★ **Multiple Camera Views** easily place, set and display multiple angle shots
- ★ **Camera Movement Controls** pan/tilt/dolly/zoom
- ★ **Shot Information** includes camera height and zoom settings
- ★ **Customizable movement arrows and frame boxes**
- ★ **Storyboard to script linking**

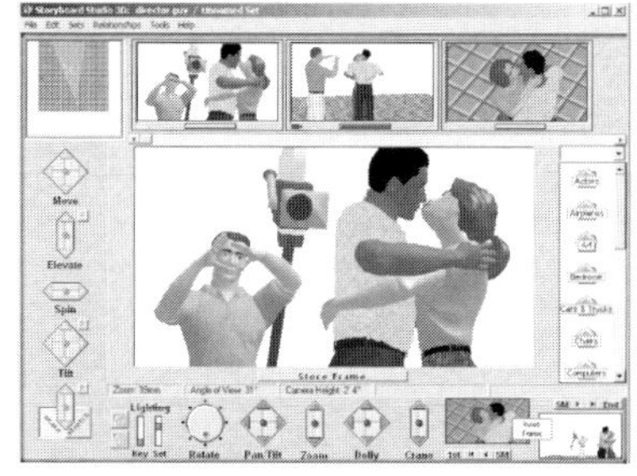
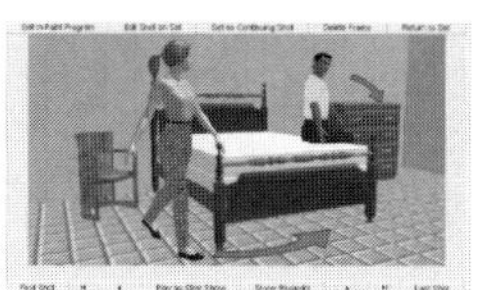
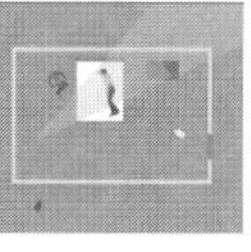

Retail Price $349.00

Save An Additional 10% When You Mention
Promotional Code HCDP51 - Expires 6/30/04

The Only Store Dedicated to the Art of Filmmaking!
WritersStore.com 800.272.8927
2040 Westwood., Los Angeles, CA 90025

A BETTER BRAND *of* LOCATIONS
(800) 553-4563 • MONTANAFILM@VISITMT.COM
WWW.MONTANAFILM.COM

NEW MEXICO

New Mexico Film Office
1100 St. Francis Dr., Ste. 1200
Santa Fe, NM 87505
Phone 505-827-9810
800-545-9871
Fax 505-827-9799
www.nmfilm.com
Frank Zuniga - Director

NEW YORK

New York State Governor's Office for Motion Picture and Television Department
633 Third Ave., 33rd Fl.
New York, NY 10017
Phone 212-803-2330
Fax 212-803-2339
www.nylovesfilm.com/index.asp
Pat Swinney Kaufman - Deputy Commissioner/Director

New York City Mayor's Office of Film, Theatre & Broadcasting
1697 Broadway, Ste. 602
New York, NY 10019
Phone 212-489-6710
Fax 212-307-6237
Email info@film.nyc.gov
www.nyc.gov/film
Katherine Oliver - Commissioner

NORTH CAROLINA

North Carolina Film Office
4324 Mail Service Center
Raleigh, NC 27699-4324
Phone 919-733-9900
800-232-9227
Fax 919-715-0151
www.ncfilm.com
Bill Arnold – Film Commissioner

NORTH DAKOTA

North Dakota Film Commission
1600 E. Century Ave., Ste. 2
Bismarck, ND 58503
Phone 701-328-2525
Fax 701-328-4878
www.ndtourism.com
Sara Otte Coleman – Film Commissioner

OHIO

Ohio Film Commission
77 S. High St., 29th Fl.
Columbus, OH 43215
Phone 614-466-2284
800-230-3523
Fax 614-466-6744
www.ohiofilm.com
Steve Cover - State Film Commissioner

OKLAHOMA

Oklahoma Film Commission
15 N. Robinson, Ste. 802
Oklahoma City, OK 73102
Phone 405-522-6760
800-766-3456
Fax 405-522-0656
www.oklahomafilm.org
Dino Lalli - Director

OREGON

Oregon Film & Video Office
One World Trade Center
121 SW Salmon St., Ste. 1205
Portland, OR 97204
Phone 503-229-5832
Fax 503-229-6869
www.oregonfilm.org
Veronica Rinard - Executive Director

PENNSYLVANIA

Pennsylvania Film Office
Commonwealth Keystone Bldg.
400 North St., 4th Fl.
Harrisburg, PA 17120-0225
Phone 717-783-3456
Fax 717-787-0687
www.filminpa.com
Brian Kreider - Director

PUERTO RICO

Puerto Rico Film Commission
355 F.D. Roosevelt Ave., Ste. 106
Hato Rey, PR 00918
Phone 787-754-7110
787-758-4747, x2251
Fax 787-756-5706
www.puertoricofilm.com
Laura A. Velez - Executive Director

RHODE ISLAND

Rhode Island Film & TV Office
RI Economic Development Corporation
One W. Exchange St.
Providence, RI 02903
Phone 401-222-2601
Fax 401-273-8270
www.rifilm.com
Rick Smith - Director

SOUTH CAROLINA

South Carolina Film Commission
1201 Main St., Ste. 1600
Columbia, SC 29201
Phone 803-737-0490
Fax 803-737-3104
Email scfilmoffice@sccommerce.com
www.scfilmoffice.com
Jeff Monks – Film Commissioner

SOUTH DAKOTA

South Dakota Film Office
711 E. Wells Ave.
Pierre, SD 57501
Phone 605-773-3301
Fax 605-773-3256
www.filmsd.com
Chris Hull - Manager

TENNESSEE

Tennessee Film, Entertainment and Music Commission
312 Eighth Avenue N.,
Tennessee Tower, 9th Fl.
Nashville, TN 37243
Phone 615-741-3456
877-818-3456
Fax 615-741-5554
www.filmtennessee.com
David Bennett - Executive Director

TEXAS

Texas Film Commission
PO Box 13246
Austin, TX 78711
Phone 512-463-9200
Fax 512-463-4114
www.texasfilmcommission.com
Tom Copeland - Director

UTAH

Utah Film Commission
324 S. State St., Ste. 500
Salt Lake City, UT 84111
Phone 801-538-8740
800-453-8824
Fax 801-538-8746
www.film.utah.org
Leigh von der Esch - Executive Director

filmbigisland.com
808 326-2663

The Film Offices of the Hawaiian Islands

hawaiifilmoffice.com 808 586-2570
filmhonolulu.com 808 527-6108
filmkauai.com 808 241-6386
filmmaui.com 808 270-7415

Waikoloa: Big Island: Hawaii
Photography: G. Brad Lewis

One Goal.

Millions of Competitors.

Only the Strong Survive.

Scr(i)ptXpert

Prepare for battle.

- Professional script coverage and brutally honest feedback
- Free access to Producers, Agents and Managers
- Analysis, notes and review by top industry professionals
- All screenplay/teleplay formats welcome
- Fast turnaround and reasonable rates

See our web site, **www.scriptxpert.com,** for more details.

VERMONT

Vermont Film Commission
10 Baldwin St., Drawer #33
Montpelier, VT 05633-2001
Phone 802-828-3618
Fax 802-828-0607
www.vermontfilm.com
Danis Regal - Executive Director

VIRGINIA

Virginia Film Office
901 E. Byrd St.
Richmond, VA 23219-4048
Phone 804-371-8204
800-854-6233
Fax 804-371-8177
www.film.virginia.org
Rita McClenny - Director

WASHINGTON

Washington State Film Office
2001 Sixth Ave., Ste. 2600
Seattle, WA 98121
Phone 206-256-6151
Fax 206-256-6154
www.filmwashington.com
Suzy Kellett - Director

WEST VIRGINIA

West Virginia Film Office
c/o West Virginia Division of Tourism
90 MacCorkle Ave. SW
South Charleston, WV 25303
Phone 304-558-2200
800-225-5982
Fax 304-558-0108
www.wvdo.org
Pamela Haynes - Director

WISCONSIN

Wisconsin Film Office
201 W. Washington Ave., 2nd Fl.
Madison, WI 53703
Phone 800-345-6947
Fax 608-266-3403
www.filmwisconsin.org
Sarah Klavas - Director, Marketing

WYOMING

Wyoming Film Office
I-25 @ College Dr.
Cheyenne, WY 82002
Phone 307-777-3400
800-458-6657
Fax 307-777-2877
www.wyomingfilm.org
Michell Phelan - Manager

INTERNATIONAL FILM COMMISSIONS

AUSTRALIA

AusFILM
2049 Century Plaza East, 19th Fl.
Los Angeles, CA 90067
Phone 310-229-4833
Fax 310-277-2258
Email tracey.montgomery@austrade.gov.au
www.ausfilm.com.au
Tracey Montgomery – Film Commissioner, L.A.

Melbourne Film Office
GPO Box 4361
Melbourne, Victoria 3001
Australia
Phone 61-3-9660-3240
Fax 61-3-9660-3201
www.film.vic.gov.au/info
Caroline Pitcher – General Manager

New South Wales Film & Television Office
GPO Box 1744
Sydney, New South Wales 2001
Australia
Phone 61-2-9264-6400
Fax 61-2-9264-4388
www.fto.nsw.gov.au
Garry Brennan – Film Commissioner

Pacific Film & Television Commission
PO Box 94, Albert St.
Brisbane, Queensland 4002
Australia
Phone 61-7-3224-4161
Fax 61-7-3224-6717
www.pftc.com.au

South Australian Film Corporation
3 Butler Dr., Hendon Common
Hendon, South Australia 5014
Australia
Phone 61-8-8348-9300
Fax 61-8-8347-0385
Email safilm@safilm.com.au
www.safilm.com.au
Nadine Hewson – Promotions & Media Liaison Officer

CANADA

Alberta Film Commission
5th Fl., Commerce Pl.
10155 – 102 St.
Edmonton, Alberta
T5J 4L6 Canada
Phone 780-422-8584
Fax 780-422-8582
www.albertafilm.ca
Dan Chugg – Film Commissioner

British Columbia Film Commision
201-865 Hornby St.
Vancouver, British Columbia
V6Z 2G3 Canada
Phone 604-660-2732
Fax 604-660-4790
www.bcfilm.bc.ca
Susan Croome – Film Commissioner

Thompson-Nicola Film Commission
300-465 Victoria St.
Kamloops, British Columbia
V2C 2A9 Canada
Phone 250-377-8673
Toll Free BC 1-877-377-8673
Fax 250-372-5048
Cell 250-319-6211
Email vweller@tnrd.bc.ca
www.tnrd.bc.ca
Victoria Weller – Executive Director of Film

Montréal Film and TV Commission
303 Notre-Dame Street East, 6th Fl.
Montréal, Québec H2Y 3Y8
Canada
Phone 514-872-2883
Fax 514-872-3409
www.montrealfilm.com
Daniel Bissonnette – Film Commissioner

Toronto Film and Television Office
Toronto City Hall
100 Queen Street West, Main Fl., West Side
Toronto, Ontario M5H 2N2
Canada
Phone 416-392-7570
Fax 416-392-0675
www.torontofilm.permits.com
Rhonda Silverstone – Film Commissioner

FRANCE

Commission Nationale du Film France
30, Avenue de Messine
Paris 75008 France
Phone 33-1-5383-9898
Fax 33-1-5383-9899
www.filmfrance.com
Benoit Caron – Executive Director

filmhonolulu.com
808 527-6108

The Film Offices of the Hawaiian Islands

hawaiifilmoffice.com 808 586-2570
filmbigisland.com 808 326-2663
filmkauai.com 808 241-6386
filmmaui.com 808 270-7415

As close as far away gets.
Kaaawa Valley: Honolulu: Hawaii
Photography: John DeMello

David Benioff
Fade In Enthusiast

FADE IN
THE FIRST WORD IN FILM
www.fadeinonline.com

ENTERTAINMENT PARTNERS

Offering Solutions for the Entertainment Industry

Los Angeles
Tokyo
Vancouver
Central Casting
New York
Orlando
London
Toronto

Movie Magic's Newest Releases,
EP Budgeting and EP Scheduling

Global Vista Accounting
Vista Exchange
Petty Cash Card
Virtual Production Office

Production Payroll
Music Payroll
Residual Payments
Talent Payments
Commercial Payroll
The Paymaster
Central Casting

You are always in the EP picture.

Give us a call or come visit.

We want to hear from you.

www.entertainmentpartners.com - Los Angeles 818.955.6000 - New York 646.473.9000 - Orlando 407.354.5900

creativescreenwriting PRESENTS

Screenwriting 

November 5-7, 2004

LOS ANGELES CONVENTION CENTER

"The best screenwriting event I ever attended, and I've been to more than a few."
—Richard Walter, chairman of UCLA Film Department

"The Expo is exactly the kind of thing they didn't have when I was coming up. I wish to hell that they had."
—Jeff Arch (Sleepless in Seattle)

"...a carnival for the aspiring screenwriter."
—The New Yorker

World's Largest Screenwriting Conference—Over 250 seminars, workshops, and panel discussions on every aspect of writing and selling your script. Something for everyone—seminars for "Beginning," "Advanced" and "Professional" writers.

Guests of Honor—A new guest of honor every two hours. Expo 2 guests included William Goldman, Aaron Sorkin, Andrew Kevin Walker, Gary Ross, Shane Black, Tom Schulman, Mike Medavoy and many others.

Pitch Your Script or Idea—Pitch your projects to more than 60 producers, development executives, managers and agents!

The "Creative Screenwriting Open"—A three-day screenwriting tournament held right at the Expo, the CS Open could jumpstart your Hollywood career. The winner receives $2,000 cash, agency consideration and other prizes.

Register now for first opportunity to register for seminars and workshops.

Complete Information at screenwritingexpo.com

SCREENWRITING EXPO 3 IS SPONSORED BY

ScreenStyle.com
THE SCREENWRITING STORE

GERMANY

Berlin Brandenburg Film Commission
August-Bebel-Str. 26-53
Potsdam-Babelsberg D-14482
Germany
Phone 49-331-743-8730
Fax 49-331-743-8799
www.filmboard.de
Christiane Raab – Film Commissioner

ITALY

Italian Film Commission
1801 Avenue of the Stars, Ste. 700
Los Angeles, CA 90067
Phone 323-879-0950
Fax 310-203-8335
www.filminginitaly.com
Celi Zullo – Film Commissioner

NEW ZEALAND

Film New Zealand
23 Frederick St.
PO Box 24142
Wellington, New Zealand
Phone 64-4-385-0766
Fax 64-4-384-5840
Eamil info@filmnz.org.nz
www.filmnz.com
Judith McCann - CEO

UNITED KINGDOM

British Film Commission
10 Little Portland St.
London W1W 7JG UK
Phone 44-020-7861-7860
Fax 44-020-7861-7864
Email info@ukfilmcouncil-us.org
www.ukfilmcouncil-us.org
www.bfc.co.uk
Steve Norris – Film Commissioner

London Film Commission
20 Euston Centre
London NW1 3JH UK
Phone 44-020-7387-8787
Fax 44-020-7387-8788
www.london-film.co.uk
Sue Hayes – Film Commissioner

UK Film Council, U.S.
8533 Melrose Ave., Ste. C
Los Angeles, CA 90060
Phone 310-652-6169
Fax 310-652-6232
Email film@ukfilmcouncil-usa.org
www.britfilmusa.com
Susna Finalyson-Stich – Director

GUILDS, UNIONS, AND ASSOCIATIONS

Academy of Motion Picture Arts and Sciences (AMPAS)
www.oscars.org
Honorary organization of motion picture professionals founded to advance the arts and sciences of motion pictures.
8949 Wilshire Blvd.
Beverly Hills, CA 90211-1972
Phone 310-247-3000
Fax 310-859-9351
310-859-9619

Academy of Television Arts & Sciences (ATAS)
www.emmys.tv
Nonprofit corporation for the advancement of telecommunications arts and sciences.
5220 Lankershim Blvd.
North Hollywood, CA 91601
Phone 818-754-2800
Fax 818-761-2827

Academy Players Directory
www.playersdirectory.com
Print and online casting directories.
1313 N. Vine St.
Hollywood, CA 90028
Phone 310-247-3058
Fax 310-550-5034
Email players@oscars.org
Su Hyatt – Associate Editor

Actors' Equity Association (AEA)
www.actorsequity.org
Labor union representing US actors and stage managers working in the professional theater.

Chicago
125 S. Clark St., Ste. 1500
Chicago, IL 60603
Phone 312-641-0393
Fax 312-641-6365

Los Angeles
Museum Square
5757 Wilshire Blvd., Ste. 1
Los Angeles, CA 90036
Phone 323-634-1750
Fax 323-634-1777

Orlando
10319 Orangewood Blvd.
Orlando, FL 32821
Phone 407-345-8600
Fax 407-345-1522

New York
National Headquarters
165 W. 46th St., 15th Fl.
New York, NY 10036
Phone 212-869-8530
Fax 212-719-9815

San Francisco
350 Sansome St., Ste. 900
San Francisco, CA 94104
Phone 415-391-3838
Fax 415-391-0102

Actors' Fund of America
www.actorsfund.org
Nonprofit organization providing for the social welfare of entertainment professionals.

Chicago
203 N. Wabash Ave., Ste. 2104
Chicago, IL 60601
Phone 312-372-0989
Fax 312-372-0272

Los Angeles
5757 Wilshire Blvd., Ste. 400
Los Angeles, CA 90036
Phone 323-933-9244
Fax 323-933-7615

New York
729 Seventh Ave., 10th Fl.
New York, NY 10019
Phone 212-221-7300
Fax 212-764-0238

Actors' Work Program
www.actorsfund.org
Career counseling for members of the Actors' Fund of America.

Los Angeles
5757 Wilshire Blvd., Ste. 400
Los Angeles, CA 90036
Phone 323-933-9244
Fax 323-933-7615

New York
729 Seventh Ave.
New York, NY 10019
Phone 212-354-5480
Fax 212-921-4295

Alliance of Canadian Cinema, Television & Radio Artists (ACTRA)
www.actra.ca
Labor union founded to negotiate, safeguard, and promote the professional rights of Canadian performers working in film, television, video, and all recorded media.
625 Church St., 3rd Fl.
Toronto, Ontario M4Y 2G1
Canada
Phone 800-387-3516
416-489-1311
Fax 416-489-8076

filmkauai.com
808 241-6386

The Film Offices of the Hawaiian Islands

hawaiifilmoffice.com 808 586-2570
filmbigisland.com 808 326-2663
filmhonolulu.com 808 527-6108
filmmaui.com 808 270-7415

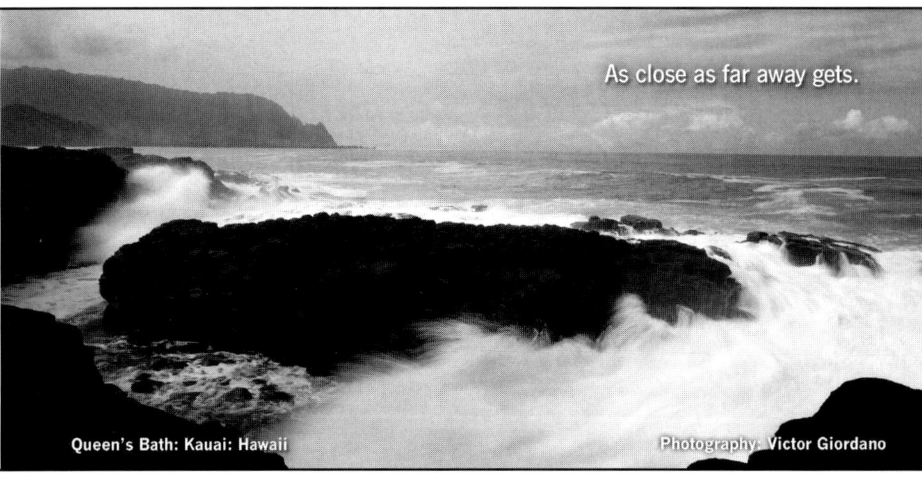

As close as far away gets.
Queen's Bath: Kauai: Hawaii
Photography: Victor Giordano

Get The Tools To Make Your Video Business More Successful

DIGITAL VIDEO EXPO WEST 2004
December 7-10, 2004
Los Angeles Convention Center
Los Angeles, CA

DIGITAL VIDEO EXPO EAST 2005
July 19-21, 2005
Jacob K. Javitz Convention Center
New York, NY

EXPO

For more information visit DV.EXPO.COM
Register with Priority Code HCD and save $10

Alliance of Motion Picture & Television Producers (AMPTP)
www.amptp.org
Trade association involved with labor issues within the motion picture and television industries.
15503 Ventura Blvd.
Encino, CA 91436
Phone 818-995-3600
Fax 818-382-1793

American Cinema Editors (ACE)
www.ace-filmeditors.org
Honorary society made up of editors deemed to be outstanding in their field.
100 Universal City Plaza,
Bldg. 2282, Rm. 234
Universal City, CA 91608
Phone 818-777-2900
Fax 818-733-5023

American Cinematheque at the Egyptian & Aero Theatres
www.egyptiantheatre.com
www.americancinematheque.com
Nonprofit cultural arts organization programming specialty film series at the Egyptian Theatre.
1800 N. Highland Ave., Ste. 717
Hollywood, CA 90028
Phone 323-461-2020
323-466-3456
(24-hour recorded information)
Fax 323-461-9737
Margot Gerber – Marketing & Publicity Manager

American Federation of Film Producers (AFFP)
www.filmfederation.com
Trade organization of creative professionals committed to excellence in filmmaking.
3000 W. Alameda Ave., Ste. 1585
Burbank, CA 91523
Phone 818-840-4924

American Federation of Musicians (AFM)
www.afm.org
Labor union representing professional musicians.

Los Angeles
3550 Wilshire Blvd., Ste. 1900
Los Angeles, CA 90010
Phone 213-251-4510
Fax 213-251-4520

New York
1501 Broadway, Ste. 600
New York, NY 10036
Phone 212-869-1330
Fax 212-764-6134

American Federation of Television & Radio Artists (AFTRA)
www.aftra.org
Labor organization representing broadcast performers.

Los Angeles
5757 Wilshire Blvd., Ste. 900
Los Angeles, CA 90036
Phone 323-634-8100
Fax 323-634-8126
Christopher de Haven - Contact

New York
260 Madison Ave., 7th Fl.
New York, NY 10016
Phone 212-532-0800
Fax 212-532-2242

American Film Institute (AFI)
www.afi.com
Organization dedicated to preserving and advancing the art of the moving image through events, exhibitions and education.

Los Angeles
2021 N. Western Ave.
Los Angeles, CA 90027
Phone 323-856-7600
Fax 323-467-4578

American Film Institute (AFI) (continued)

Washington, DC
The John F. Kennedy Center for the Performing Arts
Washington, DC 20566
Phone 202-833-2348
Fax 202-659-1970

American Guild of Musical Artists (AGMA)
www.musicalartists.org
Union representing classical artists, opera singers, ballet dancers, stage managers, and stage directors.
1430 Broadway, 14th Fl.
New York, NY 10018
Phone 212-265-3687
Fax 212-262-9088

American Guild of Variety Artists (AGVA)
Labor union representing performers in Broadway, off-Broadway, and cabaret productions, as well as theme park and nightclub performers.

Los Angeles
4741 Laurel Canyon Blvd., Ste. 208
North Hollywood, CA 91607
Phone 818-508-9984
Fax 818-508-3029

New York
363 Seventh Ave., 17th Fl.
New York, NY 10001
Phone 212-675-1003
Fax 212-633-0097

American Humane Association (AHA)
www.ahafilm.org
Watchdog organization dedicated to preventing cruelty to animal actors performing in films and television.
Western Regional Office
Film and Television Unit
15366 Dickens St.
Sherman Oaks, CA 91403
Phone 818-501-0123
800-677-3420 (Hotline)
Fax 818-501-8725

American Screenwriters Association (ASA)
www.goasa.com
Nonprofit organization promoting and encouraging the art of screenwriting as well as the support and advancement of screenwriters.
269 S. Beverly Dr., Ste. 2600
Beverly Hills, CA 90212-3807
Phone 866-265-9091

American Society of Cinematographers (ASC)
www.theasc.com
Union representing professional cinematographers, dedicated to improving the quality of motion picture presentation.
1782 N. Orange Dr.
Hollywood, CA 90028
Phone 323-969-4333
800-448-0145
Fax 323-882-6391

filmmaui.com
808 270-7415

The Film Offices of the Hawaiian Islands
hawaiifilmoffice.com 808 586-2570
filmbigisland.com 808 326-2663
filmhonolulu.com 808 527-6108
filmkauai.com 808 241-6386

As close as far away gets.
Jaws: Maui: Hawaii
Photography: Rob Ratkowki

You write the million dollar spec

we'll provide the inspiration

"...I constantly find myself hopelessly driving around, looking for a good, inspiring place to work. theOffice™ seems to be a Godsend. Finally I'll have a destination."

- J.J. Abrams (creator/exec. producer "Alias" & "Felicity")

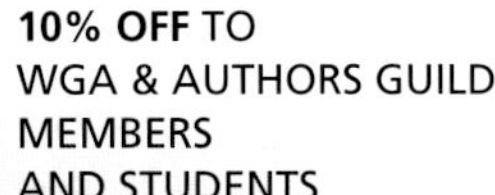

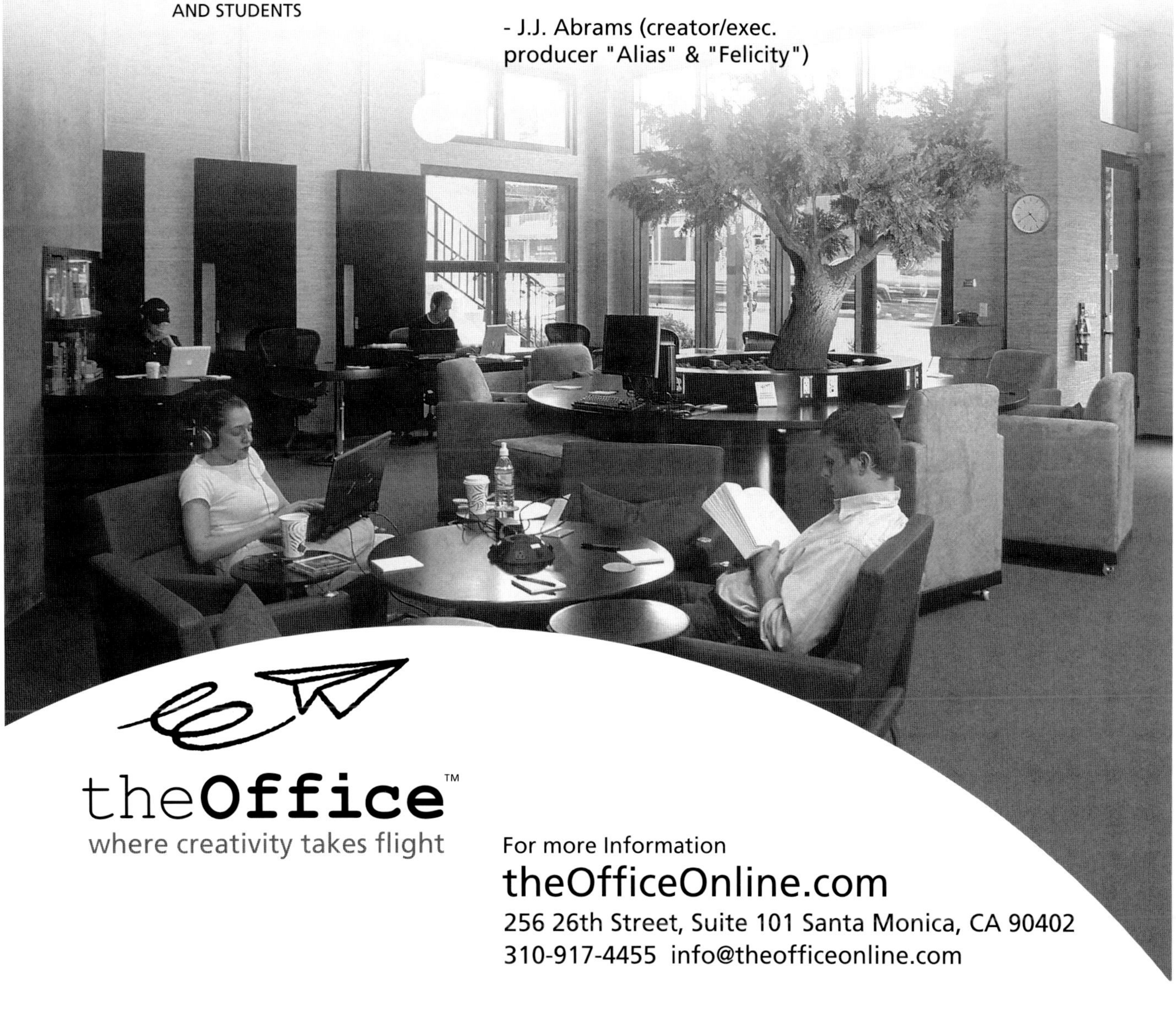

theOffice™
where creativity takes flight

For more Information
theOfficeOnline.com
256 26th Street, Suite 101 Santa Monica, CA 90402
310-917-4455 info@theofficeonline.com

American Society of Composers, Authors & Publishers (ASCAP)
www.ascap.com
Performing rights organization representing composers, lyricists, songwriters, and music publishers.

Los Angeles
7920 W. Sunset Blvd., 3rd Fl.
Los Angeles, CA 90046
Phone 323-883-1000
Fax 323-883-1049

Nashville
2 Music Square West
Nashville, TN 37203
Phone 615-742-5000
Fax 615-742-5020

New York
One Lincoln Plaza
New York, NY 10023
Phone 212-621-6000
Fax 212-724-9064

American Society of Journalists & Authors (ASJA)
www.asja.org
Organization of independent nonfiction writers.
1501 Broadway, Ste. 302
New York, NY 10036
Phone 212-997-0947
Fax 212-768-7414

American Society of Media Photographers (ASMP)
www.asmp.org
Trade organization dedicated to protecting and promoting the interests and high professional standards of photographers whose work is for publication.
150 N. Second St.
Philadelphia, PA 19106
Phone 215-451-2767
Fax 215-451-0880

American Women in Radio & Television, Inc. (AWRT)
www.awrt.org
National organization supporting the advancement of women in the communications industry.
8405 Greensboro Dr., Ste. 800
McLean, VA 22102
Phone 703-506-3290
Fax 703-506-3266

Art Directors Guild & Scenic, Title and Graphic Artists
www.ialocal800.org
Organization representing production designers, art directors, assitant art directors and scenic, title and graphic designers.
Local 800 I.A.T.S.E.
11969 Ventura Blvd., Ste. 200
Studio City, CA 91604
Phone 818-762-9995
Fax: 818-762-9997
Lydia Zimmer – Office Manager

Association of Film Commissioners International (AFCI)
www.afci.org
Organization providing representation and support to member film commissions.
314 N. Main, Ste. 308
Helena, MT 59601
Phone 406-495-8040
323-462-6092 (LA)
Fax 406-495-8039
323-462-6091 (LA)
Email info@afci.org
Bill Lindstrom - CEO

Association of Independent Commercial Producers (AICP)
www.aicp.com
Organization representing interests of US companies that specialize in producing commercials in various media (film, video, Internet, etc.) for advertisers and agencies.

Los Angeles
650 N. Bronson Ave., Ste. 223B
Los Angeles, CA 90004
Phone 323-960-4763
Fax 323-960-4766
Farah Fima – Office Manager

New York
3 W. 18th St., 5th Fl.
New York, NY 10011
Phone 212-929-3000
Fax 212-929-3359

Association of Independent Video and Filmmakers (AIVF)
www.aivf.org
Nonprofit membership organization serving local and international film and videomakers, including documentarians and experimental artists.
304 Hudson St., 6th Fl.
New York, NY 10013
Phone 212-807-1400
Fax 212-463-8519
Email info@aivf.org
Bo Mehrad – Info Services Director

Association of Talent Agents (ATA)
www.agentassociation.com
Nonprofit trade association for talent agencies representing clients in the motion picture and television industries, as well as literary, theater, radio, and commercial clients.
9255 Sunset Blvd., Ste. 930
Los Angeles, CA 90069
Phone 310-274-0628
Fax 310-274-5063
Shellie Jetton – Administrative Director

Authors Guild, The
www.authorsguild.org
Society dedicated to advocacy for fair compensation, free speech, and copyright protection for published authors.
31 E. 28th St., 10th Fl.
New York, NY 10016
Phone 212-563-5904
Fax 212-564-5363

Black Filmmaker Foundation (BFF), The
www.dvrepublic.org
Nonprofit organization of emerging Black filmmakers.
670 Broadway, Ste. 300
New York, NY 10012
Phone 212-253-1690
Fax 212-253-1689

Breakdown Services
www.breakdownservices.com
Communications network and casting system providing integrated tools for casting directors and talent representatives, as well as casting information for actors.

Los Angeles
2140 Cotner Ave.
Los Angeles, CA 90025
Phone 310-276-9166

New York
Phone 212-869-2003

Vancouver
Phone 604-943-7100

Broadcast Music, Inc. (BMI)
www.bmi.com
Nonprofit performing rights organization of songwriters, composers and music publishers.

Los Angeles
8730 Sunset Blvd., 3rd Fl. West
West Hollywood, CA 90069-2211
Phone 310-659-9109
Fax 310-657-6947

Nashville
10 Music Square East
Nashville, TN 37203-4399
Phone 615-401-2000
Fax 615-401-2707

New York
320 W. 57th St.
New York, NY 10019
Phone 212-586-2000
Fax 212-489-2368

California Arts Council (CAC)
www.cac.ca.gov
State organization encouraging artistic awareness, expression, and participation reflecting California's diverse cultures.
1300 I St., Ste. 930
Sacramento, CA 95814
Phone 916-322-6555
800-201-6201
Fax 916-322-6575
Adam Gottlieb – Communications Director

Casting Society of America (CSA)
www.castingsociety.com
Trade organization of professional film and television casting directors.

Los Angeles
606 N. Larchmont Blvd., Ste. 4B
Los Angeles, CA 90004-1309
Phone 323-463-1925
Fax 323-463-5753
Larry Raab – Office Manager

New York
C/O Bernard Telsey
145 W. 28th St., Ste. 12F
New York, NY 10001
Phone 212-868-1260
Fax 212-868-1261

Cinewomen
www.cinewomen.org
Nonprofit organization dedicated to supporting the advancement of women within the motion picture industry.

Los Angeles
9903 Santa Monica Blvd., Ste. 461
Beverly Hills, CA 90212
Phone 310-855-8720

New York
PO Box 1477, Cooper Station
New York, NY 10276
Phone 212-604-4264

Clear, Inc.
www.clearinc.org
Organization of clearance and research professionals working in the film, television, and multimedia industries.
PO Box 628
Burbank, CA 91503-0628
Fax 413-647-3380

Commercial Casting Directors Association (CCDA)
Organization dedicated to providing a level of professionalism for casting directors within the commercial industry.
c/o Jeff Gerard @ Chelsea Studios
11530 Ventura Blvd.
Studio City, CA 91604
Phone 818-782-9900

supported by the Writers Guild of America, west

scriptapalooza tv

television writing competition

accepting pilots, sitcoms and 1 hour dramas

CHANGE THE WAY YOU WATCH TV.

Production companies and agents receive winners
2 past winners have won Daytime Emmys
Another entrant is writing for Comedy Central
We are supported by the WGA, west

DEADLINE IS NOVEMBER 15

www.scriptapalooza.com

info@scriptapalooza.com

323.654.5809 office

"Despite it's frivolous name, Scriptapalooza is the best screenwriting competition I know."

- Robert McKee
Author of STORY

Costume Designers Guild (CDG)
www.costumedesignersguild.com
Union representing motion picture, television, and commercial costume designers. Promotes research, artistry and technical expertise in the field of film and television costume design.
4730 Woodman Ave., Ste. 430
Sherman Oaks, CA 91423
Phone 818-905-1557
Fax 818-905-1560
Email cdgia@earthlink.net
James J. Casey, Jr. – Executive Director

Directors Guild of America (DGA)
www.dga.org
Labor union representing film and television directors, unit production managers, first assistant directors, second assistant directors, technical coordinators, tape associate directors, stage managers and production associates.
Chicago
400 N. Michigan Ave., Ste. 307
Chicago, IL 60611
Phone 888-600-6975
312-644-5050
Fax 312-644-5776
Los Angeles
7920 Sunset Blvd.
Los Angeles, CA 90046
Phone 800-421-4173
310-289-2000
(Main Line)
323-851-3671
(Agency Listing)
Fax 310-289-2029
New York
110 W. 57th St.
New York, NY 10019
Phone 800-356-3754
212-581-0370
Fax 212-581-1441

Dramatists Guild of America, Inc., The
www.dramaguild.com
Professional association of playwrights, composers and lyricists.
1501 Broadway, Ste. 701
New York, NY 10036
Phone 212-398-9366
Fax 212-944-0420

Filmmakers Alliance
www.filmmakersalliance.com
Nonprofit collective of independent filmmakers.
453 S. Spring St.
Los Angeles, CA 90013
Phone 213-228-1152
Fax 213-228-1156

Hispanic Organization of Latin Actors (HOLA)
www.hellohola.org
Arts service organization committed to projecting Hispanic artists and their culture into the mainstream of Anglo-American industry and culture.
107 Suffolk St., Ste. 302
New York, NY 10002
Phone 212-253-1015
Fax 212-253-9651
Email holagram@hellohola.org
Manny Alfaro – Executive Director

Hollywood Radio & Television Society (HRTS)
www.hrts-iba.org
Nonprofit organization made up of West Coast executives from the entertainment (and ancillary) industries, providing mentoring and scholarship programs as well as networking opportunities. Sponsors The International Broadcasting (& Cable) Awards.
13701 Riverside Dr., Ste. 205
Sherman Oaks, CA 91423
Phone 818-789-1182
Fax 818-789-1210

Horror Writers Association
www.horror.org
Worldwide organization of horror and dark fantasy writers and publishing professionals.
PO Box 50577
Palo Alto, CA 94303
Phone 650-322-4610

Humanitas Prize, The
www.humanitasprize.org
Prestigious prizes awarded to film and television writers whose produced scripts communicate values which most enrich the human person.
17575 Pacific Coast Highway
PO Box 861
Pacific Palisades, CA 90272
Phone 310-454-8769
Fax 310-459-6549
Email humanitasmail@aol.com
Enio Sevilla – General Manager

Independent Feature Project (IFP)
www.ifp.org
Nonprofit service organization providing resources and information for independent filmmakers and industry professionals.
Chicago
33 E. Congress Parkway, Ste. 505
Chicago, IL 60605
Phone 312-435-1825
Fax 312-435-1828

Independent Feature Project (IFP) (continued)
Los Angeles (IFP/W)
8750 Wilshire Blvd., 2nd Fl.
Beverly Hills, CA 90211
Phone 310-432-1200
Fax 310-432-1203
Miami
210 Second St.
Miami Beach, FL 33139
Phone 305-538-8242
Minneapolis
401 N. Third St., Ste. 450
Minneapolis, MN 55401
Phone 612-338-0871
Fax 612-338-4747
New York
104 W. 29th St., 12th Fl.
New York, NY 10001-5310
Phone 212-465-8200
Fax 212-465-8525

Independent Film & Television Alliance (IFTA)
www.ifta-online.org
Trade association for the independent film and television industries.
10850 Wilshire Blvd., 9th Fl.
Los Angeles, CA 90024-4321
Phone 310-446-1000
Fax 310-446-1600
Jean Prewitt - President

International Alliance of Theatrical Stage Employees (IATSE)
www.iatse.lm.com
Union representing technicians, artisans and craftpersons in the entertainment industry including live theater, film and television production and trade shows.
Los Angeles
10045 Riverside Dr.
Toluca Lake, CA 91602
Phone 818-980-3499
Fax 818-980-3496
New York
1430 Broadway, 20th Fl.
New York, NY 10018
Phone 212-730-1770
Fax 212-730-7809
212-921-7699

International Press Academy
www.pressacademy.com
Association of professional entertainment journalists.
9601 Wilshire Blvd., Ste. 755
Beverly Hills, CA 90210
Phone 310-550-8209
Fax 310-550-0420
Mirjana Van Blaricom - President

Motion Picture Association Of America (MPAA)
www.mpaa.org
Trade association for the US motion picture, home video and television industries.
15503 Ventura Blvd.
Encino, CA 91436
Phone 818-995-6600
Fax 818-382-1799

Motion Picture Editors Guild
www.editorsguild.com
Union representing motion picture, television, and commercial editors, sound technicians and projectionists and story analysts.
Chicago
6317 N. Northwest Highway
Chicago, IL 60631
Phone 773-594-6598
888-594-6734
Fax 773-594-6599
Los Angeles
7715 Sunset Blvd., Ste. 200
Hollywood, CA 90046
Phone 323-876-4770
Fax 323-876-0861
New York
165 W. 46th St., Ste. 900
New York, NY 10036
Phone 212-302-0700
Fax 212-302-1091

Multicultural Motion Picture Association (MMPA)
www.diversityawards.org
Association promoting and encouraging diversity of ideas, cultures and perspectives in film; sponsor of the annual Diversity Awards.
9244 Wilshire Blvd.
Beverly Hills, CA 90212
Phone 310-285-9743
Fax 310-285-9770

Music Managers Forum (MMF)
www.mmfus.org
Organization dedicated to furthering the interests of managers and their artists in all fields of the music industry including live performance and recording and publishing matters.
PO Box 444, Village Station
New York, NY 10014
Phone 212-213-8787
Fax 212-213-9797

Music Video Production Association (MVPA)
www.mvpa.com
Nonprofit trade organization made up of music video production and post production companies, as well as editors, directors, producers, cinematographers, choreographers, script supervisors, computer animators and make-up artists involved in the production of music videos.
201 N. Occidental Blvd., Bldg. 7 Unit B
Los Angeles, CA 90026
Phone 213-387-1590
Fax 213-385-9507
Email info@mvpa.com
Andrea Clark – Executive Director

Mystery Writers of America (MWA)
www.mysterywriters.org
Organization of published mystery authors, editors, screenwriters, and other professionals in the field. Sponsors symposia, conferences and The Edgar Awards.
17 E. 47th St., 6th Fl.
New York, NY 10017
Phone 212-888-8171
Fax 212-888-8107

Nashville Association of Talent Directors (NATD)
www.n-a-t-d.com
Professional entertainment organization comprised of industry professionals involved in all aspects of the music and entertainment industries.
PO Box 23903
Nashville, TN 37202-3903
Phone 615-662-2200 (x*410)

National Association of Latino Independent Producers (NALIP)
www.nalip.org
Organization of independent Latin film producers.

Los Angeles
2425 E. Olympic Blvd., Ste. 600-E
Santa Monica, CA 90406
Phone 310-857-1657
Fax 310-453-5258

New York
32 Broadway, 14th Fl.
New York, NY 10004
Phone 646-336-6333
Fax 212-727-0549

National Association of Recording Arts & Sciences (NARAS)
www.grammy.com
Organization dedicated to improving the quality of life and cultural condition for musicians, producers, and other recording professionals. Provides outreach, professional development, cultural enrichment, education and human services programs. Sponsors The Grammy Awards.
The Recording Academy
3402 Pico Blvd.
Santa Monica, CA 90405
Phone 310-392-3777
Fax 310-399-3090

National Association of Television Program Executives (NATPE)
www.natpe.org
www.natpeonline.com
Nonprofit association of business professionals who create, develop and distribute content.
2425 Olympic Blvd., Ste. 600E
Santa Monica, CA 90404
Phone 310-453-4440
Fax 310-453-5258

National Conference of Personal Managers (NCOPM)
www.ncopm.com
Association for the advancement of personal managers and their clients.

Palm Desert
PO Box 609
Palm Desert, CA 92261-0609
Phone 760-200-5892
Fax 760-200-5896

New York
41 W. 56th St.
New York, NY 10019
Phone 212-582-1940
Fax 212-582-1942

National Council of La Raza (NCLR)
www.nclr.org
Private, nonprofit, nonpartisan, tax-exempt organization dedicated, in part, to promoting fair, accurate, and balanced portrayals of Latinos in film, television and music. Sponsor of the ALMA Awards.
1111 19th St., Ste. 1000
Washington, DC 20036
Phone 202-785-1670
Fax 202-785-7620

JUMP-START YOUR SCREENWRITING CAREER !
Please don't KISS away your chance to get the latest, up-to-date, and educational news about the screenwriting industry.
SUBSCRIBE TODAY! It's easy. You have 5 different ways to begin receiving the most informative screenwriting magazine in the industry.
HOLLYWOOD SCRIPTWRITER MAGAZINE
****
EMAIL your MasterCard/Visa information: number, expiration, full address and telephone. It's strictly confidential.
editorial@hollywoodscriptwriter.com

CALL us at (310) 530-0000 and we'll take your credit card/debit order over the phone.
FAX us your MasterCard/Visa or Debit order to (310) 530-0000.
LOG ON to www.hollywoodscriptwriter.com and subscribe there.

New Address
MAIL in your subscription form to: Hollywood Scriptwriter magazine, PO Box 11163, Carson, CA 90746

National Music Publishing Association (NMPA)
www.nmpa.org
Organization dedicated to interpreting copyright law, educating the public about licensing, safeguarding the interests of American music publishers, and protecting music copyright across all media and national boundaries.
475 Park Avenue South, 29th Fl.
New York, NY 10016-6901
Phone 646-742-1651
Fax 646-742-1779

Nosotros
www.nosotros.org
Organization established to improve the image of Latinos/Hispanics as they are portrayed in the entertainment industry, both in front of and behind the camera, as well as to expand employment opportunities within the entertainment industry. Sponsor of The Golden Eagle Awards.
650 N. Bronson Ave., Ste. 102
Hollywood, CA 90004
Phone 323-466-8566
Fax 323-466-8540

Organization of Black Screenwriters, Inc., The
www.obswriter.com
Nonprofit organization developing and supporting Black screenwriters.
1968 W. Adams Blvd.
Los Angeles, CA 90018
Phone 323-735-2050
Fax 323-735-2051

PEN
www.pen.org
Nonprofit organization made up of poets, playwrights, essayists, novelists, television writers, screenwriters, critics, historians, editors, journalists, and translators. Dedicated to protecting the rights of writers around the world, to stimulate interest in the written word and to foster a vital literary community.
Pen American Center
568 Broadway, 4th Fl.
New York, NY 10012-3225
Phone 212-334-1660
Fax 212-334-2181

Producers Guild of America (PGA)
www.producersguild.org
Organization representing the interests of all members of the producing team.
8530 Wilshire Blvd., Ste. 450
Beverly Hills, CA 90211
Phone 310-358-9020
Fax 310-358-9520

Recording Musicians Association (RMA)
www.rmala.org
Nonprofit organization of studio musicians and composers.
817 Vine St., Ste. 209
Hollywood, CA 90038-3716
Phone 323-462-4762
Fax 323-462-2406
Ximena Marin – Executive Administrator

Romance Writers of America (RWA)
www.rwanational.org
National nonprofit genre writers' association providing networking and support to published and aspiring romance writers.
16000 Stuebner Airline, Ste. 140
Spring, TX 77379
Phone 832-712-5200
Fax 832-717-5201

Screen Actors Guild (SAG)
www.sag.org
www.castsag.org - Member Contact Information
Union representing actors in feature films, short films and digital projects.

Los Angeles
5757 Wilshire Blvd.
Los Angeles, CA 90036
Phone 323-954-1600
(Main Line)
323-549-6858
(Commercial/Infomercials/ Industrial/Education)
323-549-6811
(Production Services-Extras)
323-549-6864
(Music Entertainment Contracts)
323-549-6835
(Television Contracts)
323-549-6828
(Theatrical Motion Pictures)
323-549-6737
(Actors to Locate)
323-549-6644
(Affirmative Action)
323-549-6745
(Agency/Agent Contracts)
323-549-6540
(Casting Seminars & Showcase Info)
323-549-6755
(Dues Information)
323-549-6773
(Emergency Fund)
323-549-6627
(Legal Affairs)
323-549-6778
(Membership Services)
323-549-6769
(New Memberships)
323-549-6505
(Residuals)
800-205-7716
(Residuals)

Screen Actors Guild (SAG) (continued)
323-549-6869
(Signatory Records)
818-954-9400
(SAG Pension & Health)
323-549-6855
(Stunts/Safety)
323-549-6023
(SAG Jobs Hotline)
323-549-6639
(Young Performers/ Coogan Law)
Fax 323-549-6603

New York
360 Madison Ave., 12th Fl.
New York, NY 10017
Phone 212-944-1030
(Main Line)
212-944-6715
(TTY Line)
Fax 212-944-6774

Scriptwriters Network
www.scriptwritersnetwork.com
Organization providing information and career counseling for film and television writers.
11684 Ventura Blvd., Ste. 508
Studio City, CA 91604
Phone 323-848-9477

SESAC
www.sesac.com
Nonprofit performing rights organization of songwriters, composers and music publishers.

Los Angeles
501 Santa Monica Blvd., Ste. 450
Santa Monica, CA 90401-2430
Phone 310-393-9671
Fax 310-393-6497

Nashville
55 Music Square East
Nashville, TN 37203
Phone 615-320-0055
Fax 615-329-9627

New York
152 W. 57th St., 57th Fl.
New York, NY 10019
Phone 212-586-3450
Fax 212-489-5699

Society of Children's Book Writers & Illustrators (SCBWI)
www.scbwi.org
Professional organization of writers and illustrators of children's books.
8271 Beverly Blvd.
Los Angeles, CA 90048
Phone 323-782-1010
Fax 323-782-1892

Society of Composers & Lyricists
www.filmscore.org
Nonprofit volunteer organization advancing the professional interests of lyricists and composers of film and television music.
400 S. Beverly Dr., Ste. 214
Beverly Hills, CA 90212
Phone 310-281-2812
Fax 310-284-4861

Society of Illustrators (SOI)
www.societyillustrators.org
Society made up of professional illustrators, art directors, art buyers, creative supervisors, instructors and publishers, dedicated to the well-being of individual illustrators and the industry of illustration.
128 E. 63rd St.
New York, NY 10021-7303
Phone 212-838-2560
Fax 212-838-2561

Society of Operating Cameramen (SOC)
www.soc.org
Organization promoting excellence in the fields of camera operation and the allied camera crafts.
PO Box 2006
Toluca Lake, CA 91610
Phone 818-382-7070

Society of Stage Directors & Choreographers (SSDC)
www.ssdc.org
Union representing directors and choreographers of Broadway national tours, regional theater, dinner theater and summer stock, as well as choreographers for motion pictures, television, and music videos.
1501 Broadway, Ste. 1701
New York, NY 10036-5653
Phone 212-391-1070
Fax 212-302-6195

Stunts-Ability, Inc.
www.stuntsability.com
Nonprofit organization training amputees and other disabled persons for stunts, acting, and effects for the entertainment industry.
PO Box 600711
San Diego, CA 92160-0711
Phone 619-542-7730
Fax 619-542-7731

Talent Managers Association (TMA)
www.talentmanagers.org
Nonprofit organization designed to establish credibilty for the profession of talent management.
4804 Laurel Canyon Blvd., Ste. 611
Valley Village, CA 91607
Phone 310-205-8495
Fax 818-765-2903
Betty McCormick Aggas – Contact

Women In Film (WIF)
www.wif.org
Organization dedicated to empowering, promoting and nurturing women in the film and television industries.
8857 W. Olympic Blvd., Ste. 201
Beverly Hills, CA 90211
Phone 310-657-5144
Fax 310-657-5154

Women's Image Network (WIN)
www.winfemme.com
Not-for-profit corporation encouraging positive portrayals of women in theater, television, and film.
PO Box 69-1774
Los Angeles, CA 90069
Phone 310-229-5365

Writers Guild of America (WGA)
Union representing writers in the motion pictures, broadcast, cable and new technologies industries.

Los Angeles (WGAW)
www.wga.org
7000 W. Third St.
Los Angeles, CA 90048-4329
Phone 323-951-4000 *(Main Line)*
323-782-4502 *(Agency Listing)*
Fax 323-782-4800 *(Main Fax)*

New York (WGAE)
www.wgaeast.org
555 W. 57th St., Ste. 1230
New York, NY 10019
Phone 212-767-7800
Fax 212-582-1909

LIBRARIES AND MUSEUMS

Academy of Motion Picture Arts & Sciences - Margaret Herrick Library
www.oscars.org
Extensive and comprehensive research and reference collections documenting film as an art form and an industry.
333 S. La Cienega Blvd.
Beverly Hills, CA 90211
Phone 310-247-3000 *(Main Line)*
310-247-3020 *(Reference)*
Fax 310-657-9351

American Museum of Moving Images
www.ammi.org
Permanent collection of moving image artifacts.
35th Ave. At 36th St.
Astoria, NY 11106
Phone 718-784-4520
Fax 718-784-4681

Library of Moving Images, Inc., The
www.libraryofmovingimages.com
Independent film archives including 19th Century experimental film footage, silent film footage, 20th Century newsreel footage, short subjects, education and industrial films, classic documentaries, vintage cartoons and home movies.
6671 Sunset Blvd., Bungalow 1581
Hollywood, CA 90028
Phone 323-469-7499
Fax 323-469-7559

Los Angeles Public Library – Frances Howard Goldwyn/Hollywood Regional Branch Library
www.lapl.org
Extensive collection documenting the entertainment industry including scripts, posters, and photographs.
1623 N. Ivar Ave.
Los Angeles, CA 90028
Phone 323-856-8260
Fax 323-467-5707

Museum of Television & Radio
www.mtr.org
Extensive collection of television and radio programming.

Los Angeles
465 N. Beverly Dr.
Beverly Hills, CA 90210
Phone 310-786-1000
Fax 310-786-1086

New York
25 W. 52nd St.
New York, NY 10019
Phone 212-621-6600
Fax 212-621-6700

New York Public Library for the Performing Arts
www.nypl.org
Extensive combination of circulating, reference and rare archival collections in the performing arts.
40 Lincoln Center Plaza
New York, NY 10023-7498
Phone 212-870-1630

Writers Guild Foundation Library
www.wga.org
Collection dedicated to the art, craft, and history of writing for motion pictures, radio, television and new media. Open to the public and Guild members.
7000 W. Third St.
Los Angeles, CA 90048-4329
Phone 323-782-4544
Fax 323-782-4695

LOSANGELESCOUTURE.COM

Lost your access card again?

Maybe it needs a leash.
A fabulous, sparkly one.

The perfect gift. Even if it's just for you.

Contact us for custom colors or designs.

www.losangelescouture.com 818.642.9622

It is illegal to copy any part of this book

A. Smith & Co. Productions

American Vantage Media

Atmosphere Entertainment MM, LLC

Atomic Cartoons, Inc.

Bad Boy Films

Bad Robot Productions

Baldwin Entertainment Group

BBC Worldwide America

Breakaway Films

John Brister Films

Calvin Productions, Inc.

Camelot Entertainment Group, Inc.

Chameleon Entertainment

Cine Mosaic

Class IV Productions

Clear Pictures Entertainment Inc.

Cloudbreak Productions, Inc.

CNBC

Condor Rising Entertainment/Folks Film, Inc.

Copasetic Creations

Michael De Luca Productions

Diplomatic Productions

David Eick Productions

Emerald City Production, Inc.

Fierce Entertainment, LLC

fox 21

Frederator Studios

Ghost Robot

GSN

H2F Entertainment

here! TV

Homerun Entertainment, Inc.

Integrated Films & Management

Ithaka

KLS Communications, Inc.

Michael G. Larkin Productions

Liquid Theory

Magnet Management

Maloof Television

Manville Entertainment, LLC

MGA Entertainment/MGA Entertainment Films

Mindfield

Moving Pictures, DPI

MSNBC

Murphy Boyz Productions

NBC News

NBC Universal Cable

NBC Universal Corporate

NBC Universal Television Studio

Paradigm Studio

Parallel Entertainment, Inc.

Paraskevas Studios

Pebblehut Too, Inc.

Pensé Productions

Rapid Heart Pictures, Ltd.

Riverrock Entertainment Group

Showtime Independent Films

Sony Online Entertainment

Sparky Pictures

Susie Q Productions

Tell the Truth Pictures

This is that, corp.

Thunder Road Pictures

TOKYOPOP Inc.

TriStar Pictures

The Walz/O'Malley Company

WideAwake, Inc.

WPT Enterprises, Inc.

Asterisks (*) next to companies denote new listings

THE CONCIERGE™

LOS ANGELES ✦ NEW YORK

AVJET CORPORATION

Excellence in corporate aviation

Operating one of the world's largest and most modern Gulfstream fleets.

Gulfstream Vs, IVSPs, IVs, IIIs, IIBs, IISPs, Challenger 604s, 601-3A
Falcon 2000, Gulfstream 200, Hawker 800XP, Astra, Westwind I/II

Worldwide Executive Jet Charter • Aircraft Management • Aircraft Sales and Leasing

FAA AIR CARRIER CERTIFICATE # ABFA012C // ALL AVJET FLIGHT CREWS ATTEND SEMI-ANNUAL SIMUFLITE / FLIGHT SAFETY AND MEDAIR TRAINING

24 hour dispatch

Headquarters: Los Angeles, Ca.
Toll Free 800-342.8538 / Ph 818-841-6190 / Fax 818-841-6209
email charter@avjet.com / www.avjet.com

CONTENTS

It is illegal to copy any part of this book

FOOD & DRINK

Commissaries & Executive Dining Rooms

THE WALT DISNEY COMPANY
Buena Vista Commissary 818-560-5546
Contact – Dawn Monteleone

Riverside Commissary 818-460-5777
Contact – Tracey Riddle

The Rotunda 818-560-1051
Contact - Nora Titner

PARAMOUNT PICTURES
The Cafe 323-956-5101
Contact - Mari Gutierrez

Executive Dining Room 323-956-8399
Contact – Mari Gutierrez

Special Functions 323-956-8599
Contact – Uschi Wilson

SONY PICTURES ENTERTAINMENT
The Grill 310-244-5134
Contact – Allen Artcliff

Rita Hayworth Dining Room....................................310-244-5521
Contact – Allen Artcliff

TWENTIETH CENTURY FOX
Cafeteria 310-369-2621
Executive Dining Room 310-369-2759

UNIVERSAL CITY STUDIOS
Commissary 818-777-2414
Executive Dining Room 818-777-5405
Catering 818-777-5402
Contact – Scott Ackerman

WARNER BROS.
Commissary 818-954-4203
Contact - Maurizio Binotto

Executive Dining Room 818-954-4220
Contact - Julene Rury

Restaurants

BEVERLY HILLS

BARNEY GREENGRASS 310-777-5877
Barney's, 9570 Wilshire Blvd. (Camden Dr.), Beverly Hills
General Manager - Sharon Kerbyn

CRUSTACEAN 310-205-8990
9646 Little Santa Monica Blvd.(Bedford Dr.), Beverly Hills
General Manager – Christopher Kulow

DA PASQUALE 310-859-3884
9749 Little Santa Monica Blvd. (Wilshire Blvd.), Beverly Hills
General Manager - Bruno Morra

GRILL ON THE ALLEY....................................310-276-0615
9560 Dayton Way (Wilshire Blvd.), Beverly Hills
General Manager – Arthur Meola

IL CIELO 310-276-9990
9018 Burton Way (Doheny Dr.), Beverly Hills
www.ilcielo.com
General Manager – Ivan Garcia

FOOD & DRINK

Restaurants

BEVERLY HILLS

IL CONO GELATERIA 310-285-2045
9641 Little Santa Monica Blvd., Beverly Hills

THE IVY 310-274-8303
113 N. Robertson Blvd. (Beverly Blvd.), Beverly Hills
General Manager - Ann Parker

JOSS 310-276-1886
9255 W. Sunset Blvd. (Doheny Rd.), Beverly Hills
General Manager – Cecil Tang

JOYA 310-274-4440
242 N. Beverly Dr. (Dayton Way), Beverly Hills
General Manager – Brian Schillizzi

KATE MANTILINI 310-278-3699
9101 Wilshire Blvd. (Doheny Dr.), Beverly Hills
General Manager - Patrick McCahon

MAPLE DRIVE....................................310-274-9800
345 N. Maple Dr. (Alden Rd.), Beverly Hills
General Manager – Douglas Wickard

MASTRO'S STEAKHOUSE 310-888-8782
246 N. Canon Dr. (Wilshire Blvd.), Beverly Hills
General Manager – George Giulio

MATSUHISA 310-659-9639
129 N. La Cienega Blvd. (Wilshire Blvd.), Beverly Hills
General Manager - Mark Varo

NATE 'N AL'S 310-274-0101
414 N. Beverly Dr. (Little Santa Monica Blvd.), Beverly Hills
General Manager - Mark Mendelson

NIC'S 310-550-5707
453 N. Canon Dr. (Little Santa Monica Blvd.), Beverly Hills
Operations Manager – Larry Nicola

POLO LOUNGE 310-276-2251
Beverly Hills Hotel, 9641 Sunset Blvd. (Rodeo Dr.), Beverly Hills
Director, Restaurants – Tony Maalouf

PREGO 310-277-7346
362 N. Camden Dr. (Wilshire Blvd.), Beverly Hills
General Manager – Marco Badini

THE REGENT BEVERLY WILSHIRE DINING ROOM 310-275-5200
9500 Wilshire Blvd. (Rodeo Dr.), Beverly Hills
Dining Room Manager – Christian Mandarino

SPAGO 310-385-0880
176 N. Canon Dr. (Wilshire Blvd.), Beverly Hills
General Manager – Tracey Spillane

TRADER VIC'S....................................310-276-6345
9876 Wilshire Blvd. (Santa Monica Blvd.), Beverly Hills
General Manager – Chai Rojana

DOWNTOWN

CAFÉ PINOT 213-239-6500
700 W. Fifth St. (Flower St.), Los Angeles
General Manager – Paul Tilson

A BRASSERIE BY WOLFGANG PUCK

EXPERIENCE WOLFGANG PUCK'S LATEST FINE DINING CONCEPT.

AN EXCITING MENU OF FRENCH AND ITALIAN INFLUENCES

REMINISCENT OF TRADITIONAL BRASSERIE CUISINE WITH A FRESH HOLLYWOOD BACKDROP.

6801 HOLLYWOOD BOULEVARD
FOURTH FLOOR
HOLLYWOOD, CA 90028
TEL [323] 491-1300
FAX [323] 491-1293
WWW.WOLFGANGPUCK.COM/VERT

FOOD & DRINK

Restaurants

DOWNTOWN

CICADA....213-488-9488
617 S. Olive St. (Sixth St.), Los Angeles
www.cicadarestaurant.com
Owner & General Manager - Adelmo Zarif

CIUDAD....213-486-5171
445 S. Figueroa St. (Fourth St.), Los Angeles
www.ciudad-la.com
General Manager – Iona Muir
Maitre d' - Tony Trujillo
P.M. Maitre d' - Terrance Burton

FLIX CAFÉ....213-534-2337
451 S. Beaudry

THE PALM (DOWNTOWN)....213-763-4600
1100 S. Flower St. (Eleventh St.), Los Angeles
General Manager – Jeff Ellis

SUSHI ROKU....626-683-3000
33 Miller Alley, (Union & Colorado), Pasadena
General Manager – Ken Ji

WATER GRILL....213-891-0900
544 S. Grand Ave. (Fifth St.), Los Angeles
General Manager - Harvey Friend

ZUCCA....213-614-7800
801 S. Figueroa St. (Eighth St.), Los Angeles
General Manager – Erwan Channo

HOLLYWOOD/WEST HOLLYWOOD

AGO RESTAURANT....323-655-6333
8478 Melrose Ave. (La Cienega Blvd.), West Hollywood
General Manager - Stefano Carella

AMMO....323-467-3293
1155 N. Highland Ave. (Santa Monica Blvd.), Hollywood
General Manager – Benny Bohn

ASIA DE CUBA....323-848-6000
Modrian Hotel 8440 W. Sunset Blvd. (La Cienega Blvd.), West Hollywood
General Manager – Howard Gilson

BALBOA....323-650-8383
8462 W. Sunset Blvd.(La Cienega Blvd.), West Hollywood
General Manager – Brent Berkowitz

BASTIDE....323-651-0426
8475 Melrose Ave.(La Cienega Blvd.), West Hollywood
General Manager – Donato Poto

BLOWFISH SUSHI LA, LLC....310-887-3848
9929 Sunset Blvd. (Doheny Rd.), West Hollywood
General Manager – Brad Dorsey

CA'BREA....323-938-2863
346 S. La Brea Ave. (Third St.), Los Angeles
Owner - Antonio Tommasi
General Manager – Aurora Simeone

CAFÉ STELLA....323-666-0265
3932 Sunset Blvd. (Sanborn Ave.), Silverlake
General Manager – Alain Jue

FOOD & DRINK

Restaurants

HOLLYWOOD/WEST HOLLYWOOD

CAMPANILE....323-938-1447
624 S. La Brea Ave. (Wilshire Blvd.), Los Angeles
General Manager – Neil Hedin

CHAYA BRASSERIE....310-859-8833
8741 Alden Dr. (Robertson Blvd.), Los Angeles
General Manager – Leonard Masumoto

CINESPACE....323-817-3456
6356 Hollywood Blvd.(Ivar Ave.), Los Angeles
Owner/General Manager – Errol Roussel

CRAVINGS....310-652-6103
8653 W. Sunset Blvd.(Sunset Plaza), Hollywood
General Manager – Omar Latif

DAN TANA'S....310-275-9444
9071 Santa Monica Blvd. (Doheny Dr.), West Hollywood
General Manager - Mike Miljkovic

DOLCE....323-852-7174
8284 Melrose Ave., (Sweetzer Ave.) Los Angeles
General Manager – Maurizio LaRosa

FENIX....323-848-6677
Argyle Hotel, 8358 W. Sunset Blvd. (Sweetzer Ave.), West Hollywood
www.argylehotel.com
General Manager – Steve Rothman

FORMOSA CAFÉ....323-850-9050
7156 Santa Monica Blvd. (La Brea Ave.), West Hollywood
General Manager – Vincent Jung

HOLLYWOOD CANTEEN....323-465-0961
1006 Seward St. (Santa Monica Blvd.), Los Angeles
General Manager - Tony

HOUSE OF BLUES....323-848-5100
8430 W. Sunset Blvd. (La Cienega Blvd.), West Hollywood
General Manager – Jim Uhl

HUGO'S....323-654-3993
8401 Santa Monica Blvd. (La Cienega Blvd.), West Hollywood
General Manager – Thomas Smith

JONES....323-850-1727
7205 Santa Monica Blvd. (Formosa Ave.), West Hollywood
General Manager – Harry Fradet

KATANA....323-650-8585
8439 W. Sunset Blvd. (La Cienega Blvd.), West Hollywood
General Manager – Christian Corben

LE DOME....310-659-6919
8720 Sunset Blvd. (La Cienega Blvd.), West Hollywood

LOCANDA VENETA....310-274-1893
8638 W. Third St. (Robertson Blvd.), Los Angeles
Night Manager - Carlo Marino

MINIBAR....323-882-6965
www.minbarlounge.com
Contact – Rebekah Barrow

MORTON'S....310-276-5205
8764 Melrose Ave. (Robertson Blvd.), Los Angeles
General Manager - Pamela Morton
Maitre d' - Todd Thurman

FOOD & DRINK

Restaurants

HOLLYWOOD/WEST HOLLYWOOD

MUSSO & FRANK 323-467-7788
6667 Hollywood Blvd. (Las Palmas Ave.), Hollywood
Manager – John Garcia

OFF VINE 323-962-1900
6263 Leland Way (Vine St.), Hollywood
General Manager - Richard Falzone

OPALINE 323-857-6725
7450 Beverly Blvd. (Vista St.), West Hollywood
General Manager – David Rosoff

PALADAR 323-465-7500
1651 Wilcox Ave. (Hollywood Blvd.), Hollywood
General Manager – Gilbert Nesbitt

THE PALM 310-550-8811
9001 Santa Monica Blvd. (Robertson Blvd.), West Hollywood
General Manager – Tommy Saboni

PANE E VINO 323-651-4600
8265 Beverly Blvd. (Sweetzer Ave.), Los Angeles
General Manager - Fred Thomas

PATINA 213-972-3331
Walt Disney Concert Hall
141 S. Grand (W. Third St.), Los Angeles
Director – Patrick Davila

FOOD & DRINK

Restaurants

HOLLYWOOD/WEST HOLLYWOOD

PINOT HOLLYWOOD 323-461-8800
1448 N. Gower St. (Sunset Blvd.), Los Angeles
General Manager – Faiz Mattar

THE STANDARD CAFÉ 323-650-9090
8300 W. Sunset Blvd. (Sweetzer Ave.), West Hollywood
General Manager – Alfred Bernardin

SUSHI ROKU 323-655-6767
8445 W. Third St., (La Cienega Blvd.) Los Angeles
General Manager – Jason Hardy

VERT 323-491-1300
6801 Hollywood Blvd. Fourth Fl. (Highland Ave.), Hollywood
General Manager – Klaus Puck

WHITE LOTUS...323-463-0060
1743 N. Cahuenga Blvd. (Hollywood Blvd.), Hollywood
General Manager – Natalie Beydoun

SANTA MONICA/WESTSIDE

BALLONA FISH MARKET 310-822-8979
13455 Maxella Ave.(Lincoln Blvd.), Marina del Rey
General Manager – Marcia Hrichison

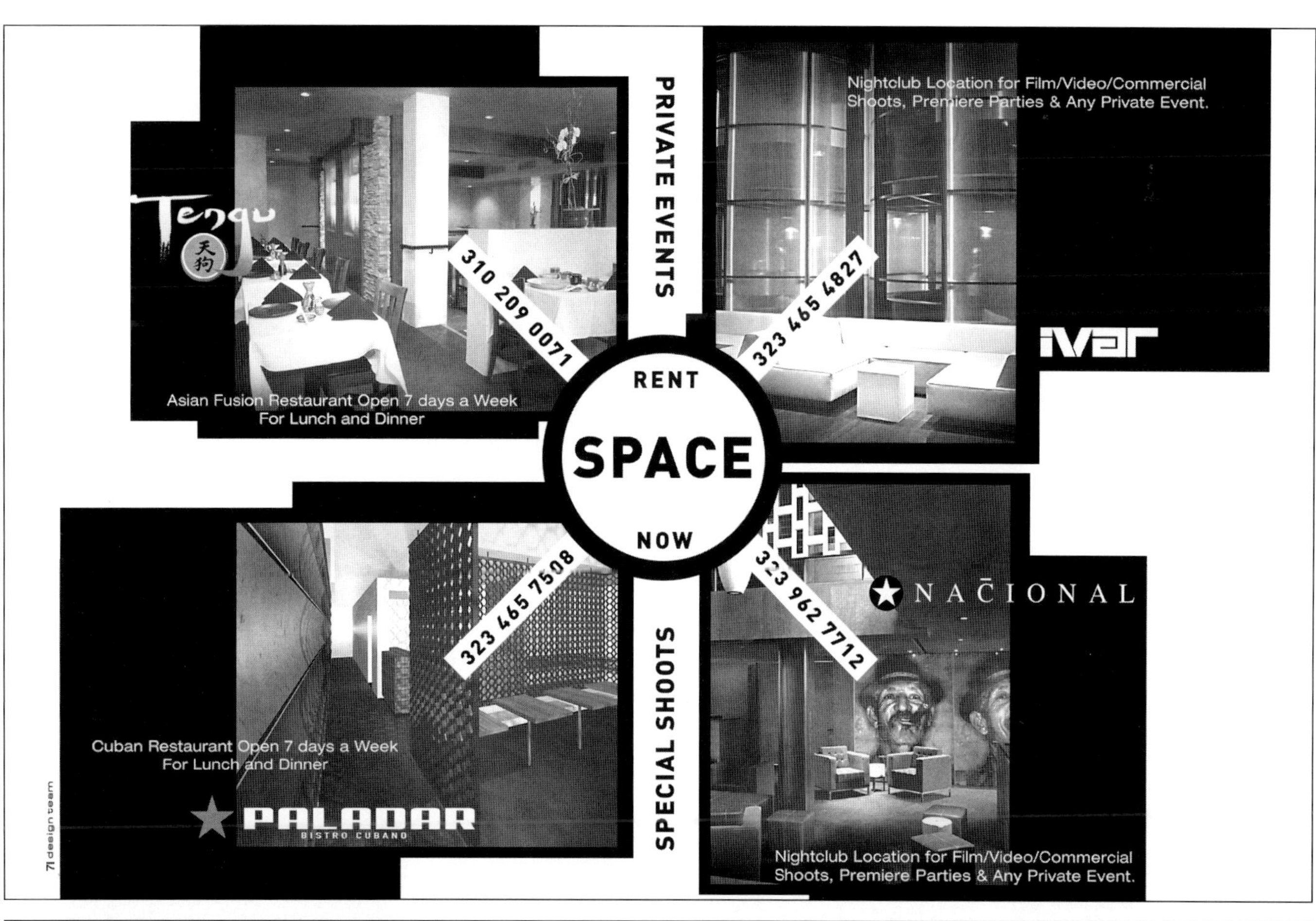

Tengu
天狗
310 209 0071
Asian Fusion Restaurant Open 7 days a Week
For Lunch and Dinner
PRIVATE EVENTS
Nightclub Location for Film/Video/Commercial
Shoots, Premiere Parties & Any Private Event.
323 465 4827
ivar
RENT
SPACE
NOW
323 465 7508
Cuban Restaurant Open 7 days a Week
For Lunch and Dinner
PALADAR
BISTRO CUBANO
SPECIAL SHOOTS
323 962 7712
NACIONAL
Nightclub Location for Film/Video/Commercial
Shoots, Premiere Parties & Any Private Event.
71 design team

It is illegal to copy any part of this book

FOOD & DRINK

Restaurants

HOLLYWOOD/WEST HOLLYWOOD

BORDER GRILL 310-451-1655
1445 Fourth St. (Broadway St.), Santa Monica
General Manager – Andrea Uyeda

BROADWAY DELI 310-451-0616
1457 Third Street Promenade (Broadway St.), Santa Monica
General Manager – Camille Marinelli

BUFFALO CLUB 310-450-8600
1520 Olympic Blvd. (15th St.), Santa Monica
General Manager - Patrick Doherty

CAFÉ BIZOU 310-582-8203
2450 Colorado Ave. (Cloverfield Blvd.), Santa Monica
General Manager – Wilfred Leon

DRAGO 310-828-1585
2628 Wilshire Blvd. (26th St.), Santa Monica
General Manager - Silvio Cicconi

EUROCHOW 310-209-0066
1099 Westwood Blvd.(Kinross St.), Westwood
General Manager – Salvatore Giorgio

GARDENS ON GLENDON 310-824-1818
1139 Glendon Ave.(Lindbrook), Westwood
General Manager – John Patterson

GRANITA 310-456-0488
23725 W. Malibu Rd. (Webb Way & Pacific Coast Highway), Malibu
General Manager – Jennifer Naylor

IVY AT THE SHORE 310-393-3113
1541 Ocean Ave. (Broadway St.), Santa Monica
General Manager - Ann Parker

JUNIOR'S DELI 310-475-5771
2379 Westwood Blvd. (Pico Blvd.), Los Angeles
General Manager - David Saul

LA FARM 310-449-4000
3000 W. Olympic Blvd. (Centinela Ave.), Santa Monica
General Manager - Jean-Pierre Peiny

PALOMINO 323-817-3456
10877 Wilshire Blvd.(Glendon & Lindbrook), Westwood
General Manager – Errol Russel

RöCKENWAGNER 310-399-6504
2435 Main St.(Ocean Park Blvd.), Santa Monica
Maitre d' – Christopher Pond

SUSHI ROKU 310-458-4771
1401 Ocean Ave. (Santa Monica Blvd.), Santa Monica
General Manager – Tiger Nakawake

TENGU 310-209-0071
10853 Lindbrook Dr. (Glendon Ave.), Westwood
General Manager – Guy Ravid

VALLEY

ART'S DELI 818-762-1221
12224 Ventura Blvd. (Laurel Canyon Blvd.), Studio City
Owner & General Manager - Art Ginsburg

BISTRO GARDEN AT COLDWATER 818-501-0202
12950 Ventura Blvd. (Coldwater Canyon Ave.), Studio City
General Manager - Greg Pappas

FOOD & DRINK

Restaurants

VALLEY

CA'DEL SOLE 818-985-4669
4100 Cahuenga Blvd. (Lankershim Blvd.), North Hollywood
General Manager - Angelo Calderan

CAFÉ BIZOU 818-788-3536
14016 Ventura Blvd. (Costello Ave.), Sherman Oaks
General Manager – Ryan Herrera

FIREFLY 818-762-1833
11720 Ventura Blvd. (Laurel Canyon Blvd.), Studio City
General Manager – Tiffany Russo

JERRY'S FAMOUS DELI 818-980-4245
12655 Ventura Blvd. (Coldwater Canyon Ave.), Studio City

MEXICALI 818-985-1744
12161 Ventura Blvd. (Laurel Canyon Blvd.), Studio City
General Manager – Glen Dobbs

PINOT BISTRO 818-990-0500
12969 Ventura Blvd. (Coldwater Canyon Ave.), Studio City
General Manager - Steve Meyer

SMOKEHOUSE 818-845-3731
4420 Lakeside Dr. (Barham Blvd.), Studio City
General Manager – Israel Eviles

Dinner Delivery

GOURMET COURIER 323-655-8666
Beverly Hills, West Hollywood, Hollywood

Catering

CHEERS CATERING, INC. 818-772-0233
www.cheerscateringinc.com

CHEF J'S KITCHEN 310-901-8671
www.chefj.com

CHRISTOPHE BERNARD CATERING 310-441-7623

DEBBIE'S DINNERS 323-936-4545
www.debbiesdinners.com

FOODWORKS 310-280-6050
www.foodworksla.com
Contact – Nora Abbott

KAI'S EUROPEAN CATERING 310-204-4450
www.eurocaters.com

MICHAEL'S EPICUREAN, INC. 818-509-0558
www.michaelsepicurean.com

MS. SHELL'S BAKERY 323-660-9757
www.msshellsbaker.com
Contact – Susie Norris-Epstein

THE PIG CATERING (Memphis-Style BBQ) 323-469-RIBS
www.labarbequeking.com
Contact - Daly Thompson

RICK ROYCE PREMIER BBQ CATERING 310-441-7427
www.rickroycebbqcatering.com
Contact - Rick Royce

WOLFGANG PUCK'S CATERING & EVENTS 323-491-1250

FOOD & DRINK

Event Planning

ALONG CAME MARY! PRODUCTIONS 323-931-9082
www.alongcamemary.com

BEAUTIFUL BARTENDERS,LLC 310-600-1077
www.beautifulbartenders.com
Contact – Ana Gallegos

CARAVENTS, INC...323-933-9993
www.caravents.com

COLIN COWIE LIFESTYLE 310-286-9600
www.colincowie.com

JEFFREY BEST 323-857-5577

LEVY, PAZANTI & ASSOCIATES.................................310-201-5033

MINDY WEISS PARTY CONSULTANTS 310-205-6000
www.mindyweiss.com

MOONDANCE EVENTS & ENTERTAINMENT...................310-287-2329
www.moondanceevents.com
Contact – Benita Karroll

SILVER BIRCHES..626-796-1431
www.silverbirches.net
Contact – Walter Hubert

ACCOMMODATIONS

Hotels

BEVERLY HILLS

AVALON.....................................310-277-5221/800-535-4715
9400 W. Olympic Blvd. (Beverly Dr.), Beverly Hills
www.avalonbeverlyhills.com
General Manager – Janne Clare

THE BEVERLY HILLS HOTEL 310-276-2251/800-283-8885
9641 Sunset Blvd. (Beverly Dr.), Beverly Hills
www.thebeverlyhillshotel.com
General Manager - Alberto del Hoyo

THE BEVERLY HILTON 310-274-7777/800-HILTONS
9876 Wilshire Blvd., (Santa Monica Blvd.), Beverly Hills
www.hilton.com
General Manager - Denny Fitzpatrick

THE CENTURY PLAZA HOTEL & SPA 310-277-2000
2025 Avenue of the Stars. (Olympic Blvd.), Century City
www.centuryplazala.com
Managing Director – Tim Loughman

FOUR SEASONS HOTEL 310-273-2222/800-332-3442
300 S. Doheny Dr. (Burton Way.), Beverly Hills
www.fourseasons.com
General Manager - William Mackay

LE MERIDIEN 310-247-0400/800-543-4300
465 S. La Cienega Blvd. (San Vicente Blvd.), Beverly Hills
www.lemeridien.com
General Manager – Lawrence Saward

MAISON 140..310-281-4000
140 Lasky Dr. (Little Santa Monica Blvd.), Beverly Hills
www.maison140.com
General Manager – Azadeh Nashat

ACCOMMODATIONS

Hotels

BEVERLY HILLS

THE PENINSULA 310-551-2888/800-462-7899
9882 S. Little Santa Monica Blvd. (Wilshire Blvd.), Beverly Hills
www.peninsula.com
General Manager - Ali Kasikci

RAFFLES L'ERMITAGE........................310-278-3344/800-800-2113
9291 Burton Way (Maple Dr.), Beverly Hills
www.lermitagehotel.com
General Manager - Jack Naderkhani

THE REGENT BEVERLY WILSHIRE 310-275-5200/800-421-4354
9500 Wilshire Blvd. (Rodeo Dr.), Beverly Hills
www.regenthotels.com
General Manager - Peter O'Colmain

DOWNTOWN

FIGUEROA HOTEL 213-627-8971/800-421-9092
939 S. Figueroa St. (Eighth St.), Los Angeles
www.figueroahotel.com
General Manager – Uno Thimansson

MILLENNIUM BILTMORE 213-624-1011/800-245-8673
506 S. Grand Ave. (Fifth St.), Los Angeles
www.millennium-hotels.com
www.thebiltmore.com
General Manager - Gunther Zweimuller

THE STANDARD (DOWNTOWN) 213-892-8080
550 S. Flower St. (Sixth St.), Los Angeles
www.standardhotel.com

WILSHIRE GRAND 213-688-7777/888-773-2888
930 Wilshire Blvd. (Figueroa St.), Los Angeles
www.thewilshiregrand.com
General Manager - John Stoddard

HOLLYWOOD/WEST HOLLYWOOD

ARGYLE 323-654-7100/800-225-2637
8358 Sunset Blvd. (La Cienega Blvd.), West Hollywood
www.argylehotel.com
General Manager – John Schulz

CHATEAU MARMONT 323-656-1010/800-CHATEAU
8221 Sunset Blvd. (Crescent Heights Blvd.), West Hollywood
www.chateaumarmont.com
General Manager - Phil Pavel

LE PARC SUITE HOTEL.......................310-855-8888/800-578-4837
733 N. West Knoll Dr. (Melrose Ave.), West Hollywood
www.leparcsuite.com
General Manager - Ira Kleinrock

MONDRIAN 323-650-8999/800-525-8029
8440 Sunset Blvd. (La Cienega Blvd.), West Hollywood
www.ianschragerhotels.com
General Manager - David Weidlich

THE STANDARD...323-650-9090
8300 Sunset Blvd. (La Cienega Blvd.), West Hollywood
www.standardhotel.com
General Manager - Laurent Fraticelli

SUNSET MARQUIS HOTEL & VILLAS 310-657-1333/800-858-9758
1200 N. Alta Loma Rd. (Sunset Blvd.), West Hollywood
www.sunsetmarquishotel.com
General Manager - Rod Gruendyke

ACCOMMODATIONS

Hotels

HOLLYWOOD/WEST HOLLYWOOD

WYNDHAM BEL AGE HOTEL 310-854-1111/800-996-3426
1020 N. San Vicente Blvd. (Sunset Blvd.), West Hollywood
www.wyndham.com
General Manager – Beth Stonelake

SANTA MONICA/WESTSIDE

HOTEL BEL-AIR 310-472-1211/800-648-4097
701 Stone Canyon Rd. (Sunset Blvd.), Bel-Air
www.hotelbelair.com
Managing Director - Carlos Lopes

LOEWS SANTA MONICA BEACH HOTEL .. 310-458-6700/866-267-4154
1700 Ocean Ave. (Colorado Ave.), Santa Monica
www.loewshotels.com
General Manager - John Thacker

PARK HYATT 310-277-1234/800-233-1234
2151 Avenue of the Stars (Olympic Blvd.), Century City
www.hyatt.com
General Manager – Ulrich Samietz

RITZ-CARLTON, MARINA DEL REY........ 310-823-1700/800-241-3333
4375 Admiralty Way (Bali Way), Marina del Rey
www.ritzcarlton.com
General Manager - Andrew Zephirin

SHUTTERS ON THE BEACH 310-458-0030/800-334-9000
1 Pico Blvd. (Ocean Front Walk), Santa Monica
www.shuttersonthebeach.com
General Manager – Henrei Birmele

ST. REGIS 310-277-6111/877-787-3452
2055 Avenue of the Stars (Olympic Blvd.), Century City
www.stregis.com
Managing Director – Timothy Loughman

W LOS ANGELES 310-208-8765/877-WHOTELS
930 Hilgard Ave. (Le Conte Ave.), Westwood
www.whotels.com/losangeles
General Manager – Robert Watson

VICEROY HOTEL 310-451-8711/800-622-8711
1819 Ocean Ave. (Pico Blvd.), Santa Monica
www.viceroysantamonica.com
General Manager – Vincent Piro

VALLEY

HILTON BURBANK 818-843-6000/800-445-8667
2500 N. Hollywood Way (Thornton Ave.), Burbank
www.hilton.com
General Manager - Joseph Kruvi

HILTON UNIVERSAL CITY....................818-506-2500/800-727-7110
555 Universal Hollywood Dr.(Lankershim Blvd.), Universal City
www.hilton.com
General Manager - Juan Aquinde

SHERATON UNIVERSAL HOTEL 818-980-1212/800-325-3535
333 Universal Hollywood Dr. (Lankershim Blvd.), Universal City
www.starwood.com/sheraton
General Manager - Wolf Walther

ACCOMMODATIONS

Corporate Retreats

DESERT TOWNS

LA QUINTA RESORT AND CLUB 760-564-4111/800-598-3828
49-499 Eisenhower Dr., La Quinta
www.laquintaresort.com
General Manager – Paul McCormick

MARRIOTT RANCHO LAS PALMAS 760-568-2727/800-228-9290
41000 Bob Hope Dr., Rancho Mirage
www.marriott.com
General Manager - Frank Garahan

THE LODGE AT RANCHO MIRAGE 760-321-8282/888-FOR-ROCK
68-900 Frank Sinatra Dr., Rancho Mirage
www.rockresorts.com
Managing Director – Herbert Spiegel

VICEROY PALM SPRINGS 760-320-4117/800-237-3687
415 S. Belardo Rd., Palm Springs
www.viceroypalmsprings.com
General Manager – Steve Cenicola

NORTH OF LA

BACARA RESORT & SPA......................805-968-0100/877-422-4245
8301 Hollister Ave., Santa Barbara
www.bacararesort.com
Public Relations Director – Oliver Unaka

FOUR SEASONS BILTMORE 805-969-2261/800-332-3442
1260 Channel Dr., Santa Barbara
www.fourseasons.com
General Manager - John Indrieri

OJAI VALLEY INN & SPA 805-646-5511/800-422-6524
905 Country Club Rd., Ojai
www.ojairesort.com
General Manager - Anna Olson

SAN YSIDRO RANCH 805-969-5046/800-368-6788
900 San Ysidro Lane, Santa Barbara
www.sanysidroranch.com

SOUTH OF LA

LA COSTA RESORT & SPA....................760-438-9111/800-854-5000
2100 Costa del Mar Rd., Carlsbad
www.lacosta.com
General Manager – April Shute

RITZ-CARLTON, LAGUNA NIGEL 949-240-2000/800-241-3333
1 Ritz-Carlton Dr., Dana Point
www.ritzcarlton.com
General Manager - John Dravinski

Corporate Housing

OAKWOOD CORPORATE HOUSING 866-327-3077
www.oakwood.com
National Account Manager – Joni Rodenbusch

PARK LA BREA APARTMENTS..................................323-549-5450
www.parklabrea.com
Corporate Housing Director – Lisa Holbrook

THE SEACASTLE IN SANTA MONICA 310-917-1998/800-295-0022
Leasing Director – Denise Phillips

TRAVEL & TRANSPORTATION

Travel Agencies

HOFFMAN/MCCORD TRAVEL SERVICES........................818-238-4400
www.worldtravel.com

MANSOUR TRAVEL..310-276-2768
www.mansourtravel.com

PRODUCTION TRAVEL & TOURS........ 818-760-0327/888-GO2-AFRICA
clubtrvl@aol.com
Contact - Sylvia Frommer-Mracky

Specialized Travel Services

BOB HOPE HEALTH CENTER 323-634-3850
335 N. La Brea Ave., Los Angeles
www.mptvfund.org

HEALTHY TRAVELER CLINIC 626-584-1200
1250 E. Green St., Pasadena
www.healthytraveler.com

THE TRAVEL MEDICINE CENTER 310-360-1331
131 N. Robertson Blvd., Beverly Hills
www.healthytravel.com

Airlines - Domestic

AIR MIDWEST/US AIRWAYS EXPRESS 800-428-4322
www.usairways.com

AIRTRAN..800-247-8726
www.airtran.com

ALASKA 800-252-7522
www.alaskaair.com

ALOHA 800-367-5250
www.alohaair.com

AMERICAN..800-433-7300
www.aa.com

AMERICAN TRANS AIR..800-435-9282
www.ata.com

AMERICA WEST...800-235-9292
www.americawest.com

CONTINENTAL...800-525-0280
www.continental.com

DELTA 800-221-1212
www.delta.com

FRONTIER 800-432-1359
www.frontierairlines.com

HAWAIIAN...800-367-5320
www.hawaiianair.com

JETBLUE 800-538-2583
www.jetblue.com

MIDWEST EXPRESS 800-452-2022
www.midwestexpress.com

NORTHWEST 800-225-2525
www.nwa.com

SOUTHWEST 800-435-9792
www.southwest.com

TRAVEL & TRANSPORTATION

Airlines - Domestic

US AIRWAYS 800-428-4322
www.usairways.com

UNITED 800-241-6522
www.ual.com

VANGUARD 800-826-4827
www.flyvanguard.com

Airlines - International

AER LINGUS 800-474-7424
www.aerlingus.ie

AIR CANADA 888-247-2262
www.aircanada.ca

AIR FRANCE...800-237-2747
www.airfrance.com

AIR NEW ZEALAND 800-262-1234
www.airnz.com

ALITALIA 800-223-5730
www.alitalia.it

AUSTRIA AIRLINES 800-843-0002
www.aua.com

AVIANCA..800-284-2622
www.avianca.com

BRITISH AIRWAYS..800-247-9297
www.british-airways.com

CATHAY PACIFIC 800-233-2742
www.cathay-usa.com

EL AL 800-223-6700
www.elal.co.il

FINNAIR 800-950-5000
www.finnair.com

IBERIA AIRLINES 800-772-4642
www.iberia.com

ICELANDAIR 800-223-5500
www.icelandair.com

KLM ROYAL DUTCH 800-374-7747
www.klm.com

KOREAN AIR 800-438-5000
www.koreanair.com

LUFTHANSA..800-645-3880
www.lufthansa.com

SWISS 877-359-7947
www.swiss.com

QANTAS 800-227-4500
www.qantas.com

VIRGIN ATLANTIC 800-862-8621
www.fly.virgin.com

Four Directions Air
Four Directions Air, Inc. is redefining how you travel for business
by telling you what we **don't** have ...
no long lines ... no cancelled flights ... no parking hassles ... no landings at
inconvenient airports ... no crowds ... no lame in-flight movies ... no mad dashes to your gate ...
and, no business meetings in yesterday's clothes because your flight went to Atlanta
and your luggage went to Albuquerque.
www.fourdirectionsair.com
an enterprise of the Oneida Indian Nation

TRAVEL & TRANSPORTATION

Charter Planes

AIRCRAFT CHARTERS & MANAGEMENT/
VIKING AVIATION 818-997-4383
www.flyviking.com; caarvik@yahoo.com
Contact - Mr. Aarvik

AVJET CORPORATION...................818-841-6190/800-342-8538
4301 Empire Ave., Burbank, CA 91505
www.avjet.com; charter@avjet.com
Contact – Mark Lefever, Executive Vice President

Avjet Corporation has provided executive jet charter services to the entertainment industry for over 25 years. Call to schedule your next flight and experience worldwide private air travel as it was meant to be.

FOUR DIRECTIONS AIR, INC................................310-301-1785
5218 Patrick Road, Verona, NY 13478
www.fourdirectionsair.com
Contact – Maggie Begley, mbegley@aol.com

Four Directions Air will change the way you look at business travel.

ELITE AVIATION 818-988-5387
www.eliteaviation.com

CLAY LACY AVIATION, INC. 818-989-2900/800-423-2904
www.claylacy.com

KOMAR AVIATION GROUP 800-555-0996
www.komaraviation.com

RAYTHEON AIRCRAFT CHARTER
AND MANAGEMENT.....................800-519-6283/818-756-2182
7240 Hayvenhurst, Van Nuys, CA 91406
www.raytheonaircraft.com; john_e_martin@rac.ray.com
Contact – John Martin

Wherever the destination, whatever the mission, we offer a complete line of aviation solutions.

SENTIENT PRIVATE JET MEMBERSHIP 866-473-6843
www.sentient.com

SKYLINK CHARTER, LLC.....................562-869-4128/888-923-7181
Skylinkllc@aol.com
Contact – Janet Concepcion

XTRAJET,INC. 310-397-1000/877-987-2538
3153 Donald Douglas Loop, South, Santa Monica
www.xtrajet.com
Contact – Mark Bethea

Car Rentals

ALAMO 800-462-5266
www.alamo.com

AVIS 800-331-1212
www.avis.com

BUDGET 800-527-0700
www.budget.com

DOLLAR 800-800-4000
www.dollar.com

ENTERPRISE 800-325-8007
www.enterprise.com

HERTZ 800-654-3131
www.hertz.com

TRAVEL & TRANSPORTATION

Car Rentals

NATIONAL 800-227-7368
www.nationalcar.com

THRIFTY 800-367-2277
www.thrifty.com

Limos

AFFORDABLE CLASS LIMOUSINE
& SEDAN SERVICE 818-881-6116/310-470-6111

BLS LIMOUSINE SERVICE 800-843-5752
www.blslimo.com

DIVA LIMOUSINE 800-427-3482
www.divalimo.com

EXOTIC LIMO 310-330-0550/866-523-9684
www.exoticlimo.com

FONTANA'S 310-366-8262/800-366-8262
www.1800fontanas.com

MUSIC EXPRESS 800-421-9494
www.musiclimo.com

Executive Car Leasing

CENTURY WEST BMW 818-505-7400/800-447-8871
4245 Lankershim Blvd. (Moorpark St.), North Hollywood
www.centurywestbmw.com

ED CAR GUY 818-563-4499
www.edcarguy.com
Contact – Ed Levitt

LAND ROVER ENCINO..818-990-9870
15800 Ventura Blvd. (Haskell Ave.), Encino
www.landroverencino.com

LOS ANGELES CLASSIC CAR SERVICE 323-290-3639/310-480-5118
5255 Veronica St. (S. La Brea Ave.), Los Angeles
www.laclassiccars.com
Contact – David Friedman

MERCEDES BENZ BEVERLY HILLS, LTD. 310-659-2980/800-497-2367
9250 Beverly Blvd. (Santa Monica Blvd.), Beverly Hills
www.bhbenz.com

ROLLS ROYCE OF BEVERLY HILLS 310-659-4050
8833 W. Olympic Blvd. (Robertson Blvd.), Beverly Hills
www.rollsroycebeverlyhills.com

GIFTS & SHOPPING

Florists

BRYAN WARK DESIGNS..310-917-1982
628 San Juan Ave. (Sixth Ave.), Venice
www.bryanwarkdesigns.com

DAVID JONES...310-659-6347
450 N. Robertson Blvd. (Melrose Ave.), West Hollywood

THE FLOWER SHOP 310-274-8491
616 N. Almont Dr., Ste. C (Melrose Ave.), West Hollywood

JACOB MAARSE FLORIST 213-629-6949
545 S. Figueroa St. (Fifth St.), Los Angeles

GIFTS & SHOPPING

Florists

MARK'S GARDEN 818-906-1718
13838 Ventura Blvd. (Woodman Ave.), Sherman Oaks

RITA FLORA 323-938-3900/800-748-2356
468 S. La Brea Ave. (Sixth St.), Los Angeles
www.ritaflora.com

TIC TOCK..323-874-3034
1603 N. La Brea Ave. (Hawthorne Ave.), Los Angeles
www.tictock.com

Gift Baskets

DEB'S DELIGHTS 323-936-4545
www.debsdelights.com

FAVOR FORTE..310-226-6959
www.favorforte.com
Contacts - Susan Leslie & Renee Lee

FIRENZE 818-832-4740
www.firenzegifts.com
Contact – Steve Gagliano

FRAICHE 888-654-7002
www.fraichegifts.com

GOURMET BY DESIGN 310-605-4955/888-982-2275
www.gourmetbydesign.com

JJ SUMMERLAND 800-610-6650
www.jjsummerlandgifts.com

K CHOCOLATIER 310-248-2626
www.dkron.com

LAH-DEE-DAH'S EDIBLE MIRACLES 818-920-1337

MINDY'S 818-947-0207
www.mindysgiftbaskets.com

MAISON CONNOISSEUR 818-346-1520
www.maisonconnoisseur.com

SCHMERTY'S GOURMET COOKIES 310-991-4345
www.schmertys.com
Contacts – Syrna & Jeffrey

WALLY'S...310-475-0606/800-9WALLYS
www.wallywine.com

Personal Shoppers

DONUM CELEBRITY &
CORPORATE GIFTS 310-317-4577/978-352-3336
www.donumgifts.com
Contacts - Kristy Barrett & Amy Frankel Nau

STAR TREATMENT GIFT SERVICES 818-781-9016/800-444-9059
www.startreatment.com
Contact - Diane

SCREENING ROOMS

BEVERLY HILLS

ACADEMY OF MOTION PICTURES ARTS & SCIENCES 310-274-3000
8949 Wilshire Blvd. (La Peer Dr.), Beverly Hills

CHARLES AIDIKOFF SCREENING ROOM 310-274-0866
150 S. Rodeo Dr. (Wilshire Blvd.), Beverly Hills
www.leaderhollywoodformat.com

CLARITY THEATRE 310-385-4092
100 N. Crescent Dr. (Wilshire Blvd.), Beverly Hills

WRITERS GUILD THEATRE.......................................323-782-4525
135 S. Doheny Dr. (Wilshire Blvd.), Los Angeles
www.wga.org

WILSHIRE SCREENING ROOM 310-659-3875
8670 Wilshire Blvd.(Willaman Dr.), Los Angeles
www.studioscreenings.com

HOLLYWOOD/WEST HOLLYWOOD

AMERICAN FILM INSTITUTE 323-856-7681
2021 N. Western Ave. (Franklin Ave.), Los Angeles
www.afi.com

DIRECTORS GUILD OF AMERICA 310-289-2021/310-289-2023
7920 Sunset BLvd. (Fairfax Ave.), Los Angeles
www.dga.org

L V
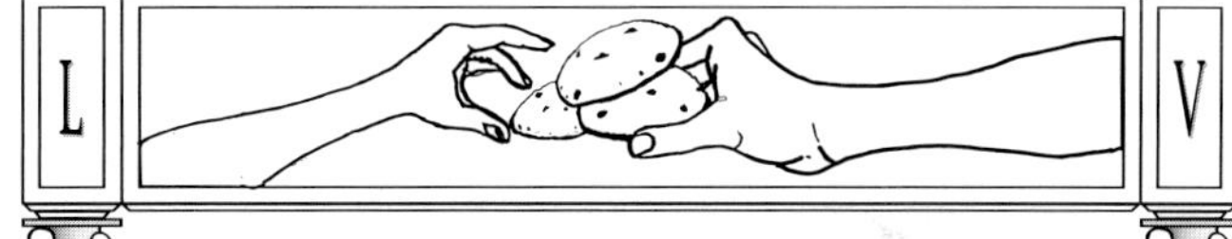

LAH-DEE-DAH'S
EDIBLE MIRACLES

- Gourmet Cookies
- Baked to Order
- Delivered Fresh to Recipient
- Gift Baskets
- Special Orders Welcome

818-920-1337
lahdeedahs@aol.com

TASTE ONE, WE DARE YOU!

SCREENING ROOMS

HOLLYWOOD/WEST HOLLYWOOD

HARMONY GOLD PREVIEW HOUSE 323-851-4900
7655 Sunset Blvd. (Fairfax Ave.), Los Angeles

PACIFIC DESIGN CENTER 310-360-6415
8687 Melrose Ave., 2nd Fl. (San Vicente Blvd.), Los Angeles
www.pacificdesigncenter.com

PARAMOUNT PICTURES 323-956-5000
5555 Melrose Ave. (Vine St.), Los Angeles
www.paramount.com

RALEIGH STUDIOS 323-871-5649
5300 Melrose Ave. (Western Ave.), Los Angeles
650 N. Bronson Ave. (Melrose Ave.), Los Angeles

SUNSET SCREENING ROOM 310-652-1933
8730 Sunset Blvd. (La Cienega Blvd.), Los Angeles

THE LOT/WARNER BROS. 818-954-2144
1041 N. Formosa Ave. (Santa Monica Blvd.), Los Angeles
www.wbpsostproduction.warnerbros.com

SANTA MONICA/WESTSIDE

ARTISAN THEATRE/LIONS GATE 310-255-4000
2700 Colorado Ave. (26th St.), Santa Monica

BENDETTI MOBILE, INC. 310-587-3377/888-834-8439
1549 11th St. (Broadway St.), Santa Monica
www.benettimobil.com

SCREENING ROOMS

SANTA MONICA/WESTSIDE

BIG TIME PICTURE COMPANY 310-207-0921
12210-1/2 Nebraska Ave. (Bundy Ave.), Los Angeles
www.bigtimepic.com

NEW DEAL STUDIOS 310-578-9929
4121 Redwood Ave. (Washington Blvd.), Los Angeles
www.newdealstudios.com

CULVER STUDIOS 310-202-3253/310-840-8589
9336 W. Washington Blvd. (Culver Blvd.), Culver City
www.theculverstudios.com

METRO-GOLDWYN-MAYER 310-449-3000
2500 Broadway St. (26th St.), Santa Monica
www.mgm.com

OCEAN SCREENING ROOM 310-576-1831
1401 Ocean Ave. (Santa Monica Blvd.), Santa Monica

SONY PICTURES STUDIOS 310-244-5721
10202 W. Washington Blvd. (Overland Ave.), Culver City
www.spe.sony.com

TODD-AO STUDIOS WEST 310-315-5000
3000 W. Olympic Blvd. (Centinela Ave.), Santa Monica

TWENTIETH CENTURY FOX 310-369-2406
10201 W. Pico Blvd. (Avenue of the Stars), Los Angeles
www.fox.com

818-788-1816
A Professional Massage Treatment Center

Your Place...

- Worksite
- Residential
- Parties & Events
- Chair or Table

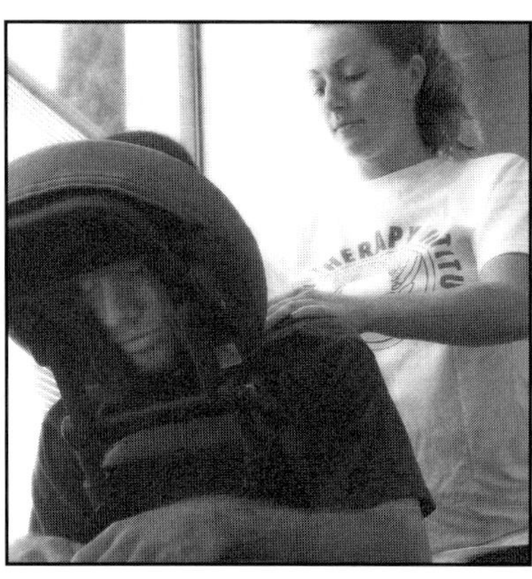

"If you receive a massage every week, you will have 2/3rds less illness." — Hans Gruenn, MD

...or Ours

- Stress-relieving
- Preventative
- Therapeutic
- Rehabilitative

15720 Ventura Blvd., Encino, CA 91436
www.touchtherapyinstitute.com

An affiliate of The Touch Therapy Institute®, L.A.'s premiere massage school.

Announcing Hollywood's Newest Fab Four

Best research tool for finding who's who in film and television

Includes contact information for:

- Studio and Network Execs
- Production Companies
- Independent Producers
- TV Shows & Staff
- Agents & Managers
- Entertainment Attorneys
- Business Affairs Depts.
- Publicity Companies
- Domestic Distributors
- International Distributors
- TV Syndication
- Financing Companies
- Direct to Video / DV
- Music Agents & Managers
- Record Companies / A&R
- Soundtrack Execs
- Music Supervisors

The New HOLLYWOOD CREATIVE DIRECTORY ONLINE

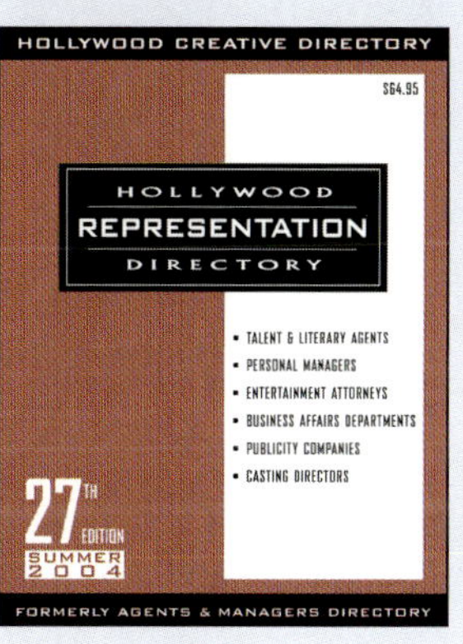

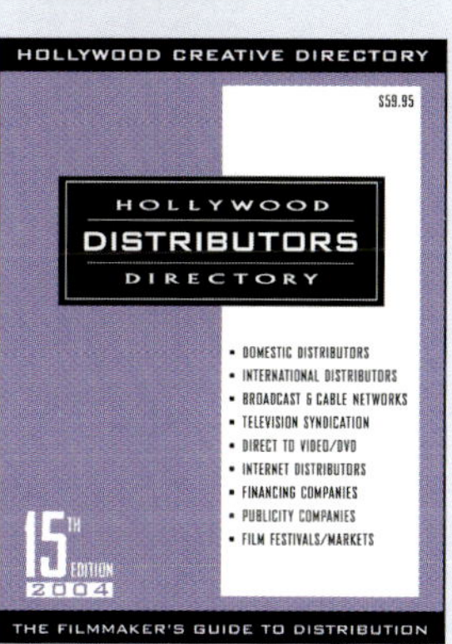

All directories in one database, just a click away

- Comprehensive, reliable and accurate
- Easy to search and navigate
- Updated daily

Now Playing

HOLLYWOOD CREATIVE DIRECTORY ONLINE is used by all major studios, networks, producers, agents, managers, distributors, and talent themselves.

For more information or to sign up today,
call **323.308.3558** or
click **www.hcdonline.com**

SCREENING ROOMS

VALLEY

ACADEMY OF TELEVISION ARTS & SCIENCES 818-754-2800
5220 Lankershim Blvd. (Magnolia Blvd.), North Hollywood
www.emmys.org

ICS SERVICES, INC. 818-242-3839
920 Allen Ave. (San Fernando Rd.), Glendale
www.icsfilm.com

SUNSET SCREENING ROOM 818-556-5190
2212 W. Magnolia Blvd. (Buena Vista St.), Burbank

UNIVERSAL STUDIOS 818-777-1000
100 Universal City Plaza (Cahuenga Blvd.), Universal City
www.universalstudios.com

THE WALT DISNEY STUDIOS 818-560-5506
500 S. Buena Vista St. (Riverside Dr.), Burbank
www.disney.go.com/studiooperations

WARNER BROS. STUDIO FACILITIES 818-954-2144
4000 Warner Blvd. (Olive Ave.), Burbank
www.wbpostproduction.warnerbros.com

VIP TICKETS

ANAHEIM ANGELS..714-940-2014
www.angelsbaseball.com
Vice President, Communications - Tim Mead

ANAHEIM MIGHTY DUCKS.......................................714-940-2911
www.mightyducks.com
Director, Public Relations - Alex Gilchrist

LOS ANGELES DODGERS 323-224-1301
www.dodgers.mlb.com
Director, Public Relations - John Olguin

LOS ANGELES CLIPPERS 213-742-7500
www.nba.com/clippers
Director, Communications - Rob Raichlen

LOS ANGELES KINGS 310-535-4545
www.lakings.com
VP, Communications - Mike Altieri

LOS ANGELES LAKERS 310-426-6004
www.nba.com/lakers
Director, Public Relations - John Black

LOS ANGELES SPARKS 310-341-1000
www.wnba.com/sparks
Director, Public Relations - Kristal Shipp

MAIL & DELIVERY

Messengers

CITY SPRINT DELIVERY........................310-258-0600/800-7DIRECT

GO-BETWEEN, INC. 310-276-6266
www.gobetween.com

THE EXPRESS GROUP 310-478-8000/800-539-7737

EXACTA MESSENGER SERVICE 310-843-4999

LE COURIER, INC. 818-848-4151
www.lecourier.com

MAIL & DELIVERY

Messengers

UNIVERSAL COURIER..310-410-4500
www.universalcourier.com

FedEx Drops

Information and Pick-up 800-463-3339
www.fedex.com

BEVERLY HILLS

9663 Santa Monica Blvd. (Bedford Dr.), Beverly Hills
345 N. Maple Dr. (Third St.), Beverly Hills
421 N. Rodeo Dr. (Burton Way), Beverly Hills
433 N. Camden Dr. (Santa Monica Blvd.), Beverly Hills
8730 W. Sunset Blvd. (Doheny Dr.), Beverly Hills

HOLLYWOOD/WEST HOLLYWOOD

6666 Lexington Ave. (Cahuenga Blvd.), Los Angeles
6201 W. Sunset Blvd. (Vine St.), Hollywood
956 Seward Ave. (Santa Monica Blvd.), Hollywood
9201 W. Sunset Blvd. (Doheny Dr.), West Hollywood
7920 W. Sunset Blvd. (Fairfax Ave.), West Hollywood
419 N. Larchmont Blvd. (Beverly Blvd.), Los Angeles

SANTA MONICA/WESTSIDE

1750 Ocean Park Blvd. (17th St.), Santa Monica
501 Colorado Ave. (Fifth St.), Santa Monica
925 Wilshire Blvd. (Ninth St.), Santa Monica
1601 Cloverfield Blvd. (Colorado Ave.), Santa Monica
10880 Wilshire Blvd. (Westwood Blvd.), Los Angeles
11041 Santa Monica Blvd. (Sepulveda Blvd.), Los Angeles
1849 Sawtelle Blvd. (Santa Monica Blvd.), Los Angeles

VALLEY

10218 Riverside Dr. (Cahuenga Blvd.), Studio City
4605 Lankershim Blvd. (Riverside Dr.), Studio City
4370 Tijunga Ave. (Moorpark St.), Studio City
14724 Ventura Blvd. (Kester Ave.), Sherman Oaks
101 N. San Fernando Blvd. (Olive Ave.), Burbank
1016 N. Hollywood Blvd. (Magnolia Ave.), Burbank

UPS Drop Boxes

Information 1-800-PICK-UPS
www.ups.com

BEVERLY HILLS

9940 Santa Monica Blvd. (Wilshire Blvd.), Beverly Hills
415 N. Crescent Dr. (Santa Monica Blvd.), Beverly Hills
9348 Civic Center Dr. (Santa Monica Blvd.), Beverly Hills
301 N. Canon Dr. (Wilshire Blvd.), Beverly Hills

HOLLYWOOD/WEST HOLLYWOOD

7901 Melrose Ave. (Fairfax Ave.), West Hollywood
8730 Sunset Blvd. (La Cienega Blvd.), West Hollywood
1040 N. Las Palmas (Santa Monica Blvd.), Hollywood
6671 Sunset Blvd. (Highland Ave.), Hollywood

SANTA MONICA/WESTSIDE

10920 Wilshire Blvd. (Centinela Ave.), Santa Monica
3015 Main St. (Marine St.), Santa Monica
1801 Avenue of the Stars (Santa Monica Blvd.), Los Angeles
10951 W. Pico Blvd. (Veteran Ave.), Los Angeles

MAIL & DELIVERY

UPS Drop Boxes

VALLEY

4024 Radford Ave. (Ventura Blvd.), Studio City
10911 Riverside Dr. (Lankershim Blvd.), North Hollywood
3500 W. Olive Ave. (Riverside Dr.), Burbank
14724 Ventura Ave. (Kester Ave.), Sherman Oaks

Post Offices

Information..800-275-8777
www.usps.com

BEVERLY HILLS

BEVERLY HILLS MAIN POST OFFICE
325 N. Maple Dr. (Third St.), Beverly Hills

BEVERLY STATION
312 S. Beverly Dr. (Olympic Blvd.), Beverly Hills

POSTAL STORE, THE
323 N. Crescent Dr. (Burton Way), Beverly Hills

WEST BRANCH STATION
820 N. San Vicente Blvd. (La Cienega Blvd.), Beverly Hills

DOWNTOWN

ALAMEDA POST OFFICE STATION
760 N. Main St. (Cesar E. Chavez Ave.), Los Angeles

ARCADE POST OFFICE STATION
508 S. Spring St. (Sixth St.), Los Angeles

ARCO POST OFFICE
505 S. Flower St. (Sixth St.), Los Angeles

BUNKER HILL MAIN POST OFFICE
350 S. Grand Ave. (Fourth St.), Los Angeles

FEDERAL POST OFFICE STATION
300 N. Los Angeles St. (Temple St.), Los Angeles

HOLLYWOOD/WEST HOLLYWOOD

BICENTENNIAL STATION
7610 Beverly Blvd. (Fairfax Ave.), Los Angeles

COLE BRANCH
1125 N. Fairfax Ave. (Santa Monica Blvd.), Los Angeles

HOLLYWOOD STATION
1615 N. Wilcox St. (Cahuenga Blvd.), Hollywood

LOS FELIZ STATION
1825 N. Vermont Ave. (Franklin Ave.), Los Angeles

SANTA WESTERN POST OFFICE STATION
1385 N. Western Ave. (Sunset Blvd.), Los Angeles

SUNSET STATION
1425 N. Cherokee Ave. (Sunset Blvd.), Hollywood

WEST BRANCH STATION
820 N. San Vicente Blvd. (Santa Monica Blvd.), West Hollywood

WILCOX STATION
6457 Santa Monica Blvd. (Cahuenga Blvd.), Hollywood

MAIL & DELIVERY

Post Offices

SANTA MONICA/WESTSIDE

CENTURY CITY MAIN POST OFFICE
9911 W. Pico Blvd. (Century Park East), Century City

OCEAN PARK STATION
2720 Neilson Way (Ocean Park Blvd.), Santa Monica

SANTA MONICA MAIN POST OFFICE
1248 Fifth St. (Arizona Ave.), Santa Monica

VENICE MAIN POST OFFICE
1601 Main St. (Venice Way), Venice

WEST LOS ANGELES STATION
11420 Santa Monica Blvd. (Sawtelle Blvd.), Los Angeles

WILL ROGERS STATION
1217 Wilshire Blvd. (12th St.), Santa Monica

VALLEY

BURBANK DOWNTOWN STATION
135 E. Olive Ave. (San Fernando Blvd.), Burbank

BURBANK MAIN POST OFFICE
2140 N. Hollywood Way (Pacific Ave.), Burbank

CHANDLER STATION
11304 Chandler Blvd. (Tijunga Ave.), North Hollywood

GLENOAKS STATION
1634 N. San Fernando Blvd. (Scott Rd.), Burbank

MAGNOLIA STATION
3810 W. Magnolia Blvd. (Hollywood Way), Burbank

STUDIO CITY STATION
3950 Laurel Canyon Blvd. (Ventura Blvd.), Studio City

TOLUCA LAKE MAIN POST OFFICE
10063 Riverside Dr. (Pass Ave.), North Hollywood

UNIVERSAL CITY MAIN POST OFFICE
4029 Lankershim Blvd. (Cahuenga Blvd.), North Hollywood

VALLEY PLAZA MAIN POST OFFICE
6242 Vantage Ave. (Laurel Canyon Blvd.), North Hollywood

VALLEY VILLAGE STATION
12450 Magnolia Blvd. (Whitsett Ave.), Valley Village

OFFICE SERVICES & SUPPLIES

Copying

BEVERLY HILLS

KINKO'S 310-271-1258
9334 Wilshire Blvd. (Doheny Dr.), Beverly Hills

DOWNTOWN

KINKO'S
835 Wilshire Blvd. (Figueroa St.), Los Angeles 213-892-1700
2723 S. Figueroa St. (Adams Blvd.), Los Angeles 213-747-8341

It is illegal to copy any part of this book

OFFICE SERVICES & SUPPLIES

Copying

HOLLYWOOD/WEST HOLLYWOOD

KINKO'S
8471 Beverly Blvd. (La Cienega Blvd.), Los Angeles ..323-782-6905
7630 Sunset Blvd. (Fairfax Ave.), Los Angeles 323-845-4501
1440 Vine St. (Sunset Blvd.), Los Angeles 323-871-1300

SANTA MONICA/WESTSIDE

KINKO'S
1875 Century Park East (Santa Monica Blvd.), Century City 310-277-0686
10924 Weyburn Ave. (Westwood Blvd.), Los Angeles ..310-443-5501
1520 Westwood Blvd. (Santa Monica Blvd.), Los Angeles 310-475-0789
11819 Wilshire Blvd. (Barrington Ave.), Los Angeles ..310-477-7756
2139 S. Bundy Dr. (Olympic Blvd.), Los Angeles 310-826-8122
601 Wilshire Blvd. (Sixth St.), Santa Monica 310-576-7710
5575 Sepulveda Blvd. (Jefferson Blvd.), Culver City ..310-313-2578
4350 Lincoln Blvd. (90 Freeway), Marina del Rey 310-827-2297

VALLEY

KINKO'S
12101 Ventura Blvd. (Laurel Canyon Blvd.), Studio City 818-980-2679
4556 Van Nuys Blvd. (Moorpark St.), Sherman Oaks....818-906-2679
5810 Sepulveda Blvd. (Hatteras St.), Van Nuys 818-780-2123
4100 Riverside Dr. (Pass Ave.), Burbank 818-567-1044
16652 Ventura Blvd. (Hayvenhurst Ave.), Encino........818-788-4243

OFFICE SERVICES & SUPPLIES

Office Supplies

DOWNTOWN

OFFICE DEPOT
401 E. Second St. (Central Ave.), Los Angeles 213-628-5000
2020 S. Figueroa St. (Washington Blvd.), Los Angeles....213-741-0576

STAPLES 213-746-6330
1701 S. Figueroa St. (Venice Blvd.), Los Angeles

HOLLYWOOD/WEST HOLLYWOOD

OFFICE DEPOT
1240 Vine St. (Fountain Ave.), Los Angeles 323-957-1274
5570 Wilshire Blvd. (La Brea Ave.), Los Angeles 323-939-0186

STAPLES
6450 Sunset Blvd. (Cahuenga Blvd.), Los Angeles 323-467-2155
5407 Wilshire Blvd. (La Brea Ave.), Los Angeles 323-965-5240
1833 La Cienega Blvd. (Venice Blvd.), Los Angeles 310-202-5343

SANTA MONICA/WESTSIDE

OFFICE DEPOT
5640 Sepulveda Blvd. (Slauson Ave.), Culver City 310-390-4023
2231 S. Barrington Ave. (Olympic Blvd.), Los Angeles 310-478-7103

STAPLES
2052 Bundy Dr. (Olympic Blvd.), Los Angeles 310-826-0442
1501 Lincoln Blvd. (California Ave.), Venice.............310-577-6740
10822 Jefferson Blvd. (Overland Ave.), Culver City 310-202-6493

VALLEY

OFFICE DEPOT
11211 Ventura Blvd. (Fulton Ave.), Studio City..........818-760-4414
228 E. Burbank Blvd. (San Fernando Blvd.), Burbank..818-848-2591
6440 Sepulveda Blvd. (Victory Blvd.), Van Nuys 818-780-9916
16571 Ventura Blvd. (Hayvenhurst Ave.), Encino........818-907-1741

STAPLES
12605 Ventura Blvd. (Whitsett Ave.), Studio City 818-753-6390
1060 W. Alameda St. (Main St.), Burbank 818-558-3350
12807 Sherman Way (Coldwater Canyon Ave.), North Hollywood...818-503-7960

CONTENTS

It is illegal to copy any part of this book

FOOD & DRINK

Restaurants

DOWNTOWN

66 212-925-0202
241 Church St. (Leonard St.)
Owner – Jean-Georges Vongerichten

71 CLINTON FRESH FOOD 212-614-6960
71 Clinton (Rivington St.)
Owner – Janet Nelson

AKA CAFÉ 212-979-6096
49 Clinton St. (Rivington St.)
General Manager – Susan Nelson

AQUAGRILL 212-274-0505
210 Spring St. (Sixth Ave.)
www.aquagrill.com
Owner & General Manager - Jennifer Marshall & Jeremy Marshall

BABBO 212-777-0303
110 Waverly Pl. (Washington Square West)
www.babbonyc.com
General Manager - Alfredo Ruiz
Maitre d' - John Mainieri

BALTHAZAR 212-965-1414
80 Spring St. (Crosby St.)
www.balthazarny.com
General Manager - Michael Lahara

BLUE RIBBON BAKERY...212-337-0404
33 Downing St. (Bedford St.)
General Manager – Sean Santamour

BLUE RIBBON SUSHI..212-343-0404
119 Sullivan St. (Prince St.)
Night Manager - Tom Wong

BLUE WATER GRILL 212-529-0900
31 Union Square West (16th St.)
General Manager – Sheena Nestor

BOND STREET..212-777-2500
6 Bond St. (Broadway & Lafayette)
General Manager - Steven Durbahn

BOULEY BAKERY..212-964-2525
120 W. Broadway (Duane St.)
www.bouley.net
Maitre d' - Didier Palange

CHEZ ES SAADA 212-777-5617
42 E. First St. (Second Ave.)
www.chezessaada.com
General Managers – Anthony Connolly

CRAFT...212-780-0880
43 E. 19th St. (Broadway)
www.craftrestaurant.com
General Manager - Katie Grieco

CRV 212-529-1700
24 Fifth Ave. (9th St.)
General Manager – Robert Bohr

DANAL 212-982-6930
90 E. 10TH St. (Third Ave.)
Owner – Danny Saltiel

FOOD & DRINK

Restaurants

DOWNTOWN

DOMINIC...212-343-0700
349 Greenwich St. (Jay St.)
Maitre d' – Patricia Orwicz

GOTHAM BAR & GRILL 212-620-4020
12 E. 12th St. (Fifth Ave.)
General Manager - Richard Hollocou
Service Director - Robin Gustafsson

GRADISCA 212-691-4886
126 W. 13th St. (Sixth Ave.)
General Manager – Massiamo

THE HARRISON 212-274-9310
355 Greenwich St. (Harrison St.)
Managing Director – Alicia Nosenzo
Service Director - Micheline Gaulin

IL BUCO 212-533-1932
47 Bond St. (LaFayette St.)
General Manager – Robert Paris

INDUSTRY 212-777-5920
509 E. 6th St. (Ave. A & B)
General Manager – Terry Carrier

JEWEL BAKO 212-979-1012
239 E. 5th St. (Second Ave.)
Owner – Jack Lamb

JIMMY'S DOWNTOWN 212-486-6400
400 E. 57TH St. (First Ave.)
General Manager – Gary Steffani

LA LUNCHONETTE 212-675-0342
130 Tenth Ave. (18th St.)
Owner – John Francios

MEET 212-242-0990
71-73 Gansevoort St. (Washington St.)
General Manager – Milana Teodorovich

MERCER KITCHEN 212-966-5454
The Mercer, 99 Prince St. (Mercer St.)
www.jean-georges.com
General Manager – Artan Ggoni

NEXT DOOR NOBU 212-334-4445
105 Hudson St. (Franklin St.)
www.myriadrestaurantgroup.com
General Manager - Richard Notar

NOBU 212-219-0500
105 Hudson St. (Franklin St.)
www.myriadrestaurantgroup.com
General Manager - Richard Notar

ONE IF BY LAND, TWO IF BY SEA 212-228-0822
17 Barrow St. (Seventh Avenue South)
www.oneifbyland.com
General Manager - Rosanne Manetta

PARIS COMMUNE 212-929-0509
411 Bleeker St. (W. 11th St.)
Owner – Hugo Uys

FOOD & DRINK

Restaurants

DOWNTOWN

THE PARK 212-352-3313
118 Tenth Ave. (17th St.)
General Manager – Kim Curlanchik

PASTIS 212-929-4844
9-11 Little W. 12th St. (Ninth Ave.)
General Manager – Michael Lahara

PROVENCE 212-475-7500
38 MacDougal St. (Prince St.)
General Managers – Michel & Marc

RAOUL'S 212-966-3518
180 Prince St. (Sullivan St.)
General Manager – Cindy Smith

SAVOY 212-219-8570
70 Prince St. (Crosby St.)
Owner – Peter Hoffman

TRIBECA GRILL 212-941-3900
375 Greenwich St. (Franklin St.)
www.myriadrestaurantgroup.com
Managing Partner - Martin Shapiro

UNION PACIFIC 212-995-8500
111 E.22nd St. (Park & Lexington)
General Manager – Thierry Sighel

VELVET RESTAURANT & LOUNGE 212-965-0439
223 Mulberry St. (Spring St.)
www.velvetnyc.com
General Manager - Louis Donato

VERITAS 212-353-3700
43 E. 20th St. (Park Avenue South)
www.veritas-nyc.com
Maitre d'Hotel - Tim Bellardo

WOO LAE OAK 212-925-8200
148 Mercer St. (Prince St.)
General Manager - Dan Reiser

YAMA 212-475-0969
122 E. 17th St. (Irving Pl.)
General Manager - Yozo Nakamura

MIDTOWN

ALAIN DUCASSE 212-265-7300
Essex House, 155 W. 58th St. (Sixth Ave.)
General Manager & Maitre d' – Herve Durozard

AQUAVIT 212-307-7311
13 W. 54th St. (Fifth Ave.)
www.aquavit.org
General Manager - David Goldstein

ASIA DE CUBA 212-726-7755
Morgans Hotel, 237 Madison Ave. (37th St.)
General Manager - Charlie Irons

ATELIER 212-521-6125
50 Central Park South
General Manager – Ronan Henaff

FOOD & DRINK

Restaurants

MIDTOWN

BARBETTA 212-246-9171
321 W. 46th St. (Eight Ave.)
Owner – Laura Maioglio

CITARELLA 212-332-1515
1240 Avenue of the Americas (49th St. & Sixth Ave.)
General Manager – Helen Guerrera

D'ARTAGNAN 212-687-0300
152 E. 46th St. (Lexington Ave.)
Owner – Ariane Daguin

DB BISTRO MODERNE 212-391-2400
City Club Hotel, 55 W. 44th St. (Sixth Ave.)
www.danielnyc.com
General Manager – JB Francois

ESTIATORIOS MILOS 212-245-7400
125 W. 55th St. (Sixth Ave.)
General Manager – Mario Zeniou

FOUR SEASONS RESTAURANT 212-754-9494
99 E. 52nd St. (Park Ave.)
General Manager – Trideep Bose

HUDSON 212-554-6000/800-444-4786
356 W. 58th St. (Eighth Ave.)
General Manager – John Beier

ILO 212-642-2255
40 W. 40th St. (Sixth Ave.)
General Manager – Patrick Littlejohn & Michel Darmon

INAGIKU 212-355-0440
111 E. 49th St. (Lexington Ave.)
General Manager – Shimura

LA CÔTE BASQUE 212-688-6525
60 W. 55th St. (Sixth Ave.)
General Manager – Loic Cadou

LA GRENOUILLE 212-752-1495
3 E. 52nd St. (Fifth Ave.)
General Manager - Charles Masson

LE CHARLOT 212-794-1628
19 E. 69th St. (Madison Ave.)
General Manager – Bruno Gelormini

LE CIRQUE 2000 212-303-7788
455 Madison Ave. (50th St.)
www.lecirque.com
General Manager - Benito Sevarin

LE PÉRIGORD 212-755-6244
405 E. 52nd St. (First Ave.)
Owner – Georges Briguet

LUTÈCE 212-752-2225
249 E. 50th St. (Second Ave.)
General Manager – Tom Serretti

MICHAEL'S 212-767-0555
24 W. 55th St. (Fifth Ave.)
General Manager – Steve Millington

It is illegal to copy any part of this book

FOOD & DRINK

Restaurants

MIDTOWN

NICOLE'S....................212-223-2288
10 E. 60th St. (Madison Ave.)
General Manager – Oscar Henquet

ONE C.P.S. BRASSERIE....................212-583-1111
The Plaza, One Central Park South (Fifth Ave.)
General Manager - Stacy Adams

PAZO....................212-752-7470
106 E. 57th St. (Park & Lexington)
General Manager – Susanne Hallen

REMI....................212-581-4242
145 W. 53rd St. (Sixth Ave.)
General Manager – Herbert Anton

RUBY FOO'S....................212-489-5600
1626 Broadway (49th St.)
General Manager – Francisco Goitia

TAO....................212-888-2288
42 E. 58th St. (Madison Ave.)
General Manager - Jennifer Rucker

TOWN....................212-582-4445
Chambers Hotel, 15 W. 56th St. (Fifth Ave.)
General Manager – Paul Guzzardo

VONG....................212-486-9592
200 E. 54th St. (Third Ave.)
www.jean-georges.com
General Manager – Joseph Lucas

EASTSIDE

540 PARK....................212-339-4050
Regency Hotel, 540 Park Ave. (61st St.)
General Manager - Stuart Schwartz

AUREOLE....................212-319-1660
34 E. 61st St. (Madison Ave.)
www.aureolerestaurant.com
General Manager - Richard Lepuzer

BARBALUC....................212-774-1999
135 E. 65th St. (Park & Lexington)
General Manager – Raffaele Antonio

DANIEL....................212-288-0033
60 E. 65th St. (Park Ave.)
www.danielnyc.com
General Manager - Michael Lawrence

KING'S CARRIAGE HOUSE....................212-734-5490
251 E. 82nd St. (Second Ave.)
General Manager – Paul King

WESTSIDE

CAFÉ DES ARTISTES....................212-877-3500
1 W. 67th St. (Central Park West)
www.cafedes.com
Managing Director - Jenifer Lang
General Manager - Ron Didner

CALLE OCHO....................212-873-5025
446 Columbus Ave. (81st St.)
General Manager - Wendy Louie

FOOD & DRINK

Restaurants

WESTSIDE

ISABELLA'S....................212-724-2100
359 Columbus Ave. (77th St.)
General Manager – Russell Nemiarche

JEAN GEORGES....................212-299-3900
1 Central Park West (60th St.)
www.jean-georges.com
General Manager – Phillipe Vongerichten

JEAN-LUC....................212-712-1700
507 Columbus Ave. (17th St.)
Managing Partner – Doug Alexander

RUBY FOO'S....................212-724-6700
2182 Broadway (77th St.)
General Manager – Francisco Goitia

TERRACE IN THE SKY....................212-666-9490
400 W. 119th St. (Amsterdam Ave.)
General Manager – Christopher Bernic

Catering

GREAT PERFORMANCES....................212-727-2424
287 Spring St. (Hudson St.)
www.greatperformances.com

NEW YORK CATERERS & PARTY PLANNERS....................212-396-9351
421 E. 65th St. (First Ave.)
www.ny-caterers.com

THOMAS PRETI CATERERS....................212-764-3188/917-667-2331
38-03 24th St., Long Island City
www.thomaspreti.com

YURA & COMPANY....................212-860-8060
1645 Third Ave. (92nd St.)

Event Planning

B. RODWIN & COMPANY, LLC....................212-255-0355
www.brodwinco.com
Partner - Brian Rodwin

BEAUTIFUL BARTENDERS, LLC....................917-488-0504
www.beautifulbartenders.com
Contact – Nilka Thomas

COLIN COWIE LIFESTYLE....................212-396-9007
www.colincowie.com

DAVID LEES PRODUCTIONS....................212-629-4321
www.davidleesproductions.com

LAWRENCE SCOTT EVENTS LTD....................516-933-7535

THE TOTAL AFFAIR....................646-230-7991
www.thetotalaffair.com

TRAVESTIES ENTERTAINMENT....................212-695-1114/800-938-6464
www.travestiesent.com

ACCOMMODATIONS

Hotels

DOWNTOWN

60 THOMPSON.................................212-431-0400/877-431-0400
60 Thompson St. (Broome St.)
www.thompsonhotels.com
General Manager - Stephen Brandman

HOLIDAY INN DOWNTOWN 212-966-8898
138 Lafayette St. (Howard St.)
www.hidowntown-nyc.com
General Manager – Sherman Chin

THE MARCEL 212-696-3800
201 E. 24th St. (Third Ave.)
www.nychotels.com
General Manager - Robert Viallta

MERCER HOTEL 212-966-6060/888-918-6060
147 Mercer St. (Prince St.)
www.mercerhotel.com
General Manager - Philip Truelove

SOHO GRAND HOTEL..........................212-965-3000/800-965-3000
310 W. Broadway (Canal St.)
www.sohogrand.com
General Manager – Brian Abel

ACCOMMODATIONS

Hotels

DOWNTOWN

TRIBECA GRAND HOTEL.....................212-519-6600/877-519-6600
2 Avenue of the Americas (Walker St.)
www.tribecagrand.com
General Manager – Brian Abel

MIDTOWN

THE BENJAMIN 212-715-2500/888-423-6526
125 E. 50th St. (Lexington Ave.)
www.thebenjamin.com
General Manager – Holly Waterbor

THE BRYANT PARK 212-642-2200
40 W. 40th St. (Sixth Ave.)
www.bryantparkhotel.com
General Manager – Bill Colombo

CHAMBERS 212-974-5656/866-204-5656
15 W. 56th St. (Fifth Ave.)
www.chambersnyc.com
General Manager – Andrew Tilley

FLATOTEL 212-887-9400/800-FLATOTEL
135 West 52nd St.
www.flatotel.com
Sales Manager – Brenda Pesce

If you prefer a typical NY hotel experience, we can put a cot in the bathroom for you.

The largest standard guest rooms of any Manhattan hotel
- Two highly rated restaurants
- 24 hr. business center
- Conference and meeting facilities

FLATOTEL
LIVE LARGE.

135 West 52nd Street, New York City 212-887-9400 1-800-FLATOTEL www.flatotel.com

ACCOMMODATIONS

Hotels

MIDTOWN

FOUR SEASONS HOTEL 212-758-5700
57 E. 57th St. (Madison Ave.)
www.fourseasons.com
General Manager - Thomas Steinhauer

HUDSON..212-554-6000/800-444-4786
356 W. 58th St. (Eighth Ave.)
www.hudsonhotel.com
General Manager – John Beier

MILLENNIUM HOTEL 212-768-4400/866-866-6455
145 W. 44th St. (Sixth Ave.)
www.millennium-hotels.com
General Manager - Per Hellman

THE MUSE 212-485-2400/877-692-6873
130 W. 46th St. (Sixth Ave.)
www.themusehotel.com
General Manager - Mark Briskin

PARAMOUNT 212-764-5500/800-225-7474
235 W. 46th St. (Broadway)
www.ianschragerhotels.com
General Manager – June Mcdougal

THE PENINSULA 212-956-2888/800-262-9467
700 Fifth Ave. (55th St.)
www.peninsula.com
General Manager - Nikalus Leuenberger

THE PLAZA 212-759-3000
Fifth Ave. & Central Park South (58th St.)
www.fairmont.com
General Manager – Len Czarnecki

RIHGA ROYAL 212-307-5000/800-937-5454
151 W. 54th St. (Seventh Ave.)
www.rihgaroyalnyc.com
General Manager – Barry Cregan

ROYALTON.......................................212-869-4400/800-635-9013
44 W. 44th St. (Fifth Ave.)
www.ianschragerhotels.com
General Manager – Jan Rozenbeld

THE ST. REGIS 212-753-4500
2 E. 55th St. (Fifth Ave.)
www.stregis.com
General Manager – Guenter Richter

THE SHOREHAM...............................212-247-6700/800-553-3347
33 W. 55th St. (Fifth Ave.)
www.shorehamhotel.com
General Manager - Jeff Harvy

THE WALDORF ASTORIA 212-355-3000/800-925-3673
301 Park Ave. (49th St.)
www.waldorf.com
General Manager - Eric Long

W NEW YORK 212-755-1200
541 Lexington Ave. (49th St.)
www.whotels.com
General Manager – Nancy Sherman

ACCOMMODATIONS

Hotels

MIDTOWN

W NEW YORK - THE TUSCANY 212-686-1600
120 E. 39th St. (Lexington Ave.)
www.whotels.com
General Manager - Jeff Darnell

EASTSIDE

THE CARLYLE 212-744-1600
Madison Ave. & 76th St.
www.rosewoodhotels.com
General Manager – James McBride

THE MARK 212-744-4300/800-843-6275
25 E. 77th St. (Madison Ave.)
www.themarkhotel.com
General Manager – Alain Negueloua

PIERRE HOTEL 212-838-8000/800-743-7734
2 E. 61st St. (Fifth Ave.)
www.fourseasons.com/pierre
General Manager – Guy Rigby

WESTSIDE

MAYFLOWER HOTEL ON THE PARK...... 212-265-0060/800-223-4164
15 Central Park West (61st St.)
www.mayflowerhotel.com
General Manager - Xavier S. Lividini

THE PHILLIPS CLUB 212-835-8800/877-854-8800
155 W. 66th St. (Broadway)
www.phillipsclub.com
General Manager - Alan Tenant

TRUMP INTERNATIONAL
HOTEL & TOWER 212-299-1000/888-448-7867
1 Central Park West (60th St.)
www.trumpintl.com
General Manager - Tom Downing

Corporate Retreats

NEW YORK

GENEVA ON THE LAKE 315-789-7190/800-3GENEVA
1001 Lochland Rd., Geneva
www.genevaonthelake.com
General Manager - William Schickel

PARC BROOK 845-677-5950
329 N. Tower Hill Rd., Millbrook
www.parcbrook.com
General Manager - Heidi Otto

SOUTHAMPTON INN 631-283-6500/800-832-6500
91 Hill St., Southampton
www.southamptoninn.com
General Manager - Barry Shatoff

VILLA ROMA RESORT HOTEL 845-887-4880/800-533-6767
356 Village Roma Rd., Callicoon
www.villaroma.com
General Manager – Paul Carlucci

ACCOMMODATIONS

Corporate Retreats

CONNECTICUT

THE INN AT NATIONAL HALL 203-221-1351/800-628-4255
Two Post Road West, Westport
www.innatnationalhall.com
General Manager – Marco Deglinnocenti

THE MAYFLOWER INN 860-868-9466
118 Woodbury Rd., Washington
www.mayflowerinn.com
General Manager - John Trevenen

WATER'S EDGE RESORT 860-399-5901/800-222-5901
1525 Boston Post Rd., Westbrook
www.watersedge-resort.com
General Manager - Paul Van Hoosier

Corporate Housing

CHURCHILL CORPORATE SERVICES 800-658-7366
www.churchillcorp.com

EMPIRE STATE PROPERTIES....................212-262-1755
www.empirestateproperties.com

ENVOY CLUB 212-481-4600/212-402-1000
www.envoyclub.com
Director, Sales – Jillian Malins
General Manager – Robert Dunker

OAKWOOD CORPORATE HOUSING 800-259-6914
www.oakwood.com

MARMARA, INC. 212-427-3100
www.marmara-manhattan.com

Real Estate

BROWN HARRIS STEVENS....................212-588-5600
www.brownharrisstevens.com

THE COCORAN GROUP 800-544-4055
www.corcoran.com

SOTHEBY'S INTERNATIONAL REALTY 212-431-2440
www.nycsothebysrealty.com

STRIBLING & ASSOCIATES 212-570-2440
www.striblingny.com

TRAVEL & TRANSPORTATION

Travel Agencies

FRENCHWAY....................212-243-3500
www.frenchwaytravel.com

TRAVELCRAFT 646-336-7081/800-777-2723
www.travelcraftusa.com

MARGO TRAVEL, INC. 212-944-1333

Airlines - Domestic

AIR MIDWEST/US AIRWAYS EXPRESS 800-428-4322
www.usairways.com

AIRTRAN....................800-247-8726
www.airtran.com

TRAVEL & TRANSPORTATION

Airlines - Domestic

ALASKA 800-252-7522
www.alaskaairlines.com

ALOHA 800-367-5250
www.alohaairlines.com

AMERICAN....................800-433-7300
www.aa.com

AMERICAN TRANS AIR....................800-435-9282
www.ata.com

AMERICA WEST....................800-235-9292
www.americawest.com

CONTINENTAL....................800-525-0280
www.continental.com

DELTA 800-221-1212
www.delta.com

FRONTIER 800-432-1359
www.frontierairlines.com

HAWAIIAN....................800-367-5320
www.hawaiianair.com

JETBLUE 800-538-2583
www.jetblue.com

MIDWEST EXPRESS 800-452-2022
www.midwestexpress.com

NORTHWEST 800-225-2525
www.nwa.com

SOUTHWEST 800-435-9792
www.southwest.com

US AIRWAYS 800-428-4322
www.usairways.com

UNITED 800-241-6522
www.ual.com

Airlines - International

AER LINGUS 800-474-7424
www.aerlingus.ie

AIR CANADA 888-247-2262
www.aircanada.com

AIR FRANCE....................800-237-2747
www.airfrance.com

AIR NEW ZEALAND 800-262-1234
www.airnewzealand.com

ALITALIA 800-223-5730
www.alitaliausa.com

AUSTRIA AIRLINES 800-843-0002
www.aua.com

AVIANCA....................800-284-2622
www.avianca.com

BRITISH AIRWAYS....................800-247-9297
www.british-airways.com

CATHAY PACIFIC 800-233-2742
www.cathaypacific.com/www.cathay-usa.com

It is illegal to copy any part of this book

TRAVEL & TRANSPORTATION

Airlines - International

EL AL 800-223-6700
www.elal.co.il

FINNAIR 800-950-5000
www.finnair.com

IBERIA AIRLINES 800-772-4642
www.iberia.com

ICELANDAIR 800-223-5500
www.icelandair.com

KLM ROYAL DUTCH 800-374-7747
www.klm.com

KOREAN AIR 800-438-5000
www.koreanair.com

LUFTHANSA 800-645-3880
www.lufthansa.com

QUANTAS 800-227-4500
www.quantas.com

SWISS 877-359-7947
www.swiss.com

VIRGIN ATLANTIC 800-862-8621
www.virgin-atlantic.com

Charter Planes

AIRNET 888-888-8463
www.airnet.com

DESERT & ISLAND AIR CHARTER 800-835-9135
www.desertislandair.com

JET EQUITY 914-761-7776
www.jetequity.com
Contact - Russ Loret

SENTIENT 866-473-6843
www.sentientjet.com

Car Rentals

ALAMO 800-462-5266
www.alamo.com

AVIS 800-331-1212
www.avis.com

BUDGET 800-527-0700
www.budget.com

DOLLAR 800-800-4000
www.dollar.com

ENTERPRISE 800-736-8227
www.enterprise.com

HERTZ 800-654-3131
www.hertz.com

NATIONAL 800-227-7368
www.nationalcar.com

THRIFTY 800-847-4389
www.thrifty.com

TRAVEL & TRANSPORTATION

Car Services/Limos

ALLSTATE PRIVATE CAR & LIMOUSINE 212-333-3333

ATTITUDE NEW YORK 212-397-0004

BERMUDA LIMOUSINE INTERNATIONAL 212-647-8400
www.bermudalimo.com

BLS LIMOUSINE INTERNATIONAL 800-843-5752
www.blslimo.com

CARMEL CAR & LIMOUSINE SERVICE 212-666-6666

DIVA 800-427-3482
www.divalimo.com

MUSIC EXPRESS 800-421-9494
www.musiclimo.com

SURREY CADILLAC LIMOUSINE SERVICE 718-937-5700

TEL AVIV 212-777-7777
www.telavivlimo.com

GIFTS & SHOPPING

Florists

ELIZABETH RYAN FLORAL DESIGNS 212-995-1111

LOTUS 212-463-0555
www.lotus212.com

RENNY AND REED 212-288-7000
www.rennyandreed.com

COUNTRY GARDENS 212-966-2015

NATURAL SURROUNDINGS 800-567-7007

WILD POPPY 212-717-5757

Gift Baskets

MANHATTAN FRUITIER 212-686-0404/800-841-5718
www.manhattanfruitier.com

THE ORCHARD 718-377-1799/800-222-0240
www.orchardfruit.com

Personal Shoppers

CONCIERGE CONNECTION OF NEW YORK 917-763-7878
www.conciergeconnectionnyc.com
Contact - Barbara

CROSS IT OFF YOUR LIST 212-725-0122/888-XOFFLIST
www.crossitoffyourlist.com

DONUM 978-352-3336
www.donumgifts.com

VISUAL THERAPY 212-315-2233
www.visual-therapy.com

When you need a car in 50 cities around the world,

When you have 20 employees that need a ride to work every day,

When you want to become familiar with cutting edge voicemail technology,

That's not us.

When you're simply looking for the best in New York City...

A·T·T·I·T·U·D·E

N E W • Y O R K

LIMOUSINES

(212) 397-0004

SCREENING ROOMS

DOWNTOWN

ANTHOLOGY FILM ARCHIVES....212-505-5181
32 Second Ave. (E. Second St.)
www.anthologyfilmarchives.org

GRAND SCREEN 212-519-6600
Tribeca Grand, 2 Sixth Ave. (Walker St.)
www.tribecagrand.com

QUAD CINEMAS 212-255-8800
34 W. 13th St. (Fifth Ave.)
www.quadcinema.com

TRIBECA SCREENING ROOM 212-941-4000
375 Greenwich St. (N. Moore St.)
www.tribecafilm.com

MIDTOWN

BROADWAY SCREENING ROOM 212-307-0990
1619 Broadway, 5th Fl. (49th St.)
www.mybsr.com

DISNEY SCREENING ROOM 212-593-8900
500 Park Ave. (59th St.)

FOX SCREENING ROOM....212-556-2406
1211 Avenue of the Americas (47th St.)

MAGNO....212-302-2505
729 Seventh Ave. (48th St.)
www.magnosoundandvideo.com

MGM 212-708-0300
1350 Sixth Ave. (55th St.)

PLANET HOLLYWOOD SCREENING ROOM 212-265-2404
1540 Broadway (45th St.)

SONY PICTURES 212-833-7654
550 Madison Ave. (55th St.)
Contact – Graham Smith

WARNER BROS. 212-484-8080
1271 Sixth Ave. (50th St.)

EASTSIDE

ALLIANCE FRANÇAIS 212-355-6100
22 E. 60th St. (Madison Ave.)
www.fiaf.org

WESTSIDE

WALTER READE THEATER 212-875-5608
165 W. 65th St. (Amsterdam Ave.)
www.filmlinc.com

VIP TICKETS

NEW JERSEY NETS....201-635-3155
www.njnets.com
Vice President, Entertainment Development & Talent Relations – Jennifer MaClure

NEW YORK GIANTS 201-935-8111
www.giants.com
President - Wellington Mara

NEW YORK ISLANDERS 516-501-6725
www.newyorkislanders.com
Vice President, Marketing & Sales – Paul Lancey

VIP TICKETS

NEW YORK JETS 516-560-8107
www.newyorkjets.com
Director, Public Relations – Ron Colangelo

NEW YORK KNICKS 212-465-6102
www.nba.com/knicks
Director, VIP Services – Anne Marie Dunleavy

NEW YORK LIBERTY....212-564-9622
www.wnba.com/liberty
Vice President, Marketing & Communications – Amy Scheer

NEW YORK METS 718-507-6387
www.mets.mlb.com
Vice President, Ticket Sales – Bill Ianciello

NEW YORK RANGERS 212-465-6405
www.newyorkrangers.com
Vice President, Marketing – Jeanie Baumgartner

NEW YORK YANKEES 718-293-4300
www.yankees.mlb.com
Director, Community Relations/Special Assistant to George M. Steinbrenner – Brian Smith

MAIL & DELIVERY

Messengers

CITIPAK DELIVERY SYSTEMS 212-265-9080

CITY EXPEDITOR, INC. 212-353-2042

GREGORY'S MESSENGER SERVICE, INC. 212-758-5506
www.gregorys-messenger.com

MOBILE MESSENGER SERVICE 212-247-7400

PERSONAL MESSENGER SERVICES....212-505-7930

SUPERSONIC MESSENGER SERVICE 212-944-6932
www.slsonline.com

FedEx Drops

Information....800-463-3339
www.fedex.com

DOWNTOWN

229 W. Fourth St. (Sheridan Square)
4 Union Square East (Fourth Ave.)
20 E. 20th St. (Broadway)

MIDTOWN

405 Park Ave. (54th St.)
880 Third Ave. (53rd St.)

EASTSIDE

1382 Third Ave. (79th St.)
1569 Second Ave. (81st St.)
1710 First Ave. (88th St.)

WESTSIDE

2372 Broadway (86th St.)
491 Amsterdam Ave. (83rd St.)

HOLLYWOOD CREATIVE DIRECTORY

HOLLYWOOD MUSIC INDUSTRY DIRECTORY Premier Edition

ISBN 1928936288
$59.95

- A & R Executives
- Soundtrack Executives
- Booking Agents
- Personal Managers
- Publishers
- Music Licensing
- Music Supervisors
- Recording Studios/ Soundstages

2004 The Hollywood Reporter BLU-BOOK PRODUCTION DIRECTORY

ISBN 192893630X
$74.95

The Hollywood Reporter Blu-Book Production Directory contains more than 200 product and service categories with thousands of listings. The directory is organized into 10 major tabbed sections that represent all the services and personnel necessary to take a film, TV, commercial or music video project from concept to completion. The Blu-Book also includes below-the-line craft professionals with credit and contact information. From camera rentals to sound stages to costumes to special effects to props to finding an animal for a production, it can all be found in this directory—truly "the yellow pages of Hollywood." Now includes expanded New York production listings.

HOLLYWOOD
CREATIVE
DIRECTORY

1024 N. Orange Drive, Hollywood, CA 90038
Phone 323.308.3490 or 800.815.0503
Fax 323.308.3493 • www.hcdonline.com

MAIL & DELIVERY

UPS Drop Boxes

Information 1-800-PICK-UPS
www.ups.com

DOWNTOWN

625 Sixth Ave. (18th St.)
421 Hudson St. (Leroy St.)
11 Madison Ave. (24th St.)
16 W. 22nd St. (Fifth Ave.)

MIDTOWN

450 Park Ave. (57th St.)
919 Third Ave. (55th St.)
500 Fifth Ave. (42nd St.)

EASTSIDE

201 E. 69th St. (Third Ave.)
1334 York Ave. (71st St.)
667 Madison Ave. (61st St.)

WESTSIDE

2112 Broadway (74th St.)
1995 Broadway (68th St.)
155 W. 72st St. (Amsterdam Ave.)

Post Offices

Information..800-275-8777
www.usps.com

DOWNTOWN

CANAL STATION
350 Canal St. (Wooster. St.)

PECK SLIP STATION
1 Peck Slip (Water St.)

VILLAGE STATION
201 Varick St. (W. Houston St.)

PRINCE STATION
124 Greene St. (Prince St.)

CANAL STREET RETAIL
6 Doyers St. (Confucius Pl.)

MIDTOWN

BRYANT STATION
23 W. 43rd St. (Fifth Ave.)

GRAND CENTRAL STATION
450 Lexington Ave. (43rd St.)

MURRAY HILL STATION
115 E. 34th St. (Lexington Ave.)

EMPIRE STATE STATION
19 W. 33rd St. (Fifth Ave.)

GREELEY SQUARE STATION
39 W. 31st St. (Seventh Ave.)

MIDTOWN STATION
223-241 W. 38th St. (Seventh Ave.)

TIMES SQUARE STATION
340 W. 42nd St. (Eighth Ave.)

MAIL & DELIVERY

Post Offices

MIDTOWN

ROCKEFELLER CENTER STATION
610 Fifth Ave. (48th St.)

RADIO CITY STATION
322 W. 52nd St. (Eighth Ave.)

EASTSIDE

CHEROKEE STATION
1483 York Ave. (79th St.)

GRACIE STATION
229 E. 85th St. (Third Ave.)

YORKVILLE STATION
1617 Third Ave. (94th St.)

LENOX HILL STATION
217 E. 70th St. (Third Ave.)

WESTSIDE

ANSONIA STATION
178 Columbus Ave. (68th St.)

PLANETARIUM STATION
127 W. 83rd St. (Columbus Ave.)

COLUMBUS CIRCLE STATION
27 W. 60th St. (Broadway)

PARK WEST STATION
693 Columbus Ave. (94th St.)

OFFICE SERVICES & SUPPLIES

Copying

DOWNTOWN

KINKO'S
21 Astor Pl. (LaFayette St.)...................................212-228-9511
250 E. Houston St. (Norfolk St.)............................212-253-9020

NEW YORK COPY CENTER
204 E. 11th St. (Third Ave.) 212-673-5628
34 E. Seventh St. (Second Ave.)............................212-473-8234

MIDTOWN

KINKO'S
191 Madison Ave. (34th St.) 212-685-3449
60 W. 40th St. (Sixth Ave.) 212-921-1060
16 E. 52nd St. (Fifth Ave.) 212-308-2679
240 Central Park South (Seventh Ave.) 212-258-3750

ABC COPY 212-949-0203
405 Lexington Ave. (E. 42nd St.)

EASTSIDE

KINKO'S 212-628-5500
1122 Lexington Ave. (78th St.)

WESTSIDE

KINKO'S 212-362-5288
221 W. 72nd St. (Columbus Ave.)

Available online at www.hcdonline.com

OFFICE SERVICES & SUPPLIES

Office Supplies

DOWNTOWN

OFFICE DEPOT 212-779-8686
540 Second Ave. (30th St.)

STAPLES
488 Broadway (Broome St.)...................................212-219-1299
345 Park Avenue South (26th St.) 212-683-3267
200 Water St. (Fulton St.)....................................212-785-9521

MIDTOWN

OFFICE DEPOT
1441 Broadway (40th St.).....................................212-764-2465
521 Fifth Ave. (43rd St.).......................................212-557-3757

OFFICE SERVICES & SUPPLIES

Office Supplies

MIDTOWN

STAPLES
16 E. 34th St. (Fifth Ave.)....................................212-683-8009
730 Third Ave. (45th St.) 212-867-9486
205 E. 42nd St. (Third Ave.) 212-697-1591
1065 Sixth Ave. (40th St.) 212-997-4446
57 W. 57th St. (Sixth Ave.) 212-308-0335
575 Lexington Ave. (51st St.) 212-644-2118
425 Park Ave. (5°6th St.) 212-753-9640

EASTSIDE

STAPLES 212-426-6190
1280 Lexington Ave. (86th St.)

WESTSIDE

STAPLES 212-712-9617
2248 Broadway (81st St.)

It is illegal to copy any part of this book

SECTION A

DEALS BY COMPANY

2929 Productions
HDNet Films 212-255-0626

44 Blue Productions, Inc.
Al Burton Productions 310-858-5511

A&E Television Networks
44 Blue Productions, Inc. 818-760-4442
Spotlight Health, Inc. 310-552-0800
Weller/Grossman Productions 818-755-4800

ABC Entertainment Television Group
The Bedford Falls Company 310-394-5022
Diplomatic Productions 323-857-6800
Harpo Films, Inc. 310-278-5559
The Landsburg Company 310-889-7112
Launa Newman Productions (LNP) 310-288-8383
Next Entertainment 818-972-0077

Orly Adelson Productions
Canvas House Films 818-558-1904
Skylark Films, Ltd. 310-396-5753

Craig Anderson Productions
Beth Grossbard Productions 310-841-2555

Ardustry Entertainment
Sam Okun Productions 310-271-0034

Armada Pictures
Filmsmith 310-260-8866

Bad Boy Films
777 Entertainment Group, Ltd. 310-824-0664

Baldwin Entertainment Group
Nick Grillo Productions 310-453-1351

BBC Worldwide America
Malcolm Leo Productions 323-464-4448

Beacon, A Division of Holding Pictures
Katalyst Films 310-907-2236

Bravo Network
Northstar Entertainment 818-762-1010

The Bubble Factory
Northstar Entertainment 818-762-1010

The Buena Vista Motion Pictures Group
Gunnfilms 818-560-6156
The Robert Simonds Company 310-789-2200

Carsey-Werner-Mandabach
The Martin/Stein Company 818-655-5730

Castle Rock Entertainment
Reiner/Greisman 310-285-2300
Zane Buzby & Conan Berkeley Productions 323-223-5566

Catch 23 Entertainment, Inc.
Avalanche! Entertainment 310-477-1464
Trevor Macy Productions 310-393-3233

CBS Entertainment
Gran Via Productions 310-777-3522
High Horse Films 323-939-8802
The Landsburg Company 310-889-7112
Michele Lee Productions 310-446-1774

Columbia Pictures
Allied Stars 310-244-5188
Michael De Luca Productions 310-244-4990
Flower Films, Inc. 310-285-0200
Gittes, Inc. 310-244-4333
The Mark Gordon Company 310-943-6401
Nuyorican 310-943-6600
Out of the Blue . . . Entertainment 310-244-7811
Parkway Productions 818-753-2323
Ricochet Entertainment 310-244-8065
Spyglass Entertainment Group 310-443-5800
Wonderland Sound and Vision 310-659-4451
Laura Ziskin Productions 310-244-7373

Comedy Central
Dakota North Entertainment/Dakota Films 818-760-0099

Cosmic Entertainment
Heller Highwater 310-275-8080, x114

Court TV
Norsemen Productions 818-753-3100

Davis Entertainment Company
Gross Entertainment 818-560-8117
Jericho Entertainment 310-709-4860

Digital Ranch Productions
Two Islands Entertainment 818-889-3902

Dimension Films
Marty Katz Productions 310-264-3948
Neo Art & Logic 323-653-6007
Platinum Studios, LLC 310-276-3900
Principato-Young Entertainment 310-274-4130

Discovery Networks, U.S.
44 Blue Productions, Inc. 818-760-4442
Norsemen Productions 818-753-3100
Weller/Grossman Productions 818-755-4800

The Walt Disney Company
Farrell Paura Productions, LLC 818-560-3000
Harpo Films, Inc. 310-278-5559
Hyde Park Entertainment 310-449-3191
Janicek-Marino Creative 303-860-0070
Junction Entertainment 818-560-2800
LivePlanet 310-664-2400
Mandeville Films . . . . . See Listing
Ricardo Mestres Productions 310-472-3242
Vanguard Films/Vanguard Animation 310-360-8039

Walt Disney Pictures/Touchstone Pictures
Beacon, A Division of Holding Pictures 310-260-7000
Boxing Cat Productions 818-765-4870
Jerry Bruckheimer Films 310-664-6260
Frontier Pictures 818-560-6970
Martin Chase Productions 818-560-3952
Mayhem Pictures 310-393-5005
Pandemonium 310-385-4088
Pfeffer Film 818-560-3177
Tollin/Robbins Productions 818-766-5004

The Donners' Company
Winchester Films 310-395-4800

Double Edge Entertainment
Cherry Road Films, LLC 310-458-6550

DreamWorks SKG

Apatow Productions 310-255-7026
Apostle Pictures 212-541-4323
Ember Entertainment Group 310-230-9759
ImageMovers 818-733-8300
The Jinks/Cohen Company 818-777-9880
The Montecito Picture Company 805-565-8590
Red Hour Films 323-602-5000
Vanguard Films/Vanguard Animation 310-360-8039
Wonderland Films 818-733-6960
Zaloom Film 818-733-7000

Echelon Entertainment

Unistar International Pictures 818-558-1820

EOE - ESPN Original Entertainment

Angotti Productions, Inc. 310-770-0718

Escape Artists

Kaplan/Perrone Entertainment, LLC 310-244-6681

Film Garden Entertainment, Inc.

Rive Gauche International TV 818-784-9912

Fine Living

44 Blue Productions, Inc. 818-760-4442
Weller/Grossman Productions 818-755-4800

Focus Features/Rogue Pictures

Back Lot Pictures 818-777-7522
Bona Fide Productions 310-273-6782
Pretty Pictures 818-733-0926
Stratus Film Company 310-689-1691
This is that, corp. 212-601-5900

Food Network

Weller/Grossman Productions 818-755-4800

Fox Television Studios

KLS Communications, Inc. 800-887-0248
Nuyorican 310-943-6600
Shevloff McKean Productions 310-369-1898
Typhoon Entertainment 310-430-1503

Franchise Pictures, Inc.

Camelot Entertainment Group, Inc. 760-759-2320
Joel Stevens Entertainment 818-509-5700

Global Media Television

The Bregman Entertainment Group 213-833-6207

Goldcrest Films International, Inc.

Peter Newman Productions, Inc. 212-897-3949

Grosso Jacobson Communications Corp.

Gloria Monty Productions, Inc. 310-274-4924

HBO Films

Avenue Pictures 310-996-6800
Blumhouse Productions 323-856-9147
Cine Mosaic 212-625-3797
Face Productions/Jennilind Productions 310-205-2746
New Redemption Pictures 310-315-4820

HBO Independent Productions

Comedy Arts Studios 310-382-3000

HBO Original Programming

Creative Players Management 310-278-0065
Ensemble 310-300-9130
PB Management 323-653-7284
Rockstone Pictures 310-260-2587

The History Channel

Weller/Grossman Productions 818-755-4800

Home & Garden Television (HGTV)

44 Blue Productions, Inc. 818-760-4442
Weller/Grossman Productions 818-755-4800

Hypnotic

Quality Filmed Entertainment 310-453-2345

Intermedia Film Equities USA, Inc.

Gran Via Productions 310-777-3522
Outlaw Production 310-777-2000

Jaffe/Braunstein Films, Ltd.

Michael G. Larkin Productions 310-826-3148
Ellyn Williams Productions 310-207-6600

Jersey Films

Hella Good Moving Pictures 310-488-9478

Lifetime Television (Los Angeles)

44 Blue Productions, Inc. 818-760-4442
Blue Raven Films 818-785-1886
Marian Rees Associates 818-508-5599

Lions Gate Entertainment

Al Burton Productions 310-858-5511
The Gurin Company 818-623-9393
Harding & Associates 818-432-4200
Ithaka 310-314-9585
Sobini Films 310-255-5115

LMNO Productions

Rive Gauche International TV 818-784-9912

Mandalay Pictures

Riche Productions 323-549-4393

Maverick Films

Concept Entertainment 310-276-6177
Zachary Feuer Films 310-729-2110

Media 8 Entertainment

Handprint Entertainment 310-481-4400

Metro-Goldwyn-Mayer Studios, Inc.

Apartment 3B Productions 310-449-3478
Atlantic Streamline 310-319-9366
Danjaq, LLC 310-449-3185
Michael Grais Productions 310-455-2699
Hyde Park Entertainment 310-449-3191
Irish DreamTime 310-449-3411
David Ladd Films 310-449-3410
Pensé Productions 310-449-3972
Arthur Sarkissian Productions 310-385-1486
SideStreet Entertainment 818-955-5240
Single Cell Pictures 310-360-7600
Trilogy Entertainment Group 310-656-9733
Mark Victor Productions 310-828-3339

Metro-Goldwyn-Mayer Worldwide Television

Maloof Television 310-452-5760
Mark Victor Productions 310-828-3339

Millennium Films

Emmett/Furla Films 310-659-9411
Dan Redler Entertainment 818-999-0786

Miramax Films
Craven/Maddalena Films 818-752-0197
Creative Light Entertainment 323-658-9166
Dancing Asparagus Productions 310-552-3333
Marty Katz Productions 310-264-3948
Outerbanks Entertainment 323-654-3700
The Todd Phillips Company 323-822-4300
Tapestry Films, Inc. 310-275-1191
Vertigo Entertainment 310-288-5160
View Askew Productions, Inc. 732-842-6933

Morgan Creek Productions
Ascendant Pictures 310-288-4600

Morningstar Entertainment
Rive Gauche International TV 818-784-9912

MPH Entertainment, Inc.
Rive Gauche International TV 818-784-9912

MTV Networks
7ponies productions 323-822-3595
Dakota North Entertainment/Dakota Films 818-760-0099
Liquid Theory 310-276-0194
Logo Entertainment, Inc. 310-276-6700
Terence Michael Productions, Inc. 310-823-3432

Mutual Film Company
Melinda Jason Company 310-274-9122

Nash Entertainment
Robert Kosberg Productions 323-468-4513

NBC Entertainment
Dark Harbor Productions 818-973-2769
The Landsburg Company 310-889-7112
Landscape Pictures 310-248-6200
Stan Rogow Productions 310-264-4199

NBC Universal Television Studio
Broadway Video (NY) 212-265-7600
Doozer 818-623-1880
Nuance Productions 818-754-5484
Untitled Burke-Tarses Project 818-840-7701
Wolf Films, Inc. 818-777-6969

Nelvana Entertainment/A Corus Entertainment Company
Paraskevas Studios 631-287-1665

Neo Art & Logic
Dimension Films 212-941-3800

New Concorde
Yellow Hat Productions, Inc 323-254-4416

New Crime Productions
Fallout Entertainment 310-571-0570

New Line Cinema
Benderspink 323-856-5500
Blue Raven Films 818-785-1886
Chick Flicks 310-967-6541
Crystal Lake Entertainment, Inc. 818-995-1585
Adam Fields Productions 310-859-9300
FilmEngine 323-960-1480
Karz Entertainment 323-785-2123
Landscape Pictures 310-248-6200
Moving Pictures, DPI 310-288-5464
Rat Entertainment/Rat TV 310-228-5000
Sandbox Entertainment 310-967-6451

New Line Television
J.D. Feigelson Productions, Inc. 310-273-7769
Trilogy Entertainment Group 310-656-9733

New Wave Entertainment
SideStreet Entertainment 818-955-5240

Newmarket Capital Group
Blue Raven Films 818-785-1886

Nickelodeon/Nick at Nite/TV Land/Spike TV
Frederator Studios 818-736-3606

Nu Image
Emmett/Furla Films 310-659-9411

Overbrook Entertainment
Liquid Theory 310-276-0194

Paramount Pictures-Motion Picture Group
Alphaville 323-956-4803
Rick Berman Productions 323-956-5037
Bull's Eye Entertainment 310-470-7500
C/W Productions 323-956-8199
Carsey-Werner-Mandabach 818-655-5598
CFP Productions 323-956-8866
The Chesterfield Film Company 213-683-3977
Robert Cort Productions 323-850-2644
Darkwoods Productions 323-850-2497
di Bonaventura Pictures, Inc. 323-956-5454
The Robert Evans Company 323-956-8800
First Light 323-956-8871
Frequency Films 323-956-5244
Guy Walks Into a Bar 323-930-9935
The Kerner Entertainment Company 310-559-5500
Klasky Csupo, Inc. 323-468-2600
Lakeshore Entertainment Corporation 323-956-4222
Latham Entertainment 323-956-8882
Lion Rock Productions 310-309-2980
A.C. Lyles Productions 323-956-5819
The Manhattan Project, Ltd. 212-258-2541
MTV Films 323-956-8023
Nickelodeon Movies 323-956-8650
Lynda Obst Productions 323-956-8744
Scott Rudin Productions 323-956-4600

Paramount Television
The Axelrod/Edwards Company 323-956-3705
Bakula Productions, Inc. 323-956-3030
Rick Berman Productions 323-956-5037
Steven Bochco Productions 310-369-2400
Braga Productions 323-956-5799
Charles Bros. 323-956-5962
Charles Floyd Johnson Productions 323-468-4520
Craftsman Films 323-956-5076
Fauci Productions 323-956-4737
Firefly Productions 323-956-8893
Grammnet Productions 323-956-5455
Grub Street Productions 323-956-4657
The Littlefield Company 323-956-8850
Simon West Productions 323-956-8994

Paramount Worldwide Television Distribution
Letnom Productions 323-857-6790

PBS
Red-Horse Productions 818-705-2588

Phoenix Pictures
Underground Film & Management 310-244-6852

Platinum Dunes
Dimension Films .212-941-3800

Radar Pictures
Frederic Golchan Productions .310-208-8525

Regency Enterprises
Nuyorican .310-943-6600
WideAwake, Inc. .310-652-9200

Regent Entertainment, Inc.
Rapid Heart Pictures, Ltd. .204-292-6066

Rehme Productions
Old Dime Box Productions, Inc. .323-876-1282

Revolution Studios
Blue Star Pictures .See Listing
Red Om Films, Inc. .212-243-2900
Roth/Arnold Productions .310-255-7005
Team Todd .310-255-7265

Riche Productions
Reelvision Entertainment .818-879-8084

RKO Pictures, LLC
Yellow Hat Productions, Inc .323-254-4416

SCI FI Channel
The Gurin Company .818-623-9393

Showtime Networks, Inc.
Elkins Entertainment .818-501-9900
Mary Ann-LaGlo Productions .818-508-5522
Platinum Studios, LLC .310-276-3900
Jon Turtle Productions .310-268-8200

Silver Pictures
Fountainhead Pictures .310-276-5583

Sony Pictures Animation
Konwiser Brothers .310-205-2477

Sony Pictures Entertainment
John Baldecchi Productions .310-244-8232
John Calley Productions .310-244-7777
Circle of Confusion Productions .310-253-7777
Escape Artists .310-244-8833
Wendy Finerman Productions .310-244-8800
Gracie Films .310-244-4222
Mandy Films .310-246-0500
Laurence Mark Productions .310-244-5239
Original Film .310-445-9000
Overbrook Entertainment .310-432-2400
Red Wagon Entertainment .310-244-4466
Revolution Studios .310-255-7000
Paul Schiff Productions .310-244-5454
Winkler Films .310-858-5780

Sony Pictures Television
David Hollander Productions .310-244-2926
Handprint Entertainment .310-481-4400
Dean Hargrove Productions .310-244-8383
Jersey Television .310-887-1176
P.A.T. Productions .310-244-8881
Storyline Entertainment .818-560-2928

Spelling Television, Inc.
Di Novi Pictures .310-581-1355

Spike TV
7ponies productions .323-822-3595
Liquid Theory .310-276-0194

The Howard Stern Production Company
Stonewerks Motion Picture Group .310-440-1954

Studio Hamburg WorldWide Pictures
Daniel Fried Productions .323-525-0023

StudioCanal (U.S.)
Cloud Productions/The Olen Company .949-719-7279
Wolfmill Entertainment .310-559-1622

Tag Entertainment
Blue Rider Pictures .310-727-3303

Telemundo Network
Galán Entertainment .310-823-2822
Nuyorican .310-943-6600

Telepictures Productions
Next Entertainment .818-972-0077

TLC (The Learning Channel)
Malcolm Leo Productions .323-464-4448

Touchstone Television
Bad Robot Productions .818-560-7064
DDJ Productions .818-560-7249
The Edelstein Company .818-560-3884
Gross Entertainment .818-560-8117
Laugh Factory Entertainment .323-848-2800
Love Spell Entertainment .818-560-5376
Mandeville Films .See Listing
Shady Acres Entertainment .818-777-4446
Silly Robin Productions .310-264-8184
Tollin/Robbins Productions .818-766-5004
Wass-Stein .818-560-1950

TRIO
World of Wonder Productions .323-603-6300

Twentieth Century Fox
Bazmark, Inq. .310-369-5448
Conundrum Entertainment .310-319-2800
Davis Entertainment Company .See Listing
Firm Films .310-860-8000
Josephson Entertainment .310-369-7501
Lightstorm Entertainment .310-656-6100
Optional Pictures, LLC .310-582-8881
Regency Enterprises .310-369-8300
Scott Free Productions .310-360-2250
Walden Media .310-887-1000
Weekend Films .310-399-9577

Twentieth Century Fox - Fox 2000
Everyman Pictures .310-369-4200
Spirit Dance Entertainment .323-512-7988
State Street Pictures .310-369-5099
Ralph Winter Productions, Inc. .310-369-4723
Zucker/Netter Productions .310-394-1644

Twentieth Century Fox - Searchlight Pictures
Everyman Pictures .310-369-4200

Twentieth Century Fox Animation
Blue Sky Studios .914-259-6500

Twentieth Century Fox Television
3 Arts Entertainment, Inc. 310-888-3200
Firm Films 310-860-8000
First Move Television Production .310-369-0094
Imagine Television 310-858-2000
Katalyst Films 310-907-2236
David E. Kelley Productions 310-727-2200
Offspring Entertainment 818-560-5645
Phase Two Productions 310-369-8555

Universal Pictures
Baer Entertainment Group 212-371-7300
Bona Fide Productions 310-273-6782
Double Feature Films 310-887-1100
Franchise Pictures, Inc. 323-848-3444
Gold Circle Films 310-278-4800
Hella Good Moving Pictures 310-488-9478
Identity Films 818-733-3378
Imagine Entertainment 310-858-2000
The Kennedy/Marshall Company .310-656-8400
Larger Than Life Productions 818-777-4004
Mandalay Pictures 323-549-4300
Barry Mendel Productions 818-733-3076
Misher Films 818-777-0555
Morgan Creek Productions 310-432-4848
Marc Platt Productions 818-777-8811
Shady Acres Entertainment 818-777-4446
Shutt-Jones Productions 818-777-9619
The Sommers Company 310-917-9200
Stratus Film Company 310-689-1691
Strike Entertainment 310-315-0550
Terra Firma Films 818-777-4457
Tribeca Productions 212-941-4000
Type A Films 818-777-6222
Working Title Films 310-777-3100
Yellow Hat Productions, Inc 323-254-4416
Zollo Productions, Inc. 212-957-1300

USA Network
Whoop Inc./One Ho Productions/Lil' Whoop Productions . . .212-941-2074

Valhalla Motion Pictures
Red-Horse Productions 818-705-2588

Vertigo Entertainment
Dimension Films 212-941-3800

VH1 (Music First)
7ponies productions 323-822-3595
Malcolm Leo Productions 323-464-4448

Viacom Entertainment Group
Alloy Entertainment 323-801-1350

VOY Pictures
Cherry Road Films, LLC 310-458-6550

Walden Media
Blue Rider Pictures 310-727-3303

Warner Bros. Entertainment Inc.
1492 Pictures 818-954-4939
Alcon Entertainment, LLC 310-789-3040
C3 Entertainment, Inc. 818-956-1337
Castle Rock Entertainment 310-285-2300
Double Nickel Entertainment 212-636-5488
Industry Entertainment 323-954-9000
Section Eight Productions 818-954-4840
Dylan Sellers Productions 818-954-4929
Spring Creek Productions, Inc. 310-270-9000
The Wolper Organization 818-954-1421

Warner Bros. Pictures
Aviator Films, LLC 323-465-4400
The Bedford Falls Company 310-394-5022
Copper Sky Productions 310-927-8150
Di Novi Pictures 310-581-1355
Fortis Films 310-659-4533
Franchise Pictures, Inc. 323-848-3444
Furthur Films 818-777-6700
Gaylord Films 818-954-3500
Gerber Pictures 310-385-5880
Green Grass Blue Sky Company, Inc. 818-787-0024
Magic Hallway Pictures 310-247-2030
Malpaso Productions 818-954-3367
Management 360 310-272-7000
Maple Shade Films 818-954-3137
Pandora Films 818-954-3600
Radiant Productions 310-656-1400
Silver Pictures 818-954-4490
Thunder Road Pictures 818-954-3130
Village Roadshow Pictures 818-260-6000
Weed Road Pictures 818-954-3771
Jerry Weintraub Productions 818-954-2500
Clifford Werber Productions 818-954-3918
Wildwood Enterprises, Inc./South Fork Pictures 310-395-5155

Warner Bros. Television Production
25 C Productions 818-954-7176
A Band Apart 323-951-4600
Alcon Entertainment, LLC 310-789-3040
Berlanti/Liddell Productions 818-954-4882
Jerry Bruckheimer Films 310-664-6260
Mark Burnett Productions 310-903-5400
Class V Productions 818-954-2796
Genrebend Productions, Inc. 310-917-1064
Good Game 818-954-3414
Hypnotic 212-809-3202
Is Or Isn't Entertainment 818-954-4842
McNamara Paper Products 818-954-5522
Miller/Boyett Productions 212-702-9779
Once A Frog Productions 818-954-7512
Section Eight Productions 818-954-4840
The Shephard/Robin Company 818-954-5719
Shoe Money Productions 818-954-2682
Tannenbaum Company 818-954-1113
True Blue Productions 323-661-9191
John Wells Productions 818-954-1687
Wonderland Sound and Vision 310-659-4451

Warner Independent Pictures
Cherry Road Films, LLC 310-458-6550
Killer Films, Inc. 212-473-3950

John Wells Productions
Harms Way Productions 818-954-2160
Killer Films, Inc. 212-473-3950

The Wolper Organization
Canvas House Films 818-558-1904

World Film Services, Inc.
Rupert Productions, Inc. 310-390-9360

It is illegal to copy any part of this book

WORKSHEET

DATE	PROJECT	CONTACT	NOTES

SECTION B

COMPANIES AND STAFF

@RADICAL.MEDIA
435 Hudson St.
New York, NY 10014
PHONE .212-462-1500/310-664-4500
FAX .212-462-1600/310-664-4600
EMAIL .info@radicalmedia.com
WEB SITE .www.radicalmedia.com
TYPES Features - New Media - Theater - TV Series
CREDITS The Fog of War - Concert for George - Shots in the Dark - Road to Paris - Erskineville Kings - The Cell - The Life - Report from Ground Zero - Eating Out Loud - A Day in the Life of Africa
SUBMISSION POLICY No unsolicited submissions
COMMENTS Willing Partners, a joint venture with Wieden & Kennedy; West Coast office: 1630 12th St., Santa Monica, CA 90404

Jon Kamen .Chairman
Frank Scherma .President
Cathy Shannon .VP, Worldwide Business Affairs
Aric Ackerman .CFO
Sabrina Padwa .General Counsel
Ray Cooper .Executive Producer (London)
Michael Davis .Executive Producer (LA)
Jack Lechner .Executive Producer (NY)
Greg Schultz .Executive Producer (NY)
Mike Bonfiglio .Producer (NY)
Jill Wakeman .Producer (LA)
Justin Wilkes .Producer (NY)
Rachel Dawson .Associate Producer (NY)
Chris Kim .Executive Assistant to Jon Kamen/Creative Executive (NY)

100 PERCENT FILM & TELEVISION, INC.
116 Spadina Ave., Ste. 701
Toronto, ON M5V 2K6 Canada
PHONE .416-304-5225
FAX .416-304-1222
EMAIL .info@onehundredpercent.ca
WEB SITE .www.onehundredpercent.ca
TYPES Features - Syndication - TV Series
CREDITS The Newsroom (PBS)
COMMENTS Coordinates film and TV productions from financing to finished product

Jan Peter Meyboom .Executive Producer
Ken Finkelman .Executive Producer
Julia Dault .No Title
Scott McEwen .No Title

100% ENTERTAINMENT
c/o Stanley Isaacs
322 S. Lucerne Blvd.
Los Angeles, CA 90020
PHONE .323-461-6360
FAX .323-934-0440
EMAIL .100percent@iname.com
WEB SITE .www.100percentent.com
TYPES Features - Direct-to-Video/DVD - Made-for-TV/Cable Movies
DEVELOPMENT Point Thunder - The Dark Ages - Ancient Blood - Raptor Island 2 - When Hell Freezes Over - Crush Depth
CREDITS Megalodon - Last Gasp - Within the Rock - Ravager - Raptor Island
COMMENTS Deal with Unreal Productions and F.W.E.

Stanley Isaacs .President
Cooper Boone .Creative Executive

1492 PICTURES
4000 Warner Blvd., Producers Bldg. 3, Ste. 18
Burbank, CA 91522
PHONE .818-954-4939
FAX .818-954-7933
TYPES Features - TV Series
DEALS Warner Bros. Entertainment Inc.
CREDITS Harry Potter and the Prisoner of Azkaban - Harry Potter and the Sorcerer's Stone - Harry Potter and the Chamber of Secrets - Bicentennial Man - Monkeybone - Stepmom - Jingle All the Way - Nine Months
SUBMISSION POLICY No unsolicited material or query letters

Chris Columbus .Writer/Director/Producer/Partner
Michael Barnathan .President/Producer/Partner
Mark Radcliffe .Producer/Partner
Paula DuPre Pesmen .Associate Producer
Jennifer Blum .Sr. VP, Production
Karen Swallow .VP
Michelle Miller .Story Editor
Elizabeth Devereux .Assistant to Mr. Columbus
Jeanne Austin .Assistant to Mr. Radcliffe

19 ENTERTAINMENT
9440 Santa Monica Blvd., Ste. 705
Beverly Hills, CA 90210
PHONE .310-777-1940
FAX .310-777-1949
TYPES Features - Reality TV - TV Series
CREDITS American Idol - From Justin to Kelly
SUBMISSION POLICY No unsolicited submissions

Simon Fuller .CEO
Tom Ennis .President, 19 Recordings Ltd.
Shonadh French .No Title
Chrissie Harwood .No Title

1ST MIRACLE PICTURES
3439 W. Cahuenga Blvd.
Hollywood, CA 90068
PHONE .323-874-6000
FAX .323-874-4252
EMAIL .sales@1stmiracleproductions.com
WEB SITE .www.1stmiracleproductions.com
TYPES Animation - Documentaries - Features - Direct-to-Video/DVD - New Media - Syndication - TV Series
DEVELOPMENT Junior Sheriff
CREDITS Freedom Deep - Never Look Back - Double Cross - Tangled - Fatal Destiny - Top of the World - Versace Murder - First Action Hero
COMMENTS Distribution

Moshe Bibiyan .CEO
Simon Bibiyan .President

25 C PRODUCTIONS
4000 Warner Blvd., Bldg. 139, Ste. 16
Burbank, CA 91522
PHONE .818-954-7176
TYPES TV Series
DEALS Warner Bros. Television Production
CREDITS The Webster Report (CBS Pilot) - Wanted (CBS Pilot)

Sarah Timberman .No Title (818-954-7176)
Carl Beverly .No Title (818-954-7250)
Chris Leanza .Manager, Development (818-954-3372)
Annie Parnell .Manager, Development (818-954-3370)

2929 PRODUCTIONS
2425 Olympic Blvd., Ste. 6040-W
Santa Monica, CA 90404
PHONE .310-309-5701
FAX .310-309-5716
WEB SITE .www.2929entertainment.com
TYPES Features
DEVELOPMENT Kingpin sequel - 342 - Infidelity for First-time Fathers
COMPLETED UNRELEASED The Jacket (Warner Independent/Section 8) - Criminal (Warner Independent/Section 8)
CREDITS Godsend (Lions Gate)

Todd Wagner .Principal/Partner
Mark Cuban .Principal/Partner
Marc Butan .President (310-309-5704)
Kent Kubena .Executive (310-309-5705, kkubena@2929productions.com)
Satsuki Mitchell .Executive (310-309-5341, smmitchell@2929productions.com)
Couper Samuelson .Assistant to Marc Butan (310-309-5701, csamuelson@2929productions.com)

2ND GENERATION FILMS
12731 Moorpark St., Ste. 9
Studio City, CA 91604
PHONE .818-985-1427
EMAIL .jquatt4827@aol.com
TYPES Documentaries - Features - Made-for-TV/Cable Movies - TV Series
DEVELOPMENT Best of Five - I'm Pretty Sure I Might Have a Fear of Committment
POST PRODUCTION Grandpa's Place
CREDITS Full Circle - True Friends - In the Kingdom of the Blind - Down and Out - The Interview - Arthur Avenue - The Father, the Son - Jesus, Mary and Joey

James Quattrochi .Director/Writer/Actor/Producer

3 ARTS ENTERTAINMENT, INC.
9460 Wilshire Blvd., 7th Fl.
Beverly Hills, CA 90212
PHONE .310-888-3200/212-905-2333
FAX .310-888-3210
TYPES Features - New Media - TV Series
DEALS Twentieth Century Fox Television
CREDITS Chris Rock Show - King of the Hill - The Hughleys - Greetings from Tucson
COMMENTS East Coast office: 451 Greenwich St., 7th Fl., New York, NY 10013

Dave Becky .No Title
Stephanie Davis .No Title
Nick Frenkel .No Title (NY)
Jeff Golenberg .No Title
Steven Greener .No Title
Howard Klein .No Title
Pam Kohl .No Title
Molly Madden .No Title
David Miner .No Title
Michael Rotenberg .No Title
Mark Schulman .No Title
Erwin Stoff .No Title
Tucker Voorhees .No Title (NY)
Scott Wexler .No Title
Steve Tann .Head, TV
Diane Gordon .Director, TV Development

3 BALL PRODUCTIONS
1600 Rosecrans Ave., Bldg. 7
Manhattan Beach, CA 90266
PHONE .310-727-3337
FAX .310-727-3339
TYPES Reality TV
CREDITS For Love or Money - Endurance - Moulah Beach

John Foy .Executive Producer
Todd Nelson .Executive Producer
J.D. Roth .Executive Producer
Troy Searer .VP, Development

3 RING CIRCUS FILMS
3699 Wilshire Blvd., Ste.1250
Los Angeles, CA 90010
PHONE .213-251-3300
FAX .213-251-3350
EMAIL .johnsid@3ringcircus.tv
WEB SITE .www.3ringcircus.tv
TYPES Features - Made-for-TV/Cable Movies - Reality TV
DEVELOPMENT Traces - Christmas City - Second Wind
CREDITS Dream with the Fishes - Tear It Down - One - Cherish - Confessions
COMMENTS Independent film production

John Sideropoulos .CEO
Johnny Wow .Producer

40 ACRES & A MULE FILMWORKS, INC.
124 DeKalb Ave.
Brooklyn, NY 11217
PHONE .718-624-3703
FAX .718-624-2008
TYPES Animation - Features - Reality TV - TV Series
POST PRODUCTION SFC (Series)
CREDITS She Hate Me - 25th Hour - 3 A.M. - Bamboozled - Original Kings of Comedy - Love and Basketball - The Best Man - Summer of Sam - He Got Game - 4 Little Girls - Get on the Bus - Girl 6 - Clockers - Crooklyn - Malcolm X - Do the Right Thing

Spike Lee .Chairman
Heather Parish .Business Manager

44 BLUE PRODUCTIONS, INC.

4040 Vineland Ave., Ste. 105
Studio City, CA 91604
PHONE .818-760-4442
FAX .818-760-1509
EMAIL .reception@44blue.com
WEB SITE .www.44blue.com

TYPES: Documentaries - Features - Reality TV - Syndication - TV Series
DEALS: A&E Television Networks - Discovery Networks, U.S. - Fine Living - Home & Garden Television (HGTV) - Lifetime Television (Los Angeles)
DEVELOPMENT: Rematch (Reality Series) - The Boudoir Girls (Reality Series) - Caesar's 24/7 (Reality Series) - Being Ben Stein (Reality Series) - Mr. Right, Right Now (Reality Series)
PRODUCTION: What Should You Do? (Lifetime) - Find & Design (A&E) - Collector Inspector (HGTV) - A Place of Our Own (KCET)
CREDITS: MSNBC Investigates - Investigative Reports (A&E) - Lock Up (MSNBC) - Headliners & Legends (MSNBC) - Small Shots (TNN) - The True Story of Black Hawk Down (History Channel) - Wide Open (A&E) - Cell Dogs (Animal Planet)

Rasha Drachkovitch .President/Executive Producer
Stephanie Drachkovitch .Executive Producer
Stuart Zwagil .Executive in Charge of Production

4TH AND GOAL ENTERTAINMENT

888 8th Ave., 2nd Fl., Ste. U
New York, NY 10019
PHONE .212-757-5127
FAX .212-757-5126
EMAIL .firstname@4thandgoalentertainment.com
WEB SITE .www.4thandgoalentertainment.com

TYPES: Documentaries - Features - New Media
DEVELOPMENT: Lucky - Tracy - Breaking Even
PRE-PRODUCTION: The Big If
POST PRODUCTION: Kiev Nites
CREDITS: Danny and Max - The Addiction
COMMENTS: Deal with Sales Inc./Producer's Resource

Scott Wartham .Producer/Partner
Brian Fischler .Producer/Partner
Jason Bright .Producer/Partner
Keith Zdrowak .Business Affairs
Yuri Rutman .No Title

4TH ROW FILMS

619 W. 54th St., 10th Fl.
New York, NY 10019
PHONE .212-974-0082
WEB SITE .www.4throwfilms.com

TYPES: Documentaries - Features - Made-for-TV/Cable Movies - TV Series
DEVELOPMENT: Teenage Kicks - Do I Look Fat in This? - The Great Date Experiment
PRE-PRODUCTION: Victor in December - Funny Peculiar - Sweet Home Chicago
POST PRODUCTION: Anytown, USA
CREDITS: A Reason to Believe - Killing Time - Twelve - The Lucky Ones
COMMENTS: Produces branding and marketing films for Fortune 500 companies

Douglas Tirola .President/Producer
Susan Bedusa .Director, Development
Robert Greene .Post Production Supervisor

6 PICTURES

14358 Magnolia Blvd., Ste. 135
Sherman Oaks, CA 91423
PHONE .818-789-7666
EMAIL .6pictures@earthlink.net

TYPES: Features - Direct-to-Video/DVD - Made-for-TV/Cable Movies
CREDITS: Tail Sting - Wes Craven Presents Carnival of Souls - Fat Man and Mr. Taco - Being Ron Jeremy - Three Shots - Captain Apache: Laugh Track Edition

Peter Soby Jr. .Producer
Kit Klehm .Partner
Scott Kimball .Director, Finance
Brad Parnell .Production Coordinator

647K PRODUCTIONS

3201 Benedict Canyon Dr.
Beverly Hills, CA 90210-1034
PHONE .310-739-7334
EMAIL .production647k@hotmail.com
WEB SITE .www.647k.com

TYPES: New Media
PRODUCTION: The Stronger
CREDITS: Bikini Car Wash - California Hot Wax - Escaping Jersey - Seat Fillers
SUBMISSION POLICY: Submit through email only
COMMENTS: Send correspondence to Jan Reesman only; Digital Shorts

Jan Marlyn Reesman .Executive Producer
Robb Reesman .Producer

777 ENTERTAINMENT GROUP, LTD.

1015 Gayley Ave., Ste. 1128
Los Angeles, CA 90024
PHONE .310-824-0664
FAX .203-886-3447
EMAIL .info@robinson-entertainment.com
SECOND EMAIL .dirdev@robinson-entertainment.com
WEB SITE .www.robinson-entertainment.com

TYPES: Features - TV Series
DEALS: Bad Boy Films
DEVELOPMENT: Ella Fitzgerald Story - Phat Gyrlz - Where There's a Will - Double Doors - Soul Feud - BC 2000
PRE-PRODUCTION: PoCo LoCo

Marcello Robinson .President/Producer
Scott Carlson .Producer
Ray Mann .Producer
Deborah Young .Producer/Writer
Brad Small .Attorney
David LoPresti .No Title
Kevin Pritchett .No Title
Rosa Turner Knapp .No Title

7PONIES PRODUCTIONS
6230 Wilshire Blvd., Ste. 2060
Los Angeles, CA 90048
PHONE 323-822-3595
FAX 323-822-3593
EMAIL .....7ponies@7ponies.com
WEB SITE www.7ponies.com
TYPES Documentaries - Features - Reality TV - TV Series
DEALS MTV Networks - Spike TV - VH1 (Music First)
DEVELOPMENT Debutantes: The Road to the Ball - Heaven's Gate Cult
POST PRODUCTION Tripped Out
CREDITS 10 Things Every Guy Should Experience - Crash Test - Sorority Life 1-3 - Fraternity Life 1&2 - Soulmates (Feature) - Instant Comedy with The Groundlings - E! True Hollywood Story: Redd Foxx, Linda Blair, Bo Derek - Heaven's Gate: The Untold Story

Sergio Myers .....Executive Producer
Catherine Finn .....Executive Producer

900 FILMS
27122-A Paseo Espada, Ste. 900
San Juan Capistrano, CA 92675
PHONE 760-477-2477
FAX 760-477-2474
EMAIL .....morgan@900films.com
SECOND EMAIL .....matt@900films.com
TYPES Documentaries - Features - Direct-to-Video/DVD - Syndication - TV Series - Reality TV
DEVELOPMENT Untitled Tony Hawk Comedy (Revolution Studios)
CREDITS Grind (Warner Bros.) - DEPSWA (Music Video/Geffen) - Making of Boom Boom Huckjam (MTV2) - Tony Hawk: Gigantic Skatepark Tour (ESPN) - Tony Hawk's Trick Tips (DVD) - Surfer TV (OLN) - King of Skate (Pay-per-view) - Jason Ellis Show (ESPN)
COMMENTS Management: Chris Fenton, MBST Entertainment, phone: 310-385-1775

Tony Hawk .....Partner/Professional Skateboarder
Morgan Stone .....Partner/Producer/Director
Matt Goodman .....Partner/Director, DP
Irene Navarro .....Production Manager
Nicole Sanchez .....Office Manager

A BAND APART
7966 Beverly Blvd., 3rd Fl.
Los Angeles, CA 90048
PHONE 323-951-4600
FAX 323-951-4601
TYPES Features - TV Series
DEALS Warner Bros. Television Production
PRODUCTION The Chumscrubber
POST PRODUCTION Casa de Carton
CREDITS Pulp Fiction - Reservoir Dogs - Good Will Hunting - Jackie Brown - The Mexican - Kill Bill Vol. 1&2 - Havana Nights

Quentin Tarantino .....Writer/Director/Partner
Lawrence Bender .....Producer/Partner
Kevin Brown .....Executive Producer, TV
Janet Jeffries .....Development
Adam Schindler .....Office Manager
Jeff Swafford .....Production
Jill Rubin .....Assistant to Mr. Bender
Justin Jacquemotte .....Assistant to Mr. Brown
Maren Olson .....Development Assistant

A-FILMS
105 Barringer Court
West Orange, NJ 07052
PHONE 973-325-2045
FAX 973-325-9668
EMAIL .....afilms@aol.com
TYPES Features - Made-for-TV/Cable Movies - TV Series
DEVELOPMENT Dead in the Center of Texas - Flatbelly - Steal Business
CREDITS Forced March - Asunder - Trapped in Silence - Murder in Coweta County - The Gift of Love: A Christmas Story - Born Beautiful - Christmas in America - Shocktrauma

Dick Atkins .....President/Producer

A WINK AND A NOD PRODUCTIONS
843 12th St., Ste. 4
Santa Monica, CA 90403
PHONE 310-394-5752
WEB SITE .....www.awinkandanod.com
TYPES Features - Made-for-TV/Cable Movies - Reality TV - TV Series
DEVELOPMENT Let 'Em Eat Cake - The Red Eye - Tiger, Tiger - Call to Courage - Welcome to My World - Unsportsmanlike Conduct - Strange Currencies
PRE-PRODUCTION Miss Cupid's Beau (Hallmark Channel) - Wedding Daze (Hallmark Channel)
CREDITS Santa Junior (Hallmark Channel)
SUBMISSION POLICY Queries will only be accepted by mail, or by email via Web site

Wendy Winks .....President
C. J. Helm .....Assistant

A&E TELEVISION NETWORKS
235 E. 45th St.
New York, NY 10017
PHONE 212-210-1400
WEB SITE .....www.aetv.com
SECOND WEB SITE .....www.biography.com
TYPES Documentaries - Direct-to-Video/DVD - Made-for-TV/Cable Movies - New Media - TV Series
CREDITS Family Plots - Growing Up Gotti - Dog the Bounty Hunter - The First 48 - Biography - Airline - American Justice - Cold Case Files - City Confidential - Investigative Reports - MI-5

Nickolas Davatzes .....President/CEO, AETN
Whitney Goit .....Sr. Executive VP, AETN
Gerard Gruosso .....CFO/Executive VP, AETN
Abbe Raven .....Executive VP/General Manager, A&E Network
Mel Berning .....Executive VP, Ad Sales, AETN
Daniel Davids .....Executive VP/General Manager, The History Channel
Jim Greiner . .Executive VP, New Enterprises, Production & Internet Services
Robert DeBitetto .....Sr. VP, Programming, A&E
Bill Harris .....Sr. VP, Production & Network Operations, AETN
Tom Heymann .....Sr. VP/General Manager, The Biography Channel
Maria Komodikis .....Sr. VP/General Manager, A&E International
Artie Scheff .....Sr. VP, Marketing, A&E
Michael Feeney .....VP, Public Affairs, AETN
Delia Fine .....VP, Film, Drama & Performing Arts, A&E
Nancy Duboc .....VP, Documentary Program Development, A&E
Jenny Hardy .....Managing Producer, The History Channel

(Continued)

A&E TELEVISION NETWORKS (Continued)

Patrice Andrews Director, Documentary Programming & Development, A&E
Laura Fleury . . . . .Director, Documentary Programming, A&E
Lynn Gardner . . . . .Director, Public Relations, The History Channel
Kerri Tarmey . . . . .Director, Corporate Communications
Marlea Willis . . . . .Director, Program Publicity, A&E
Vicky Kahn . . . . .Manager, Program Publicity
Gina Nocero . . . . .Manager, Program Publicity

***A. SMITH & CO. PRODUCTIONS**

9911 W. Pico Blvd., Ste. 250
Los Angeles, CA 90035
PHONE 310-432-4800
FAX 310-551-3085
EMAIL . . . . .info@asmithco.com
TYPES Documentaries - Reality TV - Syndication - TV Series
CREDITS The Swan 1&2 - I'm Still Alive! - Mad Mad House - Forever Eden - Come Home Alive - You Gotta See This! - Paradise Hotel - Pat Croce: Moving In

Arthur Smith . . . . .CEO
Kent Weed . . . . .President
Sean Atkins . . . . .Sr. VP
Emmy Davis . . . . .Executive in Charge of Production

ABANDON ENTERTAINMENT/ABANDON PICTURES

135 W. 50th St., Ste. 2305
New York, NY 10020
PHONE 212-246-4445
FAX 212-397-8361
EMAIL . . . . .abandonent@abandonent.com
WEB SITE . . . . .www.abandonent.com
TYPES Features - Made-for-TV/Cable Movies - New Media - TV Series
DEVELOPMENT Camelot (Miniseries) - Max Payne - Alice - Hagar the Horrible - And Soon the Darkness - Otherwise Engaged
PRE-PRODUCTION Picasso at the Lapin Agile - Lulu
CREDITS Oxygen - Pros and Cons - Time Shifters - Off the Lip - Mexico City - Scotland, PA - Glory Days
COMMENTS Partner in Mythic Entertainment; Online games

Marcus Ticotin . . . . .President/CEO
Karen Lauder . . . . .Co-President/Chairman, Abandon Pictures
Deborah Marinoff . . . . .VP, Abandon Pictures

FRANK ABATEMARCO PRODUCTIONS

74 Depot Rd.
Montecito, CA 93108
PHONE 805-969-6600
FAX 603-908-5966
EMAIL . . . . .abatemarco@aol.com
TYPES Features - Direct-to-Video/DVD - Made-for-TV/Cable Movies - Syndication - TV Series
CREDITS I Can Make You Love Me: The Stalking of Laura Black - A Tangled Web

Frank Abatemarco . . . . .President/Owner
Jay Press . . . . .Director, Development

ABBY LOU ENTERTAINMENT

1411 Edgehill Pl.
Pasadena, CA 91103
PHONE 626-795-7334
FAX 626-795-4013
EMAIL . . . . .ale@full-moon.com
TYPES Animation - Syndication - TV Series
DEVELOPMENT Adventures in Whispering Gardens (Animated Syndicated Series & Feature)
PRE-PRODUCTION A Christmas Whisper (Animated Network Special)
CREDITS Las Vegas Entertainment Award Show (NBC) - Circus Circus (Syndicated Special)
COMMENTS Distribution of family, animated and feature films

George Le Fave . . . . .Producer/President

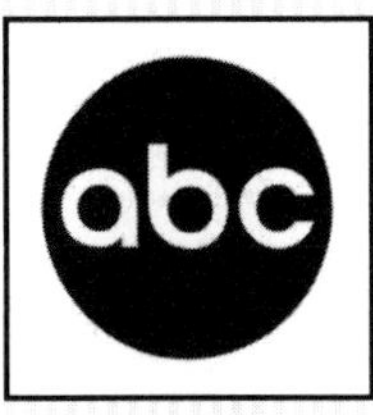

ABC CABLE NETWORKS GROUP

3800 W. Alameda Ave.
Burbank, CA 91505
PHONE 818-569-7500
WEB SITE . . . . .www.disneychannel.com
TYPES Animation - Made-for-TV/Cable Movies - New Media - TV Series

Rich Ross . . . . .President, Disney Channel Worldwide
Barry Blumberg . . . . .President, Walt Disney Television Animation
Jewell Engstrom . . . . .Sr. VP/CFO, ABC Cable Networks Group
Jonathan Barzilay . . . . .Sr. VP/General Manager, ABC Kids & Toon Disney
Deborah Blackwell . . . . .Sr. VP/General Manager, SOAPnet
Eleo Hensleigh . . . . .Executive VP, Worldwide Brand Strategy
Frederick Kuperberg . . . . .Executive VP, Business & Legal Affairs, ABC Cable Networks Group
Gary K. Marsh . . . . .Executive VP, Original Programming & Production, Disney Channel & ABC Family
Jill Casagrande . . . . .Sr. VP, Worldwide Programming Strategy
Jeff Frost . . . . .Sr. VP, Legal Affairs
Susette Hsiung . . . . .Sr. VP, Production, ABC Cable Networks Group
Matthew Palmer . . . . .Sr. VP, Marketing, Disney Channel
Vincent H. Roberts Sr. VP, Broadcast Operations, Engineering & Technology
Adina Savin . . . . .Sr. VP, Business Affairs, ABC Cable Networks Group
Patricia Wilber . . . . .Sr. VP, Advertising Sales & Promotion, ABC Cable Networks Group
Donna Ebbs . . . . .VP, Original Movies
Lynn Finley . . . . . . .VP, Broadcast Operations, ABC Cable Networks Group
Michael Healy . . . . . . .VP, Original Movies, Disney Channel & ABC Family
Karen Holm . . . . .VP, Legal Affairs, ABC Cable Networks Group
Nancy Kanter . . . . .VP, Programming, Playhouse Disney
Patti McTeague . . . . .VP, Media Relations, ABC Cable Networks Group

ABC DAYTIME

77 W. 66th St.
New York, NY 10023
PHONE 212-456-7777/818-460-1000
WEB SITE . . . . .www.abc.com
TYPES TV Series - Reality TV
COMMENTS West Coast office: 500 S. Buena Vista St., Burbank, CA 91521

Brian Frons . . . . .President
Dominick Nuzzi . . . . .Sr. VP, Production & Administration
Jana Winograde . . . . .Sr. VP, Business Affairs
Harriet Abraham . . . . .VP, Programming Operations
Sallie Schoneboom .VP, Media & Talent Relations
Julie Carruthers . . . . .Executive Producer, *All My Children*
Bill Geddie . . . . .Executive Producer, *The View*
Jill Farren Phelps . . . . .Executive Producer, *General Hospital*
Frank Valentini . . . . .Executive Producer, *One Life to Live*
Barbara Walters . . . . .Executive Producer, *The View*
Randall Barone . . . . .Director, Reality Programming
Sue Johnson . . . . .Director, Talent Development
Jennifer Turner . . . . .Director, West Coast Programming

ABC ENTERTAINMENT TELEVISION GROUP

500 S. Buena Vista St.
Burbank, CA 91521
PHONE 818-460-7777
WEB SITE . . . . .www.abc.com
TYPES Made-for-TV/Cable Movies - TV Series - Reality TV

Anne Sweeney . . . . .President, Disney/ABC Television Group
Stephen McPherson . . . . .President, ABC Entertainment
Mark Pedowitz . . . . .President, Touchstone Television
Alex Wallau . . . . .President, ABC Network Operations & Administration
James Hedges . . . . .CFO, ABC Television Network
Jeffrey Bader . . . . .Executive VP, ABC Entertainment
Gene Blythe . . . . .Executive VP, Casting, ABC Television
Francie Calfo . . . . .Executive VP, Development
Howard Davine . . . . .Executive VP, Touchstone Television
Julia Franz . . . . .Executive VP, Touchstone Television
Spencer Neumann . . . . .Executive VP, ABC Television Network
Andrea Wong . . . . .Executive VP, Alternative Programming, Specials & Latenight
Susan Binford . . . . .Sr. VP, Communications
Kevin Brockman . . . . .Sr. VP, Entertainment Communications
Olivia Cohen-Cutler . . . . .Sr. VP, Broadcast Standards & Practices
Bruce Gersh . . . . .Sr. VP, Business Development, ABC Television Network & Touchstone Television
Barry Jossen . . . . .Sr. VP, Production, Touchstone Television
Keli Lee . . . . .Sr. VP, Casting
Stephanie Leifer . . . . .Sr. VP, Comedy Programming
Jerry Longarzo . . . . .Sr. VP, Business Affairs, Touchstone Television
Jim McClintock . . . . .Sr. VP, ABC Television Network, Network Media
Suzanne Patmore-Gibbs . . . . .Sr. VP, Drama Development
Quinn Taylor . . . . .Sr. VP, Movies/Minis, *Wonderful World of Disney*
Lance Taylor . . . . .Sr. VP, Current Programming
Morgan Wandell . . . . . .Sr. VP, Drama Development, Touchstone Television
Jana Winograde . . . . .Sr. VP, Business Affairs, ABC Entertainment
Nancy D. Bennett . . . . .VP, Production Development, Movies/Minis
Sharon Williams . . . . .VP, Media Relations, Scripted Series, ABC
Josh Barry . . . . .VP, Drama Development
Shawn Blake . . . . .VP, Media Relations, Touchstone Television
Richard Claflin . . . . .VP, Comedy Series
David Cohen . . . . .VP, Legal Affairs, ABC Entertainment Group & Touchstone Television
Brian Dorfman . . . . .VP, Casting
Vicki Dummer . . . . .VP, Current & Alternative Series Programming
Annie Fort . . . . .VP, Alternative Series/Specials, Movies & Miniseries
Jim Gaston . . . . .VP, Production, Touchstone Television
Veronica Gentilli . . . . .VP, Business Affairs, Touchstone Television
Duncan Gray . . . . .VP, Alternative Series & Specials
Danielle Greene . . . . .VP, ABC Latenight
Rosalie Joseph . . . . .VP, Casting
Brenda Kyle . . . . .VP, Production, Touchstone Television
Victoria LaFortune . . . . .VP, Production, Touchstone Television
Irwin Marcus . . . . .VP, Production, Touchstone Television
Jennifer Mayo . . . . .VP, Business Affairs
Scott C. McCarthy . . . . .VP, ABC Radio Networks

(Continued)

ABC TELEVISION ENTERTAINMENT GROUP (Continued)

Deborah O'Brien . . . . .VP, Contracts Administration
Jason Saville . . . . .VP, Production
Michael Villegas . . . . .VP, Post Production, Touchstone Television
Paula Warner-Schlenker . . . . . . .VP, Post-Production, Touchstone Television
Alex Weinberger . . . . .VP, Comedy Series, Touchstone Television
Carlos Williams . . . . .VP, Business Affairs, Touchstone Television
Nina Howie . . . . .Executive Director, Comedy Series, Touchstone Television
Libby Jaynes . . . . .Executive Director, Alternative Series & Specials
Jodie Platt . . . . . .Executive Director, Comedy Series, Touchstone Television
Francisco Arias . . . . .Director, Business Affairs, Touchstone Television
Janet Murphy Butler . . . . .Director, Casting
Jocelyn Diaz . . . . .Director, Drama Development
Michael Erlinger . . . . .Director, Business Affairs
Suzanne Gordon . . . . .Director, Media Relations, Advertising, Marketing & Promotions, Children's
Mark Greenberg . . . . .Director, Production, Touchstone Television
Jean Hester . . . . . . .Director, Production Operations, Touchstone Television
Cathy Korda . . . . .Director, Program Planning & Scheduling
Adam Myman . . . . .Director, Current Programming
Nicole Norwood . . . .Director, Drama Development, Touchstone Television
Marci Philips . . . . .Director, Casting
Angela Somerville . . . . .Director, Current Series
Heather Cunningham . . . . .Manager, Comedy Development
Brian Harvey . . . . .Manager, Drama Development
Patrick Maguire . . . . .Manager, Current Programming
Greg Shephard . . . . . .Manager, Movies/Minis, *Wonderful World of Disney*

ABC FAMILY

500 S. Buena Vista St.
Burbank, CA 91521
PHONE 818-560-1000
WEB SITE . . . . .www.abcfamily.com
TYPES Made-for-TV/Cable Movies - Reality TV - TV Series
PRODUCTION Pop Rocks
POST PRODUCTION Crimes of Fashion
COMPLETED UNRELEASED Love Rules!
CREDITS Brave New Girl - Lucky 7 - See Jane Date - This Time Around - Beautiful Girl - Knock First - Switched! - Picking Up & Dropping Off - I Want to Marry Ryan Banks - My Life Is a Sitcom - Celeste in the City - Bachelor Pad - Switched Up!

Paul Lee . . . . .President
Mark Silverman . . . . .Sr. VP/General Manager

ABC SPORTS

47 W. 66th St., 13th Fl.
New York, NY 10023
PHONE 212-456-7777
FAX 212-456-4317
WEB SITE . . . . .www.abcsports.com
TYPES TV Series
COMMENTS Sports programming

George Bodenheimer . . . . .President
Loren Matthews . . . . .Sr. VP, Programming
Michael Pearl . . . . .Sr. VP, Production
Mark Mandel . . . . .VP, Media Relations
Bob Toms . . . . .VP, Production
Adam Freifeld . . . . .Sr. Publicist
Maxine Lewis . . . . .Sr. Publicist

ABOUT ENTERTAINMENT
12207 Riverside Dr., Ste. 208
Valley Village, CA 91607
PHONE . . . . See Below
EMAIL . . . . aboutentertainment@aol.com
TYPES Features - Direct-to-Video/DVD - Made-for-TV/Cable Movies - TV Series
DEVELOPMENT Tomorrow's Child (Universal) - L'arlos Guitarlos Biography - Raising Kane
CREDITS My American Vacation - Carnival of Souls - The Hidden - Up the Creek - Dead Heat
SUBMISSION POLICY Email inquiries
COMMENTS FKA Michael Meltzer Productions

Michael L. Meltzer . . . . Producer (818-766-8339, melmax@aol.com)
Frank Gargani . . . . Producer (818-892-9885, gargani@earthlink.net)
Linda Smith . . . . Associate (818-766-8339)

AC WORKS
10862 Washington Blvd.
Culver City, CA 90232
PHONE 310-345-7738
EMAIL . . . . acwrks@aol.com
TYPES Features - TV Series
DEVELOPMENT Pit Stop
CREDITS I Shot a Man in Vegas
SUBMISSION POLICY Via email

Alec Chorches . . . . Owner/Producer

ACME PRODUCTIONS
4000 Warner Blvd., Bungalow 2, Ste. 102
Burbank, CA 91522
PHONE . . . . See Below
TYPES TV Series
CREDITS Reba - Titus - Danny - Sixteen to Life (Pilot)

Mindy Schultheis . . . . Executive Producer (818-954-7779)
Michael Hanel . . . . Executive Producer (818-954-7771)

ACRONYM ENTERTAINMENT
9350 Wilshire Blvd., Ste. 328
Beverly Hills, CA 90212
PHONE 310-247-9119
FAX 310-247-9974
TYPES Documentaries - Features - Made-for-TV/Cable Movies - Syndication - TV Series - Reality TV
DEVELOPMENT Weekend Wedding - Rose and the Americans - Scammers - I Love You, I Love You NOT! - Poetry in Motion
COMPLETED UNRELEASED A Separate Peace (Showtime)
CREDITS Wintuition (Game Show Network)

Michael Sugar . . . . Partner/Producer
Laina Cohn . . . . Partner/Producer

ACT III PRODUCTIONS
100 N. Crescent Dr., Ste. 250
Beverly Hills, CA 90210
PHONE 310-385-4111
FAX 310-385-4148
TYPES Features - TV Series
CREDITS Fried Green Tomatoes - 704 Hauser - Powers That Be

Norman Lear . . . . Chairman/CEO, Act III Communications
John Baskin . . . . President
Rachel Davidson . . . . VP, TV & Motion Pictures
Marilyn Pessin . . . . Executive Assistant to Norman Lear

ACTUAL REALITY PICTURES
3524 Hayden Ave.
Culver City, CA 90232
PHONE 310-202-1272
FAX 310-202-1502
EMAIL . . . . info@actualreality.tv
WEB SITE . . . . www.actualreality.tv
TYPES Documentaries - Features - TV Series
PRODUCTION The Residents (TNT) - Going to College (Showtime) - American Candidate (FX)
CREDITS American High - Military Diaries

R.J. Cutler . . . . President
Belisa Balaban . . . . VP, Development & Current Programming
Ted Skillman . . . . VP, Production

ACTUALITY PRODUCTIONS
1640 S. Sepulveda Blvd., 4th Fl.
Los Angeles, CA 90025-7510
PHONE 310-478-1700
FAX 310-478-5929
TYPES Documentaries - Reality TV - Syndication - TV Series

Jerry Shevick . . . . Executive VP, Documentary & Reality Programming
Bari Carrelli . . . . VP, Documentary & Reality Programming

ORLY ADELSON PRODUCTIONS
12304 Santa Monica Blvd., Ste. 115
Los Angeles, CA 90025
PHONE 310-442-2012
FAX 310-442-2013
TYPES Features - Made-for-TV/Cable Movies - Reality TV - TV Series
CREDITS One True Love - God's New Plan - Ultimate Deception - The Truth About Jane - The One - The Junction Boys - The Man Who Saved Christmas - D.C. Sniper - Playmakers - Hustle: The Pete Rose Story - 3: The Dale Earnhardt Story
SUBMISSION POLICY No unsolicited submissions

Orly Adelson . . . . President
Troy Westergaard . . . . Executive Producer
Jon Eskenas . . . . Director, Development
Christine Peymani . . . . Development Assistant

AEI-ATCHITY ENTERTAINMENT INTERNATIONAL, INC.
9601 Wilshire Blvd., Box 1202
Beverly Hills, CA 90210
PHONE .323-932-0407/212-421-0256
FAX .323-932-0321
EMAIL .submissions@aeionline.com
WEB SITE .www.aeionline.com
SECOND WEB SITE .www.thewriterslifeline.com
TYPES Documentaries - Features - Direct-to-Video/DVD - Made-for-TV/Cable Movies - TV Series
DEVELOPMENT Henry's List of Wrongs (New Line) - Favorite Son - Ripley's Believe It or Not (Paramount) - Midnight Carol - The Canal Street Brothel (CBS) - Meg - Prince of Pools - Nano - War Gods - The Loch
CREDITS Features: Falling Over Backwards - Joe Somebody - Life or Something Like It; TV: Shades of Love - Amityville: The Evil Escapes - Shadow of Obsession
COMMENTS Literary management (writers and writer-directors); Book publishing; Affiliated with Writers' Lifeline, phone: 323-932-0905

Ken Atchity .Chairman/Partner
Chi-Li Wong .President/Partner
Andrea McKeown .Executive VP, Editorial
Brenna Lui .VP, Development
Michael Kuciak .Creative Executive/Associate Manager, Film/TV
Margaret O'Connor .Assistant Manager, Books
Jennifer Pope .Submissions

AETHIC PICTURES
2209 Ocean Front Walk, Ste. 4
Venice, CA 90291
PHONE .323-468-8000/416-824-2773
TYPES Features - TV Series
DEVELOPMENT When a Stranger Came - The Truth Shall Set You Free - A Solitary Blue
CREDITS The Sandy Bottom Orchestra - What Happened to Bobby Earl? - Love in the Dark Ages

Bradley Wigor .Director/Producer

AFFILIATED ENTERTAINMENT
8285 Sunset Blvd., Ste. 14
Los Angeles, CA 90046
PHONE .323-656-0390/323-656-0391
FAX .323-512-7776
EMAIL .jasonserrato@sbcglobal.net
WEB SITE .www.affiliated-ent.com
TYPES Features - Music Videos - Reality TV
DEVELOPMENT The Well - Kong - Hell's Kitchen - Swagger - Lonely Planet
PRE-PRODUCTION Baby
CREDITS Cake

Jason Serrato .Producer
Peter Chung .Director
Jin Ah Lee .Production Manager
Thomas Luong .Development
Paul Bacca .Support Services
Daniel Rogers .Editor
Scott Teti .Editor
Felix Chan .Development

AFFINITY FILMS INTERNATIONAL LTD.
6512 Hayes Dr.
Los Angeles, CA 90048
PHONE .323-571-0777/44-(0)20-7622-9219
FAX .815-361-0505/212-473-4739
EMAIL .info@affinityfilms.com
WEB SITE .affinityfilms.com
TYPES Animation - Documentaries - Features - New Media - Syndication - TV Series
DEVELOPMENT Hartley Bootlicker - Secret Agent Woman - Sufi (Documentary Series) - Poe - Hector & Harriet - Miss Moscow
PRE-PRODUCTION Island Games - Johnny Was - Dancing on the Moon
CREDITS The Boys of St. Vincent - Kayla - The Company of Strangers - The Colors of My Father (Documentary) - Kids World - Stolen Song - Stealing Heaven - That Summer of White Roses - The House That Mary Bought
SUBMISSION POLICY Email pitches limited to those periodically requested through inktip.com
COMMENTS East Coast office: PO Box 638, Cooper Station, New York, NY 10276; UK office: 2 Nelson's Row, London SW4 7JT UK

Ira Besserman .Principal
Mark Hammond .Principal
Randall Frederick .Producer
Simon MacCorkindale .Producer
Colin Neale .Producer

MINDY AFFRIME PRODUCTIONS
1429 Avon Park Terrace
Los Angeles, CA 90026
PHONE .323-661-4481
FAX .323-644-0680
EMAIL .minaffrime@aol.com
WEB SITE .www.findshivis.com
TYPES Documentaries - Features - Made-for-TV/Cable Movies - New Media - TV Series
DEVELOPMENT Golf in the Kingdom - Girlhero
CREDITS Wrestling with Alligators - Female Perversions - In the Zone - The Summer of My Deflowering
COMMENTS U.S. representative of Portman Entertainment, British film company

Mindy Affrime .President/Producer

AGAMEMNON FILMS, INC.
650 N. Bronson Ave., Ste. B-225
Los Angeles, CA 90004
PHONE .323-960-4066
FAX .323-960-4067
WEB SITE .www.agamemnon.com
TYPES Animation - Features - Made-for-TV/Cable Movies - TV Series
DEVELOPMENT The Search for Michael Rockefeller - DeMille Directs
CREDITS Treasure Island - The Crucifer of Blood - A Man for All Seasons - Mother Lode - Antony and Cleopatra - Alaska - Needful Things - The Bible - Ben Hur (Animated Feature)

Fraser C. Heston .President
John Stronach .Producer, VP
Alex Butler .Producer
Heather Thomas .Development

ROBERT AHRENS PRODUCTIONS

1134 N. Sycamore Ave., Ste. 108
Los Angeles, CA 90038
PHONE 323-464-4887/212-489-6745
FAX 212-246-5461
EMAIL . . . . .rahrensprods@aol.com

TYPES	Features - Theater
DEVELOPMENT	100 Flowers - Dixon's War - Xanadu (Theater)
POST PRODUCTION	WTC View
CREDITS	Boys Life 4: Four Play - Bumping Heads - Book of Love
COMMENTS	East Coast office: 911 Seventh Ave., Ste. 1-B, New York, NY 10019

Robert Ahrens . . . . .Producer
Eric Sanders . . . . .Assistant (NY)
Billy Snow . . . . .Assistant (LA)

SYDELL ALBERT PRODUCTIONS, INC.

6716 Hillpark Dr., Ste. 305
Los Angeles, CA 90068
PHONE 323-850-1044
FAX 323-850-7551

TYPES	Documentaries - Features - Made-for-TV/Cable Movies - Reality TV - Syndication - TV Series
DEVELOPMENT	Two untitled features
CREDITS	One of Her Own - Preppy Murder - Last Rites

Sydell Albert . . . . .Producer
Rafaell Nola . . . . .VP, Development

ALBRECHT & ASSOCIATES, INC.

3442 Dorothy Rd.
Topanga, CA 90290-4105
PHONE 818-222-4836

TYPES	Features - TV Series
CREDITS	Mickey Mouse's 60th Birthday - Scandals - CBS Comedy Bloopers - Television's Greatest Commercials 1-5 - TV Guide Preview '98

J.A. Albrecht . . . . .President/Producer/Director/Writer

ALCON ENTERTAINMENT, LLC

10390 Santa Monica Blvd., Ste. 250
Los Angeles, CA 90025
PHONE 310-789-3040
FAX 310-789-3060
EMAIL . . . . .info@alconent.com

TYPES	Animation - Features - TV Series
DEALS	Warner Bros. Entertainment Inc. - Warner Bros. Television Production
DEVELOPMENT	The Whole Pemberton Thing - Hong Kong Phooey
PRODUCTION	The Sisterhood of the Traveling Pants
POST PRODUCTION	Racing Stripes
CREDITS	Love Don't Cost a Thing - Chasing Liberty - My Dog Skip - Dude, Where's My Car? - Insomnia - The Affair of the Necklace - Lost and Found

Broderick Johnson . . . . .Co-President/Co-Founder
Andrew A. Kosove . . . . .Co-President/Co-Founder
Scott Parish . . . . .CFO
Kira Davis . . . . .VP, Production
Jamie Wager . . . . .VP, TV
Steven P. Wegner . . . . .VP, Development
Al Cuena . . . . .Director, Interactive
Robyn Harwood . . . . .Coordinator, TV
Rodney Quon . . . . .Director, Finance & Operations
Chris Alexander . . . . .Director, HR/Operations
Sunny Kim . . . . .Staff Accountant
Yolanda Cochran . . . . .Production Controller

(Continued)

ALCON ENTERTAINMENT, LLC (Continued)

Nathan Moore . . . . .Assistant to Messrs. Kosove & Johnson
Greg Rodgers . . . . .Assistant to Messrs. Kosove & Johnson
Jennifer Petruniak . . . . .Assistant to Ms. Davis
Jon Cohen . . . . .Assistant to Mr. Wegner
Zambak Tukan . . . . .Production Assistant
Kirk Shaffer . . . . .Office Runner

ALEXANDER/ENRIGHT & ASSOCIATES

201 Wilshire Blvd., 3rd Fl.
Santa Monica, CA 90401
PHONE 310-458-3003
FAX 310-393-7238

TYPES	Made-for-TV/Cable Movies - TV Series
CREDITS	Perfect Match (Lifetime) - Rain - Our Son the Matchmaker - Point Last Seen - Family Pictures - Two Babies: Switched at Birth - Outside the Law (Columbia TriStar) - Bad Dogs (Animal Planet) - Sex & the Single Mom (Lifetime) - Perfect Romance (Lifetime)

Les Alexander . . . . .Executive Producer
Don Enright . . . . .Executive Producer
Andrea Baynes . . . . .Executive Producer
Tami Gunby . . . . .Director, Administration

ALFA-FILM ENTERPRISES, INC.

264 S. La Cienega Blvd., Ste. 1138
Beverly Hills, CA 90211
PHONE 310-858-1005
FAX 310-858-1050
EMAIL . . . . .sidarfov@earthlink.net

TYPES	Features - New Media - Syndication - TV Series
DEVELOPMENT	C.H. - The Ruler of the World
PRE-PRODUCTION	Dungeons & Dragons 2
CREDITS	Masked & Anonymous - Burial of the Rats - Marquis de Sade - Black Sea 213 - Red Shoe Diaries - Business for Pleasure
COMMENTS	Mosfilm Studios, Russia; Media-Most, Russia

Anatoly A. Fradis . . . . .President

ALLIANCE ATLANTIS

808 Wilshire Blvd., 3rd Fl.
Santa Monica, CA 90401-1810
PHONE 310-899-8000/416-967-1174
FAX 310-899-8100
WEB SITE . . . . .www.allianceatlantis.com

TYPES	Animation - Documentaries - Features - Made-for-TV/Cable Movies - TV Series
CREDITS	Life with Judy Garland: Me and My Shadows - When Billie Beat Bobby - Haven - Existenz - The Sweet Hereafter - Sunshine - Joan of Arc - Nuremberg - CSI - CSI: Miami - Bowling for Columbine
COMMENTS	Toronto office: 121 Bloor Street East, Ste. 1500, Toronto, ON M4W 3M5 Canada

Peter Sussman . . . . .CEO, Alliance Atlantis Entertainment Group
Rose Marie Vega . . . . .Sr. VP, Distribution, Latin America
Janine Coughlin . . . . .Sr. VP, TV Series
Pam Wilson . . . . .Sr. VP, Publicity, Entertainment Group
Jennifer Bennett . . . . .VP, Merchandising & Licensing, Entertainment Group
Annemarie Sulatycky . . . .VP, Business & Legal Affairs, Entertainment Group

ALLIED STARS
c/o Sony Pictures
10202 W. Washington Blvd., Lean Bldg., Ste. 423
Culver City, CA 90232-3195
PHONE .310-244-5188
FAX .310-244-6499
TYPES Features
DEALS Columbia Pictures
CREDITS Peter Pan - Hook - FX 1&2 - Chariots of Fire - The Scarlet Letter

Melissa Henning .Sr. VP, Production
Kelley Jones .VP, Development

ALLOY ENTERTAINMENT
6100 Wilshire Blvd., Ste. 1500
Los Angeles, CA 90048
PHONE .323-801-1350/212-244-4307
FAX .310-234-5094/212-244-4311
TYPES Features - TV Series
DEALS Viacom Entertainment Group
DEVELOPMENT Don't Sleep with Your Drummer (HBO) - The A-List (Universal)
CREDITS TV: Alphabetical Hook-Up List (MTV) - Bakers' Dozen (Touchstone); Features: Sisterhood of the Traveling Pants (Warner Bros.) - Gossip Girl (Warner Bros.)
SUBMISSION POLICY No unsolicited material
COMMENTS East Coast office: 151 W. 26th St., 11th Fl., New York, NY 10001

Leslie Morgenstein .President
Josh Bank .VP, Books Development (NY)
Bob Levy .VP, TV Development & Production (LA)
Eddie Gamarra .Assistant to Mr. Levy (LA)

ALPHAVILLE
5555 Melrose Ave., DeMille Bldg., 2nd Fl.
Los Angeles, CA 90038-3197
PHONE .323-956-4803
FAX .323-862-1616
TYPES Features - Made-for-TV/Cable Movies
DEALS Paramount Pictures-Motion Picture Group
CREDITS The Hunted - Dark Blue - The Scorpion King - Rat Race - The Mummy - The Mummy Returns - Tombstone - Dazed and Confused - Michael - The Jackal - The Gift - Down to Earth - Intolerable Cruelty

Jim Jacks .Producer/Partner (323-956-4830)
Sean Daniel .Producer/Partner (323-956-4805)
Kate Guinzburg .Executive VP (323-956-4818)
Jennifer Moyer .VP (323-956-4293)
Rebecca Nelson .Production Executive (323-956-4890)
Chris Palmer .Assistant to Mr. Daniel
Jody Kay .Assistant to Mr. Jacks
Amy Heidish .Assistant to Ms. Guinzburg
Andrea Chu .Assistant to Ms. Moyer (323-956-4855)
Douglas Miller .Office Assistant
Carlo Hart .Reader

AM PRODUCTIONS & MANAGEMENT
8899 Beverly Blvd., Ste. 713
Los Angeles, CA 90048
PHONE .310-275-9081
FAX .310-275-9082
EMAIL .management@ammanage.com
TYPES Features - Made-for-TV/Cable Movies - TV Series
CREDITS Blonde - Tempted - A Woman's a Helluva Thing - A Place Called Home

Ann-Margret .Actor/Executive Producer
Roger Smith .Executive Producer/Writer
Alan Margulies .Executive Producer/Manager
Lori Steele .Manager/Executive Assistant

AMBUSH ENTERTAINMENT
8271 Melrose Ave., Ste. 207
Los Angeles, CA 90046
PHONE .323-951-9197
FAX .323-951-9998
WEB SITE .www.ambushentertainment.com
SECOND WEB SITE .www.dandbfilm.com
TYPES Features - Made-for-TV/Cable Movies - Reality TV - TV Series
DEVELOPMENT The Advisors - Evidence Room - Untitled Wayne Wang Project - Yummy - Untitled Matthew Leutwyler Project - The Light House - Touchback
PRE-PRODUCTION Point of Faith - Finding Jenua
COMPLETED UNRELEASED Dead & Breakfast
CREDITS This Space Between Us
SUBMISSION POLICY By referral only

Miranda Bailey .Partner/Producer/Actress
Francey Grace .Partner/Producer
Matthew Leutwyler .Partner/Prouducer/Director/Writer
Jun Tan .Partner/Producer
Julie Sandor .Producer/Development Executive
Tess Lindberg .Production Executive
Amanda Hartrey .Executive Assistant

AMERICAN ENTERTAINMENT FOUNDATION
4872 Topanga Canyon Blvd., Ste. 122
Woodland Hills, CA 91364
PHONE .818-377-5111
WEB SITE .www.miraclefilms.com
TYPES Documentaries - Features - Direct-to-Video/DVD - Made-for-TV/Cable Movies - TV Series
DEVELOPMENT The Sword of Peter - A Nation of Heroes - Aimee
PRE-PRODUCTION Summer Camp - Kept Women - First Day in Heaven
PRODUCTION Trading for God
POST PRODUCTION All God's Children
CREDITS Hometown Legend - Starpower Miracles - Heaven's Taxi

Richard Smith .President
Leslie McRay .VP, Production

AMERICAN MOVIE CLASSICS (AMC)
200 Jericho Quadrangle
Jericho, NY 11753
PHONE .516-803-3000
WEB SITE .www.amctv.com
TYPES Documentaries - New Media - TV Series
CREDITS The Lot - Hollywood Fashion Machine - The Unknown Peter Sellers - Backstory - Cinema Secrets - Reel Women: The First Women of Film - The AMC Project - Hollywood Hunt Club

Kathleen Dore .President
David Sehring .Sr. VP, Programming & Acquisitions
Rob Sorcher .Sr. VP, Programming & Production
Jessica Falcon .VP, Documentaries
Tom Halleen .VP, Programming & Scheduling
David Ladik .VP, Development & Series
Judith Orlowski .VP, Acquistions
Vlad Wolynetz .Director, Development
Joshua Berger .Director, Programming Operations
Matt Peccini .Director, Packaging Productions

AMERICAN NEW WAVE FILMS

7775 Sunset Blvd., Ste. 150
Hollywood, CA 90046
PHONE .323-850-1700
FAX .323-850-1788

TYPES	Features - Direct-to-Video/DVD - Made-for-TV/Cable Movies - TV Series
DEVELOPMENT	Cuba Libra - Wild Horses, Wild Hearts - Gas Pump Blues - Cemetary
CREDITS	Taxi Dancers - Frightmare - Midnight - King of the City (aka Club Life) - Black Room - Lola

Norman Thaddeus Vane .Writer/Director/Producer
Harlan Baird .Assistant to Producers
Gus Ramos .Assistant to Producers

*AMERICAN VANTAGE MEDIA

1547 18th St.
Santa Monica, CA 90404
PHONE .310-828-7499
FAX .310-828-1558

TYPES	Animation - Commercials - Documentaries - Features - Direct-to-Video/DVD - Made-for-TV/Cable Movies - Music Videos - New Media - Reality TV - Syndication - TV Series
DEVELOPMENT	jetBlue (Sitcom) - Firehouse TV
PRODUCTION	MasterCard Priceless Experience
POST PRODUCTION	Chrysler Million Dollar Film Festival - Cry Wolf
COMMENTS	Media Holdings: Hypnotic (Production) - Wellspring Media (Distribution) - YaYa (Marketing)

Stephen K. Bannon .CEO
David Schulte .Vice Chairman
Matt Smith .CFO
Adam Asherson .VP, Branded TV
Michael Wiese .VP, Branded Partnerships
Seth Berman .Director, Branded Partnerships
Wendy Colbert .Executive Assistant to CEO
Sophia Griffin .Office Manager

AMERICAN WORLD PICTURES

6355 Topanga Canyon Blvd., Ste. 428
Woodland Hills, CA 91367
PHONE .818-715-1480
FAX .818-715-1081
EMAIL .info@americanworldpictures.com
WEB SITE .www.americanworldpictures.com

TYPES	Features - Direct-to-Video/DVD
DEVELOPMENT	College Vice
PRODUCTION	Terror in the Sky
CREDITS	Knight Club - Tully - Menace - White Rush - Stealing Candy - The Wisher - Chopin: Desire for Love - Snow Job - Lady Jayne: Killer - Darkhunters - Two Days - Keeper of Souls - Fugitive Run - Wild Roomies
COMMENTS	Acquisitions

Mark L. Lester .President/CEO
Dana Dubovsky .President, Production
Terese Linden Kohn .Executive VP, Distribution
Carol Rossi .VP, Distribution
Dan Gold .VP, Post Production
Florian Schereck .CFO
Rafael Pujals .Director, Development
Adam Singer .Director, Acquisitions

AMERICAN ZOETROPE

6747 Milner Rd.
Los Angeles, CA 90068
PHONE .323-851-8808/415-788-7500
FAX .323-851-8803/415-989-7910
WEB SITE .www.zoetrope.com

TYPES	Features
DEVELOPMENT	Megalopolis - On the Road - Cavemen in the Hedges - Girls Guide to Hunting and Fishing - Montechristo - Black Stallion Revolts - Descent - Jeepers Creepers 3
COMPLETED UNRELEASED	Kinsey
CREDITS	Assassination Tango - Pumpkin - CQ - Virgin Suicides - Jeepers Creepers 1&2 - Lost in Translation
SUBMISSION POLICY	Accepting no submissions
COMMENTS	San Francisco office: 916 Kearny St., San Francisco, CA 94133

Jay Shoemaker .CEO (SF)
Bobby Rock .Sr. VP, Film Production & Development (LA)
Shannon Lail .Production Executive (SF)
Rachel Eckerling .Assistant to Francis Coppola (SF)
Brendan Kenney .Assistant to Bobby Rock (LA)

CRAIG ANDERSON PRODUCTIONS

9696 Culver Blvd., Meralta Plaza, Ste. 208
Culver City, CA 90232
PHONE .310-841-2555
FAX .310-841-5934
EMAIL .cappix@aol.com
WEB SITE .www.cappix.com

TYPES	Features - Made-for-TV/Cable Movies - Reality TV - Theater - TV Series
CREDITS	On Golden Pond - Songs in Ordinary Time - The Piano Lesson - The Ballad of Lucy Whipple - Midwives - True Women - The Christmas Shoes - O Pioneers! - Sally Hemings - Wilder Days - Meltdown

Craig Anderson .Executive Producer
Beth Grossbard .Producer
Kerry Bailey .Creative Executive
Dani DeJesus .Creative Executive

ANDREW LAUREN PRODUCTIONS

36 E. 23rd St., Ste. 6-F
New York, NY 10010
PHONE .212-475-1600/323-822-1343
FAX .212-529-1095
EMAIL .alpeast@yahoo.com

TYPES	Features
DEVELOPMENT	After - Blue Jean
CREDITS	G
COMMENTS	All inquiries should be directed to the New York office; West Coast office: 1355 N. Laurel Ave., Ste. 7, Los Angeles, CA 90046

Andrew Lauren .CEO
Elizabeth Bradley .Director, Development
Richard Bever .Assistant

ANGEL ARK PRODUCTIONS
5042 Wilshire Blvd., Ste. 592
Los Angeles, CA 90036
PHONE 818-981-8833
FAX 818-981-8412
TYPES: Features - Made-for-TV/Cable Movies - Reality TV - TV Series
PRODUCTION: Shut Up and Listen (CBS)
CREDITS: Agent Cody Banks 1&2 (MGM) - Bob Patterson (ABC) - Just Looking (Sony Classics) - On Edge (MGM Home Entertainment) - For Better or Worse (Castle Rock)

Jason Alexander ....Creative Partner
Jenny Birchfield-Eick ....Creative Partner/Features & TV

ANGELIKA
PO Box 4956
New York, NY 10185
PHONE 212-410-9404/213-840-6224
FAX 213-477-2004
EMAIL ....barney@angelikafilm.com
WEB SITE ....www.angelikafilm.com
TYPES: Documentaries - Features - Made-for-TV/Cable Movies - TV Series
DEVELOPMENT: Angelika TV Channel - Maniac 2 (Feature) - All Ivy (Feature) - Bloody Jocks (Feature)
PRE-PRODUCTION: WBway (Series)
PRODUCTION: Another Deep Breath (Feature)
CREDITS: Streetwise - Too Much Sleep - Metro Angelika (Cablevision)

Angelika Saleh ....President
Barney Oldfield ....General Manager
David Maquiling ....Production Manager
Thomas Bannister ....Foreign Marketing Director

ANGOTTI PRODUCTIONS, INC.
137 N. Larchmont Blvd., Ste. 274
Los Angeles, CA 90004
PHONE 310-770-0718
EMAIL ....angottiinc@aol.com
WEB SITE ....www.angottiproductions.com
TYPES: Documentaries - Industrials - Reality TV - TV Series
DEALS: EOE - ESPN Original Entertainment
CREDITS: Inside Out: Leah Remini (1&2) - Beyond the Glory (Fox Sports) - The World Stunt Awards (ABC) - The Action Sports and Music Awards - Sports Century: Year in Review - The Source Awards (UPN) - Manilow Live (PBS)
COMMENTS: Music Specials; Award Shows; Corporate & Industrial DVD Marketing

Mark Angotti ....President

ANIMAL PLANET
SEE Discovery Networks, U.S.

ANTIDOTE INTERNATIONAL FILMS, INC.
200 Varick St., Ste. 502
New York, NY 10014
PHONE 646-486-4344
FAX 646-486-5885
EMAIL ....info@antidotefilms.com
WEB SITE ....www.antidotefilms.com
TYPES: Documentaries - Features
DEVELOPMENT: Famous Long Ago - The Last Winter - Sarah - The Knockout Artist - Inland Empire - Into the Great Wide Open - Macbeth - Creeps!
PRE-PRODUCTION: The Hawk Is Dying
POST PRODUCTION: Mysterious Skin
CREDITS: High Art - Wendigo - Limon - Laurel Canyon - The Station Agent - thirteen - The Jimmy Show - Chain
SUBMISSION POLICY: No unsolicited material

Jeffrey Levy-Hinte ....Producer
Mary Jane Skalski ....Producer
Takeo Hori ....Assistant to Mr. Levy-Hinte
James Debbs ....Assistant to Ms. Skalski

APARTMENT 3B PRODUCTIONS
10250 Constellation Blvd., Ste. 2064
Los Angeles, CA 90067
PHONE 310-449-3478
FAX 310-449-3923
TYPES: Features
DEALS: Metro-Goldwyn-Mayer Studios, Inc.
DEVELOPMENT: Don't Tell My Mother - Scrawl - Selling Time - Truce - F+ - Charlie Chan - The Gentleman (TV)

Jennifer Klein ....Producer
Todd Winton ....Production Executive
Pooneh Zandazma ....Assistant to Jennifer Klein

APATOW PRODUCTIONS
2900 W. Olympic Blvd., Ste. 141
Santa Monica, CA 90404
PHONE 310-255-7026
FAX 310-255-7025
TYPES: Features - TV Series
DEALS: DreamWorks SKG
CREDITS: Anchorman: The Legend of Ron Burgundy - Undeclared - Freaks and Geeks - The Ben Stiller Show - The Larry Sanders Show - The Cable Guy - Celtic Pride - Heavyweights

Judd Apatow ....Writer/Producer
Andrew Cohen ....Story Editor

APOSTLE PICTURES
c/o The Ed Sullivan Theater
1697 Broadway, Ste. 906
New York, NY 10019
PHONE 212-541-4323
FAX 212-541-4330
TYPES: Features - TV Series
DEALS: DreamWorks SKG
CREDITS: Blow - Monument Avenue - The Job (ABC)

Denis Leary ....Actor/Director/Producer
Jim Serpico ....President, Motion Pictures & TV
Tom Sellitti ....Creative Executive
Bartow Church ....Associate
Gerard Mule ....Creative Consultant
Steve Hochmuth ....Assistant to Denis Leary
Richard Hertz ....Assistant to Steve Hochmuth
Maurice Singer ....Assistant to Producers

APPIAN WAY

9255 Sunset Blvd., Ste. 615
West Hollywood, CA 90069
PHONE .310-300-1390
TYPES Features
DEALS Initial Entertainment Group
DEVELOPMENT Cat's Cradle - Gardener of Eden - Bombshell - Firecracker Boys
POST PRODUCTION The Aviator

Leonardo DiCaprio .Owner
Bradford Simpson .President, Production
Katie Alheim .Assistant/Story Editor
John Zaozirny .Assistant

APPLE & HONEY FILM CORP.

9190 W. Olympic Blvd., Ste. 363
Beverly Hills, CA 90212
PHONE .310-556-5639
FAX .310-556-1295
WEB SITE .www.awardwinningfilms.com
TYPES Features - Made-for-TV/Cable Movies - TV Series
DEVELOPMENT Hint of Rain
CREDITS My Life as a Dog - The Quarrel - American Hero

David Brandes .Producer

APPLEDOWN FILMS, INC.

9687 W. Olympic Blvd.
Beverly Hills, CA 90212
PHONE .310-552-1833
FAX .310-552-1331
TYPES Features - Made-for-TV/Cable Movies - TV Series
DEVELOPMENT Café Berlin - The Jackie Wilson Story - Dove Against Death - Beverly Heels - Avenger
CREDITS Sunchaser - Remo Williams

Larry Spiegel .Producer/Writer
Judy Goldstein .Producer

APPLESEED ENTERTAINMENT, LLC

9801 Amestoy Ave.
Los Angeles, CA 91325
PHONE .818-718-6000
FAX .818-993-8720
EMAIL .info@appleseedent.com
TYPES Animation - Documentaries - Features - Made-for-TV/Cable Movies - TV Series
DEVELOPMENT The Shed - Gus - Notehunter - Run Away Home
PRE-PRODUCTION Little Lady Fauntleroy - Slim Chance
CREDITS Nickel & Dime - Good Morning, Vietnam - Without a Clue - What Are We Doing to Our Children? - Dying with Dignity - Not a Question of Courage - Hope Ranch - Cupid's Prey

Lynne A. Lueders .Partner/Writer
Ben Moses .Partner/Producer

LOREEN ARBUS PRODUCTIONS, INC.

8075 W. Third St., Ste. 410
Los Angeles, CA 90048
PHONE .323-930-1244
FAX .323-930-0186
EMAIL .arbusprod@arbusprod.com
SECOND EMAIL .jayme@arbusprod.com
TYPES Documentaries - New Media - Syndication - TV Series - Reality TV
CREDITS Case Closed - In the Name of Love - Crimes of Passion - Forgive or Forget
COMMENTS Emphasis on nonfiction series, movies, specials

Loreen Arbus .President/Executive Producer
Jayme Brown . .Assistant to President/Projects Coordinator/Office Manager

ARC FILMS, INC.

16070 Sunset Blvd., Ste. 207
Pacific Palisades, CA 90272
PHONE .310-804-5520
EMAIL .r.swanson15@verizon.net
TYPES Features - Direct-to-Video/DVD - Made-for-TV/Cable Movies - TV Series
DEVELOPMENT Can Do, Ohio (Series) - Protective Measures - Boogie Man & the Tooth Fairy - Homeward
CREDITS Slow Burn

Robert Swanson .Producer
Cynthia Pasco .Development

ARCHER ENTERTAINMENT

140 W. 22nd St., Ste. 7-B
New York, NY 10011
PHONE .212-741-2200
FAX .212-741-9575
WEB SITE .www.archerent.com
TYPES Documentaries - Features - Made-for-TV/Cable Movies - TV Series
DEVELOPMENT 6221 - Aging Wildly (Documentary) - The Artist - Great Unknowns - Marga - The Ministers - New York City Serenade - Silver Sixties - Sunny Day - Turning Stones
PRE-PRODUCTION Flyin' V - Gray Matters
PRODUCTION The Warrior Class
CREDITS Boys Don't Cry - Dark Harbor - Maze - Nola - Shift - You Can Count on Me

Jill Footlick .Producer/Principal
Rachel Peters .Producer/Principal
Laird Adamson .Producer
Virginia Williams .Director, Development

MARK ARCHER ENTERTAINMENT

c/o New Hollywood Studios
4717 Speedway Dr.
Fort Wayne, IN 46825
PHONE .818-303-1365/260-486-8831
FAX .260-969-9261
EMAIL .archer@newhollywoodonline.com
TYPES Commercials - Documentaries - Features - Direct-to-Video/DVD - Reality TV - TV Series
PRODUCTION Night Shift (Series) - Paper Dolls
POST PRODUCTION New Hope
CREDITS In the Company of Men - American Reel - Joe Bonamassa: A New Day Yesterday Live

Mark Archer .President/CEO

ARDEN ENTERTAINMENT
12034 Riverside Dr., Ste. 200
North Hollywood, CA 91607
PHONE ... 818-985-4600
FAX ... 818-985-3121
EMAIL ... dan@ardenentertainment.com
SECOND EMAIL ... julie@ardenentertainment.com
WEB SITE ... www.ardenentertainment.com
TYPES: Documentaries - Reality TV - TV Series
DEVELOPMENT: America's Ultimate Handyman
PRODUCTION: Extreme Surgery 2 - Growing Up Wild - Mob Scene
CREDITS: Growing Up Grizzly 1&2 - Another Way of Seeing Things - Lord of the Rings: Behind the Scenes - A Quiet Revolution - Extreme Surgery

Dan Arden ... President
John Greco ... Sr. VP
Cory Taylor ... VP, Production
Julie Uribe ... VP, Development

ARDENT ENTERTAINMENT
345 N. Maple Dr., Ste. 317
Beverly Hills, CA 90210
PHONE ... 310-550-2180
FAX ... 310-550-2178
TYPES: Features
CREDITS: Sensation - The West Side Waltz - Plato's Run

Mitch Blumberg ... Producer/Manager
Melissa Simock ... Development Executive/Assistant Manager

ARDUSTRY ENTERTAINMENT
9255 Sunset Blvd., Ste. 1000
Los Angeles, CA 90069
PHONE ... 310-281-0070
FAX ... 310-281-0050
EMAIL ... info@ardustry.com
WEB SITE ... www.ardustry.com
TYPES: Features
POST PRODUCTION: Orphan King - Pursuit of Happiness

Peter Sahagen ... President
Ehrich Van Lowe ... VP, Production

ARENAS ENTERTAINMENT
100 N. Crescent Dr., Garden Level
Beverly Hills, CA 90210
PHONE ... 310-385-4401
FAX ... 310-385-4402
EMAIL ... info@arenasgroup.com
WEB SITE ... www.arenasgroup.com
TYPES: Animation - Documentaries - Features - Direct-to-Video/DVD - New Media - TV Series
DEVELOPMENT: Macho! - El Cucuy
CREDITS: Empire - Imagining Argentina
COMMENTS: Marketing, production, distribution, talent management; Specializes in the Latino market

Santiago Pozo ... CEO
Allan Chalfin ... CFO
Larry Gleason ... President, Distribution
Amorette Jones ... President, Marketing
Ivan De Paz ... Executive VP, Talent Management
Diana Lesmez ... VP, Development, Production & Acquisitions
Marcia Daley ... VP, Legal & Business Affairs
Bobby Garcia ... Paralegal
Ignacio Manubens ... Production & Acquisitions Coordinator
Juan Gonzalez Villa ... Development & Acquisitions Coordinator
Christina Covarrubias ... Jr. Manager

ARJAY ENTERTAINMENT
1627 Pontius Ave., Ste. 100
Los Angeles, CA 90025
PHONE ... 310-481-2282
FAX ... 310-481-2287
EMAIL ... info@arjayentertainment.com
TYPES: Direct-to-Video/DVD - Reality TV - Syndication - TV Series
DEVELOPMENT: The Ultimate Weekend - The Hookup - On the DL
CREDITS: The Red Carpet - VIP Access

R.J. Williams ... CEO
Bob Williams ... Producer
Mark D. Mitchell ... Producer
Michael Vann ... VP, Production
Lauren Haggard ... Creative Executive
Becky Michieli ... Director, Marketing
Leandra Jones ... Production Coordinator

ARLINGTON ENTERTAINMENT, INC.
10866 Wilshire Blvd., Ste. 850
Los Angeles, CA 90024
PHONE ... 310-481-7190
FAX ... 310-481-7191
TYPES: Direct-to-Video/DVD - Made-for-TV/Cable Movies - Syndication - TV Series
DEVELOPMENT: Tyburn's Tales of Terror - The Aftermath - Courier - The Bloody Millennium
PRE-PRODUCTION: The Moorgate Legacy
POST PRODUCTION: Legend of the Werewolf (1975, Restoration)
CREDITS: Masks of Death - Murder Elite - One Way Ticket to Hollywood - The Ghoul (1974, Restoration)
SUBMISSION POLICY: Only consider unsolicited submissions via a recognized talent agent/agency
COMMENTS: UK office: Cippenham Court, Cippenham Lane, Cippenham, Nr Slough, Berkshire SL1 5AU UK

Anthony Palladino ... President
Kevin Francis ... Executive VP
Annette Pearse ... VP/Administrator
Bernard Thomas ... VP/Controller
Gillian Garrow ... Story & Research Editor

ARMADA PICTURES
9720 Wilshire Blvd., 5th Fl.
Beverly Hills, CA 90212
PHONE ... 310-205-9600
FAX ... 310-205-9610
TYPES: Features
DEVELOPMENT: Honor for Sale - Soldiers of Fortune - Overnight - Tamara - Family of the Year
POST PRODUCTION: Drum
CREDITS: One Point O - The Quiet American - The Wedding Planner - Blow Dry - Nurse Betty - Where the Money Is - The Crow: Salvation - Clay Pigeons - The Innocent - The Dead - Paris, Texas

Chris Sievernich ... President
Yarek Danielak ... VP, International Distribution
Matt Milich ... VP, Production
Winona Lyons ... Creative Executive

ARS NOVA PGM
511 W. 54th St.
New York, NY 10019
PHONE 212-489-9800
FAX 212-489-1908
EMAIL . . . . . info@arsnovanyc.com
WEB SITE . . . . . www.arsnovanyc.com
TYPES Features - Theater - TV Series
CREDITS Thick as Thieves - Lobby Hero - God Said `Ha!' - Julia Sweeney in the Family Way

Jon Steingart . . . . . Partner/Producer
Jenny Wiener . . . . . Partner/Producer
Jason Eagan . . . . . Producer
Gordon Greenberg . . . . . Director, Musical Development
Kacy O'Brien . . . . . Executive Assistant

ARTIST ENTERTAINMENT
PO Box 222
Beverly Hills, CA 90213
PHONE 310-770-0105
EMAIL . . . . . artistentertainment@hotmail.com
TYPES Commercials - Features - Direct-to-Video/DVD - Made-for-TV/Cable Movies - TV Series
DEVELOPMENT The Vampire Girl - The President's Physician - Bronx, NY - American Zombie
COMMENTS Management

James Asmodeo . . . . . President/CEO
Paul Withers . . . . . Head, TV
David Marciano . . . . . Manager
Malek Akkad . . . . . Consultant

THE ARTISTS' COLONY
256 S. Robertson Blvd., Ste. 1500
Beverly Hills, CA 90211
PHONE 310-720-8300
EMAIL . . . . . las@theartistscolony.com
WEB SITE . . . . . www.theartistscolony.com
TYPES Documentaries - Features - Made-for-TV/Cable Movies - New Media - TV Series
DEVELOPMENT Isabella & the Monsters - Bohemian Heart
PRE-PRODUCTION Caravaggio - Waking Up the Day - The Tenants
COMPLETED UNRELEASED Heroes
CREDITS Snow Falling on Cedars - `Til the End of Time - Shattered Image - A Girl, Three Guys and a Gun - Tidal Wave - 12

Lloyd A. Silverman . . . . . Producer
David Donnelly . . . . . Director, Development
Ginnina D'Orazio . . . . . Director, Development
Steve Grill . . . . . Director, Development (NY)
Adam Neal . . . . . Director, Development

ARTISTS PRODUCTION GROUP (APG)
2601 Colorado Ave.
Santa Monica, CA 90404
PHONE 310-300-2400
FAX 310-300-2424
TYPES Features - TV Series
DEVELOPMENT Conquest of Mexico - Rainbow Six - Red Rabbit - The Brazilian - Without Remorse - Tom Clancy's Splinter Cell - Teeth of the Tiger - Tom Clancy's Ghost Recon
CREDITS Godsend - Sidewalks of New York - You Stupid Man - A Gentleman's Game - Timeline
SUBMISSION POLICY Through agents only

Bryce Johnson . . . . . Business/Legal Affairs

ASCENDANT PICTURES
9350 Civic Center Dr., Ste. 110
Beverly Hills, CA 90210
PHONE 310-288-4600
FAX 310-288-4601
WEB SITE . . . . . www.ascendantpictures.com
TYPES Features - Interactive Games
DEALS Morgan Creek Productions
DEVELOPMENT American Knight - The Bird - Race For The Sky - Chasing Shadows - The Night We Liberated Paris
PRODUCTION Ask The Dust
POST PRODUCTION The Jacket - The Big White
CREDITS Collateral Damage - Dungeons and Dragons - Frequency - Juwanna Man - Keeping the Faith - Primal Fear - The Watcher - Wayne's World - Wing Commander - Half Past Dead - The Punisher
COMMENTS Joint venture with VIP Mediafunds

Chris Roberts . . . . . Partner/Co-CEO
Christopher Eberts . . . . . Partner/Co-CEO
Kia Jam . . . . . Partner/COO
Philip Elway . . . . . President
Hawk Koch . . . . . Partner
Deborah Aquila . . . . . Partner/Co-Head, Casting
Tricia Wood . . . . . Partner/Co-Head, Casting
John Schimmel . . . . . President, Production
Jodi Heaston . . . . . Director, Development

ASIS PRODUCTIONS
200 N. Larchmont Blvd., Ste. 2
Los Angeles, CA 90004
PHONE 323-871-4290
FAX 323-871-4847
TYPES Features - Made-for-TV/Cable Movies
DEVELOPMENT The Giver - Keller - The Moon in Two Windows
CREDITS American Heart - Hidden in America

Jeff Bridges . . . . . President
Neil Koenigsberg . . . . . Executive
Andrew Jackson . . . . . Development

TAMARA ASSEYEV PRODUCTIONS, INC.
1187 Coast Village Rd., Ste. 134
Santa Barbara, CA 93108
PHONE 323-656-4731
FAX 323-656-2211
EMAIL . . . . . tamaraprod@aol.com
TYPES Documentaries - Features - Made-for-TV/Cable Movies - TV Series
CREDITS The Shadow on the Sun: The Life of Beryl Markham - After the Promise - The Hijacking of the Achille Lauro - Penalty Phase - I Wanna Hold Your Hand - Norma Rae - Big Wednesday
SUBMISSION POLICY Email only
COMMENTS Administrator of The Woodfall Film Library

Tamara Asseyev . . . . . Producer
Constance Mead . . . . . Assistant to Producer

THE ASYLUM

6671 Sunset Blvd., Bldg. 1593
Los Angeles, CA 90028
PHONE 323-463-6575
FAX 323-463-6299
WEB SITE ....www.theasylum.cc

TYPES	Features - Direct-to-Video/DVD
DEVELOPMENT	Dinosaur Bone Wars - Alien Abduction
PRE-PRODUCTION	Unravelled
PRODUCTION	Bram Stoker's Way of the Vampire - The Bob Club
POST PRODUCTION	Evil Eyes - Bloody Bill - El Intermedio
CREDITS	King of the Ants - Max Knight - Killers 2 - The Source
SUBMISSION POLICY	Scripts: email David Michael Latt at latt@theasylum.cc; Completed Films: David Rimawi at rimawi@theasylum.cc
COMMENTS	International sales & distribution; US home video label, The Asylum Home Entertainment; 2004/5 production slate of 20 genre feature films

David Michael Latt ....Partner, Development & Production
David Rimawi ....Partner
Sherri Strain ....Partner
Kark Hirsch ....VP, Acquisitions
Rick Walker ....Distribution & Operations

ATELIER PICTURES

280 S. Beverly Dr., Ste. 500
Beverly Hills, CA 90212
PHONE 310-888-7727/805-466-4660
FAX 310-888-7726/805-466-4729
EMAIL ....atelierpictures@yahoo.com
SECOND EMAIL ....webm@atelierpix.com
WEB SITE ....www.atelierpix.com

TYPES	Features - Direct-to-Video/DVD - New Media
DEVELOPMENT	Cafe del Mundo
PRODUCTION	The Seven Deadly Sins
POST PRODUCTION	Steinbeck & Co.
CREDITS	Sealed Testimony - The Roaring 20's - Please Don't Walk Around in the Nude - Starfish - Everyman
COMMENTS	Second office: 10420 San Marcos Rd., Atascadero, CA 93422

Paul T. Gray ....Director/Executive Producer
David Rachlis ....Business Affairs
Gretchen G. Gray ....Executive VP, Creative Affairs
Tom FitzGibbon ....Director, Development
Teri Gibbons ....Development Executive
Victor Solanoy ....Webmaster

ATLANTIC STREAMLINE

1323-A Third St.
Santa Monica, CA 90401
PHONE 310-319-9366
FAX 310-319-9235
WEB SITE ....www.atlanticstreamline.com

TYPES	Features
DEALS	Metro-Goldwyn-Mayer Studios, Inc.
CREDITS	Igby Goes Down - The Thirteenth Floor - All the Queen's Men
SUBMISSION POLICY	No unsolicited submissions

Marco Weber ....CEO/President
Vanessa Coifman ....Executive VP, Creative Affairs
Hubert Hagg ....VP, Business Development
Julie Schroeder ....Executive Assistant to CEO

ATLAS ENTERTAINMENT

9200 Sunset Blvd., 10th Fl.
Los Angeles, CA 90069
PHONE 310-786-4900
FAX 310-777-2185

TYPES	Features
CREDITS	12 Monkeys - Cool Runnings - City of Angels - Three Kings - Scooby Doo 1&2 - Bulletproof Monk

Charles Roven ....Producer/Partner (310-786-4935)
Allen Shapiro ....President/Partner (310-786-4940)
Ted MacKinney ....CFO (310-786-4911)
Alan Glazer ....VP, Marketing, Publicity & Distribution (310-786-4929)
George Gatins ....VP, Production (310-786-8929)
Joan Bierman ....VP, Physical Production (310-786-4932)
Bailey Spencer-Jackson ....Director, Business Affairs (310-786-4997)
Gloria Fan ....Feature Development (310-786-4914)
Alex Ankeles ....Creative Executive (310-786-4971)
M. Riley ....Story Editor (310-786-4922)
Alexis Cohen ....Assistant to Mr. Shapiro (310-786-4944)
Paul Ton ....Assistant to Mr. Roven (310-786-4939)
Heather Dennis ....Assistant to Ms. Bierman (310-786-4934)
Mary Cybrowsky ....Assistant to Mr. Glazer (310-786-4931)
Tina Jones ....Assistant to Ms. Fan (310-786-8917)

MARILYN ATLAS MANAGEMENT

8899 Beverly Blvd., Ste. 704
Los Angeles, CA 90048
PHONE 310-278-5047
FAX 310-278-5289

TYPES	Features - Made-for-TV/Cable Movies - TV Series
DEVELOPMENT	Down River - Untitled Crime Drama - Untitled Showtime Pilot - En El Corazón de Los Montañas - Lola Goes to Roma
PRE-PRODUCTION	Add Me to the Party - Suburban Turban
CREDITS	Real Women Have Curves - A Certain Desire - Echoes
SUBMISSION POLICY	No unsolicited material accepted; Industry referrals only (actors and writers)
COMMENTS	Deal with Elysian Films

Marilyn R. Atlas ....Owner/Producer
S. Rosenthal ....Literary
Elizabeth Lopez ....Talent Assistant/Literary Development

ATMAN ENTERTAINMENT

335 N. Maple Dr., Ste. 354
Beverly Hills, CA 90210
PHONE 310-550-5127

TYPES	Features - Made-for-TV/Cable Movies - TV Series
DEVELOPMENT	Lambs of God - Ingle Woods - The Man Who Fell in Love with the Moon - Hell on Earth - Nancy Wake
CREDITS	Fight Club - Under Suspicion

Ross Grayson Bell ....Producer
Shadi Enayati ....Creative Executive

*ATMOSPHERE ENTERTAINMENT MM, LLC
9200 Sunset Blvd., Ste. 515
Los Angeles, CA 90069
PHONE 310-860-0310
FAX 310-860-0410
TYPES Animation - Features - Made-for-TV/Cable Movies - Reality TV - TV Series
DEVELOPMENT 300 - Dating Nick McBride - Books of Magic - Ride Down Mt. Morgan - Chasing the Dime - Interior Decorators - Revelation
CREDITS Taking Lives - Godsend

Mark Canton .....Chairman/CEO
Bernie Goldmann .....President
Steve Barnett .....Executive VP, Motion Picture Development & Production
Stacy Mandelberg .....Sr. VP, TV
Ray Kimsey .....Creative Executive
Chantal Lundberg .....Creative Executive
Silenn Thomas .....Creative Executive
Josh Levitan .....Assistant to Bernie Goldmann

*ATOMIC CARTOONS, INC.
928 Davie St.
Vancouver, BC V6Z 1B8 Canada
PHONE 604-734-2866
FAX 604-734-2869
EMAIL .....info@atomiccartoons.com
WEB SITE .....www.atomiccartoons.com
TYPES Animation - TV Series
CREDITS Atomic Betty (A Canada/France Co-Production, between Breakthrough Films & Television, Teleimages Kids and Atomic Cartoons, Inc.)

Trevor Bentley .....CEO
Edward Peghin .....COO
Rob Davies .....VP, Production
Jeffery Agala .....Director
Mauro Casalese .....Director/VP, Production
Ridd Sorensen .....Director
Shelby Tony .....Accountant/Coordinator

AURA ENTERTAINMENT
9350 Wilshire, Ste. 400
Beverly Hills, CA 90212
PHONE 310-278-9991
FAX 310-278-9992
EMAIL .....mail@auraent.com
WEB SITE .....www.auraent.com
TYPES Features - TV Series
COMPLETED UNRELEASED Love Comes to the Executioner
CREDITS The Big Empty

Steve Bickel .....President/Partner
Brian Stearns .....Director, Creative Affairs

AURORA PRODUCTIONS
8642 Melrose Ave., Ste. 200
Los Angeles, CA 90069
PHONE 310-854-6900
EMAIL .....auroraprod@aol.com
TYPES Features - Made-for-TV/Cable Movies
DEVELOPMENT Blue Elevator - Immortals - The Travel Writer
CREDITS The Rock - Eddie & the Cruisers - Heart Like a Wheel

William Stuart .....President
Jane Ferda .....Development Executive

AUTOMATIC PICTURES, INC.
5225 Wilshire Blvd., Ste. 525
Los Angeles, CA 90036
PHONE 323-935-1800
FAX 323-935-8040
EMAIL .....automaticpictures@hotmail.com
TYPES Animation - Features - Made-for-TV/Cable Movies - New Media - TV Series
DEALS Pathé Pictures/Pathé Distribution
DEVELOPMENT The Season
CREDITS There's Something About Mary - Wicked

Frank Beddor .....Producer
Liz Cavalier .....Creative Executive
C.J. Wrobel .....Assistant to Frank Beddor

AVALANCHE! ENTERTAINMENT
11041 Santa Monica Blvd., Ste. 511
Los Angeles, CA 90025
PHONE 310-477-1464
FAX 310-552-0549
TYPES Animation - Documentaries - Features - Reality TV - TV Series
DEALS Catch 23 Entertainment, Inc.
CREDITS Free for All (Showtime Series) - MTV's Campus Cops - She's All That - On the Line - Get Over It - American Psycho 2 - Jekyll Island - The Story of Darrell Royal - MTV's He's The Mayor

Richard Hull .....President
Rhiannon Meier .....Development

AVENUE PICTURES
11111 Santa Monica Blvd., Ste. 525
Los Angeles, CA 90025
PHONE 310-996-6800
FAX 310-473-4376
EMAIL .....avenue@avepix.com
WEB SITE .....www.avepix.com
TYPES Features - Made-for-TV/Cable Movies - TV Series
DEALS HBO Films
DEVELOPMENT The Courier - The Moviegoer - Phobic
POST PRODUCTION The Merchant of Venice - Closer
COMPLETED UNRELEASED Mindhunters
CREDITS Short Cuts - The Player - Restoration - Drugstore Cowboy - Wayward Son - Wit - Path to War - Normal - Angels in America

Cary Brokaw .....Chairman/CEO (310-996-6810)
Sheri Halfon .....Sr. VP/CFO (310-996-6815)
Aaron Geller .....VP, Production (310-996-6803)
Judy Geletko .....Controller (310-996-6818)
Randy Robinson .....Randwell Productions (310-996-6809)
Tom Kageff .....Randwell Productions (310-996-6819)
Marc Popkin .....Assistant (310-996-6808)

AVIATOR FILMS, LLC
9595 Wilshire Blvd., Ste. 900
Beverly Hills, CA 90212
PHONE 323-465-4400
TYPES Features - Made-for-TV/Cable Movies - TV Series
DEALS Warner Bros. Pictures
CREDITS Border Line - N.Y.H.C. - Don't Go Breaking My Heart - My Louisiana Sky - Die, Mommie, Die

Anthony Edwards . . . . . Partner
Dante Di Loreto . . . . . Partner
Frank Pavich . . . . . Associate

THE AXELROD/EDWARDS COMPANY
c/o Paramount Studios
5555 Melrose Ave., B Annex 1
Los Angeles, CA 90038
PHONE 323-956-3705
FAX 323-862-0079
TYPES Features - Made-for-TV/Cable Movies - TV Series
DEALS Paramount Television
DEVELOPMENT Bugmen (Fox) - City of Angels (Lifetime) - Bel Air (Lifetime) - Purple Mountains (Showtime)
CREDITS Dave's World - Can't Hurry Love - Late Bloomer - Brother's Keeper - Movie Stars - Manhattan Man - Against the Wall - The Revenge - Some of My Best Friends - Hollywood Babylon

Jonathan Axelrod . . . . . Executive Producer
Kelly Edwards . . . . . Executive Producer
Brad Vitucci . . . . . Assistant

AXELSON-WEINTRAUB PRODUCTIONS
4421 Riverside Dr., Ste. 208
Burbank, CA 91505
PHONE 818-954-8661
FAX 818-954-0468
EMAIL . . . . . aw-prods@earthlink.net
TYPES Documentaries - Features - Reality TV - Syndication - TV Series
DEVELOPMENT Project X - Movie Quest - Citizen Racer - The Mob - Martini Shot - The Book - Spin Cycle
CREDITS Diva Detectives - An Affectionate Look at Fatherhood - Really Naked Truth - The New Adventures of Robin Hood - Strip Poker

John Axelson . . . . . Executive Producer/Director
Barbara Weintraub . . . . . Executive Producer
Rosa Tran . . . . . Creative Executive
Andrew Wu . . . . . VP, Production

BABYHEAD PRODUCTIONS, INC.
434 Norwich Dr.
West Hollywood, CA 90048
PHONE 310-659-1704
FAX 310-659-8382
EMAIL . . . . . babyheadprods@aol.com
TYPES Features - Made-for-TV/Cable Movies - TV Series
DEVELOPMENT Lulu
CREDITS Bobbie's Girl - Silent Lies

Samuel Bernstein-Shore . . . . . Partner
Ronald Bernstein-Shore . . . . . Partner

BACK LOT PICTURES
c/o Universal Pictures
100 Universal City Plaza, Bldg. 2352A-3
Universal City, CA 91608
PHONE 818-777-7522
FAX 818-866-4595
TYPES Features
DEALS Focus Features/Rogue Pictures
DEVELOPMENT Truth, Justice & the American Way - The Changeling - Senor Dracula
PRE-PRODUCTION The Mules - Kill Yourself Bridge
POST PRODUCTION The Ice Harvest
COMPLETED UNRELEASED Vanity Fair
CREDITS Eternal Sunshine of the Spotless Mind
SUBMISSION POLICY Send query letter via US mail; Release required prior to submissions; No unsolicited material

Glenn Williamson . . . . . President
Margo Klewans . . . . . Development Executive
Brian Schornak . . . . . Assistant

BACON & EGGS
15 Brooks Ave.
Venice, CA 90291
PHONE 310-450-0550
FAX 310-392-9992
EMAIL . . . . . pianolaw@aol.com
TYPES Animation - Documentaries - Features - New Media - Reality TV - TV Series
PRE-PRODUCTION When the Dead Whisper
PRODUCTION Lovewrecked
CREDITS On the Line - Free for All
SUBMISSION POLICY No unsolicited material; One-sheet synopsis accepted

Joe Anderson . . . . . Partner
Lance Bass . . . . . Partner
Wendy Thorlakson . . . . . Partner

*BAD BOY FILMS
1440 Broadway, 16th Fl.
New York, NY 10018
PHONE 212-381-1540
FAX 212-381-1599
EMAIL . . . . . firstinitiallastname@badboyworldwide.com
WEB SITE . . . . . www.badboyonline.com
TYPES Reality TV - TV Series
CREDITS Making the Band 2 (MTV) - Diddy Runs the City (MTV Docu-Drama)

Sean Combs . . . . . CEO
Anthony Maddox . . . . . General Manager

*BAD ROBOT PRODUCTIONS
500 S. Buena Vista, Production Bldg., Rm. 361
Burbank, CA 91521
PHONE 818-560-7064
FAX 818-560-6325
TYPES TV Series
DEALS Touchstone Television
PRODUCTION Lost
CREDITS Alias - Felicity

J.J. Abrams . . . . . No Title
Thom Sherman . . . . . President
Bryan Burk . . . . . Executive VP

THE BADHAM COMPANY

3344 Clerendon Rd.
Beverly Hills, CA 90210
PHONE 818-990-9495
FAX 818-981-9163
EMAIL .....vruane@badhamcompany.com
WEB SITE .....www.badhamcompany.com

TYPES	Features - Made-for-TV/Cable Movies - TV Series
DEVELOPMENT	Ocean Warrior - Terror.net - Second Chance
POST PRODUCTION	Evel Knievel (TNT, MOW)
CREDITS	Nick of Time - Stakeout 1&2 - War Games - The Jack Bull
COMMENTS	Feature representation: Robert Lazar, ICM; Cable TV representation: Jill Gillett, ICM; Manager: Todd Harris (310) 276-7884

John Badham .....Director/Producer
Vanessa Ruane .....Associate Producer

BAER ANIMATION COMPANY, INC.

7743 Woodrow Wilson Dr.
Los Angeles, CA 90046-1211
PHONE 323-874-9122
FAX 323-874-7690
EMAIL .....baer@baeranimation.com
WEB SITE .....www.baeranimation.com

TYPES	Animation - Commercials - Features - Direct-to-Video/DVD - New Media - TV Series
CREDITS	Roger Rabbit - The Prince & The Pauper - Annabelle's Wish
COMMENTS	Character design; Storyboards; Cel animation; Animation with live action

Jane Baer .....President/Executive Producer
Michael Takamoto .....Creative Director
Beth Goodwin .....Production Manager

BAER ENTERTAINMENT GROUP

Steinhardt Baer Pictures Company
650 Madison Ave., 17th Fl.
New York, NY 10022
PHONE 212-371-7300

TYPES	Animation - Features - TV Series
DEALS	Universal Pictures
DEVELOPMENT	Muslim-American animated series (Nickelodeon)
CREDITS	The Long Run
COMMENTS	Division of Steinhardt Baer Pictures Company

Thomas Baer .....Producer
Michael Steinhardt .....Partner

SUSAN BAERWALD PRODUCTIONS

132 S. Anita Ave.
Los Angeles, CA 90049
PHONE 310-476-6221

TYPES	Made-for-TV/Cable Movies - TV Series
CREDITS	Inflammable - A Time to Heal - One Special Victory - Blind Faith - Lucky/Chances - Cruel Doubt

Susan Baerwald .....Executive Producer

BAIO/WHITE PRODUCTIONS

c/o Project Development
8117 Manchester Ave., Ste. 331
Playa del Rey, CA 90293
PHONE 310-712-1770, x36
FAX 310-821-6532
EMAIL .....baiowhite@yahoo.com

TYPES	Features - Direct-to-Video/DVD - Made-for-TV/Cable Movies - Syndication
DEVELOPMENT	Premonition - Switch Hitter
PRE-PRODUCTION	Sugar Wars
CREDITS	Very Mean Men - Face to Face - Race to Space - The Hunted
SUBMISSION POLICY	Only accepts scripts from previously produced writers or projects with partial financing and/or recognizable talent attached; Use fax or mail to submit log lines, brief story synopses and explanation of elements attached to project
COMMENTS	Distribution deal with Private Planet Releasing

Neil P. White .....Producer
Steven Baio .....Producer

BAKULA PRODUCTIONS, INC.

c/o Paramount Pictures
5555 Melrose Ave.
Los Angeles, CA 90038
PHONE 323-956-3030

TYPES	Features - Made-for-TV/Cable Movies - Theater - TV Series
DEALS	Paramount Television
CREDITS	What Girls Learn - Papa's Angels - Mr. & Mrs. Smith - The Bachelor's Baby - Prowler; Theater: I Do! I Do! - The Importance of Being Wilde - The Cover of Life

Scott Bakula .....CEO/Producer
Tom Spiroff .....President/Producer
Ron Cortes .....VP, Development
Rita Hollodick .....Executive Assistant/Office Manager

JOHN BALDECCHI PRODUCTIONS

10202 W. Washington Blvd.
David Lean Bldg., Ste. 333
Culver City, CA 90232
PHONE 310-244-8232
FAX 310-244-0005

TYPES	Features - Made-for-TV/Cable Movies
DEALS	Sony Pictures Entertainment
DEVELOPMENT	Hot Wheels - RPM - The Scared Guys - Argonauts - Return to Castle Wolfenstein
CREDITS	Stark Raving Mad - The Mexican - Simon Birch - Deep Rising - Adventures of Huck Finn - Oliver Twist (TV)

John Baldecchi .....Producer
Holly Rawlinson .....Producer
David Zerr .....VP, Development
Kevin Rosenberg .....Executive Assistant
Peter Sununu .....Executive Intern

*BALDWIN ENTERTAINMENT GROUP
3000 W. Olympic Blvd., Bldg. 1, Ste. 2510
Santa Monica, CA 90404
PHONE 310-453-9277
FAX 310-453-9254
TYPES Features
DEVELOPMENT Legacy of Luna - Mandrake the Magician - Second Son
CREDITS Mystery, Alaska - Sudden Death - From the Hip - Billy Galvin - The Cellar - The Patriot - Resurrection - Spellbinder - Gideon

Howard Baldwin ....Producer
Karen Baldwin ....Producer
Nick Morton ....Executive VP, Producer
Nick Ruta ....Executive VP, Business Affairs
Todd Slater ....Executive VP

BALLISTIC MEDIA GROUP
1237-1/4 Havenhurst Dr.
Los Angeles, CA 90046
PHONE 323-650-3822
EMAIL ....info@ballistic-media.com
WEB SITE ....www.ballistic-media.com
TYPES Features - Direct-to-Video/DVD - New Media
PRE-PRODUCTION Avatar
POST PRODUCTION Dandelion - The Hand Job

Molly Mayeux ....Producer

BALLPARK PRODUCTIONS
PO Box 508
Venice, CA 90294
PHONE 310-827-1328
FAX 310-577-9626
TYPES Features - TV Series
CREDITS The Four Feathers - Crimson Tide - Colors - Lean on Me - The Peacemaker - Very Bad Things - Le Divorce

Michael Schiffer ....Producer/Writer
Sally Allen ....VP, Development

BOB BANNER ASSOCIATES
5939 Hillcrest Ave.
Dallas, CA 75205
PHONE 214-526-5440
FAX 214-526-0660
WEB SITE ....www.bobbanner.com
TYPES TV Series
CREDITS Showtime at the Apollo - Happy Birthday George Gershwin - Real Kids, Real Adventures
SUBMISSION POLICY No unsolicited material

Bob Banner ....President
Chuck Banner ....VP
Andrew Barnett ....Director, Development (469-438-4484)

BANNON-OLESHANSKY PRODUCTIONS & MANAGEMENT, LLC
1313 Ninth St., Ste. 11
Santa Monica, CA 90401
PHONE 310-395-9494
FAX 310-395-6907
EMAIL ....bannonoleshansky@aol.com
TYPES Documentaries - Features - TV Series
CREDITS Amityville Horror: The True Story 1&2

Bill Bannon Jr. ....Producer/Manager
Tony Oleshansky ....Producer/Manager

BANYAN PRODUCTIONS
530 Walnut St., Ste. 276
Philadelphia, PA 19106
PHONE 215-928-1414
FAX 215-928-9944
EMAIL ....corporate@banyanprod.com
WEB SITE ....www.banyanprod.com
TYPES Syndication - TV Series - Reality TV
PRE-PRODUCTION Nice Package
CREDITS Trading Spaces - A Wedding Story - A Makeover Story - Perfect Proposal - Birthday - Ambush Makeover

Ray Murray ....President
Ben Ringe ....Head, Development

BARCELONA FILMS
707 Cardinal Lane
Austin, TX 78704
PHONE 512-443-5643/512-443-1903
FAX 512-443-5143
EMAIL ....info@barcelonafilms.com
SECOND EMAIL ....query@barcelonafilms.com
WEB SITE ....www.barcelonafilms.com
SECOND WEB SITE ....www.mjneal.com
TYPES Commercials - Documentaries - Features - Direct-to-Video/DVD - Made-for-TV/Cable Movies - Music Videos - TV Series
DEVELOPMENT Angel's Alibi - Neurotica - Not Without Our Women - Polite Society - Two Queens Cooking (TV)
PRE-PRODUCTION Kempo Karate - Ed Parker (Documentary)
PRODUCTION Hands of the Chisholm Trail - My Mother's Fire
COMPLETED UNRELEASED UTA Project - Dear Pillow
CREDITS Brayton Field - Hansel Mieth: Vagabond Photographer - McDonalds - Nicoleta
SUBMISSION POLICY Email query

Viviane Vives ....Principal
T.E. Kolenda ....Principal
M.J. Neal ....Principal
Patrick Million ....Writer
Armando Araiza ....Executive Assistant
D.J. Perkinson ....Executive Assistant

BARNET BAIN FILMS
4250 Wilshire Blvd.
Los Angeles, CA 90010
PHONE 323-656-8829
TYPES Features - Made-for-TV/Cable Movies - New Media
DEVELOPMENT Ilium - Illusions
POST PRODUCTION Celestine Prophecy
CREDITS What Dreams May Come - Quantum Project - The Linda McCartney Story - Homeless to Harvard - Jesus - Conspiracy of Fear
COMMENTS Deal with Sightsound Technologies

Barnet Bain ....Producer

ALAN BARNETTE PRODUCTIONS

c/o Universal Studios
100 Universal City Plaza, Bldg. 2352, Ste. 101
Universal City, CA 91608
PHONE 818-733-0993/818-733-1074
FAX 818-733-3172
EMAIL .... dabarnette@aol.com
TYPES: Features - Made-for-TV/Cable Movies - TV Series
CREDITS: Resurrection - Sliders - Equalizer - Off Limits - Broken Cord - LA-7 - Seeing Double

Alan Barnette .... Executive Producer
Aaron Sandler .... Director
Marie Colabelli .... Development

BARNHOLTZ ENTERTAINMENT

34133 Mulholland Hwy.
Malibu, CA 90265
PHONE 818-879-6500
FAX 818-879-5074
EMAIL .... bbarnholtz@aol.com
SECOND EMAIL .... barnholtzacquisitions@hotmail.com
TYPES: Features - Direct-to-Video/DVD
CREDITS: Drive By - Cash Crop - Party Animalz - The First 9 1/2 Weeks - RxMas - The Playaz Court - The Mangler 2 - Cutthroat Alley - The Scheme - Dracula's Curse
COMMENTS: Distribution

Barry Barnholtz .... President/CEO
Alex Kirby .... VP/CFO
Matthew Fladell .... Sr. VP, Business Affairs
Matt Cunningham .... Director, Development
Melvin Butters .... Acquisitions
Will Santa Cruz .... Supervisor, Post Production

BARNSTORM FILMS

73 Market St.
Venice, CA 90291
PHONE 310-396-5937
FAX 310-450-4988
EMAIL .... tbtb@comcast.net
TYPES: Features - Made-for-TV/Cable Movies - TV Series
CREDITS: Taxi Driver - Untamed Heart - My Bodyguard - Five Corners - The Sting - Harlan County War

Tony Bill .... Producer/Director
Helen Bartlett .... Producer

BARON PICTURES

9 Desbrosses St., 2nd Fl.
New York, NY 10013
PHONE 212-609-0939
FAX 212-609-0938
EMAIL .... caroline@baronpictures.net
TYPES: Features
CREDITS: Monsoon Wedding

Caroline Baron .... Producer

BARRACUDA PRODUCTIONS

5512 Lemona Ave.
Sherman Oaks, CA 91411
PHONE 818-749-3729
EMAIL .... tvmovies@aol.com
TYPES: Made-for-TV/Cable Movies - TV Series
DEVELOPMENT: U Send Me (Lifetime) - Same as It Never Was (ABC Family) - I'll Be You (Oxygen)
COMPLETED UNRELEASED: Danger Beneath the Sea - A Mother Waits (Lifetime)
CREDITS: The Chris Isaak Show - A Tale of Two Wives - Off Season - Rough Air - Shake Rattle & Roll - Seconds to Spare
SUBMISSION POLICY: No unsolicited mail, calls or faxes; Email only

Marc B. Lorber .... Producer

BARWOOD FILMS

321 W. 78th St., Ste. 1-A
New York, NY 10024
PHONE 212-787-4151
FAX 212-787-7418
EMAIL .... lilycor@aol.com
TYPES: Documentaries - Features - Made-for-TV/Cable Movies - TV Series
DEVELOPMENT: Julie and Romeo - Mendel's Dwarf - The Decision
CREDITS: Serving in Silence - Prince of Tides - The Mirror Has Two Faces - Yentl - Reel Models: The 1st Women in Film - Varian's War - What Makes a Family - The Living Century

Barbra Streisand .... Owner/Actress/Producer/Director
Cis Corman .... President
Gina Biscotti .... Development Assistant

BASRA ENTERTAINMENT

68444 Perez Rd., Ste. O
Cathedral City, CA 92234
PHONE 760-324-9855
FAX 760-324-9035
EMAIL .... tony@basraentertainment.com
WEB SITE .... www.basraentertainment.com
TYPES: Documentaries - Features - Direct-to-Video/DVD
DEVELOPMENT: Spirit of Paradise - Isis - Iraqi Documentary - Soccer Feature Project
CREDITS: Vlad

Tony Shawkat .... President/Producer
Daniela Ryan .... Associate Producer

BATES ENTERTAINMENT

895-1/2 S. Lucerne Blvd.
Los Angeles, CA 90005
PHONE 323-936-6117
TYPES: Documentaries - Features - Made-for-TV/Cable Movies - TV Series
DEVELOPMENT: Whacked! - Slasher Basher - Hot Property - The Butler Did It - Second Hand - No Man - Catching Hell
PRE-PRODUCTION: Holy War - The Facts About Kate - Sick Day - Kid Bang - The Enthusiast - Where Brooklyn Sleeps
CREDITS: Last Time I Committed Suicide - Kingdom Come - Fall Time
SUBMISSION POLICY: Submit Query letter in writing; No unsolicited scripts

Edward J. Bates .... Producer
Rochelle Bates .... Producer

BATJAC PRODUCTIONS, INC.
9595 Wilshire Blvd., Ste. 610
Beverly Hills, CA 90212-2506
PHONE ... 310-278-9870
FAX ... 323-272-7381
TYPES Features

Mrs. Michael A. Wayne ... President

BATTLE PLAN
4151 Prospect Ave.
Los Angeles, CA 90027
PHONE ... 323-671-5060
TYPES Features - TV Series
DEVELOPMENT The Cell Game - Resurrecting the Champ (Feature) - Soul of the Age - Flyboys
POST PRODUCTION The Jacket
CREDITS 4 Second Delay - Deterrence - The Contender - Line of Fire

Marc Frydman ... President/Producer
Rod Lurie ... President/Producer/Writer/Director
James Spies ... Producer
Brandon Hill ... Assistant to Rod Lurie
Kurt Spenser ... Assistant to Marc Frydman
Brandon Pleus ... Development Intern

THE BAUER COMPANY
9720 Wilshire Blvd., Mezzanine
Beverly Hills, CA 90212
PHONE ... 310-247-3880
FAX ... 310-247-3881
TYPES Features - Made-for-TV/Cable Movies - TV Series
DEVELOPMENT Underground - In Search of the Assassin - Patrick

Martin R. Bauer ... Producer
Robert Marsala ... Producer
Ben Tappan ... Producer
Kimberly Weithorn ... Executive Assistant

CAROL BAUM PRODUCTIONS
8899 Beverly Blvd., Ste. 721
Los Angeles, CA 90048
PHONE ... 310-550-4575
FAX ... 310-550-2088
TYPES Features - Made-for-TV/Cable Movies - Theater - TV Series
DEVELOPMENT Grace (Fox 2000) - Naomi Fomer - Slammer (Revolution) - The Cell Game (Showtime) - Tynan (Royal Shakespeare Company)
PRE-PRODUCTION Five Dollars a Day (Fine Line)
POST PRODUCTION Sexual Life (Showtime)
COMPLETED UNRELEASED Carolina (Miramax)
CREDITS Fly Away Home - Father of the Bride - Dead Ringers - Kicking & Screaming - My First Mister - IQ - The Good Girl
SUBMISSION POLICY No unsolicited submissions

Carol Baum ... Producer
Amelia Chen Miley ... Assistant

SUZANNE BAUMAN PRODUCTIONS
21901 Velicata St.
Woodland Hills, CA 91364
PHONE ... 818-348-4342
EMAIL ... filmforthought@aol.com
WEB SITE ... www.filmforthought.com
TYPES Documentaries - Features - TV Series
DEVELOPMENT In the Time of Roses - Edge of the Bonfire
PRODUCTION The Written World
POST PRODUCTION Dying in Afghanistan
CREDITS Jackie: Behind the Myth - Animal Adventures - La Belle Epoque - River of Dreams - Circling the Drain

Suzanne Bauman ... Producer/Director
Toni Pace Carstenson ... Producer
Ryan Burroughs ... Associate Producer
John Marzilli ... Director, Development

BAY FILMS
631 Colorado Ave.
Santa Monica, CA 90401
PHONE ... 310-319-6565
FAX ... 310-319-6570
TYPES Commercials - Features
CREDITS Pearl Harbor - Armageddon - The Rock - Bad Boys 1&2

Michael Bay ... Director/Producer
Matthew Cohan ... VP, Development
Joli Eberhart ... Executive Assistant to Michael Bay
Edward Albolote ... Production Assistant

BAYONNE ENTERTAINMENT
c/o MGM
10250 Constellation Blvd.
Los Angeles, CA 90067
PHONE ... 310-449-3816
FAX ... 310-586-8759
TYPES Animation - Features - Made-for-TV/Cable Movies - Reality TV - Syndication - TV Series
DEVELOPMENT V (NBC)
COMPLETED UNRELEASED Simply Irresistible (VH1)
CREDITS Crossroads (Feature) - Dancing at the Harvest Moon (MOW) - Dean Koontz's Black River (MOW) - Blow Out (Bravo) - Brave New Girl (ABC Family)

Rob Lee ... Producer
Joe Kravitz ... Executive Assistant

BAZMARK, INQ.
10201 W. Pico Blvd.
Los Angeles, CA 90035
PHONE ... 310-369-5448
FAX ... 310-969-1679
TYPES Features
DEALS Twentieth Century Fox
CREDITS Moulin Rouge - Romeo + Juliet - Strictly Ballroom - La Bohème
SUBMISSION POLICY No unsolicited material or phone calls

Baz Luhrmann ... President
Catherine Martin ... VP
Adam Silberman ... Managing Director

***BBC WORLDWIDE AMERICA**
3500 W. Olive Ave, Ste. 110
Burbank, CA 91505
PHONE .818-840-9770
FAX .818-840-9780
WEB SITE .www.bbc.co.uk
TYPES Features - Made-for-TV/Cable Movies - Miniseries - TV Series
CREDITS The Office - State of Play - The Grid

Mark Thompson .Director General
Jana Bennett .Director, Television
George McGhee .Controller, Program Acquisitions
Paul Telegdy .VP, Programming & Co-Productions
Jeremy Whitham .Programming Associate

BEACON, A DIVISION OF HOLDING PICTURES
120 Broadway, Ste. 200
Santa Monica, CA 90401
PHONE .310-260-7000
FAX .310-260-7050
WEB SITE .www.beaconpictures.com
TYPES Features
DEALS Walt Disney Pictures/Touchstone Pictures
CREDITS For Love of the Game - Commitments - Air Force One - A Thousand Acres - End of Days - The Hurricane - Bring It On - Family Man - Thirteen Days - Spy Game - Emperor's Club - Tuck Everlasting - Open Range - Raising Helen - Ladder 49

Armyan Bernstein .Chairman
Charlie Lyons .CEO
Michael Helfant .COO
Zanne Devine .President, Production
Suzann Ellis .Head, Development & Production
Cindy McWethy .Executive VP/CFO
Nancy Rae Stone .Executive VP, Production
Gregory R. Schenz .Sr. VP, Business & Legal
Jodi Zuckerman .Director, Development
Justin Lester .Creative Executive

JUNE BEALLOR PRODUCTIONS
c/o DreamWorks SKG
100 Universal City Plaza, Bungalow 477
Universal City, CA 91608
PHONE .818-777-9000
FAX .818-866-2222
TYPES Documentaries - Features - Made-for-TV/Cable Movies - Reality TV - TV Series
CREDITS Survivors of the Holocaust - The Lost Children of Berlin - The Last Days
SUBMISSION POLICY No unsolicited material

June Beallor .Producer
Susan M. Baker .VP

BEARSMOUTH ENTERTAINMENT
901 Hermosa Ave.
Hermosa Beach, CA 90254
PHONE .310-937-0243
FAX .310-406-8803
EMAIL .bearsmouth@worldnet.att.net
TYPES Features - Direct-to-Video/DVD
DEVELOPMENT Vicious - Morning Glory
CREDITS My Dark Days - A Porcelain Dream - The Journey - A Light in the Darkness

Matt Terzian .President

BEBE DELIGHT PRODUCTIONS
2600 Franklin Rd.
Nashville, TN 37204
PHONE .615-568-3460
EMAIL .mgalin2451@aol.com
TYPES Documentaries - Features - TV Series
PRE-PRODUCTION The Glory Forever
POST PRODUCTION Tahoe - The Real Sting
CREDITS Dune - Vernon Johns - Stephen King's The Stand - The Langoliers - Life on the Water - Radio Unity

Mitchell Galin .Producer
Kim Palmer .Head, Production

PAMELA BECK
345 N. Maple Dr., Ste. 280
Beverly Hills, CA 90210
PHONE .310-859-8853
EMAIL .pamelaassist@hotmail.com
TYPES Animation - Made-for-TV/Cable Movies - Features - TV Series
DEVELOPMENT Picasso Miniseries - Other Man
CREDITS Rich Men, Single Women

Pamela Beck .President
Suzanne Keilly .Assistant to Ms. Beck

THE BEDFORD FALLS COMPANY
409 Santa Monica Blvd., Penthouse
Santa Monica, CA 90401
PHONE .310-394-5022
FAX .310-394-5825
TYPES Features - TV Series
DEALS ABC Entertainment Television Group - Warner Bros. Pictures
CREDITS The Last Samurai - Traffic - Once and Again - Dangerous Beauty - Shakespeare In Love - I Am Sam - Legends of the Fall - thirtysomething
SUBMISSION POLICY Query letters only

Edward Zwick .Executive Producer/Writer/Director (310-394-2697)
Marshall Herskovitz .Executive Producer/Writer/Director (310-394-5355)
Richard Solomon .President (310-394-5643)
Robin Budd .VP, Production (310-394-7461)
Troy Putney .Creative Executive to Mr. Zwick
Joshua Gummersall .Creative Executive to Mr. Herskovitz
David Passman .Creative Executive to Mr. Solomon
Ryan F. Coleman .Creative Executive to Ms. Budd
Arlyn Richardson .Apprentice

BEDLAM MEDIA
9229 Sunset Blvd., Ste 810
Los Angeles, CA 90069
PHONE .310-550-8100
FAX .310-550-8101
EMAIL .laurenl@belammedia.net
TYPES Features - Made-for-TV/Cable Movies - TV Series
PRE-PRODUCTION Diary - Aftershock
POST PRODUCTION Cellular
SUBMISSION POLICY No unsolicited submissions

Lauren Lloyd .Producer
Todd Sharp .Partner/Manager
Afsoun Yazdian .VP, Production
Aaron Lam .Story Editor

BELISARIUS PRODUCTIONS
c/o Sunset Gower Studios
1438 N. Gower St., Box 25, Bldg. 35, 4th Fl.
Los Angeles, CA 90028
PHONE .323-468-4500
FAX .323-468-4599
TYPES TV Series
CREDITS Navy N.C.I.S. - Quantum Leap - Magnum, P.I. - JAG - Last Rites - First Monday
COMMENTS A division of Viacom

Donald P. Bellisario .Executive Producer/Director/Writer
Chas. Floyd Johnson .Co-Executive Producer
Stephen Zito .Co-Executive Producer/Writer
Dana Coen .Co-Executive Producer/Writer
Gil Grant .Co-Executive Producer/Writer
Mark Horowitz .Co-Executive Producer
Julie Watson .Coordinating Producer
Philip DeGuere .Consulting Producer
David Bellisario .Producer
Avery Drewe .Producer
Tommy Moran .Producer/Writer
Frank Cardea .Consulting Producer
George Schenk .Consulting Producer
Don McGill .Supervising Producer
Darcy Meyers .Executive Story Editor
Barbara Hecht .Script Coordinator
Patty Sachs .Executive Assistant to Mr. Bellisario
Stephen Peters .Second Assistant to Mr. Bellisario
Debra Mayfield .Executive Assistant to Mr. Johnson

DAVE BELL ASSOCIATES
3211 Cahuenga Blvd. West
Los Angeles, CA 90068
PHONE .323-851-7801
FAX .323-851-9349
EMAIL .dbamovies@aol.com
TYPES Documentaries - Features - Made-for-TV/Cable Movies - Syndication - TV Series
DEVELOPMENT The Proud & Few - Tinker - Tunnel Rats - Bikini Zombie Warrior - Tell Dolly Parton I Love Her
PRE-PRODUCTION Jury (HBO)
CREDITS Deep Red - Long Walk Home - Do You Remember Love? - Nadia - Just a Dream

David L. Bell .President
Ted Weiant .Director, Motion Pictures
Fred Putman .Director, TV

BELL-PHILLIP TV PRODUCTIONS, INC.
7800 Beverly Blvd., Ste. 3371
Los Angeles, CA 90036-2188
PHONE .323-575-4138
FAX .323-655-8760
TYPES TV Series
CREDITS The Bold and the Beautiful

William J. Bell .Creator
Lee Phillip Bell .Co-Creator
Bradley Bell .Executive Producer/Head Writer
Ron Weaver .Sr. Producer
Rhonda Friedman .Supervising Producer
Cynthia J. Popp .Producer
Erin E. Stewart .Associate Producer

BELLPORT PICTURES
1145 Wellington Ave.
Pasadena, CA 91103
PHONE .626-568-8863
FAX .626-229-9827
TYPES Features
DEVELOPMENT The Gardener's Daughter - If Six Was Nine - The Year of Frank Sinatra - Office Party
CREDITS The Cat's Meow

Carol Lewis .Producer

BENDERSPINK
MANAGEMENT & PRODUCTION

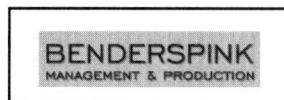

BENDERSPINK
6735 Yucca St.
Hollywood, CA 90028
PHONE .323-856-5500
FAX .323-856-5502
EMAIL .info@benderspink.com
WEB SITE .www.benderspink.com
TYPES Features - TV Series
DEALS New Line Cinema
DEVELOPMENT A History of Violence - A Fistful of Candy - Urban Townie - Just Friends - Red Eye - The Other Side of Simple
POST PRODUCTION Monster-In-Law - The Ring 2
CREDITS American Wedding - American Pie 1&2 - Cats & Dogs - Final Destination - Cheats - The Ring - The Butterfly Effect

Chris Bender .Executive
J.C. Spink .Executive
Charlie Gogolak .Executive
Brian Spink .Executive
Jill McElroy .Executive
Jake Weiner .Executive
Courtney Kivowitz .Executive
Christian Donatelli .Executive
Caryn Jacob .Executive
Melissa Hook .No Title
Marc Bretter .No Title
Neal Flaherty .No Title
Danielle Gitkin .No Title
David Phillips .No Title
Vanessa Scott .No Title

BENJAMIN PRODUCTIONS

3000 W. Olympic Blvd., Bldg. 4, Rm. 2225
Santa Monica, CA 90404
PHONE .310-264-4133
FAX .310-264-4132
EMAIL .mesahagun@yahoo.com
TYPES Features - Made-for-TV/Cable Movies - TV Series
POST PRODUCTION Unchain My Heart: Ray Charles
CREDITS La Bamba - White Nights - Everybody's All-American - The Long Walk Home - Mortal Thoughts - Against All Odds - Defenseless - Queens Logic - Street Talker - Rooftops - Testament - Billy Galvin - Shaq, the Kid in Me

Stuart Benjamin .Producer
Alise Benjamin-Mauritzson .Producer
Elena Sahagun .VP, Development
Jamie Katz .Intern

HARVE BENNETT PRODUCTIONS

PO Box 825
Culver City, CA 90232-0825
PHONE .310-306-7198
FAX .310-306-7598
TYPES Animation - Features - Made-for-TV/Cable Movies - Syndication - TV Series
CREDITS Star Trek II: The Wrath of Khan - Star Trek III: The Search for Spock - Star Trek IV: The Voyage Home - Star Trek V: The Final Frontier - Rich Man, Poor Man - A Woman Called Golda - The Mod Squad - The Six Million Dollar Man - The Bionic Woman
SUBMISSION POLICY No unsolicited material

Harve Bennett .Executive Producer/Writer
Marianne Tyler .VP, Development

BENNETT PRODUCTIONS, INC.

2032 Armacost Ave., 1st Fl.
Los Angeles, CA 90025
PHONE .310-442-6630
FAX .310-442-8235
EMAIL .scohan@bennettproductions.com
WEB SITE .www.bennettproductions.com
TYPES Music Videos - TV Series
CREDITS The Extremists - Sting Inside - Bikini Destinations
COMMENTS Post Production

Robert M. Bennett .Chairman
Casey Bennett .President
Paul Rich .Executive VP

BERGMAN LUSTIG PRODUCTIONS

3907 W. Alameda Ave., Ste. 102
Burbank, CA 91505
PHONE .818-557-7490/818-481-4302
FAX .818-557-7494
EMAIL .bergmanlustig@earthlink.net
TYPES Commercials - Documentaries - Features - Direct-to-Video/DVD - Made-for-TV/Cable Movies - Promos - TV Series
DEVELOPMENT Unknown - In the Quiet of the Evening
PRODUCTION Nomad
POST PRODUCTION The Visitors - Brick - Circle
CREDITS Dancing at the Blue Iguana - Kill Me Later - Black & White - Wedding Bell Blues - Tough Luck - Stranger Than Fiction - Long Time Since - Zoe - For Hire - Rave Review - Power 98 - Sasquatch - Heartbreak Hospital - Partners in Crime
COMMENTS IFC Image Campaign 2002/2003

Ram Bergman .Producer
Dana Lustig .Producer
Raymond Izaac .Development

BERLANTI/LIDDELL PRODUCTIONS

300 Television Plaza, Bldg. 140, Rm. 210
Burbank, CA 91505-1402
PHONE .818-954-4882
FAX .818-954-4885
TYPES Features - TV Series
DEALS Warner Bros. Television Production
PRODUCTION Jack & Bobby
CREDITS The Broken Hearts Club - Everwood

Greg Berlanti .Writer/Producer
Mickey Liddell .Producer
Robin Gurney .Sr. VP, Development

RICK BERMAN PRODUCTIONS

5555 Melrose Ave., Cooper Bldg., Ste. 232
Los Angeles, CA 90038
PHONE .323-956-5037
FAX .323-862-1076
TYPES Features - Syndication - TV Series
DEALS Paramount Pictures-Motion Picture Group - Paramount Television
CREDITS Star Trek: The Next Generation - Star Trek: Insurrection - Star Trek: Deep Space Nine - Star Trek: First Contact - Star Trek: Voyager - Enterprise - Star Trek: Nemesis

Rick Berman .Executive Producer
Dave Rossi .Supervisor, Star Trek Projects
Joanna Fuller .Assistant to Rick Berman
Ryan Simonson .Production Assistant to Mr. Berman

JAY BERNSTEIN PRODUCTIONS

PO Box 1148
Beverly Hills, CA 90213
PHONE .310-851-2126
FAX .310-858-1607
EMAIL .info@jaybernstein.com
WEB SITE .www.jaybernstein.com
TYPES Animation - Features - Direct-to-Video/DVD - Made-for-TV/Cable Movies - Syndication - TV Series
CREDITS Come Die with Me - Murder Takes All - Mike Hammer - Sunburn - Diamond Trap - Double Jeopardy - Houston Knights
COMMENTS Personal manager

Jay Bernstein .President/Producer/Director/Writer

BET - BLACK ENTERTAINMENT TELEVISION
One BET Plaza, 1235 W St. NE
Washington, DC 20018-1211
PHONE . . . 202-608-2000/818-655-6700
FAX . . . 202-608-2631/818-655-6770
WEB SITE . . . www.bet.com
TYPES Features - Made-for-TV/Cable Movies - Syndication - TV Series
CREDITS 106 & Park - Rap City - ComicView - Spring Bling - Celebration of Gospel - BET Walk of Fame - BET Awards Show - Coming to the Stage
COMMENTS Comedies; West Coast production studio: 4024 Radford Ave., R&D Bldg., 4th Fl., Studio City, CA 91604

Robert Johnson . . . Founder/CEO
Deborah L. Lee . . . President/COO, BET
Scott Mills . . . CFO
Michael Pickrum . . . COO, BET.com
Paxton Baker . . . Executive VP, BET Jazz & Digital Networks
Nina Henderson-Moore . . . Executive VP, News, Public Affairs, Programs Acquisitions
Kelli Lawson . . . Executive VP, Corporate Marketing & Communications
Byron Marchant . . . Executive VP/CAO/General Counsel
Stephen Hill . . . Sr. VP, Music Programming
Gina Holland . . . Sr. VP, Production & Network Operations
John Gordon . . . VP, Finance
Veronica Hutchinson . . . VP, Programming
Michael Lewellen . . . VP, Corporate Communications

BETTINA PRODUCTIONS, LTD.
624 S. June St.
Los Angeles, CA 90005
PHONE . . . 323-937-2101
FAX . . . 323-937-2103
EMAIL . . . wdoniger@aol.com
TYPES Features - Direct-to-Video/DVD - TV Series
DEVELOPMENT True Cross - The Last Tomorrow
CREDITS Rope of Sand - Stone Cold - Kentucky Woman

Walter Doniger . . . President

BIG EVENT PICTURES
11288 Ventura Blvd., Ste. 747
Studio City, CA 91604
PHONE . . . 818-640-8146
EMAIL . . . bigevent1@hotmail.com
TYPES Features - TV Series
DEVELOPMENT Head Cleaner - Crossing Over
CREDITS The Light of Darkness - Lay It Down - The Lesson

Michael Cargile . . . Director/Producer/Writer

BIG MOUTH PRODUCTIONS
104 W. 14th St., 4th Fl.
New York, NY 10011
PHONE . . . 646-230-6228
FAX . . . 646-230-6388
EMAIL . . . info@bigmouthproductions.com
TYPES Documentaries - Features
PRODUCTION Dishes - Arctic Waltz
CREDITS Nuyorican Dream - Outside Looking In - Innocent Until Proven Guilty - Brother Born Again - Journey to the West - Chinese Medicine Today - Deadline

Katy Chevigny . . . Producer/Director/Founder
Dallas Brennan . . . Producer
Elizabeth Mandel . . . Co-Producer
Angela Tucker . . . Outreach Director/Sound Recordist/Associate Producer

BIG PICTURE STUDIOS
16830 Ventura Blvd., Ste. 300
Encino, CA 90046
PHONE . . . 888-262-6201
EMAIL . . . info@bigpicturestudios.com
WEB SITE . . . www.bigpicturestudios.com
TYPES Commercials - Features - TV Series
CREDITS The Last Real Cowboys
COMMENTS Las Vegas office: 4625 S. Polaris, Las Vegas, NV 89103

Jeff Lester . . . CEO/Owner
Dani Parker . . . Assistant to Jeff Lester

BIGEL/MAILER FILMS
443 Greenwich St., Ste. 3-A
New York, NY 10013
PHONE . . . 212-542-3100
FAX . . . 212-542-2540
EMAIL . . . dbigel@bigelmailer.com
WEB SITE . . . www.bigelmailer.com
TYPES Features - Direct-to-Video/DVD - Made-for-TV/Cable Movies - New Media - TV Series
DEVELOPMENT The Genesis Code - The Night Job - The Great Turrell - Neanderthal - The Ultimate Ride - Accepting Aris - Josephine - Killing the Gods - Nothing to Declare - Espiritu - Break Point
PRODUCTION Devour
POST PRODUCTION Loverboy
CREDITS The Money Shot - Black and White - Two Girls and a Guy - Giving It Up - Harvard Man - Empire - The Last Producer - Lost Junction - Loverboy
SUBMISSION POLICY No unsolicited submissions

Daniel Bigel . . . CEO
Michael Mailer . . . President
Amy Rubin . . . Creative Executive

STU BILLETT PRODUCTIONS
6922 Hollywood Blvd., Ste. 300
Hollywood, CA 90028
PHONE . . . 323-462-2212
FAX . . . 323-461-1224
EMAIL . . . info@ralphedwards.com
TYPES Animation - Direct-to-Video/DVD - Syndication - TV Series - Reality TV
CREDITS Truth or Consequences - People's Court - Annabelle's Wish - This Is Your Life - Buzz

Stu Billett . . . Executive Producer

BLACK FOLK ENTERTAINMENT
1680 N. Vine St., Ste. 214
Hollywood, CA 90028
PHONE 323-466-3828
FAX 323-466-3821
EMAIL .....john@blackfolkfilms.com

TYPES	Features - TV Series
DEVELOPMENT	Fine Living
PRE-PRODUCTION	Places You'll Go
CREDITS	Ride Salley Ride - A Fare to Remember
COMMENTS	Co-Host, *The Best Damn Sports Show Period*

John Salley .....CEO
Sandra Rabbin .....Executive Assistant to CEO

BLACK SHEEP ENTERTAINMENT
4063 Radford Ave., Ste. 201-D
Studio City, CA 91604
PHONE 818-769-2227
FAX 818-769-2228
EMAIL .....blacksheepent@aol.com

TYPES	Features - TV Series
DEVELOPMENT	Cat Thief - With a Bullet - Fifty-Two
PRE-PRODUCTION	Hooking Up
CREDITS	The Cottonwood - It Had to Be You - The Big Gig
SUBMISSION POLICY	No unsolicited material

Steven Feder .....Owner/Writer/Producer/Director
Jay Beeber .....Development Executive
Jennie Na .....Assistant to Steven Feder

BLACKLIGHT FILMS
12700 Ventura Blvd., 4th Fl.
Studio City, CA 91604
PHONE 818-655-3264
FAX 818-508-1253
EMAIL .....v.ueber@blacklightfilms.com
WEB SITE .....www.blacklightfilms.com

TYPES	Features - Large Format - New Media - TV Series
CREDITS	Oceans of Air - America (26-Part Documentary Series) - Season on the Vine (Disney Theme Parks) - America's Heart and Soul (Walt Disney Pictures)
COMMENTS	Stock Footage Library

Louis Schwartzberg .....Director/Cinematographer/Executive Producer
Vincent Ueber .....Producer

BLEECKER STREET FILMS
1033 N. Carol Dr.
Los Angeles, CA 90069
PHONE 310-271-6641
FAX 310-247-0389
EMAIL .....bleeckerfilms@aol.com

TYPES	Features - Made-for-TV/Cable Movies
CREDITS	Boss of Bosses - Old Gringo - The Morning After - A Bright Shining Lie - Two for Texas - Lakota Woman - Broken Trust - She's Too Young

Lois Bonfiglio .....President
Simone Study .....Development Associate

BLUE BAY PRODUCTIONS
1119 Colorado Ave., Ste. 100
Santa Monica, CA 90401
PHONE 310-440-9904

TYPES	Features
DEVELOPMENT	Short List - Pregnant Paws - Never Say Die - Date School - Ed's Dead - Soundbite - The Train
CREDITS	Synergy - Big Momma's House - Wild Things - Dunston Checks In
COMMENTS	Independent; Development

Rodney Liber .....Producer
Rebecca Hedrick .....Producer's Assistant

BLUE RAVEN FILMS
4924 Balboa Blvd., Ste. 172
Encino, CA 91316
PHONE 818-785-1886
FAX 818-782-0307
EMAIL .....castingdiva@earthlink.net

TYPES	Features - Made-for-TV/Cable Movies - TV Series
DEALS	Lifetime Television (Los Angeles) - New Line Cinema - Newmarket Capital Group
DEVELOPMENT	Staying Afloat - The Flesh Trade - American Godess at Nanking - Training Planets - Too Good to Be True - Bubblegum Bobby
PRE-PRODUCTION	Bob the Butler - The Nice Guys Club - Max Renegade
PRODUCTION	Laren Sims Story
COMPLETED UNRELEASED	Neo Ned
SUBMISSION POLICY	Email synopsis
COMMENTS	Special consideration to contest winning scripts

Valerie McCaffrey .....Producer/Director
Steve Roeder .....Producer/Partner

BLUE RELIEF, INC.
15260 Ventura Blvd., Ste. 1040
Sherman Oaks, CA 91403
PHONE 310-822-1493
FAX 310-822-1593

TYPES	Features - Made-for-TV/Cable Movies - TV Series
DEVELOPMENT	The F Word - Dispensing with the Truth - Emmet Til - Crazy Love
CREDITS	Hanging Up - Northern Lights - Crossed Over - Pasadena (Fox, Series) - Heaven - Elephant - On Thin Ice
SUBMISSION POLICY	No unsolicited material

Diane Keaton .....No Title
Carolyn Barber .....No Title

BLUE RIDER PICTURES
1600 Rosecrans Ave., Bldg. 6-B, 3rd Fl.
Manhattan Beach, CA 90266
PHONE 310-727-3303
FAX 310-727-3334
WEB SITE .....www.blueriderpictures.com

TYPES	Documentaries - Features - Direct-to-Video/DVD - Reality TV - TV Series
DEALS	Tag Entertainment - Walden Media
DEVELOPMENT	Jaco - The Conspirator - Damien of Molotai
CREDITS	Shergar - Slow Burn - Silverwolf - Call of the Wild - Hide and Seek - Behind the Red Door - Around the World in 80 Days - Witchboard - The Incredible Mrs. Ritchie

Jeff Geoffray .....Producer/Partner
Walter Josten .....Producer/Partner

BLUE SKY STUDIOS
44 S. Broadway, 17th Fl.
White Plains, NY 10601
PHONE 914-259-6500
FAX 914-259-6499
WEB SITE ....www.blueskystudios.com
TYPES Animation - Features
DEALS Twentieth Century Fox Animation
PRE-PRODUCTION Untitled Ice Age Sequel
PRODUCTION Robots
CREDITS Ice Age
SUBMISSION POLICY No unsolicited submissions

Lisa Fragner ....Head, Feature Development
Christina Witoshkin ....Development Associate

BLUE STAR PICTURES
2900 W. Olympic Blvd., Ste. 140
Santa Monica, CA 90404
PHONE ....See Below
FAX 310-255-7020
TYPES Features - TV Series
DEALS Revolution Studios
DEVELOPMENT Mr. Lucky - Scarecrow - Holmes & Watson - Dawn Anna Story
POST PRODUCTION Little Black Book
CREDITS Comic Book Villains - Darkness Falls

William Sherak ....Producer (310-255-7018)
Jason Shuman ....Producer (310-255-7019)
Lauren Kisilevsky ....Director, Development (310-255-7047)

BLUE TULIP PRODUCTIONS
631 Wilshire Blvd., Ste. 4-C
Santa Monica, CA 90401
PHONE 310-458-2166
FAX 310-458-2188
EMAIL ....info@bluetulipprod.com
TYPES Animation - Features - TV Series
CREDITS Speed - Twister - SLC Punk - Minority Report - Equilibrium - Tomb Raider 2

Jan De Bont ....Producer/Director
Shelly Clippard ....VP, Production & Development
Christopher Stanley ....Development Associate

BLUE TURTLE, INC.
148 Green St.
New York, NY 10012
PHONE 212-274-9909
EMAIL ....yvla@aol.com
TYPES Features - TV Series
DEVELOPMENT The Thought Gang - The Red Cross
CREDITS Teknolust - Pontiac Moon - Diggstown
SUBMISSION POLICY No unsolicited material

Youssef Vahabzadeh ....Owner/Producer

BLUEBIRD HOUSE
2003 El Cerrito, Ste. 1
Los Angeles, CA 90068
PHONE 323-876-3555
TYPES Animation - Features - TV Series
DEVELOPMENT Bandits (Remake) - The Peanut People - On the Bright Side
CREDITS Disturbing the Peace - Iron Jawed Angels (HBO)
SUBMISSION POLICY No unsolicited submissions
COMMENTS Call for messenger address

Laura McCorkindale ....Producer/Writer
Marjie Schaffer ....Assistant

BLUELINE PRODUCTIONS
212 26th St., Ste. 295
Santa Monica, CA 90402
PHONE 310-319-2421
TYPES Features - Made-for-TV/Cable Movies - TV Series
CREDITS Virginia's Run - Saving Jessica Lynch - The Personals - Bat 21 - El Diablo - Nightbreaker - The Last Days of Frankie the Fly - Youngblood

Peter Markle ....Director/Producer/Writer
Melinda Culea ....Producer

BLUEPRINT ENTERTAINMENT
8840 Wilshire Blvd., Ste. 101
Beverly Hills, CA 90211
PHONE 310-358-3080/416-531-8585
FAX 310-358-3094/416-588-7276
TYPES Animation - Made-for-TV/Cable Movies - Miniseries - Reality TV - Syndication - TV Series
DEVELOPMENT Future vs. Past (Sci Fi) - Fallen Angels (CTV) - X-Quest (Sci Fi) - Missing Pieces (CTV) - I'll Be You (Oxygen) - Playing House (CTV)
PRODUCTION Impossible Heists (Court TV/Discovery Channels International) - Shoebox Zoo (CBBC/CBC/BBC Kids)
CREDITS Everybody's Doing It (MTV) - Hey, Joel (VH1/Chum) - Chasing Freedom (Court TV/CBC) - Kenny vs. Spenny (GSN/CBC) - Stripsearch (Bravo! Canada) - Wrong Coast (AMC) - Man in the Mirror: The Michael Jackson Story (VH1)
SUBMISSION POLICY No unsolicited submissions
COMMENTS Toronto office: 6 Pardee Ave., Ste. 104, Toronto, ON M6K 3H5 Canada

Noreen Halpern ....Co-President
John Morayniss ....Co-President
Joey Plager ....Executive Producer
Jeff Lynas ....Sr. VP
Christine Shipton ....Sr. VP
Elizabeth Madariaga ....Manager, Development
Kara Lindquist ....Executive Assistant

BLUMFORD ENTERPRISES, INC.
18519 Linnet St.
Tarzana, CA 91356
PHONE 818-342-3722
FAX 818-342-3096
EMAIL ....blumford@pacbell.net
TYPES Animation - Commercials - Documentaries - Features - Direct-to-Video/DVD - Made-for-TV/Cable Movies - Music Videos - New Media - Syndication - TV Series
DEVELOPMENT My Generation - Iron Mistress of Malibu - Tattoo Warrior
PRE-PRODUCTION Brothers in Arms
CREDITS Xtreme Sports TV - CIT - Wango Tango Concert at Dodger Stadium - Sport Truck Nationals - Ultimate Truck Challenge
SUBMISSION POLICY By agents only
COMMENTS Licensing

Stanford Blum ....President/CEO

BLUMHOUSE PRODUCTIONS
450 N. Rossmore Ave., Ste. 506
Los Angeles, CA 90004
PHONE 323-856-9147
TYPES Features - TV Series
DEALS HBO Films
PRE-PRODUCTION The Hottest State
POST PRODUCTION The Fever
CREDITS Hysterical Blindness (HBO) - Ethan Hawke's Hamlet - Easy Six

Jason Blum .....Producer

BOARDWALK ENTERTAINMENT/ALAN WAGNER PRODUCTIONS, INC.
210 E. 39th St.
New York, NY 10016
PHONE 212-679-3800
FAX 212-679-3816
EMAIL .....boardwalk@infohouse.com
TYPES Features - Direct-to-Video/DVD - Made-for-TV/Cable Movies - TV Series
PRE-PRODUCTION Magnificat (Feature)
CREDITS Wounded Heart - Hearts Adrift - Reasons of the Heart - Spenser Movies 1-4
SUBMISSION POLICY No unsolicited material
COMMENTS Consulting

Alan Wagner .....Chairman
Susan Wagner .....President
Elizabeth Wagner .....VP, Creative Affairs
Marti Wagner .....Director, Story Department

BOB & ALICE PRODUCTIONS, INC.
11693 San Vicente Blvd., Ste. 813
Los Angeles, CA 90049
PHONE 310-260-2959
TYPES Features - TV Series
DEVELOPMENT Anniversary - Black Book Mogul
CREDITS Return to Me - Life with Bonnie

Bonnie Hunt .....Director/Writer/Actor/Producer
Don Lake .....Writer/Actor/Producer

DANIEL BOBKER FILMS
369 N. Spaulding Ave., Ste. 1
Los Angeles, CA 90036
PHONE 323-933-5555
FAX 323-933-3908
TYPES Features
DEVELOPMENT In a Dark Wood
PRE-PRODUCTION Blood & Chocolate
PRODUCTION The Skeleton Key
POST PRODUCTION The Brothers Grimm

Daniel Bobker .....Producer

STEVEN BOCHCO PRODUCTIONS
10201 W. Pico Blvd., Bldg. 1
Los Angeles, CA 90035
PHONE 310-369-2400
FAX 310-369-3236
TYPES TV Series
DEALS Paramount Television
PRODUCTION Blind Justice
CREDITS NYPD Blue

Steven Bochco .....Chairman/CEO
Dayna Kalins Bochco .....President
Craig Shenkler .....CFO/VP
Caroline James .....VP, Production
Yemaya Royce .....Director, Media Relations

BODEGA BAY PRODUCTIONS, INC.
PO Box 17338
Beverly Hills, CA 90209-3338
PHONE 310-273-3157
WEB SITE .....www.bodegabay.biz
TYPES Features - TV Series
PRE-PRODUCTION Stone of Destiny
CREDITS Celebrity Island Videos - The Last Best Sunday - Bill & Ted's Excellent Adventure - Purpose

Michael S. Murphey .....Producer
Joel Peterson .....VP, Production
Steven St. Arnaud .....VP, Production (South Africa)
Chip Garofalo .....Producer, Large Format

BOGNER ENTERTAINMENT, INC.
4130 Cahuenga Blvd., Ste. 220
Universal City, CA 91602
PHONE 818-985-7900
FAX 818-985-7901
EMAIL .....jsbogner@aol.com
TYPES Features - Direct-to-Video/DVD - Made-for-TV/Cable Movies - TV Series
DEVELOPMENT American Black Beauty - Tell - Soccer Mom - Crankshaft - Monster Jam
PRODUCTION Supercross, the Movie
CREDITS The Retrievers - Hansel and Gretel - Miracle Dogs - The Santa Trap - Motocross Kids - Red Riding Hood

Jonathan Bogner .....Producer/President

BOKU FILMS
c/o Six Feet Productions, Inc.
1438 N. Gower St., Box 32
Hollywood, CA 90028
PHONE 323-993-7979
FAX 323-993-7071
TYPES Features - TV Series
DEVELOPMENT Babycakes - The Walker - Maps to the Stars
CREDITS Six Feet Under - Woman on Top - Further Tales of the City - More Tales of the City - Thursday - My So-Called Life - Tales of the City
SUBMISSION POLICY No unsolicited material

Alan Poul .....Producer
Jori Adler .....Assistant to Alan Poul

BONA FIDE PRODUCTIONS
8899 Beverly Blvd., Ste. 804
Los Angeles, CA 90048
PHONE 310-273-6782
FAX 310-273-7821
TYPES Documentaries - Features
DEALS Focus Features/Rogue Pictures - Universal Pictures
DEVELOPMENT Joe College - Little Children
PRE-PRODUCTION Little Miss Sunshine - Nebraska
POST PRODUCTION Bee Season - The Ice Harvest
CREDITS Cold Mountain - Election - King of the Hill - Crumb - The Wood - Jack the Bear - I Am Trying to Break Your Heart - Pumpkin

Albert Berger .....Producer
Ron Yerxa .....Producer
Carlo Martinelli .....Development
Cori Uchida .....No Title

BONDESEN-GRAUP, INC.
2211 Corinth Ave., Ste. 103
Los Angeles, CA 90064
PHONE .310-231-0123
FAX .310-231-0128
EMAIL .asst@bondesen-graup.com
TYPES Features
COMPLETED UNRELEASED If Only (Intermedia)
CREDITS Catch That Kid (Fox 2000)

Mikkel Bondesen .Partner
Jeff Graup .Partner
Alex Goldstone .Manager
Jonathan Magid .Director, Development
Josh Peters .Story Editor
Rob Rohrbach .Story Editor

BONEYARD ENTERTAINMENT
863 Park Ave., Ste. 11-E
New York, NY 10021
PHONE .212-628-8600
FAX .212-628-8615
EMAIL .boneyard_djv@yahoo.com
TYPES Documentaries - Features - Made-for-TV/Cable Movies - Reality TV - Theater - TV Series
DEVELOPMENT The Bee (TV) - Committed - Pop Star (TV) - STT (TV) - VC3 (TV) - Stealing Miss December - TMI
CREDITS Illtown - Niagara, Niagara - Slingblade - Henry Fool - The 24 Hour Woman - Frogs for Snakes - The Bumblebee Flies Anyway - Greenfingers - Go Further

Daniel J. Victor .President/CEO
Richard M. Victor .Executive VP

BOB BOOKER PRODUCTIONS
11811 W. Olympic Blvd.
Los Angeles, CA 90064
PHONE .831-626-6505
FAX .831-626-6505
SECOND EMAIL .bbooker@earthlink.net
TYPES Direct-to-Video/DVD - Syndication - TV Series - Reality TV
CREDITS Out of This World - Anything for a Laugh - Foul-Ups, Bleeps & Blunders - America's Funniest Foul-Ups (ABC)

Bob Booker .CEO
Laura Booker .VP

BOXING CAT PRODUCTIONS
11500 Hart St.
North Hollywood, CA 91605
PHONE .818-765-4870
FAX .818-765-4975
TYPES Features
DEALS Walt Disney Pictures/Touchstone Pictures
DEVELOPMENT Father Knows Best - The Santa Clause 3 - In the Pink - Shaggy Dog
CREDITS Joe Somebody - The Santa Clause 1&2 - Jungle 2 Jungle
SUBMISSION POLICY No unsolicited submissions

Tim Allen .Producer/Actor
Matt Carroll .President, Production
Lara Frerking .Director, Development

BOZ PRODUCTIONS
1632 N. Sierra Bonita Ave.
Los Angeles, CA 90046-2816
PHONE .323-876-3232
FAX .323-876-3231
EMAIL .bozenga@sbcglobal.net
TYPES Features - TV Series
DEVELOPMENT Da Miracle - Tiny's Treasure - Potter's Field - Time Jumpers - As Time Goes By - Mischief Night
CREDITS Soul Plane - Scary Movie - A Light in the Darkness - Everything's Jake

Bo Zenga .Writer/Director/Producer
Dan Wolf .Assistant to Mr. Zenga

BRADFORD ENTERPRISES & GEMMY PRODUCTIONS
450 Park Ave., Ste. 1903
New York, NY 10022
PHONE .212-308-7390
FAX .212-935-1636
EMAIL .bradford.ent@att.net
WEB SITE .www.barbarataylorbradford.com
TYPES Made-for-TV/Cable Movies - TV Series
DEVELOPMENT Where You Belong - Emma's Secret
CREDITS Everything to Gain - Love in Another Town - Voice of the Heart - Remember - To Be the Best - Her Own Rules - A Secret Affair - Hold the Dream

Robert Bradford .President/Producer
Barbara Taylor Bradford .Director/Novelist

DAVID BRADY PRODUCTIONS
10650 Front Rd.
Stella, ON K0H 2S0 Canada
PHONE .613-389-7884/613-540-0411
FAX .613-389-4877/805-241-8522
EMAIL .david@davidbradyproductions.com
WEB SITE .www.davidbradyproductions.com
TYPES Documentaries - Features - Made-for-TV/Cable Movies - Syndication - TV Series
DEVELOPMENT Features: The Ron Burton Story - Redemption - Life After Death; TV: Other Worlds - Into the Future - Mavericks & Titans
CREDITS Features: You Wish - The Grey Fox - Till Death Do Us Part - Dixie Lanes; TV: Around the World with Tippi - Counter Force - Singles Court - Life After Death
COMMENTS West Coast address: 1454 Calle Alamo, Thousand Oaks, CA 91360

David Brady .President
Milt Auruskin .VP, Co-Production/Distribution
Deborah Kimmett .VP
Jo Ann Burke .Executive Assistant/Manager (CA)

BRAGA PRODUCTIONS
c/o Paramount Pictures
5555 Melrose Ave., Hart Bldg., Ste. 205
Los Angeles, CA 90038
PHONE 323-956-5799
FAX 323-862-8503

TYPES	Animation - Documentaries - Features - Direct-to-Video/DVD - Interactive Games - Made-for-TV/Cable Movies - New Media - TV Series
DEALS	Paramount Television
DEVELOPMENT	Untitled One-Hour Dramas
CREDITS	Star Trek: Enterprise - Star Trek: Voyager - Star Trek: The Next Generation - Star Trek: Generations - Star Trek: First Contact - Mission: Impossible 2 - Tomb Raider
SUBMISSION POLICY	No unsolicited material

Brannon Braga .....President
Terry Matalas .....VP, Production & Development

BRAINSTORM MEDIA
280 S. Beverly Dr., Ste. 306
Beverly Hills, CA 90212
PHONE 310-285-0812
FAX 310-285-0772

TYPES	Documentaries - Features - Direct-to-Video/DVD - Made-for-TV/Cable Movies - New Media - Syndication - TV Series
DEVELOPMENT	Dog in the Manger - Rough - Looking Glass - Man of War - Lie with Me - Troll
PRE-PRODUCTION	Wasteland
PRODUCTION	Graveland
CREDITS	Kid Cop - Little Men (Feature) - The Truth About Lying - Little Men (Series) - Three Way Split
SUBMISSION POLICY	No submissions without written or verbal approval
COMMENTS	US Distributor & Sales Agent

Meyer Shwarzstein .....President
Trisha Robinson .....Executive VP
Seth Nagel .....Production Executive
Susan Kahn .....Controller
Gina Bono .....Sales Coordinator

BRANCATO PRODUCTIONS
8811 Burton Way, Ste. 219
West Hollywood, CA 90048
PHONE 310-271-1421
FAX 310-271-0941
EMAIL .....brancatony@aol.com
WEB SITE .....www.brancatoproductions.com

TYPES	Documentaries - Features - Made-for-TV/Cable Movies - TV Series
DEVELOPMENT	Subterfuge - Her Father's Daughter - More Crimes of Passion - Code: Fab Five
PRE-PRODUCTION	Good Mother
PRODUCTION	Never Iron Naked - Show Bunnies
POST PRODUCTION	All About Ga-Ga
CREDITS	Somewhere in the City
SUBMISSION POLICY	No unsolicited material

Paula Brancato .....CEO
Rick Albert .....Producer
John Cole .....Associate Producer
Wen Shih .....Associate Producer
George Ferris .....VP, Development
Raphael Lupercio .....Assistant to Rick Albert

BRANDED ENTERTAINMENT
333 Crestmont Rd.
Cedar Grove, NJ 07009
PHONE 973-857-6172
FAX 973-857-6174
EMAIL .....brandedentertain@aol.com
WEB SITE .....www.brandedentertainment.com

TYPES	Animation - Documentaries - Features - Direct-to-Video/DVD - New Media - TV Series
DEVELOPMENT	Shazam! - Way of the Rat - Route 666 - The Path - The Spirit - Thunder Agents
PRODUCTION	Batman Begins
POST PRODUCTION	Constantine - Catwoman - National Treasure
CREDITS	Batman 1-4 - Where on Earth Is Carmen San Diego? - Three Sovereigns for Sarah - Dinosaucers - Robin Cook's Harmful Intent - Batman: Mystery of the Batwoman
SUBMISSION POLICY	Absolutely no unsolicited submissions

Michael Uslan .....Producer
F.J. DeSanto .....VP, Development
David Uslan .....Director, Creative Affairs

BRANDMAN PRODUCTIONS
2062 N. Vine St., Ste. 5
Los Angeles, CA 90068
PHONE 323-463-3224

TYPES	Features - Made-for-TV/Cable Movies - TV Series
DEVELOPMENT	Unknown Man #89 - The Empty Land - Robert B. Parker's Stone Cold (CBS)
CREDITS	Walking Shadow - Crossfire Trail - The Heidi Chronicles - Small Vices - Last Stand at Saber River - Alone - Monte Walsh

Michael Brandman .....President
Louis Landon .....VP, Development
Joanna Miles .....VP

BRAUBACH PRODUCTIONS
3050 Airport Ave., Ste. C
Santa Monica, CA 90405
PHONE 310-230-1804

TYPES	Features - TV Series
CREDITS	A Great Bunch of Girls - Four Days in September - Last Stand at Saber River

Mary Ann Braubach .....Producer

BRAUN ENTERTAINMENT GROUP, INC.
280 S. Beverly Dr., Ste. 500
Beverly Hills, CA 90212
PHONE 310-888-7727
FAX 310-888-7726
EMAIL .....braunent@aol.com
WEB SITE .....www.braunentertainmentgroup.com

TYPES	Features - Made-for-TV/Cable Movies - TV Series
CREDITS	Edges of the Lord - Tour of Duty - Lethal Vows - Abducted: A Father's Love - Menendez: Killing in Beverly Hills

Zev Braun .....President/Executive Producer
Philip M. Krupp .....Executive VP/Producer
Ari Etkes .....Executive Assistant

DAVID BRAUN PRODUCTIONS
2530 Wilshire Blvd., 3rd Fl.
Santa Monica, CA 90403-4616
PHONE .310-453-0089
EMAIL .ls@braunco.net
TYPES Features - New Media - TV Series
CREDITS MythQuest (PBS Series) - Blind Judgement - Labyrinth: A Life of Kafka - No Good Deed
SUBMISSION POLICY No unsolicited material

David Braun .President
Lissa Sanders .VP
Peter Zinner .VP, Production
Denise Weeks .Producer/Writer
Jessica Hey .Reader/Researcher

BRAVE NEW FILMS
1948 N. Van Ness Ave.
Los Angeles, CA 90068
PHONE .323-962-9913
FAX .323-962-9903
TYPES Features - Direct-to-Video/DVD - Made-for-TV/Cable Movies - TV Series
DEVELOPMENT Last Year's River - The Minority Quarterback (ESPN)
PRE-PRODUCTION Ten Inch Hero
CREDITS The Lesser Evil - Route 9 - Black Point

David Mackay .Producer/Director
Mark Witsken .Producer

BRAVERMAN PRODUCTIONS, INC.
3000 Olympic Blvd.
Santa Monica, CA 90404
PHONE .310-264-4184
FAX .310-388-5885
EMAIL .info@braverman.net
WEB SITE .www.bravermanproductions.com
TYPES Documentaries - Direct-to-Video/DVD
DEVELOPMENT Masquerade - '58
PRODUCTION Debutantes (A&E) - Yellowstone Bison (Animal Planet) - Homeless in Paradise
COMPLETED UNRELEASED Extremely Out of Control (Discovery Channel) - Prison Doctors (Discovery Channel) - Love Behind Bars (Discovery Channel) - A Pug's Life: The Dogumentary
CREDITS Making Marines - Prison Boot Camp - Season of the Grizzly (Animal Planet) - Sextuplets (Discovery Health) - When Planes Go Down (Discovery) - Biography of Oscar® (A&E) - Broken Wings (History Channel)

Chuck Braverman .Executive Producer/Director
Marilyn Braverman .Producer/Camera/Sound
Alex Braverman .Producer/Cameraman
Rick Dowlearn .Development/Producer/Writer
Rob King .Post Production Supervisor
Ruth Fertig .Production Coordinator/Clearance Supervisor
Ash Hasen .Editor/Graphics

BRAVO NETWORK
30 Rockefeller Plaza, Fl. 14-E
New York, NY 10112
PHONE .212-664-4444/818-840-4444
WEB SITE .www.bravotv.com
TYPES Documentaries - Features - Made-for-TV/Cable Movies - Reality TV - TV Series
CREDITS Inside the Actors Studio - Broadway on Bravo - Gay Weddings - The It Factor - Page to Screen - Independent Spirit Awards - Queer Eye for the Straight Guy - Celebrity Poker Showdown - Boy Meets Boy - Bravo Profiles - Significant Others - Showbiz Moms & Dads
COMMENTS An NBC Universal Cable network; West Coast office: 3000 W. Alameda Ave., Burbank, CA 91523

Lauren Zalaznick .President, Bravo & TRIO Networks
Todd Saypoff .CFO, Bravo
Frances Berwick .Sr. VP, Programming & Production, Bravo
Mitch Salem .Sr. VP, Business Affairs, Acquisitions & Development
Dan Harrison .VP, Strategic Program Planning, Bravo Network
Jamila Hunter .VP, Development & Production (LA)
Amy Introcaso-Davis .VP, Production & Development
Christian Barcellos .Director, Packaging & Production
Carolyn Hommel .Manager, Program Planning & Scheduling

*BREAKAWAY FILMS
1191 E. Newport Center Dr., Ste. 203
Deerfield Beach, FL 33442
PHONE .954-427-2530
FAX .954-427-2538
EMAIL .info@bafilms.com
SECOND EMAIL .production@bafilms.com
WEB SITE .www.maverickentertainment.cc/breakawayfilms
TYPES Features - Direct-to-Video/DVD - Made-for-TV/Cable Movies
PRE-PRODUCTION D-Block - Low Rider Shop - Grand Opening - El Super Mercado
POST PRODUCTION Carlita's Secret - One Night in Compton - Bahama Hustle - The Evil One - Big Phat Hip Hop Family - La Migra
COMPLETED UNRELEASED Out on Parole
CREDITS I Accidentally Domed Your Son - The Hustle - Digging for Dollars - Bank Brothers - A Miami Tail - Senorita Justice - Sweet Potato Pie

Doug Schwab .Principal/Partner/Executive Producer
Pamela White .Partner/Executive Producer
J. Ronald Castell .Partner/Executive Producer
Eric Erba .Producer

PAULETTE BREEN PRODUCTIONS
6920 Texhoma Ave., Ste. 100
Van Nuys, CA 91406
PHONE 818-342-0228
FAX 818-342-0228
TYPES Features - Made-for-TV/Cable Movies - Syndication - TV Series
DEVELOPMENT Nightwatch - A Father Condemned - Stranger Beside Me - Too High a Price - Recluse
PRE-PRODUCTION Dynamite - Tomorrow Doesn't Count - Regrets
POST PRODUCTION Changing Times
CREDITS 83 Hrs. - Separated by Murder - Abducted: A Father's Love - The Stranger Within - Down Will Come Baby - Haven - A Dry Spell

Paulette Breen ....President/Producer
Randall Sanders ....VP, Creative Affairs
Kathy Page ....Creative Assistant/Office Administration

THE BREGMAN ENTERTAINMENT GROUP
1950 Sawtelle Blvd., Ste. 360
West Los Angeles, CA 90025-7014
PHONE 213-833-6207
EMAIL ....buddybregman@comcast.net
WEB SITE ....www.buddybregman.com
TYPES Features - Made-for-TV/Cable Movies - Music Videos - TV Series
DEALS Global Media Television
DEVELOPMENT Trial of Ezra Pound - Garbo - Fast Break - Happy Street - Maracas: Carmen Miranda
PRE-PRODUCTION City of Masks - All of Me: The Billie Holiday-Lester Young Encounters - What's New - Evil Shadows
CREDITS Capone: The Musical
COMMENTS Deals with Spice Factory (UK), Gen X Entertainment and International Filmed Entertainment

Buddy Bregman ....President/Executive Producer
Summer Dey Curtis ....Producer
Tracey E. Bregman ....Producer
Marie de Puthod ....Writer/Director/Producer

BREGMAN PRODUCTIONS
150 E. 57th St., Penthouse 1-A
New York, NY 10022
PHONE 212-421-6161/818-954-9988
FAX 212-223-1944/818-954-9989
TYPES Features
DEVELOPMENT The Gold Coast - Tapping the Source - The Domestic - Moe Snyder - Carlito's Way: The Beginning
CREDITS The Bone Collector - Sea of Love - Scarface - Serpico - Dog Day Afternoon - Carlito's Way - The Four Seasons - The Seduction of Joe Tynan - Nothing to Lose

Martin Bregman ....No Title
Michael Bregman ....No Title
Michael Klawitter ....No Title
Louis A. Stroller ....No Title

BRIGHT STREET PICTURES
150 Lexington Ave.
Buffalo, NY 14222-1810
PHONE 716-884-6771
TYPES Animation - Documentaries - Features - Made-for-TV/Cable Movies - New Media - Syndication - TV Series
CREDITS A Father for Brittany - Any Mother's Son - Christ in Concrete

Joseph A. DiPasquale ....Executive Producer/President
Don Elick ....VP, Production

BRIGHTLIGHT PICTURES, INC.
3500 Cornett Rd.
Vancouver, BC V5M 2H5 Canada
PHONE 604-453-4710
FAX 604-453-4711
EMAIL ....mary@brightlightpictures.com
WEB SITE ....www.brightlightpictures.com
DEVELOPMENT Peachland - Blood Rayne - Dungeon Siege - Hunter: The Reckoning - Fear Effect - Far Cry
PRODUCTION The Long Weekend
POST PRODUCTION White Noise - Going the Distance
COMPLETED UNRELEASED Alone in the Dark
CREDITS House of the Dead - Punch - Alienated - Finder's Fee

Stephen Hegyes ....Producer
Shawn Williamson ....Producer
Karyn Edwards ....VP, Legal & Business Affairs
Jonathan Shore ....VP, Distribution & Post Production
Andrew Boutilier ....Director, Development
Mary Quinn ....Assistant to Stephen Hegyes
David Chang ....Assistant, Post Production
Jane Grimston ....Legal Assistant to Karyn Edwards
Micah Kelpin ....Assistant to Shawn Williamson
Tracy Smith ....Assistant, Development
Dan West ....Assistant, Production

BRILLSTEIN-GREY ENTERTAINMENT
9150 Wilshire Blvd., Ste. 350
Beverly Hills, CA 90212
PHONE 310-275-6135
FAX 310-275-6180
TYPES Features - New Media - TV Series
CREDITS The Sopranos

Bernie Brillstein ....Consultant
Brad Grey ....Chairman
Jonathan Liebman ....Vice Chairman
Steve Blume ....CFO
Peter Traugott ....President, BGTV
Sandy Wernick ....Sr. Executive VP
Marc Gurvitz ....Executive VP
Susie Fitzgerald ....Sr. VP, BGTV
Amy Weiss ....Sr. VP, Business & Legal Affairs
Tony Carey ....VP, TV Production
Becky Clements ....VP, BGTV
Lisa Katz ....Director, BGTV
Kassie Evashevski ....Literary Manager
Sean White ....Manager, TV Production

It is illegal to copy any part of this book

BRINK FILMS, INC.

134 S. Van Ness Ave.
Los Angeles, CA 90004
PHONE .310-463-0216
EMAIL .info@brinkfilm.com
WEB SITE .www.brinkfilm.com

TYPES: Features - New Media - TV Series
DEVELOPMENT: The Last New Yorker - Capture the Flag - Prairie Girl
PRE-PRODUCTION: Nitro USA
PRODUCTION: TV Party
CREDITS: Spun - Pornstar Pets
SUBMISSION POLICY: No unsolicited mail submissions

Danny Vinik .President
Wyatt Landesmann .Producer
Mary Ann Brazil .VP, Production
Kai Eric .VP, Development
Robin Kohli .New Media
Jeff Flohr .Assistant to Mr. Vinik

*JOHN BRISTER FILMS

1211 Sunset Plaza Dr., Ste. 413
Los Angeles, CA 90069
PHONE .310-652-3800
FAX .310-652-3801
WEB SITE .www.johnbrister.com

TYPES: Features - Direct-to-Video/DVD - Made-for-TV/Cable Movies
DEVELOPMENT: Voice of Treason - Hockey Dog - Rudy's Run - Gravity - Untitled U-Boat - Soccer Dog: Down Under - First Mouse - Ship of Souls - Stealing Signs
CREDITS: In Enemy Hands - Soccer Dog: European Cup - Rocket's Red Glare - Soccer Dog: The Movie

John H. Brister .President
Erik Mountain .Sr. VP, Development

BRISTOL BAY PRODUCTIONS

132 B Lasky Dr.
Beverly Hills, CA 90212
PHONE .310-248-6360
FAX .310-248-6370
WEB SITE .www.bristolbayproductions.com

TYPES: Features - Made-for-TV/Cable Movies
DEVELOPMENT: Charm School - Atlas Shrugged
PRE-PRODUCTION: Parent Wars
POST PRODUCTION: Sahara - Swimming Upstream - Danny Deck Chair - Ray - Sound of Thunder - Game of Their Lives

Lenny Kornberg .Executive VP, Production
Chris DeMoulin .Executive VP, Marketing
Jackie Levine .VP, Production
Bill Brown .Sr. VP, Physical Production
Vicki Dee Rock .Sr. VP, Physical Production
Lindsay Fellows .VP, Music
Francesca Hickson .CFO
Gordon Tichell .Controller
Laine Kline .Associate General Counsel
Jack Lilburn .Creative Executive
Kathy Miller Kelley .Director, Development
Erica Stern .Director, Marketing
Linda Montgomery .Accounts Payable Manager
Chris Russell .Assistant to Bill Brown
Kristy Sexton .Assistant to Erica Stern
Bonnie Solomon .Assistant to L. Kornberg & K. Miller Kelly
Marsha Trainer .Assistant to Vicki Dee Rock
Marcia Wheatley .Assistant to Laine Kline

BRITISH LION

5302 Ethel Ave.
Sherman Oaks, CA 91401
PHONE .818-789-9112/44-1753-651-700
FAX .818-789-2901/44-1753-656-844
WEB SITE .www.britishlionfilms.com

TYPES: Features - Made-for-TV/Cable Movies
DEVELOPMENT: Puccini - Duel of Kings - Blithe Spirit - May Day
CREDITS: The Third Man - A Man for All Seasons - Don't Look Now - The Wicker Man - Lady Jane - Turtle Diary
COMMENTS: UK office: Pinewood Studios, Pinewood Rd., Iver Heath, Bucks SL0 0NH UK

Peter R. E. Snell .Chairman/CEO
Toni Pinnolis .VP (LA)

BROAD STROKES ENTERTAINMENT

3575 Cahuenga Blvd. West, Ste. 360
Los Angeles, CA 90068
PHONE .323-874-1648
FAX .323-874-1650

TYPES: Features - Made-for-TV/Cable Movies - Syndication - TV Series
DEVELOPMENT: The Bear and His Monkey - Bub
CREDITS: The Longshot - Little Sister - Teen Steam - Below Utopia - Safesearching.com

Lin Milano .Producer
Vanessa Torres .Producer
Tracey Washington .Producer

BROADWAY PICTURES, INC.

11835 W. Olympic Blvd., Ste. 550-E
Los Angeles, CA 90064
PHONE .310-268-8200
FAX .310-444-4101
EMAIL .ron@broadwaypictures.com
SECOND EMAIL .yianna@broadwaypictures.com

TYPES: Features - Made-for-TV/Cable Movies - TV Series
DEVELOPMENT: Enemy Within - The Tenants - Fort McCoy
PRE-PRODUCTION: Addiction - Redliners - Night Train - The Last Face
CREDITS: Off Season (Showtime) - Holy Tortilla

Ron Broadway .CEO/Producer
Yianna Apostolidis-Trewyn .Director, Development

BROADWAY VIDEO (NY)
1619 Broadway, Brill Bldg., 9th Fl.
New York, NY 10019
PHONE . . . 212-265-7600
WEB SITE . . . www.broadwayvideo.com
TYPES Animation - Documentaries - Features - New Media - TV Series
DEALS NBC Universal Television Studio
CREDITS Saturday Night Live - Kids in the Hall - Night Music - Late Night with Conan O'Brien
COMMENTS Audio/video post production, graphics, duplication; Distribution

Lorne Michaels . . . Chairman
Jack Sullivan . . . CEO
Brian Offutt . . . COO
Alex Drosin . . . President, Broadway Video Enterprises
Cristina McGinniss . . . Sr. VP

BROADWAY VIDEO ENTERTAINMENT
c/o Paramount Studios
5555 Melrose Ave., Dressing Room Bldg., Ste. 105
Los Angeles, CA 90038-3197
PHONE . . . 323-956-5655 (Film)/818-840-7532 (TV)
FAX . . . 323-862-8605 (Film)/818-840-7519 (TV)
TYPES Features - TV Series
CREDITS Wayne's World - A Night at the Roxbury - Superstar - Kids in the Hall - Lady's Man - Mean Girls - Tommy Boy - Black Sheep
COMMENTS Subsidiary of Broadway Video

Lorne Michaels . . . Chairman
JoAnn Alfano . . . President, TV
Jack Sullivan . . . CEO
Jill Messick . . . Executive VP, Features
Mark O'Connor . . . VP, Production
Hilary Marx . . . Creative Executive
Nassim Bakhtiari . . . Development Assistant

BROOKLYN FILMS
3815 Hughes Ave.
Culver City, CA 90232-2715
PHONE . . . 310-841-4300
FAX . . . 310-204-3464
TYPES Features - TV Series
DEVELOPMENT The Understudy - Land of the Blind
POST PRODUCTION The World of Tomorrow
CREDITS Uprising (Miniseries) - Things You Can Tell Just by Looking at Her - Red Corner - Up Close & Personal - The War - Fried Green Tomatoes - Boomtown

Jon Avnet . . . Director/Producer (310-841-4300)
Carol Chacamaty . . . Executive VP, Finance/Administration (310-841-4307)
Marsha Oglesby . . . Sr. VP, Development & Production (310-841-4316)
Sandy Yep . . . Creative Assistant to Jon Avnet (310-841-4304)

BROOKSFILMS LIMITED
c/o Culver Studios
9336 W. Washington Blvd.
Culver City, CA 90232
PHONE . . . 310-202-3292
FAX . . . 310-202-3225
TYPES Features
CREDITS The Fly 1&2 - Frances - Elephant Man - My Favorite Year - The Producers (Theater)

Mel Brooks . . . President
Leah Zappy . . . VP, Production Services
Jennifer Yale . . . Development

BROOKWELL MCNAMARA ENTERTAINMENT, INC.
c/o Hollywood Center Studios
1040 N. Las Palmas, Bldg. 33, 2nd Fl.
Los Angeles, CA 90038
PHONE . . . 323-860-8989
FAX . . . 323-860-8991
WEB SITE . . . www.bme-online.com
TYPES Features - Made-for-TV/Cable Movies - TV Series
DEVELOPMENT Better Watch Out - First Dogs - The Virgin - Frog Prince
POST PRODUCTION Heart of Summer
COMPLETED UNRELEASED Phil of the Future (Pilot)
CREDITS That's So Raven - Even Stevens - The Even Stevens Movie - Race to Space - The Trial of Old Drum - Treehouse Hostage - Wild Grizzly

Sean McNamara . . . Producer/Writer/Director
David Brookwell . . . Producer/Writer/Director
David Grace . . . VP, Production
Mieke Berlin . . . VP, Development
Brad Jensen . . . Director, Production
Matthew Thomas . . . Director, Development

BROTHERHOOD FILMS
1086 S. Fairfax Ave.
Los Angeles, CA 90019
PHONE . . . 323-933-4402
FAX . . . 323-933-4402
WEB SITE . . . www.brotherhoodfilms.com
SECOND WEB SITE . . . www.qd3entertainment.com
TYPES Documentaries - Features - Direct-to-Video/DVD - Made-for-TV/Cable Movies - New Media - TV Series
CREDITS The Freshest Kids
COMMENTS Deal with QD3 Entertainment

Israel . . . Director/Producer
Quincy Jones . . . Co-Producer
Quincy "QD3" Jones III . . . Executive Producer
Eric N. Brenner . . . Co-Executive Producer
Michael Sutton . . . Co-Executive Producer
Richard Colon . . . Co-Producer

JERRY BRUCKHEIMER FILMS

1631 Tenth St.
Santa Monica, CA 90404
PHONE .310-664-6260
FAX .310-664-6261
WEB SITE .www.jbfilms.com

TYPES	Features - Reality TV - Syndication - TV Series
DEALS	Walt Disney Pictures/Touchstone Pictures - Warner Bros. Television Production
PRE-PRODUCTION	Glory Road
POST PRODUCTION	National Treasure
CREDITS	TV: CSI: New York - Skin - Cold Case - CSI: Miami - Without a Trace - CSI - The Amazing Race; Features: King Arthur - Veronica Guerin - Pirates of the Caribbean - Bad Boys 1&2 - Kangaroo Jack - Pearl Harbor - Remember the Titans

Jerry Bruckheimer .Producer (310-664-6262)
Mike Stenson .President (310-664-6250)
Chad Oman .President, Production (310-664-6264)
Jonathan Littman .President, TV (310-664-6295)
KristieAnne Reed .Sr. VP, Production (310-664-6246)
Melissa Reid .Sr. VP, Production (310-664-6265)
Kimberly Metcalf .VP, TV (310-664-6267)
Charlie Banks .Creative Executive (310-664-6266)

BONNIE BRUCKHEIMER PRODUCTIONS

12439 Magnolia Blvd., Ste. 217
Valley Village, CA 91607
PHONE .818-761-0270

TYPES	Features - Made-for-TV/Cable Movies
CREDITS	Divine Secrets of the Ya-Ya Sisterhood - For the Boys - Man of the House - That Old Feeling - Beaches
SUBMISSION POLICY	No unsolicited material

Bonnie Bruckheimer .Producer

THE BUBBLE FACTORY

8840 Wilshire Blvd., 3rd Fl.
Beverly Hills, CA 90211
PHONE .310-358-3000
FAX .310-358-3299

TYPES	Features
CREDITS	The Pest - A Simple Wish - For Richer or Poorer - Playing Mona Lisa - Flipper - McHale's Navy - Stinkers - That Old Feeling - A Fate Totally Worse Than Death

Sid Sheinberg .Partner
Bill Sheinberg .Partner
Jon Sheinberg .Partner
Mitch Solomon .Executive VP, Motion Pictures
Kevin D. Forester .VP, Finance & Operations
Gwen Osborne .VP, Development
Wendy Brennan .Manager, Contract Administration
Shawna van Gils .Operations Manager
Joe Carrabba .Executive Assistant to J. Sheinberg
Melanie Chapman .Executive Assistant to S. Sheinberg
Caryn Santoro .Executive Assistant to K. Forester
Michael Connolly .Executive Assistant to M. Solomon & G. Osborne

THE BUENA VISTA MOTION PICTURES GROUP

500 S. Buena Vista St.
Burbank, CA 91521-0001
PHONE .818-560-1000
WEB SITE .www.disney.com

TYPES	Animation - Features
COMMENTS	Includes Walt Disney Pictures/Touchstone Pictures

Richard Cook .Chairman, The Walt Disney Studios
Oren Aviv .President, Buena Vista Pictures Marketing
Nina Jacobson .President, Buena Vista Motion Pictures Group
Thomas Schumacher .President, Disney Theatrical Productions, Ltd.
David J. Stainton .President, Walt Disney Feature Animation
Chuck Viane .President, Buena Vista Pictures Distribution
Bruce Hendricks .President, Physical Production, Walt Disney Pictures
Alan Bergman .Executive VP/CFO, The Walt Disney Studios
Bernardine Brandis .Executive VP, Business & Legal Affairs, The Walt Disney Studios
Susan Butterworth .Executive VP, Development, Walt Disney Feature Animation
Pam Coats .Executive VP, Creative Affairs, Walt Disney Feature Animation
Glen Lajeski .Executive VP, Music Creative/Marketing, Buena Vista Motion Pictures Group
Mitchell Leib .Executive VP/General Manager, Buena Vista Motion Pictures Group, Music & Soundtracks
Phil Lofaro .Producer, Walt Disney Feature Animation
Jeffrey Miller .Executive VP, Worldwide Post Production & Operations, The Walt Disney Studios
Phillip E. Muhl .Executive VP, Business & Legal Affairs, Walt Disney Pictures Administration
Jason T. Reed .Executive VP, Production, Walt Disney Pictures Theatrical
Marcia Ross Executive VP, Features Casting, Walt Disney Pictures Theatrical
Fred Tio .Executive VP, Worldwide Marketing
Robert W. Bacon .Sr. VP, Production, Walt Disney Feature Animation
Steve Bardwil .Sr. VP, Legal Affairs, Walt Disney Pictures Administration
Doug Carter .Sr. VP, Business Affairs, Walt Disney Pictures Administration
Tim Engel .Sr. VP, Walt Disney Feature Animation
Brad Epstein .Sr. VP, Production, Walt Disney Pictures Administration
Michele Gazica .Sr. VP, Participations & Residuals, Walt Disney Pictures Administration
Steven W. Gerse .Sr. VP, Business & Legal Affairs, Walt Disney Pictures Administration
Karen Glass .Sr. VP, Development & Production, Walt Disney Pictures Administration
Whitney Green .Sr. VP, Production, Walt Disney Pictures Administration
Scott Holtzman .Sr. VP, Music, Walt Disney Pictures Administration
Robert W. Johnson .Sr. VP, Labor Relations, Walt Disney Worldwide Services
Jerry Ketcham .Sr. VP, Production, Walt Disney Pictures
Bob Lambert .Sr. VP, Corporate New Technology & Development
Alan Levey .Sr. VP/General Manager, Disney Theatrical Productions, Ltd.
David McCann .Sr. VP, Walt Disney Pictures Theatrical Production
Duncan Orrell-Jones .Sr. VP, Finance & Planning, Walt Disney Feature Animation
Marjorie Randolph .Sr. VP, Human Resources & Administration, The Walt Disney Studios
Art Repola .Sr. VP, Visual Effects & Production, Walt Disney Theatrical Production
Dennis Rice .Sr. VP, Publicity, Buena Vista Pictures Marketing
Paul Steinke .Sr. VP, Production Finance, Walt Disney Theatrical Production
Brigham Taylor .Sr. VP, Production, Walt Disney Pictures Theatrical
Heidi Trotta .Sr. VP, Communications, The Walt Disney Studios
John Blas .VP, Animation Creative Services, Walt Disney Pictures Administration
Kristin Burr .VP, Production, Walt Disney Pictures Theatrical
Gail Goldberg .VP, Casting, Walt Disney Theatrical Production
Stephanie Harris .VP, Credit & Title Administration, Walt Disney Pictures Administration
Sylvia J. Krask .VP, Music Business & Legal Affairs, Walt Disney Pictures & Television
Iya Labunka .VP, Production, Walt Disney Pictures Production
Stephanie Mangano .VP, Casting Administration, Walt Disney Pictures & Television
Donna Morong .VP, Features Casting, Walt Disney Pictures Administration
Paige Olson .VP, Business & Legal Affairs, Walt Disney Pictures Administration
Doug Short .VP, Production, Walt Disney Theatrical Production
Calvin Tindal .VP, Production Resources, Walt Disney Theatrical Production
Jonathan Treisman .VP, Development, Walt Disney Feature Animation

(Continued)

THE BUENA VISTA MOTION PICTURES GROUP (Continued)

Kal Walthers . . . . . .VP, Business Affairs, Walt Disney Pictures Administration
Monica Zierhut . . . . . .VP, Music Production, Walt Disney Pictures Theatrical Administration
Carlton Jackson Jr. . . . . .Creative Executive, Walt Disney Pictures Theatrical
LouAnne Brickhouse . . . . . .Director, Production, Walt Disney Pictures Theatrical Administration
Jill Rachel Morris . . . . . .Director, Production, Walt Disney Pictures Theatrical Administration
Elizabeth Lynch . . . . . .Sr. Counsel
Bill Neuschaefer . . . . . .Sr. Counsel
David Trygstad . . . . . .Sr. Counsel
Vickie Cameron . . . . . .Counsel
Kobie Conner . . . . . .Counsel
Renat Engel . . . . . .Counsel
Chad Harris . . . . . .Counsel
Tom Loftus . . . . . .Counsel
Kevin Monroe . . . . . .Counsel
Jun S. Oh . . . . . .Counsel
Gamze Onur . . . . . .Counsel
Heather Wayland . . . . . .Counsel
Don Welty . . . . . .Counsel

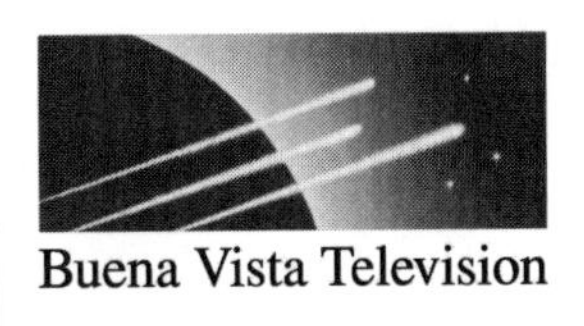

BUENA VISTA TELEVISION

500 S. Buena Vista St.
Burbank, CA 91521-0001
PHONE 818-560-1000
WEB SITE . . . . . .www.bventertainment.go.com
SECOND WEB SITE . . . . . .www.disney.com
TYPES — Reality TV - Syndication - TV Series
DEVELOPMENT — The Tony Danza Show
CREDITS — Live with Regis & Kelly - Who Wants to Be A Millionaire - Ebert & Roeper

Janice Marinelli . . . . . .President
John Bryan . . . . . .Executive VP/General Sales Manager
Mary Kellogg-Joslyn . . . . . .Executive VP, Current Programming, Buena Vista Productions
Lloyd Komesar . . . . . .Executive VP, Strategic Research
Howard Levy . . . . . .Executive VP, Ad Sales
Sal Sardo . . . . . .Executive VP, Marketing
Dan Cohen . . .Sr. VP/General Manager, Buena Vista Pay TV & Distribution
Jed Cohen . . . . . .Sr. VP/General Sales Manager, West
Tom Malanga . . . . . .Sr. VP, Finance
Robert Mendez . . . . . .Sr. VP, Business Affairs
Jennie Born . . . . . .VP, Promotions
Sandra Brewer . . . . . .VP, Affiliate Relations
Blake Bryant . . . . . .VP, Creative Services
George Gubert . . . . . .VP, Research
Kim Harbin . . . . . .VP, Press & Publicity
Rob Morhaim . . . . . .VP, Development, Buena Vista Productions
Carlos Torres . . . . . .VP, Production, Buena Vista Productions
Brooke Bowman Executive Director, Development, Buena Vista Productions

BULL'S EYE ENTERTAINMENT

10850 Wilshire Blvd.
Los Angeles, CA 90024
PHONE 310-470-7500
FAX 310-470-7550
EMAIL . . . . . .info@bullseyeent.com
TYPES — Features - TV Series
DEALS — Paramount Pictures-Motion Picture Group
PRODUCTION — Crash (Feature/Independent)
POST PRODUCTION — Employee of the Month (Feature/Independent) - Thumbsucker (Feature/Independent)

Tom Nunan . . . . . .Partner
Cathy Schulman . . . . . .Partner
Janet Salas . . . . . .VP, Development & Production
Felicia Flick . . . . . .Executive Assistant to Cathy Schulman
Ryan Vernon . . . . . .Executive Assistant to Tom Nunan

BUNGALOW 78 PRODUCTIONS

500 S. Buena Vista St.
Old Animation Bldg. 1-E, Ste. 9
Burbank, CA 91521
PHONE 323-956-4440
FAX 323-862-2090
TYPES — Features - TV Series
DEALS — Touchstone Television
CREDITS — A Minute with Stan Hooper - Coach - Catch Me If You Can - Patch Adams - Romy & Michelle's High School Reunion
COMMENTS — Moving at press time

Barry Kemp . . . . . .Executive Producer/Writer
Jill Bowles . . . . . .Assistant to B. Kemp
Wyatt Hannon . . . . . .Assistant

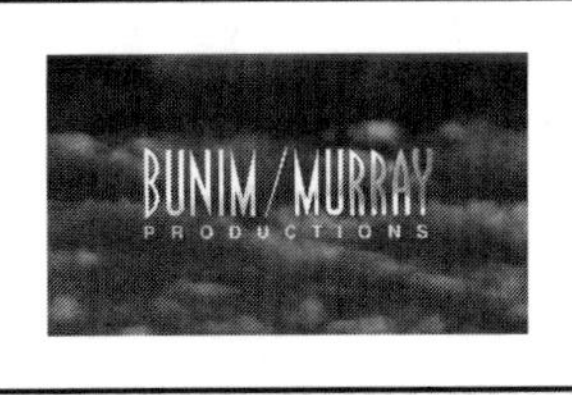

BUNIM/MURRAY PRODUCTIONS, INC.

6007 Sepulveda Blvd.
Van Nuys, CA 91411
PHONE 818-756-5100/818-756-5253
FAX 818-756-5140
WEB SITE . . . . . .www.bunim-murray.com
TYPES — Documentaries - Features - Direct-to-Video/DVD - Made-for-TV/Cable Movies - Reality TV - Syndication - TV Series
CREDITS — The Simple Life - Starting Over (Syndication) - Born to Diva - The Real Cancun - The Real World - Road Rules - The Real World/Road Rules Challenge - Class Reunion (MOW) - Making the Band - Love Cruise: The Maiden Voyage - The Billionaire

Jonathan Murray . . . . . .Executive Producer
Joey Carson . . . . . .COO
Phillip Segal . . . . . .Executive VP, Current Programming & Developmnet
Sasha Alpert . . . . . .VP, Casting
Phil Castaneda . . . . . .VP, Production Finance
Joyce Corrington . . . . . .VP, Creative Affairs
Scott Freeman . . . . . .VP, Creative Affairs
Gil Goldschein . . . . . .VP, Business & Legal Affairs
Kevin Lee . . . . . .VP, Creative Affairs
Patrick Murphy . . . . . .VP, Production
Stacey O'Donnell . . . . . .Director, Human Resources
Bart Peele . . . . . .Director, Operations
Mark Raudonis . . . . . .Director, Post Production
Dave Stone . . . . . .Music Director
Jason Toney . . . . . .Director, Web Development

BURLEIGH FILMWORKS

22287 Mulholland Hwy., Ste. 129
Calabasas, CA 91302
PHONE .818-224-4686
FAX .818-223-9089
EMAIL .steve@burleighfilmworks.com
TYPES Features - Made-for-TV/Cable Movies - TV Series
DEVELOPMENT Swimming After Midnight - Heartstrings - The Horses' Mouth
COMPLETED UNRELEASED Edge of America - Bereft
CREDITS Execution of Justice
SUBMISSION POLICY Query by email

Steve Burleigh .Owner

MARK BURNETT PRODUCTIONS

640 N. Sepulveda Blvd.
Los Angeles, CA 90049
PHONE .310-903-5400
TYPES Features - Reality TV - TV Series
DEALS Warner Bros. Television Production
DEVELOPMENT Rockstar
PRODUCTION Commando Nanny - The Contender - Global Frequency
COMPLETED UNRELEASED Recovery
CREDITS Survivor - The Apprentice - The Restaurant - The Casino
COMMENTS Warner Bros. deal for scripted TV only

Mark Burnett .Executive Producer/Showrunner/Partner
Conrad Riggs .Co-Executive Producer/Head, Reality Development & Business Operations
Cara Goldberg .Co-Producer
Diane Winkler .Controller
Lisa Hennessy .Head, Physical Production
Mike Winchester .Director, Finance
Michelle Castillo .Coordinator, Reality Development
Rachael Harrell .Coordinator, Scripted Development & Production
Michaela Starr .Coordinator, Scripted Development & Production
Susann Guercioni .Paralegal
Kristen Parks .Executive Assistant to Mr. Burnett

BURRUD PRODUCTIONS

16351 Gothard St., Unit D
Huntington Beach, CA 92647
PHONE .714-842-8422
FAX .714-842-0433
EMAIL .burrudprod@aol.com
WEB SITE .www.burrud.com
TYPES Animation - Documentaries - Features - New Media - TV Series
PRODUCTION Multiples, Multiples
CREDITS Movie Monsters Revealed - Strange Travels - Mysteries Within - Stick Men of Las Vegas - Yoga for Kids - Vegas Cops - Vegas Challenge - Mutter Museum - Shark Chasers - Mostly True Stories - Vegas Dealers - Mardi Gras Cops
SUBMISSION POLICY No unsolicited submissions

John Burrud .President/CEO
Stanley H. Green .Executive VP, Business Affairs
Valerie Chow .VP, Production
Shannon Mead .Executive Assistant to President

AL BURTON PRODUCTIONS

468 N. Camden Dr., Ste. 200
Beverly Hills, CA 90210
PHONE .310-858-5511
EMAIL .alburton22@aol.com
TYPES New Media - Syndication - TV Series
DEALS 44 Blue Productions, Inc. - Lions Gate Entertainment
PRE-PRODUCTION The Making of a Supreme Court Justice - Scott Baio Project - Graham & Tucker - Bethany Hamilton Story
PRODUCTION Ben Sein Project
CREDITS Alvin Toffler's Beyond Futureshock - The New Lassie - Charles in Charge - Win Ben Stein's Money - Turn Ben Stein On

Al Burton .Executive Producer
Adam Pliska .Executive Producer
Jerram Swartz .Producer
Nicole Langevin .General Manager/Producer
Phillip Weldele .Director, Development

BUTCHERS RUN FILMS

1041 N. Formosa Ave., Santa Monica Bldg., East 200
West Hollywood, CA 90046
PHONE .323-850-2703
FAX .323-850-2741
TYPES Features
DEVELOPMENT The Running Kind
PRE-PRODUCTION Misfortune...A Love Story
CREDITS A Family Thing - The Man Who Captured Eichmann - The Apostle - A Shot at Glory - Assassination Tango

Robert Duvall .Actor/Producer/Director
Rob Carliner .Producer/Manager
Adam Prince .Director, Development

BYRUM POWER & LIGHT

PO Box 1211
Redding, CT 06875
PHONE .310-428-5664
TYPES Features - TV Series
CREDITS Duets - The Razor's Edge - Heart Beat - Mahogany - Inserts - Middle Ages - South of Sunset - Winnetka Road
SUBMISSION POLICY No unsolicited material

John Byrum .Writer/Director
Karin Reznack-Byrum .No Title

C/W PRODUCTIONS

c/o Paramount Pictures
5555 Melrose Ave.
Hollywood, CA 90038
PHONE .323-956-8199
FAX .323-862-1250
TYPES Features
DEALS Paramount Pictures-Motion Picture Group
CREDITS Mission: Impossible 1&2 - Without Limits - The Others - Vanilla Sky - The Last Samurai - Shattered Glass

Paula Wagner .Producer
Don Granger .No Title
Gaye Hirsch .No Title
Darren Miller .No Title
Amy Stevens Hammond .No Title
Jeff Buitenveld .No Title
Mia Fenwick .No Title
Kathrina Cotner .No Title
Alex Katsnelson .No Title
Grady Lee .No Title
Chris Pyne .No Title
Robert Ripley .No Title
Nick Roe .No Title
Rebecca Tucker .No Title

C2 PICTURES

2308 Broadway
Santa Monica, CA 90404

PHONE .310-315-6000
FAX .310-828-0443

TYPES	Features - Interactive Games - TV Series
DEVELOPMENT	Terminator 4 - Evermere - Smoke and Mirrors - Aurora - Trapped
CREDITS	Evita - Die Hard 3 - Star Gate - I Spy - Terminator 3 - Rambo 1-3 - Jacob's Ladder - Angel Heart - Total Recall
SUBMISSION POLICY	No unsolicited submissions accepted
COMMENTS	MK Productions/Cinergi Pictures

Mario Kassar .Co-CEO
Andrew Vajna .Co-CEO
Samuel Falconello .CFO
James Middleton .Sr. VP, Production & Development
Joel Michaels .Production Executive
Chad Kennedy .Development
Beverly Cusack .Controller

C3 ENTERTAINMENT, INC.

1725 Victory Blvd.
Glendale, CA 91201

PHONE .818-956-1337
FAX .818-241-0122
EMAIL .corporate@c3entertainment.com
WEB SITE .www.c3entertainment.com

TYPES	Documentaries - Features - Direct-to-Video/DVD - Made-for-TV/Cable Movies
DEALS	Warner Bros. Entertainment Inc.
DEVELOPMENT	Modern Outlaws - High Strides - Disorder in the Court - The New Three Stooges
CREDITS	The 75th Anniversary of the Three Stooges (NBC) - The Three Stooges (ABC MOW) - The Three Stooges Greatest Hits (ABC Variety Special)
SUBMISSION POLICY	Via email: query@c3entertainment.com

Earl Benjamin .President/CEO
Tavi B. Benjamin .VP, Business Affairs
Elizabeth Gibbar .Director, Finance & Operations
Ryan Jordan .Director, Development
Eric Lamond .Director, Marketing
Robert N. Benjamin .General Counsel

CAIRO/SIMPSON ENTERTAINMENT, INC.

10800 Wilkins Ave.
Los Angeles, CA 90024

PHONE .310-470-9309
EMAIL .cairosimpsonent@earthlink.net

TYPES	Features - Made-for-TV/Cable Movies - TV Series
CREDITS	The Jackie Gleason Story - The Pilot's Wife - Price of a Broken Heart - Perfect Body - What We Did That Night - Vanished Without a Trace - Her Deadly Rival - Twisted Desire - Lucky 7 - Infidelity

Judy Cairo .Producer/Partner
Michael Simpson .Producer/Partner

CALDERA/DE FANTI ENTERTAINMENT

PO Box 402, 1954 N. Hillhurst Ave.
Los Angeles, CA 90027

PHONE .323-906-9500
FAX .323-906-9555
EMAIL .ccaldera@earthlink.net

TYPES	Features - TV Series
DEVELOPMENT	A Little Lower Than the Angels - Giants - Diego - Locas - The Answer to My Prayer - Jym Titans
CREDITS	Selena - The Disappearance of Garcia Lorca - 3 Blind Mice

Carolyn Caldera-De Fanti .Producer
Jean-Luc De Fanti .Producer
Laura Espejo .Assistant

JOHN CALLEY PRODUCTIONS

c/o Sony Pictures Studios
10202 W. Washington Blvd., Lean Bldg., Ste. 119
Culver City, CA 90232

PHONE .310-244-7777
FAX .310-244-4070

TYPES	Features
DEALS	Sony Pictures Entertainment
DEVELOPMENT	The Da Vinci Code - Against All Enemies - Cruel & Unusual - The Company
POST PRODUCTION	Closer
SUBMISSION POLICY	No unsolicited submissions

John Calley .Chairman/CEO/Producer
Lisa Medwid .VP, Production
Erica Hagen .Executive Assistant to Mr. Calley

CALM DOWN PRODUCTIONS, INC.

1360 N. Crescent Heights Blvd., Ste. 3-B
Los Angeles, CA 90046

PHONE .323-650-4027
FAX .323-654-1104

TYPES	Features - TV Series
CREDITS	Stop with the Kicking - Grant & Lee - The Underworld - Work with Me - Deterrence (Feature) - Martini Shot
COMMENTS	San Francisco Stage Run Theater: *All Grown Up and No Place to Go*

Kevin Pollak .CEO
Lucy Webb .President/Producer
Amy Barnes .Creative Development
Kimberly Foster .Executive Assistant

*CALVIN PRODUCTIONS, INC.

928 Hilldale Ave.
West Hollywood, CA 90069

PHONE .310-360-6323
FAX .310-358-9420
EMAIL .carl@rumbaugh.com

TYPES	Features - Theater - TV Series
DEVELOPMENT	American Darlings
PRE-PRODUCTION	Social Grace
CREDITS	Raisin in the Sun (Theater)

Carl Rumbaugh .Producer

CAMDEN PICTURES
2265 Westwood Blvd., Ste. 479
Los Angeles, CA 90064
PHONE .310-458-3906
FAX .940-234-9234
EMAIL .producer@camdenpictures.com
WEB SITE .www.camdenpictures.com
TYPES Documentaries - Features
DEVELOPMENT Magic Matt - Chiller - You're Only Young Twice
PRODUCTION Taking a Shot: A Search for the American Dream on the Poker Tournament Trail (Feature Documentary)
CREDITS Men in Scoring Position

Susan Genard .Producer
Timothy Rhys .Screenwriter/Director

*CAMELOT ENTERTAINMENT GROUP, INC.
100 E. San Marcos Blvd., Ste. 400
San Marcos, CA 92069
PHONE .760-759-2320
FAX .760-759-2321/760-759-2324
EMAIL .bob@camelotfilms.com
SECOND EMAIL .hkdyal@camelotfilms.com
WEB SITE .www.camelotfilms.com
TYPES Features - Direct-to-Video/DVD - Made-for-TV/Cable Movies - Syndication - TV Series
DEALS Franchise Pictures, Inc.
DEVELOPMENT Victims - The Cauldron
CREDITS Saved - He is My Brother - One Down, Two to Go

Robert P. Atwell .Chairman/President/CEO
H. Kaye Dyal .President, Camelot Films, Inc.
Albert Golusin .CFO
Jane Olmstead .Director
Rounsevelle Schaum .Development
Susan Sanchez .Administrator
Patrick Winn .Administrator
Alice Sarazen .Administrator

CAMELOT PICTURES
8330 W. Third St.
Los Angeles, CA 90048
PHONE .323-651-2427/212-609-9393
FAX .323-651-2430/212-609-9394
WEB SITE .www.camelot-pictures.com
TYPES Features - Made-for-TV/Cable Movies - TV Series
DEVELOPMENT Rainbow's End - Saving Casanova - Larceny Is for Lovers - Black Friday - The Line - Leave 'em Laughing - Brothel - In the Pink - Marlene - Richard Petty - Chapel Hill
COMPLETED UNRELEASED Garden State - Home of Phobia
CREDITS Beyond Borders - S.W.A.T. - Nixon - Any Given Sunday - Art of War - Virgin Suicides - Witchblade - Assassinated: The Life of Kennedy and King - The Day Reagan Was Shot - Serving Sara - Freeway
SUBMISSION POLICY No unsolicited submissions
COMMENTS East Coast office: 451 Greenwich St., 2nd Fl., New York, NY 10013

Gary Gilbert .Partner
Dan Halsted .Partner
Philip Hall .No Title
Jordan Horowitz .No Title
Nick Confalone .No Title

CANDY HEART PRODUCTIONS, LLC
8840 Wilshire Blvd.
Beverly Hills, CA 90211
PHONE .310-358-3271
FAX .310-358-3272
EMAIL .chprods@aol.com
WEB SITE .www.candyheartproductions.com
TYPES Documentaries - Features - Made-for-TV/Cable Movies
DEVELOPMENT 65 Roses - What If? - Dead Tales - The Apprentice - When the Dead Whisper - Desolate - The Couple Gene
CREDITS Fast Women
COMMENTS Screamfest Horror Film Festival

Rachel Belofsky .President/Executive Producer

CANNELL STUDIOS
7083 Hollywood Blvd., Ste. 600
Hollywood, CA 90028
PHONE .323-465-5800
FAX .323-856-7390
WEB SITE .www.cannell.com
TYPES Features - Made-for-TV/Cable Movies - New Media - Syndication - TV Series
DEVELOPMENT Final Victim - A-Team - King Con - Terror.net - Greatest American Hero - Riding the Snake - 21 Jump Street - The Devil's Workshop - Wiseguy

Stephen J. Cannell .Chairman of the Board
Douglas S. Rosen .VP, Production
Daisy Marco .CFO
Jeannie Gravley .VP, Distribution
Frank Flanagan .Sales Agent
Kathy Ezso .Assistant to Mr. Cannell
Theresa Peoples .Assistant to Mr. Rosen

REUBEN CANNON & ASSOCIATES
5225 Wilshire Blvd., Ste. 526
Los Angeles, CA 90036
PHONE .323-939-3190
FAX .323-939-7793
EMAIL .reubcan@aol.com
TYPES Features - Made-for-TV/Cable Movies - TV Series
CREDITS Down in the Delta (Feature) - Get on the Bus (Feature) - Dancing in September (HBO) - Woman Thou Art Loosed - Love Don't Cost a Thing (Feature)

Reuben Cannon .Producer/Casting Director
Kim Williams .Casting Director

MAJ CANTON PRODUCTIONS
655 Oxford Ave.
Venice, CA 90291-4724
PHONE .310-823-1917
TYPES Made-for-TV/Cable Movies - TV Series - Reality TV
CREDITS Wife, Mother, Murderer - A Mother's Revenge
COMMENTS Author, *Complete Guide to TV Movies & Miniseries 1984-2003*

Maj Canton .Producer

CANVAS HOUSE FILMS

624 E. Cedar Ave., Ste. A
Burbank, CA 91501
PHONE 818-558-1904
EMAIL ....teemley@msn.com

TYPES	Features - Direct-to-Video/DVD - Made-for-TV/Cable Movies - TV Series
DEALS	Orly Adelson Productions - The Wolper Organization
DEVELOPMENT	The Wishing Map (Animated Series) - House of Seven Gables (Feature)
PRE-PRODUCTION	Notzilla (Feature)
CREDITS	Out of Time (Showtime) - Destiny - The Limited (Independent)

Mitch Teemley ....Producer
Elizabeth Gray ....Associate

CAPITAL ARTS ENTERTAINMENT

17941 Ventura Blvd., Ste. 205
Encino, CA 91316
PHONE 818-343-8950
WEB SITE ....www.capitalarts.com

TYPES	Features - Direct-to-Video/DVD - Made-for-TV/Cable Movies - TV Series
DEVELOPMENT	Mutha's Day - On the Twelfth Day of Christmas - The Dead Key
PRE-PRODUCTION	Reveille - Room Service
PRODUCTION	Happy Endings - The Devil's Rejects
POST PRODUCTION	Down in the Valley
CREDITS	Route 9 - Casper Meets Wendy - After the Storm - Time Cop 2 - All I Want - Beethoven's 5th - The Prince and Me - The Cookout

Mike Elliott ....President
Rob Kerchner ....President
Lisa Gooding ....Development
Joe Genier ....Production
Jan Kikumoto ....Post Production
Karen Gorodetzky ....Production Executive
Kristen Morton ....Production Executive
Paul Di Franco ....Music Supervisor
Erin Royer ....Assistant

CAPO PRODUCTIONS

1726 Kelton Ave.
Los Angeles, CA 90024
PHONE 310-477-4234
EMAIL ....capoprod@earthlink.net

TYPES	Documentaries - Features - Made-for-TV/Cable Movies - TV Series
DEVELOPMENT	Shine of Rainbows - Press Club
PRE-PRODUCTION	Partition
PRODUCTION	The History and Evolution of American Harmony (Documentary)
CREDITS	Hot Spot - Other Voices - Just a Little Harmless Sex

Deborah Capogrosso ....President

ANNE CARLUCCI PRODUCTIONS

9200 Sunset Blvd., Penthouse 20
Los Angeles, CA 90069
PHONE 310-550-9545
FAX 310-550-8471
EMAIL ....acprod@sbcglobal.net

TYPES	Features - Made-for-TV/Cable Movies - TV Series
DEVELOPMENT	Female Intelligence (CBS) - Out of Control (Lifetime) - Debbie Smith Project (Court TV) - The Jurors (Court TV) - Don't Look Back (Lifetime) - Secret Lives of Second Wives (Lifetime) - Piece of Cake (ABC Family)
PRE-PRODUCTION	False Pretenses (Lifetime) - Twist (Feature/JB Media)
CREDITS	Donato and Daughter - Sex & Mrs. X - The Soul Collector - When Husbands Cheat - Dangerous Evidence - Sublet - Not Our Son - Unforgivable - Out of Sync - Wicked Minds - Guilt by Association - Dangerous Child - Going for Broke

Anne Carlucci ....Executive Producer
Robyn Snyder ....Director, Development

CARRIE PRODUCTIONS, INC.

c/o Danny Glover
2625 Alcatraz Ave., Ste. 243
Berkeley, CA 94705
PHONE 510-450-2500
FAX 510-450-2506

TYPES	Features - TV Series
CREDITS	Buffalo Soldiers - Freedom Song - America's Dream - Just a Dream
SUBMISSION POLICY	No unsolicited submissions
COMMENTS	Affiliated with Robey Theatre Company

Danny Glover ....Executive Producer
Sarisa Middelton ....VP
Karen Bolt ....Development

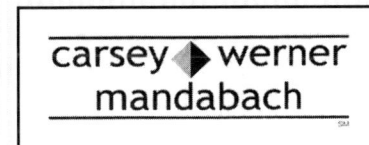

carsey werner mandabach

CARSEY-WERNER-MANDABACH

4024 Radford Ave., Bldg. 3
Studio City, CA 91604
PHONE 818-655-5598
FAX 818-655-6236
WEB SITE ....www.cwm.com

TYPES	Animation - Features - Syndication - TV Series
DEALS	Paramount Pictures-Motion Picture Group
PRODUCTION	Good Girls Don't
CREDITS	Whoopi - That 70's Show - Grounded for Life - 3rd Rock from the Sun - Roseanne - The Cosby Show

Marcy Carsey ....Partner/Executive Producer
Tom Werner ....Partner/Executive Producer
Caryn Mandabach ....Partner/Executive Producer
Bob Dubelko ....Co-President/COO
Dirk W. van de Bunt ....Co-President/COO
Matt Berenson ....President, CWM Films
Herb Lazarus ....President, CWM International
Rochelle Gerson ....Executive VP, Business Affairs
James Kraus .....Executive VP/General Sales Manager, CWM Distribution
Bret Sarnoff ....Executive VP, Finance/CFO
Norma Acland ....Sr. VP, Legal Affairs
James Anderson ....Sr. VP, Publicity/Public Relations
Kathy Busby ....Sr. VP/Head, Development
Gabriela Marino-Park ....VP, Production Finance

(Continued)

CARSEY-WERNER-MANDABACH (Continued)

Barron Postmus . . . VP, Marketing/Creative Services
Diann Shaw . . . VP, Publicity/Public Relations
Rick Pagano . . . VP, Casting
Michael Shear . . . CWM Creative Executive

CARSON SIGNATURE FILMS, INC.

10 Universal City Plaza, 20th Fl.
Universal City, CA 91608
PHONE . . . 818-753-2333
FAX . . . 818-753-2332
EMAIL . . . carson@carsonsignaturefilms.com

TYPES	Documentaries - Features - Direct-to-Video/DVD - Made-for-TV/Cable Movies - TV Series - Reality TV
DEVELOPMENT	Blue Mountain - Eyes Only
CREDITS	In the Company of Spies

Beaux Carson . . . President
Darby Connor . . . Sr. VP

THE THOMAS CARTER COMPANY

3000 W. Olympic Blvd.
Santa Monica, CA 90404
PHONE . . . 310-264-3990
FAX . . . 310-264-3991
EMAIL . . . tcc.film@verizon.net

TYPES	Features - Made-for-TV/Cable Movies - TV Series
CREDITS	Features: Coach Carter - Save the Last Dance - Metro - Swing Kids; Cable Movies: Don King: Only in America - Five Desperate Hours - The Uninvited - Trapped in a Purple Haze - Ali: An American Hero

Thomas Carter . . . President
Jennifer Buchwald . . . Manager, Development

CARTOON NETWORK

1050 Techwood Dr. NW
Atlanta, GA 30318
PHONE . . . 404-885-2263
FAX . . . 404-885-4312
WEB SITE . . . www.cartoonnetwork.com

TYPES	Animation - Features - TV Series
PRODUCTION	Hi Hi Puffy Ami Yumi - Juniper Lee - Samurai Jack - The Powerpuff Girls - The Grim Adventures of Billy and Mandy - Star Wars: Clone Wars - Johnny Bravo - Megas XLR - Foster's Home for Imaginary Friends
CREDITS	The Powerpuff Girls Movie

Jim Samples Executive VP/General Manager, Cartoon Network Worldwide
Bob Higgins . . . Sr. VP, Programming & Development
Mark Norman . . . Sr. VP, Business Operations
Michael Ouweleen . . . Sr. VP, Development & Creative Direction
Sam Register . . . Sr. VP, Original Animation
Alice Cahn . . . VP, Development
Terry Kalagian . . . VP, Programming
Brian Miller . . . VP/General Manager, Cartoon Network Studios

CARUSO VISUAL PRODUCTIONS, INC.

1951 Dundas St. East
Toronto, ON M4L 1M7 Canada
PHONE . . . 416-918-3295
EMAIL . . . carusofilms@sympatico.ca
WEB SITE . . . www.carusofilms.com

TYPES	Documentaries - Features - TV Series
DEVELOPMENT	Obsessions (Series) - Be Careful What You Wish For (TV Series) - Club Utopia (Feature)
PRODUCTION	Into the Heat (Feature)
COMPLETED UNRELEASED	Shut Up You Separatist (Feature) - Bitter Circle (Feature) - Unknown Celebrities
CREDITS	No Angel (Feature) - Love Letters: A Romantic Trilogy (Feature) - Bitter Circle (Feature) - Unknown Celebrities (Documentary) - Night Crawlers (Short Film)

Frank A. Caruso . . . CEO/Producer/Director/Writer
David Lees . . . Producer/Director/Writer
John Miller . . . Executive Producer
Andrew Star . . . Executive Producer
James Murray . . . Head Writer
Mandy Lee Jones . . . Writer
Mellisa Munroe . . . TV/Video Director

CASTLE ROCK ENTERTAINMENT

335 N. Maple Dr., Ste. 350
Beverly Hills, CA 90210-3867
PHONE . . . 310-285-2300
FAX . . . 310-285-2345
WEB SITE . . . www.castle-rock.com

TYPES	Features - TV Series
DEALS	Warner Bros. Entertainment Inc.
PRODUCTION	Miss Congeniality 2
POST PRODUCTION	Polar Express
CREDITS	Before Sunset - Miss Congeniality - A Few Good Men - City Slickers - In the Line of Fire - Misery - The Shawshank Redemption - Seinfeld - The Green Mile - When Harry Met Sally
COMMENTS	Cable

Rob Reiner . . . Producer/Director
Martin Shafer . . . Chairman/CEO
Liz Glotzer . . . President, Castle Rock Pictures
Andrew Scheinman . . . Producer/Director
Jessica Roddy . . . Sr. VP, Business Affairs
David Blasucci . . . Director, Publicity Services
Gaylyn Fraiche . . . Director, Development
Ashley Kingsley . . . Manager, Administration

CATALAND FILMS
450 W. 15th St., Ste. 602
New York, NY 10011
PHONE .212-989-5995
FAX .212-989-5505
EMAIL .richp@cataland.com
WEB SITE .www.cataland.com
TYPES Animation - Documentaries - Features - TV Series
DEVELOPMENT Time Riders - Welcome to Mayfield - Greek Road - Broken Lizard's Beer Fest
POST PRODUCTION On the One
CREDITS Club Dread - Super Troopers - Puddle Cruiser - Way Off Broadway

Richard Perello .No Title
Chloe O'Connor .No Title
Robin Reid .No Title

CATAPULT FILMS
832 Third St., Ste. 303
Santa Monica, CA 90403-1155
PHONE .310-395-1470
FAX .310-401-0122
TYPES Features - TV Series
DEVELOPMENT The Inventors of Sex - Undercover Lover - Outerberlin - Corner
CREDITS Inferno - Bride of the Wind (Paramount Classics) - Love Object (Content/Pressman Films)

Lawrence Levy .Producer
Lisa Josefsberg .Producer

CATCH 23 ENTERTAINMENT, INC.
301 N. Canon Dr., Ste. 207
Beverly Hills, CA 90210
PHONE .310-273-2734
FAX .310-273-1033
EMAIL .firstinitiallastname@catch23ent.com
TYPES Features - Made-for-TV/Cable Movies - TV Series
CREDITS One Hour Photo

Robert B. Sturm .Chairman

CATCHLIGHT FILMS
4216-3/4 Glencoe Ave.
Marina del Rey, CA 90292
PHONE .310-827-3797
FAX .310-827-2533
EMAIL .mailbox@catchlightfilms.com
WEB SITE .www.catchlightfilms.com
TYPES Commercials - Documentaries - Features
DEVELOPMENT Black Tulip - Lesser of 3 Evils - 4D - Heart of the Beholder
POST PRODUCTION Festival of the Pacific - Songs for the City of Angels
COMPLETED UNRELEASED Break a Leg - Red, White & Buddha
CREDITS Amy's Orgasm - World Festival of Sacred Music: The Americas - In the Weeds

Jeanette Volturno .Producer
Rick Osako .Production Manager

CATES/DOTY PRODUCTIONS
10920 Wilshire Blvd., Ste. 830
Los Angeles, CA 90024
PHONE .310-208-2134
TYPES Features - TV Series
CREDITS Absolute Strangers - Call Me Anna - The Academy Awards® - Tom Clancy's Net Force - Innocent Victims - Confessions: Two Faces of Evil

Gilbert Cates .Producer/Director
Dennis Doty .Producer
Peggy Griffin .Associate Producer

CATFISH PRODUCTIONS
23852 Pacific Coast Hwy., Ste. 313
Malibu, CA 90265
PHONE .310-456-6175
FAX .310-456-5276
EMAIL .catfishprods@aol.com
TYPES Animation - Commercials - Documentaries - Features - Direct-to-Video/DVD - Made-for-TV/Cable Movies - Music Videos - New Media - TV Series
DEVELOPMENT Walk the Line (aka Cash) - Luther - The Back Up Guy - Waking Up Driving - Counters - The Handyman - Jello - Jury of Her Peers
CREDITS Marriage of Convenience - The Stars Fell on Henrietta - The Absolute Truth - A Passion for Justice - Fanny Kemball - Blackout - Dr. Quinn (The Movie) - Murder in the Mirror - Submerged
SUBMISSION POLICY No unsolicited screenplays or books; One-page queries only; Finished films OK

James Keach .Actor/Producer/Director
Jane Seymour .Actress/Producer
Richard Keith .Development
Debra Pearl .Development

CBS ENTERTAINMENT
7800 Beverly Blvd.
Los Angeles, CA 90036-2188
PHONE .323-575-2345/212-975-4321
WEB SITE .www.cbs.com
TYPES Made-for-TV/Cable Movies - TV Series - Reality TV
COMMENTS East Coast office: 51 W. 52nd St., 6th Fl., New York, NY 10019

Leslie Moonves .Co-President/Co-COO, Viacom Entertainment Group
Nancy Tellem .President, CBS Entertainment
Kelly Kahl .Executive VP, Program Planning & Scheduling
Nina Tassler .Executive VP, Drama Series Development
Bela Bajaria .Sr. VP, Movies & Miniseries
Deborah Barak .Sr. VP, Business Affairs
Barbara Bloom .Sr. VP, Daytime Programs
Chris Ender .Sr. VP, Communications
Peter Golden .Sr. VP, Talent & Casting
David A. Katz .Sr. VP, Strategic Planning & Interactive Ventures
Jim McKairnes .Sr. VP, Program Planning & Scheduling
Laverne McKinnon .Sr. VP, Drama Development
Mitchell R. Semel .Sr. VP, Programming, East Coast
David Stapf .Sr. VP, Current Programs
Eric Steinberg .Sr. VP, West Coast Research

(Continued)

CBS ENTERTAINMENT (Continued)

Jack Sussman . . . . Sr. VP, Specials
Wendi Trilling . . . . Sr. VP, Comedy Series Development
Nancy Carr . . . . VP, Communications
Lucy Cavallo . . . . VP, Casting
Francis Cavanaugh . . . . VP, Photography, West Coast
Karen Church . . . . VP, Casting
Chris Davidson . . . . VP, Current Programs
Vincent P. Favale . . . . VP, Late Night Programs, East Coast
Amy Herzig . . . . VP, Casting, East Coast
Alexandra Jaffe . . . . VP, Current Programs
Dan Kupetz . . . . VP, Business Affairs
Sidney H. Lyons . . . . VP, Business Affairs, Longform Contracts & Acquisitions
Richard J. Mensing Jr. . . . . VP, Daytime Programs, East Coast
Roni Mueller . . . . VP, Business Affairs
Anne R. Nelson . . . . VP, Business Affairs
Fern Orenstein . . . . VP, Casting
Julie Pernworth . . . . VP, Comedy Development
Erica Rockler . . . . VP, Business Affairs
Jodi Roth . . . . VP, Specials
Sam Semon . . . . VP, Business Affairs
Gary Silver . . . . VP, Business Affairs
Joan Yee . . . . VP, Sponsor Programming, Movies & Miniseries
Robert Zotnowski . . . . VP, Current Programs
Cindy Badell-Slaughter . . . . Director, Music Operations
Carolyn Ceslik . . . . Director, Children's Programs, East Coast
Dorian Hannaway . . . . Director, Late Night Programming, West Coast
Edy Mendoza . . . . Director, Comedy Development
Greg Harris . . . . Director, Current Programs
Dick Kirschner . . . . Director, Current Programs
Alison Rinzel . . . . Director, Daytime Casting, East Coast
Margot Wain . . . . Director, Daytime Programs, West Coast
David Marko . . . . Director, Miniseries & Movies
Shannon O'Connor . . . . Director, Miniseries & Movies
Nancy Daniels . . . . Director, Alternative Series Development
Cynthia Brown . . . . Director, Business Affairs
Joel Goldberg . . . . Director, Business Affairs
Travis Pierson . . . . Director, Business Affairs
Christopher T. Ryan . . . . Director, Business Affairs
Roger Senders . . . . Director, Business Affairs

CBS NEWS

524 W. 57th St.
New York, NY 10019
PHONE 212-975-4321
WEB SITE . . . . www.cbsnews.com

Andrew Heyward . . . . President
John Frazee . . . . Sr. VP, News Services
Marcy McGinnis . . . . Sr. VP, News Coverage
Betsy West . . . . Sr. VP, Prime Time
Margery Baker-Riker . . . . VP, CBS News Productions
Sandra Genelius . . . . VP, Communications
Frank Governale . . . . VP, Operations
Janet Leissner . . . . VP/Bureau Manager, Washington
Linda Mason . . . . VP, Public Affairs
James McKenna . . . . VP, Finance & Administration
Harvey Nagler . . . . VP, News, CBS Radio
John Paxson . . . . VP, London Bureau Chief

CBS PRODUCTIONS

7800 Beverly Blvd.
Los Angeles, CA 90036-2188
PHONE 323-575-2345
WEB SITE . . . . www.cbs.com
TYPES Made-for-TV/Cable Movies - TV Series
CREDITS CSI - CSI: Miami - CSI: NY - Listen Up - Center of the Universe - dr. vegas - Without a Trace - Still Standing - King of Queens - Yes, Dear - Judging Amy - Joan of Arcadia - Cold Case

Maria Crenna . . . . Executive VP
Kevin Berg . . . . Sr. VP, Production
Brian Banks . . . . VP, Comedy Series
Leola Gorius . . . . VP, Talent & Guild Negotiations/Business Affairs
Michael Azzolino . . . . Director, Drama Series
Katherine Petrie . . . . Director, Movies for TV & Miniseries
Jim Donnelly . . . . Manager, Comedy
Leigh London . . . . Manager, Drama

CBS SPORTS

51 W. 52nd St.
New York, NY 10019
PHONE 212-975-4321
WEB SITE . . . . www.cbs.com
TYPES TV Series

Sean McManus . . . . President, CBS Sports
Tony Petitti . . . . Executive Producer, CBS Sports
Ken Aagaard . . . . Sr. VP, Operations & Production Services
Michael L. Aresco . . . . Sr. VP, Programming
Robert Correa . . . . Sr. VP, Programming
Arthur Harris . . . . VP, Broadcast Operations
Martin L. Kaye . . . . VP, Finance
LeslieAnne Wade . . . . VP, Communications

CECCHI GORI PICTURES

11990 San Vicente Blvd., Ste. 300
Los Angeles, CA 90049
PHONE 310-442-4777
FAX 310-442-9507
WEB SITE . . . . www.cecchigori.com
TYPES Features - TV Series
CREDITS Il Postino - The Star Maker - Mediterraneo - La Vita E'Bella (Life Is Beautiful) - Johnny Stecchino - Ciao Professore - Il Mio West - House of Cards - Seven - From Dusk Till Dawn - Man Trouble - The Blackout - Alexander
COMMENTS Motion picture development; Italian distribution/production

Gianni Nunnari . . . . President
Ludy Blasco . . . . CFO
Scott Coleman . . . . VP, Production
Craig J. Flores . . . . VP, Business & Legal Affairs

CENTAUR PRODUCTIONS

2811 Waverly Dr., Ste. 6
Los Angeles, CA 90039
PHONE 323-662-8877
WEB SITE . . . . www.godsexapplepie.com
TYPES Features
DEVELOPMENT The Experiment
CREDITS God, Sex & Apple Pie

Jerome Courshon . . . . Producer/Writer

CENTROPOLIS ENTERTAINMENT
1445 N. Stanley, 3rd Fl.
Los Angeles, CA 90046
PHONE 323-850-1212
FAX 323-850-1201
WEB SITE .....www.centropolis.com
TYPES Features
CREDITS Universal Soldier - StarGate - Independence Day - Godzilla - The Patriot - The Visitor - 13th Floor - The Day After Tomorrow
SUBMISSION POLICY No unsolicited submissions

Roland Emmerich .....Partner
Ute Emmerich .....Partner
Aaron Boyd .....Executive Assistant
Kirstin Winkler .....Assistant to Producer

CFP PRODUCTIONS
c/o Paramount Studios
5555 Melrose Ave., Lubitsch Bldg., Ste. 117
Los Angeles, CA 90038-3197
PHONE 323-956-8866/310-470-0845
FAX 310-470-0842
EMAIL .....cfpprod@aol.com
WEB SITE .....www.cfpproductions.com
TYPES Features
DEALS Paramount Pictures-Motion Picture Group
CREDITS Out-of-Towners - How to Lose a Guy in 10 Days

Christine Peters .....Producer
Bradford Smith .....President
Randy Tat .....Executive VP
Oliver Obst .....Director, Development
Adele Heydenrich .....Assistant
Frank Reina .....Assistant
Rob Stone .....Assistant

*CHAMELEON ENTERTAINMENT
1127 21st St., Ste. 2
Santa Monica, CA 90403
PHONE 310-829-7181/310-384-2711
FAX 310-829-2662/310-829-0660
EMAIL .....damon@chameleonfilms.com
SECOND EMAIL .....damon@chameleonent.com
TYPES Commercials - Music Videos - Reality TV
DEVELOPMENT MySpaceTV - Malibu Moms - Mascot - Life Makeover
CREDITS Taildaters (MTV) - Burned - Courage - Blind Date

Damon Harman .....CEO/Executive Producer
Jon Nixon .....VP, Production
Nathan Rotmenz .....VP, Post Production
Bob Gustafson .....Director, Development
Jennifer Kelley .....Manager, Womens Development
Todd Raderman .....Production Manager
Joan Vento-Hall .....Business Affairs

CHANCELLOR ENTERTAINMENT
10600 Holman Ave., Ste. 1
Los Angeles, CA 90024
PHONE 310-474-4521
FAX 310-470-9273
EMAIL .....chaentrpm@aol.com
TYPES Features - Direct-to-Video/DVD - Made-for-TV/Cable Movies - New Media - TV Series
DEVELOPMENT The Carmen Miranda Story - Sing Out - Untitled Ben Scantlin Project
CREDITS Idol Maker - The Razor's Edge - Letter to Three Wives - Smilin' Jack - Mama Dee's Den
COMMENTS Music and talent management

Robert P. Marcucci .....President/CEO
Ben Scantlin .....President, Production/Talent Manager
LaRissa Douglas .....Sr. VP, Talent & Development

CHANTICLEER FILMS
5914 Foothill Dr.
Los Angeles, CA 90068
PHONE 323-462-4705
FAX 323-462-1603
EMAIL .....antihil@aol.com
SECOND EMAIL .....yona@aol.com
TYPES Features - Documentaries - Animation - Made-for-TV/Cable Movies - TV Series
CREDITS Eddie's Million Dollar Bake-Off - Down Came a Black Bird - Tru Confessions - On the Edge - Directed by... - Lush Life

Jana Sue Memel .....President/Producer/Director
Hillary Anne Ripps .....VP, Production Administration/Producer

CHARLES BROS.
c/o Paramount Television
5555 Melrose Ave., Shulberg Bldg., Ste. 317
Los Angeles, CA 90038-3197
PHONE 323-956-5962
FAX 323-862-3407
TYPES TV Series
DEALS Paramount Television
CREDITS Cheers

Glen Charles .....Executive Producer
Les Charles .....Executive Producer

CHARLES FLOYD JOHNSON PRODUCTIONS
c/o Sunset Gower Studios
1438 N. Gower St., Bldg. 35, Ste. 451
Los Angeles, CA 90028-3197
PHONE 323-468-4520
FAX 323-468-4517
TYPES Documentaries - TV Series
DEALS Paramount Television
CREDITS The Rockford Files - Quantum Leap - Magnum P.I. - JAG - First Monday - Navy N.C.I.S.

Chas. Floyd Johnson .....Executive Producer
Anne Burford .....VP, Development
Debra Mayfield .....Assistant to Mr. Johnson
Austin Grady .....Second Assistant to Mr. Johnson

CHARTOFF PRODUCTIONS
1250 Sixth St., Ste. 101
Santa Monica, CA 90401
PHONE .310-319-1960
FAX .310-319-3469
TYPES Features - Made-for-TV/Cable Movies
DEVELOPMENT The Man Who Stole the Mona Lisa - Ender's Game - The Tutor
COMPLETED UNRELEASED In My Country
CREDITS Rocky Movies - Raging Bull - Straight Talk - The Right Stuff

Robert Chartoff .CEO
Lynn Hendee .President
Lori Imbler Vernon .Production Associate

PAYASO/CHECKMATE ENTERTAINMENT
100 Universal City Plaza, Bldg. 320, Ste. 1-D
Universal City, CA 91608
PHONE .818-733-1839/310-276-7458
FAX .818-733-1841
EMAIL .yvette@checkmatetalent.com
WEB SITE .www.checkmatestaffing.com
TYPES Features - Direct-to-Video/DVD - Made-for-TV/Cable Movies - TV Series
DEVELOPMENT Robbin Hoodz - Slob
PRE-PRODUCTION Carthief - The Original Latin Queens of Comedy - Shrinking Santa Fe
CREDITS The Original Latin Kings of Comedy

Scott Montoya .Producer
Yvette Yates .Development Executive/Producer

CHEERFUL PICTURES
1625 W. Bijou St.
Colorado Springs, CO 80904
PHONE .719-471-2605
EMAIL .cheerfulpictures@aol.com
TYPES Documentaries - Features - Direct-to-Video/DVD
DEVELOPMENT The Mermaid Latitudes - All Fall Down - Slipping Into Darkness
CREDITS The Summer Intern - Catherine's Grove - The Tramp Returns - Alano House - Video Travelogue Series: World on a String

Barry Hickey .President/CEO
Kevin Hickey .VP

CHEESEBURGER FILMS, INC.
1000 W. Washington, Ste. 541
Chicago, IL 60607
PHONE .312-226-2726
FAX .312-226-0511
EMAIL .info@cheeseburgerfilms.com
WEB SITE .www.cheeseburgerfilms.com
TYPES Commercials - Documentaries - Features - Direct-to-Video/DVD - Music Videos - Reality TV - TV Series
DEVELOPMENT The Bomb in the Suburbs - Party Animals - Where Da Party @?
PRE-PRODUCTION Gonzo - Rome
CREDITS One Shot - Dark - Great Lakes Experience (Documentary Feature)
COMMENTS Specializes in high-impact urban genre

Brad Wells .Executive Producer/CEO
John Trusk .Executive Creative Director
Jeffrey T. Brown .Director/Cinematographer
D.A. Bullock .Writer/Director
Samuel McQueen .Writer/Director
Ken Nelson .Writer/Director
Joe Williams .Cinematographer

CHERRY ROAD FILMS, LLC
1460 Fourth St., Ste. 212
Santa Monica, CA 90401
PHONE .310-458-6550
FAX .310-458-6510
EMAIL .info@cherryroadfilms.com
WEB SITE .www.cherryroadfilms.com
TYPES Features
DEALS Double Edge Entertainment - VOY Pictures - Warner Independent Pictures
DEVELOPMENT Money for Nothing - Manhattan Loverboy - Forget About it - Wild Blue - Down on the Farm - White Noise
PRE-PRODUCTION Southland Tales
POST PRODUCTION The L.A. Riots Spectacular
COMPLETED UNRELEASED Eulogy (Lions Gate) - Mail Order Bride (Summit)

Kendall Morgan .President/Co-Founder
Bo Hyde .CEO/Co-Founder
Kathleen Haase .President, Production
Tommaso Fiacchino .VP, Development
Mark Marabate .Development Assistant

CHESLER/PERLMUTTER PRODUCTIONS
15611 Ventura Blvd.
Encino, CA 91436
PHONE .818-808-0052/416-927-0016
FAX .818-808-0054/416-960-8447
EMAIL .cpproductions@chesperl.com
TYPES Features - Made-for-TV/Cable Movies - TV Series
PRE-PRODUCTION Animal Tails 2 - Public Enemies - Gruesome
CREDITS Animal Tails - PAX Mystery Movies - Hitchhiker - Welcome to Paradox - Bear with Me - Falling Through - Zebra Lounge - Tempo
COMMENTS Family entertainment; Toronto office: 129 Yorkville Ave., Ste. 200, Toronto, ON M5R 1C4 Canada

Lewis Chesler .Chairman/Executive Producer
David Perlmutter .Chairman/Executive Producer (Toronto)
Kevin Commins .Executive VP, Development
Rob Vaughn .Executive VP, Production
Hank McCann .VP, Talent
Charles Barratt .Director, Development

THE CHESTERFIELD FILM COMPANY
1351 Fourth St., Ste. 201
Santa Monica, CA 90401
PHONE .213-683-3977
EMAIL .info@chesterfield-co.com
WEB SITE .www.chesterfield-co.com
TYPES Features
DEALS Paramount Pictures-Motion Picture Group
DEVELOPMENT Smart People
CREDITS The Good Doctor - Black Circle Boys - Digging to China
COMMENTS Writer's Film Project Screenwriting Fellowship

Edward Rugoff .President
Amanda Parham .No Title
Adam Sledd .No Title
Sheri Tsukamoto .No Title

CHIARAMONTE FILMS, INC.
4330 Glencoe Ave., Ste. 4
Marina del Rey, CA 90292
PHONE 310-578-7363
FAX 310-578-1704
EMAIL . . . . . monte7117@comcast.net
TYPES Features - Syndication - TV Series
DEVELOPMENT The Perfect Candidate - Judge for a Day
PRE-PRODUCTION Ricardo del Rey
COMPLETED UNRELEASED Ex-Chronicles
CREDITS Twogether

Andrew Chiaramonte . . . . . Writer/Producer/Director

CHICAGOFILMS
101 5th Ave., 8th Fl.
New York, NY 10003
PHONE 212-645-3000
FAX 212-645-3014
TYPES Features - TV Series
CREDITS The Last Good Time - Parents - Gosford Park

Bob Balaban . . . . . Actor/Director/Producer
Kate Schumaecker . . . . . Director, Development

CHICK FLICKS
116 N. Robertson Blvd., Ste. 400
Los Angeles, CA 90048
PHONE 310-967-6541
FAX 310-854-0383
TYPES Features - Made-for-TV/Cable Movies
DEALS New Line Cinema
DEVELOPMENT Love Hurts - Bad Hair Day - Hurricane Season - Eleanor and Colette - Gridiron Girls - Stories I Couldn't Tell When I Was a Pastor - Elles Jump
PRE-PRODUCTION Harder They Come
POST PRODUCTION Heart of Summer - Unholy Ghosts (Hallmark Channel)
SUBMISSION POLICY Only through representation

Sara Risher . . . . . President
Rebecca Heller . . . . . Director, Development

CHIODO BROS. PRODUCTIONS, INC.
110 W. Providencia Ave.
Burbank, CA 91502
PHONE 818-842-5656
FAX 818-848-0891
EMAIL . . . . . klowns@chiodobros.com
WEB SITE . . . . . www.chiodobros.com
TYPES Animation - Documentaries - Features - Direct-to-Video/DVD - Made-for-TV/Cable Movies - New Media - Syndication - TV Series
DEVELOPMENT Washington/Burnes - Hutchington Square - Innards
PRODUCTION Team America (Paramount Pictures)
CREDITS Killer Klowns from Outer Space - The Crayon Box - The Amazing Live Sea Monkeys - Clay (Disney Channel)
COMMENTS Main title & stop motion animation on *Elf*

Stephen Chiodo . . . . . Director/Development
Edward Chiodo . . . . . Producer/Development
Charles Chiodo . . . . . Designer/Development
Paul Kemp . . . . . COO/Development

CHOTZEN/JENNER PRODUCTIONS
1608 N. Cahuenga Blvd., Ste. 381
Hollywood, CA 90028
PHONE 323-465-9877
FAX 323-460-6451
TYPES Features - Made-for-TV/Cable Movies - TV Series
DEVELOPMENT Love and Honor (MOW)
PRE-PRODUCTION Snapshots (Series)
CREDITS My Father's Shadow - The Rosa Parks Story - Lies He Told - Prison of Secrets - Matter of Justice - Murder in the Mirror

Yvonne Chotzen . . . . . Producer/Partner
William Jenner . . . . . Producer/Partner
Dominique Azusa . . . . . Development

CHRIS/ROSE PRODUCTIONS
3131 Torreyson Pl.
Los Angeles, CA 90046
PHONE 323-851-8772
FAX 323-851-0662
EMAIL . . . . . crprods@aol.com
TYPES Features - Made-for-TV/Cable Movies - TV Series
DEVELOPMENT Singing in the Comeback Choir - Caught on Tape (Lifetime) - An Accidental Friendship (Lifetime)
CREDITS Down in the Delta - Long Island Incident - Kingfish - The Crossing
SUBMISSION POLICY Only by agent or legal representative

Robert W. Christiansen . . . . . Executive Producer
Rick Rosenberg . . . . . Executive Producer

CHROMOSOME22 FILMS
31 Spinnaker St., Ste. 16
Marina del Rey, CA 90292
PHONE 310-823-4006
FAX 310-823-1696
EMAIL . . . . . chromosome22film@aol.com
TYPES Features - TV Series
DEVELOPMENT Hope Canyon - Wrong Route
PRE-PRODUCTION Hottie - Street Dreams
PRODUCTION Book Ends - The Taken
POST PRODUCTION Getting Played
CREDITS Destiny Turns on the Radio - Savoy - Black Circle Boys

Raquel Carreras . . . . . Producer/CEO
Ghost Kasen . . . . . Producer

CHUBBCO FILM CO.
1416 N. La Brea Ave.
Hollywood, CA 90028
PHONE 323-802-1886
FAX 310-451-4825
TYPES Features - Made-for-TV/Cable Movies
CREDITS To Sleep with Anger - Hoffa - The Crow - Eve's Bayou - Dark Blue - Pootie Tang
SUBMISSION POLICY No queries

Caldecot Chubb . . . . . Producer

CINE GRANDE ENTERTAINMENT

554 Norwich Dr.
Los Angeles, CA 90048
PHONE .310-358-2240
FAX .310-659-0071
TYPES Features - Made-for-TV/Cable Movies
CREDITS Sub Down - Talos the Mummy - New World Disorder - Point Men - The Ride - High Speed

Silvio Muraglia .Chairman/CEO
Luca Brenna .Development
Fiona Nottingham .Development

*CINE MOSAIC

9 Desbrosses St., 2nd Fl.
New York, NY 10013
PHONE .212-625-3797/212-625-3819
FAX .212-625-3571
EMAIL .ldp@cinemosaic.net
SECOND EMAIL .marcus@cinemosaic.net
TYPES Features - Made-for-TV/Cable Movies
DEALS HBO Films
DEVELOPMENT The Impressionist - Homebody Kabul - The Probable Future - The Bruce Lee Project - A Gesture Life - Culture Bandit
POST PRODUCTION Vanity Fair

Lydia Dean Pilcher .President/Producer
Ashley Rudden .Director, Development
Marcus Lansdell .Development Coordinator

CINEASTE GROUP, INC.

1248 11th St., Ste. B
Santa Monica, CA 90401
PHONE .310-395-1169
FAX .310-395-8291
EMAIL .cineaste@verizon.net
TYPES Features
DEVELOPMENT Two Thumbs Up - South of Sunset - You Must Remember This - American Woman - Hand of Fate
CREDITS Good Luck - Grim Prairie Tales

Andrew Kamrowski .Producer/President
Paul O'Lague .VP, Development

CINECITY PICTURES

1925 Century Park East, 5th Fl.
Los Angeles, CA 90067
PHONE .310-559-7410
FAX .310-559-7452
EMAIL .cinecity@cinecity.com
TYPES Features
CREDITS Bopha!

Lawrence Taubman .Producer
Stacy Katz .Director, Development

CINÉGROUPE

1010 Ste-Catherine East, 5th Fl.
Montréal, Quebec H2L 2G3 Canada
PHONE .514-849-5008
FAX .510-849-5001
WEB SITE .www.cinegroupe.com
TYPES Animation - Features - New Media - TV Series
PRODUCTION Chalie Jade
POST PRODUCTION Tripping the Rift
CREDITS P3K: Pinocchio 3000 - Tripping the Rift - 11 Somerset - Seriously Weird - Pig City - Galidor: Defenders of the Outer Dimension - Sagwa: The Chinese Siamese Cat - Mega Babies - Lion of Oz

Jacques Pettigrew .President/CEO (Montréal)
Michel Lemire .Executive VP/Creative Affairs (Montréal)
Marie-Christine Dufour .Executive VP, Distribution, Licensing & Marketing (Montréal)
Elaine Bigras .Coordinator, Distribution

CINEMA 21 GROUP

140 Butterfly Lane
Montecito, CA 93108
PHONE .805-565-5754
FAX .805-565-5795
WEB SITE .www.peterlance.com
TYPES Features - TV Series
CREDITS Blackjack - First Degree Burn - Missing Persons - The Stingray: Lethal Tactics of the Sole Survivor - 1000 Years for Revenge: International Terrorism and the FBI (The Untold Story) - The Riverman (Written by)
COMMENTS Cinema 21 Books

Peter Lance .Writer/Producer
Travis Payne .Co-Producer

CINEMA LIBRE STUDIO

8328 De Soto Ave.
Canoga Park, CA 91304
PHONE .818-349-8822
FAX .818-349-9922
EMAIL .info@cinemalibrestudio.com
WEB SITE .www.cinemalibrestudio.com
TYPES Documentaries - Features - Direct-to-Video/DVD
DEVELOPMENT Chain of Voices
PRE-PRODUCTION Mundo Mata - Sleeping on Stones - Soldier Child
PRODUCTION American Knees
POST PRODUCTION Heads N' Tailz - The Third Wish
CREDITS Uncovered: The War on Iraq - World Order (Somewhere in Africa) - Heavy Metal 2000 - St. Patrick's Day
SUBMISSION POLICY Query first via email
COMMENTS Distributor (US and International); Post production services for independent filmmakers

Philippe Diaz .Producer
Kindra Ruocco .Studio Operations/Project Analysis
Philippe Lenglet .International Sales
Beth Portello .Business Development
Rick Rosen .Legal/Business Affairs

CINEMA SEVEN PRODUCTIONS

c/o Carnegie Hall
154 W. 57th St., Ste. 112
New York, NY 10019
PHONE 212-315-1060/310-247-1444
FAX 212-315-1085/310-247-1477
EMAIL ....cin7prod@aol.com
TYPES Features
CREDITS Where Eagles Dare - Angel Heart - The Long Goodbye - Harper - Farewell, My Lovely - Equus - The Missouri Breaks
COMMENTS West Coast office: 144 S. Beverly Dr., Ste. 407, Beverly Hills, CA 90212; UK office: Pinewood Studios, Pinewood Rd., Iver Heath, Bucks SLO 0NH UK, phone: 44-1753-656-825

Elliott Kastner ....President
Dillon Kastner ....Producer (LA)
George Pappas ....Sr. VP
James Deyarmin ....VP, Business Affairs
Pasquale Botta ....Head, Production (NY)
Julius Ortiguero ....Head, Production (LA)
Emma Sinclair ....Head, Production (UK)

CINERGI PICTURES ENTERTAINMENT, INC.

2308 Broadway
Santa Monica, CA 90404-2916
PHONE 310-315-6000
FAX 310-828-0443
TYPES Features
CREDITS Die Hard: With a Vengeance - Evita - Tombstone

Andrew Vajna ....Chairman/CEO
Samuel Falconello ....Sr. VP, Finance/CFO
Beverly Cusack ....Controller
Gabriella Szegedi ....Assistant to Andrew Vajna
Elizabeth Papp ....Assistant to Samuel Falconello

CINETEL FILMS

8255 Sunset Blvd.
Los Angeles, CA 90046-2432
PHONE 323-654-4000
FAX 323-650-6400
TYPES Features - Direct-to-Video/DVD - Made-for-TV/Cable Movies - TV Series
DEVELOPMENT Story of My Life - Carnival - Beethoven Conspiracy
PRE-PRODUCTION Descent - Fire from Above - Caved In - Solar Strike - Heat Stroke
PRODUCTION Crash Landing - Cerberus
POST PRODUCTION Premonition - Subzero
COMPLETED UNRELEASED Devil Winds - Lost Treasure - I Accuse Momentum - Global Effect - Detonator - Snakehead Terror - Stingers
CREDITS Carried Away - Green Sails - A Rumor of Angels

Paul Hertzberg ....President/CEO
Lisa Hansen ....President, Production
Robert Caramanica ....CFO
Marcy Rubin ....Sr. VP, International Sales
Neal Elman ....VP, Creative Affairs
Vicki Sawyer ....VP, Production
Steve Gregeropoulous ....Business Affairs

CINEVIEW PRODUCTIONS, INC.

PO Box 2665
Hollywood, CA 90078
PHONE 323-255-5333
EMAIL ....lpbcineview@earthlink.net
WEB SITE ....www.dreammerchantstudios.com
TYPES Features - Direct-to-Video/DVD - Made-for-TV/Cable Movies - New Media
DEVELOPMENT Death Warmed Over
PRE-PRODUCTION Maximum Justice 2
PRODUCTION Indestructible
COMPLETED UNRELEASED Ginger's Rise
CREDITS Fatal Pursuit - Silent Fury - Thief & the Stripper - Maximum Justice - Flat Out - Secret Life of Jeffrey Dahmer - Margaritaville Malibu Open - Dark Force - Tomahawk - Rodrique: A Man & His Dog
COMMENTS Full-service production studio; Lighting grip, camera, production sound; Avid and Final Cut pro-editing systems

L.P. Brown III ....President/CEO
Jack Conroy ....Director/DP
Darryl Giors ....Studio Operations/Web Design/Avid Tech Support
Jeremy McCormick ....Administrative Assistant

CINEVILLE INTERNATIONAL, INC.

3400 Airport Ave.
Santa Monica, CA 90405
PHONE 310-397-7150
FAX 310-397-7155
EMAIL ....support@cineville.com
WEB SITE ....www.cineville.com
TYPES Features - Direct-to-Video/DVD
DEALS Universal Pictures International
DEVELOPMENT Buck - American - Deficit - The Gladstones
PRE-PRODUCTION Here and Hereafter
POST PRODUCTION Surviving Eden
CREDITS Gas Food Lodging - The Crew - Swimming with Sharks - Cafe Society - Hurlyburly - The Affair

Carl Colpaert ....Co-Principal
Christoph Henkel ....Co-Principal
Lee Caplin ....Partner
Lisa Larivee ....Production
Alessnadra Bizzarri ....Development
Madeline Dimaggio ....Development
Patricia Gomez-Peralta ....Development
Roy Thomasson ....Distribution
Brendan Maze ....Coordinator
Carla Olson ....Coordinator
Huston Miller ....Management
Adel Nur ....Management

CINNAMON PRODUCTIONS, INC.

19 Wild Rose Rd.
Westport, CT 06880
PHONE 203-221-0613
FAX 203-227-0840
EMAIL ....cinnaprods@aol.com
WEB SITE ....www.nativevideos.com
TYPES Commercials - Documentaries - Features - Made-for-TV/Cable Movies - Music Videos - TV Series
DEVELOPMENT Three Quarters Louie - Joplin: The Movie - Garbage World - The Waves
PRODUCTION As You Like It - Broken Treaty 3 - Stormy and the Whales - My Girlfriend's a Reptile
CREDITS Brainstorm - Broken Treaty at Battle Mountain - To Protect Mother Earth - Jeremy - Even If a Hundred Ogres... - Skezag

Joel L. Freedman ....Owner/Director/Producer
Alan Eisenberg ....Producer/Director

(Continued)

CINNAMON PRODUCTIONS, INC. (Continued)

John C. May . . . . .Producer
Alan H. Freedman . . . . .VP, Music
John Carnright . . . . .Art/Design
Lynne Otis . . . . .Director, Development
Denny Hammerton . . . . .Creative Affairs
Wendy Rothkopf . . . . .Creative Affairs/Producer
Gerald Goodness . . . . .Story Editor/Producer
Joan Prince . . . . .Office Manager

CIRCLE OF CONFUSION PRODUCTIONS

8548 Washington Blvd.
Culver City, CA 90232
PHONE 310-253-7777/718-275-1012
FAX 310-253-9065/718-997-0521
EMAIL . . . . .info@circleofconfusion.com
WEB SITE . . . . .www.circleofconfusion.com
TYPES — Animation - Features - New Media - TV Series
DEALS — Sony Pictures Entertainment
DEVELOPMENT — Bounty (Universal) - Fate of the Blade (Disney) - Zillion (Pandemonium) - Hammer of the Gods (New Regency) - The House at Awful End (Warner Bros.) - The Psycho (Universal) - Jinx (Universal) - Red (UA) - Crenshaw Boulevard (New Line)
COMMENTS — East Coast office: 107-23 71st Rd., Ste. 300, Forest Hills, NY 11375

Lawrence Mattis . . . . .Partner
David Alpert . . . . .Partner
David Engel . . . . .Partner
Jason Lust . . . . .Partner
Jesse Israel . . . . .Assistant
Bryan Millard . . . . .Assistant

CITY ENTERTAINMENT

266-1/2 S. Rexford Dr.
Beverly Hills, CA 90212
PHONE 310-273-3101
FAX 310-273-3676
TYPES — Animation - Documentaries - Features - Made-for-TV/Cable Movies - Syndication - TV Series
DEVELOPMENT — I Believe Jason Leopold (Showtime) - A Band of Angels (Paramount) - Exodus 1947 (ABC) - I'm with the Band - Broadway Joe (FX) - Howard Street - Fovever Barbie (A&E) - Paris 1919 (HBO) - Sam the Banana Man (Showtime) - The Madame C.J. Walker Story (HBO) - Women of Valour (Lifetime) - Papillon (Lion Rock) - The Outfit - U.S.A. - Strange Fruit
PRE-PRODUCTION — The Hoax (The Mark Gordon Company)
CREDITS — Dead Men Can't Dance - Introducing Dorothy Dandridge (HBO) - Dodson's Journey (CBS) - The Pentagon Papers (FX) - And Starring Pancho Villa as Himself (HBO)
SUBMISSION POLICY — No unsolicited material

Joshua D. Maurer . . . . .President/Executive Producer

CIVILIAN PICTURES

5225 Wilshire Blvd., Ste. 326
Los Angeles, CA 90036
PHONE 323-938-3220
FAX 323-938-3229
EMAIL . . . . .info@civilian.com
WEB SITE . . . . .www.civilian.com
TYPES — Features - New Media
CREDITS — American Movie

Barry Poltermann . . . . .President
Carrie Heckman . . . . .VP, Marketing
Wrye Martin . . . . .VP, Production
John Murphy . . . . .VP, Operations

CLARITY PICTURES, LLC

1107 Fair Oaks Ave., Ste. 155
South Pasadena, CA 91030
PHONE 310-226-7046
FAX 310-388-5846
EMAIL . . . . .info@claritypictures.net
WEB SITE . . . . .www.claritypictures.net
TYPES — Animation - Commercials - Documentaries - Features - Made-for-TV/Cable Movies - New Media - TV Series
DEVELOPMENT — Copying Beethoven - The Pale Horseman - Forever Quest
PRE-PRODUCTION — Blackbird Lake
PRODUCTION — Perfect Match (Lifetime)
CREDITS — 18 Shades of Dust - Love & Action in Chicago - Wish You Were Dead
SUBMISSION POLICY — Email query letter

David Basulto . . . . .President/Producer
Lorri Klein . . . . .VP, Production

DICK CLARK PRODUCTIONS, INC.

3003 W. Olive Ave.
Burbank, CA 91505-4590
PHONE 818-841-3003
FAX 818-567-4546
WEB SITE . . . . .www.dickclarkproductions.com
TYPES — Direct-to-Video/DVD - Made-for-TV/Cable Movies - Syndication - TV Series - Reality TV

Dick Clark . . . . .Chairman/CEO
Jules Haimovitz . . . . .Vice-Chairman
Francis La Maina . . . . .President/COO
Andrew E. Suser . . . . .Sr. VP, Business Affairs
Mike Richards . . . . .Sr. Development Executive/Producer
Nicole Raffanello . . . . .Director, Development, Alternative Series
Bill Simon . . . . .CFO/VP, Finance & Treasurer
R.A.C. Clark .Sr. VP, Production & Programming
Barry Adelman . . . . .Sr. VP, Creative Affairs
Brian Pope . . . . .VP, Business Affairs
Linda Stricklin-Gilbert .Director, Business Affairs & VP, Contract Administration

*CLASS IV PRODUCTIONS

c/o Warner Bros.
4000 Warner Blvd., Bldg. 138, Rm. 1201
Burbank, CA 91522
PHONE 818-954-2796
TYPES — TV Series
DEALS — Warner Bros. Television Production

Steve Pearlman . . . . .Producer
Andrew Plotkin . . . . .Executive VP, Creative Affairs

CLC PRODUCTIONS

1223 Wilshire Blvd., Ste. 404
Santa Monica, CA 90403
PHONE . . . 310-454-0664
FAX . . . 310-459-2889
WEB SITE . . . www.cathylee.com
TYPES — Features - Made-for-TV/Cable Movies - New Media - Reality TV - Syndication - TV Series
CREDITS — One Child - Let the Magic Begin: The Book - The Code - Touched - Orpheus Conspiracy

Cathy Lee Crosby . . . CEO
Susan Roberts . . . President
Brooke Channon . . . VP, Development
Robbyn Benjamin . . . Director, Development
Curt Abramson . . . CPA
Steve Breimer . . . Business Affairs

CLEAN BREAK PRODUCTIONS

14046 Aubrey Rd.
Beverly Hills, CA 90210
PHONE . . . 818-995-1221
FAX . . . 818-995-0089
WEB SITE . . . www.tomarnoldonline.com
TYPES — Features - TV Series
CREDITS — The Tom Show

Tom Arnold . . . President/Producer
Laura Kahwaji . . . Assistant/Production Manger

*CLEAR PICTURES ENTERTAINMENT INC.

12400 Ventura Blvd., Ste. 306
Studio City, CA 91604
PHONE . . . 818-980-5460
FAX . . . 818-980-4716
EMAIL . . . elizfowler@aol.com
TYPES — Features - Made-for-TV/Cable Movies - TV Series
DEVELOPMENT — Blood Trail - Half-Life - Nice Girls Don't Get the Corner Office
CREDITS — Devil's Knot (USA Network) - Frontera Street (Lifetime Television)
COMMENTS — A Division of Elizabeth Fowler Management

Elizabeth Fowler . . . President
Paula Smith . . . CFO/Executive VP, Business Development
Jenny Rankin . . . Assistant

PATRICIA CLIFFORD PRODUCTIONS

PO Box 1166
Malibu, CA 90265
PHONE . . . 310-317-1195
FAX . . . 310-317-1485
TYPES — Features - Made-for-TV/Cable Movies - TV Series
CREDITS — Secret Life of Zoey - Hysteria: The Def Leppard Story - Warden of Red Rock - To Dance with the White Dog - A Husband, a Wife & a Lover - The Elizabeth Smart Story - Pop Rocks
SUBMISSION POLICY — No unsolicited material

Patricia Clifford . . . Producer

CLOUD PRODUCTIONS/THE OLEN COMPANY

7 Corporate Plaza
Newport Beach, CA 92660
PHONE . . . 949-719-7279/949-644-OLEN
FAX . . . 949-719-7250
EMAIL . . . cloud18@aol.com
WEB SITE . . . www.cloudentertainment.com
TYPES — Features - TV Series - Direct-to-Video/DVD - Documentaries
DEALS — StudioCanal (U.S.)
DEVELOPMENT — The Bull - Tolstoy - Vegas Grand - Hitler's Olympics - Shoplifting School
PRODUCTION — Elementary, My Dear Rasputin
CREDITS — Ice Castles 1&2 - Walking the Edge - House of Terror - Midnight in St. Petersburg
COMMENTS — Co-production deals with MosFilm Studios/Russia and StudioCanal Plus

S. Rodger Olenicoff . . . President/Producer
Gary Thompson . . . VP, Development
S. Goncharoff . . . VP, Production
Lynn Holly Johnson . . . VP, Creative Affairs
Volf Vartanian . . . Head, Moscow Office

*CLOUDBREAK PRODUCTIONS, INC.

PO Box 491817
Los Angeles, CA 90049
PHONE . . . 310-451-7233
FAX . . . 310-394-0244
EMAIL . . . charlie@cloudbreakproductions.com
SECOND EMAIL . . . israel@cloudbreakproductions.com
WEB SITE . . . www.cloudbreakproductions.com
TYPES — Commercials - Documentaries - Features - Made-for-TV/Cable Movies - Music Videos - Reality TV - TV Series
DEVELOPMENT — Intellectual Property

Charlie McDowell . . . President/CEO
Alex Israel . . . VP/CFO
Mary Steenburgen . . . Advisor
Ted Danson . . . Advisor

CMT: COUNTRY MUSIC TELEVISION

330 Commerce St.
Nashville, TN 37201
PHONE . . . 615-335-8400
WEB SITE . . . www.cmt.com
TYPES — Music Videos - TV Series
CREDITS — CMT Most Wanted Live - Top 20 Countdown - Inside Fame - CMT Total Release - 100 Greatest Songs of Country Music - Controversy - Cowboy U - 40 Greatest Men of Country Music - 40 Greatest Women of Country Music

Judith McGrath . . . Chairman/CEO, MTV Networks
Brian Philips . . . Sr. VP/General Manager
Jama Bowen . . . VP, Press
Martin Clayton . . . VP/General Manager, CMT.com
James Hitchcock . . . VP, Creative & Marketing
Chris Parr . . . VP, Music & Talent
Lewis Bogach . . . Director, Program Development & Production
Sarah Brock . . . Director, Program Development & Production
John C. Feld . . . Director, Program Development & Production
Melanie Moreau . . . Director, Development

*CNBC
Global Headquarters
900 Sylvan Ave.
Englewood Cliff, NJ 07632
PHONE 201-735-2622/818-840-3214
FAX 201-585-6244
WEB SITE .... www.nbcumv.com/cnbc
TYPES TV Series
COMMENTS West Coast office: 3000 Alameda Ave., Ste. C296, Burbank, CA 91523-0001

Pamela Thomas-Graham .... President/CEO, CNBC
Richard Cotton .... President/Managing Director, CNBC Europe
David M. Zaslav .... President, NBC Universal Cable
Bridget Baker .... Sr. VP, Cable Distribution, NBC Universal Cable
David Friend .... Sr. VP, CNBC Business News
Mark Hotz .... Sr. VP, Marketing, NBC Universal Cable
Henry Ahn .... VP, Affiliate Sales, NBC Universal Cable
Brian Hunt .... VP, Affiliate Ad Sales, Promotions & National Accounts, NBC Universal Cable
Robert Meyers .... General Manager, CNBC Enterprises

COBBLESTONE FILMS
PO Box 34370
Los Angeles, CA 90034
PHONE 310-404-5959
EMAIL .... cstonefilms@aol.com
TYPES Features - Made-for-TV/Cable Movies - TV Series
DEVELOPMENT Wings of an Angel
CREDITS One Against the Wind - Dalva
SUBMISSION POLICY Query letters and submissions by email only

Ben Adler .... Producer
Jacqui Adler .... Producer

MARTIN B. COHEN PRODUCTIONS
9962 Durant Dr.
Beverly Hills, CA 90212
PHONE 310-552-2958
FAX 310-277-5031
TYPES Features
DEVELOPMENT Turn a Blind Eye - The Third Secret - Yankee Mandarin - Christine

Martin B. Cohen .... Producer/Director
Phillip B. Gittelman .... Executive VP, Creative Development
Shannon Brennan .... Creative Executive
Amie Vines .... Development Executive

COLISEUM PICTURES CORPORATION
5073 Avenida Hacienda
Tarzana, CA 91356-4222
PHONE 818-881-1515
FAX 818-881-7977
EMAIL .... submissions@coliseumpictures.com
WEB SITE .... www.coliseumpictures.com
TYPES Animation - Features - Made-for-TV/Cable Movies - TV Series
DEVELOPMENT Fast Track - Atmosphere

Robert Kesler .... Producer
Robin Lombardo .... Producer
Cheryl Campbell .... Assistant
Noah Hall .... Assistant

COLLABORATIVE ARTISTS
445 S. Beverly Dr., Ste. 100
Beverly Hills, CA 90212
PHONE 310-274-4800
FAX 310-274-4803
EMAIL .... collaborative@sbcglobal.net
WEB SITE .... www.collaborativeartists.com
TYPES Features - Made-for-TV/Cable Movies - Reality TV - Syndication - TV Series
CREDITS The Season: Red Storm Rising
COMMENTS Specials

Steve Leon .... President
Courtland Walker .... Manager, Program Development

COLLEEN CAMP PRODUCTIONS
421 S. Beverly Dr.
Beverly Hills, CA 90212
PHONE 310-282-8662
FAX 310-282-8655
EMAIL .... colleen@triplecprods.com
SECOND EMAIL .... darin@triplecprods.com
TYPES Features - TV Series
DEVELOPMENT Pre-Nup - Lady Gold - The Alibi Club - Karma - The War Magician - Napoleon
PRE-PRODUCTION Parent Wars
CREDITS An American Rhapsody - HBO Creature Features

Colleen Camp .... Producer (colleen@triplecprods.com)
Darin Pfeiffer .... Creative Executive (darin@triplecprods.com)
Ahmet Elez .... Assistant
Brett Sills .... Assistant

THE COLLETON COMPANY
137 N. Larchmont Blvd., Ste. 457
Los Angeles, CA 90004
PHONE 323-466-0770/212-673-0916
FAX 323-466-1035
TYPES Features - Made-for-TV/Cable Movies - TV Series
DEVELOPMENT Present Value - Pledged - Ferry Tales
PRE-PRODUCTION The Painted Veil
CREDITS Renaissance Man - Riding in Cars with Boys - Live from Baghdad

Sara Colleton .... President
Rene Smallwood .... Assistant to Sara Colleton

COLOMBY FILMS
2110 Main St., Ste. 302
Santa Monica, CA 90405
PHONE 310-399-8881
FAX 310-392-1323
WEB SITE .... www.colombyfilms.com
TYPES Features - Made-for-TV/Cable Movies - TV Series
DEVELOPMENT Monk (Feature) - Blue Monday (Feature)
CREDITS Body Shots (New Line) - Breakdown - One Good Cop

Harry Colomby .... No Title
Cam Roberts .... Development/Acquistions

COLOSSAL ENTERTAINMENT
1261 N. Laurel Ave., Ste. 15
Los Angeles, CA 90046
PHONE .323-656-6647
EMAIL .clsslent@aol.com
TYPES Animation - Features - Made-for-TV/Cable Movies - TV Series
DEVELOPMENT Rich Deceiver (Fox 2000, Feature) - Tracing Iris - Party Girls (Animated Series) - Henry and Ella - The Condemned - Learning Curves
CREDITS The Call of the Wild - Anya's Bell

Graham Ludlow .Producer/Writer
John Bonneau .VP, Development & Production
Art Hamilton .Assistant

COLUMBIA PICTURES
A Sony Pictures Entertainment Company
10202 W. Washington Blvd.
Culver City, CA 90232
PHONE .310-244-4000
FAX .310-244-2626
WEB SITE .www.spe.sony.com
TYPES Features
COMMENTS Includes Columbia TriStar Motion Picture Group; See also Sony Pictures

Amy Pascal .Chairman, Motion Picture Group, SPE
Ben Feingold .President, CTMPG, CTHE, DVD Distribution
Geoff Ammer .President, CTMPG Worldwide Marketing
Gareth Wigan .Vice Chairman, CTMPG
Bob Osher .COO, CPMPG
Gary Martin .President, Columbia Production Administration & SPS Operations
Doug Belgrad .Co-President, Production
Matt Tolmach .Co-President, Production
Lia Vollack .President, Worldwide Music
Amy Baer .Executive VP, Production
Robert Geary .Executive VP, Business Affairs & Operations
Andrea Giannetti .Executive VP, Production
James Honore .Executive VP, Post Production
Lori Furie .Sr. VP, Production
Jon Gibson .Sr. VP, Business Affairs
John Levy .Sr. VP, Business Affairs
Pilar McCurry .Sr. VP, Music Creative Affairs
Russ Paris .Sr. VP, Post Production
Raul Perez .Sr. VP, Music Administration
Mark Wyman .Sr. VP, Business Affairs
Ray Zimmerman .Sr. VP, Production Administration
Pete Corral .VP, Production Administration
Mark Horowitz .VP, Business Affairs Administration
Donald Kennedy .VP, Music Licensing
Larry Kohorn .VP, Music Business Affairs
Pam Kunath .VP, Business Affairs, CTMPG
Kathy McDermott .VP, Production Administration
Karen Moy .VP, Story Department
Rachel O' Connor .VP, Production
Thomas Stack .VP, Business Affairs Contract Administration
Rita Zakrzewski .VP, Music Publishing

COMEDY ARTS STUDIOS
2500 Broadway, Ste. 400
Santa Monica, CA 90404
PHONE .310-382-3000
TYPES TV Series
DEALS HBO Independent Productions
CREDITS Everybody Loves Raymond - The Mind of the Marrried Man - US Comedy Arts Festival

Stu Smiley .Owner/Executive Producer
Cameron Burr .Director, Development
Lisa Doty .Development Executive
Townsend Miller-Jones .Story Editor

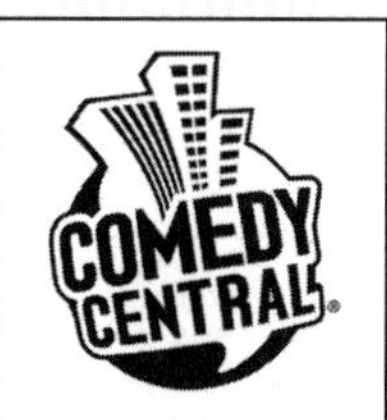

COMEDY CENTRAL
1775 Broadway, 10th Fl.
New York, NY 10019
PHONE .212-767-8600/310-407-4700
FAX .212-767-8592 (Press)/310-407-4797
WEB SITE .www.comedycentral.com
TYPES Reality TV - TV Series
CREDITS Crossballs - The Graham Norton Effect - Crank Yankers - Insomniac with Dave Attell - Reno 911 - Tough Crowd with Colin Quinn - Chappelle's Show - The Daily Show with Jon Stewart - South Park - The Man Show
COMMENTS West Coast office: 2049 Century Park East, Ste. 4170, Los Angeles, CA 90067

Doug Herzog .President/CEO
Bob Burger .CIO
Chris Pergola .CFO
Hank Close .Executive VP, Ad Sales
Tony Fox .Executive VP, Corporate Communications
Lauren Corrao .Sr. VP, Original Programming/Head, Development
Kathryn Mitchell .Sr. VP, Programming & Development
Cathy Tankosic .Sr. VP, Marketing
Joella West .Sr. VP, Business & Legal Affairs/General Counsel
Steve Albani .VP, Corporate Communications
Barry Blyn .VP, Programming Research
Zoe Friedman .VP, Current Programming, West Coast
Genise Jackson .VP, Business & Legal Affairs
Debbie Kirsh .VP, Operations, Production
Beth Lewand .VP, Digital Media
Holly Lim .VP, Enterprises & Corporate Strategy
Gary Mann .VP, Development, West Coast
Patty Newberger .VP, Comedy Central Films
Elizabeth Porter .VP, Talent & Events
Jim Sharp .VP, Development & Original Programming, West Coast
Robert Stein .VP, Production
Lou Wallach .VP, Development & Original Programming, East Coast
Jessi Klein .Director, Development, East Coast
Dave Koga .Director, Development, West Coast
Aaron Rothman .Director, Development, East Coast
Lee Barden .Controller
Dan Powell .Manager, Development, East Coast
Margaret Yuspa .Manager, Development, West Coast
William Oh .Counsel, Business Affairs

COMPANY FILMS
2629 Main St., Ste. 167
Santa Monica, CA 90405
PHONE . . . 310-399-2500
FAX . . . 310-399-2583
WEB SITE . . . www.companyfilms.com
TYPES Features
DEVELOPMENT Hunger - Napoleon - Saint Julian
PRODUCTION Echo
SUBMISSION POLICY No unsolicited material

Stephen Hamel . . . Producer
Frederika Wegman . . . Assistant

THE CON
76 Mercer St., 4th Fl.
New York, NY 10012
PHONE . . . 212-219-7617
FAX . . . 212-941-8075
EMAIL . . . contact@thecon.com
WEB SITE . . . www.thecon.com
TYPES Features - New Media - TV Series
DEVELOPMENT TV: The Instant Show - Fester - Craft - Brain Farts - The Adam Roth Show - Alpha Beta Geek - Untitled Video Game Series - It's Your Show; Film: The Phoenix - Body - Untitled Original Film
PRE-PRODUCTION 30 Days (TV)
CREDITS Super Size Me (Roadside Attractions/Samuel Goldwyn) - I Bet You Will (MTV)

Morgan Spurlock . . . Producer
Dave Pederson . . . Head, Development
Joe the Artist . . . Artistic Director
Stela Gueorguiev . . . Editor
Gueorgui Gueorguiev . . . Chief Programmer
Rainier Rodriguez . . . Chief Designer

CONCEPT ENTERTAINMENT
c/o Maverick Films
9348 Civic Center Dr., 3rd Fl.
Beverly Hills, CA 90210
PHONE . . . 310-276-6177
FAX . . . 310-276-9477
EMAIL . . . enquiries@conceptentertainment.biz
WEB SITE . . . www.conceptentertainment.biz
TYPES Features - Direct-to-Video/DVD - TV Series
DEALS Maverick Films
DEVELOPMENT Sloppy - Dreary & Naughty - TAG - Forty - Crimes of Produce - Girls Love Cadillacs
PRE-PRODUCTION Material Girls
POST PRODUCTION The Big White

David Faigenblum . . . Producer/Manager
Eve LaDue . . . Producer/Manager
Rafi Crohn . . . Creative Assistant

CONCOURSE PRODUCTIONS
171 Pier Ave., Ste. 354
Santa Monica, CA 90405
PHONE . . . 310-306-0502
FAX . . . 310-822-6633
EMAIL . . . concourseprods@comcast.net
TYPES Features - Made-for-TV/Cable Movies
DEVELOPMENT The Locked Room - Jump Shot
CREDITS James Dean - Crime of the Century - Intersection - For the Boys - On Golden Pond - The River - The Rose - Cinderella Liberty - The Fox - The Reivers

Mark Rydell . . . Producer/Director
Eric Miller . . . Producer

*CONDOR RISING ENTERTAINMENT/FOLKS FILM, INC.
400 S. Beverly Dr., Ste. 214
Beverly Hills, CA 90212
PHONE . . . 310-709-7507
EMAIL . . . folksn@aol.com
TYPES Features
CREDITS Willowbee - Last Goodbye

Nathan Folks . . . Principal
Philip Righter . . . Principal

CONNECTION III ENTERTAINMENT CORP.
8489 W. Third St.
Los Angeles, CA 90048
PHONE . . . 323-653-3400
WEB SITE . . . www.connection3.com
TYPES Features - Made-for-TV/Cable Movies - Syndication
CREDITS Phat Beach (Feature) - What About Your Friends? (UPN, Movie) - The Garage Club - Urbanflix Preview (Syndication)

Cleveland O'Neal . . . Producer
Brian O'Neal . . . Producer

CONSTANTIN FILM DEVELOPMENT, INC.
9200 Sunset Blvd., Ste. 800
Los Angeles, CA 90069
PHONE . . . 310-247-0300
FAX . . . 310-247-0305
TYPES Features
POST PRODUCTION Resident Evil Apocalpyse
CREDITS Resident Evil - House of the Spirits - Last Exit to Brooklyn - Name of the Rose - Smilla's Sense of Snow

Bernd Eichinger . . . No Title
Mitch Horwits . . . No Title
Lisa Kregness . . . No Title
Robert Kulzer . . . No Title
Laura Levinson . . . No Title
Marsha Metz . . . No Title
Johannes Schlichting . . . No Title
Heather Thomas . . . No Title

CONTENTFILM
1648 N. Wilcox Ave.
Hollywood, CA 90028
PHONE . . . 323-871-8383
FAX . . . 323-871-1870
WEB SITE . . . www.contentfilm.com
TYPES Features
CREDITS Never Die Alone - The Cooler - The Guys - The Hebrew Hammer - Party Monster - Love Object
COMMENTS East Coast office: 419 Lafayette St., 7th Fl., New York, NY 10003, phone: 212-489-3333; London office: 14/15 D'Arblay St., London WIF 8DZ UK, phone: 44-207-851-9170

Edward R. Pressman . . . CEO/Chairman
John Schmidt . . . President/COO (NY)
Alessandro Camon . . . Head, Production & Development (LA)
Sofia Sondervan . . . Head, Production & Development (NY)
Jasmine Stodel . . . Manager, Business Affairs (NY)
Jamie Carmichael . . . Managing Director (London)
Harry White . . . Sales Executive (London)
Judith Baugin . . . Marketing Manager (London)
Steven Hora . . . Assistant to Alessandro Camon (LA)
Ryan Demler . . . Assistant to John Schmidt (NY)
Patrick Russell . . . Assistant to Sofia Sondervan (NY)
Mira Shin . . . Assistant to Edward Pressman (NY)

CONTRAST ENTERTAINMENT

1545 N. Laurel Ave., Ste. 103
Los Angeles, CA 90046
PHONE .323-650-8754
FAX .323-822-0312

TYPES	Features - TV Series
DEVELOPMENT	The Kitchen - The Last Man
POST PRODUCTION	Cry Wolf
CREDITS	The Tower of Babble

Beau Bauman .Writer/Producer
Jeff Wadlow .Writer/Director

CONUNDRUM ENTERTAINMENT

325 Wilshire Blvd., Ste. 201
Santa Monica, CA 90401
PHONE .310-319-2800
FAX .310-319-2808

TYPES	Animation - Features - TV Series
DEALS	Twentieth Century Fox
DEVELOPMENT	Three Stooges
POST PRODUCTION	Ringer
CREDITS	Stuck on You - Shallow Hal - Osmosis Jones - Me, Myself & Irene - There's Something About Mary - Dumb & Dumber - Kingpin

Peter Farrelly .No Title
Bobby Farrelly .No Title
Bradley Thomas .No Title
Mark Charpentier .No Title
Clemens Franek .No Title
Kevin Barnett .No Title
Sarah Lopez .No Title
Kris Meyer .No Title

COOKIE JAR ENTERTAINMENT

4500 Wilshire Blvd.
Los Angeles, CA 90010
PHONE .323-954-4563
FAX .323-939-8933
EMAIL .toper@topertaylor.com
WEB SITE .www.topertaylor.com

TYPES	Animation - Direct-to-Video/DVD - TV Series
CREDITS	Paddington Bear - Aruthur - Caillou - Country Mouse and City Mouse Adventures - Lillte Lulu Show - Creep School - Mona the Vampire - Zoboomafoo

Toper Taylor .President & COO

COOPER'S TOWN PRODUCTIONS

302A W. 12th St., Ste. 214
New York, NY 10014
PHONE .212-255-7566
FAX .212-255-0211
EMAIL .info@cooperstownproductions.com

TYPES	Features
DEVELOPMENT	One Split Second
SUBMISSION POLICY	No unsolicited material

Philip Seymour Hoffman .CEO
Emily Ziff .President

*COPASETIC CREATIONS

11628 Chenault St., Ste. 102
Los Angeles, CA 90049
PHONE .310-995-1608
EMAIL .info@copaseticcreations.com
WEB SITE .www.copaseticcreations.com

TYPES	Features - Theater - TV Series

Eli Talbert .Partner/President, Creative Affairs
Ryan McCormick .Partner/President, Production
Shannon Clark .Partner/President, Business Relations

COPPER SKY PRODUCTIONS

714-1/2 Orchid Ave.
Corona del Mar, CA 92625
PHONE .310-927-8150
FAX .949-721-1177

TYPES	Features - TV Series
DEALS	Warner Bros. Pictures
CREDITS	With Honors

Abe Milrad .Producer
B.J. Markel .VP, Creative Affairs

CORE ENTERTAINMENT ORGANIZATION

14724 Ventura Blvd., Penthouse
Sherman Oaks, CA 91403
PHONE .818-986-8040
FAX .818-986-8041
EMAIL .core@coreentertainment.biz

TYPES	Features - Reality TV - Syndication - TV Series
POST PRODUCTION	Hollywood Tonight
CREDITS	The New Tom Green Show - The Man Show - Loveline - Open Mike - My House/My Rules - Happy as I Can Be - On Target - Mike MacDonald Christmas - Freddy Got Fingered - Stealing Harvard
COMMENTS	Formerly Siddons & Associates and Lapides Entertainment Organization; Music

Howard Lapides .President
Bill Siddons .President
Andrew Lear .VP, Comedy & Development
Julia Mays .VP/Manager
Jackie Stern .VP/Manager
David Brown .Manager
Kesila Childers .Assistant
Mona Moon .Assistant
Wendy Vinglinsky .Assistant

CORNICE ENTERTAINMENT

1640 S. Sepulveda Blvd., Ste. 218
Los Angeles, CA 90025
PHONE .310-445-1614
FAX .310-996-1892

TYPES	Features - TV Series
CREDITS	Highwaymen

Michael E. Marcus .No Title
Kathleen Rippert .No Title

CORNUCOPIA PICTURES

10989 Bluffside Dr., Ste. 3414
Studio City, CA 91604
PHONE .818-985-2720
FAX .818-985-2720
EMAIL .filmbiz@aol.com
TYPES Features - TV Series
DEVELOPMENT Kung Fu Theater - Remember Sunday - The Moe Norman Story - U.N. (TV)
CREDITS Race the Sun - The Disappearance of Vonnie - Christmas on Division Street - Switched at Birth

Barry Morrow .Writer/Producer
Paul Jay Shrater .Writer/Producer
Tom Jankiewicz .Writer
Gerard Karsenty .VP, Development

ROBERT CORT PRODUCTIONS

1041 N. Formosa Ave., Admin. Bldg., Ste. 196
West Hollywood, CA 90046
PHONE .323-850-2644
FAX .323-850-2634
TYPES Features - Made-for-TV/Cable Movies
DEALS Paramount Pictures-Motion Picture Group
CREDITS Save the Last Dance - Runaway Bride - Mr. Holland's Opus - Harlan County War - Against the Ropes - Something the Lord Made
SUBMISSION POLICY No unsolicited submissions

Robert Cort .Producer
Scarlett Lacey .VP, Production
Eric Hetzel .VP, Production
Mimi Zora .Creative

CORYMORE PRODUCTIONS

9171 Wilshire Blvd., Ste. 400
Beverly Hills, CA 90210
PHONE .310-274-7891
FAX .310-274-3496
EMAIL .dena@corymore.com
TYPES Made-for-TV/Cable Movies - TV Series
CREDITS South by Southwest - Mrs. Pollifax - Murder She Wrote - Mrs. 'Arris Goes to Paris - Positive Moves - Mrs. Santa Claus - A Story to Die For - The Last Free Man

Angela Lansbury .Actress/Producer
Anthony Shaw .Director/Producer
Shane McGrath .Development

COSGROVE-MEURER PRODUCTIONS

4303 W. Verdugo Ave.
Burbank, CA 91505
PHONE .818-843-5600
FAX .818-843-8585
TYPES Features - Made-for-TV/Cable Movies - TV Series
CREDITS Unsolved Mysteries - The Inheritance - Voice from the Grave - A Friend's Betrayal - Yesterday's Children - Ball in the House

John Cosgrove .CEO
Terry Meurer .President
Linda Berman .Sr. VP, Development
Stuart Schwartz .VP, Reality Development
Jo Levi .Feature Development
Christine Lenig .Assistant to T. Meurer & J. Cosgrove

COSMIC ENTERTAINMENT

9255 Sunset Blvd., Ste. 1010
West Hollywood, CA 90069
PHONE .310-275-8080
FAX .310-275-8081
TYPES Documentaries - Features - Made-for-TV/Cable Movies - TV Series
POST PRODUCTION Orphan King
CREDITS The Matthew Shepard Story - When Billie Beat Bobby - Dark Blue

Goldie Hawn .Partner, Clearlight
Kurt Russell .Partner, Go Mav
Kate Hudson .Partner, Birdie
Oliver Hudson .Partner, Workshed
Jay Cohen .Partner
Emily Cummins .Feature Film
Scott Martin .Birdie
Shanna Tyndall Nussbaum .TV
John Stalberg .Workshed
Carrie Van Hoy .No Title
Marianne Norris .No Title
Deloris Horn .No Title
Amanda Countner .No Title

COSSETTE PRODUCTIONS

8899 Beverly Blvd., Ste. 100
Los Angeles, CA 90048
PHONE .310-278-3366
FAX .310-278-6587
TYPES Theater - TV Series
CREDITS BET Awards Show - BET Walk of Fame - The Civil War - The Scarlet Pimpernel - Grammy Awards - Latin Grammy Awards - The Will Rogers Follies
COMMENTS TV Specials

Pierre Cossette .Chairman
John Cossette .President

COURT TV

600 Third Ave.
New York, NY 10016
PHONE .212-973-2800
FAX .212-973-3210
WEB SITE .www.courttv.com
TYPES Documentaries - Made-for-TV/Cable Movies - Syndication - TV Series
CREDITS The System - Forensic Files - Hollywood & Crime - MugShots - Dominick Dunne's Power, Privilege and Justice - Catherine Crier Live - Hollywood at Large
COMMENTS Crime and justice programming; West Coast office: 2049 Century Park East, Ste. 3330, Los Angeles, CA 90067

Henry Schleiff .Chairman/CEO
Art Bell .President/COO
Ira Fields .Executive VP/CFO
Doug Jacobs .Executive VP/General Counsel
Darren Campo .Sr. VP, Programming, Strategy & Research
Marlene Dann .Sr. VP, Daytime Programming
Jennifer Geisser .Sr. VP, Corporate Communications
Scoot MacPherson .Sr. VP, Community & Government Affairs
Mary D. Silverman .Sr. VP, Programming & Development
Andy Verderame .Sr. VP, Creative Services
Rosalie Muskatt .VP, Original Movies
Jennifer Randolph .VP, Organizational Development
Todd Schwartz .Head, Alternative Development

CINDY COWAN ENTERTAINMENT, INC.

8265 Sunset Blvd., Ste. 205
Los Angeles, CA 90046
PHONE 323-822-1082
FAX 323-822-1086
TYPES: Features - Made-for-TV/Cable Movies - TV Series
DEVELOPMENT: Ticket to the Promised Land - Dead at 27 - The Reckoning - The Kroy, Maine Incident
PRE-PRODUCTION: Slight of Hand - West Memphis Three - Knights in Manhattan
CREDITS: Dr. T & the Women - Very Bad Things - Savior - Little City - The Florentine - Changing Habits - Scorched

Cindy Cowan ....President
Sara Cline ....Director, Development

COYOTE PASS PRODUCTIONS

PO Box 6318
Altadena, CA 91003-6318
PHONE 626-794-4463
FAX 626-798-9930
EMAIL ....coyotepassbd@charter.net
WEB SITE ....http://webpages.charter.net/coyotepass
TYPES: Commercials - Documentaries - Features - Reality TV - TV Series
DEVELOPMENT: Somebody's Gotta Pay the Piper
PRODUCTION: Celebrity Tee Time
CREDITS: Out of Order - Beneath the News - Juan for All - Regreso
SUBMISSION POLICY: By email only
COMMENTS: Specialize in Latino characters and themes; Infomercials

Beth Dolan ....Writer/Producer
Luis Remesar ....Writer/Director
Gregory Cabrera ....Producer
Sheila Higgins ....Producer
Lysa Nevarrez ....Producer
Ritchie Summers ....Producer

CPC ENTERTAINMENT

840 N. Larrabee St., Ste. 2322
Los Angeles, CA 90069-4528
PHONE 310-652-8194/212-554-6447
EMAIL ....development@cpcentertainment.com
WEB SITE ....www.cpcentertainment.com
TYPES: Features - Made-for-TV/Cable Movies
DEVELOPMENT: With a Twist - Zero Hour - Miami Scoop
CREDITS: River to Greyrock - In the Eyes of a Stranger
COMMENTS: East Coast office: 353 W. 57th St., Ste. 2227, New York, NY 10019-3100

Peggy Howard Chane ....Producer/Director
Sylvie de la Riviere ....VP, Development (Paris)
Steve Nemiroff ....Director, Development

CRAFTSMAN FILMS

5555 Melrose Ave., Clara Bow Bldg., Ste. 205
Los Angeles, CA 90038
PHONE 323-956-5076
FAX 323-862-1823
TYPES: Features - TV Series
DEALS: Paramount Television
DEVELOPMENT: The Ch'o-Do Incident
CREDITS: Homeland Security

Kerry McCluggage ....Producer
Sebastian Twardosz ....VP, Development
Kimberly Koenen ....Executive Assistant

CRANE WEXELBLATT ENTERTAINMENT

6061 Galahad Dr.
Malibu, CA 90265
PHONE 310-457-4821
FAX 310-457-3888
EMAIL ....twomoguls@aol.com
TYPES: Features - Made-for-TV/Cable Movies - New Media - TV Series
DEVELOPMENT: Ticker - Darby Sabini - Free Reign (Pebble Hut) - Widow Claire (Sandcastle/Footprints/Unity Productions)
CREDITS: Lily Dale - The Passion of Ayn Rand - One-Eyed King

Peter Crane ....Producer/Director
Linda Curran Wexelblatt ....Producer

CRAVE FILMS

3312 Sunset Blvd.
Los Angeles, CA 90026
PHONE 323-669-9000
FAX 323-669-9002
WEB SITE ....www.cravefilms.com
TYPES: Features
DEVELOPMENT: Beware the Night - Wild Bunch
PRE-PRODUCTION: Harsh Times
CREDITS: Dark Blue - Training Day - The Fast and the Furious - U-571 - The Patriot - SWAT

David Ayer ....President
Jesse Felsot ....No Title

CRAVEN/MADDALENA FILMS

11846 Ventura Blvd., Ste. 208
Studio City, CA 91604
PHONE 818-752-0197
FAX 818-752-1789
TYPES: Animation - Features - Made-for-TV/Cable Movies - New Media - TV Series
DEALS: Dimension Films - Miramax Films
POST PRODUCTION: Cursed
CREDITS: Scream 1-3 - Music of the Heart

Wes Craven ....Director/Producer
Marianne Maddalena ....President/Producer
Alix Taylor ....VP, Development
Suzanne Santry ....Director, Development
Cody Zwieg ....Assistant to Ms. Maddalena

CRC ENTERTAINMENT

7260 Sunset Blvd., Ste. 203
Los Angeles, CA 90046
PHONE 323-653-6909
FAX 323-969-9060
TYPES: Features - Made-for-TV/Cable Movies - Syndication - TV Series
DEVELOPMENT: Tangled Web - The Assassination - Royal Service - The Murder Game - The Lurker - Kindness of Strangers
CREDITS: Hot Flashes - Metalbeast - Tales from the Darkside - The Shipment - The Norm Crosby Celebrity Golf Show - The Biz

T.J. Castronovo ....Producer
Michael Carazza ....Producer
Rita Cook ....Production Executive
Dan Watanabe ....Director, Development

CREATED BY
1041 N. Formosa Ave.
West Hollywood, CA 90046
PHONE 323-850-3555
FAX 323-850-3554
EMAIL .... createdby@earthlink.net
TYPES: Features - Made-for-TV/Cable Movies - TV Series
DEVELOPMENT: Foundation - Caves of Steel - Red Mars
CREDITS: Riverworld

Ralph M. Vicinanza .... President
Vincent Gerardis .... Manager
Eli Kirschner .... Director, Development

CREATIVE CAPERS ENTERTAINMENT
444 E. Broadway
Glendale, CA 91205
PHONE 818-552-2290
FAX 818-552-2296
WEB SITE .... www.creativecapers.com
TYPES: Animation - Features - Direct-to-Video/DVD - New Media - TV Series
DEVELOPMENT: The Studman Bros. - TIKIS
PRODUCTION: Bionicle: Legends of Metru-Nui
CREDITS: Nightmare Ned (ABC) - Sitting Ducks (Cartoon Network) - Bionicle: Mask of Light (Lego/Miramax)
SUBMISSION POLICY: No unsolicited material

Sue Shakespeare .... Producer/Partner
Terry Shakespeare .... Producer/Director/Partner
David Molina .... Producer/Director/Partner
Colleen Cohn .... Development Executive

CREATIVE LIGHT ENTERTAINMENT
8383 Wilshire Blvd., Ste. 212
Beverly Hills, CA 90211
PHONE 323-658-9166
TYPES: Animation - Documentaries - Features
DEALS: Miramax Films
CREDITS: Comic Book: The Movie - Stan Lee's Mutant Monsters and Marvels - Mind Meld - Hail Sid Caesar: The Golden Age of Comedy - The Spot

Scott Zakarin .... CEO/Partner
Rich Tackenberg .... COO/Partner
Ted Chalmers .... Head, World Wide Distribution
Bruce Newberg .... VP, Casting

CREATIVE MANAGEMENT GROUP, LLC
9465 Wilshire Blvd., Ste. 335
Beverly Hills, CA 90212
PHONE 310-888-0082
FAX 310-888-1848
TYPES: Features - Made-for-TV/Cable Movies - Syndication - TV Series - Reality TV
DEVELOPMENT: American Bandstand - Good Times - The Italian - Jonathan Pollard Spy Case - Straight Man
CREDITS: National Lampoon's Van Wilder - Speedway Junkie

Rodney A. Omanoff .... Partner/President
Jack Boyajian .... Partner/Business Affairs
Graham Kaye .... Executive VP
Jill Stewart .... Assistant
Sasha Vinokur .... Assistant
Edward Horowitz .... No Title

CREATIVE PLAYERS MANAGEMENT
121 S. Beverly Dr.
Beverly Hills, CA 90212
PHONE 310-278-0065
FAX 310-278-0937
TYPES: Features - Made-for-TV/Cable Movies - Reality TV - TV Series
DEALS: HBO Original Programming
PRE-PRODUCTION: The Lee Benson Story (HBO)
CREDITS: Kids in the Hall - Vacant Lot - Pretty When She Cries - I'm with Busey
COMMENTS: Specializes in comedy

Pamela Thomas .... Manager/Producer
Elizabeth Gebbia .... Manager/Producer
David Gebbia .... Producer

CREATIVE VISIONS
1223 Sunset Plaza Dr., Ste. B
West Hollywood, CA 90069
PHONE 310-652-8833
WEB SITE .... www.creativevisions.org
SECOND WEB SITE .... pbs.org/globaltribe
TYPES: Animation - Documentaries - Features - TV Series
DEVELOPMENT: G-Tribe (Animated Series) - Dan Eldon Story
COMPLETED UNRELEASED: Globaltribe South Africa
CREDITS: Dying to Tell the Story - Soldiers of Peace: A Children's Crusade - Lost in Africa - Globaltribe (PBS)
SUBMISSION POLICY: No unsolicited material

Kathleen Eldon .... President
Amy Eldon .... VP
Alison Fast .... Director, Development
Martin Williams .... Development Associate
Ethan Sawyer .... Development Associate

CREATURE ENERTAINMENT
11766 Wilshire Blvd., Ste. 1610
Los Angeles, CA 90025
PHONE 310-278-9013
FAX 310-278-8933
EMAIL .... creatureent@aol.com
TYPES: Features
DEVELOPMENT: Falling

Milla Jovovich .... Partner/Producer
Chris Brenner .... Partner/Producer
Ben Howdeshell .... Research & Development

CRESCENT SKY, INC.
1420 N. Sierra Bonita Ave., Ste. 312
Los Angeles, CA 90046
PHONE 323-876-3534
EMAIL .... info@crescentskyonline.com
WEB SITE .... www.crescentskyonline.com
TYPES: Commercials - Documentaries - Features - Music Videos - Reality TV
DEVELOPMENT: Sellout - The Last Hope - Henry's Adventure - Beauty Sleep - 24-7 - Best of Times - Justice
PRE-PRODUCTION: Creep
COMPLETED UNRELEASED: Primera Cita
CREDITS: A Galaxy Far Far Away

Tariq Jalil .... CEO
Terry Tocantins .... VP, Production

CROWN INTERNATIONAL PICTURES, INC.

8701 Wilshire Blvd.
Beverly Hills, CA 90211
PHONE .310-657-6700
FAX .310-657-4489
EMAIL .crown@crownintlpictures.com
WEB SITE .www.crownintlpictures.com
TYPES Features
CREDITS My Mom's a Werewolf - My Tutor - My Chauffeur - Lena's Holiday

Mark Tenser .President/CEO
Marilyn J. Tenser .Producer
Wilfredo P. de Leon .VP, Finance

CRPI ENTERTAINMENT

19200 Von Karman Ave., Ste. 400
Irvine, CA 92612
PHONE .949-477-8072
FAX .949-477-8079
TYPES Made-for-TV/Cable Movies - TV Series
CREDITS Celine Dion: The Concert - Celine Dion: The Colour of My Love - Lilith Fair: Sarah McLachlan & Friends - Golden Will: The Silken Laumann Story

Carol Reynolds .President/Executive Producer
David McCarthy .Executive VP

CRYSTAL LAKE ENTERTAINMENT, INC.

4420 Hayvenhurst Ave.
Encino, CA 91436
PHONE .818-995-1585
TYPES Features - TV Series
DEALS New Line Cinema
CREDITS Freddie vs. Jason - Terminal Invasion - Deep Star Six - My Boyfriend's Back - House - Friday the 13th - Jason X - Extreme Close-Up

Sean S. Cunningham .Producer/Director
Geoff Garrett .Creative Executive
Mary Liz Thomson .Creative Executive

CRYSTAL SKY, LLC

1901 Avenue of the Stars, Ste. 605
Los Angeles, CA 90067
PHONE .310-843-0223
FAX .310-553-9895
TYPES Features - TV Series
DEVELOPMENT Deathlok - Werewolf by Night - Fathers and Sons - Tekken
PRE-PRODUCTION Ghost Rider - Facade - The Secret War
CREDITS Baby Geniuses 1&2 - Murder in a Small Town - The Musketeer - Unleashed
COMMENTS Producing partner, Jon Voight Entertainment; Management division, Artists Only Management

Hank Paul .Chairman
Dorothy Koster .Co-Chairman
Steven Paul .President
Patrick Ewald .Executive VP, Production & Development
Joe Inga .Sr. VP, Finance
Jason Price .Sr. Director, Business Affairs & Co-Productions
Dede Binder .Talent Manager
Angelica Dailey .Assistant to President
Natasha Burr .Development/Talent Manager Assistant

CRYSTAL SPRING PRODUCTIONS, INC.

9713 Santa Monica Blvd.
Beverly Hills, CA 90210
PHONE .310-550-2720
FAX .310-550-2701
EMAIL .mail@crystalspringproductions.com
TYPES Animation - Documentaries - Features - Direct-to-Video/DVD - Made-for-TV/Cable Movies - New Media - Syndication - TV Series - Reality TV
CREDITS Welcome to Hollywood - The Last Game
COMMENTS Projects in development in all media

Jim Lampley .Producer
Bree Walker Lampley .Producer
Stephen Ricci .Producer
Brian Haynes .Producer

CSM/JOINT ADVENTURE FILMS

5353 Topanga Canyon Blvd.
Woodland Hills, CA 91364
PHONE .818-883-7891
FAX .818-883-7895
EMAIL .susan@csmcommunications.com
WEB SITE .www.csmcommunications.com
TYPES Reality TV
CREDITS The Restaurant - Survivor

Lori Hall .Executive Producer
John Feist .Executive Producer
Steven Chester .Sr. VP

CTONIC FLIKZ

623 N. Plymouth Blvd.
Los Angeles, CA 90004
PHONE .323-957-7824/33-13-489-6988 (Paris)
EMAIL .ctonic@sbcglobal.net
TYPES Animation - Features - New Media - TV Series
DEVELOPMENT Zombie Mom - Pedal to the Metal - Story of My Life - Pots Damer Platz - Spaggiari - Nobel Men - Mrs. President
PRE-PRODUCTION Bob Is Not Gay
CREDITS Where the Day Takes You - Butter - Carried Away

Catalaine Knell .Producer

CUBE VISION

2900 W. Olympic Blvd.
Santa Monica, CA 90404
PHONE .310-255-7100
FAX .310-255-7163
TYPES Features
CREDITS Friday - Next Friday - Friday After Next - Barbershop 1&2 - All About the Benjamins - Are We There Yet?

Ice Cube .Partner
Matt Alvarez .Partner
John Hayes .No Title
David Hebenstreit .No Title

CURB ENTERTAINMENT
3907 W. Alameda Ave.
Burbank, CA 91505
PHONE .818-843-8580
FAX .818-566-1719
WEB SITE .www.curbentertainment.com
TYPES Features
POST PRODUCTION Drop Dead Sexy
CREDITS Tough Luck - Pipe Dream - Pressure - Mexico City - Oxygen - The Proposal - Wedding Bell Blues - Kill Me Later - Zoe - Out of Line - Water's Edge - The Untold
SUBMISSION POLICY Please submit synopsis, attachments & budget

Carole Curb .President
Wendy Reeds .Executive Director/Head, Sales
Aaron Rogers .Director/Head, Marketing

CURIOUS PICTURES
440 Lafayette St., 6th Fl.
New York, NY 10003
PHONE .212-674-1400
FAX .212-674-0081
EMAIL .rwink5@curiouspictures.com
WEB SITE .www.curiouspictures.com
TYPES Animation - Commercials - Direct-to-Video/DVD - Made-for-TV/Cable Movies - Music Videos - New Media - TV Series
DEVELOPMENT Frog Boy the Manphibian - Warped
PRODUCTION Barbie Jammin' in Jamaica - Mattel Masquerade Madness
POST PRODUCTION Wrong Coast (AMC)
COMPLETED UNRELEASED Hey Joel
CREDITS Codename: Kids Next Door (Cartoon Network) - Sheep in the Big City (Cartoon Network) - A Little Curious (HBO Family) - Avenue Amy (Oxygen) - The Offbeats (Nickelodeon)

Steve Oakes .President/Director
Susan Holden .CFO
Richard Winkler .Partner/Executive Producer
David Starr .Executive Producer/Head, Marketing

CURRENT ENTERTAINMENT
1411 Fifth St., Ste. 405
Santa Monica, CA 90401
PHONE .310-260-9599
FAX .310-395-3935
WEB SITE .www.currentent.com
TYPES Features - TV Series
DEVELOPMENT D.O.A.
PRODUCTION The Transporter 2
POST PRODUCTION Taxi - Chaos - Danny the Dog
CREDITS Kiss of the Dragon - The One - Invincible - The Transporter

Steven Chasman .CEO/Producer/Manager
Emmarie Dempsey .No Title
Josh Kazdan .No Title

DAN CURTIS PRODUCTIONS
725 Arizona Ave., Ste. 301
Santa Monica, CA 90401
PHONE .310-395-9935
FAX .310-395-9936
EMAIL .dancurtisprods@aol.com
TYPES Features - TV Series
CREDITS Dark Shadows - The Love Letter - War and Remembrance - Winds of War - Our Fathers

Dan Curtis .Producer/Director
David Kennedy .President
Jim Pierson .Marketing/Promotions
Kelly Wade .Executive Assistant

CW PRODUCTIONS, LTD.
499 N. Canon Dr., Ste. 316
Beverly Hills, CA 90210
PHONE .818-880-0539
FAX .818-880-0547
EMAIL .cwprods@earthlink.net
WEB SITE .www.cindywilliams.com
TYPES Animation - Documentaries - Features - Made-for-TV/Cable Movies - TV Series
CREDITS Father of the Bride 1&2

Cindy Williams .President/Producer/Director/Writer
Charlie Brogdon .VP, Development

CYPRESS POINT PRODUCTIONS
3000 Olympic Blvd.
Santa Monica, CA 90404
PHONE .310-315-4787
FAX .310-315-4785
EMAIL .cypresspf@earthlink.net
TYPES Features - Made-for-TV/Cable Movies - Reality TV - TV Series
DEVELOPMENT See Arnold Run - The Last Vampire
PRE-PRODUCTION Over the Edge
CREDITS Black & Blue - Nuremberg - Second Honeymoon - Christmas Visitor - 44 Minutes: Shootout in North Hollywood - Out of the Ashes - Natalie Wood: Hollywood's Last Child

Gerald W. Abrams .Chairman
Michael Goldstein .Producer
Michael Waldron .Associate

DAKOTA NORTH ENTERTAINMENT/DAKOTA FILMS
4133 Lankershim Blvd.
North Hollywood, CA 91602
PHONE .818-760-0099
FAX .818-760-1070
WEB SITE .www.dakotafilms.com
TYPES Features - Direct-to-Video/DVD - Made-for-TV/Cable Movies - TV Series - Reality TV
DEALS Comedy Central - MTV Networks
CREDITS Run Ronnie, Run - Tenacious D - Oscar's Opening Film Sequence - MTV's Movie Awards Film - Mr. Show with Bob and David - The Best Commercials You've Never Seen - The Lemur - Viva La Bam (MTV) - Real Comedy (Comedy Central)
SUBMISSION POLICY No unsolicited material

Troy Miller .Producer/Director
Tracey Baird .Producer
Bruce Klassen .Coordinating Producer

DALAKLIS-MCKEOWN ENTERTAINMENT, INC.

1750 Berkeley St.
Santa Monica, CA 90404
PHONE 310-460-0200
FAX 310-460-0202
EMAIL . . . . production@dmetv.net
WEB SITE . . . . www.dmetv.net

TYPES	Documentaries - Reality TV - TV Series
PRE-PRODUCTION	Instant Weddings - Ultimate Guide to Greece
PRODUCTION	All Access: Hot Couples - All Access Spotlight: Latoya Jackson - Lenny Kravitz - Soapography (SoapNet)
POST PRODUCTION	How Stars Get Hot? 4 - Ready for The Weekend Movies - Before & Afternoon Movies
CREDITS	10 Perfect Summer Get-a-Ways (Fine Living) - All Access: Fleetwood Mac (VH1) - Babyface: Face2Face - Music Paradise - Intimate Portrait: Young Hollywood - Lisa Marie Presley - Porn to Rock - All Access Spotlight: Josh Groban - Clay Aiken - MERGE (Lifetime)

Charles Dalaklis . . . . Executive Producer
Theresa McKeown . . . . Executive Producer
Bob Asher . . . . VP, Creative Affairs
Matt Antrim . . . . Casting Director
Amy Barboor . . . . Post Production Supervisor
Joseph Ferraro . . . . Co-Executive Producer, Before and After'noon Movies
Todd Smelser . . . . Supervising Editor
Arletta Amos . . . . Production Manager
Brian Guzy . . . . Coordinator, Product Placement
Sheila Mitchell . . . . Director, Operations/Human Resources
Colin Whelan . . . . Supervising Producer, Ready for the Weekend Movie
Michael Keck . . . . Executive Assistant to Mr. Dalaklis
Wynter Mitchel . . . . Executive Assistant to Ms. McKeown

DANCING ASPARAGUS PRODUCTIONS

264 S. La Cienega Blvd., Ste. 238
Beverly Hills, CA 90211
PHONE 310-552-3333
FAX 310-552-3334

TYPES	Features
DEALS	Miramax Films
DEVELOPMENT	Weekend of the Damned - Rot Tochter - 14 Minutes and 59 Seconds - 1-0-1-7
PRODUCTION	Enfant Terribles
CREDITS	Vipor - True Blood - Buried Trust - Hungry
SUBMISSION POLICY	No unsolicited material
COMMENTS	London office: 56 Glouchester Road, Ste. 570, Kensington, London SW7 4UB UK

Terry Nemeroff . . . . Producer (LA)
B. Pogue . . . . Producer (London)

LEE DANIELS ENTERTAINMENT

39 W. 131st St., Ste. 2
New York, NY 10037
PHONE 646-548-0930
FAX 646-548-9883
EMAIL . . . . info@leedanielsentertainment.com
SECOND EMAIL . . . . firstname@leedanielsentertainment.com
WEB SITE . . . . www.leedanielsentertainment.com

TYPES	Features
DEVELOPMENT	The Narrative of Arthur Gordon Pym - Ladies' Night - ICED - The Invisible Life
PRODUCTION	Shadowboxer
POST PRODUCTION	The Woodsman
CREDITS	Monster's Ball
SUBMISSION POLICY	Send loglines/query letters to Doreen Oliver; No submissions without signed company release form

Lee Daniels . . . . Producer/CEO
David Robinson . . . . CFO/Head, International Sales
Lisa Cortés . . . . Sr. VP, Production
Doreen S. Oliver . . . . VP, Development
Liz Gately . . . . Executive Assistant to Lee Daniels

DANJAQ, LLC

c/o Colorado Center
2400 Broadway St., Ste. 310
Santa Monica, CA 90404
PHONE 310-449-3185
FAX 310-449-3189

TYPES	Features
DEALS	Metro-Goldwyn-Mayer Studios, Inc.
CREDITS	The James Bond Films - Chitty Chitty Bang Bang
SUBMISSION POLICY	No unsolicited material

Michael Wilson . . . . President/CEO
David Pope . . . . COO
Barbara Broccoli . . . . VP, Production/Development

DARK HARBOR PRODUCTIONS

3500 W. Olive Ave., Ste. 368
Burbank, CA 91505
PHONE 818-973-2769
FAX 818-973-2765

TYPES	TV Series
DEALS	NBC Entertainment
PRODUCTION	Nevermind Nirvana

David Schwimmer . . . . Principal
Larry Hancock . . . . Executive
Jenna Seiden . . . . Executive
Allison Belanger . . . . Assistant

DARK HORSE ENTERTAINMENT
8425 W. Third St., Ste. 400
Los Angeles, CA 90048
PHONE 323-655-3600
WEB SITE ....www.dhentertainment.com
TYPES Animation - Features - Direct-to-Video/DVD - Interactive Games - TV Series
DEVELOPMENT 30 Days of Night - Criminal Macabre - Grendel
PRODUCTION Son of the Mask - Alien vs. Predator
CREDITS The Mask - Time Cop - Mystery Men - Hellboy
COMMENTS Moving at press time

Mike Richardson ....President/Producer
Barry Levine ....Producer
Chris Tongue ....Creative Executive
Noel Bastien ....Assistant

DARK MATTER PRODUCTIONS
c/o SHS Management
1910 Montana Ave.
Santa Monica, CA 90403
PHONE 310-205-8401
EMAIL ....dmpscripts@cox.net
TYPES Features - TV Series
DEVELOPMENT Little Red - Black Crow
CREDITS Lewis & Clark & George - Denise Calls Up
SUBMISSION POLICY Accepts development proposals via email

Dan Gunther ....President

DARK TRICK FILMS
421 N. Beverly Dr., Ste. 280
Beverly Hills, CA 90210
PHONE 310-274-3600
FAX 310-274-3670
TYPES Features
CREDITS National Lampoon's Van Wilder

Jonathon Komack Martin ....Partner
Ryan Reynolds ....Partner
Michael K. Eitelman ....VP, Development
Jeremy Martin ....No Title

DARKWOODS PRODUCTIONS
1041 N. Formosa Ave., SME 105
West Hollywood, CA 90046
PHONE 323-850-2497
FAX 323-850-2491
TYPES Features - TV Series
DEALS Paramount Pictures-Motion Picture Group
POST PRODUCTION Collateral
CREDITS The Green Mile - The Shawshank Redemption - Black Cat Run - The Salton Sea - The Majestic
SUBMISSION POLICY No unsolicited submissions

Frank Darabont ....Director/Writer/Producer/Partner
Anna Garduño ....President, Production/Partner
Denise Huth ....VP, Production
Juan Francisco ....Assistant to Frank Darabont
Dave Johnson ....Assistant

DARKWORLD PICTURES, INC.
3727 W. Magnolia Blvd., Ste. 153
Burbank, CA 91510
PHONE 818-761-5450
EMAIL ....darkworld@dannydraven.com
WEB SITE ....www.darkworldpictures.com
SECOND WEB SITE ....www.dannydraven.com
TYPES Documentaries - Features - Direct-to-Video/DVD - Made-for-TV/Cable Movies - Music Videos - New Media
DEALS Shadow Entertainment
DEVELOPMENT Cybervamps - Plasm
CREDITS Horrorvision - Hell Asylum - Cryptz - Stuart Gordon Presents Deathbed - Darkwalker

Danny Draven ....CEO/Producer/Director
Jojo Draven ....Partner/Co-Producer

DASH FILMS/ROC FILMS
280 Park Ave., 5th Fl.
New York, NY 10017
PHONE 212-907-8031
FAX 212-907-8089
TYPES Features - TV Series
POST PRODUCTION State Property 2
CREDITS Death of a Dynasty - State Property - Paid in Full - Paper Soldiers - Streets Is Watching - Backstage

Damon Dash ....CEO, Dash/Roc Films
Beth Melillo ....Sr. VP, Production & Developmnent

DAVID HOLLANDER PRODUCTIONS
10202 W. Washington Blvd., Astaire Bldg., Ste. 2110
Culver City, CA 90232
PHONE 310-244-2926
FAX 310-244-1522
TYPES TV Series
DEALS Sony Pictures Television
CREDITS The Guardian

David Hollander ....Producer
Christian Trokey ....Assistant to David Hollander

ALAN DAVID MANAGEMENT
8840 Wilshire Blvd.
Beverly Hills, CA 90211
PHONE 310-358-3155
FAX 310-358-3256
EMAIL ....adavid@planbproductions.net
TYPES Features - Reality TV - Syndication - TV Series
DEVELOPMENT The UFC - Chief of Station - Action Hero's Handbook
PRE-PRODUCTION Ghosts
PRODUCTION American Casino

Alan David ....President
Miriam Kravitz ....Assistant

DAVIS ENTERTAINMENT COMPANY

2121 Avenue of the Stars, Ste. 2800
Los Angeles, CA 90067
PHONE .... See Below
FAX 310-556-3688
TYPES Features - Made-for-TV/Cable Movies - TV Series
DEALS Twentieth Century Fox
PRODUCTION Fat Albert
POST PRODUCTION Flight of Phoenix - Alien vs. Predator
CREDITS I, Robot - Garfield - Daddy Day Care - Behind Enemy Lines - Dr. Doolittle 1&2 - Grumpy Old Men 1&2 - Out to Sea - Predator 1&2 - The Chamber - Waterworld - The Firm - Asteroid - Heartbreakers - Life or Something Like It
COMMENTS Second office: 150 S. Barrington Pl., Los Angeles, CA 90049; phone: 310-889-8000, Feature fax: 310-889-8008, TV fax: 310-889-8011

John A. Davis .... Chairman (310-556-3550)
Wyck Godfrey .... President, Davis Entertainment (310-889-8006)
Brooke Brooks .... Executive VP (310-556-3550)
Brian D. Manis .... Executive VP, Production (310-889-8012)
Danielle Sterling .... Executive VP (310-889-8017)
Amy Palmer .... VP, Development, TV (310-889-8005)
Monnie Wills .... Director, Development (310-889-8009)
Jennifer Buzas .... Story Editor (310-889-8003)
Chris Tipton .... Assistant to John Davis (310-889-8002)
Elek Hendrickson .... Assistant to Wyck Godfrey (310-889-8004)
Marc Marcum .... Assistant to Brian Manis (310-889-8013)

DAYBREAK PRODUCTIONS

3000 W. Olympic Blvd., Bldg. 5, Ste. 2121
Santa Monica, CA 90404
PHONE 310-264-4202
FAX 310-264-4222
TYPES Features - TV Series
CREDITS Waterworld - Field of Dreams - The Rocketeer - Die Hard 1&2 - October Sky - The Girl Next Door

Charles Gordon .... Producer
James Abraham .... Director, Development

DC COMICS

1700 Broadway
New York, NY 10019
PHONE 212-636-5400
TYPES Features

Paul Levitz .... President/Publisher
Richard Bruning .... Sr. VP/Creative Director
Patrick Caldon .... Sr. VP, Finance & Operations
Cheryl Rubin .... Sr. VP, Brand Management
Lillian Laserson .... Sr. VP/General Counsel
Gregory Noveck .... Sr. VP, Creative Affairs
Georg Brewer .... VP, Design & Retail Product Development
Chris Caramalis .... VP, Finance
Terri Cunningham .... VP/Managing Editor
Dan DiDio .... VP, Editorial
Alison Gill .... VP, Manufacturing
Rich Johnson .... VP, Book Trade Sales
David McKillips .... VP, Advertising & Custom Publishing
John Nee .... VP, Business Development
Bob Wayne .... VP, Sales & Marketing
Karen Berger .... VP/Executive Editor, Vertigo
John Ficarra .... Editor, MAD
Jim Lee .... Editorial Director, WildStorm

DDJ PRODUCTIONS

500 S. Buena Vista St., Disney Studios, Stage 7
Burbank, CA 91521
PHONE 818-560-7249
TYPES TV Series
DEALS Touchstone Television
SUBMISSION POLICY Accepted through agents only

Don Reo .... Partner
Damon Wayans .... Partner
Jeff Sagansky .... Partner
Julie Miller .... Director, Development

DINO DE LAURENTIIS COMPANY

100 Universal City Plaza, Bungalow 5195
Universal City, CA 91608
PHONE 818-777-2111
FAX 818-866-5566
TYPES Features - TV Series
DEVELOPMENT The Last Legion - Alexander the Great
CREDITS Breakdown - Bound - U-571 - Hannibal - Red Dragon
SUBMISSION POLICY No unsolicited material

Dino De Laurentiis .... Producer
Martha De Laurentiis .... President/Producer
Stuart Boros .... Business Affairs
Lorenzo De Maio .... Executive Assistant to Dino De Laurentiis
Roberta Shintani .... Executive Assistant to Dino De Laurentiis

*MICHAEL DE LUCA PRODUCTIONS

c/o Columbia Pictures
10202 W. Washington Blvd.
Culver City, CA 90232
PHONE 310-244-4990
TYPES Features
DEALS Columbia Pictures

Michael De Luca .... Producer

DE PASSE ENTERTAINMENT

5750 Wilshire Blvd., Ste. 640
Los Angeles, CA 90036
PHONE 323-965-2590
FAX 323-934-2548
TYPES Features - Made-for-TV/Cable Movies - Syndication - TV Series
CREDITS Showtime at the Apollo - Essence Awards - NAACP Image Awards - Cheaters - Buffalo Girls - The Jacksons: An American Dream - Lonesome Dove - Sister Sister - The Smart Guy - The Temptations (Miniseries)
SUBMISSION POLICY No unsolicited submissions

Suzanne de Passe .... Chairman/CEO
Suzanne Coston .... President
Rose Caraet .... Director, Creative Affairs

DECODE ENTERTAINMENT
512 King St. East, Ste. 104
Toronto, ON M5A 1M1 Canada
PHONE .416-363-8034
FAX .416-363-8919
EMAIL .decode@decode-ent.com
WEB SITE .www.decode.tv
TYPES Animation - Features - Interactive Games - New Media - TV Series
PRE-PRODUCTION Animation: The Save Ums 2 - Bromwell High; Live Action: Going for Gold
PRODUCTION Animation: King 2 - Franny's Feet; Live Action: Radio Free Roscoe 2 - Kratts Brothers' Be The Creature 2

Neil Court .Partner
John A. Delmage .Partner
Steven DeNure .Partner
Beth Stevenson .Partner
Anne Loi .Sr. VP, Finance & Operations
Dominique Bazay .VP, International Sales
Dan Fill .VP, Interactive Development
Joan Fisher .VP, Legal & Business Affairs

DEEP IMAGE UNLIMITED, INC.
8265 Sunset Blvd., Ste. 200
Los Angeles, CA 90046
PHONE .323-654-9483
FAX .323-654-9492
EMAIL .info@deepimage.info
WEB SITE .www.deepimage.info
TYPES Commercials - Documentaries - Features - New Media
COMPLETED UNRELEASED One Bright Shining Moment: The Forgotten Summer of George McGovern
CREDITS Features: Hollywood Boulevard - Black & White - Keeper of the Flame (Documentary); TV: Fame - Our House - Eight Is Enough

Stephen Vittoria .Creative Director/Managing Partner
Frank Fischer .Managing Partner/Producer

DEEP RIVER PRODUCTIONS
100 N. Crescent Dr., Ste. 350
Beverly Hills, CA 90210
PHONE .310-432-1800
FAX .310-432-1801
TYPES Features
PRE-PRODUCTION The Honeymooners - Little Miss Sunshine
CREDITS Dr. Dolittle - Courage Under Fire - Big Momma's House - Laws of Attraction

David T. Friendly .Partner
Marc Turtletaub .Partner
Julie Durk .No Title
Michael McGahey .No Title
Melissa Pontious .No Title
Amy Schwarz .No Title
Felipe Linz .No Title
Meghan de Andrade .No Title

DEJA VIEW PRODUCTIONS, INC.
6700 Independence Ave., Ste. 290
Canoga Park, CA 91303
PHONE .818-888-0821
EMAIL .denneJon@aol.com
TYPES Features - Made-for-TV/Cable Movies
CREDITS Dawn of the Dead - High Crimes - The Flintstones in Viva Rock Vegas - Pacific Heights - Short Circuit

Dennis E. Jones .Producer/Line Producer

DELAWARE PICTURES
c/o Raleigh Studios
650 N. Bronson Ave., Ste. 114-B
Hollywood, CA 90004
PHONE .323-960-4552
WEB SITE .www.delawarepictures.com
TYPES Features - Made-for-TV/Cable Movies - Music Videos
DEVELOPMENT Doe - Elvis in Paradise - Blackwolf - Road Master: The George Barris Story - Pretty Boys
PRE-PRODUCTION Rough Diamonds
CREDITS Bad Jim - Pretty Boy Floyd - Hatfield & McCoys - No Drums - Stephanie - Human Error - All Your Children (Music Video)

J. Patrick Lenny .Executive Producer
Clyde Ware .Writer/Director
Pepe Serna .Producer/Actor
Stephane Mermet .Producer
Barry Donovan .Producer/Actor
Michele Turner .Producer
Dawn Nepp .Business Affairs
Linda Weyer .Executive Assistant

DENVER AND DELILAH FILMS
1041 N. Formosa Ave., Formosa Bldg., Ste. 8
Los Angeles, CA 90046
PHONE .323-850-3113
FAX .323-876-6273
EMAIL .dndfilms@aol.com
WEB SITE .www.danddfilms.com
TYPES Documentaries - Features
DEVELOPMENT Ice at the Bottom of the World - Jinx
PRE-PRODUCTION Homesick
POST PRODUCTION Head in the Clouds
CREDITS Monster
SUBMISSION POLICY No unsolicited material

Charlize Theron .Producer
Meagan Riley-Grant .Producer (323-850-3113)
Beth Kono .No Title

DEPEW PRODUCTIONS
1351 N. Crescent Heights Blvd., Ste. 116
West Hollywood, CA 90046
PHONE .323-654-5300
TYPES Commercials - Features - Direct-to-Video/DVD - Music Videos - New Media
CREDITS Children of the Corn 3&4 - The Hard Truth - The Willies - 2001: A Space Travesty - Cowboys and Angels - The Independent - Hansel & Gretel - The Retrievers - Slasher
COMMENTS Line producer and production manager; Member, DGA

Gary DePew .Producer

DESALVO PRODUCTIONS
c/o Forster Entertainment
12533 Woodgreen St.
Los Angeles, CA 90066
PHONE .323-854-5331
FAX .323-874-4049
EMAIL .uponstone@earthlink.net
TYPES Documentaries - Features - Made-for-TV/Cable Movies - TV Series
SUBMISSION POLICY Via email only
COMMENTS Seeking projects for producing and/or directing

Anne DeSalvo .Producer

DESERT HEART PRODUCTIONS
685 Venice Blvd.
Venice, CA 90291
PHONE 310-399-0013
FAX 310-396-4047
EMAIL .... ddeitchco@earthlink.net

TYPES	Features
DEVELOPMENT	Blonde Ghost - Desert Hearts Sequel
COMPLETED UNRELEASED	Angel on My Shoulder
CREDITS	Desert Hearts - Women of Brewster Place - Prison Stories - Common Ground - The Devil's Arithmetic

Donna Deitch .... Director/Producer
Vivien Bell .... Assistant to Donna Deitch

DESTINY PICTURES
1423 Second St., Ste. 411
Santa Monica, CA 90401
PHONE 310-656-1034
EMAIL .... destinypictures@hotmail.com

TYPES	Features - Direct-to-Video/DVD - Made-for-TV/Cable Movies - TV Series
DEVELOPMENT	Incoming - Second Time Around - Sanna Maaneka...It Ain't New Yawk
CREDITS	The Perfect Tenant - The Perfect Nanny
SUBMISSION POLICY	Query via email only

Mark Castaldo .... Producer

DEUTSCH/OPEN CITY FILMS
145 Avenue of Americas, 7th Fl.
New York, NY 10013
PHONE 212-255-0500
FAX 212-255-0455
EMAIL .... oc@opencityfilms.com

TYPES	Features
COMPLETED UNRELEASED	The Assassination of Richard Nixon
CREDITS	Three Seasons - Down to You - The Guys - Welcome to the Dollhouse - Lovely and Amazing - Series 7 - Coffee and Cigarettes

Jason Kliot .... Co-President/Co-Founder/Producer
Joana Vicente .... Co-President/Co-Founder/Producer
Tory Tunnell .... VP
Kristina Redick .... Manager/Coordinator
Jeffrey Fierson .... Assistant to Jason Kliot & Joana Vicente

VIN DI BONA PRODUCTIONS
12233 W. Olympic Blvd., Ste. 170
Los Angeles, CA 90064
PHONE 310-442-5600
FAX 310-442-5605
WEB SITE .... www.vdbp.com
SECOND WEB SITE .... www.afv.tv

TYPES	Syndication - TV Series
CREDITS	America's Funniest Home Videos - Meet the Marks - Sherman Oaks - Show Me The Funny - Extraordinary World of Animals - That's Funny
COMMENTS	Hollywood Licensing, LLC, 15821 Ventura Blvd., Ste. 110, Encino, CA 91436, phone: 818-906-9333, fax: 818-906-9336, www.hollywoodlicensing.com, Vin Di Bona: Co-Chairman, Tammy Treglia: Co-Chairman, Yolanda Seabourne: Director, Licensing & New Media

Vin Di Bona .... Chairman
Terry Moore .... President, Acquisitions & Production
Peter J. Schankowitz .... President, Development
Dawn Friedman .... Executive VP, Business & Legal Affairs
Cara Di Bona .... VP, Corporate
Janet Ghio .... VP, Human Resources
Sharon Arnett .... VP, Post Production

DI BONAVENTURA PICTURES, INC.
5555 Melrose Ave., Dressing Room Bldg., Ste. 112
Los Angeles, CA 90038
PHONE 323-956-5454
FAX 323-862-2288

TYPES	Documentaries - Features - Made-for-TV/Cable Movies - TV Series
DEALS	Paramount Pictures-Motion Picture Group
DEVELOPMENT	Carlos & Jeff - Sleeping with Schubert - SIS - Doomsday - Dead to Rights - Doom

Lorenzo di Bonaventura .... President/Producer
Erik Howsam .... VP, Production
Jeremy Steckler .... VP, Production
Aaron Bauer .... Development Assistant
Colleen Conroy .... Development Assistant
Toni Kalmacoff .... Development Assistant
Andrew Major .... Development Assistant

DI NOVI PICTURES
3110 Main St., Ste. 220
Santa Monica, CA 90405
PHONE 310-581-1355
FAX 310-399-0499

TYPES	Features - TV Series
DEALS	Spelling Television, Inc. - Warner Bros. Pictures
PRODUCTION	The Sisterhood of the Traveling Pants
POST PRODUCTION	Catwoman
CREDITS	Practical Magic - Little Women - Ed Wood - Edward Scissorhands - Batman Returns - A Walk to Remember - The District - What a Girl Wants - Message in a Bottle
SUBMISSION POLICY	No unsolicited material

Denise Di Novi .... Producer
Alison Greenspan .... President
Marc Resteghini .... VP
Maureen Poon Fear .... Assistant to Denise Di Novi
Nikki Levy .... Assistant to Alison Greenspan
Andy Tunnicliffe .... Assistant to Marc Resteghini

DIC ENTERTAINMENT
303 N. Glenoaks Blvd., 4th Fl.
Burbank, CA 91502
PHONE 818-955-5400
FAX 818-955-5696

TYPES	Animation - TV Series

Andy Heyward .... Chairman/CEO
Brad Brooks .... President
Michael Maliani .... CCO
Kevin O'Donnell .... Sr. VP, Creative Affairs
Cindy Davis .... VP, Domestic Licensing
Vincent Marchica .... VP, Creative
Ryan Gagerman .... Executive Director, Licensing
Heather Fuscellero .... Director, Retail
Kathy DeGennero .... Sr. Designer

LOUIS DIGIAIMO & ASSOCIATES, LTD.
214 Sullivan St., Ste. 2-C
New York, NY 10012
PHONE .212-253-5510
FAX .212-253-5540
EMAIL .l.digiaimo@att.net
TYPES Features - Made-for-TV/Cable Movies - TV Series
DEVELOPMENT Hit #29 - The Dana Bowman Story - The Booster - No Lights, No Sirens - Fort Pit - Untitled Exorcist Cop Project - America - The Truth Hurts
CREDITS Donnie Brasco - An Everlasting Piece - Falcone - Dinner Rush - The 24th Day
COMMENTS Casting director

Lou DiGiaimo .Producer
Lou DiGiaimo Jr. .Producer
Russ Lyster .Producer/Manager

DIGITAL DOMAIN, INC.
300 Rose Ave.
Venice, CA 90291
PHONE .310-314-2800
FAX .310-314-2888
WEB SITE .www.digitaldomain.com
TYPES Commercials - Features - Music Videos
DEVELOPMENT Plant Life - Shadowplay - A Thousand Cranes
PRE-PRODUCTION Instant Karma
CREDITS VFX: Titanic - What Dreams May Come - How the Grinch Stole Christmas - X-Men - Apollo 13 - O Brother, Where Art Thou? - The Time Machine - Vanilla Sky - A Beautiful Mind - We Were Soldiers - XXX - Secondhand Lions - I, Robot - The Day After Tomorrow - Peter Pan

Scott Ross .Chairman/CEO
C. Brad Call .President/COO
Nancy Bernstein .Sr. VP, Feature Films & Theme Park Attractions
Ed Ulbrich .Sr. VP, Commercial Production
Kevin K. Cooper .VP, Feature Film Development
Yvette Macaluso .VP, Finance
Gabby Gourrier .Executive Producer/Director, Commercial Production
Molly Hansen .General Counsel

DIGITAL RANCH PRODUCTIONS
14110 Riverside Dr.
Sherman Oaks, CA 91423
PHONE .818-817-9690
FAX .818-817-9699
WEB SITE .www.digitalranch.tv
TYPES Commercials - Documentaries - Direct-to-Video/DVD - New Media - Syndication - TV Series - Reality TV
CREDITS Mail Call - Shifting Gears - Dangerous Missions - Modern Marvels - James Bond's Gadgets - The System

Robert Kirk .Executive Producer
Robert Lihani .Executive Producer
Rob Beemer .Executive in Charge of Production
Valarie Sheldon .Business Affairs

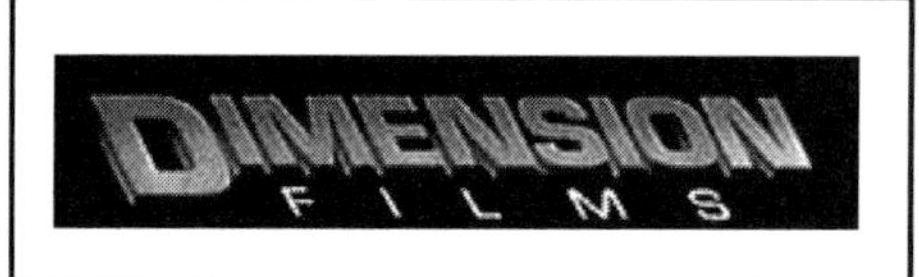

DIMENSION FILMS
c/o Miramax Films
375 Greenwich St.
New York, NY 10013-2338
PHONE .212-941-3800/323-822-4100
FAX .212-941-3949/323-822-4216
WEB SITE .www.dimensionfilms.com
TYPES Features - Direct-to-Video/DVD
DEALS Craven/Maddalena Films - Neo Art & Logic - Platinum Dunes - The Todd Phillips Company - Vertigo Entertainment
DEVELOPMENT Beaks - Manhattan Baby - Merlin - 1408 - Duke Nukem - Into the Ether - The Golden Tux - Jealous Type - Retribution - The Spy Next Door - Werewolf by Night - Shadowman - Ghost Rider - Backwater
PRE-PRODUCTION Six Million Dollar Man
POST PRODUCTION Mindhunters - Cursed - The Brothers Grimm - Darkness
CREDITS Bad Santa - The Others - Scream 1-3 - Scary Movie 1-3 - Spy Kids 1-3 - Equilibrium - My Boss's Daughter
COMMENTS West Coast office: 8439 Sunset Blvd., West Hollywood, CA 90069

Bob Weinstein .Co-Chairman (NY)
Andrew Rona .Co-Head, Production (NY)
Brad Weston .Co-Head, Production (LA)
Timothy Clawson .Executive VP, Physical & Post Production (LA)
Andrew Gumpert .Executive VP, Business & Legal Affairs (LA)
Jere Hausfater .Executive VP/Co-Head, Miramax International (LA)
Kevin Hyman .Executive VP, Physical Production (NY)
Amanda Lundberg .Executive VP, Worldwide Publicity (NY)
Emily Bear .Sr. VP, Publicity (NY)
Linda Borgeson .Sr. VP, Post Production (LA)
Brian Burkin .Sr. VP, Business & Legal Affairs (NY)
Joshua Greenstein .Sr. VP, Marketing (NY)
Dan Levine .Sr. VP, Production & Development (LA)
Jennifer Wachtell .Sr. VP, Development (NY)
Katrina Wolfe .VP, Production & Casting (NY)
Michael Zoumas .Sr. VP, Production & Development (LA)
Jane Evans .VP, Physical Production (NY)
Jim Glander .VP, Physical Production (LA)
Rachel Levy .VP, Motion Picture Music (LA)
Michael E. Marshall .VP, Business & Legal Affairs (LA)
Tracy McGrath .VP, Physical Production (LA)
Peter McPartlin .VP, Business & Legal Affairs (LA)
Nick Phillips .VP, Production & Development (LA)
Jessica Rovins .VP, Publicity (LA)
Matthew Stein . .VP, Production & Development, Home Entertainment (NY)
Andrea Wertheim .VP, Post Production (LA)
Eric Sherman .Sr. Director, Business & Legal Affairs (LA)
Sarah Sobel .Sr. Director, Business & Legal Affairs (NY)
Lumumba Mosquera .Director, Business & Legal Affairs (NY)
Donyea Rochlin .Director, Development (LA)
Michael Curry .Manager, Development (LA)
Dianne Fahey .Manager, Business & Legal Affairs (LA)
Michael Grady .Manager (NY)
Tommy Popps .Jr. Publicist (NY)

DINAMO ENTERTAINMENT

2001 S. Barrington Ave., Ste. 150
Los Angeles, CA 90025
PHONE .310-473-1311
FAX .310-473-8233
EMAIL .dinamo@earthlink.net
TYPES Features - Made-for-TV/Cable Movies - TV Series
CREDITS Suicide Kings - The Substitute - Bad Influence - Lost & Found

Morrie Eisenman .President
Jim Zaphiriou .VP, Creative Affairs

*DIPLOMATIC PRODUCTIONS

6030 Wilshire Blvd., Ste. 301
Los Angeles, CA 90036
PHONE .323-857-6800/212-456-2902
FAX .323-857-6801
TYPES Reality TV - TV Series
DEALS ABC Entertainment Television Group

Michael Davies .Producer
Ruth Caruso .Head, Scripted Series

DIRECTORS' CIRCLE FILMWORKS

2630 Lacy St.
Los Angeles, CA 90031
PHONE .323-222-1202
FAX .323-225-7815
TYPES Features - Direct-to-Video/DVD - Made-for-TV/Cable Movies - New Media - TV Series
CREDITS Masquerade - Rendezvous - Playing with Fire - Body of Evidence - Brother Future - After All - A Private Affair - Rhapsody

Roy Campanella II .President/CEO
Patrick Cunningham .Director, Talent
Akua Campanella .Director, Talent
Nikki Napier .Development Assistant
Loureva Watson .Office P.A.

DISCOVERY NETWORKS, U.S.

One Discovery Pl.
Silver Spring, MD 20910-3354
PHONE .240-662-2000
FAX .240-662-1845
EMAIL .firstname_lastname@discovery.com
WEB SITE .www.discovery.com
TYPES Documentaries - New Media - Reality TV - TV Series
COMMENTS Animal Planet, Discovery Channel, Discovery HD Theater™, Discovery en Español, Discovery Health Channel, Discovery Home Channel, Discovery Kids Channel, Discovery Times Channel, Discovery Wings Channel, FitTV, The Science Channel, TLC, Travel Channel

John S. Hendricks .Founder/Chairman, Discovery Communications, Inc.
Judith A. McHale .President/CEO, Discovery Communications, Inc.
Billy Campbell .President, Discovery Networks, U.S./Acting General Manager, Animal Planet
Joe Abruzzese .President, Advertising Sales, Discovery Networks, U.S.
Ken Dice .Executive VP, Marketing, Discovery Networks, U.S.
Bill Goodwyn .Executive VP, Affiliate Sales & Marketing, Discovery Networks, U.S.

(Continued)

DISCOVERY NETWORKS, U.S. (Continued)

Jane Root .Executive VP/General Manager, Discovery Channel
Maureen Smith .Executive VP/General Manager, Animal Planet
Bill Allman .Sr. VP, Online Content/General Manager, Discovery.com
Steve Burns .Sr. VP/General Manager, The Science Channel
Annie Howell .Sr. VP, Communications, Discovery Networks, U.S.
Marjorie Kaplan .Sr. VP/General Manager, Discovery Kids Channel
David Karp .Sr. VP/General Manager, Discovery en Español, Discovery Home & Leisure Channel, Discovery Wings Channel
Roger Marmet .Sr. VP/General Manager, TLC
Vivian Schiller .Sr. VP/General Manager, Discovery Times Channel
Clint Stinchcomb .Sr. VP/General Manager, Discovery HD Theater™
Carole Tomko .Sr. VP/General Manager, FitTV
Eileen O'Neill .Acting General Manager, Discovery Health Channel

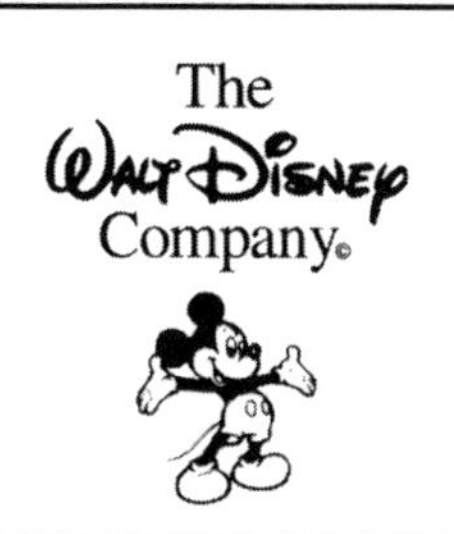

THE WALT DISNEY COMPANY

500 S. Buena Vista St.
Burbank, CA 91521
PHONE .818-560-1000
WEB SITE .www.disney.com
TYPES Features

Michael D. Eisner .CEO
Robert Iger .President/COO
Anne Sweeney .Co-Chair, Disney Media Networks
George Bodenheimer .Co-Chair, Disney Media Networks
Peter E. Murphy .Sr. Executive VP/Chief Strategic Officer
Thomas O. Staggs .Sr. Executive VP/CFO
Alan N. Braverman .Executive VP/General Counsel
John J. Garand .Executive VP, Planning & Control
Zenia Mucha .Sr. VP, Corporate Communications
Gary Foster .VP, Corporate Communications, Disney Consumer Products
John Spelich .VP, Corporate Communications
Dan Wolf .VP, Corporate Communications
Marsha L. Reed .VP/Governance Administration, Assistant Secretary

WALT DISNEY PICTURES/TOUCHSTONE PICTURES

SEE The Buena Vista Motion Pictures Group

DISNEYTOON STUDIOS

500 S. Buena Vista St.
Burbank, CA 91521
PHONE .818-560-5000
WEB SITE .www.disney.com
TYPES Animation - Features - Direct-to-Video/DVD

Sharon Morrill .President, DisneyToon Studios
Ellen Gurney .Sr. VP, Creative Affairs
Lenora Hume .Sr. VP, Worldwide Production
Brian Snedeker .Sr. VP, Creative Affairs
Matt Walker .Sr. VP, Music
Baker Bloodworth .VP, Special Projects
Karen Ferguson .VP, Digital Production & Technology
Jill Gilbert .VP, Creative Affairs
Susan Kirch .VP, Creative Affairs
Paul Rappoport .VP, Finance
Michelle Robinson .VP, Production
Brett Swain .VP, Music
Steve Swofford .VP, Post Production & Editorial
Elizabeth Wolfe .VP, Publicity
Jamie Thomason .Voice Casting & Dialog Director
Jeff Howard .Director, Creative Affairs
Eddie Khanbeigi .Attorney, Business Affairs

DISTANT HORIZON

8282 Sunset Blvd., Ste. A
Los Angeles, CA 90046
PHONE 323-848-4140
WEB SITE .....www.distant-horizon.com

TYPES	Documentaries - Features - TV Series
DEVELOPMENT	The Long Walk to Freedom - La Brassiere - Amy - Don't Look Up - Kite
CREDITS	Red Dust - Sarafina! - Cry, the Beloved Country - Face - Theory of Flight - Get Real - Black Mask - The Dish - I Capture the Castle

Anant Singh .....No Title
Brian Cox .....No Title
Tyler Steele .....No Title

DIY-DO IT YOURSELF NETWORK

9721 Sherrill Blvd.
Knoxville, TN 37932
PHONE 865-694-2700
FAX 865-531-8933
WEB SITE .....www.diynetwork.com

TYPES	New Media - Syndication - TV Series
CREDITS	Be Your Own Contractor - Classic Car Restoration - DIY to the Rescue - Kitchen Renovations - Talk2DIY Automotive - Warehouse Warriors - Tools for Women (Workshop)
COMMENTS	TV and online network providing step-by-step, do-it-yourself instructions and demonstrations

Bob Baskerville .....President
Cindy McConkey .....VP, Communications, Scripps Networks
Jeff Sears .....VP, Creative Services
Bill Sykes .....VP, Programming
Robyn Ulrich .....VP, Marketing
Freddy James .....Director, Programming

DOCKRY PRODUCTIONS

2528 Hutton Dr.
Beverly Hills, CA 90210
PHONE 310-274-0761

TYPES	Animation - Features - Direct-to-Video/DVD - Made-for-TV/Cable Movies - New Media - Syndication - TV Series
PRE-PRODUCTION	Moose - Haitian War - Cards - Rotation
PRODUCTION	Jordan Stars - Pyramids - Viva Alhambra
POST PRODUCTION	Holler - Not Me - Mynamr 2 - Solly Finders
COMPLETED UNRELEASED	Tax - Jakey - Visitors
CREDITS	Fun - Darts - Face Finders - Forget Me Not - Norwegian Moon - Jones XX - Desert Times - Bhutan Adventures
SUBMISSION POLICY	Only thru Agent
COMMENTS	Parent company, International Productions, a consortium of twenty-nine companies from twenty-nine countries; Non-English-language projects

Nancy Dockry .....President
Walter Edwards .....Executive VP
Sue Cazen .....Sr. VP, Development
Mohamad Amin .....VP, Special Projects
Tad Clancy .....VP, Comedy TV
Jonathan Farmer .....VP, Acquisitions
John Firste .....VP, Drama TV
Vivian Tarrot .....VP, Direct-to-Video
Carter Temple .....VP, Children's Projects
Victor Williams .....VP, Production
Peter Brownet .....Director, Video Projects
Jack Dillman .....Director, Features
Victoria Evans .....Director, Comedy TV
Linda Pele .....Director, Animation
Theo Vorta .....Director, Drama TV
Jeremy Chu .....Financial Consultant
Adolph Kaczynski .....Treasurer
James Mark .....Legal Affairs

DOG AND PONY PRODUCTIONS

PO Box 115
Ranco Mirage, CA 92270
PHONE 760-202-9220
FAX 760-321-6616
EMAIL .....sbzbab@yahoo.com

TYPES	Animation - Features - TV Series
CREDITS	The West Side Waltz - 1,000 Men and a Baby

Stephen L. Bedell .....Producer/Manager/Owner

DOMINANT PICTURES

7758 Sunset Blvd.
Los Angeles, CA 90046
PHONE 323-878-1111

TYPES	Features - TV Series
PRE-PRODUCTION	Valley of the Dolls Redux
POST PRODUCTION	Surviving Christmas
CREDITS	Charlie's Angels 1&2 - Private Parts - The Brady Bunch Movie - Dr. Dolittle - The Late Shift - 28 Days - Can't Hardly Wait - I Spy
COMMENTS	Moving at press time

Betty Thomas .....Owner/Director
Todd Kaufman .....Assistant to Betty Thomas

MAUREEN DONLEY PICTURES

c/o MD Pix
914 Westwood Blvd., Ste. 591
Los Angeles, CA 90024
PHONE 310-441-0834
FAX 310-441-1595
EMAIL .....mcd@mdpix.com

TYPES	Animation - Features
DEVELOPMENT	Moorchild
CREDITS	The Little Mermaid - Anastasia
COMMENTS	Specializes in live-action, mixed-media and animated motion pictures

Maureen Donley .....Producer
Lauren Sands .....VP, Development

THE DONNERS' COMPANY

9465 Wilshire Blvd., Ste. 420
Beverly Hills, CA 90212
PHONE 310-777-4600

TYPES	Animation - Features - TV Series
DEVELOPMENT	Labor Day - 12 Days of Christmas - Gregoire Moulin - Match Mutts - Sam & George - Science Fiction - Secret Life of Bees - Dude Looks Like a Lady - Unaccompanied Minors
POST PRODUCTION	Constantine
CREDITS	Timeline - Lethal Weapon 1-4 - Maverick - Free Willy 1-3 - Lady Hawke - Dave - Volcano - Consipiracy Theory - You've Got Mail - Any Given Sunday - X-Men - X2
SUBMISSION POLICY	No unsolicited submissions

Richard Donner .....No Title (310-777-6730)
Lauren Shuler Donner .....No Title (310-777-6725)
Cece Neber .....No Title (310-777-6730)
Kathy Liska .....No Title (310-777-6725)
Derek Hoffman .....No Title (310-777-6735)
Jack Leslie .....No Title (310-777-6720)
Rick Hong .....No Title (310-777-6720)
Dantram Nguyen .....No Title (310-777-6735)
Bobby Sabelhaus .....No Title (310-777-6725)

DOOZER

15030 Ventura Blvd., Ste. 779
Sherman Oaks, CA 91403
PHONE 818-623-1880
TYPES TV Series
DEALS NBC Universal Television Studio
CREDITS Scrubs - Spin City - Clone High

Bill Lawrence .... Executive Producer/Writer
Eren Celeboglu .... Assistant

DOUBLE EAGLE ENTERTAINMENT

PO Box 1268
Beverly Hills, CA 90213-1268
PHONE 310-246-1690
FAX 310-246-1693
EMAIL .... rowlandperk@earthlink.net
TYPES Features - New Media - Syndication - TV Series
CREDITS Hiroshima - Code Name: Wolverine - Psychic Chronicles

Stephen Saltzman .... Executive VP, Operations/Business Affairs

DOUBLE EDGE ENTERTAINMENT

15233 Ventura Blvd., Penthouse 9
Sherman Oaks, CA 91403
PHONE 818-205-9898
FAX 818-205-9797
EMAIL .... nina.yang@deegroup.com
WEB SITE .... www.doubleedgeentertainment.com
TYPES Animation - Features
DEVELOPMENT The Little Monk - Nanking - Dark Reign
PRE-PRODUCTION Untitled Horror Film
POST PRODUCTION Untitled Mail Order Bride Project - Sledge

Bob Sheng .... Co-Founder/CEO
Nina Yang .... Co-Founder/President/Producer
Stanley Tong .... Producer/Director
Steve Yang .... Associate/Project Manager
Scott Hui .... Office Manager/Coordinator

DOUBLE FEATURE FILMS

9465 Wilshire Blvd., Ste. 950
Beverly Hills, CA 90212
PHONE 310-887-1100
FAX 310-887-1110
TYPES Features
DEALS Universal Pictures
PRODUCTION Skeleton Key
POST PRODUCTION Be Cool

Michael Shamberg .... Co-Chair
Stacey Sher .... Co-Chair
Karen Willaman .... COO/CFO
Carla Santos Shamberg .... Executive VP, Special Projects
Kira Goldberg .... VP, Development
Erin Dicker .... Creative Executive

DOUBLE NICKEL ENTERTAINMENT

c/o Warner Bros.
1325 Avenue of the Americas, 30th Fl.
New York, NY 10019
PHONE 212-636-5488
FAX 212-636-5487
TYPES Features - Made-for-TV/Cable Movies - Reality TV - TV Series
DEALS Warner Bros. Entertainment Inc.
DEVELOPMENT Black Lightning - Pop Rocks - You Are Here - Typhoid Mary - Innocent - The Diagnosis - I. Paparazzi - Peter - Tempest
PRE-PRODUCTION Untitled Reality Show (Style Network)

Jenette Kahn .... Producer/Partner (212-636-5488)
Adam Richman .... Producer/Partner (212-636-5112)
Peter Schwerin ..... VP, Production & Development (310-273-2734 x 244)
Anna Ng .... Assistant to the Partners (212-636-5486)

JEAN DOUMANIAN PRODUCTIONS

595 Madison Ave., Ste. 2200
New York, NY 10022
PHONE 212-486-2626
FAX 212-688-6236
TYPES Documentaries - Features - Made-for-TV/Cable Movies - Theater - TV Series
DEVELOPMENT Godspeed - Fighting Fish - Fly'n V
PRODUCTION Ellie Parker
CREDITS Everyone Says I Love You - Deconstructing Harry - The Spanish Prisoner - Sweet and Lowdown - Small Time Crooks - Celebrity - Mighty Aphrodite - Women Talking Dirty - All the Real Girls - Bullets Over Broadway; Off-Broadway: *Dinah Was - Things You Shouldn't Say Past Midnight - Fuddy Meers - What the Butler Saw - Bat Boy*; Broadway: *Frankie & Johnny - Amour - Jumpers*

Jean Doumanian .... President
Etan Frankel .... VP, Development
Kimberly Jose .... VP, Production & Development
Stephen Lancellotti .... Executive Assistant
Lisa Quintela .... Executive Assistant

JEFF DOWD & ASSOCIATES

3200 Airport Ave., Ste. 1
Santa Monica, CA 90405
PHONE 310-572-1500
FAX 310-572-1501
TYPES Features
PRE-PRODUCTION The Secret Life of Huckleberry Finn
CREDITS Neil Young's Greendale - Better Luck Tomorrow - Kissing Jessica Stein - Scratch - Fern Gully - Zebrahead - Loved - Dream with the Fishes - Smiling Fish & Goat on Fire - Metallica: Some Kind of Monster - The Cockettes
COMMENTS Producers Representative

Jeff Dowd .... Partner
Sarah Rose Bergman .... Assistant

DOWNEY/TODOROFF PRODUCTIONS
c/o Bordertown Pictures
2800 Neilson Way, Ste. 911
Santa Monica, CA 90405
PHONE .310-281-8688
FAX .310-392-8669
EMAIL .todoroff@ix.netcom.com
WEB SITE .www.tomtodoroff.com
TYPES Features - Direct-to-Video/DVD - Made-for-TV/Cable Movies - TV Series
CREDITS Borrowed Hearts - Monday After the Miracle - A Test of Love - Second Honeymoon - The Sons of Mistletoe - The Survivors Club (CBS) - No Vacancy - RSC Meets USA: Working Shakespeare

Roma Downey .Producer
Tom Todoroff .Producer
Trevor Schneeberger .Assistant to Mr. Todoroff

DPS FILM ROMAN, INC.
12020 Chandler Blvd., Ste. 200
North Hollywood, CA 91607
PHONE .818-761-2544
FAX .818-985-2973
WEB SITE .www.filmroman.com
TYPES Animation - Commercials - Features - Direct-to-Video/DVD - Made-for-TV/Cable Movies - New Media - TV Series
DEVELOPMENT John Waters' Patent Leather Dream House - McShegny - Back in the Day - Junior High Tech - Cracked - Spawn
CREDITS Motocrossed - The Simpsons - King of the Hill - Johnny Tsunami - Mission Hill - The Oblongs - My First Mister - X-Men - Family Guy - Free for All - Tripping the Rift
COMMENTS Internet/Web development

John W. Hyde .CEO/President
Scott Greenberg .COO
Mike Wolf .Sr. VP, Production Animation
Sidney Clifton .Sr. VP, Creative Development
Kevin Van Hook .VP/General Manager, Forum Visual Effects
Stacey Smart .VP, Special Projects

DREAM ENTERTAINMENT, INC.
8489 W. Third St.
Los Angeles, CA 90048
PHONE .323-655-5501
FAX .323-655-5603
EMAIL .dream@dreamentertainment.net
WEB SITE .www.dreamentertainment.net
TYPES Features - Direct-to-Video/DVD
PRE-PRODUCTION Untitled Band Project - DISASTER!
CREDITS According to Spencer - Girl Fever - 100 Girls - More Dogs Than Bones - Never Again - The Journeyman - RSVP - Dahmer - Gacy - Monster Man - The Manson Family - The Manor

Ehud Bleiberg .Chairman/CEO/Producer
Yitzhak Ginsberg .President/Producer
Nadine de Barros .VP, Sales & Acquisitions
Marcia Matthew .VP, Finance
Shannon Wilson .Coordinator
Silke Wolz .Manager, Contracts & Servicing

DREAM FACTORY
2008 N. Berendo St.
Los Angeles, CA 90027
PHONE .323-665-8178
FAX .323-665-8186
TYPES Features - TV Series
CREDITS Free Willy 1-3 - Return to Me - Lethal Weapon 1-3 - Local Boys

Jennie Lew Tugend .Producer
Ricarda Ankenbrand .Producer

DREAMWORKS SKG
1000 Flower St.
Glendale, CA 91201
PHONE .818-695-5000
WEB SITE .www.dreamworks.com
TYPES Animation - Features - New Media - TV Series
PRE-PRODUCTION Talisman
PRODUCTION The Ring 2 - Shark Tale
COMPLETED UNRELEASED Collateral - Surviving Christmas
CREDITS The Terminal - Anchorman - Almost Famous - American Beauty - A.I. - A Beautiful Mind - Catch Me If You Can - Cast Away - Euro Trip - Gladiator - Minority Report - Old School - The Ring - Road to Perdition - Saving Private Ryan - Seabiscuit - Shrek 1&2 - Win a Date with Tad Hamilton

David Geffen .Co-Principal
Jeffrey Katzenberg .Co-Principal
Steven Spielberg .Co-Principal
Helene Hahn .COO
Justin Falvey .Co-Head, TV
Darryl Frank .Co-Head, TV
Laurie MacDonald .Co-Head, DreamWorks Pictures
Walter Parkes .Co-Head, DreamWorks Pictures
Ann Daly .Head, Feature Animation
Adam Goodman .Head, Theatrical Production
David Beaubaire .Theatrical Production
Michael Grillo .Theatrical Production
Marc Haimes .Theatrical Production
Andrea McCall .Theatrical Production
Grey Rembert .Theatrical Production
Claire Rudnick-Polstein .Theatrical Production
Mark Sourian .Theatrical Production
Marty Cohen .Post Production
Michael Ostin .Music
Mo Ostin .Music
Lenny Waronker .Music
Jack Bleck .Theatrical & TV Business Affairs
Tim Connors .Theatrical & TV Business Affairs
Ronni Coulter .Business/Legal Affairs
Brian Edwards .Legal Affairs
Alison Lima .Animation Business/Legal Affairs

DREYFUSS/JAMES PRODUCTIONS
c/o The Lot
1041 N. Formosa Ave., Formosa Bldg., Rm 200
West Hollywood, CA 90046
PHONE 323-850-3140
FAX 323-850-3141
TYPES Features - Made-for-TV/Cable Movies - TV Series
CREDITS Quiz Show - Mr. Holland's Opus - Having Our Say

Richard Dreyfuss .....Owner/Executive Producer
Judith James .....Owner/Executive Producer
Greg Szimonisz .....VP, Development
Audrey Bamber .....Assistant to Mr. Dreyfuss

DRIVEN ENTERTAINMENT
PO Box 6795
Burbank, CA 91510
PHONE 310-980-2882
EMAIL .....driven@drivenentertaiment.com
WEB SITE .....www.drivenentertainment.com
TYPES Features - Music Videos - TV Series
DEVELOPMENT Every Other Weekend - Legacy
CREDITS Sunday with Simon - Cravings - The Ringbearer - God Is Watching Over You - The Chickilu Ya-Ya's - Every 15 Minutes
SUBMISSION POLICY No unsolicited submissions

Celeste Wade .....Producer
Laura Hudson .....Producer

DUCKS IN A ROW ENTERTAINMENT CORPORATION
145 S. Maple Dr., Penthouse
Beverly Hills, CA 90212
PHONE 310-859-2815
FAX 310-859-2957
EMAIL .....ducksinrow@aol.com
TYPES Features - Made-for-TV/Cable Movies - New Media - Syndication - TV Series
CREDITS A Murder on Shadow Mountain (CBS)
SUBMISSION POLICY No unsolicited material

Anat Baron .....Executive Producer

DUGOW/SCHNEIDER ENTERTAINMENT
1041 N. Formosa Ave., Formosa Bldg., Rm. 4
West Hollywood, CA 90046
PHONE 323-850-3121
FAX 323-850-3196
TYPES Features - Made-for-TV/Cable Movies - TV Series
DEVELOPMENT Don't Sleep with Your Drummer - Mouthpiece - Housebroken: Confessions of a Stay-at-Home Dad

Iris Dugow .....Producer
Scott Schneider .....Producer

RONALD S. DUNAS PRODUCTIONS
10643 Selma Way
Los Angeles, CA 90077
PHONE 310-273-4712
FAX 310-275-1647
EMAIL .....rondunas@aol.com
TYPES Features - Direct-to-Video/DVD - Made-for-TV/Cable Movies - Reality TV - TV Series
DEVELOPMENT Chaos - Speakeasy - Boys of '68 - Snatched - Protective Custody
CREDITS Dr. Phibes - Scorned & Swindled - Bells - Speakeasy

Ronald Dunas .....President/Writer/Producer
Anthony Steiner .....Development Consultant
Lorrie Ryan .....Assistant to Ronald Dunas

THE DUNCAN GROUP, INC.
777 N. Jefferson St.
Milwaukee, WI 53202
PHONE 414-223-1060
WEB SITE .....www.duncanentertainment.com
TYPES Documentaries - Features - TV Series
CREDITS Eden - Cadillac Ranch - The Break Up - Row Your Boat

Chip Duncan .....Producer/Director

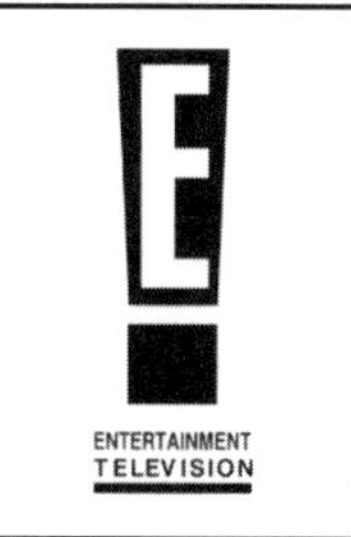

E! NETWORKS
5750 Wilshire Blvd.
Los Angeles, CA 90036
PHONE 323-954-2400
FAX .....323-954-2662 (PR)
WEB SITE .....www.eonline.com
TYPES Documentaries - Reality TV - TV Series
CREDITS 101 Series - Clean House - E! News Live - Howard Stern - E! True Hollywood Story - Scream Play - Dr. 90210 - How Do I Look? - Brini Maxwell Show - New York Nick
COMMENTS 24-hour entertainment network; E! Entertainment Television; Style Network

Ted Harbert .....President/CEO
Ken Bettsteller .....COO
Mark Sonnenberg .....Executive VP, Entertainment
David T. Cassaro .....Sr. Executive VP
Neil Baker .....Sr. VP, Sales & Distribution
Lisa Berger .....Sr. VP, Programming Development
Howard Bolter .....Sr. VP, Network & Production Operations
Jack Carey .....Sr. VP, Technology and Operations
Steve Dolcemaschio .....Sr. VP, Finance/CFO
Brad Fox .....Sr. VP, Affiliate Relations
Jeff Lai .....Sr. VP, Business & Legal Affairs
Kevin MacLellan .....Sr. VP, International
Leslee Perlstein .....Sr. VP, Human Resources
Stephen H. Schwartz .....Sr. VP, Style Programming
Jeff Shore .....Sr. VP, Production
Steven Blue .....VP, Production Management
Salaam Coleman Smith .....VP, Programming
Sarah Goldstein .....VP, Publicity & Media Relations
Ann Lewis .....VP/Executive Producer
Barry Nugent .....VP, Talent

It is illegal to copy any part of this book

E[3] ENTERTAINMENT, LLC

1067 Gayley Ave., 2nd Fl.
Los Angeles, CA 90024
PHONE .310-209-1174/310-209-1175
FAX .310-209-1164
EMAIL .jlee@e3ent.net
SECOND EMAIL .alightner@e3ent.net
WEB SITE .www.e3ent.net
TYPES Animation - Features - TV Series
DEVELOPMENT Future Force - Day of the Opera - The Roman - Marya
PRE-PRODUCTION Mermaids Singing - The Fat Man - The Sailmaker - Monkey Knife Fight
COMPLETED UNRELEASED Dizzyland
CREDITS Morning - The Last Supper - Campfire Tales - Photographing Fairies - Kiss the Girls - Apple Jack
COMMENTS Business and legal affairs consulting

Don Schneider .Principal
Larry Weinberg .Principal
Michael Korine .CFO
Jennifer Lee .Development Executive
Jeffrey Daitch .Business & Legal Affairs
Angela Lightner .Office Manager

EARTHBOURNE FILMS, INC.

713 Hampden Pl.
Pacific Palisades, CA 90272
PHONE .310-230-2031
FAX .310-230-2053
EMAIL .earthbourne@aol.com
TYPES Documentaries - Features - TV Series
DEVELOPMENT The Doctor Is Sick - Gun, with Occasional Music - Ingenious Pain
CREDITS Touch - The Minus Man
SUBMISSION POLICY No unsolicited submissions

Fida Attieh .Producer
Hampton Fancher .Writer/Director

EARTHWORKS FILMS

13527 Contour Dr.
Sherman Oaks, CA 91423
PHONE .818-990-2261
FAX .818-990-2265
EMAIL .maflorio@pacbell.net
TYPES Documentaries - Features
DEVELOPMENT Laura Nyro Documentary
PRE-PRODUCTION Venice (Documentary)
CREDITS Broken Rainbow (Documentary) - Tibet: Cry of the Snow Lion (Documentary)

Maria Florio .President
Victoria Mudd .VP

EAST OF DOHENY/LEXINGTON ROAD PRODUCTIONS

9014 Melrose Ave.
Los Angeles, CA 90069
PHONE .310-248-4880
FAX .310-248-4990
EMAIL .info@eastofdoheny.com
WEB SITE .www.eastofdoheny.com
TYPES Features - Theater
CREDITS Features: A Time for Dancing - Siegfried & Roy: The Magic Box (IMAX) - Men with Guns; Theater: *Napoleon: The Musical, The Full Monty, Art, Cressida* (West End, London), *Flower Drum Song* (Los Angeles), *The Sweet Smell of Success, Big River, Match, Not About Nightingales* (Broadway)
COMMENTS Family entertainment

Lou Gonda .Partner
Kelly Gonda .Partner
Harvey Gettleson .CFO
Kitty Olisky .Executive VP
David Hamlin .Head, Business Affairs
Lynette Howell .Office Manager/Theatrical Executive

ECHELON ENTERTAINMENT

400 S. Victory Blvd., Ste. 203
Burbank, CA 91502
PHONE .818-558-1820
FAX .818-558-1877
EMAIL .info@echelonent.com
WEB SITE .www.echelonent.com
TYPES Animation - Documentaries - Features - Direct-to-Video/DVD - TV Series
DEVELOPMENT The Sugar Wars - Bad Kitty - Pumpkinhead 3 - S.I.N. - El Destino - Bordergate - Deep Blue - Grim's Day Off
CREDITS Wisegirls (Cinemax) - Maniacts (Video/MTI) - A Light in the Forest (Ardustry); Distributor (Newmark/Echelon): CockFight - Wake - Bachelor Man - A Tale of Two Pizzas - Swimming Upstream
SUBMISSION POLICY Name talent only
COMMENTS DVD/Video label: Singa Home Entertainment

Eric Louzil .President/CEO
Gloria Morrison .President, Development & Acquisitions
Geoff Jarvis .VP, International Sales
Stacey Parks .VP, International Sales
Tommy Savich .VP, Domestic Sales
John Howard .Head, Press Relations
Mark Holdom .Pre-Sales/Theatrical Distribution
Francia Buitrago .Administrative Assistant
Ellen Roongcharoen .Sales Assistant

ECHO LAKE PRODUCTIONS

421 S. Beverly Dr., 8th Fl.
Beverly Hills, CA 90212
PHONE .310-789-4790
FAX .310-789-4791
EMAIL .contact@echolakeproductions.com
TYPES Features
DEVELOPMENT Salt of the Earth - Make Someone Happy - Son of a G Man
PRE-PRODUCTION Dreamland - Water
CREDITS The Big Empty - Things Behind the Sun - Thirteen Conversations About One Thing - Levity - La Ciudad

Doug Mankoff .President
Andrew D. Spaulding .Executive VP
Jessica Stamen .VP, Development
Amotz Zakai .Director, Development
Angela Agne .Office Manager

ABRA EDELMAN PRODUCTIONS
16170 Kennedy Rd.
Los Gatos, CA 95032
PHONE 877-630-2272
EMAIL ....abra@abraknitting.com
TYPES Features - Direct-to-Video/DVD - Made-for-TV/Cable Movies - Syndication - TV Series
CREDITS Just Ask My Children - Air Bud 1&2 - Dungeons & Dragons - Some Girls - Loving Lulu - Bulletproof Heart - Underworld - Changing Habits - According to Spencer - Snap Judgment

Abra Edelman ....Producer
Elisa Goodman ....Casting Partner

THE EDELSTEIN COMPANY
500 S. Buena Vista St., Animation Bldg., Ste. 2D4
Burbank, CA 91521-1740
PHONE 818-560-3884
FAX 818-560-4949
TYPES Made-for-TV/Cable Movies - TV Series
DEALS Touchstone Television
CREDITS Threat Matrix - Hope and Faith (Pilot) - Desperate Housewives

Michael Edelstein ....Producer
Chris Loveall ....Assistant

EDMONDS ENTERTAINMENT
1635 N. Cahuenga Blvd., 5th Fl.
Los Angeles, CA 90028
PHONE 323-860-1550
FAX 323-860-1554
WEB SITE ....www.edmondsent.com
TYPES Features - TV Series
CREDITS Soul Food (Feature) - Hav Plenty - Light It Up - Punks - Soul Food (Series) - Maniac Magee
SUBMISSION POLICY No unsolicited material

Tracey E. Edmonds ....President/CEO
Kenneth "Babyface" Edmonds ....President/CEO
Janine Jones ....Sr. VP, Television
Steve Lapuk ....VP, Development, Film
Julian Lloyd ....Director, Creative Affairs
Emerlynn Lampitoc ....Executive Assistant, TV

EDUCATIONAL COMMUNICATIONS
PO Box 351419
Los Angeles, CA 90035
PHONE 310-559-9160
EMAIL ....ecnp@aol.com
WEB SITE ....www.ecoprojects.org
TYPES Documentaries - TV Series
CREDITS ECONEWS (Series)
SUBMISSION POLICY By telephone
COMMENTS Over 500 half-hour videos and 1,500 audio programs about the environment; Produces worldwide ecotourism specials as well as Enviromental Directions radio series, PSAs and video news reports

Nancy Pearlman ....Executive Producer
Leslie Lewis ....Assistant

RONA EDWARDS PRODUCTIONS
264 S. La Cienega Blvd., Ste. 1052
Beverly Hills, CA 90211
PHONE 323-466-3013
FAX 323-467-1258
TYPES Documentaries - Features - Made-for-TV/Cable Movies - Syndication - TV Series - Reality TV
DEVELOPMENT Matchmakers (Warner Bros.)
CREDITS The Companion - One Special Victory - I Know What You Did - Out of Sync - Der Murder Meiner Mutter
COMMENTS Also ES Entertainment, Literary Consultants

Rona Edwards ....Producer
Monika Skerbelis ....Producer (ES Entertainment) (310-278-4484)
Marianne Moore ....Director, Development

RALPH EDWARDS PRODUCTIONS
6922 Hollywood Blvd., Ste. 300
Hollywood, CA 90028
PHONE 323-462-2212
FAX 323-461-1224
EMAIL ....info@ralphedwards.com
TYPES Animation - Direct-to-Video/DVD - Syndication - TV Series - Reality TV
CREDITS Truth or Consequences - People's Court - Annabelle's Wish - This Is Your Life - Bzzz

Ralph Edwards ....Chairman Emeritus
Barbara Dunn-Leonard ....President
James B. Pollock ....Vice Chairman
Gary Edwards ....Executive VP

EFB PRODUCTIONS
12233 W. Olympic Blvd., Ste. 256
Los Angeles, CA 90064
PHONE 310-979-5964
FAX 310-826-2084
TYPES Features - TV Series
DEVELOPMENT Truck 44 - 04 July - PU-239 - The Kingdom - Trap Team
POST PRODUCTION Friday Night Lights
CREDITS Very Bad Things - Wonderland (TV) - The Rundown
SUBMISSION POLICY Via Endeavor Agency

Peter Berg ....Writer/Director
Maria Williams ....Tiny Dancer

***DAVID EICK PRODUCTIONS**
100 Universal City Plaza, Bldg. 2372A, Ste. E
Universal City, CA 91608
PHONE 818-777-7567
FAX 818-733-2522
TYPES TV Series
PRODUCTION Battlestar Galactica
CREDITS Cover Me - The Agency - Spy Game - American Gothic - Hercules: The Legendary Journeys

David Eick ....President
James Halpern ....Creative Executive

It is illegal to copy any part of this book

EIGHTH SQUARE ENTERTAINMENT
606 N. Larchmont Blvd., Ste. 307
Los Angeles, CA 90004
PHONE 323-469-1003
FAX 323-469-1516
EMAIL ....eighthsq@aol.com
TYPES: Features - Made-for-TV/Cable Movies - Theater - TV Series
PRE-PRODUCTION: Before the Devil Knows You're Dead
POST PRODUCTION: Lehi's Wife
CREDITS: Psycho Beach Party - I'll See You in My Dreams
SUBMISSION POLICY: No unsolicited material

Jeff Melnick ....No Title
Janette Jensen "JJ" Hoffman ....No Title

EL DORADO PICTURES
725 Arizona Ave., Ste. 100
Santa Monica, CA 90401
PHONE 310-458-4800
FAX 310-458-4802
WEB SITE ....www.alecbaldwin.com
TYPES: Features - Made-for-TV/Cable Movies - TV Series
PRODUCTION: Lymelife
CREDITS: The Confession - Nuremberg - State and Main - Second Nature

Alec Baldwin ....Producer
Jon Cornick ....Producer
Helen Berger ....Assistant to Alec Baldwin
Tiffany Nishimoto ....Assistant to Jon Cornick

EL NORTE PRODUCTIONS
PO Box 2871
Culver City, CA 90232-2871
PHONE 310-244-2581
FAX 310-244-0550
EMAIL ....bmjelnorte@hotmail.com
TYPES: Documentaries - Features - TV Series
DEVELOPMENT: Zapata - Bordertown - Tattooed Soldier
CREDITS: American Tapestry - El Norte - Mi Familia - Selena - Why Do Fools Fall in Love - American Family (PBS)
SUBMISSION POLICY: No unsolicited submissions

Gregory Nava ....CEO/Producer
Barbara Martinez Jitner ....President/Producer

ELECTRIC ENTERTAINMENT
PO Box 46277
Los Angeles, CA 90046
PHONE 323-817-1300
FAX 323-467-7155
WEB SITE ....www.electric-entertainment.com
TYPES: Features - Made-for-TV/Cable Movies - New Media - TV Series
CREDITS: Universal Soldier - Stargate - Eight Legged Freaks - Independence Day - Godzilla - The Patriot - The Visitor - Cellular
SUBMISSION POLICY: No unsolicited submissions

Dean Devlin ....President
Marc Roskin ....VP, Development/Co-Producer
Kearie Peak ....Co-Producer
Rachel Olschan ....Associate Producer

ELEVENTH DAY ENTERTAINMENT
17003 Ventura Blvd., Ste. 200
Encino, CA 91316
PHONE 818-784-6403
FAX 818-784-6421
EMAIL ....mail@eleventhday.com
WEB SITE ....www.eleventhday.com
TYPES: Commercials - Documentaries - Direct-to-Video/DVD - New Media - TV Series
PRODUCTION: For the Love of Liberty - The Story of the New Testament
CREDITS: The Warner Bros. Story: 75 Years of Laughter - CBS: The First Fifty Years - The Wonderful World of Disney: 40 Years of Magic - MGM: When the Lion Roars - Sex, Censorship & the Silver Screen
COMMENTS: Corporate; Interactive film; Video production

Frank Martin ....Producer/Director
Rudy Poe ....Producer/Director

ELIXIR FILMS
1831 Colorado Ave., Ste. 1000
Santa Monica, CA 90404
PHONE 310-449-0120
FAX 310-449-0170
EMAIL ....info@elixirfilms.com
WEB SITE ....www.elixirfilms.com
TYPES: Features
DEVELOPMENT: The Ambidextrist - Expats
PRODUCTION: Long Way Round
COMPLETED UNRELEASED: Where the Red Fern Grows
CREDITS: Wake Up and Smell the Coffee - The Good Thief

David Alexanian ....Producer
Alexis Alexanian ....Producer
James Simak ....Creative Executive
Andrew Mer ....Development

ELKINS ENTERTAINMENT
8306 Wilshire Blvd., PMB 438
Beverly Hills, CA 90211-2382
PHONE 818-501-9900
FAX 818-501-9800
EMAIL ....elkinsent@msn.com
TYPES: Animation - Documentaries - Features - Direct-to-Video/DVD - Made-for-TV/Cable Movies - Syndication - Theater - TV Series
DEALS: Showtime Networks, Inc.
DEVELOPMENT: The Huntsman - Romeo & Juliet - Cat's Cradle - The Timothy Leary Story - The Challenger
PRE-PRODUCTION: For the Love of Liberty
CREDITS: A Doll's House - Richard Pryor Live - A New Leaf - Inside - In His Father's Shoes - Oh! Calcutta! - Golden Boy - Father for Charlie - Sex, Censorship and the Silver Screen - Stander - Pippin
COMMENTS: Management; Deal with The Mark Taper Forum

Hillard Elkins ....President/Producer
Sandi Love ....VP
Greg Hausmann ....VP, Operations

ELSBOY/SUNTAUR ENTERTAINMENT
1581 N. Crescent Heights Blvd.
Los Angeles, CA 90046
PHONE .323-656-3800
EMAIL .suntaurent@aol.com
TYPES Features - Made-for-TV/Cable Movies - TV Series
DEVELOPMENT Untitled Magic Reality Show (TV); Features: Posse Whipped - Snow in April - Impossible Dreams - Collision Course - The Party-Party
CREDITS Under One Roof (CBS, Series) - In Too Deep (Feature) - Maxie (Feature) - Laurel Avenue (HBO, Miniseries) - Grand Avenue (Miniseries) - Save the Dog (Disney Channel)

Paul Aaron .Writer/Producer/Director
James Waugh .Director, Development

EMBER ENTERTAINMENT GROUP
11718 Barrington Court, Ste. 116
Los Angeles, CA 90049
PHONE .310-230-9759
TYPES Features
DEALS DreamWorks SKG
DEVELOPMENT The Unseen - The Man from U.N.C.L.E. - The Girl from U.N.C.L.E. - Thirty Minutes or Less
CREDITS Forbidden Planet - Back to the Beach - Permanent Record - The Night Before - Tales from the Hollywood Hills

Lindsay Dunlap .Producer
Chantel Hendrickson .Manager
J.A. Keller .Finance
J.A. McGuire .Finance (UK)

EMBY EYE
243 23rd St.
Santa Monica, CA 90402
PHONE .310-264-5573
EMAIL .embyeye@hotmail.com
TYPES Features - Made-for-TV/Cable Movies - TV Series
CREDITS Sleep Easy Hutch Rimes - Edie & Pen - When the Party's Over - Three of Hearts - A Carol Christmas

Matthew Irmas .President

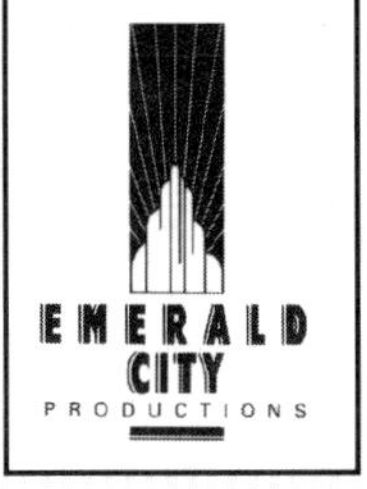

***EMERALD CITY PRODUCTION, INC.**
c/o Stankevich-Gochman, LLP
9777 Wilshire Blvd., Ste. 550
Beverly Hills, CA 90212
PHONE .310-859-8825
FAX .310-859-8830
TYPES Features
CREDITS Lord of the Rings Trilogy - The Matrix - Face/Off - The Fan - Rapa Nui - Wilder Napalm - China Moon - Dick Tracy - Child's Play - Peggy Sue Got Married - The Cotton Club
SUBMISSION POLICY No unsolicited submissions

Barrie M. Osborne .Producer

EMERALD TAPESTRY PICTURES
322 Culver Blvd., Ste. 191
Playa del Rey, CA 90293
PHONE .323-850-4456
TYPES Features
DEVELOPMENT Shortstop
CREDITS Eight Lanes in Hamilton

Ken O'Donnell .Partner
Joel Berry .Partner

EMERGING PICTURES
245 W. 55th St., 4th Fl.
New York, NY 10019
PHONE .212-245-6767
FAX .212-202-4984
EMAIL .inquiries@emergingpictures.com
WEB SITE .www.emergingpictures.com
TYPES Documentaries - Features - Made-for-TV/Cable Movies - TV Series
DEVELOPMENT A.K.A. - Love, Marriage and Marilyn Monroe - Speedology - Master and Margarita - Nickel and Dimed
PRE-PRODUCTION For Real - Superheros
POST PRODUCTION The Brothel - Forget Me Not (Fei)
COMPLETED UNRELEASED The Forgotten - Second Best - Home of the Brave - Dance Cuba - The Game of Their Lives - Tony and Tina's Wedding
CREDITS Twelve - Killing Time - The Lucky Ones - The Ballad of Bering Strait - Way Past Cool - This Old Cub - Relative Evil
SUBMISSION POLICY See Web site

Ira Deutchman .President/CEO
Barry Rebo .Chairman
Giovanni Cozzi .Vice Chairman
Josh Green .Director, Marketing & Business Development
Scott Karpf .Director, Acquisitions & Development

EMMETT/FURLA FILMS
8530 Wilshire Blvd., Ste. 420
Beverly Hills, CA 90211
PHONE .310-659-9411
FAX .310-659-9412
TYPES Features
DEALS Millennium Films - Nu Image
DEVELOPMENT Micronauts - Room Service - Abominable Snowman - The Greatest Escape - Genie with the Light Blue Hair - Pop Princess - The Contract - 88 Minutes
PRE-PRODUCTION Amityville: The Devil's Horror Within
POST PRODUCTION Control - A Love Song for Bobby Long - Blind Horizon - Lover Boy - Edison
CREDITS Wonderland - Narc - Half Past Dead - Good Advice - Speedway Junky

Randall Emmett .Producer/Co-Chair
George Furla .Producer/Co-Chair
Stanley Tepper .CFO
M. Dal Walton III .VP, Development & Business Affairs
Rosie Charbonneau .Executive Assistant to Producers
Jose Jaime .Second Executive Assistant

EMPIRE PICTURES INCORPORATED
8580 Cole Crest Dr.
Los Angeles, CA 90046
PHONE .323-656-4075
FAX .323-656-7772
TYPES Features
DEVELOPMENT Surprise Party - John Tucker Must Die - Veronica - Marvin - I Know That You Know - Art Con - Nike - Coincidence - High Maintenance - Eveless Eden
PRE-PRODUCTION Quail Hollow
POST PRODUCTION The Big White
CREDITS Keys to Tulsa - Bandits - The Last Seduction

Michael Birnbaum .President/Producer

ENCHANTMENT FILMS, INC.
105 Bryn Mawr St., SE
Albuquerque, NM 87106
PHONE .505-256-1313
TYPES Features
DEVELOPMENT Root of All Evil
PRE-PRODUCTION The Big Dump - Sandia Tram
COMPLETED UNRELEASED A Man, a Midget, and a Deck of Cards - Baby Insane & The Buddha
CREDITS Dead Men Can't Dance - South Central - Hearts of Stone - Columbia Discovery Program
COMMENTS Digital; Founder, Flicks on 66, Digital Film Festival, Albuquerque, NM; NM Distributor, Fuji Film

Steve Anderson .Writer/Director/Producer
Jim Powell .Marketing Director
Georgia Packard .Camera Manager
Marshall Bear .Administrative Executive
Dennis Geomelski .Associate Producer
Danny Wilding .Angel Set Security

ENDEMOL USA, INC.
9255 Sunset Blvd., Ste. 1100
Los Angeles, CA 90069
PHONE .310-860-9914
FAX .310-860-0073
WEB SITE .www.endemol.com
TYPES Reality TV
CREDITS Big Brother - Fear Factor - Spy TV - Performing As... - The People's Champions - Anything for Love - Extreme Makeover: Home Edition - Todd TV
SUBMISSION POLICY No unsolicited material

David Goldberg .President
Eugene Young .Sr. VP, Programming & Development
Ira Chartoff .VP, Finance & Administration
Lisa Higgins .VP, Production
Elizabeth Sherman .VP, New Media
Caroline Baumgard .Director, Development
Robert Smith .Director, Programming
Tina Hoover .Manager, Production
Cynthia Stockhammer .Manager, Programming & Development
Carrie Raisler .Coordinator, Development

ENDGAME ENTERTAINMENT
1041 N. Formosa Ave., Admin. Bldg., Ste. 195
Los Angeles, CA 90046
PHONE .323-850-2747
FAX .323-850-2754
TYPES Documentaries - Features - Made-for-TV/Cable Movies - Theater - TV Series
DEVELOPMENT Electroboy - Zombie Survival Guide - Alibi - River Queen
PRE-PRODUCTION Beyond the Sea
POST PRODUCTION Five Children & It - Proof - Beyond the Sea - The Year of the Yao
COMPLETED UNRELEASED Harold & Kumar Go to White Castle - Stage Beauty
CREDITS Pulse: A Stomp Odyssey - Michael Jordan to the Max (IMAX) - It's the Rage; Broadway: Hairspray - The Producers - Stomp - Little Shop of Horrors

James Stern .CEO
Julia Eisenman .President, Production (323-850-2738)
Doug Hansen .COO
Cindy Kirven .VP, Finance & Business Affairs
Adam Del Deo .Producer
Laura Mueller .Assistant
Eleanor Nett .Assistant

ENERGY ENTERTAINMENT
999 N. Doheny Dr., Ste. 711
Los Angeles, CA 90069
PHONE .310-274-3440
WEB SITE .www.energyentertainment.com
TYPES Features
DEVELOPMENT The Number 23 (New Line) - Turn (Radar Pictures) - Planet Terry (New Line) - Honeymoon From Hell (Paramount) - Prom (Lions Gate) - Wimpy (Alcon/WB) - Rapid (Columbia) - Bachelorette (Universal)
COMMENTS Feature literary management

Brooklyn Weaver .Owner/Manager
Jeannie Bendel .Story Department
Biana Kirk .Story Department

ENSEMBLE
9348 Civic Center Dr., Mezzanine
Beverly Hills, CA 90210
PHONE .310-300-9130/44-207-927-6525
FAX .310-300-9098/44-207-927-6526
TYPES Features - Made-for-TV/Cable Movies - TV Series
DEALS HBO Original Programming
CREDITS Band of Brothers
COMMENTS UK address: 61 Charlotte St., London, W1T 4PF UK

Jennifer Erzen .No Title
Jennifer Jackson .No Title
Lily Lester .No Title
Patrick Murray .No Title
Tony To .No Title
Angus Wood .No Title

ENSEMBLE ENTERTAINMENT
10474 Santa Monica Blvd., Ste. 380
Los Angeles, CA 90025
PHONE .310-882-8900
FAX .310-882-8901

TYPES	Animation - Documentaries - Features - Direct-to-Video/DVD - Interactive Games - New Media - TV Series
DEVELOPMENT	The Snow Goose - The Poseidon Adventure - You'll Never Eat Lunch in This Town Again - Party Animals - Cola Wars - Above Kansas
CREDITS	The Ties That Bind - Slaves to the Underground
COMMENTS	Management company; Interactive multi-media

Jon Brown .Partner
Barbara Lawrence .Partner
Jeffrey Thal .Partner
Patti Cummings .Assistant to Jeffrey Thal
Natasha Gatlin .Assistant to Barbara Lawrence
Yoni Ovadia .Assistant to Jon Brown

ENTERAKTION STUDIOS
c/o Sound City Center Stage
15466 Cabrito Rd.
Van Nuys, CA 91406
PHONE .818-994-5494
FAX .818-994-5794
EMAIL .info@enteraktion.com
WEB SITE .www.enteraktion.com

TYPES	Animation - Documentaries - Features - Direct-to-Video/DVD - Interactive Games - New Media - Syndication - TV Series
PRE-PRODUCTION	The Neighborhood
POST PRODUCTION	Kidsline - 14 Stories
CREDITS	Denial - We Dare You - Mismatch - House to House - The Arrival (CD-ROM)

Tom Walsh .CEO/Producer/Director/Co-Chairman
Ronald Hilton .Co-Chairman
Adriana Walsh .Executive VP
Chris Goger .VP, Production
Jerry Smith .Director, Digital/CGI
Paulina Guth .Animation Coordinator

ENTERTAINMENT CONSULTING GROUP
16935 Vanowen St., Ste. 203
Van Nuys, CA 91406
PHONE .818-708-0888, x23
FAX .818-708-0130

TYPES	Animation - Features - Direct-to-Video/DVD - TV Series
CREDITS	ILL-ustrated (VH1) - Firedog (Animated Feature)

Eric Treibatch .Producer

ENTERTAINMENT LICENSING ASSOCIATES
22287 Mulholland Hwy., Ste. 425
Calabasas, CA 91302
PHONE .818-225-7870
EMAIL .dankletzky@earthlink.net

TYPES	Animation - Features - TV Series
DEVELOPMENT	Dead or Alive (Feature) - Pillow People (Animated Series)
POST PRODUCTION	Resident Evil 2
CREDITS	Features: Resident Evil - House of the Dead; Animated Series: The Secret Files of the Spy Dogs - Street Fighter - Mega Man - Dark Stalkers

Daniel Kletzky .President
Michael Hack .Producer

ENTITLED ENTERTAINMENT
606 N. Larchmont Blvd., Ste. 208
Los Angeles, CA 90004
PHONE .323-469-9000
FAX .323-469-9008
WEB SITE .www.entitledentertainment.com

TYPES	Features - Theater
DEVELOPMENT	Getting Blue - My Father Had a Daughter
POST PRODUCTION	Aurora Borealis - L.A. Riot Spectacular
COMPLETED UNRELEASED	Illusion
CREDITS	Thirteen Conversations About One Thing - Levity - Long Day's Journey Into Night (Broadway)

James Burke .Partner
Scott Disharoon .Partner
Laura Citrano .VP

ENTPRO, INC.
1015 Gayley Ave., Ste. 1149
Los Angeles, CA 90024-3424
PHONE .310-440-4829

TYPES	Features - Made-for-TV/Cable Movies - Theater
DEVELOPMENT	Six Dance Lessons in Six Weeks
POST PRODUCTION	Puerto Vallarta Squeeze - The Sisters
CREDITS	Rescue Me - False Witness - A Friendship in Vienna

Richard Alfieri .Writer/Producer
Arthur Allan Seidelman .Director/Producer
Joseph Eastwood .Development

ENVISION ENTERTAINMENT
209 E. 56th St., 4th Fl.
New York, NY 10022
PHONE .212-888-6350
EMAIL .sid.feders@envisionentertainment.com
WEB SITE .www.envisionentertainment.com

TYPES	Documentaries - Features - Made-for-TV/Cable Movies - New Media - Reality TV - Syndication - TV Series
DEVELOPMENT	Wrong Is Right (Reality Game Show) - Clubhouse Rules - What's the Big Idea? (Documentary Series) - The Con Man of Abscam (TV Movie) - Nautilus Under the Ice (Feature) - Spycatcher (Feature) - CBS vs. Congress (Feature) - Red in the Face (Feature) - Abandoned: The Greely Expedition - The Voyage of the Nautilus (Documentary)
CREDITS	Cloned - Beijing to London Taxi - One Minute to Midnight - Robert F. Kennedy: The Man and the Memories - Get Music: The Television Show

Sid Feders .Executive Producer/Writer/Director

ENVISION ENTERTAINMENT, LLC
6525 Sunset Blvd., Ste. 703
Los Angeles, CA 90028
PHONE .323-957-9803
FAX .323-957-1318
EMAIL .rob_envisionent@comcast.net
SECOND EMAIL .michael_envisionent@comcast.net
TYPES: Features - Direct-to-Video/DVD - Made-for-TV/Cable Movies - New Media - TV Series
DEVELOPMENT: Personal Shopper - Williamsport - Silence
CREDITS: 10 Attitudes
SUBMISSION POLICY: Submissions by request only
COMMENTS: In Affiliation with Allan Carr Enterprises; Own rights to dance remix version of *Grease*; Main emphasis on Feature Films; Limited actor management

Rob Bonet .Producer
Michael O. Gallant .Producer
Rob Stein .Creative Executive
Tobias Daniels .Executive Assistant
David Johnson .Executive Assistant

EOE - ESPN ORIGINAL ENTERTAINMENT
ESPN Plaza
Bristol, CT 06010
PHONE .860-766-2000/212-916-9200
FAX .860-766-2415
EMAIL .footage@espn.com
WEB SITE .www.espn.com
TYPES: Documentaries - Made-for-TV/Cable Movies - TV Series
CREDITS: Playmakers - Pardon The Interruption - The Junction Boys - Dream Job - ESPY's - World Series of Poker - Streetball - A Season on the Brink - The Season - Around the Horn
COMMENTS: Sports programming; East Coast address: 605 Third Ave., 8th Fl., New York, NY 10158

George Bodenheimer .President
Mark Shapiro .Sr. VP/General Manager, Programming
Ron Semiao .Sr. VP, ESPN Original Entertainment
Michael Antinoro .Executive Producer, ESPN Original Entertainment
Will Staeger .Executive Producer, ESPN Original Entertainment
Fred Christenson .Director, Programming & Strategic Acquisitions, ESPN Original Entertainment

EPIPHANY PICTURES, INC.
10625 Esther Ave.
Los Angeles, CA 90064
PHONE .310-815-1266/310-452-0242
FAX .310-815-1269/310-452-7542
EMAIL .firstname@ephiphanypictures.com
WEB SITE .www.epiphanypictures.com
SECOND WEB SITE .www.roaddogsthemovie.com
TYPES: Animation - Documentaries - Features - Direct-to-Video/DVD - Made-for-TV/Cable Movies - TV Series
DEVELOPMENT: Eminent Domain - The African - Behind the Lines - Mayor Daley: American Pharaoh - American Standard - Cigars, Cars (and Guitars) - Caveman Robot - Deep Creek - Candy War
PRE-PRODUCTION: Sweet Home Chicago - Everlasting
PRODUCTION: Dharma (Working Title)

(Continued)

EPIPHANY PICTURES, INC. (Continued)
CREDITS: Phenomenon: The Lost Archives (PBS) - Picture Windows (Showtime) - Rosemary - Road Kings (Lions Gate Films)

Scott JT Frank .Producer/Director (scott@epiphanypictures.com)
Dan Halperin .Producer/Director (310-452-0242, dan@epiphanypictures.com)
Mark Frazel .Director, Development (773-935-8765, mark@epiphanypictures.com)
Carey Lundin .Producer/Director (312-787-3322, carey@epiphanypictures.com)

STEFANIE EPSTEIN PRODUCTIONS
427 N. Canon Dr., Ste. 206
Beverly Hills, CA 90210
PHONE .310-385-0300
FAX .310-385-0302
TYPES: Features - Made-for-TV/Cable Movies - TV Series
DEVELOPMENT: Shore Leave - What Men Want Most - Postal Police - Mad Shoes - Babygate - Vanishing Act
PRE-PRODUCTION: The Best Day
COMPLETED UNRELEASED: A Boyfriend for Christmas
CREDITS: Audrey's Rain - Abduction of Innocence

Stefanie Epstein .Producer
Jason Murtagh .Creative Executive

ESCAPE ARTISTS
c/o Sony Pictures
10202 W. Washington Blvd., Astaire Bldg., 3rd Fl.
Culver City, CA 90232
PHONE .310-244-8833
FAX .310-244-2151
EMAIL .firstname_lastname@spe.sony.com
WEB SITE .www.hollywoodlitsales.com
TYPES: Features - New Media - TV Series
DEALS: Sony Pictures Entertainment
DEVELOPMENT: Dairy - Need - Nautica
POST PRODUCTION: The Weather Man
CREDITS: A Knight's Tale - Alex and Emma

Steve Tisch .Partner/Producer (310-244-6612)
Todd Black .Partner/Producer (310-244-8683)
Jason Blumenthal .Partner/Producer (310-244-8670)
David Alper .Partner/CEO (310-244-6615)
David Bloomfield .Executive VP, Business & Legal Affairs (310-244-6631)
Chrissy Blumenthal .VP, Production (310-244-8658)
Kim Skeeters .VP, Administration & Finance (310-244-6619)
Lance Johnson .Director, Development (310-244-5053)
Kathy Rowe .Office Manager/Assistant to Todd Black (310-244-8220)
Chris Coggins .Creative Assistant (310-244-8659)
Lacy Boughn .Assistant to Steve Tisch (310-244-6620)
Jennifer Dubin .Assistant to David Alper (310-244-6632)
Anne Lopez .Assistant to David Bloomfield (310-244-7680)

ESPARZA-KATZ PRODUCTIONS

3030 Andrita St.
Los Angeles, CA 90065
PHONE 310-281-3770
FAX 310-281-3777
TYPES: Features - Made-for-TV/Cable Movies - TV Series
DEVELOPMENT: Cesar Chavez Story - Green Card Marines - Walkout - Salt of the Earth
CREDITS: Gods and Generals - Avenging Angel - Selena - Gettysburg - Rough Riders - The Cisco Kid - Milagro Beanfield War - The Disappearance of Garcia Lorca - Introducing Dorothy Dandridge
SUBMISSION POLICY: No unsolicited submissions or phone calls

Moctesuma Esparza .....Executive Producer
Robert Katz .....Executive Producer
Kim Myers .....Producer
Luis Guerrero .....Executive Assistant
Erick Garcia .....Executive Assistant

ESSENTIAL ENTERTAINMENT

5138 Sunset Blvd., Ste. 41
Hollywood, CA 90027
PHONE 323-666-4300
FAX 323-660-8068
EMAIL .....chris@essentialentertainment.com
WEB SITE .....www.essentialentertainment.com
TYPES: New Media - TV Series
CREDITS: What's Your 20? - Night Bites

Chris Tragos .....President

ETERNITY PICTURES, INC.

169 Pier Ave., 2nd Fl.
Santa Monica, CA 90405
PHONE 310-452-7313
FAX 310-452-7318
EMAIL .....production@eternitypictures.com
TYPES: Features
DEVELOPMENT: The Courier
CREDITS: Jeepers Creepers - Deuces Wild - The Contender - If You Only Knew - Afterglow - Cookie's Fortune - Laws of Deception - Shaded Places - Detour - Virgin Suicides - Partners - Enemies of Laughter

Willi E. Baer .....Producer
Carmen M. Miller .....Producer
Zana Ross .....Assistant to CMM & WEB

EUPHORIA ENTERTAINMENT

1505 Fourth St., Ste. 220
Santa Monica, CA 90401
PHONE 310-576-7500
FAX 310-576-7501
EMAIL .....euphoriafilm@aol.com
TYPES: Animation - Features - Made-for-TV/Cable Movies - New Media - TV Series
DEVELOPMENT: Our House (TNT/Johnson & Johnson) - The Trade - Golden Gate - John Doe - Blood Dreams - Man Who Saved the World

Gary Kessler .....Producer/Writer
Herman Miller .....Development

THE ROBERT EVANS COMPANY

c/o Paramount Studios
5555 Melrose Ave., Lubitsch Bldg., Ste. 117
Los Angeles, CA 90038-3197
PHONE 323-956-8800
FAX 323-862-0070
TYPES: Features - TV Series
DEALS: Paramount Pictures-Motion Picture Group
DEVELOPMENT: The Man Who Kept the Secrets - The Stranger at the Palazzo D'Oro - The Mailman
CREDITS: Kid Notorious - Chinatown - The Saint - The Godfather - How to Lose a Guy in 10 Days

Robert Evans .....Chairman
Alicia Allain .....President
James DeJulio .....Development Executive

EVERGREEN FILMS, LLC

1515 Palisades Dr., Ste. N
Pacific Palisades, CA 90272
PHONE 310-573-9978
FAX 310-573-1137
EMAIL .....monique@evergreenfilms.com
TYPES: Animation - Commercials - Documentaries - TV Series
PRODUCTION: Alien Planet
CREDITS: Dinosaur Planet (Discovery Channel)

Pierre de Lespinois .....Director
Fran LoCascio .....Executive Producer
John Copeland .....Producer

EVERYMAN PICTURES

10201 W. Pico Blvd., Bldg. 52, Rm. 105
Los Angeles, CA 90035
PHONE 310-369-4200
FAX 310-969-0883
TYPES: Features - TV Series - Reality TV
DEALS: Twentieth Century Fox - Fox 2000 - Twentieth Century Fox - Searchlight Pictures
DEVELOPMENT: Elling - Utopia Street - Niagara - Used Guys
PRODUCTION: Meet the Fockers - Hitchhiker's Guide to the Galaxy - American Candidate (Showtime)
CREDITS: Fifty First Dates - Austin Powers in Goldmember - Mystery, Alaska - Meet the Parents - Austin Powers: International Man of Mystery - Austin Powers: The Spy Who Shagged Me
SUBMISSION POLICY: No unsolicited material

Jay Roach .....Chairman/CEO
Jennifer Perini .....President, Development (310-369-3606)
Brandon Brito .....Assistant to Jay Roach
Carrye Gilliland .....Assistant to Jennifer Perini
Rheanna Bates .....Development Assistant

EVOLUTION

3310 W. Vanowen St.
Burbank, CA 91505
PHONE .818-260-0300
FAX .818-260-1333
WEB SITE .www.evolutionusa.com
TYPES Made-for-TV/Cable Movies - Promos - Reality TV - TV Series
DEVELOPMENT Search for the World's Greatest Kid Magician (Disney Channel)
PRODUCTION The Mansion (TBS) - King of the Jungle (Animal Planet) - Flab to Fab (VH1) - Movie Surfers (Disney Channel) - Clean Sweep (TLC) - Switched! (ABC Family) - Bands Reunited (VH1)
CREDITS Boy Meets Boy (Bravo) - Fear Factor - Big Brother - Bug Juice (Disney Channel) - Gay Weddings (Bravo) - You Rock With (VH1)

Douglas Ross .President
Greg Stewart .CFO
Kathleen French .Sr. VP, Production
Dean Minerd .Sr. VP
Tom Campbell .VP, Development
Bryan Hale .Director, Development

EVOLUTION ENTERTAINMENT

901 N. Highland Ave.
Los Angeles, CA 90038
PHONE .323-850-3232
FAX .323-850-0521
TYPES Features - TV Series
CREDITS Bull Durham - Set It Off - John Q - The Sandlot - Love Don't Cost a Thing - George of the Jungle 2 - SAW - Two and a Half Men - The Casino

Mark Burg .Partner/Producer
Oren Koules .Partner/Producer
Gregg Hoffman .Head, Production
Troy Begnaud .Talent
Evan Corday .Literary
Stephen Gates .Literary
Brad Kaplan .Literary
Tiffany Kuzon .Talent
Ben Levine .Talent
Stephen Marks .Literary
Paul Nicholls .Talent
Chris Ridenhour .Literary
Dan Spilo .Talent
Brian Wilkins .Literary/Talent
Andrew Wilson .Literary
David Clark .Assistant
Chad Cole .Assistant
Jonathan Leeder .Assistant
Jennifer Loyacano .Assistant
Jessica Moresco .Assistant
Justine Stevenson .Office Manager
Rebecca Boccardo .Receptionist

EVOLVING PICTURES ENTERTAINMENT

3151 Cahuenga Blvd. West, Ste. 110
Hollywood, CA 90068
PHONE .323-850-3380
FAX .323-850-3395
EMAIL .evolvingpictures@yahoo.com
WEB SITE .www.evolvingpicturesentertainment.com
TYPES Animation - Features - Made-for-TV/Cable Movies - Reality TV - TV Series
COMPLETED UNRELEASED Detention
CREDITS Mystery, Alaska - Gideon - Resurrection - Time Served - Spincycle - Where's Angelo?
SUBMISSION POLICY Representation: Submit query, logline or synopsis by email; If interested will respond with release forms
COMMENTS Infomercials

Jean Pierre Pereat .President
Jeff Beltzner .VP
Jack Gilardi Jr. .VP, Production (323-850-3388)
Peter E. Jackson .No Title

EXILE ENTERTAINMENT

732 El Medio Ave.
Pacific Palisades, CA 90272
PHONE .310-573-1523
FAX .310-573-0109
EMAIL .exile_ent@yahoo.com
SECOND EMAIL .exilesubs@yahoo.com
TYPES Features
DEVELOPMENT Mississippi Mud - Cowboy Cupid (Focus) - Mephisto's Bridge - The Fifth Woman - Criminals - Steal a Pencil for Me - Straight Up (MGM) - Mountains of Madness (DreamWorks) - The Alibi (Summit)
COMPLETED UNRELEASED Modigliani - American Wake
CREDITS Gothika - Blueberry - Hellboy
SUBMISSION POLICY Send queries only to exilesubs@yahoo.com

Gary Ungar .Producer
Gunder Kehoe .Assistant

EXXCELL ENTERTAINMENT, INC./EXXCELL FILMS

PO Box 1740
Ojai, CA 93024
PHONE .805-640-9430
FAX .805-640-9430
WEB SITE .www.exxcell.com
SECOND WEB SITE .www.dianeladd.com
TYPES Documentaries - Features - Made-for-TV/Cable Movies - Syndication - TV Series
DEVELOPMENT Hot Water Biscuits - Woman Inside - White on Rice - Last of the Bad Girls - Kicks
PRODUCTION Whispers in the Wind (Documentary)
CREDITS Mrs. Munck
COMMENTS Offices in Dallas, TX

Robert C. Hunter .Chairman/CEO
Diane Ladd .President/Actress/Director/Writer
C. Scott Alsop .Associate Producer
Fredrick A. Kleberg .Development Associate
Shirley Johnson .Executive Secretary
Bonnie White .Personal Assistant

FACE PRODUCTIONS/JENNILIND PRODUCTIONS
335 N. Maple Dr., Ste. 175
Beverly Hills, CA 90210
PHONE 310-205-2746
FAX 310-285-2386
TYPES Features - Made-for-TV/Cable Movies - TV Series
DEALS HBO
CREDITS Analyze That - America's Sweethearts - 61* - Forget Paris - Analyze This - Mr. Saturday Night - City Slickers 1&2 - My Giant
SUBMISSION POLICY No unsolicited submissions

Billy Crystal . . . . Actor/Writer/Director
Cheryl Bloch . . . . Sr. VP, Development, TV (310-888-3588)
Samantha Sprecher . . . . VP, Development, Features (310-285-2375)
Liz Goumas . . . . Development Assistant (310-205-2746)
Carol Sidlow . . . . Assistant to Mr. Crystal

FACTORY FEATURES, LLC
12735 Woodbridge St.
Studio City, CA 91604
PHONE 818-985-9805
EMAIL . . . . steven@factorfeatures.com
TYPES Documentaries - Features - Direct-to-Video/DVD - Made-for-TV/Cable Movies - Music Videos - New Media
DEVELOPMENT 47 Dead Bodies
POST PRODUCTION World Wide Glide - Hot Hot Heat
CREDITS Echo & The Bunnymen: Live in America - The Amati Girls - Carlo's Wake - Henri - Blue Sunshine - The Walkmen
COMMENTS Member, PGA

Steven C. Johnson . . . . Producer

FADE IN FILMS
287 S. Robertson Blvd., Ste. 467
Beverly Hills, CA 90211
PHONE 310-275-0287
EMAIL . . . . inquiries01@fadeinonline.com
WEB SITE . . . . www.fadeinonline.com
TYPES Features
DEVELOPMENT An American Crime
CREDITS Clay Pigeons
COMMENTS A division of Fade In Publishing Group, Inc.

Audrey Kelly . . . . President/Producer
Heather Millerton . . . . No Title

FAIR DINKUM PRODUCTIONS
6767 Forest Lawn Dr., Ste. 111
Los Angeles, CA 90068
PHONE 323-845-1776
FAX 323-845-1779
TYPES Features - TV Series

Henry Winkler . . . . Actor/Executive Producer/Director
Andrea Schell . . . . Executive Assistant to Mr. Winkler

FALLOUT ENTERTAINMENT
2260 Centinela Ave.
Los Angeles, CA 90064
PHONE 310-571-0570
FAX 310-571-0505
EMAIL . . . . fofilms@aol.com
TYPES Commercials - Features - Music Videos - TV Series
DEALS New Crime Productions - Rhino Entertainment
DEVELOPMENT Cosmic Bandito - Lucha Loco - For the Love of Joey
CREDITS Tapeheads - Car 54, Where Are You? - Posse - Desperate but Not Serious - My Dinner with Jimi

Bill Fishman . . . . Chairman
Jim Fishman . . . . President
Sundae . . . . Executive Producer
Tom Blatnik . . . . Head, Video Production

FARRELL PAURA PRODUCTIONS, LLC
500 S. Buena Vista St., Animation Bldg., Ste. 2-C
Burbank, CA 91521-1700
PHONE 818-560-3000
FAX 818-560-4070
TYPES Features
DEALS The Walt Disney Company

Joseph Farrell . . . . CEO (818-560-8000)
Catherine Paura . . . . CEO (818-560-7900)
Josie Rosen . . . . President, Production (818-560-8100)
Barry Isaacson . . . . Executive VP, Production (818-560-8400)
Wayne Kline . . VP, Liasion Office of Production/Research (818-560-4800)
Paul Jackson . . . . Executive Assistant (818-560-3200)
Eric Seppala . . . . Executive Assistant (818-560-8600)
Stephanie Watanabe . . . . Executive Assistant (818-560-8300)

FARRELL/MINOFF PRODUCTIONS
14011 Ventura Blvd., Ste. 401
Sherman Oaks, CA 91423
PHONE 818-789-5766
FAX 818-789-7459
TYPES Documentaries - Features - Direct-to-Video/DVD - Made-for-TV/Cable Movies - Syndication - TV Series
DEVELOPMENT The Wrong Man (TNT)
CREDITS Dominick & Eugene - Sins of the Mind - Patch Adams

Mike Farrell . . . . Actor/Producer/Director
Marvin Minoff . . . . Producer

FAST CARRIER PICTURES
3535 Hayden Ave.
Culver City, CA 90232
PHONE 310-836-5018
FAX 310-836-5012
EMAIL . . . . steve@fastcarrier.com
SECOND EMAIL . . . . fastcarriervp@aol.com (Pitches Only)
WEB SITE . . . . www.fastcarrier.com
TYPES Documentaries - Features - Direct-to-Video/DVD - Made-for-TV/Cable Movies - TV Series
DEVELOPMENT Cut Off - Yellow Bricks - Twilight Time - The Errand Boy - The Battle for Hollywood - A Walk in the Sun - Atom & Eve - The Prison Movie - Dragon Tracks - Round the Bend - The Trap
PRE-PRODUCTION The Suicide Project
CREDITS Bleacher Bums - Silent Night

Steve Rubin . . . . President
Rory Aylward . . . . VP, Development
Larry Landsman . . . . Development (East Coast)

FAT CHANCE FILMS

PO Box 34928
Los Angeles, CA 90034
PHONE . . . 323-882-4130
WEB SITE . . . www.beatsbythebay.com
TYPES: Documentaries - Features - TV Series
DEVELOPMENT: Chinaman - The Independent Game - Desperate Times
POST PRODUCTION: Beats by the Bay
CREDITS: One Last Time - Circle of Pain - Why Colors - Some of My Best Friends - Passing the Torch - Midnight Blue

Bobby Mardis . . . Producer/Director

FAUCI PRODUCTIONS

5555 Melrose Ave., Lucy Bungalow, Ste. 105
Hollywood, CA 90038-3197
PHONE . . . 323-956-4737
FAX . . . 323-862-2242
EMAIL . . . fauciproductions@aol.com
TYPES: Animation - Features - Made-for-TV/Cable Movies - TV Series
DEALS: Paramount Television
DEVELOPMENT: Untitled Felicia Henderson Comedy
PRE-PRODUCTION: Untitled Showtime Drama
COMPLETED UNRELEASED: On the Couch
CREDITS: Down Home - Follow Your Heart - When the Bough Breaks
SUBMISSION POLICY: Query only via fax

Dan Fauci . . . President
Tai Fauci . . . VP
Christina Fernandez . . . Assistant

THE PHIL FEHRLE COMPANY

16857 Escalon Dr.
Encino, CA 91436
PHONE . . . 818-981-6553
TYPES: Features - Made-for-TV/Cable Movies - TV Series
DEVELOPMENT: Parachute Lies - Shooters - A Message for Gracia - Short Ends - The Hungry Hour
CREDITS: Thomas and the Magic Railroad - The Secret of Roan Inish - The Whipping Boy - Curaçao - The Little Kidnappers - Thomas and Friends (Children's Series) - Jack and the Pack (Children's Series)
SUBMISSION POLICY: No unsolicited manuscripts
COMMENTS: Family movies; Children's branded properties; Independent Theatricals

Phil Fehrle . . . Producer

J.D. FEIGELSON PRODUCTIONS, INC.

9171 Wilshire Blvd., Ste. 541
Beverly Hills, CA 90210-5564
PHONE . . . 310-273-7769
TYPES: Features - Direct-to-Video/DVD - Made-for-TV/Cable Movies - TV Series
DEALS: New Line Television
CREDITS: The Lake - Dark Night of the Scarecrow - Gone to Texas - Chiller - Red Water - One of the Missing (PBS)
SUBMISSION POLICY: No submissions accepted

J.D. Feigelson . . . Owner/Executive Producer
Dick deBlois . . . Business Affairs
Thea Kerman . . . Legal Affairs (310-657-7007)
Wayne Mejia . . . Business Manager

EDWARD S. FELDMAN COMPANY

1041 N. Formosa Ave., Santa Monica East, Ste. 210
West Hollywood, CA 90046
PHONE . . . 323-850-2655
FAX . . . 323-850-2649
EMAIL . . . esfeldman@aol.com
SECOND EMAIL . . . winshipper@aol.com
TYPES: Features - Made-for-TV/Cable Movies
DEVELOPMENT: The Program (Intermedia) - Presto...Romeo - Vacancy - Michelangelo on the Run
CREDITS: K-19: The Widowmaker - 102 Dalmatians - The Truman Show - The Doctor - Witness - Green Card - Forever Young - 101 Dalmatians

Ed Feldman . . . President/Producer
Winship Cook . . . Co-Producer/VP, Development

THE FELDMAN COMPANY

c/o The Lot
1041 N. Formosa Ave., Writers Bldg., Rm. 315
West Hollywood, CA 90046
PHONE . . . 323-850-2503
FAX . . . 323-850-2506
WEB SITE . . . www.thefeldmancompany.com
TYPES: Features - Made-for-TV/Cable Movies - New Media - TV Series
DEVELOPMENT: Karski: How One Man Tried to Stop the Holocaust - Looking for Dick - Dish - The Bet - Don't Sleep with Your Drummer - Kilfee
CREDITS: Trash - Moose Mating - Planet Parenthood
COMMENTS: Management

Todd Feldman . . . Producer

FENADY ASSOCIATES, INC.

249 N. Larchmont Blvd., Ste. 6
Los Angeles, CA 90004
PHONE . . . 323-466-6375
FAX . . . 323-466-6376
TYPES: Features - TV Series
CREDITS: The Sea Wolf - Chisum - The Man with Bogart's Face - Yes Virginia, There Is a Santa Claus - The Green Journey - Jake Spanner, Private Eye; TV Series: The Rebel - Branded - Hondo

Andrew J. Fenady . . . President
John Duke Fenady . . . Sr. VP, Creative Affairs
Sean Fenady . . . VP, Creative Development
Ulysses Smith . . . Director, Development

FESTIVAL PICTURES

4711 La Villa Marina, Ste. H
Marina del Rey, CA 90292
PHONE . . . 323-461-0262
FAX . . . 323-461-3268
EMAIL . . . festivalpix@aol.com
TYPES: Features - Direct-to-Video/DVD - Made-for-TV/Cable Movies
DEVELOPMENT: Forbidden City - Hard Case - Quality of Mercy - Princess Starlight
PRE-PRODUCTION: Faster
CREDITS: The Right Temptation - Kiss Toledo Goodbye - Primary Suspect - Just Sue Me - Red Sun Rising - Sworn to Justice - Out for Blood
COMMENTS: Thrillers; Historical dramas; Imaginative genre projects

Paul Maslak . . . President
Neva Friedenn . . . VP

ZACHARY FEUER FILMS
c/o Maverick
9348 Civic Center Dr., 3rd Fl.
Beverly Hills, CA 90210
PHONE .310-729-2110
FAX .310-820-7535
TYPES Features - Made-for-TV/Cable Movies - New Media - TV Series
DEALS Maverick Films
DEVELOPMENT Mort the Dead Teenager - The Lightning Field - She Rocks - How to Be a Latino Pop Star - Chasing Fate
CREDITS All the Queen's Men - Texas Cheerleader Murdering Mom

Zachary Feuer .Producer/President

FEURY/GRANT ENTERTAINMENT
441 West End Ave., Ste. 10-A
New York, NY 10024
PHONE .212-724-9290
FAX .212-724-9297
TYPES Documentaries - Features - Made-for-TV/Cable Movies - TV Series
CREDITS What Sex Am I? - Battered - Say It! Fight It! Cure It! - Seasons of the Heart - Staying Together
SUBMISSION POLICY Submissions by query letter

Joseph Feury .Producer
Lee Grant .Actress/Director

FGM ENTERTAINMENT
301 N. Canon Dr., Ste. 328
Beverly Hills, CA 90210
PHONE .310-205-9900
FAX .310-205-9909
TYPES Features
CREDITS Stigmata - Species - Internal Affairs - Ronin
SUBMISSION POLICY No unsolicited submissions; No faxed resumés or queries

Frank Mancuso Jr. .Producer/President
Vikki Williams .Line Producer

ADAM FIELDS PRODUCTIONS
8899 Beverly Blvd., Ste. 821
West Hollywood, CA 90048
PHONE .310-859-9300
FAX .310-859-4795/818-990-1042
TYPES Features - New Media - TV Series
DEALS New Line Cinema
DEVELOPMENT Josiah's Canon - Wanted: Dead or Alive - Pamela West - Truth or Dare - NY Dive - Untitled John Milius Project - What a Man's Gotta Do - Mr. S - My Life with Frank
CREDITS Donnie Darko - Brokedown Palace - Ravenous - Money Train - Great Balls of Fire - Johnny Be Good - Vision Quest - Whoopee Boys

Adam Fields .President
Jimmy Bevilacqua .Assistant
Rob Gonzalez .Assistant
Kathleen Mullin .Assistant
Roy Rocha .Assistant

*FIERCE ENTERTAINMENT, LLC
8306 Wilshire Blvd., Ste. 904
Beverly Hills, CA 90211
PHONE .310-860-1174
FAX .310-860-9446
EMAIL .info@fierce-entertainment.com
WEB SITE .www.fierce-entertainment.com
TYPES Features - Direct-to-Video/DVD - Made-for-TV/Cable Movies
CREDITS Shadow Dancer - Marvel's Man-Thing - To Kill a King - Carolina

Christopher Petzel .CEO
Kasper Graversen .Literary Editor

FIFTY CANNON ENTERTAINMENT, LLC
12501 Gladstone Ave., Stage 3
Sylmar, CA 91342
PHONE .818-837-1493
FAX .818-837-3811
TYPES Features - TV Series
CREDITS Traffic - Huff
COMMENTS UK office: Oxford House, 76 Oxford St., London W1D 1BS UK

Mike Newell .Chairman
Cameron Jones .President
William Butler-Sloss .VP
Esther Douglas .Head, Development & Production (UK)
Marty Musatov .Story Editor

FILBERT STEPS PRODUCTIONS
200 W. 57th St., Ste. 304
New York, NY 10019
PHONE .212-246-2301
FAX .212-246-2285
EMAIL .info@filbertsteps.com
WEB SITE .www.filbertsteps.com
TYPES Features
DEVELOPMENT Scorpions in a Bottle - White Collared - Murdering Michael Malloy - The Disappearance of Daniel Klein - Almost Legal - Runaway Boys
CREDITS Two Family House - Forever Fabulous

Alan Klingenstein .President
Bernie DeLeo .VP, Creative Affairs
David Viola .Director, Development

FILM BRIDGE INTERNATIONAL
1316 Third Street Promenade, Ste. 105
Santa Monica, CA 90401
PHONE .310-656-8680
FAX .310-656-8683
EMAIL .contact@filmbridgeinternational.com
WEB SITE .www.filmbridgeinternational.com
TYPES Documentaries - Features - Made-for-TV/Cable Movies
DEVELOPMENT Headhunter - Disaster at Sea
PRE-PRODUCTION Dolan's Cadillac - Beast of Bataan - When We Were Modern - The Four Saints
POST PRODUCTION Hamlet Unzipped
CREDITS Lying in Wait - Beyond the Summit - Splitsville - Velocity of Gary - Say Nothing - Big Spender
SUBMISSION POLICY No unsolicited material

Ellen S. Wander .No Title
Isabel Pereciado Louckas .No Title
Lori Mathison .No Title

FILM CRASH
1433 Yale St., Ste. D
Santa Monica, CA 90404
PHONE .310-315-1821/212-334-6515
EMAIL .firstname@filmcrash.com
WEB SITE .www.filmcrash.com
TYPES Features - TV Series
POST PRODUCTION The Deep and Dreamless Sleep
CREDITS The Technical Writer - Kicked in the Head (Universal) - The Headhunter's Sister - Rhythm Thief - The Lost Words - Spare Me - Sex and the City (HBO) - Popular (Disney) - Dead Last (Warner Bros.)
SUBMISSION POLICY Not accepting submissions at this time
COMMENTS East Coast office: 276 Bowery, Ste. 4, New York, NY 10012

Matthew Harrison .Partner
Karl Nussbaum .Partner
Scott Saunders .Partner, NY
Daniel Blumberg .Producer

FILM FARM
1817 Stanford St., 2nd Fl.
Santa Monica, CA 90404
PHONE .310-453-0900
TYPES Features - TV Series
DEVELOPMENT Nim's Island - Generation X - Mr. Spaceman - Out of Gas - The Saints and Sinners of Okay County - The Bra
PRE-PRODUCTION Picasso at the Lapin Agile
CREDITS The Vagina Monologues - Corrina, Corrina - The Search for Signs of Intelligent Life in the Universe - Traveller - Off the Lip - Prayer of the Roller Boys
SUBMISSION POLICY No unsolicited submissions

Paula Mazur .Producer
Robert Mickelson .Director/Producer
Brandon Howe .Executive Assistant to Paula Mazur
Patrick Smith .Intern

FILM GARDEN ENTERTAINMENT, INC.
4146 Lankershim Blvd.
North Hollywood, CA 91602
PHONE .818-783-3456
FAX .818-752-8186
WEB SITE .www.filmgarden.tv
TYPES Documentaries - Reality TV - TV Series
PRODUCTION Calorie Commando - Your Reality Checked
POST PRODUCTION Insider's List - Travel Channel Specials
COMPLETED UNRELEASED Body Challenge Hollywood
CREDITS A Wedding Story - Murder Reopened - Women in Blue - Wild on the Set - Discovery Health Body Challenge - Two for Las Vegas - Ultimate Ten - Mysteries of Mating - Total Zoo - Adoption Stories - Tailgate Party

Nancy Jacobs Miller .President/Executive Producer
Michelle Van Kempen .Executive VP
Craig Golin .Executive in Charge of Production
Toni Gray .Director, Operations
Shawn Silver .Director, Development

FILMCOLONY
100 N. Crescent Dr., Ste. 125
Beverly Hills, CA 90210
PHONE .310-432-1701
FAX .310-432-1705
TYPES Features - Made-for-TV/Cable Movies
DEVELOPMENT The Nanny Diaries - The Fourth Hand - Solomon Grundy - Mulligan - Hurt - Mr. Vertigo
COMPLETED UNRELEASED J.M. Barrie's Neverland
CREDITS Levity - The Bourne Identity - The Cider House Rules - She's All That - Hurlyburly - Jackie Brown - Pulp Fiction - Reservoir Dogs

Richard N. Gladstein .President/Producer
Geoff Clark .Director, Development
Nick Nantell .Assistant to Mr. Gladstein

FILMENGINE
6735 Yucca St.
Hollywood, CA 90028
PHONE .323-960-1480
FAX .323-960-1482
TYPES Features - TV Series
DEALS New Line Cinema
DEVELOPMENT Wish You Were Here - The Rum Diary - The Whale Hunter - Octopus (TV) - Rockstars (TV) - The Other Side of Simple
PRE-PRODUCTION Lucky Slevin
PRODUCTION Heart of Summer
CREDITS The Butterfly Effect - O - Cheaters - The Real Cancun

Anthony Rhulen .No Title
A.J. Dix .No Title
Tyler Mitchell .No Title
Rich Stirling .No Title
Mike Stirling .No Title
Rick de Oliveira .TV
Steve Striegal .TV

FILMROOS
PO Box 69-1694
West Hollywood, CA 90069
PHONE 323-655-0712
FAX 323-655-8092
EMAIL ....broos@filmroos.com
TYPES Documentaries - TV Series
PRODUCTION Holy Grail
CREDITS Gods and Goddessess: A Greek Mythology - A History of God - Biblical Disasters - In Search of History - Biography - Mysteries of the Bible - Escape: True Stories of Suspense - Top Secret - Intimate Portrait
COMMENTS Cable Series, Specials

Bram Roos ....Executive Producer
Yun Lingner ....Executive in Charge of Production (323-578-4702)

FILMS BY JOVE
11325 Sunshine Terrace
Studio City, CA 91604
PHONE 818-506-0550
FAX 818-505-9730
EMAIL ....filmsbyjove@earthlink.net
WEB SITE ....www.russiananimation.com
TYPES Animation - Features - TV Series
CREDITS Cheburashka - Animated Soviet Propaganda - Mikhail Baryshnikov's Stories from My Childhood - The Jungle Book - Fairy Tales from Faroff Lands: The Animated Classic Showcase
SUBMISSION POLICY No submissions
COMMENTS Distribution

Joan Borsten ....Principal
Oleg Vidov ....Principal
Sergei Vidov ....Sales

FILMSAAVY
16931 Dearborn St.
Northridge, CA 91343
PHONE 818-895-4916
FAX 818-895-8415
EMAIL ....filmsaavy@msn.com
WEB SITE ....www.filmsaavy.saavedra.com
TYPES Features - TV Series
DEVELOPMENT Dead Money - American Icon - Fifth Avenue - Home Alone on the Range
PRE-PRODUCTION A Shattered Stage - Arrow Man - Leyendecker
CREDITS Rhapsody in Bloom - At First Sight - Two Guys Talkin' About Girls - Closer and Closer
COMMENTS East Coast office: 975 Park Ave., Ste. 10-C, New York, NY 10028

Craig M. Saavedra ....Partner
Michael Shulman ....Partner
Noelle Kramer ....Director, Development
Michael Eastin ....Story Editor
Josh Doughty ....Creative Executive

FILMSMITH
9720 Wilshire Blvd., 5th Fl.
Beverly Hills, CA 90210
PHONE 310-260-8866
EMAIL ....zmatz@armada-pictures.com
TYPES Features
DEALS Armada Pictures
CREDITS Drum - One Point 0 - Birds of Prey (IMAX) - The Price of Air - Wildflowers - Sleep Easy, Hutch Rimes - Welcome to Hollywood - Glam - French Exit

Zachary Matz ....Producer

FILMSTREET, INC.
8306 Wilshire Blvd., Ste. 331
Beverly Hills, CA 90211
PHONE 323-935-5707
EMAIL ....filmstreetinc@yahoo.com
TYPES Features - Direct-to-Video/DVD - Made-for-TV/Cable Movies - TV Series - Reality TV
DEVELOPMENT Fish & Chips - Politics of Love - Before I Met Eva
CREDITS Midnight Witness - Conversations in Limbo

Peter Foldy ....Writer/Producer/Director
Palmerston Hughes ....Creative Assistant

FINE LINE FEATURES
116 N. Robertson Blvd.
Los Angeles, CA 90048
PHONE 310-854-5811/212-649-4800
FAX 310-659-1453/212-956-1942
WEB SITE ....www.flf.com
TYPES Features - Documentaries
DEVELOPMENT M'lady - The Recipe - I Was Amelia Earhart
CREDITS Elephant - The Anniversary Party - Before Night Falls - Pecker - Shine - The Sweet Hereafter - Filth and Fury - Tumbleweeds - Dancer in the Dark - State and Main - Saving Grace - American Splendor
COMMENTS East Coast office: 888 Seventh Ave., 20th Fl., New York, NY 10016

Mark Ordesky ....Executive VP, New Line Productions
Guy Stodel ....Sr. VP, Acquisitions & Co-Productions
Ileen Maisel ....Sr. VP, European Productions & Acquisitions
Alexandra Rossi ....VP, European Acquisitions & Co-Productions
Swanna MacNair ....Creative Executive
Meredith Finn ....Director, Acquisitions & Productions
Jackie Tepper ....Director, Acquisitions & Co-Productions
Sejin Park ....Assistant to Guy Stodel
Jennifer Rogers ....Assistant to Mark Ordesky
Michael Schaefer ....Assistant to Ileen Maisel

FINE LIVING
5757 Wilshire Blvd., Museum Square
Los Angeles, CA 90036
PHONE 310-228-4500
FAX 323-931-0708
WEB SITE ....www.fineliving.com
CREDITS Born American - Best for Less - Fantasy Camp - 10 Perfect Summer Getaways - Simply Wine with Andrea Immer - Radical Sabbatical - Genuine Article - The Great Adventure
COMMENTS Original lifestyle programming

Ken Solomon ....President
Charles Segars ....Sr. VP, Programming & Production
Cindy McConkey ....VP, Communications, Scripps Networks
Robyn Miller ....VP, Marketing
Greg Neal ....VP, Creative Services

WENDY FINERMAN PRODUCTIONS

10202 W. Washington Blvd.
Culver City, CA 90232
PHONE .310-244-8800
FAX .310-244-8488
TYPES Features
DEALS Sony Pictures Entertainment
DEVELOPMENT Devil Wears Prada - Sophie and the Rising Sun - One for the Money - P.S. I Love You
CREDITS Fairy Tale...A True Story - Stepmom - Forrest Gump - The Fan - Sugar & Spice - Drumline

Wendy Finerman .Producer
David Blackman .VP (310-244-8060)
Lisa Zupan .No Title
Katie Pastore .No Title

FIREBRAND PRODUCTIONS

1524 Riverside Dr.
Burbank, CA 91506
PHONE .818-955-5711
FAX .818-955-5158
TYPES Features - Made-for-TV/Cable Movies - TV Series
CREDITS The Good Old Boys - A Slight Case of Murder - Four Eyes & Six Guns - The New Adventures of Spin and Marty: Suspect Behavior - Just Ask My Children

Salli Newman .Producer
Gina DeMasters .Assistant to Ms. Newman

FIREFLY PRODUCTIONS

c/o Paramount Pictures
5555 Melrose Ave., Dreier Bldg., Ste. 112
Los Angeles, CA 90038
PHONE .323-956-8893
FAX .323-862-1089
TYPES Made-for-TV/Cable Movies - TV Series
DEALS Paramount Television
CREDITS Dodson's Journey (CBS)

David James Elliott .President
Alixandre Witlin .VP, Development

FIREWORKS ENTERTAINMENT

421 S. Beverly Dr.
Beverly Hills, CA 90212
PHONE .310-789-4700 (TV)/310-789-4750 (Film)
FAX .310-789-4799 (TV)/310-789-4747 (Film)
WEB SITE .www.fireworksentertainment.com
TYPES Made-for-TV/Cable Movies - Syndication - TV Series
CREDITS Mutant X - Gene Roddenberry's Andromeda - La Femme Nikita - Highlander: The Raven - A Wrinkle in Time - Poison - Blonde - Zoe Busiek: Wild Card - Strange Days at Blake Holsey High
COMMENTS Toronto office: 81 Barber Greene Rd., Toronto, ON M3C 2A2 Canada, phone: 416-446-5311, fax: 416-446-5544

Adam Haight .President/COO
Greg Phillips . . .President, Fireworks International (UK) (44-207-307-6300)
Michael Weisbarth .President, Fireworks TV

FIRM FILMS

9465 Wilshire Blvd., 6th Fl.
Beverly Hills, CA 90212
PHONE .310-860-8000
FAX .310-860-8100
TYPES Animation - Documentaries - Features - TV Series - Reality TV
DEALS Twentieth Century Fox - Twentieth Century Fox Television
CREDITS After the Sunset - 11:14 - House of 1000 Corpses - The Simple Life (TV)

Julie Yorn .Head, Film & TV Production
Nicole Vorias .Firm TV
Marc Gordon .Director, Development

FIRST ENTERTAINMENT, LLC

9348 Civic Center Dr., Mezzanine
Beverly Hills, CA 90210
PHONE .310-205-6090
FAX .310-205-6093
EMAIL .firstent@aol.com
TYPES Animation - Features - TV Series
DEVELOPMENT The First Bastard (Miramax) - Not a Pretty Woman (Fox) - The Race (MGM) - Labor Day (Beacon) - Get Me Roman Faraday (DreamWorks) - House Breakers (DreamWorks) - Office Retreat (New Line) - Family Reunion (Spyglass) - American Booty (MTV) - South of the Border (Disney) - Behind the Cape (Constantin/Franchise)
COMPLETED UNRELEASED The Ringer (Fox Searchlight)
CREDITS First to Go - Married to It - Bingo - Anger Management - My Boss's Daughter
COMMENTS Comedy; Jacobs Entertainment: Personal management for writers and directors

John Jacobs .President
John Lash .Story Editor
Collin O'Reilly .Manager

FIRST KISS PRODUCTIONS

468 N. Camden Dr., Ste. 200
Beverly Hills, CA 90210
PHONE .310-860-5611
FAX .310-285-1735
TYPES Features - TV Series
CREDITS Braceface - Excess Baggage

Alicia Silverstone .Actress/Producer
Carolyn Kessler .Manager/Producer
Matt Miranda .Creative Executive
Rob Anderson .Assistant

FIRST LIGHT

c/o Paramount Pictures
5555 Melrose Ave., Clara Bow Bldg., Ste. 200
Hollywood, CA 90038
PHONE .323-956-8871
FAX .323-862-2320
TYPES Features - TV Series
DEALS Paramount Pictures-Motion Picture Group
CREDITS K-19: The Widowmaker - Strange Days - Point Break - Near Dark - The Inside

Kathryn Bigelow .Director/Producer
David Markus .VP

FIRST MOVE TELEVISION PRODUCTION
10201 W. Pico Blvd., Bldg. 71, Rm. 1
Los Angeles, CA 90035
PHONE .310-369-0094
FAX .310-969-1295
TYPES TV Series
DEALS Twentieth Century Fox Television
CREDITS Hidden Hills (NBC) - The Lone Ranger (WB)

Susanne Daniels .President/CEO
Sheila Ducksworth .Sr. VP, Development
Sean Boyle .Manager (310-369-0098)
Mollie Binkley .Assistant to Ms. Daniels

PRESTON STEPHEN FISCHER COMPANY
13078 Mindanao Way, Penthouse 313
Marina del Rey, CA 90292
PHONE .310-578-9587
FAX .310-823-3548
EMAIL .psfco@aol.com
TYPES Features - Made-for-TV/Cable Movies - TV Series
CREDITS Talking to Heaven - Intensity - White Fang 2 - Las Vegas - War Stories - Countdown (ABC Pilot)

Preston Fischer .Producer

FISHER PRODUCTIONS
269 S. Wilton Pl.
Los Angeles, CA 90004
PHONE .323-692-0991
FAX .323-692-0981
EMAIL .rickafilms@aol.com
TYPES Features - Made-for-TV/Cable Movies - TV Series
CREDITS New Suit - Family Sins - Stepsister from the Planet Weird - Follow Your Heart - In Broad Daylight
SUBMISSION POLICY No unsolicited material

Ricka Fisher .Executive Producer

FISHER TELEVISION PRODUCTIONS, INC.
269 S. Wilton Pl.
Los Angeles, CA 90004
PHONE .323-692-0991
FAX .323-692-0981
EMAIL .afisher423@aol.com
TYPES Documentaries - Reality TV - Syndication - TV Series
DEVELOPMENT The Mother of All Dogs (National Geographic Channel)
PRODUCTION Mars Rocks: A Geology of the Red Planet (Discovery-Science) - Cassini: Rendezvous With the Ringed Planet (Discovery-Science)
CREDITS Mars Rocks (Science Channel) - Flea Market Finds with the Kovels (HGTV) - Loretta Lynn's Haunted Plantation - (Travel Channel) - Harlem Hellfighters (History Channel)
COMMENTS Nonfiction programming; Syndicated and cable series and specials

Albert Fisher .President

FIVE SISTERS PRODUCTIONS
171 Pier Ave., Ste. 207
Santa Monica, CA 90405
PHONE .310-712-5443
WEB SITE .www.fivesistersproductions.com
TYPES Features - TV Series
CREDITS Just Friends - Temps - Manna from Heaven

Maria Burton .Producer/Director
Jennifer Burton .Producer/Writer
Ursula Burton .Producer/Actor
Gabrielle C. Burton .Producer/Director
Charity Burton .Producer
Roger Burton .Co-Producer
Gabrielle B. Burton .Co-Producer/Writer

FLAME TELEVISION
1416 N. La Brea Ave.
Hollywood, CA 90028
PHONE .323-802-1700
FAX .323-802-1709
TYPES Animation - Features - Reality TV - TV Series
PRE-PRODUCTION Driver: Behind the Wheel of NASCAR (FX)
PRODUCTION Bad Girl's Guide (UPN)
CREDITS Rock Me Baby (UPN) - Sports Night - The PJ's - 24 - Mulholland Drive

Tony Krantz .CEO/Executive Producer
Nina Lederman .Executive VP
Julie Bistrow .Manager, Creative Affairs
Todd Blake .No Title
Rebecca McGill .No Title

FLASHPOINT ENTERTAINMENT
1318 San Ysidro Dr.
Beverly Hills, CA 90210
PHONE .310-205-6300
TYPES Features - TV Series
DEVELOPMENT North of Sunset
CREDITS The Bourne Identity - The Bourne Supremacy
SUBMISSION POLICY No unsolicited material

Andrew R. Tennenbaum .Producer

FLAT PENNY FILMS
114 N. Mansfield, 2nd Fl.
Los Angeles, CA 90036
PHONE .323-933-0991
TYPES Features - Made-for-TV/Cable Movies - TV Series
DEVELOPMENT Anonymous Sources - Mistaken Identity - Lovers Leap (New Regency) - 100 Days of Darkness (FX) - Down to the River
CREDITS State of the Union - The Cherry Orchard - Spyglass - Micho
SUBMISSION POLICY Query letter with return postcard only

Amy Lanier .President/Owner

FLIP SIDE FILM
81 Bedford St., Ste. 3-C
New York, NY 10014
PHONE .646-201-9857
EMAIL .tcdonahue@mac.com
TYPES Documentaries - Features
DEVELOPMENT Tupperware - The Anointed One - 1&9
PRODUCTION Guest of Cindy Sherman
COMPLETED UNRELEASED Highway Courtesans
CREDITS Washington Heights - Thanksgiving

Tom Donahue .Producer
Anura Idupuganti .Producer

FLORENTINE FILMS
59 Maple Grove Rd., PO Box 613
Walpole, NH 03608
PHONE .603-756-3038
FAX .603-756-4389
WEB SITE www.florentinefilms.com
TYPES Documentaries
PRODUCTION The War - America's Best Idea: Our National Parks
POST PRODUCTION Unforgiveable Blackness: The Rise and Fall of Jack Johnson
CREDITS Thomas Jefferson - Lewis and Clark - Baseball - The Civil War - Jazz - Mark Twain - The Shakers: Hands to Work, Hearts to God - Empire of the Air: The Men Who Made Radio - Huey Long

Ken Burns .President/Producer/Director
Lynn Novick .Producer
Paul Barnes .Producer/Supervising Film Editor
Dayton Duncan .Producer/Writer
Dave Schaye .Producer
Geoffrey C. Ward .Writer
Erik Ewers .Editor
Sean Huff .Editor
Craig Mellish .Editor
Sarah Botstein .Co-Producer
Aileen Silverstone .Associate Producer
Susanna Steisel .Associate Producer
Pam Baucom .Coordinating Producer

FLOWER FILMS, INC.
9220 Sunset Blvd., Ste. 309
Los Angeles, CA 90069
PHONE .310-285-0200
FAX .310-285-0827
TYPES Features
DEALS Columbia Pictures
CREDITS Fifty First Dates - Charlie's Angels: Full Throttle - Duplex - Never Been Kissed - Charlie's Angels - Olive, the Other Reindeer - Donnie Darko
SUBMISSION POLICY By agent or manager only

Drew Barrymore .Partner
Nancy Juvonen .Partner
Gwenn Stroman .VP, Development
Alan Trezza .Director, Development
Barry Dale Johnson .Office Manager
Miri Yoon .Executive Assistant to Ms. Barrymore
Aaron Poirier .Executive Assistant to Ms. Juvonen
Kelly Kall .Office Assistant

FLYING A STUDIOS, INC.
28537 Conejo View Dr.
Agoura Hills, CA 91301
PHONE .818-706-3456
FAX .818-706-3416
EMAIL dave@flyingastudios.com
SECOND EMAIL kathy@flyingastudios.com
WEB SITE www.flyingastudios.com
TYPES Features - Direct-to-Video/DVD - Made-for-TV/Cable Movies - TV Series
DEVELOPMENT Destination West - Untarnished Valor - The Happy Bottom Riding Club
PRE-PRODUCTION Witness in the Shadows
COMPLETED UNRELEASED My Friends Call Me Moose (Direct-to-Video/DVD)
CREDITS Frequent Flyer

Dave Berthiaume .President (818-519-0705)
Kathy Leitch .VP, Development
James Talbott .VP, Business Affairs (310-980-4690)

FLYING FREEHOLD PRODUCTIONS
233 Wilshire Blvd., Ste. 600
Santa Monica, CA 90401
PHONE .310-393-8879
FAX .310-393-8479
EMAIL flyingfreehold@aol.com
TYPES Features - TV Series
DEVELOPMENT Simple City - Faust - Dr. Science
CREDITS King of Texas - A Christmas Carol - The Lion in Winter

Patrick Stewart .CEO
Wendy Neuss-Stewart .President
Jackie Edwards .Creative Executive

FOCUS FEATURES

FOCUS FEATURES/ROGUE PICTURES
A Division of Universal Pictures
100 Universal City Plaza
Universal City, CA 91608
PHONE .818-777-1000
WEB SITE www.universalstudios.com
SECOND WEB SITE www.focusfeatures.com
TYPES Features
PRODUCTION Brokeback Mountain - The Constant Gardener
POST PRODUCTION Seed of Chucky (Rogue) - Ice Harvest - Assault on Precinct 13 (Rogue)
COMPLETED UNRELEASED Vanity Fair - The Motorcyle Diaries
CREDITS Eternal Sunshine of the Spotless Mind - Ned Kelly - Sylvia - Swimming Pool - Lost in Translation - 8 Women - Far from Heaven - The Pianist - The Guys - The Shape of Things - 21 Grams - The Door in the Floor

David Linde .Co-President
James Schamus .Co-President
David Brooks .President, Marketing
Jack Foley .President, Theatrical Distribution
John Lyons .President, Production
Andrew Karpen .COO
Glen Basner .Executive VP, International Sales & Distribution
Adriene Bowles .Executive VP, Publicity & Marketing
Aveeram Eschenasy .Executive VP, Business Affairs Administration
Kevin Hyman .Executive VP, Production
Amy Kaufman .Executive VP, Production
Joe Pichirallo .Executive VP, Production
Howard Meyers .Sr. VP, Business Affairs
Gordon Ampel .VP, Operations
Susan Anderson .VP, Finance
Christopher Brescia .VP, Business & Legal Affairs
Donna Dickman .VP, Publicity
Jason Resnick .VP, Acquisitions
Jeffrey Roth .VP, Post Production
Kahli Small .VP, Production & Development
Tim Spencer .VP, International Sales
Rob Wilkinson .VP, Research

FOOD CHAIN FILMS, INC.
1393 La Granada Dr.
Thousand Oaks, CA 91362
PHONE .805-374-1913
FAX .805-374-1913
TYPES Features - TV Series
CREDITS Failure Is Not an Option
SUBMISSION POLICY No unsolicited material or queries

Kitty Radler .Producer
Robert Radler .Producer/Director

FOOD NETWORK
1180 Avenue of the Americas
New York, NY 10036
PHONE .212-398-8836
FAX .212-997-0997
EMAIL .msmith@foodnetwork.com
WEB SITE .www.foodnetwork.com
TYPES TV Series - Reality TV
CREDITS Date Plate - Boy Meets Grill - Food Fight - Roker on the Road - Into the Fire - Trivia Unwrapped - Jamie's Kitchen - How to Boil Water - Mario in America - Dweezil & Lisa
COMMENTS Programs that celebrate food and the people who love food

Brooke Bailey Johnson .President
Kathleen Finch .Sr. VP, Primetime Programming & Development
Bob Tuschman .Sr. VP, Daytime & In the Kitchen Programming
Michael Adley .VP, Creative Director
Adam Rockmore .VP, Marketing
Bruce Seidel .VP, Acquisitions & Program Planning
Michael Smith .VP, On-Air Strategy & Creative Services

FOOTHILL ENTERTAINMENT, INC.
1231 State St., Ste. 208
Santa Barbara, CA 93101
PHONE .805-965-4488
FAX .805-965-1168
EMAIL .info@foothillentertainment.com
WEB SITE .www.foothillentertainment.com
TYPES Animation - Documentaries - Features - Direct-to-Video/DVD - Made-for-TV/Cable Movies - TV Series
DEVELOPMENT Tango Express - Flavia Kids - Me & My Shadow - Wings of Angels - Kiz & Tel - Gododo - Vessels - Kid Kaiju - Boxing Betties and Boy - Snapper
PRE-PRODUCTION Pirate School - Food Chain
POST PRODUCTION Monkeez - Uncle Marvin - The Dress-Up Box
CREDITS Barney
COMMENTS Children's and family entertainment

Gregory B. Payne .CEO
Jo Kavanagh-Payne .President
Katie Simon .Executive Assistant

FORELAND PICTURES
PO Box 931058
Hollywood, CA 90093
PHONE .323-436-2868
EMAIL .studio@forelandpictures.com
TYPES Features - Music Videos - Commercials - Documentaries - New Media - Syndication - TV Series
DEVELOPMENT Quasi Goad - Sunset Hall
CREDITS Blews - Lovely

Darren A. Green .Partner
Marco De Molina .Partner
Susan Conn .Production Manager
Kevin Nevarro .Assistant to Mr. De Molina
Alexander Bergen .Assistant to Mr. Green

FORENSIC FILMS, INC.
1 Worth St., 2nd Fl.
New York, NY 10013
PHONE .212-966-1110
FAX .212-966-1125
EMAIL .forfilm@aol.com
TYPES Features
DEVELOPMENT Satan's Lee - The Man Who Was Thursday
CREDITS Raising Victor Vargas - Clean - Undefeated - Gummo - Demonlover - What Happened Was - First Love, Last Rights - Joe the King - Julien Donkey-Boy - Chasing Sleep - The Chateau - King of the Jungle - Saving Face

Scott Macaulay .Producer
Robin O'Hara .Producer

FOREST HILLS PICTURES
PO Box 1071
Fairfield, CT 06825
PHONE .203-254-3239
EMAIL .howeis@aol.com
TYPES Commercials - Documentaries - Features - Made-for-TV/Cable Movies - New Media - Syndication - TV Series
CREDITS Lovestruck - The Kazooist - Follow You, Follow Me

Howard J. Weisman .Executive Producer
Herbert Solver .Director, Development

FORTIS FILMS
8581 Santa Monica Blvd., Ste. 1
West Hollywood, CA 90069
PHONE .310-659-4533
TYPES Features - TV Series
DEALS Warner Bros. Pictures
CREDITS Practical Magic - Hope Floats - Making Sandwiches - Trespasses - Gun Shy - Miss Congeniality - Two Weeks' Notice - The George Lopez Show

Sandra Bullock .Actor/Producer
Gesine Bullock-Prado .President/CEO
Maggie Biggar .VP, Production
Lillian Dean .VP, Development
Bryan Moore .Office Manager

FORTRESS ENTERTAINMENT
6725 Sunset Blvd., Ste. 280
Hollywood, CA 90028
PHONE .323-467-4700
FAX .323-467-6425
EMAIL .info@fortress-ent.com
WEB SITE .www.fortress-ent.com
TYPES Animation - Documentaries - Features - Made-for-TV/Cable Movies - New Media - TV Series - Reality TV
DEALS Daniel L. Paulson Productions
DEVELOPMENT Dreamtective - Bull - Commercial Challenge
SUBMISSION POLICY No unsolicited submissions
COMMENTS Finance, development and production

Brett Forbes .Executive Producer/Partner
Patrick Rizzotti .Executive Producer/Partner
Bonnie Forbes .Producer
Mike Gozzard .VP, Development
David Cuddy .Development Executive
Bruce Fishelman .Business Affairs

FORWARD PASS, INC.
12233 W. Olympic Blvd., Ste. 340
Los Angeles, CA 90064
PHONE .310-207-7378
TYPES Features - TV Series
CREDITS Collateral - Ali - Last of the Mohicans - Manhunter - Thief - Drug Wars - Heat - Jericho Mile - The Insider

Michael Mann .Writer/Producer/Director

DAVID FOSTER PRODUCTIONS
c/o The Lot
4401 Wilshire Blvd., Ste. 310
Los Angeles, CA 90010
PHONE .323-965-0902
FAX .323-965-0962
EMAIL .fosterflicks@aol.com
TYPES Features
DEVELOPMENT Pompeii - Trust - Cold Fire
CREDITS McCabe & Mrs. Miller - Running Scared - Short Circuit 1&2 - The Mask of Zorro - The River Wild - The Getaway (Original & Remake) - The Thing - Collateral Damage - Hart's War - The Core

David Foster .Producer
Shane Riches .Director, Development
Chris Sobolewski .Development Assistant
Laura Terry .Development Assistant

FOUNDATION ENTERTAINMENT
3272 Motor Ave., 2nd Fl.
Los Angeles, CA 90034
PHONE .310-204-4686
FAX .310-204-4603
WEB SITE .www.foundent.com
SECOND WEB SITE .www.visionboxmedia.com
TYPES Features - Theater - TV Series
DEVELOPMENT Watermark - Cousin Ginny
CREDITS The Umbilical Brothers' THWAK! - The Basketball Diaries - Daybreak - Swing Kids - Foxfire - Tortilla Soup - Charlotte Sometimes - Teddy Bear's Picnic
SUBMISSION POLICY Synopses only, unless solicited

John Manulis .President
Randy Weiss .Coordinator, Development & Production

FOUNDATION MANAGEMENT
100 N. Crescent Dr., Ste. 323
Beverly Hills, CA 90210
PHONE .See Below
FAX .310-385-4338
TYPES Features - New Media - Syndication - TV Series
DEVELOPMENT Centerfold (Mandalay Pictures)

Reagan Silber .Chairman (310-385-4317)
Adam Kolbrenner .Manager (310-385-4321)
Brady McKay .Manager (310-385-4321)
Christine Stafford .Executive Assistant to Mr. Silber
Tom Legath .Assistant

FOUNTAIN PRODUCTIONS
12312 W. Olympic Blvd.
Los Angeles, CA 90064
PHONE .310-979-5001
FAX .310-979-5100
TYPES Features - Made-for-TV/Cable Movies - TV Series
CREDITS The Jennie Project (Disney Channel) - The Wonderful World of Disney - Miracle Worker - Ladies and the Champ - Inspector Gadget 2

Charles Hirschhorn .Founder/CEO
Peter Green .President

FOUNTAINHEAD PICTURES
8670 Burton Way, Ste. 319
Los Angeles, CA 90048
PHONE .310-276-5583
FAX .310-276-5583
EMAIL .fountpix@pacbell.net
TYPES Features - Made-for-TV/Cable Movies - TV Series
DEALS Silver Pictures
DEVELOPMENT The Time Patrol - The Bank Job
CREDITS Pictures at the Beach - Baraba - Sandor - Straight and Narrow

Aaron J. Shuster .Director/Writer/Producer
Kimberly Norton .Producer/Manager
Brandon Wright .Creative Affairs
Morgan Daniels .Assistant

FOUR BOYS FILMS
200 N. Larchmont Blvd., 2nd Fl.
Los Angeles, CA 90004
PHONE .323-957-0366
FAX .323-957-0388
EMAIL .fourboysfilms@sbcglobal.net
TYPES Features - Made-for-TV/Cable Movies - Theater - TV Series
DEVELOPMENT Engagement Ring - Florence, Not Italy - Wilberforce - Crossing the Line - Wendover Whale - Laddie - Mother's Day - Theo - Affairs of Men
CREDITS And So to Bedlam...
COMMENTS Produced series of telefilms in partnership with 1A Productions and BBC; Representation, UTA; Partnership with the Play Company and Edgemar Center for the Arts

David Hunt .President/CEO
Patricia Heaton .VP
Anna Kim .Creative Executive

FOUR POINT ENTERTAINMENT

14945 Ventura Blvd., Ste. 300
Sherman Oaks, CA 91403
PHONE . . . 818-528-1461
FAX . . . 818-528-1466
EMAIL . . . info@fourpoint.tv
WEB SITE . . . www.fourpointentertainment.com
TYPES Animation - Features - Made-for-TV/Cable Movies - Reality TV - Syndication - TV Series
DEVELOPMENT Bo Derek's Colorado
PRODUCTION A Day in the Life - Secrets of Superstar Fitness - Winning Women - Extreme Sports
CREDITS Amazing America - American Gladiators - Beyond Reality - Case Closed - Great Drives - Likely Suspects - Missing Reward - The Other Side - Real Ghosts 1-3 - That's Amore - Saved by the Light
COMMENTS Large feature, MOW's and TV library

Shukri Ghalayini . . . Chairman/CEO
Jackie Watson . . . Producer
Louis George . . . VP, Sales & Acquisitions
Rich Procter . . . VP, Creative Development
Luca Barbareschi . . . Executive Producer
Doris Keating . . . Executive Producer
Raegan Matthews . . . Associate Producer
Michael Meyer . . . Business & Legal Affairs

*FOX 21

1847 Centinela Ave.
Santa Monica, CA 90404
PHONE . . . 310-315-7890
FAX . . . 310-315-7878
WEB SITE . . . www.fox.com
TYPES TV Series
COMMENTS A division of Twentieth Century Fox Television

Jane Leisner . . . Sr. VP
Brett Weitz . . . VP, Creative Affairs
Shaleen Desai . . . Director, Creative Affairs
Marci Wiseman . . . Consultant, Business Affairs

FOX BROADCASTING COMPANY

10201 W. Pico Blvd.
Los Angeles, CA 90035
PHONE . . . 310-369-1000/212-556-2400
WEB SITE . . . www.fox.com
TYPES TV Series - Reality TV
COMMENTS Mailing address: PO Box 900, Beverly Hills, CA 90213

K. Rupert Murdoch . . . Chairman/CEO, News Corporation
Peter Chernin . . . Chairman/CEO, The Fox Group/President & COO, News Corporation
Tony Vinciquerra . . . President/CEO, Fox Networks Group
Gail Berman . . . President, Entertainment
Ed Wilson . . . President, Fox Television Network
Robert Quicksilver . . . President, Network Distribution
Ira Kurgan . . . President, Network Business Operations
Andrew Setos . . . President, Engineering Fox Group
Preston Beckman . . . Executive VP, Strategic Program Planning
Mike Darnell . . . Executive VP, Specials & Alternative Programming
Craig H. Erwich . . . Executive VP, Programming
Del Mayberry . . . Executive VP, Finance & Administration
Roberta Mell . . . Executive VP, Marketing
Marcia Shulman . . . Executive VP, Casting

(Continued)

FOX BROADCASTING COMPANY (Continued)

Eric Yeldell . . . Executive VP, Legal Affairs
Kathy Atkinson . . . Sr. VP, Finance
Melva Benoit . . . Sr. VP, Research
Joe Earley . . . Sr. VP, Publicity & Corporate Communications
Karen Fox . . . Sr. VP, Business Affairs
Jeremy Gold . . . Sr. VP, Comedy Development
Ted Gold . . . Sr. VP, Drama Development
Missy Halperin . . . Sr. VP, Talent Relations
Bob Huber . . . Sr. VP, Casting
Kary McHoul Gatens . . . Sr. VP, Alternative Programming
George Oswald . . . Sr. VP, Creative Services
Donna Redier-Linsk . . . Sr. VP, Business Affairs
Marcy Ross . . . Sr. VP, Current Programming
Tom Sheets . . . Sr. VP, Special Programming
Minna Taylor . . . Sr. VP, Legal Affairs
Mitsy Wilson . . . Sr. VP, Diversity Development
Kathy Edrich . . . VP, Business Affairs
Scott Grogin . . . VP, Corporate Communications
Michelle Hooper . . . VP, Entertainment Publicity
Sabrina Bonet Ishak . . . VP, Alternative Programming & Specials
Samie Kim . . . VP, Comedy Development
Susan Levison . . . VP, Drama Development
Alan Rast . . . VP, Creative Services
Wenda Fong . . . VP, Alternative Programming
Kristen Guertin Graham . . . VP, Talent Relations
MJ LaVaccare . . . VP, Scheduling
Pauline O'Con . . . VP, Drama Casting
Gerald Alcantar . . . VP, Diversity Development
Amy Christopher . . . Director, East Coast Casting
Jonathan Davis . . . Director, Alternative Programs & Late Night
Jane Greenstein . . . Director, Comedy Development
Stefani Relles . . . Director, Non-Traditional Development
Russell Rothberg . . . Director, Current Programming
Anne Schwarz . . . Director, Scheduling
Jonathan Wax . . . Director, Current Programming
Suzanna Makkos . . . Manager, Current Programming
Zack Olin . . . Manager, Current Programming
Yvette Urbina . . . Manager, Current Programming

FOX NEWS CHANNEL

1440 S. Sepulveda Blvd.
Los Angeles, CA 90025
PHONE . . . 310-444-8751
FAX . . . 310-444-8665
WEB SITE . . . www.foxnews.com
TYPES TV Series
CREDITS The O'Reilly Factor - Hannity & Colmes - The Fox Report with Shepard Smith
COMMENTS News Programming

Kevin Magee . . . VP, Programming
Bill Shine . . . VP, Production
Bert Solivan . . . VP, News Information/General Manager, Foxnews.com

TED FOX PRODUCTIONS

8491 Sunset Blvd., Ste. 248
Hollywood, CA 90069
PHONE 310-659-5016
EMAIL .....info@tedfoxproductions.com
WEB SITE .....www.tedfoxproductions.com

TYPES	Features - Direct-to-Video/DVD - Made-for-TV/Cable Movies - Music Videos - New Media - Syndication - TV Series
DEVELOPMENT	Harvest - Killer Ride
PRE-PRODUCTION	Dead Awake
PRODUCTION	Succubus
CREDITS	Soulmates - Love Is Like That - Deadfall - Little Cobras - Monkey Business - Dark Nova - Quick & Easy - Liquid Dreams - Mo' Poe - Treasure Hunter - Runaway Dream - Supernatural
COMMENTS	Digital video; TV and feature music production; Distribution

Ted Fox .....President/Producer
Sharon Craig .....Director, Development
Jeff Carlis .....Acquisitions
Joy Freeman .....Story Editor
Johanna Trias .....Story Editor

FOX SPORTS NETWORK

10201 W. Pico Blvd., Bldg. 101
Los Angeles, CA 90035
PHONE 310-369-1000
WEB SITE .....www.foxsports.com

TYPES	TV Series
CREDITS	The Best Damn Sports Show Period - Beyond the Glory
COMMENTS	National and regional sports networks providing 24-hour sports and entertainment programming

Bob Thompson .....President
Randy Freer .....COO
George Greenberg .....Executive VP, Programming & Production
David Rone .....Sr. VP, Regional Network Development & Rights Acquisitions
Zig Gauthier .....VP, Development
Read Jackson .....VP, Programming & Production
Michael Feller .....Director, Programming & Scheduling
Doug Levy .....Director, Production & Operations
Geoff Suddleson .....Director, Development

FOX TELEVISION STUDIOS

10201 W. Pico Blvd., Bldg. 41
Los Angeles, CA 90035
PHONE 310-369-1000
FAX 310-369-7378
WEB SITE .....www.fox.com
SECOND WEB SITE .....www.newscorp.com

TYPES	Documentaries - Made-for-TV/Cable Movies - Reality TV - TV Series
CREDITS	Malcolm in the Middle - The Bernie Mac Show - Method & Red - Listen Up - Shacking Up - Redemption - Anonymous Rex - The Grid - The Shield - Family Forensics - Twelve Mile Road - Prince William - Sins of the Father - Biography - Cleopatra: The Film That Changed Hollywood - Temptation Island 3

Angela Shapiro .....President, Fox Television Studios
David Madden .....Executive VP, Fox Television Pictures
David Martin .....Executive VP, Fox Alternative Productions
Daniela Welteke .....Executive VP/Head, Fox World Productions
Aaron Meyerson .....Sr. VP, Non-Fiction Programming
Lisa Demberg .....Sr. VP, Fox Television Pictures
Kevin J. Burns .....President, Prometheus Entertainment
Scott Hartford . . .VP, Development & Production, Prometheus Entertainment
Rich Vokulich .....Executive VP
Bob Lemchen .....Sr. VP, Fox Television Studios, Physical Production
Justin Pierce .....Sr. VP, Corporate Communications
Edward Sabin .....Sr. VP, Business & Legal Affairs
Hayley Babcock .....VP, Fox World Productions
Tim Crescenti .....Producer/Executive, Fox World Productions
Martin Carlson .....VP, Business & Legal Affairs
Marney Hochman .....VP, Creative Affairs, Fox Alternative Productions
Naomi Martinez .....VP, Finance & Administration
Eric Poticha .....VP, Fox Television Pictures
Gary Shapiro .....VP, Creative Affairs, Fox Alternative Productions
Stacy Kreisberg .....VP, Business & Legal Affairs
Andrew Durham Executive Director, Production, Fox Alternative Productions
Dean Barnes .....Director, Post Production
Vinette Bond .....Director, Business & Legal Affairs
Cheryl Buysse .....Director, Business & Legal Affairs
Valerie Eads .....Director, Business & Legal Affairs, Fox Television Studios/Regency Television
Ronit Koren .....Director, Marketing
Cathy Viesel .....Director, Creative Affairs, Fox Alternative Productions

FR PRODUCTIONS

2980 Beverly Glen Circle, Ste. 200
Los Angeles, CA 90077
PHONE 310-470-9212
FAX 310-470-4905

TYPES	Features
DEVELOPMENT	The Black Stallion Revolts (UA)
CREDITS	Lost in Translation - The Young Black Stallion (Disney) - Black Stallion - Barfly - Godfather 2&3 - Apocalypse Now - The Secret Garden - Town and Country - Virgin Suicides - The Conversation - The Outsiders

Fred Roos .....Producer/President
Kara Mazzola .....Director, Development
Jessica Janos .....Story
David Lawrence .....Story

FRANCHISE PICTURES, INC.

8228 Sunset Blvd.
Los Angeles, CA 90046
PHONE 323-848-3444
FAX 323-848-9612

TYPES	Features
DEALS	Universal Pictures - Warner Bros. Pictures
DEVELOPMENT	Special Interest - Void Moon - Psychic - Wing and a Prayer
POST PRODUCTION	Half Past Dead - Avenging Angelo - The Foreigner - A Hairy Tale - A Sound of Thunder - The Whole Ten Yards
CREDITS	Heist - The Whole Nine Yards - The Pledge - Angel Eyes - Get Carter - Ballistic: Ecks vs. Sever - City by the Sea - Alex and Emma - The In-Laws

Elie Samaha ....Chairman/CEO
Tracee Stanley ....President, Development
Mimi Steinbauer ....President, International Distribution
Hans Turner ....Executive VP/CFO
Rick Kwak ....Executive VP, Business Affairs
Tiffany Boehmke ....VP, Business & Legal Affairs
Leeza-Maria el Khazen ....VP, Business Development
James Holt ....VP, Production Finance
Erik Anderson ....Creative Executive
David Ducar ....Director, Business & Legal Affairs
Nolan Pielak ....International Distribution

PETER FRANKOVICH PRODUCTIONS, INC.

1525 Ensley Ave.
Los Angeles, CA 90024
PHONE 310-551-6650
FAX 310-551-6509
EMAIL ....pfprod@earthlink.net

TYPES	Features - Made-for-TV/Cable Movies - TV Series
DEVELOPMENT	Dollars - From Noon Till Three - Cactus Flower - Bob & Carol, Ted & Alice
CREDITS	The Lake - Ride the Wind - The Unspoken Truth - Her Costly Affair - Donor (CBS)

Peter Frankovich ....President/Producer

FRANZKE ENTERTAINMENT INC.

6206 Langdon Ave.
Van Nuys, CA 91411
PHONE 818-414-0245
FAX 818-373-4846
EMAIL ....davidfranzke@yahoo.com

TYPES	Reality TV - Syndication
DEVELOPMENT	Homecoming Queen - The Replacement - X-Treme Punishment
CREDITS	Punk'd (MTV) - Granted (MTV) - Jamie Kennedy Experiment (WB) - Braniac

David Franzke ....Executive Producer/CEO

FRAZIER | CHIPMAN ENTERTAINMENT

11825 Laurelwood Dr., Ste. 6
Studio City, CA 90046
PHONE 323-974-9730/818-980-9104
FAX 818-487-0634
EMAIL ....info@frazierchipman.com
WEB SITE ....www.frazierchipman.com

TYPES	Commercials - Documentaries - Features - Made-for-TV/Cable Movies - Music Videos - Syndication - TV Series - Reality TV
COMPLETED UNRELEASED	One Door Down - Money Trouble
CREDITS	The Zeros

Garett Chipman ....Director/Producer/Partner
Kelly Frazier ....Executive Producer/Partner

*FREDERATOR STUDIOS

231 W. Olive Ave.
Burbank, CA 91502
PHONE 818-736-3606
FAX 818-736-3449
EMAIL ....hey@frederator.kz
WEB SITE ....www.frederator.kz

TYPES	Animation - TV Series
DEALS	Nickelodeon/Nick at Nite/TV Land/Spike TV
CREDITS	Oh Yeah! Cartoons - ChalkZone - The Fairly OddParents - My Life as a Teenage Robot

Fred Seibert ....President
Eric Homan ....VP, Creative Affairs

JACK FREEDMAN PRODUCTIONS

1093 Broxton Ave., Ste. 228
Los Angeles, CA 90024
PHONE 310-208-2200
EMAIL ....freedmanfilms@aol.com

TYPES	Features - Made-for-TV/Cable Movies - TV Series
CREDITS	Killers in the House - Mother's Boys - Toy Soldiers - Body Parts

Jack Freedman ....Chairman of the Board
Patricia Herskovic ....President

JOEL FREEMAN PRODUCTIONS, INC.

15323 Weddington St., Ste. 102
Sherman Oaks, CA 91411
PHONE 818-995-1189
FAX 818-995-1638
EMAIL ....jprods@pacbell.net
WEB SITE ....www.joelfreemanproductions.com

TYPES	Features - Made-for-TV/Cable Movies - TV Series
DEVELOPMENT	Booker - Woof - Romantics, Misfits and Fools - Marti
CREDITS	The Heart Is a Lonely Hunter - Shaft - Love at First Bite - The Octagon - Soapdish

Joel Freeman ....Producer

It is illegal to copy any part of this book

FREMANTLEMEDIA NORTH AMERICA (LA)
2700 Colorado Ave., Ste. 450
Santa Monica, CA 90404
PHONE .310-255-4700
FAX .310-255-4800
EMAIL .firstname.lastname@fremantlemedia.com
WEB SITE .www.fremantlemedia.com
TYPES Reality TV - TV Series
PRE-PRODUCTION The Block - Liar - How Clean Is Your House - Property Ladder
PRODUCTION American Idol 3 - Date Patrol - Canadian Idol - Behind Bars
CREDITS Family Feud - The Price Is Right - 100 Centre Street - Nero Wolfe - Whammy - The All New Press Your Luck - Oliver's Twist - American Idol - The Swan
COMMENTS Deals with Chaos Theory and Story Go Round

Tom Gutteridge .CEO (255-4701)
Cecile Frot-Coutaz .COO/Production (255-4779)
David Shall .Executive VP, Business & Legal Affairs (255-4729)
Anne Bartnett .Sr. VP, Business & Legal Affairs (255-4732)
Gaby Johnson .Sr. VP, Entertainment (255-4722)
Jeff Mirkin .Sr. VP, Development (255-4750)
Tracy Verna .Sr. VP, Lifestyle Programming
Jill Schwartz-McKiernan .VP, Acquisitions (255-4764)
Jason Daniel .Head, Drama Development (255-4704)
Michael Jafta .VP, Business & Legal Affairs (255-4725)
Molly Van Vleck .Director, Executive Office (255-4702)
Hugh Wright .Director, Development (255-4746)
Michael Katz .Director, Development, Reality
Nigel Caaro Evans .Manager, Acquisitions & Development (255-4715)
Mandel Ilagen .Manager, Development (255-4719)

FREMANTLEMEDIA NORTH AMERICA (NY)
1540 Broadway
New York, NY 10036
PHONE .212-541-2800
FAX .212-541-2810
EMAIL .firstname.lastname@fremantlemedia.com
WEB SITE .www.fremantlemedia.com
TYPES Made-for-TV/Cable Movies - TV Series - Reality TV
COMMENTS Game shows

Tom Gutteridge .CEO, North America
Lou Festa .CFO

FREQUENCY FILMS
5555 Melrose Ave., Lubitsch 106/108
Hollywood, CA 90038
PHONE .323-956-5244
FAX .323-862-2249
WEB SITE .www.frequencyfilms.com
TYPES Features - TV Series
DEALS Paramount Pictures-Motion Picture Group
CREDITS The Mexican - RPM - The Warriors - Keen Eddie - Harry Green and Eugene

J.H. Wyman .Writer/Director/Executive Producer
Judy Dent .Executive Assistant to J.H. Wyman

FRESH PRODUCE FILMS
417 N. Orange Dr.
Los Angeles, CA 90036
PHONE .323-934-5500
FAX .323-933-6463
EMAIL .mpfpc@aol.com
TYPES Features - Made-for-TV/Cable Movies - TV Series
DEVELOPMENT I Know You Really Love Me - Cease Fire - Hair Salon Documentary - Annika - More Than a Woman - The Crystal Skull - The Sky Is Green
POST PRODUCTION Z Channel/The Uncommon Denominator (IFC)
CREDITS Amos and Andrew - Still Breathing - Kill the Man - Twin Falls Idaho - Cherry Falls - Wild Iris - Expert Witness (CBS)

Marshall Persinger .President/Producer

DANIEL FRIED PRODUCTIONS
c/o Studio Hamburg International Production
5225 Wilshire Blvd., Ste. 626
Los Angeles, CA 90036
PHONE .323-525-0023
FAX .323-417-5083
EMAIL .info@dfprods.com
TYPES Features - Made-for-TV/Cable Movies - TV Series
DEALS Studio Hamburg WorldWide Pictures
POST PRODUCTION The Illusion
CREDITS O

Daniel Fried .Producer

BUDD FRIEDMAN DIGITAL
12200 W. Olympic Blvd.
Los Angeles, CA 90064
PHONE .310-806-4400
FAX .310-806-4401
TYPES TV Series
DEVELOPMENT Playboy All-Star Comedy Bash
CREDITS 40 Years of Laughter at the Improv (NBC) - Comedians Unleashed (Animal Planet) - National Lampoon's Funny Money (GSN)
COMMENTS Joint venture with TMC Entertainment

Budd Friedman .Founder/CEO
Marc Price .Partner/Producer
Tip McPartland .Partner/Producer

FRIES FILM GROUP, INC.
22817 Ventura Blvd., Ste. 909
Woodland Hills, CA 91364
PHONE .818-888-3052
FAX .818-888-3042
TYPES Features - TV Series
DEVELOPMENT Dr. Lopez
PRE-PRODUCTION Alien Agent - Canes - Hunt for the Devil
CREDITS Bandios - New Adventures of Pinocchio - Fatal Blade - Bleeders - LAPD

Charles M. Fries .President
Tony Brewster .COO (asbrewster@earthlink.net)
Michael Stone .Executive VP, Worldwide Distribution
Theodore Elman .Office Manager

CHUCK FRIES PRODUCTIONS, INC.
1880 Century Park East, Ste. 315
Los Angeles, CA 90067
PHONE .310-203-9520
FAX .310-203-9519
TYPES Features - Direct-to-Video/DVD - Made-for-TV/Cable Movies - TV Series
DEVELOPMENT The Flying Nun - Petals on the Wind - Chicken and the Cheerleader - The Big Ride - Woman on the Ledge 2
CREDITS Screamers - Deadly Web - Troop Beverly Hills
COMMENTS Fries Film Company, Inc.; Fries Enterprises, Inc.; Avanti Enterprises

Charles W. Fries .Chairman/President/CEO
Ava Fries .President, Avanti Enterprises
Jeff Swanson .Executive Assistant

FRONT STREET PRODUCTIONS, LLC
1620 Broadway, Ste. E
Santa Monica, CA 90404
PHONE .310-264-1400
FAX .310-264-6688
TYPES Features - TV Series
POST PRODUCTION The Deal
CREDITS Pressure - Water's Edge - The Proposal - Out of Line - The Break Up - Eden - We Don't Live Here Anymore

Harvey Kahn .Producer/Partner
Jonas Goodman .Producer
Michael Carlin .Director, Development

FRONTIER PICTURES
500 S. Buena Vista St., Animation Bldg., Ste. 2-D9
Burbank, CA 91521
PHONE .818-560-6970
FAX .818-560-6503
EMAIL .frontierpics@aol.com
TYPES Features - TV Series
DEALS Walt Disney Pictures/Touchstone Pictures
DEVELOPMENT Girl Scout in Paradise - Buzzkill - Fab Girl - X-Girls - Port O' Call (Disney) - The Wild - The Jane Plan - Alpha Male - The Santa Clause 3
CREDITS Head Over Heels - The New Guy

John J. Strauss .President
Ed Decter .President
Kate Purdy .Director, Development

MARK FROST
2934-1/2 Beverly Glen Circle, PMB 251
Bel Air, CA 90077
PHONE .818-986-0821
FAX .818-990-4449
TYPES Features - TV Series
CREDITS All Souls - Buddy Faro - Twin Peaks - American Chronicles - Storyville

Mark Frost .Executive Producer
Kevin Danczak .Assistant to Mr. Frost

FTM PRODUCTIONS
10866 Wilshire Blvd., Ste. 850
Los Angeles, CA 90024
PHONE .310-481-9911
FAX .310-481-9909
EMAIL .ftmprod@aol.com
TYPES Features - Made-for-TV/Cable Movies - Syndication - TV Series
DEVELOPMENT Year One - Head Games - XXL - Crash Site
CREDITS Scoring - The Girl Next Door - Voyage to Terror - Flinch - Passport to Murder

Tony Masucci .Founder

FULLER FILMS, INC.
1008 Fifth Ave.
Venice, CA 90291
PHONE .310-717-8842
EMAIL .gopics@sympatico.ca
TYPES Features - Theater - TV Series
PRE-PRODUCTION Who You Know - Noise
CREDITS The Believer - K Street - Internal Affairs - Rabbit Head - Deep Cover
SUBMISSION POLICY By query letter

Henry Bean .Writer/Director/Producer
Leora Barish .Writer/Director/Producer
Paul De Souza .Producer

FUNNY BOY FILMS
346 N. Detroit St.
Los Angeles, CA 90036
PHONE .323-993-0000
FAX .323-993-0060
WEB SITE .www.funnyboyfilms.com
TYPES Features
DEVELOPMENT Adam & Steve
CREDITS Latter Days

Kirkland Tibbels .President/CEO
Darryl Anderle .CFO
George Bendele .VP, Development
Jonathan Weber .Assistant to Mr. Tibbels

FURST FILMS
8954 W. Pico Blvd., 2nd Fl.
Los Angeles, CA 90035
PHONE .310-278-6468
FAX .310-278-7401
EMAIL .info@furstfilms.com
TYPES Features - Made-for-TV/Cable Movies - TV Series
DEVELOPMENT Sluts - The Precious Few - Between the Covers - Clean - Rain Falls - Conviction
PRE-PRODUCTION First Snow
PRODUCTION The Matador
POST PRODUCTION The Woods
CREDITS The Cooler - Owning Mahowny - Blue Ridge Fall - Everything Put Together

Sean Furst .Producer
Bryan Furst .Producer
Shauna Phelan .Creative Executive

FURTHUR FILMS
100 Universal City Plaza, Bldg. 1320/4G
Universal City, CA 91608
PHONE 818-777-6700/212-333-1421
FAX 818-866-1278/212-333-8163
TYPES Features
DEALS Warner Bros. Pictures
CREDITS It Runs in the Family - The In-Laws - SwimFan - Don't Say a Word - One Night at McCool's
COMMENTS East Coast office: 825 Eighth Ave., 30th Fl., New York, NY 10019

Michael Douglas .....Producer
Marcy Drogin .....President, Production (NY)
Allen Burry .....Publicist (LA)
Angela Congelose .....Controller (LA)
James LaVigne .....Director, Development (NY)
Julianne Berkowitz .....No Title (NY)
Robert Mitas .....No Title (LA)
Carley Thayer .....No Title (NY)

FUSE
11 Penn Plaza, 15th Fl.
New York, NY 10001
PHONE 212-324-3400
FAX 212-324-3445
WEB SITE .....www.fuse.tv
TYPES New Media - TV Series
CREDITS Tastemaker - Oven Fresh - Dedicate Live - Mixtape Mixdown - Soundtrack to Your Life - Uranium - Celebrity Tastemaker - Rockzilla - No. 1 Countdown - Chunky Beat - Kung Faux
COMMENTS Cable channel; Digital cable music network; Internet

Marc Juris .....President
Mary Corigliano .....VP, Marketing
Norman Schoenfeld .....VP, Programming
Robert Weiss .....Head, Programming

FX NETWORKS, LLC
10000 Santa Monica Blvd.
Los Angeles, CA 90067
PHONE 310-286-3800
FAX 310-789-4688
EMAIL .....jsolberg@fxnetworks.com
WEB SITE .....www.fxnetworks.com
TYPES Made-for-TV/Cable Movies - Reality TV - TV Series
CREDITS Redemption - Rescue Me - RFK - Son of the Beach - Deliberate Intent - A Glimpse of Hell - Sins of the Father - The Shield - Bigshot: Confessions of a Campus Bookie - The Pentagon Papers - 44 Minutes - The North Hollywood Shootout - Nip/Tuck

Peter Liguori .....President/CEO
John Landgraf .....President, Entertainment
Lee Bartlett .....Sr. VP, Legal & Business Affairs
Gerard Bocaccio .....Sr. VP, Entertainment
Nick Grad .....Sr. VP, Series Development
Steve Leblang .....Sr. VP, Strategic Planning & Research
Chuck Saftler .....Sr. VP, Programming (310-789-4652)
John Solberg .....Sr. VP, Public Relations (310-789-4689)
Matt Cherniss .....VP, Series Development
Eric Schrier VP, Current Series & Alternative Programming (310-789-4699)

G4 MEDIA, INC.
12312 W. Olympic Blvd.
Los Angeles, CA 90064
PHONE 310-979-5000
FAX 310-979-5099
EMAIL .....info@g4tv.com
WEB SITE www.g4techtv.com
TYPES Documentaries - New Media - TV Series
CREDITS TV Series: X-Play - G4tv.com - The Screen Savers - Pulse - Filter - Arena - Portal - Judgment Day - Cinematech - Sweat; Documentaries: Icons - Players - Specials: G-Phoria - The Award Show 4 Gamers - EA Sports Madden Challenge
COMMENTS Cable and satellite TV network; Video gaming, technology and lifestyle programming

Charles Hirschhorn .....Founder/CEO
Debra Green .....COO
Alan Duke .....Sr. VP, Business & Legal Affairs
Vinnie Longobardo .....Sr. VP, Programming
Dale Hopkins .....Sr. VP, Ad & Affiliates Sales
Gaynor Strachan Chun .....Sr. VP, Marketing
Gil Breakman .....VP, Finance
Soheila Ataei .....VP, Human Resources
Peter Green .....VP, Programming
Peter Hammersly .....VP, Programming
Laura Civiello .....VP, Program Acquisitions & Development
Julie Fields .....VP, Creative
Frank Voci .....VP, Internet Services
David Shane .....VP, Publicity & Media Relations
Benita Husband .....VP, Production Management
Tina Kowalewski .....VP, Program Development
Rob Hause .....VP, Broadcast Operations
Lauren de la Fuente .....VP, Ad & Affiliate Marketing
Jason Liebowitz .....VP, Ad Sales, East Coast
Gloria Jolley .....VP, Affiliate Relations
Mark O'Connell .....VP, Affiliate Relations, East Coast
Hubert T. Smith Jr. .....VP, Business & Legal Affairs
Scot Rubin .....VP, Editorial

GALÁN ENTERTAINMENT
523 Victoria Ave.
Venice, CA 90291
PHONE 310-823-2822
FAX 310-823-7361
WEB SITE .....www.galanent.com
TYPES Documentaries - Features - Made-for-TV/Cable Movies - New Media - Syndication - TV Series
DEALS Telemundo Network
PRODUCTION The Swan
CREDITS Loco Slam - Bravo Awards - Los Beltran - Solo en America - Padre Alberto - Viva Vegas - True Love Stories - La Cenicienta

Nely Galán .....President/CEO
Chevy Hernandez .....VP, Development
Norma Carballo .....Coordinator, Development

GALLANT ENTERTAINMENT

16161 Ventura Blvd., Ste. 664
Encino, CA 91436
PHONE 818-905-9848
FAX 818-906-9965
EMAIL .....gallantent@aol.com
TYPES Features - Direct-to-Video/DVD - Made-for-TV/Cable Movies - Syndication - TV Series
DEVELOPMENT Williamsport - Silence
PRODUCTION Journeys Below the Line (DVD)
CREDITS 10 Attitudes - Stompin' at the Savoy - Bionic Ever After

Michael O. Gallant .....President/Producer
Kathleen Gallant .....VP, Business Affairs

GALLO ENTERTAINMENT, INC.

1421 Ambassador St., Ste. 101
Los Angeles, CA 90035
PHONE 310-277-8107
FAX 310-277-1828
TYPES Features - Made-for-TV/Cable Movies
CREDITS Hustling - The Lookalike - Princess Daisy

Lillian Gallo .....Producer/Partner

GARLIN PICTURES, INC.

11728 Dorothy St., Ste. 103
Los Angeles, CA 90049
PHONE 310-488-9092
FAX 310-826-9366
TYPES Features - Reality TV - TV Series
DEVELOPMENT The Shape of Fear - Sue Me - Without a Net - Disneyland 2 Miles - Valedictorian - Love Stats - My Brother's Fiancee's Sister
PRE-PRODUCTION Dreamgirl - Life to Come
PRODUCTION Relative Strangers
COMPLETED UNRELEASED The Godfather of Green Bay - Untitled VH1 Reality Pilot
CREDITS Shacking Up (WB) - Malibu's Most Wanted - Tough Luck - The Jamie Kennedy Experiment - Blowback

Brian R. Etting .....Producer/Director
Josh Etting .....Producer/Writer

THE GARY-PAUL AGENCY

1549 Main St.
Stratford, CT 06615
PHONE 203-375-2636
FAX 203-345-6167
EMAIL .....maynard@optonline.net
WEB SITE .....www.thegarypaulagency.com
SECOND WEB SITE .....www.ouchtv.net
TYPES Documentaries - Features - Direct-to-Video/DVD - Made-for-TV/Cable Movies - TV Series
DEVELOPMENT Protecting Their Nest
PRE-PRODUCTION -18 ° : The Temperature at Which Blood Freezes
POST PRODUCTION The Ranchers
CREDITS The Water's Edge - Through the Lens
SUBMISSION POLICY Email queries only
COMMENTS Animatronics facility; Below-the-line technicians; Sports cinematography; WGA

Garret C. Maynard .....Owner/Producer
Philip Curney .....Post Production Manager
Timothy Perniciaro .....Production Manager

GAYLORD FILMS

4000 Warner Blvd.
Burbank, CA 91522
PHONE 818-954-3500
TYPES Features
DEALS Warner Bros. Pictures
DEVELOPMENT The Emperor of Ocean Park - White Out - Dreamer - My Losing Season - Wonder Twins
POST PRODUCTION Cinderella Story - Untitled Carroll Ballard Project
CREDITS Divine Secrets of the Ya-Ya Sisterhood - What a Girl Wants
COMMENTS Pandora is a specialty division of Gaylord Films

Hunt Lowry .....President/CEO
Steven C. Smith .....CFO
Dana Ginsburg .....Executive VP, Business Affairs
Stacy Cohen .....Sr. VP, Production
Paula Marcus .....VP, Physical Production & Finance
Casey La Scala .....Producer
Patty Reed .....Director, Development
Matt Hutaff .....Assistant to Dana Ginsburg

GEKKO FILM CORPORATION

c/o MGM Worldwide Television, Inc.
2500 Broadway St.
Santa Monica, CA 90404
PHONE 604-292-8525
FAX 604-292-8550
TYPES Animation - Documentaries - Features - Direct-to-Video/DVD - Large Format - Made-for-TV/Cable Movies - Syndication - TV Series
CREDITS MacGyver - Legend - Stargate-SG1
COMMENTS Canadian office: 2400 Boundary Rd., Burnaby, BC V5M 3Z3 Canada

Richard Dean Anderson .....CEO
Michael Greenburg .....President
Gregory D. Almas .....Production

JANNA E. GELFAND PRODUCTIONS

960 S. Westgate, Ste. 108
Los Angeles, CA 90049
PHONE 310-826-2345
FAX 310-826-6268
EMAIL .....jegprods@earthlink.net
TYPES Features - TV Series
DEVELOPMENT Cherokee Heist - Material Girl - Monestary Blues - Just Play Dead - The Big Turnaround
CREDITS Kissing Miranda - Beethoven's 5th

Janna E. Gelfand .....Producer
Amy Andelson .....Development

GENDECE FILM COMPANY
4150 Arch Dr., Ste. 403
Studio City, CA 91604
PHONE . . . 818-623-9242
TYPES Features - Made-for-TV/Cable Movies - Theater - TV Series
DEVELOPMENT Stars and Angels
PRE-PRODUCTION Dancer in the Wings
PRODUCTION The Paul Jabara Story
CREDITS Runaway Train - Salsa - 6 Pac: The Musical - Selena - The American Choreography Awards - Tina Landon: Behind the Moves (DreamWorks)
COMMENTS Soundtracks; Stage musicals

Brian Gendece . . . Producer/Partner/Manager
Bob Esty . . . Partner/Music Director

GENERATION ENTERTAINMENT
75 Grand St., Ste. 2W
New York, NY 10013
PHONE . . . 212-966-1444
FAX . . . 212-966-3137
EMAIL . . . info@generationentertainment.com
TYPES Features - TV Series
DEVELOPMENT Subliminal - Racing Time - Sandcastle - Central Casting - Paranoia - The Crossing - Crime of the Century
CREDITS The Photographer - Mugshots: Dr. Richard Sharpe - Mugshots: Robert Blake
SUBMISSION POLICY Query by fax only

Jeremy Stein . . . Producer/Writer/Director
Potter Lewis . . . Director, Development
Trent Masters . . . Creative Executive

GENREBEND PRODUCTIONS, INC.
233 Wilshire Blvd., 4th Fl.
Santa Monica, CA 90401
PHONE . . . 310-917-1064
FAX . . . 310-917-1065
TYPES Features - Made-for-TV/Cable Movies - New Media - TV Series
DEALS Warner Bros. Television Production
POST PRODUCTION Jack & Bobby
CREDITS Tarzan - Without a Trace - Band of Brothers - West Wing - Smallville - ER - Millennium - X-Files

David Nutter . . . Director/President
Tom Lavagnino . . . Writer/VP, Creative Affairs

GERBER PICTURES
9465 Wilshire Blvd., Ste. 318
Beverly Hills, CA 90212
PHONE . . . 310-385-5880
FAX . . . 310-385-5881
TYPES Features - Direct-to-Video/DVD - Made-for-TV/Cable Movies - TV Series
DEALS Warner Bros. Pictures
CREDITS Juwanna Man - James Dean - Queen of the Damned - What a Girl Wants - The In-Laws - Grind

Bill Gerber . . . President
Taylor Latham . . . Director, Development (310-385-1416)
Jay Polidoro . . . Assistant to Bill Gerber (310-385-9606)

GHOST HOUSE PICTURES
315 S. Beverly Dr., Ste. 216
Beverly Hills, CA 90212
PHONE . . . 310-785-3900
FAX . . . 310-785-9176
TYPES Features
DEALS Senator International
DEVELOPMENT 30 Days of Night - Scarecrow
POST PRODUCTION Boogeyman - The Grudge

Sam Raimi . . . Director/Executive Producer
Robert Tapert . . . Executive Producer
Michael Kirk . . . VP, Development
Sue Binder . . . Business Manager
David Pollison . . . Assistant

*GHOST ROBOT
373 Broadway, Ste. F-3
New York, NY 10013
PHONE . . . 212-343-0900
FAX . . . 212-898-1119
EMAIL . . . man@ghostrobot.com
WEB SITE . . . www.ghostrobot.com
TYPES Animation - Commercials - Features - Music Videos
DEVELOPMENT Ecstasy Club - Original Glory - Kingston
POST PRODUCTION Road
CREDITS Hell House - Breath Control - The Federation of Black Cowboys

Zachary Mortensen . . . Producer
Tommy Pallotta . . . Producer
Joshua Zeman . . . Producer
Mitch Schultz . . . Producer/Director, Development

LEEZA GIBBONS ENTERPRISES (LGE)
3340 Ocean Park Blvd., Ste. 3045
Santa Monica, CA 90405
PHONE . . . 310-581-6380
FAX . . . 310-581-3516
TYPES Made-for-TV/Cable Movies - Radio - Reality TV
DEVELOPMENT A Boy I Once Knew - Curl Up and Dye - Senior Moments - The Kirk Franklin Show
PRODUCTION Leeza Gibbons: Hollywood Confidential (Radio)
CREDITS The Michael Essany Show - MTV's Verdict - Leeza - Intimate Portrait of JFK Jr. - Straight from the Heart - The Teen Files - E! Specials: Hollywood Youth - Gay Hollywood - Celebrities and Their Causes - Leeza Gibbons Hollywood Confidential

Leeza Gibbons . . . CEO
Vincent J. Arcuri . . . Creative Executive
Rick Bradley . . . Marketing, Licensing & Endorsements
Jerry Sharell . . . Publicity & PR

AL GIDDINGS IMAGES, INC.
75 Bridger Hollow Rd.
Pray, MT 59065
PHONE . . . 406-333-4300
FAX . . . 406-333-4308
EMAIL . . . stocklibrary@algiddings.com
WEB SITE . . . www.algiddings.com
TYPES Documentaries - Features
CREDITS Blue Whale: Largest Animal on Earth - Galapagos: Beyond Darwin - Titanic - Galapagos: IMAX 3D - Secrets of the Humpback Whale - Water: Gift of Life - In Celebration of Trees
COMMENTS Stock footage library

Al Giddings . . . President/Director/Producer
Donna Pace . . . General Manager

GIGANTIC PICTURES
16065 Jeanne Lane
Encino, CA 91436
PHONE .310-488-1195
FAX .270-574-8024
EMAIL .giganticpix@attglobal.net
TYPES Features
DEVELOPMENT First Descent - Close Your Eyes - Emergence - Cajun Night Before Christmas - Dishdogz
CREDITS Thick as Thieves

Glenn Zoller .Producer

GILLEN & PRICE
7425 Oakwood Ave.
Los Angeles, CA 90036
PHONE .See Below
TYPES Features - TV Series
DEVELOPMENT Eye of the Raven - The Geography of Paradise - The Purification Ceremony - Lost in Translation
CREDITS Fried Green Tomatoes - Mercy Point
SUBMISSION POLICY No unsolicited material

Anne Marie Gillen .Producer (310-390-3923)
Jody Price .Producer (323-655-8047)

ROGER GIMBEL PRODUCTIONS, INC.
1675 Old Oak Rd.
Los Angeles, CA 90049
PHONE .310-459-3838
FAX .310-459-6940
TYPES Features - Made-for-TV/Cable Movies
DEVELOPMENT Synanon - Rachel Carson (Silent Spring)
CREDITS Montana - Chernobyl: The Final Warning - Murder Between Friends - The Perfect Mother

Roger Gimbel .President/Executive Producer
Leeza Watstein .Director, Development

GINTY FILMS INTERNATIONAL
16255 Ventura Blvd., Ste. 625
Encino, CA 91436
PHONE .310-277-1408/353-1-676-1044
FAX .818-981-5943/353-1-676-2155
EMAIL .rwginty@aol.com
WEB SITE .www.robertginty.com
TYPES Commercials - Features - Direct-to-Video/DVD - Made-for-TV/Cable Movies - Music Videos - Syndication - TV Series
DEVELOPMENT Green Shadows - White Whale - Robyn Hood - The Cotton Club Murders - Elaine & Bill: Portrait of a Marriage - Mrs. Warren's Profession - Elvis and Red - Churchill at Harrow
CREDITS China Beach - Dream On - Early Edition - Fame L.A. - Charmed - V.I.P. - Exterminator 3 - Nash Bridges - Xena - Honey, I Shrunk the Kids - MTV's 2gether - Tracker
COMMENTS Irish Theatre Art Center (New York/Dublin/London); Deals with The Irish Film Board, RTE (Ireland), Stage 5 Productions (Rome), Cinecitta Studios (Rome) and Ardmore Studios (Dublin); Ireland office: 20 Upper Merrion St., Dublin 2 Ireland

Robert Ginty .Producer/Director/CEO
Cindy Brace .Company Representative (Paris)
Suzanne Depoe .Company Representative (Toronto)
Stefano Fava .Company Representative (Rome)
Justin Moore-Lewy .Company Representative (Dublin)

GIRAFFE PRODUCTIONS
4406 Vantage Ave.
Studio City, CA 91604
PHONE .818-755-0900
FAX .818-755-0902
EMAIL .giraffeprods@aol.com
WEB SITE .www.jaymohrlive.com
TYPES Features - Reality TV - TV Series
DEVELOPMENT Diamond - East of Cielo - Never the Bride - Rehab - Singlea - On the Table - Dude Food - Destination Unknown - Life Behind Bars - Soul Surfer
PRE-PRODUCTION Lonely Street
PRODUCTION Last Comic Standing 2
CREDITS Mohr Sports (ESPN) - Last Comic Standing (NBC)

Jay Mohr .President
Cori L. Fry .Director, Development
Charles Genercer .Creative Executive

GITTES, INC.
c/o Columbia Pictures
10202 W. Washington Blvd., Poitier Bldg., Ste. 1200
Culver City, CA 90232-3195
PHONE .310-244-4333
FAX .310-244-1711
TYPES Features
DEALS Columbia Pictures
DEVELOPMENT American Caesar - The Chet Baker Project - The Ladies' Man
CREDITS Little Nikita - Breaking In - Goin' South - About Schmidt - The Girl Next Door

Harry Gittes .Producer
Edward C. Wang .Director, Development (310-244-4334)

GLATZER PRODUCTIONS
c/o Villains
9247 Alden Dr.
Beverly Hills, CA 90210
PHONE .310-888-8900
TYPES Features - TV Series
DEVELOPMENT First Born - The Princess of Paradise Park
PRE-PRODUCTION The Laird - Un-American
CREDITS In the Weeds (Series) - The Grave - Deceiver - In the Weeds (Feature) - Blue Ridge Fall
COMMENTS Deal with Villians

Peter Glatzer .Producer
Emerson Bruns .Business Affairs
Beau J. Genot .Post Production

It is illegal to copy any part of this book

GLOBAL ENTERTAINMENT MEDIA

122-1/2 S. Sweetzer Ave.
Los Angeles, CA 90048
PHONE 310-748-8580
FAX 323-658-5501
EMAIL ....walter.morgan@ubutv.com
WEB SITE ....www.ubutv.com

TYPES	Animation - Commercials - Documentaries - Features - Direct-to-Video/DVD - Made-for-TV/Cable Movies - Syndication - TV Series
DEVELOPMENT	Unnamed Animation Features - RSVP (TV Pilot)
PRE-PRODUCTION	Rio Love Story - Puppy Love
PRODUCTION	Supplier Diversity (TV Special)
POST PRODUCTION	Mardi Gras vs. Carnival
COMPLETED UNRELEASED	Cotton Tales
CREDITS	Down and Dirty
COMMENTS	Deal with UBU TV Network

Walter Morgan ....President/CEO
Roger Mende ....President, Production
Cheryl Morgan ....VP, Development
Wendy Teal ....VP, Programming

GLOBAL ENTERTAINMENT NETWORK EAST, INC.

34 Harbor Heights Dr.
Centerport, NY 11721
PHONE 631-262-1757
FAX 631-262-1760
EMAIL ....geneast@erols.com
WEB SITE ....www.globalentertainmentnet.com

TYPES	Features - Made-for-TV/Cable Movies - TV Series
DEVELOPMENT	Michael McPherson: Luminaire - Flip Orley Live at the Celebrity Theater - Finis Henderson Live at the Millenium Theater - AGA-BOOM: Comic Performance Art
CREDITS	Just Your Luck - Pink as the Day She Was Born

Stan Bernstein ....President
JoAnn Maccarone ....Office Manager
Mary Hughes ....Assistant to President

GLOBAL MEDIA TELEVISION

3535 Hayden Ave., 1st Fl.
Culver City, CA 90232
PHONE 310-553-5870
FAX 310-553-5897
WEB SITE ....www.globalmediatelevision.com

TYPES	Made-for-TV/Cable Movies - Syndication - TV Series - Reality TV
DEVELOPMENT	Win Me Over - Gallup Extreme Hidden Video - Something About Janice
PRE-PRODUCTION	As Seen on TV (VH1)
PRODUCTION	Sin City (VH1) - Curb Appeal (USA)

Joe Scotti ....President
Tony Scotti ....CEO
Gary Kurtz ....Executive VP, Development
Jon Noel Bert ....Managing Director, London
Leonard Breijo ....Business Affairs
Anthony Scotti ....Program Development
Deanna Taylor ....Executive Assistant
Mona Cushing ....Executive Assistant

GMG FILMS

3000 W. Olympic Blvd.
Santa Monica, CA 90404
PHONE 310-315-4850
FAX 310-315-4851

TYPES	Features - Made-for-TV/Cable Movies - TV Series
DEVELOPMENT	Jingle Belle (Revolution) - Prisoner in Paradise (Feature) - Bang the Drum Slowly (Feature) - Two Untitled Features (Lions Gate)
CREDITS	Bad Company

Gary Goodman ....Partner
Josh Thomashow ....Development Executive

GO GIRL MEDIA, SLK

11733 Montana Ave., Ste. 107
Los Angeles, CA 90049
PHONE 310-472-8910/818-481-8444
FAX 310-889-9034/818-893-9560
EMAIL ....info@gogirlmediatv.com
WEB SITE ....www.gogirlmediaslk.com

TYPES	Features - Made-for-TV/Cable Movies - Reality TV - Syndication - TV Series
DEVELOPMENT	B-Band Mogul: The Lou Pearlman Story - Ruby - The Rex - Potential of a Superman - Diamonds in the Ruff (Jane Carter) - ACDC (Hearst Entertainment) - I'm Mom (Jerry Offsay/Parkchester Pictures) - FUBAR - The Rock and Road Tour (Global Media Television) - The Gamers' Lounge - Pajamarama - Chicks with Attitude
PRODUCTION	Doggie Style (Pilot-Lifetime) - It's Just a Movie (Pilot-E!) - Back in the Day (Pilot-Film Roman) - Street Monk
COMMENTS	Ongoing development deal with Film One Holdings; Second address: 9062 Havenhurst Ave., North Hills, CA 91343

Susie Singer Carter ....Partner/Producer/Writer
Laura Keats ....Partner/Producer/Director
Kelly Kapp ....Partner/Producer/Writer
Don Priess ....Executive VP, Creative & Production
Deborah Zimmerly ....Story Editor
Joey Singer ....Executive Assistant
Michael Touna ....Development Assistant

GO TIME ENTERTAINMENT

3981 Weslin Ave.
Sherman Oaks, CA 91423
PHONE 818-681-1677
FAX 818-981-7986
EMAIL ....gotime@earthlink.net

TYPES	TV Series
DEVELOPMENT	King Arthur's Courts - The Breakroom - Simon Says
CREDITS	Let's Bowl (Comedy Central)
COMMENTS	Specializes in comedy

Tim Scott ....Executive Producer/Director
Nick Schenk ....Executive Producer/Writer

THE GOATSINGERS

177 W. Broadway, 2nd Fl.
New York, NY 10013
PHONE 212-966-3045
FAX 212-966-4362

TYPES	Made-for-TV/Cable Movies - Features - TV Series
CREDITS	The Grey Zone - Three Seasons

Harvey Keitel ....President
Helen Habtemariam ....Executive Assistant/Production Office Manager

GOD'S DREAM LLC

11217 Old Rockford Rd.
Minneapolis, MN 55441
PHONE .763-559-9086
FAX .763-559-9089
EMAIL .godsdream@msn.com
WEB SITE .www.godsdreamllc.com
TYPES Features - Animation - Made-for-TV/Cable Movies
DEVELOPMENT Jericho/My Master's Voice - My Best Friend - Time Jumper
CREDITS The Personals - The Cellar - Youngblood - I Love You to Death - Herman USA

Patrick Wells .President/Producer
Valerie O'Conor .VP, Creative Development
Ken Reiner .Producer/Screenwriter
John Bradford Goodman .Writer/Director

GOEPP CIRCLE PRODUCTIONS

10990 Wilshire Blvd., 16th Fl.
Los Angeles, CA 90024
PHONE .310-273-8535
TYPES Features - TV Series
DEVELOPMENT Steve Was Here - Phrackers - Illusion
POST PRODUCTION The Thunderbirds
CREDITS Clockstoppers - Dying to Live - Roswell - Star Trek: Insurrection - Star Trek: First Contact

Jonathan Frakes .Director/Producer

GOFF-KELLAM PRODUCTIONS

8491 Sunset Blvd., Ste. 1000
West Hollywood, CA 90069
PHONE .323-656-2001
FAX .323-656-1002
EMAIL .goffkellam@aol.com
WEB SITE .www.goffkellam.com
TYPES Features
DEVELOPMENT Lovesick - Beauty and the Brains - Deprivation - Teen Bitch - Cool Girl Hate Club - Out at the Wedding
COMPLETED UNRELEASED Girl Play
CREDITS Kartenspieler - Children of the Struggle - Roberta Loved - Seventy - Heavy Put-Away

Gina G. Goff .Producer
Laura A. Kellam .Producer

FREDERIC GOLCHAN PRODUCTIONS

c/o Radar Pictures
10900 Wilshire Blvd., 14th Fl.
Los Angeles, CA 90024
PHONE .310-208-8525/310-854-3030
FAX .310-208-1764/310-854-6060
EMAIL .fgfilm@aol.com
TYPES Features - Made-for-TV/Cable Movies
DEALS Radar Pictures
DEVELOPMENT Family Values - Divorce Club - Fandorin
PRE-PRODUCTION Bad Dog - The Way the Dead Love - Random
CREDITS In the Deep Woods - Kimberly - Intersection - Quick Change - The Associate - Dream Date

Frederic Golchan .President

GOLD CIRCLE FILMS

9420 Wilshire Blvd., Ste. 250
Beverly Hills, CA 90212
PHONE .310-278-4800
FAX .310-278-0885
WEB SITE .www.goldcirclefilms.com
TYPES Features
DEALS Universal Pictures
DEVELOPMENT The Last Two People on Earth - The Benny Factor - Jupiter's Mom - Flypaper - 2:22
POST PRODUCTION White Noise - Jiminy Glick in Lalawood - Something Borrowed - The Long Weekend
CREDITS My Big Fat Greek Wedding - The Man from Elysian Fields - Poolhall Junkies - Sonny

Paul Brooks .President
Scott Niemeyer .CFO
Jeff Levine .Producer
Joanna Jones .VP, Post Production & Worldwide Distribution
Wendy Rhoads .Director, Development
Zak Kadison .Creative Executive

GOLDCREST FILMS INTERNATIONAL, INC.

1240 Olive Dr.
Los Angeles, CA 90069
PHONE .323-650-4551/44-207-437-8696
FAX .323-650-3581/44-207-437-4448
EMAIL .mailbox@goldcrest-films.com
WEB SITE .www.goldcrest.org
TYPES Animation - Features - Made-for-TV/Cable Movies
CREDITS To End All Wars - Space Truckers - No Way Home - Rock-A-Doodle - Black Rainbow - Clockwatchers
COMMENTS UK office: 65/66 Dean St., London W1D 4PL UK; East Coast office: 799 Washington St., New York, NY 10014, phone: 212-243-4700

John Quested .Chairman (NY)
Stephen R. Johnston .President (LA)
Peter McRae .COO (London)
Tony Murphy .Sr. VP, Business Affairs (London)
Patty Tapanes .Director, Business Affairs (LA)
Susan England .Production & Acquisitions

GOLDEN QUILL

8899 Beverly Blvd., Ste. 702
Los Angeles, CA 90048
PHONE .310-274-5016
FAX .310-274-5028
TYPES Features
CREDITS The In-Laws - Love Story - The Babe - Outrageous Fortune
SUBMISSION POLICY No unsolicited submissions

Arthur Hiller .Director/Producer
Brenda White .Executive Assistant

GOLDENRING PRODUCTIONS

11271 Ventura Blvd., Rm. 506
Studio City, CA 91604
PHONE .818-508-7425
FAX .818-508-7428
TYPES: Features - Made-for-TV/Cable Movies - TV Series
DEVELOPMENT: Free B-92 (HBO) - MAD Project (HBO) - I Know That You Know (Landscape Pictures) - $5 a Day (Fine Line) - Fatal Error (Lifetime) - Verona (ABC Family) - Kindred Spirits (ABC Family)
PRE-PRODUCTION: I Do, But I Don't (Lifetime)
CREDITS: On the Second Day of Christmas - My First Mister - Widows - Heart of a Stranger

Jane Goldenring .President
Ryan Coleman .Development

GOLDSMITH ENTERTAINMENT COMPANY

11718 Barrington Court, Ste. 766
Los Angeles, CA 90049
PHONE .310-440-3711
EMAIL .goldsmec@aol.com
TYPES: Features - Made-for-TV/Cable Movies
PRE-PRODUCTION: Home for the Holidays 5 (CBS)
CREDITS: Dalva - In the Mood - One Against the Wind - Home for the Holidays

Karen Mack .President

THE GOLDSTEIN COMPANY

1644 Courtney Ave.
Los Angeles, CA 90046
PHONE .310-659-9511
FAX .775-637-6684
TYPES: Features - Large Format - Reality TV - TV Series
PRE-PRODUCTION: The Other Side of Simple - Africa: The Rituals of Life
CREDITS: The Mothman Prophecies - Ringmaster - Under Siege - Pretty Woman - The Hunted

Gary W. Goldstein .Producer
Sandra Tomita .Associate Producer
Catherine Wachter .Development

GOLDSTREET PICTURES, INC.

1930 Ocean Ave., Ste. 307
Santa Monica, CA 90405
PHONE .310-452-0262
FAX .310-452-7349
TYPES: Documentaries - Features - TV Series
DEVELOPMENT: A Low Life in High Heels - Damned Strong Love - My Rotten Life - She Tried to Be Good: The Dorris Wishman Story
CREDITS: HBO's Real Sex - Vampire's Kiss - Motorama - Wigstock: The Movie

Barry Shils .Producer/Director
Doran George .VP

GOOD GAME

4000 Warner Blvd., Bldg. 34, Ste. 101
Burbank, CA 91522
PHONE .818-954-3414
FAX .818-954-3415
TYPES: Animation - Features - Made-for-TV/Cable Movies - TV Series
DEALS: Warner Bros. Television Production

Lauren Graham .President
Kathy Ebel .VP
Veronica Becker .Development Associate

THE GOODMAN COMPANY

8491 Sunset Blvd., Ste. 329
Los Angeles, CA 90069
PHONE .323-655-0719
EMAIL .ilyssagoodman@yahoo.com
TYPES: Features - Reality TV - TV Series
DEVELOPMENT: Star Struck - The Wish - Jeremy Thatcher - Dragon Hatcher - The Paw
PRE-PRODUCTION: Princess
COMPLETED UNRELEASED: The Hidden Realm - Mall or Nothing
CREDITS: A Cinderella Story - Moolah Beach - Summer of the Monkeys

Ilyssa Goodman .President/Producer

GOODMAN/ROSEN PRODUCTIONS

3000 W. Olympic Blvd.
Santa Monica, CA 90404
PHONE .310-315-4850/973-535-1313
FAX .310-315-4851/973-548-1601
EMAIL .goodrosen@aol.com
TYPES: Features - Made-for-TV/Cable Movies - Syndication - TV Series
DEVELOPMENT: Cryptopia (Graphic Novel) - Annie
CREDITS: TV: Highlander - Police Academy - The Lost World - Zorro; Features: The Virginian - The Cisco Kid - Wagons East
COMMENTS: East Coast office: 200 Fifth Ave., 12th Fl., New York, NY 10010

Gary Goodman .Partner
Barry Rosen .Partner
Amy Rodriguez .Assistant to Barry Rosen

THE MARK GORDON COMPANY

12200 W. Olympic Blvd., Ste. 250
Los Angeles, CA 90064
PHONE .310-943-6401
FAX .310-943-6402
TYPES: Features - Made-for-TV/Cable Movies - TV Series
DEALS: Columbia Pictures
CREDITS: The Day After Tomorrow

Mark Gordon .No Title
Betsy Beers .No Title
Lawrence Inglee .No Title
Conor Copeland .No Title
Christina Johnson .No Title
Lindsey Liberatore .No Title
Josh McLaughlin .No Title
Ashley Salisbury .No Title
Jordan Wynn .No Title

DAN GORDON PRODUCTIONS

2060-D Avenue Los Arboles, Ste. 256
Thousand Oaks, CA 91362-1361
PHONE .805-496-2566
WEB SITE .www.zaki.yc.edu
TYPES: Features - TV Series
DEVELOPMENT: Two Guys on the Job - Little War of Our Own - On Wings of Eagles - The Day of the Opera - Samurai Girl - The Third Terrorist - Just Plain Dead
CREDITS: Gotcha - Passenger 57 - Wyatt Earp - Murder in the First - The Assignment - The Hurricane
SUBMISSION POLICY: No unsolicited submissions

Dan Gordon .Writer/Producer
Brad Benjamin .VP

GOTHAM ENTERTAINMENT GROUP
304 Hudson St., 6th Fl.
New York, NY 10013
PHONE 443-269-1405
FAX 860-795-8243
EMAIL .....infoplease@gothamcity.com
WEB SITE .....www.gothamcity.com
TYPES Features - Direct-to-Video/DVD - Made-for-TV/Cable Movies - Syndication - TV Series
DEVELOPMENT Howard Stern's Porky's
CREDITS Goodbye Lover (Warner Bros.) - The Blood Oranges (Lions Gate)
SUBMISSION POLICY See Web site

Eric Kopeloff .....Partner
Joel Roodman .....Partner
Andy Myers .....Partner

GRACIE FILMS
c/o Sony Pictures Entertainment
10202 Washington Blvd., Poitier Bldg.
Culver City, CA 90232
PHONE 310-244-4222
FAX 310-244-1530
TYPES Animation - Features - TV Series
DEALS Sony Pictures Entertainment
CREDITS Riding in Cars with Boys - What About Joan? - As Good as It Gets - Big - Bottle Rocket - Broadcast News - Jerry Maguire - The Simpsons

James L. Brooks .....Producer/Writer/Director
Richard Sakai .....President
Julie Ansell .....President, Motion Pictures
Denise Sirkot .....Executive VP

GRADE A ENTERTAINMENT
368 N. La Cienega Blvd.
Los Angeles, CA 90048
PHONE 310-358-8600
FAX 310-919-2998
EMAIL .....development@gradeaent.com
TYPES Features - Made-for-TV/Cable Movies - TV Series
DEVELOPMENT Union Transfer - Midnight Voices - Granny - Miracle Cars - Magic Kingdom - Five Ancestors
PRE-PRODUCTION Untraceable
POST PRODUCTION Guide to Guys
CREDITS Captain Ron - It Takes Two - A Chance of Snow

Andy Cohen .....Producer/Manager

GRAHAM/ROSENZWEIG FILMS
6399 Wilshire Blvd., Ste. 510
Los Angeles, CA 90048
PHONE 323-782-6888
FAX 323-782-6967
EMAIL .....grfilms@gocybernet.com
TYPES Features - Made-for-TV/Cable Movies - TV Series
DEVELOPMENT Manifestant - Darksiders - Where's the Party At? - The Reincarnation of Peter Proud
CREDITS Windtalkers - Phoenix - Dumb and Dumber - The War at Home - Threesome

Tracie Graham .....Producer
Alison Rosenzweig .....Producer

GRAINY PICTURES
PO Box 122
Cold Spring, NY 10516
PHONE 845-265-2241
EMAIL .....info@grainypictures.com
SECOND EMAIL .....fijijohn2002@yahoo.com
WEB SITE .....www.grainypictures.com
TYPES Documentaries - Features - TV Series
POST PRODUCTION Fiji: Reel Paradise
CREDITS How's Your News? - Split Screen - Chasing Amy
SUBMISSION POLICY No unsolicited submissions

Janet Pierson .....Co-President
John Pierson .....Co-President

MICHAEL GRAIS PRODUCTIONS
395 S. Topanga Canyon Blvd., Ste. 203
Topanga, CA 90290
PHONE 310-455-2699
FAX 310-455-2685
EMAIL .....submissions@michaelgraisproductions.com
TYPES Features - Made-for-TV/Cable Movies - Syndication - TV Series
DEALS Metro-Goldwyn-Mayer Studios, Inc.
DEVELOPMENT Outer Limits (Feature) - Manticore - Void Moon - Watching the Detective - Lakeshore Drive
CREDITS Poltergeist 1&2 - Marked for Death - Stephen King's Sleepwalkers - Great Balls of Fire - Who Killed Atlanta's Children? - The Immortal

Michael Grais .....Writer/Producer
Barbara Carswell .....CEO
Mary Rickard .....Director, Development

GRAMMNET PRODUCTIONS
c/o Paramount Pictures
5555 Melrose Ave., Wilder Bldg., Ste. 114
Los Angeles, CA 90038-3197
PHONE .....323-956-5455 (TV)/323-956-5840 (Features)
FAX .....323-862-2284 (TV)/323-862-1433 (Features)
TYPES Animation - Features - New Media - TV Series
DEALS Paramount Television
DEVELOPMENT This Way Madness Lies - Uncle Mame - Lost Soul - The Case of the Halloween Hangman - The Interrogator (ABC) - Cloak (ABC) - Ripple Effect (Sci Fi)
PRODUCTION Medium (NBC)
CREDITS Kelsey Grammer Salutes Jack Benny - Fired Up - The Innocent - Girlfriends - Gary the Rat - In-Laws
SUBMISSION POLICY No unsolicited material
COMMENTS Features office: 5555 Melrose Ave., Wilder Bldg., Ste. 116, Los Angeles, CA 90038-3197

Kelsey Grammer .....Actor/Producer/CEO (323-956-5547)
Steve Stark .....President (323-956-5455)
Joanne Weiss .....Sr. VP, Feature Development (323-956-5840)
Jessica Hochman .....Director, Feature Development (323-956-5832)
Julie Mondimore .....Director, TV Development (323-956-5420)
Chris Maul .....Manager, Programming (323-956-5423)
Xochitl L. Olivas .....Production Manager (323-956-5547)
Jon Norwood .....Grammnet Assistant (323-956-5547)
Joe Rohrlich .....Features Assistant (323-956-5587)

It is illegal to copy any part of this book

GRAN VIA PRODUCTIONS
9350 Civic Center Dr., Ste. 100
Beverly Hills, CA 90210
PHONE .310-777-3522
FAX .310-777-0008
TYPES Features - TV Series
DEALS CBS Entertainment - Intermedia Film Equities USA, Inc.
CREDITS The Guardian (TV) - Galaxy Quest - My Dog Skip - Donnie Brasco - A Little Princess - Bugsy - Rain Man - Good Morning, Vietnam - Dragonfly - The Rookie - The Banger Sisters - Moonlight Mile - The Alamo - The Notebook
SUBMISSION POLICY No unsolicited submissions

Mark Johnson .No Title
Susan Kaufman .No Title
Bryan Seabury .No Title
Tom Williams .No Title
Melissa Scrivner .No Title

GRANADA AMERICA
15303 Ventura Blvd., Ste. 800
Sherman Oaks, CA 91403
PHONE .818-455-4600
FAX .818-455-4700
TYPES Made-for-TV/Cable Movies - Reality TV - TV Series
DEVELOPMENT Son of Pocahontas - Fort Bragg's Deadly Summer - Identity Theft - Lovesick - Box Full of Everything - Mrs. Bigamy - Lovers Are Not People - Kidnapping the American Dream
PRODUCTION Hell's Kitchen (Fox) - Identity Theft
CREDITS Danger Beneath the Sea - Rough Air: Danger on Flight 534 - Seconds to Spare - Scent of Murder - Second Nature - Rush of Fear - Rudy: The Rudy Giuliani Story - Maiden Voyage - I'm a Celebrity: Get Me Out of Here (ABC) - American Princess (NBC) - Airline (A&E) - Room Raiders (MTV) - First 48 (A&E) - Brainiac (The WB) - Ultimate Tree House (Discovery) - House of Dreams (A&E) - Caught! (Court TV)

Paul Jackson .CEO
Stephen J. Davis .President
Linda S. Ross .CFO
Jody Brockway .Sr. VP, Scripted Development
Craig McNeil .Sr. VP, Scripted Production
Curt Northrup .Sr. VP, Non-Scripted Development
Sam Zoda .Sr. VP, Non-Scripted Production
Ivan Garel-Jones .Sr. VP, Commercial Affairs

GRAND PRODUCTIONS, INC.
10201 W. Pico Blvd., Bldg. 51
Los Angeles, CA 90035
PHONE .310-369-5027
FAX .310-969-3142
TYPES Features - Made-for-TV/Cable Movies - TV Series
DEALS Touchstone Television
DEVELOPMENT Mi Familia - Cat's Cradle - The Amazing Carlo - Golden Hour
CREDITS Any Day Now - Beauty - A Song from the Heart - The Round Table - Leaving L.A. - Adventure, Inc. - An Unexpected Love - John Grisham's The Street Lawyer
SUBMISSION POLICY No unsolicited material

Gary A. Randall .President/Owner
Alexandra Bleckner .Director, Development

GRAY ANGEL PRODUCTIONS
74 Market St.
Venice, CA 90291
PHONE .310-581-0010
FAX .310-396-0551
TYPES Features
DEVELOPMENT A Time to Be Born - The White Rose
CREDITS Bastard Out of Carolina - Agnes Browne

Anjelica Huston .President
Jaclyn Bashoff .Director, Development

GRB ENTERTAINMENT
c/o Michael Branton
13400 Riverside Dr., Ste. 300
Sherman Oaks, CA 91423
PHONE .818-728-7600
FAX .818-728-7601
EMAIL .mbranton@grbtv.com
WEB SITE .www.grbtv.com
TYPES Reality TV - TV Series
PRODUCTION Next Action Star (NBC) - Second Chance (TLC) - Untold Stories from the ER (TLC) - Beauty Shop Secrets (CMT) - Mr. Justice (A&E) - Simply Irresistible (VH1) - Expeditions to the Edge (National Geographic) - Intervention (A&E) - Growing Up Gotti (A&E)
CREDITS Cannonball Run - ConQuest - The Last Mission - War Dogs - Hollywood's Greatest Stunts - Travel Scams & Rip-Offs Revealed - World of Wonder - Movie Magic
COMMENTS International Distribution; Unscripted Drama, Incredible Clip Shows, Hidden Camera

Gary R. Benz .President
Michael Branton .Executive VP, Creative Affairs
Debby Reid Levin .Sr. VP, Production

MICHAEL GREEN & ASSOCIATES
4020 Towhee Dr.
Calabasas, CA 91302
PHONE .818-222-8466
FAX .818-222-2589
TYPES Features - Made-for-TV/Cable Movies - TV Series
CREDITS The Perfect Getaway - Coming Unglued

Michael C. Green .Executive Producer

GREEN COMMUNICATIONS
255 Parkside Dr.
San Fernando, CA 91340
PHONE .818-557-0050
FAX .818-557-0056
EMAIL .info@greenfilms.com
WEB SITE .www.greenfilms.com
TYPES Features - Made-for-TV/Cable Movies - Miniseries - TV Series
DEVELOPMENT Air Rage - Happy Landings - Flight of Fear - Yellow Airbus
PRE-PRODUCTION Junior Pilot
CREDITS Ground Control - Living in Peril - Space Marines - The Time of Her Time - Dark Prince - The Last Producer - Sordid - Mambo Cafe - G-men from Hell - Outpatient - Lucky Town

Talaat Captan .President
D'Arcy Conrique .President, International Sales & Distribution

SARAH GREEN FILM CORP.
451 Greenwich St., 7th Fl.
New York, NY 10013
PHONE .646-214-7929
FAX .646-214-7920
EMAIL .sgfilmcorp@prodigy.net
TYPES Features
DEVELOPMENT The New World - Wise Child - Murder Most Foul - My Bones Are All I Keep - Machine Dreams - Monopolis
CREDITS Frida - State and Main - Girlfight - The Winslow Boy - The Spanish Prisoner - The Secret of Roan Inish - Havana Nights
SUBMISSION POLICY No unsolicited material

Sarah Green .Producer
Ivan Bess .Development
Peter Liegel .No Title

GREEN GRASS BLUE SKY COMPANY, INC.
10153-1/2 Riverside Dr., Ste. 283
Toluca Lake, CA 91602
PHONE .818-787-0024/39-6-331-4045
EMAIL .greengrassblueskycompany@adelphia.net
TYPES Features
DEALS Warner Bros. Pictures
DEVELOPMENT Angels of Aachen - Falling Off the Floor - Myths and Tangos - Sleeping with Lorenzo
CREDITS Almost Classix - Bedtime Stories - Icarus Mission - Adventures of Dynamo Duck - Autumn Sweet - The Resting Place
COMMENTS Italy office: Centro Settoriale Belsito, Via Sappada 5, Rome 00135 Italy

Frank Catalano .President
Anthony Catalano .Business Affairs/International Co-Productions (LA)
Gregory Snegoff .Writer/Producer (Italy)
Ronald J. Wong .Creative Development

JOAN GREEN MANAGEMENT & PRODUCTIONS
1836 Courtney Terrace
Los Angeles, CA 90046
PHONE .323-878-0484
FAX .323-878-0492
TYPES Features - TV Series
CREDITS Mother, May I Sleep with Danger - Dare to Love

Joan Green .President/Manager
Amy Slomovits .Manager

GREEN MOON PRODUCTIONS
11718 Barrington Court, Ste. 827
Los Angeles, CA 90049
PHONE .310-471-8800
FAX .310-471-8022
TYPES Animation - Documentaries - Features - Made-for-TV/Cable Movies - TV Series
DEVELOPMENT Conquistadors - Billy Two Sugars - Infidel - Killing Pablo - Yonkers Joe - The Other Side
CREDITS Crazy in Alabama - The Body - Along for the Ride - Tart - Imagining Argentina - Pancho Villa

Antonio Banderas .No Title
Melanie Griffith .No Title
Diane Sillan Isaacs .No Title
Luis Fernandez .No Title

GREENESTREET FILMS
9 Desbrosses St., 2nd Fl.
New York, NY 10013
PHONE .212-609-9000
FAX .212-609-9099
EMAIL .general@gstreet.com
WEB SITE .www.greenestreetfilms.com
TYPES Features - TV Series
DEVELOPMENT One Bad Sistah - The Percy Towne Fifth - Tenderness - The Pleasure of Your Company - Gromo - Jack Tucker - My Wife Is an Actress
PRE-PRODUCTION Fade Out
PRODUCTION Romance & Cigarettes - Once in a Lifetime
POST PRODUCTION Slow Burn - Yes
CREDITS Pinero - Just a Kiss - The Chateau - A Price Above Rubies - Illuminata - Company Man - I'm Not Rappaport - Lisa Picard Is Famous - In the Bedroom - Swimfan - Uptown Girls

John Penotti .President/Founding Partner
Debbie Johnson .General Manager
Vicki Cherkas .Head, Legal & Business Affairs
Jamie Gordon .Head, Development
Cedric Jeanson .Head, Production Finance
Tim Williams .Head, Production
Miles Ferguson .Director, Post Production
Courtney Potts .Director, Development
Fisher Stevens .Creative Director/Founding Partner
Jared Goldman .Manager, Production
Mary Lawless .Manager, Business & Legal Affairs
Lori Lazar .Manager, Development

ROBERT GREENWALD PRODUCTIONS
10510 Culver Blvd.
Culver City, CA 90232-3400
PHONE .310-204-0404
FAX .310-204-0174
TYPES Features - TV Series - Made-for-TV/Cable Movies - Documentaries - Direct-to-Video/DVD
PRODUCTION The Dead Will Tell - Plain Truth
CREDITS The Book of Ruth - Disappearance - Redeemer - Steal This Movie - Audrey Hepburn - Deadlocked - Sharing the Secret - Blonde - Livin' for Love: The Natalie Cole Story - The Crooked E. - Uncovered

Robert Greenwald .Producer/Director
Philip Kleinbart .Producer/Executive VP
Alys Shanti .Producer/Sr. VP
MaShona Hobbs .Development Associate
Devin Smith .Development Associate
Monica Khudan .Production Coordinator
Aaron Gershman .Office Administrator
Michael Curran .Production Assistant

GREENWOOD AVENUE ENTERTAINMENT
2004 Palisades Dr.
Pacific Palisades, CA 90272
PHONE .310-454-9984
FAX .310-454-9984
EMAIL .dwyercat@aol.com
SECOND EMAIL .davesprod@aol.com
TYPES Documentaries - Direct-to-Video/DVD - Made-for-TV/Cable Movies - Syndication - TV Series
CREDITS Deep Diver: Tiger Shark Odyssey - Baywatch (1989-2002) - Thunder in Paradise - Avalon: Beyond the Abyss

David W. Hagar .Executive Producer/Director
Cathy Dwyer .Executive Producer

GREIF COMPANY
9233 W. Pico Blvd., Ste. 218
Los Angeles, CA 90035
PHONE 310-385-1200
FAX 310-385-1207
WEB SITE ....www.greifcompany.com
TYPES: Documentaries - Features - Made-for-TV/Cable Movies - TV Series
DEVELOPMENT: Baby for Sale (Lifetime) - Funny Money - A&E Biography - Steve McQueen Documentary (TCM)
COMPLETED UNRELEASED: The Manual (Fine Living)
CREDITS: Walker: Texas Ranger - Keys to Tulsa - Sins - Intimate Portraits - Headliners & Legends - Monday Night Mayhem - Opening the Tombs of the 10,000 Mummies - Weddings of a Lifetime - Taboo - World Class with Frederique - Word of Honor (TNT)
SUBMISSION POLICY: No unsolicited material

Leslie Greif ....President/Executive Producer/Director/Writer
Kathy Williamson ....Executive Producer
Julie Frankel ....Producer
Mimi Freedman ....Co-Producer
Joanne Rubino ....VP, Production

GREYSTONE TELEVISION AND FILMS
5200 Lankershim Blvd., Ste. 800
North Hollywood, CA 91601
PHONE 818-762-2900
FAX 818-762-1626
EMAIL ....info@greystonetv.com
WEB SITE ....www.greystonetv.com
TYPES: Documentaries - Features - Direct-to-Video/DVD - TV Series - Reality TV
CREDITS: Conquest - TR: An American Lion - Tales of the Gun - Fine Living: Breathing Room - Left Luggage - Spirit of Yosemite

Craig Haffner ....President/CEO
Donna E. Lusitana ....President, Greystone Television
Shinaan Krakowsky ....COO/General Counsel
Rick Brookwell ....CFO/Corporate Counsel
Glenn Kirschbaum ....VP, Greystone Television
Louis Tarantino ....VP, Greystone Television/Supervising Producer
Rhys Thomas ....VP, Greystone Television
Sara Hutchinson ....VP, Development
Seth Isler ....VP, Development
Debra Cunningham ....Executive Assistant to Mr. Haffner

MERV GRIFFIN ENTERTAINMENT
130 S. El Camino Dr.
Beverly Hills, CA 90212
PHONE 310-385-2700
FAX 310-385-2701
WEB SITE ....www.merv.com
TYPES: Features - Made-for-TV/Cable Movies - Syndication - TV Series - Reality TV
CREDITS: The Ainsley Harriott Show - The Christmas List - Click! - Men Are from Mars, Women Are from Venus - Murder at the Cannes Film Festival - Inside the Osmonds - Gilda Radner: It's Always Something - Shade

Merv Griffin ....Chairman
Lawrence Cohen ....President/CEO
Ernest Chambers ....Sr. VP, Production
Ron Ward ....VP

NICK GRILLO PRODUCTIONS
3000 Olympic Blvd., Bldg. 1, Ste. 2510
Santa Monica, CA 90404
PHONE 310-453-1351
FAX 310-453-9255
TYPES: Features - Made-for-TV/Cable Movies - TV Series
DEALS: Baldwin Entertainment Group
DEVELOPMENT: Nothing Like It in the World - McNally's Risk - Defender of the People - Orangeburg Massacre - Honor for Sale
CREDITS: Gods and Generals - Deacons for Defense - Conviction

Nick Grillo ....President/Producer

GRINNING DOG PICTURES
c/o Passion River
GreeneStreet Film Center
9 Desbrosses St., 2nd Fl.
New York, NY 10013
PHONE 212-966-5877
FAX 212-966-5914
EMAIL ....connie@grinningdogpictures.com
WEB SITE ....www.grinningdogpictures.com
TYPES: Documentaries - Reality TV - TV Series
DEVELOPMENT: The Postcard Geisha - Cowboy: The Life of a Legend - Bogie & Me: A Beautiful Friendship - Precious Cargo
PRE-PRODUCTION: Jail Journey - Youth Alert: Child Find
PRODUCTION: Map of the Missing (Documentary)
CREDITS: Wolfman: Myth & Science - Jessica Savitch Bio - The Curse of Tutankhamen - Medical Detectives - Forensic Files - Science Frontiers
COMMENTS: Feature length IMAX films in development with series attached

Connie Bottinelli ....CEO/Executive Producer
Gary Parker ....Writer

GRISHAM FILMS USA
477 E. Freehold Rd.
Freehold, NJ 07728
PHONE 723-303-1764
FAX 732-303-8534
EMAIL ....emile.savia@grishamfilms.com
WEB SITE ....www.grishamfilms.com
TYPES: Commercials - Features - Made-for-TV/Cable Movies
DEVELOPMENT: The Gucci Wars - Further Lane - Bookie - Seven Five Nine - Angel on My Shoulder
CREDITS: Cuban Fire - The Big Bang

Emile Savia ....Producer
Ed Christie ....Executive Producer
Francesca Cupi ....Business Affairs
Keith R. Hiatt ....Executive Internet Specialist

DAN GRODNIK PRODUCTIONS
9916 Santa Monica Blvd.
Beverly Hills, CA 90212
PHONE 310-277-1231
FAX 310-277-1299
EMAIL ....grodzilla@earthlink.net
TYPES: Features - Made-for-TV/Cable Movies - TV Series
CREDITS: Who Is Cletis Tout? - Uncorked - Powder - National Lampoon's Christmas Vacation
COMMENTS: Deal with Trademark Entertainment

Daniel L. Grodnik ....Producer
Wendy Moore ....Assistant

GROSS ENTERTAINMENT
500 S. Buena Vista St., Old Animation Bldg., Rm. 3B-8
Burbank, CA 91521-1850
PHONE .818-560-8117
FAX .818-560-8180
EMAIL .matthew.gross@abc.com
TYPES Features - Reality TV - TV Series
DEALS Davis Entertainment Company - Touchstone Television
PRE-PRODUCTION The Middleman
COMPLETED UNRELEASED Sherman's March
CREDITS Joe Somebody - Bronx Cheers
SUBMISSION POLICY No unsolicited material

Matthew Gross .President
Ben Haber .Feature Development
Robert Hull Jr. .Executive Assistant

KEN GROSS MANAGEMENT
7720 Sunset Blvd., 2nd Fl.
Los Angeles, CA 90046
PHONE .323-512-2999
FAX .323-512-2699
EMAIL .kgmla@pacbell.net
TYPES Features - Made-for-TV/Cable Movies - TV Series
DEVELOPMENT A Christmas Wish - The Lost Christmas
CREDITS Murder at Midnight - A Town Without Christmas - Stealing Sinatra - Finding John Christmas
COMMENTS Management

Kenneth H. Gross .President/Producer/Manager
Jenz Bergren .Development/Management

BETH GROSSBARD PRODUCTIONS
9696 Culver Blvd., Ste. 208
Culver City, CA 90232
PHONE .310-841-2555
FAX .310-841-5934
EMAIL .bethgcap@aol.com
TYPES Features - Made-for-TV/Cable Movies - TV Series
DEALS Craig Anderson Productions
DEVELOPMENT The Christmas Blessing - A Blistering Frost - Joey Pigza - Virtue & Vice: The Frank Barnaba Story
CREDITS Meltdown - The Christmas Shoes - Passion & Prejudice - Range of Motion - No One Could Protect Her
SUBMISSION POLICY Query with treatment

Beth Grossbard .Executive Producer
Karen Jacobs .Development Executive

GROSSBART KENT PRODUCTIONS
9255 Sunset Blvd., Ste. 500
Los Angeles, CA 90069
PHONE .310-275-5800
FAX .310-275-5818
TYPES Features - Syndication - TV Series
CREDITS Unforgivable - Any Mother's Son - The Preppie Murder - The Alison Gertz Story - Personally Yours

Jack Grossbart .President/Executive Producer
Linda L. Kent .Sr. VP, Development
Sarah Hoover .Executive Assistant

GROSSO JACOBSON COMMUNICATIONS CORP.
1801 Avenue of the Stars, Ste. 911
Los Angeles, CA 90067
PHONE .310-788-8900/212-644-6909
FAX .310-788-8914/212-355-3178
TYPES Documentaries - Features - Made-for-TV/Cable Movies - Reality TV - TV Series
DEVELOPMENT Untitled FX Series - Untitled FX Movie - Untitled Sci Fi Series - Untitled NBC Series
CREDITS Ten Mary Higgins Clark Movies - The Big Easy - The French Connection 30th Anniversary Special - Top Cops - All American Girl: Mary Kay Letourneau - Judgment Day
COMMENTS East Coast office: 767 Third Ave., 27th Fl., New York, NY 10017

Sonny Grosso .Co-Chairman/Executive Producer (NY)
Lawrence S. Jacobson .Co-Chairman/Executive Producer (LA)
Keith Johnson .Sr. VP, Development (NY)
Christina Avis Krauss .Development & Casting (NY)
Lena Saban .Controller (NY)
Wendy Slutsky .Development & Production (LA)
Van Vandegrift .Development (LA)

GROSS-WESTON PRODUCTIONS
10560 Wilshire Blvd., Ste. 801
Los Angeles, CA 90024
PHONE .310-777-0010
FAX .310-777-0016
EMAIL .gross-weston@sbcglobal.net
TYPES Features - Direct-to-Video/DVD - Made-for-TV/Cable Movies - Syndication - TV Series
DEVELOPMENT Louis Armstrong Project (HBO) - Road Taken (CBS) - Rat-Dog Dick (Lifetime/Hearst) - Billie's Blues (Showtime) - All the Good Ones Are Married (Lifetime) - The Fountainhead (Paramount/Warner Bros.)
CREDITS A Place for Annie (ABC) - I Love You Perfect (ABC) - Always Remember I Love You (CBS) - Firestorm (ABC) - Highway Heartbreaker (CBS) - Jonathan, The Boy Nobody Wanted (NBC) - Big & Hairy (Showtime) - Country Gold (CBS) - Forbidden Love (CBS) - Miss All American Beauty (CBS)
SUBMISSION POLICY From agent or lawyer, or with a release form

Marcy Gross .Executive Producer
Ann Weston .Executive Producer

GRUB STREET PRODUCTIONS
c/o Paramount TV
5555 Melrose Ave., Wilder Bldg., Ste. 101
Los Angeles, CA 90038-3197
PHONE .323-956-4657
TYPES Syndication - TV Series
DEALS Paramount Television
CREDITS Wings - Frasier - Pursuit of Happiness - Encore! Encore!
COMMENTS Development

Peter Casey .Creator/Executive Producer
David Lee .Creator/Executive Producer

GRYPHON FILMS
13042 Rose Ave.
Los Angeles, CA 90069
PHONE .310-861-5383
FAX .310-388-3012
WEB SITE www.gryphonfilms.com
TYPES Features
DEVELOPMENT Thunderhead - The Cloak and the Breach - Steele's Island - Call of Cthulhu - Five Generations of Jerks - House of Shadows - Parallel Kiss
CREDITS The Cooler - Betrayal

Robert Gryphon .Chairman/Executive Producer
Brett Morrison .Producer
Patrick Aluise .Producer
Wil Forbis .Genre Development

*GSN
A Sony Pictures/Liberty Media Company
2150 Colorado Ave.
Santa Monica, CA 90404
PHONE .310-255-6800
FAX .310-255-6810
WEB SITE www.gsn.com
TYPES Reality TV - TV Series
DEVELOPMENT American Dream Derby (Reality)
COMMENTS The Network for Games; Additional genre: Casino

Rich Cronin .President/CEO
Brent Willman .CFO, Finance
Ian Valentine .Head, Programming
Michael Kohn .Sr. VP, Business & Legal Affairs
John P. Roberts .Sr. VP, Interactive & Online Entertainment
Kevin Belinkoff .VP, Programming
David Primuth .VP, Research
Cindy Ronzoni .VP, Publicity & Corporate Communications
Ryan Tredinnick .VP, Operations
Linnea Hemenez .Executive Director, Creative Services
Jennifer Michaels .Director, Corporate Communications

GUNNFILMS
500 S. Buena Vista St., Old Animation Bldg., Ste. 3-A7
Burbank, CA 91521
PHONE .818-560-6156
FAX .818-842-8394
TYPES Features - TV Series
DEALS The Buena Vista Motion Pictures Group
DEVELOPMENT Untitled Shaolin Project - Renegade - Untitled Viking Project - Sugar Rum Cherry - Spaulding Gets Nothing - Defense - Maid of Honor - All Access - Ruprecht - Once Upon a Prairie - South China Sea - War Dogs - Candleshoe
PRE-PRODUCTION Sky High
CREDITS Freaky Friday - The Haunted Mansion - The Country Bears
SUBMISSION POLICY Send synopsis or treatment by fax

Andrew Gunn .Producer
Ann Marie Sanderlin .Executive Producer (818-560-6284)
Kit Giordano .Assistant to Andrew Gunn
Justin Maurice .Assistant to Ann Marie Sanderlin

THE GURIN COMPANY
11846 Ventura Blvd., Ste. 303
Studio City, CA 91604
PHONE .818-623-9393
FAX .818-623-9595
TYPES Documentaries - Features - Syndication - TV Series
DEALS Lions Gate Entertainment - SCI FI Channel
DEVELOPMENT America's Sexiest - The Big Mission - Crowbar - The Human Clock - 24 Hours - Mission: Improvement - The Lost Episodes - Superhuman - The Mind Game - Minds of Steel
CREDITS Extreme World Records - Weakest Link - Lingo - Voice of a Child - Only Joking - Twenty One - Now or Never - On Thin Ice - KISS Live - Miss USA - Miss Universe - Miss Teen USA - Queen for a Day - Survival Test - Settle the Score - Test the Nation
COMMENTS First look deal with Chip Butterman and Brad Wollack; Deal with Carlton/ActionTime

Phil Gurin .President
Ilyse Curtis .Executive in Charge of Production
Jeannie Koenigsberg .Director, Development
Marc Jansen .Creative Consultant
Jeff Ellingson .Assistant to President

GURNEY PRODUCTIONS
124 Idaho Ave., Ste. 303
Santa Monica, CA 90403
PHONE .310-434-1049
FAX .310-899-0212
EMAIL .hotlinestv@earthlink.net
WEB SITE www.hotlinestv.com
TYPES Commercials - Features - Direct-to-Video/DVD - Made-for-TV/Cable Movies - TV Series - Reality TV
DEVELOPMENT TV Series: Fantasy Camp - Scholarship - Juiced - Spying on Sharks; Features: Pipe Dreams - All Talk - Gumbo
CREDITS Hotlines (Spike TV/HD Net, TV Series) - Fish On (ESPN, Series)

Scott Gurney .Producer/Director/President
Deirdre Delaney .Producer/Director/VP
Michael Berk .Producer/Writer

GUY WALKS INTO A BAR
7421 Beverly Blvd., Ste. 4
Los Angeles, CA 90036
PHONE .323-930-9935/212-941-1509
FAX .323-930-9934/212-941-1557
EMAIL .info@guywalks.com
TYPES Documentaries - Features - TV Series
DEALS Paramount Pictures-Motion Picture Group
DEVELOPMENT Number One Girl - Fat Chance - Dillinger - The Retreat - The Manny - The User
CREDITS Elf - Out of Time

Todd Komarnicki .Partner/Producer
Jon Berg .Partner/Producer
Matthew Weinberg .Manager
Ross Siegel .Development Assistant
Jennifer Preston .Assistant

H. BEALE COMPANY
PO Box 5356
Beverly Hills, CA 90209
PHONE 310-278-1762
FAX 310-278-6971
TYPES Features - Made-for-TV/Cable Movies - Syndication - TV Series
CREDITS Bladesquad - Beggars and Choosers

Lilly Tartikoff .....President

H.R.D. PRODUCTIONS
3940 Laurel Canyon Blvd., Ste. 706
Studio City, CA 91604
PHONE 818-760-8907
FAX 818-763-7049
TYPES Features - TV Series
DEVELOPMENT The Girl Who Invented Kissing
PRE-PRODUCTION The Beginning of Wisdom
CREDITS The Whole 10 Yards

Howard Deutch .....Director
Kelly Rae Kenan .....Assistant

H2 PRODUCTIONS
212 San Vicente Blvd., Ste. H
Santa Monica, CA 90402
PHONE 310-394-8127
EMAIL .....sbakalar@alumni-gsb.stanford.edu
TYPES Documentaries - Features - Direct-to-Video/DVD - Made-for-TV/Cable Movies - TV Series
DEVELOPMENT Hypersonic - We Should Beat Stink's Ass - Against the Wind - Queen of the East - Perfect Partner
CREDITS The Substitute 1&2 - Peacock Blues - Tell About the South

Devorah Cutler-Rubenstein .....Producer/Writer/Director
Steven Bakalar .....Producer/Writer
Ariel Schoolsky .....VP, Development
Kamafi Adio-Byrd .....Development

***H2F ENTERTAINMENT**
1264 Ozeta Terrace, Ste. 301
West Hollywood, CA 90069
PHONE 310-203-8350
TYPES Features - TV Series
DEVELOPMENT Wulf - Inner Circle
PRODUCTION Waiting - Ryan Pinkston Thing

Chris Fenton .....Partner
Walter Hamada .....Partner
Jonathan Hung .....Partner

H2O MOTION PICTURES
1648 Wilcox Ave.
Los Angeles, CA 90028
PHONE 323-769-9007
FAX 323-871-1870
DEVELOPMENT People Who Knock - Running Wild
CREDITS Max - Owning Mahowney
COMMENTS Deal with Brightlight Pictures (Vancouver)

Andras Hamori .....President/Producer

HAFT ENTERTAINMENT
130 W. 57th St., Ste. 13A
New York, NY 10019
PHONE 212-586-3881
FAX 212-459-9798
EMAIL .....haft@bellatlantic.net
TYPES Features - Made-for-TV/Cable Movies - TV Series
DEVELOPMENT Waging Peace - MIR - Complicity
PRE-PRODUCTION Earthworks - Five Quarters - An Almost Perfect Kill
POST PRODUCTION Eulogy
CREDITS The Singing Detective - Dead Poets Society - Emma - Pirates of Silicon Valley - Tigerland - Jakob the Liar - Third Miracle - Hocus Pocus - Last Dance - Beyond Therapy

Steven Haft .....Producer
Eileen Burke .....Development

RANDA HAINES COMPANY
c/o The Broder • Webb • Chervin • Silbermann Agency
9242 Beverly Blvd., Ste. 200
Beverly Hills, CA 90210
PHONE 818-760-1173
FAX 818-760-1175
TYPES Features
CREDITS A Family Thing - Dance with Me - Antwone Fisher - Los Zafiros: Music from the Edge of Time (Documentary)

Randa Haines .....Director/Producer

HALCYON ENTERTAINMENT
1510 11th St., Ste. 101
Santa Monica, CA 90401
PHONE 310-899-6900
FAX 310-899-6909
EMAIL .....borrelli@halcyonentertainment.com
WEB SITE .....www.halcyonentertainment.com
TYPES Features
DEVELOPMENT Wishful Thinking - Love and Music - The Sett - Madeleine's Ghost - Mind Games - Lone Survivor - 66 - Dog World
PRE-PRODUCTION Breakback (Millennium/Dan Redler)
POST PRODUCTION Deepwater

Chris Coen .....President
Jason Karten .....Creative Executive
Chris Borrelli .....VP

HALLMARK ENTERTAINMENT
1325 Avenue of the Americas, 21st Fl.
New York, NY 10019
PHONE .212-977-9001
FAX .212-977-9049
WEB SITE .www.hallmarkent.com
TYPES: Animation - Made-for-TV/Cable Movies - Miniseries - TV Series
CREDITS: King of Texas - Dinotopia (Miniseries) - Noah's Ark - Alice in Wonderland - Cleopatra - Arabian Nights - Animal Farm - Temptations - Merlin - Snow White - Prince Charming - Snow Queen - The Lion in Winter - Dream Keeper
COMMENTS: West Coast distribution office: 4201 Wilshire Blvd., Ste. 304, Los Angeles, CA 90010

Robert Halmi Sr. .Chairman
Robert Halmi Jr. .President/CEO
Peter von Gal .Executive VP/COO
Tony Guido .Executive VP, Legal & Business Affairs
Janet Jacobson .Executive VP, Co-Production Programming
Dan Martin .Executive VP, Production
Lynn Holst .Sr. VP, Development
Kelly Coogan Swanson .Sr. VP, Marketing

HALLMARK HALL OF FAME PRODUCTIONS, INC.
12001 Ventura Pl., Ste. 300
Studio City, CA 91604
PHONE .818-505-9191
FAX .818-505-9842/818-505-8379 Production
TYPES: Made-for-TV/Cable Movies
CREDITS: Brush with Fate - A Painted House - Fallen Angel
COMMENTS: 2-Hour TV Dramas; Post Production fax: 818-505-9394

HALLWAY PICTURES
535 S. Curson Ave., Ste. 6-H
Los Angeles, CA 90036
PHONE .805-969-5068
FAX .805-969-7418
TYPES: Documentaries - Features
DEVELOPMENT: Richard Pryor Documentary - The Bomb
CREDITS: Johnson Family Vacation - Soul Plane - Higher Learning - Why Do Fools Fall in Love? - Shaft

Paul Hall .Producer
Wesley Jones .Assistant to Paul Hall

THE HAMPTONS FILM COMPANY
4455 Los Feliz Blvd.
Los Angeles, CA 90027
PHONE .323-663-2565
TYPES: Features - Made-for-TV/Cable Movies - New Media
DEVELOPMENT: The Silver Bridge - The Pissing Contest - Treehouse
PRE-PRODUCTION: A Moment of Grace
CREDITS: Cheyenne Warrior - Up Above the World So High - Mariette in Ecstasy - Cyber Policy - Privacy - EEO - Stepmonster - Ultraviolet
COMMENTS: Producer/Director for ELT Interactive Courseware

Alba Francesca .Producer/Director
Gary DePew .VP, Production

HANDPRINT ENTERTAINMENT
1100 Glendon Ave., Ste. 1000
Los Angeles, CA 90024
PHONE .310-481-4400
FAX .310-481-4419
TYPES: Features - TV Series
DEALS: Media 8 Entertainment - Sony Pictures Television
DEVELOPMENT: 16 Pleasures (First Look Media) - The Crib (Touchstone/ABC) - Wedding Daze (Media 8) - In The Game (Touchstone/ABC) - Fast Movie (Media 8)
PRODUCTION: Havoc
CREDITS: Fresh Prince of Bel Air - Above the Rim - Booty Call - The Fighting Temptations - Monster - Maid in Manhattan

Benny Medina .Partner
Jeff Pollack .Partner
Steve Kay .General Manager
Evan Weiss .Head, TV
Michael Baum .Manager
Jenny Frankfurt .Manager
Jill Littman .Manager
Dario Svidler .Manager
Dannielle Thomas .Manager

HAPPY DAGGER PICTURES
2240 N. New Hampshire Ave.
Los Angeles, CA 90027
PHONE .323-660-0757
TYPES: Features
DEVELOPMENT: Lincoln Trio
CREDITS: Life Without Dick
SUBMISSION POLICY: No unsolicited submissions

Emily Stevens .Producer
Bix Skahill .Writer/Director
Micah Schifman .Assistant

HAPPYTOGETHER CORP. FILM & TV
6080 Center Dr., 5th Fl.
Los Angeles, CA 90045
PHONE .310-846-5077/310-846-5040
FAX .310-846-5002
EMAIL .info@happytogether.us
SECOND EMAIL .sales@happytogether.us
WEB SITE .www.happytogether.us
TYPES: Features - Direct-to-Video/DVD - Made-for-TV/Cable Movies - TV Series
DEVELOPMENT: Dangerous Switch-Up - He Is Back

Anthony TeJumson . .President/CEO/Producer (anthony@happytogether.us)
Sanford Fleishman .President/Producer
Melody Lee .CFO
Biggi Zielo .COO (biggi@happytogether.us)

HARBOR LIGHTS PRODUCTIONS
8634 Oak Park Ave.
Northridge, CA 91325
PHONE 818-993-5255
FAX 818-993-5266
EMAIL . . . . . moviерock@aol.com

TYPES	Features - Made-for-TV/Cable Movies - Syndication - TV Series - Reality TV
PRE-PRODUCTION	The Babe Who Struck Out Ruth
CREDITS	White Squall - Titanic - Nervous Ticks - Race for Glory - All's Fair

Rocky Lang . . . . . Writer/Producer/Director

HARDING & ASSOCIATES
c/o Dave Harding
14622 Ventura Blvd., Ste. 461
Sherman Oaks, CA 91403
PHONE 818-432-4200

TYPES	Documentaries - Features - TV Series
DEALS	Lions Gate Entertainment
PRODUCTION	Criss Angel Supernatural - Unsolved History
CREDITS	Celebrity Undercover - A Century of Living - Yes, Virginia, There Is a Santa Claus - Secrets Revealed - World's Most Dangerous...
COMMENTS	Deal with Termite Art Productions

Dave Harding . . . . . Executive Producer

DEAN HARGROVE PRODUCTIONS
10202 W. Washington Blvd.
Culver City, CA 90232
PHONE 310-244-8383
FAX 310-244-0303

TYPES	TV Series
DEALS	Sony Pictures Television
CREDITS	Matlock - Diagnosis Murder - Perry Mason Movies

Dean Hargrove . . . . . Executive Producer
Doris Stockstill . . . . . Executive Assistant to Mr. Hargrove

HARMS WAY PRODUCTIONS
4000 Warner Blvd., Bldg. 17, Rm. 111
Burbank, CA 91522
PHONE 818-954-2160
FAX 818-954-7033

TYPES	Features - Made-for-TV/Cable Movies - TV Series
DEALS	John Wells Productions
POST PRODUCTION	Duma
CREDITS	White Oleander - The Good Thief - Third Watch - West Wing

Kristin Harms . . . . . Producer
Matt Billingsly . . . . . Creative Executive (818-954-3295)

HARPO FILMS, INC.
345 N. Maple Dr., Ste. 315
Beverly Hills, CA 90210
PHONE 310-278-5559/312-633-1000

TYPES	Features - Made-for-TV/Cable Movies - TV Series
DEALS	ABC Entertainment Television Group - The Walt Disney Company
POST PRODUCTION	Their Eyes Were Watching God
CREDITS	Beloved - Before Women Had Wings - The Wedding - David & Lisa - Tuesdays with Morrie - Amy & Isabelle
SUBMISSION POLICY	No unsolicited material
COMMENTS	Chicago office: 110 N. Carpenter, Chicago, IL 60607

Oprah Winfrey . . . . . Chairman/CEO
Kate Forte . . . . . President
Scott Stein . . . . . Executive
Melody Fowler . . . . . Creative Executive
Lisa Halliday . . . . . Media & Corporate Relations
Todd Davis . . . . . Office Manager
Alison Treleaven . . . . . Executive Assistant to President
Donna Raimondi . . . . . Assistant to Scott Stein

THE HARRIS COMPANY
1260 S. Beverly Glen, Ste. 305
Los Angeles, CA 90024
PHONE 310-273-5350
FAX 310-273-7177
EMAIL . . . . . info@theharriscompany.com

TYPES	Features - Direct-to-Video/DVD - Made-for-TV/Cable Movies - Syndication - TV Series
DEVELOPMENT	The Girl with the Golden Gun - The Dream Detective - Posessed
PRE-PRODUCTION	Dance Machine - Conversations with Other Women
PRODUCTION	My Dad's a Famous Film Star
POST PRODUCTION	Crash
CREDITS	Gods & Monsters - Twilight of the Golds - Family Law (TV) - EZ Streets (TV) - Maze

Mark R. Harris . . . . . CEO
Dan Harris . . . . . Creative Director

HART ENTERTAINMENT
15030 Ventura Blvd., Ste. 905
Sherman Oaks, CA 91403
PHONE 818-504-4864
FAX 818-673-1894

TYPES	Features - TV Series
CREDITS	Final Decision - Two Shades of Blue - The Greatest Walks of Life

Geno Hart . . . . . Chairman/CEO
Steve Larson . . . . . Sr. VP, Production

HART SHARP ENTERTAINMENT, INC.

575 Broadway, 6th Fl.
New York, NY 10012
PHONE 212-475-7555
FAX 212-475-1717
WEB SITE ....www.hartsharp.com
SECOND WEB SITE ....www.hartsharpvideo.com
TYPES Features
DEVELOPMENT Revolutionary Road - Two Guys from Verona - Snake Hips - Women's Maintenance Club - Taboo
PRE-PRODUCTION Evening - Night Listener
POST PRODUCTION Proof - P.S. - A Home at the End of the World
CREDITS Dark Harbor - Boys Don't Cry - You Can Count on Me - Lift - Nicholas Nickleby - Undefeated - Just Another Story
SUBMISSION POLICY No unsolicited submissions

John N. Hart Jr. ....Partner
Jeffrey Sharp ....Partner
Michael Hogan ....COO
Robert Kessel ....Head, Production
Brett Williams ....Director, Production
Daniel Feiner ....Director, Business Affairs
Nina Wolarsky ....Director, Development
Eileen Choi ....Assistant to John Hart

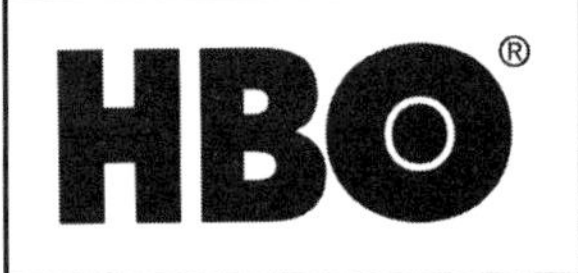

HBO FILMS

2500 Broadway, Ste. 400
Santa Monica, CA 90404
PHONE 310-382-3000
WEB SITE ....www.hbo.com/films
TYPES Features - Made-for-TV/Cable Movies
POST PRODUCTION Mrs. Harris - Lackawana Blues - The Ballad of Bettie Page - Dirty War - Sometimes in April - Empire Falls
COMPLETED UNRELEASED The Life and Death of Peter Sellers - Yesterday
CREDITS Angels in America - American Splendor - Elephant - Everyday People - And Starring Pancho Villa as Himself - Iron Jawed Angels - Something the Lord Made - Maria Full of Grace
COMMENTS Premium cable movies

Colin Callender ....President
Keri Putnam ....Sr. VP, Development & Production
Glenn Whitehead ....Sr. VP, Business Affairs & Production
Kary Antholis ....VP, Development & Production
Janet Graham Borba ....VP, Production
Carrie Frazier ....VP, Casting
Jeffrey Guthrie ....VP/Sr. Counsel (West Coast Programming)
Cynthia Davis Kanner ....VP, Post Production
Jonathan Krauss ....VP, Development & Production
Maud Nadler ....VP, Independent Films
Jay Roewe ....VP, Production
Molly Wilson ....VP/Chief Counsel (West Coast Programming)
Suzanne Young ....VP, Business Affairs
Dennis O'Connor ....Head, Theatrical Releasing, HBO Films
Amy Berman ....Director, Casting
Elaine Chin ....Director, Development & Production
Mark Levenstein ....Director, Production
Sam Martin ....Director, Development & Production
Ginny Nugent ....Director, Production
Miranda Thompson ....Director, Development & Production
Pam Winn ....Director, Post Production
Bettina Moss ....Sr. Story Editor
Donna Pearlmutter Reichman ....Production Manager
Dottie Simmons ....Operations Manager
Kandace Williams ....Story Editor
Marc Thomas King ....Coordinator

HBO INDEPENDENT PRODUCTIONS

2500 Broadway, Ste. 400
Santa Monica, CA 90404
PHONE 310-382-3000
WEB SITE ....www.hbo.com
TYPES TV Series
CREDITS Everybody Loves Raymond

Tracy Katsky ....Head, HBO Independent Productions
Russell Schwartz ....Head, Business Affairs
Casey Bloys ....Director, Creative Affairs

HBO ORIGINAL PROGRAMMING

2500 Broadway, Ste. 400
Santa Monica, CA 90404
PHONE 310-382-3000/212-512-1000
WEB SITE ....www.hbo.com
TYPES Documentaries - TV Series
CREDITS Carnivàle - K Street - Six Feet Under - Curb Your Enthusiasm - Sex and the City - Sopranos - The Wire
COMMENTS East Coast office: 1100 Avenue of the Americas, New York, NY 10036

Chris Albrecht ....Chairman/CEO, HBO, Inc.
Sheila Nevins ....President, HBO Documentary & Family (NY)
Carolyn Strauss ....President, HBO Entertainment
Michael Lombardo ....Executive VP, Business Affairs & Production
Carmi Zlotnik ....Executive VP, Creative Operations, Business Development & New Media
Sarah Condon ....Sr. VP, Comedy Series
Susan Ennis ....Sr. VP, Planning & Operations, Original Programming & Films (NY)
Nancy Geller ....Sr. VP, Original Programming (NY)
Anne Thomopoulos ....Sr. VP, Miniseries & Dramatic Events
Nancy Abraham ....VP, Original Programming, Documentaries (NY)
David Goodman ....VP, Business Affairs
Miranda Heller ....VP, Drama Series
Lisa Heller ....VP, Documentary Programming (NY)
Dolores Morris ....VP, HBO Family & Documentary Programming (NY)
Lisa Pongracic ....VP, Business Affairs
Beth White ....VP, Business Affairs
Mike Garcia ....Director, Drama Series
Jada Miranda ....Director, Comedy Series
John Murchison ....Director, Dramatic Miniseries & Events
Nina Rosenstein ....Director, Development (NY)
Gina Balian ....Manager, Comedy, Drama, Miniseries

HDNET FILMS

145 Avenue of Americas, 7th Fl.
New York, NY 10013
PHONE 212-255-0626
FAX 212-255-0602
EMAIL ....oc@opencityfilms.com
TYPES Features
DEALS 2929 Productions
PRE-PRODUCTION Over the Mountains - Quid Pro Quo
PRODUCTION Enron: Black Magic
COMMENTS Digital features

Jason Kliot ....Co-President/Producer
Joana Vicente ....Co-President/Producer
Will Battersby ....Head, Development
Gretchen McGowan ....Head, Production
Kristina Redick ....Manager, Finance
Jeffrey Fierson ....Assistant to Jason Kliot & Joana Vicente
Quentin Little ....Development Assistant

THE HECHT COMPANY

3607 W. Magnolia, Ste. L
Burbank, CA 91505
PHONE . . . 310-989-3467
EMAIL . . . hechtco@aol.com

TYPES — Features - Made-for-TV/Cable Movies - TV Series
DEVELOPMENT — Count 3 and Pray - Dreamers - Rehab - The Catacombs
CREDITS — First, Last and Deposit - King of the Ants

Duffy Hecht . . . Producer

HEEL & TOE FILMS

2058 Broadway
Santa Monica, CA 90404
PHONE . . . 310-264-1866
FAX . . . 310-264-1865

TYPES — Features - TV Series
DEVELOPMENT — House
CREDITS — Century City - Quiz Show - Donnie Brasco - Homicide: Life on the Street - Gideon's Crossing - Sum of All Fears

Paul Attanasio . . . Writer/Producer
Katie Jacobs . . . Producer
Brian Pines . . . VP, Development & Production
Matthew Lewis . . . Executive Assistant to Paul Attanasio
Jenny Paul . . . Assistant to Katie Jacobs & Brian Pines

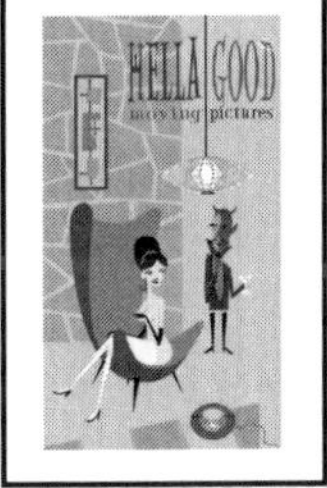

HELLA GOOD MOVING PICTURES

PO Box 97
Venice, CA 90294
PHONE . . . 310-488-9478
EMAIL . . . hella-good@earthlink.net

TYPES — Features - TV Series - Animation
DEALS — Jersey Films - Universal Pictures
DEVELOPMENT — The Marx Brothers - Fenwick's Suit - Sleepless Beauty - King of Crash - Spike Jones - Waxing Macabre - The Other Side - Taxi Dog - Guardian Angels - Ingrid Bergman - Sunburnt Angels - Birdmen - Jack B. Nimble - On the Table - Joe Made Guy - Elephants - Renaissance Men - Standard Life - Sexploitation Cinema - Rainbow Man - Vanishing Planet - Dry Fire
CREDITS — The Reunion - Murder at the Cannes Film Festival - Shelter Island - Macabre Theatre (KDOC) - Napoleon Dynamite
COMMENTS — Partnerships with Good Medicine Films, Inc., Smashing Entertainment

David Michaels . . . Writer/Producer/Director
Jory Weitz . . . Producer
Chris Douridas . . . President, Music
Dino Magis . . . VP, Creative Development
Tim Ranson . . . VP, Creative Development
Mark Alexander . . . VP, Creative Development

HELLER HIGHWATER

c/o Cosmic Entertainment
9255 Sunset Blvd., Ste. 1010
West Hollywood, CA 90069
PHONE . . . 310-275-8080, x114
FAX . . . 310-275-8081
EMAIL . . . peterheller@earthlink.net

TYPES — Features - Made-for-TV/Cable Movies - TV Series
DEALS — Cosmic Entertainment
DEVELOPMENT — The Authority - The Little Lord - Breathtaker
PRE-PRODUCTION — Dreamland
CREDITS — Like Mike - Barb Wire - Hotel de Love - Caught Up - Bones - Brown Sugar - Full Ride
COMMENTS — Management company specializes in writers and directors

Peter Heller . . . Producer

PAUL HELLER PRODUCTIONS

1666 N. Beverly Dr.
Beverly Hills, CA 90210
PHONE . . . 310-275-4477
FAX . . . 310-275-4714
EMAIL . . . pheller@earthlink.net
WEB SITE . . . www.pheller.no-ip.com

TYPES — Documentaries - Features - Made-for-TV/Cable Movies - New Media
DEVELOPMENT — O.B.E.(Out of Body Experience) - Xavier's Folly
PRODUCTION — Skirball Cultural Center Exhibits: Personal Journeys: Synagogues
CREDITS — Withnail & I - David & Lisa - My Left Foot - The Annihilation of Fish - Enter the Dragon - The First Monday in October
COMMENTS — Museum audio and video; Skirball Cultural Center: New Exhibits; Hong Kong Museum of History; US Department of State: New Exhibits

Paul Heller . . . Producer
Kathy Zebrowski-Heller . . . President
Trevor Pressman . . . Director, Development Editor

ROSILYN HELLER PRODUCTIONS

2237 Nichols Canyon Rd.
Los Angeles, CA 90046
PHONE . . . 323-876-2820
EMAIL . . . rozheller@aol.com

TYPES — Features - Made-for-TV/Cable Movies
DEVELOPMENT — The Girls Next Door
PRE-PRODUCTION — The Defiant
CREDITS — Ice Castles - Beans of Egypt, Maine - Who's That Girl - American Heart
SUBMISSION POLICY — No unsolicited material

Rosilyn Heller . . . President/Producer

HENNESSEY ENTERTAINMENT, LTD.
PO Box 9054
Baltimore, MD 21222
PHONE 410-284-7759
EMAIL .... TeamHennessey@aol.com
SECOND EMAIL .... NewzSpy@aol.com
WEB SITE .... www.thephixer.com
SECOND WEB SITE .... www.newzspy.com
TYPES — Features - Made-for-TV/Cable Movies - New Media - TV Series
DEVELOPMENT — CIA/FBI (Untitled Feature) - Undercover Girl (Cable Movie)
CREDITS — Dangerous Evidence (Lifetime) - Love, Mary (CBS) - First Steps (CBS) - Aunt Mary (CBS)
SUBMISSION POLICY — No unsolicited material; Query letter by agent, attorney or manager; No loglines
COMMENTS — Book publishing; Criminal investigative journalism; Entertainment public relations and marketing; Affiliate offices in Los Angeles, New York, London

Ellis A. Cohen .... President/CEO/Producer
Jake Baron .... Sr. Creative Executive
Leonard H. Cohen .... Sr. Creative Executive/Associate Producer (Emeritus)
Stephen Resnick .... Creative Executive
Kelly Kristopher .... Assistant to Ellis A. Cohen/Creative Executive

THE JIM HENSON COMPANY
1416 N. La Brea Ave.
Hollywood, CA 90028
PHONE 323-802-1500/212-794-2400
FAX 323-802-1825/212-570-1147
WEB SITE .... www.henson.com
TYPES — Animation - Commercials - Features - Direct-to-Video/DVD - Made-for-TV/Cable Movies - Music Videos - New Media - Syndication - TV Series
DEVELOPMENT — Astroboy - The Moon and the Sun - Thumb - Time Dogs - King of the Elves - Let It Rain - Neverwhere - Parasyte
PRE-PRODUCTION — Frances
POST PRODUCTION — MirrorMask - Five Children and It - Farscape: The Peacekeeper Wars
CREDITS — Good Boy! - Farscape - Mopatop's Shop - Jim Henson's The Hoobs - Jim Henson's Animal Jam - Bambaloo
COMMENTS — UK office: 30 Oval Rd., Camden, London NW1 7DE, UK, phone: 44-207-428-4000, fax: 44-207-428-4001

Lisa Henson .... Co-Chair/Co-CEO
Brian Henson .... Co-Chair/Co-CEO
Peter Schube .... President/COO
Michael R. Polis .... Sr. VP, Marketing, Worldwide & Jim Henson Home Entertainment
Laurie Don .... VP, Financial Operations
Joe Henderson .... VP, Administration
John McGuire .... VP, Business & Legal Affairs
Kelly Oien Perez .... VP, Creative Affairs
Kristine Belson .... Producer, Jim Henson Pictures
Pete Coogan .... Managing Director, Jim Henson's Creature Shop

JIM HENSON PICTURES
1416 N. La Brea Ave.
Hollywood, CA 90028
PHONE 323-802-1500
FAX 323-802-1835
WEB SITE .... www.henson.com
TYPES — Animation - Features - Direct-to-Video/DVD - Made-for-TV/Cable Movies - TV Series
DEVELOPMENT — Astroboy - Neverwhere - Moon and the Sun - Thumb - Only Human
POST PRODUCTION — Mirror Mask - Five Children and It
CREDITS — Buddy - The Adventures of Elmo in Grouchland - Muppets from Space - Rat - Good Boy!

Lisa Henson .... Co-Chairman/CEO
Kristine Belson .... Producer
Melissa Eaton .... Project Coordinator

***HERE! TV**
10990 Wilshire Blvd., Penthouse
Los Angeles, CA 90024
PHONE 310-998-4298
FAX 310-998-4268
WEB SITE .... www.heretv.com
TYPES — Documentaries - Features - Direct-to-Video/DVD - Made-for-TV/Cable Movies - TV Series
DEVELOPMENT — House of Usher - Jekyll and Hyde - Third Man Out - Young Van Helsing
PRE-PRODUCTION — Cynthia Rothrock Project
PRODUCTION — The Complex
POST PRODUCTION — Dante's Cove
COMPLETED UNRELEASED — The Sisterhood
CREDITS — Merci Docteur Rey - Yes Nurse! No Nurse! - Callas Forever - Beautiful Boxer

Paul Colichman .... President, here! TV
Mark Reinhart .... Executive VP
Meredith Kadlec .... Director, Development

VICKY HERMAN PRODUCTIONS
3641 Glenridge Dr.
Sherman Oaks, CA 91423
PHONE 818-981-2034
TYPES — Features - Made-for-TV/Cable Movies - TV Series
CREDITS — Dirty Pictures - A Dangerous Affair - Trial by Fire - Holiday Affair - The Baby Dance - All She Ever Wanted - Elvis Meets Nixon

Vicky Herman .... Producer

JOSSELYNE HERMAN & ASSOCIATES/MOVING IMAGE FILMS

345 East 56th St., Ste. 3-C
New York, NY 10022
PHONE . . . 212-355-3033/917-721-4747
FAX . . . 212-937-5270
EMAIL . . . info@jhermanassociates.com
SECOND EMAIL . . . jhatalent@aol.com
WEB SITE . . . www.jhermanassociates.com
SECOND WEB SITE . . . www.annebreal.com
TYPES Animation - Commercials - Documentaries - Features - Direct-to-Video/DVD - Made-for-TV/Cable Movies - Music Videos
DEVELOPMENT Very Very Naked - The Little Prince - Kids Cooking with Comedy - The Pack - Olivia - The Representative - The Market
PRE-PRODUCTION The Making of...
POST PRODUCTION Tollbooth
CREDITS A&E Biography - Anne B. Real - Caged

Josselyne Herman-Saccio . . . Owner/Producer
Michael Saccio . . . Producer
Harvey Herman . . . Director
Don Rodgers . . . Music Division Manager
Eric Jacobs . . . Project Manager
Sonya Kolba . . . Development Associate
Melissa Sommer . . . Musical Theatre Division
Elaine Herman . . . Casting Director

BRYAN HICKOX PICTURES, INC.

c/o Jacksonville Production Center
851 N. Market St.
Jacksonville, FL 32202-2742
PHONE . . . 904-509-4790
FAX . . . 904-354-5753
EMAIL . . . b.hickox@comcast.net
TYPES Documentaries - Features - Direct-to-Video/DVD - Made-for-TV/Cable Movies - Reality TV - Syndication - TV Series
DEVELOPMENT Tidings of Comfort and Joy - Sunday's Love - X-Treme Reality (Series)
PRE-PRODUCTION The Tentmaker
PRODUCTION Changing the Face of Poverty
CREDITS The Painting - Conquering Hollywood - Spring Fling - Safe Harbor - Ride - Stand for What Is Right - Sudden Terror: The Hijacking of School Bus #17 - CCPD - Family Reunion

S. Bryan Hickox . . . Producer/Owner
Joanne Kraemer . . . CFO
Dan H. Hinds . . . VP, Business Affairs
Michael Stark . . . Casting
Terry VanDerwier . . . Casting

HIGH HORSE FILMS

c/o Santa Clarita Studios
25135 Anza Dr., Stage 5
Santa Clarita, CA 91355
PHONE . . . 323-939-8802
FAX . . . 323-939-8832
TYPES Features - TV Series
DEALS CBS Entertainment
CREDITS CSI: Crime Scene Investigation - Keep the Change - Hard Promises - Baby It's You

Cynthia Chvatal . . . Producer
William Petersen . . . Actor/Producer
Beth Robinowitz . . . Director, Development

HIGH MAINTENANCE FILMS

365 S. Cloverdale Ave.
Los Angeles, CA 90036
PHONE . . . 323-697-8895
FAX . . . 928-395-8943
EMAIL . . . karen@highmaintenancefilms.com
WEB SITE . . . www.highmaintenancefilms.com
TYPES Features - TV Series
DEVELOPMENT Messages Deleted - Downloading Nancy - The Magic Egg - Asleep at the Switch
PRE-PRODUCTION She Died Twice
PRODUCTION Ghost Soldier
COMPLETED UNRELEASED Black Cloud
CREDITS Pool Hall Junkies

Karen Beninati . . . President/Producer
Bryan Howe . . . Executive Producer

HIGH ROAD PRODUCTIONS

5750 Wilshire Blvd., Ste. 580
Los Angeles, CA 90036
PHONE . . . 323-276-0349
TYPES Features - TV Series
CREDITS Pontiac Moon - Diggstown - Jacknife - Table for Five
SUBMISSION POLICY Direct submissions and inquiries to Sharon Roesler

Robert Schaffel . . . Producer/Writer
Sharon Roesler . . . Producer
E.J. Campfield . . . Writer

HIPPOFILMS

1721 Colby Ave., Ste. 5
Los Angeles, CA 90025
PHONE . . . 310-445-9157
FAX . . . 310-445-9403
EMAIL . . . hippofilms@aol.com
TYPES Documentaries - Features - Made-for-TV/Cable Movies
DEVELOPMENT Gin and Tonic - Pepper in the Blood
CREDITS Rent Control

David Eric Brenner . . . President
Bob McGinness . . . Sr. Director, Production
Sherman Toy . . . Director, Operations
Tex Wall . . . Director, Creative Affairs
Gina C. Roland . . . Director, Development
Martin Santacruz Jr. . . . Assistant

S. HIRSCH COMPANY, INC./SEEMORE FILMS

15456 Ventura Blvd., Ste. 300
Sherman Oaks, CA 91403
PHONE . . . 818-990-1212
FAX . . . 818-990-1824
TYPES Features
DEVELOPMENT Winter in America - Seville Communion - Midnight Call - The Overworld - The Heretic
COMMENTS Acquisitions consulting

Steven Hirsch . . . President/CEO
Darius Kapfer . . . Sr. VP
Mark Padilla . . . Executive Assistant

THE HISTORY CHANNEL
235 E. 45th St.
New York, NY 10017
PHONE 212-210-1400
FAX 212-907-9481
WEB SITE . . . . www.historychannel.com
TYPES Documentaries
CREDITS Remember the Alamo - Barbarians - Quest for King Arthur - First Invasion: The War of 1812 - The True Story of Alexander - Ben Franklin - Tactical to Practical - Wild West Tech - Mail Call - Deep Sea Detectives - Modern Marvels - Investigating History
SUBMISSION POLICY No unsolicited proposals

Daniel Davids . . . . Executive VP/General Manager
Charles Maday . . . . Sr. VP, Programming
Michael Mohamad . . . . Sr. VP, Marketing
Beth Dietrich . . . . VP, Historical Programming
Peter Gaffney . . . . VP, Program Acquisitions & Scheduling
Carl Lindahl . . . . VP, Historical Programming
Susan Werbe . . . . VP, Historical Programming
Dolores Gavin . . . . Director, Historical Programming
Peggy Kim . . . . Director, Historical Programming
Marc Etkind . . . . Director, Historical Programming

HIT & RUN PRODUCTIONS, INC.
222 Riverside Dr., Ste. 8-B
New York, NY 10025
PHONE 212-974-8400
FAX 212-974-8443
EMAIL . . . . firstname@hitandruninc.com
TYPES Features
DEVELOPMENT The Husband I Bought - Children of Men - Confessions of a Dogwalker - The Last Audition - Black Oasis - Sanctuary
CREDITS Eye of the Beholder - Beautopia

Tony Smith . . . . Chairman
Hilary Shor . . . . President, Production

HOFFMAN FILMS
c/o Flutie Entertainmnet
9300 Wilshire Blvd., Ste. 333
Beverly Hills, CA 90212
PHONE 310-422-5922
EMAIL . . . . hoffmanfilms@juno.com
TYPES Features - TV Series
CREDITS Hometown Legend

Shawn Hoffman . . . . Actor/Writer/Producer
Teresa Klorer . . . . Director, Development

GARY HOFFMAN PRODUCTIONS
3931 Puerco Canyon Rd.
Malibu, CA 90265
PHONE 310-456-1830
FAX 310-456-8866
EMAIL . . . . garyhofprods@charter.net
TYPES Features - Made-for-TV/Cable Movies - TV Series
CREDITS Bastard Out of Carolina - Soul of the Game - Bonnie & Clyde: The True Story - The Fitzgeralds & the Kennedys - WWIII - The Big Heist - National Lampoon's Thanksgiving Reunion

Gary Hoffman . . . . Producer/President
Ann Ryan . . . . Development

HOLLYWOOD NETWORK, INC.
433 N. Camden Dr., Ste. 600
Beverly Hills, CA 90210
PHONE 310-288-1882
FAX 310-288-0060
EMAIL . . . . hollyinfo@hollywoodnetwork.com
WEB SITE . . . . www.hollywoodnetwork.com
TYPES Features - Direct-to-Video/DVD - New Media
CREDITS Power Brokers - Justice...On Trial
COMMENTS A division of CCS Entertainment

Carlos de Abreu . . . . President/Producer
Janice de Abreu . . . . Producer
Michael Almeida . . . . VP, International
John Jacobson . . . . VP, New Media

HOME & GARDEN TELEVISION (HGTV)
9721 Sherrill Blvd.
Knoxville, TN 37932
PHONE 865-694-2700
FAX 865-531-1588
WEB SITE . . . . www.hgtv.com
TYPES TV Series
CREDITS Debbie Travis' Facelift - Mission: Organization - Designers' Challenge - Decorating Cents - Designed to Sell - Outer Spaces - Room by Room - Curb Appeal - House Hunters - Sensible Chic - Weekend Warriors
COMMENTS Helpful information and insights from hosts who are recognized experts in their field

Burton Jablin . . . . President
Michael Dingley . . . . Sr. VP, Programming
Mary Ellen Iwata . . . . VP, Development

HOMEGROWN PICTURES, INC.
5042 Wilshire Blvd., Ste. 585
Los Angeles, CA 90036
PHONE 323-930-0349
FAX 323-930-0348
EMAIL . . . . homegrownpics@aol.com
SECOND EMAIL . . . . ccolumbina@aol.com
TYPES Features
DEVELOPMENT The Harlem Shake - The Dying Ground - 42.4% - Buck Wild - Step in the Name of Love
PRODUCTION Hustle and Flow
CREDITS Buddy - Muppets from Space - Elmo in Grouchland - Biker Boyz - Good Boy!
SUBMISSION POLICY No unsolicited material

Stephanie Allain . . . . Producer
Jenny Klion . . . . Producer (212-206-3648)

*HOMERUN ENTERTAINMENT, INC.

5800 Hannum Ave., Ste. B
Culver City, CA 90230
PHONE .310-338-1500
FAX .310-338-1490
EMAIL .homeplate@homerunent.com
WEB SITE .www.homerunent.com
TYPES Documentaries - New Media - Reality TV - TV Series
CREDITS DIY: Blueprint for Home Building - Be Your Own Contractor - Weekend Gardening - Weekend Landscaping; Food Network: The Best Of... - Food Finds; Fine Living: Top 5 Food & Wine Adventures - Homes of the Wine Country; WE Women's Entertainment: Line on Design
COMMENTS Multiple projects for various cable networks in development

Barry Gribbon .Executive Producer/CEO/Founder
Jennifer Gribbon .General Manager/Founder
Stuart Crowner .Executive Producer
Randall Andrews .Producer
Tanya Green .Producer
Lynn Jordan .Producer
Veronica Penn .Producer
Brent Pierson .Producer
Sharon Clinton .Associate Producer
Don Jones .Associate Producer
Blaine Pate .Associate Producer
Steve Plutte .Coordinating Producer
Belma Johnson .Supervising Producer/Development
Jordan Ruden .Production Manager
Aaron Goldstein .Production Coordinator

HOPE ENTERPRISES, INC.

210 N. Pass Ave., Ste. 101
Burbank, CA 91505
PHONE .818-841-2020
FAX .818-841-2028
EMAIL .hei@bobhope.com
WEB SITE .www.bobhope.com
TYPES Documentaries - TV Series
DEVELOPMENT Various Bob Hope Projects
CREDITS Bob Hope Archives
COMMENTS Company established by Bob Hope in 1946

Linda Hope .Producer/Writer
Jim Hardy .Post Production Supervisor/Editor/Archivist

HOPSCOTCH PICTURES

9220 Sunset Blvd., Ste. 305
Los Angeles, CA 90069
PHONE .310-860-2680
FAX .310-860-2681
TYPES Features - TV Series
DEVELOPMENT 2.2 -Just for Fun - Bedford and Park - Meet Jane Doe - Rushing - The Life and Times of HJ Hermin
CREDITS My First Mister

Sukee Chew .Producer
Jesse Hara .Development

HORSEPOWER ENTERTAINMENT

4063 Radford Ave., Ste. 206
Studio City, CA 91604
PHONE .818-506-4300
TYPES Features - TV Series - Reality TV
DEVELOPMENT No Fear (Independent)
PRE-PRODUCTION Dreadnaught (Columbia)
CREDITS The Core (Paramount) - Emperor's Club (Universal)

Cooper Layne .Writer/Producer
Tina Velvet .Creative Executive

HUMANOIDS, INC.

12001 Ventura Pl., Ste. 310
Studio City, CA 91604
PHONE .818-655-9800
FAX .818-655-9811
WEB SITE .www.humanoids.com
TYPES Animation - Features - TV Series
DEVELOPMENT Book of Jack - Metal - Sanctum
POST PRODUCTION Immortal
CREDITS Thomas in Love - Rolie Polie Olie
COMMENTS Subsidiary of Humanoids Group

Fabrice Giger .Chairman/Publisher
Justin Connolly .Producer
Paul Benjamin .Producer/Publishing

HUMBLE JOURNEY FILMS

7656 W. Sunset Blvd.
Los Angeles, CA 90046
PHONE .323-882-6376
FAX .323-882-6386
TYPES Features - Made-for-TV/Cable Movies - Reality TV - TV Series
DEVELOPMENT 25 to Life (TV) - M'Lady (Feature)
CREDITS Crazy as Hell - Rebound - Mind Prey - Psalms from the Underground - The Salton Sea
SUBMISSION POLICY No unsolicited submissions

Eriq La Salle .No Title
Butch Robinson .No Title
Terri Feldman Lubaroff .No Title
Allison Davis .No Title
Ben Roberts .No Title
Jasmine D. Waters .No Title

HUNGRY MAN

428 Broadway, 6th Fl.
New York, NY 10013
PHONE .212-625-5600
FAX .212-625-5699
EMAIL .mail@hungryman.com
WEB SITE .www.hungryman.com
TYPES Commercials - Features
COMMENTS Primarily commercials

Bryan Buckley .Partner/Director
Steve Orent .Partner/Executive Producer
Hank Perlman .Partner/Executive Producer

PETER HYAMS PRODUCTIONS, INC.

1453 Third Street Promenade, Ste. 315
Santa Monica, CA 90401-2397
PHONE .310-393-1553
FAX .310-393-1554
EMAIL .hyamsproductions@aol.com
TYPES Features - TV Series
POST PRODUCTION Sound of Thunder

Peter Hyams .Director/Writer
Jonathan Steinberg .Director, Development

HYDE PARK ENTERTAINMENT

2450 Broadway St., Ste. 400
Santa Monica, CA 90404
PHONE 310-449-3191
FAX 310-449-3356
EMAIL ....hpe411@hydeparkentertainment.com
TYPES Features - Made-for-TV/Cable Movies - TV Series
DEALS Metro-Goldwyn-Mayer Studios, Inc. - The Walt Disney Company
DEVELOPMENT The Dark Fields - The Other End of the Line - Bringing Down the House 2 - Premonition - Endgame - Mandrake - Emperor Zehnder
POST PRODUCTION Shopgirl
CREDITS Bringing Down the House - Raising Helen - Walking Tall - Moonlight Mile - Bandits - Original Sin - Anti-Trust

Ashok Amritraj ....Chairman/CEO (310-449-3085)
Jon Jashni ....President (310-449-3224)
Matt Baer ....Producer (310-586-8834)
Joe D'Angelo ....VP, Finance (310-449-3108)
Ezra Hudson ....Creative Executive (310-449-3094)
Ben Dietz ....Assistant to Ashok Amritraj (310-586-8137)
Amanda Bromberg ....Assistant to Matt Baer (310-449-3094)
Bryan Stamp ....Assistant to Jon Jashni (310-449-3183)

HYPERION STUDIO

6725 Sunset Blvd., Ste. 240
Hollywood, CA 90028
PHONE 323-871-0022
FAX 323-871-0044
WEB SITE ....www.hyperionpictures.com
TYPES Animation - Features - Direct-to-Video/DVD - TV Series
CREDITS The Proud Family - Playing by Heart - Life with Louie - Tom's Midnight Garden - Brave Little Toaster - Bebe's Kids - Marigold

Tom Wilhite ....President
Willard Carroll ....Co-Owner/Writer/Director/Producer
Bruce Smith ....Executive Producer/Director
Chris Young ....Producer/Director

HYPNOTIC

80 South St., 3rd Fl.
New York, NY 10038
PHONE 212-809-3202/310-453-2345
FAX 212-809-3209/310-453-0075
EMAIL ....info@hypnotic.com
WEB SITE ....www.hypnotic.com
TYPES Commercials - Documentaries - Features - Direct-to-Video/DVD - Music Videos - New Media - TV Series
DEALS Warner Bros. Television Production
DEVELOPMENT Living the Lie - Nick Tungsten - Shadow Man
POST PRODUCTION Mail Order Bride
CREDITS The O.C. - Terry Tate: Office Linebacker - The Bourne Identity - The Bourne Supremacy
COMMENTS West Coast office: 1520 Cloverfield Blvd., Ste. D, Santa Monica, CA 90404

David Bartis ....CEO
Daniel Gossels ....COO
Doug Liman ....Vice Chairman
John Christie ....VP, Internet
Gene Klein ....VP, Acquisitions & Development
Susan Petersen ....VP, Distribution
Michael Wiese ....VP, Brand Partnerships

ICON PRODUCTIONS, INC.

808 Wilshire Blvd., 4th Fl.
Santa Monica, CA 90401
PHONE 310-434-7300
FAX 310-434-7377
TYPES Features - Made-for-TV/Cable Movies - TV Series
PRODUCTION Clubhouse
CREDITS Maverick - Hamlet - Braveheart - Payback - The Three Stooges - What Women Want - We Were Soldiers - The Passion of the Christ

Bruce Davey ....President
Vicki Christianson ....COO
Steve McEveety ....Features Producer
Nancy Cotton ....Sr. VP, TV
Kevin Lake ....Sr. VP, Features
Eveleen Bandy ....VP, TV & Features
Stefanie Huie ....VP, Features
Elizabeth Kennedy ....Story Editor
Amy Pocha ....Story Editor

IDEAL ENTERTAINMENT, INC.

8787 Shoreham Dr., Ste. 1206
Los Angeles, CA 90069
PHONE 323-939-3399
FAX 323-939-3009
EMAIL ....info@ideal-entertainment.com
TYPES Animation - Features - Large Format - TV Series
PRE-PRODUCTION American Road
PRODUCTION Curious George - NFL 3D IMAX
COMPLETED UNRELEASED Chick Corea: Rendezvous in New York
CREDITS All Access: Front Row. Backstage. LIVE! (IMAX) - Richie Rich - The Big Brass Ring
COMMENTS IMAX films; Music-related films; 3D films; East Coast office: 175 W. 12th St., Ste. 14F, New York, NY 10011

Jon Shapiro ....President/Producer
Peter Shapiro ....VP/Producer

IDENTITY FILMS

100 Universal City Plaza, Bungalow 4144
Universal City, CA 91608
PHONE 818-733-3378
FAX 818-733-5424
TYPES Features
DEALS Universal Pictures
DEVELOPMENT Gregoire Moulin Against Humanity - Two-Way Stretch

Seann William Scott ....Producer
Graham Larson ....Producer
Geoff Pattison ....Creative Executive

IDIOM FILMS & ENTERTAINMENT

1041 N. Formosa Ave., Santa Monica Bldg. East
West Hollywood, CA 90046
PHONE 323-850-2778
FAX 323-850-2779
EMAIL ....info@idiom-films.com
TYPES Features - Made-for-TV/Cable Movies - TV Series
DEVELOPMENT The Nice Guys Club - Forever Man
PRE-PRODUCTION Laws of Nature

Quay Hays ....President
Michael Dragotto ....International Sales Consultant
Zack Graham ....Assistant
Fred Medick ....Assistant

IFM FILM ASSOCIATES, INC.

1328 E. Palmer Ave.
Glendale, CA 91205
PHONE 818-243-4976
FAX 818-550-9728
EMAIL ....contact@ifmfilm.com
WEB SITE ....www.ifmfilm.com
TYPES: Features - Direct-to-Video/DVD - Made-for-TV/Cable Movies - TV Series
DEVELOPMENT: Soulfinder - James's Garden - Islanders
PRE-PRODUCTION: Sally Marshall Is Not an Alien (Series)
CREDITS: Sally Marshall Is Not an Alien (Feature) - The Whole of the Moon - The Hit
SUBMISSION POLICY: Synopsis only; No unsolicited scripts

Antony I. Ginnane ....President
Ann Lyons ....Executive VP
Anthony J. Lyons ....VP, International
David Makhlout ....Director, International Sales
Patrick Cochran ....Executive Assistant

ILLUMINATI ENTERTAINMENT

11901 Santa Monica Blvd., Ste. 494
Los Angeles, CA 90025
PHONE 310-820-5613
FAX 310-826-0465
EMAIL ....info@illuminatientertainment.com
WEB SITE ....www.illuminatientertainment.com
TYPES: Animation - Features - New Media - TV Series
DEVELOPMENT: The Interman - Jingle Belle - Cryptopia (TV) - Dark Ride

Ford Lytle Gilmore ....President/Producer

IMAGE PRODUCTIONS

200 42nd Ave. North
Nashville, TN 37209
PHONE 615-297-4410/310-281-8000
FAX 615-298-4420
EMAIL ....tlneff@documentarychannel.com
SECOND EMAIL ....inquiry@fabfootage.com
WEB SITE ....www.documentarychannel.com
SECOND WEB SITE ....www.fabfootage.com
TYPES: Documentaries - Features - TV Series
DEALS: The Documentary Channel
PRODUCTION: Generations of Elvis (IMAX)
CREDITS: Broker's Choice - Red Grooms: Sunflower in a Hothouse - Running Mates - Blood Brothers - Gates of Pearl - Beatrice Wood: Mama of Dada - Stories in the Sand - Herb Albert: Music for Your Eyes - Our Country (IMAX)
COMMENTS: Archived footage

Tom Neff ....President

IMAGEMAKER FILMS

561 28th Ave.
Venice, CA 90291
PHONE 310-302-1001
FAX 310-302-1002
EMAIL ....steven@imagemakerfilms.com
WEB SITE ....www.imagemakerfilms.com
TYPES: Features - Made-for-TV/Cable Movies - TV Series
DEVELOPMENT: The House of the Scorpion - Upbeat - Untraceable - Coincidence - 49 - RFB - Oops the Beagle - Paducah (TV) - Gimme Shelter (TV)
CREDITS: Attraction - Lone Star State of Mind - The Dog Ate It - At First Sight

Steven Pearl ....Producer/Writer

IMAGEMOVERS

100 Universal City Plaza, Bldg. 484
Universal City, CA 91608
PHONE 818-733-8300
FAX 818-733-8301
TYPES: Features
DEALS: DreamWorks SKG
COMPLETED UNRELEASED: The Polar Express
CREDITS: Romancing the Stone - Used Cars - Forrest Gump - Back to the Future 1-3 - Who Framed Roger Rabbit? - Death Becomes Her - Contact - 1941 - What Lies Beneath - Cast Away - Matchstick Men

Robert Zemeckis ....Writer/Director/Producer
Steve Starkey ....Producer
Jack Rapke ....Producer
Bennett Schneir ....Head, Creative Affairs

IMAGERIES ENTERTAINMENT

2815 Coldwater Canyon Dr.
Beverly Hills, CA 90210
PHONE 310-278-7297
FAX 310-278-5085
TYPES: Features - Made-for-TV/Cable Movies - TV Series
DEVELOPMENT: Straight Ballin' - The Tension Ring - Elixir - Once in a Lifetime
PRE-PRODUCTION: North of Sunset
POST PRODUCTION: The Water Giant
CREDITS: Deep Freeze - Eyes of the Beholder - Men of Respect - Friday the 13th, Part VII - Curse of the Forty-Niner - The New Adventures of Pippi Longstocking - A Light in the Forest

Gary Mehlman ....Producer/Partner
Alexandra Mehlman ....Director, Development
John Buechler ....Writer/Director/Partner

IMAGINARIUM ENTERTAINMENT GROUP

723 Ocean Front Walk
Venice, CA 90291
PHONE 310-314-6400
FAX 310-388-5855
WEB SITE ....www.imaginariumeg.com
TYPES: Documentaries - Features - TV Series
DEVELOPMENT: A Rhinestone Alibi (Paramount) - American Empire: A Documentary
POST PRODUCTION: Collateral (DreamWorks)

Julie Richardson ....Producer/Partner
Nathan Holtz ....Producer/Partner
Theo Lacey ....Staff
Caitlin Lochridge ....Staff
John Orozco ....Staff

It is illegal to copy any part of this book

IMAGINARY FORCES
6526 Sunset Blvd.
Hollywood, CA 90028
PHONE .323-957-6868/646-486-6868
FAX .323-957-9577/646-486-4700
EMAIL .information@imaginaryforces.com
WEB SITE .www.imaginaryforces.com
TYPES — Animation - Commercials - Features - Interactive Games - Large Format - Music Videos - New Media - Promos
POST PRODUCTION — Blade: Trinity
CREDITS — Blade 1&2 - Juice - Boys - The Last Minute
COMMENTS — Conceptual design, marketing, main title design, corporate branding, environmental site design; East Coast office: 530 W. 25th St., 5th Fl., New York, NY 10001

Peter Frankfurt .Managing Partner/Creative Director
Chip Houghton .Managing Partner/Executive Producer
Saffron Kenny .Partner/Head, Production (NY)
Karin Fong . Partner/Creative Director
Mikon van Gastel .Partner/Creative Director (NY)
Stephanie Kemp .Head, Sales
Anita Olan .Head, Production (LA)
Ahmet Ahmet .Sr. Art Director
Brandy Armendariz .Marketing Director
Michelle Dougherty .Sr. Art Director
Sara Marandi .Sr. Art Director

IMAGINATION PRODUCTIONS, INC.
3000 W. Olympic Blvd.
Santa Monica, CA 90404
PHONE .310-315-4760
FAX .310-471-4597
WEB SITE .www.imaginationprods.com
TYPES — Features - Made-for-TV/Cable Movies - TV Series
DEVELOPMENT — High Alert - Larry Gelbart's Power Failure - Diary of an Immortal Man - Undercover Actress - Plenty of Money & You
CREDITS — The Don's Analyst - National Lampoon's Favorite Deadly Sins - Public Enemy #2 - Mastergate - The Ratings Game

David Jablin .Executive Producer/Director
Lee Biondi .Creative Executive

IMAGINE ENTERTAINMENT
9465 Wilshire Blvd., 7th Fl.
Beverly Hills, CA 90212
PHONE .310-858-2000
FAX .310-858-2020
WEB SITE .www.imagine-entertainment.com
TYPES — Features
DEALS — Universal Pictures
CREDITS — Cinderella Man - Friday Night Lights - A Beautiful Mind - 8 Mile

Brian Grazer .Chairman
Ron Howard .Chairman
Karen Kehela Sherwood .Co-Chairman, Imagine Films
Michael Rosenberg .President, Entertainment
Jim Whitaker .President, Production
Robin Barris .Sr. VP, Administration & Operations
Erica Huggins .Sr. VP, Motion Pictures
Kim Roth .Sr. VP, Motion Pictures
David Bernardi .VP, Motion Pictures
Christy Sterling .Controller
Sarah Bowen .Director, Development

(Continued)

IMAGINE ENTERTAINMENT (Continued)
Anna Culp .Creative Executive
Ittay Arad .Creative Associate
Kristen Bihr .Creative Associate
Brad Grossman .Special Projects
Chris Wade .Story Editor

IMAGINE TELEVISION
9465 Wilshire Blvd., 7th Fl.
Beverly Hills, CA 90212
PHONE .310-858-2000
FAX .310-858-2011
TYPES — TV Series
DEALS — Twentieth Century Fox Television
PRODUCTION — Quintuplets - The Inside
CREDITS — 24 - Arrested Development - Felicity

Brian Grazer .Chairman
Ron Howard .Chairman
David Nevins .President
Skip Chasey .Executive VP, Business Affairs
Katie O'Connell .Executive VP, Creative Affairs
Erin Nowocinski .Director, Current Programming
Elio Chavez Jr. .Coordinator, Business Affairs
Bianca Chern .Coordinator, Drama
Melanie Grodanz .Coordinator, Comedy

IMAX CORPORATION
3003 Exposition Blvd.
Santa Monica, CA 90404
PHONE .310-255-5500
FAX .310-315-1759
WEB SITE .www.imax.com
TYPES — Features - Animation - Documentaries - Large Format
DEVELOPMENT — Magnificent Desolation 3D - Denizens of the Deep 3D
CREDITS — NASCAR 3D - Harry Potter and the Prisoner of Azkaban: The IMAX Experience - Matrix Revolutions: The IMAX Experience - Matrix Reloaded: The IMAX Experience - Apollo 13: The IMAX Experience - Space Station 3D - Star Wars: Attack of the Clones - Santa vs. the Snowman 3D

Greg Foster .President, Filmed Entertainment
Meg Wilson .Sr. VP, Film Entertainment
Phil Groves .VP, Film Distribution & Development

IMPACT ENTERTAINMENT
468 N. Camden Dr., Ste. 200
Beverly Hills, CA 90210
PHONE .310-860-7669
FAX .310-860-7600
EMAIL .info@impactent.com
WEB SITE .www.impactent.com
TYPES — Features - New Media - TV Series
DEVELOPMENT — Abominable - Fortress 3000 - Conspiracy X - Ninja Burger - Monster Island - The Illusionist - Heart of Africa - Elsie Hooper
CREDITS — Fortress 1&2
SUBMISSION POLICY — No unsolicited submissions

Troy Neighbors .President
Brandon Thomas .VP, Development
Karla Huff .Creative Executive
Nick Mashkin .Production Assistant

IN MOTION PICTURES, INC.

8291 Presson Pl.
Los Angeles, CA 90069
PHONE .323-654-8662
FAX .323-654-0196
TYPES Features
CREDITS The Other Sister - Overboard - Frankie and Johnny - Norma Rae

Nabila Khashoggi .President
Alex Rose .President

INCOGNITO ENTERTAINMENT

9440 Santa Monica Blvd., Ste. 302
Beverly Hills, CA 90210
PHONE .310-246-1500
FAX .310-246-0469
EMAIL .incognito@pacbell.net
TYPES Features - Reality TV - TV Series
CREDITS Three to Tango - Morning - Freeway 2 - Modern Vampires

Lawrence Abramson .Owner/CEO
Andrew Howard .Executive
Christian Vigeland .Development

THE INDEPENDENT FILM CHANNEL (IFC)

200 Jericho Quadrangle
Jericho, NY 11753
PHONE .516-803-4500
FAX .516-803-4506
WEB SITE .www.ifctv.com
TYPES Features - Made-for-TV/Cable Movies - TV Series
CREDITS Dinner for Five - Rocked with Gina Gershon - Ultimate Film Fanatic - Film School

Joshua Sapan .CEO, Rainbow Programming Holdings, Inc.
Kathleen Dore .President, Entertainment Services
Jonathan Sehring .President, IFC Entertainment
Ed Carroll .Executive VP/General Manager, IFC Companies
Evan Shapiro .Sr. VP, Marketing
Caroline Kaplan .Sr. VP, Production & Development
Alison Bourke .Director, Original Programming
Debbie De Montreux .Director, Production & Development

INDIE GENIUS PRODUCTIONS

3230 N. Hall St.
Dallas, TX 75201
PHONE .214-526-0288
EMAIL .westmemphisthree@sbcglobal.net
WEB SITE .www.cxothemovie.com
TYPES Documentaries - Features - Made-for-TV/Cable Movies - Reality TV - TV Series
DEVELOPMENT The Duke - Walk On - Priority One
PRE-PRODUCTION West Memphis Three
CREDITS Thoth - The X-Files - Roswell - Stories from the Quilt
COMMENTS Drama, true stories, romantic comedies; Consulting producers

Curt Johnson .Producer

INDIGO FILMS

999 Andersen Dr., Ste. 110
San Rafael, CA 94901
PHONE .415-460-4870
FAX .415-460-0170
EMAIL .info@indigofilms.com
WEB SITE .www.indigofilms.com
TYPES Documentaries - Syndication - TV Series
PRE-PRODUCTION The Untold Story of Richard Nixon - Secrets of Voodoo - Exploding History!
PRODUCTION To the Shores of Tripoli - America's Best Haunted Places - Live Volcanoes! - Stormchasers
CREDITS Travel Channel's Best Of - History Undercover - Weird Places - City Cops
COMMENTS Los Angeles office: 11901 Santa Monica Blvd., Ste. 329, Los Angeles, CA 90025

David M. Frank .President
Rosemary Wall .Supervising Producer
Bree Ann Van Praag .Series Producer
Paul Sauer .Producer
Laurie Brian .Series Producer
Kim Hawkins .Series Producer
Sarah Kass .Producer
Julie Nelson .Producer
Lisa Mao .Manager, Program Development
Maida Counts .Production Supervisor

INDUSTRY ENTERTAINMENT

955 S. Carrillo Dr., 3rd Fl.
Los Angeles, CA 90048
PHONE .323-954-9000
FAX .323-954-9009
TYPES Features - Direct-to-Video/DVD - Made-for-TV/Cable Movies - Syndication - TV Series
DEALS Warner Bros. Entertainment Inc.
CREDITS 25th Hour - The Player - Sex, Lies, and Videotape - Drugstore Cowboy - The Yards - Fifteen Minutes - Requiem for a Dream - Quills - Becker (CBS) - Live from Baghdad (HBO) - War Stories (NBC)
COMMENTS Formerly Addis-Wechsler & Associates

Keith Addis .Managing Partner
Nick Wechsler .Managing Partner
Eryn Brown .Feature/TV Production
Sandra Chang .Feature/TV Production
Andrew Deane .Feature/TV Production
Scott Fish .TV Production
Helena Heyman .TV Production
Brad Mendelsohn .Feature/TV Production
Jeff Sommerville .Feature Production
Rosalie Swedlin .Feature/TV Production

INFINITY MEDIA, INC.

8000 Sunset Blvd., #B-310
Los Angeles, CA 90046
PHONE .323-848-8966
FAX .323-848-8727
EMAIL .watt@infinitymediainc.com
WEB SITE .www.infinitymediainc.com
TYPES Features
DEVELOPMENT Eye of the Raven - 99 Days
PRE-PRODUCTION Alicia's Book
PRODUCTION The Cave
CREDITS Mr. Ripley's Return - The Woods - Saved - The Final Cut - Confidence - Evelyn - Dead Heat - Frailty - The Human Stain - The Snow Walker

Michael Ohoven .CEO
Bill Vince .President
Joe Hobel .COO/Head, Production
Andrew Mann .CFO
Kerry Rock .VP, Acquisitions
Rob Merilees .Producer

It is illegal to copy any part of this book

INFRONT PRODUCTIONS

c/o Gary Loder/The Gersh Agency
232 N. Canon Dr.
Beverly Hills, CA 90210
PHONE 310-205-5828

TYPES	Features - Theater - TV Series
DEVELOPMENT	Makeover (Warner Bros., Feature) - Anonymous (Carsey-Werner-Mandabach, Pilot)
PRODUCTION	Honeymooners (Paramount, Feature) - Bang Room (Pasadena Playhouse)
CREDITS	Mad About You - Good Advice - Two Guys and a Girl - Roseanne - Davis Rules - Simon
SUBMISSION POLICY	All submissions must go to Gary Loder at the Gersh Agency

Danny Jacobson ....Writer/Producer
Marc Brener ....Associate Producer

INITIAL ENTERTAINMENT GROUP

3000 W. Olympic Blvd., Bldg. 2, Ste. 1550
Santa Monica, CA 90404
PHONE 310-315-1722
FAX 310-315-1723

TYPES	Features
DEALS	Appian Way
PRE-PRODUCTION	The Accidental Husband - The Good Sheperd
POST PRODUCTION	The Aviator - The Ballad of Jack and Rose - An Unfinished Life
CREDITS	Gangs of New York - Ali - The Dangerous Lives of Altar Boys - Traffic - Dr. T & the Women - Desert Saints - Joe the King - Savior - Little City - Montana
COMMENTS	Specializes in international distribution

Graham King ....President/CEO
Colin Cotter ....COO
Stephanie Denton ....President, International Distribution
Schuyler Ha ....VP, Marketing & Publicity
James Putt ....VP, Post Production Services

*INTEGRATED FILMS & MANAGEMENT

c/o The Lot
1041 N. Formosa Ave., Ste. 17
West Hollywood, CA 90046
PHONE 323-850-2668
FAX 323-850-2648

TYPES	Features - Made-for-TV/Cable Movies - TV Series
DEVELOPMENT	The Liberty (FX Studios)
PRE-PRODUCTION	The Amityville Horror - Tamara

Andy Trapani ....Principal
Steve Whitney ....Principal
Brendan Bragg ....Creative Executive
Chris Winvick ....Creative Executive

INTERMEDIA

INTERMEDIA FILM EQUITIES USA, INC.

9350 Civic Center Dr., Ste. 100
Beverly Hills, CA 90210
PHONE 310-777-0007/44-207-593-1630
FAX 310-777-0008/44-207-593-1639
EMAIL ....info@intermediafilm.com
WEB SITE ....www.intermediafilm.com

TYPES	Features
DEVELOPMENT	T4 - Tom Mix & Pancho Villa - Sleepwalker - Me Again - Shift - Number One Girl - Skeletons of the Sahara - Untitled DJ - Project - Fear Itself - Iron Curtain - Liberty - Abyssinia - In the Heart of the Sea - Time and Chance - Killer's Game - The Eleventh Hour - Viking - The Baghdad Blog - Shelter
POST PRODUCTION	Alexander
COMPLETED UNRELEASED	Mindhunters - Suspect Zero - If Only
CREDITS	Adaptation - Dark Blue - The Life of David Gale - K-PAX - Nurse Betty - The Wedding Planner - Iris - Sliding Doors - Playing by Heart - Hilary and Jackie - Terminator 3: The Rise of the Machines
SUBMISSION POLICY	No unsolicited submissions
COMMENTS	Munich office: Cuvilliésstraße 25, München 81679 Germany, phone: 49-89-9810-7100, fax: 49-89-9810-7199

Moritz Borman ....Chairman
Jon Gumpert ....Vice Chairman/Head, Motion Picture Operations
Bahman Naraghi ....COO
Scott Kroopf ....President, Motion Picture Group
Joel Sill ....President, Intermedia Music Group
Noel Lohr ....General Counsel
Gavin James ....Managing Director, UK Operations (London)
Linda Benjamin ....Executive VP, Business & Legal Affairs
Mary Beth Bambridge ....Sr. VP, Distribution & Finance
Dennis Higgins ....Sr. VP, Marketing & Corporate Communications
Robert Lacy ....Sr. VP, Controller
Mark McNair ....Sr. VP, Physical Production
Seana Adair ....VP, Human Resources
Tony Alessi ....VP, Film Finance
Saeed Daeenejad ....VP, Operations
Lindsey Dold ....VP, Development
Steve Freedman ....VP, Production Finance
Katya Kleiner ....VP, Corporate Affairs & Development
Alex Litvak ....VP, Development
Jason Sachs ....VP, Credit & Collections/Participants & Residuals
Michele Sanders ....VP, Accounting
Alison Haskovec ....Creative Executive
Devon Schiff ....Creative Executive
Sarah Harvey ....Development Executive (London)

INTERNATIONAL ARTS ENTERTAINMENT

8899 Beverly Blvd., Ste. 800
Los Angeles, CA 90048
PHONE 310-550-6760
FAX 310-550-8839
EMAIL ....info@internationalartsentertainment.com
WEB SITE ....www.internationalartsentertainment.com

TYPES	Features - TV Series
DEVELOPMENT	To Come Again - Untitled Sebastian Junger Project - Hand Me Down
PRE-PRODUCTION	Fever Pitch (Fox 2000)
POST PRODUCTION	A Good Woman
COMPLETED UNRELEASED	Bookies - My Little Eye
CREDITS	High Fidelity - Donnie Brasco - Best Laid Plans - 200 Cigarettes - My Little Eye - Pushing Tin

Alan Greenspan ....Owner/Producer
Kathryn Beck ....Creative Executive

INTERNATIONAL TELEVISION GROUP (ITG) - EPIX FILMS
1322 Second St.
Santa Monica, CA 90401
PHONE 310-656-9100
FAX 310-656-9104
EMAIL . . . . .info@epixfilms.com
WEB SITE . . . . .www.epixfilms.com
TYPES Commercials - Features - Music Videos - TV Series
DEVELOPMENT 8 Ball Chicks
CREDITS Cat on a Hot Tin Roof - Uncle Wally's General Store

Lou LaMonte . . . . .President/Executive Producer
Ish Muniz . . . . .Head, Music Video Division/Executive Producer
Teresa Campbell . . . . .VP, Production & Development

INTUITION PRODUCTIONS
1635 Cahuenga Dr., 5th Fl.
Los Angeles, CA 90028
PHONE 323-464-1682
EMAIL . . . . .intuitionamy@yahoo.com
TYPES Features - Made-for-TV/Cable Movies - TV Series
DEVELOPMENT Passengers - Spy Girl (Warner Bros.) - Marathon Guy
PRE-PRODUCTION Summer of '77 (UPN)
CREDITS The Stepford Wives (Paramount) - Three to Tango (Warner Bros.) - In the Company of Spies (Showtime) - Harlan County War (Showtime) - After the Rain (Capella International) - Point of Origin (HBO) - Mafia Doctor (CBS) - It Must Be Love (CBS)

Keri Selig . . . . .President/Producer
Amy Ficken . . . . .Assistant/Director

IRISH DREAMTIME
2450 Broadway, Ste. E-420
Santa Monica, CA 90404
PHONE 310-449-3411
FAX 310-586-8138
TYPES Features
DEALS Metro-Goldwyn-Mayer Studios, Inc.
DEVELOPMENT Lover's Leap - Mexicali
POST PRODUCTION The Matador
CREDITS Laws of Attraction - Evelyn - The Thomas Crown Affair (1999) - The Match - The Nephew
SUBMISSION POLICY No unsolicited material

Pierce Brosnan . . . . .Producer/Partner
Beau St. Clair . . . . .Producer/Partner
Angelique Higgins . . . . .Executive VP, Development
Amanda Scarano . . . . .Production Executive
Chris Charalambous . . . . .Creative Executive

IRONWORKS PRODUCTION
295 Greenwich St., Ste. 391
New York, NY 10007
PHONE 212-486-9829
FAX 212-486-9829
EMAIL . . . . .ironworksproductions@pobox.com
TYPES Documentaries - Features - Direct-to-Video/DVD - TV Series
DEVELOPMENT The Professionals - Plunge - Lions & Foxes - Heart of a Dog - Charlie Victor Romeo - Home Swap - Joyful Noise - 1-900 - Persons Living and Dead - Salon - Psychic Tea Party - In Darwin's Footsteps
CREDITS Trust - Curse of the Starving Class - Side Streets - Island of the Dead

Bruce Weiss . . . . .President
Isa Freeling . . . . .Executive VP, Development

IS OR ISN'T ENTERTAINMENT
4000 Warner Blvd., Bldg. 34, Rm. 100
Burbank, CA 91522
PHONE 818-954-4842
TYPES Features - TV Series
DEALS Warner Bros. Television Production
CREDITS Untitled Aisha Tyler Project (CBS Pilot) - Beck and Call (UPN Pilot)

Lisa Kudrow . . . . .Partner
Dan Bucatinsky . . . . .Partner
Danica Ross . . . . .Development Associate

ISHTAR FILMS
11333 Moorpark St., Ste. 460
Studio City, CA 91602
PHONE 800-428-7136/818-985-0567
FAX 818-753-0040
EMAIL . . . . .ishtarfilms@sbcglobal.net
WEB SITE . . . . .www.ishtarfilms.com
TYPES Documentaries - Made-for-TV/Cable Movies
PRODUCTION Untitled May Sarton Project - The Art of Aging
CREDITS Berenice Abbott: A View of the 20th Century - Votes for Women - Thistle Hotel - A Ring of Endless Light (Disney)
COMMENTS Independent filmmakers; Distributor; Producer of a dozen documentaries for educational and TV release

Martha Wheelock . . . . .President
Kay Weaver . . . . .CFO
Iris Caplan . . . . .Associate
Marita Giovanni . . . . .Associate

ITB CINEGROUP/TELEVISION
947 Nordica Dr.
Los Angeles, CA 90065
PHONE 323-258-5564
FAX 323-258-6634
EMAIL . . . . .quixotic@att.net
TYPES Features - TV Series
DEVELOPMENT Fusong - Sword Searchers - Slow Boat to China
PRE-PRODUCTION Ladies Coupé - Dragon Breath
PRODUCTION No More Señor Nice Guy
CREDITS Road to Hope - The Treatment - Dream Parlor - Criminal Act - Race, Religion & Racism - Family Mancuso - A Reason to Remember - The Price of Freedom
COMMENTS Deals with Timeless Entertainment, Micah Filmworks, Financeart, Asian Movie Works, Castle Peak Pictures, What If Entertainment, Adam Productions

Frank Antonelli . . . . .Writer/Producer
Mark Byers . . . . .Director/Producer/Writer
Heather Ashley . . . . .VP, Development
Ma Wai Yan . . . . .Production Executive

***ITHAKA**
4553 Glencoe Ave., Ste. 320
Marina del Rey, CA 90292
PHONE 310-314-9585/310-314-9588
FAX 310-399-0462
EMAIL . . . . .firstname_ithaka@lgecorp.com
TYPES Features - TV Series
DEALS Lions Gate Entertainment
DEVELOPMENT Amarillo Slim
PRE-PRODUCTION Man and Wife
PRODUCTION Untitled Jonathan Ames Show (Showtime)
COMPLETED UNRELEASED Mail Order Bride

Braxton Pope . . . . .Producer (braxton_ithaka@lgecorp.com)
Andrew Weiner . . . . .Producer (andrew_ithaka@lgecorp.com)

IVY FILMS
2677 Rutherford Dr.
Los Angeles, CA 90068
PHONE 323-464-2220
FAX 323-464-2226
EMAIL . . . . .contact@ivyfilms.com
WEB SITE . . . . .www.ivyfilms.com
SECOND WEB SITE . . . . .www.ivymediagroup.com
TYPES Features - New Media - TV Series
DEVELOPMENT Sally & Angela (Series) - Digital Classical Theatre
CREDITS Dischord
SUBMISSION POLICY No unsolicited material

Mark Wilkinson . . . . .Writer/Director/Producer
Nancy Trombacco . . . . .Producer

IXTLAN
1207 Fourth St., Penthouse 1
Santa Monica, CA 90401
PHONE 310-395-0525
FAX 310-395-1536
EMAIL . . . . .ixtlancorp@aol.com
TYPES Documentaries - Features
POST PRODUCTION Alexander
CREDITS Born on the Fourth of July - JFK - Nixon - Any Given Sunday - Heaven and Earth - Salvador - People vs. Larry Flynt - Comandante - The Corruptor - Assassinated - Gravesend - Killer - Freeway - Indictment: The McMartin Trial - The New Age - The Joy Luck Club - Wild Palms - Zebrahead - South Central - Iron Maze - Blue Stell - Reversal of Fortune
SUBMISSION POLICY No unsolicited material

Oliver Stone . . . . .Writer/Director
Rob Wilson . . . . .No Title
Takae Shimizu . . . . .No Title

J2 ENTERTAINMENT, INC.
11684 Ventura Blvd., Ste. 968
Studio City, CA 91604
PHONE 818-980-8114
FAX 818-980-8115
EMAIL . . . . .J2asst@aol.com
TYPES Animation - Features - Reality TV - TV Series
DEVELOPMENT His Roof, Her Rules - Reality Check - Down & Out - Larger Than Life - Bare Necessities - Untitled Foreman Project - Romance & Cigarettes

Justin Berfield . . . . .Partner/Actor/Producer
Jason Felts . . . . .Partner/Writer/Producer
Brad Alesi . . . . .Partner/elevate
Kurt Fedderson . . . . .VP, Finance
Leslie Boydt . . . . .Assistant to K. Fedderson

JACK ANGEL PRODUCTIONS INC.
2044 Stanley Hills Dr.
Los Angeles, CA 90046
PHONE 323-650-3392
EMAIL . . . . .lisajolin@aol.com
TYPES Features - Made-for-TV/Cable Movies - TV Series
DEVELOPMENT Illusion - Phrackers - Casey's Fort - Lena Sharpe
CREDITS Roswell - Dying to Live

Lisa J. Olin . . . . .Producer

JAFFE/BRAUNSTEIN FILMS, LTD.
12301 Wilshire Blvd., Ste. 110
Los Angeles, CA 90025
PHONE 310-207-6600
TYPES Made-for-TV/Cable Movies - TV Series
DEVELOPMENT The Great Escape - Elvis
PRODUCTION Evel Knievel - The Brooke Ellison Story
CREDITS Nero Wolfe (A&E) - 100 Centre Street (A&E) - The Rosa Parks Story - It's Always Something: The Gilda Radner Story - Sounder - Martha, Inc. - Behind the Camera: The Unauthorized Story of Charlie's Angels - 10.5 - Word of Honor - Undercover Christmas
SUBMISSION POLICY Must have representation by an agent and/or lawyer

Michael Jaffe . . . . .Partner
Howard Braunstein . . . . .Partner
John Hassig . . . . .Business Affairs Attorney
Kerry Wagner . . . . .Business Affairs Associate
Lynn Delaney . . . . .Assistant to Mr. Jaffe/Office Manager
Victor Boutrous . . . . .Assistant to Mr. Braunstein

JAFFILMS, LLC
745 Fifth Ave., Ste. 1604
New York, NY 10151
PHONE .212-262-4700/310-860-0595
FAX .212-223-0032/310-860-0566
TYPES Features - Made-for-TV/Cable Movies
DEVELOPMENT Crossing to Safety - Madness
CREDITS Four Feathers - I Dreamed of Africa - Madeline - The Accused - Fatal Attraction - Kramer vs. Kramer - Taps

Stanley R. Jaffe .Producer
Bob Jaffe .Producer
Megan Cannan .Assistant to Stanley Jaffe (NY)

JANICEK-MARINO CREATIVE
600 Ogden St.
Denver, CO 80218
PHONE .303-860-0070
FAX .303-837-8451
EMAIL .cre8vtv@aol.com
WEB SITE .www.janicekmarino.com
TYPES Commercials - Documentaries - Features - Direct-to-Video/DVD - TV Series
DEALS Buena Vista Home Entertainment - Starz Encore Group, LLC - The Walt Disney Company
DEVELOPMENT Baby Einstein Series - UTV Channel Launch
PRE-PRODUCTION Features: Black Swallow; TV: Guys Guide - Life ED - Rock by Baby - Family Tree - Bunford T.E. Bunny - Expecting Adam Feature
PRODUCTION Baby Monet
POST PRODUCTION Baby Safari
CREDITS Baby Neptune - Ancient Secrets of Life - Winnie the Pooh/Book of Pooh Documentary - ABC TGIF - Baby Einstein Videos - ABC Specials - Baby Einstein's Numbers Nursery - Baby McDonald
SUBMISSION POLICY No unsolicited submissions
COMMENTS Branding; Agent: Innovative Artists, Marcia Hurwitz, 310-656-5144; Deal with The Baby Einstein Company

Jim Janicek .President/Executive Producer
Len Marino .Partner/Executive Producer
Jane Pahl .Production Assistant

JANUS FILMS, LLC
265 E. 66th St., Ste. 16-D
New York, NY 10021
PHONE .212-396-9209
FAX .212-327-0541
WEB SITE .www.janusfilms.net
TYPES Features
DEVELOPMENT By Grand Central Station I Sat Down and Wept - Sell by Date - Bodies - Change
COMPLETED UNRELEASED Romance and Cigarettes
CREDITS Kart Racer - Among Giants - Investigating Sex - Advice from a Caterpillar - Top of the Foodchain - The Incredible Mrs. Ritchie

Jana Edelbaum .President
Robin Gold .Development Executive

JARET ENTERTAINMENT
6973 Birdview Ave.
Malibu, CA 90265
PHONE .310-589-9600
FAX .310-589-9602
EMAIL .info@jaretentertainment.com
WEB SITE .www.jaretentertainment.com
TYPES Features - TV Series
DEVELOPMENT Face First - Girl in the Curl
PRE-PRODUCTION The Cold
CREDITS 10 Things I Hate About You
COMMENTS Publishing

Seth Jaret .CEO/Producer
Adam Jaret .Creative Executive

MELINDA JASON COMPANY
1011 N. Alfred St., Ste. 100
West Hollywood, CA 90069
PHONE .310-274-9122
TYPES Features - Made-for-TV/Cable Movies - TV Series
DEALS Mutual Film Company
DEVELOPMENT Sweet Talk - Love Spell - We Make Your Dreams Come True (Fox TV/Mark Gordon)
PRE-PRODUCTION Secrets (Showtime/Mark Gordon/Love Spell)
PRODUCTION Untitled Dramedy (Paramount Pictures)
CREDITS The First Power - Eve of Destruction - Body of Evidence - Killer
SUBMISSION POLICY No unsolicited submissions

Melinda Jason .President

JAZZ PICTURES, INC.
202 N. Beverly Dr.
Beverly Hills, CA 90210-5303
PHONE .310-888-2412
FAX .310-888-2454
TYPES Features
CREDITS Mercy - Bad Company - Little Boy Blue - Claudine's Return

Amedeo A. Ursini .President/Producer

JCS ENTERTAINMENT II
12400 Wilshire Blvd., Ste. 1500
Los Angeles, CA 90025
PHONE .213-999-3019
EMAIL .jcsent2@aol.com
TYPES Documentaries - Made-for-TV/Cable Movies - TV Series - Reality TV
DEVELOPMENT The Challengers - Coco Chanel (MOW) - Earth Angels
PRODUCTION P.S.I. for Young Teens (Documentary)
CREDITS America's Greatest Pets - Ripley's Believe It or Not - Stay the Night - Something Borrowed/Blue - P.S.I. for Teens (Documentary)

J.C. Shardo .Executive Producer/President
Lisa Ferrell .Director, Development

It is illegal to copy any part of this book

JENKINS ENTERTAINMENT

6080 Center Dr., 6th Fl.
Los Angeles, CA 90045
PHONE .310-242-6662
FAX .310-242-5201
EMAIL dallas@jenkins-entertainment.com
WEB SITE www.jenkins-entertainment.com
TYPES Features - Direct-to-Video/DVD - Made-for-TV/Cable Movies
DEVELOPMENT Twas the Night Before - The Man Who Moved a Mountain
PRE-PRODUCTION Though None Go with Me
CREDITS Hometown Legend

Dallas Jenkins .President/Producer
Jerry B. Jenkins .CEO/Executive Producer

JERICHO ENTERTAINMENT

c/o A Pictures
3015 Main St., 4th Fl.
Santa Monica, CA 90405
PHONE .310-709-4860
FAX .310-455-6114
EMAIL jericho@jerichoentertainment.com
TYPES Features - Made-for-TV/Cable Movies - TV Series
DEALS Davis Entertainment Company
PRE-PRODUCTION Five Fingers - Living & Breathing
CREDITS Bobbie's Girl - The Hebrew Hammer

Josh Kesselman .Partner
Dustin White .CFO
Greg Corbin .VP, Development

JERSEY FILMS

PO Box 491246
Los Angeles, CA 90049
PHONE .310-550-3200
FAX .310-550-3210
TYPES Features
CREDITS Along Came Polly - Erin Brockovich - Man on the Moon - Living Out Loud - Out of Sight - Gattaca - Feeling Minnesota - Sunset Park - Get Shorty - Reality Bites - Pulp Fiction - Hoffa - 8 Seconds

Danny DeVito .No Title
Nikki Allyn Grosso .Business Manager

JERSEY TELEVISION

9465 Wilshire Blvd., Ste. 950
Beverly Hills, CA 90212
PHONE .310-887-1176
FAX .310-887-1110
TYPES TV Series
DEALS Sony Pictures Television
CREDITS Reno 911 (Comedy Central) - Karen Sisco (ABC) - American Embassy (Fox) - UC Undercover (NBC) - Kate Brasher (CBS)

Danny DeVito .Partner
Michael Shamberg .Partner
Stacey Sher .Partner
Ellie Hannibal .Sr. VP, TV
Ryanne Kim .Manager

JIGSAW PICTURES

1645 Mohawk St.
Los Angeles, CA 90026
PHONE .213-484-0486/213-864-2307
FAX .323-927-1810
EMAIL jrohn@jigsawpictures.net
SECOND EMAIL spark@jigsawpictures.net
WEB SITE www.jigsawpictures.net
TYPES Animation - Documentaries - Features
DEVELOPMENT Viva la Mega Babe - Liberty
COMPLETED UNRELEASED Hale Bopp
CREDITS Anne B. Real - Amerikan Passport

Jeanine Rohn .Producer
Steve Parker .Producer

THE JINKS/COHEN COMPANY

100 Universal City Plaza, Bldg. 1320, Ste. 3-E
Universal City, CA 91608
PHONE .818-777-9880
FAX .818-866-9843
TYPES Features - TV Series
DEALS DreamWorks SKG
POST PRODUCTION The Forgotten
CREDITS American Beauty - Big Fish - Down with Love

Dan Jinks .Producer
Bruce Cohen .Producer
Sam Hansen .Director, Development
Bree Tichy .Assistant to Dan Jinks & Bruce Cohen

JOADA PRODUCTIONS, INC.

1437 Rising Glen Rd., Ste. 423
Los Angeles, CA 90069
PHONE .310-652-6263
FAX .310-652-2995
EMAIL joadaproductions@cs.com
TYPES Features - Made-for-TV/Cable Movies
DEVELOPMENT The Bell Ringer - Bring Her Back Alive - Love Related
PRE-PRODUCTION Lift Every Voice - Double Dutch (Co-Production with Letnom Productions)
CREDITS Grizzly Adams and the Legend of Dark Mountain - Secrets of a Small Town - Sheba Baby - Grizzly - The Guardian - Predator - Lovely but Deadly - Just Before Dawn
COMMENTS Owns and operates The Hollywood Writers Studio

David Sheldon .Producer/Director/CEO
Joan McCall .President, Production & Development
Boyd Aug .VP, Business Affairs
Ed Roberts .Director, Development
China Winston .Creative Executive
William Meringoff .Director, Marketing

JOEL FILMS

11718 Gwynne Lane
Los Angeles, CA 90077
PHONE .310-476-4041/310-880-9692
FAX .310-889-0060
EMAIL .joelfilms@aol.com

TYPES	Features
DEVELOPMENT	Useless Eaters - Alone (Empty World) - The End - Sicario 2 - Clifford Un-Authorized
PRE-PRODUCTION	A Distant Place
POST PRODUCTION	The Boss
COMPLETED UNRELEASED	A Step Forward (Punto y Raya)
CREDITS	The Big World - Pedro Navaja - Borrowed Land - Agony - Sicario (Assassins for Hire) - Glue Sniffer - Devil Gold

Joseph Novoa .Director/Producer
Elia Schneider .Director/Producer
Joel Novoa .Director/Producer
Santiago Rindel .Producer
Isabel N. Meneses .International Relations
Rafael Schneider .Associate Producer
Ibi Schneider .Associate Producer
Gaby Rindel .Associate

JOHN FOGEL ENTERTAINMENT GROUP

612 S. Flower St.
Los Angeles, CA 90017
PHONE .310-441-5906
EMAIL .jafent@aol.com

TYPES	Features
DEVELOPMENT	Protection (Twentieth Century Fox) - Switcheroo (Revolution) - Second Time Around (DreamWorks) - 7th Game (MGM-UA) - The Confidence Game
COMMENTS	Formerly JAF Entertainment; Develops high-concept features from scratch only

John Fogel .Producer
Joel Newton .Director, Development
Adam Barnes .Assistant

MAGIC JOHNSON ENTERTAINMENT

9100 Wilshire Blvd., Ste. 700-E
Beverly Hills, CA 90212
PHONE .310-247-2033/310-247-2030
FAX .310-786-8796

TYPES	Animation - Documentaries - Features - Direct-to-Video/DVD - Made-for-TV/Cable Movies - TV Series
DEVELOPMENT	Keep It Cool - The Tour - Hit Squad - A Little Magic
PRODUCTION	Crossover (Showtime Documentary)
POST PRODUCTION	Untitled Beauty Shop Movie
CREDITS	Passing Glory (TNT) - Brown Sugar (Fox Searchlight) - Who's Got Game? (MTV)

Earvin Johnson .CEO
Nikkole Denson .President

BRIDGET JOHNSON FILMS

1416 N. La Brea Ave.
Hollywood, CA 90028
PHONE .323-802-1749

TYPES	Features - Made-for-TV/Cable Movies
DEVELOPMENT	The Basic Eight - Going Public - Meet John Trow - An American Love Story - For Better, for Worse - I'm a Tiger - The Paisley Years - Smart People
PRODUCTION	Ice Princess (aka Skate)
CREDITS	As Good As It Gets - Riding in Cars with Boys - Joy Ride
SUBMISSION POLICY	No unsolicited material

Bridget Johnson .Producer
Kendra Oat-Judge .Creative Executive

DON JOHNSON PRODUCTIONS

9876 Wilshire Blvd., Ste. 33
Beverly Hills, CA 90210
PHONE .310-887-6001

TYPES	Features - TV Series
CREDITS	In the Company of Darkness - The Horatio Alger Awards - The Marshall - Nash Bridges - Word of Honor

Don Johnson .CEO/Executive Producer
J.B. Moresco .Assistant

JOSEPHSON ENTERTAINMENT

10201 W. Pico Blvd., Bldg. 50
Los Angeles, CA 90035
PHONE .310-369-7501
FAX .310-969-0898

TYPES	Features - TV Series
DEALS	Twentieth Century Fox

Barry Josephson .Producer
Ami Vitori .VP, Production & Development
Bridget Humphrey .Creative Executive
Alex Young .Assistant to Barry Josephson

JPH PRODUCTIONS

3469 Wonder View Pl.
Los Angeles, CA 90068
PHONE .323-874-7254

TYPES	Features - Made-for-TV/Cable Movies - TV Series
DEVELOPMENT	Devil May Care (Series) - Babe in Paradise
POST PRODUCTION	Unauthorized (VH1)
CREDITS	Rockstrology - Legalese - Truth or Consequences, N.M.

J. Paul Higgins .Producer

JTN PRODUCTIONS
13743 Ventura Blvd., Ste. 200
Sherman Oaks, CA 91423
PHONE .818-789-5891
FAX .818-789-5892
EMAIL .staff@jtnproductions.com
WEB SITE .www.jtnproductions.com
TYPES Documentaries - Made-for-TV/Cable Movies - New Media - Reality TV - Syndication - TV Series
PRE-PRODUCTION Great Synagogues of the World - For Better or Worse - The Jewish Americans - The Road to Peace - The Old Neighborhood - Yearnings
CREDITS PBS: A Chanukah Celebration - A Passover Celebration - Simple Wisdom with Irwin Kula - New Jewish Cuisine - No Safe Place - The 92nd Street Y Presents - Alef...Bet...Blast-off! - HomeStyles

Jay Sanderson .CEO
Harvey Lehrer .VP, Production

JUDGE-BELSHAW ENTERTAINMENT, INC.
4655 Kingswell Ave., Ste. 208
Los Angeles, CA 90027
PHONE .323-662-3365
FAX .323-662-3313
EMAIL .mail@judgebelshaw.com
WEB SITE .www.judgebelshaw.com
TYPES Features - TV Series
DEVELOPMENT The Last Truce - The Bride - Untitled TV Pilots
PRODUCTION Dirtysomethings
POST PRODUCTION Food for Thought
CREDITS Actual Jokes (HBO) - Urban Myths (Hypnotic) - Shanhan's Army (CBS) - Office Party (HBO) - Ratchet (Feature)

George Belshaw .Partner
Jonathan Judge .Partner

JUNCTION ENTERTAINMENT
500 S. Buena Vista St., Animation Bldg., Ste. 1-B
Burbank, CA 91521-1616
PHONE .818-560-2800
FAX .818-841-3176
TYPES Features
DEALS The Walt Disney Company
DEVELOPMENT Fraternity Brothers
POST PRODUCTION National Treasure
CREDITS Instinct - Phenomenon - While You Were Sleeping - The Kid

Jon Turteltaub .Producer/Director
Christina Steinberg .President/Producer
Dominique Fichera .Director, Development
Karim Zreik .Director, Development
Dan Shotz .Creative Associate
Trisha Ward .Creative Associate

JUNCTION FILMS
9615 Brighton Way, Ste. 320
Beverly Hills, CA 90210
PHONE .310-246-9799
FAX .310-246-3824
EMAIL .bwhibbs@aol.com
TYPES Features - New Media - TV Series - Reality TV
DEVELOPMENT Triptych - Street Racer - Gray
PRE-PRODUCTION .45
POST PRODUCTION Tiptoes - The Method - Blessed
CREDITS Case of Evil - Freeway - Trees Lounge - Love & Sex - Barb Wire - Monster

Brad Wyman .Producer
Donald Kushner .Producer
Salome Breziner .VP
David Alvarado .Creative Executive

JURIST PRODUCTIONS
215 W. 20th St.
New York, NY 10011
PHONE .212-627-4660
FAX .212-242-9056
TYPES Features - Made-for-TV/Cable Movies - TV Series
CREDITS Without Warning: Terror in the Towers - Stolen from the Heart

Madelon Rosenfeld .Producer/President
Ira Block .VP

JUST SINGER ENTERTAINMENT
4242 Tujunga Ave.
Studio City, CA 91604
PHONE .818-506-2400
FAX .818-506-2409
TYPES Features - Made-for-TV/Cable Movies - Miniseries - TV Series
DEVELOPMENT The Accidental Virgin - Stick It - Out of Time
PRE-PRODUCTION One Minute Soaps
POST PRODUCTION Halloweentown 3 - Crimes of Fashion
CREDITS The Luck of the Irish - Halloweentown 1&2 - Jackie, Ethel, Joan: Women of Camelot - Double Teamed - Right on Track - One Minute Soap
SUBMISSION POLICY Through signatory reps only

Sheri Singer .Executive Producer/Owner
Dena Hysell .Manager, Development

K2 PRODUCTIONS
c/o Electric Entertaiment
5707 Melrose Ave.
Los Angeles, CA 90038-3807
PHONE .323-817-1308
FAX .323-467-7280
TYPES Features - TV Series
CREDITS Wild America (Warner Bros.) - Dear God (Paramount) - American History X (New Line Cinema)
COMMENTS Foreign co-productions for theatrical release and overseas TV

Kearie Peak .Producer
Josef Steinberger .Producer, German Office
Thomas Leong .IPA, Hong Kong
Jonathan Strauss .Associate

KAHN POWER PICTURES

818 N. Doheny Dr., Ste. 1003
West Hollywood, CA 90069
PHONE . . . 310-550-0770/310-550-8708
FAX . . . 310-550-6292
EMAIL . . . iampower2003@yahoo.com
WEB SITE . . . www.artists4film.com
TYPES Features - Made-for-TV/Cable Movies
CREDITS Gia - Stalin - Fatherland - Roswell - White Mile - Buffalo Soldiers - Out of the Gate: The Sirr Parker Story - Hot Spot - The Dead Hollywood Moms Society - Traffic - Open House - Traffic: The Miniseries
SUBMISSION POLICY No unsolicited submissions

Derek Power . . . Chairman
Ilene Kahn Power . . . President/Executive Producer (310-550-8708)
Jeremy Kahn . . . New Media

RONALD J. KAHN PRODUCTIONS

87 Old Mill Rd.
Great Neck, NY 11023
PHONE . . . 516-466-8394/323-665-7443
TYPES Features - Made-for-TV/Cable Movies - Theater - TV Series
DEVELOPMENT The Spy - Blood Diamonds - The Freak Box - Surrender - The Golf War
CREDITS The Lawrenceville Stories (aka The Prodigious Hickey)

Ronald J. Kahn . . . Producer
Sasha Kahn . . . Writer/Producer

KANPAI PICTURES

7807 Sunset Blvd.
Los Angeles, CA 90046
PHONE . . . 323-883-0725
EMAIL . . . mail@kanpaipictures.com
WEB SITE . . . www.kanpaipictures.com
TYPES Animation - Documentaries - Features - Reality TV - TV Series
DEVELOPMENT A Trip to the Inn
PRODUCTION Channel 101 (FX, Pilot) - Women in Hollywood (AMC Special) - Gordian (Sci-Fi, Animated Pilot)
CREDITS Osbourne Family Christmas Special (MTV) - Under Exposed (Bravo Pilot) - My VH1 Music Awards 2000/2001 - VH1 Fashion Awards 2000 - VH1 ILLUSTRATED - WB Presents Teen People's What's Next

Jay Karas . . . Executive Producer/Director
Andee Kuroda . . . Executive Producer/Director

MARTY KAPLAN

3502 Watt Way
Los Angeles, CA 90089-0281
PHONE . . . 213-740-9945
FAX . . . 213-740-3772
EMAIL . . . mkaplan@aol.com
TYPES Features - TV Series
CREDITS Noises Off - The Distinguished Gentleman - Max Q

Marty Kaplan . . . President

KAPLAN/PERRONE ENTERTAINMENT, LLC

10202 W. Washington Blvd., Astaire Bldg., Ste. 3003
Culver City, CA 90232
PHONE . . . 310-244-6681
FAX . . . 310-244-2151
WEB SITE . . . www.kaplanperrone.com
TYPES Features - TV Series
DEALS Escape Artists
DEVELOPMENT Knowing

Aaron Kaplan . . . No Title
Sean Perrone . . . No Title

KAREEM PRODUCTIONS

5458 Wilshire Blvd.
Los Angeles, CA 90036
PHONE . . . 310-201-7960
FAX . . . 310-201-7964
TYPES Features - TV Series
COMMENTS Theatrical agent, Mike Eisenstadt, phone: 323-939-1188

Kareem Abdul-Jabbar . . . President
Hanna Broda . . . Assistant

KARST PRODUCTIONS

PO Box 2606
Malibu, CA 90265
PHONE . . . 818-880-4299
FAX . . . 818-880-5399
EMAIL . . . patricekarst@aol.com
TYPES Documentaries - Features - TV Series
DEVELOPMENT In the Beginning
COMMENTS Looking for spiritual, metaphysical and inspirational properties

Patrice Karst . . . President

KARZ ENTERTAINMENT

1149 N. Gower St., Ste. 201
Los Angeles, CA 90038
PHONE . . . 323-785-2123
FAX . . . 323-785-2117
TYPES Features - Made-for-TV/Cable Movies - TV Series
DEALS New Line Cinema
CREDITS Malibu's Most Wanted - Max Keeble's Big Move - The Jamie Kennedy Experiment - Joe and Max - Geppetto - My Date with the President's Daughter - Model Behavior - Spring Break Lawyer
SUBMISSION POLICY Through representation only

Mike Karz . . . Producer
Russell Hollander . . . Sr. VP, Production
Katherine Brown . . . Creative Executive
Josh Weinstock . . . Development Associate

KASSIRER AV PICTURES
4669 Del Moreno Dr.
Woodland Hills, CA 91364
PHONE 818-340-9800/44-207-758-1484
FAX 818-346-5276
TYPES: Features - Direct-to-Video/DVD - Syndication - TV Series
DEALS: MAC Releasing
PRE-PRODUCTION: Dead Run - Filmmaker - Wild Country - Dead Wrong
PRODUCTION: The Last Ride - Sex Machine - Cabbages and Queens
POST PRODUCTION: School for Seduction
COMPLETED UNRELEASED: Capital Punishment - The Driver - Dog
CREDITS: North Shore Fish - Double Edge - In God We Trust - Dog Soldiers - The Real Howard Spitz - House! - Death Machine
COMMENTS: Packaging and financing of studio and independent films and TV; UK office: 102 Dean St., 3rd Fl., London W1D 3TQ UK

Allan M. Kassirer ....Producer
Victor Bateman ....Producer
Angad Paul ....Producer

KATALYST FILMS
1633 26th St., 2nd Fl.
Santa Monica, CA 90404
PHONE 310-907-2236
FAX 310-907-2456
TYPES: Features - TV Series
DEALS: Beacon, A Division of Holding Pictures - Twentieth Century Fox Television
DEVELOPMENT: Overtime (Tapestry/WB) - Breakups Are Their Business - Random Acts of Kindness (Beacon) - The Dinner Party (Sony)
CREDITS: Punk'd - The Butterfly Effect
SUBMISSION POLICY: No unsolicited submissions

Ashton Kutcher ....Partner
Jason Goldberg ....Partner
Ilana Darsky ....Creative Executive
TJ Jefferson ....Executive Assistant to Jason Goldberg

KATIE FACE PRODUCTIONS
13351 Riverside Dr., Ste. 610
Sherman Oaks, CA 91423
PHONE 818-986-0634
FAX 818-986-0913
TYPES: Made-for-TV/Cable Movies - TV Series
DEVELOPMENT: The Governor George Ryan Story (Showtime)
PRODUCTION: The Tony Danza Show (Talk Show)
CREDITS: Hudson Street - Before They Were Stars - Bermuda Triangle - Crowned and Dangerous - The Tony Danza Show (Sitcom)

Tony Danza ....Principal
Tamara Holmes ....Sr. VP, TV
George Sealey ....VP, Development

MARTY KATZ PRODUCTIONS
3000 Olympic Blvd.
Santa Monica, CA 90404
PHONE 310-264-3948
FAX 310-264-3949
EMAIL ....martykatzproductions@earthlink.net
TYPES: Features
DEALS: Dimension Films - Miramax Films
PRE-PRODUCTION: Revolver
POST PRODUCTION: The Great Raid
CREDITS: Man of the House - Lost in America - Mr. Wrong - Reindeer Games - Impostor - The Four Feathers

Marty Katz ....Producer
Tiffany Tiesiera ....VP, Development
Campbell Katz ....Director, Development

PERRY KATZ PRODUCTIONS
3917 Van Noord Ave.
Studio City, CA 91604
PHONE 818-981-0232
FAX 818-981-6451
EMAIL ....pkatz1@aol.com
TYPES: Features
CREDITS: Flipper - McHale's Navy - Crocodile Dundee in Los Angeles

Perry Katz ....President

JON KATZMAN PRODUCTIONS
509 Westbourne Dr.
West Hollywood, CA 90048
PHONE 310-652-5902
FAX 310-652-0579
TYPES: Features - Made-for-TV/Cable Movies - TV Series
PRE-PRODUCTION: Family Values (VH1)
CREDITS: You're Killing Me - Redemption (FX)

Jon Katzman ....President/Executive Producer
Brian Jones ....Director, Development

THE KAUFMAN COMPANY
15030 Ventura Blvd., Ste. 510
Sherman Oaks, CA 91403
PHONE 818-990-1240
EMAIL ....info@thekaufmancompany.com
WEB SITE ....www.thekaufmancompany.com
TYPES: Features - Made-for-TV/Cable Movies - TV Series
DEVELOPMENT: Billy Liar - The Last Safari - The Owen Hart Story - Appointment with Dr. Death
CREDITS: Return to the Batcave - Surviving Gilligan's Island - Run the Wild Fields - Jewel

Paul A. Kaufman ....Executive Producer

KDD PRODUCTIONS, LLC

156 S. Irving Blvd.
Los Angeles, CA 90004
PHONE 323-461-3379

TYPES	Documentaries - Features - Made-for-TV/Cable Movies - TV Series
DEVELOPMENT	Hostile Hallways (Documentary) - Big Trouble (A&E) - The Infamous Harris Boys (Hearst/Lifetime) - Consider This Señora (Handprint/Lifetime)
CREDITS	Scattering Dad (CBS) - Somebody's Daughter (ABC) - Special Bulletin (NBC) - Under Siege (NBC) - Anya's Bell (CBS) - Blackout (NBC) - Cold Sassy Tree (TNT) - Crazy in Love (TNT) - Devil's Child (ABC) - Nickel & Dimed (Showtime)
SUBMISSION POLICY	No unsolicited material

Karen Danaher-Dorr ....Executive Producer
Lynne Bover ....VP, Development

KECKINS PROJECTS, LTD.

Attorney Allen Arrow/Shugett and Arrow
111 W. 57th St.
New York, NY 10107
PHONE 212-645-0049
EMAIL ....keckinsprojects@aol.com

TYPES	Features - Made-for-TV/Cable Movies - TV Series
DEVELOPMENT	The Other Woman - Timed Out Credentials
PRE-PRODUCTION	The Hive
CREDITS	The Simian Line - Northern Lights - Parallel Lives - Everybody Wins - Chantilly Lace - Playing for Time - End of Summer - Second Serve - Mayflower - Looking Up
SUBMISSION POLICY	No unsolicted material

Linda Yellen ....Director/Writer
Martin Yellen ....Executive VP
James Reifenberg ....Development

KEDZIE PRODUCTIONS

8615 Tamarack Ave.
Sun Valley, CA 91352
PHONE 818-252-6129
FAX 818-504-3508

TYPES	Made-for-TV/Cable Movies - TV Series
CREDITS	The Division - Any Day Now - Dawson's Creek (Pilot) - Courthouse - Lois and Clark

Deborah Joy LeVine ....Executive Producer/Writer
David Lloyd ....Assistant

KEEVE PRODUCTIONS

12727 Mitchell Ave., Ste. 102
Los Angeles, CA 90066
PHONE 310-390-8311
EMAIL ....fred@keeveproductions.com
WEB SITE ....www.keeveproductions.com

TYPES	Animation - Documentaries - Features - Made-for-TV/Cable Movies - TV Series
DEVELOPMENT	Letters from Heaven - Suddenly Last Summer - Designated Caretaker - When the Fat Girl Sings - Naked Speed - Rogue - Apartment Zero - Drifters - Bottom of the Barrel - Life as a Whole Note - The Oasis - Adventures of a Stick
CREDITS	From Russia to Hollywood - Florida City

Frederick Keeve ....President/Owner/Filmmaker
Tristen Cutler ....Director, Imagination
Brad Chmielewski ....Webmaster

KELLER ENTERTAINMENT GROUP

c/o Micheline Keller
1093 Broxton Ave., Ste. 246
Los Angeles, CA 90024
PHONE 310-443-2226
FAX 310-443-2194
EMAIL ....kirt@kellerentertainment.com
WEB SITE ....www.kellerentertainmentgroup.com

TYPES	Features - Made-for-TV/Cable Movies - Syndication - TV Series
DEVELOPMENT	Tug of War (Feature) - Gypsy of the Silk Road (TV) - Ramses (TV)
PRE-PRODUCTION	Wyland's World (TV) - Blood Brothers (Feature)
POST PRODUCTION	Bug Spreaders (Short Film)
CREDITS	Conan - Tarzan - Acapulco Heat - Summer of Fear - Women of Valor - Kent State

Max Keller ....Chairman
Micheline Keller ....President
Kirt Eftekhar ....VP
Alex King ....Administrator
David Keller ....Writer/Director

DAVID E. KELLEY PRODUCTIONS

1600 Rosecrans Ave., Bldg. 4-B
Manhattan Beach, CA 90266
PHONE 310-727-2200

TYPES	Features - TV Series
DEALS	Twentieth Century Fox Television
CREDITS	Picket Fences - Chicago Hope - The Practice - Lake Placid - Ally McBeal - Mystery, Alaska - Snoops - Boston Public - girls club - The Brotherhood of Poland, New Hampshire - Boston Legal

David E. Kelley ....CEO/Writer/Executive Producer
Rick Silverman ....COO
Bob Breech ....Sr. VP
Veronica Wilson ....Sr. VP, Legal Affairs
Neely Swanson ....VP, Business Affairs
Stacey M. Luchs ....VP, Media Relations & Publicity

THE KENNEDY/MARSHALL COMPANY

619 Arizona Ave.
Santa Monica, CA 90401
PHONE 310-656-8400
FAX 310-656-8430

TYPES	Features - Large Format
DEALS	Universal Pictures

Frank Marshall ....Producer/Director
Kathleen Kennedy ....Producer
Mary Radford ....Assistant to Frank Marshall
Elyse Klaits ....Assistant to Kathleen Kennedy
Gregg Taylor ....Sr. VP, Development
Michelle Sy ....VP, Development
Tara Grace ....Story Editor
Kyle Radford ....Office Manager

KENNETH JOHNSON PRODUCTIONS
4461 Vista Del Monte Ave.
Sherman Oaks, CA 91403
PHONE 818-905-5255
FAX 818-905-6114
EMAIL . . . . kennycjohnson@aol.com
TYPES Features - Made-for-TV/Cable Movies - TV Series
DEVELOPMENT V: The Second Generation (NBC/Warner Bros.) - The Ripple Effect (Grammnet Prods.)
CREDITS The Incredible Hulk (TV) - Bride of the Incredible Hulk - Alien Nation (Six TV Movies) - The Liberators - Shadow Chasers - Hot Pursuit - V

Kenneth Johnson . . . . Writer/Director/Executive Producer
Susan Appling . . . . VP
Brenda Griffin . . . . Research Assistant

DIANA KEREW PRODUCTIONS
2036 Hillsboro Ave.
Los Angeles, CA 90034
PHONE 310-838-3931
TYPES Made-for-TV/Cable Movies - TV Series
CREDITS The Perfect Husband: The Laci Peterson Story (USA) - Hitler: The Rise of Evil (CBS) - When Billie Beat Bobby - Stepsister from Planet Weird - Fifteen and Pregnant - Paris Trout - Ed McBain's 87th Precinct - Crossed Over - Jenifer

Diana Kerew . . . . Producer

THE KERNER ENTERTAINMENT COMPANY
8522 National Blvd., Ste. 109
Culver City, CA 90232
PHONE 310-559-5500
FAX 310-559-9780
TYPES Features - TV Series
DEALS Paramount Pictures-Motion Picture Group
CREDITS Snow Dogs - Inspector Gadget - When a Man Loves a Woman - George of the Jungle - Fried Green Tomatoes - Less Than Zero - Mighty Ducks 1-3
SUBMISSION POLICY No unsolicited submissions

Jordan Kerner . . . . President (310-815-5100)
Paul Neesan . . . . Executive VP (310-815-5105)
Matt Vogel . . . . Creative Executive (310-815-5108)
Lydia Montano . . . . Controller (310-815-5109)
Lindsay Devlin . . . . Director, Development (310-815-5107)
Dorothy Davis . . . . Office Manager (310-815-5111)
Andrea Butterfield . . . . Executive/Creative Assistant (310-815-5103)
Kyle Peck . . . . Production Assistant (310-815-5115)

KETCHAM FILMS
610 Santa Monica Blvd.
Santa Monica, CA 90401
PHONE 310-656-0070
EMAIL . . . . ketchamfilms@aol.com
TYPES Features - Made-for-TV/Cable Movies - TV Series
CREDITS The Hurricane - I Accuse

John Ketcham . . . . Producer

KEY CREATIVES, LLC
9595 Wilshire Blvd., Ste. 800
Berverly Hills, CA 90212
PHONE 310-273-3004
FAX 310-273-3006
TYPES Features - TV Series
COMMENTS Also management company

Ken Kamins . . . . Chairman/CEO
David Greenblatt . . . . Partner
Bill Block . . . . COO
Paul Hanson . . . . VP/CFO
Pam Silverstein . . . . Manager

KEY ENTERTAINMENT, INC.
8447 Wilshire Blvd., Ste. 206
Beverly Hills, CA 90211
PHONE 323-651-9977
FAX 323-651-9976
EMAIL . . . . emckey@aol.com
TYPES Features
DEVELOPMENT Solace (New Line) - Moth Smoke - Riot
CREDITS The Alarmist - Judas Kiss - Coming Soon - Girls on Top - Slap Her, She's French - Love and a Bullet - Till Human Voices Wake Us

Matthias Emcke . . . . CEO
Will Bratten . . . . Assistant to Mr. Emcke

KEYLIGHT ENTERTAINMENT GROUP
244 Fifth Ave., 11th Fl.
New York, NY 10001
PHONE 212-725-2090
FAX 212-725-1588
TYPES Features
DEVELOPMENT Miss Pettigrew Lives for a Day - Coal - Olivia and the Cowboy - Dead in the Center of Texas - Apes and Angels
COMPLETED UNRELEASED J.M. Barrie's Neverland
SUBMISSION POLICY No unsolicited material

Nellie Bellflower . . . . No Title
Natalie Altshuler . . . . No Title
Michael Mislove . . . . No Title

T'KEYAH KEYMAH, INC.
10061 Riverside Dr., Ste. 714
Toluca Lake, CA 91602
PHONE 818-569-5456/773-509-5108
WEB SITE . . . . www.tkeyah.com
TYPES Features - Theater
DEVELOPMENT Untitled romantic comedy
COMPLETED UNRELEASED One Last Time
CREDITS Circle of Pain; Theater: T'Keyah Live!. . . Mostly: A True Variety Show
COMMENTS Chicago office: 3473 S. King Dr., Ste. 438, Chicago, IL 60616

T'Keyah Crystal Keymah . . . . Producer/Actress/Writer/Director

KEYSTONE ENTERTAINMENT, INC.
23410 Civic Center Way, Ste. E-9
Malibu, CA 90265
PHONE .310-317-4883
FAX .310-317-4903
EMAIL .malibu@keypics.com
WEB SITE .www.keypics.com

TYPES	Features
DEVELOPMENT	Air Bud 6: Aussie Rules - Spymate 2 - Tooth Fairy - Hairy Putter
PRE-PRODUCTION	Chesnut - Indian Rubber
COMPLETED UNRELEASED	Spymate
CREDITS	Air Bud - Air Bud: World Pup - Air Bud: Spikes Back - Air Bud: Seventh Inning Fetch - Air Bud: Golden Receiver - Hero of Central Park - The Duke - MVP - Final Cut - Underworld - Bulletproof Heart - MXP 3

Robert Vince .Producer/CEO
Michael Strange .President
Anna McRoberts .Producer

KG PRODUCTIONS, INC.
c/o Sunset Gower Studios
1438 N. Gower St., Box 56, Bldg. 42
Hollywood, CA 90028
PHONE .323-463-6000
WEB SITE .www.kgproductions.com

TYPES	Documentaries - Direct-to-Video/DVD - TV Series
CREDITS	Making of Traffic (Showtime) - Far from Heaven: Behind the Scenes (Bravo) - The Pianist: Behind the Scenes (Bravo) - Intolerable Cruetly: Behind the Scenes - The Ladykillers: Behind the Scenes

Kevin Gill .President
Joe Russo .Managing Producer
John Price .Producer

KILLER FILMS, INC.
380 Lafayette St., Ste. 202
New York, NY 10003
PHONE .212-473-3950
FAX .212-473-6152
WEB SITE .www.killerfilms.com

TYPES	Features - New Media - TV Series
DEALS	John Wells Productions - Warner Independent Pictures
POST PRODUCTION	A Dirty Shame - A Home at the End of the World - Mrs. Harris - The Ballad of Bettie Page
CREDITS	The Company - Far from Heaven - One Hour Photo - Hedwig and the Angry Inch - Boys Don't Cry - The Grey Zone - Storytelling - Safe - I Shot Andy Warhol - Camp - Party Monster - Kids - Velvet Goldmine - Happiness - Series 7
SUBMISSION POLICY	No unsolicited material or queries

Christine Vachon .Principal/Producer
Pamela Koffler .Principal/Producer
Katie Roumel .Principal/Producer
Jocelyn Hayes .Producer
Chika Chukudebelu .Development Coordinator
Charles Pugliese .Coordinator
Meghan Wicker .Coordinator
Michael Wiggins .Business Affairs

KILLERPIX GLOBAL MEDIA FILMCO
1413 Sanborn Ave.
Los Angeles, CA 90027
PHONE .323-666-4911
FAX .323-666-0313
WEB SITE .www.killerpix.net

TYPES	Features - Made-for-TV/Cable Movies - TV Series
DEVELOPMENT	The Devil Made Her Do It - In the Groove - Out There - Tiger Team - Platinum Bikini - Stairway to Heaven
PRODUCTION	Oceanside - Hot Chicks
COMPLETED UNRELEASED	The Taste of Dirt - Hubby/Wifey
CREDITS	Stranger Inside - Straight Right - Death in Venice, CA - The New Women - Violation
SUBMISSION POLICY	No unsolicited scripts or treatments; No email inquiries

P. David Ebersole .Writer/Director/Producer (323-666-4911)
Todd Hughes .Writer/Director/Producer (323-666-0313)
Tristen Tuckfeld .Assistant

KINETIC FILMWORKS
6880 Sunset Blvd., Ste. L193
Hollywood, CA 90028
PHONE .323-462-6355
EMAIL .kineticfilmworks@aol.com
WEB SITE .www.kineticfilmworks.com

TYPES	Features - Direct-to-Video/DVD
DEVELOPMENT	The Last Horror Picture Show
CREDITS	Frostbiter - Hellblock 13 - Head Cheerleader, Dead Cheerleader
SUBMISSION POLICY	Email queries only, no drop-offs
COMMENTS	Also finishing funds

Gary Jones .Producer/Partner
Jeff Miller .Producer/Partner

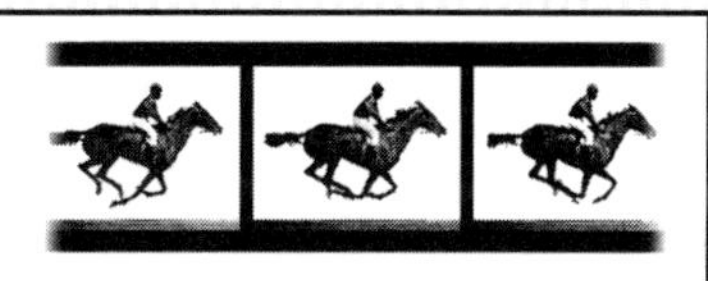

KINETIC PICTURES
1680 N. Vine St., Ste. 316
Hollywood, CA 90028
PHONE .323-468-8340
FAX .323-468-3830
WEB SITE .www.kineticpictures.com

TYPES	Features - Made-for-TV/Cable Movies - TV Series
CREDITS	A Season on the Brink - Beer Money - Prancer Returns - Clive Barker's Saint Sinner - Deathlands

Joshua Butler .Partner
Chet Fenster .Partner

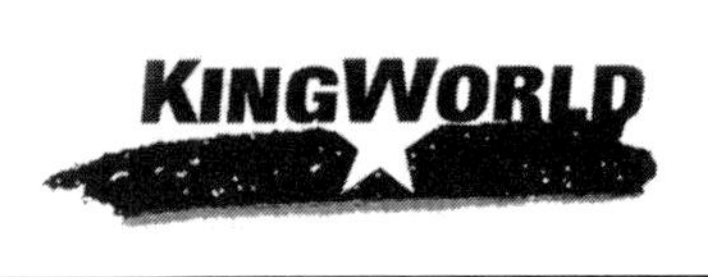

KING WORLD PRODUCTIONS, INC./A UNIT OF CBS ENTERPRISES

2401 Colorado Ave., Ste. 110
Santa Monica, CA 90404
PHONE 310-264-3300/212-315-4000
WEB SITE . . . . . www.kingworld.com
TYPES Syndication - TV Series
CREDITS Living it Up! with Ali & Jack - Dr. Phil - Hollywood Squares - Jeopardy - Wheel of Fortune
COMMENTS East Coast office: 1700 Broadway, 32nd & 33rd Fls., New York, NY 10019

Roger King . . . . . Chairman/CEO
Robert Madden . . . . . Executive VP, CBS Enterprises
Armando Nuñez Jr. . . . . . President, CBS Broadcast International/Executive VP, CBS Enterprises
Steven LoCascio . . . . . Sr. VP/CFO, CBS Enterprises & King World Productions, Inc. (973-376-1313)
Arthur R. Sando . . . . . Sr. VP, Communications
Mike Stornello . . . . . Sr. VP, Development
Jonathan Birkhahn . . . . . Sr. VP, Business Affairs
Rich Cervini . . . . . VP, Production & Technical Operations (NY)
Ralph Goldberg . . . . . VP, Legal Affairs, Reality-Based Programming (NY)
Veronika Lineberry . . . . . VP, Creative Services, West Coast
Sylvester Russo . . . . . VP/Controller (973-376-1313)

KINGMAN FILMS INTERNATIONAL

c/o Kingman International
14010 Live Oak Ave.
Baldwin Park, CA 91706
PHONE 626-430-2300 x123
FAX 626-851-8069
WEB SITE . . . . . www.kingman.net
TYPES Features - TV Series
CREDITS Frontline - Good Advice - The Kiss - To Protect and Serve

Arthur Chang . . . . . Founder/CEO

KINGSGATE FILMS, INC.

8954 W. Pico Blvd., 2nd Fl.
Los Angeles, CA 90035
PHONE 310-281-5880
FAX 310-281-2633
TYPES Features - TV Series
DEVELOPMENT White Jazz - Official Assassins
CREDITS Affliction - Simpatico - Investigating Sex - Rules of Attraction

Nick Nolte . . . . . Actor/Producer
Greg Shapiro . . . . . Producer

DAVID KIRSCHNER PRODUCTIONS

400 S. June St.
Los Angeles, CA 90020
PHONE 323-939-0230
FAX 323-930-0753
EMAIL . . . . . dkps@pacbell.net
TYPES Animation - Features - Made-for-TV/Cable Movies - TV Series
DEVELOPMENT Immortals - Undone - Wooly Bully - Martian Child - Peony
PRE-PRODUCTION 5 Days (Miniseries) - Curious George - Miss Potter - Child's Play 5
CREDITS An American Tail 1-3 - Hocus Pocus - Titan A.E. - Bride of Chucky - Frailty - The Flintstones - Secondhand Lions
SUBMISSION POLICY No unsolicited material

David Kirschner . . . . . Producer
Corey Sienega . . . . . VP, Production & Development
Ian Moore . . . . . Story Editor

KISMET ENTERTAINMENT GROUP

16830 Ventura Blvd., Ste. 260
Encino, CA 91436
PHONE 818-990-4900
FAX 818-990-4901
TYPES Features
DEVELOPMENT Amphibian
PRE-PRODUCTION Dog Soldiers 2
COMPLETED UNRELEASED Kidnapped - Cemetery Gates - Mojave - Boo! - Neo Ned
CREDITS Dog Soldiers - No Good Deed - Asylum (Paramount Classics) - Stander (Newmarket)

David E. Allen . . . . . Chairman/CEO
Harman M. Kaslow . . . . . President/COO
Todd Knowlton . . . . . VP, Promotion & Marketing
Brian Patrick O'Toole . . . . . VP, Creative Development
Sheri Bryant . . . . . Producer

KLASKY CSUPO, INC.

6353 Sunset Blvd.
Los Angeles, CA 90028
PHONE 323-468-2600
WEB SITE . . . . . www.klaskycsupo.com
SECOND WEB SITE . . . . . www.globaltantrum.com
TYPES Animation - Commercials - Features - Direct-to-Video/DVD - New Media - TV Series
DEALS Paramount Pictures-Motion Picture Group
CREDITS The Wild Thornberrys Movie - The Rugrats Go Wild - Stressed Eric - Rugrats - The Wild Thornberrys - Rocket Power - As Told by Ginger - Duckman - The Simpsons - The Rugrats Movie - Rugrats in Paris: The Movie
COMMENTS Tone Casualties Records

Gabor Csupo . . . . . Co-Chairman
Arlene Klasky . . . . . Co-Chairman
Terry Thoren . . . . . President/CEO
John Andrews . . . . . Sr. VP, Commercials & Internet
Cella Harris . . . . . Sr. VP, TV Animation Production
Hal Waite . . . . . Sr. VP, Feature Animation
Doug Willard . . . . . Sr. VP, Finance & Operations
Paul Yamamoto . . . . . Sr. VP, Global Tantrum Creative Affairs
Michael Faulkner . . . . . VP, Creative Affairs

RANDAL KLEISER PRODUCTIONS

3050 Runyon Canyon Rd.
Los Angeles, CA 90046
PHONE 323-850-5511
FAX 323-850-1074
EMAIL ....rkproductions@earthlink.net
WEB SITE ....www.directorsnet.com/kleiser

TYPES: Features
POST PRODUCTION: Red Riding Hood
CREDITS: Grease - Getting It Right - White Fang - It's My Party

Gregory Hinton ....Executive Producer

*KLS COMMUNICATIONS, INC.

5430 Oakdale Ave.
Woodland Hills, CA 91364
PHONE 800-887-0248
EMAIL ....lschiller@klscomm.com

TYPES: Documentaries - Features - Made-for-TV/Cable Movies - Reality TV - TV Series
DEALS: Fox Television Studios
DEVELOPMENT: Why America Slept (Showtime) - First Hours (CBS) - Jessie Hollywood (USA Network)
CREDITS: CBS Miniseries: Master Spy - American Tragedy; CBS MOW: Double Jeopardy - The Plot to Kill Hitler; ABC MOW: Marilyn, The Untold Story - Hey I'm Alive; NBC Miniseries: Peter the Great - The Executioner's Song

Lawrence Schiller ....President
Bruce A. Pobjoy ....Producer

THE KNIGHT COMPANY

1401 Ocean Ave., Ste. 305
Santa Monica, CA 90401
PHONE 310-395-7100
FAX 310-395-7099
EMAIL ....cknight@knight-co.com

TYPES: Animation - Features - Made-for-TV/Cable Movies - New Media - TV Series
DEVELOPMENT: Paper or Plastic - Blood Money - Creature
CREDITS: Winners Take All - The Dream Team

Christopher W. Knight ....President
Jennifer Wahoff ....Director, Development

KATHRYN KNOWLTON PRODUCTIONS

4235-B Colfax Ave.
Studio City, CA 91604
PHONE 818-509-9776
FAX 818-762-8238
EMAIL ....info@thescript.com

TYPES: Animation - Features - Made-for-TV/Cable Movies - New Media - Syndication - TV Series
DEVELOPMENT: The Deceiver - Chromium Yellow - Sight Unseen
CREDITS: Jacknife - An Eye for an Eye
COMMENTS: Management company; Division of CSS

Kathryn Knowlton ....President/Producer/Manager
Stephanie Cooper ....Story Editor

THE KONIGSBERG-SMITH COMPANY

7919 Sunset Blvd., 2nd Fl.
Los Angeles, CA 90046
PHONE 323-845-1000
FAX 323-845-1020
EMAIL ....konigsbergsmith@pacbell.net

TYPES: Features - Made-for-TV/Cable Movies - TV Series
CREDITS: The Last Don - Titanic - Bella Mafia - Like Mother, Like Son: The Strange Story of Sante and Kenny Kimes - Caught in the Act

Frank Konigsberg ....No Title
Drew Smith ....No Title
Neal Doherty ....No Title

KONWISER BROTHERS

9000 Sunset Blvd., Ste. 710
Los Angeles, CA 90069
PHONE 310-205-2477
FAX 310-273-6092
EMAIL ....rogers@konwiserbros.com
WEB SITE ....www.konwiserbros.com

TYPES: Animation - Commercials - Documentaries - Features - Direct-to-Video/DVD - Made-for-TV/Cable Movies - Reality TV - Theater - TV Series
DEALS: Sony Pictures Animation - Warner Home Video
DEVELOPMENT: The Reel Deal - The Last Game (Feature) - Pancho Gonzalez Story (Feature)
PRE-PRODUCTION: Step-Up (Broadway) - Roy Rogers (Sony)
PRODUCTION: Smile
POST PRODUCTION: Underground Poets Railroad - Crossover (aka Dynasties) - Back in the Day
COMPLETED UNRELEASED: Dallas 362 (aka Dallas & Rusty)
CREDITS: Miss Evers' Boys - On Hallowed Ground - Focus - The Wash - Maze - Quest for Nutrition - The Last Game (Documentary) - Pancho Gonzales (TV)

Kip Konwiser ....Partner
Kern Konwiser ....Partner
J. Rogers Marquess III ....Creative Development

KOPELSON ENTERTAINMENT

1900 Avenue of the Stars, Ste. 500
Los Angeles, CA 90067
PHONE 310-407-1500
FAX 310-407-1501

TYPES: Features
CREDITS: Don't Say a Word - A Perfect Murder - U.S. Marshals - Devil's Advocate - Eraser - Seven - Outbreak - The Fugitive - Falling Down - Platoon - Twisted

Arnold Kopelson ....Producer/Co-Chairperson/President (310-407-1522)
Anne Kopelson ....Producer/Co-Chairperson (310-407-1532)
Sherryl Clark ....President (310-407-1540)
Evan Kopelson ....Sr. VP, TV (310-407-1560)
Chris Cowles ....VP, Production (310-407-1570)
Claudia O'Hehir ....Executive Assistant to Anne Kopelson (310-407-1544)
Ryan Engle ....Assistant to Sherryl Clark (310-407-1535)
Kevin Jarzynski ....Executive Assistant to Arnold Kopelson (310-407-1533)

ROBERT KOSBERG PRODUCTIONS

c/o Nash Entertainment
1438 N. Gower St., Box 10
Hollywood, CA 90028
PHONE .323-468-4513
FAX .530-483-3257
WEB SITE .www.moviepitch.com
TYPES Features - Made-for-TV/Cable Movies - New Media - TV Series - Reality TV
DEALS Nash Entertainment
DEVELOPMENT Surrender Dorothy (Warner Bros.) - The Hardy Men (Fox 2000)
CREDITS Commando - In the Mood - Man's Best Friend - Twelve Monkeys - Mr. Personality

Robert Kosberg .Producer
Marisa Forrest .Director, Development

KRAININ PRODUCTIONS, INC.

25211 Summerhill Lane
Stevenson Ranch, CA 91381
PHONE .661-259-9700
EMAIL .krainin@comcast.net
WEB SITE .www.kraininproductions.com
TYPES Documentaries - Features - Made-for-TV/Cable Movies
DEVELOPMENT TV Movies: Reality Check; Features: Tube Wars - Lovers, Liars, and Thieves - Ota Benga - Jerry Lewis
PRE-PRODUCTION Cut to the Heart (HBO)
CREDITS To America - Disaster at Silo 7 - George Wallace - Quiz Show - John Glenn: Return of the Hero - Something the Lord Made

Julian Krainin .Producer/Director/President
Joel Adams .Development Executive
Jason Hart .Special Projects
Martha Wineblatt .Production & Development
Todd Philips .TV & Feature Development

THE JONATHAN KRANE GROUP

8033 W. Sunset Blvd., Rm. 6750
Hollywood, CA 90046
PHONE .323-650-0942
FAX .323-650-9132
WEB SITE .www.kraneonproducing.com
TYPES Features
CREDITS Look Who's Talking - Chocolate War - Michael - Blind Date - Face/Off - The General's Daughter - Swordfish - Domestic Disturbance

Jonathan D. Krane .Producer/CEO/Chairman
Maria Gustafsson .Assistant to Mr. Krane

SID & MARTY KROFFT PICTURES CORPORATION

c/o CBS Studio Center
4024 Radford Ave., Bldg. 5, Ste. 102
Studio City, CA 91604
PHONE .818-655-5314
FAX .818-655-8235
TYPES Features - Direct-to-Video/DVD - TV Series
DEVELOPMENT Sigmund & the Seamonsters (Feature) - Land of the Lost (Feature) - H.R. Pufnstuf (Feature) - Concierge Confidential (TV)
CREDITS Family Affair (WB)

Marty Krofft .President
Sid Krofft .Executive VP

FRED KUEHNERT PRODUCTIONS

10550 Wilshire Blvd., Ste. 1001
Los Angeles, CA 90024
PHONE .310-470-3363
FAX .310-470-0060
EMAIL .fkuehnert@earthlink.net
TYPES Features - Direct-to-Video/DVD
DEVELOPMENT Sicilian Love Story - Free Falling - The Girl Warrior
PRE-PRODUCTION The Fallen Ones - Winner
COMPLETED UNRELEASED 29 and Holding
CREDITS Buddy Holly Story - Grey Night (aka The Killing Box) - Cold Night Into Dawn - Cypress Edge - Beneath Loch Ness
COMMENTS Financial consulting; Producers Representative; Expert witness

Fred T. Kuehnert .Managing Partner
Robert Birmingham .Partner/Producer
Grant Guthrie .Partner/Producer
Sandra Chouinard .Executive Assistant

KURTIS PRODUCTIONS, LTD.

400 W. Erie St., Ste. 500
Chicago, IL 60610
PHONE .312-951-5700
FAX .312-951-8251
TYPES Documentaries - TV Series
CREDITS Investigative Reports - Cold Case Files - Investigating History
COMMENTS HD documentaries

Megan Murphy .General Manager

THE KUSHNER-LOCKE COMPANY

280 S. Beverly Dr., Ste. 205
Beverly Hills, CA 90212
PHONE .310-275-7508
FAX .310-275-7518
TYPES Features - Direct-to-Video/DVD - TV Series
CREDITS Pinocchio (New Line) - Andre (Paramount) - Brave Little Toaster 1-3 (Disney) - Gun (ABC) - Freeway 1&2 - Harvard Man - Basil - Whole Wide World - Picking Up the Pieces - Ringmaster - Harts of the West (CBS)

Alice Neuhauser .Responsible Officer

KUSTOM ENTERTAINMENT

1427 Third Street Promenade, Ste. 201
Santa Monica, CA 90401
PHONE .310-587-2200
FAX .310-587-2230
TYPES Features - Reality TV - TV Series
DEVELOPMENT The Translator (Intermedia) - Russian Brides (Dimension) - Town Creek (WB) - Dean Tate Wants My Girlfriend (New Regency) - Jonestown - Suckernucks (Senator) - '87 Fleer
PRE-PRODUCTION American Candidate (Showtime) - First Snow (El Camino Pictures)
POST PRODUCTION Stay (New Regency/Fox)

Tom Lassally .No Title
Robyn Meisinger .No Title
Fred Lidskog .No Title
Kevin Breay .No Title
Neda Niroumand .No Title

KUZUI ENTERPRISES, INC.
888 Seventh Ave., 35th Fl.
New York, NY 10116
PHONE 845-469-2863
FAX 845-496-9180
TYPES Features - TV Series
CREDITS Telling Lies in America - Orgazmo - Buffy the Vampire Slayer - Tokyo Pop

Kaz Kuzui ....Co-President
Fran Rubel Kuzui ....Co-President

LA LUNA FILMS
9350 Civic Center Dr.
Beverly Hills, CA 90210
PHONE 310-550-3800
FAX 310-550-3801
EMAIL ....jtimon@pacificafilm.com
TYPES Features - Made-for-TV/Cable Movies - TV Series
DEALS Pacifica Film Development, Inc.
DEVELOPMENT Abyssinia - Carried Away - Constantinople - Cuba and the Night - Taking Out the Cat - Thirst - Trigger - Winter Woke Up - In 2 Win - The Prince - The Lion of Crete - The Battle Horse - Friendly Fire - Perfect Cover - Session Men
CREDITS Mermaids - Butcher's Wife - Drop Zone - Dream Lover - Fires Within - Shadow Ops - 6 Days/7 Nights

Wallis Nicita ....Producer
Jeff Timon ....Writer/Associate Producer (310-550-3834)

THE LADD COMPANY
9465 Wilshire Blvd., Ste. 910
Beverly Hills, CA 90210
PHONE 310-777-2060
FAX 310-777-2061
TYPES Features
DEVELOPMENT Beach Music - Gone Baby Gone - The Andrew's Project - Who's Your Nanny - Hunting Down Amanda
POST PRODUCTION An Unfinished Life
CREDITS Chariots of Fire - Blade Runner - The Right Stuff - Police Academy - Braveheart

Alan Ladd Jr. ....President
Amanda Lamb ....Producer (310-777-2064)

DAVID LADD FILMS
c/o MGM
2450 Broadway St., Ste. 400
Santa Monica, CA 90404
PHONE 310-449-3410
FAX 310-586-8272
TYPES Features
DEALS Metro-Goldwyn-Mayer Studios, Inc.
DEVELOPMENT Godspeed, Lawrence Mann - I Want Kandee - Man on 3rd - Men & Other Mammals - Stealing Johnny Dead
CREDITS The Serpent and the Rainbow - Mod Squad - Hart's War - A Guy Thing
SUBMISSION POLICY No unsolicited submissions

David Ladd ....President
Megan Dunleavy ....VP (310-449-3190)
David Steinberg ....Assistant to David Ladd/Story Editor
Brian Wetherby ....Assistant to Megan Dunleavy/Story Editor

LAKESHORE ENTERTAINMENT CORPORATION
c/o Paramount Pictures
5555 Melrose Ave., Gloria Swanson Bldg.
Los Angeles, CA 90038
PHONE 323-956-4222
FAX 323-862-1190
TYPES Features
DEALS Paramount Pictures-Motion Picture Group
DEVELOPMENT The Last Kiss - Lucky Stars - Serpentine - R.S.V.P. - Dying Animal - The Ugly Truth - American Pastoral - Ivanhoe - The Straight Man - School Spirit - Crank - Boy Meets Girl - Janis - Exorcism of Anneliese Michel
PRE-PRODUCTION Aeon Flux - Underworld 2
PRODUCTION Cave - Million Dollar Baby
COMPLETED UNRELEASED Wicker Park
CREDITS The Human Stain - The Mothman Prophecies - The Gift - Autumn in New York - Runaway Bride - Arlington Road

Tom Rosenberg ....Chairman/CEO
Gary Lucchesi ....President, Lakeshore Entertainment
Eric Reid ....COO
Marc Reid ....CFO
Richard Wright ....Executive VP/Head, Production
Robert Benun ....Sr. VP, Business & Legal Affairs
Robert McMinn ....Sr. VP, Development
Virginia Longmuir Sr. VP, International Business, Legal Affairs & Operations
Andre Lamal ....VP, Physical Production
Renee Mancuso ....VP, Finance
Christine Buckley ....VP, Music, Business & Legal Affairs
Bic Tran ....VP, Acquistions & Co-Productions
Kjose Elliott ....Office Manager
Elizabeth Schlater ....Assistant to Mr. Rosenberg
Ilsa Berg ....Assistant to Mr. Lucchesi
Bonnie Brocatto ....Assistant to Ms. Longmuir
Jason Payne ....Assistant to Mr. Reid & Mr. Benun
Grant Grabowski ....Assistant to Mr. Wright

LANCASTER GATE ENTERTAINMENT
4702 Hayvenhurst Ave.
Encino, CA 91436
PHONE 818-995-6000
FAX 818-905-8164
TYPES Features - Made-for-TV/Cable Movies
DEVELOPMENT Tough Cookie - Sumo Mouse
CREDITS Secret Cutting - December - Grumpy Old Men - Angel Flight Down - Grumpier Old Men - The Four Chaplains

Richard C. Berman ....Producer
Brian K. Schlichter ....Executive VP, Development & Production

It is illegal to copy any part of this book

DAVID LANCASTER PRODUCTIONS

3356 Bennett Dr.
Los Angeles, CA 90068-1704
PHONE . . . 323-874-1415
FAX . . . 323-874-7749
EMAIL . . . laninco@earthlink.net

TYPES	Features
POST PRODUCTION	Infinite Darkness - A Love Song for Bobby Long - Riding the Bullet - Slipstream
CREDITS	'Night Mother - Sadness of Sex - Loving Jezebel - Don't Look Under the Bed - Federal Protection - Borderline - Pavement - Consequence - Blast
SUBMISSION POLICY	Query letters accepted; No unsolicited material or drop-offs

David Lancaster . . . Producer
Chad Marting . . . Production Executive

LANCE ENTERTAINMENT, INC.

9107 Wilshire Blvd., Ste. 625
Beverly Hills, 90210
PHONE . . . 310-888-3494
FAX . . . 310-859-7173
EMAIL . . . pierre@lance-ent.com

TYPES	Features - Made-for-TV/Cable Movies
POST PRODUCTION	Saving Emily
COMPLETED UNRELEASED	Stranger at the Door
CREDITS	A Woman Hunted - The Perfect Nanny - The Perfect Wife - Yesterday's Children - Blind Obsession - Rain - Living with Fear - Seduced by a Thief - Internal Affairs - Platoon - Deep Cover - Scanners - The Perfect Husband
SUBMISSION POLICY	No unsolicited submissions

Pierre David . . . President
Ken Sanders . . . Creative Affairs & Production
Kendall Nowlin . . . Associate

THE LANDSBURG COMPANY

PO Box 49920
Los Angeles, CA 90049-0920
PHONE . . . 310-889-7112
FAX . . . 310-889-7116

TYPES	Features - TV Series
DEALS	ABC Entertainment Television Group - CBS Entertainment - NBC Entertainment
CREDITS	Living Dolls: The Making of a Child Beauty Queen (HBO) - The Lottery (NBC) - Country Justice (CBS) - If Someone Had Known (NBC) - A Mother's Right: The Elizabeth Morgan Story (ABC)
SUBMISSION POLICY	No unsolicited material
COMMENTS	Specials

Alan Landsburg . . . Chairman/CEO
Howard Lipstone . . . President/COO
Linda Otto . . . In House Producer
Diane Skwarek . . . Manager, Business Affairs

LANDSCAPE PICTURES

9465 Wilshire Blvd., Ste. 308
Beverly Hills, CA 90212
PHONE . . . 310-248-6200
FAX . . . 310-248-6300

TYPES	Features - Made-for-TV/Cable Movies - TV Series
DEALS	NBC Entertainment - New Line Cinema
DEVELOPMENT	Leisureworld - Fearless - Surprise Party - John Tucker - I Know That You Know What I Know - Billy Liar - The Hypnotist - Man on a Train - Barry & Stan - Fly on the Wall
PRE-PRODUCTION	Quail Hollow
CREDITS	Sleepover
SUBMISSION POLICY	No unsolicited material

Bob Cooper . . . Chairman/CEO
Karen Lunder . . . Sr. VP, Features
Gregg Goldman . . . VP, TV
Scott Vila . . . Head, Series TV
Ariana D. Harris . . . Assistant to Mr. Cooper
David Quinalty . . . Assistant to Mr. Cooper
Cheryl Delao . . . Assistant to Karen Lunder
Lindsay Mediagovich . . . Assistant to Mr. Vila

LANGLEY PRODUCTIONS

2225 Colorado Ave.
Santa Monica, CA 90404
PHONE . . . 310-449-5300
FAX . . . 310-449-5330
WEB SITE . . . www.cops.com

TYPES	Documentaries - Features - TV Series - Reality TV
CREDITS	Code 3 - Anatomy of Crime - Cops - Reality Check - Vampire Clan - Dogwatch - Wildside - Tiptoes
SUBMISSION POLICY	Through representation only

John Langley . . . President/Executive Producer/Director/Writer
Doug Waterman . . . Supervising Producer, COPS
Elie Cohn . . . Producer, Features
Karen Hori . . . VP, TV Production

LANTANA PRODUCTIONS

9701 Wilshire Blvd., Ste. 1111
Beverly Hills, CA 90212
PHONE . . . 310-247-7400
FAX . . . 310-247-7404

TYPES	Features - TV Series
CREDITS	Swing Shift - Circle of Friends - Stanley & Iris

Arlene Sellers . . . Producer
Alex Winitsky . . . Producer

LARCO PRODUCTIONS, INC.

2111 Coldwater Canyon
Beverly Hills, CA 90210
PHONE . . . 323-350-5455
EMAIL . . . info@itsalive.biz
WEB SITE . . . www.itsalive.biz

TYPES	Animation - Features - Reality TV - Theater - TV Series
DEVELOPMENT	Captivity
PRODUCTION	Cellular
CREDITS	Phonebooth - Invasion of Privacy - Original Gangstas - Guilty as Sin - Body Snatchers - Best Seller - The Invaders (TV Series) - Q - Private Files of J. Edgar Hoover - It's Alive - Gold Told Me - Bone
SUBMISSION POLICY	No unsolicited mail accepted

Larry Cohen . . . Writer/Producer/Director
Jill Gatsby . . . VP, Development/Producer

LARGER THAN LIFE PRODUCTIONS

100 Universal City Plaza, Bldg. 5138
Universal City, CA 91608
PHONE . . . 818-777-4004
FAX . . . 818-866-5677

TYPES	Features
DEALS	Universal Pictures
DEVELOPMENT	Creature from the Black Lagoon - The Deal (aka Bye-Bye Brooklyn) - Zero Game - Tale of Despereaux - Moth Diaries
CREDITS	Pleasantville - Seabiscuit
SUBMISSION POLICY	No unsolicited submissions

Gary Ross . . . Writer/Director/Principal
Allison Thomas . . . Producer
Robin Bissell . . . Producer
Maggie Malone . . . Director, Development
Michelle Steffes . . . Director, Development

*MICHAEL G. LARKIN PRODUCTIONS

12301 Wilshire Blvd., Ste. 110
Los Angeles, CA 90025
PHONE . . . 310-826-3148/310-994-0797
FAX . . . 310-207-6069
EMAIL . . . capecod114@aol.com

TYPES	Features - Made-for-TV/Cable Movies - TV Series
DEALS	Jaffe/Braunstein Films, Ltd.
CREDITS	Behind the Camera: The Unauthorized Story of Charlie's Angels - Red Water - Murder in the Heartland

Michael G. Larkin . . . Producer

THE LARODA GROUP

18320 Keswick St.
Reseda, CA 91335
PHONE . . . 818-342-6500
FAX . . . 818-344-8801
EMAIL . . . info@laroda.com
WEB SITE . . . www.laroda.com

TYPES	Documentaries - Features - Direct-to-Video/DVD - New Media - TV Series
DEVELOPMENT	Swingin' (Feature)
PRE-PRODUCTION	Sammy Davis Jr. Story (Feature)
POST PRODUCTION	Sammy & Company (DVD-Series)
CREDITS	The Sammy Davis Jr. Show (DVD)

Barrett LaRoda . . . CEO
Indira LaRoda . . . President
Clinton Galloway . . . CFO
Garnet Morris . . . COO
Matin Sed . . . VP, Production
Brian Galloway . . . Development

LASALLE HOLLAND

141 W. 28th St., Ste. 300
New York, NY 10001
PHONE . . . 212-541-4443
FAX . . . 212-563-9655
WEB SITE . . . www.lasalleholland.com

TYPES	Documentaries - Features - Music Videos - TV Series
DEVELOPMENT	The Wright Brothers - No Lights No Sirens
PRE-PRODUCTION	Everything's Fine
COMPLETED UNRELEASED	Pagans
CREDITS	Hurricane Streets - Spring Forward - Desert Blue - Martin and Orloff - Bobby 6 Can't Swim - Loggerheads
SUBMISSION POLICY	Open

Gill Holland . . . Partner
Lillian Lasalle . . . Partner
Raymond DeMarco . . . Managing Partner
Mike Morley . . . Managing Partner
Matt Parker . . . Director, Development
Kyle Luker . . . Jr. Manager

THE LATE BLOOMER COMPANY, LTD.

56 W. 56th St., 3rd Fl.
New York, NY 10019
PHONE . . . 212-247-4945
FAX . . . 212-247-4945
EMAIL . . . lejen@prodigy.net

TYPES	Animation - Features - Made-for-TV/Cable Movies - Syndication - TV Series
DEVELOPMENT	Don't Ask, Don't Tell - The Colonel: The Colonel Tom Parker Story - Feel the Thunder: The Dick Dale Story - Time's Up - Vampire City - The Electra Conspiracy - Games without Frontiers - Whatever Happened to Randolph Scott?
CREDITS	Out of the Ashes (Showtime) - Skeezer (NBC) - The Legend of Walks Far Woman (NBC) - Playing with Fire (NBC) - Runaway Father (CBS)
SUBMISSION POLICY	Query letters for books and screenplays via email only; Include logline and synopsis
COMMENTS	Member, PGA

Lee Levinson . . . Partner/Producer
Jena Levinson . . . Partner/Producer

LATHAM ENTERTAINMENT

5555 Melrose Ave., Dressing Room Bldg., Rm. 117
Hollywood, CA 90038
PHONE . . . 323-956-8882
FAX . . . 323-862-2289

TYPES	Animation - Features - Direct-to-Video/DVD - Syndication - TV Series
DEALS	Paramount Pictures-Motion Picture Group
CREDITS	The Original Kings of Comedy - The Queens of Comedy
SUBMISSION POLICY	No unsolicited submissions

Walter Latham . . . President/Producer
Christopher Balonek . . . No Title
David Higgins . . . No Title
Patricia Jones . . . No Title
Tom Just . . . No Title

LATIN HOLLYWOOD FILMS

2934-1/2 Beverly Glen Circle, Ste. 262
Bel Air, CA 90077
PHONE . . . 310-451-2799
EMAIL . . . latinafilm@aol.com
WEB SITE . . . www.kikikiss.com

TYPES	Documentaries - Features - New Media - TV Series
DEVELOPMENT	Exonerating Evidence (Lalu Prouctions) - The Other Side of the Rainbow - The Kiki Melendez Show
PRE-PRODUCTION	Influenced by Glory
POST PRODUCTION	Dominican Baseball with Manny Mota (Documentary)
CREDITS	Salsa Desde Hollywood - Kiki Desde Hollywood - The Effects of Vicodin in Hollywood - Hot Tamales Live!
COMMENTS	Latin themes for the general market; Hollywood segments for BBC and international markets; AOL coverage of Latin Grammys; La Musica.com; Deal with Western International Syndication

Christian "Kiki" Melendez . . . CEO/Executive Producer
David Baum . . . Partner
Eva Longoria . . . Producer
Lupe Ontiveros . . . Producer
Anthony Lopez . . . Head Writer
John Berry . . . International Sales
Lillian Casares . . . Promotions & Marketing
Sandy Fairall . . . Development
Nancy Tiballi . . . Talent Coordinator

LAUGH FACTORY ENTERTAINMENT
8001 Sunset Blvd.
West Hollywood, CA 90046
PHONE .323-848-2800
FAX .323-848-2810
EMAIL .management@laughfactory.com
WEB SITE .www.laughfactory.com
TYPES Features - Made-for-TV/Cable Movies - TV Series
DEALS Touchstone Television
DEVELOPMENT The Bob Marley Show
CREDITS Rocket Man

Jamie Masada .Owner/President
Shaina Traunfeld .No Title

LAUNA NEWMAN PRODUCTIONS (LNP)
10390 Wilshire Blvd., Ste. 1407
Los Angeles, CA 90022
PHONE .310-288-8383
FAX .310-288-8306
TYPES Documentaries - Features - New Media - Reality TV - Syndication - TV Series
DEALS ABC Entertainment Television Group
DEVELOPMENT Happy Hour
POST PRODUCTION Kids R Funny
CREDITS I Survived a Disaster 1-4

Launa Newman-Minson .Executive Producer
Erik Fleming .VP, Development
Whitney-Anne Minson .VP, Creative Affairs

LAUNCHPAD PRODUCTIONS
c/o Latham Entertainment
5555 Melrose Ave., Dressing Room Bldg., Ste. 117
Los Angeles, CA 90038
PHONE .323-956-8882
FAX .323-862-2289
EMAIL .dwh@launchpadprods.com
TYPES Features
DEVELOPMENT Stacked - Big Momma's House 2
PRODUCTION Hard Candy
CREDITS Big Momma's House - Here on Earth

David W. Higgins .Producer

LAVIN ENTERTAINMENT GROUP
411 S. Front St.
Wilmington, NC 28401
PHONE .910-772-9916
TYPES Features - Syndication - TV Series
CREDITS Stolen Memories: Secrets from the Rose Garden - A Place to Call Home

Linda Lavin .Actress/Director/Producer

ROBERT LAWRENCE PRODUCTIONS
2017 Pacific Ave., Ste. 2
Venice, CA 90291
PHONE .310-883-2426
FAX .310-822-0835
TYPES Features
DEVELOPMENT Gates of Fire - Pet Peeves - Top Dog - Chavez Ravine
PRODUCTION Mozart & the Whale
CREDITS The Last Castle - Rock Star - Clueless - Rapid Fire - A Kiss Before Dying - Die Hard: With a Vengeance - Down Periscope

Robert Lawrence .Producer
Sean Robins .VP, Production
Robb Aguirre .Development Associate

LEACH ENTERTAINMENT ENTERPRISES, INC.
122 E. 42nd St., Ste. 1518
New York, NY 10168-1599
PHONE .212-557-6900
FAX .212-557-6901
TYPES Syndication - TV Series
CREDITS Lifestyles - Gourmet Getaways - TVFN - Heroes America - Miracles & Wonders - Penthouse Vegas

Robin Leach .Executive Producer
Nick LaPenna .Producer

MICHELE LEE PRODUCTIONS
10866 Wilshire Blvd., Ste. 1100
Los Angeles, CA 90024
PHONE .310-446-1774
TYPES Features - Made-for-TV/Cable Movies - TV Series
DEALS CBS Entertainment
CREDITS Color Me Perfect - When No One Would Listen - Scandalous Me: The Jacqueline Susann Story - Big Dreams & Broken Hearts: The Dottie West Story

Michele Lee .President
Ken Dusick .Development/Director, Business Affairs
Linda Howard .Administration

LEFRAK PRODUCTIONS
40 W. 57th St., Ste. 409
New York, NY 10019
PHONE .212-541-9444
FAX .212-974-8205
TYPES Features - Made-for-TV/Cable Movies - New Media - TV Series
DEVELOPMENT 100 Days of Darkness - Betrayal.com
CREDITS Miss Rose White - Mi Vida Loca - The Infiltrator - Shot Through the Heart - Life of the Party - Student Seduction

Francine LeFrak .President
Sean Castles .Assistant

ARNOLD LEIBOVIT ENTERTAINMENT

PO Box 261
Cedar City, UT 84721
PHONE 435-867-6414
WEB SITE .... www.scifistation.com
TYPES Animation - Features - TV Series
DEVELOPMENT The Time Machine (Miniseries) - Untitled Arnold Leibovit Sci-Fi Project - 7 Faces of Dr. Lao
CREDITS The Time Machine - Puppetoon Movie - Fantasy Film Worlds of George Pal
COMMENTS Puppetoon animation studios

Arnold Leibovit .... Producer/Director
Barbara Schimpf .... VP, Production

THE JERRY LEIDER COMPANY

11661 San Vicente Blvd., Ste. 505
Los Angeles, CA 90049
PHONE 310-820-3161
FAX 310-820-4323
EMAIL .... gjleider@pacbell.net
TYPES Features - Made-for-TV/Cable Movies - TV Series
DEVELOPMENT Mayday - Ladies Man - I Love You Again - Sunday to Sunday
PRODUCTION Mythquest
CREDITS Confessions of a Teen Aged Drama Queen - Coast to Coast - Cadet Kelly - My Favorite Martian - Trucks - Payne

Jerry Leider .... President
Gerald Rubin, Esq. .... Legal Affairs

LEMON SKY PRODUCTIONS, INC.

2282 El Contento Dr.
Los Angeles, CA 90068
PHONE 323-957-9620
FAX 323-957-9699
TYPES Features - TV Series
DEVELOPMENT A Mother's Recompense - Magic Malik
CREDITS Lemon Sky - Living in Oblivion - The Real Blonde - Double Whammy

Marcus Viscidi .... President
Samantha Bell .... VP, Development
John Parker .... VP, Finance

LEO FILMS AND URBAN MOVIES

6249 Langdon Ave.
Van Nuys, CA 91411
PHONE 818-782-6541
FAX 818-782-3320
EMAIL .... lustgar@pacbell.net
WEB SITE .... www.leofilms.com
TYPES Documentaries - Features - Direct-to-Video/DVD - Made-for-TV/Cable Movies - TV Series
DEVELOPMENT Radio Kill - Edith Wharton's Summer - Vampz 2 - Welcome to Gangworld
COMPLETED UNRELEASED Vampz
CREDITS American Taboo - Power Slide - The Bewitching - Fury - Evil Sister 2
SUBMISSION POLICY Email query

Steve Lustgarten .... President

MALCOLM LEO PRODUCTIONS

6536 Sunset Blvd.
Hollywood, CA 90028
PHONE 323-464-4448
FAX 323-462-1428
EMAIL .... malcolmleoprods@aol.com
WEB SITE .... malcolmleoproductions.com
TYPES Documentaries - Features - Direct-to-Video/DVD - New Media - Syndication - TV Series
DEALS BBC Worldwide America - TLC (The Learning Channel) - VH1 (Music First)
DEVELOPMENT Otis Redding Story - American Cool - The Secret Life of Rock'n'Roll - British Invasion
PRE-PRODUCTION Sound of the Cities
CREDITS This Is Elvis - Rock 'n' Roll Moments - Rolling Stone Anniversary - Beach Boys: An American Band (DVD) - Brady Bunch Reunion - Happy Days Reunion - Rock 'n' Roll Christmas - Will Rogers Look Back in Laughter - Cole Porter Red, Hot & Blue
COMMENTS Archive licensing source footage for film, TV, music, pop culture, rock'n'roll

Malcolm Leo .... Executive Producer/Director
David Fairfield .... Development/Editorial
A. Mills .... Librarian/Research

LETNOM PRODUCTIONS

1104 S. Hayworth Ave.
Los Angeles, CA 90035
PHONE 323-857-6790
FAX 323-933-0737
TYPES Features - Direct-to-Video/DVD - Made-for-TV/Cable Movies - New Media - TV Series
DEALS Paramount Worldwide Television Distribution
CREDITS Little Pieces
COMMENTS Montel Williams's production company

Angela Lee .... President, Production
Guy Rocourt II .... Director, Development
Judy T. Marcelline .... Development Associate

LETT/REESE INTERNATIONAL PRODUCTIONS

1910 Bel Air Rd.
Los Angeles, CA 90077
PHONE 310-472-7387
FAX 310-476-5043
EMAIL .... lettreese@earthlink.net
TYPES Made-for-TV/Cable Movies
DEVELOPMENT Mahalia & Me - Grandma's Hand - The Truth Virus
CREDITS The Secret Path (CBS) - Anya's Bell (CBS) - The Moving of Sophia Myles (CBS)

Franklin Lett .... Chairman/CEO
Della Reese-Lett .... Vice Chairman
Frank T. Lett III .... Producer
Billie E. Hall .... Assistant to Chairman

LEVEL 1 ENTERTAINMENT
9100 Wilshire Blvd., Ste. 503
Beverly Hills, CA 90212
PHONE .310-777-7600
FAX .310-777-7608
TYPES Features - TV Series
DEVELOPMENT Games of the Hangman - King Con - Ring World - Angel City Bullet - Nobody's Safe - Bad Dogs - NASCAR Cabbie - The Covenant - The Seven
CREDITS The In-Laws - Hard to Kill - Diabolique - Bad Moon - Wild America - Incognito - Wild, Wild West - X-Men (Fox) - Married to the Mob (Orion/MGM) - The Innocent (NBC) - The People Next Door - The Owl

Edward L. Milstein . .Co-Chairman/CEO (edwardlmilstein@level1ent.com)
Bill Todman Jr. .Co-Chairman/CEO (billtodmanjr@level1ent.com)
Paul Schwake .COO (paulschwake@level1ent.com)
Erin Newell .Creative Executive (erin@level1ent.com)
Tracey Fiorito .Executive Assistant (tfiorito@level1ent.com)

LEVEL SEVEN FILMS
634 S. Spring St., Ste. 812
Los Angeles, CA 90014
PHONE .213-438-0317
FAX .213-694-2846
EMAIL .vincentf@gabriela.net
TYPES Features - Made-for-TV/Cable Movies - TV Series
DEVELOPMENT Blood Ties - Freddie - Double Cross - Captain Blood - The Sleeper - Brothers - The Wheelman
PRE-PRODUCTION Level 7 - The Wheelman - The Grave - Day After Day
CREDITS Gabriela

Vincent J. Francillon .Producer

RON LEVINSON PRODUCTIONS
7000 Raintree Circle, Ste. 201
Culver City, CA 90230
PHONE .310-559-2470
TYPES Features - TV Series
CREDITS Gene Roddenberry's Earth: Final Conflict - In the Arms of a Killer - Relic Hunter - Pink Panther

Ron Levinson .Producer/Writer

THE LEVINSON/FONTANA COMPANY
185 Broome St.
New York, NY 10002
PHONE .212-206-3585
FAX .212-206-3581
WEB SITE .www.tomfontana.com
SECOND WEB SITE .www.levinson.com
TYPES Made-for-TV/Cable Movies - TV Series
CREDITS Homicide: Life on the Street - Oz - The Beat - The Jury - Strip Search (HBO) - Shot in the Heart (HBO)
SUBMISSION POLICY Through agent only

Barry Levinson .Executive Producer/Director/Writer
Tom Fontana .Executive Producer/Writer
James Finnerty .Executive Producer
Kevin Deiboldt .Assistant to Mr. Fontana
Brant Englestein .Assistant to Mr. Fontana

ZANE W. LEVITT PRODUCTIONS/ZETA ENTERTAINMENT
3422 Rowena Ave.
Los Angeles, CA 90027
PHONE .323-668-2108
EMAIL .zwlprod@aol.com
TYPES Features - TV Series
PRE-PRODUCTION Tree Crosses
CREDITS Blast - Montana - Guncrazy - Shiloh - Shiloh Season - Amityville - Fist of the North Star - Liquid Dreams - The Big Squeeze - One Good Turn - Mortuary Academy - Out of the Dark - A Sea Apart - Puerta Vallarta Squeeze

Zane W. Levitt .CEO/Producer
Rowena Murphy .CFO/Producer

MICHAEL I. LEVY ENTERPRISES
12210-1/2 Nebraska Ave.
Los Angeles, CA 90025
PHONE .310-954-0175
FAX .310-826-0071
TYPES Documentaries - Features - Direct-to-Video/DVD - Made-for-TV/Cable Movies - New Media - Reality TV - Syndication - TV Series
CREDITS O - Gardens Of Stone - Prelude To A Kiss - Gotcha - Article 99 - Masquerade
COMMENTS Management company; Corporate consulting

Michael I. Levy .Producer/Manager
Tony Heffner .Development Executive

LICHT/MUELLER FILM CORPORATION
132 S. Lasky Dr., Ste. 200
Beverly Hills, CA 90212
PHONE .310-205-5500
FAX .310-205-5590
WEB SITE .www.licht-mueller.com
TYPES Features - Made-for-TV/Cable Movies - TV Series
CREDITS Idle Hands - The Cable Guy - Waterworld - Spinning Boris (Showtime)

Andrew Licht .Producer
Jeffrey Mueller .Producer
Chris Kachel .Creative Assistant

BARBARA LIEBERMAN PRODUCTIONS
c/o Robert Greenwald Productions, Inc.
10510 Culver Blvd.
Culver City, CA 90232
PHONE .310-204-0404
FAX .310-204-0174
TYPES Features - Made-for-TV/Cable Movies - TV Series
CREDITS The Dead Will Tell - Ann Rule Presents The Stranger Beside Me - Gleason - Obsessed - Fever - And Never Let Her Go - Til Death Us Do Part

Barbara Lieberman .Executive Producer
Quinn Saunders .Development Associate

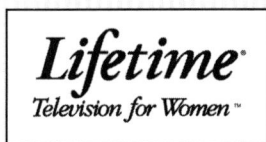

LIFETIME TELEVISION (LOS ANGELES)
2049 Century Park East, Ste. 840
Los Angeles, CA 90067
PHONE .310-556-7500
WEB SITE .www.lifetimetv.com
TYPES Made-for-TV/Cable Movies - Reality TV - TV Series
CREDITS Homeless to Harvard - Gracie's Choice - We Were the Mulvaneys - Sex and the Single Mom - The Truth About Jane - Strong Medicine - The Division - Wild Card - Missing - Any Day Now - What Should You Do? - Speaking of Women's Health - Intimate Portrait - Merge - Head 2 Toe

Carole Black .President/CEO
Rick Haskins .Executive VP/General Manager, Lifetime Entertainment Services
Louise Henry-Bryson .Executive VP, Affiliate Relations
Bill Brand .Sr. VP, Reality Programming
Kelly Goode .Sr. VP, Scripted Programming
Trevor Walton .Sr. VP, Original Movies
Libby Beers .VP, Original Movies
Theresa Edy .VP, Scripted Programming
Marian Effinger .VP, Reality Programming
Marianne Goode .VP, Music
Rick Jacobs .VP, Talent
Colleen McCormick .VP, Production, Scripted Programming
Charisse McGhee-Lazarou .VP, Current Series Programming
Dorian Winship .VP, Production, Reality Programming
Arturo Interian .Director, Original Movies
Rebecca Whittington .Director, Original Movies
Mark Petulla .Director, Production, Scripted Programming
Colette Shelton .Director, Reality Programming
Jennifer Jenkins .Manager, Original Movies

LIFETIME TELEVISION (NEW YORK)
c/o Worldwide Plaza
309 W. 49th St.
New York, NY 10019
PHONE .212-424-7000/718-706-3600
WEB SITE .www.lifetimetv.com
TYPES TV Series - Reality TV
CREDITS See Lifetime Television (Los Angeles)
COMMENTS Studio address: 34-12 36th St., Astoria, NY 11106

Carole Black .President/CEO
Lynn Picard .Executive VP/General Manager, Lifetime Television Network
James Wesley .CFO/Executive VP, Finance
Tim Brooks .Executive VP, Research
Pat Langer .Executive VP, Business & Legal Affairs/Human Resources
Meredith Wagner .Executive VP, Public Affairs
Leslie Glenn-Chesloff .Sr. VP, Acquisitions, Planning & Scheduling
Val Boreland .VP, Scheduling, Planning & Acquisitions
Ron Plante .VP, Strategic Planning & Scheduling
Allison Wallach .VP, Original Programming
Kristine Hunsinger .Director, Scheduling & Acquisitions

LIGHTHOUSE ENTERTAINMENT
409 N. Camden Dr., Ste. 202
Beverly Hills, CA 90210
PHONE .310-246-0499
FAX .310-246-0899
EMAIL .amijb@lighthousela.com
TYPES Features - TV Series
DEVELOPMENT A Violent Act - Family Business - Joy of Living - Isle of Women
PRE-PRODUCTION Hollywood Valentine - Searching for John Wayne - Caught in the Act - Chaos Theory
POST PRODUCTION A Good Woman
CREDITS Cherish - A Foreign Affair - The Rookie - Gridlock'd - Fun - Dream with the Fishes

Steven Siebert .Producer/President
Ami J. Baldwin .Development/Management
Elle Fisher .Executive Assistant

LIGHTHOUSE PRODUCTIONS
120 El Camino Dr., Ste. 212
Beverly Hills, CA 90212
PHONE .310-859-4923
FAX .310-859-7511
EMAIL .lighthouse38@hotmail.com
TYPES Features - Direct-to-Video/DVD - New Media - TV Series
DEVELOPMENT Mimzy - Tropic of Night - Little Boy Blue
CREDITS The Flamingo Kid - The Sting - Close Encounters of the Third Kind - Taxi Driver - Mimic - Impostor
SUBMISSION POLICY No unsolicited submissions; Synopses only

Michael Phillips .Producer/President
Juliana Maio .Producer (310-859-2309)
John Frank Rosenblum .Producer (310-859-0670)
Toni Baffo .Producer
Lucy Mukerjee .Director, Development

LIGHTMOTIVE, INC.
10351 Santa Monica Blvd., Ste. 402
Los Angeles, CA 90025
PHONE .310-282-0660
FAX .310-282-0990
TYPES Features - New Media - TV Series
CREDITS The Killing Fields - The Mission - Undressed - Vatel
SUBMISSION POLICY No unsolicited material

Roland Joffe .CEO/Chairman
Brian Lhee .Production Executive

LIGHTSTONE ENTERTAINMENT, INC.
6430 Sunset Blvd., 10th Fl.
Los Angeles, CA 90028
PHONE .323-301-4250
FAX .323-301-4202/323-301-4204
EMAIL .lightfilms@sbcglobal.net
SECOND EMAIL .lightfilms@aol.com
WEB SITE .www.lightstoneentertainment.com
TYPES Commercials - Features - Music Videos - TV Series
DEVELOPMENT Bullfighter - Dragster - Goliath - Bounty
PRE-PRODUCTION Bobby Zero
CREDITS 3000 Miles to Graceland - Lowball - Chix on Flix (New Media) - Venus & Vegas - Love & Suicide - The Unseen

Demian Lichtenstein .President
Scott Lochmus .Producer
Luis Moro .Producer
Lisa Collins .Creative Executive
Jesse Guma .Creative Executive
Miklos Wright .Creative Development
David Coplan Schneider .Development

It is illegal to copy any part of this book

LIGHTSTORM ENTERTAINMENT

919 Santa Monica Blvd.
Santa Monica, CA 90401
PHONE 310-656-6100
FAX 310-656-6102
TYPES Features
DEALS Twentieth Century Fox
CREDITS Strange Days - Titanic - Aliens - Abyss - Terminator - T2 - True Lies
SUBMISSION POLICY No unsolicited material

James Cameron . . . . Chairman/CEO
Jon Landau . . . . Partner
Rae Sanchini . . . . Partner/President
Curtis Burch . . . . VP, Development
Greg Frankovich . . . . VP, Production & Development
Tom Cohen . . . . Creative Executive

LINE DRIVE PRODUCTIONS

12222 Wilshire Blvd., Penthouse 3
Los Angeles, CA 90025
PHONE 310-571-0195
FAX 310-571-9150
TYPES Features - Made-for-TV/Cable Movies
DEVELOPMENT Stopping Power - Nightlife - Containment
CREDITS Bad Moon - Body Parts - The Hitcher - Near Dark - Blue Steel - Cohen and Tate - Undertow - The Last Outlaw

Eric Red . . . . Writer/Director/Producer
Meredith Casey . . . . Director, Development
John Fallon . . . . Creative Executive

LINKLETTER/ATKINS/KRITZER

8484 Wilshire Blvd., Ste. 205
Beverly Hills, CA 90211
PHONE 323-655-5696
FAX 323-655-5173
EMAIL . . . . producedby@aol.com
WEB SITE . . . . www.eddiekritzer.com
TYPES Animation - Documentaries - Features - Direct-to-Video/DVD - Made-for-TV/Cable Movies - New Media - Radio - Syndication - TV Series
DEVELOPMENT The New Kids Say the Darndest Things (Nick@Nite) - Television Week - Movie Call - Gmen & Gangsters - We Are the Champions
CREDITS High Voltage (KDP Productions) - Kids Say the Darndest Things (CBS, Syndication) - False Witness (NBC) - Shattered: If Your Kid's on Drugs (USA/Universal Home Video)
COMMENTS Created and produced Rockline; Founded Global Satellite Network, part of Clear Channel

Art Linkletter . . . . Partner
Irvin Atkins . . . . Partner
Eddie Kritzer . . . . Partner

LION EYES ENTERTAINMENT

12210-1/2 Nebraska Ave.
Los Angeles, CA 90025
PHONE 310-943-4354
FAX 310-954-0171
TYPES Features - New Media - TV Series
DEVELOPMENT Shi - Paper Dragon - W.A.S.P. - Subterranean
CREDITS White Squall - Thelma & Louise - The Browning Version - Trapped

Mimi Polk Gitlin . . . . Producer/President
Richard Gitlin . . . . Producer
Anthony Baker . . . . Story Editor/Assistant to Mimi Polk Gitlin

LION ROCK PRODUCTIONS

2120 Colorado Ave., Ste. 225
Santa Monica, CA 90404
PHONE 310-309-2980
FAX 310-309-6151
TYPES Features - TV Series
DEALS Paramount Pictures-Motion Picture Group
CREDITS Paycheck - The Big Hit - Face/Off - Broken Arrow - Windtalkers - Bulletproof Monk - Mission Impossible 2
COMMENTS Video game studio: Tiger Hill

John Woo . . . . Director/Producer
Terence Chang . . . . Producer
Caroline Macaulay . . . . Executive VP
Suzanne Zizzi . . . . Sr. VP
Annie Hughes . . . . VP
Brittany Philion . . . . Executive Assistant to Mr. Woo
Casey Collins . . . . Assistant to Mr. Woo
Todd Weinger . . . . Assistant to Mr. Chang
Tom W. Metz III . . . . Assistant to Ms. Macaulay & Ms. Zizzi

LIONS GATE ENTERTAINMENT

2700 Colorado Ave.
Santa Monica, CA 90404
PHONE 310-449-9200
FAX 310-255-3870
EMAIL . . . . recep@lgecorp.com
WEB SITE . . . . www.lionsgatefilms.com
TYPES Animation - Features - Direct-to-Video/DVD - Made-for-TV/Cable Movies - TV Series
CREDITS Features: Monster's Ball - Farenheit 9/11 - The Cooler - Girl With A Pearl Earring - The Punisher - Cabin Fever - American Psycho - Requiem for a Dream - Reservoir Dogs - Shattered Glass - Confidence - Blair Witch Project - National Lampoon's Van Wilder; Television: The Dead Zone - 1-800 Missing - 5 Days to Midnight
COMMENTS Diversified entertainment production and distribution company operating four core businesses: Motion pictures, TV, animation and studio facilities; Majority ownership of CinemaNow Video-on-Demand business

Jon Feltheimer . . . . CEO
Mark Amin . . . . Vice Chairman
Michael Burns . . . . Vice Chairman
Steve Beeks . . . . President, Lions Gate Entertainment, Inc.
Jim Keegan . . . . CAO/CFO
Wayne Levin . . . . General Counsel/Executive VP, Corporate Operations
John Dellaverson . . . . Executive VP
Marni Wieshofer . . . . Executive VP, Corporate Development

(Continued)

LIONS GATE ENTERTAINMENT (Continued)

Tom Ortenberg . . . . President, Lions Gate Films Releasing
Steve Rothenberg . . . . Executive VP, Domestic Theatrical Distribution
Michael Paseornek . . . . President, Lions Gate Films Production
Donna Sloan . . . . Sr. VP, Lions Gate Films Production
Jonathan Ruiz . . . . VP, Lions Gate Films Production
John Sacchi . . . . VP, Lions Gate Films Production
Robert Melnik . . . . Sr. VP, Business Affairs, Lions Gate Films Production
Carl Pedregal . . . . VP, Feature Post Production
Nick Meyer . . . . Co-President, Lions Gate International Films
Sergei Yershov . . . . Co-President, Lions Gate International Films
Peter Block . . . . President, Home Entertainment, Acquisitions & New Media
Jason Constantine . . . . Sr. VP, Acquisitions
Glenn Ross . . . . President, Lions Gate Family Home Entertainment
Ron Schwartz . . . . Executive VP, Home Video Sales
Kevin Beggs . . . President, Lions Gate Television Programming & Production
Sandra Stern . . . . Executive VP, TV Business & Legal Affairs
Joanna Klein . . . . VP, Series TV
Richard Jordan . . . . Executive VP, Physical Operations
Sarah Greenberg . . . . Executive VP, Publicity
Tim Palen . . . . Sr. VP, Marketing
Anne Parducci . . . . Executive VP, Retail & Consumer Marketing
Curt Marvis . . . . CEO, CinemaNow

JAMES LIPTON PRODUCTIONS

159 E. 80th St.
New York, NY 10021
PHONE 212-535-9500
FAX 212-772-1126
TYPES: Made-for-TV/Cable Movies - TV Series
CREDITS: Inside the Actors' Studio - Copacabana - Mirrors - Bob Hope Specials

James Lipton . . . . Writer/Producer

*LIQUID THEORY

8981 Sunset Blvd., Ste. 102
Los Angeles, CA 90046
PHONE 310-276-1094
FAX 310-276-1093
EMAIL . . . . info@liquid-theory.com
WEB SITE . . . . www.liquid-theory.com
TYPES: Animation - Commercials - Music Videos - TV Series
DEALS: MTV Networks - Overbrook Entertainment - Spike TV
CREDITS: Spike Likes Movies - Roger That (Spike TV) - MTV Reality Awards - MTV Video Music Awards - MTV Movie Awards - VH1 Big in '03 Awards - GQ Awards - MusiCares: Person of the Year - VH1 Fashion Awards - Rock and Roll Hall of Fame Ceremony - 52 Most Irresistible Women (Spike TV)
COMMENTS: Deal with Guild/Kelly Productions

Austin Reading . . . . No Title
Julie Kellman Reading . . . . No Title
Michael Lang . . . . No Title

THE LITTLEFIELD COMPANY

c/o Paramount Studios
5555 Melrose Ave., Cooper Bldg., Ste.115
Hollywood, CA 90038
PHONE 323-956-8850
FAX 323-862-2252
TYPES: TV Series
DEALS: Paramount Television
CREDITS: Keen Eddie (Fox) - Like Family (WB) - Do Over (WB)

Warren Littlefield . . . . Principal
Andrew Bourne . . . . VP, Development (x8857)
Chad Gervich . . . . Manager, Talent & Development (x8862)
Patricia Mann . . . . Executive Assistant to Mr. Littlefield (x8861)

GEORGE LITTO PRODUCTIONS, INC.

c/o Warner Bros.
4000 Warner Blvd., Bldg. 138, Rm. 1103
Burbank, CA 91522
PHONE 818-954-1627
FAX 818-954-6584
TYPES: Features
DEVELOPMENT: Hawaii Five-0 - Any Four Women Could Rob the Bank of Italy - Accidental Soldier
CREDITS: Over the Edge - Dressed to Kill - Kansas - Blow Out - Obsession - The Crew - Thieves Like Us - Drive In - Night Game

George Litto . . . . CEO/Owner
Andria Litto . . . . Partner/President
Linda Lee . . . . Executive Assistant

LIVEPLANET

2644 30th St., Ste. 101
Santa Monica, CA 90405
PHONE 310-664-2400
FAX 310-664-2401
EMAIL . . . . info@liveplanet.com
WEB SITE . . . . www.liveplanet.com
TYPES: Features - New Media - TV Series - Reality TV
DEALS: The Walt Disney Company
CREDITS: American Wedding - Project Greenlight 1&2 - Push, Nevada - The Core - Emperor's Club - American Pie 1&2 - Joy Ride - Stolen Summer - Best Laid Plans - Matchstick Men - Battle of Shaker Heights
SUBMISSION POLICY: No unsolicited material

Larry Tanz . . . . CEO, President
Marc Joubert . . . . Director, Strategic Partnerships
Amanda White . . . . VP, Special Projects
Amanda Hayward . . . . Creative Executive
Michelle Nigro . . . . Creative Executive

LMNO PRODUCTIONS

15821 Ventura Blvd., Ste. 320
Encino, CA 91436
PHONE 818-380-8000
FAX 818-995-5544
WEB SITE . . . . www.lmnotv.com
TYPES: Documentaries - New Media - Reality TV - Syndication - TV Series
CREDITS: Kids Say the Darndest Things - Travel Channel's Secrets - Final Justice with Erin Brockovich (Lifetime) - The Littlest Groom - Babies: Special Delivery - Amazing Medical Stories - Travel Channel World's Best - Behind Closed Doors with Joan Lunden

Eric Schotz . . . . President/CEO/Executive Producer
Bill Paolantonio . . . . Executive VP, Creative Affairs/Executive Producer
Kirk Schenck . . . . Sr. VP, Business Affairs
Lisa Bourgoujian . . . . VP, Cable Group
Larry Goldman . . . . VP, Corporate Communications
Ed Horwitz . . . . VP, Production
Tracey Green . . . . Director, Development

MIKE LOBELL PRODUCTIONS

1424 N. Crescent Heights Blvd., Ste. 21
Los Angeles, CA 90046
PHONE 323-822-2910
TYPES: Features
CREDITS: Striptease - It Could Happen to You - The Freshman - Honeymoon in Vegas - White Fang - Journey of Natty Gann - Tears of the Sun

Mike Lobell . . . . Producer
Kent Anderson . . . . Assistant to Mike Lobell

PETER LOCKE PRODUCTIONS
846 Woodacres Rd.
Santa Monica, CA 90402
PHONE 310-395-3433
FAX 310-458-1241
EMAIL ....peter@peterlocke.net
TYPES — Features - Direct-to-Video/DVD - Made-for-TV/Cable Movies - TV Series
DEVELOPMENT — The Hills Have Eyes (Dimension) - A Man with a Camera (T&D Productions)
CREDITS — Pinocchio (New Line) - Andre (Paramount) - Brave Little Toaster 1-3 (Disney) - Divorce Court - First & Ten (HBO) - Gun (ABC) - Freeway - Harvard Man - Basil - Whole Wide World - Picking Up the Pieces

Peter Locke ....President
Nanette Munro ....Assistant

LOGO ENTERTAINMENT, INC.
1875 Century Park East, Ste. 600
Los Angeles, CA 90067
PHONE 310-276-6700
TYPES — Animation - Documentaries - Features - Direct-to-Video/DVD - Made-for-TV/Cable Movies - Reality TV - Syndication - TV Series
DEALS — MTV Networks
CREDITS — For Love of Olivia - To Dance with Olivia - The Inspectors - The Color of Love: Jacey's Story

Louis Gossett Jr. ....Actor/Executive Producer
Dennis Considine ....Executive Producer

LONDINE PRODUCTIONS
1626 N. Wilcox Ave., Ste. 480
Hollywood, CA 90028-6273
PHONE 310-281-7540
FAX 310-822-9025
EMAIL ....cassiusii@aol.com
TYPES — Commercials - Features - Direct-to-Video/DVD - Made-for-TV/Cable Movies - Music Videos - TV Series
DEVELOPMENT — Runnin' Down Crenshaw - Mall Crazy - At the Movies
PRE-PRODUCTION — Crazy House - The Daydreams and a Man Named Jimmy - Karma
PRODUCTION — Marquest Houston Music Video
POST PRODUCTION — B2K Music Video
CREDITS — D.C. Cab - House Party 4 - High Frequency - You Got Served
SUBMISSION POLICY — By email only
COMMENTS — Internet streaming video; Produced over 70 music videos that have aired on MTV and BET

Cassius Vernon Weathersby ....President/Producer
Nadine Weathersby ....VP/Producer
Joshua Weathersby ....VP

MICHAEL LONDON PRODUCTIONS
1041 N. Formosa Ave., SM East Bldg., Ste. 205
West Hollywood, CA 90046
PHONE 323-850-3530
TYPES — Features
DEALS — Paramount Pictures-Motion Picture Group
DEVELOPMENT — Fortune's Fools - Passengers - The Illusionist
POST PRODUCTION — Sideways
CREDITS — House of Sand and Fog - Thirteen - The Guru - 40 Days and 40 Nights - Second String

Michael London ....Producer
Jane Garnett ....Producer
Khristina Kravas ....Executive Assistant

LONETREE ENTERTAINMENT
23852 Pacific Coast Hwy., Ste. 741
Malibu, CA 90265
PHONE 310-589-6016
FAX 310-589-1506
EMAIL ....lonetreez@aol.com
TYPES — Documentaries - Features - Made-for-TV/Cable Movies - New Media - TV Series
DEALS — TF1 International
DEVELOPMENT — The War Magician - Kiddie Ride - Soul Catchers - Hard Evidence
PRE-PRODUCTION — The Vixens - Chi-Chian
PRODUCTION — The Naked Truth
CREDITS — The Ghost - Code of the Dragon
SUBMISSION POLICY — No unsolicited submissions

Tony Eldridge ....President/Producer
Michele Barbera ....Producer
Roger Davis ....Producer
Victoria Woodbeck-Natkin ....Director, Development
Ian Austin ....Development
Ellen Fitzmaurice ....Development
Rob Lee ....Development Assistant

LONGBOW PRODUCTIONS
15340 Longbow Dr.
Sherman Oaks, CA 91403-4907
PHONE 818-762-6600
EMAIL ....mail@longbowfilms.com
TYPES — Features - Direct-to-Video/DVD - Made-for-TV/Cable Movies - Syndication - Reality TV
DEVELOPMENT — Smoke & Mirrors - The Battle of Hastings - Mt. Weather
PRE-PRODUCTION — World Champions
POST PRODUCTION — Hollywood Hold 'Em
CREDITS — Secret Cutting - The Summer of Ben Tyler - A Private Matter - A League of Their Own - The Last Brickmaker in America - Forever & Always

Bill Pace ....Partner (x10)
Ronnie D. Clemmer ....Partner (x26)
Richard Kughn ....Partner
Herman Hong ....Technological Operations (x31)

LONGFELLOW PICTURES
250 Hudson St., 10th Fl.
New York, NY 10013
PHONE .212-431-5550
FAX .212-431-5822
EMAIL .longfellow@mindspring.com
TYPES Features - Direct-to-Video/DVD
CREDITS Princess Caraboo - The Prince of Tides - The Rachel Papers - Curtain Call - Town and Country - The Perfect You - The Emperor's Club
SUBMISSION POLICY No unsolicited material

Rachel Horovitz .Producer
Andrew Karsch .Producer
John Fireman .Assistant
Elizabeth Marvin .Assistant

LOOKING GLASS PRODUCTIONS
2118 Wilshire Blvd., Ste. 760
Santa Monica, CA 90403-5784
PHONE .310-281-7598
FAX .323-663-6270
WEB SITE .www.lookingglassproductions.com
TYPES Animation - Documentaries - Features - New Media - Theater - TV Series
CREDITS Sand Trap - The Thing at Pete and Julie's - Shiny Objects - R&H Educational Films - Moving Alan

Jerry Rapp .Writer/Director/Producer
Karen Hayden-Jaffe .Director, Development
Daedalus Howell .Writer/Director

LYNN LORING PRODUCTIONS
2313 Canyonback Rd.
Los Angeles, CA 90049
PHONE .310-472-5050
FAX .310-476-2828
EMAIL .lynn3939@aol.com
TYPES Features - Direct-to-Video/DVD - Made-for-TV/Cable Movies - New Media - Syndication - TV Series
DEVELOPMENT I Love You Tomorrow
CREDITS Mr. Mom - Best Little Girl in the World - Taking Gary Feldman

Lynn Loring .President/Executive Producer
Brett Tracy .Creative Assistant

LOTUS PICTURES
10433 Wilshire Blvd., Ste. 602
Los Angeles, CA 90024
PHONE .310-474-7803
FAX .310-474-7452
EMAIL .lotuspics@aol.com
TYPES Features - Made-for-TV/Cable Movies
DEVELOPMENT Seeing Red - Jinetera - The Haole Substitute - The Rig - Tark the Shark - Binion Murder Story
PRE-PRODUCTION Double the Danger - Aurora Island
CREDITS Blacktop - Legacy - Bandits - Baywatch (TV) - Stateside - Downtown: A Street Tale

Michele Berk .Owner/Producer
Joseph Salemi .VP, Production
Sidney Kiwitt .Business Affairs

LOVE SPELL ENTERTAINMENT
500 S. Buena Vista St., Animation 1-E, Rm. 24
Burbank, CA 91521
PHONE .818-560-5376
FAX .818-560-6430
TYPES Features - TV Series
DEALS Touchstone Television
DEVELOPMENT Bunny - My Romance - Secrets - 13 Seconds
POST PRODUCTION If Only

Jennifer Love Hewitt .President
Kim Kovac .VP, Development & Production
Matt Ferrone .Creative Executive

LUCKY CROW FILMS
4335 Van Nuys Blvd., Ste. 335
Sherman Oaks, CA 91403
PHONE .818-783-7529/818-990-8030
FAX .818-783-7594
EMAIL .luckycrow@aol.com
TYPES Documentaries - Features - Made-for-TV/Cable Movies
DEVELOPMENT 65 Roses - Flight - God Box - The Californias - Code - She's a Rich Girl - Unnatural Selection
PRE-PRODUCTION Closer to Fine
POST PRODUCTION Perfect Match
COMPLETED UNRELEASED My Date with Drew
CREDITS Agent Cody Banks 1&2 - The Usual Suspects (Special Edition DVD) - Mercy Streets

Kerry David .Producer
Jon Gunn .Producer/Director
Christine Norton .President, Production
Robin Pruzansky .Creative Executive
Jianna Maarten .No Title

LOIS LUGER PRODUCTIONS, INC.
10542 Whipple St.
Toluca Lake, CA 91602
PHONE .818-487-6950
TYPES Features - Direct-to-Video/DVD - TV Series
CREDITS Terror in the Shadows - The Danger of Love - Lion of Africa

Lois Luger .President/Producer
Wendy Arthur .Creative Executive

LUMINOUS ENTERTAINMENT
5820 Wilshire Blvd., Ste 400
Los Angeles, CA 90036
PHONE .323-931-3700
FAX .323-931-8649
TYPES Features
DEVELOPMENT Untitled Revolution Studios Project - A Thousand Days - Untitled Surf Documentary
COMPLETED UNRELEASED Admissions - Guarding Eddy
CREDITS Twin Falls Idaho - Still Breathing - Kill the Man - Cherry Falls - The Breed - Wild Iris

Annette Vait .Producer
Joyce Schweickert .Executive Producer

LUNARIA FILMS
2922 Second St., Ste. E
Santa Monica, CA 90405-5433
PHONE .310-581-9212
FAX .310-581-9512
EMAIL .lunariafilms@mindspring.com
TYPES Features - Made-for-TV/Cable Movies - TV Series
DEVELOPMENT Saint-Ex - John Steinbeck's Travels with Charley - The War Junkie - The Sunday Wife - Breathing Recommended - Sing Fat and the Imperial Duchess of Woo - The Star Detective Agency
CREDITS Kicking & Screaming - Black Circle Boys - The Only Thrill - Vig - Lakeboat

Erin E. Martin .Producer

DAN LUPOVITZ PRODUCTIONS
1501 S. Holt Ave.
Los Angeles, CA 90035
PHONE .310-276-4923
FAX .310-385-0196
TYPES Features - Made-for-TV/Cable Movies - TV Series
CREDITS Simpatico - Search and Destroy - The Velocity of Gary - Mrs. Cage - Late for Dinner

Dan Lupovitz .Producer
Randy Albelda .Head, Development

A.C. LYLES PRODUCTIONS
c/o Paramount Pictures
5555 Melrose Ave., Hart Bldg.
Hollywood, CA 90038-3197
PHONE .323-956-5819
TYPES Features - TV Series
DEALS Paramount Pictures-Motion Picture Group
CREDITS Deadwood (HBO) - Conversations with the President - The Last Day - Dear Mr. President - Here's Boomer

A.C. Lyles .Executive Producer

THE TOM LYNCH COMPANY
421 South Beverly Dr., 7th Fl.
Beverly Hills, CA 90212
PHONE .310-789-4727
FAX .310-282-9176
WEB SITE .www.tomlynchco.com
TYPES TV Series - Features - Made-for-TV/Cable Movies - Direct-to-Video/DVD - Animation - Syndication - Reality TV - New Media
PRODUCTION Secret Central
CREDITS Red Sneakers - The Jersey - Journey of Allen Strange - 100 Deeds for Eddie McDowd - Night Tracks - Kids Inc. - Secret World of Alex Mack - Caitlin's Way - Just Deal - Skate - Scout's Safari - Romeo!

Thomas W. Lynch .CEO/Writer/Executive Producer/Director
Gary Stephenson .Sr. VP
Keith Fay .Director, Development
Brenda Bisner . .Production Dept. Coordinator/Co-Director, Development
Andy Fiedler .Executive Assistant

LYNCH SIDEROW PRODUCTIONS
11500 W. Olympic Blvd., Ste. 364
Los Angeles, CA 90064
PHONE .310-473-4733
FAX .310-473-7174
TYPES Features - TV Series
PRE-PRODUCTION The Hollow Men
CREDITS Spyder Games - The Andy Dick Show - Jackass, the Movie - Virgin Chronicles

Norman Siderow .CEO
John D. Lynch .President
Darren Wadyko .Development & Production

THE LYNN COMPANY
1611 Abbot Kinney Blvd.
Venice, CA 90291
PHONE .310-581-2000
FAX .310-581-2010
EMAIL .jonathan@jonathanlynn.com
WEB SITE .www.thelynncompany.net
TYPES Features - TV Series

Jonathan Lynn .Producer
Edward Lynn .Producer

TAMI LYNN PRODUCTIONS
20411 Chapter Dr.
Woodland Hills, CA 91364
PHONE .818-888-8264
FAX .818-888-8267
EMAIL .tamilynn8264@aol.com
TYPES Documentaries - Features - TV Series
DEVELOPMENT CASA - Dead Day - The Man That God Forgot - Not Scarred for Life - 90 Miles to Bakersfield - Sleeping with the Lion
CREDITS Kiss of Fire - Claudine's Return - Jesse - Vibrations - Given a Chance... A Little Girl's Journey - Given a Chance... I'm Just Like You

Tami Lynn .President/Producer
Kim Marriner .Producer/Writer/Avid Editor
Marc Alexander .Producer/Writer
John Tamiazzo .Writer
Kassie Marriner .Co-Producer
Humaira Arsalan .Assistant to Ms. Lynn
Linda Gomez .Assistant to Ms. Lynn

MACARIEDELSTEIN FILMS
112 N. Mansfield Ave.
Los Angeles, CA 90036
PHONE .323-938-7007/323-936-1967
TYPES Features
DEVELOPMENT Manila Bay (Disney) - No Place Like Home (New Line) - Le Trou - The Big Blow (Scott Free/Fox Production) - Gideon (Fox) - Resurrection (Disney) - Shelter (InterMedia)
PRE-PRODUCTION The Invisible - No Place Like Home - Cold Hand in Mine
PRODUCTION The Ring 2
CREDITS Mulholland Drive - The Straight Story - Lumiere Campaign - The Ring

Neal Edelstein .Producer (323-938-7007)
Mike Macari .Producer (323-936-1967)

MACGILLIVRAY FREEMAN FILMS
PO Box 205
Laguna Beach, CA 92652
PHONE 949-494-1055
FAX 949-494-2079
WEB SITE .....www.macfreefilms.com
TYPES Documentaries - Large Format
DEVELOPMENT Space Journey - Ocean Planet
PRODUCTION Greece: Secrets of the Past
CREDITS Everest - Dolphins - The Living Sea - To Fly! - Coral Reef Adventure - Top Speed
COMMENTS IMAX Documentaries

Greg MacGillivray .....President/Producer/Director
Alec Lorimore .....Producer/VP, Production & Development

TREVOR MACY PRODUCTIONS
1048 4th St.
Santa Monica, CA 90403
PHONE 310-393-3233
FAX 310-393-3243
EMAIL .....trevormacy1@aol.com
TYPES Features - Made-for-TV/Cable Movies
DEALS Catch 23 Entertainment, Inc.
DEVELOPMENT Vanishing Acts - Breathing Underwater - The First Year's a Bitch
PRE-PRODUCTION Dolan's Cadillac - Going Cold
CREDITS Autofocus - The Badge - Bark

Trevor Macy .....Producer

MAD CHANCE
9021 Melrose Ave., Ste. 202
West Hollywood, CA 90069
PHONE 310-285-2077
FAX 310-285-2078
EMAIL .....firstname@madchance.com
TYPES Features
DEVELOPMENT Dramarama - Lisa Andersen - IQ83 - Get Smart - Diva - Hergatory - Fellini Black and White
CREDITS Catch That Kid - Confessions of a Dangerous Mind - Death to Smoochy - Cats and Dogs - Panic - Space Cowboys - Lucky Numbers - Ten Things I Hate About You - Bound - Assassins - The Astronaut's Wife

Andrew Lazar .....Producer
Far Shariat .....Sr. VP
Gym Hinderer .....Viceroy, Production
Lindsey Worgul .....Assistant

MADAHORNE ENTERTAINMENT, INC.
150 E. Olive, Ste. 305
Burbank, CA 91502
PHONE 818-841-0455
FAX 818-841-4106
TYPES Made-for-TV/Cable Movies - Syndication - TV Series - Reality TV
CREDITS That's Life - Suburban Sleuths - Rock Gardens - The Architecture of Wine Country

Maddy Horne .....Executive Producer
Bree LeMasters .....Director, Development

BILL MADSEN PRODUCTIONS
10200 Pico Blvd.
Los Angeles, CA 90025
PHONE 310-444-5575
TYPES Features
CREDITS Citizen Hero - Lady Lake

Bill Madsen .....Producer
Ann Forester-Jacobsen .....Director, Development

MADSTONE FILMS
85 Fifth Ave., 12th Fl.
New York, NY 10003
PHONE 212-989-4500
FAX 212-989-7744
EMAIL .....info@madstonefilms.com
WEB SITE .....www.madstonefilms.com
TYPES Features
COMPLETED UNRELEASED Rhinoceros Eyes
CREDITS One Day Crossing

Tom Gruenberg .....Co-CEO
Chip Seelig .....Co-CEO
Chris Davis .....CFO
Michael Kuhn .....Sr. VP, Marketing & Publicity

GUY MAGAR FILMS
7185 Woodrow Wilson Dr.
Los Angeles, CA 90068
PHONE 323-461-9009
FAX 323-876-9809
EMAIL .....filmmaking@actioncut.com
WEB SITE .....www.actioncut.com
TYPES Features - Direct-to-Video/DVD - TV Series
DEVELOPMENT Medusa - Encounter from Beyond - The Offspring - Justice Denied - Bounty Hunter
PRE-PRODUCTION The Myth
CREDITS Children of the Corn: Revelation - Dark Avenger - Showdown - Stepfather 3 - Retribution

Guy Magar .....Director/Writer/Producer

MAGIC HALLWAY PICTURES
9100 Wilshire Blvd., Ste. 700-E
Beverly Hills, CA 90212
PHONE 310-247-2030
FAX 310-786-8796
TYPES Features - Made-for-TV/Cable Movies - TV Series
DEALS Warner Bros. Pictures
DEVELOPMENT Manchild in the Promised Land - He Say She Say - Step - Untitled Wedding Project

Earvin Johnson .....Partner
Paul Hall .....Partner
Nikkole Denson .....President
Wesley Jones .....Assistant to Paul Hall

MAGIC LIGHT PICTURES
Pinewood Studios, Pinewood Rd.
Iver, Buckinghamshire SLO 0NH UK
PHONE .44-1753-652778
FAX .44-1753-655043
EMAIL .emma@magiclightpictures.com
TYPES Animation - Features
COMPLETED UNRELEASED Touch of Pink
CREDITS Chicken Run - The Heart of Me - The Lawless Heart - Alive and Kicking
SUBMISSION POLICY Unsolicited submissions not accepted
COMMENTS Comedy; Family

Martin Pope .Producer
Michael Rose .Producer
Chloe Sizer .Head, Development
Emma Edwards .Assistant

*MAGNET MANAGEMENT
6380 Wilshire Blvd., Ste. 915
Los Angeles, CA 90048
PHONE .See Below
FAX .323-658-8646
EMAIL .magnetasst@magnetmanagement.com
TYPES Features
DEVELOPMENT Parasomnia - Housemom
COMMENTS Deal with Matinee Pictures

Jennie Frankel .Producer/Manager (323-658-8123)
Zach Tann .Producer/Manager (323-658-8095)
Bob Sobhani .Producer/Manager (323-658-8095)
Steve Freedman .Manager (323-658-8953)
Darren Yesser .Manager (323-658-8345)
Chris Robinson .Creative Executive (323-658-8706)

MAGNETIC FILM
310 N. Stanley Ave.
Los Angeles, CA 90036
PHONE .323-933-6066
FAX .323-933-6866
TYPES Features - Reality TV
DEVELOPMENT T.U.F.F. - Dice - Underdog - Fourteen 40
CREDITS The United States of Leland

Bernie Morris .CEO/Producer
Bryan Meyers .Creative Executive
Susie Rosen .Executive Assistant

MAIN LINE PICTURES
7920 Sunset Blvd., Ste. 250
Los Angeles, CA 90046
PHONE .323-851-5555
WEB SITE .www.mainlinepictures.com
TYPES Features
DEVELOPMENT White Deer Lake - The Back Nine - USS Indianapolis
CREDITS Boxing Helena - Body Count - Good Advice - Run Ronnie Run! - 3 Amigos - Dumb and Dumberer

James Schaeffer .Chairman
Carl Mazzocone .President
Liz Hecht-Ward .Controller

MAINLINE RELEASING
301 Arizona Ave., Ste. 400
Santa Monica, CA 90401
PHONE .310-255-1200
FAX .310-255-1201
TYPES Documentaries - Features - Direct-to-Video/DVD - TV Series
PRODUCTION Wild Things 3 - Ides of March
CREDITS Indiscreet - Hangman - Wild Things 2

Rich Goldberg .President
Marc Greenberg .President
Tannaz Anisi .VP, International Sales
Marc Bienstock .VP, Production
Joe Dickstein .VP, Acquisitions
Steve Putnam .Director, Post Production

MAKE BELIEVE MEDIA USA
PO Box 2032
Los Angeles, CA 90078
PHONE .323-960-5500
FAX .323-960-5587
TYPES Documentaries - Features - Syndication
DEVELOPMENT American Soldier (Feature) - Islandia (Feature)
COMPLETED UNRELEASED The Works (Feature)

Thomas Sammon .Producer
Marlon Giles .Development
Ann O'Leary .Assistant to Thomas Sammon

MAKEMAGIC PRODUCTIONS
8489 W. Third St., Ste. 1044
Los Angeles, CA 90048
PHONE .323-653-3108
FAX .323-653-3144
EMAIL .ddavid@makemagicproductions.com
WEB SITE .www.makemagicproductions.com
SECOND WEB SITE .www.mydinnerwithovitz.com
TYPES Features
DEVELOPMENT Family for Sale - Vampire's Paradise - The Clairvoyant
PRE-PRODUCTION A Good American - Uvalde - Oscar Divo
CREDITS My Dinner with Ovitz
COMMENTS Script consulting available

Denise David .President/Producer
Steve B. Young .Writer/Director
Chris Duarte .Development Assistant

*MALOOF TELEVISION
3110 Main St., Ste. 205
Santa Monica, CA 90405
PHONE .310-452-5760
FAX .310-396-7401
WEB SITE .www.maloof-tv.com
TYPES Features - Made-for-TV/Cable Movies - New Media - Reality TV - Syndication - TV Series
DEALS Metro-Goldwyn-Mayer Worldwide Television
DEVELOPMENT Score
SUBMISSION POLICY No unsolicited material

Phil Maloof .Owner/Chairman
Gavin Maloof .Owner
Joe Maloof .Owner
George Maloof .Owner
Adrienne Maloof .Owner
Andrew Jameson .President
Ben Pratt .Director, Development

MALPASO PRODUCTIONS

c/o Warner Bros.
4000 Warner Blvd., Bldg. 81
Burbank, CA 91522-0811
PHONE 818-954-3367/818-954-2567
FAX 818-954-4803
TYPES Features
DEALS Warner Bros. Pictures
CREDITS Mystic River - The Bridges of Madison County - Bird - Unforgiven - Space Cowboys - Blood Work

Clint Eastwood . . . . Producer/Actor/Director
Judie Hoyt . . . . Producer
Robert Lorenz . . . . Producer/1st AD
Joel Cox . . . . Film Editor

MANAGED PASSION FILMS

PO Box 491202
Los Angeles, CA 90049
PHONE 310-777-8860
FAX 310-777-8864
EMAIL . . . . mgdpassion@aol.com
TYPES Features - Direct-to-Video/DVD - Made-for-TV/Cable Movies
DEVELOPMENT Big Mutt - Dinky (The Train) - Three Wild Ones - The Shouting Duke - Rainmaker - The Looters
CREDITS The Hungry Bachelors Club - Deadly Little Secrets

Kimberly Becker . . . . President

MANAGEMENT 360

9111 Wilshire Blvd.
Beverly Hills, CA 90210
PHONE 310-272-7000
FAX 310-272-0070
TYPES Features - Reality TV - TV Series
DEALS Warner Bros. Pictures

Suzan Bymel . . . . Partner
Guymon Casady . . . . Partner
Eric Kranzler . . . . Partner
Evelyn O'Neill . . . . Partner
Daniel Rappaport . . . . Partner
David Seltzer . . . . Partner
William Choi . . . . Manager
Doug Johnson . . . . Manager
Peter Kiernan . . . . Manager
Bradley Lefler . . . . Manager
Christie Smith . . . . Manager
Darin Friedman . . . . Director, Development

MANDALAY PICTURES

4751 Wilshire Blvd., 3rd Fl.
Los Angeles, CA 90010
PHONE 323-549-4300
FAX 323-549-9832
TYPES Features
DEALS Universal Pictures

Peter Guber . . . . Chairman/CEO
Paul Schaeffer . . . . Vice Chairman/COO
Randy Hermann . . . . CFO/Executive VP
Shelly Riney . . . . Executive VP, Corporate Operations
Elizabeth Guber Stephen . . . . Executive VP, Motion Picture Production
Peter Strauss . . . . Executive VP
Darrell Walker . . . . Executive VP, Business Affairs
David Zelon . . . . Executive VP, Motion Picture Production
Michelle DiRaffaele . . . . Sr. VP, Motion Picture Administration
Brian Spain . . . . Director, Accounting & Administration

MANDALAY SPORTS ACTION ENTERTAINMENT

4751 Wilshire Blvd., 3rd Fl.
Los Angeles, CA 90010
PHONE 323-549-4300
FAX 323-549-9844
WEB SITE . . . . www.mandalay.com
TYPES Documentaries - Made-for-TV/Cable Movies - Reality TV - Syndication - TV Series
DEVELOPMENT Five Seconds (Feature) - American Street Muscle (TV) - Addicted to Speed (Reality)
COMPLETED UNRELEASED Chowder Heads (Animated)
CREDITS First Daughter - Shutter Speed - First Target - WCW Superstar Series - Go for It (ABC Family) - First Shot - MIA Solved (History Channel) - The Quest for Nutrition (Discovery)
COMMENTS Specials; Branded entertainment

David G. Salzberg . . . . President
Martin Trejo . . . . Director, Development

MANDALAY TELEVISION

4751 Wilshire Blvd., 3rd Fl.
Los Angeles, CA 90010
PHONE 323-549-4300
FAX 323-549-9832
WEB SITE . . . . www.mandalay. com
TYPES Made-for-TV/Cable Movies - TV Series
PRE-PRODUCTION Southie
CREDITS Blood Crime
SUBMISSION POLICY No unsolicited material

Elizabeth Guber Stephen . . . . President (323-549-4370)
Shirley Lima . . . . Creative Executive (323-549-4371)

MANDEVILLE FILMS

500 S. Buena Vista St., Animation Bldg., 2-G
Burbank, CA 91521-1783
PHONE . . . . See Below
FAX 818-842-2937
TYPES Features - TV Series
DEALS The Walt Disney Company - Touchstone Television
CREDITS Mr. Wrong - The Other Sister - George of the Jungle - The Negotiator - Ryan Caufield - Bandits - Bringing Down the House - Antitrust - What's the Worst That Could Happen? - Monk - Raising Helen - The Last Shot - Walking Tall

David Hoberman . . . . CEO (818-560-4077)
Todd Lieberman . . . . President (818-560-4113)
Albert Page . . . . VP, Development (818-560-7903)
Dorian Howard . . . . VP, Development (818-560-7745)
Kim Meade . . . . Executive Assistant to David Hoberman (818-560-4077)
Jenny Marchick . . . . Assistant to Todd Lieberman (818-560-4113)
Boz Adams . . . . Office Assistant (818-560-7662)

MANDOLIN ENTERTAINMENT

12210-1/2 Nebraska Ave.
Los Angeles, CA 90025
PHONE 310-943-4354
FAX 310-954-0171
TYPES Features - New Media - TV Series
CREDITS Trapped - Angel Eyes - Thelma and Louise - White Squall - When a Man Loves a Woman

Mimi Polk Gitlin . . . . Producer/President
Luis Mandoki . . . . Director/Producer
Anthony Baker . . . . Story Editor/Assistant to Mimi Polk Gitlin
Rebecca Husain . . . . Assistant to Luis Mandoki

MANDY FILMS
9201 Wilshire Blvd., Ste. 206
Beverly Hills, CA 90210
PHONE .310-246-0500
FAX .310-246-0350
TYPES Features - Made-for-TV/Cable Movies - TV Series
DEALS Sony Pictures Entertainment
DEVELOPMENT Wonder Woman - The Adaptive Ultimate - Fantasy Island (Feature) - The Sleeping Detective
CREDITS Sleeping with the Enemy - War Games - Distinguished Gentleman - Double Jeopardy - Charlie's Angels 1&2 - Ground Zero

Leonard Goldberg .President
Amanda Goldberg .VP, Development/Production
Mimi Miller .Executive Assistant to Leonard Goldberg
Leslie Kolb .Assistant to Amanda Goldberg
Will Pilgrim .Assistant

THE MANHATTAN PROJECT, LTD.
1775 Broadway, Ste. 410
New York, NY 10019-1903
PHONE .212-258-2541
FAX .212-258-2546
TYPES Features - Made-for-TV/Cable Movies
DEALS Paramount Pictures-Motion Picture Group
DEVELOPMENT Appointment in Samarra - Renato's Luck - Peace Like a River - Roses Are Red
CREDITS Jaws - The Verdict - The Player - Deep Impact - Chocolat - Along Came a Spider - A Few Good Men - Sweet Smell of Success (Theater) - Mr. Goldwyn (Theater) - Framed (TV)

David Brown .Owner/Producer
Kit Golden .President, Production (212-258-2543)

THE MANHEIM COMPANY
23852 Pacific Coast Hwy., Ste. 924
Malibu, CA 90265
PHONE .310-456-7272
FAX .310-456-3790
TYPES Features - Made-for-TV/Cable Movies - TV Series
CREDITS Dirty Pictures - Leap of Faith - Roe vs. Wade - Zooman

Michael Manheim .President

MANIFEST FILM COMPANY
619 18th St.
Santa Monica, CA 90402
PHONE .310-899-5554
FAX .310-899-5553
EMAIL .manifilm@aol.com
TYPES Features - TV Series
CREDITS High Crimes - The People vs. Larry Flynt - The Joy Luck Club - Zero Effect - The Weight of Water

Janet Yang .Founder/Producer
Josh Cowing .Executive Assistant to Janet Yang
Mira Lew .Executive Assistant to Janet Yang

MANIFESTOVISION
63 W. 17th St., Ste. 5-A
New York, NY 10011
PHONE .212-966-7686
FAX .212-675-2009
EMAIL .info@manifestovision.com
WEB SITE .www.manifestovision.com
TYPES Commercials - Features - TV Series
DEVELOPMENT Black Butterflies (Feature) - Blu Tomato (TV)
POST PRODUCTION Come Away with Me (Feature)
CREDITS Acts of Worship - Perfume - Hostage

Nadia Leonelli .CEO
Fredrik Sundwall .CEO
Rob Feld .Head, Production

JAMES MANOS PRODUCTIONS, INC.
5410 Wilshire Blvd., Ste. 602
Los Angeles, CA 90036
PHONE .323-857-1630
FAX .323-857-1465
TYPES Features - Made-for-TV/Cable Movies - TV Series
CREDITS Apollo 2 - The Ditchdigger's Daughters - The Positively True Adventures of the Alleged Texas Cheerleader Murdering Mom - The Sopranos: College Episode - The Shield

James Manos Jr. .Writer/Producer
Michelle Trump .Director, Creative Affairs

*MANVILLE ENTERTAINMENT, LLC
4217 Admiralty Way
Marina del Rey, CA 90740
PHONE .310-567-6654
TYPES Made-for-TV/Cable Movies - Syndication - TV Series - Reality TV
DEVELOPMENT The Wedding Planner - Foreign Exchange - Family Vacation - The David Francis Story
COMMENTS Deal with Sennet-Gernstein Entertainment, LLC

Scott Manville .Producer

MAPLE SHADE FILMS
c/o Warner Bros.
4000 Warner Blvd.
Burbank, CA 91522
PHONE .818-954-3137
TYPES Features
DEALS Warner Bros. Pictures
PRE-PRODUCTION Catwoman
CREDITS Insomnia - A Walk to Remember - Three Kings

Ed McDonnell .President
Carolyn Manetti .VP, Production
Dan Stone .Director, Development

LAURENCE MARK PRODUCTIONS
c/o Columbia Pictures
10202 W. Washington Blvd., Poitier Bldg., Ste. 3111
Culver City, CA 90232
PHONE 310-244-5239

TYPES	Features - TV Series
DEALS	Sony Pictures Entertainment
DEVELOPMENT	Basket Case - Six Shooters - Twist of Fate - Last Holiday - Salem - Sammy
PRE-PRODUCTION	The Look-Out
CREDITS	I, Robot - Finding Forrester - Riding in Cars with Boys - As Good As It Gets - Romy & Michele - Jerry Maguire - Anywhere But Here - Center Stage - The Object of My Affection - Hanging Up - Simon Birch - Working Girl

Laurence Mark .....President/Producer
Jonathan King .....President, Production (310-244-5236)
Ilene Amy Berg .....President, TV, Long-Form (310-244-3597)
Abram Hatch .....VP, TV, Series (310-244-5144)
Terrence Myers .....VP, Production (310-244-2443)
Petra Alexandria .....Production Office Manager (310-244-3962)
Marlene Begg .....TV Story Editor
Kevin McCann .....Features Story Editor
Judy Faulkner .....Story Analyst
Tamara Chestna .....Assistant to Laurence Mark
Chad Ahrendt .....Assistant to Laurence Mark
Chad Keller .....Assistant to Terrence Myers

MARMONT PRODUCTIONS, INC.
c/o Jolene Wolff
1543 Dog Team Rd.
New Haven, VT 05472
PHONE 802-388-2461
FAX 802-388-2555
EMAIL .....marprod@earthlink.net

TYPES	Features - Made-for-TV/Cable Movies - TV Series
CREDITS	No Good Deed - Mountains of the Moon - Blood & Wine - Poodle Springs - The Postman Always Rings Twice - Porn.com
COMMENTS	Representation for all submissions to Cassian Elwes, WMA, phone: 310-859-4310

Bob Rafelson .....Director/Producer
Jolene Wolff .....VP

THE MARSHAK/ZACHARY COMPANY
8840 Wilshire Blvd., 1st Fl.
Beverly Hills, CA 90211
PHONE 310-358-3191
FAX 310-358-3192
EMAIL .....alan@themzco.com

TYPES	Features - Direct-to-Video/DVD - Made-for-TV/Cable Movies - Reality TV - Syndication - TV Series
DEVELOPMENT	High Rollers - Glamorous
PRE-PRODUCTION	Beginning of Wisdom - In the Company of Heroes
POST PRODUCTION	Blessed
CREDITS	Tiptoes - Tie That Binds - Carriers - For All Time
SUBMISSION POLICY	Referral only

Darryl Marshak .....Producer/Manager
Susan Zachary .....Producer/Manager
Mitch Clem .....Associate
Alan W. Mills .....Associate

MARSTAR PRODUCTIONS
8840 Wilshire Blvd., Ste. 102
Beverly Hills, CA 90211
PHONE 310-358-3210
FAX 310-358-3227

TYPES	Documentaries - Features - Theater - TV Series
CREDITS	Mask - Sophie's Choice - Escape from Sobibor - Love Letters - On Golden Pond

Martin Starger .....President
Hildegarde Duane .....Development Associate
Kathy Reese .....Executive Assistant to President

MARTIN CHASE PRODUCTIONS
500 S. Buena Vista St.
Burbank, CA 91521-1757
PHONE 818-560-3952

TYPES	Features - Direct-to-Video/DVD - Made-for-TV/Cable Movies - TV Series
DEALS	Walt Disney Pictures/Touchstone Pictures
PRODUCTION	The Sisterhood of the Traveling Pants (Warner Bros.)
CREDITS	The Princess Diaries 1&2 (Disney) - 1-800 MISSING (Lifetime) - The Cheetah Girls (Disney Channel) - Rodgers & Hammerstein's Cinderella (ABC)
SUBMISSION POLICY	No unsolicited submissions

Debra Martin Chase .....President/Producer
Melissa Wiechmann .....Creative Executive
Nancy Duff .....Executive Assistant

THE MARTIN/STEIN COMPANY
4024 Radford Ave., Bldg. 3
Studio City, CA 91604
PHONE 818-655-5730

TYPES	TV Series
DEALS	Carsey-Werner-Mandabach
DEVELOPMENT	Mr. & Mr. Nash (ABC) - Untitled Mark Perez Project (Fox)
CREDITS	The Downer Channel
SUBMISSION POLICY	No unsolicited material

Steve Martin .....Partner/Executive Producer
Joan Stein .....Partner/Executive Producer
Cheryl Rizzo .....Manager, Development

MARVEL STUDIOS, INC.
10474 Santa Monica Blvd., Ste. 206
Los Angeles, CA 90025
PHONE 310-234-8991
FAX 310-234-8481
WEB SITE .....www.marvel.com

TYPES	Animation - Features - New Media - Syndication - TV Series
CREDITS	Spider-Man - X-Men - Blade - Hulk - Iron Man - Fantastic Four

Stan Lee .....Chairman Emeritus
Avi Arad .....Chairman/CEO
David Maisel .....President/COO
Rick Ungar .....President, Marvel Character Group
Kevin Feige .....Executive VP
Ari Arad .....VP, Production
Craig Kyle .....Manager, Creative Development
Jason Miller .....Story Editor
Michael Kelly .....Executive Assistant to Mr. Lee
Chelsea Rutter .....Executive Assistant to Avi Arad
Emily Silver .....Executive Assistant to Rick Ungar & Kevin Feige

NIKI MARVIN PRODUCTIONS, INC.

8919 Harratt St., Ste. 304
Los Angeles, CA 90069
PHONE .310-274-6320
FAX .310-274-3890
TYPES Documentaries - Features
CREDITS Nightmare on Elm Street 3 - Buried Alive 1&2 - The Shawshank Redemption - Private Islands - Flying High

Niki Marvin .Producer/Director/Writer

MARVIN WORTH PRODUCTIONS

9784 Drake Lane
Beverly Hills, CA 90210
PHONE .310-273-0181/310-273-0182
FAX .310-274-7378
TYPES Animation - Features - Made-for-TV/Cable Movies - Theater - TV Series
DEVELOPMENT Chet Baker - Miles Davis; Theater: Where's Poppa - Lenny
CREDITS Falling in Love - Gia - Diabolique - Malcolm X - Where's Poppa - See No Evil, Hear No Evil - The Rose - Lenny - James Dean: An Invented Life

Joan Worth .Producer
Marty Binder .No Title

MARVISTA ENTERTAINMENT

12519 Venice Blvd.
Los Angeles, CA 90066
PHONE .310-737-0950
FAX .310-737-9115
EMAIL .info@marvista.net
WEB SITE .www.marvista.net
TYPES Animation - Documentaries - Features - Direct-to-Video/DVD - Made-for-TV/Cable Movies - Syndication - TV Series
PRE-PRODUCTION Core: Boiling Point - Frozen Tundra - Night of Terror - Love Thy Neighbor

Joseph Szew .President/CEO
Michael Jacobs .President, Production & Distribution
Fernando Szew .Managing Director/COO
George Port .Executive VP
JJ Lopez .Distribution Supervisor
Michelle D. Katz .Production & Distribution Coordinator

TIMOTHY MARX PRODUCTIONS, INC.

17177 Adlon Rd.
Encino, CA 91436
PHONE .818-789-4344
TYPES Documentaries - Features - Made-for-TV/Cable Movies - TV Series
CREDITS Neil Simon's The Goodbye Girl (TNT) - Arli$$ - Citizen X - Passed Away - Smooth Talk - Entourage (HBO)

Timothy Marx .Producer

MARY ANN-LAGLO PRODUCTIONS

4007 Sunswept Dr.
Studio City, CA 91604
PHONE .818-508-5522
FAX .818-508-1616
EMAIL .ma-lgprod@sbcglobal.net
TYPES Features - TV Series
DEALS Showtime Networks, Inc.
DEVELOPMENT The Golden 13 - Myrtle Faye Rumph - The Arthur Ashe Story - Run for Your Life - North Star - The Final Chapter
PRE-PRODUCTION Chasing a Lite
CREDITS Mandela and de Klerk - Free of Eden - To Sir, with Love 2 - Cutters Dream - The Club - Hope

Cedric Scott .CEO/Producer
Emmanuel Knowles .Director, Creative Affairs
Joy Thale .Executive Assistant

MASE/KAPLAN PRODUCTIONS, INC.

5314 Wortser Ave.
Sherman Oaks, CA 91401
PHONE .213-304-5267
FAX .310-388-5264
EMAIL .filmator@aol.com
TYPES Features - Made-for-TV/Cable Movies - TV Series
DEVELOPMENT Going After Cacciato
POST PRODUCTION Heart of Summer
COMPLETED UNRELEASED The Assasination of Richard Nixon
CREDITS Red Shoe Diaries - Strangers - She's So Lovely - Buffalo 66 - Dark Prince - John Q. - Trapped - The Notebook
COMMENTS Deal with Alpha Company Films, LLC

Avram Butch Kaplan .Producer
Suzanna Lezama .Director, Development

JOHN MASIUS PRODUCTIONS, INC.

c/o Rick Rosen, Endeavor Agency
9701 Wilshire Blvd., 10th Fl.
Beverly Hills, CA 90212
PHONE .310-248-2000
FAX .310-248-2032
TYPES TV Series
CREDITS Providence - Touched by an Angel

John Masius .Executive Producer/Creator/Writer

MATADOR PICTURES

12021 Wilshire Blvd., Ste. 117
Los Angeles, CA 90025
PHONE .310-472-6220/44-20-7025-8028
FAX .310-472-6223
EMAIL .info@matadorpictures.com
WEB SITE .www.matadorpictures.com
TYPES Features
DEVELOPMENT The Snow Prince - Hank - After Billy - Russell - Little Ashes - Shadow Walker - Double Vision
POST PRODUCTION Ae Fond Kiss
COMPLETED UNRELEASED Ashes and Sand - Chaos and Cadavers
CREDITS Mad Dogs and Englishmen - The Fall - Dead Funny - Mortal Kombat - Princess in Love - Another Life - Ten Minutes Older: The Trumpet - Ten Minutes Older: The Cello
SUBMISSION POLICY No unsolicited material
COMMENTS UK office: 18 Soho Square, London, W1D 3QL UK

Lauri Apelian .Producer/Partner (LA)
Nigel Thomas .Producer/Partner (UK)
Peter Watson-Wood .Producer/Partner (UK)

MATERIAL
73 Market St.
Venice, CA 90291
PHONE .310-396-5937
FAX .310-450-4988

TYPES	Features
PRODUCTION	The Midnight Meat Train
CREDITS	Red Planet - Queen of the Damned - Showtime - Time Machine - The Big Bounce

Jorge Saralegui .Producer

MATOVICH PRODUCTIONS
PO Box 5744
Beverly Hills, CA 90209
PHONE .805-813-0644
EMAIL .matpro@earthlink.net

TYPES	Features - Direct-to-Video/DVD - Made-for-TV/Cable Movies - TV Series
DEVELOPMENT	Swing Dreams - Babes in the Woods - Last Discoverer - The Mummy Formula - The Fourth Reich - The Last Californian - The Super Penguins (Animated Feature) - Santa's Grounded - I Danced For The Devil - Rosie
CREDITS	Deadly Delusions - Lightning in a Bottle - I Don't Buy Kisses Anymore - Social Suicide

Mitchel Matovich .President/Director/Producer
Steve Zupkas .VP, Animation
C. Yorston .Production

MATRIXX ENTERTAINMENT
223 W. Lancaster Ave.
Devon, PA 19333
PHONE .610-688-9212
FAX .610-688-1062
EMAIL .contact@mecfilms.com
WEB SITE .www.mecfilms.com

TYPES	Documentaries - Features
DEVELOPMENT	Tesla - Splash of Red - The Immortal Cell
PRE-PRODUCTION	Creature from Jekyll Island - Fair Weather Friends
PRODUCTION	Comedy Showcase
POST PRODUCTION	Bunny Cousins
COMPLETED UNRELEASED	Snapshot Blues
CREDITS	Money Matters - Cricket Club - Over Exposed - The Noah Fund - Morgan Stanley Presents Suzanne
SUBMISSION POLICY	See Web site
COMMENTS	Home of Pay-Per-View.com and the Lee Garmes Cinema Institute

James Jaeger .President/CEO
Paul Gibbons .Executive VP, Operations/COO
Dan Kingsley .Sr. VP, Marketing
Matt Huntington .VP, Development
Lorraine Sterling .Director, Public Relations (800-576-2001)
John Cones . .Special Counsel, Entertainment/Securities (949-706-2093)
Carol Schneider .Secretary/Treasurer

THE MATTHAU COMPANY, INC.
11661 San Vicente Blvd., Ste. 609
Los Angeles, CA 90049
PHONE .310-454-3300
WEB SITE .www.matthau.com

TYPES	Features - Made-for-TV/Cable Movies - TV Series
DEVELOPMENT	Joy - Double Trouble - Dracula - The Desert Fox
PRODUCTION	Her Minor Thing
CREDITS	Hanging Up - Mrs. Lambert Remembers Love - The Grass Harp - Grumpier Old Men - The Marriage Fool - Dennis the Menace - Doin' Time on Planet Earth

Charles Matthau .President
Lana Morgan .Director, Creative Affairs
Ashley Anderson .Creative Executive
Jason Cooper .Creative Executive
Sara Rhodes .Story Editor
Veronica Palacios .Business Affairs
Jessica Cooper .Business Affairs

SCOTT MAURO ENTERTAINMENT, INC.
4311 Wilshire Blvd.
Los Angeles, CA 90010
PHONE .323-650-0001, x23
FAX .323-692-1944
EMAIL .shmauro@aol.com

PRE-PRODUCTION	Let Me Entertain You: The Music of Jule Styne (PBS)
CREDITS	The Seventh & Eighth Annual Soap Opera Update Awards (Lifetime) - Rosemary Clooney's Golden Anniversary: An All Star Salute (A&E) - The Whimsical World of Oz (PBS) - Night of 100 Stars (NBC) - Grand Opening of Disney/MGM Studios (NBC)
COMMENTS	TV Specials only; Cable, network and syndication

Scott Mauro .President/Producer

MAVERICK FILMS
9348 Civic Center Dr., 3rd Fl.
Beverly Hills, CA 90210
PHONE .310-276-6177
FAX .310-276-9477

TYPES	Features
DEVELOPMENT	Queen of the Rodeo - Bear Force - My Sassy Girl - Feels Like the First Time - The Whale - Twilight - This Is America - The 80's Miniseries - She Rocks - The Phone - Material Girls
PRODUCTION	Sakura: Blue Eyed Samurai
CREDITS	Turn It Up - Agent Cody Banks 1&2 - 30 Days Until I'm Famous

Madonna .Principal/Producer
Guy Oseary .Principal/Producer
Mark Morgan .CEO
Milton Kim .Co-Head/Producer
Marc Vermut .CFO
Caresse Henry .Manager/Producer
David Faigenblum .Producer/Manager
Rick Joseph .Producer/Manager

(Continued)

MAVERICK FILMS (Continued)

Eve LaDue . . . . Producer/Manager
Doug Morton . . . . Producer
Martina Papinchak . . . . Producer
Jay Polstein . . . . Producer
Stephanie Pottruck . . . . Producer
Michael Rosenberg . . . . Producer, TV
Rachel Rothman . . . . Producer
Mark Saffian . . . . Producer
Eric Thompson . . . . Producer
Brent Emery . . . . Sr. VP
Greg Mooradian . . . . Producer
Jonathan Schwartz . . . . Consultant
Yael Oestreich . . . . VP, Development
Lynne Morrish . . . . Assistant to Mark Morgan

MAYA PICTURES

3030 Andrita St.
Los Angeles, CA 90065
PHONE 310-281-3770
FAX 310-281-3777
WEB SITE . . . . www.mayapictures.net

TYPES	Features - Made-for-TV/Cable Movies
SUBMISSION POLICY	No phone calls; See Web site for details
COMMENTS	Seeking first-time professional writers, directors and original complete screenplays (comedy, drama and thrillers) about the contemporary American Latino experience; Latino directors from backgrounds including film, music videos, commercials and TV series will be considered

Moctesuma Esparza . . . . Executive Producer
Kim Myers . . . . Development
Tery Lopez . . . . Development
Tonantzin Esparza . . . . Development
Andres Faucher . . . . Development
Andrew Orci . . . . Development
Luis Guerrero . . . . Executive Assistant

MAYHEM PICTURES

725 Arizona Ave., Ste. 302
Santa Monica, CA 90401
PHONE 310-393-5005
FAX 310-393-5017

TYPES	Features - TV Series
DEALS	Walt Disney Pictures/Touchstone Pictures
CREDITS	The New Guy - The Rookie - Miracle

Mark Ciardi . . . . Producer
Gordon Gray . . . . Producer
Jonathan Mone . . . . VP, Production
Nichole Millard . . . . Development Executive
Courtney Schorr . . . . Assistant

MBST ENTERTAINMENT, INC.

345 N. Maple Dr., Ste. 200
Beverly Hills, CA 90210
PHONE 310-385-1820
FAX 310-385-1834

TYPES	Features - TV Series
DEVELOPMENT	Modern Bride - Prodigy - Ghostwalker - The Club - Ride Along - Finishing School
PRODUCTION	The Greatest Game Ever Played
CREDITS	Arthur - Throw Momma from the Train - Good Morning, Vietnam - Krippendorf's Tribe - Angie - Freddy Got Fingered - Sorority Boys - The Last Shot

Larry Brezner . . . . Partner
David Steinberg . . . . Partner
Stephen Tenenbaum . . . . Partner
Jonathan Brandstein . . . . No Title
Meegan Kelso . . . . No Title
Andrew D. Tenenbaum . . . . No Title

MCNAMARA PAPER PRODUCTS

c/o Warner Bros. Television
300 Television Plaza, Bldg. 140, Rm. 207
Burbank, CA 91505
PHONE 818-954-5522
FAX 818-954-7848

TYPES	TV Series
DEALS	Warner Bros. Television Production
DEVELOPMENT	The Normals
PRODUCTION	Eyes
CREDITS	Fastlane - The Fugitive - Profit

John McNamara . . . . President/Executive Producer
Case Krell . . . . Creative Consultant
Laura Brew . . . . Administrative Director
Beata Henrichs . . . . Development Executive
Geoff Aull . . . . Researcher

MD2 PICTURES

310 S. Almont Dr.
Los Angeles, CA 90048
PHONE 310-562-9308
FAX 310-247-0182
EMAIL . . . . chrisdaniel@md2group.com
WEB SITE www.md2pictures.com

TYPES	Features
PRODUCTION	Kid Spaghetti
CREDITS	Goodbye Lover - Blood Oranges

Chris Daniel . . . . Partner
Diane Moser . . . . Partner
Felix Danciu . . . . Partner

media8
entertainment

MEDIA 8 ENTERTAINMENT

1875 Century Park East, Ste. 2000
Los Angeles, CA 90067
PHONE 310-226-8300
FAX 310-226-8350
WEB SITE www.media8entertainment.com

TYPES	Features
DEVELOPMENT	Untitled Streetball Project - Wedding Daze - The Duke of Deception - The Sixteen Pleasures - Red Lips, White Lies
PRODUCTION	Running Scared - Lovewrecked
POST PRODUCTION	The Upside of Anger - Santa's Slay - Havoc
COMPLETED UNRELEASED	11:14
CREDITS	Monster (Newmarket) - Jungle Book (Disney) - The Musketeer (Universal) - The United States of Leland (Paramount Classics) - Extreme Ops (Paramount) - Fear Dot Com (Warner Bros.) - The Body (TriStar) - Eye of the Beholder (Destination)
SUBMISSION POLICY	No unsolicited submissions
COMMENTS	Formerly MDP Worldwide

Mark Damon . . . . Chairman & CEO
Sammy Lee . . . . Vice Chairman of the Board
Richard Kiratsoulis . . . . President/COO
Stewart Hall . . . . Producer/Board Member
David Gaynes . . . . Sr. VP, Marketing & Publicity
Brian O'Shea . . . . Sr. VP, Worldwide Distribution
Jenna Piccolo . . . . Sr. VP, Business & Legal Affairs
Tatyana Joffe . . . . VP, Administrative Affairs
Jimmy Li . . . . VP, Strategic & Financial Planning
Roman Kopelevich . . . . Director, Distributor Services
Pierre Kurland . . . . Director, Financial Reporting
Matthew Waldman . . . . Director, Administrative Operations

(Continued)

MEDIA 8 ENTERTAINMENT (Continued)

Christa Zofcin . . . . .Director, Business & Legal Affairs
Audrey Delaney . . . . .Manager, Marketing & Publicity
Jelena Tadic . . . . .Manager, International Distribution
Randy Dannenberg . . . . .Creative Executive
Katherine Chang . . . . .Development Executive
Tamara Stuparich De La Barra . . . . .Development Executive
D.J. Goldberg . . . . .Development Executive
Philip Hall . . . . .Development Executive

MEDIA FOUR

8840 Wilshire Blvd., 2nd Fl.
Beverly Hills, CA 90211
PHONE 310-358-3288
FAX 310-358-3188
TYPES Features - Made-for-TV/Cable Movies - TV Series
DEVELOPMENT Julie Andrews/Carol Burnett Special
CREDITS Before They Were Stars - George - Whereabouts of Jenny

Steve Sauer . . . . .Founding Partner
Jane McKnight .Executive Assistant to Steve Sauer

MEDIA-SAVVY

6767 Forest Lawn Dr., Ste. 212
Los Angeles, CA 90068
PHONE 323-882-8008
FAX 323-882-8138
WEB SITE . . . . .www.media-savvy.com
TYPES Documentaries - Made-for-TV/Cable Movies - Syndication - TV Series - Reality TV
DEVELOPMENT Jessica! (Telepictures) - Us Weekly (VH1) - Jane of All Trades - Joyride
CREDITS Crossing Over with John Edward (Pilot)
COMMENTS Media-coaching; Brand Development; Personality Branding

Ramey Warren Black . . . . .Co-President/Executive Producer
Adora English .Co-President/Executive Producer
J. William Reardin . . . . .Executive in Charge of Production
Jess Ponce .Director, Production & Development

MEDIAVEST

1675 Broadway, 14th Fl.
New York, NY 10019
PHONE 212-468-4000
FAX 212-468-4181
TYPES Made-for-TV/Cable Movies - Syndication - TV Series
CREDITS Murder on the Orient Express - About Sarah - The Staircase - Having Our Say - The Inheritance - The Color of Love: Jacey's Story - Picnic - For Love of Olivia - What About Your Friends?

Jeffrey S. Grant . . . . .President, Programming
Nancy Beard . . . . .Manager, Programming

MEERSON-KRIKES

427 N. Canon Dr., Ste. 216
Beverly Hills, CA 90210
PHONE 310-858-0552
FAX 310-858-0554
TYPES Features
CREDITS Anna and the King - Star Trek IV - Back to the Beach - Double Impact

Steve Meerson . . . . .Writer/Producer

MELEE ENTERTAINMENT

331 N. Maple Dr.
Beverly Hills, CA 90210
PHONE 310-288-7475
FAX 310-288-7476
WEB SITE . . . . .www.melee.com
TYPES Documentaries - Features - Direct-to-Video/DVD
PRODUCTION Prison Ball
COMPLETED UNRELEASED Soul Steppin' - Outlaw Street Cars - Love Chronicles
CREDITS You Got Served - Friday - I Got the Hook Up - Riding in Vans with Boys - NASCAR
SUBMISSION POLICY No unsolicted submissions

Bryan Turner . . . . .No Title
Scott Aronson . . . . .No Title
Shellie Fontana . . . . .No Title
Michael McLeod . . . . .No Title
Michael Regen . . . . .No Title
Azar Zavvar . . . . .No Title
Mignon Carr . . . . .No Title
Ryan Urie . . . . .No Title
Christopher Dehau Lee . . . . .No Title

BILL MELENDEZ PRODUCTIONS

13400 Riverside Dr., Ste. 201
Sherman Oaks, CA 91423-2501
PHONE 818-382-7382
FAX 818-382-7377
EMAIL . . . . .billmelprod@aol.com
WEB SITE . . . . .www.billmelendez.tv
TYPES Animation - Commercials - Features - Direct-to-Video/DVD - TV Series
DEALS Paramount Home Entertainment
CREDITS A Charlie Brown Valentine - It's the Great Pumpkin, Charlie Brown - A Charlie Brown Christmas - A Charlie Brown Thanksgiving - Cathy - Garfield
COMMENTS Peanuts characters worldwide; Commercials: Met Life Campaign, Nissay Insurance (Japan), Calbee Cereals (Japan), McDonalds (Japan), Hallmark - I Want a Dog for Christmas, Charlie Brown

Bill Melendez . . . . .President
Carol Neal . . . . .CEO
Warren Taylor . . . . .Production Coordinator/Line Producer
Sandy Arnold . . . . .Casting/Recording
Joanna Coletta . . . . .Office Manager, Budgets/Accounting

BARRY MENDEL PRODUCTIONS

100 Universal City Plaza, Bungalow 5163
Universal City, CA 91608
PHONE 818-733-3076
FAX 818-733-4070
TYPES Features
DEALS Universal Pictures
CREDITS The Royal Tenenbaums - The Sixth Sense - Rushmore - Flora Plum - Unbreakable

Barry Mendel . . . . .No Title (818-733-3070)
Alisa Tager . . . . .No Title (818-733-3074)
Sarah Schechter . . . . .No Title (818-733-3086)
Billy Rosenberg . . . . .No Title (818-733-0207)
Jake Burnbaum . . . . .No Title (818-733-3073)
Patrick Walmsley . . . . .No Title (818-733-3072)

MERCER FILM GROUP INC.
3575 Cahuenga Blvd. West, Ste. 450
Los Angeles, CA 90068
PHONE 323-462-4184
EMAIL . . . . development@mercerfilm.tv
WEB SITE . . . . www.mercerfilm.tv
TYPES Features - Made-for-TV/Cable Movies - TV Series
DEVELOPMENT Valhalla
CREDITS Ambush of Ghosts - I Woke Up Early the Day I Died - The Gold Cup

Jennifer Arundale . . . . President
Scott Arundale . . . . Producer

MERCHANT-IVORY
250 W. 57th St., Ste. 1825
New York, NY 10107
PHONE 212-582-8049
FAX 212-459-9201
WEB SITE . . . . www.merchantivory.com
TYPES Documentaries - Features - Made-for-TV/Cable Movies - TV Series
DEVELOPMENT Indians Win the Empire - Made in France - Giovanni's Room
PRODUCTION The White Countess
COMPLETED UNRELEASED Merci Dr. Rey - Heights
CREDITS Le Divorce - The Mystic Masseur - The Golden Bowl - Cotton Mary - A Soldier's Daughter Never Cries - The Proprietary - Jefferson in Paris - Slaves of New York - Maurice - Howards End - A Room with a View - Surviving Picasso - The Remains of the Day - The Bostonians
SUBMISSION POLICY No unsolicited material; Fax queries

Ismail Merchant . . . . Co-President/Producer/Director
James Ivory . . . . Co-President/Director
Richard Hawley . . . . Executive VP/Producer/Director
Pierre Proner . . . . Director, Production
Melanie Shanley . . . . Coordinator

MERIDIAN FILMS
233 Wilshire Blvd., Ste. 400
Santa Monica, CA 90401
PHONE 310-394-1617
EMAIL . . . . merfilms@aol.com
SECOND EMAIL . . . . meridianrb@aol.com
TYPES Features - Direct-to-Video/DVD - TV Series
PRE-PRODUCTION Parting Gifts
CREDITS Twice Dead - Mom - Post Mortem

Bernard Demers . . . . President
Rideaux A. Baldwin . . . . VP, Production/Partner
Robert McDonnell . . . . Executive Producer/Partner

RICARDO MESTRES PRODUCTIONS
115 Barrington Walk
Los Angeles, CA 90049
PHONE 310-472-3242
FAX 310-472-3215
TYPES Features
DEALS The Walt Disney Company
CREDITS 101 Dalmations - Jack - Flubber - Just Visiting - The Hunted

Ricardo Mestres . . . . Producer
Dominic Shiach . . . . Creative Executive

METAFILMICS, INC.
4250 Wilshire Blvd.
Los Angeles, CA 90010
PHONE 323-656-8829
TYPES Features - Made-for-TV/Cable Movies - New Media
CREDITS What Dreams May Come - Quantum Project - The Linda McCartney Story - Homeless to Harvard

Barnet Bain . . . . Producer
Stephen Simon . . . . Producer

METRO-GOLDWYN-MAYER STUDIOS, INC.
10250 Constellation Blvd.
Los Angeles, CA 90067
PHONE 310-449-3000
WEB SITE . . . . www.mgm.com
TYPES Features
CREDITS Soul Plane - Barbershop 1&2 - Walking Tall - Die Another Day - Windtalkers - Crocodile Hunter - Original Sin - Legally Blonde 1&2 - Hannibal - Heartbreakers - Autumn in New York - Antitrust - The Thomas Crown Affair - The World Is Not Enough - Supernova - Return to Me - Good Boy - Out of Time

Alex Yemenidjian . . . . Chairman/CEO
Chris McGurk . . . . Vice Chairman/COO
Michael Nathanson . . . . President, MGM Pictures
Daniel Rosett . . . . President, United Artists
Peter Adee . . . . President, Worldwide Marketing
Darcie Denkert . . . . President, Entertainment Business Group
Erik Lomis . . . . President, Domestic Distribution
Dan Taylor . . . . Sr. Executive VP/CFO
William Jones . . . . Sr. Executive VP/Secretary
Jay Rakow . . . . Sr. Executive VP/General Counsel
Christopher Aronson . . . . Executive VP/General Sales Manager, Distribution
Jonathan Bader . . . . Executive VP, Business Affairs
Elizabeth Cantillon . . . . Executive VP, Features, Creative Affairs & Production
Charles Cohen . . . . Executive VP, Finance & Corporate Development
Andrew Z. Davis . . . . Executive VP, Physical Production, MGM Pictures
Joseph Fitzgerald . . . . Executive VP, Investor Relations & Corporate Communications
Elizabeth Ingold . . . . Executive VP, Production
Tobias Jaffe . . . . Executive VP, Production
Jeffrey Karbowiak Executive VP, Operations & Finance, Home Entertainment
Bruce Markoe . . . . Executive VP, Feature Post Production
Kim Spenchian . . . . Executive VP/CIO
Bruce Tuchman . . . . Executive VP, MGM Networks
Brian Yell . . . . Executive VP, International Operations
Deborah Arvesen . . . . Sr. VP/Operational Controller
Michael Glick . . . . Sr. VP, Physical Production
Stephen Hendry . . . . Sr. VP, Financial Planning
John Hertenstein . . . . Sr. VP, Estimating
Janet Janjigian . . . . Sr. VP, Corporate Communications
Scott Packman . . . . Sr. VP/Deputy General Counsel
Steve Rath . . . . Sr. VP/Financial Controller
Julie Spielberg . . . . Sr. VP, Legal Affairs
David Bloom . . . . VP, Corporate Communications
Quentin Curtis . . . . VP, Production
Eric Paquette . . . . VP, Production
Peter Chiarelli . . . . Creative Executive, Creative Affairs
DeVon Franklin . . . . Creative Executive, Creative Affairs
Erik Baiers . . . . Director, Creative Affairs
Stephanie Palmer . . . . Director, Creative Affairs
Donna Choo . . . . Executive Story Editor

METRO-GOLDWYN-MAYER WORLDWIDE TELEVISION
10250 Constellation Blvd.
Los Angeles, CA 90067
PHONE .310-449-3000
WEB SITE www.mgm.com
TYPES TV Series
CREDITS Jeremiah - Outer Limits - Stargate SG-1 - National Enquirer - Dirty Pictures

Hank Cohen .President, MGM Television Entertainment
Shelley Brown .Sr. VP, Finance & Administration
Hudson Hickman .Sr. VP, Production
Scott Spungin .Sr. VP, Business Affairs
Gloria Reich .VP, Business Affairs
Stephanie Johnson .Executive Director, Production

PATRICIA K. MEYER PRODUCTIONS
511 Hill St., Ste. 313
Santa Monica, CA 90405
PHONE .310-392-0422
FAX .310-264-3979
EMAIL pk.meyer@verizon.net
TYPES Features - Made-for-TV/Cable Movies - TV Series
CREDITS The Women of Brewster Place - This Is My Life - Menu for Murder (CBS) - Beyond Suspicion (NBC) - The Other Woman (NBC) - Home Song - Take Me Home Again - The List (Short)

Patricia K. Meyer .Writer/Producer/Director

*MGA ENTERTAINMENT/MGA ENTERTAINMENT FILMS
16380 Roscoe Blvd.
Van Nuys, CA 91406-1221
PHONE .818-894-2525
FAX .818-892-2255
WEB SITE www.mgae.com
TYPES Animation - Commercials - Features - Direct-to-Video/DVD - New Media - TV Series
DEVELOPMENT Alien Racers: The Series - Princesses (DVD) - 4Ever Best Friends (DVD) - Bratz Petz: The Series - 5-sies (DVD)
PRE-PRODUCTION Bratz: The Video! II
CREDITS Bratz: The Video! Starrin' & Stylin'

Isaac Larian .CEO, MGA Entertainment
Jay Fukuto .VP, Entertainment
Dave Malacrida .VP, Public & Media Relations
Ellen Levy-Sarnoff .Sr. Director, Creative, Bratz Entertainment
Rachel Griffin .Public & Media Relations Manager

TERENCE MICHAEL PRODUCTIONS, INC.
421 Waterview St.
Playa del Rey, CA 90293
PHONE .310-823-3432
FAX .310-861-9093
EMAIL tm@terencemichael.com
WEB SITE www.terencemichael.com
TYPES Features - Made-for-TV/Cable Movies - Reality TV
DEALS MTV Networks
COMPLETED UNRELEASED According to Spencer - Mind the Gap - Love for Rent
CREDITS Never Again (Universal/Focus) - I Shot a Man in Vegas (Lakeshore) - If Lucy Fell (TriStar) - Wirey Spindell - Chill Factor (Warner) - 100 Girls (Lions Gate) - The Pact (Lifetime TV) - Going Greek (Showtime) - Duets (MTV) - Road to Ironman (NBC) - The Skateboard Show (WB)
SUBMISSION POLICY Via email

Terence Michael .Producer
Jeanne Trepanier .Assistant

MIDDLE FORK PRODUCTIONS
301 N. Canon Dr., Ste. 228
Beverly Hills, CA 90210
PHONE .310-271-4200
FAX .310-271-8200
TYPES Features - TV Series
DEVELOPMENT The Watch
PRODUCTION Anacondas
COMPLETED UNRELEASED Who's Your Daddy? - Stealing Bess - The Hunt for the Blood Orchid
CREDITS Anaconda

Verna Harrah .Chairman
Betsy Sullenger .No Title
Richard Harrah .No Title

MIDNIGHT SUN PICTURES
9350 Civic Center Dr., Ste. 110
Beverly Hills, CA 90210
PHONE .310-432-4890
TYPES Features - TV Series
CREDITS Die Hard 2 - Blast from the Past - Deep Blue Sea - Speechless - Cliffhanger - The Long Kiss Goodnight - T.R.A.X. - Driven - Mindhunters - Exorcist: The Beginning

Renny Harlin .Director/Producer
Rebecca Spikings .Producer
Allison Rintala .Assistant to Renny Harlin
Nikki Stanghetti .2nd Assistant to Renny Harlin

MIKE'S MOVIES/MICHAEL PEYSER PRODUCTIONS
627 N. Las Palmas
Los Angeles, CA 90004
PHONE .323-462-4690
FAX .323-462-4699
TYPES Animation - Documentaries - Features
DEVELOPMENT The Mentalist - Florence - St. Vincent - Everheart Pass - Lover's Leap - Hand 'n' Glove - Golden State - Orphan Train - The Wedding Dress - Paris Trance - High Risk - The Flyer - Tricks of the Trade - The Projectionists - Dot or Feather?
CREDITS Matilda - The Distinguished Gentleman - Big Business - Ruthless People - FX - Desperately Seeking Susan - The Purple Rose of Cairo - Hackers - Camp Nowhere - The Night We Never Met - SLC Punk! - Imagining Argentina

Michael Peyser .Producer
Elizabeth Mitchell .Director, Development

MILLENNIUM FILMS
6423 Wilshire Blvd.
Los Angeles, CA 90048
PHONE .310-388-6900
FAX .310-388-6901
EMAIL .info@nuimage.net
TYPES Features - Direct-to-Video/DVD - Made-for-TV/Cable Movies
DEALS Miramax Films
DEVELOPMENT Little Sister - Undisputed 2 - Endgame
PRODUCTION 88 Minutes
POST PRODUCTION Edison - Mozart and the Whale
CREDITS Guinevere - How to Kill Your Neighbor's Dog - Replicant - Nobody's Baby - Undisputed - Prozac Nation - Grey Zone

Avi Lerner .CEO

ROBERT ELLIS MILLER FILMS
9255 Doheny Rd., Ste. 904
Los Angeles, CA 90069
PHONE .310-550-1224
FAX .310-550-1103
TYPES Features
CREDITS Reuben, Reuben - Any Wednesday - Sweet November - Hawks - The Heart Is a Lonely Hunter - Bed and Breakfast
SUBMISSION POLICY Agent/Attorney/Representation

Robert Ellis Miller .Producer/Director
Ted Billick .Director, Development

MILLER/BOYETT PRODUCTIONS
745 Fifth Ave., Ste. 3500
New York, NY 10151
PHONE .212-702-9779/212-702-8721
FAX .212-702-0899
TYPES Features - Syndication - Theater - TV Series
DEALS Warner Bros. Television Production
CREDITS Two of a Kind - Family Matters - Full House - Laverne & Shirley - Happy Days - Mork & Mindy - Perfect Strangers; Theater: Sweet Smell of Success - The Crucible - A Year with Frog and Toad - Jumpers - Democracy
COMMENTS Broadway and Off-Broadway; Musical Theater; Robert Boyett Theatricals; Theater in development: *Once Around the City*, *Dance of the Vampires*, *Funny Girl*, *Hedda Gabler*, *Boston Marriage*

Thomas L. Miller .Executive Producer
Robert L. Boyett .Executive Producer
Diane Murphy .VP, Miller/Boyett

DONNA MILLS PRODUCTIONS
253 26th St., Ste. 259
Santa Monica, CA 90402
PHONE .310-471-0398
FAX .310-471-6510
CREDITS World's Oldest Bridesmaid - My Name Is Kate - Element of Truth

Donna Mills .President/Producer

*MINDFIELD
4221 Redwood Ave.
Los Angeles, CA 90066
PHONE .310-301-3100
FAX .310-301-3199
WEB SITE .www.mindfield-la.com
TYPES Animation - Commercials - Features - Direct-to-Video/DVD - Made-for-TV/Cable Movies - Music Videos - New Media - Reality TV
DEVELOPMENT The Elements with Julio G (TV) - Ruthless (Feature) - Lowriders (Feature)
POST PRODUCTION Consequences (Def Jam/Universal)
CREDITS Retroactive - Who Killed the Idea?

Michael Nadeau .Partner
Jimmy Greenway .Partner
Anne Montalvo .Executive Assistant

MINDFIRE ENTERTAINMENT
3740 Overland Ave., Ste. E
Los Angeles, CA 90034
PHONE .310-204-4481
FAX .310-204-5882
EMAIL .info@mindfireentertainment.com
WEB SITE .www.mindfireentertainment.com
TYPES Features - Made-for-TV/Cable Movies - TV Series
DEVELOPMENT True Lust - Crazy Taxi
PRE-PRODUCTION All Souls Day
PRODUCTION Dead or Alive - House of the Dead 2
CREDITS Free Enterprise - The Specials - The House of the Dead

Mark Gottwald .Chairman
Mark A. Altman .CEO
Phil Botana .VP, Sales
Ellie Gottwald .VP, Creative Affairs
Sean Jordan .Story Analyst

MINDLESS ENTERTAINMENT
5482 Wilshire Blvd.
Los Angeles, CA 90036
PHONE 323-965-0388
EMAIL ....mindlesstv@earthlink.net
WEB SITE ....www.mindlessentertainment.com
TYPES Animation - Reality TV - Syndication - TV Series
CREDITS Hurt Bert (FOX) - Cram! (Game Show Network) - Beat the Geeks (Comedy Central) - The X Show (FX) - The New Movie Show with Chris Gore (FX) - Surreal Life (WB)

Mark Cronin ....President
James Rowley ....Executive Producer
Laurie Muslow ....VP, Development
Christie Williams ....Production Coordinator

MINDSTORM CREATIVE
1434 Sixth St., Ste. 1
Santa Monica, CA 90401
PHONE 310-393-1183
FAX 310-393-6622
TYPES Documentaries - Features - New Media - Reality TV - TV Series
DEVELOPMENT The Planet - The KT - Determinator - The Gathering
PRE-PRODUCTION Streets - Land to Sea - 30 Days - Home Skooled - Surfers Island
POST PRODUCTION The Healers
COMPLETED UNRELEASED Joe Head Goes Hollywood
COMMENTS TV and feature finance

Karina Duffy ....CEO/Executive Producer
Jason Cornwall ....Producer
Matt Dawson ....Producer

MIRAGE ENTERPRISES
233 S. Beverly Dr., Ste. 200
Beverly Hills, CA 90212
PHONE 310-888-2830/44-207-284-5588
FAX 310-888-2825/44-207-284-5599
TYPES Features - TV Series
DEVELOPMENT I Don't Know How She Does It - Bartimaeus - Michael Clayton - Columbian Gold - Liberty - The Ninth Life of Louis Drax - The Number One Ladies Detective Agency
PRE-PRODUCTION Margaret
CREDITS Cold Mountain - Sliding Doors - The Talented Mr. Ripley - Random Hearts - Up at the Villa - Heaven - Blow Dry - Iris - Birthday Girl - The Quiet American
COMMENTS UK Office: Old Chapel Studios, 19 Fleet Rd., London NW3 2QR UK

Sydney Pollack ....Producer/Director
Anthony Minghella ....Producer/Director
Bruna Papandrea ....Producer
Laurie Webb ....Director, Development
Tim Bricknell ....Executive Assistant to Mr. Minghella
Todd Malta ....Office Coordinator
Caroline Harvey ....Executive Assistant to Ms. Papandrea
Cassius Matthias ....Assistant to Mr. Minghella
Jenny McLaren ....Office Manager
Ralph Millero ....Assistant to Mr. Pollack
Donna Ostroff ....Executive Assistant to Mr. Pollack
Keri Wilson ....Creative Assistant to Mr. Pollack

MIRAMAX

MIRAMAX FILMS
375 Greenwich St.
New York, NY 10013-2338
PHONE 212-941-3800/323-822-4100
FAX 212-941-3949/323-822-4216
WEB SITE ....www.miramax.com
TYPES Features - TV Series
DEVELOPMENT Nanny Diaries - Derailed - Pippin - Damn Yankees
PRODUCTION Underclassman - Cursed
POST PRODUCTION The Aviator - Bride and Prejudice - Bridget Jones 2: Edge of Reason - Proof - Shall We Dance - Unfinished Life - JM Barrie's Neverland
CREDITS Cold Mountain - Chicago - Gangs of New York - The Barbarian Invasions - Kill Bill Vol. 1 - Scary Movie 3 - The Human Stain
COMMENTS West Coast office: 8439 Sunset Blvd., West Hollywood, CA 90069

Harvey Weinstein ....Co-Chairman
Bob Weinstein ....Co-Chairman
Meryl Poster ....Co-President, Production
Randy Spendlove ....President, Music
Rick Sands ....COO
Jeffrey Fink ....Sr. Executive VP, Miramax Home Entertainment
Ross Landsbaum ....Executive VP, Finance & Operations/CFO
Timothy Clawson ....Executive VP, Physical & Post Production
Alan Friedman ....Executive VP, Business Affairs & General Counsel
Julie Goldstein ....Executive VP, Development & European Production
Jon Gordon ....Executive VP, Production
John Hadity ....Executive VP, Motion Picture & TV Production Finance
Jere Hausfater ....Executive VP/Co-Head, Miramax International
Steven Hutensky ....Executive VP, Business Affairs
Charles Layton ....Executive VP, Office of the Co-Chairman
Michael Luisi ....Executive VP/Co-Head, Business & Legal Affairs
Agnes Mentre ....Executive VP, Acquisitions & Co-Production
Irwin Reiter ....Executive VP, Accounting & Financial Reporting
Colin Vaines ....Executive VP, European Production & Development
Jennifer Berman ....Sr. VP, Production & Development
Arianna Bocco ....Sr. VP, Acquisitions
Matt Brodlie ....Sr. VP, Acquisitions (LA)
Maeva Gatineau ....Sr. VP, Acquisitions (UK)
Jennifer Horowitz ....Sr. VP/Controller
Jeremy Kramer ....Sr. VP, Production
Dan Levine ....Sr. VP, Production & Development, Dimension Films
Mark Lindsay ....Sr. VP, Distribution/Head, Sales
Barry Littman ....Sr. VP, Business & Legal Affairs
Scott Martin ....Sr. VP, Post Production/VP, Production
Shannon McIntosh ....Sr. VP, Broadcast Video/Post Production
Christian McLaughlin ....Sr. VP, Production
David Miercort ....Sr. VP, Acquisitions & Business Affairs
Michelle Raimo ....Sr. VP, Production & Development
Eric Roth ....Sr. VP, Business & Legal Affairs
Larry Angrisani ....VP, International Publicity
Kim Berman ....VP, Broadcast & Video Post Production
Eli Holzman ....VP, TV
Heather Johnson ....VP, Publicity
Michelle Krumm ....VP, Acquisitions (LA)
Matthew Landon ....VP, Post Production
Jennifer Lane ....VP, Post Production
Rachel Levy ....VP, Motion Picture Music
Scott Maziroff ....VP, Production Finance
Michael Rothstein ....VP, Sales & Distribution
Susan Schaefer ....VP, Home Entertainment
Tim Schmidt ....VP, Business & Legal Affairs
Erica Steinberg ....VP, Creative Affairs
Jeffrey Tahler ....VP, Acquisitions
Jennifer Wachtell ....VP, Development
Thomas Zadra ....VP, Business & Legal Affairs
Kelly Carmichael ....Creative Executive

(Continued)

MIRAMAX FILMS (Continued)
Gina Gardini . . . . Production Executive
Carla Gardini . . . . Creative Executive
Hannah Minghella . . . . Creative Executive
Brent Baker . . . . Director, Finance
Frances Erickson . . . . Director/Assistant Controller
Matthew Garner . . . . Director, Post Production
David Greenbaum . . . . Director, Production & Development
Andy Kim . . . . Director, Finance
Sean McPhillips . . . . Director, Acquisitions
Joe Rangel . . . . Director, Motion Picture Music
Tracy Rieth . . . . Director, Broadcast Video/Post Production
Matthew Ritter . . . . Director, Post Production
Eric Robinson . . . . Director, Production & Development
Barbara Schneeweiss . . . . Director, TV
Gary Wax . . . . Director, Acquisitions

MIRANDA ENTERTAINMENT
7337 Pacific View Dr.
Los Angeles, CA 90068
PHONE 323-874-3600
FAX 323-851-5350
EMAIL . . . . clorenz1@aol.com
TYPES Features
POST PRODUCTION The Grudge
COMPLETED UNRELEASED Boogeyman
CREDITS Trapped - Harold and Kumar Go To White Castle

Carsten Lorenz . . . . Producer
Tobin Adams . . . . Executive Assistant to Carsten Lorenz

THE MIRISCH CORPORATION
100 Universal City Plaza, Bldg. 1320, Ste. 2C
Universal City, CA 91608-1085
PHONE 818-777-1271
FAX 818-866-1422
TYPES Animation - Features - Made-for-TV/Cable Movies - TV Series
CREDITS West Side Story - Pink Panther Movies - The Apartment

Walter Mirisch . . . . Producer
Bonnie Blume . . . . Assistant

MISHER FILMS
100 Universal City Plaza, Bungalow 5162
Universal City, CA 91608
PHONE 818-777-0555
FAX 818-733-5709
TYPES Features - TV Series
DEALS Universal Pictures
CREDITS Scorpion King - The Rundown

Kevin Misher . . . . No Title (777-8796)
Patrick Baker . . . . No Title (777-4166)
Tiffany Baker . . . . No Title (777-4166)
Andrew Berman . . . . No Title (777-5635)
Kevin Chang . . . . No Title (777-9900)
Savannah Neely . . . . No Title (777-9900)
Emily Peska . . . . No Title (777-6473)

RENEE MISSEL PRODUCTIONS
201 W. Eucalyptus, Ste. 4
Ojai, CA 93023
PHONE 805-640-0333
FAX 805-669-4511
EMAIL . . . . filmtao@aol.com
TYPES Features
DEVELOPMENT Zus and Zo - The Prodigal Spy - Another Life - Rogue Scholar - Milarepa
CREDITS Resurrection - Nell - Defenseless - The Main Event - Guy - My Man Adam

Renee Missel . . . . Producer
Bridget Stone . . . . Story Editor

MISSION ENTERTAINMENT
601 W. 26th St., Ste. 1315
New York, NY 10001
PHONE 646-336-9628
FAX 646-336-9638
EMAIL . . . . info@missionnyc.com
WEB SITE . . . . www.missionnyc.com
TYPES Features
DEVELOPMENT 211 Master Thief - Speed Kills - Abaddon
CREDITS Requiem for a Dream - Pi
COMMENTS Video Games

M. Scott Vogel . . . . CEO/Producer
David Levine . . . . Development Executive
Sam Cole . . . . Story Editor

MLW PRODUCTIONS
23640 Park Belmonte
Calabasas, CA 91302
PHONE 818-222-7787
FAX 818-222-0474
EMAIL . . . . mlweisbarth@earthlink.net
TYPES Made-for-TV/Cable Movies - TV Series

Michael L. Weisbarth . . . . Principal

MOD3PRODUCTIONS
10390 Wilshire Blvd., Ste. 1104
Los Angeles, CA 90024
PHONE 310-285-8036
EMAIL . . . . mod3productions@aol.com
WEB SITE www.mod3productions.com
TYPES Documentaries - Features - Direct-to-Video/DVD - Reality TV - TV Series
CREDITS MTV's Prom Date - Bible Code 1&2 - Agent Cody Banks 1&2 - Love and Action in Chicago - Wish You Were Dead - Hiroshima; DVD Releases: Mary Tyler Moore Show Season 1 - Kung Fu Season 1 - The Thorn Birds Special Edition - The Dukes of Hazzard Season 1

Danny Gold . . . . Partner
Matthew Asner . . . . Partner
Bruce Levine . . . . Producer
Debbie Axle . . . . Production Executive

MOFFITT-LEE PRODUCTIONS
1438 N. Gower St., Ste. 558
Hollywood, CA 90028-8306
PHONE 323-463-6646
FAX 323-467-2946
TYPES Reality TV - Syndication - TV Series
CREDITS Not Necessarily the News - U.S. Comedy Arts Festival - Hollywood Squares - Comic Relief - Dennis Miller: Citizen Arcane (HBO) - Bill Maher: Victory Begins at Home (HBO)
COMMENTS Specials

John Moffitt . . . . Executive Producer
Pat Tourk Lee . . . . Executive Producer

MONAREX HOLLYWOOD CORPORATION

11605 W. Pico Blvd., Ste. 200
Los Angeles, CA 90064
PHONE .310-478-6666
FAX .310-478-6866
EMAIL .monarexcorp@aol.com
TYPES Documentaries - Features - Direct-to-Video/DVD - Made-for-TV/Cable Movies - TV Series
DEVELOPMENT Bellarosa - Radicals - Madame Goldenflower - Bodytalk
PRE-PRODUCTION She Saw Red - The House
CREDITS Heartbreaker - Last of the Caravans - The Heroin Highway - Attack at Dawn - America Extreme - Screaming Metal - World War II - Attack Without Warning - The Naked Cage - Bloodlust - Urban Nightmare
COMMENTS Production services in the People's Republic of China and Europe, especially Germany

Chris D. Nebe .President

MONTAGE ENTERTAINMENT

2118 Wilshire Blvd., Ste. 297
Santa Monica, CA 90403-5784
PHONE .310-966-0222
FAX .310-966-0223
EMAIL .montage.ent@usa.net
TYPES Features - TV Series
CREDITS Mi Vida Loca - Gas, Food, Lodging - Red Letters - Poolhall Junkies - Frozen Impact - Bereft - Landslide

David Peters .Producer
Bill Ewart .Producer
Jim Mercurio .Director, Development

THE MONTECITO PICTURE COMPANY

1482 E. Valley Rd., Ste. 477
Montecito, CA 93108
PHONE .805-565-8590/310-247-9880
FAX .805-565-1893/310-247-9498
TYPES Features
DEALS DreamWorks SKG
CREDITS Beethoven - Ghostbusters - Dave - Space Jam - 6 Days/7 Nights - Private Parts - Road Trip - Evolution - Old School - Killing Me Softly - Eurotrip
COMMENTS Beverly Hills office: 9465 Wilshire Blvd., Ste. 920, Beverly Hills, CA 90212

Ivan Reitman .No Title
Tom Pollock .No Title
Joe Medjuck .No Title
Dan Goldberg .No Title
Jacqueline Marcus .No Title
Ken Holdren .No Title
Andrea Hirschegger .Assistant to Mr. Reitman
Jennie Reinish .Assistant to Mr. Pollock
Karl Mefford .Assistant to Mr. Medjuck
Kelly Brannen .Assistant to Ms. Marcus

MONTIVAGUS PRODUCTIONS

13930 Burbank Blvd., Ste. 100
Sherman Oaks, CA 91401-5046
PHONE .818-782-1212
FAX .818-782-1931
EMAIL .mail@montivagus.com
WEB SITE .www.montivagus.com
TYPES Features
DEVELOPMENT Crooked Creek - Throwing Bones
CREDITS Along for the Ride - The Second Room
SUBMISSION POLICY No email or fax submissions

Timothy T. Miller .President/Producer
Bryan W. Simon .Director/Producer
Marjorie Engesser .Associate Producer/Writer

GLORIA MONTY PRODUCTIONS, INC.

3550 Wilshire Blvd., Ste. 840
Los Angeles, CA 90010-2409
PHONE .310-274-4924/213-380-7130
FAX .213-383-0932
TYPES Made-for-TV/Cable Movies - TV Series
DEALS Grosso Jacobson Communications Corp.
CREDITS The Hamptons - The Imposter - Remember Me - While My Pretty One Sleeps

Gloria Monty .President

MOONSTONE ENTERTAINMENT

PO Box 7400
Studio City, CA 91614
PHONE .818-985-3003
FAX .818-985-3009
TYPES Features
PRE-PRODUCTION Company of Heroes
PRODUCTION The Promise
POST PRODUCTION Toolbox Murders
CREDITS Together - Hotel - Dancing at the Blue Iguana - Pandaemonium - Twin Falls Idaho - Miss Julie - Cookie's Fortune - Afterglow - Digging to China

Ernst "Etchie" Stroh .CEO
Yael Stroh .President
Luz Moretti .Executive VP
Greg Majerus .VP, Finance
Michael Grant .Director, Production & Marketing
Christine Meissner .Manager

MOR ENTERTAINMENT, LLC

639 First St., Ste. 1
Hermosa Beach, CA 90254
PHONE .310-937-8900
EMAIL .info@mor-ent.com
WEB SITE .www.mor-ent.com
TYPES Features
CREDITS Home Room

Ben Ormand .Producer
Russ Matthews .Director/Producer
Paul Ryan .Director/Producer

It is illegal to copy any part of this book

JAMES MOREL ENTERTAINMENT

232 N. Almont Dr.
Beverly Hills, CA 90211
PHONE .310-247-9588
EMAIL .creative@jamesmorel.com
WEB SITE .www.jamesmorel.com
TYPES Documentaries - Features - Made-for-TV/Cable Movies - Syndication - TV Series
DEVELOPMENT Risky Business - Armchair Warrior - Senior Moments - Comic Genius - Jinx! - Ultimate Weekend Party
CREDITS Star Dates - POPsmear Magazine

James Morel .Producer/Partner
Noah Jones .Creative Assistant

MORGAN CREEK PRODUCTIONS

10351 Santa Monica Blvd., Ste. 200
Los Angeles, CA 90025
PHONE .310-432-4848
FAX .310-432-4844
WEB SITE .www.morgancreek.com
TYPES Features
DEALS Universal Pictures
DEVELOPMENT Flying Tigers - The Northmen - The In-Between - Babus Americanus
POST PRODUCTION Exorcist: The Beginning
CREDITS Robin Hood - Ace Ventura 1&2 - Major League 1-3 - Diabolique - Wild America - Chill Factor - American Outlaws - Juwanna Mann

James G. Robinson .Chairman/CEO
Guy McElwaine .President
Howard Kaplan .CFO
Brian Robinson .Sr. VP, Worldwide Marketing
Beth Babyak .VP, Development
Jonathan Deckter .VP, International Sales
Ira Goldklang .VP, Legal/Business Affairs
Greg Mielcarz .VP, Worldwide Publicity
David C. Robinson .VP
Andy Bohn .Creative Executive
Mona Panchal .Creative Executive
Chris Lytton .Director, Legal/Business Affairs

MORGENSTERN ENTERTAINMENT

775 Via Colinas
Westlake Village, CA 91362
PHONE .805-497-4420
FAX .805-497-4450
EMAIL .jarrettblake@aol.com
TYPES Features - Made-for-TV/Cable Movies - Theater
DEVELOPMENT Liuzzo (Walt Disney Pictures) - Max (Paramount Television) - Modligiani (Columbia Pictures)
CREDITS Too Much Sun (New Line Cinema) - Breakin' Through (Disney Channel) - Scream for Help (Warner Bros.)
COMMENTS Theater: *In the Belly of the Beast* (Mark Taper, The Goodman, Berkeley Rep, Cleveland Rep), *The Beautiful Lady* (Mark Taper), *Modigliani* (Off Broadway)

Seymour Morgenstern .Producer

MORNINGSTAR ENTERTAINMENT

350 N. Glenoaks Blvd., Ste. 300
Burbank, CA 91502
PHONE .818-559-7255
FAX .818-559-7551
EMAIL .mstar@morningstarentertainment.com
WEB SITE .www.morningstarentertainment.com
TYPES Documentaries - Features - Direct-to-Video/DVD - Made-for-TV/Cable Movies - Reality TV - Syndication - TV Series
DEVELOPMENT The Plumber (Feature) - Relationship Series - Black Jet (Feature)
PRE-PRODUCTION BattleGround: Waterloo - Battleground: Battle of the Bulge
PRODUCTION Battlegrond: Alexander the Great - Lizzie Borden
POST PRODUCTION Untitled HGTV
CREDITS Statue of Liberty - Stealth Secrets - Sports Century: Top 50 & Beyond - Operation Thunderbolt - Super Surgery - Fire at Sea - I Survived! - The Texas Seven - The Enforcers - Chicago's Lifeline - Billy the Kid Unmasked - Theme Park Secrets
COMMENTS Direct response

Gary Tarpinian .President/CEO
Paninee Theeranuntawat .VP/Executive Producer
Dylan Tilley .Director, Development

JOHN MORRISSEY PRODUCTIONS

1875 Century Park East, Ste. 2000
Los Angeles, CA 90067
PHONE .310-226-8333
FAX .310-226-8350
TYPES Features - Made-for-TV/Cable Movies
DEVELOPMENT Red Lips, White Lies - And 1
POST PRODUCTION Havoc
CREDITS American History X - What's the Worst That Could Happen? - Kingdom Come - Booty Call - The Badge - 11:14

John Morrissey .Producer

JEFF MORTON PRODUCTIONS

5027 Noeline Ave.
Encino, CA 91436
PHONE .310-467-1123
FAX .818-981-4152
EMAIL .scoutspence@mindspring.com
TYPES Features - Made-for-TV/Cable Movies - TV Series
DEVELOPMENT Shining Woman - Are We There Yet?
PRODUCTION Blitt Happens
CREDITS Elizabeth Smart Story - Oliver Beene - Caracara - Second Skin - Don't Look Under the Bed - Double Jeopardy - Firestarter

Jeff Morton .Producer

MOSAIC MEDIA GROUP

9200 Sunset Blvd., 10th Fl.
Los Angeles, CA 90069
PHONE .310-786-4900
FAX .310-777-2185
TYPES Features - New Media - TV Series

Allen Shapiro .President
Eric Gold .Partner
Jimmy Miller .Partner
Charles Roven .Partner
Pat Magnarella .Partner, Music
Scott Welch .Partner, Music
Ted MacKinney .CFO
George Gatins .VP, Production
Lionel Conway .President, Music Publishing
Bailey Spencer-Jackson .Director, Business Affairs
Bill Bender .Director, Human Resources
Alan Glazer .VP, Marketing, Publicity & Distribution
Erika Conner .Urban Film Development
Gloria Fan .Feature Development
M. Riley .Story Editor/Production Executive
Alex Ankeles .Creative Executive/Manager
Julie Darmody .Manager
David Fleming .Manager
Paul Nelson .Manager
Caryn Weingarten .Manager

MOSHAG PRODUCTIONS, INC.

c/o Mark Mower
1531 Wellesley Ave.
Los Angeles, CA 90025
PHONE .310-820-6760
FAX .310-820-6960
EMAIL .moshag@aol.com
TYPES Features - TV Series
DEVELOPMENT I Caught Flies for Howard Hughes - '57, Chicago - '46, Chicago - The Queen's Mark - Snowblind - The Greatest Game - Gallantyne - Unbridled - Fremantle - Jane Blonde
PRE-PRODUCTION The Payback All-Star Revue - The Family - Players - Wanted
CREDITS Spun - Bully - The Bogus Witch Project (Trimark) - April's Shower

Mark Mower .Producer
Seth A. Miller .Producer
Edward Mejia .Executive Assistant

MOTION PICTURE CORPORATION OF AMERICA

1401 Ocean Ave., Ste. 301
Santa Monica, CA 90401
PHONE .310-319-9500
FAX .310-319-9501
WEB SITE .www.mpcafilm.com
TYPES Features - Direct-to-Video/DVD - Made-for-TV/Cable Movies
POST PRODUCTION Blast - Barely Legal - Slipstream - Riding the Bullet
CREDITS Pavement - Consequence - Borderline - Undisputed - Boat Trip - Joe and Max - Dumb and Dumber - B.H. Ninja - Kingpin - Annie - The Breed
SUBMISSION POLICY No unsolicited material

Brad Krevoy .Chairman/CEO
Victoria Nevinny .Sr. VP, Production & Development
Reuben Liber .VP, Production & Development

MOTOR CITY FILMS

468 N. Camden Dr., Ste. 200
Beverly Hills, CA 90210
PHONE .310-860-5667
TYPES Features - TV Series
DEVELOPMENT Waist Deep - Virtue - Jesus on Line 4
CREDITS Gridlock'd - Glitter

Vondie Curtis Hall .Producer/Director

MOUNT FILM COMPANY

9169 Sunset Blvd.
Los Angeles, CA 90069
PHONE .310-288-5990
FAX .310-288-5991
TYPES Documentaries - Features - Made-for-TV/Cable Movies
DEVELOPMENT Bloodsugar - Common Ground - Untitled Mickey Cohen project - Ecstasy - 40 Days of Musa Dagh
PRODUCTION Papa
CREDITS Night Falls on Manhattan - Death and the Maiden - Bull Durham - Tequila Sunrise - Frantic - Can't Buy Me Love - Natural Born Killers

Thom Mount .Partner/President
Craig Osborne .Partner
Joe DiMaio .Head, Physical Production
Morna Ciraki .Creative Executive
Jon Hamner .Creative Executive
Helen Bollman .Executive Assistant
Serge Juric .Assistant

MOUNTAINAIR FILMS, INC.

PO Box 4097
Santa Fe, NM 87502
PHONE .505-471-9293
FAX .505-438-0294
EMAIL .alton@mountainairfilms.com
WEB SITE .www.mountainairfilms.com
TYPES Commercials - Documentaries - Features - Made-for-TV/Cable Movies
CREDITS Rx Sin Receta - Blind Horizon - Winter Break - Unspeakable - Baraka - Hand of Fate - The Tao of Steve - Tortilla Heaven - Passion in the Desert - Soundman - Nokia *Listen* (Industrial)

Alton Walpole .Producer
Mark Duran .Artistic Director

MOVICORP HOLDINGS, INC.

1875 Century Park East, Ste. 600
Los Angeles, CA 90067
PHONE .310-553-4300
FAX .310-553-1159
WEB SITE .www.movicorp.com
TYPES New Media - Syndication - TV Series
COMMENTS Owns cable network Oasis TV and Oasistv.com; Deals with Microsoft, Comcast, Real Networks, Time Warner Cable, Akimbo

Robert Schnitzer .Chairman/CEO (x10, rschnitzer@movicorp.com)
Toni Serritello .VP, Creative Affairs
Larry Haber .Executive Committee Chair

*MOVING PICTURES, DPI
9100 Wilshire Blvd., Ste. 345 East
Beverly Hills, CA 90212
PHONE .310-288-5464
FAX .310-859-4728
WEB SITE www.dennispublishing.com
TYPES Documentaries - Features - Direct-to-Video/DVD - Made-for-TV/Cable Movies - TV Series
DEALS New Line Cinema
CREDITS Maxim Hot 100 - Blender and VH1's 50 Most Awesomely Bad Songs
COMMENTS Represents Maxim, Stuff, Blender and The Week magazines; Forthcoming Maxim Radio channel on Sirius Satellite Radio

Peter Jaysen .Executive Producer

MOXIE FIRECRACKER FILMS
39 Lincoln Pl.
Brooklyn, NY 11217
PHONE .718-230-5111
EMAIL .info@moxiefirecracker.com
WEB SITE www.moxiefirecracker.com
TYPES Documentaries - Features
CREDITS Nazi Officer's Wife - Girlhood - A Boy's Life - The Farm: Angola, USA - American Hollow - Different Moms - Epidemic Africa - Juvies - The Travelers - Up in Arms - All Kinds of Families - Healthy Start - Sixteen - Together: Stop Violence Against Women - Pandemic: Facing Aids - Indian Point: Imagining the Unimaginable (HBO)

Liz Garbus .Producer/Director/Co-Owner
Rory Kennedy .Producer/Director/Co-Owner
Julie Gaither .Business Manager
Beth Callas .Assistant to Rory Kennedy
Jessica Perez .Assistant to Liz Garbus

MOZARK PRODUCTIONS
4024 Radford Ave., Bldg. 5, Ste. 104
Studio City, CA 91604
PHONE .818-655-5779
FAX .818-655-5129
EMAIL .mozark@mptp.com
TYPES Features - TV Series
CREDITS Woman of the House - Hearts Afire - Designing Women - Evening Shade - Emeril

Linda Bloodworth-Thomason .Executive Producer/Writer
Harry Thomason .Executive Producer/Director

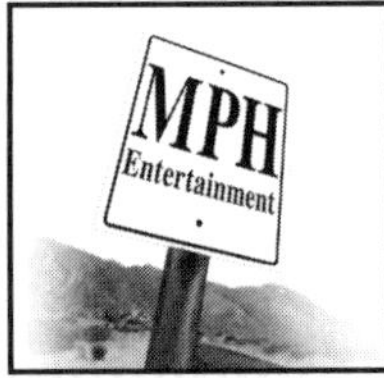

MPH ENTERTAINMENT, INC.
1033 N. Hollywood Way, Ste. F
Burbank, CA 91505
PHONE .818-441-5040
FAX .818-441-5050
WEB SITE www.mphent.com
TYPES Documentaries - Features - Made-for-TV/Cable Movies - TV Series
DEVELOPMENT Hometown: Alcatraz - Rat Girl - Executioners - Leonardo - The Mummy Dinosaur - Takedown
PRE-PRODUCTION Fortune Files - Leader of the Pack
PRODUCTION Hannibal - Untitled Sci Fi Specials
CREDITS My Big Fat Greek Wedding - Inside Islam - Founding Brothers - Sex in the 20th Century - War of the Worlds - The Real Las Vegas - The History of Sex - In the Footsteps of Jesus: Digging for the Truth - The Roswell Crash: Startling New Evidence

Jim Milio .Co-Chair
Mark Hufnail .Executive, Co-Chair
Melissa Jo Peltier .Executive, Co-Chair
Bonnie Peterson .VP, Nonfiction Programming
Teri Freeman .Director, Development

MR. MUDD
5225 Wilshire Blvd., Ste. 604
Los Angeles, CA 90036
PHONE .323-932-5656
TYPES Documentaries - Features - New Media - Theater - TV Series
CREDITS Ghost World - The Dancer Upstairs - The Libertine - How to Draw a Bunny

John Malkovich .Producer/Director
Lianne Halfon .Producer
Russ Smith .Producer
Shelly Darden .Assistant

SAM MRAOVICH PRODUCTIONS
4250 Coldwater Canyon Ave., Ste. 111
Studio City, CA 91604
PHONE .818-288-4267/818-980-9519
EMAIL .steamingdreaming@aol.com
SECOND EMAIL .moviemakerinhollywood@yahoo.com
WEB SITE www.angelfire.com/falcon/benandarthur
TYPES Animation - Features - Direct-to-Video/DVD
PRODUCTION Money Money Money
CREDITS Ben and Arthur - Expression (Short) - Steve's Hollywood Story - Sight Seeing (Short) - Making Contact with Yearbook Friends (Short)

Sam Mraovich .Producer/Director
Holly Mraovich .Producer/Script Finder
Chris Mraovich .Producer/Post Supervisor
Robert Mraovich .Post Production Agent
Leeann Mraovich .Web Design Supervisor

MRI, INC.

26500 W. Agoura Rd., Stes. 102-611
Calabasas, CA 91302
PHONE .818-878-0441
FAX .703-832-8033
EMAIL .moviereps@yahoo.com
WEB SITE .www.princeoflightmovie.com
TYPES Animation - Features - Direct-to-Video/DVD - Made-for-TV/Cable Movies - Music Videos - TV Series - Reality TV
CREDITS The Prince of Light - Raiders of the Sacred Stone - Hyderabad Blues - Cinema Cinema - Sleepaway Camp

Krishna Shah .President

*MSNBC

One MSNBC Plaza
Secaucus, NJ 07094
PHONE .201-583-5000
WEB SITE .www.msnbc.com
TYPES TV Series
CREDITS Imus in the Morning - Hardball - Countdown with Keith Olbermann - The Abrams Report - Deborah Norville - Lester Holt Live - Scarborough Country - MSNBC Investigates - Headliners & Legends - National Geographic Explorer
COMMENTS News programming

Richard Kaplan .President, MSNBC
Mark Effron .VP, MSNBC Live News Programming
Jeremy Gaines .VP, Communications
Phil Griffin .VP, Primetime Programming

MTV FILMS

c/o Paramount Studios
5555 Melrose Ave., Modular Bldg., 2nd Fl.
Los Angeles, CA 90038
PHONE .323-956-8023
FAX .323-862-1386/323-862-8020 (Production)
WEB SITE .www.mtv.com
TYPES Features
DEALS Paramount Pictures-Motion Picture Group
DEVELOPMENT The Warriors - Skip Day - Car Show - Hot Dog Movie
PRE-PRODUCTION Aeon Flux - The Longest Yard
POST PRODUCTION Coach Carter
CREDITS Napoleon Dynamite - Election - Original Kings of Comedy - Beavis & Butthead - Better Luck Tomorrow - Save the Last Dance - Varsity Blues - Orange County - The Wood - Fighting Temptations - Tupac: Resurrection - jackass: the movie

David Gale .Executive VP (323-956-4390)
Momita Sengupta .VP, Physical Production (323-956-8005)
Susan Lewis .VP, Development (323-956-4291)
Troy Craig Poon VP, Business Development & Acquisitions (323-956-8005)
Heather Parry .VP, News & Films (323-956-3229)
Kevin Mangini .Sr. Director, Soundtracks & Integrated Marketing (310-752-8485)
Gregg Goldin .Director, Development (323-956-8023)
Loretha Jones .Head, DVD Division (323-956-1695)

MTV NETWORKS

1515 Broadway
New York, NY 10036
PHONE .212-258-8000/310-752-8000
WEB SITE .www.mtv.com
TYPES Animation - Made-for-TV/Cable Movies - Reality TV - TV Series
CREDITS Pimp My Ride - Newlyweds - The Ashlee Simpson Show - I Want a Famous Face - Punk'd - Wild Boys - Rich Girls - BAM - Camp Jim - Making Da Band - The Osbournes - Real World - Road Rules - TRL - True Life - MTV's Cribs - Diary - MTV Icon - MTV Movie Awards - MTV Video Music Awards - Making the Video - Made - Doggy Fizzle Televizzle
COMMENTS West Coast office: 2600 Colorado Ave., Santa Monica, CA 90404

Tom Freston .Co-President/Co-COO, Viacom Entertainment Group
Judith McGrath .Chairman/CEO, MTV Networks
Brian Graden .President, Entertainment, MTV/VH1
Bill Roedy .President, MTV Networks International
Van Toffler .President, MTV/MTV2/MTV Films
David Cohn .General Manager, MTV2
Stephen Friedman .General Manager, mtvU
John Cucci .Executive VP/CFO, MTV Networks
Alex R. Ferrari .Executive VP/COO, MTV International
Thomas Calderone .Executive VP, Music & Talent, MTV/MTV2
Lois Curren .Executive VP, Series, Entertainment Development
Richard Eigendorff .Executive VP/COO, MTV/VH1/MTV2/Comedy Central/CMT
Tina Exarhos .Executive VP, Marketing, MTV/MTV2
Betsy Frank .Executive VP, Research & Planning
David Gale .Executive VP, MTV Films
JoAnne Adams Griffith .Executive VP, Human Resources
Leslie Leventman .Executive VP, Creative Services, Special Events, Travel Management & Convention Planning
John Shea .Executive VP, Sponsorship Development & Integrated Marketing, MTVN Music Group
David Sirulnick .Executive VP, News & Production
David Sussman . .Executive VP/General Counsel, Business & Legal Affairs
Rod Aissa .Sr. VP, Talent & Series Development
George Cheeks .Sr. VP, Business Affairs/General Counsel
Paul DeBenedettis .Sr. VP, Programming Planning & Scheduling
Tony DiSanto .Sr. VP, MTV Production
Michele Dix .Sr. VP, Music & Talent Programming
Anthony G. Dunaif .Sr. VP, MTV Business Development & Strategy
Carol Eng .Sr. VP, MTV2 Programming
Bill Flanagan .Sr. VP/Editorial Director, MTVNI
Salli Frattini .Sr. VP/Executive in Charge, MTV
M. Janet Hill .Sr. VP, Corporate Communications
Jason Hirschorn .Sr. VP, MTVN Digital Music & Media
Catherine Houser .Sr. VP, Human Resources (LA)
Cristian Jofre .Sr. VP/Creative Director, International
Jeannie Kedas .Sr. VP, Communications & Public Affairs
Jeffrey Keyton .Sr. VP, Off-Air Creative, On-Air Design, MTV
Lauren Lazin .Sr. VP, MTV News & Documentaries
Maggie Malina .Sr. VP, Original Movies for TV & Scripted Series, VH1
Nicholas Rockwell .Sr. VP/Programming & Interactive Services, Information Services & Technology
Eric Sherman . . .Sr. VP/General Manager, VH1 Classic/MTV Digital Suites
Lisa Silfen .Sr. VP, Program Enterprises
Elizabeth Skoler .Sr. VP, VH1 Business & Legal Affairs/Co-Productions
Michael Alex .VP, Online News
Peter Baron .VP, Music & Label Relations
Marnie Black .VP, MTV Communications
Michael Cole .VP, Productions, MTV Films
Marian Davis .VP, Development, Animation
Robyn Demarco .VP, Programming, MTV/MTV2/mtvU
Anthony Dibari Jr. .VP, Production
Amy Doyle .VP, Music Programming Initiative/360
Joelle Charlot Duffy .VP, Studio Production & Administration
Nusrat Durrani .VP, MTV E-Commerce
David Felton .VP/Editor at Large
Liz Gateley .VP, Production Development
Fernando Hernandez .VP, Music Series Development
Andrew Hunter .VP, Network Development
Jesse Ignjatovic .VP, Music & Talent Development

(Continued)

MTV NETWORKS (Continued)

Nicholas Lehman . . . VP, Interactive Business Development
Joi Rideout . . . VP, Business & Legal Affairs, MTVN
Michele Roberts . . . VP, MTV/VH1/CMT Radio
Jessica Samet . . . VP, Development & Original Programming, MTV Music Television
Jane Sangster . . . VP, MTV News
Kathleen Sparanese . . . VP, Administration
Lisi Harrison . . . Sr. Director, Production Development
Vanessa Reyes Smith . . . Sr. Director, Corporate Communications
Ariana Urbont . . . Sr. Director, Corporate Communications
Carolyn Everson . . . Director, Advertising Sales, mtvU
Lauren Dolgen . . . Manager, Orginal Series Development & Programming

*MURPHY BOYZ PRODUCTIONS

270 Sparta Ave., Ste. 104
Sparta, NJ 07871

PHONE	973-702-9000/973-702-9043
FAX	973-702-1550
EMAIL	ray@murphyboyz.com
WEB SITE	www.murphyboyz.com
TYPES	Animation - Features - Direct-to-Video/DVD
DEALS	Twentieth Century Fox Home Entertainment
DEVELOPMENT	Fleece - Hampton Horror - Bros and Arrow - The Latin Comedy Review
PRE-PRODUCTION	Big Black Comedy Show (Volumes 2&3)
POST PRODUCTION	Big Black Comedy Show (Volume 1)
CREDITS	Vampire in Brooklyn - Beverly Hills 3 - Holy Man - Metro

Ray Murphy Jr. . . . Partner/Producer
Bill Murphy . . . Partner/Producer
Stevie "Black" Lockett . . . Partner/Producer
Baron St. John . . . Partner/Producer

MUSE PRODUCTIONS, INC.

15-B Brooks Ave.
Venice, CA 90291

PHONE	310-306-2001
FAX	310-574-2614
WEB SITE	www.musefilm.com
TYPES	Documentaries - Features - New Media
DEVELOPMENT	The Family - Killer Inside Me - The Heart Is Deceitful Above All Things - Gardens of the Night - London Fields - Going Down - Music for Torching
CREDITS	I Love Your Work - This Girl's Life - Tiptoes - Spun - Love, Liza - Bully - Freeway - Trees Lounge - Two Girls and a Guy - This World, Then the Fireworks - Girl - Buffalo '66 - Virgin Suicides - American Psycho
COMMENTS	Interactive digital film

Chris Hanley . . . President
Roberta Hanley . . . Co-President
Tim Peternel . . . Producer/VP
David Hillary . . . Producer/VP
Michael Burress . . . Chief Administrative Officer

MUTUAL FILM COMPANY

MUTUAL FILM COMPANY

8560 W. Sunset Blvd., Ste. 800
West Hollywood, CA 90069

PHONE	310-855-7355
FAX	310-855-7356
TYPES	Features - TV Series
DEVELOPMENT	The Authority - Killing Floor - Lone Wolf and Cub - Snakes on a Plane
CREDITS	Timeline - Lara Croft Tomb Raider: The Cradle of Life - Paulie - Tomb Raider - Saving Private Ryan - 12 Monkeys - The Patriot - Primary Colors - The Jackal - A Simple Plan - Man on the Moon - Wonder Boys - Virus
COMMENTS	Foreign distribution; Financing; International sales

Gary Levinsohn . . . Principal
Edward Frumkes . . . Principal
Lesly Gross . . . VP, Operations & Administration, Mutual Film International
Paul Villarreal . . . Director, Finance & Accounting
Libby Bancroft . . . Manger, Operations
Paul Doble . . . Assistant to G. Levinsohn
Ryan Zaharako . . . Assistant to E. Frumkes
Robert Uyeda . . . Receptionist

MWG PRODUCTIONS

8075 W. Third St., Ste. 402
Los Angeles, CA 90048

PHONE	323-937-8313
FAX	323-937-5239
EMAIL	wynne9@aol.com
TYPES	Documentaries - Features - Made-for-TV/Cable Movies - New Media - TV Series
DEVELOPMENT	Hear My Testimony - Women in War - Cynthia - Proxy Warriors
CREDITS	Nine - Alaska - American Veteran Awards 2001/2002
SUBMISSION POLICY	Representation only

Max Goldenson . . . President/Producer
Ausanta Beasley . . . Executive Assistant to the President

MY2CENTENCES

9229 Sunset Blvd., Ste. 601
West Hollywood, CA 90069

PHONE	310-777-0323/212-966-0602
FAX	310-777-0324
EMAIL	info@my2centences.com
WEB SITE	www.my2c.com
TYPES	Features - New Media - Reality TV - TV Series
DEVELOPMENT	Branded - Jury of 5 - Affair Haven - Gargoyle
PRE-PRODUCTION	Untitled Fall Project - Dark Ride - Laws of Nature
COMPLETED UNRELEASED	Dead Dogs Lie - Kill Charlie
CREDITS	Animal Room - A Good Night to Die
SUBMISSION POLICY	Please submit via email to: submissions@my2c.com

Chris Williams . . . Founder/CEO (310-288-0975)
Craig Singer . . . Founder (212-966-0602)
David Williams . . . Sr. VP, Product Development
Robert Dean Klein . . . Creative

MYRIAD PICTURES

405 S. Beverly Dr., 5th Fl.
Beverly Hills, CA 90212
PHONE 310-279-4000
FAX 310-279-4001
EMAIL . . . . info@myriadpictures.com
WEB SITE . . . . www.myriadpictures.com

TYPES	Features - TV Series
PRODUCTION	The River King
POST PRODUCTION	Being Julia - Kinsey - Piccadilly Jim
COMPLETED UNRELEASED	Eulogy - Trauma
CREDITS	Jeeper Creepers 2 - The Good Girl - National Lampoon's Van Wilder - People I Know - Imagining Argentina
SUBMISSION POLICY	Scripts through agent only

Kirk D'Amico . . . . President
John Shiffman . . . . CFO
Marion Pilowsky . . . . Head, International Production
Debbie Reissman . . . . Director, Production
J.C. Rappaport . . . . Manager, Acquisitions

N/V

PO Box 52
Short Hills, NJ 07078
PHONE 973-564-5692
EMAIL . . . . nocturnalvaudeville@comcast.net

TYPES	Features - Theater - TV Series
CREDITS	Balloon Farm - Whiteboyz

Jesse Kaye . . . . Producer

NAAILA ENTERTAINMENT

2110 Broadway, Ste. A
Santa Monica, CA 90404
PHONE 310-255-0111
FAX 310-255-0112
EMAIL . . . . marvsworld@tmail.com

TYPES	Commercials - Features - Music Videos - TV Series

Hype Williams . . . . President/Director
Abdur Rahman . . . . Producer
Marvin St.Macary . . . . Executive Assistant

NAMESAKE ENTERTAINMENT

7608 West Hwy. 146, English Manor II, Ste. 100
Pewee Valley, KY 40056
PHONE 502-243-3185
FAX 502-243-3187
EMAIL . . . . info@namesakeentertainment.com
SECOND EMAIL . . . . dbailey@namesakentertainment.com
WEB SITE . . . . www.namesakeentertainment.com

TYPES	Features - Direct-to-Video/DVD - Made-for-TV/Cable Movies - TV Series
DEVELOPMENT	Eli - Pontius Pilate - Left Behind (TV Series) - The Visitation - Nightmare Academy
CREDITS	Every Mother's Worst Fear - Left Behind - Can of Worms - Hangman's Curse
SUBMISSION POLICY	Submit logline via email with contact info, including fax number; Only Faith-based/evangelical family entertainment

Joe Goodman . . . . CEO/Producer
Bobby Neutz . . . . COO/Producer
Kelly Neutz . . . . VP, Development
Tiffany Wallach . . . . Producer
Debi Bailey . . . . Director, Casting/Executive Administrator
Elliott Wallach . . . . Director, Marketing & Promotion

NANAS HART ENTERTAINMENT

14622 Ventura Blvd., Ste. 746
Sherman Oaks, CA 91403
PHONE 818-342-9800
FAX 818-342-1741
EMAIL . . . . mnh319@aol.com

TYPES	Features - Made-for-TV/Cable Movies - TV Series
CREDITS	2 Days in the Valley - Mother - Defending Your Life - The Muse - No Good Deed
SUBMISSION POLICY	No unsolicited material

Scott Hart . . . . Personal Manager
Herb Nanas . . . . Producer/Personal Manager
Fran Messer . . . . Office Manager/Assistant to Scott Hart & Herb Nanas

NASH ENTERTAINMENT

c/o Sunset Gower Studios
1438 N. Gower St., Box 10
Hollywood, CA 90028
PHONE 323-993-7384
FAX 323-993-7385

TYPES	Features - Reality TV - TV Series
CREDITS	For Love or Money (NBC) - Who Wants to Marry My Dad? (NBC) - Meet My Folks (NBC) - For Better or For Worse (TLC) - Totally Outrageous Behavior (Fox) - Outback Jack (TBS) - Wanna Come Inside? (MTV)

Bruce Nash . . . . President/CEO
Andrew Jebb . . . . VP, Production
Robyn Nash . . . . VP
Roz Taylor-Jordan . . . . VP, Casting
Ross Weintraub . . . . Director, Operations
Robert Kosberg . . . . Executive Producer
Scott Satin . . . . Executive Producer
Karen Nusbaum . . . . Assistant to President
Jo Sharon . . . . Assistant to President

NASSER ENTERTAINMENT GROUP

11350 Ventura Blvd., Ste. 101
Studio City, CA 91604
PHONE 818-505-8030
EMAIL . . . . nassent@pacbell.net
WEB SITE . . . . www.moviesfortv.com
SECOND WEB SITE . . . . www.animalworldnetwork.com

TYPES	Documentaries - Features - Direct-to-Video/DVD - Made-for-TV/Cable Movies - New Media - Syndication - TV Series
CREDITS	A Stranger to Love - Father's Choice - Forever Love - Last Brickmaker in America - Hostage Negotiator
COMMENTS	Distribution

Jack Nasser . . . . President
Steve Pine . . . . CFO
Brian Bloom . . . . VP
Joe Nasser . . . . VP
Rita Saigh . . . . Accounting
Christina Debeenie . . . . Assistant

NATIONAL GEOGRAPHIC FEATURE FILMS
9100 Wilshire Blvd., Ste. 401-E
Beverly Hills, CA 90212
PHONE 310-858-5800
FAX 310-858-5801
WEB SITE . . . . www.nationalgeographic.com
TYPES Features - Made-for-TV/Cable Movies - TV Series
DEVELOPMENT Undaunted Courage - Endurance - Aloft
PRE-PRODUCTION Emperor Zehnder
CREDITS K-19: The Widowmaker - Snow Dogs - Forbidden Territory: Stanley's Search for Livingstone

Jake Eberts . . . . Chairman
Adam Leipzig . . . . President, Production
Laura Lodin . . . . Development
Kattie Evans . . . . Development & Acquistions

NATIONAL GEOGRAPHIC KIDS' PROGRAMMING & PRODUCTION
9100 Wilshire Blvd., Ste. 401E
Beverly Hills, CA 90212
PHONE 310-858-5222
FAX 310-858-5801
TYPES Animation - Features - Direct-to-Video/DVD - Made-for-TV/Cable Movies - TV Series - Reality TV

Donna Friedman Meir . . . . President

NATIONAL LAMPOON
10850 Wilshire Blvd., Ste. 1000
Los Angeles, CA 90024
PHONE 310-474-5252
FAX 310-474-1219
WEB SITE . . . . www.nationallampoon.com
TYPES Animation - Features - Direct-to-Video/DVD - New Media - Syndication - TV Series
COMPLETED UNRELEASED National Lampoon's Thanksgiving Reunion
CREDITS National Lampoon's Van Wilder - Loaded Weapon 1 - Senior Trip - Vacation - Animal House - National Lampoon's Thanksgiving Reunion

James P. Jimirro . . . . President/CEO
Dan Laikin . . . . COO
Douglas Bennett . . . . Executive VP
Scott Rubin . . . . Editor in Chief, Nationallampoon.com
Randi Siegel . . . . Executive VP, Talent/Development
Orin Woinsky . . . . VP, National Lampoon Films

NBC UNIVERSAL

NBC ENTERTAINMENT
3000 W. Alameda Ave.
Burbank, CA 91523-0001
PHONE 818-840-4444
WEB SITE . . . . www.nbcuni.com
TYPES Made-for-TV/Cable Movies - TV Series - Reality TV

Jeff Zucker . . . . President, NBC Universal Television Group
Jeff Gaspin . . . . President, NBC Universal Cable Entertainment & Cross-Platform Strategy
Kevin Reilly . . . . President, NBC Entertainment
Vince Manze . . . . President/Creative Director, The NBC Agency
John Miller . . . . Chief Marketing Officer
Ted Frank . . . . Executive VP, Current Programs, NBC Entertainment

(Continued)

NBC ENTERTAINMENT (Continued)
Marc Graboff . . . . Executive VP, Television Group
Marc Hirschfeld . . . . Executive VP, Casting, NBC Entertainment
Ghen Maynard . . Executive VP, Primetime Development, NBC Entertainment
Beth Roberts . . . Executive VP, Business Affairs, NBC Entertainment & Cable
Howard Averill . . . . Sr. VP/CFO, West Coast
Sumithra Barry . . . . Sr. VP, NBC West Coach Program Research, NBC Entertainment
Thomas Cairns . . . . Sr. VP, Human Resources
Christopher Conti . . . . Sr. VP, Drama Development, NBC Entertainment
Cheryl Dolins . . . . Sr. VP, Comedy Development, NBC Entertainment
Andrea Hartman . . . . Sr. VP/Deputy General Counsel, NBC
Sheraton Kalouria . . . . Sr. VP, Daytime Programs, NBC Entertainment
Rick Ludwin . . . . Sr. VP, Late Night & Primetime Series, NBC Entertainment
Rebecca Marks . . . . Sr. VP, NBC Universal Television Group
Mitch Metcalf . . Sr. VP, Program Planning & Scheduling, NBC Entertainment
Craig Plestis Sr. VP, Alternative Programs & Development, \NBC Entertainment
Frank Radice . . . . Sr. VP, Advertising & Promotion, The NBC Agency
Erin Gough Wehrenberg . . . . Sr. VP, Current Series, NBC Entertainment
Vivi Zigler . . . . Sr. VP, Marketing & Advertising Services, The NBC Agency & Bravo
Gina Girolamo . . . . VP, Comedy Development, NBC Entertainment
Lisa Melching . . . . VP, Scheduling & Strategic Analysis
Jennifer O'Connell . . . . VP, Alternative Programs, NBC Entertainment
Michael Thorn . . . . VP, Drama Development, NBC Entertainment
Edwin Chung . . . . Director, Current Series, NBC Entertainment
Justin Levy . . . . Manager, Comedy Development, NBC Entertainment
Meredith Ahr . . . . Programming Associate, Alternative Programming, NBC Entertainment
Yelena Chak . . . . Programming Associate, Comedy Development, NBC Entertainment
Marina Nieto . . . . Programming Associate, Drama Development, NBC Entertainment
Mary Ann Wolf . . . . Programming Associate, Current Series, NBC Entertainment

*NBC NEWS
30 Rockefeller Plaza
New York, NY 10112
PHONE 212-664-4444
WEB SITE . . . . www.nbcuni.com
TYPES Documentaries - TV Series
CREDITS Dateline NBC - Decision 2004 - Early Today - Meet the Press - NBC Nightly News with Tom Brokaw - NBC Nightly News, Weekend Edition - The Chris Matthews Show - Today - Today, Weekend Edition
COMMENTS News programming

Jeff Zucker . . . . President, NBC Universal Television Group
Neal Shapiro . . . . President, NBC News
Allison Gollust . . . . VP, NBC News Communications & Media Relations
Lisa Hsia . . . . VP, NBC News
Elena Nachmanoff . . . . VP, Talent Development, NBC News
Bill Wheatley . . . . VP, NBC News
Barbara Levin . . . . Director, NBC News Communications & Media Relations
Lauren Kapp Sr. Manager, NBC News Communications & Media Relations
Jenny Tartikoff . . . . Press Manager, NBC News Communications & Media Relations
Lindsay Fitz . . . . Coordinator, NBC News
Megan Kopf . . . . Publicist, NBC News Media Relations

*NBC UNIVERSAL CABLE

3000 W. Alameda Ave.
Burbank, CA 91523-0001
PHONE 818-840-4444/818-777-1000
WEB SITE . . . . .www.nbcuni.com
TYPES TV Series
COMMENTS Additional office: 100 Universal City Plaza, Universal City, CA 91608

David M. Zaslav .President, NBC Universal Cable
Randel A. Falco . . . . .President, NBC Universal Television Networks Group
Jeff Gaspin . . . . .President, NBC Universal Cable Entertainment & Cross-Platform Strategy
Bonnie Hammer . . . . .President, USA & SCI FI Networks
Lauren Zalaznick . . . . .President, Bravo & TRIO Networks
Dave Howe . . . . .Executive VP, Marketing & Creative, SCI FI
Mark Stern . . . . .Executive VP, Original Programming, SCI FI Channel
Bridget Baker . . . . .Sr. VP, Cable Distribution, NBC Universal Cable
Mark Hotz . . . . .Sr. VP, Marketing, NBC Universal Cable
Jason Klarman . . . . .Sr. VP, Marketing, TRIO
Kat Stein . . . . .Sr. VP, SCI FI Channel Corporate Communications
Thomas Vitale . . . . . . .Sr. VP, Acquisitions, Scheduling & Program Planning, SCI FI Channel
Henry Ahn . . . . .VP, Affiliate Sales, NBC Universal Cable
Andrew Cohen . . . . .VP, Original Programming, Trio
Erica Conaty . . . . .VP, Marketing, NBC Universal Cable
Brian Hunt . . . . . . .VP, Affiliate Ad Sales, Promotions & National Accounts, NBC Universal Cable
Lynette Pinto . . . . .VP, Marketing, NBC Universal Cable
Kris Slava . . . . .VP, Acquisitions & Program Planning

*NBC UNIVERSAL CORPORATE

3000 W. Alameda Ave.
Burbank, CA 91523-0001
PHONE 818-840-4444/818-777-1000
WEB SITE . . . . .www.nbcuni.com
TYPES Features - TV Series
COMMENTS Additional office: 100 Universal City Plaza, Universal City, CA 91608

Roy Brandon Burgess . .Executive VP, Digital Media, International Channels & Business Development, NBC Universal
Lynn Calpeter .Executive VP/CFO, NBC Universal
Richard Cotton . . . . .Executive VP/General Counsel, NBC Universal
John Damiano . . . . .Executive VP, Affiliate Relations
Dick Ebersol . . . . .Chairman, NBC Universal Sports & Olympics
John Eck . . . .President, Technical Operations & Integration, NBC Universal
Eddie Egan . . . . .Co-President, Marketing, Universal Pictures
Tom Emrey .CFO, Universal Studios Home Video
Randel A. Falco . . . . .President, NBC Universal Television Networks Group
Rick Finkelstein . . . . .President, Universal Pictures
Adam Fogelson . . . . .President, Marketing, Universal Pictures
Jeff Gaspin . . . . .President, NBC Universal Cable Entertainment & Cross-Platform Strategy
Robert G. Gault Jr. . . . . .President/CEO, Universal Orlando
Bonnie Hammer . . . . .President, USA & SCI FI Networks
Frederick Huntsberry . . . . .Executive VP, NBC Universal Television Distribution/CFO, NBC Universal Television Group
Jay Ireland . . . . .President, NBC Universal Television Stations
Michael Jack . . . . .VP, NBC Diversity/President/General Manager, WRC-TV NBC4
Daniel R. Jensen . . . . .Executive VP/COO, Universal Studios Japan
Richard Kaplan . . . . .President, MSNBC
David Kissinger . . . . .Co-President, NBC Universal Television
Craig Kornblau . . . . .President, Universal Studios Home Video (USHV)
Larry Kurzweil . . . . .President/COO, Universal Studios Hollywood
David Linde . . . . .Co-President, Focus Features
Jay Linden . . . . .Executive VP, NBC Connect
Ron Meyer . . . . .President/COO, Universal Studios
Kathy Nelson . . . . .President, Film Music, Universal Music Group (UMG) & Universal Pictures
H. David Overbeeke . . . . .Executive VP/CIO, NBC Universal
Mary Parent . . . . .Vice Chairman, Worldwide Production, Universal Pictures
Anna Perez . . . . .Executive VP, Communications, NBC Universal
Deborah Reif . . . . .Executive VP, Financial Structuring, NBC Universal
Kevin Reilly . . . . .President, NBC Entertainment
Wyman Roberts . . . . .Executive VP/Chief Marketing Officer, Universal Parks & Resorts
Nikki Rocco . . . . .President, Universal Pictures Distribution

(Continued)

NBC UNIVERSAL CORPORATE (Continued)

Marc J. Saperstein . .Sr. Executive VP, Human Resources & Communications
James Schamus . . . . .Co-President, Focus Features
Kenneth Schanzer . . . . .President, NBC Sports
Neal Shapiro . . . . .President, NBC News
Marc Shmuger .Vice Chairman, Universal Pictures
Peter Smith . . . . .President, Universal Pictures International (UPI)
Stacey Snider . . . . .Chairman, Universal Pictures
Scott Stuber . . . . .Vice Chairman, Worldwide Production, Universal Pictures
Pamela Thomas-Graham . . . . .President/CEO, CNBC
Keith Turner . . . . .President, NBC Universal Sales & Marketing
Jim Watters . . . . .President/General Manager, Universal Operations Group
Eileen Whelley . . . . .Executive VP, Human Resources, NBC Universal
Thomas L. Williams . . . . .Chairman/CEO, Universal Parks & Resorts
Bob Wright . . . . .Vice Chairman/Executive Officer, GE & Chairman/ CEO, NBC Universal
Alan Wurtzel . . . . .President, Research & Media Development, NBC
David M. Zaslav .President, NBC Universal Cable
Jeff Zucker . . . . .President, NBC Universal Television Group

*NBC UNIVERSAL TELEVISION STUDIO

100 Universal City Plaza
Universal City, CA 91608
PHONE 818-777-1000/818-840-4444
WEB SITE . . . . .www.nbcuni.com
TYPES TV Series
COMMENTS Latenight, daytime and longform specials; Additional offices: 3000 W. Alameda Ave., Burbank, CA 91523-0001

Jeff Zucker . . . . .President, NBC Universal Television Group
Angela Bromstad . . . . .Co-President, NBC Universal Television
David Kissinger . . . . .Co-President, NBC Universal Television
Charles Engel . . . . .Executive VP, Programming
Robert Fitzpatrick . . . . .Executive VP, Business & Legal Affairs, NBC Universal Television Studio
Arthur Hasson . . . . .Executive VP, Sales & New Business, NBC Universal Television Studio
Elizabeth Herbst-Brady . . . . .Executive VP, Advertiser Sales, NBC Universal Television Studio
Rick Olshansky . . . . .Executive VP, Business Affairs
Juliana Carnessale . . . . .Sr. VP, Business & Legal Affairs, NBC Universal Television Studio
Paulo de Oliveira . . . . .Sr. VP, Cable Programming, NBC Universal Television Studio
Phil Martzolf . . . . .Sr. VP/National Sales Manager, NBC Universal Television Studio
Shelley McCrory . . . . .Sr. VP, Comedy Development, NBC Universal Television Studio
Nancy Perkins . . . . .Sr. VP, Casting, NBC Universal Television Studio
Katherine Pope . . . . .Sr. VP, Drama Development, NBC Universal Television Studio
Jeff Ingold . . . . .VP, Comedy Programming, NBC Universal Television Studio
Curt King . . . . .VP, Publicity
Laura Lancaster VP, Drama Programming, NBC Universal Television Studio
Elisa Roth . . . . .VP, Drama, Network & Cable Programming, NBC Universal Television Studio
Vernon Sanders . . . . .VP, Comedy Programming, NBC Universal Television Studio
Grace Wu . . . . .VP, Casting
Jerry DiCanio . . . . .Head, Production, NBC Universal Television Studio
Lucia Cottone . . . . .Director, Cable Programming, NBC Universal Television Studio
Renate Radford . . . . . . .Director, Comedy, NBC Universal Television Studio
Lauren Stein . . . . .Director, Drama Development, NBC Universal Television Studio

NELSON MADISON FILMS
4820 San Fernando Rd.
Los Angeles, CA 91204
PHONE . . . 818-550-6213
EMAIL . . . info@nelsonmadisonfilms.com
WEB SITE . . . www.nelsonmadisonfilms.com
TYPES Features
DEVELOPMENT Forewarned - Asphalt Cowboys - A Fate Worse Than Death
PRODUCTION Shifted
CREDITS NSYNC Bigger Than Live
COMMENTS Development and production of 35mm, DV and IMAX giant screen independent films; Production, film editing and consulting services

Michael Madison . . . Executive Producer
Linda Nelson . . . Executive Producer

NELVANA ENTERTAINMENT/A CORUS ENTERTAINMENT COMPANY
4500 Wilshire Blvd.
Los Angeles, CA 90010
PHONE . . . 323-850-9380/416-588-5571
FAX . . . 323-549-4232
WEB SITE . . . www.nelvana.com
SECOND WEB SITE . . . www.corus-ent.com
TYPES Animation - Features - Direct-to-Video/DVD - TV Series
CREDITS Little Bear - Babar - Franklin - Rolie-Polie-Olie - PBS Bookworm Bunch - Bob & Margaret - Cardcaptors - Medabots - Beyblade - Braceface - Cyberchase
COMMENTS Toronto office: 32 Atlantic Ave., Toronto, ON M6K 1X8 Canada

Doug Murphy . . . Sr. VP, Business Development
Scott Dyer . . . Sr. VP, Production & Development
Irene Weibel . . . VP, Development
Christie Dreyfuss . . . VP, Development
Sid Kaufman . . . Executive VP, Merchandising & Licensing

NEO ART & LOGIC
8315 Beverly Blvd.
Los Angeles, CA 90048-2607
PHONE . . . 323-653-6007
FAX . . . 323-653-0409
WEB SITE . . . www.neoartandlogic.com
TYPES Documentaries - Features - Direct-to-Video/DVD - Made-for-TV/Cable Movies - TV Series
DEALS Dimension Films
PRODUCTION Project Greenlight Season 3
CREDITS Wes Craven's Dracula 2000 Franchise - The Prophecy Franchise - Trekkies Franchise - Hellraiser 5-8
SUBMISSION POLICY Via phone or mail, logline only

Joel Soisson . . . Partner/Producer
Mike Leahy . . . Partner/Producer
W.K. Border . . . Partner/Producer
Simone DeCamargo . . . Finance
Kirk Morri . . . VP, Post Production
Aaron Ockman . . . Development

NET EFFECT MEDIA, INC.
4966 El Camino Real, Ste. 101
Los Altos, CA 94022
PHONE . . . 650-938-6600
FAX . . . 650-938-6400
EMAIL . . . info@neteffectmedia.com
SECOND EMAIL . . . vijay@neteffectmedia.com
WEB SITE . . . www.neteffectmedia.com
TYPES Features - Direct-to-Video/DVD
CREDITS Green Card Fever

Vijay Vaidyanathan . . . Chairman
Kapil Sethi . . . President, Distribution
Sheena Vaidyanathan . . . Supervising Producer

MACE NEUFELD PRODUCTIONS
9100 Wilshire Blvd., Ste. 517, East Tower
Beverly Hills, CA 90212
PHONE . . . 310-401-6868
FAX . . . 310-401-6866
TYPES Features - Made-for-TV/Cable Movies - TV Series
DEVELOPMENT Pathfinder - Seconds - Powers - Outrider - Ice Station Zebra
PRODUCTION Sahara
POST PRODUCTION Asylum
CREDITS The Saint - Clear and Present Danger - Patriot Games - Hunt for Red October - The General's Daughter - Sum of All Fears

Mace Neufeld . . . Principal (310-401-6868)
Kel Symons . . . VP, Development (310-401-6869)
Kathy Day . . . Executive Assistant to Mr. Neufeld/Office Manager (310-401-6868)
Ryan Patterson . . . Assistant to Mr. Symons (310-401-6869)

NEU-MAN-FILMS, INC.
21321 Lighthill Dr.
Topanga, CA 90290-4442
PHONE . . . 818-346-9004
FAX . . . 818-346-1023
EMAIL . . . submissions@neumanfilms.com
TYPES Features - Made-for-TV/Cable Movies - New Media - TV Series - Reality TV
DEVELOPMENT Pandora - Rocked - Markers - Tempting Fate - Grooming Holly
POST PRODUCTION Hidden Adventures
CREDITS Under Siege 2: Dark Territory - Never Talk to Strangers - Sunstroke - Islanders - Across Apple Lake - Chill Factor
SUBMISSION POLICY Email synopsis only; Screenplays only by request via WGA agent or our release

Jeffrey R. Neuman . . . President/Producer
Susan Clary . . . Executive VP, Business Affairs

NEVER A DULL MOMENT PRODUCTIONS, INC.
1406 N. Topanga Canyon Blvd.
Topanga, CA 90290
PHONE . . . 310-455-1651
FAX . . . 310-455-1893
EMAIL . . . ndull@aol.com
TYPES Documentaries - Features - TV Series
CREDITS The Child Abuse Projects - Deadly Love - Midnight's Child - Synapse - It's Not Me, It's My OCD - The School Violence Projects - Backyard Conservation in Arid Lands - Conservation Delivery in the West
SUBMISSION POLICY Writers and agents, email loglines

David N. Gottlieb . . . Producer/Director

NEVERLAND FILMS, INC.
10323 Santa Monica Blvd., Ste. 106
Los Angeles, CA 90025
PHONE .310-772-0008
FAX .310-772-0006
WEB SITE .www.neverlandfilms.com
TYPES Features
DEVELOPMENT Caught in the Act - The Gravedancers
POST PRODUCTION Noel
CREDITS Scorched - Drowning Mona - Cowboy Up - Palmetto - A Brother's Kiss

Al Corley .Partner/Producer
Eugene Musso .Partner/Producer
Bart Rosenblatt .Partner/Producer
Rick Berg .Partner/Management Division
Jim Mulay .VP, Production
Dave Feldman .Literary Coordinator
Karen Irvin .Story Editor
Kim Olsen .Business Affairs

NEW AMSTERDAM ENTERTAINMENT, INC.
675 Third Ave., Ste. 2521
New York, NY 10017
PHONE .212-922-1930
FAX .212-922-0674
EMAIL .mail@newamsterdamnyc.com
WEB SITE .www.newamsterdamnyc.com
TYPES Features - Made-for-TV/Cable Movies - TV Series
DEVELOPMENT Keller - Dune: The Series - Dune Prequels - He, She and It - The Merciful Women - Stephen King's The Night Flier 2
CREDITS Frank Herbert's Children of Dune - Dawn of the Dead (2004) - Pet Sematary - The Stand - The Vernon Johns Story - Frank Herbert's Dune - Dawn of the Dead (1979) - Martin

Richard P. Rubinstein .President
Michael Messina .VP, Development
Emily V. Austin-Bruns .Executive Assistant

NEW CITY PICTURES, INC.
955 Second St., Ste. 18
Santa Monica, CA 90403
PHONE .310-395-6611/604-732-7677
FAX .604-732-7693
WEB SITE .www.newcityfilms.com
SECOND WEB SITE .www.newcitypictures.net
TYPES Features - Made-for-TV/Cable Movies
CREDITS Mr. Rice's Secret
COMMENTS Vancouver office: 1005 Cypress St., Vancouver, BC, V6J 3K6 Canada

Colleen Nystedt .President
David Rockwell .CFO
Christopher Courtney .VP, Production
Lindsay Moffat .VP, Operations
Quinn Bender .Story Editor

NEW CONCORDE
11600 San Vicente Blvd.
Los Angeles, CA 90049
PHONE .310-820-6733
FAX .310-207-6816/310-207-8825
WEB SITE .www.newconcorde.com
TYPES Features - Direct-to-Video/DVD - Made-for-TV/Cable Movies - TV Series
DEVELOPMENT Storm - Firewall - Cheyenne Warrior 2 - DinoCroc 2
PRODUCTION Bloodfist 2050 - Scorpius Gigantus
POST PRODUCTION Rolling Thunder
COMPLETED UNRELEASED Rage and Discipline
CREDITS Shakedown - Treasure Island - Lethal Force - Disappearance - DinoCroc - The Keeper of Time - When Eagles Strike

Roger Corman .President/CEO/Executive Producer
Julie Corman .Sr. Executive VP/Executive Producer
Gary Jones .President, Worldwide Distribution
Frank Moreno .Vice Chairman
Catherine Corman .Producer (NY)
Thomas Krentzin .Executive VP
Frances Doel .VP, Development
Max Yoshikawa .VP, Finance
Lars Canty .Director, Marketing
Sarah Esberg .Director, Creative Affairs
Germaine Simiens .Director, Business Affairs

NEW CRIME PRODUCTIONS
555 Rose Ave.
Venice, CA 90291
PHONE .310-396-2199
FAX .310-396-4249
EMAIL .newcrime@aol.com
TYPES Features - Made-for-TV/Cable Movies
COMPLETED UNRELEASED Never Get Outta the Boat
CREDITS Grosse Pointe Blank - The Jack Bull - High Fidelity

John Cusack .Writer/Producer
Steve Pink .Writer/Producer
Grace Loh .VP, Development/Production
Aurelie Levy .Assistant to Mr. Cusack
Christen McArdle .Assistant to Ms. Loh

NEW ENGLAND PRODUCTIONS, INC.
3430 Barry Ave.
Los Angeles, CA 90066-2002
PHONE .310-390-6567
FAX .310-397-3070
TYPES Features - Made-for-TV/Cable Movies - TV Series
PRE-PRODUCTION Desperate Housewives (ABC Series)
CREDITS Motocrossed - Medusa's Child - King of the World - Out of Darkness - Metro - James Dean - Live from Baghdad - Threat Matrix (ABC Series)

George W. Perkins .Producer

NEW GENERATION FILMS, INC.

304 N. Edinburgh Ave.
Los Angeles, CA 90048
PHONE 323-655-7705/323-655-7702
FAX 323-655-7706
EMAIL . . . . . ngf@newgenerationfilmsinc.com
WEB SITE . . . . . www.newgenerationfilmsinc.com
TYPES: Animation - Features - Direct-to-Video/DVD - TV Series
DEVELOPMENT: Hana's Ring - M
PRE-PRODUCTION: Booty and the Beast
PRODUCTION: Oy Vey, My Son Is Gay! - Gunga Din
CREDITS: Crime & Punishment - Death Game - Days of Love - The Return from India - Open Heart
COMMENTS: Distribution

Evgeny Afineevsky . . . . . Co-Chairman/President
Benjamin Nof . . . . . Executive VP/Producer
Svetlana Anufrieeva . . . . . VP, Production/Producer
Victor Freilich . . . . . VP, Development/Producer
Dr. Joseph Mamaliger . . . . . VP, Finance
Alexander H. Walker Jr. . . . . . General Counsel
Alexander H. Walker III . . . . . Legal Department

NEW LINE CINEMA

116 N. Robertson Blvd., Ste. 200
Los Angeles, CA 90048
PHONE 310-854-5811/212-649-4900
FAX 310-659-2459/212-649-4966
WEB SITE . . . . . www.newline.com
TYPES: Features - Made-for-TV/Cable Movies - TV Series
POST PRODUCTION: The Wedding Crashers - Cellular - After the Sunset - Blade: Trinity - Upside of Anger
CREDITS: The Lord of the Rings Trilogy - Elf - The Butterfly Effect - Texas Chainsaw Massacre - The Notebook - Harold & Kumar Go to White Castle
COMMENTS: East Coast office: 888 Seventh Ave., 20th Fl., New York, NY 10106

Robert K. Shaye . . . . . Co-Chairman/Co-CEO
Michael Lynne . . . . . Co-Chairman/Co-CEO
Rolf Mittweg . . . . . President/COO, New Line Worldwide Distribution & Marketing
Toby Emmerich . . . . . President, New Line Productions
Stephen D. Abramson . . . . . CFO
Stephen L. Einhorn . . . . . President, New Line Home Video
Mark Ordesky . . . . . COO/Executive VP, New Line Productions
Camela Galano . . . . . President, New Line International Releasing, Inc.
James K. Rosenthal . . . . . President, New Line Television
Russell Schwartz . . . . . President, New Line Domestic Marketing
David Tuckerman . . . . President, New Line Domestic Theatrical Distribution
Benjamin Zinkin . . . . . Sr. Executive VP, Business & Legal Affairs
Erik Holmberg . . . . . Co-President, Physical Production
Paul Prokop . . . . . Co-President, Physical Production
Michael Spatt . . . . . Sr. Executive VP, Finance
Jayne Bieber . . . . . Executive VP, TV Production
Richard Brener . . . . . Executive VP, Production
Paul B. Broucek . . . . . Executive VP, Music
Diane Charbanic . . . . . Executive VP, Media & Co-Op Advertising
David Eichler . . . . . Executive VP/Controller
Sara Frith . . . . . Executive VP, International/Sr. VP, Business & Legal Affairs
Judd Funk . . . . . Executive VP, Business & Legal Affairs
Marsha Hook Haygood . . . . . Executive VP, Administration
Susannah Juni . . . . . Executive VP, Participation & Contract Accounting

(Continued)

NEW LINE CINEMA (Continued)

Christina Kounelias . . . . . Executive VP, Publicity & Promotions
Raymond J. Landes . . . . . Executive VP, Corporate Accounting
Jody A. Levin . . . . . Executive VP, Film Post Production
Jason Linn . . . . . Executive VP, Music Development
Andrew Matthews . . . . . Executive VP, Finance & International Affairs/ Sr. VP, Business & Legal Affairs
Gordon Paddison . . . . . Executive VP, Integrated Marketing
Lori Silfen . . . . . Executive VP, Music/Sr. VP, Business & Legal Affairs
Karen S. Zimmer . . . . . Executive VP, Information Services
Kent Alterman . . . . . Sr. VP, Production
Katherine Beyda . . . . . Sr. VP, Physical Production
Carolyn Blackwood . . . . . Sr. VP, Business Affairs
Stokely Chaffin . . . . . Sr. VP, Production
Jon Davidson . . . . . Sr. VP, Production Finance
Michael Del Nin . . . . . Sr. VP, Business Development
Leon Dudevoir . . . . . Sr. VP, Physical Production
Erik Ellner . . . . . Sr. VP, Business & Legal Affairs
Teri Fournier . . . . . Sr. VP, Business & Legal Affairs
Amy Goodman . . . . . Sr. VP, Business Affairs
Elissa Greer . . . . . Sr. VP, Publicity & Promotions
Michelle Guglielmelli . . . . . Sr. VP, Human Resources
Tracy Karagianis . . . . . Sr. VP, Application Development
Kevin Kasha . . . . . Sr. VP, Acquisitions & Programming
Mark S. Kaufman . . . . . Sr. VP, Music Affairs/VP, Production
Brent Kaviar . . . . . Sr. VP, Post Production
Jon Kroll . . . . . Sr. VP, New Line Television
Warren Lenard . . . . . Sr. VP, Technology & Network Services
Jacqueline R. Moskow . . . . . Sr. VP, Financial Planning & Forecasting
Joshua Ravetch . . . . . Sr. VP, Production Resources
Lauren A. Ritchie . . . . . Sr. VP, Visual Effects
Mitchell Rotter . . . . . Sr. VP, Soundtracks & Music Development
Julie A. Shapiro . . . . . Sr. VP, Business & Legal Affairs (TV)
Ron Signorotti . . . . . Sr. VP, Participation & Contracts
Richard Socarides . . . . . Sr. VP, Corporate Communications
Lance Still . . . . . Sr. VP, National Promotions
Craig Alexander . . . . . VP, Business & Legal Affairs
Erica Beier . . . . . VP, Production Services
Dana M. Belcastro . . . . . VP, Physical Production
Cale Boyter . . . . . VP, Production
Jack Deutchman . . . . . VP, Feature Post Production
Bobby L. Doyle . . . . . VP, International Post Production
Charles J. Freericks . . . . . VP, TV Creative Affairs
John Giraldo . . . . . Group VP/Assistant Controller
Emily Glatter . . . . . VP, Production Administration
Michael Grizzi . . . . . VP, Business & Legal Affairs
Brendan Kelly . . . . . VP, TV Business Administration
Kevin Kertes . . . . . VP, Music Promotions
Virginia Martino . . . . . VP, Business Affairs
Matthew Moore . . . . . VP, Production & Development
Louise M. Ransil . . . . . VP, Administration
Eric Reynolds . . . . . VP, Post Production
Sara D. Romilly . . . . . VP, Feature Post Production
Frank Salvino . . . . . VP, Feature Post Production
David Sporn . . . . . VP, Business Affairs
George Waud . . . . . VP, Production & Development
Michele Weiss . . . . . VP, Development
Magnus Kim . . . . . Creative Executive
Luke Ryan . . . . . Creative Executive
Michael Disco . . . . . Story Editor
Keith Goldberg . . . . . Director, Development

NEW LINE TELEVISION
116 N. Robertson Blvd., Ste. 710
Los Angeles, CA 90048
PHONE 310-854-5811/212-649-4900
FAX 310-289-8313/212-649-4966
WEB SITE .....www.newline.com
TYPES Made-for-TV/Cable Movies - New Media - TV Series - Reality TV
COMMENTS East Coast office: 888 Seventh Ave., 20th Fl., New York, NY 10106

Jim Rosenthal .....President, New Line Television
David Spiegelman .....Sr. Executive VP, TV Syndication
Jayne Bieber .....Executive VP, Production
Vicky Gregorian .....Sr. VP, National Sales Manager
David Imhoff .....Sr. VP, Worldwide Licensing & Merchandising
Jon Kroll .....Sr. VP, New Line Television
Julie A. Shapiro .....Sr. VP, Business & Legal Affairs
Charles J. Freericks .....VP, Creative Affairs
Robin Seidner .....VP, National TV Promotions & Marketing
Mark Costa .....Director, Production
Lori Huck .....Director, Creative Affairs
Erin Cristall .....Manager, Alternative Programming
Jaret Keller .....Coordinator, New Line Television

NEW RAY FILMS
PO Box 1335
McMurray, PA 15317
PHONE 724-969-2565
EMAIL .....newray1@aol.com
WEB SITE .....www.newray.com
SECOND WEB SITE .....www.newrayfilms.com
TYPES Features
PRE-PRODUCTION Chasing Windmills - Rachel
CREDITS The Journey

Harish Saluja .....Producer/Director
Jane Aseniero .....Co-Producer

NEW REDEMPTION PICTURES
3000 W. Olympic, Bldg. 3, Rm. 1437
Santa Monica, CA 90404
PHONE 310-315-4820
FAX 310-315-4821
TYPES Features - Made-for-TV/Cable Movies - Reality TV - TV Series
DEALS HBO Films
DEVELOPMENT Glad All Over - Jersey - Whitebread
COMPLETED UNRELEASED Safe & Sound (Reality Pilot)
CREDITS Point of Origin - 15 Minutes - Don King: Only in America - 2 Days in the Valley - The Ryan White Story - The Preppy Murder - Daddy - Stoned - A Father's Revenge

John Herzfeld .....No Title
Aundrea Hearn .....No Title
Chris Knutson .....No Title

NEW REGENCY PRODUCTIONS
SEE Regency Enterprises

NEW SCREEN CONCEPTS, INC.
84 W. Park Pl.
Stamford, CT 06901
PHONE 203-961-0670
FAX 203-961-0831
EMAIL .....newscreenconcepts@newscreenconcepts.com
WEB SITE .....www.newscreenconcepts.com
TYPES Documentaries - TV Series
CREDITS Body Human 2000 Series - Yearbook - I Am Your Child - Siegfried & Roy - Brazelton on Parenting - Houston Medical (ABC) - Extreme Makeover

Charles Bangert .....Chairman
Louis Gorfain .....President
Hank O'Karma .....Producer/Director
Janis Biewend .....Producer
Amy McCampbell .....Producer
Tommy Brown .....Post Production Supervisor
David Schewel .....Supervising Editor
Edna Calastro .....Finance/Business Affairs
Becka Slade .....Editor

NEW WAVE ENTERTAINMENT
2660 W. Olive Ave.
Burbank, CA 91505
PHONE 818-295-5000
FAX 818-295-5099
EMAIL .....bkatz@nwe.com
WEB SITE .....www.nwe.com
TYPES Features - TV Series - Reality TV
DEVELOPMENT Fairhope, USA - Fevertrail - Eyes of the Street
PRODUCTION Last Comic Standing - Trash to Cash - Hurt Bert
COMPLETED UNRELEASED Gray in Between - 8 Guys
CREDITS Action - Hype - Welcome to New York - Mohrsports

Barry Katz .....No Title
Brian Volk-Weiss .....No Title
Mark Rousso .....Manager
Julie Ayers .....Executive Assistant
Jeff Puskar .....Executive Assistant

VINCENT NEWMAN ENTERTAINMENT
8840 Wilshire Blvd., 3rd Fl.
Beverly Hills, CA 90211
PHONE 310-358-3050
FAX 310-358-3289
EMAIL .....vnentertainment@aol.com
TYPES Features - TV Series
DEVELOPMENT Features: Red-Eye - No Man's Land - Mexicali; TV: Hot Property (Series)
CREDITS A Man Apart - Poolhall Junkies - Sol Goode

Vincent Newman .....No Title
Nancy Lanham .....Development/Production
Ronene Ettinger .....Associate
Vaun Wilmott .....Writer

It is illegal to copy any part of this book

PETER NEWMAN PRODUCTIONS, INC.

799 Washington St., Ste. 201
New York, NY 10014
PHONE 212-897-3949/212-897-3979
FAX 212-624-1737
EMAIL ....pnproduction@aol.com

TYPES	Features - TV Series
DEALS	Goldcrest Films International, Inc.
DEVELOPMENT	Veeck as in Wreck - Janis Joplin - Strom Thrumond's Daughter - The Squid and the Whale
POST PRODUCTION	The Game of Their Lives
CREDITS	Smoke - The Secret of Roan Inish - Swimming to Cambodia - Lord of the Flies

Peter Newman ....President
Chelsea Horenstein ....Production Executive

NEWMARKET CAPITAL GROUP

202 N. Canon Dr.
Beverly Hills, CA 90210
PHONE 310-858-7472
FAX 310-858-7473
EMAIL ....brittany@newmarketfilms.com
WEB SITE ....www.newmarketfilms.com

TYPES	Features
CREDITS	Memento - The Mexican - Topsy-Turvy - Cruel Intentions - Stark Raving Mad - Donnie Darko - The Skulls - Real Women Have Curves - SPUN - Monster - Whale Rider
SUBMISSION POLICY	Through representation only

Chris Ball ....Partner/Co-Founder
William Tyrer ....Partner/Co-Founder
Rene Cogan ....CFO
Linda Hawkins ....Production
Brittany Ballard ....Acquisitions
Robert Fyvolent ....Business Affairs

NEXT ENTERTAINMENT

c/o Telepictures
15301 Ventura Blvd., Bldg. E
Sherman Oaks, CA 91403
PHONE 818-972-0077
FAX 818-972-0250

TYPES	TV Series - Reality TV
DEALS	ABC Entertainment Television Group - Telepictures Productions
PRODUCTION	High School Reunion
CREDITS	The Bachelor 1&2 - Million Dollar Mysteries - Public Property (Pilot) - Smartest Kid in America 1&2 - Before They Were Stars - Real Funny - World's Worst Drivers 1&2 - The Bachelorette

Mike Fleiss ....President/Executive Producer (818-972-0122)
Scott Einziger ....Co-Executive Producer (818-972-0193)
Scott Jeffress ....Co-Executive Producer (818-972-0179)
Lisa Levenson ....Co-Executive Producer (818-972-0045)
Tawnya Brown ....Executive Assistant (818-972-0122)
Nikki Pattison ....Executive Assistant (818-972-0815)

NEXUS ENTERTAINMENT, INC.

8033 Sunset Blvd., Ste. 1018
Los Angeles, CA 90046
PHONE 323-874-1648
FAX 323-650-6033

TYPES	Features - Made-for-TV/Cable Movies - Reality TV - Syndication - TV Series
DEVELOPMENT	For the Price of a Mule (CBS/WBTV)
PRODUCTION	Wedding Daze (Hallmark)
COMPLETED UNRELEASED	Home for Christmas
CREDITS	The Long Shot - Stuck with Each Other - Kids Like These - Bobby Garwood, the Last POW? - Vietnam War Story

Georg Stanford Brown ....Producer/Director
Tracey Washington ....No Title

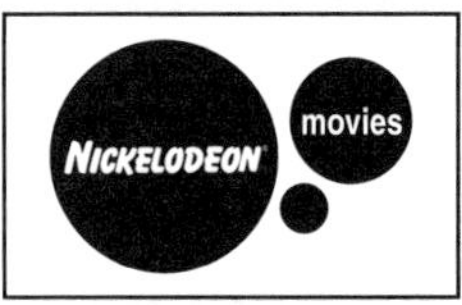

NICKELODEON MOVIES

c/o Paramount Studios
5555 Melrose Ave., Lubitsch Annex, Ste. 119
Los Angeles, CA 90038
PHONE 323-956-8650
FAX 323-862-1663
WEB SITE ....www.nick.com

TYPES	Animation - Features
DEALS	Paramount Pictures-Motion Picture Group
PRODUCTION	Sponge Bob Square Pants, the Movie - Series of Unfortunate Events
CREDITS	The Wild Thornberrys Movie - Hey Arnold! The Movie - Clockstoppers - Jimmy Neutron: Boy Genius - Rugrats in Paris - Snow Day - The Rugrats Movie - Good Burger - Harriet the Spy - Rugrats Go Wild
SUBMISSION POLICY	Unsolicited material not accepted
COMMENTS	Animation and Live Action Features; East Coast office: 1515 Broadway, 38th Fl., New York, NY 10036, phone: 212-258-7550, fax: 212-846-1873

Julia Pistor ....Sr. VP, Nickelodeon Movies
Ramsey Naito ....VP, Nickelodeon Movies
Damon Ross ....VP, Nickelodeon Movies
Ali Bell ....Creative Executive, Development
Niki Williams ....Development/Production
Michael Zermeno ....Marketing
Tarsus Jackson ....Executive Assistant, Development

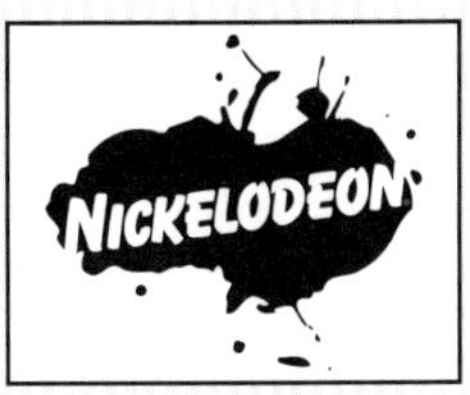

NICKELODEON/NICK AT NITE/TV LAND/SPIKE TV

1515 Broadway, 38th Fl.
New York, NY 10036
PHONE 212-258-7500
WEB SITE .....www.nick.com
SECOND WEB SITE .....www.nickatnite.com

TYPES	Animation - Features - Direct-to-Video/DVD - TV Series
DEVELOPMENT	Unfabulous (Live-Action Comedy)
PRE-PRODUCTION	Zoey 101 (Live-Action)
CREDITS	All Grown Up - Jimmy Neutron - The FairlyOdd Parents - Hey Arnold! - The Wild Thornberrys - As Told by Ginger - Rocket Power - Dora the Explorer - The Brothers Garcia - Oswald - Little Bill - All That - The Amanda Show - Blue's Clues - SpongeBob SquarePants - Rugrats
COMMENTS	Additional Web site: www.tvland.com; West Coast offices: 2600 Colorado Ave., Santa Monica, CA 90404, phone: 310-752-8000; 231 Olive Ave., Burbank, CA 91502, phone: 818-736-3000

Herb Scannell .....MTV Networks Group President, Nickelodeon, TV Land, Noggin & Spike TV
Cyma Zarghami .....President, Nickelodeon TV
Albie Hecht .....President, Spike TV
Larry W. Jones .....President, Nick at Nite/TV Land
Jeff Dunn .....Group COO, Nickelodeon Networks (Nick/Nick at Nite/Spike TV)/President, Nickelodeon Films & Enterprises
Keith Dawkins .....General Manager, Nicktoons
Marjorie Cohn .....Executive VP, Original Programming & Development, Nickelodeon
Brown Johnson .....Executive VP, Production & Development, Nick Jr.
Kevin Kay .....Executive VP, Programming & Development, Spike TV
Andra Shapiro .....Executive VP, Business Affairs/General Counsel, Nick/TV Land/Spike TV
Jim Burns .....Sr. VP, Programming & Development, Spike TV
Alison Dexter .....Sr. VP, Operations & Planning, Nickelodeon
Russell Hicks .....Sr. VP, Creative Resources, Nick/Spike TV/Nick at Nite/TV Land
Paula Kaplan .....Sr. VP, Talent, MTV Networks/Nickelodeon/Spike TV
Pam Kaufman .....Sr. VP, Promotions Marketing, Nick Movies, Nickelodeon
Dan Martinsen .....Sr. VP, Corporate Communications, Nick/Spike TV/Nick at Nite/TV Land
Melissa Polaner Sr. VP, Law & Business Affairs, MTV Networks/Nickelodeon
Kim Rosenblum .....Sr. VP, Creative, Nick at Nite/TV Land
Paul Ward .....Sr. VP, Communications, Nick at Nite/TV Land
Laura Wendt .....Sr. VP, Research & Planning, Nick/Spike TV/Nick at Nite/TV Land
Lee Tsu Aries .....VP, Animation Productions, Nickelodeon, Spike TV
Peilin Chou .....VP, Production & Development, Spike TV
Jaclyn Cohen .....VP, Programming, Nick at Nite/TV Land
Eric Coleman .....VP, Animation Development & Production, Nickelodeon Animation Studios
Tanya Giles .....VP, Research & Planning, Nick at Nite/TV Land
Jeff Goldberg .....VP, Program Planning & Acquisitions, Spike TV
Steve Keller ..VP, Live-Action Development, Nickelodeon Animation Studios
Chris Linn .....VP, Production, Nickelodeon
Sal Maniaci .....VP, Development, Nick at Nite/TV Land
Shelly Sumpter .....VP, Talent, MTV Networks/Nickelodeon/Spike TV
Mark Taylor .....VP/General Manager, Nicktoons Animation Studios
Peter Gal .....Director, Animation Development, Nickelodeon Animation Studios

TINA NIDES PRODUCTIONS

4120 Dixie Canyon Ave.
Sherman Oaks, CA 91423
PHONE 818-788-3935
FAX 818-783-8698

TYPES	Features
CREDITS	Hardball

Tina Nides .....Producer

NIGHTSTAR PRODUCTIONS, INC

1256 Devon Ave.
Los Angeles, CA 90024
PHONE 310-271-2402
EMAIL .....nightstarprods@aol.com

TYPES	Features - Made-for-TV/Cable Movies
DEVELOPMENT	Lynelle by the Sea (CBS) - Augusta, Gone (Lifetime) - Corcoran Project (Fox)
CREDITS	Disappearance (TBS) - Sharing the Secret (CBS Made-for-TV Movie) - Evolution's Child (USA)
COMMENTS	Emphasis on true stories, uplifting comedies and drama; Inspirational movies that are a testament to the human spirit

Laurie Goldstein .....Executive Producer
Diane Becker .....Director, Development

NINE BY NINE

859 Hollywood Way, PMB 431
Burbank, CA 91505
PHONE 323-464-8930
EMAIL .....info@ninebynine.com
WEB SITE .....www.ninebynine.com

TYPES	Features
PRE-PRODUCTION	Heavens Fall
POST PRODUCTION	Brothel
CREDITS	Blue Skies Are a Lie - George B. - Hollywood (and Vine) - Mama D. - Almost Salinas

Wade W. Danielson .....Partner/Producer
Gregory Ruzzin .....Partner/Writer/Director
Susan Karasic .....Director, Development

NINE YARDS ENTERTAINMENT

8530 Wilshire Blvd., 5th Fl.
Beverly Hills, CA 90211
PHONE 310-289-1088
FAX 310-289-1288

TYPES	Features - Made-for-TV/Cable Movies - TV Series
COMMENTS	Management

Alex Murray .....Producer/Manager
Aaron Ray .....Producer/Manager
Larry Schapiro .....Producer/Manager
Matt Luber .....Producer/Manager
Rachel Bati .....Manager
Steve Crawford .....Manager
Jamie Freed .....Manager

It is illegal to copy any part of this book

NITELITE ENTERTAINMENT
9255 Doheny Rd., Ste. 1904
West Hollywood, CA 90069
PHONE 310-271-1774
FAX 310-271-1934
TYPES Features - Made-for-TV/Cable Movies - New Media - TV Series
POST PRODUCTION Dynasty: Behind the Sex, Greed and Manipulation (ABC)
CREDITS Behind the Drama: Dynasty (ABC) - Beautiful Girl (ABC Family) - The Legend of Butch & Sundance (NBC) - Living with the Dead (CBS) - The Perfect Getaway - Nightmare in Big Sky Country - Cheaters (HBO) - Behind the Camera: The Unauthorized Story of Three's Company (NBC)

Greg Gugliotta . . . . Executive Producer
Korbi Ghosh . . . . Development Assistant

NO HANDS PRODUCTIONS
9 Desbrosses St., 2nd Fl.
New York, NY 10013
PHONE 212-609-0940
FAX 212-609-0947
EMAIL . . . . email@nohandsproductions.com
WEB SITE . . . . www.nohandsproductions.com
TYPES Features - Made-for-TV/Cable Movies - TV Series
PRE-PRODUCTION Keith (Miramax)
CREDITS Blue's Clues
SUBMISSION POLICY www.nohandsproductions.com/submissions

Todd Kessler . . . . President
Rebecca Goldstein . . . . Director, Development

NO RESTRICTIONS ENTERTAINMENT/CINEMA BRAVO
1274 Midvale Ave.
Los Angeles, CA 90024
PHONE 310-477-1192
EMAIL . . . . info@norestrictionsentertainment.com
WEB SITE . . . . www.norestrictionsentertainment.com
TYPES Features
DEVELOPMENT Creatures Within - On the Clouds of Rio - Not Until the War's Over - The Conquest of Mexico - A Million by Twenty-One - Wedding Bloody Wedding - The Immune Center
PRE-PRODUCTION The Boy Who Couldn't Say No
POST PRODUCTION The Three Stages of Stan
CREDITS I'll Love You Forever...Tonight

John Paul Rice . . . . Producer
Edgar Michael Bravo . . . . Producer
Charles Raison . . . . Business Affairs

NOBLE HOUSE ENTERTAINMENT, INC.
c/o Big Time Picture Co.
12210-1/2 Nebraska Ave.
Los Angeles, CA 90025
PHONE 310-943-4378
FAX 310-826-0071
EMAIL . . . . info@thescriptbroker.com
WEB SITE . . . . www.noblehouseentertainment.com
SECOND WEB SITE . . . . www.thescriptbroker.com
TYPES Features - Direct-to-Video/DVD - Made-for-TV/Cable Movies - New Media - Reality TV - TV Series
DEVELOPMENT Truth? or Dare! - Scar Lover - Hollywood Tattoo (Series) - Dancing Bandit - Hypersonic - Queen of the East - Against the Wind
PRE-PRODUCTION Bum Deal - One Big Happy Family - Number Two Pencils & Stellina
CREDITS The Substitute (Live Entertainment) - Substitute 2 (HBO) - Peacock Blues (Showtime) - Tell About the South (PBS) - Not Afraid to Laugh (Video) - What's the Big Deal: Making Shorts (DVD) - Tattoo U (FX) - Funny You Should Ask (WNEZ Talk Show)

Devorah Cutler-Rubenstein . . . . President
Kris White . . . . Director, Development
Karin Spritzler . . . . Creative Executive
Bernadette Armstrong . . . . Creative Executive
Trey Green . . . . Story Analyst
Alex Hayes . . . . Story Analyst

NOBODY PRODUCTIONS
3373 Rowena, Ste. 8
Los Angeles, CA 90027
PHONE 323-662-7976/213-448-7326
FAX 323-662-7976
EMAIL . . . . tompaul@earthlink.net
WEB SITE . . . . www.sleepacrossamerica.com
TYPES Documentaries - Features - Direct-to-Video/DVD - Made-for-TV/Cable Movies - TV Series
DEVELOPMENT Side III (Talk Show)
PRE-PRODUCTION The Legend of Sloppy Joe (Feature)
COMPLETED UNRELEASED Sleep Across America
CREDITS They Shoot Movies Don't They?

Tom Wilson . . . . President
Adele B. Wilson . . . . Sr. VP
Craig Lachman . . . . VP, Production

NOCI PICTURES ENTERTAINMENT
6421 N. St. Louis
Lincolnwood, IL 60712
PHONE 773-381-6433
FAX 847-983-4702
EMAIL . . . . filmhedge@aol.com
WEB SITE . . . . www.noci.com
TYPES Commercials - Features - Direct-to-Video/DVD - Music Videos - New Media
DEVELOPMENT Kiev Nites - Blown - The Destruction - P-2 - Between - Black and Gold - Shiny Crystal Balls
CREDITS Mr. Id

Yuri Rutman . . . . CEO/Producer/Writer/Actor
Joe Montanaro . . . . Producer/Legal Affairs
Scott J. Wartham . . . . Producer
R.P. White . . . . Executive Producer

NOON ATTACK PICTURES

1423 Reeves St.
Los Angeles, CA 90035
PHONE 310-278-3316
FAX 310-278-6388
EMAIL ....mail@noonattack.com

TYPES	Made-for-TV/Cable Movies - Features - TV Series
CREDITS	The Truth About Cats & Dogs - Heart and Souls - Love Is Strange

Cari-Esta Albert ....Producer

NORSEMEN PRODUCTIONS

4705 Laurel Canyon Blvd., Ste. 400
Valley Village, CA 91607
PHONE 818-753-3100
FAX 818-753-3101
EMAIL ....info@norsemen.tv
WEB SITE ....www.norsemen.tv

TYPES	Commercials - Documentaries - Features - Made-for-TV/Cable Movies - Promos - Reality TV - TV Series
DEALS	Court TV - Discovery Networks, U.S.
PRODUCTION	Dude Space (Discovery Channel) - Saturday Night Solution (Court TV)
CREDITS	War Games - Eco-Challenge - Dinner and a Movie - The Man Made Movie - The Movie Break - The Movie Bowl - Movie and a Makeover - Big Playstation Movie

Mike Sears ....Chairman/CEO
Seth Blair ....Executive in Charge of Production
Matt Domanski ....CFO
Michelle Davis ....VP, Development
Phil Davis ....Supervising Producer, SNS
Jeff Berk ....Producer
Todd Lachniet ....Producer, SNS
Murray Oden ....Head Writer
Eric Smith ....Writer, SNS
Mike Gross ....Project Coordinator
Ray Klein ....Director, Operations, Knight Lights
Matt Walker ....Director
Scott Young ....Post Production Supervisor, SNS
Christine Corboy ....Production Manager
Mark Henderson ....Legal Affairs
Daniel Wincentsen ....Editor, SNS
Elizabeth Krott ....Researcher, SNS
Melissa Reichner ....Production Coordinator
Bernard Edelen ....Production Assistant, SNS
Mike Sulprizio ....Assistant Production Accountant
Damian Weisbach-Leach ....Post Production Assistant, SNS

NORTHSTAR ENTERTAINMENT

4315 Coldwater Canyon Ave., Ste. 9
Studio City, CA 91604
PHONE 818-762-1010
WEB SITE ....www.bryanmichaelstoller.com

TYPES	Features - Direct-to-Video/DVD - TV Series
DEALS	Bravo Network - The Bubble Factory
DEVELOPMENT	Paul's Intergalactic Adventure - Second Chance - Home of the Angels - The Dragon's Candle - Island Girl - They Cage the Animals at Night - Miss Cast Away
PRODUCTION	Filmmaking for Dummies
POST PRODUCTION	Movie Central Goes to the People's Choice Awards - Jackie Chan's J-Team (Promo) - Miss Cast Away
CREDITS	Hollywood Goes to Las Vegas - Undercover Angel - The Random Factor - Turn of the Blade - American Comedy Awards - Animal Crackers - Dragon Fury 2 - A Canadian Werewolf in Hollywood
SUBMISSION POLICY	No unsolicited calls
COMMENTS	Deals with The Movie Network and MJJ Productions

Bryan Michael Stoller ....President

NORWOOD ENTERTAINMENT GROUP

22817 Ventura Blvd., Ste. 432
Woodland Hills, CA 91367
PHONE 818-716-7047
FAX 818-716-9909

TYPES	Features - TV Series
CREDITS	Double Platinum - Cinderella

Sonja B. Norwood ....Principal
Willie R. Norwood Sr. ....Principal

NOVA PICTURES

6496 Ivarene Ave.
Los Angeles, CA 90068
PHONE 323-462-5502
EMAIL ....pbarnett@novapictures.com
WEB SITE ....www.novapictures.com

TYPES	Commercials - Features - Made-for-TV/Cable Movies - New Media - TV Series
DEVELOPMENT	Fit Eye for the Fat Guy - Enemy at Large
CREDITS	Extraordinary Visitor - The Yellow Badge of Courage - The Life and Times of Charlie Putz
SUBMISSION POLICY	Submit synopsis via email
COMMENTS	PSAs; Member, PGA and ATAS

Peter J. Barnett ....Producer
Chris Debiec ....Line Producer

NU IMAGE

6423 Wilshire Blvd.
Los Angeles, CA 90048
PHONE 310-388-6900
FAX 310-388-6901
EMAIL ....info@nuimage.net

TYPES	Features - Direct-to-Video/DVD - Made-for-TV/Cable Movies
DEVELOPMENT	Capoeira - The Griffin
PRODUCTION	Submerged
POST PRODUCTION	Raving Sharks
CREDITS	Rats - Mansquito - Larva - Avalanche - Earthquake - Ticker - Shark Attack - Spiders - Delta Force - US Seals
COMMENTS	International distribution

Avi Lerner ....Co-Chairman/CEO
Danny Dimbort ....Co-Chairman/CEO
Trevor Short ....CFO
Boaz Davidson ....Head, Production and Creative Affairs

NUANCE PRODUCTIONS

4049 Radford Ave.
Studio City, CA 91604
PHONE . . . 818-754-5484
FAX . . . 818-754-5485
TYPES: Features - TV Series
DEALS: NBC Universal Television Studio
PRODUCTION: My 11:30 (NBC Pilot)
CREDITS: Mad About You
SUBMISSION POLICY: No unsolicited submissions

Paul Reiser . . . Partner
Craig Knizek . . . Producer
Mitch Semel . . . Consultant

NUMENOREAN FILMS

12930 Ventura Blvd., Ste. 820
Studio City, CA 91604
PHONE . . . 818-763-3797
FAX . . . 818-980-5170
TYPES: Features - Direct-to-Video/DVD - Made-for-TV/Cable Movies - New Media - Syndication - TV Series
DEVELOPMENT: Inferno - Bad Karma - Dead Again - Femizons - The Green
CREDITS: Point Blank - TNT - The Immortal - Race Against Time - HBO Creature Features: The Spider

Cary Solomon . . . Producer/Director
Chuck Konzelman . . . Producer/Director
Carol Smith . . . Office Manager

NUYORICAN

1100 Glendon Ave., Ste. 920
Los Angeles, CA 90024
PHONE . . . 310-943-6600
FAX . . . 310-943-6609
TYPES: Features
DEALS: Columbia Pictures - Fox Television Studios - Regency Enterprises - Telemundo Network
CREDITS: The Cell - 3 Strikes - Molly - Siesta
SUBMISSION POLICY: No unsolicited material

Simon Fields . . . No Title
David Shaye . . . No Title
Aida Bernal . . . No Title

NYT TELEVISION

609 Greenwich St.
New York, NY 10014
PHONE . . . 212-905-2000
FAX . . . 212-905-2050
WEB SITE . . . www.nytco.com/television
TYPES: Documentaries - TV Series
CREDITS: Trauma: Life in the ER - Maternity Ward - A Cook's Tour
COMMENTS: Nonfiction and documentary programming

Thomas K. Carley . . . President, The New York Times News Services
Michael Oreskes . . . Assistant Managing Editor/Director, Electronic News
William M. Abrams . . . President, NYT Television
Christian Gwinn . . . Sr. VP, International Sales
Ann Derry . . . Executive Director, NYT TV/Director, Program Production
Veronique Bernard . . . Director, Program Development
Lawrie Mifflin . . . Director, TV Programming
Jane Bornemeier . . . Editorial Director, TV

LYNDA OBST PRODUCTIONS

c/o Paramount Pictures
5555 Melrose Ave., Bldg. 210
Los Angeles, CA 90038
PHONE . . . 323-956-8744
FAX . . . 323-862-2287
WEB SITE . . . www.lyndaobst.com
TYPES: Features - TV Series
DEALS: Paramount Pictures-Motion Picture Group
CREDITS: How to Lose a Guy in Ten Days - Sleepless in Seattle - The Fisher King - One Fine Day - Contact - Hope Floats - The Siege - The 60's - Someone Like You - Abandon

Lynda Obst . . . Producer
Elizabeth Hooper . . . Sr. VP, Physical Production
Michael Nash . . . Sr. VP, Development
Kelly Studer . . . Story Editor
Cindy Villa . . . Executive Assistant to Lynda Obst
Christina Won . . . Executive Assistant

OCEAN PICTURES

c/o Jim Berkus/UTA
9560 Wilshire Blvd.
Beverly Hills, CA 90212
PHONE . . . 847-266-9530, Ext. 223
TYPES: Features
POST PRODUCTION: Ice Harvest
CREDITS: Analyze That - Analyze This - Bedazzled - Groundhog Day - Caddyshack - Multiplicity - National Lampoon's Vacation

Harold Ramis . . . Director/Writer/Producer
Suzanne Herrington . . . Development/Production
Laurel Ward . . . Development/Production

ODD LOT ENTERTAINMENT

368 N. La Cienega Blvd.
Los Angeles, CA 90048-1925
PHONE . . . 310-652-0999
FAX . . . 310-652-0718
EMAIL . . . info@oddlotent.com
TYPES: Features
DEVELOPMENT: Family Pictures - Hello Charlie - Return to Sender - Trap for Cinderella - Imaginary Larry - Suburban Girl - Lavender Hill Mob - The Reckoning
POST PRODUCTION: Hooligans
CREDITS: The Wedding Planner - Simple Justice - Ricochet River - Hostile Intent - Mean Creek
SUBMISSION POLICY: Accepts solicited material from WGA signatories only

Gigi Pritzker . . . CEO/Partner
Deborah Del Prete . . . COO/Partner
Laura Ivey . . . Sr. VP, Business & Legal Affairs
Linda McDonough . . . Sr. VP, Production & Development
Andrea Arria-Devoe . . . Assistant to Linda McDonough
Marcie Friedman . . . Assistant to Gigi Pritzker
Sara Kutney . . . Assistant to Deborah Del Prete

OFFERMAN ENTERTAINMENT
8601 Falmouth Ave., Ste. 407
Los Angeles, CA 90293
PHONE .310-823-4242
FAX .310-823-0014
EMAIL .g.ob@dslextreme.com
TYPES Documentaries - Features - Made-for-TV/Cable Movies
DEVELOPMENT USS Pueblo Story (Feature) - Detour: A Hollywood Story (Feature) - Norma and Irving (Documentary)
PRE-PRODUCTION The Fairbanks Men (Feature Documentary)
PRODUCTION West Side Story (Documentary) - Untitled A&E Documentary
CREDITS Amateur Detectives - Images of Life - When Disasters Strike

Gina Offerman Boyd .Producer

OFFROAD ENTERTAINMENT
c/o Paramount Pictures
5555 Melrose Ave., Drier Bldg., Ste. 209
Los Angeles, CA 90038
PHONE .323-956-4425
TYPES Features - TV Series
CREDITS 3 Ninjas Kick Back - Jury Duty - 200 Cigarettes

Steven L. Bernstein .Producer
Pat Bernard .VP
Lucky Baxter .Director, Development

OFFSPRING ENTERTAINMENT
500 S. Buena Vista St.
Burbank, CA 91521
PHONE .818-560-5645
FAX .818-560-5642
TYPES Features - TV Series
DEALS Twentieth Century Fox Television
DEVELOPMENT Sugar Rum Cherry - Topper - Enchanted - The Jetsons - The Other Guy - Four Christmases - Premonition - Pet Store
PRODUCTION The Pacifier
CREDITS The Wedding Planner - Bringing Down the House - A Walk to Remember

Adam Shankman .Director/Partner
Jennifer Gibgot .Producer/Partner
Matthew Mizel .VP, Production (818-560-6017)
Lucas Meyers .Production Coordinator
Matt Robertson .Story Editor

OIL & WATER PRODUCTIONS
8033 W. Sunset Blvd., Ste. 922
Los Angeles, CA 90046
PHONE .310-276-7690
FAX .310-276-3195
EMAIL .info@thegirlsroom.net
WEB SITE .www.thegirlsroom.net
TYPES Features
CREDITS Billy's Hollywood Screen Kiss - The Girls' Room

Irene Turner .Producer/Director

SAM OKUN PRODUCTIONS
1010 Hammond St., Ste. 115
Los Angeles, CA 90069
PHONE .310-271-0034
FAX .310-271-0334
TYPES Features - Made-for-TV/Cable Movies - TV Series
DEALS Ardustry Entertainment
DEVELOPMENT Rich Deceiver (20th Century Fox) - The Lenseman (Series) Swimming to Atlantis - Rendezvous in Black - Stolen Life - Virgin Holiday
CREDITS Anya's Bell - The Call of the Wild
COMMENTS Formerly Erratic Entertainment, Inc.

Sam Okun .Chairman/Producer
Ron Hart .VP, Literary Acquisitions
Tony Kolotzis .Creative Executive
Arlene Pachasa .Assistant to Sam Okun

OLD DIME BOX PRODUCTIONS, INC.
1999 N. Sycamore Ave., Ste. 503
Los Angeles, CA 90068
PHONE .323-876-1282
TYPES Documentaries - Features - TV Series
DEALS Rehme Productions
CREDITS Escape: Human Cargo - Creating the Future
SUBMISSION POLICY No unsolicited faxes or emails

Anne E. Curry .President/Producer/Writer
Aaron H. Sanchez .Consultant
Elizabeth Common .Executive Assistant

OLD SCHOOL PICTURES, LLC
12438 Houston St.
Valley Village, CA 91607
PHONE .323-640-2258
EMAIL .johnsavs@sbcglobal.net
TYPES Features - Direct-to-Video/DVD - Made-for-TV/Cable Movies - TV Series
DEVELOPMENT The Warning - Trancas - Puckheads - Night in Rio - With the Fishes
PRE-PRODUCTION Dr. October
POST PRODUCTION Wicked Prayer
COMPLETED UNRELEASED Sin - Lucky 13
CREDITS Normal Life - Deceiver - Girl - The Suburbans - Beyond City Limits - Con Express - Sand

John Saviano .President/Producer

LIN OLIVER PRODUCTIONS
8271 Beverly Blvd.
Los Angeles, CA 90048
PHONE .323-782-1495
FAX .323-782-1892
EMAIL .info@linoliverproductions.com
WEB SITE .www.linoliverproductions.com
TYPES Animation - Features - Direct-to-Video/DVD - Made-for-TV/Cable Movies - TV Series
DEVELOPMENT Wayside School - Hank Zipzer: The Television Series - Bingo and Bongo - Down a Dark Hall - Trumpet of the Swan (Theater)
CREDITS Harry & the Hendersons - Corduroy - Trumpet of the Swan - Finding Buck McHenry - Aliens Ate My Homework
COMMENTS Children's TV and publishing; Family feature films

Lin Oliver .Producer/Executive
Sara Rutenberg .Sr. VP, Business & Creative Affairs
Kim Turrisi .Director, Development
Kim Stratton .Manager

OMEGA ENTERTAINMENT
8760 Shoreham Dr.
Los Angeles, CA 90069
PHONE .310-855-0516
FAX .310-652-2044
EMAIL .omegap@aol.com
WEB SITE .www.omegapic.com
TYPES Features - Direct-to-Video/DVD - Made-for-TV/Cable Movies
CREDITS .com for Murder - Hired to Kill - In the Cold of the Night - The Naked Truth
COMMENTS Distribution

Nico Mastorakis .President/CEO/Writer/Producer/Director
Monty McMahon .Executive Assistant

OMNIBUS
5007 Arundel Dr.
Woodland Hills, CA 91364
PHONE .818-716-7043
FAX .818-716-1842
EMAIL .scheid3333@sbcglobal.net
TYPES Features - Made-for-TV/Cable Movies - Reality TV - TV Series
DEVELOPMENT Beached (20th Century Fox) - Mickey (TNT) - The Third Terrorist (FX)
CREDITS Cousin Bette - Sports Night (TV) - Speaking of Sex - The Crash of Flight 323 (TV) - The Court (TV)

Rob Scheidlinger .Producer/President

OMS - ONE MIND SOUND PRODUCTIONS
22817 Ventura Blvd., Ste. 984
Woodland Hills, CA 91364
PHONE .310-963-2358
FAX .818-222-2389
TYPES Features - New Media - TV Series
DEVELOPMENT Pancakes and Underwear - Voices - Second Coming of Sammy
CREDITS Parallel Lives - Chantilly Lace - Suicide Prevention Line - MLK 2K: We Still Have the Dream

Kathy Zotnowski .Producer
Philip Nemy .Producer

ON STILTS PRODUCTIONS
9699 N. Hayden Rd., Ste. 108, PMB 233
Scottsdale, AZ 85258-5808
PHONE .310-391-6053/480-991-2142
EMAIL .osp14@aol.com
TYPES Features - Made-for-TV/Cable Movies
CREDITS An Affectionate Look at Fatherhood (NBC) - Miss Evers' Boys (HBO) - On Promised Land (Disney Channel) - Mercy Mission: The Rescue of Flight 771 (NBC)

Peter Stelzer .Producer

ONCE A FROG PRODUCTIONS
c/o Warner Bros.
4000 Warner Blvd., Bldg. 140, Ste. 214
Burbank, CA 91522
PHONE .818-954-7512
TYPES Features - Made-for-TV/Cable Movies - TV Series
DEALS Warner Bros. Television Production
CREDITS American Dreams (NBC) - My Life Is a Sitcom (ABC)

Jonathan Prince .Executive Producer/Writer/Director
Pamela Bruce .VP, Development
Kristin Brunner .Assistant to Jonathan Prince

ONCE UPON A TIME FILMS, LTD.
2314 Michigan Ave.
Santa Monica, CA 90404-3930
PHONE .310-582-1220
FAX .310-582-0098
EMAIL .oncupnatim@aol.com
TYPES Features - Made-for-TV/Cable Movies - TV Series
PRE-PRODUCTION Confessions of a Sociopathic Social Climber
PRODUCTION Ladies Night
COMPLETED UNRELEASED Dynasty (ABC) - The Legend of Butch & Sundance (NBC)
CREDITS Beautiful Girl (ABC Family) - On Thin Ice (Lifetime) - Living with the Dead (CBS, Miniseries) - A Season on the Brink - Atomic Twister - Jailbait! - The Opposite Sex - Submerged - Behind the Camera: The Unauthorized Story of Three's Company (NBC) - Call Me: The Rise and Fall of Heidi Fleiss (USA)

Stanley M. Brooks .Executive Producer
Scott W. Anderson .Producer
Damian Ganczewski .Producer
Kimberly Oesterling .Director, Production
Fernando Alessandri .Manager, Development
Nimo Mathenge .Development Assistant
Daniel Rauth .Production Assistant

ONE ROOF ENTERTAINMENT
1201 W. Fifth St., Ste. M-250
Los Angeles, CA 90017
PHONE .213-534-3450
FAX .213-534-3463
EMAIL .info@oneroofentertainment.com
WEB SITE .www.oneroofentertainment.com
TYPES Commercials - Features - Music Videos - New Media - Reality TV
DEVELOPMENT Ghetto-Licious - Xmas in da Hood
PRE-PRODUCTION Three Hunters - Coldwater - Ephraim's Song - Unsung Heros
COMPLETED UNRELEASED Midsummer Night's Rave
COMMENTS Special Events

Andrew Levy .CEO/Producer
Steve Eggleston .President/Producer
Amy Gunzenhauser .Executive VP, Development
Cynthia Vinney .Assistant

ONE STEP PRODUCTIONS

12188 Laurel Terrace Dr.
Studio City, CA 91604-3644
PHONE .818-762-1624
FAX .818-763-1955
EMAIL .judy@judychaikin.com
WEB SITE .www.onestepproductions.com

TYPES	Documentaries - Features - TV Series
DEVELOPMENT	The Secret Life of Madame Domange (Feature) - Welcome to Tierra Del Humo - The Silence
CREDITS	Legacy of the Hollywood Blacklist (PBS) - Stolen Innocence (CBS) - Los Pastores (PBS) - Cotillion '65
SUBMISSION POLICY	No unsolicited material accepted

Judy Chaikin .Executive Producer
Loren Stephens .Co-Executive Producer

ONE VOICE ENTERTAINMENT, INC.

14926 Moorpark St., Ste. 101
Sherman Oaks, CA 91403
PHONE .310-203-1526

TYPES	Features - TV Series
DEVELOPMENT	Mama Got Back - Dead Beats - Kool Media Bounce - Record Men - Under Pressure
CREDITS	Elegies - Storm Warning - AEIOU Sometimes Y - I Witness (aka God's Witness)
COMMENTS	Representation: Liz Robinson & Ilan Breil, LMRK, phone: 310-446-1466; Amy Schiffman, Gersh Agency, phone: 310-274-6611

Robert Ozn .Writer/Producer

OPTIONAL PICTURES, LLC

1712 Berkeley St.
Santa Monica, CA 90404
PHONE .310-582-8881
FAX .310-582-8991

TYPES	Features
DEALS	Twentieth Century Fox
DEVELOPMENT	Piper Alpha - The Swap - Yeager
POST PRODUCTION	Flight of the Phoenix
CREDITS	Behind Enemy Lines

T. Alex Blum .Producer/President
John Moore .Director
Michael M. Hall .Assistant to T. Alex Blum/Associate
Peter Veverka .Assistant to John Moore

ORCHARD FILMS

119 W. 23rd St., Ste. 409
New York, NY 10011
PHONE .212-229-3770
FAX .212-229-3772

TYPES	Documentaries - TV Series
DEVELOPMENT	Battle of the Sexes: Billie vs. Bobby - Queer Cinema Documentary (IFC)
COMPLETED UNRELEASED	Queer Cinema Documentary (IFC)
CREDITS	Hope in a Jar (A&E) - Indie Sex: Taboos (IFC) - Miss America (PBS, *American Experience*) - Who Is Alan Smithee? (AMC) - Are You Comfortable? (Pilot) - In the Company of Women (IFC)

Lisa Ades .Producer/Director
Lesli Klainberg .Producer/Director
Chandra Simon .Associate Producer

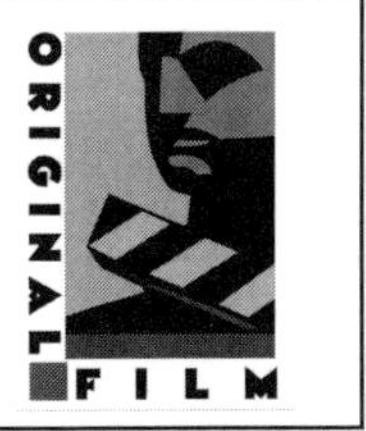

ORIGINAL FILM

2045 S. Barrington Ave.
Los Angeles, CA 90025
PHONE .310-445-9000
FAX .310-445-9191

TYPES	Features - Direct-to-Video/DVD
DEALS	Sony Pictures Entertainment
DEVELOPMENT	Static - RPM
PRODUCTION	XXX 2
POST PRODUCTION	Stealth
CREDITS	S.W.A.T. - 2 Fast 2 Furious - Not Another Teen Movie - The Fast and the Furious - Cruel Intentions 1&2 - I Know What You Did Last Summer 1&2 - Blue Streak - The Rat Pack - Saving Silverman - Urban Legend 1&2 - Torque - Out of Time - Juice - Volcano - Sweet Home Alabama - XXX
SUBMISSION POLICY	No unsolicited material

Neal Moritz .Owner/Producer
Elizabeth Buraglio .Production Executive
Amanda Cohen .Production Executive
Tania Landau .Production Executive
Heather Lieberman .Production Executive
Ori Marmur .Production Executive
Jonas Barnes .Production Assistant
Keith Dinielli .Assistant to Ms. Landau
Richelle Hassell .Assistant to Ms. Cohen
Nikki King .Assistant to Mr. Moritz

THE ORPHANAGE

6725 Sunset Blvd., Ste. 220
Hollywood, CA 90028
PHONE .323-469-6700/415-561-2570
FAX .323-469-6701/415-561-2575
EMAIL .sari@theorphanage.com
WEB SITE .www.theorphanage.com

TYPES	Features - TV Series - Made-for-TV/Cable Movies - Animation - Commercials - Music Videos
DEVELOPMENT	Blackwater - City of Darkness - The Madman's Kiss - Powered by Digby (aka Cipher) - Twenty First Century Blues - Prodigy - Pirates - Blackdeer - Stray Toasters
PRE-PRODUCTION	Griffin and Phoenix
POST PRODUCTION	Sky Captain and the World of Tomorrow (Paramount) - The Forgotten (Sony Imageworks)
COMPLETED UNRELEASED	Hero (Miramax, VFX)
CREDITS	Ten Tiny Love Stories (Lions Gate) - Hysterical Blindness (HBO) - Hellboy (Revolution Studios, VFX) - Day After Tomorrow (Fox) - Garfield: The Movie (20th Century Fox)
COMMENTS	High-end VFX; San Francisco office: C/O The Presidio, 39 Mesa St., Ste. 201, San Francisco, CA 94129

Amy Israel .Head, Production/Producer
Paul Grimshaw .VP, Orphanage Commercials
Marc Sadeghi .VP, Feature Post & VFX
John Benson .Executive Producer, Orphanage Commercials
Carsten Sorenson .CEO
Scott Stewart .Co-Founder
Jonathan Rothbart .Co-Founder/Sr. VFX Supervisor
Stuart Maschwitz .CTO
Sari Stewart .Assistant, Production
Brian Stone .Assistant

OSTROW & COMPANY

100 S. Doheny Dr., Ste. 210
Los Angeles, CA 90048
PHONE .310-276-5007
EMAIL .themoviepages@hotmail.com
WEB SITE .www.themoviepages.com
TYPES Documentaries - Features - Direct-to-Video/DVD - TV Series
DEVELOPMENT Some Assembly Required - Eli
PRE-PRODUCTION Pumpkin Jack - The Knight
PRODUCTION Home of the Brave
POST PRODUCTION The Town That Outlawed Christmas
COMPLETED UNRELEASED The Stand In - No Regrets - American Addiction
CREDITS Shadowlands - Angels with an Attitude
COMMENTS Producers Rep; Arranged financing and negotiated distribution for over 80 feature films

Page B. Ostrow .President/Producers Representative
Michael Iskra .Head, Development
Natasha Baumgarten .Executive Assistant
Matthew Daniels .Acquisitions
Jessie Kennedy .Acquisitions
Chris Morgan .Acquisitions
Jenn Page .Acquisitions
Ernie Silva .Acquisitions
Paul Neuman .Webmaster
Mark Phillips .Marketing
Alex Coscas .Development
Stephanie Yook .Development
T.K. Fordly .Reader
Michael Ireland .Reader
Mitch Moore .Reader
Jason Reed .Reader
Mindy White .Reader

OUT OF THE BLUE . . . ENTERTAINMENT

c/o Sony Pictures Entertainment
10202 W. Washington Blvd., Astaire Bldg., Ste. 1200
Culver City, CA 90232-3195
PHONE .310-244-7811
FAX .310-244-1539
TYPES Features
DEALS Columbia Pictures
CREDITS Mr. Deeds - Master of Disguise - Big Daddy - Deuce Bigalow

Sid Ganis .No Title
Alex Siskin .No Title
Mandy Safavi .No Title
Jill Noel .No Title
Nicholas Crisafi .No Title
Joyce San Pedro .No Title

OUTERBANKS ENTERTAINMENT

8000 Sunset Blvd., Ste. 301-A
Los Angeles, CA 90046
PHONE .323-654-3700
FAX .323-654-3797
EMAIL .firstname@outerbanks-ent.com
TYPES Features - TV Series
DEALS Miramax Films
DEVELOPMENT Her Leading Man - Retribution - Backwater
CREDITS Scream 1&2 - Dawson's Creek - I Know What You Did Last Summer - Wasteland - Glory Days - Halloween H20 - Cursed

Kevin Williamson .President
Jennifer Breslow .VP, Development & Production
Sarah Kucserka .Creative Executive
Eric Altman .Development Assistant
Alexis Bayoud .Assistant to Mr. Williamson
Zack Hall .Office Assistant

OUTLAW PRODUCTION

9350 Civic Center Dr.
Beverly Hills, CA 90210
PHONE .310-777-2000
FAX .310-777-2010
EMAIL .outlaw@outlawfilm.com
WEB SITE .www.outlawfilm.com
TYPES Features
DEALS Intermedia Film Equities USA, Inc.
DEVELOPMENT DJ - Joe's Last Chance - Season in Central Park - Wanna-be - Ace In the Hole - Crackerjack - The Santa Clause 3 - Wet - Regulator - 27 Dresses - Lost Boys - Space Between - Lucid - 11th Hour - Face-Time - Iron Curtain - Jupiter's Mom
PRE-PRODUCTION Phat Girlz
POST PRODUCTION The Thing About My Folks
COMPLETED UNRELEASED If Only - Mindhunters
CREDITS The Santa Clause 1&2 - National Security - Training Day - Gossip - Ready to Rumble - Three to Tango - Addicted to Love - Don Juan DeMarco - sex, lies and videotape - The Opposite Sex

Robert Newmyer .Producer
Jeffrey Silver .Producer
Scott Strauss .Producer
Dominic Ianno .Executive VP, Business Development & Strategic Marketing
Michael Glassman .No Title
Justin Springer .No Title
Sam Nam .No Title

THE OVER THE HILL GANG

520 Washington Blvd., Ste. 214
Marina del Rey, CA 90292
PHONE .310-578-2040
FAX .310-388-4617
EMAIL .tvproduc@att.net
TYPES Features - Direct-to-Video/DVD - Made-for-TV/Cable Movies - New Media - Syndication - TV Series
DEVELOPMENT The Great Christmas Train Robbery
CREDITS Sir Arthur Conan Doyle's The Lost World

Peter Bergmann .Executive Producer
Todd Makler .CFO
Arnold Soloway .Executive Producer

OVERBROOK ENTERTAINMENT

450 N. Roxbury Dr., 4th Fl.
Beverly Hills, CA 90210
PHONE .310-432-2400
FAX .310-432-2401
TYPES Features - New Media - TV Series
DEALS Sony Pictures Entertainment
CREDITS Wild Wild West Soundtrack - Love & Basketball Soundtrack - Ali - All of Us (Series) - I, Robot - Last First Kiss
COMMENTS Soundtracks; Music

Will Smith .Partner
James Lassiter .Partner
Teddy Zee .President, Motion Pictures
Jana Babatunde-Bey .General Manager
John Dukakis .Executive VP, Music
Omarr Rambert .A&R Executive, Music
Miguel Melendez .Music Management

OXYGEN MEDIA
75 Ninth Ave.
New York, NY 10011
PHONE 212-651-2000/323-860-3500
FAX 212-651-2099/323-860-3501
WEB SITE ....www.oxygen.com
TYPES Features - TV Series
CREDITS The Issac Mizrahi Show - Oprah: After the Show - Conversations from the Edge with Carrie Fisher - Girls Behaving Badly - Nice Package - Good Girls Don't - Naked Josh - Talk Sex WIth Sue Johanson
COMMENTS Cable and Internet network; West Coast office: 6650 Romaine Ave., Lot D, Bldg. 40, Hollywood, CA 90038

Geraldine Laybourne ....Founder/CEO
Marcy Carsey ....Co-Founder/Partner
Tom Warner ....Co-Founder/Partner
Caryn Mandabach ....Co-Founder/Partner
Oprah Winfrey ....Co-Founder
Lisa Gersh Hall ....COO/President
Debby Beece ....President, Programming & On-Air
Geoffrey Darby ....President, Production & Convergence
Daniel Taitz ....Chief Administrative Officer
Courtney Conte ....Sr. VP, Production (LA)
Jennifer Cotter ....Sr. VP, Development
Julie Insogna ....Sr. VP, Talent Relations & Music Programming
Brigitte McCray ....Sr. VP, Programming (NY)
Kristen Connolly Vadas ....VP, West Coast Development (LA)
Elizabeth Cullen ....VP, Program Acquisitions & Co-Production
Nikki Donen ....VP, Development
Stephanie Ziev ....VP, Development (NY)

P.A.T. PRODUCTIONS
10202 W. Washington Blvd., David Lean, Ste. 230
Culver City, CA 90232
PHONE 310-244-8881
FAX 310-244-1210
EMAIL ....patprod@spe.sony.com
TYPES Animation - Features - Reality TV - Syndication - TV Series
DEALS Sony Pictures Television
CREDITS Games: Blackjack Bowling - Run for the Money; Animation: Leo the Late Bloomer - Space Case - Merry Christmas, Space Case; Live Action: Angus and the Ducks - Pat Sajak's American League Ballpark Tour - Pat Sajak's National League Ballpark Tour
SUBMISSION POLICY No unsolicited submissions accepted

Pat Sajak ....President
David S. Williger ....Executive VP
Gary Templeton ....Director, Children's Programming
Gwen Klemann ....Executive Assistant

P.O.V. COMPANY
3033 Three Springs Dr.
Westlake Village, CA 91361
PHONE 818-707-2644
FAX 818-707-3557
TYPES Features - Made-for-TV/Cable Movies - TV Series
CREDITS American Tragedy - Two Against Time - A Town Without Christmas - Glory & Honor - The Love Letter - The Kennedys of Massachusetts - Double Platinum - The Virginian - Falcone - Fallen Angel - The Reagans

Lynn Raynor ....Producer

PACIFICA FILM DEVELOPMENT, INC.
9350 Civic Center Dr., Ste. 100
Beverly Hills, CA 90210
PHONE 310-550-3800
FAX 310-550-3801
EMAIL ....info@pacificafilm.com
TYPES Features
DEALS La Luna Films
DEVELOPMENT Abyssinia - Time and Chance - Tom Mix and Pancho Villa
POST PRODUCTION Alexander
CREDITS Terminator 3 - Nurse Betty - Clay Pigeons - Where the Money Is - The Wedding Planner - K-Pax - K-19: The Widowmaker - The Quiet American

Moritz Borman ....Chairman
Linda Benjamin ....President
Laura K. Miller ....Business Affairs Coordinator
Joe Henderson ....Executive Assistant to Mr. Borman
Jeanette Barrozo ....Assistant to Mr. Borman
Matthew Williams ....Office Assistant

PACIFICA INTERNATIONAL FILM AND TV CORPORATION
PO Box 6265
Woodland Hills, CA 91365
PHONE 818-884-8234
FAX 818-884-1349
EMAIL ....pacifica@pacifica.la
TYPES Documentaries - Features - Reality TV - TV Series
DEVELOPMENT Cure
PRE-PRODUCTION Antarctica - Phone - Turn
PRODUCTION The Ring 2
CREDITS The Ring - Cop on a Mission

Christine Iso ....Producer
Tiffany Peckosh ....Assistant, Acquisitions

THE PACK
PO Box 352194
Los Angeles, CA 90035
PHONE 323-782-8540
EMAIL ....intheirownwords@aol.com
WEB SITE ....www.celebritybioshow.com
TYPES Features - TV Series
DEVELOPMENT Something Flexible with Meaning - Elinor Adjusting
PRODUCTION In Their Own Words: Celebrity Autobiographies (E!)
CREDITS The A List - Signs of Life
SUBMISSION POLICY No unsolicited material

Eugene Pack ....Executive Producer/Writer
Dale Rehfeld ....Executive Producer
Kimberly A. Steer ....Producer

GEORGE PAIGE ASSOCIATES, INC.
25244 Malibu Rd., Ste. A
Malibu, CA 90265
PHONE 310-397-1746
FAX 310-397-1748
EMAIL ....gpacorp@aol.com
TYPES Animation - Documentaries - Features - Direct-to-Video/DVD - Made-for-TV/Cable Movies - New Media - TV Series
DEVELOPMENT The 3 Stooges Movie (Warner Bros.)
PRODUCTION Brer Rabbit
POST PRODUCTION TV's Greatest Sidekicks
CREDITS Gilda Radner's Greatest Moments - Martin & Lewis - Abbott & Costello Meet Jerry Seinfeld - The Three Stooges 75th Anniversary (NBC)

George Paige ....President
James Tumminia ....Producer

PALNICK PRODUCTIONS
c/o Judy Palnick Productions
2401 Pearl St.
Santa Monica, CA 90405
PHONE .310-450-4136
FAX .310-450-4306
TYPES Features - Made-for-TV/Cable Movies
CREDITS Murder in My Mind
SUBMISSION POLICY No unsolicited submissions

Judy Palnick .President
Harrison Cohen .Creative Executive

PAMPLIN FILM COMPANY
c/o Universal Studios Florida
1000 Universal Studios Plaza, Bldg. 22-A, Ste. 250
Orlando, FL 32819-7610
PHONE .407-224-6671
FAX .407-224-6672
EMAIL .pfcfilm@aol.com
TYPES Documentaries - Features
DEVELOPMENT Crimebusters - City of God - A Beautiful Life
PRODUCTION Orlando Like a Pro
COMPLETED UNRELEASED Hoover - 'N Sync: 24/7
CREDITS Michael Winslow Live - Magic 4 Morons

Rick Pamplin .Producer/Writer/Director
William L. Whitacre .Producer, UPM
Maggie Pamplin .Director, Operations

PANDEMONIUM
100 N. Crescent Dr., Ste. 125
Beverly Hills, CA 90210
PHONE .310-385-4088
FAX .310-385-4232
TYPES Features
DEALS Walt Disney Pictures/Touchstone Pictures

Bill Mechanic .President
Matthew Velks .COO
Lindsey Bayman .Executive VP
Ashley Kramer .Executive VP
Kerry Foster .VP
Raquel Rubio .Contract Administrator
Susan Ray .Assistant to Bill Mechanic
Neil Parris .Assistant to Ashley Kramer

PANDORA
a gaylord films company

PANDORA FILMS
4000 Warner Blvd.
Burbank, CA 91522
PHONE .818-954-3600
FAX .818-954-7713
TYPES Features
DEALS Warner Bros. Pictures
DEVELOPMENT South of the Border, West of the Sun - Sophie and the Rising Sun - Paris Underground - Capa - 29 Palms
COMPLETED UNRELEASED Cypher
CREDITS A Walk to Remember - White Oleander - Welcome to Collinwood - Grind - Blue Collar Comedy Tour - Donnie Darko
COMMENTS Specialty division of Gaylord Films

Hunt Lowry .President/CEO
Steven C. Smith .CFO
Dana Ginsburg .Executive VP, Business Affairs

(Continued)

PANDORA FILMS (Continued)
Shebnem Askin .Sr. VP, Worldwide Sales
Stacy Cohen .Sr. VP, Production
Paula Marcus .VP, Physical Production
Marc Wuertemburg .VP, Post Production
Casey La Scala .Producer
Diane Heggen .Director, Sales Operations
Patty Reed .Director, Development
Matt Hutaff .Assistant to Dana Ginsburg

PAPAZIAN-HIRSCH ENTERTAINMENT/RAY-ART STUDIOS
6625 Variel Ave., Ste. 200
Canoga Park, CA 91303
PHONE .818-887-2400
FAX .818-887-2450
TYPES Features - TV Series
CREDITS A Mother's Testimony - Determination of Death - Face Value - The Burning Zone - Nash Bridges - Oliver Beene

Robert Papazian .Executive Producer
James Hirsch .Executive Producer/Writer

***PARADIGM STUDIO**
2701 Second Avenue North
Seattle, WA 98109
PHONE .206-282-2162/866-682-4315
FAX .206-283-6433
EMAIL .paradigmstudio1@aol.com
WEB SITE .www.paradigmstudio.com
TYPES Features - TV Series
DEVELOPMENT The Secret Life of Huckleberry Finn - Uncommon Romance - Icons Among Us: Jazz in Present Tense (TV)
CREDITS Around the Fire
COMMENTS Los Angeles office: 3200 Airport Ave., Ste. 1, Santa Monica, CA 90405, phone: 310-915-9700, fax: 310-572-1501

John Comerford .President
B Dahlia .Manager

PARADOX PRODUCTIONS, INC.
801 Tarcuto Way
Los Angeles, CA 90077
PHONE .310-440-8133
FAX .310-472-6467
EMAIL .doubledox@aol.com
TYPES Features - TV Series
CREDITS The Santa Clause - Home Improvement - Roseanne - L.A. Law - Jungle 2 Jungle - Joe Somebody - thirtysomething - George Lopez Show - Miss Congeniality 2

John Pasquin .Director/President

***PARALLEL ENTERTAINMENT, INC.**
9255 Sunset Blvd., Ste. 1040
Los Angeles, CA 90069
PHONE .310-279-1123
FAX .310-279-1147
WEB SITE .www.parallelentertainment.com
TYPES TV Series
PRE-PRODUCTION Blue Collar Comedy Tour 2: Rides Again
PRODUCTION Blue Collar TV

J.P. Williams .Partner/Manager
John MacDonald .Partner/Manager
Maggie Houlehan .Manager
Maria Kerrigan .No Title
Yani Woods .No Title

PARAMOUNT CLASSICS
5555 Melrose Ave., Chevalier Bldg., 2nd Fl.
Los Angeles, CA 90038-3197
PHONE .323-956-2000
FAX .323-862-1212 (Acquisitions)/323-862-1103 (Distribution)
WEB SITE .www.paramountclassics.com
TYPES Features
CREDITS Man on the Train - Love Me If You Dare - Northfork - The Singing Detective - Bloody Sunday - Mostly Martha - The Virgin Suicides - You Can Count on Me - The Gift
COMMENTS Publicity fax: 323-862-1012

Ruth Vitale .Co-President
David Dinerstein .Co-President
Eden Salenger Rosenfelt .VP, Publicity & Promotions
Susan Wrubel .VP, Acquisitions & Co-Productions
Joe Matukewicz .Director, Acquisitions

PARAMOUNT INTERNATIONAL TELEVISION
c/o Paramount Pictures
5555 Melrose Ave.
Los Angeles, CA 90038-3197
PHONE .323-956-5000
FAX .323-862-3938
WEB SITE .www.paramount.com
TYPES Made-for-TV/Cable Movies - Syndication - TV Series
DEVELOPMENT Hindenberg
CREDITS Higher Ground - Largo - Dead Zone - Messiah

Gary Marenzi .President
Susan Akens .Executive VP, Business Affairs
Joe Lucas .Executive VP, Sales & Marketing
Isis Moussa .Sr. VP, Marketing
Christopher Ottinger .Sr. VP, Business Development & Co-Productions
Cece Braun .VP, Finance
Michael Keller .Director, Creative Affairs

PARAMOUNT PICTURES-MOTION PICTURE GROUP
5555 Melrose Ave.
Los Angeles, CA 90038-3197
PHONE .323-956-5000
FAX .323-862-1204
WEB SITE .www.paramount.com
TYPES Features

Sherry Lansing .Chairman, Motion Picture Group, Paramount Pictures
Robert G. Friedman .Vice Chairman, Motion Picture Group/ COO, Paramount Pictures
Donald De Line .Vice Chairman, Motion Picture Group/ President, Paramount Pictures
Tom Jacobson .Co-President, Paramount Pictures
Burt Berman .President, Music Division
William Bernstein .Executive VP, Special Projects
Bruce Tobey .Executive VP, Viacom Entertainment Group/ Executive VP, Paramount Motion Picture Group
Susan Glatzer .Sr. VP, Acquisitions, Motion Picture Group

PARAMOUNT PICTURES-PRODUCTION DIVISION
5555 Melrose Ave.
Los Angeles, CA 90038-3197
PHONE .323-956-5000
WEB SITE .www.paramount.com
TYPES Features

Karen Rosenfelt .President, Production
Fred T. Gallo .President, Feature Production Management Worldwide
Mark Bakshi .Executive VP, Feature Production Management
Allison Brecker-Shearmur .Executive VP, Production
Paul Haggar .Executive VP, Post Production
Brian Witten .Executive VP, Production
Richard Fowkes .Sr. VP in Charge of Business Affairs
Alan B. Heppel .Sr. VP, Motion Picture Business & Legal Affairs
Michael Hill .Sr. VP, Production Finance
Wendy Japhet .Sr. VP, Production
Kevin Koloff .Sr. VP, Business Affairs, Music
Gail Levin .Sr. VP, Features Casting
Karen Magid .Sr. VP, Motion Picture Legal
Scott Martin .Sr. VP, Intellectual Property/Associate General Counsel
Linda Wohl .Sr. VP, Music Legal
Pamela Abdy .VP, Production
Fran M. Black .VP, Motion Picture Legal
Patricia Burke .VP, Literary Affairs (NY)
Marc Evans .VP, Production
Jeff Freedman .VP, Business Affairs
Andrew Haas .VP, Production
Alexandra Koch .VP, Feature Production Management
Lee E. Rosenthal .VP, Feature Production Management
Sara Spring .VP, Feature Production Management
Linda Springer .VP, Music Production
Eldridge Walker .VP, Music Clearance
Brian Wensel .VP, Production Finance
John Wiseman .VP, Post Production

PARAMOUNT TELEVISION
5555 Melrose Ave.
Los Angeles, CA 90038-3197
PHONE .323-956-5000
WEB SITE .www.paramount.com
TYPES Made-for-TV/Cable Movies - TV Series

Garry Hart .President
Milinda McNeely .Executive VP, Legal
Reid Shane .Executive VP, Production
John A. Wentworth .Executive VP, Marketing & Media Relations
David Grossman .Sr. VP, TV Music
Sheila Guthrie .Sr. VP, Talent & Casting
Hal Harrison .Sr. VP, Post Production
Rose Catherine Pinkney .Sr. VP, Comedy Development
Tom Russo .Sr. VP, Current Programs
Craig Wagner .Sr. VP, Business Affairs
Ralph Berge .VP, Production
Marshall Coben .VP, Longform & Alternative Programming
Kim Conant .VP, Marketing & Media Relations
Brett King .VP, Current Programs
David Lavin .VP, Business Affairs
Marilyn Loncar .VP, Production
Celest Ray .VP, TV Music
Jennifer Weingroff .VP, Marketing & Media Relations
Mark Weissman .VP, Production Finance
Manfred Westphal .VP, Media Relations

PARAMOUNT WORLDWIDE TELEVISION DISTRIBUTION
5555 Melrose Ave.
Los Angeles, CA 90038-3197
PHONE . . . 323-956-5000
WEB SITE . . . www.paramount.com
TYPES Syndication - TV Series

Joel Berman . . . President, Paramount Worldwide Television Distribution
Marc Hirsch . . . President, Paramount Advertising Services
Greg Meidel . . . President, Programming, Domestic TV
Jack Waterman . . . President, Worldwide Pay TV
John Nogawski . . . President, Paramount Domestic TV
Gary Marenzi . . . President, International TV
Susan Akens . . . Executive VP, Business Affairs, International TV
Steven Madoff . . . Executive VP, Business Affairs & Legal, Pay TV
Reed Manville . . . Executive VP, International Channels, Worldwide Pay TV
Bruce Pottash . . . Executive VP, Business & Legal Affairs, Domestic TV
Robert Sheehan . . . Executive VP, Finance & Business Affairs
Terry Wood . . . Executive VP, Programming, Domestic TV
Dawn Abel . . . Sr. VP, Research
James Brehm . . . Sr. VP, Worldwide Pay TV
Cary Clew . . . Sr. VP, Business Affairs & Legal, Pay TV
Peter Kane . . . Sr. VP, Business Affairs & Legal, Domestic TV
John Kohler . . . Sr. VP, Creative Affairs, Domestic TV
Winnie Lun Leung . . . Sr. VP, Business Systems & Controls, Pay TV
Phil Murphy . . . Sr. VP, TV Group Operations
Christopher Ottinger . . . Sr. VP, Business Development & Co-Productions, International TV
Margie Pacacha . . . Sr. VP, Business Affairs & Legal, Pay TV
Steve Selover . . . Sr. VP, Business Affairs & Legal, Pay TV
David Theodosopoulos . . . Sr. VP, Business & Legal Affairs, Domestic TV
Bill Weber . . . Sr. VP, TV Systems & Archive Services
Mallory Baker . . . VP, Contract Administration
Linda Carrasquillo . . . VP, Programming, Domestic TV
Nicole Choper . . . VP, Finance, Domestic TV
Mark Bennett Corbin . . . VP/Controller, Pay TV
Lynn Fero . . . VP, Business Affairs Administration, Domestic TV
Kim Fitzgerald . . . VP, Business Affairs & Legal, Domestic TV
Brad Hart . . . VP, Programming & Production, Domestic TV
Cynthia Lieberman . . . VP, Off-Network & Special Projects, Domestic TV
Kristin Peace . . . VP, Development, Domestic TV
Giovanni Pedde . . . VP, European Operations, Rome, International TV
Garrett Smith . . . VP, Digital Mastering Operations
Cortez Smith . . . VP, Business & Legal Affairs, Domestic TV
Mara Sternthal . . . VP, Business Development, Worldwide Pay TV
Ron Sufrin . . . VP, Business Affairs, Pay TV
Cynthia Teele . . . VP, Legal, Domestic TV
David Thomas . . . VP, Creative Services & Design, Domestic TV
Richard Yannich . . . VP, International Operations, International TV

*PARASKEVAS STUDIOS
157 Tuckahoe Lane.
Southampton, NY 11968
PHONE . . . 631-287-1665
FAX . . . 631-287-4469
EMAIL . . . jrkroll@aol.com
SECOND EMAIL . . . jrkroll@mac.com
WEB SITE . . . www.thegreenmonkeys.com
SECOND WEB SITE . . . www.cartoondiner.com
TYPES Animation - Features - Direct-to-Video/DVD - TV Series
DEALS Nelvana Entertainment/A Corus Entertainment Company
DEVELOPMENT Leo Spats Ratcatcher - The Cheap Show - Cartoon Diner - Red Moon Beach - Wacky Shellhammer - Nibbles O'Hare
PRE-PRODUCTION Green Monkeys - Jerolemon Street (Nelvana)
CREDITS Maggie and the Ferocious Beast - Marvin the Tap Dancing Horse - Kids From Room 402 - The Tangerine Bear

Michael Paraskevas . . . Producer
Betty Paraskevas . . . Producer

PARIAH
9465 Wilshire Blvd., Ste. 890
Beverly Hills, CA 90212
PHONE . . . 310-276-3500
FAX . . . 310-432-4539
TYPES Features - TV Series
PRODUCTION Revelations - D.O.T.'s
CREDITS Curb Your Enthusiasm - Gilmore Girls - Stir of Echoes - Panic Room - Hack - The Ortegas - P.I. - Secret Window

Gavin Polone . . . Owner
Jessika Borsiczky . . . VP
Vivian Cannon . . . VP
Vibiana Molina . . . VP, Business Affairs
Jonathan Frank . . . Creative Executive
J.J. Klein . . . Creative Executive

PARK EX PICTURES
1001, rue Lenoir, Ste. B 2-37
Montréal, QC H4C 2Z6 Canada
PHONE . . . 514-933-4133
FAX . . . 514-933-3199
EMAIL . . . info@parkexpictures.ca
TYPES Features - Made-for-TV/Cable Movies - TV Series
CREDITS Twist (Feature) - Choice: The Henry Morgentaler Story (CTV) - Varian's War (Showtime) - Bonanno (Showtime) - P.T. Barnum (A&E) - More Tales of the City (Showtime)

Kevin Tierney . . . President
Andrea Stanford . . . Assistant to the Producer

PARKWAY PRODUCTIONS
10 Universal City Plaza, 20th Fl.
Universal City, CA 91608
PHONE . . . 818-753-2323
TYPES Features - TV Series
DEALS Columbia Pictures
CREDITS Riding in Cars with Boys - The Preacher's Wife - Awakenings - Renaissance Man - A League of Their Own - Big

Penny Marshall . . . Director
Sean Corrigan . . . President
Caryn Mamrack . . . Assistant to Ms. Marshall
Terry Trahan . . . Assistant to Ms. Marshall
Nicole Cassidy . . . Assistant to Ms. Marshall

PATCHETT KAUFMAN ENTERTAINMENT
8621 Hayden Pl.
Culver City, CA 90232
PHONE . . . 310-838-7000
FAX . . . 310-838-8430
TYPES Features - Made-for-TV/Cable Movies - TV Series - Reality TV
PRE-PRODUCTION Welcome to Twenty-Nine Palms
CREDITS Dean Koontz's Mr. Murder - The Patron Saint of Liars - In the Line of Duty - Franchise - Dean Koontz's Black River
COMMENTS Thrillers; Have stage and executive office for production

Tom Patchett . . . Chairman
Kenneth Kaufman . . . President/COO
Debra Cannold . . . VP, Production Services
Brian McKeaney . . . Director, Development

PATHFINDER PICTURES, LLC.

801 Ocean Front Walk, Ste. 7
Venice, CA 90291
PHONE .310-664-1500
FAX .310-664-0400
EMAIL .info@pathfinderpictures.com
WEB SITE .www.pathfinderpictures.com
TYPES Features
PRE-PRODUCTION Pam/Pam - Ambushes From 12 Sides - Basic Jane
CREDITS Until the Night - Shadow Fury - Yellow - Double Deception - Tweeked
COMMENTS Distributes and produces theatrical, TV/cable, video/DVD releases with budgets of $500,000 and up

Taka Arai .Producer
Gregory Hatanaka .Executive Producer
Jeff Milne .Operations
Norith Soth .Development

PATRIOT PICTURES, LLC

9065 Nemo St.
West Hollywood, CA 90069
PHONE .310-274-0745
FAX .310-274-0925
EMAIL .sduff@patriotadvisors.com
TYPES Features - New Media - TV Series
DEVELOPMENT White House Secret Service - My Gay Ghost - Animal Hotel - Crenshaw Blvd. - Weapon of Choice
PRE-PRODUCTION Tempting Pandora - Open Mic - Maledictus

Michael Mendelsohn .Chairman/CEO
Samantha Duff .Executive Assistant

PAULIST PRODUCTIONS

17575 Pacific Coast Hwy.
Pacific Palisades, CA 90272-1057
PHONE .310-454-0688
FAX .310-459-6549
EMAIL .paulistmail@paulistproductions.org
WEB SITE .www.paulistproductions.org
TYPES Documentaries - Features - Direct-to-Video/DVD - Made-for-TV/Cable Movies - TV Series
DEVELOPMENT The Fourth Wiseman (Animated) - Yoga Prayer
CREDITS The Jesus Experience - St. Peter - Judas, A Documentary - Stigmata - Judas - Entertaining Angels: The Dorothy Day Story - St. James, Brother of Jesus? - Paul, The Man Who Turned the World Upside Down

Father Frank Desiderio, C.S.P. .President
Enid N. Sevilla .General Manager/Financial Officer
Father Greg Apparcel, C.S.P. .VP, Development
Joseph Kim .VP, Business Affairs
Barbara Gangi .Producer

DANIEL L. PAULSON PRODUCTIONS

9056 Santa Monica Blvd., Ste. 203-A
West Hollywood, CA 90069
PHONE .310-278-9747
FAX .310-278-9751
EMAIL .dlpprods@sbcglobal.net
TYPES Features - Made-for-TV/Cable Movies - Reality TV - TV Series
DEALS Fortress Entertainment
POST PRODUCTION Staffers (Discovery Times)
COMPLETED UNRELEASED Jack (Showtime)
CREDITS Sunset Park - Passenger 57 - Comes a Horseman - A Cooler Climate - Saving Jessica Lynch

Daniel L. Paulson .President
Bob Chmiel .VP, Creative Affairs
Steve A. Kennedy .Director, Administration
Ben Lamoso .Development Associate

PAX

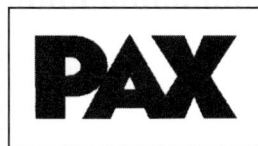

PAX TV/PAXSON COMMUNICATIONS

10880 Wilshire Blvd., Ste. 1200
Los Angeles, CA 90024
PHONE .310-234-2200/561-659-4122
FAX .310-474-7095
WEB SITE .www.pax.net
TYPES Reality TV - TV Series
CREDITS America's Funniest - Animal Tails - Balderdash - Bonanza - Candid Camera - Diagnosis Murder - Doc - Early Edition - Family Feud - It's a Miracle - Miracle Pets - On the Cover - Shop 'Til You Drop - Sue Thomas: F.B.Eye - Weakest Link
COMMENTS Game shows; Florida office: 601 Clearwater Park Rd., West Palm Beach, FL 33401

S. William Scott .President, Pax TV Network
Rob Word .Sr. VP, Program Development & Production (310-234-2267)
Barry Schulman .Sr. VP, Programming (561-682-4218)

PB MANAGEMENT

6449 W. Sixth St.
Los Angeles, CA 90048
PHONE .323-653-7284
FAX .323-653-5285
EMAIL .capnett@hotmail.com
TYPES Features - TV Series
DEALS HBO Original Programming
DEVELOPMENT The Schell Game - Grimm Repo - Brass - Magic Man - Rock, Ink

Paul Bennett .President
Barbara Caplan .VP, Development

PBS
1320 Braddock Pl.
Alexandria, VA 22314-1698
PHONE .703-739-5000
FAX .703-739-0775
WEB SITE .www.pbs.org
TYPES Documentaries - Reality TV - TV Series
CREDITS American Experience - American Masters - Antiques Roadshow - ExxonMobil Masterpiece Theatre - Frontline - Independent Lens - Mister Rogers' Neighborhood - The NewsHour with Jim Lehrer - NOVA - Now with Bill Moyers - Reading Rainbow - Wall Street Week with Fortune - Washington Week - Great Performances - Nature; Children's Programming: Arthur - Barney - Between the Lions - Clifford the Big Red Dog - Reading Rainbow - Sesame Street - Teletubbies - Zoom

Pat Mitchell .President/CEO
Wayne Godwin .Executive VP/COO
Judy Harris .Executive VP, PBS Businesses & Development
Jacoba Atlas .Sr. VP/Co-Chief Programming Executive
John F. Wilson .Sr. VP/Co-Chief Programming Executive
Pat Hunter .Sr. VP, Programming Services
Cindy Johanson .Sr. VP, PBS Interactive
Katherine Lauderdale .Sr. VP/General Counsel
Lesli Rotenberg .Sr. VP, Brand Management, Promotion & Media Relations
Tracey Beeker .VP, Marketing & Consumer Products
Jack Dougherty .VP, Business Affairs
Steven Gray .VP, Program Scheduling & Editorial Management
Paul Greco .VP/Deputy General Counsel
Gustavo Sagastume .VP, Programming
Elizabeth Suarez .VP, Development
Sylvia Bennett .Sr. Director, Fundraising Programming
John Ruppenthal .Sr. Creative Director
Sandy Heberer .Sr. Director, Factual Programming
Caryn Gutierrez-Ginsberg .Director, Program Management
Lauren Kalos .Director, Program Operations

PDI/DREAMWORKS
1800 Seaport Blvd.
Redwood City, CA 94063
PHONE .650-562-9000
FAX .650-562-9100
EMAIL .info@pdi.com
WEB SITE .www.dreamworks.com
TYPES Animation - Features
PRODUCTION Madagascar
CREDITS Shrek 1&2 - AI - Evolution - Legend of Bagger Vance - Mission: Impossible 2 - The Peacemaker - Forces of Nature - Batman & Robin - Antz - The Simpsons Homer 3-D
COMMENTS Digital

Patti Burke .Head, Studio

PDQ DIRECTIONS, INC.
4316 Marina City Dr., Ste. 729 CTN
Marina del Rey, CA 90292
PHONE .310-823-6374
FAX .310-823-2374
EMAIL .pdq01@earthlink.net
TYPES Documentaries - Features - Direct-to-Video/DVD - TV Series
DEVELOPMENT Malibu Bikini Shop 2 - Escape to Shanghai - Oscar Divo - The Gardner
COMPLETED UNRELEASED Funny Valentine
CREDITS Malibu Bikini Shop - Kandyland - Listen to the Music
COMMENTS Deal with Oasis TV

Leo Leichter .Owner/Producer
Barbra Hudson .Creative Development
Jon Leichter .Business Affairs

PEACE ARCH ENTERTAINMENT GROUP INC.
407-124 Merton St.
Toronto, ON M4S 2Z2 Canada
PHONE .416-487-0377
FAX .416-487-6141
EMAIL .info@peacearch.com
WEB SITE .www.peacearch.com
TYPES Features - Made-for-TV/Cable Movies - Reality TV - TV Series
DEVELOPMENT The Chet Baker Story - The Count - Going with Grace - Hack - Helga: A True Story - Keep Away From Me, Sorcerers - Love It or Lose It - Disaster Dogs - Tuner Madness
PRE-PRODUCTION Marlow: The Great Hoax, - Vanishing Act - The Boathouse - Campus Vets Season 2 - Kumite
PRODUCTION The Shadow Dancer - Prisoners of Age
POST PRODUCTION The Good Shepherd - Nature Unleashed: Earthquake - Nature Unleashed: Fire - Nature Unleashed: Tornado - Nature Unleashed: Volcano
COMPLETED UNRELEASED Direct Action - Hollywood Flies - Nature Unleashed: Avalanche
CREDITS GFT Entertainment: The Keeper - Absolon - Crime Spree - Detention - The Limit - Partners in Action; The Eyes Project Development Corp.: Animal Miracles - Campus Vets - Whistler Stories - Raven in the Sun - The Keeper - Heroines

Gary Howsam .CEO/President
Lewin Webb .President, GFT Entertainment
Blair Reekie .President, The Eyes Project Development Corp.
John Flock .President, Peace Arch LA, Inc.
Mara Di Pasquale .CFO
Charlie Bloye .Managing Director

PEAK PRODUCTIONS
c/o North Carolina School of the Arts
1533 S. Main St.
Winston-Salem, NC 27127
PHONE .336-770-1333
FAX .336-770-1339
EMAIL .peakprodns@aol.com
TYPES Documentaries - Features - Made-for-TV/Cable Movies - TV Series
DEVELOPMENT Bunny Kill
CREDITS Set It Off - Blaze - Midnight Clear - The Mighty Quinn - Mrs. Winterbourne - The Beast

Dale Pollock .President

PEARL PICTURES

10956 Weyburn Ave., Ste. 200
Los Angeles, CA 90024
PHONE .310-443-7773
FAX .310-443-7753
EMAIL .info@pearlpics.com

TYPES	Features - TV Series
DEVELOPMENT	The Line - OPJB - The Field - Full Cleveland - Kindred
CREDITS	A Chance of Snow - Liberty Stands Still - 10.5
COMMENTS	Production and management

Gary Pearl .No Title
Peter Marshall .No Title
J.J. Feldman .No Title

*PEBBLEHUT TOO, INC.

629 Eastern Ave., Bldg. A, Ste. 100
Toronto, ON M4M 1E4 Canada
PHONE .416-778-6800
FAX .416-778-0945
WEB SITE .www.pebblehut.com

TYPES	Documentaries - Features - Made-for-TV/Cable Movies - New Media - TV Series
DEVELOPMENT	Raven - A Violent Act - Frozen - Level Four
PRODUCTION	Doc (Season 4) - Sue Thomas (Season 2)
CREDITS	Johnny 2.0 (Feature) - Daydream Believers - The Monkees Story (MOW); TV: Sue Thomas: F.B. Eye - Doc - Twice in a Lifetime

Marilyn Stonehouse .President/Producer
Edythe Hall .VP, Business Affairs
Susan Murdoch .VP/Producer
Deborah Nathan .Development Executive
Terri Ann Myers .Director, Development
Patricia Curmi .Business Affairs

PECULIAR FILMS

15237 Sunset Blvd., Ste. 14
Pacific Palisades, CA 90272
PHONE .310-859-4630

TYPES	Features - Direct-to-Video/DVD - TV Series - Animation
DEVELOPMENT	Thornley and Oswald - Fool That I Am - Ella
PRE-PRODUCTION	Hard Hearts - Sweet Talk
CREDITS	Fight Club - Permanent Midnight - Semper Fi
SUBMISSION POLICY	No unsolicited submissions

Jim Uhls .Producer/Writer
Yalda Tehranian Uhls .Producer

ZAK PENN'S COMPANY

1416 N. La Brea
Los Angeles, CA 90028
PHONE .323-802-1790
FAX .323-802-1832

TYPES	Features
DEVELOPMENT	Man Out of Time
POST PRODUCTION	Suspect Zero
COMPLETED UNRELEASED	Incident at Loch Ness
CREDITS	X2 - Inspector Gadget - PCU - Osmosis Jones - Behind Enemy Lines - Last Action Hero - Antz

Zak Penn .Writer/Producer/Director
Lance Stockton .No Title

*PENSÉ PRODUCTIONS

10250 Constellation Blvd.
Los Angeles, CA 90067
PHONE .310-449-3972

TYPES	Features
DEALS	Metro-Goldwyn-Mayer Studios, Inc.

Scott Sander .Producer
Arthur Hair .Producer
Jessica Kill .Creative Executive

PERILOUS PICTURES

909 N. Gardner St., Ste. 301
West Hollywood, CA 90046
PHONE .323-851-5289

TYPES	Features
DEVELOPMENT	Michiganders
CREDITS	Stuart Bliss
SUBMISSION POLICY	No unsolicited submissions

Michael Zelniker .Actor/Producer/Writer
Neil Grieve .Director/Producer/Writer
Jens Sturup .Producer

PERMUT PRESENTATIONS

9150 Wilshire Blvd., Ste. 247
Beverly Hills, CA 90212
PHONE .310-248-2792
FAX .310-248-2797

TYPES	Features - TV Series
DEVELOPMENT	The Desmond Doss Story - Allegiance - Kings for a Day - The Sam Kinison Story - Money to Burn - Friends Again - Blind Sided - Julia Pastrana - Rewind
CREDITS	Face/Off - Eddie - Dragnet - Blind Date - Double Take - Consenting Adults - Three of Hearts - Richard Pryor Live in Concert - DysFunkTional Family

David Permut .Producer/President
Steven A. Longi .VP, Production
Christopher Kosfeld .Development Associate

PERSISTENT ENTERTAINMENT

8000 Sunset Blvd., 3rd Fl., East Penthouse
Los Angeles, CA 90046
PHONE .323-337-1055
FAX .323-337-1079
EMAIL .mail@persistentpictures.com
WEB SITE .www.persistentpictures.com

TYPES	Features - Made-for-TV/Cable Movies - TV Series
PRODUCTION	The Sisters
POST PRODUCTION	An Unfinished Life - Home of Phobia - A Different Loyalty - Freediver
COMPLETED UNRELEASED	September Tapes
CREDITS	Auggie Rose - The Amati Girls - Starf*cker - The Alarmist

Matthew Rhodes .Producer
Judd Payne .Producer
Jim Dominello .Assistant
Nick Myles .Assistant

PERSON TO PERSON FILMS
5000 Coldwater Canyon Ave., Ste. 12-A
Sherman Oaks, CA 91423
PHONE .818-766-4023
FAX .818-766-4034
EMAIL .afilmworks@aol.com
WEB SITE .www.ronmaxwell.com
TYPES Features - Made-for-TV/Cable Movies - TV Series
DEVELOPMENT Last Full Measure (Feature) - Joan of Arc: Virgin Warrior
PRE-PRODUCTION Untitled Mt. Vernon Project
CREDITS Gods and Generals (Ted Turner Pictures) - Gettysburg - Sioux City - Verna: USO Girl
SUBMISSION POLICY Upon request only

Ronald Maxwell .President/Writer/Director (818-766-4023)
L. Virginia Browne .Director, Development (818-766-4024)
Vivian Anderson .Business Affairs (310-645-1554)

PET FLY PRODUCTIONS
5510 Lincoln Blvd., 3rd Fl.
Los Angeles, CA 90094
PHONE .310-754-7256
FAX .310-754-7100
EMAIL .buzz@petfly.com
TYPES Features - Interactive Games - TV Series
CREDITS Features: The Rocketeer - The Wrong Guys - Trancers - Zone Troopers; TV: Viper - The Sentinel - The Flash; Games: The Sims - Harry Potter - James Bond - Metal of Honor

Danny Bilson .Writer/Executive Producer/Director
Paul De Meo .Writer/Executive Producer
Joe Lauer .President
Lisa Beard .Production Associate

DANIEL PETRIE JR. & COMPANY
18034 Ventura Blvd., Ste. 445
Encino, CA 91319-3516
PHONE .818-708-1602
FAX .818-774-0345
WEB SITE .www.danielpetriejrandcompany.com
TYPES Features - Made-for-TV/Cable Movies - TV Series
CREDITS Framed (TNT) - In the Army Now - Toy Soldiers - Turner & Hooch - Beverly Hills Cop - Dead Silence - The 6th Day

Dan Petrie Jr. .Director/Writer/Producer
Rick Dugdale .Producer

DOROTHEA G. PETRIE PRODUCTIONS, INC.
13201 Haney Pl.
Los Angeles, CA 90049
PHONE .310-394-2608
FAX .310-395-8530
TYPES Features - Made-for-TV/Cable Movies - TV Series
DEVELOPMENT Untitled CBS Movie
CREDITS The Song of the Lark - Echo of Thunder - Captive Heart - Getting Out - Caroline

Dorothea G. Petrie .Executive Producer/Producer
June Petrie .Producer/Co-Producer

STEPHEN PEVNER, INC.
382 Lafayette St., 8th Fl.
New York, NY 10003
PHONE .212-674-8403
FAX .212-529-3692
EMAIL .stephen@stephenpevnerinc.com
TYPES Features - Made-for-TV/Cable Movies - TV Series
CREDITS In the Company of Men - Your Friends & Neighbors - Nurse Betty - Possession - Bash

Stephen Pevner .Producer
Doug Silbert .Development Associate

PFD, INC.
16002 Meadowcrest Rd.
Sherman Oaks, CA 91403-4716
PHONE .818-906-7677
FAX .818-906-2836
TYPES Features - TV Series
CREDITS Look Who's Talking - The Chocolate War - Age Old Friends - C.H.U.D. 2 - Slipping Into Darkness - You Can't Hurry Love

Simon R. Lewis .President

PFEFFER FILM
c/o Walt Disney Studios
500 S. Buena Vista Blvd., Animation Bldg., Ste. 2F-8
Burbank, CA 91521
PHONE .818-560-3177
FAX .818-843-7485
TYPES Features
DEALS Walt Disney Pictures/Touchstone Pictures
DEVELOPMENT Temping Fate - Hell on Wheels - Pants on Fire - Matriphobia - Marine Electric - Vargack Paw
CREDITS Crazy/Beautiful - Malice - Grand Avenue - A Civil Action - The Horse Whisperer - A Few Good Men

Rachel Pfeffer .Producer
Asha Kurian .VP
Lindy Louis .Development Assistant

PHANTOM FOUR FILMS
1416 N. La Brea Ave.
Los Angeles, CA 90028
PHONE .323-802-1530
TYPES Features - TV Series
DEVELOPMENT The Descent - Murder Mysteries - The Fall - Mucho Mojo - Unique - Y: The Last Man
PRE-PRODUCTION Alone
POST PRODUCTION Blade: Trinity
CREDITS Features: Zig Zag - Blade 1&2 - Mission to Mars - Dark City; TV: Freakylinks - Sleepwalkers

David S. Goyer .Producer/Director/Writer
Glynis Lynn .Story Editor

PHASE TWO PRODUCTIONS
c/o Twentieth Century Fox
10201 W. Pico Blvd., Bldg. 3, Rm. 101
Los Angeles, CA 90035
PHONE 310-369-8555
FAX 310-369-8980
TYPES TV Series
DEALS Twentieth Century Fox Television
SUBMISSION POLICY No unsolicited submissions

Sandy Grushow ....Producer
Paul Shapiro ....Executive VP, Development
Holly Thro ....Manager, Development
Jono Golding ....Manager, Development

PHILIPICO PICTURES COMPANY
8737 Carlitas Joy Court
The Lakes, NV 89117
PHONE 702-255-9314/702-255-9999
TYPES Features - Direct-to-Video/DVD - Made-for-TV/Cable Movies
CREDITS Blind Terror - The Hired Heart - The Haunting of Lisa - Shoot to Kill
SUBMISSION POLICY Must query first
COMMENTS Affiliate, Century Park Pictures Corp.; Management and consulting, Stephanie Rogers & Associates; CinemaStar Partners, LLC

Phil Rogers ....Principal/Producer
Stephanie Rogers ....Principal/Producer

THE TODD PHILLIPS COMPANY
8439 Sunset Blvd., 1st Fl.
West Hollywood, CA 90069
PHONE 323-822-4300
FAX 323-822-4590
TYPES Documentaries - Features
DEALS Dimension Films - Miramax Films
CREDITS Road Trip - Old School - Starsky & Hutch

Todd Phillips ....Director/President
Scott Budnick ....VP, Production
Annette Savitch ....Creative Executive

PHOENIX PICTURES
10202 W. Washington Blvd., Frankovich Bldg.
Culver City, CA 90232
PHONE 310-244-6100
FAX 310-839-8915
TYPES Features - Direct-to-Video/DVD - Made-for-TV/Cable Movies - TV Series
DEVELOPMENT Werewolf - Damnation Game - Bad News - Yeager - Hardcourt - Destination Unknown - Dangerous Waters - Black Autumn - Flower Girl
PRE-PRODUCTION All The Kings Men - Zodiac - Miss Potter
POST PRODUCTION Stealth
CREDITS Country of My Skull - Basic - Holes - The Thin Red Line - The People vs. Larry Flynt - U-Turn - Apt Pupil - Urban Legend

Mike Medavoy ....Chairman/CEO (310-244-6106)
Arnold Messer ....President/COO (310-244-6101)
Brad Fischer ....VP, Production (310-244-6540)
Lou Phillips ....Sr. VP, Physical Production/Post Production (310-244-6455)
Scott Sebasty ....Director, Business & Legal Affairs (310-244-4134)
David Thwaites ....Director, Development (310-244-6815)
Anne Rodman ....Executive, Development (310-244-3542)
Diego Airaldi ....Creative Affairs (310-244-6187)
Christine Cabana ....Creative Affairs (310-244-2051)
Amy Carr ....Story Editor (310-244-6110)
Aaron Merrell ....Physical Production/Post Production Coordinator (310-244-6533)

PICO CREEK PRODUCTIONS
1112 Montana Ave.
Santa Monica, CA 90403
PHONE 310-394-7522
FAX 310-451-7586
TYPES Features - Made-for-TV/Cable Movies - TV Series
DEVELOPMENT Infidelity - The Plague (FX)
PRODUCTION Grey's Anatomy
CREDITS Brimstone - The Cure - Murder Live

Peter Horton ....Writer/Director/Actor/Producer

PIE TOWN PRODUCTIONS
5433 Laurel Canyon Blvd.
North Hollywood, CA 91607
PHONE 818-255-9300
FAX 818-255-9333
EMAIL ....pietown@pietown.tv
WEB SITE ....www.pietown.tv
TYPES Documentaries - Reality TV - TV Series
CREDITS Designed to Sell - Homes Across America - Weekend Warriors - House Hunters - Design on a Dime - $40 a Day - Designers' Challenge - Landscapers' Challenge - Take It Off - Take My Kids, Please - reDesign - Tune Up Your Man (Pilot)
SUBMISSION POLICY No unsolicited submissions

Tara Sandler ....Executive Producer
Jennifer Davidson ....Executive Producer
Scott Templeton ....Executive Producer
Sean Fitzgibbons ....Executive in Charge of Production
Eric Black ....Creative Director
Greg Spring ....Director, Development
Dana Besnoy ....Director, Post Production
Stina Thomas ....Post Production Supervisor
Samantha Leonard ....Production Manager
Betsy Allman ....Supervising Producer
Ellen Bauman-Kennedy ....Supervising Producer
Maxine Gray ....Supervising Producer
Drew Hallmann ....Supervising Producer
Vicky Landin ....Supervising Producer
Kim Pflieger ....Supervising Producer
Ellen Philips ....Supervising Producer
Andrea Pilat ....Supervising Producer
Stacy Schneider ....Supervising Producer
Beth Suskind ....Supervising Producer
Lesley Taylor ....Supervising Producer
Peter Field ....Coordinating Producer

THE FREDERICK S. PIERCE COMPANY
10061 Riverside Dr., Ste. 1005
Toluca Lake, CA 91602
PHONE 323-465-5588/323-964-7800
FAX 323-465-5599/323-964-7818
EMAIL ....piercefilms@earthlink.net
WEB SITE ....www.piercefilms.com
TYPES Features - Made-for-TV/Cable Movies - TV Series - Reality TV
CREDITS Substitute Wife - Cheerleader - The Absolute Truth - Moneytrain - 20,000 Leagues - In a Heartbeat
COMMENTS aka The Pierce Company

Frederick S. Pierce ....Chairman/CEO
Keith Pierce ....Executive Producer
Richard Pierce ....Executive Producer

PILGRIM FILMS & TELEVISION, INC.

4730 Woodman Ave., Ste. 300
Sherman Oaks, CA 91423
PHONE .818-728-8800
FAX .818-728-8810
TYPES Reality TV - TV Series - Syndication - Features - Documentaries
PRODUCTION American Casino: The Series (Discovery)
CREDITS Survivor 1: Borneo (CBS) - Survivor 2: The Australian Outback (CBS) - Survivor 3: Africa (CBS) - Worst-Case Scenario (TBS) - CIA Secrets (Discovery) - Cupid (CBS) - American Chopper: The Series (Discovery) - American Hot Rod: The Series (Discovery)

Craig M. Piligian .Owner/Executive Producer

PILLER²/THE SEGAN COMPANY

7025 Santa Monica Blvd.
Hollywood, CA 90038
PHONE .323-464-6201
FAX .323-464-6529
TYPES Features - Made-for-TV/Cable Movies - TV Series
CREDITS TV: The Dead Zone (USA) - Star Trek: Voyager - Star Trek: Deep Space Nine - Star Trek: The Next Generation; Features: Swimfan - Bones - Star Trek: Insurrection - Saving Private Ryan - Broken Arrow - Speed

Michael Piller .Producer/Writer
Shawn Piller .Producer/Writer
Allison Segan .Producer
Lloyd Segan .Producer
Adam Fratto .VP, Development
Eric A. Stillwell .VP, Operations
Ingrid Behrens .Associate
Georgyne LaLone .Associate

PINK SLIP PICTURES

1314 N. Coronado St.
Los Angeles, CA 90026
PHONE .213-483-7100
FAX .213-483-7200
EMAIL .pinkslip@earthlink.net
TYPES Features - TV Series
DEVELOPMENT Red Hollow - Windfall - Case of the Halloween Hangman - The Tucker Max Show
PRE-PRODUCTION Capture the Flag - The Crossing - Rumble - Snakebite
CREDITS The Bumblebee Flies Anyway - Bring It On - Tuck Everlasting
SUBMISSION POLICY No unsolicited material

Karen Firestone .Producer
Max Wong .Producer

PIRANHA PICTURES, INC.

347 W. 36th St., 15th Fl.
New York, NY 10018
PHONE .212-216-9470
FAX .212-216-9317
EMAIL .info@piranhapix.com
WEB SITE .www.piranhapix.com
TYPES Animation - Commercials - Features - Direct-to-Video/DVD - Made-for-TV/Cable Movies - Music Videos - New Media
DEVELOPMENT Untitled Sony Pictures Project
PRE-PRODUCTION Places of Greater Safety - J.B. Project
POST PRODUCTION United Nations Project (Documentary)
CREDITS Dead Beat - Breaking Up - An Occasional Hell - Scorpion Spring - The Obit Writer

George Moffly .Producer
Kim Wittenburg .Development
Ian Etra .Animation

PIRROMOUNT PICTURES

PO Box 7520
Van Nuys, CA 91409
PHONE .818-994-3262
FAX .253-276-9509
WEB SITE .www.pirromount.com
TYPES Commercials - Documentaries - Features - Direct-to-Video/DVD - Industrials - Made-for-TV/Cable Movies - Music Videos
DEVELOPMENT Root of All Evil (Feature)
CREDITS Behind the Fangs - Color Blinded - Polish Vampire in Burbank - Nudist Colony of the Dead - Curse of the Queer Wolf - Deathrow Game Show - My Mom's a Werewolf - Rectuma

Mark Pirro .Writer/Producer/Director
Lee Neville .VP, Distribution
John Cipolla .Development
Louis Gerstel .Promotion/Publicity
John Ahern .Associate Producer
Jim Rainey .Associate Producer
Steve Neimand .Legal Affairs

THE PITT GROUP

9465 Wilshire Blvd., Ste. 480
Beverly Hills, CA 90212
PHONE .310-246-4800
FAX .310-275-9258
TYPES Features - Made-for-TV/Cable Movies - TV Series
DEVELOPMENT Wynn vs. Trump (HBO) - Untitled Romantic Comedy (Revolution) - Untitled Montecito Picture Company
COMPLETED UNRELEASED Carolina
CREDITS Hollywood Homicide

Lou Pitt .President
Sophie Waterhouse .Director, Development
Ryan Vernon .Assistant to Mr. Pitt

PIXAR ANIMATION STUDIOS

1200 Park Ave.
Emeryville, CA 94608
PHONE .510-752-3000
FAX .510-752-3151
WEB SITE .www.pixar.com
TYPES Animation
PRODUCTION The Incredibles - Cars - Boundin'
CREDITS Finding Nemo - Mike's New Car - Monsters, Inc. - For the Birds - Toy Story 1&2 - A Bug's Life - Geri's Game - Tin Toy - Red's Dream - Luxo Jr. - Knickknack
COMMENTS Feature and short film computer animation

Steven P. Jobs .Chairman/CEO
Dr. Edwin E. Catmull .President
Simon Bax .Executive VP/CFO
John Lasseter .Executive VP, Creative
Sarah McArthur .Executive VP, Production
Lois Scali .Executive VP/General Counsel

PLAN B PRODUCTIONS®
1440 Dutch Valley Pl., Ste. 105
Atlanta, GA 30324
PHONE .404-881-8878
EMAIL .info@planbproductions.com
WEB SITE .www.planbproductions.com
TYPES Commercials - Features - Direct-to-Video/DVD - Industrials - Music Videos - New Media - Promos - Reality TV - TV Series
PRODUCTION The Cole Nobody Knows: The Life and Music of Freddy Cole
COMPLETED UNRELEASED Performance Anxiety - Alpha & Omega
CREDITS Contributions - How the Day Begins - Love & Fate - Squirrel Nut Zippers: Musical Candy - Post No Bills

Clay Walker .President

PLANET GRANDE PICTURES
23440 Civic Center Way, Ste. 104
Malibu, CA 90265
PHONE .310-317-1545
FAX .310-317-0256
TYPES Animation - Documentaries - New Media - Reality TV - TV Series
PRE-PRODUCTION File 86 - One Day at a Time Reunion - Country's Most Shocking
PRODUCTION Arbor Springs R.I.P. - Fifty Years of TV's Funniest Families (Museum of TV and Radio)
POST PRODUCTION InStyle Celebrity Weddings 2004
CREDITS The Andy Griffith Show Reunion: Back to Mayberry - Breaking the News - Deadwood Mysteries - InStyle Celebrity Weddings 2001-2003 - InStyle Celebrity Moms - Cirque du Soleil - Bond Girls Are Forever - TV Guide's 50 Best Shows of All Time
COMMENTS Network Specials

John Watkin .Owner
Eamon Harrington .Owner
Ron Harbin .Production Manager
Rosa Gonzalez .Production Accountant
Malaika Whitaker .Executive Assistant to Owners/Office Manager

PLASTERCITY PRODUCTIONS
6500 Sunset Blvd.
Los Angeles, CA 90028
PHONE .323-469-8500 (Production)/323-469-9800 (Post Production)
FAX .323-469-7500
EMAIL .info@plastercity.com
WEB SITE .www.plastercity.com
TYPES Features - Direct-to-Video/DVD - New Media - TV Series
DEVELOPMENT Biker Chef - Black Stallion - MacBeth - Duck Duck Goose
CREDITS Bloodhead - G-Men from Hell - Gunfighter - Palmer's Pick-up - Bel Air
COMMENTS Digital films; In-house deal with ARS NOVA XXI

Christopher Coppola .President, PlasterCITY Productions/ARS NOVA XXI
Adrienne-Stout Coppola .VP, PlasterCITY Productions
Deana McDaniel .VP, ARS NOVA XXI
Alain Silver .Producer
Nicholas Paine .Head, Production, PlasterCITY Productions
Evelyn Belasco .Head, Development ARS NOVA XXI
Michael Cioni .Post Production Supervisor, PlasterCITY Digital Post
Edward Green .Executive Assistant to Head, Production, PlasterCITY Productions
Nadalie Vajda .Executive Assistant , ARS NOVA XXI
Ian Vertovec .Head Technician/Online Editor, PlasterCITY Digital Post
Otto Arsenault .Editor/Graphic Designer, PlasterCITY Digital Post
Tony Wise .Editor, PlasterCITY Digital Post
Jody Leggio .Editor, PlasterCITY Digital Post

PLATFORM ENTERTAINMENT
10451 W. Jefferson Blvd.
Culver City, CA 90232
PHONE .310-204-3232
FAX .310-204-2877
TYPES Features - TV Series
PRE-PRODUCTION The Hard Easy - Brew
CREDITS Dante's View - Morgan's Ferry - The Job - The Hollow

Daniel Levin .Producer
Larry Gabriel .Producer
Scott Sorrentino .Producer
Mark Frank .Production
Garrett Wheeler .Production

PLATINUM DUNES
631 Colorado Ave.
Santa Monica, CA 90401
PHONE .310-394-9200
TYPES Features
DEVELOPMENT The Well - Superstition - Horsemen - The Amityville Horror - Untitled Hayes Brothers Project - The Surrogate - Untitled Texas Chainsaw Massacre Prequel
CREDITS Texas Chainsaw Massacre

Michael Bay .Partner
Andrew Form .Partner
Brad Fuller .Partner
Michele Soefer .Development Coordinator

PLATINUM STUDIOS, LLC
9744 Wilshire Blvd., Ste. 210
Beverly Hills, CA 90212
PHONE .310-276-3900
FAX .310-276-2799
EMAIL .info@platinumstudios.com
WEB SITE .www.platinumstudios.com
TYPES Animation - Features - New Media - Syndication - TV Series
DEALS Dimension Films - Showtime Networks, Inc.
DEVELOPMENT Million $ Heroes - Cowboys & Aliens - Nathan Never - Trace of Chalk - Mal Chance - Blackjack - Unique - Dark Fringe - Atlantis Rising - Final Orbit - Ghost Bullet - Book of Mercury - Ghosting
CREDITS Men in Black - Night Man - Ultraforce (Animated Series) - Jeremiah
COMMENTS Sponsoring deals with Col. John Alexander, Karen Brown, Fog Studios, Handheld Games and Blue Shift Inc.

Scott Mitchell Rosenberg .Chairman/CEO
Jay Burns .Creative Executive
Aaron Severson .Director, Development
Ron Friedman .Online Syndication
Monica Macera .Accounting
Lee Nordling .Executive Editor to Staff
Amanda Haughs .Assistant to Mr. Rosenberg

PLATONIC FILMS, INC.
176 Ocean Dr. West
Stamford, CT 06902
PHONE .203-348-2500
FAX .203-348-5200
EMAIL .ksegalla@platonicfilms.net
TYPES Features
DEVELOPMENT Fantasy Land - Chrysalis - Two Guys - Home
CREDITS The Testimony of Taliesin Jones - Whatever - Quattro Noza

Kevin Segalla .President
Benjamin Patton .Creative Executive

MARC PLATT PRODUCTIONS
100 Universal City Plaza, Bungalow 5184
Universal City, CA 91608
PHONE . . . . . 818-777-8811/818-777-1201 (Production)
FAX 818-866-6353
TYPES Features - Theater - TV Series
DEALS Universal Pictures
DEVELOPMENT About the Author - Quarterback's Tale - Nappily Ever After - Jesus Christ Superstar - Natural Man - Absolutely American - Bailey Weggins
PRODUCTION The Perfect Man
POST PRODUCTION Empire Falls
CREDITS Legally Blonde 2: Red, White & Blonde - Josie and the Pussycats - Legally Blonde - Honey
COMMENTS Theater: *Wicked*

Marc Platt . . . . . No Title (818-777-1122)
Abby Wolf . . . . . President (818-777-2259)
Joey Levy . . . . . No Title (818-777-7866)
Adam Siegel . . . . . No Title (818-777-9544)
Nicole Brown . . . . . No Title (818-777-5705)
Israel Gordan . . . . . No Title (818-777-5808)
Jared LeBoff . . . . . No Title (818-777-9961)

PLAYBOY ENTERTAINMENT GROUP, INC.
2706 Media Center Dr.
Los Angeles, CA 90065
PHONE 323-276-4000
FAX 323-276-4500
WEB SITE . . . . . www.playboy.com
TYPES Features - Direct-to-Video/DVD - Made-for-TV/Cable Movies - TV Series - Reality TV

Jim Griffiths . . . . . Sr. Executive VP, Playboy Enterprises
Ned Nalle . . . . . President, Programming
Mark Rudolph . . . . . Managing Director, PTVI/Executive VP, PEGI
Barry Leshtz . . . . . Sr. VP/General Manager, Worldwide Home Video
Alexandra Shepard . . . . . Sr. VP, Business & Legal Affairs
Sol Weisel . . . . . Sr. VP, Production & Operations
Seth Chasin . . . . . VP, Business Planning & Analysis
Eric S. Deutsch . . . . . VP, Worldwide Production
Stuart Kricun . . . . . VP, Business & Legal Affairs
Catherine Zulfer . . . . . VP/Controller
Olenka Wos . . . . . Manager, Worldwide Home Video

PLAYTIME PRODUCTIONS
311 N. Robertson Blvd., Ste. 283
Beverly Hills, CA 90211
PHONE 310-203-1360
FAX 413-778-2150/253-650-3470
WEB SITE . . . . . www.playtimeproductions.com
TYPES Animation - Features - TV Series
COMMENTS Second office: Raleigh Studios, 5400 Melrose Ave., Los Angeles, CA 90038

Brett A. Liebman . . . . . Producer/Writer
Danny Goldwyn . . . . . VP, Production
Sarah Levinson . . . . . Production Executive
Annie Simon . . . . . Development Executive
Abbie Brooks . . . . . Development Executive/Animation
Tom Hilman . . . . . Executive Assistant
Jill Tannenbaum . . . . . Executive Assistant

PLOTPOINT, INC.
12600 Kling St.
Studio City, CA 91604
PHONE 818-509-9464
TYPES Animation - Features - TV Series
CREDITS Rugrats - Becoming Dick - Lazytown

Rick Gitelson . . . . . Producer

PLUMERIA ENTERTAINMENT
4023 Stoneriver Court
Westlake Village, CA 91362
PHONE 805-496-3533
FAX 805-520-0335
EMAIL . . . . . jayenron@aol.com
TYPES Features - Made-for-TV/Cable Movies - TV Series
DEVELOPMENT Dearly Beloved - Dragon Season - A Very Good Wish
CREDITS Made-for-TV Movies: Broken Promises: Taking Emily Back - Separated by Murder - Replacing Dad - Floating Away - Legion of Fire Killer Ants - Give or Take an Inch

Rhonda Bloom . . . . . Producer/Manager
Jaye Lewis . . . . . Office Manager

PLUS ENTERTAINMENT, INC.
20 W. 23rd St., 3rd Fl.
New York, NY 10010
PHONE 212-206-8160
FAX 212-206-8168
EMAIL . . . . . info@plusentertainment.net
WEB SITE . . . . . www.plusentertainment.net
TYPES Features - Made-for-TV/Cable Movies - New Media - Theater
DEVELOPMENT Pioneer Town - Bat Boy: The Musical - Matt & Ben: The Movie - Stopping in Mansfield
CREDITS Macbeth in Manhattan - Chaos Theory - Dark Tides - Perfect Lies (The Last Lie) - Fountain of Death; Theater: Matt & Ben - Listen to My Heart: The Songs of David Friedman - Johnny Guitar: The Musical

Victoria Lang . . . . . Co-President
Pier Paolo Piccoli . . . . . Co-President
Jared Fine . . . . . Director, Project Development
Brian Baba . . . . . Director, Special Projects

POETRY & PICTURES INC.
13366 Huston, Ste. C
Sherman Oaks, CA 91423
PHONE 818-788-9900
FAX 818-788-9902
EMAIL . . . . . dclaybourn@aol.com
WEB SITE . . . . . www.dougclaybourne.com
TYPES Documentaries - Features
DEVELOPMENT Black Ball - The Carolers - The Cruelest Winter - The House of Romeo Cavalli - Victory Girl - The Haunt - Orange Surf - Emma Freud & Jung - Poe
POST PRODUCTION Duma
CREDITS Class Action - The Fast and the Furious - The Mask of Zorro - Jack - Money Train - D2: The Mighty Ducks - V.I. Warshawski - Hearts of Darkness: A Filmmaker's Apocalypse - War of the Roses - Rumble Fish - The Black Stallion Returns - Apocalypse Now
SUBMISSION POLICY No unsolicited material

Doug Claybourne . . . . . Producer
Tava Maloy Sofsky . . . . . Producer/VP, Development
Valerie Flueger . . . . . Producer/Development Executive
Aida Ghidey . . . . . Development Associate

POGUEFILM
824 N. Kilkea Dr.
Los Angeles, CA 90046
PHONE 323-658-5041
FAX 323-651-3536
TYPES Features - TV Series
CREDITS The Fast and the Furious - U.S. Marshals - The Skulls - Ghost Ship

John Pogue ....Writer/Producer
Marilyn Roberts ....Director, Development

MARTIN POLL FILMS, LTD.
PO Box 17137
Beverly Hills, CA 90209-3137
PHONE 323-876-8873/212-223-2881
FAX 323-876-8892/212-223-2897
TYPES Features - Made-for-TV/Cable Movies - TV Series
CREDITS Nighthawks - The Lion in Winter - Diana, Her True Story

Martin Poll ....President/Producer
Shirley Mellner ....Executive VP, Creative
Jason Dolan ....VP, Creative
Aliana Scurlock ....Executive Assistant

POLLYWOG ENTERTAINMENT, INC.
PO Box 2969
Beverly Hills, CA 90213
PHONE 323-651-5005
FAX 323-651-5851
WEB SITE ....www.andydick.com
TYPES Commercials - Documentaries - Features - Music Videos - New Media - Reality TV - TV Series
DEVELOPMENT Untitled Andy Dick Film - Untitled Reality TV Pilot (w/Endemol)
CREDITS The Andy Dick Show (MTV) - The Assistant (MTV)
COMMENTS Also managing actors, models and musicians; Currently collaborating with The Long Beach Shortbus (Formerly Sublime)

Andy Dick ....Director
Geoffrey Clark ....Producer (562-787-1133)
Shawn Geer ....Web Design (310-498-4409)

THE POLSON COMPANY
391 S. Madison Ave.
Pasadena, CA 91101
PHONE 626-405-0080
FAX 626-795-9039
TYPES Features - Made-for-TV/Cable Movies - TV Series
CREDITS Go Toward the Light - The Christmas Box - The Christmas Wish - Going Home - The Last Dance - Miss Lettie and Me - Secret Santa

Beth Polson ....Executive Producer
Leah Goodman ....Development

POPPIX, LLC
c/o Richard Brophy
PO Box 93117
Los Angeles, CA 90093
PHONE 323-874-8809
FAX 323-669-2893
WEB SITE ....www.poppix.com
SECOND WEB SITE ....www.littledoodle.com
TYPES Features - Direct-to-Video/DVD - Made-for-TV/Cable Movies - New Media
DEVELOPMENT 4 Below
CREDITS The Boneyard - Dark:30 - Harbinger
COMMENTS Publishes children books

Richard F. Brophy ....Producer/Publisher (richardbrophy@poppix.com)
James Cummins ....Writer/Director (jamescummins@poppix.com)

POPULAR ARTS ENTERTAINMENT, INC.
2006 W. Olive Ave.
Burbank, CA 91506
PHONE 818-562-6366
FAX 818-562-6373
EMAIL ....contactus@populararts.com
TYPES Animation - Direct-to-Video/DVD - Made-for-TV/Cable Movies - New Media - Reality TV - Syndication - TV Series
PRE-PRODUCTION Strip Club
PRODUCTION Famous (Syndicated) - On the Set (Syndicated) - Cine News (Syndicated) - Screenwriters (Syndicated) - Mondo Magic (A&E) - Life in the Fast Lane with Steve Natt (Fine Living) - Hollywood HD (HD Net) - Where in the World (History Channel)
CREDITS Going Wild with Jeff Corwin - Dr. Katz - Entertainment News Service - The Jeff Corwin Experience

Gordon (Tim) Braine ....Co-CEO/Executive Producer
Kevin Meagher ....Co-CEO/Executive Producer
Thomas Guttry ....VP, Business Affairs
Marc Wolloff ....Director, Production

POPULUXE PICTURES
9601 Wilshire Blvd., Ste. 1150
Beverly Hills, CA 90210
PHONE 323-272-5537
FAX 310-275-1853
EMAIL ....broad@earthlink.net
TYPES Features - Direct-to-Video/DVD
DEVELOPMENT Ray Gunn: Virtual Detective - Johnny B. Dead
PRE-PRODUCTION Earth Creature
CREDITS Sexbomb - Area 51 - The Last Patient
SUBMISSION POLICY No unsolicited submissions
COMMENTS Digital features; 24P HD filmmaking; DVD extras producer

Jeff Broadstreet ....Director/Producer
R.C. Rosenbalm ....Writer/Development

It is illegal to copy any part of this book

PORCHLIGHT ENTERTAINMENT
11777 Mississippi Ave.
Los Angeles, CA 90025
PHONE .310-477-8400
FAX .310-477-5555
EMAIL .distribution@porchlight.com
WEB SITE .www.porchlight.com
TYPES Animation - Features - Direct-to-Video/DVD - Made-for-TV/Cable Movies - New Media - TV Series
PRODUCTION Four Eyes - Landslide - Combustion - The Christmas Dinosaur
CREDITS Tutenstein - Night of the Twisters - Adventures from the Book of Virtues - Wild Grizzly - Jay Jay the Jet Plane - Treehouse Hostage - The Trial of Old Drum - The Brainiacs.com

Bruce D. Johnson .President/CEO
William T. Baumann .Executive VP/CFO/COO
Joe Broido .Sr. VP, Filmed Entertainment
Stephanie Slack .Sr. VP, Worldwide Sales
Adam Wright .Sr. VP, Worldwide Sales
Tom Gleason .VP, Post Production
Fred Schaefer .VP/Producer, Children's Programming
Zac Reeder .Head, Acquisitions
Rene Rodman .Director, Marketing & Licensing
D. Douglas Hill .Controller, Finance

PORT MAGEE PICTURES, INC.
c/o E! Networks
5750 Wilshire Blvd.
Los Angeles, CA 90036
PHONE .323-692-6455
FAX .323-954-2770
EMAIL .danriley@portmageepictures.com
SECOND EMAIL .peterjclark@portmageepictures.com
TYPES Documentaries - Features - Made-for-TV/Cable Movies - Reality TV - TV Series
DEVELOPMENT The Peter Fitzpatrick Story - Traitors Among Us - Tangled Web - A Kind Man and a Good Lover - My Fractured Life
PRODUCTION Surprise! (Pilot)
POST PRODUCTION Probies
COMPLETED UNRELEASED True Love (Pilot)
CREDITS The 5th Wheel - Kid Stuff - Ex-treme Dating - Lloyd & Lee - E!'s 101 Reasons the 90's Ruled - E!'s 101 Best Kept Hollywood Secrets
SUBMISSION POLICY No phone calls

Dan Riley .Partner
Peter J. Clark .Partner

THE POST OFFICE BROADCAST SERVICES
3779 Cahuenga Blvd. West
Studio City, CA 91604
PHONE .818-508-2422
FAX .818-508-2442
EMAIL .generaldelivery@tpollc.com
WEB SITE .www.tpollc.com
TYPES Animation - Commercials - Documentaries - Features - Direct-to-Video/DVD - Industrials - Interactive Games - Large Format - Made-for-TV/Cable Movies - Promos - Reality TV - Syndication - TV Series
CREDITS Clean and Narrow - Do You Wanna Know a Secret?
COMMENTS Audio, video and music post production

Edward Lopatin .CEO
Glen Matisoff .President

POW! ENTERTAINMENT
9440 Santa Monica Blvd., Ste. 620
Beverly Hills, CA 90210
PHONE .310-275-9933
FAX .310-285-9955
TYPES Features - TV Series - Animation
DEVELOPMENT Double Man - Stealing Tomorrow - Nightbird - Earth Walker - Heroes at Large - Demons - Time Trap - Nick Ratchett
PRE-PRODUCTION Hef's Super Bunnies
PRODUCTION Stan Lee's Phantom Five

Stan Lee .Chief Creative Officer
Gill Champion .Chief Operating Officer
Arthur Lieberman .Chief Business Affairs
Junko Kobayashi .Chief Financial Officer
Michael Kelly .Chief Executive Assistant

POWER ENTERTAINMENT
12200 W. Olympic Blvd., Ste. 490
Los Angeles, CA 90064
PHONE .310-481-0004
FAX .310-481-3980
TYPES Animation - Features - Direct-to-Video/DVD - Made-for-TV/Cable Movies - Syndication - TV Series - Reality TV
CREDITS One on One (UPN)

David Goldman .President/CEO
Robert Hartmann .Producer
Judi Brown .Producer
Joel Zadak .Manager
Ben Feigin .Manager
Bill Bowley .Manager
Charles Montgomery .Manager
Michael Mayne .Director, Development
Matthew Schuler .Assistant
Jesse Shapiro .Assistant

POWER UP
419 N. Larchmont, Ste. 283
Los Angeles, CA 90004
PHONE .323-463-3154
EMAIL .joinpowerup@aol.com
WEB SITE .www.power-up.net
TYPES Features - TV Series
DEVELOPMENT 2004 Film Grant Program
COMPLETED UNRELEASED Starcrossed - Billy's Dad is a Fudgepacker - Fade In
CREDITS Stuck - Breaking Up Really Sucks - Chicken Night - Fatal Instinct - Under the Hula Moon - To Kill For - In Search of Holden Caulfield - Fly Cherry - Give or Take an Inch - D.E.B.S. - Little Black Boot - Intent - The Nearly Unadventurous Life of Zoe Caudwalder

Stacy Codikow .Producer/Writer
Amy Shomer .Producer
Lisa Thrasher .Producer
Kevin Vermilion .VP

PREMIER ATTRACTIONS, INC.

8306 Wilshire Blvd., Ste. 1030
Beverly Hills, CA 90211
PHONE 310-281-7308
EMAIL .... iproduce@hotmail.com
TYPES Commercials - Documentaries - Features - Direct-to-Video/DVD - Made-for-TV/Cable Movies - Music Videos
CREDITS Changing Hearts - Destiny - Solitude Point - Running from the Shadows - Bounty Hunter - Cane Fighter
COMMENTS Limited theatrical distribution; Cable deal with Atlantic Syndication Network; Infomercials

Michael Edwards .... Producer/Director/President

EDWARD R. PRESSMAN FILM CORPORATION

1648 N. Wilcox Ave.
Hollywood, CA 90028
PHONE 323-871-8383/646-602-5700
FAX 323-871-1870/212-489-2103
TYPES Features - TV Series
CREDITS Owning Mahowny - City Hall - The Crow - Conan - Reversal of Fortune - Wall Street - Two Girls and a Guy - Black & White - American Psycho
COMMENTS East Coast office: 419 Lafeyette St., 7th Fl., New York, NY 10001

Edward R. Pressman .... CEO/Chairman
Gregory Woertz .... COO/CFO
Jon Katz .... Business Affairs
Steve Simpson .... Controller
Phil Montgomery .... Assistant to Mr. Pressman (LA)
Mira Shin .... Assistant to Mr. Pressman (NY)

PRETTY PICTURES

100 Universal City Plaza, Bldg. 2352-A, 3rd Fl.
Universal City, CA 91608
PHONE 818-733-0926
FAX 818-866-0847
TYPES Features - TV Series
DEALS Focus Features/Rogue Pictures
DEVELOPMENT dem - The Keys to the Street - Wickerman - Lilac Lane - Monster - Nic's Way - The Danish Girl
CREDITS Kinsey The Shape of Things - Possession - Nurse Betty - In the Company of Men - Donnie Brasco - Quiz Show

Neil LaBute .... Director/Writer/Producer
Gail Mutrux .... Producer
Valerie Dean .... Sr. VP, Production
Tim Harms .... Story Editor
Steven Jacobson .... Assistant to Gail Mutrux

PRINCIPAL ENTERTAINMENT

1964 Westwood Blvd., Ste. 400
Los Angeles, CA 90025
PHONE 310-446-1466/212-997-9191
FAX 310-446-1566/212-997-9280
TYPES Documentaries - Features - TV Series
DEVELOPMENT Duffy Deeter - Hightide - Wipeout - The Girl Who Struck Out Babe Ruth - Six Bullets from Now - Five Fingers
CREDITS The Last Time I Committed Suicide - Outreach (Pilot) - The Killing Yard - Monster Island (MTV)
COMMENTS Personal management; East Coast office: 130 W. 42nd St., Ste. 614, New York, NY 10036

Estelle Lasher .... Principal
Marsha McManus .... Principal
Elizabeth Robinson .... Principal

(Continued)

PRINCIPAL ENTERTAINMENT (Continued)

Ilan Breil .... Manager/Producer
Josh Kesselman .... Manager/Producer
Jill Kaplan .... Manager
Stacey McLaughlin .... Manager
Meg Mortimer .... Manager
Jennifer Glaser .... Associate (NY)
Jacy Merson .... Associate (NY)
Michael Smith .... Associate (LA)
Colin Wilhm .... Associate (LA)

VICTORIA PRINCIPAL PRODUCTIONS

120 S. Spalding Dr., Ste. 205
Beverly Hills, CA 90212
PHONE 310-278-3097
FAX 310-278-1870
WEB SITE .... www.victoriaprincipal.com
TYPES Made-for-TV/Cable Movies - TV Series
CREDITS Don't Touch My Daughter - Sparks - Inner Sanctum - Midnight's Child

Victoria Principal .... Actress/Producer
Delia Isabel Soto .... Executive Assistant

PRINCIPATO-YOUNG ENTERTAINMENT

9465 Wilshire Blvd., Ste. 430
Beverly Hills, CA 90212
PHONE 310-274-4130/310-274-4474
FAX 310-274-4108
TYPES Features - TV Series
DEALS Dimension Films
DEVELOPMENT Just Like a Woman - You Are Going to Prison - Resolution - Nanjo (Dimension) - Making Daddy a Man
PRODUCTION Reno 911 (Series)
CREDITS Wet Hot American Summer

Peter Principato .... Partner (310-274-4130)
Paul Young .... Partner (310-274-4474)
E. Brian Dobbins .... No Title (310-274-2294)
Ted Bender .... No Title (310-274-4457)
Allen Fischer .... No Title (310-274-4180)
David Gardner .... No Title (310-274-4677)
Brian Steinberg .... No Title (212-582-4255)

PRODUCE MEDIA GROUP

5912 Alcove Ave.
North Hollywood, CA 91607
PHONE 818-980-3641
FAX 818-980-4180
EMAIL .... jbunzel@producemediagroup.com
TYPES Features - Made-for-TV/Cable Movies - TV Series
DEVELOPMENT Complexity - Death of a Buick - The Agency
PRE-PRODUCTION Me and You and Everyone We Know
CREDITS STAT (Series) - Born to Be Wild

John Bunzel .... CEO

PRODUCERS GROUP STUDIOS

3016 N. Stone
Colorado Springs, CO 80907
PHONE 719-632-2463
FAX 719-634-6987
EMAIL .... directorpgs@aol.com
SECOND EMAIL .... dpsflan@aol.com
WEB SITE .... www.producersgroupstudios.com
TYPES Features - TV Series
DEVELOPMENT Rocket Squad - 7th City of Gold
CREDITS Planet Gone Mad - Spittin' Image - Pools of Anger

Russell S. Kern .... Producer/Director
Steven R. Flanigan .... Producer/Director, Photography

THE PRODUCERS
1313 Ninth St., Ste. 11
Santa Monica, CA 90401
PHONE . . . 310-395-9494
FAX . . . 310-395-6907
EMAIL . . . theproducersla@aol.com
TYPES Documentaries - Features - Made-for-TV/Cable Movies - TV Series - Reality TV
CREDITS The Amityville Horror, Part One: The Haunting - The Amityville Horror, Part Two: Horror or Hoax

Bill Bannon Jr. . . . Producer/Manager
SueAnne Fincke . . . Producer

PRODUCTION LOGISTICS, INC.
c/o Louis G. Friedman, DGA/PGA
23615 Long Valley Rd.
Hidden Hills, CA 91302
PHONE . . . 818-884-1880
FAX . . . 818-884-1820
EMAIL . . . productionlogistics@msn.com
WEB SITE . . . www.geocities.com/ProductionLogistics
TYPES Features
DEVELOPMENT Reading, Writing, & Relativity or How I Learned to Displace Matter and Raise the Dead Before Breakfast
CREDITS Into the Blue - American Wedding - Blue Crush - American Pie - The Third Wheel - Slackers - How High - Titanic - Starship Troopers - Return of the Jedi - Hexed - Raiders of the Lost Ark

Louis G. Friedman . . . Executive Producer

PRODUCTION PARTNERS, INC.
4421 Riverside Dr., Ste. 206
Burbank, CA 91505
PHONE . . . 818-556-5065
FAX . . . 818-556-5069
EMAIL . . . contact@productionpartners.com
WEB SITE . . . www.productionpartners.com
TYPES Features - TV Series
CREDITS Comedy Specials: Chris Rock, David Spade, Bill Maher; Comedy Series: Curb Your Enthusiasm

Sandy Chanley . . . Executive Producer
Tom Bull . . . Producer
Keith Truesdell . . . Director

PROMARK ENTERTAINMENT GROUP
3599 Cahuenga Blvd. West, 3rd Fl.
Los Angeles, CA 90068
PHONE . . . 323-878-0404
FAX . . . 323-878-0486
EMAIL . . . promark@promarkgroup.com
TYPES Features - Direct-to-Video/DVD - Made-for-TV/Cable Movies - TV Series
PRE-PRODUCTION Ghost Monkey
COMPLETED UNRELEASED I Witness - Black Tie Nights
CREDITS Pilgrim - After Alice - Contaminated Man - Styx - The Enemy - Last Run - The Shipment - The Stick-Up - Greenmail - One Way Out - Miami Sands - Lone Hero - Black Point - Federal Protection

Jonathan Kramer . . . President
Jay Behling . . . CFO
Steve Beswick . . . Sr. VP, Production
David Bixler . . . Sr. VP, Production
Amy Krell . . . VP, Production
Gil-Adrienne Wishnick . . . VP, Development

PROMETHEUS ENTERTAINMENT
10201 W. Pico Blvd., Bldg. 41, Ste. 202
Los Angeles, CA 90035
PHONE . . . 310-369-1709
FAX . . . 310-369-4507
EMAIL . . . scott.hartford@fox.com
TYPES Documentaries - Made-for-TV/Cable Movies - Syndication - TV Series
CREDITS A&E Biography - Behind the Planet of the Apes - Rodgers & Hammerstein: The Sound of Movies
COMMENTS Foxstar Productions; Van Ness Films

Kevin J. Burns . . . President
Scott Hartford . . . VP, Development & Production
Amy Canales . . . Executive Assistant to President & VP, Development & Production

PROSPECT PICTURES
9229 Sunset Blvd., Ste. 415
Los Angeles, CA 90069
PHONE . . . 310-205-3456
FAX . . . 310-205-3450
WEB SITE . . . www.prospectpictures.com
TYPES Documentaries - Features - TV Series
CREDITS My Baby's Daddy - Sol Goode - Rock the House

Matthew Weaver . . . Partner
Marcos Siega . . . Partner
Carl Levin . . . Partner
Jason Barhydt . . . Film/TV
Joel Rubin . . . Development Assistant
Melinda Sustin . . . Development Assistant
David Taylor . . . Development Assistant

PROTOZOA PICTURES
438 W. 37th St., Ste. 5-G
New York, NY 10018
PHONE . . . 212-244-3369
FAX . . . 212-244-3735
TYPES Animation - Features - TV Series
DEVELOPMENT Flicker - Lonewolf & Cub - Song of Kali
PRE-PRODUCTION The Fountain
CREDITS Pi - Requiem for a Dream - Below

Darren Aronofsky . . . Partner
Eric Watson . . . Partner
Ari Handel . . . President
Elizabeth Raposo . . . Director, Development
Cuffe Owens . . . No Title
Will Rowbotham . . . No Title

PROUD MARY ENTERTAINMENT
433 N. Camden Dr., Ste. 600
Beverly Hills, CA 90210
PHONE . . . 310-288-1886
FAX . . . 310-288-1801
EMAIL . . . proudmaryent@earthlink.net
TYPES Features - Made-for-TV/Cable Movies - Syndication - TV Series - Reality TV
DEVELOPMENT The Snitch - Ecstasy - Kicking Ash - Ballentine - Wow
PRE-PRODUCTION Girl from Ipenema (Feature)
COMPLETED UNRELEASED Downtown: A Street Tale
CREDITS Caught in the Act - Full Metal Racket - The Princess & the Marine

Mary L. Aloe . . . Executive Producer
Jay Jacobs . . . Executive Producer
Frank Chindamo . . . VP, Development

PTERODACTYL/KEW
2541 Canyon Oak Dr.
Los Angeles, CA 90068
PHONE 323-469-5778
FAX 323-469-5778
TYPES Features - TV Series
DEVELOPMENT Heathcliff the Cat - Creepshow
CREDITS Sabrina, the Teenage Witch - Doom Runners

Barney Cohen .....Partner
Ivan Cohen .....Partner (323-461-6167)
Kathryn Wallack .....Partner (212-627-9811)

PUNCH PRODUCTIONS
11661 San Vicente Blvd., Ste. 222
Los Angeles, CA 90049
PHONE 310-442-4880
FAX 310-442-4884
TYPES Features
CREDITS Tootsie - Mad City - Wag the Dog - Walk on the Moon - Devil's Arithmatic - Outbreak - Death of a Salesman - American Buffalo - Boys and Girls - Clubland

Dustin Hoffman .....Owner
Julie Benson .....Office Manger/Executive Assistant to Mr. Hoffman
Jackie Smith .....Second Assistant to Mr. Hoffman

QUALITY FILMED ENTERTAINMENT
c/o Hypnotic
1520 Cloverfield Blvd., Ste. D
Santa Monica, CA 90404
PHONE 310-453-2345
FAX 310-453-0075
EMAIL .....info@qualityfilmedent.com
WEB SITE .....www.qualityfilmedent.com
TYPES Features - New Media - TV Series
DEALS Hypnotic
CREDITS Boogeyman - Terry Tate: Office Linebacker - Save Virgil - George Lucas in Love
COMMENTS Management

Steven Hein .....Producer/Manager
Gary Bryman .....Producer/Manager

QUINN PRODUCTIONS
2285 Michael Faraday Dr., Ste. 12
San Diego, CA 92154
PHONE 800-468-7224/310-422-3039
EMAIL .....johnquinn2001@yahoo.com
TYPES Features - Direct-to-Video/DVD - TV Series
DEVELOPMENT Cyber-Scream - Cheerleader Camp 2
CREDITS Secret Cellar - Cheerleader Camp - Board Heads - Key to Sex - Beach Movie - Fast Lane to Vegas - The Magic of the Golden Bear

John Quinn .....President
Tiffany Jacobs-Quinn .....Director, Development

QUINTA COMMUNICATIONS USA
3000 Olympic Blvd.
Santa Monica, CA 90404
PHONE 310-264-3978
FAX 310-264-3979
TYPES Features
DEVELOPMENT The Black Dahlia - Toyer - Florentines
CREDITS Femme Fatale - Avenging Angelo - Ballistic: Ecks vs. Sever - Boys on the Run - Pirates
COMMENTS Distributor; Paris office: Quinta Communications S.A., 16 Avenue Hoche, Paris 75008 France, phone: 331-4076-0454, fax: 331-4076-0455

Tarak Ben Ammar .....Chairman (Paris)
Mark Lombardo .....President (Paris)
Paul Mitchell Rosenblum .....President (LA)
Brigitte Segal .....Legal & Business Affairs (LA)

R.L. ENTERTAINMENT, INC.
9595 Wllshire Blvd., Ste. 900
Beverly Hills, CA 90212
PHONE 310-406-0802
FAX 310-406-0902
EMAIL .....rlfilms@aol.com
TYPES Features - TV Series
DEVELOPMENT The Duelist - Adagio - Unknown - Estranged
CREDITS Kissing a Fool - Trading Favors

Rick Lashbrook .....Producer
Darby Parker .....Producer (310-863-4888)

RADAR PICTURES
10900 Wilshire Blvd., Ste. 1400
Los Angeles, CA 90024
PHONE 310-208-8525
FAX 310-208-1764
WEB SITE .....www.radarpictures.com
TYPES Features
DEVELOPMENT Heartbreak Kid - Waist Deep - The Brutus Complex - Twelve - In Search of Captain Zero
PRE-PRODUCTION Zathura - Amityville Horror
PRODUCTION Son of the Mask
CREDITS Chronicles of Riddick - The Last Samurai - Le Divorce - How to Deal - Pitch Black - Runaway Bride - Jumanji - Mr. Holland's Opus
COMMENTS Formerly Interscope Communications

Ted W. Field .....Chairman/CEO
David Boyle .....Executive VP, Business/Legal
Joe Rosenberg .....Executive VP/Producer
David Kroes .....Director, Administration/Human Resources
Jennifer Worley .....Director, Development
Davida Heller .....Creative Executive
Mike Weber .....Creative Executive

RADIANT PRODUCTIONS
914 Montana Ave., 2nd Fl.
Santa Monica, CA 90403
PHONE 310-656-1400
FAX 310-656-1408
TYPES Features
DEALS Warner Bros. Pictures
CREDITS Troy - The Perfect Storm - Air Force One - Outbreak - In the Line of Fire - Das Boot - The Agency

Wolfgang Petersen .....Director/Producer (310-656-1401)
Diana Rathbun .....Producer, Radiant Productions (310-656-1405)
Samuel Dickerman .....President, Radiant Productions (310-656-1403)
Kimberly Miller .....Creative Executive (310-656-1400)
Barbara Huber .....Assistant to Mr. Petersen (310-656-1401)

It is illegal to copy any part of this book

THE RADMIN COMPANY
9201 Wilshire Blvd., Ste. 305
Beverly Hills, CA 90210
PHONE .310-274-9515
FAX .310-274-0739
EMAIL .info@radmincompany.com
SECOND EMAIL .queries@radmincompany.com
TYPES Features - TV Series
DEVELOPMENT One Neck
CREDITS Next Best Thing - The Fantasticks - Twisted
SUBMISSION POLICY Fax or email

Linne Radmin .Producer
Ashley Berns .Development Executive
Susanna Bieger .Creative Executive
Ben Stebor .Story Editor
Jason Rich .Administrative Assistant

RAFFAELLA PRODUCTIONS, INC.
14320 Ventura Blvd., Ste. 617
Sherman Oaks, CA 91423
PHONE .310-472-0466
FAX .310-471-6315
TYPES Features - Direct-to-Video/DVD - Made-for-TV/Cable Movies - TV Series
CREDITS Prancer Returns - Daylight - Dragonheart - Dragon: Bruce Lee Story - Dragonheart: A New Beginning - Uprising - Skypilot and the World of Tomorrow

Raffaella De Laurentiis .President/Producer
Hester Hargett .Executive VP/Co-Producer

RAINBOW FILM COMPANY/RAINBOW RELEASING
9165 Sunset Blvd., Ste. 300
Los Angeles, CA 90069
PHONE .310-271-0202
FAX .310-271-2753
EMAIL .rainbow@rainbowfilms.com
WEB SITE .www.rainbowreleasing.com
TYPES Features
CREDITS Monty Python and the Holy Grail (Re-Release) - Deja Vu - Mistress - Eating - Last Summer in the Hamptons - Love After Love - New Year's Day - Babyfever
COMMENTS Distribution; Deal with Revere Entertainment, London

Henry Jaglom .President
Judith Wolinsky .Producer/Development
Sharon Lester Kohn .VP, Distribution

RAINDANCE PICTURES
45 N. Broad St., Ste. 402
Ridgewood, NJ 07450
PHONE .201-444-9700
FAX .201-444-6486
TYPES Features
DEVELOPMENT Hanomag - The Big Promise - Anna Down East
CREDITS American Saint - A Chill in the Air - Detention

Fred Strype .Producer/President
Joe Dishner .Producer

RAINSTORM ENTERTAINMENT, INC.
16027 Ventura Blvd., Ste. 600
Encino, CA 91436
PHONE .818-784-7500/818-382-3450
FAX .818-382-3445/818-382-3451
EMAIL .gldaniel@rainstormentertainment.com
SECOND EMAIL .steve@rainstormentertainment.com
WEB SITE .www.rainstormentertainment.com
SECOND WEB SITE .www.thebigempty.com
TYPES Documentaries - Features
DEVELOPMENT The Green Falcon - Kingz - Juggernaut - Sometimes Life is Hard
PRE-PRODUCTION Frost Bites
PRODUCTION F***: The Documentary
CREDITS Terror Tract - The Big Empty

Steven G. Kaplan .President/Producer
Gregg L. Daniel .Creative Executive/Producer

PEGGY RAJSKI PRODUCTIONS
918 Alandele Ave.
Los Angeles, CA 90036
PHONE .323-634-7020
FAX .323-634-7021
EMAIL .rajskip@sbcglobal.net
TYPES Features
CREDITS Home for the Holidays - Used People - Little Man Tate - Matewan - The Brother from Another Planet - The Scoundrel's Wife - The Grifters - Eight Men Out

Peggy Rajski .Producer/Director

RAKONTUR
11111 Biscayne Blvd., Ste. 222
Miami, FL 33181
PHONE .305-788-9676
FAX .253-660-3594
EMAIL .alfred@rakontur.com
TYPES Documentaries - Features - TV Series
PRODUCTION Dont' Let Them F*** with You (Documentary)
POST PRODUCTION Cocaine Cowboys (Documentary)
CREDITS Raw Deal: A Question of Consent
SUBMISSION POLICY By agent or manager only

Billy Corben .Co-Chairman
Alfred Spellman .Co-Chairman
David Cypkin .Head, Development/Production

DAVID RAMBALDI ENTERPRISES
PO Box 1149
Sugarloaf, CA 92386
PHONE .909-584-2453
FAX .909-584-7404
TYPES Documentaries - Features - Direct-to-Video/DVD - Made-for-TV/Cable Movies - New Media - Syndication - TV Series
DEVELOPMENT Fresh Water Terror - The John Brown Story - Gulf Command
PRODUCTION Mermaid Stories
POST PRODUCTION Ancient Petroglyphs of California
CREDITS Slave Master - Eyes of the Beholder - Celebrity Fishing the West

David Rambaldi .President
Neil Rambaldi .Executive Sr. VP
Stacey Jones .VP, Creative Affairs

RANDAN PRODUCTIONS, INC.
10424 Cheviot Dr.
Los Angeles, CA 90064-4408
PHONE .310-838-8883
FAX .310-842-4884

TYPES	Animation - Features - New Media - TV Series
CREDITS	Suspect - Race for Glory - Impromptu - Donor - All Lies End in Murder
COMMENTS	Seeking distribution and co-production partners

Daniel A. Sherkow .President
Randi Sunshine .VP, Development

RANDWELL PRODUCTIONS
11111 Santa Monica Blvd., Ste. 525
Los Angeles, CA 90025
PHONE .310-996-6809
FAX .310-473-4376
EMAIL .randwellprods@yahoo.com
WEB SITE .www.randwell.com

TYPES	Features - Made-for-TV/Cable Movies
CREDITS	The Pact - Profoundly Normal - Amelia Earhart: The Final Flight - Sealed with a Kiss - See You in My Dreams - Two Mothers for Zachary

Randy Robinson .President/Executive Producer
Tom Kageff .VP

*RAPID HEART PICTURES, LTD.
776 Corydon Ave., Ste. 746
Winnipeg, Manitoba R3M 0Y1 Canada
PHONE .204-292-6066
EMAIL .rapidheart2003@yahoo.com
WEB SITE .www.rapidheart.com

TYPES	Features - TV Series
DEALS	Here! Films - Regent Entertainment, Inc.
DEVELOPMENT	The Brotherhood 4 - Voodoo Academy 2 - Freakshow - Killer Bash
PRE-PRODUCTION	Too Cool for Christmas
POST PRODUCTION	The Sisterhood - Witches of the Caribbean
COMPLETED UNRELEASED	Ring of Darkness
CREDITS	Puppetmaster 3 - Leather Jacket Love Story - The Brotherhood - Final Stab - The Frightening - Speed Demon - Prehysteria 3 - The Brotherhood 2: Young Warlocks
SUBMISSION POLICY	No unsolicted manuscripts; Via email only

David DeCoteau .Director/Producer
K.C. Murray .Assistant to Mr. DeCoteau

BONNIE RASKIN PRODUCTIONS
c/o Jaffe/Braunstein Films
12301 Wilshire Blvd., Ste. 110
Los Angeles, CA 90025
PHONE .310-826-3171
FAX .310-207-6069
EMAIL .bonnie@jbfl.net

TYPES	Made-for-TV/Cable Movies - TV Series
DEVELOPMENT	Toxic Love - Lost at Sea - Murder in Mississippi
CREDITS	Killing Mr. Griffin - The Tempest - Prince William - America's Prince: The John F. Kennedy, Jr. Story

Bonnie Raskin .Executive Producer

RAT ENTERTAINMENT/RAT TV
9255 Sunset Blvd., Ste. 310
Los Angeles, CA 90069
PHONE .310-228-5000
FAX .310-860-9251

TYPES	Features - TV Series
DEALS	New Line Cinema
CREDITS	After the Sunset - Red Dragon - Rush Hour 1&2 - The Family Man - Money Talks

Brett Ratner .Director/Producer/Chairman
Jay Stern .President
John Cheng .Head, Feature Development
Jennifer Nieves .Story Editor
Anita S. Chang .Executive Assistant to Mr. Ratner
Frank Slesinski .Office Manager/Executive Assistant to Mr. Stern
Lauren Abrahams .Assistant to Mr. Cheng

RAW/PROGRESSIVE FILMS
6430 Sunset Blvd., 10th Fl.
Hollywood, CA 90028
PHONE .323-301-4200
FAX .323-301-4201

TYPES	Commercials - Features - Music Videos
CREDITS	AutoFocus - A Man Apart
COMMENTS	Finance

Joseph Nittolo .CEO
Guy Pham .COO/Partner
Brian Oliver .President, Co-Chairman/Feature Division
Rubin Mendoza .President, Music Video Division/Partner
Marshall Rawlings .President, Commercial Division/Partner
Diana Vance .President, Production
Tracy Mercer .Sr. VP, Production & Development
Brent Coert .Executive Producer, Music Videos
Dana Marshall .Producer, Music Videos
John Randolph .Producer, Music Videos
Rob Johnson .Directors' Representative
Tommy LaBuda .Directors' Representative
Sabrina Rivera .Directors' Representative
Kathy Bickel .Director, Finance
Robyn Heath .Creative Executive
Melissa Everett .Coordinator, Commercials
Claude Maluenda .Accounting
David Benjamin .Vault Manager
Gina Corona .Assistant Directors' Representative
Tiffany Dejillo .Assistant
Cecy Galvan .Assistant
Kat O'Connell .Assistant
Alex Patton .Office Assistant

RAYGUN PRODUCTIONS
6565 Sunset Blvd., Ste. 416
Hollywood, CA 90028
PHONE .323-993-0080
FAX .323-993-0088

TYPES	Features
DEVELOPMENT	The Prestige - Revolver
CREDITS	Memento - Donnie Darko - The Mexican

Aaron Ryder .Producer
Carolyn Harris .Creative Executive

REARGUARD PRODUCTIONS, INC.
8306 Wilshire Blvd., Ste. 488
Beverly Hills, CA 90211-2382
PHONE .323-937-1570

TYPES	Features - Made-for-TV/Cable Movies
CREDITS	Tales from the Crypt - Dr. Who and the Daleks - Dr. Terror's House of Horrors - Survive the Savage Sea - Land That Time Forgot - Rock, Rock, Rock! - Langrishe, Go Down - The Wannsee Conference
SUBMISSION POLICY	Call first

Max J. Rosenberg .President/Producer
Julie G. Moldo Jones .VP

RECORDED PICTURE COMPANY
7001 Melrose Ave.
Los Angeles, CA 90038
PHONE . . . 323-937-0733/44-207-636-2251
FAX . . . 323-936-4913/44-207-636-2261
EMAIL . . . rpc@recordedpicture.com
TYPES Features
DEVELOPMENT Stray - Super-Cannes - Synchro - Tideland - The System
CREDITS Sexy Beast - The Last Emperor - Rabbit Proof Fence - Stealing Beauty - The Brave - Crash - Beseiged - All the Little Animals - Brother - The Cup - The Triumph of Love - The Dreamers - Young Adam
COMMENTS London office: 24 Hanway St., London W1T 1UH UK

Jeremy Thomas . . . Producer/Chairman
Peter Watson . . . CEO/Business Affairs
Stephan Mallman . . . COO/Finance
Alexandra Stone . . . Sr. VP/Head, Development
Hercules Bellville . . . Head, Development
Florence Larsonneur . . . Business Affairs Executive
Richard Mansell . . . Business Affairs Executive
Stuart Cooke . . . Company Accountant
Karin Padgham . . . Executive Assistant to Jeremy Thomas
Matthew Baker . . . Assistant to Alexandra Stone
Julia Willis . . . Assistant to Peter Watson & Stephan Mallman
Sue Peacock . . . Assistant to Stuart Cooke
Simone Study . . . LA Office
Dan Gill . . . Runner

RED BIRD PRODUCTIONS
3623 Hayden Ave.
Culver City, CA 90232
PHONE . . . 310-202-1711
TYPES Features - Theater - TV Series
DEVELOPMENT Behind the Glass - I Sought My Brother
PRE-PRODUCTION Pepito's Story
POST PRODUCTION Fame
CREDITS Amistad - Out of Sync - Cool Women - Pepito's Story (Theater)

Debbie Allen . . . President/Actor/Director/Producer

RED BOARD PRODUCTIONS
3000 W. Olympic, Bldg. 4, Ste. 1200
Santa Monica, CA 90404
PHONE . . . 310-264-4285
FAX . . . 310-264-4286
TYPES TV Series
DEALS Paramount Television
CREDITS Big Apple - Deadwood

David Milch . . . Executive Producer/Writer
Zack Whedon . . . Assistant to Mr. Milch

RED DIAMOND COMPANY
270 N. Canon Dr., Ste. 1845
Beverly Hills, CA 90210
PHONE . . . 310-228-3105
FAX . . . 310-274-7957
EMAIL . . . reddiamond12@hotmail.com
TYPES Features - Syndication - TV Series

Rene Sheridan . . . Producer

RED HEN PRODUCTIONS
3607 W. Magnolia, Ste. L
Burbank, CA 91505
PHONE . . . 818-563-3600
FAX . . . 818-787-6637
EMAIL . . . goridich@aol.com
TYPES Features - Direct-to-Video/DVD - Made-for-TV/Cable Movies - New Media - Syndication
DEVELOPMENT Envy - Stuart Gordon Presents - Ladies Night - Edmond
CREDITS King of the Ants - Deathbed - Dagon - Space Truckers - The Wonderful Ice Cream Suit - Honey, I Shrunk/Blew Up the Kid(s) - Re-Animator - Fortress
SUBMISSION POLICY Send a brief synopsis

Stuart Gordon . . . Director/Writer/Producer

RED HORSE FILMS
432 N. Sycamore Ave., Ste. 4
Los Angeles, CA 90036
PHONE . . . 323-937-9626
EMAIL . . . gbiddle@redhorsefilms.com
TYPES Features
DEVELOPMENT Tug of War - Tetro
CREDITS 2 by 4 - Psycho Beach Party

Virginia Biddle . . . Producer/Partner
John Hall . . . Producer/Partner

RED HOUR FILMS
629 N. La Brea
Los Angeles, CA 90036
PHONE . . . 323-602-5000
TYPES Features
DEALS DreamWorks SKG
CREDITS Duplex - Zoolander - The Ben Stiller Show - Reality Bites - The Cable Guy - Dodge Ball - Starsky and Hutch
SUBMISSION POLICY No unsolicited material

Ben Stiller . . . Writer/Director/Producer
Stuart Cornfeld . . . Producer
Rhoades Rader . . . Director, Development
Lara Hannay . . . Development
Will Klein . . . Story Editor
Liz Mahoney . . . Assistant to Ben Stiller
Helen Harlan . . . 2nd Assistant to Ben Stiller
Jim Doyle . . . Assistant to Stuart Cornfeld

RED OM FILMS, INC.
16 W. 19th St., 12th Fl.
New York, NY 10011
PHONE . . . 212-243-2900
FAX . . . 212-243-2973
TYPES Documentaries - Features - Made-for-TV/Cable Movies - Reality TV - TV Series
DEALS Revolution Studios
DEVELOPMENT Without a Net - What Price Beauty - Perfect Stranger - Strange Son - Slammer - Maid in Manhattan (TV Series) - Butterfly - Apartment 4C
PRODUCTION American Girl
CREDITS Little Black Book - Mona Lisa Smile - Stepmom - Maid in Manhattan
SUBMISSION POLICY No unsolicited submissions

Julia Roberts . . . Actor/Producer
Deborah Schindler . . . President/Partner
Marisa Yeres . . . Development

RED STROKES ENTERTAINMENT
9465 Wilshire Blvd., Ste. 319
Beverly Hills, CA 90212
PHONE 310-786-7887
FAX 310-786-7827
TYPES Features - TV Series
CREDITS Call Me Claus (TNT)

Garth Brooks ....Talent/Producer
Lisa Sanderson ....CEO/Producer/Partner
Cindy Tarassoly ....Executive Assistant to Ms. Sanderson

RED WAGON ENTERTAINMENT
c/o Sony Pictures Studios
10202 W. Washington Blvd., Hepburn Bldg.
Culver City, CA 90232-3195
PHONE 310-244-4466
FAX 310-244-1480
TYPES Animation - Features - TV Series
DEALS Sony Pictures Entertainment
DEVELOPMENT American Caesar - Lone Ranger - Flint - Hannibal - Gladiator 2 - Don't Ask - RV - Alien Prison - Fertig - Dreadnought - Man Camp
PRE-PRODUCTION Memoirs of a Geisha - Bye Bye Birdie - Bewitched - Jarhead
CREDITS Wolf - Working Girl - The Craft - Hollow Man - Girl, Interrupted - Gladiator - Spy Game - Stuart Little 1&2 - Stuart Little (HBO Animated Series) - Peter Pan - Win a Date with Tad Hamilton

Douglas Wick ....Producer
Lucy Fisher ....Producer
Bobby Cohen ....President
Rachel Shane ....Executive VP, Creative Affairs
Michael Milberg ....Creative Executive
Tia Maggini ....Story Editor
Amy Peltonen ....Assistant to D. Wick
Natasha Klibansky ....Assistant to D. Wick
Meghan Snyder ....Assistant to L. Fisher
Sarah Blain ....Assistant to L. Fisher
Stacey Beck ....Assistant to B. Cohen
Rachel Miller ....Assistant to R. Shane
Ashley Jordan ....Receptionist
Lulu Frasquillo ....Runner

RED-HORSE PRODUCTIONS
6028 Calvin Ave.
Tarzana, CA 91356
PHONE 818-705-2588/818-705-4905
FAX 818-705-4969
EMAIL ....redhorse88@aol.com
WEB SITE ....www.naturallynative.com
TYPES Documentaries - Features - Made-for-TV/Cable Movies - New Media - TV Series
DEALS PBS - Valhalla Motion Pictures
DEVELOPMENT First Plant - Seventh Generation - Lozen - True Whispers: The Story of the Navajo Code Talkers
POST PRODUCTION Pop Hunter's Dew Drop Inn
CREDITS True Whispers - Naturally Native - Windows on Mars - Living Voices
COMMENTS Deal with Native American Public Telecommunications/PBS

Valerie Red-Horse ....President/Writer/Director/Producer/Actor
Dawn Jackson ....VP/Development/Producer
Pam Auer ....Business/Legal
Audrey Felton ....Executive Assistant

DAN REDLER ENTERTAINMENT
5303 Penfield Ave.
Woodland Hills, CA 91364
PHONE 818-999-0786
TYPES Features - Direct-to-Video/DVD - Made-for-TV/Cable Movies - New Media - Syndication - TV Series
DEALS Millennium Films
DEVELOPMENT Trust No One - Nowhere Man - Breakback - Brothers in Arms
PRE-PRODUCTION Proving Ground - Ice Men - The Delivery
CREDITS Profile for Murder - In His Father's Shoes - Pygmalion

Dan Redler ....Producer

REELVISION ENTERTAINMENT
299 Ocho Rios Way
Agoura, CA 91377
PHONE 818-879-8084
FAX 818-706-2878
WEB SITE ....www.reelvisionentertainment.com
TYPES Features - Made-for-TV/Cable Movies - Music Videos - New Media - Reality TV - Syndication - TV Series
DEALS Riche Productions
DEVELOPMENT Abominable - Beyond the Fields - Into the Groove - The Black Seam - Sleuth - Roadies
PRE-PRODUCTION Illegal Music - Homeland
CREDITS Fortress 1&2

Steven Feinberg ....Co-Chairman (310-927-8611)
Zane Zidel ....Co-Chairman
Josh Richmond ....Assistant to the Producers

MARIAN REES ASSOCIATES
12400 Ventura Blvd., Box 225
Studio City, CA 91604
PHONE 818-508-5599
FAX 818-508-8012
EMAIL ....vantageave@aol.com
TYPES Features - Direct-to-Video/DVD - Made-for-TV/Cable Movies
DEALS Lifetime Television (Los Angeles)
DEVELOPMENT Bet Me - Lighthouse at the End of the World - Meant to Be - Doña Ana's Funeral - Just Breathe
CREDITS In Pursuit of Honor (HBO) - Miss Rose White - Decoration Day - Love is Never Silent (Hallmark) - Ruby Bridges (Wonderful World of Disney) - Papa's Angels (CBS) - Sign of the Beaver - ExxonMobil Masterpiece Theatre - The American Collection

Marian Rees ....CEO/Executive Producer
Anne Hopkins ....President/Producer
Dyan Austin Conway ....Business Affairs
Alisa Gosselin ....Assistant

REGANMEDIA
10 E. 53rd St.
New York, NY 10022
PHONE 212-207-7400
FAX 212-207-7973
EMAIL ....reganbooks@harpercollins.com
WEB SITE ....www.reganbooks.com
TYPES Features - TV Series
CREDITS Microserfs - The Dive - I Know This Much Is True - The Other Man - Growing Up Gotti

Judith Regan ....President/Publisher
Jason Puris ....VP Development/Production (212-207-7204)

REGENCY ENTERPRISES
10201 W. Pico Blvd., Bldg. 12
Los Angeles, CA 90035
PHONE .310-369-8300
FAX .310-969-0470
WEB SITE www.newregency.com
TYPES Features
DEALS Twentieth Century Fox
PRODUCTION Elektra - Little Manhattan
POST PRODUCTION Mr. & Mrs. Smith - The Onion - Bee Season - First Daughter - Stay
CREDITS L.A. Confidential - The Client - Entrapment - A Time to Kill - Fight Club - Heat - Big Momma's House - Don't Say a Word - Unfaithful - Daredevil - Man on Fire

Arnon Milchan .Producer
David Matalon .President/CEO
Sanford Panitch .President, Filmed Entertainment
Louis Santor .Executive VP/CFO
William S. Weiner .Executive VP, Business & Legal Affairs/General Counsel
Peter Cramer .Executive VP, Production
Thomas Imperato .Executive VP/Head, Physical Production
Robert S. Corzo .Sr. VP, Finance
Kara Francis .Sr. VP, Production
Elissa Loparco .Sr. VP, Post Production
Michael H. Brown .VP, Marketing
Alexandra Milchan-Lambert .VP, Acquisitions
Andrea Shay .VP, Development & Current Programming
Stacy Maes .VP, Production
Alexa Amin .Director, Production
Heidi Sherman .Creative Executive
Alexandra Sundell .Creative Associate
Chad Freet .Production Administrator

REGENT ENTERTAINMENT, INC.
10990 Wilshire Blvd., Penthouse
Los Angeles, CA 90024
PHONE .310-806-4288
FAX .310-806-4268
WEB SITE www.regententertainment.com
TYPES Features - Direct-to-Video/DVD - Made-for-TV/Cable Movies
DEVELOPMENT Mad Crush - Too Cool for Christmas - Urgency - The Enforcer - Chupacabra
PRE-PRODUCTION Witches of the Caribbean
PRODUCTION The Legend of Pitfighter
CREDITS Brittanic - Gen-Y Cops - Gods & Monsters - I'll Remember April - Nostradamus - Hot Zone - Xtreme Mountain - Friends & Family - Sordid Lives - Tom & Viv - Cave In - Tornado Warning - Paradise Virus - A Good Night to Die - The Hunting of the President
COMMENTS 12-18 TV/Cable movies per year; Thrillers, Action, Horror, Family

Paul Colichman .Chairman
Stephen P. Jarchow .CEO
Jeff Schenck .President, Regent Studios
Gene L. George .President, Regent International
John Lambert .President, Acquisitions/Theatrical Distribution
Mark Reinhart .Executive VP
Judith Merians .Sr. VP, Business & Legal Affairs, International
Meredith Kadlec .Director, Development

REHME PRODUCTIONS
1007 Broxton Ave., Ste. 210
Los Angeles, CA 90024
PHONE .310-824-3371
FAX .310-824-5459
EMAIL rehmeprod@earthlink.net
TYPES Features - Made-for-TV/Cable Movies - TV Series
CREDITS Gettysburg - Patriot Games - Clear & Present Danger - Deacons for Defense - Gods and Generals

Robert Rehme .Principal

TIM REID PRODUCTIONS, INC.
One New Millennium Dr.
Petersburg, VA 23805-8907
PHONE .804-957-4200
FAX .804-862-1200
EMAIL jarene@nmstudios.com
WEB SITE www.nmstudios.com
SECOND WEB SITE www.timreidproductions.com
TYPES Commercials - Documentaries - Features - Direct-to-Video/DVD - New Media - Syndication - TV Series
PRE-PRODUCTION American Legacy
CREDITS American Legacy Television - About Sarah - Linc's - Blue Moon - The Contender - For Real (Feature)
SUBMISSION POLICY No unsolicited submissions
COMMENTS Additional Web site: www.americanlegacy.tv

Tim Reid .President
Daphne Reid .VP
Jarene Fleming .Production Executive

REINER/GREISMAN
335 N. Maple Dr., Ste. 135
Beverly Hills, CA 90210
PHONE .310-285-2300
TYPES Features
DEALS Castle Rock Entertainment
CREDITS A Few Good Men - American President - When Harry Met Sally - Soap Dish - Alex and Emma

Rob Reiner .Director/Producer (310-285-2328)
Alan Greisman .Producer (310-205-2766)
Keith Lesser .No Title (310-205-2776)
Pam Jones .Assistant to Rob Reiner (310-285-2352)

RELISH PRODUCTIONS
212 S. Rexford Dr.
Beverly Hills, CA 90212
PHONE .310-275-2540
FAX .310-276-6955
EMAIL mk@karzen.com
WEB SITE www.karzen.com
TYPES Features - Reality TV - TV Series
DEVELOPMENT Click Clack - Twine - Rolling - Coffee Please
POST PRODUCTION Montgomery - Home Shopping
CREDITS MAD TV (Fox) - Polo (Fox) - Steeplechase (Outdoor Life Network) - Letterman (NBC)

Marc Karzen .Director/Writer/Producer

RENAISSANCE PICTURES
315 S. Beverly Dr., Ste. 216
Beverly Hills, CA 90212
PHONE 310-785-3900
FAX 310-785-9176
TYPES Features - Direct-to-Video/DVD - Syndication - TV Series
CREDITS Evil Dead - Hard Target - A Simple Plan - The Gift - Hercules - Xena - Cleopatra 2525 - Jack of All Trades - Spider-Man

Sam Raimi . . . . Director/Executive Producer
Robert Tapert . . . . Executive Producer
Michael Kirk . . . . VP, Development
Sue Binder . . . . Business Manager
David Pollison . . . . Assistant

RENEGADE 83
5700 Wilshire Blvd., 6th Fl.
Los Angeles, CA 90046
PHONE 323-954-9077
FAX 323-954-9075
TYPES TV Series - Reality TV
DEVELOPMENT Cover Girl - The 4400 - The Complete Asshole's Guide to Life
CREDITS Blind Date - The 5th Wheel - The Surreal Life

David Garfinkle . . . . Partner
Jay Renfroe . . . . Partner
Maira Suro . . . . Head, Scripted TV
Greg Goldman . . . . Director, Development

RENEGADE ANIMATION, INC.
116 North Maryland Ave., Lower Level
Glendale, CA 91206
PHONE 818-551-2351
EMAIL . . . . ashley@renegadeanimation.com
WEB SITE . . . . www.renegadeanimation.com
SECOND WEB SITE . . . . www.renegadecartoons.com
TYPES Animation - Commercials - TV Series
CREDITS Captain Sturdy in Back in Action - Captain Sturdy in The Originals
SUBMISSION POLICY By query letter only
COMMENTS Flash animation

Darrell Van Citters . . . . President/Director
Ashley Q. Postlewaite . . . . VP/Executive Producer

RENFIELD PRODUCTIONS
c/o The Lot
1041 N. Formosa Ave., Writer's Bldg., Ste. 321
West Hollywood, CA 90046
PHONE 323-850-3905
FAX 323-850-3907
TYPES Features - New Media - TV Series
CREDITS Looney Tunes: Back in Action - Gremlins 1&2 - Innerspace - Deceived - Matinee - 2nd Civil War - Small Soldiers

Michael Finnell . . . . Producer/President
Joe Dante . . . . Director
Betty Moos . . . . Assistant to Joe Dante & Michael Finnell

REPERAGE
333 S. Beverly Dr., Ste. 100
Beverly Hills, CA 90212
PHONE 310-552-1275
FAX 310-552-1276
TYPES Features
DEVELOPMENT Future Evolution - Mary Read - Tripoli
COMPLETED UNRELEASED Two Brothers
CREDITS Enemy at the Gates - Seven Years in Tibet - Wings of Courage - The Lover - The Bear
COMMENTS Paris office: 12 rue Lincoln, Paris 75008 France

Jean-Jacques Annaud . . . . Director/Producer/Writer
Ben Spector . . . . Director, Development

REVEAL ENTERTAINMENT
1663 Euclid St.
Santa Monica, CA 90404
PHONE 310-581-5914
TYPES Commercials - Features - TV Series
POST PRODUCTION Lemony Snicket's A Series of Unfortunate Events
CREDITS Moonlight Mile - City of Angels - Casper

Brad Silberling . . . . Director/Producer/Writer
Minor Childers . . . . VP, Production
Sarah Hendler . . . . Assistant to Brad Silberling
Brian Buller . . . . Assistant

REVEILLE, LLC
100 Universal City Plaza, Bungalow 5180/5170
Universal City, CA 91608
PHONE 818-733-1218/212-413-5515
FAX 818-733-3303/212-413-6554
TYPES Documentaries - Features - Reality TV - Syndication - TV Series
CREDITS The Restaurant - Coupling - Nashville Star - Blow Out - Adrenaline X - The Office - House Wars
COMMENTS East Coast office: 1230 Sixth Ave., 20th Fl., New York, NY 10020

Benjamin Silverman . . . . CEO
Dave Mayer . . . . Executive VP, Business Affairs
Howard Owens . . . . Sr. VP, Creative Affairs/Intl. Distribution
Mark Koops . . . . VP, Creative Affairs & Distribution
Teri Weinberg . . . . VP, Current Programming
Christopher Grant . . . . Director, International Distribution

It is illegal to copy any part of this book

REVELATIONS ENTERTAINMENT

301 Arizona Ave., Ste. 303
Santa Monica, CA 90401
PHONE .310-394-3131
FAX .310-394-3133
EMAIL .ytaylor@revelationsent.com
WEB SITE .www.revelationsent.com

TYPES: Features - Made-for-TV/Cable Movies - New Media - TV Series
DEVELOPMENT: 761st Tank Battalion Project - Straight Up! - Simple City (TV/Cable) - Circle William - Ellis Jump - Rendezvous with Rama - Roses Are Red - The Long Ride - Long Walk to Freedom
CREDITS: Along Came a Spider - Bopha! - Mutiny - Under Suspicion - Levity
COMMENTS: Morgan Freeman's Publicist: Bizcuit Publicity, Inc., 2918 Santa Monica Blvd., Ste. D, Santa Monica, CA 90404, 800-523-3155, dlee@selahmedia.com

Morgan Freeman .President/Actor/Producer
Lori McCreary .CEO/Producer
Yvette Taylor .Executive VP
Kelly Mendelsohn .Manager, Production
Jill Goularte .Assistant to Yvette Taylor
Geanne Frank .Business Consultant
Stuart Hammer .Business Manager
Meg Madison .Production Photographer

REVOLUTION STUDIOS

2900 W. Olympic Blvd.
Santa Monica, CA 90404
PHONE .310-255-7000/212-243-2900
EMAIL .info@revolutionstudios.com
WEB SITE .www.revolutionstudios.com

TYPES: Features
DEALS: Sony Pictures Entertainment
COMMENTS: East Coast office: 16 W. 19th St., 12th Fl., New York, NY 10011

REYNOLDS ENTERTAINMENT

2938 Oakhurst Ave.
Los Angeles, CA 90034
PHONE .310-836-9000
FAX .310-836-9292
EMAIL .info@reynoldsent.com
WEB SITE .www.reynoldsent.com

TYPES: Features - Made-for-TV/Cable Movies
DEVELOPMENT: Rain on the Wind - Icefields - Greensleeves
PRE-PRODUCTION: Five Fingers
POST PRODUCTION: Fly Boys
CREDITS: Soul Assassin - Retroactive - Silent Hearts - Princess of Thieves - The Unsaid

Kelley Feldsott Reynolds .Partner
Patrick F. Reynolds .Partner
John Caire .Writer/Director
Ra'uf Glasgow .Writer/Director
Jackie Feldman .Assistant, Development/Acquistions

RH FACTOR

8491 Sunset Blvd., Ste. 329
Los Angeles, CA 90069
PHONE .323-860-6637
FAX .707-788-4927
EMAIL .rh-factor@earthlink.net

TYPES: Documentaries - Features - Made-for-TV/Cable Movies - Syndication - TV Series - Reality TV
DEVELOPMENT: Caravan - Sea Dog - Berg - Southbound - W.T. Knob
PRE-PRODUCTION: Untitled Horror Project
CREDITS: The Trial of Old Drum (Feature) - Emergency Vets (Series) - Lover Girl (Feature) - Jack London's Call of the Wild (Series) - Vendetta (Feature) - Kindred Spirits (Documentary)

Ross Hammer .Producer/Writer

RHYTHM & HUES STUDIOS

5404 Jandy Pl.
Los Angeles, CA 90066
PHONE .310-448-7500
FAX .310-448-7603
EMAIL .jonic@rhythm.com
WEB SITE .www.rhythm.com

TYPES: Animation - Commercials - Features - New Media - TV Series
DEVELOPMENT: 100 Bullets - Armour Star - Walnut
PRE-PRODUCTION: The Lion, The Witch and The Wardrobe
PRODUCTION: The Ring 2
POST PRODUCTION: Friday Night Lights
CREDITS: VFX: Cat in the Hat - Elf - Daredevil - Babe 1&2 - Cats & Dogs - Scooby-Doo - Sum of All Fears - X2 - The Rundown - Intolerable Cruelty - Garfield - Scooby Doo 2 - Around the World in 80 Days - Chronicles of Riddick
SUBMISSION POLICY: No unsolicited submissions
COMMENTS: Character animation; Visual effects; Theme parks

Richard E. Hollander .President, Film Division
Lee Berger .VP, Production/Executive Producer
Mark Brown .VP, Technology
Pauline Ts'o .VP, Development
Scot Byrd .Public Relations
Judi Affleck .Assistant to Richard Hollander
Joni Cantrell .Assistant to Lee Berger

RICE & BEANS PRODUCTIONS

30 N. Raymond, Ste. 605
Pasadena, CA 91103
PHONE .626-792-9171
FAX .626-792-9171
EMAIL .vin88@pacbell.net

TYPES: Animation - Features - Made-for-TV/Cable Movies - New Media - TV Series
DEVELOPMENT: Animated Pilot (Disney Channel)
CREDITS: In the House - Night Court - Roc - Growing Pains - Married with Children - Empty Nest - Between Brothers - The Steve Harvey Show - Greetings from Tucson
COMMENTS: Internet entertainment

Vince Cheung .Writer/Producer
Ben Montanio .Writer/Producer

RICHE PRODUCTIONS

4171 Wilshire Blvd., 3rd Fl.
Los Angeles, CA 90010
PHONE 323-549-4393
FAX 323-549-9821
TYPES Features
DEALS Mandalay Pictures
DEVELOPMENT Tarzan - Books of Magic - Human Target - Where's Waldo - Cannon Ball Run - Aquaman
CREDITS Starsky and Hutch - Tomcats - The Family Man - Deep Blue Sea - Sweet Water - Mouse Hunt - The Mod Squad - Empire Records

Alan Riche ....Partner
Peter Riche ....Partner
Jennifer Smith ....Development Associate
Jeanne Thompson ....Creative Executive

RICOCHET ENTERTAINMENT

10202 W. Washington Blvd., Poitier Bldg., Ste. 3214
Culver City, CA 90232
PHONE 310-244-8065
FAX 310-244-1720
TYPES Features - TV Series
DEALS Columbia Pictures
DEVELOPMENT Guilty Pleasure - Honeymoon - Unseen - Trouble in Toyland - Viva Lefty - The Swap - Grown Ups - Henry Trotter and the Sorcerer's Balls - Ten on Sunday - Dean's List
CREDITS The Sweetest Thing - Double Vision

Ricky Strauss ....Producer
Lisa Ullmann ....VP, Development
Karen Switzenbaum ....Assistant
Brian Miller ....Assistant

RIDINI ENTERTAINMENT CORPORATION

c/o Raleigh Studios
650 N. Bronson Ave.
Los Angeles, CA 90004
PHONE 323-960-8071/818-884-0104
FAX 818-884-7902
WEB SITE ....www.ridinientertainment.com
TYPES Features - Made-for-TV/Cable Movies - Syndication - TV Series
DEVELOPMENT When Life Begins
PRE-PRODUCTION The Last Valentine
CREDITS Future Fear - Shepherd - Falling Fire - Convict 762
COMMENTS Public Relations; Talent Management

Maryann Ridini ....President

ANTHONY RIDIO PRODUCTIONS, INC.

500 Avenue G
Redondo Beach, CA 90277
PHONE 310-316-8652
TYPES Features - Made-for-TV/Cable Movies - TV Series
DEVELOPMENT Some Rainy Day - Astral Agent - Runaround - Deadly Exchange - Clone Rebels - Clear Shot
PRE-PRODUCTION Billy Hatchett
CREDITS Free Jack - Hellbound

Anthony Ridio ....CEO/Producer
R. Ellis Frazier ....Writer/Production Executive
Ian Rabin ....VP/Director, Development
Philip Georgious ....Manager, Development
Ed Golden ....Development
Stephanie Nichols ....Development
Kelly Ridio ....Development
Rosemary Torigian ....Story Editor

RIGHT ANGLE STUDIOS

4712 Admiralty Way, Ste. 244
Marina del Rey, CA 90232
PHONE 310-823-3764
FAX 310-823-3164
WEB SITE ....www.rightanglestudios.com
TYPES Features - Made-for-TV/Cable Movies - New Media
DEVELOPMENT He Will Come - The Select - Trick or Treat

Jon Fitzgerald ....President
Cindy Green ....Marketing

RITA FILMS

1044 S. Hayworth Ave.
Los Angeles, CA 90035
PHONE 323-935-8666
EMAIL ....veraanderson@comcast.com
WEB SITE ....www.thedogwalker.com
TYPES Documentaries - Features - Reality TV
DEVELOPMENT The Shark - Feeling Randy - Antarctica - A Woman Like You - Fresh - The Go-Go Boys
CREDITS The Dogwalker
SUBMISSION POLICY No unsolicited submissions

Vera Anderson ....Partner/Producer
Paul Duran ....Partner/Writer/Director

RIVE GAUCHE INTERNATIONAL TV

15442 Ventura Blvd., Ste. 101
Sherman Oaks, CA 91403
PHONE 818-784-9912
FAX 818-784-9916
EMAIL ....rivegaucheint@cs.com
WEB SITE ....www.rgitv.com
TYPES Documentaries - Reality TV - TV Series
DEALS Film Garden Entertainment, Inc. - LMNO Productions - Morningstar Entertainment - MPH Entertainment, Inc.
CREDITS Wild Weddings 3 - DNA: Guilty or Innocent - Amazing Animal Videos - The World's Wildest Commercials - Battleground - Forty Deuce - Wild on the Set - 101 Things Removed from the Body - The Littlest Groom - That's Just Wrong
COMMENTS Termite Art Productions; Kaos Entertainment; Hallock Healey Productions; Renegade Productions; Tri Crown Productions

Ronald Glazer ....President
Mark Rafalowski ....COO
Christiane Nicolini ....VP
Sharon Beverly ....Director, Development

RIVER ONE FILMS
132 W. 23 St., Ste. 1
New York, NY 10011
PHONE 917-748-6834
FAX 212-929-1848
EMAIL . . . . riveronefilms@yahoo.com
TYPES Features - Made-for-TV/Cable Movies
DEVELOPMENT The Member-Guest - La Boda Negra - Blue Lips - Miss Christina
PRE-PRODUCTION Spring Break Chain Gang - A Tale of Two Horses
COMPLETED UNRELEASED Sunburn
CREDITS Tumbleweeds - The Jack Bull - Watch It

Thomas J. Mangan IV . . . . President

***RIVERROCK ENTERTAINMENT GROUP**
3974 Cloverleaf St.
Westlake Village, CA 91362
PHONE 805-778-0224/805-778-0225
FAX 805-496-0915
TYPES Documentaries - Features
DEVELOPMENT Staying Fat for Sarah Byrnes - The Style of Integrity: Martin Ritt

Martina Ritt . . . . Owner/Producer/Director
Betsy Fels . . . . Producer/Development

RIVET ENTERTAINMENT, LLC
221 Rose Ave.
Venice, CA 90291
PHONE 310-452-9830
FAX 310-450-1277
EMAIL . . . . info@rivetentertainment.com
WEB SITE . . . . www.rivetentertainment.com
TYPES Documentaries - Made-for-TV/Cable Movies - TV Series
DEVELOPMENT The Decision to Drop the Bomb (Discovery)
POST PRODUCTION Deconstruction: The Science of Building a House (Science Channel)
CREDITS Before We Ruled the Earth (Discovery Docudrama Series) - Walking with Cavemen (Discovery)

Bill Latka . . . . Executive Producer
Nicoline Storey . . . . Production Coordinator

RJN PRODUCTIONS, INC.
2934-1/2 Beverly Glen Circle, Ste. 394
Bel Air, CA 90077
PHONE 310-859-2770
FAX 310-859-2946
EMAIL . . . . rjnproductions@adelphia.net
TYPES Features
DEVELOPMENT Slouching Towards L.A. (Feature) - Tag You're It
CREDITS Double Exposure - Executive Power - Totally Blonde
COMMENTS 35mm and digital feature films

Richard J. Naegele . . . . President
Diane Driscoll . . . . Producer
Brian Trausch . . . . Producer
William R. Murray . . . . VP, Operations

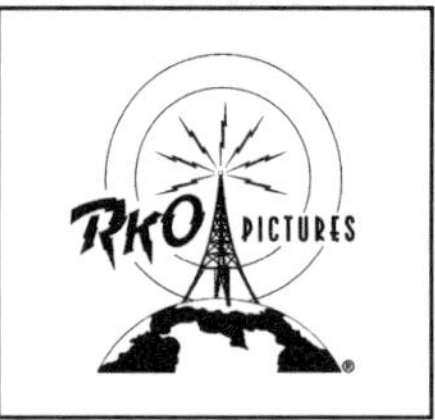

RKO PICTURES, LLC
1875 Century Park East, Ste. 2140
Los Angeles, CA 90067
PHONE 310-277-0707/212-644-0600
FAX 310-226-2490
EMAIL . . . . info@rko.com
WEB SITE . . . . www.rko.com
TYPES Animation - Documentaries - Features - Direct-to-Video/DVD - Made-for-TV/Cable Movies - New Media
DEVELOPMENT The Locked Room - Beyond a Reasonable Doubt - Suspicion - Mr. Blandings Builds His Dream House - The Rig - The Monkey's Paw
COMPLETED UNRELEASED Shade
CREDITS Mighty Joe Young - The Magnificent Ambersons - Milk & Money - A Holiday Affair - Ritual
COMMENTS East Coast office: 3-E. 54th St., 12th Fl., New York, NY 10022

Ted Hartley . . . . Chairman/CEO
Dina Merrill . . . . Vice Chairman
Aaron Ray . . . . Chief Strategy Officer/Board Member
Jonathan Marshall . . . . COO/General Counsel
Kevin Harris . . . . Sr. VP, Finance
Ray Reyes . . . . Attorney, Business & Legal Affairs
Sam Marshall . . . . Manager, Business Development

ROBBINS ENTERTAINMENT
75 Second Ave., Ste. 200
Needham, MA 02494
PHONE 781-449-8800
FAX 781-449-6573
EMAIL . . . . mitchell@robbinsentertainment.com
TYPES Features
DEVELOPMENT A Certain Smile
CREDITS Squeeze - The Darien Gap - Next Stop Wonderland - XX/XY

Mitchell B. Robbins . . . . President
Susan L. Welsh . . . . VP, Production

DOLORES ROBINSON ENTERTAINMENT
9250 Wilshire Blvd., Ste. 220
Beverly Hills, CA 90212
PHONE 310-777-8777
FAX 310-777-8780
TYPES Features - Made-for-TV/Cable Movies - TV Series
CREDITS Matt Waters - Southern Fried Ice - Between Brothers
COMMENTS Talent manager

Dolores Robinson . . . . President/Partner/Producer
Ben Hasler . . . . Development
Aichi Ali . . . . Assistant

AMY ROBINSON PRODUCTIONS

101 Fifth Ave., 8th Fl., Ste. R
New York, NY 10003
PHONE .212-645 9811
FAX .212-645-9810
EMAIL .amyrobinsonprod@aol.com
TYPES Features
CREDITS Chilly Scenes of Winter - With Honors - Once Around - Running on Empty - Drive Me Crazy - For Love of the Game - Autumn in New York - From Hell - White Palace - Baby It's You - After Hours

Amy Robinson .Producer
Gabrielle Cran .Director, Development

ROCKET SCIENCE LABORATORIES

8441 Santa Monica Blvd.
West Hollywood, CA 90069
PHONE .323-802-0500
FAX .323-802-0599
EMAIL .rsl@rocketsciencelabs.com
TYPES Documentaries - Features - Made-for-TV/Cable Movies - Syndication - TV Series - Reality TV
CREDITS My Big Fat Obnoixous Fiance - Joe Millionaire 1&2 - Married by America - M*A*S*H: 30th Anniversary - Temptation Island 1&2 - Images of Life: Photographs That Changed the World
COMMENTS Formerly ZM & ZMC Productions

Jean-Michel Michenaud .Partner/Executive Producer
Chris Cowan .Partner/Executive Producer
Charles Duncombe .Head, Production
Tracy Geyer .Production Supervisor
Charles Steenveld .Head, Business Affairs
Alex Demyanenko .Head, Development

ROCKING HORSE PRODUCTIONS

2934-1/2 Beverly Glen Circle, Ste. 445
Bel Air, CA 90077
PHONE .310-315-4868
EMAIL .rockinghorse7@earthlink.net
TYPES Features - Made-for-TV/Cable Movies - TV Series
DEVELOPMENT Crossing the Line
PRE-PRODUCTION Undercurrent - Crook Factory
CREDITS Stranger in the Kingdom - Hollywood Sign - The Last Tzaddik - In the Kingdom of the Blind - The Man with One Eye Is King - FearX
SUBMISSION POLICY Email synopsis

Eugene Davis .Partner
Penny Perry Davis .Partner

ROCKSTONE PICTURES

1800 Century Park East, Ste. 600
Los Angeles, CA 90067
PHONE .310-260-2587
FAX .310-260-2588
EMAIL .info@rockstonepics.com
WEB SITE .www.rockstonepics.com
TYPES Features - TV Series
DEALS HBO Original Programming
DEVELOPMENT Rice & Peas - Jimmy Wounderful - S.E.X. - The Family Stone
PRE-PRODUCTION Holla
CREDITS Sister Sessions - Ten Benny - Restaurant

H.M. Coakley .Partner
Camille Irons .Partner
James Wong .Director, Development
Skye Smith .Assistant to Producers

STAN ROGOW PRODUCTIONS

3000 Olympic Blvd., Bldg. 3, Rm. 1436
Santa Monica, CA 90404
PHONE .310-264-4199
TYPES Features - Made-for-TV/Cable Movies - TV Series
DEALS NBC Entertainment
CREDITS Nowhere Man - The Defenders - Nowhere to Hide - Shannon's Deal - Middle Ages - Lizzie McGuire - State of Grace

Stan Rogow .Executive Producer
Robin Lippin .Casting Director

ROGUE CREATIVE/VFX

30 Irving Pl., 6th Fl.
New York, NY 10003
PHONE .212-475-4466/212-475-4463
FAX .212-475-8671
EMAIL .dan@rogue-creative.com
SECOND EMAIL .nick@rogue-creative.com
WEB SITE .www.rogue-creative.com
TYPES Animation - Commercials - Features - Direct-to-Video/DVD - Music Videos - New Media - Promos - Reality TV - TV Series
COMMENTS Special Effects

Nick Litwinko .Executive Producer
Dan O'Brien .Sr. Producer
Fran Roberts .Director

PHIL ROMAN ENTERTAINMENT

4450 Lakeside Dr., Ste. 250
Burbank, CA 91505
PHONE .818-985-1200
FAX .818-985-2668
EMAIL .sales@romanent.com
WEB SITE .www.philromanent.com
TYPES Animation - Features - Direct-to-Video/DVD - New Media - TV Series
CREDITS Howdi Gaudi - Atomic Betty - Grandma Got Run Over by a Reindeer - Christmas in Gaudinia
COMMENTS Development and production of Spanish language projects

Phil Roman .President/CEO

ROMANO SHANE PRODUCTIONS

2893 Sea Ridge
Malibu, CA 90265
PHONE .310-456-3444
FAX .310-456-1166
EMAIL .michel@romanoshaneproductions.com
WEB SITE .www.romanoshaneproductions.com
TYPES Features - Made-for-TV/Cable Movies - Reality TV - TV Series
DEVELOPMENT Outfit - Me & My Cannoli's - Leonardo - Fixed - Dog Eat Dog
PRE-PRODUCTION Friends Again - Band on the Run - The Italian - Vinyl
CREDITS Catch Me If You Can - North Fork - Stealing Time - The Lost Treasures of the Titanic - Dracula: Live from Transylvania - I, Robot
COMMENTS Co-financing; Foreign Sales; Deal with Brass Hat (UK)

Anthony Romano .Co-President/Producer
Michel Shane .Co-President/Producer
Nadine Maren Schoenweitz .Head, Development

It is illegal to copy any part of this book

ROPE THE MOON PRODUCTIONS
421 N. Rodeo Dr.
Beverly Hills, CA 90210
PHONE .310-276-9559
FAX .310-276-9449
TYPES Documentaries - Features - Made-for-TV/Cable Movies
CREDITS Grand Champion - In a Whisper

Amanda Micallef .Producer
Lawren Sunderland .Creative Executive
Julie Cannon .Development

ALEX ROSE PRODUCTIONS, INC.
8291 Presson Pl.
Los Angeles, CA 90069
PHONE .323-654-8662
FAX .323-654-0196
TYPES Features - TV Series
DEVELOPMENT The Wonder 5 - Greased - I'm Pretty Sure I Might Have a Fear of Committment
CREDITS The Other Sister - Exit to Eden - Frankie & Johnny - Quigley Down Under - Overboard - Nothing in Common - Norma Rae - Big Wednesday - Nothing in Common (Series) - Just Us Kids (TV)

Alexandra Rose .President
Manuela Goulden .Development

LEE ROSE PRODUCTIONS
421 N. Robertson Blvd.
West Hollywood, CA 90048
PHONE .310-659-2050
TYPES Features - Made-for-TV/Cable Movies - TV Series
DEVELOPMENT My Last Day on Earth (Feature)
COMPLETED UNRELEASED Jack (Showtime)
CREDITS What Girls Learn - A Mother's Prayer - Nothing Personal - An Unexpected Family - The Color of Courage - The Truth About Jane - An Unexpected Life - A Girl Thing - An Unexpected Love

Lee Rose .Executive Producer/Writer/Director
Justine O'Neill .Director, Development

ROSEMONT PRODUCTIONS INTERNATIONAL, LTD.
6625 Variel Ave., Ste. 204
Canoga Park, CA 91303
PHONE .818-676-3606
TYPES Made-for-TV/Cable Movies - TV Series
DEVELOPMENT Night Over Water
PRODUCTION Into the West (Miniseries)
CREDITS The Winning Season - Door to Door - Purgatory - The Secret Garden - What Love Sees - High Noon - For All Time - The Wool Cap

Norman Rosemont .Executive Producer
David A. Rosemont .Executive Producer
Sheri Williams (aka Brummond) .Director, Development

ZVI HOWARD ROSENMAN PRODUCTIONS
635-A Westbourne Dr.
Los Angeles, CA 90069
PHONE .310-659-2100
EMAIL .bigzr@aol.com
TYPES Documentaries - Features - Made-for-TV/Cable Movies - TV Series
DEVELOPMENT Eagle's Wings - Foul Play - Ten Good Men - Park Avenue Ghost - Life of an Honest Man - Gloria & Doria Gray - Trapped - Fenwick's Suit - Slammer - American Neurotic - Cat 'n' Mouse - Grace Metallious - Trophy Boys - Crim Law
PRE-PRODUCTION Master of Longwood
POST PRODUCTION Noel

Zvi Howard Rosenman .President

GAY ROSENTHAL PRODUCTIONS
1438 N. Gower St., Box 16
Hollywood, CA 90028
PHONE .323-468-3300
FAX .323-468-3301
TYPES Documentaries - Reality TV - TV Series
CREDITS TV's Most Memorable Weddings (NBC) - Child Stars: Then and Now (NBC) - VH1's Behind the Music - Inside TV Land - TNN's Fame for 15 - NBC's 20 Years of Must See TV - Friends Season Finale Special - Frasier Season Finale Special

Gay Rosenthal .President/Executive Producer
Paul Barrosse .Executive Producer
Nicholas Caprio .Executive VP, Programming & Production
Robyn Olson .Finance
Robert Zimmerman .Associate Producer
Eric Almaguer .Executive Assistant
Troy Combs .Executive Assistant

ROSSWWMEDIA, CORPORATION
11444 Washington Blvd., Ste. C227
Los Angeles, CA 90066
PHONE .310-276-5160
WEB SITE .www.rosswwmedia.com
TYPES Features - Direct-to-Video/DVD - Made-for-TV/Cable Movies - New Media - Theater - TV Series
DEVELOPMENT Hangman's Point - Unleashed - Murder in China Red
PRE-PRODUCTION DeSade - The List
CREDITS The Buddy Holly Story - Beneath Loch Ness

Alex Ross .CEO
Fred T. Kuehnert .President, Production
Brandon A. Lopez .Story Editor
Martin Gostanian .Story Department
Elizabeth Villalobos .Story Department
Lisa Vogel .Story Department

HEIDI ROTBART MANAGEMENT
1810 Malcolm Ave., Ste. 207
Los Angeles, CA 90025
PHONE .310-470-8339/310-880-7656
FAX .310-446-8610
EMAIL .hrotbartmgt@aol.com
TYPES Features - Made-for-TV/Cable Movies - Syndication - TV Series - Reality TV
DEVELOPMENT Debbie Puente Untitled Project
COMMENTS Specializes in the Hispanic market

Heidi Rotbart .Partner/President
Lori Morrison .Assistant to Heidi Rotbart

ROTH/ARNOLD PRODUCTIONS
2900 W. Olympic Blvd., Ste. 132
Santa Monica, CA 90404
PHONE .310-255-7005
FAX .310-255-7004

TYPES	Features
DEALS	Revolution Studios
DEVELOPMENT	Dinner for Two - Our Man in Indiana - Christmas in Connecticut - Avon Ladies of the Amazon - Bring on the Bling
CREDITS	Grosse Pointe Blank - Unstrung Heroes - Benny & Joon - Forces of Nature - America's Sweethearts - 13 Going on 30

Donna Arkoff Roth .Principal (310-255-7005)
Susan Arnold .Principal (310-255-7005)
Desi Van Til .Director, Development (310-255-7014)
David Saltzman .Development (310-255-7005)

ROUGH DIAMOND PRODUCTIONS
1424 N. Kings Rd.
Los Angeles, CA 90069
PHONE .323-848-2900
FAX .323-848-8142

TYPES	Features
DEVELOPMENT	Mighty John L. - Confidence Game - Lola Montez - Jumper - Wavelength
PRE-PRODUCTION	The Last Lagoon
POST PRODUCTION	Blast - Riding the Bullet - Slipstream
COMPLETED UNRELEASED	I Witness
CREDITS	Stander - Temptation - The Set Up - Past Perfect - A Matter of Trust - A Breed Apart - Detour - The Contaminated Man - In Pursuit - Styx - The Shipment - Greenmail - Pavement - Consequence

Julia Verdin .President/Partner/Producer
Bill Kravitz .President, Production
Zachary Weintraub .Director/Producer

ROUGH DRAFT STUDIOS
209 N. Brand Blvd.
Glendale, CA 91203
PHONE .818-507-0491
FAX .818-507-0486
WEB SITE .www.roughdraftstudios.com

TYPES	Animation - Commercials - Features - TV Series
DEVELOPMENT	Vinyl Cafe (CBS Pilot) - Nancy Stellar (Cartoon Network)
CREDITS	Drawn Together (Comedy Central) - Futurama (Fox) - Baby Blues (WB) - The Maxx (MTV) - Star Wars Clone Wars (Cartoon Network & Lucasfilm Ltd.)
COMMENTS	Emmy Award winning animation studio, specializing in the blend of traditional and computer animation

Gregg Vanzo .President
Claudia Katz .Producer/Partner
Rich Moore .Director/Partner
Scott Vanzo .Director, CGI/Partner

ROUNDTABLE INK
1720-1/2 Whitley Ave.
Los Angeles, CA 90028
PHONE .323-466-4646
FAX .323-466-1884

TYPES	Features - TV Series
DEVELOPMENT	Deep Core - Greek Girl's Guide to War - Phobic - Untitled USA Network Project (TV) - The Suck (TV)
POST PRODUCTION	The Mountain (TV)
CREDITS	Jake 2.0 - What Women Want - The Chronicle (TV) - Urban Legend 1&2 - Summer's End - The Wishing Tree - Popular (TV) - 13 Going on 30

Gina Matthews .Partner/Producer
Grant Scharbo .Partner/Producer

RSF PRODUCTIONS
11105 Acama St., Ste. 19
Studio City, CA 91602
PHONE .213-399-1700
FAX .707-982-0745
EMAIL .rsfproductions@aol.com

TYPES	Features - Direct-to-Video/DVD - Made-for-TV/Cable Movies - Syndication - TV Series - Reality TV
CREDITS	Dark Wolf - Redemption of the Ghost - Ground Zero - Can't Be Heaven - Street Knight

Richard Friedman .Director/Writer/Producer
Richard Sindell .Producer

RUBIN * BURKE PRODUCTIONS
c/o The Studio
636 12th St.
Manhattan Beach, CA 90266
PHONE .323-276-4052/310-702-2703

TYPES	Made-for-TV/Cable Movies - Features - TV Series

Shawn Burke-Kawabe .Producer/Partner
Marjorie Rubin .Producer/Partner
Dagney Cardinale .Assistant

RUBY-SPEARS PRODUCTIONS
3500 W. Olive Ave., Ste. 300
Burbank, CA 91505
PHONE .818-840-1234
FAX .818-885-6251
EMAIL .rsproductions@earthlink.net
WEB SITE .www.rubyspears.com

TYPES	Animation - Features - Syndication - TV Series
DEVELOPMENT	Cannibal - Rubbadubba - The Arm - Speed Grunge - The Super T's
CREDITS	Rumpelstiltskin - Jirimpimbira - Slammin' Sammy: The Sammy Sosa Story
COMMENTS	Animation consultants; Production services

Joseph Ruby .President/Executive Producer
Kenneth Spears .VP/Executive Producer

SCOTT RUDIN PRODUCTIONS

c/o Paramount Pictures
5555 Melrose Ave., DeMille Bldg., Ste. 100
Los Angeles, CA 90038
PHONE .323-956-4600/212-704-4600
FAX .323-862-0262
TYPES Features
DEALS Paramount Pictures-Motion Picture Group
CREDITS Iris - The Royal Tenenbaums - The Hours - Zoolander - First Wives Club - Clueless - The Firm - In and Out - The Truman Show - Sleepy Hollow - Wonder Boys - Shaft - South Park: Bigger, Longer & Uncut - School of Rock
COMMENTS East Coast office: 120 W. 45th St., 10th Fl., New York, NY 10036

Scott Rudin .Producer (NY)
Scott Aversano .President (LA) (323-956-5911)
Mark Roybal .Sr. VP (LA)
John Delaney .VP (NY)
Chris Cussen .Director, Development (NY)
Michael Ellenberg .Director, Development (LA) (323-956-4662)
Kelly McCormick .Story Editor (NY)
Connor Price .Executive Assistant to Scott Rudin (NY)
Will Russell-Shapiro .Executive Assistant to Scott Aversano (LA)
Jules Eggli .Assistant to Scott Rudin
Ted Cella .Assistant to Scott Rudin
Adam Rosenberg .Assistant to Scott Rudin
Aaron Janus .Assistant to Scott Rudin
Paul Roemen .Assistant to Scott Rudin
Sam Cassel .Story Editor (LA)

RUPERT PRODUCTIONS, INC.

3760 Grandview Blvd.
Los Angeles, CA 90066
PHONE .310-390-9360
FAX .310-390-9620
EMAIL .ooglerupe@aol.com
WEB SITE .www.grandviewfilms.com
TYPES Documentaries - Features - Direct-to-Video/DVD - Made-for-TV/Cable Movies - New Media - Syndication - TV Series - Reality TV
DEALS World Film Services, Inc.
DEVELOPMENT Happy Faces - A Simple Road - Community Property
PRE-PRODUCTION Roseto, Roseto
CREDITS Nowhere Land - Electra Glide in Blue - Last Dragon - Wolfen - Snakes and Ladders - Liar, Liar - NASCAR's Victory Lane (Foxsports Net) - The Squeeze - Happy Birthday Gemini - JAWS 3-D - Much Ado About Nothing
COMMENTS Game shows

Rupert Hitzig .President

S PICTURES, INC.

4420 Hayvenhurst Ave.
Encino, CA 91436
PHONE .818-995-1585/310-866-7977
FAX .818-995-1677
EMAIL .chuck.simon@stoneworkstv.com
WEB SITE .www.stoneworkstv.com
TYPES Features - Direct-to-Video/DVD - Made-for-TV/Cable Movies - Reality TV - Syndication - TV Series
DEVELOPMENT Wrongfully Accused (CBS) - The Whale - Weekly World News - LOL - The Asylum - Furnace
PRE-PRODUCTION Stealing Tennessee - Dead in the West - Tributemania
CREDITS Terminal Invasion (SCI FI Channel) - Control Factor (SCI FI Channel)
SUBMISSION POLICY Release required

Chuck Simon .President/Producer
Christine M. Torres .VP, Creative Affairs
Mary-Liz Thomson .Director, Development

ALAN SACKS PRODUCTIONS, INC.

11684 Ventura Blvd., Ste. 809
Studio City, CA 91604
PHONE .818-752-6999
FAX .818-752-6985
EMAIL .asacks@pacbell.net
TYPES Documentaries - Features - Made-for-TV/Cable Movies - TV Series
CREDITS Pixel Perfect - The Color of Friendship - Smart House - The Other Me - You Wish - Welcome Back Kotter

Alan Sacks .Producer

SALTY FEATURES

104 W. 14th St., 4th Fl.
New York, NY 10011
PHONE .212-924-1601
FAX .212-924-2306
EMAIL .info@saltyfeatures.com
WEB SITE .www.saltyfeatures.com
TYPES Features
DEVELOPMENT Jernigan - Bam Bam and Celeste - Valparaiso - Signs of Life - The Brutal Language of Love
COMPLETED UNRELEASED Evergreen
CREDITS Boys Don't Cry - Rhinoceros Eyes - Breaker - My Architect
SUBMISSION POLICY No unsolicited submissions

Eva Kolodner .Producer
Yael Melamede .Producer

SAMOSET, INC./SACRET, INC.

127 Broadway, Ste. 220
Santa Monica, CA 90401
PHONE .310-458-1618
FAX .310-458-4037
TYPES Features - Made-for-TV/Cable Movies - TV Series
DEVELOPMENT Untitled JSY Military Series (Showtime)
CREDITS Bronx County - Sirens - Orleans - Texarkana - VR5 - Romero - Testament - China Beach - Thanks of a Grateful Nation - Level 9 - King of the World - Champions - Rumor of War - Keys - Pentagon Papers - The West Wing - Deceit (Lifetime)
SUBMISSION POLICY No unsolicited submissions

John Sacret Young .Writer/Director/Producer
Jacqueline Horn .CFO
Sean Molloy .Researcher/Executive Assistant to Mr. Young

SAMUEL GOLDWYN FILMS
9570 W. Pico Blvd., Ste. 400
Los Angeles, CA 90035
PHONE .310-860-3100/212-367-9435
FAX .310-860-3195/212-367-0853
TYPES Features
DEVELOPMENT Goshawk Squadron - The Secret Life of Walter Mitty
CREDITS Super Size Me - He Loves Me, He Loves Me Not - Raising Victor Vargas - Japanese Story
COMMENTS East Coast office: 1133 Broadway, Ste. 926, New York, NY 10010

Samuel Goldwyn Jr. .Chairman of the Board/CEO
Meyer Gottlieb .President
Julie Huey .VP, Development
Peter Goldwyn .Director, Acquisitions
Tamara Lecker .Manager, Development/Acquisitions (NY)
Rorri Feinstein Executive Assistant to Samuel Goldwyn Jr. & Meyer Gottlieb

RON SAMUELS ENTERTAINMENT, INC.
120 El Camino Dr., Penthouse
Beverly Hills, CA 90212
PHONE .310-273-8964
FAX .310-273-9208
TYPES Features - TV Series
CREDITS Downtown (CBS) - Jane Doe (USA) - Ravenhawk - Iron Eagle 1-3 - Scruples - A Different Affair

Ron Samuels .Producer

SAMUELSON PRODUCTIONS LIMITED
10401 Wyton Dr.
Los Angeles, CA 90024-2527
PHONE .310-208-1000/44-207-439-4900
FAX .310-208-2809/44-207-439-4901
EMAIL .petersam@who.net
SECOND EMAIL .mjwsam@aol.com
WEB SITE .www.oscarwilde.com
SECOND WEB SITE .www.firststar.org
TYPES Features
CREDITS Wilde - Revenge of the Nerds - Tom & Viv - Turk 182 - Arlington Road - Dog's Best Friend - The Commissioner - Gabriel and Me - Playmaker - The Gathering - Things to Do Before You're 30
COMMENTS See also www.starlight.org, www.star-bright.org; London head office: 13 Manette St., London W1V 5LB UK

Peter Samuelson .No Title
Marc Samuelson .No Title
Saryl Hirsch .Controller
Viktorjia Parr .Producers' Assistant
Jessica Parker .Producers' Assistant
Renato Celani .Assistant

SANCTUARY
7221 Pacific View Dr.
Los Angeles, CA 90068
PHONE .323-850-7550
EMAIL .sanctuarymedia@hotmail.com
TYPES Documentaries - Features
SUBMISSION POLICY No unsolicited submissions

Charles Daguerre Alvaré .President/Producer
Carrie Rudolf .Production Executive

SANDBOX ENTERTAINMENT
116 N. Robertson Blvd., Ste. 400
Los Angeles, CA 90048
PHONE .310-967-6451
FAX .310-854-0383
TYPES Features - TV Series
DEALS New Line Cinema
DEVELOPMENT Action Abramowitz - Killer Instinct - Graff - Connecting with Jack Gabriel - Humbuggin'

Noah Emmerich .Producer
Daniel Schnider .Director, Development

SANDER/MOSES PRODUCTIONS, INC.
4695 White Oak Ave.
Encino, CA 91316
PHONE .818-906-7074
FAX .818-906-7170
EMAIL .ian@sandermoses.com
SECOND EMAIL .kim@sandermoses.com
WEB SITE .www.sandermoses.com
TYPES Features - Made-for-TV/Cable Movies - New Media - Reality TV - TV Series
DEVELOPMENT Chitown - The Surgeon - Basement Boys
CREDITS Frankenstein - For the People - Profiler - The Beast - How to Marry a Billionaire - Brimstone - Ali: An American Hero - Chasing The Dragon - New York News - Stolen Babies - I'll Fly Away - D.O.A. - Everybody's All American - How'd They Do That? - Extreme Edge - Comic Strip Live/Primetime MTV Awards
COMMENTS Internet Programming

Ian Sander .Executive Producer/Writer/Director
Kim Moses .Executive Producer/Writer/Director

SANDSTORM FILMS
3733 Motor Ave., Ste. 200
Los Angeles, CA 90034
PHONE .310-838-8004
FAX .310-838-8065
TYPES Features
COMPLETED UNRELEASED Sniper 3 - Vampires: Temple of Blood - Mummy an' the Armadillo - The Nutcracker and Mouseking
CREDITS Sniper 2 - Alien Hunter - True Blue - The Forsaken - Outside - Ozona - Black Day Blue Night - Shadowhunter - Exit in Red - Climate for Killing - Thunder Alley - Shadowzone - The Slayer - Crash and Burn

J.S. Cardone .Partner
Scott Einbinder .Partner
Carol Kottenbrook .Partner
Dylan Tarason .Production Associate
Daniel Manus .Development Associate

SANFORD/PILLSBURY PRODUCTIONS

2932 Wilshire Blvd., Ste. 202
Santa Monica, CA 90403
PHONE .310-449-4520
FAX .310-899-9809
TYPES Features - Made-for-TV/Cable Movies - New Media - TV Series
PRE-PRODUCTION Cherries - Quid Pro Quo
CREDITS Desperately Seeking Susan - River's Edge - Eight Men Out - And the Band Played On - How to Make an American Quilt - The Love Letter

Sarah Pillsbury .Producer
Midge Sanford .Producer
Deborah Goodwin .Director, Development

SAPHIER PRODUCTIONS

4245 Valley Meadow Rd.
Encino, CA 91436
PHONE .818-501-3531
FAX .818-995-6554
EMAIL .psaphier@mindspring.com
TYPES Features - TV Series
DEVELOPMENT Creation - Chippendales - The Devil's Breath - Amateur Night at the Apollo - Birdmen - Smoke and Mirrors (TV Pilot) - Siren's Dance
CREDITS Black Dog - Scarface - Eddie Macon's Run - Four Seasons (TV)

Peter Saphier .Principal

SARABANDE PRODUCTIONS

715 Broadway, Ste. 210
Santa Monica, CA 90401
PHONE .310-395-4842
FAX .310-395-7079
TYPES Made-for-TV/Cable Movies - Features - Syndication - TV Series
CREDITS Birdy - Bring on the Night - Mad Love - Nothing Sacred - Thicker Than Blood - Nightjohn - Baby - The Wedding Dress

David Manson .President
Arla Sorkin Manson .Executive VP
Aaron Graff .Director, Development

ARTHUR SARKISSIAN PRODUCTIONS

9255 Sunset Blvd., Ste. 340
West Hollywood, CA 90069
PHONE .310-385-1486
FAX .310-385-1171
TYPES Features - TV Series
DEALS Metro-Goldwyn-Mayer Studios, Inc.
DEVELOPMENT Rush Hour 3 - Starring Vic - Defiant Ones - Red Circle - El Cid - Red Sun - Christmas Robbers - Champagne - You Must Remember This - Again - Weddingville - The Street - Hi Dharma - Between the Covers - Two Lucky People - Prince Test - Nobody's Home
CREDITS Rush Hour 1&2 - Last Man Standing - While You Were Sleeping - Wanted Dead or Alive

Arthur Sarkissian .Producer
Peter Sussman .VP, Development
Tina Sutakanat .Creative Executive
Brad Baker .Development Assistant

SATURN FILMS

9000 Sunset Blvd., Ste. 911
West Hollywood, CA 90069
PHONE .310-887-0900
FAX .310-248-2965
TYPES Features
PRODUCTION Lord of War
CREDITS Sonny - Shadow of the Vampire - The Life of David Gale - Family Man

Nicolas Cage .CEO/Producer
Norm Golightly .President/Producer
Seth Schur .Director, Development
Jen Bosworth .Office Manager
Matt Summers .Story Editor/Assistant to Norm Golightly
Stephen Bures .Assistant to Nicolas Cage
Houston Parker .Assistant to Nicolas Cage

SAVOIR FAIRE PRODUCTIONS

1025 Chautauqua Blvd.
Pacific Palisades, CA 90272
PHONE .310-459-6191
FAX .310-459-6491
EMAIL .savfair@earthlink.net
TYPES Documentaries - Features - New Media - Theater - TV Series
CREDITS Wee Singdom - Hanimals - Landslide - A Bissele Nacht Musik - God
COMMENTS Affiliated with Team Studio/European Film Partners; Opera

Rebekah Jorgensen .Producer/Director/Co-Chair, Women In Film Int'l

SCARAB PRODUCTIONS

PO Box 4617
North Hollywood, CA 91617-0617
PHONE .818-766-6418
FAX .818-487-0584
TYPES Animation - Features - TV Series
DEVELOPMENT Goosetown - Borrowed Time - Just My Luck - Little Legends - The Jester's Son - The Amazing Henry
CREDITS Cats Don't Dance - Disney's House of Mouse - Disney's 101 Dalmations (Series)
SUBMISSION POLICY No unsolicited material

Rick Schneider .Producer/Writer/Director
Terry Notary .Producer
Jason Lethcoe .Writer
Joann Estoesta .Assistant

SCARLET FIRE ENTERTAINMENT

9401 Alcott St.
Los Angeles, CA 90035
PHONE .310-281-3369
FAX .775-255-6928
EMAIL .fireflix@aol.com
TYPES Animation - Features - Direct-to-Video/DVD - TV Series
DEVELOPMENT Birds of a Feather - Par 4 the Course
CREDITS Breathe - Resolution - Fore!

Robert Steinberg .Executive Producer/President
Wayne L. Green .VP, New Media
Sara Dobson .Director, Development

SCHACHTER ENTERTAINMENT

1157 S. Beverly Dr.
Los Angeles, CA 90035
PHONE 310-712-3730
FAX 310-277-6602
EMAIL .....ted@schachterent.com
TYPES Features - TV Series
DEVELOPMENT The Pleasure of Your Company - Run, Fat Boy, Run - Raritan Valley Line - Destination: Moon - Sweetness - Diggers - Salt Lake City
CREDITS Homeboys in Outer Space - Bela Donna
COMMENTS Comedy

Ted Schachter .....Principal
Molly Randall .....Executive Assistant
Hogan Carter .....Assistant

EDGAR J. SCHERICK ASSOCIATES, INC.

1950 Sawtelle Blvd., Ste. 282
Los Angeles, CA 90025
PHONE 310-996-2376
FAX 310-996-2392
EMAIL .....info@scherick.com
TYPES Features - Made-for-TV/Cable Movies - TV Series
CREDITS The Stepford Wives - Sleuth - Rambling Rose - Ruby Ridge - The Wall - Path to War - The Stepford Wives (Remake)

Edgar J. Scherick .....Executive Producer/President
Bradford Scherick .....VP
Stephen Abronson .....Director, Development

PAUL SCHIFF PRODUCTIONS

10202 W. Washington Blvd., Astaire Bldg., Ste. 2210
Culver City, CA 90232
PHONE 310-244-5454
TYPES Features - TV Series
DEALS Sony Pictures Entertainment
CREDITS Maid in Manhattan - My Cousin Vinny - Young Guns 1&2 - Rushmore - Black Knight - Mona Lisa Smile - Walking Tall

Paul Schiff .....President/Producer
Tai Duncan .....VP, Production
Sam Alipour .....Creative Executive

GEORGE SCHLATTER PRODUCTIONS

8321 Beverly Blvd.
Los Angeles, CA 90048
PHONE 323-655-1400
FAX 323-852-1640
TYPES TV Series
CREDITS Laugh In - Real People - Sinatra: 80 Years My Way - AFI Life Achievement in Honor of Dustin Hoffman - AFI Life Achievement in Honor of Harrison Ford - Muhammad Ali 60th Birthday Celebration

George Schlatter .....Executive Producer
Maria S. Schlatter .....Co-Producer
Donn Hoyer .....Co-Producer
Gary Necessary .....Executive in Charge of Production
Nathan Golden .....Accounting
Suzzanne Stangel .....Production Manager
James Hunt .....Production Coordinator

SCHOLASTIC ENTERTAINMENT

524 Broadway
New York, NY 10012-3999
PHONE 212-343-7554
FAX 212-343-7888
EMAIL .....cpitsirilos@scholastic.com
WEB SITE .....www.scholastic.com
TYPES Animation - Features - New Media - Syndication - TV Series
PRE-PRODUCTION His Dark Materials
PRODUCTION I Spy
CREDITS Goosebumps - Indian in the Cupboard - The Magic School Bus - Clifford the Big Red Dog - Dear America - Horrible Histories - Clifford's Really Big Movie

Deborah Forte .....President
Ken Olshansky .....Sr. VP, TV Programming
Martha Atwater .....VP, Programming

ADAM SCHROEDER ENTERTAINMENT

1041 N. Formosa Ave., Santa Monica Bldg., Ste. C
Los Angeles, CA 90046
PHONE 323-850-2525
FAX 323-850-2524
TYPES Features
DEVELOPMENT The Fraud Prince - The College Experience - Kleopatra - Kung Fu - Clash of the Titans
PRE-PRODUCTION Emperor Zehnder - Bobby
CREDITS The Truman Show - Sleepy Hollow - A Simple Plan - South Park: Bigger, Longer & Uncut - The First Wives Club - Wonder Boys - Clueless

Adam Schroeder .....President
Micah D. Smith .....Creative Executive

JOEL SCHUMACHER PRODUCTIONS

c/o Warner Bros.
4000 Warner Blvd., Bldg. 139, Rm. 26
Burbank, CA 91522
PHONE 818-954-6100
FAX 818-954-4642
TYPES Features
POST PRODUCTION Phantom of the Opera
CREDITS Director: Batman & Robin - A Time to Kill - Batman Forever - 8mm - Flawless - Tigerland - Bad Company - Phone Booth - Veronica Guerin
SUBMISSION POLICY No unsolicited submissions

Joel Schumacher .....Owner
Eli Richbourg .....Associate Producer
Claire Baker .....Executive Assistant to Joel Schumacher

FAYE SCHWAB PRODUCTIONS/MMA, INC.

9461 Charleville Blvd., Ste. 367
Beverly Hills, CA 90212
PHONE 310-278-4738
FAX 310-278-5006
EMAIL .....fayeschwab@aol.com
WEB SITE .....www.fayeschwab.com
TYPES Features - Made-for-TV/Cable Movies - TV Series
DEVELOPMENT Red Lips, White Lies - The Machinist - PO Box 134 - The Cut-Out Man - Higher - Jay J. Armes - Chris Lucky - Olympus - Betrayal - A Course in Murder - Billy's Voice - The Wedding Dress
CREDITS The Morning After - Chattahoochee - Demolition Man - Love Comes Softly (Hallmark)

Faye Schwab .....President/Producer
Stephanie Seidan .....Director, Development

It is illegal to copy any part of this book

SCHWARTZ & COMPANY, INC.
1223 Wilshire Blvd., Ste. 283
Santa Monica, CA 90403
PHONE 310-394-8227
FAX 310-394-7871
EMAIL . . . . bill@schwartzcompany.com
WEB SITE . . . . www.schwartzcompany.com
TYPES: Animation - Documentaries - Features - Direct-to-Video/DVD - TV Series
DEVELOPMENT: The Rat Pack in Lost Vegas - Me and My Shadows
PRE-PRODUCTION: Secret of Zack's Gullwing - Alexander the Great (Documentary) - Little Mermaid Goes to Hollywood (Animated Feature)
COMPLETED UNRELEASED: Howard Hughes (Documentary)
CREDITS: Snow White & the Magic Mirror - Young Pocahontas - Moses: Egypt's Great Prince - Terror on the Titanic - Secret of Anastasia - Secret of Mulan - Operation Dalmation: The Big Adventure

William A Schwartz . . . . CEO
Sabrina Bassman . . . . Director, Research
Page Ostraw . . . . Finance Director
Diane Breen . . . . Administrative Assistant

STEVEN SCHWARTZ PRODUCTIONS
906 Howard St.
Marina del Rey, CA 90292
PHONE 310-305-8542
TYPES: Features - TV Series
CREDITS: Critical Care - 100 Centre Street - The Practice - A Raisin in the Sun - Likely Stories
SUBMISSION POLICY: No unsolicited submissions

Steven Schwartz . . . . Writer/Producer
Nicki Miller . . . . Director, Development

KRISTINE SCHWARZ PRODUCTIONS
216 W. Quinto St., Ste. 3
Santa Barbara, CA 93105
PHONE 805-565-1625
WEB SITE . . . . www.kristineschwarzproductions.com
TYPES: Documentaries - Features - Direct-to-Video/DVD - Made-for-TV/Cable Movies - New Media - Reality TV - TV Series
DEVELOPMENT: The Deception - The September Alternate - Wolf and Blood - The Roman - Waiting for Good Joe
CREDITS: Kalifornia - Another Stakeout - Disorganized Crime - Raid Gauloises: Race Across the Himalayas
SUBMISSION POLICY: No unsolicited material
COMMENTS: Adventure programming; Psychology consultation for motion picture and TV development and production

Kristine J. Schwarz . . . . Producer

SCI FI CHANNEL
1230 Avenue of the Americas
New York, NY 10020
PHONE 212-413-5000/818-777-1000
FAX 212-413-6509/818-866-1420
WEB SITE . . . . www.scifi.com
SECOND WEB SITE . . . . www.nbcuni.com
TYPES: Animation - Documentaries - Features - Made-for-TV/Cable Movies - Reality TV - TV Series
DEVELOPMENT: Nine Lives Trilogy - The Triangle - The Twelve - Dead Lawyers - Anonymous Rex - Witchhunter Robin - Eureka - Motel Man
CREDITS: Battlestar Galactica - Stargate SG-1 - Stargate Atlantis - Tripping the Rift - Scare Tactics - Proof Positive - Andromeda - Earthsea - Farscape: The Peacekeeper Wars
COMMENTS: West Coast office: 100 Universal City Plaza, Bldg. 1440, 32nd Fl., Universal City, CA 91608

Bonnie Hammer . . . . President, SCI FI Channel & USA Network
David Howe . . . . Executive VP, Marketing & Brand Strategy, SCI FI Channel
Mark Stern . . . . Executive VP, Original Programming, SCI FI Channel
Thomas Vitale . . . . Sr. VP, Programming & Scheduling, SCI FI Channel
Richard Lynn . . . . Sr. VP, Business Affairs/General Counsel, USA Cable
Tony Optican . . . . VP, Development & Current Programming, SCI FI Channel
Erik Storey . . . . VP, Development & Current Programming, SCI FI Channel
Craig Engler . . . . General Manager, SCIFI.COM
Nora O'Brien . . . . Director, Original Scripted Programming, SCI FI Channel
Chris Regina . . . . Director, Programming, SCI FI Channel
Robyn Lattaker-Johnson Director, Alternative Programming, SCI FI Channel
Stuart Swezey . . . . Director, Alternative Programming, SCI FI Channel

SCOTT FREE PRODUCTIONS
634 N. La Peer Dr.
West Hollywood, CA 90069
PHONE 310-360-2250
FAX 310-360-2251
TYPES: Documentaries - Features - Interactive Games - Made-for-TV/Cable Movies - TV Series
DEALS: Twentieth Century Fox
DEVELOPMENT: Emma's War - Domino Diamond Dead
PRODUCTION: The Kingdom of Heaven - In Her Shoes
POST PRODUCTION: Tristan & Isolde
CREDITS: Man on Fire - Black Hawk Down - The Gathering Storm - Crimson Tide - Thelma & Louise - Enemy of the State - Gladiator

Ridley Scott . . . . Co-Chairman
Tony Scott . . . . Co-Chairman
Lisa Ellzey . . . . President
Zach Schiff-Abrams . . . . VP, Production
David Zucker . . . . VP, TV
Erin Upson . . . . Director, Development
Anne Lai . . . . Director, Development
Jordan Sheehan . . . . Executive Assistant to Ridley Scott
Bain McEldowney . . . . Assistant to Ridley Scott
Peter Toumasis . . . . Executive Assistant to Tony Scott
Tom Moran . . . . Assistant to Tony Scott
Ersin Pertan . . . . Assistant to Zach Schiff-Abrams
Shane Starr . . . . Assistant to Lisa Ellzey

SCOUT PRODUCTIONS

119 Braintree St.
Boston, MA 02134
PHONE 617-782-7722/212-581-8200
FAX 617-782-7799/212-581-8310
EMAIL . . . . . info@scoutvision.com
WEB SITE . . . . . www.scoutvision.com
TYPES Documentaries - Features - TV Series - Reality TV
CREDITS The Fog of War - Session 9 - Dead Dog - Private Lies - Mr. Death - Six Ways to Sunday - Home Before Dark - Never Met Picasso - First Person (IFC/Bravo) - Queer Eye for the Straight Guy (Series) - Knock First

David Collins . . . . . Producer/Partner
Michael Williams . . . . . Producer/Partner
Robert Curran . . . . . Head, Production

SCREEN DOOR ENTERTAINMENT

6312 Variel Ave., Ste. 201
Woodland Hills, CA 91367
PHONE 818-887-3001
FAX 818-887-3002
WEB SITE . . . . . www.sdetv.com
TYPES TV Series
CREDITS Insider's Garden - Seasoned Gardener - Room by Room - Outer Spaces - Nitty Gritty - The Look for Spring
SUBMISSION POLICY No phone calls

Joel Rizor . . . . . President/Executive Producer
Nicole Block . . . . . Production Manager
Alessandra Ascoli . . . . . Director, Development & Production
Kevin Mercier . . . . . Post Production Supervisor

SCREEN GEMS

A Sony Pictures Entertainment Company
10202 W. Washington Blvd.
Culver City, CA 90232
PHONE 310-244-4000
TYPES Features

Clinton Culpepper . . . . . President
Benedict Carver . . . . . Sr. VP, Acquisitions & Co-Productions
Stacy Kolker Cramer . . . . . Sr. VP, Production
Gilbert Dumontet . . . . . Sr. VP, Production
Gary Hirsch . . . . . Sr. VP, Business Affairs

SCREENMAGIC ENTERTAINMENT, INC.

PO Box 25164
Los Angeles, CA 90025
PHONE 310-473-4737
FAX 310-473-4927
TYPES Documentaries - Features
DEVELOPMENT Starving Hysterical Naked - The King of B's - Karma Loop - Jamoke - A Journey Through Time (Documentary) - Grace Notes - The Life and Times of Anthony Quinn (Documentary) - Here to Nowhere (Documentary) - Something Different About the Neighbors
CREDITS The Woman Chaser
COMMENTS Independent development and production

Soly Haim . . . . . Producer
Mark Haber . . . . . Director
Josh White . . . . . Development

SEA CLIFF ENTERTAINMENT

431 S. Bedford Dr.
Beverly Hills, CA 90212
PHONE 323-308-3411
TYPES Features - TV Series
DEVELOPMENT Wilbur - Paper or Plastic - Industry Referral Only
PRE-PRODUCTION Under a Satin Sky - The Last Authentic Man in Los Angeles
PRODUCTION Alan Dale's Neighbors
SUBMISSION POLICY No unsolicited submissions

Dana Gold . . . . . President
Anne Shrager . . . . . Director, Development
Jamie Black . . . . . Assistant

SECTION EIGHT PRODUCTIONS

c/o Warner Bros.
4000 Warner Blvd., Bldg. 15
Burbank, CA 91522
PHONE 818-954-4840
FAX 818-954-4860
TYPES Features - TV Series
DEALS Warner Bros. Entertainment Inc. - Warner Bros. Television Production
COMPLETED UNRELEASED The Jacket - Criminal
CREDITS Oceans Eleven - Welcome to Collinwood - Insomnia - Far from Heaven - K Street

George Clooney . . . . . CEO/Partner
Steven Soderbergh . . . . . CEO/Partner
Ben Cosgrove . . . . . President
Jennifer Fox . . . . . President
Grant Heslov . . . . . President, TV
Erika Armin . . . . . Creative Executive
Rachel Eggebeen . . . . . Creative Executive
Amy Minda Cohen . . . . . Assistant to Mr. Clooney
Tara Duncan . . . . . Assistant to Mr. Heslov

SEGUE PRODUCTIONS, INC.

11150 Santa Monica Blvd., Ste. 1200
Los Angeles, CA 90025
PHONE 310-312-1828
FAX 310-231-7014
TYPES Features
CREDITS Restoration - Ransom

Kip Hagopian . . . . . Chairman/President
Pat Papero . . . . . Executive Assistant

SEKRETAGENT PRODUCTIONS

1608 Argyle Ave.
Los Angeles, CA 90028
PHONE 323-462-9900
FAX 323-462-9911
EMAIL . . . . . info@sekretagents.com
WEB SITE . . . . . www.sekretagents.com
TYPES Animation - Features - TV Series
DEVELOPMENT The Wind in the Willows - The Dogs of Babel

Corey May . . . . . Producer
Dooma Wendschuh . . . . . Producer

DYLAN SELLERS PRODUCTIONS

4000 Warner Blvd.
Burbank, CA 91522
PHONE 818-954-4929
TYPES: Features - Made-for-TV/Cable Movies - TV Series
DEALS: Warner Bros. Entertainment Inc.
DEVELOPMENT: The Expendables - Jailhouse Lawyer - Redline - Domestic Affairs - Kung Fu Kids - The Greatest Escape - Fishing for Moonlight - Escape from Libby Prison
POST PRODUCTION: A Cinderella Story
CREDITS: Out to Sea - Passenger 57 - The Paper - The Replacements - Valentine - Agent Cody Banks 1&2

Dylan Sellers .....Producer
Bonny Giardina .....VP
Jesse Ehrman .....Director, Development
Christopher Hogenson .....Creative Assistant

LIZ SELZER-LANG PRODUCTIONS

2801 Ocean Park Blvd., Ste. 215
Santa Monica, CA 90405
PHONE 310-745-0414
FAX 310-745-0413
EMAIL .....lizlangprods@aol.com
TYPES: Features - Made-for-TV/Cable Movies
DEVELOPMENT: Poster Child (Showtime) - My Dark Places (Myriad Pictures) - Morning Meltdown (USA) - Rabbit Stew (Showtime)
CREDITS: Blonde (CBS, Miniseries) - Livin' for Love: The Natalie Cole Story (NBC) - Deadlocked (TNT) - Steal This Movie (Lions Gate)

Liz Selzer-Lang .....Executive Producer

SENATOR INTERNATIONAL

8666 Wilshire Blvd.
Beverly Hills, CA 90211
PHONE 310-360-1441
FAX 310-360-1447
EMAIL .....info@senatorinternational.com
TYPES: Features
DEALS: Ghost House Pictures
DEVELOPMENT: 30 Days of Night - With This Ring - Jonestown Suckernucks - Rise - Scarecrow - Stranger Than Fiction
PRODUCTION: The Grudge
COMPLETED UNRELEASED: Boogeyman
CREDITS: Trapped - Das Experiment - Nothing - Harold and Kumar Go to White Castle
COMMENTS: Distribution

Joe Drake .....President (310-300-2062)
Brian Goldsmith .....CFO/Executive VP, Operations (300-2057)
Nathan Kahane .....Executive VP, Motion Pictures (300-2053)
Pierre Weisbein Executive VP, International Sales & Distribution (300-2064)
Aubrey Henderson .....VP, Motion Pictures (300-2047)
Rob McEntergart .....VP, Business & Legal Affairs (300-2078)
Jack Schuster .....VP, Post Production & Servicing (300-2054)
Brent Jack .....VP, International Marketing (300-2056)
Andrew Boyd .....Director, International Marketing (300-2052)
Delphine Perrier .....Sr. Manager, Legal Affairs & Contract Administration (300-2051)
Mickey Guerin .....Sr. Coordinator, Business & Legal Affairs (300-2067)
Jim Miller .....Creative Executive (300-2073)
Lorita Shepherd .....Controller (300-2048)
Maureen Mottram .....Accounting Manager (300-2046)
Dina Valenzuela .....Staff Accountant (300-2072)
Rosanna Canonigo .....Sr. Financial Analyst (300-2050)
Mali Kinberg .....Director, International Sales (300-2071)
Chiara Telarucci .....Sales Coordinator (300-2075)
Patricia Rivera .....Executive Assistant to Joe Drake (300-2063)
Monika Ramnath .....Executive Assistant to Brian Goldsmith (300-2058)

(Continued)

SENATOR INTERNATIONAL (Continued)

Matthew Milam .....Executive Assistant to Nathan Kahane (300-2055)
Dayna Feldman .....Executive Assistant to Pierre Weisbein (300-2065)
Pauline Metzler .....Executive Assistant to Aubrey Henderson (300-2069)
Jennifer Regan .....Executive Assistant to Rob McEntegart (300-2079)

SERAPHIM FILMS

1606 Argyle St.
Hollywood, CA 90028
PHONE 323-462-0840
FAX 323-462-9911
WEB SITE .....www.clivebarker.com
TYPES: Features - New Media - TV Series
DEVELOPMENT: Tortured Souls
CREDITS: Saint Sinner - Salome - The Forbidden - Nightbreed - Candyman - Candyman: Farewell to the Flesh - Lord of Illusions - Hellraiser 1-4 - Gods & Monsters

Clive Barker .....President
Joe Daley .....Executive VP, Production
Anthony DiBlasi .....VP, Production
David Armstrong .....Merchandising, Dogfish
Michael Hadley .....Merchandising, Dogfish
David J. Dodds .....Office Manager

SERENADE FILMS

2901 Ocean Park Blvd., Ste. 217
Santa Monica, CA 90405
PHONE 310-452-3335
FAX 310-452-0108
EMAIL .....serenadefilms@aol.com
TYPES: Features

Leslie Urdang .....Producer/Partner
Michael Hoffman .....Producer/Partner
Michael Nozik .....Producer/Partner
Amy Robinson .....Producer/Partner
Nick Goodwin Self .....Co-Producer
Julia Wells .....Production Coordinator

SERENDIPITY PRODUCTIONS, INC.

15260 Ventura Blvd., Ste. 1040
Sherman Oaks, CA 91403
PHONE 818-789-3035
FAX 818-789-0213
EMAIL .....serendipityprod@earthlink.net
WEB SITE .....http://home.earthlink.net/~danheffner
TYPES: Features - Direct-to-Video/DVD - Made-for-TV/Cable Movies
DEVELOPMENT: Run
POST PRODUCTION: Anonymous Rex
CREDITS: Highway 395 - Holy Matrimony - The Good Mother - Cocktail - George of the Jungle 2 (Walt Disney Pictures) - Saw

Daniel Jason Heffner .....Producer/Principal

SESAME WORKSHOP
One Lincoln Plaza, 4th Fl.
New York, NY 10023
PHONE .212-595-3456
FAX .212-875-6175
WEB SITE .www.sesamestreet.com
SECOND WEB SITE .www.sesameworkshop.org
TYPES Animation - TV Series
CREDITS Sesame Street - Dragon Tales - Sagwa, the Chinese Siamese Cat - Tiny Planets
COMMENTS www.stickerworld.org; Live action

Gary E. Knell .President/CEO
Melvin Ming .COO
Michael Lombardi .CFO
Lewis Bernstein .Executive Producer
Karen Gruenberg .Executive VP, Operations
Liz Kalodner .Executive VP, Global Consumer Products & International TV Distribution
Terry Fitzpatrick .Sr. VP, Business Operations
Nancy Steingard .Sr. VP, Creative Development
Jennifer Chrein .VP, Global TV Distribution
Anne Gorfinkel .VP/Executive Director, Educational Outreach
Jamie Greenberg .VP, Philanthropic Development
Lynn Lehmkuhl .VP, Corporate Sponsorship
Anita Stewart .VP, Corporate Sponsorship
Julian Scott .Group VP, European Operations

SEVEN ARTS PICTURES
10202 W. Washington Blvd.
David Lean Bldg., Ste. 430
Culver City, CA 90232
PHONE .310-244-6767
FAX .310-244-0567
EMAIL .salesinfo@saspix.com
TYPES Features
DEVELOPMENT Wavelength - Serenade - Neuromancer - Molly Deeds - Lost Lagoon
PRE-PRODUCTION Pool Hall Prophets - Noise
POST PRODUCTION Asylum
CREDITS An American Rhapsody - The Believer - Johnny Mnemonic - No Good Deed - I'll Sleep When I'm Dead - Stander

Peter M. Hoffman .President/CEO
Susan Hoffman .Co-President/Producer
Daniel Diamond .Consultant
Kate Hoffman .Executive VP
Cassia Hoffman .Production Executive
Kelli Sturges .Production Executive
Erik Smith .Consultant

SHADOWCATCHER ENTERTAINMENT
1001 Fourth Ave. Plaza, Ste. 4408
Seattle, WA 98154
PHONE .206-328-6266
FAX .206-389-1708
TYPES Features - Made-for-TV/Cable Movies - Theater
PRODUCTION The Skeleton Key (Universal)
CREDITS Smoke Signals - The Book of Stars - Getting to Know You

David Skinner .Producer
Roger Baerwolf .Producer
Tom Gorai .Producer

SHADY ACRES ENTERTAINMENT
c/o Universal Pictures
100 Universal City Plaza, Bldg. 6111
Universal City, CA 91608
PHONE .818-777-4446
FAX .818-866-6612
TYPES Features - TV Series
DEALS Touchstone Television - Universal Pictures
CREDITS Bruce Almighty - Liar Liar - Patch Adams - The Nutty Professor - Dragonfly - 8 Simple Rules for Dating My Teenage Daughter
SUBMISSION POLICY No unsolicited submissions

Michael Bostick .No Title
Ginny Durkin .No Title
Dagan Handy .No Title
Jacq Lesko .No Title
Amanda Morgan Palmer .No Title
Tom Shadyac .No Title
Glenda Storm .No Title
Jason Wilson .No Title
Greta Bramberg .No Title
Jordan Wolfe .No Title

SHANNON & COMPANY
23151 Plaza Point Dr., Ste. 110
Laguna Hills, CA 92653
PHONE .949-855-0844
WEB SITE .www.historyquestvideo.com
TYPES Documentaries - Direct-to-Video/DVD
DEVELOPMENT A Time for Heros - The Final Journey - Hotel Laguna - The Studio Club
COMMENTS Docudramas

R.J. Adams .Owner/Director
Diane C. Adams .Producer

RICHARD & ESTHER SHAPIRO ENTERTAINMENT, INC.
5700 Wilshire Blvd., Ste. 355
Los Angeles, CA 90036
PHONE .323-934-2202
FAX .323-934-2203
TYPES Features - TV Series

Richard Shapiro .Chairman
Esther Shapiro .President/CEO
Florie Shapiro .Director, Development

SHAPIRO/GRODNER PRODUCTIONS
12925 Riverside Dr., 4th Fl.
Sherman Oaks, CA 91423
PHONE .818-325-6900
FAX .818-379-4721/818-379-4722
TYPES Documentaries - Reality TV
PRODUCTION Situation: Comedy (Bravo) - Missy Elliott Project (UPN)
CREDITS Big Brother 2-5 (CBS) - Blow Out (Bravo) - The Family (ABC) - DNA: Guilty or Innocent - Family Business - Flipped - The Teen Files - Rescue 911 - Scared Straight! - The Story of Santa Claus - Scared Straight! 20 Years Later
SUBMISSION POLICY No unsolicited material
COMMENTS Currently producing reality series for CBS, UPN, Bravo, Showtime

Arnold Shapiro .Executive Producer
Allison Grodner .Executive Producer
Jeff Anderson .Executive in Charge, Production
Amy Bailey .Director, Development & Production
Rickey Ackerman .Director, Finance
Becky Blitz .Assistant to Arnold Shapiro

SHATTER GLASS PRODUCTIONS, INC.
4012 Tracy St.
Los Angeles, CA 90027
PHONE 323-662-4201
FAX 323-661-6943
EMAIL .....spencertee@aol.com
TYPES: Documentaries - Features - Direct-to-Video/DVD - New Media - TV Series - Reality TV
DEVELOPMENT: Evolution Gone Bad - Hometown - Rock & Roll Animals - Payback - Scott Free
PRE-PRODUCTION: Name It, Buy It, Drink It
CREDITS: Hollywood Squares - Screenwriters: On Film - Pump It Up (Fox) - Menace - Music in High Places (MTV)
COMMENTS: Music series; Deal with Innovative Media Productions, Inc.

Spencer Thornton .....Producer/Director
Valli Kleven .....Writer
Sam Hill .....Production Manager

THE SHEPHARD/ROBIN COMPANY
4000 Warner Blvd., Bldg. 138, Ste. 1106
Burbank, CA 91505
PHONE 818-954-5719
TYPES: Features - Made-for-TV/Cable Movies - TV Series
DEALS: Warner Bros. Television Production
CREDITS: Popular - Brutally Normal - Bailey's Mistake (ABC MOW) - Nip/Tuck (FX) - The D.A. (ABC)
SUBMISSION POLICY: No unsolicited submissions

Greer Shephard .....Executive Producer/Owner
Michael Robin .....Executive Producer/Owner

SHEVLOFF MCKEAN PRODUCTIONS
10201 W. Pico Blvd., Trailer 721
Los Angeles, CA 90035
PHONE 310-369-1898
FAX 310-969-3141
TYPES: TV Series - Reality TV
DEALS: Fox Television Studios
DEVELOPMENT: The Royals
PRODUCTION: Family Forensics (A&E)

Michael Shevloff .....Executive Producer
Gerry McKean .....Executive Producer
Gabriela Tavakoli .....Manager, Creative Affairs

SHOE MONEY PRODUCTIONS
4000 Warner Blvd., Bldg. 138, Rm. 1101
Burbank, CA 91522
PHONE 818-954-2682
FAX 818-954-1660
EMAIL .....shoemoney@warnerbros.com
TYPES: Features - TV Series
DEALS: Warner Bros. Television Production
CREDITS: West Wing - Sports Night - Jack & Bobby

Thomas Schlamme .....Executive Producer/Director
AJ Marcantonio .....Executive
Julie De Joie .....Executive
Alejandra Pedemonte .....Assistant to Thomas Schlamme

SHORELINE ENTERTAINMENT
1875 Century Park East, Ste. 600
Los Angeles, CA 90067
PHONE 310-551-2060
FAX 310-201-0729
EMAIL .....info@shorelineentertainment.com
SECOND EMAIL .....macy@shorelineentertainment.com
WEB SITE .....www.shorelineentertainment.com
TYPES: Features - Direct-to-Video/DVD - Made-for-TV/Cable Movies - TV Series
DEVELOPMENT: Judge Dredd: Possession - Stinger - Parasite 2
PRE-PRODUCTION: Conversation with a Monster - Kalamazoo
PRODUCTION: Constellation
POST PRODUCTION: Marilyn Hotchkiss' Ballroom Dancing & Charm School
COMPLETED UNRELEASED: Beeper - Irish Eyes - Real Time
CREDITS: The Godson - Detour - Flight of Fancy - The Man from Elysian Fields - A Crack in the Floor - Clubland - Dark Asylum - Beeper - Tail Sting - The Visit - The King's Guard - A Matter of Trust - Glengarry Glen Ross

Morris Ruskin .....President
Sam Eigen .....Director, World-Wide Distribution
Steve Chicorel .....Head, Marketing
Steve Macy .....Manager, Delivery of Materials
Fabrizio DeLeo .....International Marketing
Brian Sweet .....Sales Manager
Gretchen Von Tongien .....Acquisitions

SHOWBUZZ
PO Box 15324
Beverly Hills, CA 90209
PHONE 323-936-8300
EMAIL .....gloria_everett@hotmail.com
TYPES: Features
DEVELOPMENT: They Cage the Animals at Night
PRE-PRODUCTION: Heavens Fall
PRODUCTION: If
COMPLETED UNRELEASED: Miss Cast Away
CREDITS: Stage Ghost - Echos of Enlightenment - Charmed & Dangerous - Silent Lies - George B - The Random Factor - Beach Beverly Hills

Gloria Everett .....Producer

*SHOWTIME INDEPENDENT FILMS
1633 Broadway
New York, NY 10019
PHONE 212-708-1600/310-234-5200
WEB SITE .....www.sho.com
TYPES: Features - Made-for-TV/Cable Movies
CREDITS: The Best Thief in the World - Speak - Gettin' the Man's Foot Outta Your Baadasssss!
COMMENTS: West Coast office: 10880 Wilshire Blvd., Ste. 1600, Los Angeles, CA 90024

Robert Greenblatt .....President, Entertainment, Showtime Networks, Inc.
Matthew Duda .....Executive VP, Acquisitions, Planning & Distribution, Showtime Networks, Inc.
Ann Foley .....Executive VP, Programming, Showtime Networks, Inc.

SHOWTIME NETWORKS, INC.

1633 Broadway
New York, NY 10019
PHONE 212-708-1600/310-234-5200
WEB SITE ....www.sho.com
TYPES Documentaries - Made-for-TV/Cable Movies - TV Series
CREDITS !Huff - American Candidate - Cavedweller - Dead Like Me - The L Word - Penn & Teller: Bullshit! - Queer As Folk
COMMENTS West Coast office: 10880 Wilshire Blvd., Ste. 1600, Los Angeles, CA 90024

Matthew C. Blank ....Chairman/CEO (NY)
Robert Greenblatt ....President, Entertainment (LA)
Melinda Benedek ....Executive VP, Business Affairs (LA)
Matthew Duda ....Executive VP, Program Acquisitions & Planning (LA)
Ann Foley ....Executive VP, East Coast Programming (NY)
Gary Levine ....Executive VP, Original Programming (LA)
Richard Licata ....Executive VP, Entertainment Public Relations (LA)
Michael Rauch ....Executive VP, Production (LA)
Joan Boorstein ....Sr. VP, Creative Affairs (LA)
Patrick Burks ....Sr. VP, Field Operations (NY)
Tim Delaney ....Sr. VP, Production Operations (NY)
Sara Fischer ....Sr. VP, Motion Picture Production (LA)
Gary Garfinkel ....Sr. VP, Program Acquisitions (LA)
Danielle Gelber ....Sr. VP, Original Programming (LA)
Beth Klein ....Sr. VP, Talent & Casting, Showtime/Viacom (LA)
Pancho Mansfield ....Sr. VP, Development, Original Programming (LA)
Carol Mechanic ....Sr. VP, Programming (LA)
Frank Pintauro ......Sr. VP/Sr. Creative Director, Original Programming & Creative Services (NY)
Marica Chacona ....VP, Programming Scheduling (NY)
Nikki Ferraro ....VP, Talent Relations & Special Events (LA)
Pearlena Igbokwe ....VP, Original Programming (LA)
Anne Kurrasch ....VP, Business Affairs (LA)
John Moser ....VP, Family Programming (NY)
Jamie Padnos ....VP, Program Planning (LA)
Judith Pless ....VP, International Business Development (NY)
Vince Porter ....VP, Production (LA)
Tom Christie ....Sundance Channel (NY)

SHUKOVSKY ENGLISH ENTERTAINMENT

4605 Lankershim Blvd., Ste. 510
North Hollywood, CA 91602
PHONE 818-763-9191
FAX 818-763-9878
TYPES Features - TV Series
CREDITS Murphy Brown - Love & War - Double Rush - The Louie Show - Ink - Living in Captivity

Diane English ....Writer/Executive Producer
Joel Shukovsky ....Executive Producer
Erin Hill ....Executive Assistant to Diane English & Joel Shukovsky

THE SHUMAN COMPANY

3815 Hughes Ave., 4th Fl.
Culver City, CA 90232
PHONE 310-841-4344
FAX 310-204-3578
TYPES Features - TV Series
DEVELOPMENT Far Side of Victory - Money Shot - The Decision
CREDITS Sweethearts - Kissing Miranda

Lawrence Shuman ....Producer
Craig Grella ....Professor of Biology
David Wolthoff ....Consulting Exegete

SHUTT-JONES PRODUCTIONS

100 Universal City Plaza, Bldg. 6111, Ste. 100
Universal City, CA 91608
PHONE 818-777-9619
FAX 818-866-5006
TYPES Features - Direct-to-Video/DVD - TV Series
DEALS Universal Pictures
DEVELOPMENT False Advertising - 32 Candles - The Surgeon - The Basement Boys - Madame President - One Nation Under Bob
CREDITS Blue Crush
SUBMISSION POLICY No unsolicited material

Buffy Shutt ....Producer
Kathy Jones ....Producer
Lalo Vasquez ....Story Editor

SIDESTREET ENTERTAINMENT

2660 W. Olive Ave.
Burbank, CA 91505
PHONE 818-955-5240
FAX 818-955-5299
TYPES Animation - Features - Made-for-TV/Cable Movies - TV Series - Reality TV
DEALS Metro-Goldwyn-Mayer Studios, Inc. - New Wave Entertainment
CREDITS The Wade Robson Project

Michael Gruber ....Partner
Matt Walden ....Partner
Mara Jacobs ....Head, Production
Benjamin Heywood ....Creative Executive
Jim Albarano ....Assistant
Branon Coluccio ....Assistant

SIERRA CLUB PRODUCTIONS

1041 N. Formosa Ave., Writers Bldg., Ste. 301
West Hollywood, CA 90046
PHONE 323-850-2737
FAX 323-850-2734
WEB SITE ....www.sierraclub.org
TYPES Documentaries - Features - TV Series
DEVELOPMENT Moose - Sierra Club Adventures
PRE-PRODUCTION Hope's Edge - Getting There: Transportation of the Future
PRODUCTION On the Brink: Solutions to Global Warming
COMPLETED UNRELEASED Vertical Frontier
CREDITS Lethal Swarms: Killer Bees - Ansel Adams: A Documentary Film

Adrienne Bramhall ....Executive Producer
Kristopher Michel ....Production/Development Manager

SIGNATURE PICTURES
725 Arizona Ave., Ste. 202
Santa Monica, CA 90401
PHONE .310-394-1000
FAX .310-394-1001
EMAIL .frontdesk@signaturepictures.com
WEB SITE .www.signaturepictures.com

TYPES	Features
DEVELOPMENT	In Search of Ina Byers - Cover Me
PRE-PRODUCTION	The Black Dahlia - Lords of Dogtown
POST PRODUCTION	Hairy Tale - Tristan & Isolde - Sound of Thunder
COMPLETED UNRELEASED	Imaginary Heroes
CREDITS	Extreme Ops - The Musketeer - Maximum Risk - Time Cop - Double Team - The Body - Feardotcom - Spartan
SUBMISSION POLICY	No unsolicited materials

Rudy Cohen .Producer
Moshe Diamant .Producer
Illana Diamant .Producer
Art Linson .Producer
John Linson .Producer
David Lamping .President, International
Edo Cohen .VP, International
Rene Gil-Besson .Production Executive
Sammy Goldsmith .Development Executive
James Portolese .Development Executive
Carolyn Miller .Assistant to Art Linson

SILLY ROBIN PRODUCTIONS
3000 Olympic Blvd.
Santa Monica, CA 90404
PHONE .310-264-8184
FAX .310-315-4800

TYPES	Features - TV Series
DEALS	Touchstone Television
DEVELOPMENT	Bunny Bunny (HBO Films) - Untitled David Hoberman Project (Touchstone TV) - The Ambassador (Robert Cort Productions) - Rotisserie Life (Comedy Central)
PRE-PRODUCTION	The Furst Family (Touchstone TV)
CREDITS	Saturday Night Live - Curb Your Enthusiasm - The Story of Us - It's Garry Shandling's Show (Creator) - Dragnet - North - The Please Watch the Jon Lovitz Special (Fox)
COMMENTS	Stageplays, novels, magazine fiction, essays

Alan Zweibel .Writer/Producer/Director
John Robertson .Director, Development

SILVER DREAM PRODUCTIONS
1499 Huntington Dr., Ste. 500
South Pasadena, CA 91030
PHONE .626-799-3880
FAX .626-799-5363
EMAIL .luoyan@silverdreamprods.com

TYPES	Features
CREDITS	Pavillion of Women

Luo Yan .Actress/Producer
Chris Liu .General Manager
Wen Gong .Assistant

SILVER LION FILMS
701 Santa Monica Blvd.
Santa Monica, CA 90401
PHONE .310-393-9177
FAX .310-458-9372
WEB SITE .www.silverlionfilms.com

TYPES	Animation - Features - Made-for-TV/Cable Movies - TV Series
DEVELOPMENT	Resolution - A Call from L.A. - Storm Warning - Sunstroke - Freeze Frame - The Caretakers - Two Men and a Moving Truck - The Knack - Sweetwater Flyers
PRODUCTION	Monkey King
POST PRODUCTION	Club Dread - Man on Fire - Caught in the Act
CREDITS	Flashfire - The Air Up There - Pure Luck - Steel Dawn - Flipper - Gunmen - McHale's Navy - One Man's Hero - Crocodile Dundee in L.A.

Lance Hool .Producer/Director
Conrad Hool .Producer
Chase Mellen .VP, Business Affairs
Belinda White .Executive Assistant

SILVER PICTURES
c/o Warner Bros.
4000 Warner Blvd., Bldg. 90
Burbank, CA 91522-0001
PHONE .818-954-4490
FAX .818-954-3237

TYPES	Features - New Media - Reality TV - TV Series
DEALS	Warner Bros. Pictures
DEVELOPMENT	Wonder Woman - Speed Racer - Superfly - WXYZ - Year of the Ram - Dodging Bullets - Bad Ronald
POST PRODUCTION	House of Wax - Kiss Kiss, Bang Bang
CREDITS	Predator 1&2 - The Matrix - The Matrix Reloaded - The Matrix Revolutions - Die Hard 1&2 - Lethal Weapon 1-4 - Action - Tales from the Crypt - Cradle 2 the Grave - Gothika - Next Action Star (Reality TV Series)

Joel Silver .Chairman
Steve Richards .COO
Susan Levin .Executive VP, Production
Jennifer Gwartz .Sr. VP, TV
Danielle Stokdyk .Sr. VP, TV
Adam Kuhn .VP, Finance
Pam Martin .VP, Operations
Erik Olsen .VP, Development
David Gambino .Creative Executive

CASEY SILVER PRODUCTIONS
506 Santa Monica Blvd., Ste. 322
Santa Monica, CA 90401
PHONE .310-566-3750
FAX .310-566-3751

TYPES	Features - TV Series
DEVELOPMENT	Rebels - Cruel & Unusual
POST PRODUCTION	Ladder 49
CREDITS	Gigli - Hidalgo
SUBMISSION POLICY	Through agent or attorney only

Casey Silver .Chairman
Afshin Ketabi .Creative Executive
Fleming Brooks .Operations Manager
Matthew Reynolds .Story Editor

SILVERCREEK ENTERTAINMENT
87 Upper Lake Rd.
Lake Sherwood, CA 91361
PHONE 805-370-3630
FAX 805-370-3631
TYPES Features - Made-for-TV/Cable Movies - TV Series
DEVELOPMENT The Confidant: The Robert Blake-Leebonny Bakley Story (Feature) - In His Best Interest (MOW) - The Money Trail (Feature)
CREDITS Like Mother/Like Son: The Strange Story of Sante and Kenny Kimes - The Shield (FX) - Caught in the Act - Sweet Justice - Hill Street Blues - Every Mother's Nightmare - Cracker - L.A. Docs - Gideon's Crossing
COMMENTS Music and literary properties; Author of *Breaking into Acting for Dummies;* Garrison Productions Inc. produces segments for prime-time news magazine shows

Larry Garrison ....President/Executive Producer/Author/Actor
Scott Brazil ....Executive Producer/Director

SILVERLINE ENTERTAINMENT, INC.
22837 Ventura Blvd., Ste. 205
Woodland Hills, CA 91364
PHONE 818-225-9032
FAX 818-225-9053
EMAIL ....admin@silverlineentertainment.com
WEB SITE ....www.silverlineentertainment.com
TYPES Features - Direct-to-Video/DVD - Made-for-TV/Cable Movies
DEVELOPMENT Deadline
COMPLETED UNRELEASED Lethal
CREDITS The Last Warrior - Dusting Cliff 7 - Where Truth Lies - Angels Don't Sleep Here

Leman Cetiner ....CEO/Producer
Axel Munch ....President/Producer
Robert Yap ....VP, Development & Distribution
Amila Giducos ....VP, Finance

THE FRED SILVERMAN COMPANY
1648 Mandeville Canyon Rd.
Los Angeles, CA 90049
PHONE 310-471-4676
FAX 310-471-6536
EMAIL ....fsprods@aol.com
TYPES Made-for-TV/Cable Movies - TV Series
CREDITS Diagnosis Murder - Perry Mason - Matlock - In the Heat of the Night - 21

Fred Silverman ....President
Linsey Hubbard ....Assistant

SILVERS/KOSTER PRODUCTIONS, INC.
219 S. Willaman Dr.
Beverly Hills, CA 90211
PHONE 310-652-5288
FAX 310-652-5351
EMAIL ....skfilmco@aol.com
WEB SITE ....www.silvers-koster.com
TYPES Animation - Features - Direct-to-Video/DVD - New Media - TV Series
DEVELOPMENT The Adventures of Mutt and Jeff - Love You to Death - Man with a Mission - Love Slave - Amanda's Girls
PRE-PRODUCTION Invisible Kids
PRODUCTION Perfect Partners
CREDITS Hugo Pool - Dead End - My Gardner
COMMENTS Worldwide production company

Tracey Silvers ....Chairman
Iren Koster ....President
Karen Corcoran ....VP, Development
Louis Koyatch ....VP, Finance

THE GENE SIMMONS COMPANY
PO Box 16075
Beverly Hills, CA 90210
PHONE 310-859-1694
FAX 310-859-2631
TYPES Features - Made-for-TV/Cable Movies - TV Series
DEVELOPMENT Tim Allen Project - Neal Bogart Story - Sex, Drugs and Rock 'n' Roll - November Files - Tennessee Waltz - Jon Sable - Smash - Chillerama - Rena Mero Story - Terry and the Pirates - Hitmen
CREDITS Detroit Rock City
SUBMISSION POLICY No unsolicited material

Gene Simmons ....Producer

THE ROBERT SIMONDS COMPANY
1999 Avenue of the Stars, Ste. 2350
Los Angeles, CA 90067
PHONE 310-789-2200
FAX 310-201-5998
TYPES Features
DEALS The Buena Vista Motion Pictures Group
PRE-PRODUCTION Shaggy D.A. (Disney)
PRODUCTION Pink Panther - Herbie - Untitled Martin Lawrence Project
POST PRODUCTION Taxi
CREDITS Just Married - The Water Boy - Big Daddy - Happy Gilmore - Problem Child 1&2 - Billy Madison - The Wedding Singer - Half Baked - Corky Romano - See Spot Run - Cheaper by the Dozen

Robert Simonds ....Producer
Ira Shuman ....President, Physical Production
Tracey Trench ....President, Creative Affairs
Aaron Wilder ....VP, Development
Lily Chang ....Executive Assistant to Mr. Simonds
Amber Defrancis ....Development Assistant
Alison Luzietti ....Creative Affairs Assistant

BRENT SIMS FILMS
5817 Gettysburg Dr.
Baton Rouge, LA 70817
PHONE 225-751-2894/310-993-8024
WEB SITE ....www.brentsims.com
TYPES Features
DEVELOPMENT Evil Squirrel - Double Dutch
CREDITS Gutter Punks - Silence - Becoming Vex
SUBMISSION POLICY No queries

Brent Sims ....Director/Writer/Producer
Jason Buuck ....Development (LA)

SIMSIE FILMS/MEDIA SAVANT PICTURES
1977 Coldwater Canyon Dr.
Beverly Hills, CA 90210
PHONE 310-271-0777
FAX 310-271-7439
EMAIL ....simsie@earthlink.net
TYPES Features - Made-for-TV/Cable Movies - TV Series
DEVELOPMENT Water's Edge - Ordinary Miracles - The End of the Real World, Russell - Full Cleveland - Spacey Movie
PRE-PRODUCTION Oceanside
CREDITS Patti Rocks - Reflections in the Dark - Mortal Passions - Young Blades - Charlton Heston Presents the Bible
SUBMISSION POLICY Via email query only
COMMENTS Deal with Evertrade Pictures

Gwen Field ....Partner
Christopher Sepulveda ....Assistant

JOSEPH SINGER ENTERTAINMENT
3000 W. Olympic Blvd., Bldg. 3, Ste. 1466
Santa Monica, CA 90404
PHONE .310-284-4066
TYPES: Features
CREDITS: Dr. Doolittle 1&2 - Courage Under Fire - Dante's Peak - Mercury Rising

Joseph Singer .Producer
Dan Teebor .Sr. VP
Jeff Levy .Creative Executive
Philip Westgren .Creative Executive

CARLA SINGER PRODUCTIONS
133 E. 58th St., Ste. 301
New York, NY 10022
PHONE .212-755-6690
FAX .212-888-6470
TYPES: Features - TV Series
COMPLETED UNRELEASED: Just for Laughs (Pilot)
CREDITS: A Marriage of Convenience - 36 Hours to Die - Test of Love - Love Lessons - Straight from the Heart

Carla Singer .Executive Producer
Allyson Giard .Creative Executive

SINGLE CELL PICTURES
1016 N. Palm Ave.
West Hollywood, CA 90069
PHONE .310-360-7600
FAX .310-360-7011
TYPES: Features
DEALS: Metro-Goldwyn-Mayer Studios, Inc.
CREDITS: Velvet Goldmine - Being John Malkovich - Freak City - Thirteen Conversations About One Thing - Saved!

Michael Stipe .Producer
Sandy Stern .Producer
Justin Marks .Assistant

SISTERLEE PRODUCTIONS, INC.
4024 Radford Ave., Bldg. 5
Studio City, CA 91604
PHONE .818-655-5909
TYPES: TV Series
CREDITS: A Different World - Hangin' with Mr. Cooper - Living Single - Lush Life - For Your Love - Half and Half (UPN)
SUBMISSION POLICY: No unsolicited material

Yvette Lee Bowser .Executive Producer

SITTING DUCKS PRODUCTIONS
2578 Verbena Dr.
Los Angeles, CA 90068
PHONE .323-461-2095
EMAIL .sittingducks@earthlink.net
TYPES: Animation - Features - Direct-to-Video/DVD - Made-for-TV/Cable Movies - New Media - TV Series
DEVELOPMENT: Noah's Blimp - Mambo - Nelvana - Kindinsky's Kat Band - Cinar
CREDITS: Sitting Ducks - The Mouse and Monster - The Santa Claus Brothers (Disney Channel)

Michael Bedard .Executive Producer
Elizabeth Daro .Executive Producer

SITV
3030 Andrita St., Bldg. A
Los Angeles, CA 90065
PHONE .323-256-8900
FAX .323-256-9888
WEB SITE .www.sitv.com
TYPES: Animation - Made-for-TV/Cable Movies - Syndication - TV Series
CREDITS: The Brothers Garcia (Series) - Funny Is Funny - Café Olé - Latino Laugh Festival

Jeff Valdez .Co-Chairman
Leo Perez .COO
Albert Chavez .VP, Finance
Betty Gower .VP, Marketing
Ed Leon .VP, Production
Rita Morales Patton .VP, Programming
Steve Levin .Advertising/Sales
Montse Garriga .Assistant to Jeff Valdez
Jennifer Vigil .Assistant to Rita Morales Patton

MARY JANE SKALSKI
c/o Antidote International Films, Inc.
200 Varick St., Ste. 502
New York, NY 10014
PHONE .646-486-4344
FAX .646-486-5885
EMAIL .maryjane@antidotefilms.com
TYPES: Documentaries - Features - TV Series
DEVELOPMENT: The F*** Up - Long Division for Lunatics - Macbeth - Sarah - Creeps!
PRE-PRODUCTION: The Hawk Is Dying
POST PRODUCTION: Mysterious Skin
COMPLETED UNRELEASED: Chain
CREDITS: The Jimmy Show - Trick - The Myth of Fingerprints - Wonderland - Brothers McMullen - The Lifestyle - The Station Agent
SUBMISSION POLICY: No unsolicited material

Mary Jane Skalski .Producer
James Debbs .No Title

SKIPPY DOG PRODUCTIONS
150 W. 15th St., Ste. 4
New York, NY 10010
PHONE .212-929-7770
EMAIL .info@skippydog.net
TYPES: Features - Made-for-TV/Cable Movies - Theater - TV Series
CREDITS: Dancing in the Shadows - 2nd Wind

Riley Weston .Actress/Writer/Producer

SKYE ISLAND ENTERTAINMENT
4509 Cato St.
Los Angeles, CA 90032
PHONE .323-227-6618/323-804-8999
FAX .323-227-9985
EMAIL .skyeislandent@aol.com
TYPES: Features - Direct-to-Video/DVD
DEVELOPMENT: Victory Red - Red Hot Charlie - Lola Goes to Roma
PRE-PRODUCTION: The Wonder Five - O, Jerusalem
SUBMISSION POLICY: No unsolicited material
COMMENTS: Open to co-production deals, including international co-productions

Diane Cornell .General Partner/Producer/Director/Writer
Jenny Fitzgibbons .General Partner/Writer/Co-Producer
Scott Campbell .Production Designer/Software & Website Design
Reinhard Schriener .Post Production Supervisor

SKYLARK FILMS, LTD.
1123 Pacific St., Ste. G
Santa Monica, CA 90405-1525
PHONE .310-396-5753
FAX .310-396-5753
EMAIL .skyfilm@aol.com
TYPES Features - Made-for-TV/Cable Movies - TV Series
DEALS Orly Adelson Productions
DEVELOPMENT Earth Anthem
PRODUCTION Positive Spin (Syndication, Radio)
CREDITS Terminal Justice - The Styx - Chasing Justice - Coal of the Heart
SUBMISSION POLICY No unsolicited material; Query first

Bradford Pollack .Producer
Annelouise Verboan .Development Associate/Story Analyst

SKYLINE PICTURES, LLC
10037 Reevesbury Dr.
Beverly Hills, CA 90210
PHONE .310-949-9222
TYPES Features - Made-for-TV/Cable Movies
PRE-PRODUCTION Del Rio
CREDITS Basic - The 7th Coin
SUBMISSION POLICY No unsolicited materials

Dror Soref .Producer/Director
Grant Cardone .Executive Producer
Yoram Barzilai .Producer
Erica De La Paz .VP, Creative Development

DANIEL SLADEK ENTERTAINMENT CORPORATION
8306 Wilshire Blvd., Ste. 510
Beverly Hills, CA 90211
PHONE .323-934-9268
FAX .323-934-7362
EMAIL .dansladek@aol.com
WEB SITE .www.danielsladek.com
TYPES Features - Direct-to-Video/DVD - Made-for-TV/Cable Movies - New Media - TV Series - Reality TV
DEVELOPMENT Prayers for Bobby - The Road to Gandolfo - Romance by Design
CREDITS Tale of the Mummy - Sub Down - Silent Trigger - Hidden Assassin - Thank Heaven

Daniel Sladek .Producer/President
Chris Taaffe .Producer
Marian Salas .Financial Affairs

SLIPNOT! PRODUCTIONS/SPG
3762 Willow Crest Ave.
Studio City, CA 91604
PHONE .818-753-5965
FAX .818-753-0569
EMAIL .slipnotspg@aol.com
WEB SITE .www.slipnotproductions.com
TYPES Commercials - Documentaries - Features - Direct-to-Video/DVD - Made-for-TV/Cable Movies - Music Videos - Reality TV - TV Series
DEVELOPMENT Delinquent - White Elephant - Double Jointed - Looking Back
POST PRODUCTION Lost in Transit
CREDITS The Pros and Cons of Breathing - Breaking Point - Point Blank - Out of Time - Love Crimes - Murder by Numbers - Stay on Point - Narcosys - Evicted
SUBMISSION POLICY Contact before submitting
COMMENTS Cable and home video distribution

David Penn .Writer/Producer
Scott Simons .Writer/Producer
Michael Stahlberg .Writer/Director

SMOKIN' GUN PRODUCTIONS
3003 W. Olive Ave.
Burbank, CA 91505
PHONE .661-299-4806
FAX .661-299-1569
EMAIL .dannohanks@sbcglobal.net
WEB SITE .www.smokin-gun-productions.com
TYPES Features - New Media - TV Series - Reality TV
DEVELOPMENT Heart of Oak - T - The Kissena Crew - Prisoner in Paradise (GMG Films)
PRE-PRODUCTION Vermin & Pestilence (TV Series)
CREDITS Caught in the Act (NBC TV Special) - Fox Undercover (Fox TV News)

Dan "Danno" Hanks .Co-Owner/Producer
Fred Valis .Co-Owner/Producer/Writer
Andrew Smith .Business Affairs
Kimbyrly Valis .Executive Assistant

SNAPDRAGON FILMS, INC.
23852 Pacific Coast Hwy., Ste. 373
Malibu, CA 90265
PHONE .310-456-0101
FAX .310-456-7504
EMAIL .bpalef@earthlink.net
TYPES Documentaries - Features - Made-for-TV/Cable Movies - New Media - TV Series
DEVELOPMENT Wired for Sound (Feature)
CREDITS Marvin's Room - Cemetary Club - Parents - Moonstruck

Bonnie Palef .Director/Producer/Writer
Manuel Granado .Producer Assistant

SNEAK PREVIEW ENTERTAINMENT, INC.
1604 Vista del Mar St.
Hollywood, CA 90028
PHONE .323-962-0295
FAX .323-962-0372
EMAIL .indiefilm@sneakpreviewentertain.com
WEB SITE .www.sneakpreviewentertain.com
TYPES Features - Made-for-TV/Cable Movies - TV Series
DEVELOPMENT The Preacher's Son - Arrow Man - Blanca Rosa - Situation Wanted
PRE-PRODUCTION Queer Fear
PRODUCTION When Do We Eat?
POST PRODUCTION Hellbent
COMPLETED UNRELEASED The Civilization of Maxwell Bright
CREDITS Circuit - Relax...It's Just Sex - Twin Falls Idaho - Tollbooth - The Clean and Narrow - Scorchers - Bird of Prey - Fast Sofa
COMMENTS Talent management

Michael J. Roth .Manager/Producer
Josh Silver .Manager/Producer
Brad Warshaw .Manager/Producer
Steven J. Wolfe .Manager/Producer
Adam Fike .Executive Assistant
Scott Hyman .Executive Assistant
Melissa Moss .Executive Assistant

It is illegal to copy any part of this book

SNOWFALL FILMS
2321 W. Olive Ave., Ste. A
Burbank, CA 91506
PHONE .818-558-5917
FAX .818-842-4112
WEB SITE .www.snowfallfilms.com
TYPES Features
DEVELOPMENT A Dead Man in Deptford - Fox Hunt - Chaperone - Clockmore
PRE-PRODUCTION Danger Zone - The Drowner
PRODUCTION Mr. Silvester
COMPLETED UNRELEASED Bailey's Billions - The Heart Is Deceitful Above All Things
CREDITS Undertaking Betty (AKA Plots With a View) - Jericho Mansions
COMMENTS Deal with Spice Factory (UK)

Suzanne Lyons .Producer
Kate Robbins .Producer
Ruby Lopez .Creative Executive

SOBINI FILMS
2700 Colorado Ave., Ste. 510B
Santa Monica, CA 90404
PHONE .310-255-5115
FAX .310-255-5110
WEB SITE .www.sobini.com
TYPES Features
DEALS Lions Gate Entertainment
DEVELOPMENT Julia Pastrana - Dark Sister - Poster Boy - Peaceful Warrior
CREDITS Framed - The Prince and Me

Mark Amin .Producer/Chairman
Robin Schorr .President, Production
Cami Winikoff .President
Jason W. Cooper .Administrative Assistant

SOLO ENTERTAINMENT GROUP
9350 Wilshire Blvd., Ste. 212
Beverly Hills, CA 90212
PHONE .310-205-6280
FAX .310-205-6281
TYPES Animation - Features - TV Series
DEVELOPMENT Hunted Hunter - Gene Pool - Pony Kids - Itz - Suspicious Minors - Purple Land - Sector 7 - Knights of the Sea
PRE-PRODUCTION Carlo & Frankie
CREDITS American Psycho - Rollerball - Igby Goes Down - Hansel & Gretel - Vidas Privadas - Historias Minimas
COMMENTS Formerly Helkon International Pictures

Christian Halsey Solomon .President/CEO
Lee Solomon .Executive VP/COO
Lucas Jarach .VP, Sales & Acquisitions

SOLO ONE PRODUCTIONS
8205 Santa Monica Blvd., Ste. 1279
Los Angeles, CA 90046-5912
PHONE .323-658-8748
FAX .323-658-8749
EMAIL .solo1productions@aol.com
WEB SITE .www.marleeonline.com
TYPES Features - Made-for-TV/Cable Movies - New Media - TV Series
DEVELOPMENT Sound and Fury - The Decorators
CREDITS Where the Truth Lies - Eddie's Million Dollar Cookoff
COMMENTS Deal with One World Live Network

Marlee Matlin .Actress/Producer
Jack Jason .Producer

ANDREW SOLT PRODUCTIONS
9121 Sunset Blvd.
Los Angeles, CA 90069
PHONE .310-276-9522
FAX .310-276-0242
EMAIL .sofaent@aol.com
WEB SITE .www.sofa4u.com
TYPES TV Series
CREDITS The NBC 75th Anniversary Special - NBC's 50 Years of Late Night - The History of Rock 'n' Roll - The Best of Ed Sullivan - First 50 Years of CBS - The Hunt for Amazing Treasure - D.J. Games

Andrew Solt .Producer/Writer/Director
Greg Vines .Sr. VP, Production

THE SOMMERS COMPANY
204 Santa Monica Blvd., Ste. A
Santa Monica, CA 90401
PHONE .310-917-9200
FAX .310-917-5036
EMAIL .info@sommerscompany.com
TYPES Features - TV Series
DEALS Universal Pictures
DEVELOPMENT The Argonauts - Razors - Flame Over India - Flash Gordon - Break It Up - Who Was Claire Jallu? - Transylvania - Delaware McChood
CREDITS Van Helsing - The Mummy - The Mummy Returns - The Scorpion King - The Jungle Book - Huck Finn - Deep Rising
SUBMISSION POLICY No unsolicited submissions

Stephen Sommers .Chairman
Robert Ducsay .President, Production
Matthew Stuecken .Director, Development
Jennifer Ceballos .Assistant to Mr. Stuecken
Ryan Landels .Assistant to Mr. Ducsay
Jesse Peckham .Assistant to Mr. Sommers
Dinah Hutson .Assistant
Dikran Ornekian .Assistant

*SONY ONLINE ENTERTAINMENT
8958 Terman Court
San Diego, CA 92121
PHONE .858-577-3100
FAX .858-577-3200
WEB SITE .www.sonypictures.com
TYPES Features - New Media

John Smedley .President
Adam Joffe .CTO
Ralph Koster .CCO
John Needham .CFO/Sr. VP, Finance
Russell Shanks .COO
Donald Vercelli .Sr. VP, Sales & Marketing
Ken Dopher .VP, Finance

SONY PICTURES ANIMATION
9050 W. Washington Blvd.
Culver City, CA 90232
PHONE .310-840-8000
FAX .310-840-8100
WEB SITE .www.spe.sony.com
TYPES Animation - Features
COMMENTS Feature digital animation

Penney Finkelman Cox .Executive VP
Sandra Rabins .Executive VP
Barbara Zipperman .Sr. VP, Business Affairs
Nate Hopper .VP, Creative Affairs
Michelle Murdocca .VP, Animation

SONY PICTURES DIGITAL
3960 Ince Blvd.
Culver City, CA 90232
PHONE .310-840-8676
FAX .310-840-8390
WEB SITE .www.spe.sony.com
TYPES Features
COMMENTS Includes Sony Pictures Integrated Network (SPIN) and Sony Pictures Digital Networks

Yair Landau .President, Sony Pictures Digital
Corii Berg .Executive VP, Legal & Business Affairs
Patrick Kennedy .Executive VP
Michael Arrieta .Sr. VP, Strategic Alliances
Steven Banfield .Sr. VP, Technology
Tim Chambers .Sr. VP/General Manager, Advanced Platforms Group
Doug Chey .Sr. VP, Technology
Mary Coller .Sr. VP/General Manager, SoapCity
Ron Geller .Sr. VP, SPD Europe
Don Levy .Sr. VP, Media Relations
Curtis Palmer .Sr. VP/Chief Technologist
Ira Rubenstein .Sr. VP, Sony Pictures Integrated Network (SPIN)
Nazir Allibhoy .VP, Strategic Alliances
Andra Anderson .VP, Operations
Emmanuelle Borde .VP, Sony Pictures Integrated Network (SPIN)
Rio Caraeff .VP, Wireless Services
Marie Davis .VP, Production Services
Eric Gaynor .VP, Business Affairs
Paul Jensen .VP, Strategic Alliances
Shalom Mann .VP, Advanced Platforms
Audrey Marco .VP, Strategic Alliances
Andrew Mosson .VP, Screenblast
Michael Paull .VP, Business Development
Caleb Pourchot .VP, Engineering
Geoffrey Springer .VP, Technology, Sony Pictures Integrated Network (SPIN)

SONY PICTURES ENTERTAINMENT
10202 W. Washington Blvd.
Culver City, CA 90232
PHONE .310-244-4000
FAX .310-244-2626
WEB SITE .www.spe.sony.com
TYPES Features - TV Series
COMMENTS See also Columbia Pictures

Michael Lynton .Chairman/CEO
Amy Pascal .Chairman, Motion Picture Group, SPE/Vice Chairman, SPE
Jeff Blake .Vice Chairman/President, CTMPG Worldwide Marketing & Distribution
Yair Landau .Vice Chairman/President, Sony Pictures Digital
Beth Berke .Executive VP/CAO
David Hendler .Executive VP/CFO
Leah Weil .Executive VP/General Counsel
Simon Baker .Sr. VP/Corporate Treasurer
Suzanne Criley .Sr. VP, Human Resources
Susan Tick .Sr. VP, Corporate Communications
Karen L. Halby .VP
Jared Jussim .Assistant Secretary
Lynne R. Shulim .Assistant Treasurer

SONY PICTURES IMAGEWORKS
A Sony Pictures Entertainment Company
9050 W. Washington Blvd.
Culver City, CA 90232
PHONE .310-840-8000
FAX .310-840-8100
WEB SITE .www.imageworks.com
TYPES Animation - Features - New Media - TV Series
COMMENTS See also Sony Pictures Digital Entertainment; Full-service visual effects and digital animation

Tim Sarnoff .President
Debbie Denise .Sr. VP/Executive Producer, Production Infrastructure
Jenny Fulle .Sr. VP, Production
Thomas Hershey .Sr. VP, Operations
George Joblove .Sr. VP, Technology
Stanley Szymanski .Sr. VP, Digital Production
Barry Weiss .Sr. VP, Animation Production
Mae Turner-Moody .VP, Digital Operations
William Villarreal .VP, Technical Operations

SONY PICTURES TELEVISION
A Sony Pictures Entertainment Company
10202 W. Washington Blvd.
Culver City, CA 90232
PHONE .310-244-4000
WEB SITE .www.sonypicturestelevision.com
TYPES Made-for-TV/Cable Movies - TV Series - Reality TV
COMMENTS Regional offices: 550 Madison Ave., 12th Fl., New York, NY 10022, phone: 212-833-8354, fax: 212-833-8360; 2859 Paces Ferry Rd., Ste. 1130, Atlanta, GA 30339, phone: 770-434-5400, fax: 770-431-0202; 455 N. Cityfront Plaza Dr., Ste. 3120, Chicago, IL 60611, phone: 312-644-0770, fax: 312-644-0781

Steve Mosko .President
Russ Krasnoff .President, Programming & Production
Jeanie Bradley .Executive VP, Programming
Richard Frankie .Executive VP, Business Operations
Edward Lammi .Executive VP, Production
Don Loughery .Executive VP, Strategic Operations
David Mumford .Executive VP, Planning & Operations
Helen Verno .Executive VP, Movies & Miniseries
John Weiser .Executive VP, Syndication/Feature Films Library
Melanie Chilek .Sr. VP, Reality Programming
Jamie Erlicht .Sr. VP, Development
Robert Hunka .Sr. VP, Music
Joanne Mazzu .Sr. VP, Business Affairs
John Morrissey .Sr. VP, Production
Winifred White Neisser .Sr. VP, Movies for TV & Miniseries
Doug Roth .Sr. VP, Research
Phil Squyres .Sr. VP, Technical Operations
Dawn Steinberg .Sr. VP, Talent & Casting
Zackary Van Amburg .Sr. VP, Development
Jeff Weiss .Sr. VP, Business Affairs, Syndication
Glenn Adilman .VP, Development
Gerette Allegra .VP, Current Programming
Howard Bauer .VP, TV Production
Ellen Cohen .VP, Business Affairs
Jim Dietle .VP, Business Affairs
Sarah Finn .VP, Production
Christina Friedgen .VP, Post Production
Andy House .VP, Production
Stephanie Keane .VP, Current Programming
Melissa Kellner .VP, Development
Patrick Kelly .VP, Business Affairs
Diane Oldham .VP, Research
Margaret Paris .VP, Music Licensing
James Petretti .VP, Research
Craig Smith .VP, Special Events
Charles Smolsky .VP, Business Affairs
John Spector .VP, Production
Karen Tatevosian .VP, Business Affairs
Andy Teach .VP, Network & Cable Research
Sarah Weidman .VP, Development

SONY PICTURES TELEVISION INTERNATIONAL

A Sony Pictures Entertainment Company
10202 W. Washington Blvd.
Culver City, CA 90232
PHONE 310-244-4000
WEB SITE ....www.sonypicturestelevision.com
TYPES   Syndication - TV Series

Michael Grindon ....President
Hyuk-Jo Kwon ....President, Columbia TriStar Films of Korea
Andy Kaplan ....Sr. Executive VP, International Networks
John McMahon ....Sr. Executive VP/Managing Director, Europe
Steven Kent ....Executive VP, International TV Production
Darren Childs ....Sr. VP, International Networks
Nathalie Civrais ....Sr. VP, Southern European Production
Donna Cunningham ....Sr. VP, Business Affairs, Production
Martha Eberts ....Sr. VP, International Networks
Dewy Ip ....Sr. VP/Managing Director, Asia
Marie Jacobson ....Sr. VP, Programming
Daniel McCaffrey ....Sr. VP, International Production
Fran McConnell ....Sr. VP, Production
Todd Miller ....Sr. VP/Managing Director, Asia
Ross Pollack ....Sr. VP, Business Development, Asia
T.C. Schultz ....Sr. VP, International Channels
Sunder Aaron ....VP, International Networks
Mark Bluestone ....VP/General Manager
Jiande Chen ....VP/General Manager, Asia
Claudio DiPersia ....VP/General Manager, AXN Latin America
Brendan Fitzgerald ....VP, International Production
Jack Ford ....VP/Managing Director, Australia
Natalie Garcia ....VP, Distribution & Production, Spain
Paul Gilbert ....VP, International Program Development & Format Sales
Ross Hair ....VP, International Networks
Ann Harris ....VP, Production
Jeffrey Lerner ....VP, International Production
Gabriela Mondragon ....VP, Development & Production, Mexico
Pamela Parker ....VP, Business Affairs
Sergio Pizzolante ....VP/General Manager, AXN
Jesus Torres ....VP/General Manager, Latin America
Keith Le Goy ....Managing Director, Latin America

SOUTH PRODUCTIONS, LLC

41-018 Wailea St.
Waimanalo, HI 96795
PHONE 808-259-0490
FAX 808-259-0487
TYPES   Features - TV Series
CREDITS   Melrose Place - Hyperion Bay - Baywatch Hawaii - Almost Grown - Equal Justice - Models Inc. - Going to Extremes - Beaches - For the Boys - Man of the House
SUBMISSION POLICY   No unsolicited material
COMMENTS   Developing TV and film projects in Hawaii for national and worldwide distribution

Frank South ....Producer
Margaret South ....Producer

SOUTH SHORE ENTERTAINMENT

8840 Wilshire Blvd., Ste 207
Beverly Hills, CA 90211
PHONE 818-990-2016/310-266-6511
FAX 818-990-5039
EMAIL ....southshoreprod@aol.com
TYPES   Features - Made-for-TV/Cable Movies - Syndication - TV Series
DEVELOPMENT   Save Our Child (Lifetime) - Man Bites Dog (Showtime) - Playing God (USA) - The Alamo (USA, Miniseries) - The Burzynski Breakthrough (Fox Studios, MOW)
CREDITS   An American Daughter - My Little Assassin - Final Justice - Santa Who? - Brimstone

Robert A. Schwartz ....Executive Producer (818-990-6251)
Don Klein ....Executive Producer
Dylan Shields ....Director, Creative Affairs

SOUTH SIDE FILMS

26039 Mulholland Hwy.
Calabasas, CA 91302
PHONE 818-878-5748
FAX 818-878-5759
TYPES   Features - Made-for-TV/Cable Movies - TV Series
DEVELOPMENT   Naked Warriors - Vision - Waco
CREDITS   Judas and Jesus - Blind Fury - Vanishing Point - The Fixer - Crossfire Trail - Who Killed Atlanta's Children? - Christmas Rush - Red Water

Charles Robert Carner ....Writer/Director
Debra Sharkey ....Writer
Mark Shields ....Storyboard Artist
Jonathan Vermer ....Assistant

SOUTHERN SKIES, INC.

1104 S. Holt Ave., Ste. 302
Los Angeles, CA 90035
PHONE 310-855-9833
FAX 310-855-0220
EMAIL ....edman2000@comcast.com
TYPES   Features - Made-for-TV/Cable Movies - TV Series
CREDITS   For the Boys - Major League 1&2 - City Slickers - Alien 3 - The Great Santini

Ed Markley ....Producer

SOUTHPAW ENTERTAINMENT

1250 Sixth St., Ste. 305
Santa Monica, CA 90401
PHONE 310-587-3537
FAX 310-319-1897
TYPES   Features - Made-for-TV/Cable Movies - TV Series
POST PRODUCTION   Eulogy - House Of D
COMMENTS   FKA Ovation Entertainment

Richard Barton Lewis ....CEO
Corey Ackerman ....VP, Development
Gaby Jerou ....Director, Development
Jamie Gregor ....Assistant to Richard Barton Lewis

*SPARKY PICTURES

10040 Meritage Court
Sun Valley, CA 91352
PHONE 818-632-4603
FAX 818-351-0164
EMAIL ....info@sparkypictures.com
WEB SITE ....www.sparkypictures.com
TYPES   Features - Direct-to-Video/DVD - Made-for-TV/Cable Movies - Reality TV - TV Series
DEVELOPMENT   The Quarry - Snakevamp - The Mist - Locusts - Extensions - Weather Woman - Dream Girl - All-Stars - Granted - The Orange Tree - Bones!
POST PRODUCTION   Harbinger
CREDITS   Immortal
SUBMISSION POLICY   Unsolicited material not accepted

Walter Michael Bost ....Partner/Producer
Liisa Kyle ....Partner/Producer

SPECTACOR FILMS

10724 Moorpark St.
Los Angeles, CA 91602
PHONE .818-980-9994
FAX .818-980-9939
TYPES Features
DEVELOPMENT Zinger - Vortex
CREDITS Johnny 2.0 - The Shadow Men - Thick & Thin - Raw Nerve

Ed Snider .Partner
David Newlon .President/CEO
Jeff Foster .Controller

SPELLING TELEVISION, INC.

5700 Wilshire Blvd.
Los Angeles, CA 90036-3696
PHONE .323-965-5700
FAX .323-965-5895
TYPES Made-for-TV/Cable Movies - TV Series
PRODUCTION Clubhouse
CREDITS Summerland - 7th Heaven - Charmed

Aaron Spelling .Chairman/CEO
E. Duke Vincent .Vice Chairman
Jonathan C. Levin .President
Renate Kamer .Sr. VP
Gail Patterson .Sr. VP, Production
Kenneth Miller .Sr. VP, Post Production
Pamela Shae .Sr. VP, Talent
Rachel Bendavid .VP, Series Development
Julie Morse .VP, Controller
Shannon Knight .VP, Business & Legal Affairs
Bret Garwood .Executive Director, Video Operations
Jennifer Grisanti .Executive Director, Current Programming
Kelly McDonald .Executive Director, Talent

Spike TV

SPIKE TV

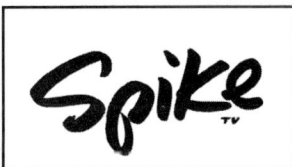

1515 Broadway
New York, NY 10036
PHONE .212-258-8000
WEB SITE .www.spiketv.com
TYPES Animation - Documentaries - Made-for-TV/Cable Movies - Syndication - TV Series - Reality TV

Herb Scannell .MTV Networks Group President, Nickelodeon, TV Land, Noggin & Spike TV
Albie Hecht .President, Spike TV
Kevin Kay .Executive VP, Programming & Development, Spike TV
Jim Burns .Sr. VP, Current Series, Spike TV
Marc Edwards .Sr. VP, Marketing, Spike TV
David Lawenda .Sr. VP, Ad Sales, Spike TV
Dan Martinsen .Sr. VP, Corporate Communications, Spike TV, Nickelodeon, TV Land
Niels Schuurmans .Sr. VP, Branding, Spike TV
Keith Brown .VP, News & Documentaries, Spike TV
Peilin Chou .VP, Production & Development, Spike TV
Jeff Goldberg .VP, Program Planning & Acquisitions, Spike TV
Jessica Heacock .VP, Affiliate Sales, MTVN
Robert Pini .VP, Communications, Spike TV
Dario Spina .VP, Marketing, Spike TV
Ivana Shechter-Garcia .Producer
Debra Fazio .Director, Press, Spike TV
David Schwarz .Director, Press, Spike TV

DARIN SPILLMAN PRODUCTIONS

1814 Idaho Ave.
Santa Monica, CA 90403
PHONE .310-592-8269
TYPES Features
DEVELOPMENT Skins Game
CREDITS Civil Brand - Turbulence 2 - Diplomatic Siege - Leprechaun in the Hood - Hide and Seek
COMMENTS No unsolicited submissions

Darin Spillman .Principal

SPIRIT DANCE ENTERTAINMENT

1023 N. Orange Dr.
Los Angeles, CA 90038
PHONE .323-512-7988
FAX .323-512-7996
TYPES Features - Made-for-TV/Cable Movies - TV Series
DEALS Twentieth Century Fox - Fox 2000
DEVELOPMENT Bow Wow Club - Head Hunters - The Facts About Kate - The First Family (TV) - Powder Blue - American Gun
CREDITS Chasing Papi - Door to Door - Green Dragon - Feast of All Saints

Forest Whitaker .President/Producer/Director
Michael Connor .VP, Affairs
Arlene Gibbs .VP, Development
James Boyd .Director, Nodance Film Festival
Alysha Augort .Office Manager
Stephanie Lim .Assistant to Arlene Gibbs

SPIRIT HORSE PRODUCTIONS

1601 San Elijo Rd.
San Marcos, CA 92078-1002
PHONE .888-429-0777/310-562-9608
FAX .310-362-8969
EMAIL .spirithorse@usa.com
SECOND EMAIL .spirithorse@asia.com
TYPES Animation - Commercials - Documentaries - Features - Made-for-TV/Cable Movies - New Media - Reality TV - Syndication - TV Series
DEVELOPMENT Interstate - The U.N.I.T. - Lightning in a Jar - Lake Bob - The Ninth Order
PRE-PRODUCTION The Bounty - Envoy - The Point - Extreme Pizza
PRODUCTION Bunkhouse - Planet XYZ
POST PRODUCTION Planet X - Fire Dog - Silent Images
CREDITS Operation Sethos: High Tech in the Tomb of the Pharoah - Don't Explain - Heaven's Pond - Secret Tunnel Hidden Treasure (NBC) - The Two Henrys - War of China's Fate - KoreaGate - Operation SETI (Discovery)
SUBMISSION POLICY Query first by email

Shari Hamrick .Producer (310-849-1957)
Michelle Hartly .Producer (310-562-9608)
Scott Duthie .Producer (818-517-7283)
Alex Williams .VP, Acquisitions & Co-Productions (631-224-7221)
Paige Dillon .Director, Development (631-224-7221)
Jeffrey L. Costell .Business & Legal Affairs (310-458-5959)

SPITFIRE PICTURES
9348 Civic Center Dr., Mezzanine
Beverly Hills, CA 90210
PHONE . . . 310-300-9000
FAX . . . 310-300-9001
EMAIL . . . info@spitfirepix.com
TYPES — Documentaries - Features - Made-for-TV/Cable Movies - TV Series
CREDITS — The Quiet American - K-19 - Adaptation - K-Pax - The Life of David Gale - National Security - Sliding Doors - Hilary and Jackie - Iris - Enigma - The Wedding Planner - Masked & Anonymous - Terminator 3

Guy East . . . No Title (UK)
Nigel Sinclair . . . No Title (LA)
Alex Brunner . . . No Title (LA)
Ben Holden . . . No Title (UK)
Debi Zornes . . . No Title (UK)
Lauren McClard . . . No Title (LA)
Barry Price . . . No Title (LA)

SPOTLIGHT HEALTH, INC.
1940 Century Park East, 4th Fl.
Los Angeles, CA 90067
PHONE . . . 310-552-0800
FAX . . . 310-552-6213
EMAIL . . . info@spotlighthealth.com
WEB SITE . . . www.spotlighthealth.com
TYPES — Documentaries - New Media - Syndication - TV Series
DEALS — A&E Television Networks
CREDITS — Carnie Wilson: Snapshots of Success - Larry King: King of Hearts - Montel Williams: MS Picked The Wrong Person - Lighthearted: Heart's Ann Wilson's Weight Loss Journey - Rodney Dangerfield: Rodney Wants Respect for AAA
COMMENTS — Marketing and communications firm specializing in the healthcare industry; Deals with USAToday.com, World Now, Inc. and eUniverse; Books; Periodicals

Dr. Jonathan Sackier . . . Chairman
Tyler Spring . . . CFO
Mick Kleber . . . Chief Creative Officer
Dr. Stephen Shoop . . . Chief Medical Officer
Richard James . . . Sr. VP, Account Services
Len Sherk . . . Sr. VP, Account Services
Brad Feldman . . . Director, Digital Marketing Services
Albert Meggers . . . Director, Technology Services

SPRING CREEK PRODUCTIONS, INC.
335 N. Maple Dr., Ste. 209
Beverly Hills, CA 90210
PHONE . . . 310-270-9000
FAX . . . 310-270-9001
TYPES — Features - Made-for-TV/Cable Movies
DEALS — Warner Bros. Entertainment Inc.
POST PRODUCTION — Envy
CREDITS — Loony Tunes - Analyze This - Liberty Heights - The Perfect Storm - An Everlasting Piece - Bandits - Possession - Analyze That
COMMENTS — Formerly Baltimore/Spring Creek Pictures, Inc.

Paula Weinstein . . . Producer
Len Amato . . . President (310-270-9080)
Jeffrey Levine . . . VP (310-270-9050)
Palak Patel . . . Director, Development (310-270-9040)
Kristen McGuiness . . . Story Editor (310-270-9030)

SPROCKETDYNE ENTERTAINMENT
5707 Melrose Ave.
Los Angeles, CA 90038
PHONE . . . 323-817-1336
FAX . . . 323-467-7280
TYPES — Animation - Features - TV Series
CREDITS — Happy Texas - Stuart Little 1&2 - Haunted Mansion - Killer Diller

Rob Minkoff . . . Director/Partner
Jason Clark . . . Producer/Partner
Warren Davis . . . VP, Development
Teryn Fogel . . . VP, Development
Kerry Derzius . . . Creative Executive
Nancy Walker . . . Assistant to Rob Minkoff

SPUMCO
10859 Burbank Blvd., Ste. A
North Hollywood, CA 91601
PHONE . . . 818-623-1955
FAX . . . 818-623-1958
EMAIL . . . kkolde@thegrid.net
TYPES — Animation - Features - New Media - TV Series
PRODUCTION — The New Ren & Stimpy Show
CREDITS — The Ren & Stimpy Show - Bjork: I Miss You - Ranger Smith - The Goddamn George Liquor Program - The Ripping Friends
COMMENTS — Cartoons on the Internet

John Kricfalusi . . . Producer/Director/President
Kevin Kolde . . . VP/General Manager

SPYGLASS ENTERTAINMENT GROUP
10900 Wilshire Blvd., 10th Fl.
Los Angeles, CA 90024
PHONE . . . 310-443-5800
FAX . . . 310-443-5912
WEB SITE . . . www.spyglassentertainment.com
TYPES — Features - TV Series
DEALS — Columbia Pictures
PRE-PRODUCTION — Mute Witness - Static - The Invisible
PRODUCTION — Hitchhiker's Guide to the Galaxy - The Pacifier
CREDITS — Seabiscuit - Bruce Almighty - The Recruit - Shanghai Knights - The Count of Monte Cristo - The Sixth Sense - The Insider - Keeping the Faith - Shanghai Noon - Unbreakable - Reign of Fire - Miracles (ABC/Touchstone) - Connie and Carla

Gary Barber . . . Co-Chairman/CEO
Roger Birnbaum . . . Co-Chairman/CEO
Jonathan Glickman . . . President
Derek Evans . . . Executive VP, Production
Paul Neinstein . . . Executive VP
Karen Sortito . . . Executive VP, Worldwide Marketing
Jeffrey Chernov . . . Sr. VP, Physical Production
Rebekah Rudd . . . Sr. VP, Post Production
Megan Wolpert . . . Sr. VP, TV
Jose Gutierrez . . . VP, Finance
Erin Stam . . . VP, Production
Ivan Oyco . . . Creative Executive
Kim Buttlar . . . Executive Director
Marlena Thomas . . . Executive Director

SPYWORM
1009 Abbot Kinney Blvd.
Venice, CA 90291
PHONE .310-399-6600
FAX .310-399-4530
EMAIL .info@spyworm.tv
WEB SITE .www.spyworm.tv
TYPES Documentaries - Features - New Media - TV Series
DEVELOPMENT What Were You Thinking? - Shoot America - The Los Angeles Underground
POST PRODUCTION The Mechanical Bride - Chocolate
COMPLETED UNRELEASED Real Life PI's - Stuffed
CREDITS The Pavilion - Sex* Like You've Never Seen Before - Burned

Jack C. Merrick .Producer/Partner
C. Grant Mitchell .Producer/Director/Partner
Kevin Lee Barrere .Production Manager

SRG PRODUCTIONS
c/o Sandy Russell Gartin
6543 Commodore Sloat Dr.
Los Angeles, CA 90048
PHONE .323-935-3052
FAX .323-935-3052
TYPES Animation - Made-for-TV/Cable Movies - Features - Syndication - TV Series
CREDITS Cats Don't Dance - The Perfect Getaway - Bad Attitudes - A Billion for Boris - No Big Deal

Sandy Russell Gartin .Producer

ST. AMOS PRODUCTIONS
3480 Barham Blvd., Ste. 108
Los Angeles, CA 90068
PHONE .323-850-9872
TYPES Features - Made-for-TV/Cable Movies - TV Series - Reality TV
DEVELOPMENT Meet Jane Doe - Butterflies Are Free - Mary Surratt - Saving Shakespeare - Leaving Hopeful - The Man That God Forgot - The Dog's Meow - America's Favorite Couples (Special)
CREDITS The Beach Boys (ABC) - Grown Ups - Thieves (ABC) - The Virgin Chronicles (MTV) - The Martin & Lewis Story (CBS)

John Stamos .Producer/Actor
Marc Alexander .Producer/Writer/Development

STAMPEDE ENTERTAINMENT
3000 W. Olympic Blvd.
Santa Monica, CA 90404
PHONE .310-552-9977
FAX .310-552-9324
WEB SITE .www.stampede-entertainment.com
TYPES Features - TV Series
DEVELOPMENT Supernatural Law - Tremors 5
CREDITS City Slickers - Heart and Souls - Tremors 1-4 - Tremors (Sci Fi Channel)

Nancy Roberts .Partner/Co-Chairman/CEO
S.S. Wilson .Partner/Co-Chairman
Brent Maddock .Partner
Greg Stevens .VP
Margaret Shields .No Title

STAR ENTERTAINMENT GROUP, INC.
13547 Ventura Blvd., Ste. 140
Sherman Oaks, CA 91423
PHONE .818-988-2200
FAX .818-988-2202
WEB SITE .www.findinghomemovie.com
TYPES Features
DEVELOPMENT Shifting Sands - Young Warriors (Remake) - Memories of the Heart - Malibu High (Remake)
POST PRODUCTION Finding Home
CREDITS Young Warriors - Malibu High - Prima Donnas - Night Force - Don't Go Near the Park - The Great Skycopter Rescue - Lovely, but Deadly

Lawrence D. Foldes .Chairman
Victoria Paige Meyerink .President
Denis Hoffman .Production Executive
Michael Sloan .Production Executive
Grafton S. Harper .Director, Development
Luigi Marchesi .Production Coordinator
Sean Blodgett .Post Production Coordinator
Robert C. Rosen, Esq. .Legal Counsel

STAR LAND ENTERTAINMENT, INC.
8306 Wilshire Blvd., Ste. 7032
Beverly Hills, CA 90211
PHONE .323-651-1625
TYPES Features - Syndication - TV Series
CREDITS The Stand Off - Love & War 2 - All's Fair in Love & War - July 4th Triangle
COMMENTS Features for worldwide theatrical release

James Tyler .Producer/Director/Writer/Actor
Steven Halpern .Writer/Producer
Richard LaMarr .Executive
Sharon Choi .VP, Acquisitions
Gary Sohl .Director, Operations

STARGAZER ENTERTAINMENT, INC.
11828 La Grange Ave.
Los Angeles, CA 90025
PHONE .310-479-1200
FAX .310-473-9166
EMAIL .wmrc1@aol.com
TYPES Features - Direct-to-Video/DVD - TV Series
CREDITS Perfect Witness - Money Plays - Age Old Friends - AMC's Hollywood Report Series - Charlie Rose Specials

Wayne Rogers .Executive Producer
Amy Rogers .Executive Producer
William Tannen .Executive Producer
Linda Black .Production Assistant

JANE STARTZ PRODUCTIONS, INC.
244 Fifth Ave., 11th Fl.
New York, NY 10001
PHONE .212-545-8910
FAX .212-545-8909
EMAIL .jsp@janestartzproductions.com
TYPES Features - Direct-to-Video/DVD - TV Series
DEVELOPMENT Son of the Mob - The Night Room - I Want to Buy a Vowel - This Is Not a Toy - Two Princesses of Bamarre - North Shore Ninja - Pushcart War - The Orphans Club - Lord of the Nutcracker Men - Judy Blume's Deenie
CREDITS The Mighty - Indian in the Cupboard - The Magic Schoolbus - The Baby-Sitters Club - Tuck Everlasting - Ella Enchanted

Jane Startz .President/Producer
Gillian MacKenzie .VP, Creative Affairs
Billy Mulligan .Director, Development

STATE STREET PICTURES

c/o Twentieth Century Fox
10201 W. Pico Blvd., Bldg. 52, Rm. 123
Los Angeles, CA 90064
PHONE 310-369-5099
FAX 310-369-8613
TYPES Features - TV Series
DEALS Twentieth Century Fox - Fox 2000
DEVELOPMENT A Conversation with the Mann - Criminal Minded - Two Year Mark - Some Kind of Blue - Frontin' - Untitled Derwin Henderson project
PRE-PRODUCTION Roll Bounce
CREDITS Soul Food (Feature) - Men of Honor - Soul Food (Series) - Barbershop 1&2

Robert Teitel ....Producer
George Tillman Jr. ....Director
Heather Courtney ....VP, Production & Development
Poppy Hanks ....Director, Development
Kimberly Barton ....Assistant to VP
Chuck Hayward ....Assistant to Producer
George Tarrant ....Assistant to Director

STEAMROLLER PRODUCTIONS, INC.

4117-1/2 Radford Ave.
Studio City, CA 91604
PHONE 818-505-6635
FAX 818-505-6636
EMAIL ....steamrollerprod@aol.com
TYPES Documentaries - Features - Direct-to-Video/DVD - New Media - TV Series
DEVELOPMENT Under Siege 3 - Untitled Mercenary Project
PRE-PRODUCTION Submerged
POST PRODUCTION Into the Sun
COMPLETED UNRELEASED Out of Reach
CREDITS The Glimmer Man - Fire Down Below - On Deadly Ground - Under Siege 1&2 - Above the Law - Steven Seagal's Aikido: The Path Beyond Thought - Exit Wounds - Half Past Dead

Steven Seagal ....CEO/Director/Writer/Producer/Actor
Phillip Goldfine ....COO
Binh Dang ....Production Executive
Tracy Irvine ....Executive Assistant
Patrice Messina ....Executive Assistant

MITCHELL STEIN PRODUCTIONS

PO Box 426
Corte Madera, CA 94976
PHONE 415-924-4546
EMAIL ....msp@poolside.com
TYPES Animation - Documentaries - Features - New Media - TV Series
DEVELOPMENT The Pact - 48 Shades of Brown - Boneheads - Untitled IMAX Project
CREDITS Dream with the Fishes - Christmas in the Clouds - The Earth Will Swallow You
COMMENTS Independent producer; Produced and/or on production team of LucasArts, Commercial Pictures, Walt Disney Productions, New World InterPlay, Electronic Arts

Mitchell Stein ....Producer

THE HOWARD STERN PRODUCTION COMPANY

10 E. 44th St.
New York, NY 10017
PHONE 212-867-1200
FAX 212-867-2434
TYPES Animation - Features - TV Series
DEVELOPMENT Porky's - Rock 'n' Roll High School - Howard Stern's Teenage Years (SpikeTV) - Schimmel & Schimmel (The WBTV) - ABC Interview Special
CREDITS The Howard Stern E! Show - Son of the Beach - Doomsday - The Howard Stern Radio Show

Howard Stern ....President
Don Buchwald ....Agent
Mark Grande ....Director, Development

STEVENS & ASSOCIATES

9454 Wilshire Blvd., Ste. 600
Beverly Hills, CA 90212
PHONE 310-275-7541
FAX 310-275-5929
TYPES Animation - Documentaries - Features - Made-for-TV/Cable Movies - TV Series
PRE-PRODUCTION Lord Byron - Praying for Rain
CREDITS Gunshy - This Is L.S.A. - Money Shot - What Alice Found

Neal Stevens ....President
Arastao Maree ....Development Executive
Chris Regner ....Associate
Lisa Barden ....Development Associate
Jacob Dikhow ....Development Associate
Stephen Roe ....Development Associate

THE STEVENS COMPANY

c/o Jess Morgan & Company
5750 Wilshire Blvd., Ste. 590
Los Angeles, CA 90036-3697
PHONE 323-634-2400/202-416-7960
FAX 323-937-6532
EMAIL ....newlibertydot@aol.com
TYPES Documentaries - Features - TV Series
DEVELOPMENT American Requiem - Ghost of Jack Gilette - Chasing Rainbows
PRE-PRODUCTION Kennedy Center Honors (CBS) - Christmas in Washington (TNT)
CREDITS Thin Red Line - Kennedy Center Honors - Christmas in Washington - Sin
COMMENTS East Coast office: JFK Center, Washington, DC 20566

George Stevens Jr. ....Partner/Writer/Producer/Director
Michael Stevens ....Partner/Writer/Producer/Director
Dottie McCarthy ....Assistant to George Stevens Jr.

JOEL STEVENS ENTERTAINMENT

206 S. Brand Blvd.
Glendale, CA 91204
PHONE 818-509-5700
FAX 818-509-6734
TYPES Features - Made-for-TV/Cable Movies - TV Series
DEALS Franchise Pictures, Inc.
DEVELOPMENT David & the Devil - Liar - Full Ride - A Funny Life - Yosemite National - Denmark: Hotel and Casino
CREDITS Elvis & Me (ABC Miniseries)

Joel Stevens ....President/CEO
Adam Neal ....Director, Talent & Development
John Will ....Office Manager/Associate
Ian Baca ....Talent & Development Associate

STEWART TELEVISION, INC.
5525 Oakdale Ave., Ste. 275
Woodland Hills, CA 91364
PHONE 818-313-9394
FAX 818-313-9514
EMAIL . . . . company@stewarttelevision.com
WEB SITE . . . . www.stewarttelevision.com
TYPES TV Series
CREDITS Sports on Tap - Remember This - Inquizition - Hollywood Showdown - Missouri Lottery: Fun & Fortune - Multi-State Lottery: Powerball Instant Millionaire

Sande Stewart . . . . Executive Producer
Molly Gray . . . . Producer
Bruce Burmester . . . . Director

STILLWATER FILMS
311 N. Robertson Blvd., Ste. 737
Beverly Hills, CA 90211
PHONE 310-273-3525
FAX 310-273-3526
EMAIL . . . . stillwaterfilms@hotmail.com
TYPES Documentaries - Features - TV Series
DEVELOPMENT Self Serve - Lost Not Found - Coyote Highway
POST PRODUCTION Punk's Not Dead - Brick
CREDITS Good Housekeeping

Susan Dynner . . . . Partner/Producer
Mark Mathis . . . . Partner/Producer

STONE STANLEY ENTERTAINMENT
c/o Hollywood Center Studios
1040 N. Las Palmas, Bldg. 1
Hollywood, CA 90038
PHONE 323-960-2599
FAX 323-860-3145
EMAIL . . . . mmarcus@stonestanley.com
WEB SITE . . . . www.stonestanley.com
TYPES Syndication - TV Series - Reality TV
CREDITS Celebrity Mole: Yucatan - The Joe Schmo Show - Fame - The Man Show - Shop 'til You Drop - Legends of the Hidden Temple - Oblivious

Scott A. Stone . . . . Partner
David Decker . . . . Sr. VP, Business & Legal Affairs
Jennifer Decker . . . . VP, Production Finance
Eliot Goldberg . . . . VP, Current Programming
Sharon Levy . . . . VP, Development
Matthew Marcus . . . . VP, Marketing & Corporate Communications
Michael Frederick . . . . Director of Development

STONE VILLAGE PICTURES, LLC
9200 Sunset Blvd., Ste. 520
West Hollywood, CA 90069
PHONE 310-777-2163/310-777-2162
FAX 310-777-2150
TYPES Features - TV Series
DEVELOPMENT The Hundredth Man - Nobody True - J. Edgar Hoover - Tortilla Curtain - MODOC
POST PRODUCTION Empire Falls
CREDITS The Human Stain - Las Vegas (NBC/Dreamworks)
COMMENTS Las Vegas shows

Scott Steindorff . . . . No Title
Andrew Molasky . . . . No Title
Danny Greenspun . . . . No Title
Robin Greenspun . . . . No Title
Valeska Ramet . . . . No Title (310-777-2180)
Dylan Russell . . . . No Title (310-777-2176)
Scott LaStaiti . . . . No Title (310-777-2162)
Anne Quin-Harkin . . . . No Title (310-777-2165)
Sarah Scott . . . . No Title (310-777-2181)

STONE VS. STONE
213 Rose Ave., The Firehouse, 2nd Fl.
Venice, CA 90291
PHONE 310-664-1999/212-334-8228
TYPES Features - TV Series
CREDITS Citizen X - The Negotiator - Gone in 60 Seconds
COMMENTS Publisher: Rugged Land: 401 West St., New York, NY 10014

Robert Stone . . . . Producer/Writer
Webster Stone . . . . Producer/Writer

STONELOCK PICTURES
18590 Ventura Blvd., Ste. 205
Tarzana, CA 91356
PHONE 818-716-6356/310-858-7286
FAX 818-716-6866
EMAIL . . . . info@stonelockpictures.com
WEB SITE . . . . www.stonelockpictures.com
TYPES Features
DEVELOPMENT The Last Seduction of Mata Hari
PRE-PRODUCTION Gilgamesh
CREDITS In Dark Places - The Spreading Ground - The Jimmy Show - Thirteen Conversations About One Thing
COMMENTS Fully integrated finance and production company

Beni Tadd Atoori . . . . CEO/CFO
Sabrina Atoori . . . . President, Production
Adrian Vina . . . . Executive Assistant
Andrew Schoellkopf . . . . Administrative Assistant

STONEWERKS MOTION PICTURE GROUP
500 S. Sepulveda Blvd., Ste. 600
Los Angeles, CA 90049
PHONE 310-440-1954
FAX 310-440-7842
TYPES Features
DEALS The Howard Stern Production Company
DEVELOPMENT Porky's - Rock 'n' Roll High School - Little Gridfellas

H. Daniel Gross . . . . President, Production & Development
Steve Squillante . . . . Sr. VP, Production & Development
Steven Weigle . . . . Development Assistant

STONEWORKS TELEVISION
4420 Hayvenhurst Ave.
Encino, CA 91436
PHONE 818-995-1585/310-475-3201
WEB SITE . . . . www.stoneworkstv.com
TYPES TV Series
DEVELOPMENT Weekly World News - Dead in the West - The Whale
CREDITS Terminal Invasion - Control Factor - Find a Fortune
SUBMISSION POLICY No unsolicited submissions or drop-offs

Chris Cusack . . . . Partner/Producer
Chuck Simon . . . . Partner/Producer

It is illegal to copy any part of this book

STORM ENTERTAINMENT
127 Broadway, Ste. 200
Santa Monica, CA 90401
PHONE .310-656-2500
FAX .310-656-2510
EMAIL .storment95@aol.com
WEB SITE .www.stormentertainment.com
TYPES Animation - Features - Made-for-TV/Cable Movies
PRE-PRODUCTION Outlanders - Coyote! - Preacher - Emma Thompson's Johnny Hit and Run Pauline - Crusade in Jeans - Sweet Talk - Ghett'a Life - Heidi
CREDITS Modern Vampires - Hurlyburly - The Criminal - Fast Sofa - Big City Blues - Lovelife - Nevada - Kart Racer - Glam - Heaven or Vegas

H. Michael Heuser .President/CEO
Kourosh Esmailzadeh .Manager, International Distribution

STORYLINE ENTERTAINMENT
500 S. Buena Vista St.
Old Animation Bldg., Ste. 3-C
Burbank, CA 91521
PHONE .818-560-2928
FAX .818-560-5145
WEB SITE .www.storyline-entertainment.com
TYPES Features - Made-for-TV/Cable Movies - TV Series
DEALS Sony Pictures Television
PRODUCTION Empire
CREDITS Chicago - The Music Man (ABC) - Annie - Footloose - The Beach Boys - The Three Stooges - Life with Judy Garland: Me and My Shadows - Martin and Lewis (CBS) - Lucy (CBS)

Craig Zadan .Executive Producer
Neil Meron .Executive Producer
Travis Knox .VP, Feature Development
Dave Mace .VP, Production & Development, TV
Laine Bateman .Assistant to Mr. Zadan & Mr. Meron
Lorry Costello .Assistant to Mr. Mace
Andrew Wang .Assistant to Mr. Zadan & Mr. Meron

STORYTIME ENTERTAINMENT
544 Lillian Way
Los Angeles, CA 90004
PHONE .323-468-9101
FAX .323-369-7633
EMAIL .storytimeentertainment@comcast.net
TYPES Made-for-TV/Cable Movies
DEVELOPMENT Baby Makes Three (CBS, Trilogy) - Golden Code (FX)
CREDITS Jewel (CBS)

Helene Lynn-Nash .Producer

STORYWORKS ENTERTAINMENT, INC.
4301 Baronsgate Rd.
Westlake Village, CA 91361
PHONE .818-618-4322/818-620-7983
EMAIL .heather@storyworksentertainment.net
SECOND EMAIL .shelly@storyworksentertainment.net
WEB SITE .www.storyworksentertainment.net
SECOND WEB SITE .www.theindustry.la
TYPES Commercials - Documentaries - Features - Made-for-TV/Cable Movies - TV Series
DEVELOPMENT Been There, Came Back - Chasing Honus - Mad Moms in a Mini Van - Cat Dancing
CREDITS The Perfect Husband
COMMENTS Seeking development and production funds, co-production partnerships and distribution alliances

Heather Hale .President
Shelly Howell .CEO

BERT STRATFORD PRODUCTIONS, INC.
662 Millbrook Rd.
River Edge, NJ 07661
PHONE .212-757-2211
FAX .201-265-0963
TYPES Animation - Features - Direct-to-Video/DVD - Made-for-TV/Cable Movies - Syndication - TV Series
DEVELOPMENT Smothers Brothers Movie (Showtime) - Pony Kids (Feature) - Burkie - UnDead (Feature) - Men Wanted (Feature)
CREDITS 12 Days of Christmas - White Fang - Bingo & Molly - Noel - Peppermint Rose - The Christmas Secret

Bert Stratford .Producer/Owner
Aura Sujaritchan .Director, Development

STRATUS FILM COMPANY
10850 Wilshire Blvd., 6th Fl.
Los Angeles, CA 90024
PHONE .310-689-1691
FAX .310-234-8975
TYPES Features
DEALS Focus Features/Rogue Pictures - Universal Pictures
DEVELOPMENT Painted Veil - Killing Pablo
PRODUCTION Hostage - Haven - Jump Shot
POST PRODUCTION Laws of Attraction - Winter Passing - Crash - House of D - A Love Song for Bobby Long - Sueno - Employee of the Month

Bob Yari .Partner (310-689-1691)
Mark Gordon .Partner (310-943-6404)
Richard Lewis .CFO
Neil Sacker .COO/General Counsel
Brad Jenkel .Executive VP, Production
Robert Katz .Executive VP, Production
Robyn Roth .Sr. VP, Business & Legal Affairs
Shelly Strong .VP, Production & Finance
Dan Stutz .VP, Business & Legal Affairs
Meredith Grindlinger .Business Affairs
Rick Gold .Assistant to Neil Sacker
Andrea Hanson .Assistant to Bob Yari
Ian Watermeier .Assistant to Robert Katz

STRIKE ENTERTAINMENT
3000 W. Olympic Blvd., Bldg. 5, Ste. 1250
Santa Monica, CA 90404
PHONE .310-315-0550
FAX .310-315-0560
TYPES Features
DEALS Universal Pictures
DEVELOPMENT Beautiful Killer - Children of Men - You Are Going to Prison - Lucky Jim - Miss Fortune
CREDITS The Rundown - Dawn of the Dead

Marc Abraham .No Title
Tom Bliss .No Title
Eric Newman .No Title
Phil Altmann .No Title
Josh Bratman .No Title
Kristel Laiblin .No Title
Amanda Murphy .No Title
Mark Barclay .No Title
Tracey Averett .No Title

MEL STUART PRODUCTIONS, INC.
1551 S. Robertson Blvd., Ste. 204
Los Angeles, CA 90035
PHONE .310-785-9080
FAX .310-785-9179
EMAIL .melfilm@aol.com
TYPES Documentaries - Features - TV Series
CREDITS Willy Wonka & the Chocolate Factory - Man Ray - Four Days in November - Running on the Sun - The Rise and Fall of the Third Reich - Wattsax - Ripley's Believe It or Not - W.S. Mervin: A Poet's View

Mel Stuart .President

STUDIO HAMBURG WORLDWIDE PICTURES
9200 Sunset Blvd., Ste. 330
Los Angeles, CA 90069
PHONE .310-246-6533/49-40-6688-5561
FAX .310-246-6535/49-40-6688-5550
EMAIL .wwp@studio-hamburg.de
WEB SITE .www.studio-hamburg.de
TYPES Features - Direct-to-Video/DVD
PRE-PRODUCTION Dungeons & Dragons: The Sequel
POST PRODUCTION Chestnut: Hero of Central Park
COMPLETED UNRELEASED The Boys from County Clare
COMMENTS An equity film fund financing and producing feature films up to $20 million

Wolfgang Esenwein .CEO
David Korda .LA Representative
Alexandra Heneka .Creative Executive
Melanie Lotsch .Assistant to Wolfgang Esenwein

STUDIOCANAL (U.S.)
301 N. Canon Dr., Ste. 210
Beverly Hills, CA 90210
PHONE .310-247-0994
FAX .310-247-0998
TYPES Features

Robert Chamberlain .No Title
Barbara DiNallo .No Title

STUN
5225 Wilshire Blvd., Ste. 909
Los Angeles, CA 90036
PHONE .323-954-6464
FAX .323-954-7464
EMAIL .info@stunproductions.com
TYPES Features - New Media - TV Series
DEVELOPMENT A Public Affair - Darger - Dolomites - Heart of the Matter
CREDITS The Gun Seller - Found in the Street - The Magic Shop - IOU

Susan Adler .Chairman/President

STUNTMAN, INC.
c/o Laura Lizer & Associates
PO Box 46609
Los Angeles, CA 90046
PHONE .323-876-4040
FAX .323-876-5109
TYPES Features - Made-for-TV/Cable Movies - New Media - TV Series

Hal Needham .Director/Writer/Producer
Laura Lizer .Business Manager

SUB ROSA PRODUCTIONS, INC.
8721 Santa Monica Blvd., Ste. 460
Los Angeles, CA 90069-4511
PHONE .323-650-4466
FAX .323-650-4448
EMAIL .sr@sub-rosa-productions.com
WEB SITE .www.isubrosa.com
SECOND WEB SITE .www.subrosabooks.com
TYPES Features - Made-for-TV/Cable Movies - New Media - Reality TV - Syndication - TV Series
CREDITS Love at First Bite - Check Is in the Mail - How to Beat the High Cost of Living - People TV
SUBMISSION POLICY Do not send scripts; Email a logline and no more than one paragraph, with contact info; Write "Submission" in subject line

Robin Krause .President/CEO/Producer
Karen G. Jackovich .President, Worldwide TV (NY) (212-682-3195)
Sherilyn Moore .Sr. VP, Development
Liz Amsden .VP, Production
Charles Terry Goldstein, Esq. .VP, Business Affairs
Kit Westman .Head, Production
Tena Montoya .Producer
Jon Andersen .Creative Executive
Nikki Donahue .Creative Executive
Shannon Jacobson .Creative Executive
A.D. Crane .Director, Operations
Tanya Sharma .Director, Online Marketing
Jarrett Widman .Director, New Media
Suzanne Cross .Executive Assistant
Michelle Loparo .Development Assistant
Fleur Henry .Assistant

ANDREW SUGERMAN
c/o Allied Cinema Corporation
3576 Dixie Canyon Ave.
Sherman Oaks, CA 91423
PHONE .213-891-2670
WEB SITE .www.hometown.aol.com/absuger
TYPES Features - Made-for-TV/Cable Movies
POST PRODUCTION Shopgirl
CREDITS Love Kills - Working Trash - Kimberly - Basic Training - Payoff - Spiders - Prozac Nation - Undisputed - Ballistic - Boat Trip - The Whole Ten Yards - Johnson Family Vacation

Andrew Sugerman .Producer

MIKE SULLIVAN PRODUCTIONS, INC.

2314 Michigan Ave.
Santa Monica, CA 90404-3930
PHONE .310-315-7315
FAX .310-582-0041
EMAIL .mikhsul@aol.com
TYPES Features - Made-for-TV/Cable Movies - TV Series - Reality TV
CREDITS Growing Pains - Just the Ten of Us - The Growing Pains Movie

Mike Sullivan .President/Executive Producer
Paul Spadone .Sr. VP, Development
Craig Young .Story Editor

SUMMERLAND ENTERTAINMENT

17939 Chatsworth St., Ste. 260
Granada Hills, CA 91344
PHONE .818-368-3208
EMAIL .bruce@sumrland.com
TYPES Features - Made-for-TV/Cable Movies - TV Series
DEVELOPMENT The Girl from Hollywood - London, Texas - American Triumph - Fable for Two
CREDITS The Dream Team - Baywatch Nights - Nightmare Café - Fatal Memories - In the Heat of the Night - The Dirty Dozen - Police Story: The Freeway Killings - George Washington
COMMENTS Deal with Angelic Entertainment

Bruce A. Pobjoy .President/Producer
Brianne Michelle .VP, Development

SUMMERS ENTERTAINMENT

31708 Broad Beach Rd.
Malibu, CA 90265
PHONE .310-589-2189
FAX .310-457-1662
EMAIL .july4bu@charter.net
TYPES Documentaries - Features - Made-for-TV/Cable Movies - New Media - Syndication - TV Series
CREDITS Slow Burn - Who Knew? - Stakeout 1&2 - Sandlot - Mystery Date - Vital Signs - Dogfight - DOA

Cathleen Summers .Producer

SUMMIT ENTERTAINMENT

1630 Stewart St., Ste. 120
Santa Monica, CA 90404
PHONE .310-309-8400
FAX .310-828-4132
TYPES Features
DEVELOPMENT Black Sabbath - The Watcher - Time Travel for Dumies - The Fat Man - Untitled Doug Liman Project - Forget About It - Me Again
PRODUCTION Mr. & Mrs. Smith - The Alibi
CREDITS Wrong Turn - Dot the I - Memento - Vanilla Sky

Patrick Wachsberger .President/CEO
Bob Hayward .COO
David Garrett .Executive VP (UK)
Erik Feig .President, Production & Acquisitions
Adrienne Biddle .VP, Development & Acquisitions
Meredith Milton .Director, Development & Acquisitions

SUNDANCE INSTITUTE

8857 W. Olympic Blvd.
Beverly Hills, CA 90211
PHONE .310-360-1981
FAX .310-360-1969
EMAIL .la@sundance.org
WEB SITE .www.sundance.org
TYPES Documentaries - Features - New Media
COMMENTS Nonprofit arts organization

Kenneth Brecher .Executive Director
Pat Dandonoli .Director, Strategic Initiatives
Geoffrey Gilmore .Director, Programming, Sundance Film Festival
Peter Golub .Director, Film Music Program/Composers Lab Coordinator
Philip Himberg .Artistic Director, Theater Program
Michelle Satter .Director, Feature Film Program
John Cooper .Associate Director, Film Festival Programming
Debby Stover .Associate Producer, Theater
Alesia Weston .Sr. Manager, Feature Film Program, International
Ilyse McKimmie .Manager, Feature Film Program
Judith Wexler .Manager, Administrative Services
Trevor Groth .Programmer, Sundance Film Festival
Bird Runningwater .Programmer, Native American Initiatives
Shari Frilot .Associate Programmer, Sundance Film Festival
Elizabeth Richardson .Programming Coordinator
Lane Kneedler .Administrative Coordinator
Joseph Beyer .Assistant to Director, Film Festival Programming
Michael Bodie .Assistant to Director, Feature Film Program
Jonathan Korn .Receptionist

SUNLIGHT PRODUCTIONS

854-A Fifth St.
Santa Monica, CA 90403
PHONE .310-899-1522
FAX .310-899-1262
EMAIL .info@sunlightproductions.com
WEB SITE .www.sunlightproductions.com
TYPES Features - TV Series
CREDITS The Search for John Gissing - The Mind of the Married Man (HBO) - Indian Summer - Crossing the Bridge - Londinium - The Sex Monster - Coupe de Ville - The Upside of Anger

Mike Binder .Writer/Director/Actor
Jack Binder .Producer
Nicole Sacker .Assistant to Jack Binder
Rachel Zimmerman .Assistant to Mike Binder

RONALD SUPPA PRODUCTIONS, INC.

32063 Canterhill Pl.
Westlake Village, CA 91361-4817
PHONE .818-879-1383
EMAIL .rsprodinc@aol.com
TYPES Features
DEVELOPMENT Brothers - Lord Byron's Daughter - The Shining Path
CREDITS Defense Play - Riding the Edge - Paradise Alley - Maui Heat

Ronald Suppa .Writer/Producer
Eric Harrington .VP, Development
Jolene Rae .VP, New Media

***SUSIE Q PRODUCTIONS**
117 Perry St., Ste. 20
New York, NY 10014
PHONE .646-221-4581
EMAIL .leber2000@yahoo.com
WEB SITE .www.susieqproductions.com
TYPES Features
DEVELOPMENT Hello and Goodnight - 17 Stitches - The Last Rites of Joe May - Born Again - I Love New York
PRE-PRODUCTION Bittersweet Place
POST PRODUCTION The Roost
COMPLETED UNRELEASED Down to the Bone
CREDITS Margarita Happy Hour - The Technical Writer

Susan Leber .Producer

SWEENEY ENTERTAINMENT
8755 Lookout Mountain Ave.
Los Angeles, CA 90046
PHONE .323-822-3000
FAX .323-822-3020
EMAIL .sweedavid@aol.com
TYPES Animation - Documentaries - Features - Made-for-TV/Cable Movies - TV Series
DEVELOPMENT Destiny
CREDITS Wigstock: The Movie
SUBMISSION POLICY No unsolicited submissions

David Sweeney .Partner/Producer
Gary Light .Associate

SYMPHONY PICTURES, INC.
1148 Fourth St., Ste. 116
Santa Monica, CA 90403
PHONE .310-656-9040
FAX .310-656-9046
EMAIL .mail@sympics.com
TYPES Features - Made-for-TV/Cable Movies - TV Series
DEVELOPMENT Cannibus Club - Pegasus - Marin Family Court - False Heart - Film School
PRE-PRODUCTION National Lampoon's The Trouble With Frank
CREDITS Seduced by a Thief - Clover Bend - Da - Nightbreaker - Judgement in Berlin - She Stood Alone: The Tailhook Scandal - Target Earth - Mickey and Dommy - Doomsday Man - Above Suspicion

William R. Greenblatt .President
Jeffrey Carrara .Producer
Gizza Elizondo .Director, Creative Affairs
Jessica Kollar .Director, Development

SYNCHRONICITY PRODUCTIONS
6363 Santa Monica, 2nd Fl. West
Los Angeles, CA 90038
PHONE .310-246-1477/212-704-0515
FAX .323-465-1914
TYPES Animation - Commercials - Documentaries - Features - Direct-to-Video/DVD - Made-for-TV/Cable Movies - New Media - Syndication - Theater - TV Series
CREDITS Holy Joe - In Pursuit of Honor - Element of Truth
COMMENTS East Coast office: 500 Fifth Ave., Ste. 1825, New York, NY 10110

Larry Peerce .No Title
Adam Peck .No Title

SYNERGY ENTERTAINMENT GROUP
PO Box 902
Corona Del Mar, CA 92625
PHONE .949-933-9721
EMAIL .marialane_2020@yahoo.com
WEB SITE .www.synergyentertainmentgroupllc.com
TYPES Features - TV Series
CREDITS Jason's Lyric

Marilla Lane Ross .Executive VP

T.V. REPAIR
857 Castac Pl.
Pacific Palisades, CA 90272
PHONE .310-459-3671
FAX .310-459-4251
EMAIL .davidjlatt@earthlink.net
TYPES New Media - TV Series
DEVELOPMENT Dr. Dave (Showtime)
CREDITS Citizen Baines (CBS) - EZ Streets - ATF - Under Suspicion - Hill Street Blues - Gramercy Park (ABC)

David J. Latt .Producer/Writer

TACTICS
8740 Dorrington Ave.
West Hollywood, CA 90048-1724
PHONE .310-657-6642
FAX .310-657-5904
TYPES Features - Made-for-TV/Cable Movies
DEVELOPMENT The Honeymoon - SOS Doctors - Partners in Crime - Try to Remember - Hysterical Pregnancy
CREDITS Peroxide Passion - End of the Line - Reunion - Nine Months - North Star - Operation Splitsville

Anne Francois .CEO/Producer

TAE PRODUCTIONS/MEDEACOM PRODUCTIONS
4741 E. Palm Canyon Dr., Ste. 171
Palm Springs, CA 92264
PHONE .760-321-6683
FAX .760-328-3366
TYPES Documentaries - Features - Direct-to-Video/DVD - New Media - Syndication - TV Series
DEVELOPMENT Warriors of the Rainbow: The Greenpeace Movie - Directors' Cuts 2 (Hearst) - Vanishing Voices (Rhino) - Wealth (The Kuhn Foundation) - Closer to Truth (The Kuhn Foundation)
PRODUCTION Harley-Davidson: The Spirit of America - Day of the Dead - Hootenanny Reunion (Shout)
CREDITS Operation Enduring Freedom (Artisan) - Crossing the Line (Lifetime) - Heaven & Earth (Warner Bros.) - Victory in the Desert: General Colin Powell (Artisan) - First Works 1&2 (Showtime/Rhino) - Princess Grace (ABC) - Terrorism (Series/The Discovery Channel)

Robert D. Kline .President/CEO
Stephanie Heredia .VP/Producer
Armando Diaz .VP, Production
Roger Diaz .VP, Internet
Johnnie Tidwell .Creative Affairs
Ann Kelly .Assistant to President/CEO

TAFFNER ENTERTAINMENT, LTD.
17925 Tarzana St.
Encino, CA 91316
PHONE .323-937-1144
FAX .310-284-3290
TYPES Documentaries - Features - Syndication - TV Series
CREDITS Rumpole at the Bailey - Too Close for Comfort - Three's Company - Wanted

Don Taffner Jr. .Executive VP/CEO (NY/LA)
Jeff Cotugno .CFO (NY)
Emmet Lavery Jr. .VP, Business Affairs (LA)

TAG ENTERTAINMENT
4130 Cahuenga Blvd., 2nd Fl.
Universal City, CA 91602
PHONE .818-985-7900
FAX .818-985-7901
EMAIL .info@tagentertainment.com
WEB SITE .www.tagentertainment.com
TYPES Features - Made-for-TV/Cable Movies - New Media
POST PRODUCTION Red Riding Hood
CREDITS No Place Like Home - Hansel & Gretel - Miracle Dogs - The Santa Trap - Dumb Luck - The Retrievers - Castle Rock - Motocross Kids
COMMENTS Focus on family entertainment

Steve Austin .CEO/Chairman/Producer
Michael Amato .Head, Production
Nzinga Garvey .Associate Producer
Suzanne Holland .Associate Producer
Rena Tonelli .Production Executive

MARTIN TAHSE PRODUCTIONS
360 S. Burnside Ave., Ste. 5-L
Los Angeles, CA 90036
PHONE .323-965-5029
FAX .323-965-5039
EMAIL .nkhv@aol.com
WEB SITE .www.newkidhomevideo.com
TYPES Animation - Features - Made-for-TV/Cable Movies - Theater
DEVELOPMENT Too-Toot Tootsie, Goodbye - Dog Daze
CREDITS Kukla, Fran and Ollie - The Night Swimmers - The Lookalike - Matters of the Heart - Words by Heart; Theater: Oldest Living Confederate Widow Tells All

Martin Tahse .President
Michael Vodde .VP, Development

TAILFISH PRODUCTIONS
PO Box 491584
Brentwood, CA 90049
PHONE .310-453-4105
FAX .310-829-3908
EMAIL .kgolod@aol.com
TYPES Features - TV Series
DEVELOPMENT Diamond Kings - Earthbound
CREDITS Circus - Darkness Falls

James Gibb .Producer
Ksana Golod .Producer (310-289-0170, kgolod@aol.com)
Taylor Van Arsdale .Writer/Producer
Bria Little .Creative Executive

TAKES ON PRODUCTIONS
1547 18th St.
Santa Monica, CA 90404
PHONE .310-264-2474
EMAIL .takeson@mac.com
TYPES TV Series
PRODUCTION Tracey Takes On DVD series
CREDITS Tracey Takes On - Tracey Ullman's Visible Panty Line - Ruby Romaine's Trailer Tales
COMMENTS Distributor of sixty-two half-hour shows, five one-hour shows and twenty-two half-hour talk shows

Allan McKeown .Chairman/CEO
Stephanie Cone .Producer

TALISMAN PACIFIC
20802 Hillside Dr.
Topanga, CA 90290
PHONE .310-455-2808/44-207-603-7474
EMAIL .talpacific@aol.com
TYPES Features - TV Series
CREDITS Rob Roy - Box of Moonlight - The Tic Code - The Secret Adventures of Jules Verne (TV)
COMMENTS UK office: 5 Addison Pl., London W11 4RJ UK

Steven Sherman .No Title

TALKING WALL PICTURES, INC.
850 Seventh Ave., Ste. 805
New York, NY 10019
PHONE .212-397-8686
FAX .212-397-0282
TYPES Features - Made-for-TV/Cable Movies - TV Series
CREDITS Darrow - Wonderland

John David Coles .Director/President

TALL PINE PRODUCTIONS
4000 Warner Blvd., Bldg. 138, Rm. 1104-A
Burbank, CA 91522
PHONE .818-954-4706
FAX .818-954-1239
TYPES Features - Made-for-TV/Cable Movies - TV Series
CREDITS Salton Sea - Taking Lives - Black Cat Run

D. J. Caruso .Director/Producer
Ken Aguado .Producer

TALLULAH FILMS, INC.
8031 Woodland Lane
Los Angeles, CA 90046
PHONE .310-271-0291
EMAIL .arufusisaacs@aol.com
TYPES Features
DEVELOPMENT Vanishing Point - TUSK - Beryl Markham - Into the Sun - David Stirling - Paradise Pages
PRE-PRODUCTION Mad, Bad and Dangerous to Know
CREDITS The Blockhouse - 9 1/2 Weeks - Cohen & Tate - Victory by Design - Porsche - The Boys from County Clare

Antony Rufus Isaacs .Producer/Partner
Claire Brown .VP, Development

TANNENBAUM COMPANY

c/o Warner Bros. Television
4000 Warner Blvd., Bldg. 133, Rm. 209
Burbank, CA 91522
PHONE .818-954-1113
FAX .818-954-7830
TYPES TV Series
DEALS Warner Bros. Television Production

Eric Tannenbaum .Producer
Kim Tannenbaum .Producer
Mike Dussault .Assistant

TAPESTRY FILMS, INC.

9328 Civic Center Dr.
Beverly Hills, CA 90210
PHONE .310-275-1191
FAX .310-275-1266
TYPES Features - Direct-to-Video/DVD
DEALS Miramax Films
DEVELOPMENT Overtime - Electric God - Voodoo U. - A Horse's Tale
PRODUCTION Underclassman
CREDITS Point Break - A Kid in King Arthur's Court - She's All That - The Wedding Planner - Pay It Forward - Serendipity - National Lampoon's Van Wilder

Peter Abrams .Producer/Partner
Robert L. Levy .Producer/Partner
Andrew Panay .Partner
Natan Zahavi .Producer
Terry Guerin .Director, Literary Affairs (NY) (212-822-8520)
Michael Schreiber .Director, Development
Alicia Hopkins .Business Affairs
Sherwood Jones .Post Production Supervisor
Trever Stewart .Development Assistant
Molly Tripp .Executive Assistant to Messrs. Abrams & Levy

THE TARAN COMPANY

270 Lafayette St., Ste. 1308
New York, NY 10012
PHONE .212-226-5333
FAX .212-229-2397
TYPES TV Series
CREDITS Welcome to New York
COMMENTS Manager

Maureen Taran .President/CEO

TARMAC FILMS

PO Box 4705
Horseshoe Bay, TX 78657-4705
PHONE .830-598-1096
FAX .830-598-1097
EMAIL .tarmacfilm@aol.com
TYPES Features
DEVELOPMENT Empire State - Love and the Art of Destiny
PRE-PRODUCTION West of Texas
CREDITS Pigeonholed - The Woman Chaser - The Art of Insanity

Joe McSpadden .Producer
Matt Davis .Special Assistant to Producer

TAURUS ENTERTAINMENT COMPANY

c/o Hollywood Production Center
1149 N. Gower St.
Hollywood, CA 90038
PHONE .323-785-2500
FAX .323-785-2501
EMAIL .taurusec@aol.com
WEB SITE .www.taurus-entertainment.com
TYPES Features - Direct-to-Video/DVD - Syndication - Theater - TV Series
DEVELOPMENT George Romero Presents Sharing Joy and Sorrow
PRE-PRODUCTION Creepshow
POST PRODUCTION Day of the Dead - Horror 102
CREDITS Killing Point - Mastermind - Morella - Hot Springs Hotel - Horror 101 - Lesson of an Assassin - Girls Fight Tonight - Museum of the Dead
COMMENTS International Distribution

Stanley E. Dudelson .Chairman
James G. Dudelson .President/CEO
Robert F. Dudelson .President/COO
Ana Clavell .VP, Production & Post Production
Stephen Kripner .Director, Online Services

TAVEL ENTERTAINMENT

9171 Wilshire Blvd., Ste. 406
Beverly Hills, CA 90210
PHONE .310-278-6700
FAX .310-278-6770
TYPES Features - TV Series
CREDITS Judging Amy - The Wishing Tree - Ride the Wind - Summers End - Fever - Due East

Connie Tavel .Owner
Vera Mihailovich .No Title
Adrianne Sandoval .Assistant to Ms. Tavel
Sharon King .Assistant to Ms. Mihailovich

TAYLOR MADE FILMS

1270 Stone Canyon Rd.
Los Angeles, CA 90077
PHONE .310-472-1763
FAX .310-472-8698
EMAIL .tmadefilms@aol.com
TYPES Documentaries - Features - TV Series
CREDITS Moscow on the Hudson - Down and Out in Beverly Hills - The Tempest - Taking Care of Business - Moon Over Parador - Faithful

Geoffrey Taylor .President/Producer

GRAZKA TAYLOR PRODUCTIONS

1311 Broadway
Santa Monica, CA 90404
PHONE .310-201-0806
FAX .310-393-9162
EMAIL .grazkat@aol.com
TYPES Features - Documentaries - Made-for-TV/Cable Movies
PRE-PRODUCTION Touched (Feature) - Forgiveness (Documentary)
CREDITS The Burning Season - Tricks - The Operation - Voice in Exile - Rage - Mahalia Jackson - The Power and the Glory - Prophecies

Grazka Taylor .Producer

It is illegal to copy any part of this book

MICHAEL TAYLOR PRODUCTIONS

2370 Bowmont Dr.
Beverly Hills, CA 90210
PHONE . . . 213-821-3113/310-273-6040
FAX . . . 213-740-3395/310-273-5698
EMAIL . . . taycoprod@aol.com
TYPES Features - Made-for-TV/Cable Movies
DEVELOPMENT Moving Elliott (Universal) - Once a Thief - Unforgettable - Swiss Family Robinson - Warriors of Tsin
PRE-PRODUCTION Copying Beethoven
CREDITS Princess of Thieves - Instinct - Phenomenon - The Hi-Line - Bottle Rocket - Mrs. Munck - Blue Steel - Hider in the House - Pursuit of D.B. Cooper - Last Embrace - Phenomenon 2

Michael Taylor . . . Producer
David Clawson . . . Assistant

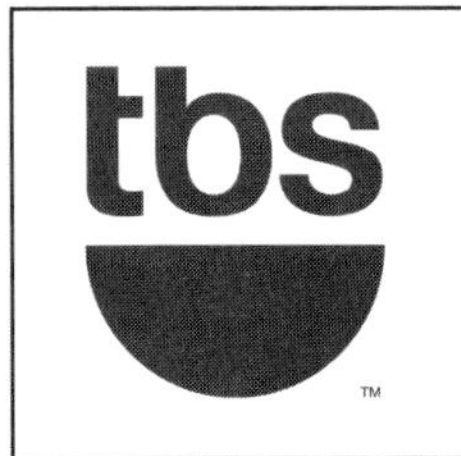

TBS

3500 W. Olive Ave., 15th Fl.
Burbank, CA 91505
PHONE . . . 818-977-5500/404-885-4370
WEB SITE . . . www.tbs.tv
TYPES TV Series - Reality TV
CREDITS House Rules - Untitled Bruce Nash Project - Gilligan's Island - The Trumpet Awards
COMMENTS Atlanta office: 1050 Techwood Drive NW, Atlanta, GA 30318

Mark Lazarus . . . President, Turner Entertainment Group
Steve Koonin . . . Executive VP/COO, TBS & TNT
Sandra Dewey . . . Sr. VP, Business Operations, TBS & TNT
Ken Schwab . . . Sr. VP, Programming, TBS & TNT
David Hudson . . . VP, Original Programming, Production
Christy Kwon Kreisberg . . . VP, Original Programming, Series, Franchises & Specials
Sara Auspitz . . . Manager, Original Programming, Series, Franchises & Specials
Susan Birrell . . . Legal Affairs
William Sy . . . Assistant to Christy Kwon Kreisberg

TEAM TODD

c/o Revolution Studios
2900 W. Olympic Blvd.
Santa Monica, CA 90404
PHONE . . . 310-255-7265
FAX . . . 310-255-7222
EMAIL . . . teamtodd@aol.com
TYPES Features - Made-for-TV/Cable Movies - TV Series
DEALS Revolution Studios
CREDITS Austin Powers 1-3 - If These Walls Could Talk 1&2 - Boiler Room - Memento

Suzanne Todd . . . Producer
Jennifer Todd . . . Producer
Jessica Blatt . . . Production Assistant
Brian Malone . . . Production Assistant

TEITELBAUM ARTISTS GROUP

8840 Wilshire Blvd.
Beverly Hills, CA 90211
PHONE . . . 310-358-3250
FAX . . . 310-358-3251
WEB SITE . . . www.teitelbaumartists.com
TYPES Features - Made-for-TV/Cable Movies - TV Series - Reality TV
DEVELOPMENT Tortilla Soup (Touchstone/CBS) - Untitled Rick Reynolds Project (Sony) - Crawling and Flying (Sony TV)
CREDITS Bonds of Love (CBS MOW) - Valdez (NBC Pilot) - Life...and Stuff (CBS) - Hacienda Heights (NBC Pilot)

Mark Teitelbaum . . . President
Kimley Blanks . . . Manager
David Herd . . . Manager

TELEMUNDO NETWORK

2290 W. Eighth Ave.
Hialeah, FL 33010
PHONE . . . 305-884-8200/800-688-8851
FAX . . . 305-889-7980
WEB SITE . . . www.telemundo.com
TYPES TV Series

James M. McNamara . . . President/CEO, Telemundo Communications Group, Inc.
Ibra Morales . . . President, Telemundo Television Stations
Don Browne . . . COO, Telemundo Communications Group, Inc.
Vincent Sadusky . . . CFO/Treasurer
Ramón Escobar . . . Executive VP, Programming & Production
Jorge Hidalgo . . . Executive VP, Sports
Steven Mandala . . . Executive VP, Sales
Joe Peyronnin . . . Executive VP, News & Information Programming
Millie Carrasquillo . . . Sr. VP, Research
Glenn Dryfoos . . . Sr. VP/General Counsel
Emilce Elgarresta . . . Sr. VP, Entertainment Specials
Alejandro Garcia . . . Sr. VP, Programming, Telemundo Network
Mauricio Gerson . . . Sr. VP, Programming, Telemundo Network
Adriana Ibañez . . . Sr. VP, Scheduling
José Pérez . . . Sr. VP, Daytime Programming
Mimi Belt . . . VP, Program Development, Telemundo Network
Arnaldo Limansky . . . Sr. Director, Production

TELEPICTURES PRODUCTIONS

3500 W. Olive Ave., 10th Fl.
Burbank, CA 91505
PHONE . . . 818-972-0777
WEB SITE . . . www.telepicturestv.com
TYPES New Media - Syndication - TV Series
CREDITS The Bachelor - Judge Mathis - ElimiDate - Celebrity Justice - Extra - Street Smarts - Steve Harvey's Big Time - The Ellen DeGeneres Show - The Larry Elder Show

Jim Paratore . . . President
Hilary Estey McLoughlin . . . Executive VP/General Manager
David Auerbach . . . Sr. VP, Programming
David Benavente . . . Sr. VP, Finance & Administration
Howard Borim . . . Sr. VP, Marketing/Creative Director
Lisa Hackner . . . Sr. VP, Development
Kevin Hamburger . . . Sr. VP, Production
Chris Circosta . . . VP, Production
David McGuire . . . VP, Development
Leslie Oren . . . VP, Consumer Publicity
Sheila Rosenbaum . . . VP, Production
Vivienne Vella . . . VP, Legal & Business Affairs

*TELL THE TRUTH PICTURES
4308 Hendrickson Rd.
Ojai, CA 93023
PHONE 805-646-7655
FAX 805-646-7724
EMAIL .....info@tttpictures.com
WEB SITE .....www.tttpictures.com
TYPES — Commercials - Documentaries - Features - Reality TV
POST PRODUCTION — The Magic City
CREDITS — Mighty Times: The Legacy of Rosa Parks - A Place at the Table - Little Secret - Rock the Boat

Robert Hudson .....Producer
Bobby Houston .....Director

TELLING PICTURES, INC.
2261 Market St., Ste. 506
San Francisco, CA 94114
PHONE 415-864-6714
EMAIL .....tellingpix@aol.com
WEB SITE .....www.tellingpictures.com
TYPES — Documentaries - Features - TV Series
CREDITS — Crime and Punishment - Life 360 - The Celluloid Closet - Times of Harvey Milk - Common Thread: Stories from the Quilt - Where Are We - Paragraph 175 - Xtreme: Sports to Die For

Rob Epstein .....Producer/Director
Jeffrey Friedman .....Producer/Director
Michael Ehrenzweig .....Producer, *Paragraph 175*
James Chan .....Production Manager

TEMPEST ENTERTAINMENT
850 N. Harper Ave.
Los Angeles, CA 90046
PHONE 323-653-1757
FAX 323-653-8764
EMAIL .....info@tempestfinancing.com
WEB SITE .....www.tempestfinancing.com
TYPES — Animation - Features
DEVELOPMENT — Northern Borders - Irene & Willie
CREDITS — Education of Little Tree - Chicken Run - Grey Owl - Snow in August
COMMENTS — Deal with Allied Filmmakers

Lenny Young .....President
Andrew Gould .....Director, Development

NANCY TENENBAUM FILMS
15 Cannon Rd.
Wilton, CT 06897
PHONE 203-761-4995
EMAIL .....ntfilms2@aol.com
TYPES — Features - New Media
DEVELOPMENT — The Chill - Inside View - It's Lonely on Top - The Winowers - The Truest Story of a Girl Ever Told - Life of the Party - City of the Dead - Horror Hotel - Assisted Living - The Scary Boys
PRE-PRODUCTION — The Drive
PRODUCTION — Meet the Fockers
CREDITS — Meet the Parents - The Daytrippers - Mac - Rapture - sex, lies and videotape

Nancy Tenenbaum .....President
Meredith Hall .....Director, Development
Sean Barrett .....Assistant
Michael Durette .....Assistant

TENTH PLANET PRODUCTIONS
833 N. La Cienega Blvd., Ste. 200
Los Angeles, CA 90069
PHONE 310-659-8001
FAX 310-659-8029
WEB SITE .....www.tenthplanet.net
TYPES — TV Series
CREDITS — MTV Movie Awards - Pepsi SMASH - Countdown to Oscars® 2004 - The Nick and Jessica Variety Hour - Chris Rock: Never Scared - Ellen DeGeneres: Here and Now - An Evening with the Dixie Chicks - America: A Tribute to Heroes - Super Bowl XXXVII Halftime Show - NFL Kickoff Live - Rock and Roll Hall of Fame Induction Ceremony - A Very Special Christmas From Washington, D.C. - VH1 Fashion Awards

Joel Gallen .....No Title
Ryan Pinette .....No Title
Gino Falsetto .....No Title

TEOCALLI ENTERTAINMENT
6001 Creekwood Pass
Spring Branch, TX 78070
PHONE 830-228-5950
FAX 830-228-5904
TYPES — Animation - Documentaries - Features - Direct-to-Video/DVD - Made-for-TV/Cable Movies - TV Series
DEVELOPMENT — ENIAC - Elephantitis - Times Like These
POST PRODUCTION — A Circle on the Cross
CREDITS — The Legend of Billy the Kid - The Radicals - The Top of the Bottom Half: An Evening with the Keeper of All Knowledge - Killing Time
SUBMISSION POLICY — No unsolicited submissions

Robert A. Nowotny .....President
Lynda Lorraine .....Development Executive

ARIELLE TEPPER PRODUCTIONS
1501 Broadway, Ste. 1301
New York, NY 10036
PHONE 212-944-9696
FAX 212-944-8999
EMAIL .....info@atpnyc.com
WEB SITE .....www.atpnyc.com
TYPES — Theater
DEVELOPMENT — Swimming
PRE-PRODUCTION — Bounce - Ball
PRODUCTION — De La Guarda Villa Villa - Jumpers - The Moonlight Room - Democracy
CREDITS — 30 Days - Theater: The Last Five Years - Freak - Sandra Bernhard's I'm Still Here Damn It - James Joyce's The Dead - Hollywood Arms - Harlem Song - Dance of the Vampire

Arielle Tepper .....Producer
Rachel Neuburger .....Associate Producer
Kim Montelibano .....Theater Associate
Paul Zahn .....Theater Associate

TERRA FIRMA FILMS
100 Universal City Plaza, Bungalow 5164
Universal City, CA 91608
PHONE . . . 818-777-4457
FAX . . . 818-733-4289
TYPES Features
DEALS Universal Pictures
CREDITS American Pie 1&2 - American Wedding

Adam Herz . . . Writer/Producer (818-777-5487)
Greg Lessans . . . Co-President (818-777-9545)
Josh Shader . . . Co-President (818-777-4771)
Craig Ferguson . . . No Title (818-777-7197)

***THIS IS THAT, CORP.**
417 Canal St.
New York, NY 10013
PHONE . . . 212-601-5900
FAX . . . 212-601-5916
TYPES Documentaries - Features - Made-for-TV/Cable Movies
DEALS Focus Features/Rogue Pictures
DEVELOPMENT The Hawk Is Dying - Fast Track - Family Planning - Sector 7 - The Parker Grey Show - A Very Private Gentleman
POST PRODUCTION A Dirty Shame - Thumbsucker
CREDITS The Door in the Floor - Eternal Sunshine of the Spotless Mind - 21 Grams - American Splendor
SUBMISSION POLICY No unsolicited material

Ted Hope . . . Partner/Producer
Anthony Bregman . . . Partner/Producer
Anne Carey . . . Partner Producer
Diana Victor . . . Partner/Head, Business Affairs
Stefanie Azpiazu . . . Production/Creative Executive
Claire Pacacha . . . Production/Creative Executive
Eric Papa . . . Production/Creative Executive
Jesse Sanchez . . . Office Manager

LARRY THOMPSON ORGANIZATION
9663 Santa Monica Blvd., Ste. 801
Beverly Hills, CA 90210
PHONE . . . 310-288-0700
FAX . . . 310-288-0711
EMAIL . . . ltbeverlyhills@aol.com
WEB SITE . . . www.larrythompsonorg.com
TYPES Features - Made-for-TV/Cable Movies - Reality TV - Syndication - TV Series
PRODUCTION Celebrity Home Video
CREDITS Lucy & Desi: Before the Laughter - Crimes of Passion - The Woman He Loved - And the Beat Goes On: The Sonny & Cher Story - Murder in the Mirror - Iron Chef USA: Showdown in Las Vegas - A Date with Darkness: The Trial and Capture of Andrew Luster

Larry Thompson . . . Chairman/CEO
Robert G. Endara II . . . Director, Development
Kelly Thompson . . . Director, Development

THOMPSON STREET ENTERTAIMENT
754 N. Kilkea Dr.
Los Angeles, CA 90046
PHONE . . . 323-651-5813
TYPES Documentaries - Features - Direct-to-Video/DVD - Made-for-TV/Cable Movies - TV Series
CREDITS All Over the Guy - Princess of Thieves - An Ideal Husband - Get Bruce - Cool Runnings - Mary and Rhoda
SUBMISSION POLICY No unsolicited material

Susan B. Landau . . . Producer

THOUSAND WORDS
9100 Wilshire Blvd., Ste. 404-E
Beverly Hills, CA 90212
PHONE . . . See Below
FAX . . . 310-859-8333
EMAIL . . . info@thousand-words.com
WEB SITE . . . www.thousand-words.com
TYPES Features
PRODUCTION A Scanner Darkly
COMPLETED UNRELEASED The Clearing
CREDITS Saturn - Waking Life - Requiem for a Dream - The United States of Leland

Palmer West . . . Co-President/Founder (310-859-8330)
Jonah Smith . . . Co-President (310-859-8330)
Jesse Johnston . . . Director, Development (310-859-8331)
Stephanie Lewis . . . Creative Executive (310-859-8331)
Erin Hagerty . . . Assistant (310-859-8330)

THREE STRANGE ANGELS, INC.
9720 Wilshire Blvd., 4th Fl.
Beverly Hills, CA 90212
PHONE . . . 310-777-3114
TYPES Features
POST PRODUCTION Nanny McPhee

Lindsay Doran . . . Producer
Jinyi Chong . . . Executive Assistant

THRESHOLD ENTERTAINMENT
1649 11th St.
Santa Monica, CA 90404
PHONE . . . 310-452-8899
FAX . . . 310-452-0736
EMAIL . . . hanna@threshold-digital.com
WEB SITE . . . www.threshold.tv
TYPES Animation - Features - Direct-to-Video/DVD - New Media - Syndication - TV Series
DEVELOPMENT Heroes - Ninja Scroll - Duke Nukem - Mortal Kombat: Devastation - Only Love Is Real
PRODUCTION Food Fight!
CREDITS Mortal Kombat - Mortal Kombat: Annihilation - Beowulf - Mortal Kombat: Conquest
COMMENTS Computer graphics/visual effects facility: TDRL

Larry Kasanoff . . . Producer/Chairman/CEO
George Johnsen . . . CTO
Joshua Wexler . . . CIO
Kristy Scanlan . . . VP, Development
Hanna Schmieder . . . VP, Marketing/Publicity

*THUNDER ROAD PICTURES

4000 Warner Blvd.
Burbank, CA 91522
PHONE .818-954-3130
FAX .818-954-3321
TYPES Features - Made-for-TV/Cable Movies - TV Series
DEALS Warner Bros. Pictures
CREDITS Alexander the Great - Welcome to Mooseport - Basic - K-19

Basil Iwanyk .No Title
Tobin Armbrust .No Title
Mary Viola .No Title
Mark Burrell .No Title
Heather Montgomery .No Title
Alysia Cotter .No Title

TIDEWATER ENTERTAINMENT, INC.

926 2nd St., Ste. 202
Santa Monica, CA 90403
PHONE .310-458-9554
FAX .310-458-9554
TYPES Features - TV Series
CREDITS Excellent Cadavers - Life Size - Crimson Tide - True Romance - The Fan

Bill Unger .President

TIG PRODUCTIONS, INC.

4450 Lakeside Dr., Ste. 225
Burbank, CA 91505
PHONE .818-260-8707
FAX .818-260-0440
TYPES Features
DEVELOPMENT Taming Ben Taylor
COMPLETED UNRELEASED Whirlygirl - Encore Presentation: 500 Nations - Laffit Pincay Documentary
CREDITS Open Range - Thirteen Days - Dances with Wolves - The Bodyguard - Wyatt Earp - Message in a Bottle - Head Above Water
SUBMISSION POLICY Through agent only

Kevin Costner .Partner
Jim Wilson .Partner
Soraya Dancsecs .VP
Jasa Abreo .Creative Executive
Sara Geiger .No Title

TIMELINE FILMS

9725 Culver Blvd.
Culver City, CA 90232-2739
PHONE .310-287-3702
FAX .310-287-1370
EMAIL .hugh@timelinefilms.com
WEB SITE .www.timelinefilms.com
TYPES Documentaries - TV Series
DEVELOPMENT Uncle Tom's Cabin (Documentary) - Fire and Ice
POST PRODUCTION Lionel Hampton (Documentary)
CREDITS Captured on Film: True Story of Marion Davies - Clara Bow: Discovering the *It* Girl - Louise Brooks: Looking for Lulu - The DeMille Dynasty - Yosemite - Complicated Women (TCM) - Masters of Production (KCET)

John Flynn .Partner
Hugh Munro Neely .Partner
Andi Hicks .Producer

THE STEVE TISCH COMPANY

10202 W. Washington Blvd., Astaire Bldg., 3rd Fl.
Culver City, CA 90232
PHONE .310-244-6612
FAX .310-204-2713
TYPES Features - TV Series
CREDITS Long Kiss Goodnight - Forrest Gump - The Postman - American History X - Corrina, Corrina - Lock, Stock and Two Smoking Barrels - Snatch

Steve Tisch .Chairman (310-244-6612)
Kim Skeeters .VP, Administration & Finance (310-244-6619)
Lacy Boughn .Assistant to Steve Tisch (310-244-6620)

TLC (THE LEARNING CHANNEL)

SEE Discovery Networks, U.S.

TLC ENTERTAINMENT

c/o CBS Studio Center
4024 Radford Ave.
Studio City, CA 91604-2101
PHONE .818-655-6155
FAX .818-655-6254
EMAIL .tlc@tlcentertainment.com
WEB SITE .www.tlcentertainment.com
TYPES Animation - Direct-to-Video/DVD - TV Series
CREDITS The Kids' Ten Commandments - McGee and Me! - Secret Adventures - The ALL NEW Captain Kangaroo - Mister Moose's Fun Time - The Christmas Lamb - The Legend of the Three Trees
COMMENTS Focus on kids' and family entertainment; Single-camera film, multi-camera tape; Live action/animation combo; 2D/3D animation

George Taweel .Co-Founder/Partner
Rob Loos .Co-Founder/Partner
Maureen Smith .Partner

*TOKYOPOP INC.

5900 Wilshire Blvd., Ste. 2000
Los Angeles, CA 90036
PHONE .323-692-6700
FAX .323-692-6701
EMAIL .susanh@tokyopop.com
WEB SITE .www.tokyopop.com
TYPES Animation - Features - Direct-to-Video/DVD - TV Series
DEVELOPMENT Love Hina - Mysterians - Priest - Princess Ai - Karma Club - Stray Sheep - Real Bout High School
CREDITS Rave Master - Reign: The Conqueror - Inital D - Street Fury - GTO - Brigadoon - Marmelade Boy - Spring & Chaos - Saint Tail - Vampire Princess Miyu

Stuart J. Levy .Chairman
John Parker .President/COO
Mark Lebowitz .CFO
Bill Josey .General Counsel/VP, Business Affairs
Victor Chin .VP, Inventory Control
René Garcia .VP, Film & TV
Mike Kiley .VP, Operations
Ron Klamert .VP, Production & Manufacturing
Steve Kleckner .Sr. VP, Sales & Distribution
John Powers .VP, Marketing
Steve Galloway .Executive Director, Development
Susan Hale .Director, Public Relations
Jeremy Ross .Director, Editiorial
Jennifer Wagner .Creative Director
Kathryn Klingler .Licensing & Merchandise Sales Director

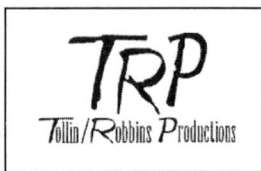

TOLLIN/ROBBINS PRODUCTIONS

10960 Ventura Blvd., 2nd Fl.
Studio City, CA 91604
PHONE 818-766-5004
FAX 818-766-8488
TYPES — Documentaries - Features - TV Series
DEALS — Touchstone Television - Walt Disney Pictures/Touchstone Pictures
CREDITS — Hardwood Dreams - The Show - Big Fat Liar - Hardball - Summer Catch - Varsity Blues - Good Burger - Smallville - Arli$$ - The Nick Cannon Show - The Nightmare Room - All That - The Amanda Show - What I Like About You - I'm with Her - One Tree Hill - The Perfect Score - Radio - Hardwood Dreams: Ten Years Later

Mike Tollin .... Co-President/Executive Producer/Director
Brian Robbins .... Co-President/Executive Producer/Director
Joe Davola .... Executive Producer/Head, TV
Sharla Sumpter .... Executive VP, Film
Chris Castallo .... Sr. VP, TV Development
Shelley Zimmerman .... Sr. VP, TV Development
Jonny Fink .... Producer
Berna Levin .... VP, Feature Development
Lauren Wagner .... Creative Executive
Suzanne Craig .... Assistant to Mike Tollin
Susie Esparza .... Assistant to Brian Robbins
Ryan Hunt .... Assistant to Joe Davola
Mike Nunes .... Assistant to Chris Castallo
Chris Armstrong .... Assistant to Shelley Zimmerman
Meghann Collins .... Assistant to Sharla Sumpter

TOMORROW FILM CORPORATION

16250 Ventura Blvd., Ste. 400
Encino, CA 91436
PHONE 818-788-8776
FAX 818-788-8782
EMAIL .... admin@tomorrowfilms.com
WEB SITE .... www.tomorrowfilms.com
TYPES — Features
CREDITS — The Third Wheel - Double Bang - Just the Ticket - Till Human Voices Wake Us - American Girl

Yoram Pelman .... President/Producer
Diane Miller .... Director, Servicing
Incoronata "Inc" Pagliuca .... No Titlle

TOOLEY PRODUCTIONS

101 S. Robertson Blvd., Ste. 203
Los Angeles, CA 90048
PHONE 310-777-8733
FAX 310-777-8730
EMAIL .... tooleyproduction@aol.com
TYPES — Features - TV Series
DEVELOPMENT — Features: The Courier - Monty - Outward Bound - We're the Millers; TV: Sol Goode - Hot Property - Posers
PRE-PRODUCTION — By Virtue Fall - Mexicali - Past Tense - Redline
POST PRODUCTION — Shadowboxer
CREDITS — A Man Apart - Blind Horizon - Poolhall Junkies - Sol Goode - In the Shadows - A Better Way to Die

Tucker Tooley .... Producer
Christopher Wilhem .... Creative Executive/Executive Assistant

TOP COW PRODUCTIONS, INC.

10350 Santa Monica Blvd., Ste. 100
Los Angeles, CA 90025
PHONE 310-286-0758
FAX 310-286-2128
WEB SITE .... www.topcow.com
TYPES — Animation - Features - Direct-to-Video/DVD - Interactive Games - New Media - TV Series
DEVELOPMENT — Inferno - A-Team - Fathom - The Cleaner - Rising Stars - Wanted
CREDITS — Witchblade

Marc Silvestri .... CEO
Chris Carlisle .... VP, Creative Affairs

TORNELL PRODUCTIONS

80 Varick St., Ste. 10C
New York, NY 10013
PHONE 212-625-2530/310-581-0422
FAX 212-625-2532/310-399-2901
TYPES — Features
DEVELOPMENT — August and Everything After - Live! - Bad Dog - High Tide - Carnivore - Zero to Sixty - The Artist's Wife
CREDITS — Igby Goes Down - Jawbreaker - The Big Split - The Craft - Breakin' All the Rules
COMMENTS — West Coast address: 149 Fraser Ave., Santa Monica, CA 90405

Lisa Tornell .... Producer

TOTEM PRODUCTIONS

8009 Santa Monica Blvd.
Los Angeles, CA 90046
PHONE 323-650-4994
FAX 323-650-1961
EMAIL .... totempro@aol.com
TYPES — Features
CREDITS — Enemy of the State - Man on Fire

Tony Scott .... Co-Chairman
Tom Moran .... Executive Assistant to Mr. Scott
Peter Toumasis .... Executive Assistant to Mr. Scott

TOUCHSTONE TELEVISION

SEE ABC Entertainment Television Group

TRANCAS INTERNATIONAL FILMS

1875 Century Park East, Ste. 1145
Los Angeles, CA 90067
PHONE 310-553-5599
FAX 310-553-0536
TYPES — Features
CREDITS — The Halloween Movies - The Message - Lion of the Desert

Moustapha Akkad .... President/Producer/Director
Malek Akkad .... Director, Creative Development
Christi Sinkus .... Office Manager

TRAVEL CHANNEL

SEE Discovery Networks, U.S.

TRAVELER'S REST FILMS
Bergamot Station, 2525 Michigan Ave., Bldg. J5
Santa Monica, CA 90404
PHONE .310-829-1972
FAX .310-264-0766
TYPES Features - TV Series
DEVELOPMENT Bury My Heart at Wounded Knee (HBO) - The Andromeda Strain (Sci Fi) - Alfred Hitchcock and the Making of Psycho
PRODUCTION Kojak (USA)
CREDITS Firestarter: Rekindled - A&E's The Great Gatsby - The Darkling

Tom Thayer .President
Linda Messier .Development Associate

TREASURE ENTERTAINMENT
468 N. Camden Dr., Ste. 200
Beverly Hills, CA 90210
PHONE .310-860-7490
FAX .310-943-1488
EMAIL .info@treasureentertainment.net
WEB SITE .www.treasureentertainment.net
TYPES Commercials - Documentaries - Features - Direct-to-Video/DVD - Made-for-TV/Cable Movies - Music Videos - New Media
DEVELOPMENT High Midnight (Anonymous Content) - Move The Crowd (Parkchester Films) - Johnny Pinstripes (Cindy Cowan Entertainment) - Lazenby Lane (Cube Vision) - Don Mckay
PRE-PRODUCTION Harsh Times (Crave Films)
PRODUCTION Little Athens (Legaci Pictures)
POST PRODUCTION Flint Town Kids (Documentary)
COMPLETED UNRELEASED Rock Fresh (Documentary) - Cycles - Fault
CREDITS Personal Vendetta - Scorched
SUBMISSION POLICY Query letter or script by referral with release form (available on Web site)

Mark Heidelberger .Co-Chairman/COO
J.M. Felsot .Co-Chairman/President
Ian Vishnevsky .CFO
Kevin Asbell .VP, Business & Legal Affairs
Kevin Aschman .VP, Music Management
Jonathan Hoffberg .VP, New Media
Andrew Yoo .VP, Finance
Kyle Lundberg .VP, Marketing & Distribution

TREE LINE FILM
1708 Berkeley St.
Santa Monica, CA 90404
PHONE .310-883-7220
TYPES Features
DEVELOPMENT Follow Me
CREDITS Scream - Cop Land - Identity

Cathy Konrad .President/Owner
James Mangold .President/Owner
Scott Nemes .VP

TREZZA ENTERTAINMENT
39 E. 78th St., Ste. 603
New York, NY 10021
PHONE .212-327-2218
FAX .212-504-2618
TYPES Documentaries - Features - Made-for-TV/Cable Movies
DEVELOPMENT My Pal Rinker - Piaf
PRE-PRODUCTION Headlong - Beautiful View
COMPLETED UNRELEASED Cut and Dry
CREDITS Pollock - Georgia

James Francis Trezza .Producer
Barbara Turner .Producer/Writer
Ellen Segal .Associate Producer

TRIAGE ENTERTAINMENT
c/o John Bravakis
15260 Ventura Blvd., Ste. 700
Sherman Oaks, CA 91403
PHONE .818-386-6800
FAX .818-386-9889
EMAIL .jbravakis@triageinc.com
WEB SITE .www.triageinc.com
TYPES Animation - Documentaries - Reality TV - Syndication - TV Series
CREDITS Iron Chef America - Home for the Holidays - The Mentalist - Cowboy U - Scariest Places on Earth

Stu Schreiberg .President
John Bravakis .Executive VP
Steve Kroopnick .Sr. VP
Stacy Hashimoto .Production Executive
Myra Byrnes .Post Production Supervisor

TRIBE
310 Main St.
Chatham, NJ 07928
PHONE .973-635-2660
FAX .973-635-2654
EMAIL .mail@tribepictures.com
WEB SITE .www.tribepictures.com
TYPES Documentaries - Features - New Media - TV Series
DEVELOPMENT Extra Innings - Month of Sundays - Briar Rose
CREDITS A Modern Affair - Acts of Love - Birth Mother Portraits
COMMENTS Seeking humanistic drama or comedy scripts that are entertaining, uplifting and project positive values

Vern Oakley .Director/Producer/President

TRIBECA PRODUCTIONS
375 Greenwich St., 8th Fl.
New York, NY 10013
PHONE .212-941-4000
FAX .212-941-4044
WEB SITE .www.tribecafilm.com
SECOND WEB SITE .www.tribecafilmfestival.org
TYPES Features - Made-for-TV/Cable Movies - New Media - TV Series
DEALS Universal Pictures
DEVELOPMENT The Good Shepherd
PRODUCTION Meet the Fockers
POST PRODUCTION House of D - Compleat Female Stage Beauty
CREDITS A Bronx Tale - Wag the Dog - Analyze This - Marvin's Room - Thunderheart - Rocky & Bullwinkle - Meet the Parents - About a Boy - Showtime - Analyze That - We Will Rock You (Tribeca Theatrical Production)

Robert De Niro .Partner
Jane Rosenthal .Partner
Naomi Despres .Executive VP, Production
Rachel Cohen .VP, Development & Production
Hardy Justice .VP, Development
Geoffrey Isenman .Creative Executive
Angela Robinson .Creative Executive

It is illegal to copy any part of this book

TRIBUNE ENTERTAINMENT COMPANY

5800 Sunset Blvd., TEC Bldg., Ste. 10
Los Angeles, CA 90028
PHONE .323-460-5800
FAX .323-460-3858
WEB SITE .www.tribtv.com
TYPES Syndication - TV Series
CREDITS Mutant X - Gene Roddenberry's Earth: Final Conflict - BeastMaster - Soul Train - Gene Roddenberry's Andromeda - Soul Train Music Awards - Soul Train Lady of Soul Awards - Soul Train Starfest - Family Feud - Dreamworks Movie Package - Hearst Entertainment Movie Package - DIC's Kids Network
COMMENTS Off-net syndication

Richard H. Askin Jr. .President/CEO (323-460-3955)
David Berson .Sr. VP, Business Affairs (323-460-3802)
Donna Harrison Sr. VP, Unscripted & Reality Programming (323-460-3834)
Richard Inouye .Sr. VP, Finance & Administration (323-460-3852)
William Hamm VP, Scripted Programming & Development (323-460-3817)
George NeJame .VP, Production & Operations (323-460-3894)
Mashawn Nix .Director, Development, Reality (323-460-3890)
Jim Toten .Chief Engineer (323-460-5911)

TRICOAST STUDIOS

6374 Arizona Circle
Los Angeles, CA 90045
PHONE .310-641-7888
FAX .310-641-9888
EMAIL .tricoast@tricoast.com
WEB SITE .www.tricoast.com
TYPES Commercials - Documentaries - Features - Direct-to-Video/DVD - Made-for-TV/Cable Movies - New Media - TV Series
DEVELOPMENT Southern Comfort - 9 - Mortal Half
CREDITS Never Talk to Stangers - The Set Up - Escape from Atlantis - Under Seige 2 - The Chill Factor - Madison - The Proposition - The Pact
COMMENTS A full service studio, including distribution, marketing, production and post production facilities

Marcy Levitas Hamilton .CEO/President/Development
Strath Hamilton .Executive Producer/Director
Martin Wiley .Executive Producer/Director
Adam Rodriguez .General Manager
Liza Field .Production Manager
Yusaku Mizoguchi .Supervising Editor
Cara Oberfoell .Main Title Designer
John Charles .DVD Authoring
Phillip Raves .Sound Supervisor

TRICOR ENTERTAINMENT

1613 Chelsea Rd.
San Marino, CA 91108
PHONE .818-763-0699/626-282-5184
FAX .626-441-0033/626-282-5185
EMAIL .tricorent@aol.com
TYPES Features - Made-for-TV/Cable Movies - TV Series
PRODUCTION The Bridge of San Luis Rey - The Devil & Daniel Webster
CREDITS Extreme Days - The Amati Girls - Carlo's Wake - The Homecoming of Jimmy Whitecloud
COMMENTS Distributor

Craig Darian .Co-Chairman/CEO (626-282-5184)
Howard Kazanjian .Co-Chairman (818-763-0699)

TRI-ELITE ENTERTAINMENT, LTD.

8601 Wilshire Blvd., Ste. 700
Beverly Hills, CA 90211
PHONE .310-358-8300
FAX .310-358-8304
EMAIL .trielite@cs.com
TYPES Made-for-TV/Cable Movies - Syndication
DEVELOPMENT Hollywood Live - 11th Annual House of Blues Spring Benefit Concert & Awards
CREDITS The Diversity Awards (The WB) - The American Society of Young Musicians - Cable Channel Awards

Jarvee Hutcherson .President/Executive Producer
Kemani Bandy .VP
Gordon Kenney .Producer/Development
Dionicio Virvez .Producer
Steve Gold .Business Affairs
Bev Shavers .Executive Assistant to President

TRILLION ENTERTAINMENT, INC.

650 N. Bronson Ave., Ste. 134
Los Angeles, CA 90004
PHONE .323-871-4456
FAX .323-960-4759
EMAIL .sd@trillion-ent.com
WEB SITE .www.trillion-ent.com
SECOND WEB SITE .www.newsuitmovie.com
TYPES Features - Documentaries
DEVELOPMENT The Nazi Officer's Wife (Feature) - Bright Young Things - Friends & Lovers - The Gold of Malabar - The Porch
CREDITS Joyride - The Item - Jane Bond (Short) - New Suit - The Nazi Officer's Wife (Documentary)

Laurent Zilber .Co-President
Christina Zilber .Co-President
Scott Duncan .Sr. VP, Operations
Kathryn Tyus-Adair .Sr. VP, Production
Trisha Hoving .Executive Assistant
Julie Ann Wight .Executive Assistant

TRILLIUM PRODUCTIONS, INC.

PO Box 1560
New Canaan, CT 06840
PHONE .203-966-5540
FAX .203-972-9175
TYPES Documentaries - Features - Made-for-TV/Cable Movies - TV Series
DEVELOPMENT The Breadwinner
CREDITS South Pacific - Sarah Plain and Tall 1-3 - Serving in Silence - Journey - Ballad of Lucy Whipple - Baby - Do You Mean There Are Still Real Cowboys? - Broken Hearts, Broken Homes
SUBMISSION POLICY Unsolicited submissions are not accepted

Glenn Close .President
Nancy Evans Cox .Executive Assistant

TRILOGY ENTERTAINMENT GROUP

325 Wilshire Blvd., Ste. 203
Santa Monica, CA 90401
PHONE .310-656-9733
FAX .310-656-9737
TYPES Features - TV Series
DEALS Metro-Goldwyn-Mayer Studios, Inc. - New Line Television
DEVELOPMENT Jones - Brown Eyed Girl - Sweet Smell of Success - Outer Limits (Feature) - Taj Mahal - If Not for You - Blue Eden - Monster - Flying Tigers - An Infinity of Mirrors - Lighthouse - UFO - Papa - Blood Crazy - For the People - See Jane Run - Between the Lines - Crusade - Black Ice - Allies
PRE-PRODUCTION Outer Limits - Blue Eden
CREDITS The Dangerous Lives of Altar Boys - Robin Hood: Prince of Thieves - Backdraft - Blown Away - Moll Flanders - Larger Than Life - Tank Girl - The Kiss; TV: Outer Limits - The Magnificent Seven - The Twilight Zone - Carrie - Breaking News - Houdini

Pen Densham .Partner
Neil Kaplan .Partner
John Watson .Partner
Bryan Flam .Development Executive, Features & TV
Nevin Densham .Creative Executive/Head, Development, Project X
Alex Daltas .Creative Executive
Julie Fitzgerald .Manager, Development
Howard Han .Creative Consultant
Jonathan Hughes .Creative Assistant

TRINITY PICTURES, INC.

11600 San Vicente Blvd.
Los Angeles, CA 90049
PHONE .310-820-6733
FAX .310-207-6816
WEB SITE .www.concord-newhorizons.com
SECOND WEB SITE .www.trinitypix.com
TYPES Features - Direct-to-Video/DVD
CREDITS A Cry in the Wild - The Westing Game - The Dirt Bike Kid - Legend of the Lost Tomb - Da

Julie Corman .Chairman/CEO
Catherine Corman .Development Associate (NY)

TRIO

1230 Avenue of the Americas
New York, NY 10020
PHONE .212-413-5000
FAX .212-413-6545
WEB SITE .www.triotv.com
TYPES Documentaries - TV Series
COMPLETED UNRELEASED Final Cut: The Making of Heaven's Gate and the Unmaking of a Studio - The N Word - Fat City - Texas: America Supersized
CREDITS Outlaw Comedy: The Censoring of Bill Hicks - New Orleans Jazz Festival - Mozart: Lost & Found - Death of a Princess - Easy Riders, Raging Bulls - The Golden Globes: Hollywood's Dirty Little Secret - Journalists: Casualties of War

Lauren Zalaznick .President, Bravo & TRIO Networks
Jason Klarman .Sr. VP, Marketing
Andrew Cohen .VP, Original Production
Kris Slava .VP, Acquisitions
Elma Cremin .Director, Acquisitions
Sam Paul .Director, Production
Dave Serwatka .Director, Documentary Programming

*TRISTAR PICTURES

10202 W. Washington Blvd.
Culver City, CA 90232
PHONE .310-244-4000
FAX .310-244-2626
WEB SITE .www.spe.sony.com
TYPES Features

Valerie Van Galder .President
Marc Weinstock .Sr. VP, Marketing
Danielle Rosenfeld .VP, Publicity

TRIUMPH PICTURES, INC.

19528 Ventura Blvd., Ste. 182
Tarzana, CA 91356-2917
PHONE .818-708-1384/310-266-6617
WEB SITE .www.triumphpictures.com
TYPES Features - Made-for-TV/Cable Movies - TV Series
CREDITS Lone Wolf McQuade - Sheena - The Man Who Broke a Thousand Chains - Jury Duty - Stone Cold - 3 Ninjas Kick Back - 3 Ninjas: High Noon at Mega Mountain - Lion of Africa - Steal the Sky

Yoram Ben-Ami .President
Anni Nedivi .VP, Production

It is illegal to copy any part of this book

TRIVISION PICTURES, LLC
c/o Raleigh Studios
5300 Melrose Ave, Ste. B-255
Hollywood, CA 90038
PHONE .310-470-0095/310-358-9007
FAX .310-470-0225
EMAIL .alextab@aol.com
SECOND EMAIL .alex@dh1.tv
TYPES Animation - Features - Made-for-TV/Cable Movies - Music Videos - Reality TV - TV Series
DEVELOPMENT The Hybrid - Love and Hate - Switching Souls - Army Men - High Risk - Stonewall Jackson - Nightwalk - Trainer
PRE-PRODUCTION Before the Devil Knows You're Dead
PRODUCTION Into a Far Country - Switching Souls - Love vs. Hate - Pool Hall Prophets - Army Men - Double Play
POST PRODUCTION Framed (TNT/Lions Gate)
COMPLETED UNRELEASED Cyborg - Exterminator - The Last Emperor Screwballs - A Time to Die
CREDITS Red American - I, Mexicali - And It Is Only Love - The Last Cowboy - Deadly Dance - Bloodsport 2 - Stranger in the House - Strip Search - Universal Cop - Set Up - Trouble - Justice - Partners - Save Me - Perfect Target
COMMENTS DH1 Studio/Trivision Pictures office: 8730 Sunset Blvd., 6th Fl., West Los Angeles, CA 90069

Alexander Tabrizi .Chairman
Pliny Porter .President
Richard Style .Producer/Writer
John Windfield .Producer/Finance
Ross Hammer .Executive VP
Steven Mendelson .Head, TV Production & Development
Steve Rockmael .Head, Talent
George Saunders .Head, Production
Michael Gulian .Producer/Writer
Jeaque Haitkin .Producer/Writer
Spiro Razatos .Director/Writer/Stunt Coordinator
Steve Saxton .Producer
Peter Yuval .Producer
Joe Zito .Producer/Director
Jon Broderick .In-House Producer/UPM
Rebecca Morrison .Creative Consultant
David Poland .Creative Consultant
Teressa Tunney .Creative Consultant
Peter Laipis .Writer/Director

TROMA, INC.
Troma Bldg., 733 Ninth Ave.
New York, NY 10019
PHONE .212-757-4555
FAX .212-399-9885
EMAIL .webmaster@troma.com
WEB SITE .www.troma.com
TYPES Features - Direct-to-Video/DVD
DEVELOPMENT Poultrygeist - Schlock and Schlockability
POST PRODUCTION Parts of the Family
CREDITS Toxic Avenger - Citizen Toxie - Terror Firmer - Sgt. Kabukiman NYPD - Tromeo & Juliet - Cannibal! The Musical - Rowdy Girls - Def by Temptation - Decampitated - Bloodsucking Freaks - Tales From the Crapper - Suicide - Trailer Town

Lloyd Kaufman .President
Michael Herz .VP
Jeremy Howell .VP, Sales
Rob Sundermann .Director, Events & Publicity

TROUBLEMAKER STUDIOS
c/o Robert Newman/ICM
8942 Wilshire Blvd.
Beverly Hills, CA 90211
PHONE .310-550-4000
FAX .310-550-4100
TYPES Features
CREDITS Once Upon a Time in Mexico - Spy Kids 1-3 - Game Over - From Dusk Till Dawn - Desperado - El Mariachi
SUBMISSION POLICY No unsolicited submissions

Robert Rodriguez .Producer/Writer/Director

TRUE BLUE PRODUCTIONS
PO Box 27127
Los Angeles, CA 90027-0127
PHONE .323-661-9191
FAX .323-661-9190
EMAIL .trueblueprod@earthlink.net
TYPES Animation - Features - Made-for-TV/Cable Movies - TV Series
DEALS Warner Bros. Television Production
COMMENTS Offers should be directed to Jason Weinberg at Untitled Management 323-966-4400

Kirstie Alley .Actor/Producer
LeeAnn Vasquez .Assistant to Ms. Alley

TRUE FRIEND PRODUCTIONS
1112 Montana Ave., Ste. 535
Santa Monica, CA 90403
PHONE .310-230-9807
FAX .310-230-9667
EMAIL .trufrn@aol.com
TYPES Features - Made-for-TV/Cable Movies - Reality TV - TV Series
DEVELOPMENT Six Impossible Things - The Magic Club - The Accomplished Magician - Your Psychic Makeover - Bob's Sense of Humor - Snow Job - Your Intuitive Life
CREDITS The Effects of Magic (Showtime)
SUBMISSION POLICY Submit logline via email
COMMENTS Looking for feature comedies, films with strong musical elements and family features

Belinda Casas-Wells .Producer/Partner
Chuck Martinez .Producer/Partner

SIMON TSE PRODUCTIONS
9060 Santa Monica Blvd., Ste. 330
West Hollywood, CA 90069
PHONE .310-385-9331
FAX .310-385-9347
TYPES Animation - Features - TV Series
DEVELOPMENT Virtua Fighter - Pacific Edge - Shenmue 2 - Headhunter
CREDITS Shenmue - Gedo - Fatal Blade - The Yakuza Way - New York Cop - Distant Justice - Sweet Evil - Silencer (aka Body Count)

Simon Tse .Producer/CEO
Jill Nowak .Director, Development
Anita Yoneda .Executive Assistant

T-SQUARED PRODUCTIONS
3496 Wade St.
Los Angeles, CA 90066
PHONE 310-915-0055
FAX 310-915-9109
TYPES Features - New Media - TV Series
CREDITS Kissing Miranda - Fried Green Tomatoes - Sweethearts - Kids World

Tom Taylor . . . . Producer/Attorney

TUDOR MANAGEMENT GROUP
18 Sunset Ave., Ste. 1
Venice, CA 90291
PHONE 310-401-2020
TYPES Features - Direct-to-Video/DVD - Made-for-TV/Cable Movies - TV Series
DEVELOPMENT Red Sneakers
CREDITS Getting Personal - The Fixer - Heads - Sahara - Next Door - BUGS

Marty Tudor . . . . No Title
Mieke ter Poorten Berlin . . . . No Title
Maria K. Aspinwall . . . . No Title
Liberty Convoy . . . . No Title

TUFFIN ENTERTAINMENT
302A W. 12th St., Ste. 153
New York, NY 10014
PHONE 877-684-5045
FAX 212-656-1715
EMAIL . . . . info@tuffinentertainment.com
WEB SITE . . . . www.tuffinentertainment.com
TYPES Features
DEVELOPMENT Dragon Slayer's Academy - Across the Border - The Flying Circus
PRE-PRODUCTION The Basement
PRODUCTION Moscow Chill
POST PRODUCTION 2001 Maniacs
CREDITS Chapter Zero - Open Mic - Medquest (TV)

Christopher Tuffin . . . . Producer

TULCHIN ENTERTAINMENT
11377 W. Olympic Blvd., 2nd Fl.
Los Angeles, CA 90064
PHONE 310-914-7900
FAX 310-914-7927
EMAIL . . . . entesquire@aol.com
SECOND EMAIL . . . . info4tulchenent@yahoo.com
WEB SITE . . . . www.medialawyer.com
TYPES Animation - Documentaries - Features - Direct-to-Video/DVD - Made-for-TV/Cable Movies - New Media - Reality TV - TV Series
CREDITS Guy - To Sleep with Anger - Mona Must Die - The Mouse - Chicks, Man - Barbara Kopple Cannes Documentary - Private Property - Peak Experience - Blind - Rogues - Elvira's Haunted Hills - The Gristle
COMMENTS Producers Representative; Entertainment law firm

Harris Tulchin . . . . Owner/President
Robert Yu . . . . VP, Sales
Ed Brancheau . . . . Director, Sales & Acquisitions

TULE RIVER FILMS
940 W. Alameda Ave.
Burbank, CA 91506
PHONE 818-556-2666
FAX 818-556-2667
WEB SITE . . . . www.tuleriverfilms.com
TYPES Features
DEVELOPMENT Otto - Botany Bay - Rumble in the Jungle
PRE-PRODUCTION She Died Twice - Downloading Nancy
COMPLETED UNRELEASED Black Cloud

David Moore . . . . Producer
Adam Batz . . . . Executive Producer
Igor Kovacevich . . . . Head, Development

THE TURMAN PICTURE COMPANY INC.
12220 Dunoon Lane
Los Angeles, CA 90049
PHONE 213-740-3307
FAX 213-745-6652
EMAIL . . . . pstark@usc.edu
TYPES Features - Made-for-TV/Cable Movies
CREDITS Kingdom Come - American History X - The River Wild - Running Scared - Short Circuit - Great White Hope - The Graduate - The Best Man
SUBMISSION POLICY No unsolicited material

Lawrence Turman . . . . Producer

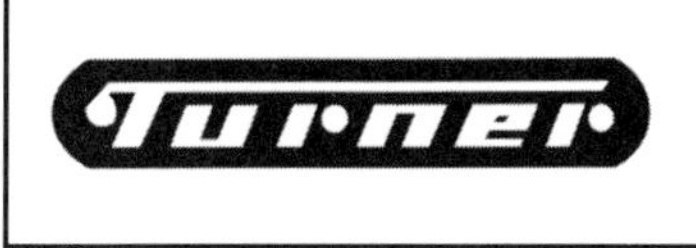

TURNER ENTERTAINMENT GROUP
1050 Techwood Dr. NW
Atlanta, GA 30318-5604
PHONE 404-827-1500
WEB SITE . . . . www.turner.com
TYPES Animation - Documentaries - Made-for-TV/Cable Movies - New Media - Syndication - TV Series - Reality TV

Philip Kent . . . . Chairman/CEO, Turner Broadcasting System, Inc.
Terence McGuirk . . . . Vice Chairman, TBS, Inc.
Mark Lazarus . . . . President, Turner Entertainment Group, TBS, Inc.
Vicky Miller . . . . Executive VP/CFO, TBS, Inc.
Kelly Regal . . . . Executive VP, Corporate Communications & Human Resources, TBS, Inc.
Louise Sams . . Executive VP/General Counsel, Turner Broadcasting System, Inc./President, Turner Broadcasting System International, Inc.
Jonathan Katz . . . . Executive VP, Program Planning & Acquisitions, TEG
Shirley Powell . . . . Sr. VP, Corporate Communications, TBS, Inc.
Terri Tingle . . . . Sr. VP, Standards & Practices, TEN

TURNER NETWORK TELEVISION (TNT)

1050 Techwood Dr.
Atlanta, GA 30318
PHONE 404-827-1700/818-977-5500
WEB SITE ....www.tnt.tv
TYPES Made-for-TV/Cable Movies - TV Series
DEVELOPMENT Into the West (Working Title) - The Librarian - Night Over Water - Clandestine - Elsewhere - Wait Until Dark - Pleading Guilty - Rampart
COMPLETED UNRELEASED The Wool Cap
CREDITS The Grid - Salem's Lot - Evel Knievel - The Winning Season - Bad Apple - The Goodbye Girl - Word of Honor - Wilder Days - Caesar - Door to Door - King of Texas - The 10th Annual SAG Awards - Monte Walsh - Second Nature
COMMENTS West Coast office: 4000 Warner Blvd., Bldg. 160, Burbank, CA 91505

Mark Lazarus ....President, Turner Entertainment Group (Atlanta)
Steve Koonin ....Executive VP/COO, TBS & TNT (Atlanta)
Michael Wright ....Sr. VP, Original Programming (Burbank)
Sandra Dewey ....Sr. VP, Business Operations, TBS & TNT (Burbank)
Sharon Byrens ....VP, Sponsored Films (Burbank)
Sam Linsky ....Director, Original Programming (Burbank)
Lainie Gallers ....Manager, Original Programming (Burbank)
Ken Schwab ....Sr. VP, Programming, TBS & TNT (Atlanta)
Michael Borza ....Sr. VP, On-Air Creative, TNT (Atlanta)
Nicholas Bogner ....VP, Original Programming, TNT (Burbank)
Karen Cassell ....Sr. VP, Public Relations, TBS & TNT (Atlanta)

JON TURTLE PRODUCTIONS

11835 W. Olympic Blvd., Ste. 550-E
Los Angeles, CA 90064
PHONE 310-268-8200
FAX 310-444-4101
EMAIL ....srajltd@aol.com
TYPES Features - Made-for-TV/Cable Movies - Syndication - TV Series
DEALS Showtime Networks, Inc.
DEVELOPMENT Redliners - Pablo Escobar - Who You Know - Red Ocean - The Quarterback - Tree of Fire - Celestial Battle
PRE-PRODUCTION Night Train
CREDITS Time at the Top - Arrival 2 - Fluke - Freak City - In a Class of His Own - They Call Me Sirr
SUBMISSION POLICY No unsolicited material

Jon Turtle ....President
Jeff Steele ....Development & Acquisitions

TURTLEBACK PRODUCTIONS, INC.

11736 Gwynne Lane
Los Angeles, CA 90077
PHONE 310-440-8587
FAX 310-440-8903
TYPES Features - Made-for-TV/Cable Movies - TV Series
PRODUCTION The Brooke Ellison Story
CREDITS Witness Protection - The Pentagon Wars - Remember WENN - Hell on Heels: The Battle of Mary Kay (CBS)

Howard Meltzer ....President/Executive Producer

TVA PRODUCTIONS

3950 Vantage Ave.
Studio City, CA 91604
PHONE 818-505-8300
FAX 818-505-8370
EMAIL ....info@tvaproductions.com
WEB SITE ....www.tvaproductions.com
TYPES Animation - Commercials - Documentaries - New Media - Syndication - TV Series
DEVELOPMENT The Explorer - Entertainment World News
CREDITS Healthy Living (PBS) - Health World News - Business World News - Cessna Citation X (DVD)

Jeffery Goddard ....Executive Producer
Patrice Jordan ....Sr. VP, Production
Mark Mannshreck ....Editor/Videographer

NORMAN TWAIN PRODUCTIONS

250 W. 54th St., Ste. 604
New York, NY 10019
PHONE 212-397-6605
FAX 212-397-6609
EMAIL ....ntprods@aol.com
TYPES Features - Made-for-TV/Cable Movies - TV Series
DEVELOPMENT Spinning Into Butter - Within Range
CREDITS Boycott - Curveballs Along the Way - Lean on Me
SUBMISSION POLICY Script submissions accepted

Norman Twain ....Producer
Tanya Doyle ....Development Associate

TWENTIETH CENTURY FOX

10201 W. Pico Blvd.
Los Angeles, CA 90035
PHONE 310-369-1000
WEB SITE ....www.fox.com
TYPES Features
CREDITS X2 - Master and Commander: The Far Side of the World - Cheaper by the Dozen - The Day After Tomorrow - Garfield - Dodgeball: A True Underdog Story - I, Robot - Alien vs. Predator
COMMENTS Mailing address: PO Box 900, Beverly Hills, CA 90213

James Gianopulos ....Chairman
Tom Rothman ....Chairman
Robert Harper ....Vice Chairman
Ted Gagliano ....President, Feature Post Production
Joe Hartwick ....President, Physical Production
Robert Kraft ....President, Fox Music, Inc.
Hutch Parker ....President, Production, TCF
Steven Bersch ....COO, Fox Home Entertainment
Bob Cohen ....Executive VP, Legal Affairs
J.R. DeLang ....Executive VP, Studio Operations
Greg Gelfan ....Executive VP, Fox Filmed Entertainment
Dean Hallett ....Executive VP, Finance/CFO, FFE
Donna Isaacson ....Executive VP, Feature Talent
Deborah Liebling ....Executive VP, Production, TCF
Steve Plum ....Executive VP, Business Affairs
Mark Resnick ....Executive VP, Business Affairs
Gary D. Roberts ....Executive VP, Litigation
Jim Tauber ....Executive VP, Co-Productions & Aquisitions
Fred Baron ....Sr. VP, Physical Production

(Continued)

TWENTIETH CENTURY FOX (Continued)

Robbie Brenner . . . . . Sr. VP, Production, TCF
Fred Chandler . . . . . Sr. VP, Post Production
Kimberly Cooper . . . . . Sr. VP, Physical Production
Ted Dodd . . . . . Sr. VP, Creative Affairs
Mike Hendrickson . . . . . Sr. VP, Physical Production
Thomas Imperato . . . . . Sr. VP, Physical Production
Vanessa Morrison . . . . . Sr. VP, Production, TCF
Victoria Rossellini . . . . . Sr. VP, Business Affairs
Tony Safford . . . . . Sr. VP, Acquisitions
David Starke . . . . . Sr. VP, Physical Production
Emma Watts . . . . . Sr. VP, Production, TCF
Alex Young . . . . . Sr. VP, Production, TCF
Steve Asbell . . . . . VP, Production, TCF
Aisha Coley . . . . . VP, Feature Casting
Michael Heard . . . . . VP, Physical Production
Paul Hoffman . . . . . VP, Business Affairs
Peter Kang . . . . . VP, Production, TCF
Christian Kaplan . . . . . VP, Feature Casting
Adam Moos . . . . . VP, Physical Production
Tom Siegrist . . . . . VP, Production, Fox Home Entertainment
Michael Hothorn . . . . . Director, Feature Casting
Aaron Williams . . . . . Director, Production Development Accounting
Ray Strache . . . . . Manager, Acquisitions
Jean Song . . . . . Creative Executive, TCF
Jason Young . . . . . Creative Executive, TCF
Riley Kathryn Ellis . . . . . Literary Scout, Young Adult & Children's

TWENTIETH CENTURY FOX - FOX 2000

10201 W. Pico Blvd., Bldg. 78
Los Angeles, CA 90035
PHONE 310-369-2000
FAX 310-369-4258
WEB SITE . . . . . www.fox.com
TYPES Features
CREDITS Unfaithful - Phone Booth - Man on Fire

Elizabeth Gabler . . . . . President, Production
Carla Hacken . . . . . Executive VP, Production
Maria Faillace . . . . . Director
Rodney Ferrell . . . . . Director
Erin Lindsey . . . . . Creative Executive
Drew Reed . . . . . Literary Consultant

TWENTIETH CENTURY FOX - SEARCHLIGHT PICTURES

10201 W. Pico Blvd., Bldg. 38
Los Angeles, CA 90035
PHONE 310-369-4402
FAX 310-369-2359
WEB SITE . . . . . www.foxsearchlight.com
TYPES Features
CREDITS Bend It Like Beckham - The Dancer Upstairs - The Good Thief - L'Auberge Espagnole - Le Divorce - 28 Days Later - Thirteen - In America - The Dreamers - Never Die Alone - Johnson Family Vacation - Napoleon Dynamite - The Clearing - Garden State
COMMENTS East Coast office: 1211 Sixth Ave., 16th Fl., New York, NY 10036

Peter Rice . . . . . President, Production
Joseph De Marco . . . . . Executive VP, Business Affairs
Claudia Lewis . . . . . Executive VP, Production
Julia Dray . . . . . Sr. VP, Production
Chris Maxwell . . . . . Sr. VP, Legal Affairs
Liz Sayre . . . . . Sr. VP, Physical Production
Jamie Taylor . . . . . Sr. VP, Legal Affairs
Joshua Deighton . . . . . VP, Production

(Continued)

TWENTIETH CENTURY FOX - SEARCHLIGHT PICTURES (Continued)

Lawrence Grey . . . . . VP, Production
Jill Gwen . . . . . VP, Finance & Operations
Zola Mashariki . . . . . Director, Production
Susan O'Leary . . . . . Director, Fox Searchlab
Jeff Arkuss . . . . . Creative Executive
Charlotte Koh . . . . . Creative Executive
Brendan Countee . . . . . Assistant to Lawrence Grey & Jeff Arkuss
Jason Hargrove . . . . . Assistant to Joshua Deighton & Zola Mashariki
Christine Kilyk . . . . . Assistant to Peter Rice
Mirjam Kositchek . . . . . Assistant to Julia Dray
Veronica Lemcoff . . . . . Assistant to Claudia Lewis
Felipe Marino . . . . . 2nd Assistant to Peter Rice

TWENTIETH CENTURY FOX - TCF

SEE Twentieth Century Fox

TWENTIETH CENTURY FOX ANIMATION

10201 W. Pico Blvd., Bldg. 58
Los Angeles, CA 90035
PHONE 310-369-1000
FAX 310-369-3907
WEB SITE . . . . . www.fox.com
TYPES Animation - Features
CREDITS Anastasia - Titan A.E. - Ice Age - Robots
COMMENTS Formerly known as Fox Family Films

Christopher Meledandri . . . . . President, Animation
John Cohen . . . . . Creative Executive
Lisa Fragner . . . . . Head, Development, Blue Sky Studios

TWENTIETH CENTURY FOX TELEVISION

10201 W. Pico Blvd.
Los Angeles, CA 90035
PHONE 310-369-1000
FAX 310-369-2970
TYPES TV Series
CREDITS Reba - 24 - Bernie Mac - Judging Amy - The Simpsons - King of the Hill - Yes, Dear - Still Standing - Arrested Development - Tru Calling - The Simple Life 2 - Method & Red - Quints - The Jury - North Shore - American Dad - Family Guy - Fleet Street - The Inside - Untitled John Stamos Project (Mid Season) - Kelsey Grammer Presents: The Sketch Show

Gary Newman . . . . . President, Twentieth Century Fox Television
Dana Walden . . . . . President, Twentieth Century Fox Television
Robert Barron . . . . . CFO/Executive VP
Howard Kurtzman . . . . . Executive VP, Business & Legal Affairs
Pam Baron . . . . . Sr. VP, Business Affairs
Neal Baseman . . . . . Sr. VP, Business Affairs
Sam Bramhall . . . . . Sr. VP, Business Affairs
Kelly Cline . . . . . Sr. VP, Legal Affairs
Jeffrey Glaser . . . . . Sr. VP, Current Programming
Joel Hornstock . . . . . Sr. VP, TV Production
Janie Kleiman . . . . . Sr. VP, TV Production
Sharon Klein . . . . . Sr. VP, Casting
Bruce Margolis . . . . . Sr. VP, Production
Steven Melnick . . . . . Sr. VP, Marketing
Quan Phung . . . . . Sr. VP, Comedy Development
Jennifer Nicholson Salke . . . . . Sr. VP, Drama
Jim Sharp . . . . . Sr. VP, TV Production
Chris Alexander . . . . . VP, Media Relations
Wendy Bartosh . . . . . VP, Legal Affairs
Jodi Clancy . . . . . VP, Marketing & Research
Gary Hall . . . . . VP, Post Production
Eileen Ige . . . . . VP, Production Accounting
Ann Maney . . . . . VP, Casting, Comedy
Patrick Moran . . . . . VP, Drama
Jacquie Perryman . . . . . VP, Creative Music
Marci Proietto . . . . . VP, TV Production
Janet Savage . . . . . VP, Business Affairs
Steve Sicherman . . . . . VP, Current Programming

(Continued)

TWENTIETH CENTURY FOX TELEVISION (Continued)

Lianne Siegel Shattuck . . . . . VP, Current Programming
Mike Walsh . . . . . VP, Finance
Jo Gard . . . . . Executive Director, Production Accounting
Lynn Barrie . . . . . Director, Comedy Development
Arlene Getman . . . . . Director, Talent Relations
Amy Hartwick . . . . . Director, Comedy Development
Bridget Hegarty . . . . . Director, Current Programming
Beth Hoffman . . . . . Director, Business Affairs
Stacey Levin . . . . . Director, Media Relations
Tony Martinelli . . . . . Director, Casting, Drama
Tracey Raab . . . . . Director, Media Relations
Dana Shelburne . . . . . Director, Current Programming
Nicholas Weinstock . . . . . Director, Comedy Development
Susannah Jeffers . . . . . Sr. Counsel
James Dunn . . . . . Counsel
Brad Bertner . . . . . Manager, Comedy Development
Grace Coffey . . . . . Manager, Business Affairs Administration
Casey Kyber . . . . . Manager, Marketing & Research
Adriana Lemus . . . . . Manager, Media Relations
Larry Vallario . . . . . TV Post Production Supervisor
Jenny Loomis . . . . . Consultant, Business Affairs
Pam Smith . . . . . Coordinator, Business Affairs
Jake Vonk . . . . . Administration, Business Affairs

TWENTIETH TELEVISION

2121 Avenue of the Stars
Los Angeles, CA 90067
PHONE 310-369-1000
FAX 310-369-1718
WEB SITE . . . . . www.fox.com

TYPES: Syndication - TV Series
CREDITS: Classmates - Ambush Makeover - On-Air with Ryan Seacrest - Good Day Live - Divorce Court - Ex-treme Dating - Texas Justice

Bob Cook . . . . . President/COO
Robb Dalton . . . . . President, Programming & Production
Marisa Fermin . . . . . Executive VP, Business Affairs & Development
Elaine Bauer-Brooks . . . . . Sr. VP, Programming & Development
Joanne Burns . . . . . Sr. VP, Research, Marketing & New Media
Cheri Vincent . . . . . Sr. VP, Finance & Administration
Les Eisner . . . . . VP, Media Relations
Daniel Tibbets . . . . . VP, Production

TWILIGHT PICTURES, INC.

580 N. Kinglsey Dr.
Los Angeles, CA 90004
PHONE 877-255-2528
FAX 403-286-3240
EMAIL . . . . . twilight.pictures@shaw.ca
WEB SITE . . . . . www.twilight-pictures.com

TYPES: Documentaries - Features - TV Series
DEVELOPMENT: Series: The Greatest of Them All - The Twilight Years - The Middle Child
CREDITS: Features: Cheerful Tearful - Stone Coats - Check it Out (Six Part Series); Documentaries: Project Cougar - Suzuki's World
COMMENTS: Offices in Calgary and Vancouver

Signe Olynyk . . . . . Writer/Producer
Lorene Lacey . . . . . Producer
Neo Edmund . . . . . Associate Producer
Bob Schultz . . . . . Associate Producer
Andrea Spiegel . . . . . Development

TWIN BROS. PRODUCTIONS, INC.

11661 San Vicente Blvd., Ste. 609
Los Angeles, CA 90049
PHONE 310-275-1300
EMAIL . . . . . development@twinbros.com

TYPES: Features - Made-for-TV/Cable Movies - New Media - TV Series
DEVELOPMENT: Bonhoeffer and Canaris - Bogart's Brother - The Expert
CREDITS: Das Boot: The Director's Cut - Shattered - Carlito's Way
SUBMISSION POLICY: No unsolicited submissions

Ortwin Freyermuth . . . . . President/CEO
Nik P. Grohne . . . . . Assistant to President/CEO

TWO ISLANDS ENTERTAINMENT

31008 Old Colony Way
Westlake Village, CA 91361
PHONE 818-889-3902/818-383-6233
EMAIL . . . . . twoislandsmail@aol.com
WEB SITE . . . . . www.twoislands.com

TYPES: Documentaries - Features - Direct-to-Video/DVD - New Media - TV Series
DEALS: Digital Ranch Productions
DEVELOPMENT: Disaster Squad - Searching for Bedford Falls - Paint Party - Grizzly Jr. - Hiding in Hibbing - Haunting at Sea Horse Farm - Jersey Devil - Tooth & Nail
PRE-PRODUCTION: Waiting for April - Kalamazoo
COMPLETED UNRELEASED: Down By the Sea
CREDITS: Edge of Honor - Test Pilots: Full Tilt - Test Pilots: Flying the Wing - Basic Training - Gear - Safe at Home
SUBMISSION POLICY: Through recognized agents only
COMMENTS: Deal with TMAC (The Magazines Alive Channel); Deal with Londinium Productions

David O'Malley . . . . . Producer
Michael Spence . . . . . Producer
Jeffrey Conlon . . . . . Acquisitions & Development
Karen O'Malley . . . . . Director, Development
Agi Orsi . . . . . Foreign Distribution & Marketing

TWO OCEANS ENTERTAINMENT GROUP

2017 Lemoyne St.
Los Angeles, CA 90026
PHONE 323-669-0824
FAX 323-669-0527
EMAIL . . . . . twoceans@aol.com

TYPES: Animation - Documentaries - Features - Made-for-TV/Cable Movies - TV Series
DEVELOPMENT: Virginia Uribe Project (Showtime)
CREDITS: Sail Away (Discovery Kids) - Happily Ever After: Fairy Tales for Every Child (HBO) - Baby Monitor: Sound of Fear (USA Network) - Reading Your Heart Out (HBO) - Middle School Confessions (HBO)

Meryl Marshall-Daniels . . . . . President/Executive Producer
Susan Whittaker . . . . . Executive VP, Development/Executive Producer

TWO STEPP PRODUCTIONS

2717 W. Clark Ave.
Burbank, CA 91505
PHONE .818-841-0243
EMAIL .asteppprod@aol.com
TYPES Features - Made-for-TV/Cable Movies
DEVELOPMENT Seeing Spotz - Coronado's Gold
CREDITS Dancer, Texas Pop. 81 - Willing to Kill: The Texas Cheerleader Story - The Boy David - Undertaking Betty

Alan Stepp .Producer
James Allen Bradley .Producer
Chase Chenowith .Producer

TYPE A FILMS

100 Universal City Plaza, Bldg. 1320, Ste. 2-E
Universal City, CA 91608
PHONE .818-777-6222
FAX .818-866-2866
TYPES Features
DEALS Universal Pictures
DEVELOPMENT Sports Widow - Whiteout - Penelope
CREDITS Legally Blonde 2: Red, White & Blonde

Reese Witherspoon .Producer
Jennifer Simpson .President
Elinor Vizio .Director, Development
Pamela Palmer Doqui .Assistant to Reese Witherspoon
Tula Jeng .Assistant
Rachael Robertson .Assistant

TYPHOON ENTERTAINMENT

MTV Bldg., 1633 26th St., 3rd Fl.
Santa Monica, CA 90404
PHONE .310-430-1503
EMAIL .steve@typhoonentertianment.com
WEB SITE .www.typhoonentertainment.com
TYPES Commercials - Features - Direct-to-Video/DVD - Made-for-TV/Cable Movies - Music Videos - Reality TV - TV Series
DEALS Fox Television Studios
DEVELOPMENT The Shop - The Kevin Mitnick Movie - Lucky Strike - There's Something About Anna - Emerald City - Sangraal - The Hunter
PRE-PRODUCTION After the Fall - The Shores of Tripoli - The Napster Movie
PRODUCTION I'm in the...
POST PRODUCTION Rome (HBO) - Inked (A&E)
CREDITS Molly - Rough Riders - One Man's Hero - Sliver - Jade - The Saint - Gettysburg - A Date with Anna - VH1's Driven

Jeff Bowler .Founder/Executive Producer
William J. MacDonald .President/Producer
Steve Bowler .Associate Producer/Writer/Development
Brahm Taylor .Creative Director/Website
Steve Clarke .Music Development

UFLAND PRODUCTIONS

534 21st St.
Santa Monica, CA 90402
PHONE .310-656-3031
FAX .310-656-3073
EMAIL .ufland.productions@verizon.net
TYPES Features
CREDITS Night and the City - The Last Temptation of Christ - Not Without My Daughter - Snow Falling on Cedars - One True Thing - Crazy/Beautiful

Mary Jane Ufland .Producer
Harry J. Ufland .Producer

UNDERGROUND FILM & MANAGEMENT

10202 W. Washington Blvd.
Frankovich Bldg., Stes. 115-117
Culver City, CA 90232
PHONE .310-244-6852/310-244-6380
FAX .310-842-7530
EMAIL .trevor@mission-underground.com
SECOND EMAIL .nick@mission-underground.com; will@mission-underground.com
WEB SITE .www.mission-underground.com
TYPES Features - New Media - Reality TV - TV Series
DEALS Phoenix Pictures
DEVELOPMENT The Section - Lowroaders - Road to Freaknik - Venus Kincaid - Flower Girl - Destination Unknown - Black Autumn - Zoom's Academy - Range Rats - Soccer Mom - Pariah
CREDITS Urban Legend 2: The Final Cut
COMMENTS Management division: Underground Management

Nick Osborne .Founding Partner/Producer (310-244-6194)
Trevor Engelson .Partner/Producer (310-244-6380)
Will Lowery .Associate/Manager (310-244-6339)

UNGER PRODUCTIONS, INC.

6606 W. Sixth St.
Los Angeles, CA 90048-4606
PHONE .323-651-9381
FAX .323-651-9386
EMAIL .tonyunger@sbcglobal.net
TYPES Features
DEVELOPMENT Innocent Times - Triptych - Big Bad John
CREDITS Dark Side of Hollywood - Silent Rage - Don't Look Now - Force 10 from Navarone

Anthony B. Unger .President

UNION ENTERTAINMENT

1337 Ocean Ave., Ste. B
Santa Monica, CA 90401
PHONE .310-395-1040
FAX .310-395-1065
WEB SITE .www.unionent.com
TYPES Features - New Media
DEVELOPMENT Nothing But the Truth - Chameleon - Criminalympics - Devil's Island - Priest - Second Life
PRODUCTION Crusty Demons
COMPLETED UNRELEASED Godsend
COMMENTS Solicited submissions only

Sean O'Keefe .President, Film
Richard Leibowitz .President, Games
Dan Jevons .Creative Executive, Games
Will Staples .Creative Executive, Film
Howard Bliss .Business & Legal Affairs
Ethan Malykont .Graphic Designer
Mike Weber .Assistant, Games

It is illegal to copy any part of this book

UNION SQUARE ENTERTAINMENT

9595 Wilshire Blvd., Ste. 900
Beverly Hills, CA 90212
PHONE .310-300-8410
FAX .310-300-8411
EMAIL .info@unionsquareent.com
WEB SITE .www.unionsquareent.com
TYPES Features
COMMENTS Production & Financing

Jason Berk .Principal/Producer
Matt Lane .Principal/Producer
Sidney Sherman .Principal/Producer

UNISTAR INTERNATIONAL PICTURES

400 S. Victory Bvd., Ste. 203
Burbank, CA 91502
PHONE .818-558-1820
FAX .818-558-1877
EMAIL .unistarpix@aol.com
TYPES Features - Direct-to-Video/DVD - Made-for-TV/Cable Movies - Syndication - TV Series
DEALS Echelon Entertainment
DEVELOPMENT El Destino - True Detective (Series/Feature)
PRE-PRODUCTION Grim's Day Off - Bad Kitty
CREDITS Midnight - Firestorm - True Story - Whatever Happened to Bobby Earl? - Contagious - A Light in the Forest (Feature) - Nobody Knows Anything

Gloria Morrison .President/Executive Producer

UNITY COMMUNICATIONS

538 N. Louise St., Ste. 2
Glendale, CA 91206
PHONE .818-243-5244/818-506-5865
FAX .818-243-5202/818-506-5935
EMAIL .sjogun@aol.com
SECOND EMAIL .harrydace@sbcglobal.net
TYPES Features - Direct-to-Video/DVD - Made-for-TV/Cable Movies - Theater - TV Series
DEVELOPMENT Three the Hard Way (2004) - Karma - El Sid - El Diluvio Que Viene (Beyond the Rainbow) - Bonhoeffer - Change of Heart - The Edna St. Vincent Millay Story - Destiny - Abelard & Heloise
PRE-PRODUCTION Retribution - On the Level - The Boys in Autumn - Beyond the Rainbow - To Light One Candle - Family Portrait
CREDITS TV: The Awakening Land - Two Women Abroad; Film: Three the Hard Way - Fatal Inheritance - Take a Hard Ride

Harry Bernsen .President/Producer
Marinka Sjoberg .Co-President/Producer
Collin Bernsen .VP, Production
Roger N. Golden .VP, Legal & Financial
Dace Obrascovs .VP, Development
Caren Wilson .VP, Development

UNITY PRODUCTIONS

8593 Lookout Mt. Ave.
Los Angeles, CA 90046
PHONE .323-654-6299
FAX .323-654-4231
EMAIL .unityprods@hotmail.com
WEB SITE .www.unityproductions.com
TYPES Documentaries - Features - Syndication - Theater - TV Series
DEVELOPMENT A Private War - Pushing Daisy
PRE-PRODUCTION Before the Devil Knows You're Dead - A Perfect Family
CREDITS Den of Lions - Deuces Wild - City of Ghosts; Theater: Act One - Floating Rhoda & the Glue Man

Michael Cerenzie .Producer
Brian Linse .Producer

UNIVERSAL HOME ENTERTAINMENT PRODUCTIONS

100 Universal City Plaza, Bldg. 1320-3M
Universal City, CA 91608
PHONE .818-777-1000
WEB SITE .www.universalstudios.com
TYPES Direct-to-Video/DVD

Louis A. Feola .President, Universal Worldwide Entertainment
Suzie Peterson .Executive VP, Production
Robert W. Rubin .Executive VP
Nancy Eagle .Sr. VP, Business & Legal Affairs
Tom Ruzicka .Sr. VP, Cartoon Productions, Universal Cartoon Studios
Ellen Cockrill .VP, TV
Naomi Gagliano .VP, Finance
Philip Goore .VP, Business & Legal Affairs
Patricia Jackson .VP, Production
Traci Nishida .VP, Finance

UNIVERSAL PICTURES

100 Universal City Plaza
Universal City, CA 91608
PHONE .818-777-1000
WEB SITE .www.universalstudios.com
TYPES Features
CREDITS The Cat in the Hat - Intolerable Cruelty - Bruce Almighty - The Hulk - 2 Fast 2 Furious - American Wedding - Seabiscuit - Honey - Peter Pan - Van Helsing

Stacey Snider .Chairman, Universal Pictures
Marc Shmuger .Vice Chairman, Universal Pictures
Mary Parent .Vice Chairman, Worldwide Production, Universal Pictures
Scott Stuber .Vice Chairman, Worldwide Production, Universal Pictures
Rick Finkelstein .President, Universal Pictures
James D. Brubaker .President, Physical Production
Adam Fogelson .President, Marketing, Universal Pictures
Kathy Nelson .President, Film Music, Universal Music Group (UMG) & Universal Pictures
Nikki Rocco .President, Universal Pictures Distribution
Peter Smith .President, Universal Pictures International (UPI)
Louis Feola .President, Universal Home Video
Eddie Egan .Co-President, Marketing, Universal Pictures
Beth Lauren Goss .Executive VP, Universal Studios Consumer Products Group, Worldwide
James M. Horowitz .Executive VP, Business & Legal Affairs
Donna Langley .Executive VP, Production
Michael Moses .Executive VP, Publicity
William A. Sutman .Executive VP/CFO, Technical Operations
Holly Bario .Sr. VP, Production

(Continued)

UNIVERSAL PICTURES (Continued)

Jeffrey Brauer . . . . Sr. VP
Frank Chiocchi . . . . Sr. VP, Creative Advertising
Philip Cohen . . . . Sr. VP
Andrew Fenady . . . . Sr. VP, Physical Production, Universal Pictures
Harry Garfield . . . . Sr. VP, Film Music
Charles Gaylord . . . . Sr. VP, Market Research
Laura Kesler . . . . Sr. VP, Human Resources
Stephanie Kluft . . . . Sr. VP, Publicity
Greig McRitchie . . . . Sr. VP, Post Production
Paul Pflug . . . . Sr. VP, Media Relations
Gerald Pierce . . . . Sr. VP, Technology
Dan Wolfe . . . . Sr. VP, Creative Advertising
Alissa Andrews-Grayson . . . . VP, Publicity
Scott Bernstein . . . . VP, Production
Gary Chong . . . . VP, Operations
Jerry Clark . . . . VP, Finance
Dylan Clark . . . . VP, Production
Gavin Feinberg . . . . VP, Corporate Planning
Aida Gaboyan . . . . VP, Film Music
Tony Grana . . . . VP, Production Resources
Bob Holmes . . . . VP, Human Resources
Julie Hutchison . . . . VP, Feature Casting
Bret Johnson . . . . VP, Physical Production
Romy Kaufman . . . . VP, Story Department
Jennifer Kirschenbaum . . . . VP, International Finance
Jeff LaPlante . . . . VP, Production Finance
Bill Mandel . . . . VP, Broadband Technology
Dan Martinez . . . . VP, Group Controller, Filmed Entertainment
Jerry Pettit . . . . VP, Production Support
Damien Saccani . . . . VP, Production
Rod Smith . . . . VP, Production Finance
Pamela Speak . . . . VP, Administration
Michele Stratton . . . . VP/Controller
Lawrence Weier . . . . VP, Feature Production Services
Alan Youngstein . . . . VP, Financial Systems Planning & Ultimates

UNIVERSAL STUDIOS

100 Universal City Plaza
Universal City, CA 91608
PHONE 818-777-1000
WEB SITE . . . . www.nbcuni.com
TYPES Features
COMMENTS Theme Parks

Ron Meyer . . . . President/COO, Universal Studios
Patti Hutton . . . . CFO/Executive VP
Kenneth L. Kahrs . . . . Executive VP, Human Resources
Karen Randall . . . . Executive VP/General Counsel
Susan Fleishman . . . . Sr. VP, Corporate Media Affairs, Universal Studios/ Sr. VP, Community Affairs, NBC Universal
Maren Christensen . . . . Sr. VP, Intellectual Property
Linda Bloss-Baum . . VP, Public Policy/Government Relations, NBC Universal
Keith Gorham . . . . Sr. VP, Industrial Relations
Paul Pflug . . . . Sr. VP, Media Relations, Universal Pictures
Mark Wooster . . . . Sr. VP, Legal Affairs
Nestor Barrero . . . . VP, Employment Counsel
Stephanie Caprielian . . . . VP, Labor Relations
Primo Custodio . . . . VP, Human Resources
Karen Elliott . . . . VP, Anti-Piracy Operations
Samuel Flowers . . . . VP, Corporate Development & Strategic Planning
Cindy Gardner . . . . VP, Internal Communications, NBC Universal
Sheldon Kasdan . . . . VP/Sr. Labor Counsel
Ellen Nichols . . . . VP, Human Resources Development
Anne Nielsen . . . . VP/Sr. Trademark Counsel
Ann O'Connor . . . . VP, Government Affairs
Marc Palotay . . . . VP, General Tax Counsel
William Phillips Jr. . . . . VP, Labor & Legal Affairs
Mark Pinkerton . . . . VP, Corporate Planning
Virginia Tanawong . . . . VP, Compensation & Benefits
Crystal Wright . . . . VP, Legal

UNIVERSAL TELEVISION GROUP

SEE NBC Universal Television Studio

UNTITLED BURKE-TARSES PROJECT

330 Bob Hope Dr., C-113
Burbank, CA 91523
PHONE 818-840-7701
FAX 818-840-7789
TYPES Made-for-TV/Cable Movies - TV Series
DEALS NBC Universal Television Studio

Karey Burke . . . . Co-Partner
Jamie Tarses . . . . Co-Partner
Melissa Loy . . . . Executive Assistant

UNTITLED ENTERTAINMENT

8436 W. Third St., Ste. 650
Los Angeles, CA 90048
PHONE 323-966-4400/212-777-7786
FAX 323-966-4401/212-777-8642
TYPES Features - TV Series
COMMENTS East Coast office: 23 E. 22nd St., 3rd Fl., New York, NY 10010

Jason Weinberg . . . . Partner
Stephanie Simon . . . . Partner
Beth Holden-Garland . . . . Partner
Gene Parseghian . . . . Partner (NY)
Johnnie Planco . . . . Partner (NY)
Elise Konialian . . . . VP (NY) (212-777-1214)
Jennifer Levine . . . . Head, Production
Evan Hainey . . . . Manager
Jason Moore . . . . Associate
Jason Newman . . . . Manager
Alissa Vradenburg . . . . Manager
Brian Young . . . . Manager
Scott Zimmerman . . . . Manager
Mimi Di Trani . . . . Associate
David Koth . . . . Associate
Katie Rhodes . . . . Associate
Adam Griffin . . . . Assistant to Jason Newman
Jennifer Merlino . . . . Assistant to Jennifer Levine
Oubansack Pouiphanvongxay . . . . Assistant to Scott Zimmerman
Matt Weiss . . . . Assistant to Alissa Vradenburg
Tosha Lewis . . . . Assistant to Evan Hainey
Nicky Talmadge . . . . Assistant to Stephanie Simon

UPN

11800 Wilshire Blvd.
Los Angeles, CA 90025
PHONE 310-575-7000
WEB SITE . . . . www.upn.com
TYPES TV Series

Leslie Moonves . . . . Co-President/Co-COO, Viacom Entertainment Group
Dawn Ostroff . . . . President, Entertainment, UPN
Kelly Kahl . . . . Executive VP, Program Planning & Scheduling, CBS
Kim Fleary . . . . Sr. VP, Comedy Development
Maggie Murphy . . . . Sr. VP, Drama Development
Jack Sussman . . . . Sr. VP, Specials, CBS
Nicole Ungerman-Levinsohn . . . . Sr. VP, Business & Legal Affairs
Judith Weiner . . . . Sr. VP, Talent & Casting
Laurie Zaks . . . . Sr. VP, Current Programming
Larry Barron . . . . VP, Alternative Programs
Rebecca Stay . . . . VP, Drama Development
Steve Veisel . . . . VP, Comedy Development
Eric Kim . . . . Director, Current Programs
Kevin Levy . . . . Director, Scheduling
Michael McDonald . . . . Director, Drama Development
Beth Miyares . . . . Director, Current Programs
Dana Theodoratos . . . . Manager, Casting

UPSTART ENTERTAINMENT
10433 Wilshire Blvd., Penthouse F
Los Angeles, CA 90024
PHONE .310-475-6025
FAX .310-475-9844
EMAIL .mjnathanson@earthlink.net
TYPES Features - Syndication - TV Series
CREDITS She's Out of Control - The Bulkin Trail - Mom's Got a Date with a Vampire - The Miller Guide

Michael J. Nathanson .Writer/Producer

URBAN ENTERTAINMENT
9200 Sunset Blvd., Ste. 510
Los Angeles, CA 90069
PHONE .310-724-5630
FAX .310-724-5635
EMAIL .info@urbanent.com
WEB SITE .www.urbanentertainment.com
TYPES Features - TV Series - Direct-to-Video/DVD - Animation
DEVELOPMENT Whitebread (New Line) - Diesel Debutantes (New Line) - Ralph (Universal) - Tour De Soul (Universal) - Step in the Name of Love (CMG)
PRE-PRODUCTION Beanstalk in Brooklyn (Animated Feature)
POST PRODUCTION The Golden Blaze (Animated Feature)
CREDITS Undercover Brother (Universal/Imagine)

Michael Jenkinson .CEO
Nichelle Protho .Sr. VP, Production & Development
Helena Echegoyen .Sr. VP, Development & Production
Christopher Brown .Coordinator, Development & Production

USA NETWORK
1230 Avenue of the Americas
New York, NY 10020
PHONE .212-413-5000/818-777-1000
WEB SITE .www.universalstudios.com
SECOND WEB SITE .www.usanetwork.com
TYPES Made-for-TV/Cable Movies - TV Series
CREDITS USA Network Original Programming: Call Me: The Rise and Fall of Heidi Fleiss - The Dead Zone - Monk - Nashville Star - Spartacus - Touching Evil
COMMENTS West Coast office: 100 Universal City Plaza, Universal City, CA 91608

Jeff Wachtel .Executive VP, Programming
Gordon Beck .Sr. VP, Production
Jane Blaney .Sr. VP, Programming
Jackie de Crinis .Sr. VP, Programming
Laurette Hayden .Sr. VP, Programming
John Kelley .Sr. VP, Press
Richard Lynn .Sr. VP, Business Affairs & General Counsel
Chris McCumber .Sr. VP, On-Air Promotions
Melissa Alcruz .VP, Marketing
Christof Bove .VP, Longform Programming
John Cronopulos .VP, Sales
Lorenzo De Guttadauro .VP, Creative
Sonya Joo .VP, Business Development
Kevin Landy .VP, Programming
William McGoldrick .VP, Business Development
Marla Newborn .VP, Programming
Kim Reed .VP, Publicity
Alexandra Shapiro .VP, Marketing
Wendy Weatherford .VP, Promotion

USA-INTERTAINMENT
8560 Sunset Blvd., Ste. 800
Los Angeles, CA 90069
PHONE .310-860-5000
FAX .310-860-5001
WEB SITE .www.intertainment.de
TYPES Features

Barry Baeres .Chairman
Stephen Brown .President
Meghan Treese .VP
Sandra Prassel .Director, Business Affairs

UTOPIA PICTURES & TELEVISION
205 S. Beverly Dr., Ste. 209
Beverly Hills, CA 90212
PHONE .310-550-8746
FAX .310-550-8714
TYPES Animation - Documentaries - Features - Direct-to-Video/DVD - Made-for-TV/Cable Movies - Syndication - TV Series - Reality TV
DEVELOPMENT Saving Shiloh - Cardinal Sins - Evan's Crime - Hearts - Flow My Tears - Radio Free Albemuth - Valis
PRODUCTION Incarnation
CREDITS Shiloh - Shiloh Season - Reckless Indifference - Eight Days a Week - Instant Karma - Across the Tracks - Jack London's Call of the Wild - The Second Day of Christmas
COMMENTS Management

Declan O'Brien .President (310-550-7336)
Dale Rosenbloom .Director/Producer
Merrilu Gordon .Director, Development

RENÉE VALENTE PRODUCTIONS
13547 Ventura Blvd., Ste. 195
Sherman Oaks, CA 91423
PHONE .323-969-1541/941-493-1587
FAX .941-493-1792
EMAIL .valenteprod@aol.com
TYPES Features - Made-for-TV/Cable Movies - TV Series
CREDITS A Storm in Summer (Showtime) - A Man Upstairs - Poker Alice - Around the World in 80 Days (Miniseries) - Contract on Cherry Street - Blind Ambition
SUBMISSION POLICY Release must accompany; No email submissions accepted
COMMENTS Florida office: 1811 Englewood Rd., Englewood, FL 34223

Renée Valente .Executive Producer

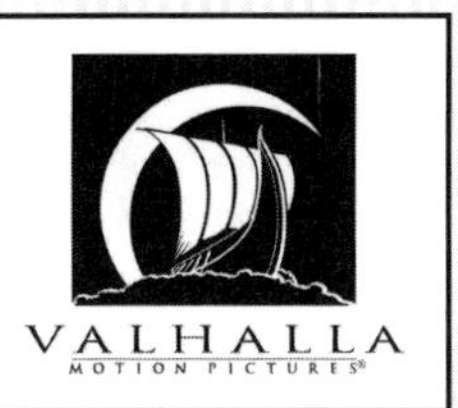

VALHALLA MOTION PICTURES

8530 Wilshire Blvd., Ste. 400
Beverly Hills, CA 90211
PHONE .310-360-8530
FAX .310-360-8531
EMAIL .vmp@valhallapix.com

TYPES: Documentaries - Features - Made-for-TV/Cable Movies - TV Series
PRE-PRODUCTION: Aeon Flux
CREDITS: The Hulk - Dick - Terminator 1&2 - Aliens - Armageddon - Tremors - Dante's Peak - Clockstoppers - Water Dance - No Escape - Abyss - Safe Passage - Virus - The Punisher
SUBMISSION POLICY: No unsolicited submissions

Gale Anne Hurd .CEO/Producer
Bryan Hickel .President
Julie Thomson .CFO
Stephen Emery .Director, Development
Stephen Tao .Executive, TV
Christine Forgo .Accountant
Kevin Boyle .Assistant to Bryan Hickel
Anne Hong .Assistant, TV
Michelle Reihel .Assistant to Gale Anne Hurd

VANDERKLOOT FILM STUDIO

750 Ralph McGill Blvd. NE
Atlanta, GA 30312
PHONE .404-221-0236/404-688-3348
FAX .404-221-1057
EMAIL .bv@vanderkloot.com
SECOND EMAIL .bv@magicklantern.com
WEB SITE .www.vanderkloot.com

TYPES: Documentaries - Features - Direct-to-Video/DVD - New Media - TV Series
DEVELOPMENT: The Chaldean Affair - Secret Sky: The Story of the Ferry Command - Bio-Invaders - The Know Show
PRE-PRODUCTION: The BIG Theme Park - The BIG Ocean Liner
PRODUCTION: The BIG Airshow (DVD) - The BIG Plane Trip
POST PRODUCTION: The BIG Rescue
CREDITS: Cumberland: Island in Time - The BIG Adventure Series
COMMENTS: Little Mammoth Media (www.littlemammoth.com); Magick Lantern Post (www.magicklantern.com)

William VanDerKloot .President/Producer/Director
Lisa Lewis .Executive Producer, Post Production
Todd Schaffer .Executive Producer, Commercials
Paul A. Johns .Controller
Jennifer Mador .Director, Post Production
Jim Mouton .Business Development
James Powell .Sr. Editor
Nancy Rosette .Editor
Adrienne Watts .Little Mammoth Sales Manager
Jesenko Fazlagic .Sr. Designer/Editor
Bazyl Dripps .Editor

VANGUARD FILMS/VANGUARD ANIMATION

8703 W. Olympic Blvd.
Los Angeles, CA 90035
PHONE .310-360-8039
FAX .310-888-8012
EMAIL .mail@vanguardfilms.com
WEB SITE .www.vanguardfilms.com
SECOND WEB SITE .www.vanguardanimation.com

TYPES: Animation - Features - TV Series
DEALS: DreamWorks SKG - The Walt Disney Company
DEVELOPMENT: After Man - On the Road - Galaxy High - The Twits - Space Chimps - Toad Trip
PRE-PRODUCTION: Pet Boy - Gateway to the Gods
PRODUCTION: Valiant (Disney) - Happily N'Ever After
CREDITS: 7 Years in Tibet - Sarafina - Thin Blue Line - Shrek 1&2 - The Tuxedo

John H. Williams .CEO/Producer (john@vanguardfilms.com)
Neil Braun .President (neil@vanguardfilms.com)
Eric Bennett .VP (212-766-4486, eric@vanguardfilms.com)
Rob Moreland .Creative (robmoreland@yahoo.com)
Venecia Duran .Creative (venecia@vanguardfilms.com)
Christopher Bird .Creative (310-392-4622)

VANGUARD PRODUCTIONS

12111 Beatrice St.
Culver City, CA 90230
PHONE .310-306-4910
FAX .310-306-4910
EMAIL .vanguard.productions@verizon.net

TYPES: Commercials - Documentaries - Features - Direct-to-Video/DVD - Made-for-TV/Cable Movies - Music Videos - Reality TV - TV Series
DEVELOPMENT: Treasure of Devil Island - Border Lords - They Also Served (Series) - Alpine Horror - Sea of Demons (Series) - Canyon Gate - Regrettable Error
PRE-PRODUCTION: Dead Rail
CREDITS: We the People - The Bad Pack - Cross Dreams - Wanted - Closing the Deal - Route 666

Terence M. O'Keefe .Writer/Producer/Director
Bennett J. Fidlow .VP, Creative Affairs
Bruce Miyaki .VP, Development
Kay Thaiwadhana .Executive Assistant

VANTAGE ENTERPRISES, INC.

3724 Vantage Ave.
Studio City, CA 91604
PHONE .818-509-8967

TYPES: Documentaries - Features - Direct-to-Video/DVD - Made-for-TV/Cable Movies - Syndication - TV Series
CREDITS: Hollywood's Best Kept Secrets - Convict Cowboy - The Lazarus Man - Black Fox - Orleans - National Desk - The Lot - Darkness at High Noon: The Carl Foreman Documents - American Valor

Norman S. Powell .Partner
Ellen Levine .Partner

VANTAGE ENTERTAINMENT®
22431 Miranda St.
Woodland Hills, CA 91367
PHONE 818-999-0119
EMAIL . . . . vantageenter@aol.com
TYPES — Features - Direct-to-Video/DVD - Made-for-TV/Cable Movies - TV Series
DEVELOPMENT — Running Dark - Marapa - From the Heart - Into the West - Straight as an Arrow
PRE-PRODUCTION — Kidnapping Grapes
SUBMISSION POLICY — No unsolicited material

Courtney Silberberg . . . . Producer/Writer
Jacquelyn Kinkade Silberberg . . . . Producer/Writer

THE VAULT, INC.
1831 Centinela Ave., 2nd Fl.
Santa Monica, CA 90404
PHONE 310-315-0012
FAX 310-315-9322
TYPES — Features
POST PRODUCTION — Perfect Opposites
CREDITS — The Last Supper - Campfire Tales - Panic

Matt Cooper . . . . Producer/Director/Writer
David Cooper . . . . Executive Producer
Lori Miller . . . . Producer

JOSEPH S. VECCHIO ENTERTAINMENT
811 Euclid Ave., Ste. 5
Santa Monica, CA 90403
PHONE 310-917-1515
FAX 310-393-7979
EMAIL . . . . jettv@aol.com
TYPES — Documentaries - Features - Direct-to-Video/DVD - Made-for-TV/Cable Movies - New Media - Syndication - TV Series
DEVELOPMENT — Fighting Black Lions - Night Magic - The Wanderer - Wild Card - In Deadly Earnest
PRE-PRODUCTION — Stranger in a Strange Land - Dante & the Debutante
CREDITS — Oscar - Sunchaser
COMMENTS — Entertainment Guidance Company: Consultation services for all aspects of the entertainment industry

Joseph S. Vecchio . . . . Producer

VENTANA FILMS
7440 Palo Vista Dr., Ste. 100
Los Angeles, CA 90046-1311
PHONE 323-876-3331
EMAIL . . . . lafilm@aol.com
TYPES — Commercials - Features - Music Videos
DEVELOPMENT — Isabel - Way of the Beast
CREDITS — Better Watch Out - Cabeza de Vaca - Cronos
COMMENTS — Four picture deal with The Mine, LLC

Julio Solorzano . . . . Chairman
Arthur H. Gorson . . . . President/Head, Production
Bernard Nussbaumer . . . . Sr. VP

VERDON-CEDRIC PRODUCTIONS
PO Box 2639
Beverly Hills, CA 90213
PHONE 310-274-7253
TYPES — Features
SUBMISSION POLICY — No unsolicited scripts

Sidney Poitier . . . . Producer/Director/Writer/Actor

VERTIGO ENTERTAINMENT
9348 Civic Center Dr., Mezzanine Level
Beverly Hills, CA 90210
PHONE 310-288-5160
FAX 310-278-5295
TYPES — Features - TV Series
DEALS — Miramax Films
DEVELOPMENT — My Wife Is a Gangster - My Sassy Girl - Il Mare - Chaos
POST PRODUCTION — Dark Water - The Grudge
CREDITS — The Ring

Roy Lee . . . . Producer
Doug Davison . . . . Producer
Sonny Mallhi . . . . VP
Gabriel Mason . . . . Director, Development
Irene Yeung . . . . Assistant

VH1 (MUSIC FIRST)
1515 Broadway
New York, NY 10036
PHONE 212-846-8000/310-752-8000
WEB SITE www.vh1.com
TYPES — Documentaries - Made-for-TV/Cable Movies - TV Series - Reality TV
CREDITS — Before They Were Rock Stars - Behind the Music - Fan Club - Legends - Storytellers - Top 20 Countdown - Ultimate Albums - Where Are They Now? - Becoming - Driven - Bands Reunited
COMMENTS — West Coast office: 2600 Colorado Ave., Santa Monica, CA 90404

Judith McGrath . . . . Chairman/CEO, MTV Networks
Christina Norman . . . . President, VH1
Brian Graden . . . . President, Entertainment, MTV/VH1
Rick Krim . . . . Executive VP, Talent & Music Relations
Elyse Zaccaro . . . . Executive Producer, Series & Specials
Nigel Cox-Hagen . . . . Sr. VP/Creative Director
Bruce Gillmer . . . . Sr. VP, Music & Talent Relations
Michael Hirschorn . . . . Sr. VP, News & Production
Mimi James . . . . Sr. VP, West Coast Talent & Creative Development
Cliff Lachman . . . . Sr. VP, West Coast Production & Development
Maggie Malina . . . . Sr. VP, Original Movies & Scripted Series
Colleen Fahey Rush . . . . Sr. VP, Research & Planning
Ben Zurier . . . . Sr. VP, Programming Strategy
Melissa Cobb . . . . VP, West Coast Motion Pictures for TV
Jerry Leo . . . . VP, Program Planning & Scheduling
Kim Rozenfeld . . . . VP, West Coast Original Programming & Series Development
Jeff Olde . . . . Executive Consultant, West Coast Current Programming
Stacy Alexander . . . . Director, West Coast Casting
Alex Campbell . . . . Director, East Coast Programming & Development
Lauren Gellert . . . . Director, East Coast Programming & Development
Julio Kollerbohm . . . . Director, West Coast Original Programming & Series Development
Eli Lehrer . . . . Director, East Coast Programming & Development
Jill Modabber . . . . Director, West Coast Current Programming
Stella Stolper . . . . Director, West Coast Talent
Danielle Woodrow . . . . Director, Development, Original Movies & Scripted Series
David Allensworth . . . . Manager, East Coast Programming & Development
Damla Dogan . . . . Manager, West Coast Original Programming & Series Development
Kim Guidone . . . . Manager, West Coast Pictures for TV
Stacey Jenkins . . . . Manager, East Coast Programming & Development
Brandon Riegg . . . . Manager, West Coast Original Programming & Series Development
Claire McCabe . . . . Executive Creative Consultant, West Coast Current Programming

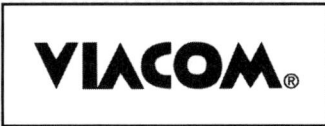

VIACOM ENTERTAINMENT GROUP
5555 Melrose Ave.
Los Angeles, CA 90038
PHONE 323-956-5000
TYPES Features - TV Series

Tom Freston .....Co-President/Co-COO
Leslie Moonves .....Co-President/Co-COO
Thomas McGrath .....President, Paramount Enterprises/ Executive VP, Viacom Entertainment Group
Mike Bartok .....Executive VP, Legal & Business Affairs
Isaac Palmer .....Sr. VP, Corporate Development
Ana Loehnert .....VP, Business Development

VIALTA
48461 Fremont Blvd.
Fremont, CA 94538
PHONE 510-870-3088
FAX 510-870-3899
WEB SITE .....www.vialta.com
TYPES Animation - Documentaries - Features - Direct-to-Video/DVD - New Media - Syndication - TV Series
COMMENTS Produces and distributes DVD content

Didier Pietri .....CEO/President
Lisa Burger .....Manager, Content
Kevin Beauchamp .....Post Production Supervisor

MARK VICTOR PRODUCTIONS
2932 Wilshire Blvd., Ste. 202
Santa Monica, CA 90403
PHONE 310-828-3339
FAX 310-828-9588
EMAIL .....markvictorproductions@hotmail.com
TYPES Animation - Features - Direct-to-Video/DVD - Made-for-TV/Cable Movies - Reality TV - Syndication - TV Series
DEALS Metro-Goldwyn-Mayer Studios, Inc. - Metro-Goldwyn-Mayer Worldwide Television
DEVELOPMENT Synbat - The Wrath of Grapes - Rifting - Rough Night - The Mine - Bounty - Ditch - Ashley Bleu & the G-Girls
PRE-PRODUCTION Outer Limits
POST PRODUCTION States of Grace - God's Army 2
CREDITS Poltergeist 1&2 - Stephen King's Sleepwalkers - Marked for Death - Cool World - Immortals (Series) - Great Balls of Fire - Who Killed Atlanta's Children?

Mark Victor .....Producer/Writer
Mark Skelly .....Producer
Anne Russell .....Director, Development

VIENNA PRODUCTIONS
3940 Laurel Canyon Blvd., Ste. 212
Studio City, CA 91604
PHONE 818-702-6760
FAX 818-501-8474
EMAIL .....vienna1@pacbell.net
TYPES Documentaries - Features - New Media - TV Series
PRODUCTION The Thunderbirds
POST PRODUCTION In the Zone - The Legacy of Sir William Osler
CREDITS Blue Angels - Thunder Over the Pacific - One Vision - Into the Wild Blue

Rob Stone .....President
Mark Garner .....Development Executive

VIEW ASKEW PRODUCTIONS, INC.
116 Broad Street
Red Bank, NJ 07701
PHONE 732-842-6933
FAX 732-842-3772
WEB SITE .....www.viewaskew.com
TYPES Features
DEALS Miramax Films
CREDITS Jay and Silent Bob Strike Back - Dogma - Clerks - Mallrats - Chasing Amy - Jersey Girl

Kevin Smith .....President
Scott Mosier .....VP
Gail Stanley .....Development Executive

VILLAGE ROADSHOW PICTURES
3400 Riverside Dr., Ste. 900
Burbank, CA 91505
PHONE 818-260-6000
FAX 818-260-6001
WEB SITE .....www.villageroadshowpictures.com
TYPES Features
DEALS Warner Bros. Pictures
PRODUCTION Ocean's 12 - Charlie and the Chocolate Factory - Happy Feet
CREDITS The Matrix - The Matrix Reloaded - The Matrix Revolutions - Mystic River - Ocean's Eleven - Training Day - Two Weeks Notice - Miss Congeniality - Three Kings - Analyze This - Deep Blue Sea - Space Cowboys - Swordfish - Cats & Dogs - Don't Say a Word - Catwoman
SUBMISSION POLICY No unsolicited submissions

Bruce Berman .....Chairman/CEO
Steve Krone .....President/COO
Reid Sullivan .....Executive VP/CFO
Dana Goldberg .....Executive VP/Head of Production
Michael Lake .....Executive VP, Worldwide Feature Production
Kevin Berg .....VP, Legal & Financial Affairs
Anna Dergan .....VP, Administration & Operations
Jordanna Fraiberg .....VP, Production
Joel Goldstein .....VP, Business & Legal Affairs
Joseph Hanratty .....VP, Controller
Gina Kilberg .....Sr. VP, Worldwide Marketing & Distribution
Kellie Maltagliati .....Director, Marketing & Publicity
Tim Whitcome .....Manager, Marketing & Distribution
Fred Klein .....Story Editor
Suzy Figueroa .....Executive Assistant to B. Berman
Remi Guyton .....Executive Assistant to D. Goldberg
David Rossi .....Executive Assistant to S. Krone & R. Sullivan

DIMITRI VILLARD PRODUCTIONS
8721 Santa Monica Blvd., Ste. 100
Los Angeles, CA 90069-4507
PHONE .310-229-4545
FAX .310-362-8898
EMAIL .dsvillard@earthlink.net
TYPES Features - Made-for-TV/Cable Movies
DEVELOPMENT Headhunter - Where's Harry?
CREDITS Say Nothing - Flight of the Navigator - Once Bitten - In Love & War

Dimitri Villard .President
Susan Danforth .Assistant

VINTON STUDIOS
1100 Glendon Ave., 17th Fl.
Los Angeles, CA 90024
PHONE .310-689-7222/503-225-1130
FAX .310-689-7244/503-226-3746
WEB SITE .www.vinton.com
TYPES Animation - Features - Direct-to-Video/DVD - Made-for-TV/Cable Movies - New Media - TV Series
DEVELOPMENT Various
PRE-PRODUCTION Tim Burton's Corpse Bride
CREDITS The PJs - Gary & Mike
COMMENTS Animation studio: 1400 NW 22nd Ave., Portland, OR 97210

Jeff Farnath .CEO
Jeffrey Auerbach .President, Entertainment Division/Producer
Sarah Feeley .Director, Development
Kathy Radcliffe .Assistant to Jeff Farnath
Gabrielle Ginter .Assistant to Jeffrey Auerbach

VISIONARY ENTERTAINMENT
1558 N. Stanley Ave.
Los Angeles, CA 90046
PHONE .323-874-4875
FAX .323-845-9722
TYPES Features - TV Series
DEVELOPMENT Major Domo - Untitled Action/Boat Comedy - Never a Bride
PRE-PRODUCTION Don't Ask
CREDITS Wigstock: The Movie
SUBMISSION POLICY No unsolicited submissions
COMMENTS Management

Tom Parziale .Manager/Producer
Derek Kent .Associate
Rustie Burris .Executive Assistant

VISIONBOX MEDIA GROUP
3272 Motor Ave., 2nd Fl.
Los Angeles, CA 90034
PHONE .310-204-4686
FAX .310-204-4603
EMAIL .info@visionboxmedia.com
WEB SITE .www.visionboxmedia.com
TYPES Animation - Documentaries - Features - TV Series
DEVELOPMENT Morningstar - Hush - Black and White - Immaculate Conception - The Last Date Movie - Cousin Ginny
PRE-PRODUCTION Believe In Me
PRODUCTION The Chosen One (Animation)
POST PRODUCTION The L.A. Riot Spectacular
CREDITS Falling Like This - Teddy Bears' Picnic - Charlotte Sometimes - The Invisibles - The Cooler - Love Object - Tortilla Soup - Never Die Alone
SUBMISSION POLICY Synopses only unless solicited

John Manulis .CEO
Chris Miller .President, Post Production
Lulu Zezza .COO/Managing Producer
Andrea Mia .Film Sales, Marketing & Development
Randy Weiss .Coordinator, Development & Production

VISTA STREET ENTERTAINMENT
1720 20th St., Ste. 202
Santa Monica, CA 90404
PHONE .310-453-1013
FAX .310-453-2724
EMAIL .vistastreet@anet.net
WEB SITE .www.videotrash.com
TYPES Features - Direct-to-Video/DVD - New Media - TV Series
CREDITS Witchcraft 1-12 - Dead by Dawn - Strangers - Sisters - Bloodbath - Blood Revenge - The Medicine Show - Beaver Creek - Vampire Blood - Pussywillow

Jerry Feifer .President
Heather Branch .Development

VIVIANO ENTERTAINMENT
9255 Sunset Blvd., Ste. 1000
Los Angeles, CA 90069
PHONE .310-281-0070
FAX .310-281-0050
TYPES Features - TV Series
DEVELOPMENT Freedom House - Happy Jack
CREDITS Three to Tango - Caught in the Act - Nightmare Man - Alibi - Strange Love - Pitfall - Magic Hour - Letters from Joe - Mom's Got a Date - Strange Hearts - Family Sins

Bettina Sofia Viviano .Producer/President/Literary Manager
Susan Levitan .Producer/Manager
Brent Travers .Producer
Marc Verresen .Creative Executive
David Rock .Story Editor

JON VOIGHT ENTERTAINMENT
1901 Avenue of the Stars, Ste. 605
Los Angeles, CA 90067
PHONE .310-843-0223
FAX .310-553-9895
EMAIL .develop@crystal-sky.com
CREDITS Baby Geniuses 1&2 - Unleashed

Patrick Ewald .Executive VP, Development
Angelica Dailey .Assistant to Mr. Voight

VON ZERNECK-SERTNER FILMS

13425 Ventura Blvd., Ste. 301
Sherman Oaks, CA 91423
PHONE .818-789-2766
FAX .818-789-2768
EMAIL .kellygarrett@vzsfilms.com
TYPES Features - Made-for-TV/Cable Movies - TV Series
DEVELOPMENT Natalie Wood - Scott Turow's Reversible Errors - Dynasty: Behind The Scenes
CREDITS Crazy Horse - Robin Cook's Acceptable Risk - Wes Craven Presents Don't Look Down - Three Days - No Ordinary Baby - We Were the Mulvaneys

Robert Sertner .Partner
Frank von Zerneck .Partner
Danielle von Zerneck Fearnley .Producer
Ira Pincus .Producer
Randy Sutter .Sr. VP, Production
Ted Babcock .VP, Post Production
Peter Sadowski .VP, Production
Kelly Garrett .Manager, Development
Nancy Mouton .Executive Assistant

VOY PICTURES

1800 Century Park East, 6th Fl.
Los Angeles, CA 90067
PHONE .877-785-5368/212-204-8331
FAX .310-388-0775/212-202-5240
EMAIL .contact@voygroup.com
WEB SITE .www.voygroup.com
SECOND WEB SITE .www.voy.tv
TYPES Features - TV Series
COMMENTS English-language Latino films

Brian Field .COO
Emilio Diez Barrosso .CEO, VOY Pictures
Andrew Thau .CEO, VOY Network

VOYAGE ENTERTAINMENT

9350 Wilshire Blvd., Ste. 224
Beverly Hills, CA 90212
PHONE .310-273-9520
FAX .310-248-3604
TYPES Documentaries - Features - TV Series
PRODUCTION Thanks to Gravity
CREDITS The Anarchist Cookbook - Sam & Joe - Something More - Lady Killers - The Hunting of the President

Amy Greenspun .Partner
Gina Philips .Partner
Evan Rimer .Assistant to Amy Greenspun

THE ROBERT D. WACHS COMPANY

345 N. Maple Dr., Ste. 179
Beverly Hills, CA 90210
PHONE .310-276-1123
FAX .310-276-5572
EMAIL .wachsmgr@aol.com
TYPES Features - Theater
DEVELOPMENT Last Dance: The Life, Times and Music of Paul Jabara - Blind-Sided - Bride's Night Out
PRE-PRODUCTION Light Sensitive (Broadway) - According to Goldman
CREDITS Raw - Coming to America - Delirious - The Golden Child - Harlem Nights - Beverly Hills Cop 1&2 - Another 48 Hours
SUBMISSION POLICY Referrals preferred; Written, faxed or email submissions accepted
COMMENTS Personal Management

Robert Wachs .No Title

RAYMOND WAGNER PRODUCTIONS, INC.

10377 Rochester Ave.
Los Angeles, CA 90024
PHONE .310-278-1970
FAX .310-274-2662
TYPES Features - Made-for-TV/Cable Movies - TV Series
CREDITS Turner & Hooch - Run - Snow Day - Maniac Magee

Raymond Wagner .President/Producer
Christine McBride .Director, Development

BRAD WAISBREN ENTERPRISES

PO 1928
Studio City, CA 91614
PHONE .818-506-3000
TYPES Animation - Features - TV Series
CREDITS Just for the Record - World Star Quiz - MTV Thursday Special - Amazing Animals
COMMENTS Member, PGA

Brad Waisbren .Producer
Marci Higer .Development
Philip Kramer .Business Affairs

WALD/KAHANE ENTERTAINMENT LLC

15260 Ventura Blvd., Ste. 1240
Sherman Oaks, CA 91403
PHONE .818-382-2515
FAX .818-990-2038/818-382-6216
EMAIL .ursulavari@aol.com
SECOND EMAIL .josielamberth@aol.com
TYPES Features - Made-for-TV/Cable Movies - Reality TV - Syndication - TV Series
DEVELOPMENT Rampart Scandal (HBO) - The Power of Joy (George Foreman) - George Foreman Biopic
PRE-PRODUCTION The Contender (NBC)
CREDITS Pensacola - Two Days in the Valley - Beyond Gang Lines - The Gong Show - The All New Dating Game - The Newlywed Game - Quiz Kids Challenge - El Show De Paul Rodriguez - Switched At Birth - Elvis: The Tribute - Roseanne - The Reagans

Jeff Wald .Co-Chairman
Rob Kahane .Co-Chairman
Jeff Ballenberg .VP, Sales
Angela Bures .Director, Marketing
John Alderson .Artist Manager
Josie Lamberth .Development Executive
Dennis Vacca .Controller
Sue Atkinson .Accounts Payable
Ursula Vari .Assistant to Mr. Wald
Steven Waldstein .Assistant to Mr. Wald
Manni Barrientos .Head of Mailroom

WALDEN FILMS

953 Fourth St., Ste. 305
Santa Monica, CA 90403
PHONE .310-394-1662
EMAIL .waldencine@aol.com
TYPES Features - TV Series
DEVELOPMENT Poe - Expedition - Liecatcher
CREDITS A&E Biography - The Napoleon Murder Mystery - White House: 200th Anniversary - Crime & Punishment

Noah Morowitz .Executive Producer/Director

WALDEN MEDIA

9916 Santa Monica Blvd., 2nd Fl.
Beverly Hills, CA 90212
PHONE .310-887-1000
FAX .310-887-1001
WEB SITE .www.walden.com
TYPES Features
DEALS Twentieth Century Fox
DEVELOPMENT The Giver - Wilberforce - Biblionauts - Bridge to Terabithia - Carlisle School - Nim's Island
PRE-PRODUCTION Chronicles of Narnia: The Lion, The Witch and The Wardrobe
COMPLETED UNRELEASED I Am David
CREDITS Around the World in 80 Days - Holes - Ghosts of the Abyss - Pulse: a STOMP Odyssey
COMMENTS Walden Family Playhouse: 555 17th St., Ste. 2400, Denver, CO 80202, phone: 303-298-1000; East Coast office: 294 Washington St., 7th Fl., Boston, MA 02108, phone: 617-451-5420

Cary Granat .CEO
David Weil .CEO, Anschutz Film Group
Micheal Flaherty .Co-Founder/President (Boston)
Jess Wittenberg .COO
Francesa Hickson .CFO
Frances X. Flaherty .Executive VP, General Counsel
Larry Bernstein .Executive VP, Finance
Alex Schwartz .Executive VP, Production
Tom Prince .Executive VP, Physical Production
Karin Le Maire Crounse .VP, Project Development (Boston)
Joe del Hierro .VP, Motion Picture Development & Production
Lindsay Fellows .VP, Music
Boris Katsnelson .VP, Business Development
Debbie Kovacs .VP, Publishing (Boston)
Frank Smith .VP, Business & Legal Affairs
Martin Sorger .VP/Creative Director (Boston)
Randy Testa .VP, Education & Professional Development
Gordon Tichell .Controller
Barbara Byrne .Director, Educational Outreach
Brian Crounse .Director, Research & Large Format Projects
Julie Daggett .Director, Development
Tommy Finkelstein .Director, Business & Legal Affairs
Jean Kwon .Director, Educational Content
Evan Turner .Director, Development
David Kaufmann .Creative Executive
Gordon Kaywin .Creative Executive

WALKER/FITZGIBBON TV/FILMS

1019 Kane Concourse, Ste. 201
Miami Beach, FL 33154
PHONE .888-284-3456 (Film)/305-864-9390
FAX .305-864-9833
EMAIL .walkerfitz@aol.com
WEB SITE .www.walkerfitzgibbon.com
TYPES Commercials - Documentaries - Features - Made-for-TV/Cable Movies - Music Videos - TV Series
DEVELOPMENT The True Story of the Miami River Cops - CENTAC 26 - INK: Crime Beat
POST PRODUCTION Tributo A Nuestros Heroes (TV Special)
CREDITS Intimate Portrait: Gloria Estefan (Lifetime) - Sony Music/MTV Latin America Documentaries: Shakira - Andy Garcia/Cachao
COMMENTS West Coast office: 2306 Ronda Vista Dr., Los Angeles, CA 90027; Specials; Independent development and production; Docu-dramas

Mo Fitzgibbon .Producer/Director
Robert W. Walker .Executive Producer
Fernando Viquez .Director, Production
Victoria Rose .Development & Business Affairs (NY)
Nora Castillo .Production Manager

WALLETSIZE PICTURES

12103 Maxwellton Rd.
Studio City, CA 91604
PHONE .818-753-9080
FAX .818-753-9481
WEB SITE .www.walletsizepictures.com
TYPES Features - Made-for-TV/Cable Movies - TV Series
CREDITS Stephen King's It - And the Sea Will Tell - Doublecrossed - One Special Night - A Father's Son - Breaking the Surface

Jim Green .Partner/Executive Producer
Mark Bacino .Partner/Executive Producer
Val McLeroy .VP, Production & Development
Jamie Green .Executive Assistant
Jack S. Kimball .Executive Assistant/LA Production Coordinator

WALTZING CLOUDS, INC.

3001 Heavenly Ridge St.
Thousand Oaks, CA 91362
PHONE .805-553-9094
TYPES Documentaries - Features - Made-for-TV/Cable Movies - TV Series
DEVELOPMENT The Investigation - Dual - The Searchers - Black Dragon
PRE-PRODUCTION Ernest Hemingway's The Old Man and the Sea
CREDITS Dead Ahead - The Ticket - The Hunted - Overlord
COMMENTS Deal with Streamfilms AG

Stuart Cooper .President/Writer/Director
Kelly Korzon .VP, Development & Production

*THE WALZ/O'MALLEY COMPANY

3000 W. Olympic Blvd., Ste. 2376
Santa Monica, CA 90404
PHONE .310-315-4706
FAX .310-315-4800
EMAIL .info@walzomalley.com
WEB SITE .www.walzomalley.com
TYPES Documentaries - Made-for-TV/Cable Movies - Music Videos - Reality TV - TV Series
PRE-PRODUCTION Out of My Mind - Open Bar - The Off Season
PRODUCTION Cocktails with Tony Abou-Ganim (Fine Living Network)
CREDITS Drive She Said - Baggage - Mardi Gras Cops - Max Knight: Ultra Spy - Chameleon
COMMENTS Scripted and non-scripted television programming

Sean O'Malley .Producer/Writer
Jon Alon Walz .Producer/Writer
John Duffy .Line Producer
Cheryl Pacino .Executive Assistant

WAR & WISDOM ENTERTAINMENT

345 S. Doheny Dr., Ste. 204
Beverly Hills, CA 90212
PHONE .310-271-7325
TYPES Features - Direct-to-Video/DVD - New Media - TV Series - Reality TV
DEVELOPMENT Rosa (Feature) - A Man Named Crispus (Feature) - Francois (Feature) - Refocus (Reality TV)
CREDITS The Elevator (HBO) - The Theory of the Leisure Class (Vanguard Cinema)
SUBMISSION POLICY No unsolicited material or calls

Athena Stensland .Producer/Writer
Matthew Ashburn .Writer/Producer

WARDENCLYFFE ENTERTAINMENT
8899 Beverly Blvd., Ste. 603
Los Angeles, CA 90048
PHONE .310-273-9664
FAX .310-273-9658
TYPES Features
DEVELOPMENT The Alchemist - Nobody Nowhere - Mockingbird - U.S.S. Pueblo
PRODUCTION Dave Barry's Complete Guide to Guys
COMPLETED UNRELEASED Kart Racer - Blizzard
CREDITS Iron Will - Survivors - Wooly Boys - With You or Without You - Virginia's Run
SUBMISSION POLICY No unsolicited material

Robert Schwartz .Producer/President
Brandon Kienzle .Director, Development
Alejandro Laguette .Creative Executive

WARNER BROS. ANIMATION
15303 Ventura Blvd., Bldg. E
Sherman Oaks, CA 91403
PHONE .818-977-8700
EMAIL .firstname.lastname@warnerbros.com
WEB SITE .www.warnerbros.com
TYPES Animation - Features - Direct-to-Video/DVD - Syndication - TV Series

Sander Schwartz .President
Christopher Keenan .Sr. VP, Creative Affairs
Andy Lewis .Sr. VP/General Manager
Roland Poindexter .Sr. VP, Action-Adventure Properties
Howard Schwartz .Sr. VP, Domestic Production
Kim Christianson .VP, Creative Affairs
Dan Crane .VP, Feature Production
Toshi Hiruma .VP, International Production
Tim Iverson .VP, Post Production
Frank Keating .VP, Marketing
Peter Steckelman .VP, Business & Legal Affairs

WARNER BROS. ENTERTAINMENT INC.
4000 Warner Blvd.
Burbank, CA 91522-0001
PHONE .818-954-6000
WEB SITE .www.warnerbros.com
TYPES Animation - Documentaries - Features - Direct-to-Video/DVD - New Media - Syndication - TV Series

Barry M. Meyer .Chairman/CEO
Alan Horn .President/COO
Barbara S. Brogliatti .Executive VP/Chief Corporate Communications Officer
Gary Credle .Executive VP, Administration & Studio Operations
Richard J. Fox .Executive VP, International
Diane Nelson .Executive VP, Global Brand Management
Bruce Rosenblum .Executive VP, Warner Bros. Television Group
John A. Schulman .Executive VP/General Counsel
Edward A. Romano .Executive VP/CFO
Kevin Tsujihara .Executive VP, Corporate Business Development & Strategy
Darcy Antonellis .Sr. VP, Worldwide Anti-Piracy Operations
John Calkins .Sr. VP, Corporate Business Development & Strategy
Leigh Chapman .Sr. VP/Chief Employment Counsel
Michael Goodnight .Sr. VP/Assistant Corporate Controller
James L. Halsey .Sr. VP/CIO
Reginald Harpur .Sr. VP/Controller
Dean Marks .Sr. VP, Intellectual Property, Corporate Business Development & Strategy
Gary Meisel .Sr. VP, Corporate Business Development & Strategy
(Continued)

WARNER BROS. ENTERTAINMENT INC. (Continued)
Steven Mertz .Sr. VP/General Counsel, Europe
Zazi Pope .Sr. VP/Deputy General Counsel
Sheldon Presser .Sr. VP/Deputy General Counsel
Lisa Rawlins .Sr. VP, Studio & Production Affairs
Laura Valan .Sr. VP, TV Financial Management
Kiko Washington .Sr. VP, Worldwide Human Resources
Clarissa Weirick .Sr. VP/General Counsel, Corporate Business Development & Strategy
Jeremy Williams .Sr. VP/Deputy General Counsel
Scott Rowe .VP, Corporate Communications

WARNER BROS. PICTURES
4000 Warner Blvd.
Burbank, CA 91522-0001
PHONE .818-954-6000
WEB SITE .www.warnerbros.com
TYPES Features

Jeff Robinov .President, Production
Steven Papazian .President, Physical Production
Doug Frank .President, Music Operations
Bob Brassel .Executive VP, Production
Lynn Harris .Executive VP, Production
Kevin McCormick .Executive VP, Production
Courtenay Valenti .Executive VP, Production
Marc Solomon .Executive VP, Post Production & Visual Effects
Keith Zajic .Executive VP, Business Affairs, Music
Steve Spira .Executive VP, Worldwide Business Affairs
Patti Connolly .Executive VP, Business Affairs
Polly Cohen .Sr. VP, Production
Jessica Goodman .Sr. VP, Production
Lora Kennedy .Sr. VP, Casting
Lionel Wigram .Sr. VP, Production
Chris De Faria .Sr. VP, Physical Production & Visual Effects
Frank J. Urioste .Sr. VP, Feature Production
William Young .Sr. VP, Feature Production
Lisa Margolis .Sr. VP, Business & Legal Affairs, Music
Bob Fisher .Sr. VP, Financial Investments & Analysis
Dan Furie .Sr. VP, Business Affairs
Jodi Levinson .Sr. VP, Business Affairs
Pam Kirsh .Sr. VP/General Counsel, Legal
David Sagal .Sr. VP/General Counsel, Business & Legal Affairs
Jeffrey Clifford .VP, Production
Dan Lin .VP, Production
Greg Silverman .VP, Production
Aditya Sood .VP, Production
Teresa Wayne .VP, Story & Creative Administration
Mark Scoon .VP, Feature Production
Suzi Civita .VP, Music
Ellen Schwartz .VP, Music Development
Eileen Hale .VP/Associate General Counsel
Virginia Tweedy .VP, Business Affairs

WARNER BROS. TELEVISION PRODUCTION
4000 Warner Blvd.
Burbank, CA 91522-0001
PHONE .818-954-6000
WEB SITE .www.warnerbros.com
TYPES New Media - TV Series

Peter Roth .President
Craig Hunegs .Executive VP
Leonard Goldstein .Executive VP, Development
Brett Paul .Executive VP, Business Affairs
Judith Zaylor .Executive VP, Production
Mary V. Buck .Sr. VP, Casting
Melinda Hage .Sr. VP, Current Programming
Hank Lachmund .Sr. VP, Labor Relations
Roxanne Lippel .Sr. VP, TV Music
Gregg Maday .Sr. VP, Movies & Miniseries
Sharan Magnuson .Sr. VP, Publicity
Marianne Cracchiolo Mago .Sr. VP, Comedy Development
Geriann McIntosh .Sr. VP, Administration
Marjorie Neufeld .Sr. VP/General Counsel, Legal Affairs
Susan Rovner .Sr. VP, Drama Development
David Sacks .Sr. VP, Current Programming
Christina Smith .Sr. VP, Financial Administration
(Continued)

WARNER BROS. TELEVISION PRODUCTION (Continued)

Tony Amatullo . . . . VP, Network Production
Clancy Collins . . . . VP, Current Programming
Nannette Diacovo . . . . VP, Legal Affairs
Jay Gendron . . . . VP, Business Affairs
Adam Glick . . . . VP, Business Affairs
Phil Gonzales . . . . VP, Publicity
Vicky Herman . . . . VP, Production
Henry Johnson . . . . VP, Production
Heather Kadin . . . . VP, Drama Development
Rachel Kaplan . . . . VP, Drama Development
Lisa Lang . . . . VP, Comedy Development
Lisa Lewis . . . . VP, Production
Mara Lopez . . . . VP, Post Production
Mimi Magnuson-Carson . . . . VP, Legal Affairs
Wendi Matthews . . . . VP, Casting
Sue Palladino . . . . VP, Business Affairs
Ellen Rauch . . . . VP, Production
Bronwyn Savasta . . . . VP, Music
Tony Sepulveda . . . . VP, Casting
Meg Simon . . . . VP, Casting
Adrienne Turner . . . . VP, Current Programming
Sam Wolfson . . . . VP, Labor Relations
Jody Zucker . . . . VP, Legal
Barbara Zuckerman . . . . VP, Legal
Jeanne Cotton . . . . Director, Current Programming
Stephanie Groves . . . . Director, Current Programming
Wendy Steinhoff . . . . Director, Comedy Development
Odetta Watkins . . . . Director, Current Programming
Amy Byer . . . . Manager, Comedy Development
Rachel Filippelli . . . . Manager, Current Programming
Rebecca Franko . . . . Manager, Current Programming
Lisa Roos . . . . Manager, Drama Development

WARNER BROS. THEATRE VENTURES

4000 Warner Blvd.
Burbank, CA 91522-0001
PHONE 818-954-6000
WEB SITE . . . . www.warnerbros.com
COMMENTS Live Entertainment

Gregg Maday . . . . Executive VP

WARNER INDEPENDENT PICTURES

4000 Warner Blvd.
Burbank, CA 91522-0001
PHONE 818-954-6000
WEB SITE . . . . www.warnerbros.com
TYPES Features

Mark Gill . . . . President
Michael Andreen . . . . Executive VP, Production
Steven Friedlander . . . . Executive VP, Distribution
Laura Kim . . . . Executive VP, Marketing & Publicity
Andrew Kramer . . . . Executive VP, Business Affairs & Operations
Paul Federbush . . . . Sr. VP, Production & Acquisitions
Despina Beazoglou . . . . VP, Business & Legal Affairs
Tracey Bing . . . . VP, Production & Acquisitions
Erin O'Neil . . . . VP, Creative Advertising

WARREN MILLER ENTERTAINMENT

2540 Frontier Ave., Bldg. 104
Boulder, CO 80301
PHONE 303-442-3430
FAX 303-998-7208
WEB SITE . . . . www.warrenmiller.com
TYPES Documentaries - Features - Direct-to-Video/DVD - Made-for-TV/Cable Movies - TV Series
PRE-PRODUCTION Pop Sci's Tech Adventures - Warren Miller's 56th Annual
PRODUCTION This Happened to Me (Series)
COMPLETED UNRELEASED X Team
CREDITS World's Best: Top Ten Ski Resorts (Travel Channel) - Warren Miller's Impact - Superior Beings (ESPN) - Global Adventures (OLN) - Inside: Avalanches (Discovery) - Toyota: There & Back (OLN) - Warren Miller's Thrills & Spills - Wild Survival with Corbin Bernsen - Amstel Light Iceland Open (OLN) - Guy's Guide to Colorado (Spike TV)
COMMENTS Division of Time Warner

Perkins Miller . . . . VP/General Manager
Gary Hines . . . . Executive in Charge of Production
Chris Keig . . . . Head, Production
Jeff Moore . . . . Director, New Business Development

WASS-STEIN

500 S. Buena Vista St., Animation 2B-4
Burbank, CA 91521
PHONE 818-560-1950/818-560-1985
FAX 818-563-9889
TYPES TV Series
DEALS Touchstone Television
CREDITS Less Than Perfect

Nina Wass . . . . Partner (818-560-1950)
Gene Stein . . . . Partner (818-560-1985)
Catherine Dunn . . . . Assistant to Nina Wass
Lori Schaffhauser . . . . Assistant to Gene Stein

WATERSHED FILMS

833 Moraga Dr., Ste. 1
Los Angeles, CA 90049
PHONE 310-472-8750
EMAIL . . . . jbrooke@earthlink.net
WEB SITE . . . . www.watershedfilms.com
TYPES Documentaries - Features - TV Series
PRE-PRODUCTION The Wellness Detective
CREDITS Plato's Run - The Dinosaur Hunter - Tall Tales - One in Eight - VH1 50 Greatest Album Covers
COMMENTS Deal with Paradise FX

James Brooke . . . . Producer
Neil DeGroot . . . . Producer
Wally Parks . . . . Producer

THE WB TELEVISION NETWORK

4000 Warner Blvd., Bldg. 34-R
Burbank, CA 91522
PHONE .818-977-5000
FAX .818-977-2282
WEB SITE .www.thewb.com
TYPES Made-for-TV/Cable Movies - TV Series - Reality TV

Garth Ancier .Chairman, The WB Television Network
David Janollari .President, Entertainment
Bob Bibb .Co-President, Marketing
Lewis Goldstein .Co-President, Marketing
Carolyn Bernstein .Executive VP, Drama Development
Michael Clements .Co-Executive VP, Comedy Development
Suzanne Kolb .Executive VP, Marketing
Kathleen Letterie .Executive VP, Talent & Casting
John Maatta .Executive VP & General Counsel, Legal
Mitch Nedick .Executive VP, Finance & Operations
Tracey Pakosta .Co-Executive VP, Comedy Development
Michael Ross .Executive VP, Business Affairs
Brad Turell .Executive VP, Network Communications
Ken Werner .Executive VP, Network Distribution
Keith Cox .Sr. VP, Alternative Programming
Maria Grasso .Sr. VP, Drama Development
Mary Hall .Sr. VP, Research
Tana Nugent Jamieson .Sr. VP, Programming, Movies of the Week
Rick Mater .Sr. VP, Broadcast Standards
Betsy McGowen .Sr. VP/General Manager, Kids WB!
Paul McGuire .Sr. VP, Network Communications
Rusty Mintz .Sr. VP, Scheduling
Michael Roberts .Sr. VP, Current Programming
Chris Sanagustin .Sr. VP, Current Programming
Claudia Ramsumair .VP, Casting
Clay Spencer .VP, Drama Development
Wendy Baxter .Director, Current Programming
Jennifer Levi .Director, Alternative Programming
Jay Potashnick .Director, Scheduling
Tal Rabinowitz .Director, Comedy Development
Tess Sanchez .Director, Casting

WE: WOMEN'S ENTERTAINMENT

200 Jericho Quadrangle
Jericho, NY 11753
PHONE .516-803-3000
WEB SITE .www.we.tv
TYPES Documentaries - New Media - TV Series
PRODUCTION When I Was a Girl - She House
CREDITS Royal Families of the World - Everyday Elegance with Colin Cowie - Real Simple - Cinematherapy - Cool Women - Winning Women - Agenda - Astrology Show - Young, Sexy & Royal - Rock N' Moms

Elizabeth Doree .VP, Programming
Jeff Eisenberg .VP, Production
Judith Orlowski .VP, Acquisitions
Gary Pipa .Director, Scheduling

JIM WEDAA PRODUCTIONS

6399 Wilshire Blvd., Ste 1011
Los Angeles, CA 90004
PHONE .323-852-6966
FAX .323-852-6969
EMAIL .jim@jimwedaaproductions.com
WEB SITE .www.jimwedaaproductions.com
TYPES Features - Made-for-TV/Cable Movies - TV Series
DEVELOPMENT Juggernaut - The Blue Wall - Eleven-99 - Public Displays of Affection (PDA) - Fixxer - Whispers in Bedlam - The Demonologists - Saint Ex
PRE-PRODUCTION Juggernaut - Terrington Prep
CREDITS Mission to Mars - Big Trouble - Black Dog - Red Team - Nine Lives

Jim Wedaa .President
Jared Patrick .Assistant to Jim Wedaa

WEED ROAD PICTURES

4000 Warner Blvd., Bldg. 81, Ste. 115
Burbank, CA 91522
PHONE .818-954-3771
FAX .818-954-3061
EMAIL .weedroad@earthlink.net
TYPES Features
DEALS Warner Bros. Pictures
DEVELOPMENT The Revenant - Le Voyeur - Tonight He Comes - 100 Bullets - The Dark - Shibumi - The Exec
POST PRODUCTION Mindhunters - Constantine - Mr. & Mrs. Smith
CREDITS Deep Blue Sea - Starsky & Hutch

Akiva Goldsman .Producer
Stephanie Gisondi .VP
Wes Rowe .Creative Executive
Viruna Cutler .Assistant to Akiva Goldsman
Jane Kelly Kosek .Assistant to Akiva Goldsman
Ashley Epting .Assistant to Stephanie Gisondi & Wes Rowe

WEEKEND FILMS

2654 Main St.
Santa Monica, CA 90405
PHONE .310-399-9577
FAX .310-399-9515
TYPES Features
DEALS Twentieth Century Fox
DEVELOPMENT Walk of Fame - Mr. Magorium's Wonder Emporium - Silver Strike - Slowman - Where You Are - Lying on the Couch - Run for Your Wife
POST PRODUCTION Because of Winn Dixie
CREDITS The First $20 Million - Bedazzled - Multiplicity - Groundhog Day - The League of Extraordinary Gentlemen
SUBMISSION POLICY No query letters

Trevor Albert .Producer
Kym Bye .Development Executive
Troy Benjamin .Assistant

WEINSTOCK PRODUCTIONS

140 S. Irving Blvd.
Los Angeles, CA 90004
PHONE .323-465-1976
TYPES Features
CREDITS Sleepover - Joe Gould's Secret - Where the Money Is

Charles Weinstock .Producer

JERRY WEINTRAUB PRODUCTIONS

c/o Warner Bros.
4000 Warner Blvd., Bungalow 1
Burbank, CA 91522-0001
PHONE .818-954-2500
FAX .818-954-1399

TYPES	Features
DEALS	Warner Bros. Pictures
PRODUCTION	Ocean's Twelve
CREDITS	Ocean's Eleven - Vegas Vacation - The Specialist - Diner - Nashville - Soldier - Avengers - Karate Kid 1-4

Jerry Weintraub .Producer
Mark Vahradian .President
Susan Ekins .VP, Physical Production
Leigh Boniello .Creative Executive
Kimberly Pinkstaff .Executive Assistant to Jerry Weintraub

LLOYD WEINTRAUB PRODUCTIONS

11771 Preston Trails Ave.
Northridge, CA 91326
PHONE .818-831-7774

TYPES	Features - Made-for-TV/Cable Movies - TV Series
CREDITS	For the Love of Nancy - Chicken Soup for the Soul - Voices from Within - Touched by Evil - Opposites Attract

Lloyd Weintraub .President

WEINTRAUB/KUHN PRODUCTIONS

1821 Wilshire Blvd., Ste. 645
Santa Monica, CA 90403
PHONE .310-453-4222
FAX .310-453-4211

TYPES	Documentaries - Features - Direct-to-Video/DVD - Made-for-TV/Cable Movies - Syndication - TV Series
DEVELOPMENT	Patton and His Dog Soldiers (Feature) - Bruce Lee: The Final Days (Documentary)
PRE-PRODUCTION	Angels on Horseback (Feature) - Vampire on the Orient Express (Feature) - They Only Come Out at Midnight (Feature)
POST PRODUCTION	La Femme Musketeer (Miniseries)
CREDITS	High Road to China - The New Adventures of Robin Hood - Enter the Dragon - The Devil's Arithmetic - Perilous - Amazons and Gladiators - Endangered Species - Dream Warrior - Curse of the Dragon

Fred Weintraub .Producer
Tom Kuhn .Producer
Jackie Weintraub .VP, Development
Maxwell Meltzer .Business Affairs
Tony Roman .Post-Production Supervisor
Tyrrell Shaffner .Executive Assistant

WELLER/GROSSMAN PRODUCTIONS

5200 Lankershim Blvd., Ste. 500
North Hollywood, CA 91601
PHONE .818-755-4800
FAX .818-755-4820
WEB SITE .www.wellergrossman.com

TYPES	Documentaries - New Media - Reality TV - Syndication - TV Series
DEALS	A&E Television Networks - Discovery Networks, U.S. - Fine Living - Food Network - Home & Garden Television (HGTV) - The History Channel
COMPLETED UNRELEASED	A&E Pilot
CREDITS	Wolfgang Puck (TV Food Network) - The Carol Duvall Show (HGTV) - Radical Sabbatical (Fine Living Network) - Berman & Berman (Discovery Health) - It's a Miracle (PAX) - Bar B Que with Bobby Flay

Gary H. Grossman .Executive Producer
Robb Weller .Executive Producer
Steve Lange .Executive Producer
Noel Poole .CFO
Dave Shikiar .Executive in Charge of Production
Debbie Supnik .Director, Development

JOHN WELLS PRODUCTIONS

c/o Warner Bros. Studios
4000 Warner Blvd., Bldg. 1
Burbank, CA 91522-0001
PHONE .818-954-1687
FAX .818-954-3657

TYPES	Features - TV Series
DEALS	Warner Bros. Television Production
CREDITS	The Good Thief - White Oleander - ER - The West Wing - Third Watch - China Beach - Presidio Med - The Big Time - Citizen Baines - Trinity

John Wells .Writer/Producer (818-954-1687)
Andrew Stearn .Executive VP, TV (818-954-7568)
Ned Haspel .Executive VP, Finance & Business Affairs (818-954-5115)
Laura Holstein .Executive VP, Features (818-954-5341)
John Levey .Sr. VP, Casting (818-954-4080)
Chris Selak .Sr. VP, TV (818-954-3629)
Tracy Underwood .VP, Features (818-954-2721)
Reeva Mandelbaum .VP, Research (818-954-4135)
Joy Daffern .VP, Human Resources & Administration (818-954-5276)
Lisa Morales .Director, Features (818-954-3542)
Shelagh M. O'Brien .Director, Production (818-954-5441)
Dan Hadl .Director, Finance & Business Affairs (818-954-3609)
Philip Ross .Manager, TV (818-954-2309)
Heather Zuhlke .Executive Assistant to John Wells (818-954-1687)
Walter Hong .Assistant to Andrew Stearn (818-954-7568)
Jared Geoffroy .Assistant to Ned Haspel (818-954-5115)
Matt Skiena .Assistant to Laura Holstein (818-954-5341)
Erin Lowrey .Assistant to Chris Selak (818-954-3629)
Jonathan Stopek .Assistant to Tracy Underwood (818-954-2721)
Sara Isaacson .Assistant to John Levey (818-954-4080)

CLIFFORD WERBER PRODUCTIONS

c/o Warner Bros.
4000 Warner Blvd.
Burbank, CA 91522
PHONE .818-954-3918
FAX .818-954-3903

TYPES	Features
DEALS	Warner Bros. Pictures
DEVELOPMENT	Sydney White and the Seven Dorks
COMPLETED UNRELEASED	A Cinderella Story

Clifford Werber .Producer
Dara Resnik .Creative Executive

WEST EGG STUDIOS, INC.

c/o JB Films, Ltd.
12301 Wilshire, Ste. 110
Los Angeles, CA 90025
PHONE .310-207-1021
FAX .310-207-6069
EMAIL .gstelzner@weggstudios.com
WEB SITE .www.weggstudios.com

TYPES: Documentaries - Features - Made-for-TV/Cable Movies - TV Series
DEVELOPMENT: The Apostles (CBS) - You Send Me (Lifetime) - Too Young to Marry (Lifetime) - PUNCH! (Animated Series/Nelvana) - A Midsummer Night's Magic (MTV)
PRE-PRODUCTION: Hidden Jesus
CREDITS: Jackie Bouvier Kennedy Onassis (CBS) - Reluctant Saint: The Life of Francis of Assisi (Hallmark Channel, Documentary) - Nightscreams (NBC)

George Stelzner .Executive Producer

SIMON WEST PRODUCTIONS

5555 Melrose Ave., Dressing Room Bldg., Rm. 109
Hollywood, CA 90038
PHONE .323-956-8994
FAX .323-862-2205

TYPES: Features - TV Series
DEALS: Paramount Television
CREDITS: Blackhawk Down - Con Air - The General's Daughter - Lara Croft: Tomb Raider - Keen Eddie (Paramount/Fox) - Harry Green and Eugene (Paramount/ABC)

Simon West .Director/Producer
Jib Polhemus .President, Production
Marta Bartholomew .Assistant

WESTERN SANDBLAST

3780 Wilshire Blvd., 7th Fl.
Los Angeles, CA 90010
PHONE .213-637-8633
FAX .213-637-0110
WEB SITE .www.sandblast.com

TYPES: Features - Made-for-TV/Cable Movies - TV Series

Dan Pyne .No Title
John Mankiewicz .No Title
Susan Ruskin .No Title
Neil Ingram .No Title
Erich Anderson .No Title
Aaron Lipstadt .No Title
Kim Simi .No Title
Eyde Belasco .No Title
Max Flynn .No Title

WHAMAPHRAM PRODUCTIONS

146 N. San Fernando Blvd., Ste. 214
Burbank, CA 91502
PHONE .818-846-2261
FAX .866-861-1918
WEB SITE .www.whamaphram.com

TYPES: Animation - Features
DEVELOPMENT: G-Force

Hoyt Yeatman .No Title
David James .No Title
Ed Kashiba .No Title
Jeff Mahn .No Title

THE WHEELHOUSE

15464 Ventura Blvd.
Sherman Oaks, CA 91403-3002
PHONE .818-461-3599
FAX .818-907-0819
WEB SITE .www.thewheelhouse.com

TYPES: Features - TV Series
CREDITS: Braveheart - The Man in the Iron Mask - Pearl Harbor - We Were Soldiers

Randall Wallace .Director/Writer/Producer
Danielle Lemmon .VP, Production & Development
Stephen Zapotoczny .VP, Production & Development
Jill Rytie .Coordinator, Production & Development
Jason Tracey .Coordinator, Production & Development

WHITELIGHT ENTERTAINMENT

5200 Lankershim Blvd., Ste. 350
North Hollywood, CA 91601
PHONE .818-655-9747
FAX .818-763-8121

TYPES: Animation - Features - TV Series
DEVELOPMENT: Lupin 3 - Brimstone - Way of the Warrior
PRE-PRODUCTION: The Best Christmas Pageant Ever
CREDITS: Minority Report - Lost World: Jurassic Park - Schindler's List - Jurassic Park - Hook

Gerald R. Molen .Chairman/CEO
Chet Thomas .President, Production
David Ranes .VP, Development
Shaun Jorgensen .Assistant
Chris Taylor .Assistant

WHITEWATER FILMS

2232 S. Cotner Ave.
Los Angeles, CA 90064
PHONE .310-575-5800
FAX .310-575-5802
EMAIL .info@whitewaterfilms.com
WEB SITE .www.whitewaterfilms.com

TYPES: Features - TV Series
DEVELOPMENT: Burnt Bridge Road - Bulldogs
PRODUCTION: Nearing Grace
POST PRODUCTION: Mean Creek
CREDITS: Halloween: Resurrection - Bad Boys - Distant Thunder - American Dreamer - Life Goes On - Just a Little Harmless Sex
SUBMISSION POLICY: No unsolicited material

Rick Rosenthal .President
Susan Johnson .VP, Production
Ryan Peterson .Director, Development
Doug Sutherland .No Title

WHOOP INC./ONE HO PRODUCTIONS/LIL' WHOOP PRODUCTIONS

375 Greenwich St.
New York, NY 10013
PHONE .212-941-2074

TYPES: Features - Made-for-TV/Cable Movies - TV Series
DEALS: USA Network
DEVELOPMENT: Destined to Witness - Tumbling - Sullivan's Travels - Rush Home Road
PRODUCTION: Untitled Nickelodeon Pilot (Girls' Soccer Show) - Whoopi's Littleburg
CREDITS: Hollywood Squares - Strong Medicine - Ruby's Bucket of Blood - Call Me Claus - What Makes a Family - Whoopi (NBC)

Whoopi Goldberg .Executive Producer
Tom Leonardis .President/Executive Producer/Director, Development
Shannon McCandless .Assistant

WHYADUCK PRODUCTIONS, INC.
4804 Laurel Canyon Blvd., PMB 502
North Hollywood, CA 91607
PHONE ... 818-980-5355
EMAIL ... duckprods@aol.com
WEB SITE ... www.duckprods.com
TYPES: Documentaries - Features - TV Series
DEVELOPMENT: The Sirens of Titan
PRODUCTION: Dick Gregory: The Color of Funny - Kurt Vonnegut: American Made
CREDITS: Lenny Bruce: Swear to Tell the Truth - Mother Night - W.C. Fields Straight Up - Curb Your Enthusiasm - Mort Sahl: The Loyal Opposition - The Marx Brothers in a Nutshell

Robert B. Weide ... President/Producer

WICKED MONKEY PRODUCTIONS
6404 Hollywood Blvd., Ste. 324
Hollywood, CA 90028
PHONE ... 323-461-6665
TYPES: Features - Direct-to-Video/DVD - Made-for-TV/Cable Movies - TV Series
DEVELOPMENT: The Immortals
CREDITS: Candyman 3 - Sleepstalker

Al Septien ... Writer/Producer
Turi Meyer ... Writer/Director
Sterling Quinn ... Development

*WIDEAWAKE, INC.
8752 Rangely Ave.
Los Angeles, CA 90048
PHONE ... 310-652-9200
TYPES: Features - Reality TV - TV Series
DEALS: Regency Enterprises
DEVELOPMENT: Destiny - Big Brother - Untitled Dating Project - The Holiday Club - Soulmates
CREDITS: The Girl Next Door

Luke Greenfield ... Writer/Director/Producer
Juan Castro ... Producer
Matthew Seigel ... Producer
Joseph Garner ... Assistant

DAN WIGUTOW PRODUCTIONS
534 La Guardia Pl., Ste. 3
New York, NY 10012
PHONE ... 212-477-1328
FAX ... 212-254-6902
TYPES: Features - Made-for-TV/Cable Movies
DEVELOPMENT: Murder in Medina County
PRODUCTION: Revenge of the Middle-Aged Woman
CREDITS: Raising Waylon (MOW) - In a Child's Name (Miniseries) - Brave New World - Hunt for the Unicorn Killer (Miniseries) - Peter Benchley's The Beast (Miniseries) - Guilty Hearts (Miniseries)

Dan Wigutow ... Executive Producer
Laura Brownson ... Producer
Monika Ingram ... Story Editor

WILD AT HEART FILMS, LLC
10100 Santa Monica Blvd., Ste. 1300
Los Angeles, CA 90067
PHONE ... 310-205-0550
FAX ... 310-229-4494
TYPES: Features - Made-for-TV/Cable Movies - TV Series
DEVELOPMENT: Personal Foul (Showtime) - Ooh LA LA - The New York Christmas Movie (Sony/Revolution) - Harlem Prince - Heart of the Atom - A Not So Royal Wedding - War Paint
PRE-PRODUCTION: The 12 - Fractured - Speed Freaks (Spike TV)
CREDITS: Jackpot - Northfork - In and Out

James Egan ... CEO/Producer/Writer
Marlise Karlin ... President/Producer
Boris Geiger ... Business Affairs

WILDRICE PRODUCTIONS
12439 Magnolia Blvd., Ste. 173
North Hollywood, CA 91607
PHONE ... 818-487-2765
FAX ... 818-753-9830
EMAIL ... joelrice@wildriceproductions.com
TYPES: Made-for-TV/Cable Movies - TV Series
DEVELOPMENT: Pierre Heist - Babygate - Mad Shoes - Just Rewards - Vanishing Act
PRE-PRODUCTION: Ghost of a Chance - Family Room (Pilot)
POST PRODUCTION: Boyfriend for Christmas
COMPLETED UNRELEASED: This Time Around (Pilot)
CREDITS: Love Rules! - I Want to Marry Ryan Banks - Picking Up & Dropping Off - Audrey's Rain - This Time Around - Code 1114 - One Kill - About Sarah - Half a Dozen Babies - Sleeping with the Devil

Joel S. Rice ... Executive Producer

WILDWELL FILMS
1516 Rosalia Rd., Loft 7
Los Angeles, CA 90027
PHONE ... 323-662-4050
WEB SITE ... www.m4our.com/wake
TYPES: Documentaries - Features
DEVELOPMENT: Sleepwalking - Venus - The Dead Girls - The Lucky Day - Dark Corner
PRE-PRODUCTION: Magic Hour
CREDITS: Spirit of '76 - Bram Stoker's Dracula - Traveling Light - Wake
SUBMISSION POLICY: Agent submission or legal representative only
COMMENTS: Fiercely independent

Susan Landau Finch ... Producer/Writer
Henry LeRoy Finch ... Director/Writer
Joe Hendrix ... Assistant

WILDWOOD ENTERPRISES, INC./SOUTH FORK PICTURES
1101 Montana Ave., Ste. E
Santa Monica, CA 90403
PHONE ... 310-395-5155
FAX ... 310-395-3975
TYPES: Features
DEALS: Warner Bros. Pictures
COMPLETED UNRELEASED: The Motorcycle Diaries
CREDITS: Quiz Show - A River Runs Through It - Ordinary People - The Horse Whisperer - The Legend of Bagger Vance
SUBMISSION POLICY: No unsolicited material

Robert Redford ... Owner
Karen Tenkhoff ... Producer
Connie Wethington ... No Title
Bill Holderman ... No Title

ELLYN WILLIAMS PRODUCTIONS

c/o Jaffe/Braunstein Films, Ltd.
12301 Wilshire Blvd., Ste. 110
Los Angeles, CA 90025
PHONE 310-207-6600
FAX 310-207-6069

TYPES	Made-for-TV/Cable Movies - Syndication - TV Series
DEALS	Jaffe/Braunstein Films, Ltd.
DEVELOPMENT	Reunited Twins - Night Over Water - DROOD - An Empty Plate - A Home for the Holidays - Blackout
CREDITS	A Mother's Testimony - The Third Twin - Boot Camp - The Stalking of Laurie Show - Hunger Point

Ellyn Williams ....Executive Producer

WILMARK ENTERTAINMENT, INC.

200 N. Catalina Ave., Ste. B
Redondo Beach, CA 90277
PHONE 310-379-7533
FAX 310-801-0633
EMAIL ....wilibaronet@yahoo.com

TYPES	Documentaries - Features - Made-for-TV/Cable Movies - TV Series
DEVELOPMENT	Battledance - Deity - Interrogator (ABC)
PRODUCTION	Live or Die
CREDITS	Any Day Now - Beauty - Vendetta - Intimate Portraits - Trapped (USA, MOW) - CSI: Miami - Medical Investigation (NBC)

Mark Israel ....President
Wili Baronet ....VP

BRAD WILSON PRODUCTIONS, INC.

4120 Burbank Blvd.
Burbank, CA 91505
PHONE 818-845-8811
FAX 818-845-8868
EMAIL ....brad@bradwilson.biz
WEB SITE ....www.bradwilson.biz

TYPES	Features - Direct-to-Video/DVD - Made-for-TV/Cable Movies - TV Series
DEVELOPMENT	The Country Series - Breeders - Kissing a Dream - Believers Among Us
CREDITS	A Family Thing - Left Luggage - Don't Let Go - The Ghost Club - One of Them - Undercover Kids

Brad Wilson ....Producer
Laura Roberts ....Head, Development

WILSON/WOODS PRODUCTIONS

10641 La Grange Ave., Ste. 304
Los Angeles, CA 90025
PHONE 310-470-6924
FAX 310-470-8990
EMAIL ....robtwoods@att.net

TYPES	Features - Made-for-TV/Cable Movies
DEVELOPMENT	Krystal Turns 18
CREDITS	The Elf Who Saved Christmas (USA) - The Elf and the Magic Key (USA) - The Miracle of the Cards (PAX)

Lee Wilson ....Producer
Robert Woods ....Producer

WINCHESTER FILMS

701 Santa Monica Blvd., Ste. 230
Santa Monica, CA 90401
PHONE 310-395-4800/44-207-851-6500
FAX 310-395-8578/44-207-851-6505
WEB SITE ....www.winchesterfilms.com

TYPES	Features - Made-for-TV/Cable Movies
DEALS	The Donners' Company
DEVELOPMENT	Li'l Homies - The Yes Man - The Divide - Sixteen Blocks - Sam & George - Forever and a Day - Daughter of the Queen of Sheba - Harv the Barbarian
COMPLETED UNRELEASED	The Night We Called It A Day
CREDITS	Shooting Fish - Divorcing Jack - Lighthouse - Heartbreakers - Last Orders - A Christmas Carol - Jane Doe - Scotland, PA - Lantana (UK) - Scorched
SUBMISSION POLICY	No unsolicited material
COMMENTS	UK office: 19 Heddon St., London W1B 4BG UK

Hadeel Reda ....Producer
Simone Bennett ....VP, Business & Legal Affairs

MARGOT WINCHESTER PRODUCTIONS, INC.

15479 La Maida St.
Sherman Oaks, CA 91403
PHONE 818-907-8162
FAX 818-907-1162
EMAIL ....mwinch@pacbell.net

TYPES	Documentaries - Made-for-TV/Cable Movies - TV Series - Reality TV
PRODUCTION	Los Angeles Free Clinic Video - n2n Brain Research Video - PA Foundation Video
CREDITS	A Strange Affair - Brotherhood of Justice

Margot Winchester ....President/Producer

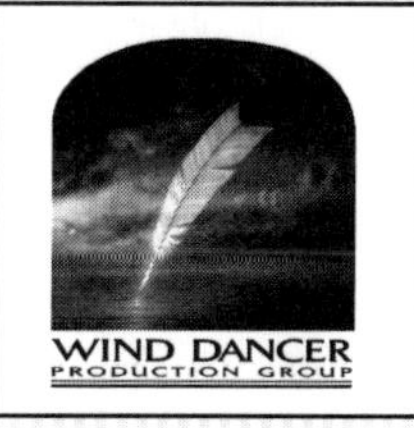

WIND DANCER PRODUCTIONS INC. (EAST)

200 W. 57th St., Ste. 601
New York, NY 10019-3211
PHONE 212-765-4772
FAX 212-765-4775

TYPES	Features - TV Series
DEVELOPMENT	Daughter of the Queen of Sheba - Dilligaf
PRE-PRODUCTION	Harv the Barbarian
CREDITS	What Women Want - Where the Heart Is - Firelight - Home Improvement - Thunder Alley - Soul Man - Costello

Matt Williams ....Principal
David McFadzean ....Principal
Carmen Finestra ....Principal
Dete Meserve ....Executive VP

WIND DANCER PRODUCTIONS INC. (WEST)
745 S. Marengo Ave., Ste. 204
Pasadena, CA 91106
PHONE . . . 626-356-4618
FAX . . . 626-356-4619

TYPES	Features - TV Series
DEVELOPMENT	Daughter of the Queen of Sheba - Dilligaf
PRE-PRODUCTION	Harv the Barbarian
CREDITS	What Women Want - Where the Heart Is - Firelight - Home Improvement - Thunder Alley - Soul Man - Costello

Matt Williams . . . Principal
David McFadzean . . . Principal
Carmen Finestra . . . Principal
Dete Meserve . . . Executive VP

THE WINER COMPANY
4636 Van Nuys Blvd.
Van Nuys, CA 91403
PHONE . . . 310-395-0058
FAX . . . 310-395-8850
EMAIL . . . hwinerco@aol.com

TYPES	Features - Made-for-TV/Cable Movies
DEVELOPMENT	In Hiding - Addict - Custom of the Country - Weapon Zero - Justice - Ground Zero
CREDITS	Lucky 7 - Damaged Care - Jeremiah - Riot - House Arrest - Space Camp - Infidelity

Harry Winer . . . President

WINGNUT FILMS LTD.
PO Box 15-208
Miramar, Wellington 6003 New Zealand
PHONE . . . 64-4-388-9939
FAX . . . 64-4-388-9449

TYPES	Features
PRE-PRODUCTION	King Kong
CREDITS	The Lord of the Rings - The Frighteners - Heavenly Creatures - Meet the Feebles - Braindead - Bad Taste
SUBMISSION POLICY	No unsolicited submissions accepted

Peter Jackson . . . Director/Producer

WINKLER FILMS
211 S. Beverly Dr., Ste. 200
Beverly Hills, CA 90212
PHONE . . . 310-858-5780

TYPES	Features
DEALS	Sony Pictures Entertainment
CREDITS	Rocky - Goodfellas - Raging Bull - The Right Stuff - The Net - At First Sight - Life as a House - The Shipping News - Enough - De-Lovely

Irwin Winkler . . . CEO
Rob Cowan . . . President
June Czerwinski . . . VP, Production & Development
Selina Gomeau . . . Assistant to Irwin Winkler
Julie Milstead . . . Assistant to Rob Cowan

STAN WINSTON PRODUCTIONS
7028 Valjean Ave.
Van Nuys, CA 91406
PHONE . . . 818-902-5639
FAX . . . 818-902-3856
WEB SITE . . . www.stanwinstonproductions.com

TYPES	Features - Made-for-TV/Cable Movies - TV Series
DEVELOPMENT	Courtney Crumrin - The Deaths of Ian - Me & My Monster
CREDITS	The Day the World Ended - Deader - Earth vs. the Spider - How to Make a Monster - She Creature - Teenage Caveman - Wrong Turn

Stan Winston . . . President/Director/Producer (818-782-0870)
Brian J. Gilbert . . . Producer (briang@stanwinston.com)
Ryan Murphy . . . Story Editor (ryan@stanwinston.com)

RALPH WINTER PRODUCTIONS, INC.
c/o Twentieth Century Fox Film Corporation
10201 W. Pico Blvd., Bldg. 6, Ste. 101
Los Angeles, CA 90035
PHONE . . . 310-369-4723
FAX . . . 310-969-0727

TYPES	Features - Direct-to-Video/DVD - Made-for-TV/Cable Movies - TV Series
DEALS	Twentieth Century Fox - Fox 2000
DEVELOPMENT	Pontius Pilate - The Fantastic Four - Breaking the Box - X-Men 3
PRE-PRODUCTION	The Visitation
CREDITS	X-Men - X2: X-Men United - Planet of the Apes - Inspector Gadget - Left Behind: The Movie - Mighty Joe Young - Hackers - Star Trek 4-6 - Shoot or Be Shot - Hangman's Curse - Blizzard

Ralph Winter . . . Producer (310-369-4723)
David Gorder . . . Development Executive/Producer (310-369-2526)
Allison Calleri . . . Assistant to Mr. Winter (310-369-4723)

WISENHEIMER FILMS
139 S. Kilkea Dr.
Los Angeles, CA 90048
PHONE . . . 323-653-5545
WEB SITE . . . www.wisenheimerfilms.com

TYPES	Documentaries - Features - TV Series
DEVELOPMENT	Ajax Amsterdam - Director's Girlfriend
POST PRODUCTION	Waiting
CREDITS	Stolen Summer - The Third Wheel - Super Great & Wonderful - Speakeasy - Battle of Shaker Heights

Jeff Balis . . . Producer
Elva Rivas . . . Staff

DAN WITT PRODUCTIONS
4337 Shadyglade Ave.
Studio City, CA 91604
PHONE . . . 818-508-6912
FAX . . . 818-508-9814
EMAIL . . . danwitt@earthlink.net

TYPES	Features - TV Series
CREDITS	Zebra Lounge - A Killing in a Small Town - An Unfinished Affair - Summer of Ben Tyler - The Runaway - Nightmare Street

Dan Witt . . . Producer/Writer

WITT-THOMAS FILMS

11901 Santa Monica Blvd., Ste. 596
West Los Angeles, CA 90025
PHONE .310-472-6004
FAX .310-476-5015
EMAIL .pwittproductions@aol.com
TYPES Features
CREDITS Insomnia - Three Kings - Final Analysis - Dead Poets Society
COMMENTS Witt-Thomas Productions: 11240 Magnolia Blvd., Ste. 201, North Hollywood, CA 91601

Paul Junger Witt .Producer
Tony Thomas .Producer
Marlene Fuentes .Assistant to Mr. Thomas
Ellen Benjamin .Assistant to Mr. Witt

WITT-THOMAS-HARRIS PRODUCTIONS

11901 Santa Monica Blvd., Ste. 596
West Los Angeles, CA 90025
PHONE .310-472-6004/818-762-7500
FAX .310-476-5015/818-762-7540
EMAIL .pwittproductions@aol.com
SECOND EMAIL .tthom1438@aol.com
TYPES Features
CREDITS Soap - Benson - Empty Nest - John Larroquette Show - The Golden Girls - Blossom
COMMENTS Second office: 11240 Magnolia Blvd., Ste. 201, North Hollywood, CA 91601

Paul Junger Witt .Partner
Tony Thomas .Partner (818-762-7500)
Susan Harris .Partner
Marlene Fuentes .Assistant to Tony Thomas
Ellen Benjamin .Assistant to Mssrs. Witt and Harris

FRED WOLF FILMS

4222 W. Burbank Blvd.
Burbank, CA 91505
PHONE .818-846-0611
FAX .818-846-0979
EMAIL .administration@fredwolffilms.com
WEB SITE .www.fredwolffilms.com
TYPES Animation - Features - Direct-to-Video/DVD - Syndication - TV Series
DEVELOPMENT Zoe and Moe - Brittany the Cyber-Chick - Judge Courtney
CREDITS The Fantastic Voyages of Sinbad - Teenage Mutant Ninja Turtles - Zorro

Fred Wolf .President
Cheryl Wadsworth .Director, Administration
Liz Wolf .Production Supervisor

WOLF FILMS, INC.

100 Universal City Plaza, Bldg. 2252
Universal City, CA 91608-1085
PHONE .818-777-6969/212-627-0088
FAX .818-866-1446/212-627-0957
TYPES Features - Syndication - TV Series
DEALS NBC Universal Television Studio
DEVELOPMENT Bury My Heart at Wounded Knee
CREDITS Law & Order - Law & Order: Special Victims Unit - Law & Order: Criminal Intent - Law & Order: Trial By Jury - Crime and Punishment

Dick Wolf .Executive Producer, Creator, *Law & Order/Law & Order: SVU/ Law & Order: Criminal Intent, Law & Order: Trial By Jury*
Peter Jankowksi .Executive Producer, *Law & Order/Law & Order: SVU/ Law & Order: Criminal Intent, Law & Order: Trial By Jury*
Nena Rodrigue .Head, Development
Tony Ganz .Features
Esrin Gozukizil .Director, Programming
Neal Baer .Executive Producer, *Law & Order: SVU* (LA)
Rene Balcer .Executive Producer, *Law & Order: Criminal Intent* (LA)
Walon Green .Executive Producer, *Law & Order: Trial By Jury*
Ted Kotcheff .Executive Producer, *Law & Order: SVU* (NY)
Eric Overmyer .Executive Producer, *Law & Order*
Fred Berner .Executive Producer, *Law & Order: Criminal Intent*
Matthew Penn .Executive Producer, *Law & Order*

WOLFMILL ENTERTAINMENT

9027 Larke Ellen Circle
Los Angeles, CA 90035-4222
PHONE .310-559-1622
FAX .310-559-1623
EMAIL .craig@wolfmill.com
WEB SITE .www.wolfmill.com
TYPES Animation - Features - Syndication - TV Series
DEALS StudioCanal (U.S.)
DEVELOPMENT Elfquest - Ponytailers - Astounding Space Thrills
CREDITS Pocket Dragon Adventures - T.H.U.N.D.E.R. Agents
COMMENTS Deals with Sceneries International and Pictor Media

Craig Miller .Partner
Marv Wolfman .Partner
Richard Rosen .Business Affairs

THE WOLPER ORGANIZATION

4000 Warner Blvd., Bldg. 14, Rm. X
Burbank, CA 91522-0001
PHONE .818-954-1421
FAX .818-954-1593

TYPES	Features - Made-for-TV/Cable Movies - Miniseries - Reality TV - Syndication - TV Series
DEALS	Warner Bros. Entertainment Inc.
DEVELOPMENT	The Witching Hour - Travels with Charley - Bettie Page (Feature) - Stephen King's It - Time Thief (Feature) - G.A.M.E. - Blueprint - For the Price of a Mule - The Year Without a Santa Claus - 1000 Years for Revenge - On the Brinks
CREDITS	L.A. Confidential - Murder in the 1st - Surviving Picasso - Thornbirds - Roots - Mists of Avalon - Queen - Penn & Teller: Bullshit (Seasons 1&2) - Evil Never Dies - Helter Skelter - Stephen King's Salem's Lot
SUBMISSION POLICY	No unsolicited material
COMMENTS	Development office: 4000 Warner Blvd., Bldg. 14, Rm. V, Burbank, CA 91522-0001

David L. Wolper .Chairman
Mark M. Wolper .President/Executive Producer
Kevin Nicklaus .VP, Development
Murad Hussain .Story Editor
Laura Elizabeth Cannon .Office Manager

WONDERLAND FILMS

100 Universal City Plaza, Bldg. 5171
Universal City, CA 91608
PHONE .818-733-6960
FAX .818-733-6988

TYPES	Features
DEALS	DreamWorks SKG
DEVELOPMENT	American Gothic - Liberty - Modern Mates - Dark Grace - Black Diamond - The Kite Runner - Queen's Gambit - Viva Miss Browne - Flim Flam Man - Peep World - Ti Shoringo Blues
COMPLETED UNRELEASED	The Motorcycle Diaries
CREDITS	Searching for Bobby Fischer - Sliding Doors - The Talented Mr. Ripley - Blow Dry - Heaven - The Quiet American - Cold Mountain
SUBMISSION POLICY	Agency represented material only

Bill Horberg .Producer
Rebecca Yeldham .Producer

WONDERLAND SOUND AND VISION

8739 Sunset Blvd.
West Hollywood, CA 90069
PHONE .310-659-4451
FAX .310-659-4482

TYPES	Features - TV Series
DEALS	Columbia Pictures - Warner Bros. Television Production
DEVELOPMENT	Radiant
CREDITS	Fastlane (Series) - Charlie's Angels: Full Throttle - The O.C. - The Mountain

McG .Partner
Stephanie Savage .Partner
David Manpearl .VP, Development
Anna Mastro .Executive Assistant to McG
Laura Moran .Assistant to David Manpearl
Andy Shapiro .Assistant to McG

THE WOOFENILL WORKS, INC.

516 E. 81st St., Ste. 3
New York, NY 10028-2530
PHONE .212-734-2578
FAX .212-734-3186
EMAIL .prymeva@earthlink.net
WEB SITE .home.earthlink.net/~prymeva/

TYPES	Features - Made-for-TV/Cable Movies - New Media - TV Series
DEVELOPMENT	The Ganymede Project - Wheel of the Jaguar - Thunder from Rain - Dark Millennium - The Prymeva Chronicles - Who the Hell is Neil Robertson? - The Jovian Dilemma - Two Readheads and a Dead Blonde
CREDITS	Murder Between Friends - Exit - All American Murder - Double Crossed: The Barry Seales Story - Catch Me Killer - Man Outside
SUBMISSION POLICY	Send query with synopsis, prefer email

Joseph K. Landsman .Chairman/CEO
Jan A. Koster .President/Creative Director
Barbara Assante .CFO/Executive Producer
Ronald Tanet .Executive Producer/Corporate Counsel
Robert L. Cohen .VP, Production/Supervising Producer
Robert J. Nichols .VP/Corporate Counsel
Jonathan Stathakis .Production/Distribution Consultant
Carlton D. Baker II .Producer

WORKING TITLE FILMS

9720 Wilshire Blvd., 4th Fl.
Beverly Hills, CA 90212
PHONE .310-777-3100/44-207-307-3000
FAX .310-777-5243
WEB SITE .www.workingtitlefilms.com

TYPES	Features
DEALS	Universal Pictures
CREDITS	Bean - Dead Man Walking - Fargo - Four Weddings and a Funeral - Notting Hill - Elizabeth - Bridget Jones's Diary - About a Boy - O Brother Where Art Thou? - The Big Lebowski - Billy Elliot - High Fidelity - Love Actually - Thirteen - Thunderbirds - Wimbledon
SUBMISSION POLICY	No unsolicited submissions
COMMENTS	UK office: Oxford House, 76 Oxford St., London W1D 1BS UK

Tim Bevan .Co-Chairman
Eric Fellner .Co-Chairman
Liza Chasin .President, Production (US)
Debra Hayward .Head, Film (UK)
Michelle Wright .Head, Production (UK)
Daniel Pipski .VP, Development (US)
Chris Clark .Development Executive (UK)
Amelia Granger .Literary Acquisitions Executive (UK)

WORLD FILM SERVICES, INC.

630 Fifth Ave., Ste. 1505
New York, NY 10111
PHONE .212-632-3456
FAX .212-632-3457

TYPES	Features - TV Series
CREDITS	A Passage to India - The Dresser - Beautiful Thing

John Heyman .CEO
Pamela Osowski .VP
Roy Krost .Canada

WORLD INTERNATIONAL NETWORK
811 N. Catalina Ave., Ste. 2304
Redondo Beach, CA 90277
PHONE 310-937-9967
FAX 310-937-8401
TYPES Features - Made-for-TV/Cable Movies
CREDITS The Perfect Nanny - The Perfect Wife - Yesterday's Children - Blind Obsession - Rain - A Mother's Testimony - She's No Angel - Living with Fear - Seduced by a Thief - Redemption of the Ghost - Cloverbend - Perilous - Spirit

Larry Gershman ....Chairman/CEO
Anita R. Gershman ....President/COO
Martha Mikita ....Executive VP/CFO
Zana Thompson ....Contoller

WORLD OF WONDER PRODUCTIONS
6650 Hollywood Blvd., Ste. 400
Hollywood, CA 90028
PHONE 323-603-6300
FAX 323-603-6301
EMAIL ....wow@worldofwonder.net
WEB SITE ....www.worldofwonder.net
TYPES Documentaries - Features - TV Series
DEALS TRIO
PRODUCTION Linda Lovelace Documentary (Imagine) - Rock Around the Block - Man's Best Friend - House of Clues - Housebusters
CREDITS Party Monster (Strand Releasing) - Shock Video: Too Hot for the Box (HBO) - Gay Hollywood (AMC) - Women on Top: Hollywood Power (AMC) - School's Out: The Life of a Gay High School (MTV) - Monica in Black and White (HBO) - Brilliant But Cancelled (Trio) - The Eyes of Tammy Faye (Lions Gate)

Fenton Bailey ....Executive Producer/Co-Director
Randy Barbato ....Executive Producer/Co-Director
David Schiff ....Head, Production
Thairin Smothers ....Producer
Eduardo Magana ....Post Production Supervisor
Robin Nelson ....Post Production Manager
Devon Schneider ....Production Manager
Jim Galasso ....Head, Development
David Lott ....Office Manager

WORLDWIDE PANTS, INC.
1697 Broadway
New York, NY 10019
PHONE 212-975-5300/323-575-5600
FAX 212-975-4780
EMAIL ....lswdl@aol.com
WEB SITE ....www.cbs.com
TYPES Features - TV Series
CREDITS The Late Late Show with Craig Kilborn - Everybody Loves Raymond - The Late Show with David Letterman - Ed
COMMENTS West Coast office: 7800 Beverly Blvd., Ste. 244, Los Angeles, CA 90036

Rob Burnett ....President/CEO
Valerie Shaer ....Executive VP/COO
David Letterman ....Comptroller
Steve Burnett ....Director, Creative Affairs
Kelly Kulchak-Robinson ....Sr. VP, Development

WOVIE, INC.
106 E. Fifth Ave
Olympia, WA 98501
PHONE 360-236-1605
FAX 360-528-2398
EMAIL ....info@wovie.com
WEB SITE ....www.wovie.com
SECOND WEB SITE ....www.groupthemovie.com
TYPES Animation - Features - New Media
DEVELOPMENT Sophisticated - In the Way of Intimacy
CREDITS Group (Feature)

Marilyn Freeman ....Strategic Director
Anne de Marcken ....Creative Director

***WPT ENTERPRISES, INC.**
1041 N. Formosa Ave., Formosa Bldg., Ste. 99
West Hollywood, CA 90046
PHONE 323-850-2888
FAX 323-850-2870
EMAIL ....wpt@worldpokertour.com
WEB SITE ....www.worldpokertour.com
TYPES Documentaries - Features - TV Series
CREDITS World Poker Tour

Steven Lipscomb ....CEO
Audrey Kania ......Executive VP/Consumer Products, Corporate Alliances
Robyn Moder ....Executive VP, WPT Studios
Eric Leemon ....Head, Development
Adam Pliska ....Director, Legal Affairs

LINDA WRIGHT PRODUCTIONS
2465 Pleasant Grove Circle
Thousand Oaks, CA 91362
PHONE 805-493-2999
EMAIL ....lin5280@aol.com
TYPES Made-for-TV/Cable Movies - TV Series
DEVELOPMENT The Step-Family - Portrait of Love - The Longest Night
CREDITS A Champion's Fight - A New Beginning
SUBMISSION POLICY Only quality family material welcome; Mail queries only

Linda M. Wright ....Creator/Writer/Producer
Stephanie Gomes ....Assistant

NORTON WRIGHT PRODUCTIONS
13331 Moorpark St., Ste. 308
Sherman Oaks, CA 91423
PHONE 818-990-3058
TYPES Features - Made-for-TV/Cable Movies - New Media - TV Series
DEVELOPMENT Intentional Injustice - Christmas in Nowhere - A Stolen Mind
CREDITS Night of the Wolf - Murderous Intent - Angel Flight Down - Rescue of Flight 232 - Sadie & Son - Haunted by Her Past
SUBMISSION POLICY Script submissions via agent only

Norton Wright ....Executive Producer/Writer
Susan Watson ....Director, Development

WWE FILMS
345 N. Maple Dr., Ste. 201
Beverly Hills, CA 90210
PHONE .310-285-5300
FAX .310-285-9914
WEB SITE .www.wwe.com
TYPES Features - Direct-to-Video/DVD - Syndication - TV Series

Joel Simon .President (310-285-5301)
Jed Blaugrund .VP (310-285-5303)
Richie Lowell .Executive Assistant to Joel Simon/Office Manager (310-285-5302)
Sharyn Stele .Executive Assistant to Jed Blaugrund (310-285-5313)

THE WYLE/KATZ COMPANY
1041 N. Formosa, Writers Bldg., Ste. 311
West Hollywood, CA 90046
PHONE .323-850-2777
FAX .323-850-2776
TYPES Features - Made-for-TV/Cable Movies - TV Series
DEVELOPMENT Blood Lines

Noah Wyle .Actor/Producer
James Katz .Producer
Ben Mandelker .Director, Development

XINGU FILMS LTD.
12 Cleveland Row, St. James's
London, SW1A 1DH UK
PHONE .44-0-20-7451-0600
FAX .44-0-20-7451-0601
EMAIL .anita@xingufilms.com
TYPES Documentaries - Features
DEVELOPMENT Pedigree Chums - A Guide to Recognizing Your Saints - Alpha Male - Entertaining Angels - Hungry
COMPLETED UNRELEASED Cheeky (Feature)
CREDITS The Grotesque; Documentaries: Boys from Brazil - Moving the Mountain - The Sweatbox - A Kind of Childhood

Trudie Styler .Chairman/Producer/Director
Anita Sumner .CEO/Associate Producer
Travis Swords .Producer
Alex Francis .Head, Development
Dorothee Inderfurth .Production Assistant

MARK YELLEN PRODUCTIONS
183 S. Orange Dr.
Los Angeles, CA 90036
PHONE .323-935-5525
FAX .323-935-5755
EMAIL .mypfilms@earthlink.net
TYPES Commercials - Features - Direct-to-Video/DVD - Made-for-TV/Cable Movies - Music Videos
DEVELOPMENT Wolftrap - Stoneface: The Buster Keaton Story - Between a Rock and a Hard Place - The Yards Between Us - Alter Arrangement - Rev
POST PRODUCTION Puerto Vallarta Squeeze
CREDITS Montana - Shiloh - Where the Rivers Flow North - Shiloh Season - Fist of the North Star - Blast - The Big Squeeze - One Good Turn

Mark Yellen .Producer
Brook Philips .Director, Development
Liz Reed .Assistant

YELLOW HAT PRODUCTIONS, INC
350 S. Center St., Ste. 500
Reno, NV 89501
PHONE .323-254-4416
FAX .323-254-2547
EMAIL .starrynightmovie@aol.com
WEB SITE .www.pauldavids.com
SECOND WEB SITE .www.starrynightmovie.com
TYPES Animation - Documentaries - Features - Direct-to-Video/DVD - Made-for-TV/Cable Movies
DEALS New Concorde - RKO Pictures, LLC - Universal Pictures
DEVELOPMENT Demon Gun - The Stud Who Saved the World - Let's Fall in Love Until Wednesday - This Magic Moment - Stand Up and Run - Mark My Words
PRE-PRODUCTION Just Be Claus - Hidden Mission
POST PRODUCTION The Sci-Fi Boys
CREDITS Timothy Leary's Dead - The Artist & The Shaman - Starry Night - Roswell (Showtime Original Movie)
SUBMISSION POLICY No unsolicited submissions

Paul Davids .President/Producer
Hollace Davids .VP/Producer

THE YORK COMPANY
2027 N. Lake Ave., Ste. 5
Altadena, CA 91001
PHONE .626-296-0300
EMAIL .dwyork@sbcglobal.net
TYPES Features - TV Series
CREDITS Flashfire (HBO) - La Cucaracha - Dragon: The Bruce Lee Story - Midnight Run - Seven Days

Dan York .Producer/Writer

BUD YORKIN PRODUCTIONS
250 Delfern Dr.
Los Angeles, CA 90077
PHONE .310-274-8260
FAX .310-276-0757
TYPES Features - New Media - Syndication - TV Series
CREDITS Intersection - Twice in a Lifetime - Blade Runner - All in the Family

Bud Yorkin .President
Damon Carr .Producer

YORKTOWN PRODUCTIONS, LTD.
18 Gloucester Lane, 4th Fl.
Toronto, ON M4Y 1L5 Canada
PHONE .416-923-2787
FAX .416-923-8580
EMAIL .kimbriggs@yorktownfilms.com
TYPES Features
POST PRODUCTION The Statement
CREDITS Moonstruck - The Hurricane - A Soldier's Story - In the Heat of the Night - Thomas Crown Affair (1968) - Fiddler on the Roof - Jesus Christ Superstar - Only You

Norman Jewison .Director/Producer
Michael Jewison .Producer
Elizabeth Broden .Assistant to Norman Jewison
Kim Briggs .Office Manager

MIKE YOUNG PRODUCTIONS

20335 Ventura Blvd., Ste. 225
Woodland Hills, CA 91364
PHONE 818-999-0062
FAX 818-999-0172
TYPES Animation - TV Series
CREDITS He-Man and the Master of the Universe (Cartoon Network) - Clifford's Puppy Days (PBS) - Pet Alien - Jaker's! The Adventures of Piggley Winks (PBS)

Mike Young . . . . . Owner
Bill Schultz . . . . . Owner
Liz Young . . . . . Owner

YOUR HALF PICTURES

760 N. Cahuenga Blvd.
Hollywood, CA 90038
PHONE 323-466-3679
FAX 323-466-3648
EMAIL . . . . . submissions@yourhalf.com
SECOND EMAIL . . . . . ryan@yourhalf.com
WEB SITE . . . . . www.yourhalf.com
TYPES Documentaries - Features - Reality TV - TV Series
DEVELOPMENT Shores of Light - Eddie Would Go
PRE-PRODUCTION Rookies - Steel City
PRODUCTION Camgirls
POST PRODUCTION The Pick-Up
CREDITS World Festival of Sacred Music
SUBMISSION POLICY See Web site

Josh R. Jaggars . . . . . Producer
Ryan Harper . . . . . Producer/Director
Eric Arlt . . . . . Producer/Development
Rusty Gray . . . . . Producer/Development
Brian Jun . . . . . Director/Producer
Andrew Dignan . . . . . Development

Z FILMS

7024 Hawthorn Ave., Ste. 200
Los Angeles, CA 90028
PHONE 323-466-7448
TYPES Features
DEVELOPMENT Bright Midnight - With Love, Brendan - Blind Spot - Another Life - My Clementine - Love Her Madly
PRE-PRODUCTION Vinyl
CREDITS Fix - A Test of Will (Short)

Richard Zelniker . . . . . Writer/Director/Producer
Tram Nguyen Zelniker . . . . . Writer

THE SAUL ZAENTZ COMPANY

2600 Tenth St.
Berkeley, CA 94710
PHONE 510-549-1528
TYPES Features
CREDITS One Flew Over the Cuckoo's Nest - Amadeus - The English Patient

Saul Zaentz . . . . . Producer

ZALOOM FILM

1000 Flower St.
Glendale, CA 91201
PHONE 818-733-7000
TYPES Animation - Features - Made-for-TV/Cable Movies - TV Series
DEALS DreamWorks SKG
CREDITS Encino Man - Hearts of Darkness - H-E-Double Hockey Sticks - The Cape (Series) - The Sports Pages - The Whole Shebang - Wonderful World of Disney Telefilm Series - PAX Network Family Film Series
SUBMISSION POLICY No unsolicited submissions

George Zaloom . . . . . Producer
Bruno Fortuna . . . . . VP, Development
Robin Goodfellow . . . . . Director, Development

ZANE BUZBY & CONAN BERKELEY PRODUCTIONS

2658 Griffith Park Blvd., Ste. 299
Los Angeles, CA 90039
PHONE 323-223-5566
FAX 323-225-6668
EMAIL . . . . . zmail@earthlink.net
TYPES Features - TV Series - Animation - Syndication
DEALS Castle Rock Entertainment
DEVELOPMENT What Men Don't Want Women to Know - Renegades - The Big Guys - Hard Rockin' Girls - Percival Everett Project - Kyle Baker Project - High Maintenance
PRE-PRODUCTION Massacre in Ivenitz - Cowboy Wally: The Movie
CREDITS Adam Ferrara's Have Some - David Lassley's Back to Blue Eyed Soul - Missin' Twenty Grand
COMMENTS Music and comedy CD production; Deal with Honeyland Productions

Zane Buzby . . . . . Director/Executive Producer
Conan Berkeley . . . . . Executive Producer
Teri Coleman . . . . . VP, Development
Peter Barton . . . . . Director, Development
Sally Porterfield . . . . . Development Executive
Irwin J. Tenenbaum . . . . . Legal Affairs, Loeb & Loeb

THE ZANUCK COMPANY

9465 Wilshire Blvd., Ste. 930
Beverly Hills, CA 90212
PHONE 310-274-0261
FAX 310-273-9217
EMAIL . . . . . zanuckco@aol.com
TYPES Features - TV Series
PRODUCTION Charlie and the Chocolate Factory
POST PRODUCTION Dead Lawyers
CREDITS Big Fish - Road to Perdition - Planet of the Apes - Deep Impact - The Verdict - Cocoon - The Sting - Driving Miss Daisy - Jaws - Rush - True Crime - Rules of Engagement - Academy Awards 2000 - Reign of Fire
SUBMISSION POLICY No unsolicited submissions

Richard D. Zanuck . . . . . Producer (310-274-0261)
Lili Fini Zanuck . . . . . Producer/Director (310-274-0209)
Dean Zanuck . . . . . Producer (310-274-5929)
Harrison Zanuck . . . . . Producer (310-274-5929)

ZEPHYR PRODUCTIONS

516 Gretchen Court
Greensboro, NC 27410
PHONE .336-855-1960
FAX .336-855-1960
EMAIL .zephyrfilms@aol.com
TYPES Documentaries - Features
DEVELOPMENT Magnus (aka Divine Obsession) - Cocksure - Hog Wild Dog Child - The FRUITeeNIES (Animated Feature) - War Vintage - Foodies - The Velvet Hour - Impossible Triangle
CREDITS The Culture of Apple (Documentary) - Echoes - Inside the World of Jesse Allen (Vorpal) - Eidolons
COMMENTS Shorts; ASA member; WGA Registered; NCSAF; Foreign funding: Edgar Diem CFI Austria

Barbara R. Davis .Producer/Writer
Matt Davis .Producer/Director/Writer

ZERO PICTURES

171 Pier Ave., Ste. 317
Santa Monica, CA 90405
PHONE .310-450-9040
EMAIL .info@zeropictures.com
WEB SITE .www.zeropictures.com
PRODUCTION The Bar Code
POST PRODUCTION The Blue Door - Phoenix Point
CREDITS Lucinda's Spell - Hero, Lover, Fool - The Wooden Gun - Dogstar - Lou Lou - Self Storage - Mic and the Claw - The Invisibles - Welcome Says the Angel - Prometheus Bound - Is That All There Is? - Charlotte Sometimes

Michael Kastenbaum .Filmmaker
Marc Ambrose .Filmmaker
Jon Jacobs .Filmmaker
Louise Fenton .Filmmaker
John Clemens .Web Designer

ZINKLER FILMS

9000 Sunset Blvd., Ste. 1101
West Hollywood, CA 90069
PHONE .310-285-1840/310-288-0482
FAX .310-285-0440/310-288-0470
WEB SITE .www.zinklerfilms.com
TYPES Features - Direct-to-Video/DVD
DEVELOPMENT Beady - All American Game (Quality Urban Theatrical) - Sight for Sore Eyes (Features)
PRE-PRODUCTION Significant Other
POST PRODUCTION Messiah
CREDITS Wisegirls - Heartland - Forever 21 - Boys Klub
SUBMISSION POLICY Email synopsis and package info to submissions@zinklerfilms.com or visit company website; Unrepresented/published singers/songwriters for house soundtracks may send us demos (no website inquiries)
COMMENTS Screenplays with packaged attachments only for co-productions; Indie festival productions up to $500,000, major motion pictures up to $15 million; Music/talent and urban concept screenplays welcome if clean; Mailing address: PO Box 629, Beverly Hills, CA 90213

Jessica Russell .Producer/President
Arrika Russell .Producer/Writer
Dennis Holahan .Attorney
Michael Holtz .Attorney
Kate Miller .Assistant Producer/Head, Development
Richard Ginsberg .Music Attorney
Jacopo Stecchini .Marketing Director
Camilo Silva .Development Coordinator

RON ZISKIN PRODUCTIONS, INC.

3575 Cahuenga Blvd., Ste. 620
Los Angeles, CA 90068
PHONE .323-883-0882
FAX .323-883-0812
TYPES Features - Syndication - TV Series
CREDITS Stealing Sinatra - The Courage to Love - Winning Women - SoapCenter - Futuresport - Born American - The Goodbye Girl - Comfort and Joy

Ron Ziskin .President
Donald Pfister .VP, Production
Maddie Miyoshi .Director, Development

LAURA ZISKIN PRODUCTIONS

10202 W. Washington Blvd.
Astaire Bldg., Ste. 1310
Culver City, CA 90232
PHONE .310-244-7373/212-512-5197
FAX .310-244-0073/212-512-5009
TYPES Features - Made-for-TV/Cable Movies - TV Series
DEALS Columbia Pictures
DEVELOPMENT Deus Ex - Katharine Graham Project - Me & My Monster
POST PRODUCTION Stealth
CREDITS Spider-Man 2 - Dinner with Friends - Pretty Woman - To Die For - As Good As It Gets - Fail Safe - Spider-Man - Tarzan (Series)
COMMENTS East Coast office: 1100 Avenue of the Americas, Ste. G2625, New York, NY 10036; TV division: 4000 Warner Blvd., Bldg. 133, Rm. 203, Burbank, CA 91522, phone: 818-954-6595, fax: 818-954-6520

Laura Ziskin .Producer
Leslie Morgan .Sr. VP
Renee Witt .Sr. VP, Creative Affairs (NY)
Pam Oas Williams .VP, TV
Kristin Lewandowski .Story Editor (NY)
Ryan Behnke .Assistant to Ms. Ziskin
Jessie Blatt .Assistant to Ms. Morgan
Danie Pavone .Assistant to Ms. Williams
Henry Gayden .Office Assistant

ZOKALO ENTERTAINMENT

5840 S. Van Ness Ave.
Los Angeles, CA 90047
PHONE .323-295-0000
EMAIL .info@zokalo.com
WEB SITE .www.zokalo.com
TYPES Documentaries - Features - TV Series
DEVELOPMENT Muneera (Feature) - The Naked Truth (Documentary)
PRE-PRODUCTION Tears in the Dark (Feature)
PRODUCTION Tea with Jesús and Susana (Cable Talk Show)
CREDITS No Turning Back (Feature)

Jesús Nebot .Filmmaker/Actor/Principal
John Bradford Goodman .VP, Development
Susana Santiago .VP, Marketing
Gilbert Orozco .Executive

ZOLLO PRODUCTIONS, INC.
257 W. 52nd St., 2nd Fl.
New York, NY 10019
PHONE 212-957-1300
FAX 212-957-1315
EMAIL ....zpi@aol.com
WEB SITE ....www.members.aol.com/zpi/index.html
TYPES Documentaries - Features - Made-for-TV/Cable Movies - Theater - TV Series
DEALS Universal Pictures
DEVELOPMENT Untitled Wright Brothers (Paramount) - Untitled Philo Farnsworth (HBO)
PRE-PRODUCTION Little Fugitive - Untitled Dan Algrant Film
CREDITS The Paper - Quiz Show - In the Gloaming - Mississippi Burning - Hurly Burly - Ghosts of Mississippi - Lansky - Naked in New York - Could Be Worse; Theater: The Goat (New York) - Chitty Chitty Bang Bang (London)

Frederick Zollo ....Producer
Nicholas Paleologos ....Producer
Jono Gero ....Creative Affairs, NY

ZOPIX
887 Chattanooga Ave.
Pacific Palisades, CA 90272
PHONE 310-454-6954
TYPES Features - Made-for-TV/Cable Movies - Miniseries
DEVELOPMENT The Milestone Club - Kulani - Buzz - Endor
CREDITS The Mists of Avalon (TNT, Miniseries)

Lisa Alexander ....President

ZUCKER PRODUCTIONS
1250 Sixth St., Ste. 201
Santa Monica, CA 90401
PHONE 310-656-9202
FAX 310-656-9220
TYPES Features
DEVELOPMENT Henry & Gwen - Time & Chance - You Are Here
CREDITS Rat Race - Unconditional Love - My Best Friend's Wedding - My Life - Ghost - Ruthless People - Airplane! - First Knight

Jerry Zucker ....No Title
Janet Zucker ....No Title
Marion Douglas ....No Title
Tavis Larkham ....No Title
Michael Feldman ....No Title

ZUCKER/NETTER PRODUCTIONS
1411 Fifth St., Ste. 402
Santa Monica, CA 90401
PHONE 310-394-1644
FAX 310-899-6722
TYPES Features
DEALS Twentieth Century Fox - Fox 2000
DEVELOPMENT The Life of Pi - Rule #3 - Fever Pitch
POST PRODUCTION The Untitled Onion Sketch Movie
CREDITS My Boss's Daughter - Dude, Where's My Car? - Phone Booth - Scary Movie 3
SUBMISSION POLICY Through agency only

Gil Netter ....President/Producer
David Zucker ....Producer/Director/Writer
Alissa Ferguson ....VP
Tom Carstens ....Assistant to Mr. Netter
Phil Dornfeld ....No Title
Myles Nye ....Runner

ZUCKERMAN ENTERTAINMENT
c/o Donald Zuckerman
343 N. Orange Dr.
Los Angeles, CA 90036
PHONE 310-452-4410
FAX 323-692-0126
EMAIL ....donaldzucker@earthlink.net
TYPES Documentaries - Features - Made-for-TV/Cable Movies
PRODUCTION Dishdogz
POST PRODUCTION Hooligans (aka The Yank)
CREDITS Mayor of Sunset Strip - The Man from Elysian Fields - Thick as Thieves - Big Brass Ring - Beat - Say Nothing - Dogtown - The Low Life - The Adventures of Tom Sawyer

Donald Zuckerman ....Producer
Katy Cooper ....Assistant

WORKSHEET

DATE	PROJECT	CONTACT	NOTES

SECTION C

TV SHOWS AND STAFF

24 (Fox/60 mins.)
21050 Lassen St.
Chatsworth, CA 91311
PHONE .818-717-5400
FAX .818-717-5450
PRODUCTION COMPANIES Imagine Television - Twentieth Century Fox Television

Joel Surnow .Executive Producer/Showrunner/Creator
Robert Cochran .Executive Producer/Showrunner/Creator
Brian Grazer .Executive Producer
Howard Gordon .Executive Producer
Evan Katz .Co-Executive Producer
Stephen Kronish .Co-Executive Producer
Michael Loceff .Co-Executive Producer
Keifer Sutherland .Co-Executive Producer
Jon Cassar .Producer/Director
Tim Iacofano .Line Producer
Duppy Demetrius .Story Editor
Matt Michnozetz .Staff Writer
Debi Manwiller .Casting Director

7TH HEAVEN (WB/60 mins.)
c/o Spelling Television
5700 Wilshire Blvd., Ste. 575
Los Angeles, CA 90036
PHONE .310-998-5700
PRODUCTION COMPANY Spelling Television, Inc.

Aaron Spelling .Executive Producer
Brenda Hampton .Executive Producer/Creator
E. Duke Vincent .Executive Producer
Sue Tenney .Co-Executive Producer
Pam Cotton .Coordinating Producer
Chris Olsen .Producer
Jeff Olsen .Producer
Shawn Kostanian .Associate Producer/Co-Producer
Jeff Rogers .Story Editor
Vicki Huff .Casting Director

8 SIMPLE RULES (ABC/30 mins.)
500 S. Buena Vista St., Stage 6, 5th Fl.
Burbank, CA 91521
PHONE .818-560-8635
FAX .818-560-5715
PRODUCTION COMPANIES Shady Acres Entertainment - Touchstone Television

Judd Pillot .Executive Producer/Showrunner
John Peaslee .Executive Producer/Showrunner
Tom Shadyac .Executive Producer
Michael Bostick .Executive Producer
James Widdoes .Executive Producer/Director
Steve Baldikoski .Co-Executive Producer
Bryan Behar .Co-Executive Producer
Rob Hanning .Co-Executive Producer
Seth Kurland .Co-Executive Producer
Kathy Stumpe .Co-Executive Producer
Marty Weiss .Co-Executive Producer
Tracy Gamble .Creator
Laurie Gelman .Consulting Producer
Hayes Jackson .Supervising Producer
Bonnie Kallman .Supervising Producer
Paul Ciancarelli .Producer
David DiPietro .Producer
Alan Padula .Producer
Tamiko Brooks .Staff Writer
Lori Openden .Casting Director

ACCORDING TO JIM (ABC/30 mins.)
4024 Radford Ave., Norvet Bldg., 3rd Fl.
Studio City, CA 91604
PHONE .818-655-5094
FAX .818-655-8668
PRODUCTION COMPANIES Touchstone Television - Brad Grey TV

Suzanne Bukinik .Executive Producer
Jonathan Stark .Executive Producer/Creator/Showrunner
Marc Gurvitz .Executive Producer
Nastaran Dibai .Executive Producer
Jeffrey Hodes .Executive Producer
Warren Bell .Co-Executive Producer
Mitch Hunter .Co-Executive Producer
Jana Hunter .Co-Executive Producer
Howard Morris .Co-Executive Producer
Bob Nickman .Co-Executive Producer
John Beck .Supervising Producer
David Feeney .Supervising Producer
Ron Hart .Supervising Producer
Bob Heath .Supervising Producer/UPM
Harry Hannigan .Executive Story Editor
Sylvia Green .Story Editor
Chris Nowak .Staff Writer
Jeff Greenberg .Casting Director

ALIAS (ABC/60 mins.)
c/o Touchstone Television
500 S. Buena Vista St., Bldg. 22-23
Burbank, CA 91521
PHONE .818-560-7000
PRODUCTION COMPANIES Bad Robot Productions - Touchstone Television

J.J. Abrams .Executive Producer/Creator/Showrunner
Jeff Melvoin .Executive Producer/Showrunner
Ken Olin .Executive Producer
Jesse Alexander .Co-Executive Producer
Jeffrey Bell .Co-Executive Producer
Jeff Pinkner .Co-Executive Producer
Sarah Caplan .Producer
Brian Bark .Associate Producer
Nicole Carrasco .Associate Producer
Meighan Offield .Associate Producer
Rick Orci .Story Editor
April Webster .Casting Director

ALL MY CHILDREN (ABC/60 mins.)
320 W. 66th St.
New York, NY 10023
PHONE .212-456-0800
PRODUCTION COMPANY ABC Daytime

Julie Carruthers .Executive Producer
Ginger Smith .Supervising Producer
Karen Johnson .Producer
Judy Wilson .Casting Director

ALL OF US (UPN/30 mins.)
4024 Radford Ave., Admin. Bldg., Ste. 210
Studio City, CA 91604
PHONE .818-655-5561/818-655-5800
FAX .818-655-8003
PRODUCTION COMPANIES Overbrook Entertainment - Warner Bros. Television Production
COMMENTS Writers' office: 4024 Radford Ave., Admin. Bldg., Ste. 290, Studio City, CA 91604

Betsy Borns .Executive Producer/Showrunner
James Lassiter .Executive Producer
Jada Pinkett Smith .Executive Producer
Will Smith .Executive Producer
Arthur Harris .Co-Executive Producer
Stacy A. Littlejohn .Producer
Ralph Paredes .Associate Producer
Leo Clarke .Line Producer
Jared Bush .Staff Writer
Bryon Hord .Staff Writer
Lori Lakin .Staff Writer
Ray Lancon .Staff Writer
Terence Paul Winter .Staff Writer
Josh Wolf .Staff Writer
Monica Swann .Casting Director

THE AMAZING RACE (CBS/60 mins.)
c/o World Race Productions, Inc.
7800 Beverly Blvd.
Los Angeles, CA 90036
PHONE .310-577-9381
FAX .310-577-9473
PRODUCTION COMPANY Bruckheimer Productions

Jerry Bruckheimer .Executive Producer
Bertram van Munster .Executive Producer/Co-Creator
Elise Doganieri .Sr. Producer/Co-Creator
Scott Owens .Executive in Charge of Production

***AMERICAN DAD (Fox/30 mins.)**
5700 Wilshire Blvd., Ste. 475
Los Angeles, CA 90036
PHONE .323-857-8900
FAX .323-857-8945
PRODUCTION COMPANY Twentieth Century Fox Television
COMMENTS Animated

Seth MacFarlane .Executive Producer/Creator
Mike Barker .Executive Producer
Matt Weitzman .Executive Producer
Dave Hemingson .Co-Executive Producer
Kenny Schwartz .Co-Executive Producer
Rick Wiener .Co-Executive Producer
David Zuckerman .Co-Executive Producer
Carter Bays .Supervising Producer
Craig Thomas .Supervising Producer
Ron Hughart .Supervising Director
Kara Vallow .Producer
Dan Vebber .Producer
Brian Boyle .Co-Producer
Diana Ritchey .Animation Producer
Neal Boushell .Executive Story Editor
Nahnatchka Khan .Executive Story Editor
Sam O'Neal .Executive Story Editor
Steve Hely .Staff Writer
Alison McDonald .Staff Writer
Chris McKenna .Staff Writer
Matt McKenna .Staff Writer
Linda Lamontagne .Casting Director

AMERICAN DREAMS (NBC/60 mins.)
1438 N. Gower St., Box 1
Hollywood, CA 90028
PHONE .323-468-3200
FAX .323-468-3201
PRODUCTION COMPANY NBC Universal Television Studio

Jonathan Prince .Executive Producer/Creator/Showrunner
Dick Clark .Executive Producer
David Semel .Executive Producer/Showrunner
Jim Chory .Co-Executive Producer
Becky Hartman-Edwards .Co-Executive Producer
Josh Reims .Co-Executive Producer
Emily Whitesell .Co-Executive Producer
John Romano .Consulting Producer
Rama Stagner .Supervising Producer
Gigi Coello Bannon .Co-Producer
Paul Linden .Co-Producer
Nancy Won .Executive Story Editor
Mike Foley .Story Editor
Liz Tigelaar .Story Editor
Natalie Hart .Casting Director
Jason La Padura .Casting Director

AMERICAN IDOL/AMERICAN JUNIORS (Fox/60 mins.)
7800 Beverly Blvd., Ste. 251
Los Angeles, CA 90036
PHONE .323-575-8000
WEB SITE .www.idolonfox.com
PRODUCTION COMPANIES 19 Entertainment - FremantleMedia North America (LA)

Simon Fuller .Executive Producer/Creator
Cecile Frot-Coutaz .Executive Producer
Nigel Lithgow .Executive Producer
Ken Warrick .Executive Producer

AMERICA'S FUNNIEST HOME VIDEOS (ABC/60 mins.)
12233 W. Olympic Blvd., Ste. 170
Los Angeles, CA 90064
PHONE .310-442-5600
FAX .310-442-5604
WEB SITE .www.afv.tv
SECOND WEB SITE .www.vindibona.com
PRODUCTION COMPANY Vin Di Bona Productions

Vin Di Bona .Executive Producer
Terry Moore .Co-Executive Producer
Todd Thicke .Co-Executive Producer
J. Elvis Weinstein .Consulting Producer/Writer
Michele Nasraway .Producer
Trace Beaulieu .Writer
Michael Palleschi .Writer
Gina Di Bona .Production Consultant
Gerald Jaskulski .Line Producer
Richard Connor Sr. .Sr. Coordinating Producer
Joe Bellon .Coordinating Producer
Greg Bellon .Coordinating Producer

ARRESTED DEVELOPMENT (Fox/30 mins.)
c/o Culver Studios
10201 W. Pico Blvd.
Culver City, CA 90232
PHONE .310-369-4720
FAX .310-969-3264
PRODUCTION COMPANIES Imagine Television - Twentieth Century Fox Television

Mitch Hurwitz .Executive Producer/Creator/Showrunner
Brian Grazer .Executive Producer
Ron Howard .Executive Producer
David Nevins .Executive Producer
John Levenstein .Co-Executive Producer
Richard Rosenstock .Co-Executive Producer
Jim Vallely .Consulting Producer
Chuck Martin .Supervising Producer
Barbie Feldman .Producer
Victor Hsu .Producer
Brad Copeland .Co-Producer
Christine Larson-Nitzsche .UPM
Abraham Higginbotham .Story Editor
Courtney Lilly .Staff Writer
Geraldine Leder .Casting Director

AS THE WORLD TURNS (CBS/60 mins.)
c/o JC Studios
1268 E. 14th St.
Brooklyn, NY 11230
PHONE .718-780-6450
FAX .718-780-7660
WEB SITE .www.astheworldturnstv.com
PRODUCTION COMPANY Procter & Gamble Productions, Inc.

Chris Goutman .Executive Producer
Carole Shure .Sr. Producer
Vivian Gundaker .Producer
Hogan Sheffer .Head Writer
Jean Passanante .Co-Head Writer
Chris Whitesell .Associate Head Writer
Kelsey Bay .Coordinating Producer
Jennifer Maloney .Associate Producer
Paula Cwickly .Associate Writer
Susan Dansby .Associate Writer
Judith Donato .Associate Writer
Charlotte Gibson .Associate Writer
Craig Heller .Associate Writer
Meg Kelly .Associate Writer
Lynn Martin .Associate Writer
Elizabeth Page .Associate Writer
Judy Tate .Associate Writer
Courtney Simon .Script Editor
Mary Clay Boland .Casting Director
LaMont Craig .Associate Casting Director

THE BACHELOR/THE BACHELORETTE (ABC/60 mins.)
15301 Ventura Blvd., Bldg. E
Sherman Oaks, CA 91403
PHONE .818-972-0077
FAX .818-972-0250
PRODUCTION COMPANIES Next Entertainment - Telepictures Productions

Mike Fleiss .Executive Producer
Scott Jeffress .Co-Executive Producer
Lisa Levenson .Co-Executive Producer
Lacey Pemberton .Casting Director

***BAD GIRL'S GUIDE (UPN/30 mins.)**
c/o Paramount Network Television
5555 Melrose Ave.
Los Angeles, CA 90038-3197
PHONE .323-956-1718
FAX .323-862-1007
PRODUCTION COMPANIES Flame Television - Paramount Television Production

Jennifer Heath .Executive Producer/Creator
Cameron Tuttle .Executive Producer/Creator
Michele J. Wolff .Executive Producer/Creator
Tony Krantz .Executive Producer
Nina Lederman .Co-Executive Producer
Jenny McCarthy .Producer

BEHIND THE MUSIC (VH1/60 mins.)
c/o MTV Networks
2600 Colorado Ave., 3rd. Fl.
Santa Monica, CA 90404
PHONE .310-752-8000
FAX .310-907-2317
WEB SITE .www.vh1.com
PRODUCTION COMPANY VH1 (Music First)

George Moll .Executive Producer
Justin Sturken .Executive Producer

THE BERNIE MAC SHOW (Fox/30 mins.)
4024 Radford Ave., Bungalow 16
Studio City, CA 91604
PHONE .818-655-5870
FAX .818-655-8496
PRODUCTION COMPANY Twentieth Century Fox Television
COMMENTS Writers' office: Bungalow 12

Peter Aronson .Executive Producer/Showrunner
Warren Hutcherson .Executive Producer
Marc Abrams .Co-Executive Producer
Rich Appel .Co-Executive Producer
Michael Benson .Co-Executive Producer
Bernie Mac .Co-Executive Producer
Teri Schaffer .Co-Executive Producer
Jerry Collins .Producer
Steven Greener .Producer
Marshall Boone .Co-Producer
Michael Petok .Line Producer
Eileen Mack Knight .Casting Director

***BLIND JUSTICE (ABC/60 mins.)**
c/o Steven Bochco Productions
10201 W. Pico Blvd., Bldg. 1
Los Angeles, CA 90035
PHONE .310-369-2400
FAX .310-369-3236
PRODUCTION COMPANIES Paramount Television Production - Steven Bochco Productions

Steven Bochco .Executive Producer
Matt Olmstead .Executive Producer/Co-Creator
Nick Wootten .Executive Producer/Co-Creator

It is illegal to copy any part of this book

BLUES CLUES (Nickelodeon/30 mins.)
1633 Broadway, 4th Fl.
New York, NY 10019
PHONE .212-654-6400
FAX .212-654-4720
COMMENTS Animated

Traci Paige Johnson .Executive Producer/Creator
Todd Ellis Kessler .Executive Producer/Creator
Angela Santomero .Executive Producer/Creator
Jennifer Twomey .Executive Producer
Wendy Harris .Supervising Producer
David Palmer .Supervising Director, Animation/Producer
Dr. Alice Wilder .Director, Research & Development/Producer
Marcy Pritchard .Line Producer

THE BOLD AND THE BEAUTIFUL (CBS/30 mins.)
7800 Beverly Blvd., Ste. 3371
Los Angeles, CA 90036
PHONE .323-575-4138
FAX .323-655-8760
PRODUCTION COMPANY Bell-Phillip TV Productions, Inc.

William J. Bell .Creator
Lee Phillip Bell .Co-Creator
Bradley Bell .Executive Producer
Rhonda Friedman .Supervising Producer
Ron Weaver .Sr. Producer
Cynthia J. Popp .Producer
Erin E. Stewart .Associate Producer
Christy Elaine Dooley .Casting Director

***BOSTON LEGAL (ABC/60 mins.)**
c/o David E. Kelley Productions
1600 Rosecrans Ave., Bldg. 4-B
Manhattan Beach, CA 90266
PHONE .310-727-2200
PRODUCTION COMPANIES David E. Kelley Productions - Twentieth Century Fox Television

David E. Kelley .Executive Producer/Creator
Bill D'Elia .Executive Producer
Scott Kaufer .Executive Producer
Jeff Rake .Executive Producer
Mike Listo .Co-Executive Producer
Lukas Reiter .Supervising Producer
Steve Robin .Supervising Producer
Jonathan Shapiro .Supervising Producer
Bob Breech .Sr. VP, Kelley Productions/Consulting Producer
Kerry Ehrin .Consulting Producer
Peter Ocko .Consulting Producer
Janet Knutsen .Producer/UPM
Anne Uemura .Associate Producer
Ken Miller .Casting Director
Nikki Valko .Casting Director

CARNIVÀLE (HBO/60 mins.)
25135 Anza Dr., Stage 1
Santa Clarita, CA 91355
PHONE .661-294-2025
FAX .661-294-2033
PRODUCTION COMPANIES Carny, Inc. - HBO Original Programming

Howard Klein .Executive Producer/Showrunner
Daniel Knauf .Executive Producer/Creator
David Knoller .Co-Executive Producer
Dawn Prestwich .Co-Executive Producer
Nicole Yorkin .Co-Executive Producer
John McLaughlin .Consulting Producer
Tracy Torme .Consulting Producer
Dan Hassid .Supervising Producer
Bill Schmidt .Supervising Producer
Bernie Caulfield .Producer
John Papsidera .Casting Director
Wendy O'Brien .Casting Director

***CENTER OF THE UNIVERSE (CBS/30 mins.)**
c/o CBS Productions
7800 Beverly Blvd.
Los Angeles, CA 90036
PHONE .818-954-5032
PRODUCTION COMPANIES CBS Productions - Tannenbaum Company - Warner Bros. Television Production

Nat Bernstein .Executive Producer
Mitchel Katlin .Executive Producer
Eric Tannenbaum .Executive Producer
Kim Tannenbaum .Executive Producer
Brett Baer .Co-Executive Producer
Dave Finkel .Co-Executive Producer
Eric Zicklin .Co-Executive Producer
Bruce Rasmussen .Consulting Producer
Shira Zeltzer .Staff Writer

***CHALKZONE (Nickelodeon/30 Mins.)**
231 W. Olive Ave.
Burbank, CA 91502
PHONE .818-736-3606
FAX .818-736-3449
EMAIL .hey@frederator.kz
WEB SITE .www.frederator.kz
PRODUCTION COMPANIES Frederator Studios - Nickelodeon Animation Studios

Larry Huber .Creator/Executive Producer/Writer
Bill Burnett .Creator/Executive Producer/Writer
Fred Seibert .Executive Producer
Debby Hindman .Line Producer
Jenny Nissenson .Writer
Ford Riley .Writer
Aydrea Walden .Writer
Ginny McSwain .Casting Director

CHARMED (WB/60 mins.)
5555 Melrose Ave., Bungalow 11
Los Angeles, CA 90038
PHONE .323-956-2600
FAX .323-862-2626
PRODUCTION COMPANY Spelling Television, Inc.

Aaron Spelling .Executive Producer
Brad Kern .Executive Producer
E. Duke Vincent .Executive Producer
Jim Conway .Co-Executive Producer
Jon Pare .Producer
Cameron Litvak .Staff Writer
Leslee Dennis .Casting Director

***CLUBHOUSE (CBS/60 mins.)**
15001 Calvert St.
Van Nuys, CA 91411
PHONE .818-778-2330
FAX .818-373-4121
PRODUCTION COMPANIES Icon Productions, Inc. - Spelling Television, Inc.

Daniel Cerone .Executive Producer/Creator
Mel Gibson .Executive Producer
Aaron Spelling .Executive Producer
E. Duke Vincent .Executive Producer
Ken Topolsky .Executive Producer
Bruce Davey .Executive Producer

CODENAME: KIDS NEXT DOOR (Cartoon Network/30 mins.)

c/o Curious Pictures
440 Lafayette St., 6th Fl.
New York, NY 10003
PHONE .212-674-1400
FAX .212-674-0081
WEB SITE .www.curiouspictures.com
PRODUCTION COMPANY Curious Pictures
COMMENTS Animated; Two stories per half-hour

Tom Warburton .Executive Producer/Creator
Susan Holden .Executive Producer
Steve Oakes .Executive Producer
David Starr .Executive Producer
Richard Winkler .Executive Producer
Bruce Knapp .Producer
Collette Sunderman .Casting Director

COLD CASE (CBS/60 mins.)

4000 Warner Blvd., Bldg. 185
Burbank, CA 91522
PHONE .818-954-3399
FAX .818-954-2832
PRODUCTION COMPANIES Bruckheimer Productions - CBS Productions - Warner Bros. Television Production

Meredith Stiehm .Executive Producer/Creator/Showrunner
Jerry Bruckheimer .Executive Producer
Jonathan Littman .Executive Producer
Jan Oxenberg .Consulting Producer
Mark Pellington .Consulting Producer
Tyler Bensinger .Supervising Producer
Chis Mundy .Supervising Proudcer
Sean Whitesell .Supervising Producer
Perry Husman .Producer
Veena Sud .Story Editor
Rebecca Mangieri .Casting Director
Barbara Fiorentino .Casting Director

*COMMANDO NANNY (WB/30 mins.)

4000 Warner Blvd., Bldg. 190, Rm. 201
Burbank, CA 91505
PHONE .818-954-1453
FAX .818-954-1111
PRODUCTION COMPANIES Mark Burnett Productions - Warner Bros. Television Production

Mark Burnett .Executive Producer
Rachel Sweet .Executive Producer/Showrunner
Tim Kelleher .Co-Executive Producer
Tom Palmer .Consulting Producer
J.J. Paulsen .Consulting Producer
Richard Goodman .Supervising Producer
Alex Barnow .Co-Producer
Marc Firek .Co-Producer
Amanda Lasher .Co-Producer
Faye Oshima Belyeu .Line Producer
Joe Rubin .Staff Writer
George White .Staff Writer
Tamara Billik .Casting Director

*THE CONTENDER (NBC/60 mins.)

c/o Mark Burnett Productions
640 N. Sepulveda Blvd.
Los Angeles, CA 90049
PHONE .310-903-5400
PRODUCTION COMPANIES DreamWorks Television - Mark Burnett Productions

Mark Burnett .Executive Producer
Jeffrey Katzenberg .Executive Producer
Slyvester Stallone .Executive Producer

*CRAZY FOR YOU (NBC/30 mins.)

100 Universal City Plaza, Bldg. 2128, Ste. C
Universal City, CA 91608
PHONE .818-733-1966
FAX .818-733-1967
PRODUCTION COMPANY NBC Universal Television Studio

Eileen Heisler .Executive Producer/Co-Creator
DeAnn Heline .Executive Producer/Co-Creator
Rob Bragin .Co-Executive Producer
Rodney Rothman .Supervising Producer
Katy Ballard .Producer
Bill Daly .Producer
Werner Walian .Producer
Greg Behrendt .Consultant
Judah Miller .Executive Story Editor
Murray Miller .Executive Story Editor
Vincent Brown .Staff Writer
Justin Spitzer .Staff Writer

CROSSING JORDAN (NBC/60 mins.)

100 Universal City Plaza, Bldg. 5225, 2nd Fl.
Universal City, CA 91608
PHONE .818-733-5588
FAX .818-733-3710
PRODUCTION COMPANY Tailwind Productions

Tim Kring .Executive Producer/Creator
Dennis Hammer .Executive Producer
Allan Arkush .Co-Executive Producer/Director
Skip Beaudine .Co-Executive Producer/UPM
Kathy McCormick .Co-Executive Producer
Jon Cowan .Supervising Producer
Linda Gase .Supervising Producer
Robert Rovner .Supervising Producer
Andi Bushell .Producer
Sharon Lee Watson .Co-Producer
Kira Arne .Story Editor
Natalie Hart .Casting Director
Jason La Padura .Casting Director

CSI (CBS/60 mins.)

25135 Anza Dr., Stage 6
Santa Clarita, CA 91355
PHONE .661-294-2070
FAX .661-294-4925
PRODUCTION COMPANIES Alliance Atlantis - Bruckheimer Productions - CBS Productions

Jerry Bruckheimer .Executive Producer
Carol Mendelsohn .Executive Producer/Showrunner
Danny Cannon .Executive Producer
Ann Donahue .Executive Producer
Naren Shankar .Executive Producer
Anthony Zuiker .Executive Producer/Creator
Jonathan Littman .Executive Producer
Cynthia Chvatal .Executive Producer
William Petersen .Executive Producer
Josh Berman .Co-Executive Producer
Elizabeth Devine .Consulting Producer
Louis Milito .Producer
Sarah Goldfinger .Executive Story Editor
Carol Kritzer .Casting Director
Andy Henry .Casting Associate

CSI: MIAMI (CBS/60 mins.)
1600 Rosecrans Ave., Bldg. 2B, 2nd Fl.
Manhattan Beach, CA 90266
PHONE 310-727-5959
FAX 310-727-5960
PRODUCTION COMPANIES Alliance Atlantis - Bruckheimer Productions - CBS Productions

Jerry Bruckheimer . . . . Executive Producer
Danny Cannon . . . . Executive Producer
Ann Donahue . . . . Executive Producer/Showrunner/Creator
Jonathan Littman . . . . Executive Producer
Carol Mendelsohn . . . . Executive Producer/Creator
Anthony Zuiker . . . . Executive Producer/Creator
Jonathan Glassner . . . . Consulting Producer
Shane Brennan . . . . Supervising Producer
Steve Maeda . . . . Producer
Elizabeth Devine . . . . Producer
Scott Shiffman . . . . Producer
Sunil Nayar . . . . Co-Producer
Mike Ostrowski . . . . Executive Story Editor
Ildy Modrovich . . . . Story Editor
Marc Dube . . . . Staff Writer
Corey Miller . . . . Staff Writer
Nan Dutton . . . . Casting Director

***CSI: NEW YORK (CBS/60 mins.)**
4024 Radford Ave., Bldg. 7, 2nd Fl. Center
Studio City, CA 91604
PHONE 818-655-5511
FAX 818-655-8247
PRODUCTION COMPANIES Alliance Atlantis - Bruckheimer Productions - CBS Productions

Jerry Bruckheimer . . . . Executive Producer
Anthony Zuiker . . . . Executive Producer
Ann Donahue . . . . Executive Producer
Carol Mendelsohn . . . . Executive Producer
Jonathan Littman . . . . Executive Producer
Danny Cannon . . . . Executive Producer
Andrew Lipsitz . . . . Executive Producer

THE DAILY SHOW WITH JON STEWART (Comedy Central/30 mins.)
513 W. 54th St.
New York, NY 10019
PHONE 212-468-1700
FAX 212-468-1890

Jon Stewart . . . . Executive Producer
Stewart Bailey . . . . Co-Executive Producer
Ben Karlin . . . . Co-Executive Producer
Kahane Corn . . . . Supervising Producer
DJ Javerbaum . . . . Head Writer
Hilary Kun . . . . Talent Booker

DANNY PHANTOM (Nickelodeon/30 mins.)
c/o Nickelodeon
231 W. Olive Ave.
Burbank, CA 91502
PHONE 818-736-3000
COMMENTS Animated

Butch Hartman . . . . Executive Producer/Creator
Bob Boyle . . . . Producer
Steve Marmel . . . . Producer

***THE DAYS (ABC/60 mins.)**
c/o Tollin/Robbins Productions
10960 Ventura Blvd., 2nd Fl.
Studio City, CA 91604
PHONE 604-420-3660/818-766-5004
FAX 604-420-3638/818-766-8488
PRODUCTION COMPANY Tollin/Robbins Productions

Mike Tollin . . . . Executive Producer
Brian Robbins . . . . Executive Producer
Joe Davola . . . . Executive Producer
Peter Tortorici . . . . Executive Producer
John Scott Shepherd . . . . Executive Producer/Creator
Tim Johnson . . . . Supervising Producer
Michael Pendell . . . . Line Producer
Layne Wong . . . . Staff Writer
Mara Casey . . . . Casting Director
Jami Rudofsky . . . . Casting Director

DAYS OF OUR LIVES (NBC/60 mins.)
3000 W. Alameda Ave.
Burbank, CA 91523
PHONE 818-840-4089
FAX 818-840-4968
PRODUCTION COMPANIES Corday Productions, Inc. - Sony Pictures Television

Ken Corday . . . . Executive Producer
Steve Wyman . . . . Co-Executive Producer
James E. Reilly . . . . Consulting Producer/Head Writer
Janet Spellman-Rider . . . . Sr. Coordinating Producer
Tom Walker . . . . Sr. Coordinating Producer
Roy Steinberg . . . . Producer
Jane Atkins . . . . Writer
Peter Brash . . . . Writer
Rick Draughon . . . . Writer
Sofia Landon Geier . . . . Writer
Victor Gialonella . . . . Writer
Renee Godelia . . . . Writer
Jeanne Marie Grunwell . . . . Writer
Dena Higley . . . . Writer
Mark Higley . . . . Writer
Bruce Neckels . . . . Writer
John Newman . . . . Writer
Jodie Scholz . . . . Writer
Fran Bascom . . . . Casting Director
Linda Poindexter . . . . Casting Director

DEAD LIKE ME (Showtime/60 mins.)
2400 Boundary Rd.
Vancouver, BC V5M 3Z3 Canada
PHONE 604-292-8360/310-452-3148
FAX 604-292-8678/310-452-2854
PRODUCTION COMPANY Metro-Goldwyn-Mayer Worldwide Television

John Masius . . . . Executive Producer
Stephen Godchaux . . . . Executive Producer
Steven Beers . . . . Co-Executive Producer
Pascal Verschooris . . . . Producer
Ben Brafman . . . . Producer
J.J. Philbin . . . . Story Editor
Paul Weber . . . . Casting Director (LA)
Michelle Allen . . . . Casting Director (Vancouver)

THE DEAD ZONE (USA/60 mins.)
3330 Bridgeway St.
Vancouver, BC V5K 5E9 Canada
PHONE 604-296-2000/323-464-6201
FAX 604-296-2020
WEB SITE www.piller2.com
PRODUCTION COMPANIES Lions Gate Entertainment - Paramount International Television - Piller^2/The Segan Company
COMMENTS Writers' office: 7025 Santa Monica Blvd., Los Angeles, CA 90038

Michael Piller .....Executive Producer/Creator (323-817-1100)
Lloyd Segan .....Executive Producer (323-817-1113/604-296-2018)
Harold Tichenor .....Consulting Producer (604-983-5803)
Shawn Piller .....Supervising Producer/Creator (604-296-2009/323-817-1101)
Robert Petrovicz .....Producer (604-296-2008)
Kira Domaschuk .....Co-Producer (604-296-2006)
Anthony Michael Hall .....Co-Producer
Eric A. Stillwell .....Associate Producer
Amber Woodward .....Associate Producer
Sue Brouse .....Casting Director (Vancouver) (604-990-9543)
Eric Dawson .....Casting Director (LA) (818-623-1818)
Shawn Dawson .....Casting Director (LA) (818-623-1818)

DEADWOOD (HBO/60 mins.)
c/o Roscoe Productions, Inc.
Melody Ranch
24715 Oak Creek Ave.
Newhall, CA 91321
PHONE 661-259-0073
FAX 661-259-5078
PRODUCTION COMPANIES HBO Original Programming - Red Board Productions - Roscoe Productions, Inc.

David Milch .....Executive Producer/Creator
Gregg Fienberg .....Co-Executive Producer/Showrunner
Ed Bianchi .....Producer/Director
A.C. Lyles .....Producer
Scott Stephens .....Producer
Ted Mann .....Co-Producer
Elizabeth Sarnoff .....Co-Producer
Steve Turner .....Co-Producer
Jody Worth .....Co-Producer
Hilton Smith .....Associate Producer
Bernadette McNamara .....Staff Writer
Peter Ocko .....Staff Writer
Steven Shill .....Staff Writer
Libby Goldstein .....Casting Director
Junie Lowry-Johnson .....Casting Director

*DESPERATE HOUSEWIVES (ABC/60 mins.)
c/o Touchstone Television
3800 W. Alameda Ave.
Burbank, CA 91505
PHONE .....818-733-3773/310-369-1296 (Casting)
FAX 818-733-3775
PRODUCTION COMPANY Touchstone Television
COMMENTS Writers' office: 100 Universal City Plaza, Bldg. 2128, Universal City, CA 91608

Marc Cherry .....Executive Producer/Creator
Tom Spezialy .....Executive Producer
Michael Edelstein .....Executive Producer
Oliver Goldstick .....Consulting Producer
Joey Murphy .....Consulting Producer
John Pardee .....Consulting Producer
Charles Pratt .....Consulting Producer
Alex Cunningham .....Producer
Patty Lin .....Producer
Tracey Stern .....Producer
David Schulner .....Co-Producer
Jenna Bans .....Staff Writer
Scott Genkinger .....Casting Director
Junie Lowry-Johnson .....Casting Director

THE DIVISION (Lifetime/60 mins.)
8615 Tamarack Ave.
Sun Valley, CA 91352
PHONE 818-252-6100
FAX 818-504-3505

Deborah Joy LeVine .....Executive Producer/Creator
Aaron Lipstadt .....Executive Producer
Dan Levine .....Co-Executive Producer
Anne Kenney .....Consulting Producer
Judy Feldman .....Supervising Producer
Sarah Gallagher .....Supervising Producer
Penny Adams .....Producer
John T. Walker .....Producer
Ashley Gable .....Co-Producer
Hynndie Wali .....Co-Producer
Stewart A. Lyons .....Co-Producer/UPM
Lorna Johnson .....Casting Director

DORA THE EXPLORER (Nickelodeon/30 mins.)
231 W. Olive Ave.
Burbank, CA 91502
PHONE 818-736-3000
FAX 818-736-3421
WEB SITE .....www.nickjr.com
PRODUCTION COMPANY Nickelodeon/Nick at Nite/TV Land/Spike TV
COMMENTS Animated

Chris Gifford .....Executive Producer/Writer/Creator
Valerie Walsh .....Co-Executive Producer/Writer/Creator
Jeff DeGrandis .....Supervising Producer
Eric Weiner .....Executive Story Editor/Producer
Miken Wong .....Line Producer
Cathy Galeota .....Coordinating Producer
Nicola Gayle .....Production Manager
Melissa Chusid .....Casting Director
Kia Riddick .....Casting Director

*DR. VEGAS (CBS/60 mins.)
c/o Warner Bros. Television
4000 Warner Blvd.
Burbank, CA 91522
PHONE 818-977-6820
PRODUCTION COMPANY Warner Bros. Television Production

Jack Orman .....Executive Producer
Steve Pearlman .....Executive Producer
Ira Behr .....Consulting Producer
Jill Goldsmith .....Supervising Producer
Lance Gentile .....Producer
Rob Lowe .....Producer
Ted Humphrey .....Story Editor
Craig Sweeney .....Staff Writer
Dan Shaner .....Casting Director
Michael Testa .....Casting Director

It is illegal to copy any part of this book

THE ELLEN DEGENERES SHOW (Syndicated/60 mins.)
3000 W. Alameda Ave., Ste. 2700
Burbank, CA 91523
PHONE 818-260-5600
FAX 818-260-5601
WEB SITE ....www.ellendegeneres.com
PRODUCTION COMPANIES NBC Entertainment - Telepictures Productions - Warner Bros. Television Production

Mary Connelly ....Executive Producer
Ellen DeGeneres ....Executive Producer
Ed Glavin ....Executive Producer
Andy Lassner ....Co-Executive Producer
Greg Gorden ....Executive in Charge
Derek Westervelt ....Coordinating Producer
Bradford Brillowski ....Producer
Melissa Costello ....Producer
Jason Gabel ....Producer
Christine Schomer ....Producer
Melissa Geiger Schrift ....Producer
Christopher Miele ....Production Manager
Karen Kilgariff ....Head Writer
Karen Anderson ....Writer
Danny Breen ....Writer
Greg Ftizsimmons ....Writer
Margaret Smith ....Writer
Michelle Gross ....Publicist
Lori Blackman ....Talent Executive

*EMPIRE (ABC/30 mins.)
c/o Storyline Entertainment
500 S. Buena Vista St.
Old Animation Bldg., Ste. 3C
Burbank, CA 91521
PHONE 818-560-2928
FAX 818-560-5145
PRODUCTION COMPANIES Storyline Entertainment - Touchstone Television

Chip Johannessen ....Executive Producer
Tom Wheeler ....Executive Producer
Tony Jonas ....Executive Producer
Neil Meron ....Executive Producer
Craig Zadan ....Executive Producer
Sara Cooper ....Consulting Producer
Carrie Henderson ....Line Producer

ENTERPRISE (UPN/60 mins.)
c/o Paramount Network Television
5555 Melrose Ave., Cooper Bldg., Rm. 205
Los Angeles, CA 90038-3197
PHONE 323-956-5951
PRODUCTION COMPANY Paramount Television Production

Rick Berman ....Executive Producer/Creator
Brannon Braga ....Executive Producer/Creator
Manny Coto ....Co-Executive Producer
Merri Howard ....Supervising Producer
Peter Lauritson ....Supervising Producer
Libby Goldstein ....Casting Director

*ENTOURAGE (HBO/30 mins.)
c/o HBO
2500 Broadway, Ste. 400
Santa Monica, CA 90404
PHONE 310-382-3000
WEB SITE ....www.hbo.com
PRODUCTION COMPANY HBO Original Programming

Larry Charles ....Executive Producer
Doug Ellin ....Executive Producer
Steve Levinson ....Executive Producer
Mark Wahlberg ....Executive Producer
Timothy Marx ....Co-Executive Producer
Rob Wise ....Co-Producer
Sheila Jaffe ....Casting Director
Georgianne Walken ....Casting Director

ER (NBC/60 mins.)
c/o Warner Bros. Television
4000 Warner Blvd., Bldg. 133, Rm. 204
Burbank, CA 91522
PHONE 818-954-3830
FAX 818-954-3847
PRODUCTION COMPANIES Amblin Entertainment - Constant C. Productions - Warner Bros. Television Production

John Wells ....Executive Producer
Michael Crichton ....Executive Producer
Christopher Chulack ....Executive Producer/Showrunner
R. Scott Gemmill ....Executive Producer
Dee Johnson ....Executive Producer
Jonathan Kaplan ....Co. Executive Producer
Bruce Miller ....Supervising Producer
Joe Sachs ....Supervising Producer
David Zabel ....Supervising Producer
Julie Hebert ....Producer
Wendy Spence Rosato ....Producer
Richard Thorpe ....Producer
Tommy Burns ....Co-Producer/UPM
Yahlin Chang ....Executive Story Editor
Lisa Zwerling ....Story Editor
Mark Morocco ....Staff Writer
Sonya Steele ....Staff Writer
John Levey ....Casting Director

EVE (UPN/30 mins.)
1438 N. Gower, Bldg. 62, Rm. 115
Hollywood, CA 90028
PHONE 323-468-7889
FAX 323-468-7750
PRODUCTION COMPANY Warner Bros. Television Production

Robert Greenblatt ....Executive Producer
David Janollari ....Executive Producer
Meg DeLoatch ....Executive Producer
Troy Carter ....Co-Executive Producer
David W. Duclon ....Co-Executive Producer
Eve Jeffers ....Co-Executive Producer
Michael Ajakwe Jr. ....Consulting Producer
Janice Hirsch ....Consulting Producer
Jim Tripp-Haith ....Line Producer
Trish Baker ....Producer
Torian Hughes ....Producer
Holy Powell ....Casting Director
Elizabeth Melcher ....Casting Director

EVERWOOD (WB/60 mins.)
1000 West/2610 South
Salt Lake City, UT 84119
PHONE 801-908-8800/818-977-7557
FAX 801-908-8836/818-977-7501
PRODUCTION COMPANIES Everwood Utah, Inc. - Warner Bros. Television Production
COMMENTS Writers' office: 4000 Warner Blvd., Bldg. 160, Ste. 700, Burbank, CA 91522

Greg Berlanti ....Executive Producer/Creator/Showrunner
Mickey Liddell ....Executive Producer
Rina Mimoun ....Executive Producer
Andrew A. Ackerman ....Co-Executive Producer
Michael C. Green ....Co-Executive Producer
Bruce Miller ....Supervising Producer
Anna Fricke ....Co-Producer
Sherri Cooper ....Executive Story Editor
John E. Pogue ....Executive Story Editor
David Hudgins ....Story Editor
Patrick Rush ....Casting Director

EVERYBODY LOVES RAYMOND (CBS/30 mins.)
4000 Warner Blvd., Bldg. 131
Burbank, CA 91522
PHONE 818-954-7770
FAX 818-954-7905
PRODUCTION COMPANIES HBO Independent Productions - Worldwide Pants, Inc.

Ray Romano ....Executive Producer
Philip Rosenthal ....Executive Producer/Showrunner
Rory Rosegarten ....Executive Producer
Stu Smiley ....Executive Producer
Tucker Cawley ....Executive Producer
Lew Schneider ....Executive Producer
Steve Skrovan ....Executive Producer
Jeremy Stevens ....Executive Producer
Mike Royce ....Executive Producer
Tom Caltabiano ....Co-Executive Producer
Leslie Caveny ....Co-Executive Producer
Lisa Helfrich-Jackson ....Co-Executive Producer
Aaron Shure ....Co-Executive Producer
Holli Gailen ....Producer
Ken Ornstein ....Producer/UPM
Lisa Miller Katz ....Casting Director
Maggie Sherman ....Casting Associate

EVIL CON CARNE (Cartoon Network/30 mins.)
c/o Cartoon Network
300 N. Third St.
Burbank, CA 91502
PHONE 818-729-4000
EMAIL ....cnsjobs@turner.com
COMMENTS Animated

Maxwell Atoms ....Executive Producer/Creator
Brian Miller ....Executive Producer
Louis J. Cuck ....Line Producer
Laura A. Dalesandro ....Production Manager
Kris Zimmerman ....Casting Director

***EYES (ABC/60 mins.)**
1438 N. Gower St., Box 30
Hollywood, CA 90028
PHONE 323-468-7800
FAX 323-468-7801
PRODUCTION COMPANIES McNamara Paper Products - Warner Bros. Television Production

John McNamara ....Executive Producer/Showrunner
Chris Long ....Co-Executive Producer/Director
Bonnie Mark ....Co-Executive Producer
Lewis Abel ....Producer
Aaron Zelman ....Producer
Case Krell ....Creative Consultant
Tom Smuts ....Story Editor
John Belluso ....Staff Writer
Sera Gamble ....Staff Writer
Evangeline Orday ....Staff Writer
Raelle Tucker ....Staff Writer
Eric Dawson ....Casting Director

FAIRLY ODD PARENTS (Nickelodeon/30 mins.)
c/o Nickelodeon
231 W. Olive Ave.
Burbank, CA 91502
PHONE 818-736-3000
COMMENTS Animated

Butch Hartman ....Executive Producer/Creator
Fred Seibert ....Executive Producer
Bob Boyle ....Producer
Steve Marmel ....Producer

FAMILY GUY (Fox/30 mins.)
c/o Twentieth Century Fox
10201 W. Pico Blvd.
Los Angeles, CA 90035
PHONE 323-857-8800
FAX 323-857-8835

Seth MacFarlane ....Executive Producer/Creator/Showrunner
David Goodman ....Executive Producer/Showrunner
Chris Sheridan ....Executive Producer
Danny Smith ....Co-Executive Producer
Mark Hentemann ....Consulting Producer
Mike Rowe ....Supervising Producer
Shannon Smith ....Animation Producer
Kara Vallow ....Producer
Alex Borstein ....Co-Producer
Steve Callaghan ....Co-Producer
Mike Henry ....Co-Producer
Patrick Henry ....Co-Producer
Alec Sulkin ....Co-Producer
Wellesley Wild ....Co-Producer
Kim Ferhman ....Associate Producer
Tom Devanney ....Consultant
Kirker Butler ....Staff Writer
Patrick Meighan ....Staff Writer
John Viener ....Staff Writer

FATHER OF THE PRIDE (NBC/30 mins.)
1000 Flower St., Lakeside Basement
Glendale, CA 91201
PHONE 818-695-3726
PRODUCTION COMPANY DreamWorks Television
COMMENTS Animated CGI

Jonathan Groff . . . . Supervising Executive Producer/Showrunner
Jeffrey Katzenberg . . . . Executive Producer/Creator
Jon Pollack . . . . Executive Producer
Joe Aguilar . . . . Co-Executive Producer
Cheryl Holliday . . . . Co-Executive Producer
Rob Cohen . . . . Consulting Producer
Klay Hall . . . . Supervising Director
Ron Weiner . . . . Producer
Mary Sandell . . . . Line Producer
David Goodman . . . . Staff Writer
Glasgow Phillips . . . . Staff Writer
Jon Ross . . . . Staff Writer
Jean Yu . . . . Staff Writer
Laura Gutin . . . . Script Coordinator
Leslee Feldman . . . . Casting Director
Alison Flierl . . . . Assistant to Jonathan Groff & Jon Pollack

FEAR FACTOR (NBC/60 mins.)
1149 N. Gower St., Ste. 105
Hollywood, CA 90038
PHONE 323-785-2242
FAX 323-785-2243
WEB SITE . . . . www.fearfactor.com
PRODUCTION COMPANIES Endemol USA, Inc. - Lock and Key Productions

Matt Kunitz . . . . Executive Producer
David Hurwitz . . . . Executive Producer
J. Rupert Thompson . . . . Director
Brian Veskosky . . . . Supervising Producer
Perry Barndt . . . . Sr. Producer
Scott Larsen . . . . Producer
Tom Herschko . . . . Segment Producer
Kevin Wehrenberg . . . . Line Producer
Rebecca Shumsky . . . . Supervising Casting Producer
Jason Henry . . . . Associate Segment Producer
Erin O'Brien . . . . Associate Segment Producer
Brad Car . . . . Associate Producer
Felicia Nainoa . . . . Associate Producer
Laurie Zink . . . . Associate Producer

FRANKLIN (Nickelodeon/30 mins.)
42 Pardee Ave.
Toronto, ON M6K 3H5 Canada
PHONE 416-535-0935
WEB SITE . . . . www.nelvana.com
PRODUCTION COMPANY Nelvana Entertainment/A Corus Entertainment Company
COMMENTS Animated

Paulette Bourgeois . . . . Executive Producer/Creator
Brenda Clark . . . . Executive Producer
Scott Dyer . . . . Executive Producer
Paul Robertson . . . . Executive Producer
Gary Hurst . . . . Director
Patricia Burns . . . . Supervising Producer
Jocelyn Hamilton . . . . Supervising Producer
Bob Ardiel . . . . Story Editor

GENE RODDENBERRY'S ANDROMEDA (Syndicated/60 mins.)
8651 Eastlake Dr.
Burnaby, BC V5A 4T7 Canada
PHONE 604-421-8220
FAX 604-421-8215
WEB SITE . . . . www.andromedatv.com
PRODUCTION COMPANIES Andromeda Productions, Ltd. - Fireworks Entertainment - Tribune Entertainment Company

Majel Roddenberry . . . . Executive Producer
Jay Firestone . . . . Executive Producer
Adam Haight . . . . Executive Producer
Stuart Aikins . . . . Casting Director

GENERAL HOSPITAL (ABC/60 mins.)
4151 Prospect Ave.
Los Angeles, CA 90027
PHONE 323-671-5563
PRODUCTION COMPANY ABC Daytime

Jill Farren Phelps . . . . Executive Producer
Bob Guza Jr. . . . . Head Writer
Charles Pratt Jr. . . . . Head Writer
Mercer Barrows . . . . Producer
Michelle Henry . . . . Producer
Mary O'Leary . . . . Producer
Deborah Genovese . . . . Coordinating Producer
Mark Teschner . . . . Casting Director

THE GEORGE LOPEZ SHOW (ABC/30 mins.)
c/o Warner Bros. Television
4000 Warner Blvd., Bldg. 19, Rm. 229
Burbank, CA 91522
PHONE 818-954-3332
FAX 818-954-3371
PRODUCTION COMPANIES Fortis Films - Mohawk Productions - Warner Bros. Television Production

Robert Borden . . . . Executive Producer/Creator
Sandra Bullock . . . . Executive Producer
Bruce Helford . . . . Executive Producer/Creator/Showrunner
Dave Caplan . . . . Executive Producer
Deborah Oppenheimer . . . . Executive Producer
Paul Kaplan . . . . Co-Executive Producer
Mark Torgove . . . . Co-Executive Producer
Allen Zipper . . . . Creative Consultant
Jim Hope . . . . Supervising Producer
George Lopez . . . . Producer/Creator
Rick Nyholm . . . . Producer
Frank Pace . . . . Producer
Luisa Leschin . . . . Co-Producer
John Morey . . . . Co-Producer
Michael Loftus . . . . Punch-up
Bonnie Zane . . . . Casting Director

GILMORE GIRLS (WB/60 mins.)
4000 Warner Blvd., Bldg. 193, Rm. 200
Burbank, CA 91522
PHONE 818-954-3115
PRODUCTION COMPANY Warner Bros. Television Production

Amy Sherman-Palladino . . . . Executive Producer/Creator/Showrunner
Daniel Palladino . . . . Executive Producer
Bill Prady . . . . Co-Executive Producer
Jim Berg . . . . Consulting Producer
Stan Zimmerman . . . . Consulting Producer
Patricia Fass Palmer . . . . Producer
Rebecca Kirshner . . . . Producer
Helen Pai . . . . Producer
Jessica Queller . . . . Co-Producer
Mara Casey . . . . Casting Director
Jami Rudofsky . . . . Casting Director

GIRLFRIENDS (UPN/30 mins.)
c/o Paramount Network Television
5555 Melrose Ave., Balaban Bldg., Ste. D
Los Angeles, CA 90038
PHONE 323-956-1803/323-956-4500
FAX 323-862-1118
PRODUCTION COMPANIES Grammnet Productions - Paramount Television Production
COMMENTS Writers' office: Balaban Bldg., Ste. B

Kelsey Grammer ....Executive Producer
Mara Brock Akil ....Executive Producer
Regina Hicks ....Co-Executive Producer
Michael Kaplan ....Co-Executive Producer
Mark Brown ....Consulting Producer
Dee La Duke ....Consulting Producer
Norman Vance Jr. ....Supervising Producer
Dan Dugan ....Producer/UPM
Tim Edwards ....Co-Producer
Mary Fukuto ....Co-Producer
Susie Johnson ....Production Coordinator
Karin Gist ....Story Editor
Veronica Chambers ....Staff Writer
Michele Marburger ....Staff Writer
Kevin Marburger ....Staff Writer

***GLOBAL FREQUENCY (WB/60 mins.)**
c/o Mark Burnett Productions
640 N. Sepulveda Blvd.
Los Angeles, CA 90049
PHONE 310-903-5400/604-639-1812
FAX 310-903-5592
PRODUCTION COMPANIES Mark Burnett Productions - Warner Bros. Television Production
COMMENTS Midseason

Mark Burnett ....Executive Producer
John Rogers ....Executive Producer

***GREY'S ANATOMY (ABC/60 mins.)**
c/o The Mark Gordon Company
12200 W. Olympic Blvd., Ste. 250
Los Angeles, CA 90064
PHONE 310-943-6401
FAX 310-943-6402
PRODUCTION COMPANIES The Mark Gordon Company - Touchstone Television

Mark Gordon ....Executive Producer
James Parriott ....Executive Producer/Showrunner
Shonda Rhimes ....Executive Producer/Creator
Betsy Beers ....Executive Producer
Peter Horton ....Co-Executive Producer
Ann Hamilton ....Consulting Producer
Krista Vernoff ....Supervising Producer
Mimi Schmir ....Producer
Gabrielle Stanton ....Producer
Harry Werksman ....Producer
Zoanne Clack ....Story Editor
Stacey McKee ....Staff Writer

THE GRIM ADVENTURES OF BILLY & MANDY (Cartoon Network/30 mins.)
c/o Cartoon Network
300 N. Third St.
Burbank, CA 91502
PHONE 818-729-4000
FAX 818-729-4026
COMMENTS Animated

Maxwell Atoms ....Executive Producer/Creator
Brian Miller ....Executive Producer
Louis J. Cuck ....Line Producer
Laura A. Dalesandro ....Production Manager
Kris Zimmerman ....Casting Director

GROUNDED FOR LIFE (WB/30 mins.)
c/o CBS Radford
4024 Radford Ave., Bldg. 4, Rm. 101
Studio City, CA 91604
PHONE 818-655-5967
FAX 818-655-8002
PRODUCTION COMPANY Tujunga Productions, LLC

Marcy Carsey ....Executive Producer
Caryn Mandabach ....Executive Producer
Tom Werner ....Executive Producer
Jeff Astrof ....Executive Producer/Showrunner
Bill Martin ....Executive Producer/Co-Creator
Mike Schiff ....Executive Producer/Co-Creator
Mike Sikowitz ....Executive Producer/Showrunner
Ned Goldreyer ....Co-Executive Producer
Chris Kelly ....Co-Executive Producer
Jim Armogida ....Producer
Steve Armogida ....Producer
Denis Biggs ....Producer
Erica Rivinoja ....Co-Producer
Rebecca Hughes ....Staff Writer
Meg Lieberman ....Casting Director
Cami Patton ....Casting Director

GUIDING LIGHT (CBS/60 mins.)
c/o CBS
222 E. 44th St.
New York, NY 10017
PHONE 212-986-5330
FAX 212-697-7143
WEB SITE ....www.guidinglighttv.com
PRODUCTION COMPANY Procter & Gamble Productions, Inc.

Ellen Wheeler ....Executive Producer
Jan Conklin ....Coordinating Producer
Maria Macina ....Coordinating Producer
David Kreizman ....Head Writer
Alexandra Johnson ....Producer
Dana Halber ....Assistant Producer
Rob Decina ....Casting Director
Melanie Haseltine ....Associate Casting Director
Darlene Failla ....Casting Assistant

HALF & HALF (UPN/30 mins.)
4024 Radford Ave., Bldg. 5, 2nd Fl.
Studio City, CA 91604
PHONE 818-655-5496
FAX 818-655-8404
PRODUCTION COMPANIES CBS Productions - SisterLee Productions, Inc.

Yvette Lee Bowser ....Executive Producer/Showrunner
Jamie Wooten ....Co-Executive Producer
Winifred Hervey ....Consulting Producer
Heather MacGillvray ....Supervising Producer
Linda Mathious ....Supervising Producer
David Matthews ....Supervising Producer
Gina Scheerer ....Co-Producer
Beth Seriff ....Co-Producer
Geoff Tarson ....Co-Producer
Carla Waddles ....Co-Producer
Beverly Rose ....Line Producer
Michaela Feeley ....Executive Story Editor
Chauncy B. Raglin-Washington ....Story Editor
Kevin Scott ....Casting Director

***HAWAII (NBC/60 mins.)**
c/o NBC Studios
3000 W. Alameda Ave.
Burbank, CA 91523
PHONE 818-526-6284
PRODUCTION COMPANY NBC Universal Television Studio

Jeff Eastin ....Executive Producer/Showrunner

HOPE & FAITH (ABC/30 mins.)
c/o Silvercup Studios East
3402 Starr Ave.
Long Island, NY 11101
PHONE .718-906-3200
FAX .718-906-3222
PRODUCTION COMPANY Touchstone Television

Joanna Johnson .Executive Producer/Creator
Emile Levisetti .Executive Producer
Gil Junger .Executive Producer/Director
Peter Murrieta .Co-Executive Producer
David Rosenthal .Co-Executive Producer
Tom Leopold .Consulting Producer
Jenna Bruce .Supervising Producer
Elysse Bezahler .Producer/UPM
Tod Hammel .Producer
Bobby Gaylor .Co-Producer
Dara Schnapper .Associate Producer
Taylor Hamra .Story Editor
Jenny Snider .Story Editor
Victoria Webster .Story Editor
James Calleri .Casting Director

*HOUSE (Fox/60 mins.)
10201 W. Pico Blvd., Bldg. 89
Los Angeles, CA 90035
PHONE .310-369-3100
FAX .310-969-1100
PRODUCTION COMPANY Heel & Toe Films

Paul Attanasio .Executive Producer
Katie Jacobs .Executive Producer
David Shore .Executive Producer
Bryan Singer .Executive Producer
Amy Lippens .Casting Director

HUFF (Showtime/60 mins.)
12501 Gladstone Ave., Stage 2
Sylmar, CA 91342
PHONE .818-837-3810
FAX .818-837-3811
PRODUCTION COMPANIES Allenford Productions Inc. - Sony Pictures Television

Bob Lowry .Executive Producer/Creator/Showrunner
Scott Winant .Executive Producer
Cameron Jones .Executive Producer
Thania St. John .Co-Executive Producer
Hank Azaria .Producer
Lori-Etta Paub .Producer
Nancy Sanders .Producer
Dauri Chase .Co-Producer
David Maples .Co-Producer
Mark Richard .Co-Producer
Byron Balasco .Staff Writer
Jessica Mecklenburg .Staff Writer
Nicole Mirante .Staff Writer
Tim Payne .Casting Director

*THE INSIDE (Fox/60 mins.)
c/o Imagine Television
9465 Wilshire Blvd., 7th Fl.
Beverly Hills, CA 90212
PHONE .310-858-2000/310-579-5100
FAX .310-858-2011
PRODUCTION COMPANIES Imagine Television - Twentieth Century Fox Television

Kathryn Bigelow .Executive Producer
Brian Grazer .Executive Producer
Ron Howard .Executive Producer
Glenn Kessler .Executive Producer
Todd Kessler .Executive Producer
David Nevins .Executive Producer
Hart Hanson .Consulting Producer
Gay Walch .Producer
Daniel Zelman .Producer
Mark Fish .Staff Writer
Ahmed Lavalais .Staff Writer

*JACK & BOBBY (WB/60 mins.)
1041 N. Formosa Ave., Santa Monica West, Ste. 5
West Hollywood, CA 90046
PHONE .323-850-3939
FAX .323-850-3949
PRODUCTION COMPANIES Berlanti/Liddell Productions - Warner Bros. Television Production

Greg Berlanti .Executive Producer/Creator
Mickey Liddell .Executive Producer
Thomas Schlamme .Executive Producer
Vanessa Taylor .Co-Executive Producer/Creator
Andrew A. Ackerman .Co-Executive Producer
Maggie Friedman .Consulting Producer
Michael C. Green .Consulting Producer
Marc Guggenheim .Supervising Producer
Jonathan Lisco .Supervising Producer
Steven "Scoop" Cohen .Co-Producer
Brad Meltzer .Co-Producer
Paul Marks .Line Producer
Barbie Kligman .Story Editor
Erik Oleson .Story Editor
Liz Dean .Casting Director
Robert Ulrich .Casting Director

JAG (CBS/60 mins.)
c/o Paramount Television Production
1438 N. Gower St., Box 25
Hollywood, CA 90028
PHONE .323-468-4500
FAX .323-468-4599
PRODUCTION COMPANIES Belisarius Productions - Paramount Television Production

Donald P. Bellisario .Executive Producer
Chas. Floyd Johnson .Co-Executive Producer
Stephen Zito .Co-Executive Producer
Dana Coen .Co-Executive Producer
Philip DeGuere .Consulting Producer
Don McGill .Supervising Producer
David Bellisario .Producer
Avery Drewe .Producer
Darcy Meyers .Producer
Larry Moskowitz .Producer
Peter Dunne .Producer
Julie Watson .Coordinating Producer
Megan Mascena Gaspar .Associate Producer
Chip Vucelich .UPM
Susan Bluestein .Casting Director

JEREMIAH (Showtime/60 mins.)
c/o Platinum Studios
9744 Wilshire Blvd., Ste. 210
Los Angeles, CA 90212
PHONE .310-276-3900

Luke Perry .Executive Producer
J. Michael Straczynski .Executive Producer
Scott Mitchell Rosenberg .Executive Producer
Ervin Rustemagic .Executive Producer
Joe Dante .Executive Producer
Mike Finnell .Executive Producer
Grant Rosenberg .Co-Executive Producer
George Horie .Producer
Sara Barnes .Co-Producer
Ben Brafman .Co-Producer
Stephanie Germain .Co-Producer
Gregory Noveck .Co-Producer
Paul Weber .Casting Director (Vancouver)
Bette Chadwick .Casting Director
Candice Elzinga .Casting Director

JIMMY KIMMEL LIVE (ABC/60 mins.)
6834 Hollywood Blvd., 6th Fl.
Hollywood, CA 90028
PHONE .323-860-5900

Duncan Gray .Executive Producer
Jimmy Kimmel .Executive Producer
Jason Schrift .Executive Producer
Steve O'Donnell .Head Writer
Tony Barbieri .Writer
Jacob Lentz .Writer

JIMMY NEUTRON: BOY GENIUS (Nickelodeon/30 mins.)
c/o DNA Productions
2201 W. Royal Lane, Ste. 275
Irving, TX 75063
PHONE .214-352-4694
FAX .214-496-9333
PRODUCTION COMPANY Nickelodeon/Nick at Nite/TV Land/Spike TV
COMMENTS Animated

Steve Oedekerk .Executive Producer
Keith Alcorn .Co-Executive Producer/Director
Jed Spingarn .Co-Executive Producer
Mike Gasaway .Director
John A. Davis .Co-Producer/Creator

JOAN OF ARCADIA (CBS/60 mins.)
10202 W. Washington Blvd., Tracy West Bldg.
Culver City, CA 90232
PHONE .310-244-3500
FAX .310-244-1565
PRODUCTION COMPANIES CBS Productions - Sony Pictures Television

Barbara Hall .Executive Producer/Creator/Showrunner
James Hayman .Executive Producer
Stephen Nathan .Executive Producer
Peter Schindler .Co-Executive Producer
Tom Garrigus .Supervising Producer
Joy Gregory .Co-Producer
David Grae .Story Editor
Lindsay Sturman .Staff Writer
Vicki Rosenberg .Casting Director

***JOEY (NBC/30 mins.)**
c/o Warner Bros. Television
4000 Warner Blvd.
Burbank, CA 91522
PHONE .818-954-6600
FAX .818-954-6926
PRODUCTION COMPANY Warner Bros. Television Production

Scott Silveri .Executive Producer
Shana Goldberg-Meehan .Executive Producer
Kevin Bright .Executive Producer
Sherry Bilsing-Graham .Co-Executive Producer
Ellen Plummer .Co-Executive Producer
Brian Buckner .Consulting Producer
Brian Kelley .Consulting Producer
Robert Carlock .Supervising Producer
Vanessa McCarthy .Executive Story Editor
John Quaintance .Story Editor
Craig DeGregorio .Staff Writer
Matt Hubbard .Staff Writer
Brian Myers .Casting Director

JOHNNY BRAVO (Cartoon Network/30 mins.)
300 N. Third St.
Burbank, CA 91502
PHONE .818-729-4000
FAX .818-729-4086
COMMENTS Animated

Van Partible .Producer/Creator
Diana Ritchey .Line Producer

***JONNY ZERO (Fox/60 mins.)**
516 W. 36th St., 2nd Fl.
New York, NY 10018
PHONE .212-279-3433/818-954-3093
FAX .212-279-4348
PRODUCTION COMPANIES John Wells Productions - Warner Bros. Television Production

John Wells .Executive Producer
R. Scott Gemmill .Executive Producer/Creator
Llewellyn Wells .Executive Producer
Mimi Leder .Executive Producer

JUDGING AMY (CBS/60 mins.)
c/o Twentieth Century Fox
10201 W. Pico Blvd., Trailer 773
Los Angeles, CA 90035
PHONE .310-369-0704
FAX .310-969-1222
PRODUCTION COMPANIES CBS Productions - Twentieth Century Fox Television

Joseph Stern .Executive Producer/Showrunner
Amy Brenneman .Executive Producer
Connie Tavel .Executive Producer
Karen Hall .Executive Producer
Alex Taub .Executive Producer
Barbara Hall .Executive Consultant/Creator
James Frawley .Co-Executive Producer
Rob Fresco .Consulting Producer
Carol Barbee .Supervising Producer
Thomas R. Moore .Producer
Lyla Oliver .Producer
Paul Guyot .Co-Producer
Val Joseph .Co-Producer
Barry O'Brien .Executive Story Editor
Stephanie Ripps .Staff Writer
Vicki Rosenberg .Casting Director

***KELSEY GRAMMER PRESENTS: THE SKETCH SHOW (Fox/30 mins.)**
c/o Grammnet Productions
5555 Melrose Ave., Wilder Bldg., Ste. 114
Los Angeles, CA 90038
PHONE 323-956-5455
FAX 323-862-2284
PRODUCTION COMPANIES Grammnet Productions - Twentieth Century Fox Television

Kelsey Grammer .....Executive Producer
Steve Stark .....Executive Producer
John Thoday .....Executive Producer
Dan Patterson .....Executive Producer

***KEVIN HILL (UPN/60 mins.)**
175 Queens Quay East, Ste. 300
Toronto, ON M5A 1B6 Canada
PHONE 416-368-0087/818-526-4208
FAX 416-368-0093/818-526-4299
PRODUCTION COMPANIES Icon Productions, Inc. - Touchstone Television
COMMENTS Writers' office: 800 S. Main St., 3rd Fl., Burbank, CA 91506

Bruce Davey .....Executive Producer
Mel Gibson .....Executive Producer
Jorge A. Reyes .....Executive Producer/Creator
Alex Taub .....Executive Producer
Todd Ellis Kessler .....Supervising Producer
Adam Armus .....Producer
Kay Foster .....Producer
Michael Reisz .....Staff Writer
Shana Landsberg .....Casting Director

KIM POSSIBLE (Disney Channel/30 mins.)
c/o Walt Disney TV Animation
500 S. Buena Vista St.
Burbank, CA 91524
PHONE 818-560-0560
COMMENTS Animated

Mark McCorkle .....Executive Producer
Bob Schooley .....Executive Producer
Steve Loter .....Director
Kurt Weldon .....Line Producer
Tom Hart .....Writer

THE KING OF QUEENS (CBS/30 mins.)
c/o Sony Pictures Entertainment
10202 W. Washington Blvd., Lean Bldg., Ste. 410
Culver City, CA 90232
PHONE 310-244-3343
FAX 310-244-0443
PRODUCTION COMPANIES CBS Productions - Sony Pictures Television

Tom Hertz .....Executive Producer/Showrunner
Kevin James .....Executive Producer
Tony Sheehan .....Executive Producer
Jeff Sussman .....Executive Producer
Michael J. Weithorn .....Creator/Executive Consultant
David Bickel .....Co-Executive Producer
Chris Downey .....Co-Executive Producer
Michelle Nader .....Co-Executive Producer
Rob Schiller .....Co-Executive Producer/Director
Ilana Wernick .....Co-Executive Producer
Nick Bakay .....Consulting Producer
Liz Astroff .....Supervising Producer
Rock Reuben .....Supervising Producer
Annette Davis .....Producer/UPM
Owen Ellickson .....Story Editor
Mike Soccio .....Story Editor
Dennis Regan .....Staff Writer
Cami Patton .....Casting Director

KING OF THE HILL (Fox/30 mins.)
1875 Century Park East, 4th Fl.
Los Angeles, CA 90067
PHONE 310-229-2476
FAX 310-229-2477
PRODUCTION COMPANIES 3 Arts Entertainment, Inc. - Twentieth Century Fox Television
COMMENTS Animated

Greg Daniels .....Executive Producer/Creator
Mike Judge .....Executive Producer/Creator
John Altschuler .....Executive Producer/Showrunner
David Krinsky .....Executive Producer/Showrunner
Howard Klein .....Executive Producer
Michael Rotenberg .....Executive Producer
John Collier .....Co-Executive Producer
Sivert Glarum .....Co-Executive Producer
Michael Jamin .....Co-Executive Producer
Dan McGrath .....Co-Executive Producer
Garland Testa .....Co-Executive Producer
Aron Abrams .....Consulting Producer
Jim Dauterive .....Consulting Producer
Greg Thompson .....Consulting Producer
Kit Boss .....Supervising Producer
Dan Sterling .....Supervising Producer
Joe Boucher .....Producer
Etan Cohen .....Producer
Mark McJimsey .....Producer
Greg Cohen .....Co-Producer
J.B. Cook .....Co-Producer
Kenny Micka .....Co-Producer
Tony Gama-Lobo .....Story Editor
Becky May .....Story Editor
Christy Stratton .....Story Editor
Wyatt Cenac .....Staff Writer
Julie Mossberg .....Casting Director
Scott Muller .....Casting Coordinator

THE L WORD (Showtime/60 mins.)
8275 Manitoba St.
Vancouver, BC V5X 4L8 Canada
PHONE 604-419-1300/310-234-5200

Ilene Chaiken .....Executive Producer
Steve Golin .....Executive Producer
Larry Kennar .....Executive Producer
Beth Klein .....Casting Director (LA)
Coreen Mayrs .....Casting Director (Vancouver)

LAS VEGAS (NBC/60 mins.)
8660 Hayden Pl.
Culver City, CA 90232
PHONE 310-840-7499
FAX 310-840-7409
PRODUCTION COMPANIES DreamWorks Television - NBC Universal Television Studio

Gary Scott Thompson .....Executive Producer/Creator/Showrunner
Gardner Stern .....Executive Producer/Showrunner
Justin Falvey .....Executive Producer
Darryl Frank .....Executive Producer
Scott Steindorff .....Executive Producer
Michael Berns .....Co-Executive Producer
Kim Newton .....Co-Executive Producer
Matt Pyken .....Co-Executive Producer
Dan Sackheim .....Consulting Producer
Stephen Sassen .....Producer
Tracey D'Arcy .....Co-Producer
Lorie Zerweck .....Co-Producer/UPM
Adele Lim .....Executive Story Editor
Kyle Harimoto .....Story Editor
Vanessa Reisen .....Story Editor
Cami Patton .....Casting Director
Jennifer Lare .....Casting Director

*LAST CALL WITH CARSON DALY (NBC/30 mins.)

c/o NBC Studios
30 Rockefeller Plaza, Ste. 1755-E
New York, NY 10112
PHONE 212-664-5550
FAX 212-664-4011

Carson Daly . . . . Producer/Host
David Friedman . . . . Executive Producer
Guy Oseary . . . . Executive Producer
Steve Paley . . . . Director
Geoff Addeo . . . . Line Producer
Jason Ryan . . . . Segment Producer
Rob Crabbe . . . . Segment/Associate Producer
Nicole Yaron . . . . Associate Producer
Steve Lookner . . . . Head Writer
David King . . . . Writer
Alan Yang . . . . Writer
Mike Hammeke . . . . Production Manager
Jamie Granet . . . . Executive Talent Booker
Diana Miller . . . . Jr. Talent Booker
Adam Underhill . . . . Jr. Talent Booker
Sheeelagh Lynch . . . . Talent Coordinator
Jessica Nolan . . . . Assistant to Carson Daly

*THE LATE LATE SHOW WITH CRAIG KILBORN (CBS/60 mins.)

7800 Beverly Blvd., Ste. 244
Los Angeles, CA 90036
PHONE 323-575-5600
FAX 323-575-5656
WEB SITE . . . . www.cbs.com

Craig Kilborn . . . . Host/Writer
Todd Yasui . . . . Executive Producer
Brian McAloon . . . . Director
Mike Gibbons . . . . Producer/Head Writer
Cathy Hoeven . . . . Supervising Producer
Alisa Gichon . . . . Talent Executive
Ross Abrash . . . . Writer
Peter Charkalis . . . . Writer
Chris DeLuca . . . . Writer
Dan French . . . . Writer
Jonathan "Goldy" Goldblatt . . . . Writer
Ted Jessup . . . . Writer
Ted Mulkerin . . . . Writer
David Nickoll . . . . Writer
David Harte . . . . Segment Producer
Michael Naidus . . . . Segment Producer

LATE NIGHT WITH CONAN O'BRIEN (NBC/60 mins.)

c/o NBC Studios
Rockefeller Center, Studio 6-A
New York, NY 10112
PHONE 212-664-3737
FAX 212-664-4622
PRODUCTION COMPANY Broadway Video Entertainment

Lorne Michaels . . . . Executive Producer
Jeff Ross . . . . Executive Producer
Mike Sweeney . . . . Head Writer
Allan Kartun . . . . Director
Cecelia Pleva . . . . Talent Booker

LAW & ORDER (NBC/60 mins.)

100 Universal City Plaza, Bldg. 2252
Universal City, CA 91608
PHONE 818-777-6969
FAX 818-866-1226/212-627-0957
PRODUCTION COMPANY Wolf Films, Inc.
COMMENTS East Coast office: Pier 62, Hudson River at W. 23rd St., New York, NY 10011

Dick Wolf . . . . Executive Producer
Eric Overmyer . . . . Executive Producer
Matthew Penn . . . . Executive Producer
Wendy Battles . . . . Co-Executive Producer
William N. Fordes . . . . Co-Executive Producer
Arthur Forney . . . . Co-Executive Producer
Peter Jankowski . . . . Co-Executive Producer
Richard Sweren . . . . Co-Executive Producer
Roz Weinman . . . . Co-Executive Producer
Gary Karr . . . . Supervising Producer
Kati Johnson . . . . Producer
Lois Johnson . . . . Producer
Nick Santora . . . . Producer
Kathy O'Connell . . . . Associate Producer
Alfredo Barrios Jr. . . . . Executive Story Editor
Davey Holmes . . . . Staff Writer
Lynn Kressel . . . . Casting Director
Suzanne Ryan . . . . Casting Director

LAW & ORDER: CRIMINAL INTENT (NBC/60 mins.)

100 Universal City Plaza, Bldg. 5166
Universal City, CA 91608
PHONE 818-777-6969/212-336-6350
PRODUCTION COMPANY Wolf Films, Inc.
COMMENTS East Coast office: Pier 62, Hudson River at W. 23rd St. New York, NY 10011

Dick Wolf . . . . Executive Producer
Rene Balcer . . . . Executive Producer/Showrunner
Peter Jankowksi . . . . Executive Producer
Fred Berner . . . . Executive Producer
Gerry Conway . . . . Co-Executive Producer
Arthur Forney . . . . Co-Executive Producer
Warren Leight . . . . Co-Executive Producer
Marlane Meyer . . . . Co-Executive Producer
Michael Kewley . . . . Supervising Producer
John L. Roman . . . . Producer
Stephanie Sengupta . . . . Producer
Diana Son . . . . Co-Producer
Mary Rae Thewlis . . . . Co-Producer
Jim Sterling . . . . Executive Story Editor
Elizabeth Benjamin . . . . Story Editor
Lynn Kressel . . . . Casting Director

LAW & ORDER: SPECIAL VICTIMS UNIT (NBC/60 mins.)
100 Universal City Plaza, Bldg. 2252
Universal City, CA 91608
PHONE 818-777-6969/201-662-7170
FAX 818-733-2742/201-662-7175
PRODUCTION COMPANIES Universal Network Television - Wolf Films, Inc.
COMMENTS East Coast office: 5801 West Side Ave., North Bergen, NJ 07047

Dick Wolf . . . . .Executive Producer
Neal Baer . . . . .Executive Producer/Showrunner
Peter Jankowksi . . . . .Executive Producer
Ted Kotcheff . . . . .Executive Producer
Tara Butters . . . . .Co-Executive Producer
Dawn DeNoon . . . . .Co-Executive Producer
Michele Fazekas . . . . .Co-Executive Producer
Arthur Forney . . . . .Co-Executive Producer
Jonathan Greene . . . . .Co-Executive Producer
Patrick Harbinson . . . . .Co-Executive Producer
Robert Nathan . . . . .Co-Executive Producer
Lisa Marie Petersen . . . . .Co-Executive Producer
Roz Weinman . . . . .Co-Executive Producer
Randy Roberts . . . . .Supervising Producer
David DeClerque . . . . .Producer
Peter Leto . . . . .Producer
Gail Barringer . . . . .Co-Producer
Jose Molina . . . . .Co-Producer
Amanda Voytek . . . . .Co-Producer
Lynn Kressel . . . . .Casting Director
Jonathan Strauss . . . . .Casting Director

***LAW & ORDER: TRIAL BY JURY (NBC/60 mins.)**
c/o Wolf Films, Inc.
100 Universal City Plaza, Bldg. 2252
Universal City, CA 91608-1085
PHONE 818-777-6969
FAX 818-866-1446
PRODUCTION COMPANIES Universal Network Television - Wolf Films, Inc.

Dick Wolf . . . . .Executive Producer/Creator
Walon Green . . . . .Executive Producer/Creator
Mark Rydell . . . . .Executive Producer

***LAX (NBC/60 mins.)**
100 Universal City Plaza, Bldg. 2128, Ste. E
Universal City, CA 91608
PHONE 818-733-2134
FAX 818-733-2965
PRODUCTION COMPANY NBC Universal Television Studio

Mark Gordon . . . . .Executive Producer
Nick Thiel . . . . .Executive Producer/Creator
Russ Friend . . . . .Co-Executive Producer
Garrett Lerner . . . . .Co-Executive Producer
Paul Redford . . . . .Co-Executive Producer
Anthony Russo . . . . .Co-Executive Producer/Director
Joe Russo . . . . .Co-Executive Producer/Director
Kayla Alpert . . . . .Supervising Producer
Andy Dettmann . . . . .Supervising Producer
Dan Fesman . . . . .Producer
Harry Victor . . . . .Producer
Jill Blotevogel . . . . .Story Editor
Alex Woo . . . . .Staff Writer

LESS THAN PERFECT (ABC/30 mins.)
c/o CBS Radford
4024 Radford Ave., Bungalow 18
Studio City, CA 91604
PHONE 818-655-5422
FAX 818-655-8740
PRODUCTION COMPANIES Touchstone Television - Wass-Stein

Christine Zander .Executive Producer/Showrunner
Gene Stein . . . . .Executive Producer
Nina Wass . . . . .Executive Producer
Rob LaZebnik . . . . .Co-Executive Producer
Chuck Tatham . . . . .Co-Executive Producer
Ted Wass . . . . .Director
Terri Minsky . . . . .Creator
Dan Cohen . . . . .Consulting Producer
F.J. Pratt . . . . .Consulting Producer
J.J. Wall . . . . .Consulting Producer
Claudia Lonow . . . . .Consulting Producer
Justin Adler . . . . .Supervising Producer
Cynthia Greenburg . . . . .Supervising Producer
Trevor Kirschner . . . . .Co-Producer
Dionne Kirschner . . . . .Line Producer/UPM
Mike Dieffenbach . . . . .Story Editor
Earl Davis . . . . .Staff Writer
Julie Mossberg . . . . .Casting Director
Jill Anthony . . . . .Casting Director

***LIFE AS WE KNOW IT (ABC/60 mins.)**
555 Brooksbank Ave., Bldg. 9, Ste. 240
North Vancouver, BC V7J 3S5 Canada
PHONE 604-983-5577
FAX 604-983-5587
PRODUCTION COMPANY Touchstone Television

Jeff Judah . . . . .Executive Producer/Co-Creator
Gabe Sachs . . . . .Executive Producer/Co-Creator
Stu Bloomberg . . . . .Executive Producer
Allison Adler . . . . .Co-Executive Producer
Michael Engler . . . . .Co-Executive Producer
Donald Todd . . . . .Co-Executive Producer
Joel Madison . . . . .Consulting Producer
Richard Heus . . . . .Producer
Adam Horowitz . . . . .Producer
Eddy Kitsis . . . . .Producer
Melissa Carter . . . . .Co-Producer
Leila Gurstein . . . . .Staff Writer
Luvh Raake . . . . .Staff Writer
Allison Jones . . . . .Casting Director (Los Angeles)
Coreen Mayrs . . . . .Casting Director (Vancouver)

***LISTEN UP (CBS/30 mins.)**
c/o Regency Television
10201 W. Pico Blvd., Trailer 795
Los Angeles, CA 90035
PHONE 310-369-3355
FAX 310-969-0361
PRODUCTION COMPANY CBS Productions

Jeff Martin . . . . .Executive Producer/Creator/Showrunner
Lindy DeKoven . . . . .Executive Producer
David Litt . . . . .Co-Exective Producer
Daphne Pollon . . . . .Co-Executive Producer
Dan O'Keefe . . . . .Consulting Producer
Dan Kopelman . . . . .Supervising Producer
Linda Figueiredo . . . . .Co-Producer
Kenya Barris . . . . .Executive Story Editor
Leslie Litt . . . . .Casting Director

LITTLE BEAR (Nickelodeon/30 mins.)
42 Pardee Ave.
Toronto, ON M6K 3H5 Canada
PHONE .416-535-0935
WEB SITE .www.nelvana.com
PRODUCTION COMPANY Nelvana Entertainment/A Corus Entertainment Company
COMMENTS Animated

Maurice Sendak .Executive Producer/Creator
John B. Carls .Executive Producer
Scott Dyer .Executive Producer
Ted Bastien .Director
Patricia Burns .Supervising Producer

***LOST (ABC/60 mins.)**
c/o Touchstone Television
3800 W. Alameda Ave.
Burbank, CA 91505
PHONE .818-560-7223
PRODUCTION COMPANIES Bad Robot Productions - Touchstone Television

J.J. Abrams .Executive Producer/Co-Creator
Damon Lindelof .Executive Producer/Co-Creator
Bryan Burk .Executive Producer
David Fury .Co-Executive Producer
Jennifer M. Johnson .Consulting Producer
Lynne E. Litt .Consulting Producer
Javier Grillo-Marxuach .Supervising Producer
Christian Taylor .Supervising Producer
Sarah Caplan .Producer
Paul Dini .Story Editor
Monica Macer .Staff Writer
April Webster .Casting Director

MAD TV (Fox/60 mins.)
c/o Hollywood Center Studios
1040 N. Las Palmas, Bldg. 2
Hollywood, CA 90038
PHONE .323-860-8999
FAX .323-860-8997
EMAIL .info@madtv.com
WEB SITE .www.madtv.com
PRODUCTION COMPANY Girl Group Company

Dick Blasucci .Executive Producer
Quincy Jones .Executive Producer
David Salzman .Executive Producer
Lauren Dombrowski .Co-Executive Producer
Steven Haft .Co-Executive Producer
Scott King .Co-Executive Producer
Bryan Adams .Supervising Producer
Steven Cragg .Supervising Producer
Michael Hitchcock .Supervising Producer
Chris Cluess .Producer
Jennifer Joyce .Producer
Bruce McCoy .Producer
Scott Sites .Producer
Maiya Williams .Producer
John Crane .Co-Producer
Jim Wise .Co-Producer

MALCOLM IN THE MIDDLE (Fox/30 mins.)
c/o CBS Radford
4024 Radford Ave., Bungalow 19
Studio City, CA 91604
PHONE .818-655-5562
COMMENTS Writers' office: 4024 Radford Ave., Norvet Bldg., Ste. 402, Studio City, CA 91604

Linwood Boomer .Executive Producer/Creator/Showrunner
Matthew Carlson .Co-Executive Producer
Michael Glouberman .Co-Executive Producer
Eric Kaplan .Co-Executive Producer
Jay Kogen .Co-Executive Producer
Gary Murphy .Co-Executive Producer
Alex Reid .Co-Executive Producer
Rob Ulin .Co-Executive Producer
David Sacks .Consulting Producer
Neil Thompson .Consulting Producer
Jen Celotta .Supervising Producer
Jimmy Simons .Producer/UPM
Andy Bobrow .Staff Writer
Geraldine Leader .Casting Director

***MEDICAL INVESTIGATION (NBC/60 mins.)**
5555 Melrose Ave., Bungalow 1
Los Angeles, CA 90038
PHONE .323-956-1400
FAX .323-862-1330
PRODUCTION COMPANIES Landscape Pictures - Paramount Television Production

Larry Andries .Executive Producer/Showrunner
Marc Buckland .Executive Producer
Bob Cooper .Executive Producer
Scott Vila .Executive Producer
Jim Hart .Co-Executive Producer
Jason Horwitch .Co-Executive Producer/Creator
Mark Israel .Co-Executive Producer
Barry Schkolnick .Co-Executive Producer
Dan Arkin .Supervising Producer
Sharon Bialy .Casting Director
Sherry L. Thomas .Casting Director

***MEDIUM (NBC/60 mins.)**
1600 Rosecrans Ave., Bldg. 2A, 3rd Fl.
Manhattan Beach, CA 90266
PHONE .310-727-2121
FAX .310-727-2122
PRODUCTION COMPANIES Grammnet Productions - Paramount Television Production
COMMENTS Midseason

Glenn Gordon Caron .Executive Producer
Kelsey Grammer .Executive Producer
Steve Stark .Executive Producer
Rene Echevarria .Executive Producer
Ronald L. Schwary .Executive Producer
Michael Angeli .Co-Executive Producer
Moira Kirland .Supervising Producer
Chris Dingess .Co-Producer
Meg Liberman .Casting Director

MEGAS XLR (Cartoon Network/30 mins.)
c/o Cartoon Network
300 N. Third St.
Burbank, CA 91502
PHONE 818-729-4000
PRODUCTION COMPANY Cartoon Network
COMMENTS Animated

Jody Schaeffer ....Executive Producer/Creator
George Krstic ....Executive Producer/Creator
Chris Prynoski ....Supervising Director
Alian Matz ....Head Writer
Kelly Crews ....Line Producer
Kelsey Mann ....Storyboard
Edward Artinian ....Art Director
Jack Monaco ....Staff Writer

***THE MEN'S ROOM (NBC/30 mins.)**
c/o NBC Studios
4024 Radford Ave., Scoring Bldg., 2nd Fl.
Burbank, CA 91604
PHONE 818-655-5807
FAX 818-655-8408

Danny Zuker ....Executive Producer
Wil Calhoun ....Co-Executive Producer
David Walpert ....Consulting Producer
Franco E. Bario ....Supervising Producer
Paul Corrigan ....Supervising Producer
Brad Walsh ....Supervising Producer
Joe Port ....Producer
Joe Wiseman ....Producer
Rich Dahm ....Story Editor
Kourtney Kang ....Story Editor
Zack Rosenblatt ....Story Editor
Michele Hirsch ....Production Coordinator
Joy Dickson ....Casting Director
Nicole Arbusto ....Casting Director

***METHOD & RED (Fox/30 mins.)**
10201 W. Pico Blvd., Bldg. 99, Ste. 430
Los Angeles, CA 90035
PHONE 310-369-5527
FAX 310-969-1639
PRODUCTION COMPANIES Regency Enterprises - Twentieth Century Fox Television

Will Gluck ....Executive Producer
Method Man ....Executive Producer
Kell Cahoon ....Executive Producer/Showrunner
Ira Ungerleider ....Co-Executive Producer
James Ellis ....Producer
Shauna Garr ....Producer
Robert Lloyd ....Producer
Jeff Melman ....Producer
Redman ....Producer
Robert Lewis ....Line Producer
Liz Marks ....Casting Director

MISSING (Lifetime/60 mins.)
c/o Missing Productions
629 Eastern Ave., Bldg. A, Ste. 202
Toronto, ON M4M 1E4 Canada
PHONE 416-406-2654
FAX 416-406-1982
PRODUCTION COMPANY Lions Gate Entertainment

William Laurin ....Executive Producer/Creator
Glenn Davis ....Executive Producer/Creator
Debra Martin Chase ....Executive Producer
Vivica A. Fox ....Co-Executive Producer
Shawn Dawson ....Casting Director (US)
Stephanie Gorin ....Casting Director (Canada)

MONK (USA/60 mins.)
846 N. Cahuenga Blvd.
Los Angeles, CA 90038
PHONE 323-993-5304
FAX 323-993-5395
PRODUCTION COMPANY O.C.P.I. Productions, Inc.

David Hoberman ....Executive Producer
Andy Breckman ....Executive Producer/Writer
Tony Shalhoub ....Executive Producer
Randy Zisk ....Executive Producer/Director
Fern Field ....Co-Executive Producer
Anthony Santa Croce ....Producer/UPM
Tom Sharpling ....Supervising Producer
David Breckman ....Producer
Scott Collins ....Associate Producer
Daniel Dratch ....Executive Story Editor
Hy Conrad ....Story Editor
Joe Toplyn ....Story Editor
Sheridan Thayer ....Production Supervisor
Amy Britt ....Casting Director
Anya Colloff ....Casting Director

***THE MOUNTAIN (WB/60 mins.)**
4210 Phillips Ave.
Burnaby, BC V5A 2X2 Canada
PHONE 604-420-1341/818-977-4411
FAX 604-420-0816
PRODUCTION COMPANIES Warner Bros. Television Production - Wonderland Sound and Vision

McG ....Executive Producer
Shaun Cassidy ....Executive Producer/Showrunner
Stephanie Savage ....Executive Producer/Co-Creator
Gina Matthews ....Consulting Producer/Co-Creator
Grant Scharbo ....Consulting Producer/Co-Creator
Laurie Arent ....Co-Producer
JP Finn ....Producer
Joe Lazarov ....Producer
Jesse Stern ....Story Editor
Karen Barna ....Staff Writer

***MY LIFE AS A TEENAGE ROBOT (Nickelodeon/30 mins.)**
231 W. Olive Ave.
Burbank, CA 91502
PHONE 818-736-3606
FAX 818-736-3449
EMAIL ....hey@frederator.kz
WEB SITE ....www.frederator.kz
PRODUCTION COMPANIES Frederator Studios - Nickelodeon Animation Studios
COMMENTS Animated

Rob Renzetti ....Creator/Executive Producer
Fred Seibert ....Executive Producer
Debby Hindman ....Line Producer
Scott Peterson ....Story Editor
Margaret Tang ....Casting Director

MY WIFE AND KIDS (ABC/30 mins.)
500 S. Buena Vista St., Stage 7, 5th Fl.
Burbank, CA 91521
PHONE 818-560-6614
FAX 818-560-3426
PRODUCTION COMPANIES Touchstone Television - Wayans Brothers Entertainment

Damon Wayans ....Executive Producer
Don Reo ....Executive Producer
David Himelfarb ....Executive Producer
Dean Lorey ....Executive Producer
Kevin Rooney ....Co-Executive Producer
Jim Vallely ....Co-Executive Producer
Kim Wayans ....Producer
Craig Wayans ....Producer
Susan Crank ....Producer/UPM
Mark Nasser ....Co-Producer
Annice Parker ....Co-Producer
Rodney Barnes ....Executive Story Editor
Damien Wayans ....Executive Story Editor
Valencia Parker ....Staff Writer
Damon Wayans Jr. ....Staff Writer
Kevin Scott ....Casting Director
Jill Uyeda ....Casting Director

NAVY N.C.I.S. (CBS/60 mins.)
c/o Paramount Television Production
1438 N. Gower St., Box 25
Hollywood, CA 90028
PHONE 323-468-4500
FAX 323-468-4599
PRODUCTION COMPANIES Belisarius Productions - Paramount Television Production

Donald P. Bellisario ....Executive Producer
Chas. Floyd Johnson ....Co-Executive Producer
Gil Grant ....Co-Executive Producer
Mark Horowitz ....Co-Executive Producer
Roger Director ....Supervising Producer
Frank Cardea ....Consulting Producer
Juan Carlos Coto ....Consulting Producer
George Schenck ....Consulting Producer
David Bellisario ....Producer
Avery Drewe ....Producer
John C. Kelley ....Producer
Frank Military ....Producer
Mark R. Schilz ....Producer
Julie Watson ....Coordinating Producer
Josh Rexon ....Associate Producer
Susan Bluestein ....Casting Director

NIP/TUCK (FX/60 mins.)
5555 Melrose Ave., Modular Bldg., 1st Fl.
Los Angeles, CA 90038
PHONE 323-956-2400
PRODUCTION COMPANY The Shephard/Robin Company

Ryan Murphy ....Executive Producer/Creator
Greer Shephard ....Executive Producer
Michael Robin ....Executive Producer

***NORTH SHORE (Fox/60 mins.)**
1800 Stewart St.
Santa Monica, CA 90404
PHONE 310-579-5251/808-733-4141
FAX 310-579-5307
PRODUCTION COMPANY Twentieth Century Fox Television

Chris Brancato ....Executive Producer/Showrunner
Bert Salke ....Executive Producer/Showrunner
Gretchen Berg ....Co-Executive Producer
Ken Biller ....Co-Executive Producer
Peter Elkoff ....Co-Executive Producer/Creator
Aaron Harberts ....Co-Executive Producer
Kim Costello ....Consulting Producer
Kevin Falls ....Consulting Producer
Dana Baratta ....Supervising Producer
Liz Heldens ....Producer
Matt McGuinness ....Story Editor
Amy Berg ....Staff Writer
Andrew Colville ....Staff Writer
Colleen McGuinness ....Staff Writer
Barbara Stordahl ....Casting Director
Angela Terry ....Casting Director

NYPD BLUE (ABC/60 mins.)
10201 W. Pico Blvd., Bldg. 1
Los Angeles, CA 90035
PHONE 310-369-2400/310-369-0581
FAX 310-369-3236
EMAIL ....yemaya.royce@bochcomedia.com
PRODUCTION COMPANY Steven Bochco Productions

Steven Bochco ....Executive Producer
Mark Tinker ....Executive Producer
Bill Clark ....Executive Producer
Matt Olmstead ....Executive Producer
Nicholas Wootton ....Executive Producer
Bill Finkelstein ....Executive Producer
Bob Doherty ....Co-Executive Producer/UPM
Caroline James ....VP, Production
Tom Szentgyorgyi ....Supervising Producer
Jesse Bochco ....Producer
Keith Eisner ....Producer
John Hyams ....Producer
Joanne McCool ....Producer
Maureen Milligan ....Co-Producer
Greg Plageman ....Co-Producer
Joyce Davis ....Associate Coordinating Producer
David Glazier ....Associate Producer
Scott Genkinger ....Casting Director
Junie Lowry Johnson ....Casting Director
Holly Baker-Kreiswirth ....Assistant to M. Tinker
Michelle Debbaudt ....Assistant to S. Bochco
Bridgid Scofield ....Assistant to B. Clark
Sonny Postiglione ....Assistant to Producers
Jan Payne ....Assistant to Writers

THE O.C. (Fox/60 mins.)
1600 Rosecrans Ave., Bldg. 6-A, 2nd Fl.
Manhattan Beach, CA 90266
PHONE .310-727-2838
FAX .310-727-2839
PRODUCTION COMPANIES Hypnotic - Warner Bros. Television Production - Wonderland Sound and Vision

McG .Executive Producer
Josh Schwartz .Executive Producer/Creator
Robert DeLaurentis .Executive Producer/Showrunner
David Bartis .Executive Producer
Doug Liman .Executive Producer
Allan Heinberg .Co-Executive Producer
Stephanie Savage .Co-Executive Producer
Ian Toynton .Supervising Producer
John Stephens .Producer
Loucas George .Line Producer
Drew Greenberg .Co-Producer
J.J. Philbin .Story Editor
Patrick Rush .Casting Director

***THE OFFICE (NBC/30 mins.)**
c/o Reveille, LLC
100 Universal City Plaza, Bungalow 5180/5170
Universal City, CA 91608
PHONE .818-733-1218
FAX .818-733-3303
PRODUCTION COMPANY Reveille, LLC

Greg Daniels .Executive Producer
Ricky Gervais .Executive Producer
Howard Klein .Executive Producer
Stephen Merchant .Executive Producer
Ben Silverman .Executive Producer

ONE LIFE TO LIVE (ABC/60 mins.)
56 W. 66th St.
New York, NY 10023
PHONE .212-456-3582
FAX .212-456-2755
PRODUCTION COMPANY ABC Daytime

Frank Valentini .Executive Producer
Suzanne Flynn .Producer
John Tumino .Producer
Shelley Honigbaum .Associate Producer
Josh Griffith .Head Writer
Michael Malone .Head Writer
Shelly Altman .Associate Head Writer
Richard Backus .Associate Head Writer
Ron Carlivati .Associate Head Writer
Anna Teresa Cassio .Associate Head Writer
Michelle Poteet Lisanti .Writer
Leslie Nipkow .Writer
Ginger Redmon .Script Writer
David Cherrill .Script Editor
Julie Madison .Casting Director

ONE ON ONE (UPN/30 mins.)
c/o Paramount Television Production
5555 Melrose Ave., Mae West Bldg., Ste. 10
Los Angeles, CA 90038
PHONE .323-956-8900
FAX .323-862-2223
PRODUCTION COMPANIES Daddy's Girl Production - Paramount Television Production

Eunetta T. Boone .Executive Producer

ONE TREE HILL (WB/60 mins.)
1223 N. 23rd St.
Wilmington, NC 28405
PHONE .910-343-3770/818-954-1883
FAX .910-343-3777/818-954-3314
PRODUCTION COMPANIES Tollin/Robbins Productions - Warner Bros. Television Production
COMMENTS Writers' office: 4000 Warner Blvd., Bldg. 260, Burbank, CA 91522

Joe Davola .Executive Producer
Mark Perry .Executive Producer/Showrunner
Brian Robbins .Executive Producer
Mark Schwahn .Executive Producer/Creator
Mike Tollin .Executive Producer
Jennifer Cecil .Supervising Producer
Greg Prange .Producer
R. Lee Fleming Jr. .Co-Producer
David Hartley .Co-Producer/UPM
Chad Fiveash .Executive Story Editor
James Stoteraux .Executive Story Editor
Terrence Coli .Staff Writer
Stacy Rukeyser .Staff Writer
Anna Lotto .Writers' Assistant
Craig Fincannon .Casting Director
Lisa Mae Fincannon .Casting Director
Susan Glickman .Casting Director
Alex Wald .Casting Director

PASSIONS (NBC/60 mins.)
4024 Radford Ave.
Studio City, CA 91604
PHONE .818-655-5454
FAX .818-655-8375
WEB SITE .www.nbc.com/passions
PRODUCTION COMPANY Outpost Farms, Inc.

James E. Reilly .Creator/Head Writer/Consulting Producer
Lisa de Cazotte .Executive Producer
Richard Schilling .Supervising Producer
Mary-Kelly Weir .Producer
Jeanne Haney .Coordinating Producer
Denise Mark .Associate Producer
Eva Demirjian .Publicity
Jackie Briskey .Casting Director (Principals)
Don Phillip Smith .Casting Director (Under Fives/Extras)

THE POWERPUFF GIRLS (Cartoon Network/30 mins.)
300 N. Third St.
Burbank, CA 91502
PHONE .818-729-4000
FAX .818-729-4114
COMMENTS Animated

Craig McCracken .Executive Producer/Creator
Lauren Faust .Supervising Director
Bryan Andrews .Art Director
Chris Savino .Producer
Shareena Carlson .Line Producer
Mike Kim .Storyboard/Writer
Chris Reccardi .Storyboard/Writer
Amy Rogers .Outline Editor
Collette Sunderman .Casting Director

QUEER AS FOLK (Showtime/60 mins.)
c/o Dufferin Gate Productions
20 Butterick Rd.
Toronto, ON M8W 3Z8 Canada
PHONE .416-255-4811/416-255-2260
FAX .416-255-7488
PRODUCTION COMPANY QAF IV Productions Ltd.

Ron Cowen .Executive Producer/Showrunner
Daniel Lipman .Executive Producer/Showrunner
Tony Jonas .Executive Producer
Sheila Hockin .Producer
Del Shores .Consulting Producer
Michael MacLennan .Supervising Producer
Brad Fraser .Co-Producer
Adam Newman .Coordinating Producer
Shawn Postoff .Executive Story Editor
Ross Clydesdale .Casting Director

***THE QUEER EYE FOR THE STRAIGHT GUY (Bravo/60 mins.)**
c/o Scout Productions
119 Braintree St.
Boston, MA 02134
PHONE .617-782-7722/212-581-8200
FAX .617-782-7799/212-581-8310
WEB SITE .www.bravotv.com
PRODUCTION COMPANY Scout Productions

Dorothy Aufiero .Executive Producer
Christian Barcellos .Executive Producer
Frances Berwick .Executive Producer
David Collins .Executive Producer/Creator
Amy Introcaso-Davis .Executive Producer, Bravo
Michael Williams .Executive Producer
Linda Lea .Co-Executive Producer/Showrunner
David Metzler .Co-Executive Producer

***QUINTUPLETS (Fox/30 mins.)**
c/o Twentieth Century Fox Television
10201 W. Pico Blvd., Trailer 732
Los Angeles, CA 90035
PHONE .310-369-5444
FAX .310-969-3248
PRODUCTION COMPANIES Imagine Television - Twentieth Century Fox Television

Mark Reisman .Executive Producer/Creator
Brian Grazer .Executive Producer
David Nevins .Executive Producer
Michael Borkow .Consulting Producer
Stephen Engel .Consulting Producer
Jim Bernstein .Supervising Producer
Stephen Lloyd .Supervising Producer
Michael Shipley .Supervising Producer
Jesse Ward .Line Producer/UPM
Jennifer Fisher .Producer
Don Signar .Producer
Gloria Calderon Kellett .Staff Writer
Rick Millikan .Casting Director

***REAL TIME WITH BILL MAHER (HBO/60 mins.)**
7800 Beverly Blvd.
Los Angeles, CA 90036
PHONE .323-575-7700
EMAIL .tickets@realtimehbo.com
WEB SITE .www.hbo.com
PRODUCTION COMPANY Brad Grey TV

Brad Grey .Executive Producer
Marc Gurvitz .Executive Producer
Scott Carter .Executive Producer
Bill Maher .Executive Producer
Sheila Griffiths .Executive Producer
Dean Johnson .Supervising Producer
Billy Martin .Producer

REBA (WB/30 mins.)
10201 W. Pico Blvd., Bldg. 38, Rm. 125
Los Angeles, CA 90035
PHONE .310-369-7322
FAX .310-969-3323
PRODUCTION COMPANIES Acme Productions - Twentieth Century Fox Television

Kevin Abbott .Executive Producer/Showrunner
Matt Berry .Executive Producer
Michael Hanel .Executive Producer
Mindy Schultheis .Executive Producer
Don Beck .Co-Executive Producer
Pat Bullard .Co-Executive Producer
Patti Carr .Co-Executive Producer
Chris Case .Co-Executive Producer
Reba McEntire .Co-Executive Producer
Lara Runnels .Co-Executive Producer
Jason Shubb .Producer
Sabrina Wind .Co-Producer
Steve Stajich .Story Editor
Chris Atwood .Staff Writer
Greg Orson .Casting Director

***RELATED BY FAMILY (Fox/30 mins.)**
c/o Paramount Network Television
5555 Melrose Ave., Wilder Bldg., 2nd Fl.
Los Angeles, CA 90038
PHONE .323-956-1800
FAX .323-862-4301
PRODUCTION COMPANY Paramount Television Production
COMMENTS Garfield Grove Productions

Victor Fresco .Executive Producer/Creator
Maggie Bandur .Co-Executive Producer
Michael Ross .Co-Executive Producer
Michael Teverbaugh .Co-Executive Producer
Miriam Trogdon .Co-Executive Producer
Adam Chase .Consulting Producer
Marc Solakian .Producer
John Hoberg .Story Editor
Kat Likkel .Story Editor
John Westbrook .Story Editor
Anand Chulani .Staff Writer

***THE RESTAURANT (NBC/60 mins.)**
c/o Mark Burnett Productions
640 N. Sepulveda Blvd.
Los Angeles, CA 90049
PHONE .310-903-5400
PRODUCTION COMPANIES Mark Burnett Productions - Reveille, LLC

Mark Burnett .Executive Producer
Ben Silverman .Executive Producer
Robert Riesenberg .Executive Producer
Jamie Bruce .Executive Producer
Henrietta Conrad .Executive Producer
Sebastian Scott .Executive Producer

***REVELATIONS (NBC/60 mins.)**
175 Queen's Quay, Ste. 400
Toronto, ON M5A 1B6 Canada
PHONE .416-368-4999
FAX .416-368-6555
PRODUCTION COMPANY Pariah

Gavin Polone .Executive Producer
David Seltzer .Executive Producer/Creator

It is illegal to copy any part of this book

***RODNEY (ABC/30 mins.)**
c/o Touchstone Television
4024 Radford Ave., Bungalow 8
Studio City, CA 91604
PHONE .818-655-5906
FAX .818-655-8451
PRODUCTION COMPANY Touchstone Television

David Himelfarb .Executive Producer
Ric Swartzlander .Executive Producer
Gayle Abrams .Co-Executive Producer
Bob Myer .Consulting Producer
Phil Baker .Supervising Producer
Drew Vaupen .Supervising Producer
Jason Fisher .Producer/UPM
Robert Berlinger .Producer/Director
Mark Gross .Producer
Steve Joe .Producer
Greg Schaffer .Producer
Maisha Closson .Co-Producer
Bonnie Zane .Casting Director

ROMEO! (Nickelodeon/30 mins.)
8351 Ontario St.
Vancouver, BC V5X 3E8 Canada
PHONE .604-322-1262
FAX .604-322-1135
PRODUCTION COMPANIES Pieces Productions, Inc. - The Tom Lynch Company

Tom Lynch .Executive Producer
Master P .Executive Producer
Fracaswell Hyman .Executive Producer

SAMURAI JACK (Cartoon Network/30 mins.)
300 N. Third St.
Burbank, CA 91502
PHONE .818-729-4000
FAX .818-729-4086
WEB SITE .www.cartoonnetwork.com
COMMENTS Animated

Genndy Tartakovsky .Producer/Creator
Todd Garfield .Line Producer
Dan Krall .Art Director
Scott Wills .Art Director
Collette Sunderman .Casting Director

SATURDAY NIGHT LIVE (NBC/90 mins.)
30 Rockefeller Plaza, 17th Fl.
New York, NY 10112
PHONE .212-664-4511
FAX .212-664-2485
PRODUCTION COMPANY Broadway Video (NY)

Lorne Michaels .Executive Producer
Ken Aymong .Supervising Producer
Steve Higgins .Producer
Marci Klein .Producer
Mike Shoemaker .Producer
Tina Fey .Head Writer
Dennis McNicholas .Head Writer

***SAVAGES (ABC/30 mins.)**
100 Universal City Plaza, Bldg. 3213
Universal City, CA 91608
PHONE .818-733-1717
FAX .818-733-3359
PRODUCTION COMPANY Icon Productions, Inc.

Bruce Davey .Executive Producer
Mel Gibson .Executive Producer
Mike Scully .Executive Producer
Julie Thacker-Scully .Executive Producer
Andy Gordon .Co-Executive Producer
Brian Scully .Co-Executive Producer
Donick Cary .Consulting Producer
Tom Gammill .Consulting Producer
George Meyer .Consulting Producer
Max Pross .Consulting Producer
Coral Hawthorne .Producer/UPM
Nancy Cotton .Producer
Lissa Levin .Producer
Claudia Hitchcock .Associate Producer
Steve Molaro .Story Editor
Barbie Block .Casting Director
Sally Steiner .Casting Director

SCRUBS (NBC/30 mins.)
c/o Touchstone Television
500 S. Buena Vista St.
Burbank, CA 91521
PHONE .818-623-1880
FAX .818-623-2552
PRODUCTION COMPANY Touchstone Television

Bill Lawrence .Executive Producer/Creator/Showrunner
Tim Hobert .Co-Executive Producer
Matt Tarses .Co-Executive Producer
Eric Weinberg .Co-Executive Producer
Gabrielle Allan .Supervising Producer
Garrett Donovan .Supervising Producer
Neil Goldman .Supervising Producer
Mike Schwartz .Co-Producer
Randall Winston .Line Producer
Janae Bakken .Executive Story Editor
Deb Fordham .Executive Story Editor
Mark Stegemann .Executive Story Editor
Angela Nissel .Story Editor
Brett Benner .Casting Director
Debby Romano .Casting Director

***SECOND TIME AROUND (UPN/30 mins.)**
c/o Paramount Network Television
5555 Melrose Ave., Fleischer Brothers Bldg.
Los Angeles, CA 90038
PHONE .323-956-4100
FAX .323-862-2030
PRODUCTION COMPANY Paramount Television Production

Claude Brooks .Executive Producer
Ralph Farquhar .Executive Producer
Michelle Listenbee Brown .Co-Executive Producer
Efrem Seeger .Consulting Producer
Kenny Smith .Supervising Producer
Nancy Sprows .Producer
Eileen McKnight .Casting Director

***SHACKING UP (WB/30 mins.)**
10202 W. Washington Blvd., Jimmy Stewart Bldg., Ste. 26
Culver City, CA 90232
PHONE .310-244-4242
PRODUCTION COMPANY Regency Enterprises
COMMENTS Midseason

Jamie Kennedy .Executive Producer
Michael Longworthy .Executive Producer
David Garrett .Co-Executive Producer
Jason Ward .Co-Executive Producer

THE SHIELD (FX/60 mins.)
4151 Prospect Ave., Silverlake Bldg.
Los Angeles, CA 90027
PHONE .323-671-4161
FAX .323-671-5511
PRODUCTION COMPANIES Fox Television Studios - Sony Pictures Television

Shawn Ryan .Executive Producer/Creator
Scott Brazil .Executive Producer/Director
Charles H. Eglee .Co-Executive Producer
Glen Mazzara .Co-Executive Producer
Scott Rosenbaum .Supervising Producer
Kurt Sutter .Supervising Producer
Michael Chiklis .Producer
Adam E. Fierro .Producer
Liz Craft .Co-Producer
Sarah Fain .Co-Producer

SIGNIFICANT OTHERS (Bravo/30 mins.)
c/o NBC Studios
330 Bob Hope Dr., Ste C-227
Burbank, CA 91523
PHONE .818-840-7671
FAX .818-840-7681

Peter Tortorici .Executive Producer
Robert Roy Thomas .Executive Producer
Michael Pendell .Producer
Jordana Arkin .Co-Producer
Francene Selkirk-Ackerman .Casting Director

THE SIMPSONS (Fox/30 mins.)
10201 W. Pico Blvd.
Los Angeles, CA 90035
PHONE .310-369-3959
FAX .310-369-3852
PRODUCTION COMPANIES DPS Film Roman, Inc. - Gracie Films - Twentieth Century Fox Television
COMMENTS Animated

James L. Brooks .Executive Producer
Matt Groening .Executive Producer
Al Jean .Executive Producer/Showrunner
Stewart Burns .Co-Executive Producer
Kevin Curran .Co-Executive Producer
John Frink .Co-Executive Producer
Dana Gould .Co-Executive Producer
Dan Greaney .Co-Executive Producer
Tim Long .Co-Executive Producer
Ian Maxtone-Graham .Co-Executive Producer
Carolyn Omine .Co-Executive Producer
Don Payne .Co-Executive Producer
Michael Price .Co-Executive Producer
Matt Selman .Co-Executive Producer
Larina Adamson .Supervising Producer
Marc Wilmore .Supervising Producer
Joel Cohen .Producer
Tom Gammill .Producer
Ron Hauge .Producer
George Meyer .Producer
David Mirkin .Producer
Bonnie Pietila .Producer/Casting Consultant
Max Pross .Producer
Richard Raynis .Producer
Mike Reiss .Producer
Richard Sakai .Producer
Denise Sirkot .Producer
Matt Warburton .Co-Producer
Richard Chung .Animation Co-Producer
Dominique Braud .Associate Producer
Felicia Nalivansky .Associate Producer
Danny Chun .Story Editor

SIX FEET UNDER (HBO/60 mins.)
1438 N. Gower St., Box 32
Hollywood, CA 90028
PHONE .323-993-7070
FAX .323-993-7071
PRODUCTION COMPANY Six Feet Productions, Inc.

Alan Ball .Executive Producer/Showrunner/Creator
Robert Greenblatt .Executive Producer
David Janollari .Executive Producer
Bruce Eric Kaplan .Executive Producer
Alan Poul .Executive Producer
Scott Buck .Co-Executive Producer
Rick Cleveland .Co-Executive Producer
Jill Soloway .Supervising Producer
Robert Del Valle .Producer
Lori Jo Nemhauser .Producer
Kate Robin .Producer
Craig Wright .Executive Story Editor
Nancy Oliver .Story Editor
Libby Goldstein .Casting Director
Junie Lowry Johnson .Casting Director

SMALLVILLE (WB/60 mins.)
4000 Warner Blvd., Bldg. 160, Ste. 200
Burbank, CA 91522
PHONE .818-977-4050
FAX .818-977-2404
PRODUCTION COMPANIES Smallville Studios, Inc. - Tollin/Robbins Productions - Warner Bros. Television Production

Alfred Gough .Executive Producer/Showrunner/Co-Creator
Miles Millar .Executive Producer/Showrunner/Co-Creator
Ken Horton .Executive Producer
Greg Beeman .Executive Producer
Brian Robbins .Executive Producer
Mike Tollin .Executive Producer
Joe Davola .Executive Producer
Jeph Loeb .Consulting Producer
Steven DeKnight .Supervising Producer
Bob Hargrove .Producer
Brian Peterson .Producer
Todd Slavkin .Producer
Kelly Souders .Producer
Darren Swimmer .Producer
Tim Scanlan .Co-Producer
Luke Schelhaas .Co-Producer
Holly Harold .Staff Writer
Dee Dee Bradley .Casting Director (US)
Coreen Mayrs .Casting Director (Canada)

THE SOPRANOS (HBO/60 mins.)
c/o Silvercup Studios
42-22 22nd St., 3rd Fl.
Long Island City, NY 11101
PHONE .212-512-1000
FAX .212-512-1053
PRODUCTION COMPANY HBO Original Programming

David Chase .Executive Producer/Creator
Ilene Landress .Co-Executive Producer

SOUTH PARK (Comedy Central/30 mins.)
c/o Comedy Central
2049 Century Park East, Ste. 4170
Los Angeles, CA 90067
PHONE .310-407-4700
FAX .310-407-4797
WEB SITE www.southparkstudios.com
PRODUCTION COMPANY Comedy Central
COMMENTS Animated

Trey Parker .Executive Producer/Creator
Matt Stone .Executive Producer/Creator
Anne Garefino .Executive Producer
Jennifer Howell .Supervising Producer
Frank Agnone .Producer

***SPELLBOUND (Fox/30 mins.)**
c/o Warner Bros. Television
4000 Warner Blvd.
Burbank, CA 91522
PHONE .818-954-6000
PRODUCTION COMPANY Warner Bros. Television Production

Rob Greenberg .Executive Producer/Creator
Suzanne Martin .Executive Producer/Creator

STARGATE SG-1 (SCI FI/60 mins.)
2400 Boundary Rd.
Burnaby, BC V5M 3Z3 Canada
PHONE .604-292-8500
FAX .604-292-8550
PRODUCTION COMPANY Kawoosh! Productions VIII, Inc.

Robert Cooper .Executive Producer
Brad Wright .Executive Producer
Michael Greenburg .Executive Producer
Richard Dean Anderson .Executive Producer
Joseph Mallozzi .Executive Producer
Paul Mullie .Executive Producer
N. John Smith .Co-Executive Producer
Peter DeLuise .Supervising Producer
Damian Kindler .Supervising Producer
Andy Mikita .Co-Producer
Aikins-Cossey .Casting Director (Canada)
Paul Weber .Casting Director (US)

STILL STANDING (CBS/30 mins.)
4024 Radford Ave., Mack Sennett Bldg.
Studio City, CA 91604
PHONE .818-655-5504
FAX .818-655-8492
PRODUCTION COMPANIES CBS Productions - Twentieth Century Fox Television

Diane M. Burroughs .Executive Producer/Showrunner/Co-Creator
Joey Gutierrez .Executive Producer/Showrunner/Co-Creator
Tim Doyle .Executive Producer
Richard J. Gurman .Co-Executive Producer
Regina Stewart .Co-Executive Producer
Ben Wexler .Co-Executive Producer
Ed Yeager .Co-Executive Producer
Ellen Byron .Consulting Producer
Lissa Kapstrom .Consulting Producer
Randy Cordray .Producer/UPM
Adam Goldberg .Executive Story Editor
Carla Filisha .Story Editor
Jayne Hamil .Story Editor
Deborah Barylski .Casting Director

STRONG MEDICINE (Lifetime/60 mins.)
c/o Columbia TriStar Television
10202 W. Washington Blvd.
Culver City, CA 90232
PHONE .310-482-3200
FAX .310-313-6699
WEB SITE www.lifetimetv.com
PRODUCTION COMPANY Sony Pictures Television

Whoopi Goldberg .Executive Producer
Tammy Ader .Executive Producer
John Perrin Flynn .Co-Executive Producer
Dianne Messina Stanley .Co-Executive Producer
Jim Stanley .Co-Executive Producer
Jeremy Littman .Consulting Producer
Joe DeOliveira .Producer
Jim Weis .Co-Producer
Laura Wolner .Co-Producer
Tom Leonardis .Associate Producer
Susie Schelling .Associate Producer
Lori Sugar .Casting Director

SUMMERLAND (WB/60 mins.)
5300 Melrose Ave.
Los Angeles, CA 90038
PHONE .323-960-4770
FAX .323-960-4771
PRODUCTION COMPANY Spelling Television, Inc.

Remi Aubuchon .Executive Producer/Showrunner
Aaron Spelling .Executive Producer
Stephen Tolkin .Executive Producer
E. Duke Vincent .Executive Producer
Lori Loughlin .Producer

SURVIVOR (CBS/60 mins.)
c/o Mark Burnett Productions
640 N. Sepulveda Blvd.
Los Angeles, CA 90049
PHONE .310-903-5400
PRODUCTION COMPANY Mark Burnett Productions

Mark Burnett .Executive Producer
Tom Shelly .Co-Executive Producer

TEMPTATION ISLAND INTERNATIONAL (Fox/60 mins.)
10201 W. Pico Blvd., Bldg. 41
Los Angeles, CA 90035
PHONE .310-369-5361
WEB SITE www.fox.com

Gregory Vanger .Executive Producer

THAT 70'S SHOW (Fox/30 mins.)
4024 Radford Ave., Bldg. 1
Studio City, CA 91604
PHONE .818-655-5161
WEB SITE www.that70sshow.com
PRODUCTION COMPANY Carsey-Werner-Mandabach

Marcy Carsey .Executive Producer
Tom Werner .Executive Producer
Caryn Mandabach .Executive Producer
Jackie Filgo .Executive Producer
Jeff Filgo .Executive Producer
Dean Batali .Co-Executive Producer
Rob Des Hotel .Co-Executive Producer
Mark Hudis .Co-Executive Producer
Gregg Mettler .Co-Executive Producer
Dave Schiff .Co-Executive Producer
Philip Stark .Co-Executive Producer
Bryan Moore .Producer
Kristin Newman .Producer
Melanie Patterson .Producer
Chris Peterson .Producer
G. Charles Wright .Casting Director

THAT'S SO RAVEN (Disney Channel/30 mins.)

1040 N. Las Palmas, Bldg. 33, 2nd Fl.
Los Angeles, CA 90038
PHONE .323-860-8989
FAX .323-860-8990
PRODUCTION COMPANY Brookwell McNamara Entertainment, Inc.

David Brookwell .Executive Producer
Sean McNamara .Executive Producer
Dennis Rinsler .Executive Producer
Marc Warren .Executive Producer
Dava Savel .Co-Executive Producer
Patty Gary-Cox .Producer
Pixie Wespiser .Co-Producer
Joey Paul Jensen .Casting Director

THIRD WATCH (NBC/60 mins.)

196 Diamond St., 2nd Fl.
Brooklyn, NY 11222
PHONE .718-609-9616
FAX .718-609-0461
PRODUCTION COMPANIES John Wells Productions - Warner Bros. Television Production

John Wells .Executive Producer
Christopher Chulack .Executive Producer
Ed Bernero .Executive Producer
Brooke Kennedy .Executive Producer
Scott Williams .Co-Executive Producer
John Ridley .Consulting Producer
Janine Sherman Barrois .Producer
Charles S. Carroll .Producer
Kristin Harms .Producer
Siobhan Byrne O'Connor .Producer
Andrew Stearn .Producer
Grant Anderson .Co-Producer
Glenn Kershaw .Co-Producer
Vicki Voltarel .Co-Producer
Charles Murray .Story Editor
Angela Amato Velez .Creative Consultant
Beth Bowling .Casting Director
Kim Miscia .Casting Director

THIS OLD HOUSE (PBS/30 mins.)

c/o This Old House Productions, Inc.
PO Box 130
Concord, MA 01742
PHONE .978-202-3000
FAX .978-202-3058
WEB SITE .www.thisoldhouse.com
COMMENTS Productions include This Old House, Ask This Old House, Find!, Inside This Old House

Bruce Irving .Executive Producer
Russell Morash .Executive Producer/Director, *Find!*

THE TONIGHT SHOW WITH JAY LENO (NBC/60 mins.)

c/o NBC Studios
3000 W. Alameda Ave.
Burbank, CA 91523
PHONE .818-840-4444

Debbie Vickers .Executive Producer
Larry Goitia .Supervising Producer
Patti M. Grant .Supervising Producer
Ellen Brown .Director

*TRADING SPACES (TLC/60 mins.)

c/o Banyan Productions
530 Walnut St., Ste. 276
Philadelphia, PA 19106
PHONE .215-928-1414
FAX .215-928-9944
PRODUCTION COMPANY Banyan Productions

Susan Cohen-Dickler .Executive Producer
Kathy Davidov .Executive Producer
Jan Dickler .Executive Producer
Tom Farrell .Executive Producer
Ray Murray .Executive Producer

TRU CALLING (Fox/60 mins.)

c/o Millenium Canadian Productions, Ltd.
10/210 555 Brooksbank Ave.
North Vancouver, BC V7J 3S5 Canada
PHONE .604-983-5880/310-579-5190
FAX .604-983-5475/310-579-5360
PRODUCTION COMPANIES Original Film - Twentieth Century Fox Television

Marty Adelstein .Executive Producer
Jon Feldman .Executive Producer/Creator/Showrunner
Neal Moritz .Executive Producer
Dawn Parouse .Executive Producer
Doris Egan .Co-Executive Producer
Jane Espenson .Co-Executive Producer
Michael Katleman .Co-Executive Producer
Scott Shepherd .Consulting Producer
Zack Estrin .Supervising Producer
Rich Hatem .Supervising Producer
Robert Doherty .Producer
Kathy Gilroy-Sereda .Line Producer/Production Manager
Karine Rosenthal .Staff Writer
Sue Brouse .Casting Director
Barbara Stordahl .Casting Director
Angela Terry .Casting Director

TWO AND A HALF MEN (CBS/30 mins.)

c/o Warner Bros. Television
4000 Warner Blvd., Bldg 160, Rm. 7002
Burbank, CA 91522
PHONE .818-977-1777
FAX .818-977-3737
PRODUCTION COMPANIES Tannenbaum Company - Warner Bros. Television Production

Chuck Lorre .Executive Producer/Showrunner
Kim Tannenbaum .Executive Producer
Eric Tannenbaum .Executive Producer
Lee Aronsohn .Executive Producer
Don Foster .Co-Executive Producer
Jeff Abugov .Co-Executive Producer
Susan Beavers .Supervising Producer
Eddie Gorodetsky .Supervising Producer
Michael Collier .Producer
Mark Roberts .Co-Producer
Ken Miller .Casting Director
Nikki Valco .Casting Director

***VERONICA MARS (UPN/60 mins.)**
4705 Ruffin Rd., Stages Bldg. 4&5
San Diego, CA 92123
PHONE .858-715-6405/818-752-5471
FAX .858-627-9370/818-754-8848
PRODUCTION COMPANIES Silver Pictures - Warner Bros. Television Production
COMMENTS Writers' office: 5542 Satsuma Ave., North Hollywood, CA 91601

Joel Silver .Executive Producer
Rob Thomas .Executive Producer/Creator
Jennifer Gwartz .Co-Executive Producer
Danielle Stokdyk .Co-Executive Producer
Jed Seidel .Co-Executive Producer/Writer
Diane Ruggiero .Supervising Producer
Dan Etheridge .Co-Producer
Phil Klemmer .Staff Writer
Dayna Lynne North .Staff Writer
Aury Wallington .Staff Writer
Dee Dee Bradley .Casting Director (LA)
D. Candis Paule .Casting Director (San Diego)

THE WEST WING (NBC/60 mins.)
c/o Warner Bros. Television
4000 Warner Blvd., Bldg. 136, Rm. 255
Burbank, CA 91522
PHONE .818-954-7303
FAX .818-954-7357
PRODUCTION COMPANIES John Wells Productions - Warner Bros. Television Production

John Wells .Executive Producer/Showrunner
Alex Graves .Co-Executive Producer
Christopher Misiano .Co-Executive Producer
Llewellyn Wells .Co-Executive Producer
Carol Flint .Consulting Producer
Peter Noah .Consulting Producer
Lawrence O'Donnell .Consulting Producer
John Sacret Young .Consulting Producer
Thomas Schlamme .Consulting Producer
Kristin Harms .Producer
Eli Attie .Co-Producer
Mindy Kanaskie .Co-Producer
Patrick Ward .Co-Producer
Debora Cahn .Story Editor
Mark Goffman .Story Editor
Josh Singer .Staff Writer
Laura Schiff .Casting Director

WHAT I LIKE ABOUT YOU (WB/30 mins.)
c/o Warner Bros. Television
4000 Warner Blvd., Bldg. 136, Rm. 132
Burbank, CA 91522
PHONE .818-954-5470
FAX .818-954-7958
PRODUCTION COMPANIES Tollin/Robbins Productions - Warner Bros. Television Production

Caryn Lucas .Executive Producer/Showrunner
Joe Davola .Executive Producer
Brian Robbins .Executive Producer/Creator
Mike Tollin .Executive Producer/Creator
Rosalind Moore .Co-Executive Producer
Marco Pennette .Co-Executive Producer
Peter Marc Jacobson .Consulting Producer
Amy Engelberg .Supervising Producer
Wendy Engelberg .Supervising Producer
Drew Brown .Producer
Casey Johnson .Co-Producer
Lesley Wake-Webster .Co-Producer
David Windsor .Co-Producer
Brett Benner .Casting Director
Debby Romano .Casting Director

WHATEVER HAPPENED TO ROBOT JONES (Cartoon Network/30 mins.)
300 N. Third St.
Burbank, CA 91502
PHONE .818-729-4000
FAX .818-729-4026
COMMENTS Animated

Greg Miller .Creator
Mike Stern .Art Director
Janet Dimon .Line Producer
Margaret Tang .Casting Director

WHO WANTS TO BE A MILLIONAIRE? (Syndicated/30 mins.)
30 W. 67th St.
New York, NY 10023
PHONE .212-456-3500
FAX .212-456-4300
WEB SITE .www.millionairetv.com

Michael Davies .Executive Producer
Leigh Hampton .Executive Producer
Paul Smith .Executive Producer
Vincent Rubino .Co-Executive Producer

WHO WANTS TO MARRY MY DAD? (NBC/60 mins.)
c/o Nash Entertainment
Sunset Gower Studios
1438 N. Gower St., Box 10, Bldg. 35
Hollywood, CA 90028
PHONE .323-993-7384
FAX .323-468-4791
PRODUCTION COMPANY Nash Entertainment

Bruce Nash .Executive Producer
Scott Satin .Executive Producer
Andrew Jebb .Co-Executive Producer
Todd Jensen .Executive in Charge of Production
Sean Perez .Associate Producer of Production

WILD CARD (Lifetime/60 mins.)
c/o Fireworks Entertainment
421 S. Beverly Dr., 5th Fl.
Beverly Hills, CA 90212
PHONE .310-789-4582
PRODUCTION COMPANY Fireworks Entertainment

Lynn Marie Latham .Executive Producer/Creator
Bernard Lechowick .Executive Producer/Creator
Douglas Steinberg .Executive Producer
Kevin Inch .Co-Executive Producer
Sandy Isaac .Co-Executive Producer
Bill Schrwartz .Co-Executive Producer
Greg Ball .Supervising Producer
Steve Blackman .Supervising Producer
Michael Weisbarth .Supervising Executive
Darin Goldberg .Staff Writer
Shelley Meals .Staff Writer
Robin Bernheim .Writer
Karen Rea .Casting Director (LA)
Deirdre Bowen .Casting Director (Toronto)

WILL & GRACE (NBC/30 mins.)
4024 Radford Ave., Bungalow 3
Studio City, CA 91604
PHONE . . . 818-655-5642
FAX . . . 818-655-8690
PRODUCTION COMPANIES KoMut Entertainment - NBC Universal Television Studio

David Kohan . . . Executive Producer/Creator
Max Mutchnick . . . Executive Producer/Creator
James Burrows . . . Executive Producer
David Flebotte . . . Executive Producer/Showrunner
Alex Herschlag . . . Executive Producer/Showrunner
Gary Janetti . . . Co-Executive Producer
Tim Kaiser . . . Co-Executive Producer
Jon Kinnally . . . Co-Executive Producer
Greg Malins . . . Co-Executive Producer
Tracy Poust . . . Co-Executive Producer
Bill Wrubel . . . Co-Executive Producer
Laura Kightlinger . . . Consulting Producer
Jhoni Marchinko . . . Consulting Producer
Jeff Greenstein . . . Creative Consultant
Bruce Alden . . . Producer
Sally Bradford . . . Producer
Peter Chakos . . . Producer
Gail Lerner . . . Producer
Steve Sandoval . . . Producer
Sonja Warfield . . . Story Editor
Tracy Lilienfield . . . Casting Director

THE WIRE (HBO/60 mins.)
1801 S. Clinton St.
Baltimore, MD 21224
PHONE . . . 410-537-6550
FAX . . . 410-537-6588
PRODUCTION COMPANY HBO Original Programming

David Simon . . . Executive Producer/Creator
Robert F. Colesbury . . . Executive Producer
Nina K. Noble . . . Executive Producer
Joe Chappelle . . . Co-Executive Producer
Ed Burns . . . Producer
George Pelecanos . . . Producer
Karen Thorson . . . Producer
Bill Zorzi . . . Staff Writer
Rafael Alvarez . . . Writer
Dennis Lehane . . . Writer
Joy Lusco Kecken . . . Writer
Richard Price . . . Writer
Alexa Fogel . . . Casting Director (NY)
Pat Moran . . . Casting Director (Baltimore)

WITHOUT A TRACE (CBS/60 mins.)
c/o Warner Bros. Television
4000 Warner Blvd.
Burbank, CA 91522
PHONE . . . 818-954-1707
FAX . . . 818-954-6165
PRODUCTION COMPANIES Bruckheimer Productions - CBS Productions - Warner Bros. Television Production

Jerry Bruckheimer . . . Executive Producer
Jonathan Littman . . . Executive Producer
Ed Redlich . . . Executive Producer/Showrunner
Hank Steinberg . . . Executive Producer/Creator
David Amann . . . Co-Executive Producer
Jennifer Levin . . . Co-Executive Producer
Jan Nash . . . Co-Executive Producer
Greg Walker . . . Co-Executive Producer
Simon Mirren . . . Producer
Scott White . . . Producer
Allison Abner . . . Co-Producer
David Goodman . . . Executive Story Editor
Maria Maggenti . . . Executive Story Editor
Mary V. Buck . . . Casting Director
Gary Zuckerbrod . . . Casting Director

***WORLD CUP COMEDY (PAX/60 mins.)**
c/o Hollywood Center Studios
1040 N. Las Palmas Ave., Bldg. 6, 2nd Fl.
Los Angeles, CA 90038
PHONE . . . 323-860-5030
FAX . . . 323-860-5031
PRODUCTION COMPANY Grammnet Productions

Kelsey Grammer . . . Executive Producer
Wayne Page . . . Executive Producer
Dan O'Connor . . . Co-Executive Producer
Adam Peck . . . Co-Executive Producer
Steve Stark . . . Co-Executive Producer
Richard G. King . . . Supervising Producer
Steve Atinsky . . . Segment Producer
Jeff McCarthy . . . Segment Producer
Carol Kritzer . . . Casting Director

YES, DEAR (CBS/30 mins.)
4024 Radford Ave., Bldg. 7, 2nd Fl.
Studio City, CA 91604
PHONE . . . 818-655-5121
FAX . . . 818-655-8430

Alan Kirschenbaum . . . Executive Producer/Showrunner/Creator
Greg Garcia . . . Executive Producer/Showrunner/Creator
Bobby Bowman . . . Co-Executive Producer
Ralph Greene . . . Consulting Producer
Gigi McCreery . . . Consulting Producer
Perry Rein . . . Consulting Producer
Fred Shafferman . . . Consulting Producer
Jay Kleckner . . . Supervising Producer/UPM
Erika Kaestle . . . Producer
Patrick McCarthy . . . Producer
Mike Pennie . . . Co-Producer
Jamie Rhonheimer . . . Co-Producer
Rick Redick . . . Co-Producer, Post Production
David Hartle . . . Associate Producer, Production
Michael Mariano . . . Executive Story Editor
Bob Smiley . . . Staff Writer
Dava Waite . . . Casting Director

THE YOUNG AND THE RESTLESS (CBS/60 mins.)
7800 Beverly Blvd., Ste. 3305
Los Angeles, CA 90036
PHONE . . . 323-575-2532
FAX . . . 323-653-0361
PRODUCTION COMPANY Sony Pictures Television

William J. Bell . . . Executive Producer
John F. Smith . . . Co-Executive Producer
Edward J. Scott . . . Supervising Producer
John C. Fisher . . . Coordinating Producer
Kathryn Foster . . . Producer
Joshua O'Connell . . . Associate Producer
Marnie Saitta . . . Casting Director

It is illegal to copy any part of this book

WORKSHEET

DATE	PROJECT	CONTACT	NOTES

Available online at www.hcdonline.com

SECTION D

INDEX BY TYPE

Animation

Animation (continued)

Animation (continued)

It is illegal to copy any part of this book

Direct-to-Video/DVD (continued)

Direct-to-Video/DVD (continued)

Direct-to-Video/DVD (continued)

Documentaries

It is illegal to copy any part of this book

Documentaries (continued)

Documentaries (continued)

Documentaries (continued)

Documentaries (continued)

Documentaries (continued)

Features

Features (continued)

Features (continued)

Features (continued)

Features (continued)

Features (continued)

Features (continued)

It is illegal to copy any part of this book

Features (continued)

Features (continued)

Features (continued)

Features (continued)

Features (continued)

Features (continued)

Features (continued)

Features (continued)

Features (continued)

Features (continued)

Quinta Communications USA
R.L. Entertainment, Inc.
Radar Pictures
Radiant Productions
The Radmin Company
Raffaella Productions, Inc.
Rainbow Film Company/Rainbow Releasing
Raindance Pictures
Rainstorm Entertainment, Inc.
Peggy Rajski Productions
Rakontur
David Rambaldi Enterprises
Randan Productions, Inc.
Randwell Productions
Rapid Heart Pictures, Ltd.
Rat Entertainment/Rat TV
RAW/Progressive Films
Raygun Productions
Rearguard Productions, Inc.
Recorded Picture Company
Red Bird Productions
Red Diamond Company
Red Hen Productions
Red Horse Films
Red Hour Films
Red Om Films, Inc.
Red Strokes Entertainment
Red Wagon Entertainment
Red-Horse Productions
Dan Redler Entertainment
Reelvision Entertainment
Marian Rees Associates
ReganMedia
Regency Enterprises
Regent Entertainment, Inc.
Rehme Productions
Tim Reid Productions, Inc.
Reiner/Greisman
Relish Productions
Renaissance Pictures
Renfield Productions
Reperage
Reveal Entertainment
Reveille, LLC
Revelations Entertainment
Revolution Studios
Reynolds Entertainment
RH Factor
Rhythm & Hues Studios
Rice & Beans Productions
Riche Productions
Ricochet Entertainment
Ridini Entertainment Corporation
Anthony Ridio Productions, Inc.
Right Angle Studios
Rita Films
River One Films
Riverrock Entertainment Group
RJN Productions, Inc.
RKO Pictures, LLC
Robbins Entertainment
Dolores Robinson Entertainment
Amy Robinson Productions
Rocket Science Laboratories
Rocking Horse Productions
Rockstone Pictures
Stan Rogow Productions
Rogue Creative/VFX
Phil Roman Entertainment
Romano Shane Productions
Rope The Moon Productions
Alex Rose Productions, Inc.

Features (continued)

Lee Rose Productions
Zvi Howard Rosenman Productions
rossWWmedia, Corporation
Heidi Rotbart Management
Roth/Arnold Productions
Rough Diamond Productions
Rough Draft Studios
Roundtable Ink
RSF Productions
Rubin * Burke Productions
Ruby-Spears Productions
Scott Rudin Productions
Rupert Productions, Inc.
S Pictures, Inc.
Alan Sacks Productions, Inc.
Salty Features
Samoset, Inc./Sacret, Inc.
Samuel Goldwyn Films
Ron Samuels Entertainment, Inc.
Samuelson Productions Limited
Sanctuary
Sandbox Entertainment
Sander/Moses Productions, Inc.
Sandstorm Films
Sanford/Pillsbury Productions
Saphier Productions
Sarabande Productions
Arthur Sarkissian Productions
Saturn Films
Savoir Faire Productions
Scarab Productions
Scarlet Fire Entertainment
Schachter Entertainment
Edgar J. Scherick Associates, Inc.
Paul Schiff Productions
Scholastic Entertainment
Adam Schroeder Entertainment
Joel Schumacher Productions
Faye Schwab Productions/MMA, Inc.
Schwartz & Company, Inc.
Steven Schwartz Productions
Kristine Schwarz Productions
SCI FI Channel
Scott Free Productions
Scout Productions
Screen Gems
ScreenMagic Entertainment, Inc.
Sea Cliff Entertainment
Section Eight Productions
Segue Productions, Inc.
SekretAgent Productions
Dylan Sellers Productions
Liz Selzer-Lang Productions
Senator International
Seraphim Films
Serenade Films
Serendipity Productions, Inc.
Seven Arts Pictures
Shadowcatcher Entertainment
Shady Acres Entertainment
Richard & Esther Shapiro Entertainment, Inc.
Shatter Glass Productions, Inc.
The Shephard/Robin Company
Shoe Money Productions
Shoreline Entertainment
ShowBuzz
Showtime Independent Films
Shukovsky English Entertainment
The Shuman Company
Shutt-Jones Productions
SideStreet Entertainment
Sierra Club Productions

Features (continued)

Signature Pictures
Silly Robin Productions
Silver Dream Productions
Silver Lion Films
Silver Pictures
Casey Silver Productions
SilverCreek Entertainment
Silverline Entertainment, Inc.
Silvers/Koster Productions, Inc.
The Gene Simmons Company
The Robert Simonds Company
Brent Sims Films
Simsie Films/Media Savant Pictures
Joseph Singer Entertainment
Carla Singer Productions
Single Cell Pictures
Sitting Ducks Productions
Mary Jane Skalski
Skippy Dog Productions
Skye Island Entertainment
Skylark Films, Ltd.
Skyline Pictures, LLC
Daniel Sladek Entertainment Corporation
Slipnot! Productions/SPG
Smokin' Gun Productions
Snapdragon Films, Inc.
Sneak Preview Entertainment, Inc.
Snowfall Films
Sobini Films
Solo Entertainment Group
Solo One Productions
The Sommers Company
Sony Online Entertainment
Sony Pictures Animation
Sony Pictures Digital
Sony Pictures Entertainment
Sony Pictures Imageworks
South Productions, LLC
South Shore Entertainment
South Side Films
Southern Skies, Inc.
Southpaw Entertainment
Sparky Pictures
Spectacor Films
Darin Spillman Productions
Spirit Dance Entertainment
Spirit Horse Productions
Spitfire Pictures
Spring Creek Productions, Inc.
Sprocketdyne Entertainment
Spumco
Spyglass Entertainment Group
Spyworm
SRG Productions
St. Amos Productions
Stampede Entertainment
Star Entertainment Group, Inc.
Star Land Entertainment, Inc.
Stargazer Entertainment, Inc.
Jane Startz Productions, Inc.
State Street Pictures
Steamroller Productions, Inc.
Mitchell Stein Productions
The Howard Stern Production Company
Stevens & Associates
The Stevens Company
Joel Stevens Entertainment
Stillwater Films
Stone Village Pictures, LLC
Stone vs. Stone
Stonelock Pictures
Stonewerks Motion Picture Group

Features (continued)

Features (continued)

Features (continued)

Made-for-TV/Cable Movies (continued)

Made-for-TV/Cable Movies (continued)

Made-for-TV/Cable Movies (continued)

Made-for-TV/Cable Movies (continued)

Made-for-TV/Cable Movies (continued)

Made-for-TV/Cable Movies (continued)

Music Videos (continued)

New Media

New Media (continued)

New Media (continued)

It is illegal to copy any part of this book

Reality TV (continued)

Reality TV (continued)

Syndication

Syndication (continued)

It is illegal to copy any part of this book

Syndication (continued)

Syndication (continued)

Theater

TV Series

TV Series (continued)

TV Series (continued)

TV Series (continued)

TV Series (continued)

TV Series (continued)

TV Series (continued)

TV Series (continued)

TV Series (continued)

TV Series (continued)

TV Series (continued)

TV Series (continued)

TV Series (continued)

TV Series (continued)

The Post Office Broadcast Services
POW! Entertainment
Power Entertainment
Power Up
Edward R. Pressman Film Corporation
Pretty Pictures
Principal Entertainment
Victoria Principal Productions
Principato-Young Entertainment
Produce Media Group
Producers Group Studios
The Producers
Production Partners, Inc.
Promark Entertainment Group
Prometheus Entertainment
Prospect Pictures
Protozoa Pictures
Proud Mary Entertainment
Pterodactyl/KEW
Quality Filmed Entertainment
Quinn Productions
R.L. Entertainment, Inc.
The Radmin Company
Raffaella Productions, Inc.
Rakontur
David Rambaldi Enterprises
Randan Productions, Inc.
Rapid Heart Pictures, Ltd.
Bonnie Raskin Productions
Rat Entertainment/Rat TV
Red Bird Productions
Red Board Productions
Red Diamond Company
Red Om Films, Inc.
Red Strokes Entertainment
Red Wagon Entertainment
Red-Horse Productions
Dan Redler Entertainment
Reelvision Entertainment
ReganMedia
Rehme Productions
Tim Reid Productions, Inc.
Relish Productions
Renaissance Pictures
Renegade 83
Renegade Animation, Inc.
Renfield Productions
Reveal Entertainment
Reveille, LLC
Revelations Entertainment
RH Factor
Rhythm & Hues Studios
Rice & Beans Productions
Ricochet Entertainment
Ridini Entertainment Corporation
Anthony Ridio Productions, Inc.
Rive Gauche International TV
Rivet Entertainment, LLC
Dolores Robinson Entertainment
Rocket Science Laboratories
Rocking Horse Productions
Rockstone Pictures
Stan Rogow Productions
Rogue Creative/VFX
Phil Roman Entertainment
Romano Shane Productions
Alex Rose Productions, Inc.
Lee Rose Productions
Rosemont Productions International, Ltd.
Zvi Howard Rosenman Productions
Gay Rosenthal Productions
rossWWmedia, Corporation

TV Series (continued)

Heidi Rotbart Management
Rough Draft Studios
Roundtable Ink
RSF Productions
Rubin * Burke Productions
Ruby-Spears Productions
Rupert Productions, Inc.
S Pictures, Inc.
Alan Sacks Productions, Inc.
Samoset, Inc./Sacret, Inc.
Ron Samuels Entertainment, Inc.
Sandbox Entertainment
Sander/Moses Productions, Inc.
Sanford/Pillsbury Productions
Saphier Productions
Sarabande Productions
Arthur Sarkissian Productions
Savoir Faire Productions
Scarab Productions
Scarlet Fire Entertainment
Schachter Entertainment
Edgar J. Scherick Associates, Inc.
Paul Schiff Productions
George Schlatter Productions
Scholastic Entertainment
Faye Schwab Productions/MMA, Inc.
Schwartz & Company, Inc.
Steven Schwartz Productions
Kristine Schwarz Productions
SCI FI Channel
Scott Free Productions
Scout Productions
Screen Door Entertainment
Sea Cliff Entertainment
Section Eight Productions
SekretAgent Productions
Dylan Sellers Productions
Seraphim Films
Sesame Workshop
Shady Acres Entertainment
Richard & Esther Shapiro Entertainment, Inc.
Shatter Glass Productions, Inc.
The Shephard/Robin Company
Shevloff McKean Productions
Shoe Money Productions
Shoreline Entertainment
Showtime Networks, Inc.
Shukovsky English Entertainment
The Shuman Company
Shutt-Jones Productions
SideStreet Entertainment
Sierra Club Productions
Silly Robin Productions
Silver Lion Films
Silver Pictures
Casey Silver Productions
SilverCreek Entertainment
The Fred Silverman Company
Silvers/Koster Productions, Inc.
The Gene Simmons Company
Simsie Films/Media Savant Pictures
Carla Singer Productions
SisterLee Productions, Inc.
Sitting Ducks Productions
SiTV
Mary Jane Skalski
Skippy Dog Productions
Skylark Films, Ltd.
Daniel Sladek Entertainment Corporation
Slipnot! Productions/SPG
Smokin' Gun Productions
Snapdragon Films, Inc.

TV Series (continued)

Sneak Preview Entertainment, Inc.
Solo Entertainment Group
Solo One Productions
Andrew Solt Productions
The Sommers Company
Sony Pictures Entertainment
Sony Pictures Imageworks
Sony Pictures Television
Sony Pictures Television International
South Productions, LLC
South Shore Entertainment
South Side Films
Southern Skies, Inc.
Southpaw Entertainment
Sparky Pictures
Spelling Television, Inc.
Spike TV
Spirit Dance Entertainment
Spirit Horse Productions
Spitfire Pictures
Spotlight Health, Inc.
Sprocketdyne Entertainment
Spumco
Spyglass Entertainment Group
Spyworm
SRG Productions
St. Amos Productions
Stampede Entertainment
Star Land Entertainment, Inc.
Stargazer Entertainment, Inc.
Jane Startz Productions, Inc.
State Street Pictures
Steamroller Productions, Inc.
Mitchell Stein Productions
The Howard Stern Production Company
Stevens & Associates
The Stevens Company
Joel Stevens Entertainment
Stewart Television, Inc.
Stillwater Films
Stone Stanley Entertainment
Stone Village Pictures, LLC
Stone vs. Stone
Stoneworks Television
Storyline Entertainment
Storyworks Entertainment, Inc.
Bert Stratford Productions, Inc.
Mel Stuart Productions, Inc.
Stun
Stuntman, Inc.
Sub Rosa Productions, Inc.
Mike Sullivan Productions, Inc.
Summerland Entertainment
Summers Entertainment
Sunlight Productions
Sweeney Entertainment
Symphony Pictures, Inc.
Synchronicity Productions
Synergy Entertainment Group
T.V. Repair
TAE Productions/Medeacom Productions
Taffner Entertainment, Ltd.
Tailfish Productions
Takes On Productions
Talisman Pacific
Talking Wall Pictures, Inc.
Tall Pine Productions
Tannenbaum Company
The Taran Company
Taurus Entertainment Company
Tavel Entertainment
Taylor Made Films

TV Series (continued)

TV Series (continued)

TV Series (continued)

SECTION **E**

INDEX BY STATE

Arizona

California

California (continued)

California (continued)

California (continued)

California (continued)

California (continued)

California (continued)

California (continued)

California (continued)

It is illegal to copy any part of this book

California (continued)

California (continued)

California (continued)

California (continued)

California (continued)

California (continued)

California (continued)

California (continued)

California (continued)

New York (continued)

New York (continued)

North Carolina

Pennsylvania

Tennessee

Texas

Utah

Vermont

Virginia

Washington

Wisconsin

It is illegal to copy any part of this book

WORKSHEET

DATE	PROJECT	CONTACT	NOTES

SECTION F

INDEX BY NAME

It is illegal to copy any part of this book

It is illegal to copy any part of this book

It is illegal to copy any part of this book

It is illegal to copy any part of this book